# ENCYCLOPAEDIA

## OF

# MEDICAL ASTROLOGY

## *By*

### HOWARD LESLIE CORNELL, M.D., LL.D.

(Honorary Professor of Medical Astrology at the First National
University of Naturopathy and Allied Sciences, Newark, N. J.)

*Author Of*
"Astrology and the Diagnosis of Disease", 1918
A Bound Volume of His
"Magazine Articles on Medical and Biblical Astrology", 1924

*Member Of*
The New York Psychical Research Society; National Geographic Society;
The British Institute of Medical Astrology and Metaphysical Science;
Permanent Member of the National Eclectic Medical Association.

*Formerly*
National Secretary of the National Astrological Society of the United States,
and of the American Astrological Society.

Published By
THE CORNELL PUBLISHING COMPANY
3108 Humboldt Street
Los Angeles, California, U. S. A.
1933

LONDON
L. N. Fowler & Co.
7, Imperial Arcade, Ludgate Circus, E. C. 4

*Astrologically Yours,*

*H. L. Cornell, M. D., D. A.*

# Volume 1

# LETTER OF INTRODUCTION

**FIRST NATIONAL UNIVERSITY OF NATUROPATHY**
AND
**ALLIED SCIENCES**
143 ROSEVILLE AVENUE
NEWARK. N. J.

COMBINING
N. J. COLLEGE OF OSTEOPATHY
MECCA COLLEGE OF CHIROPRACTIC
U. S. SCHOOL OF NATUROPATHY
U. S. SCHOOL OF PHYSIOTHERAPY

February 3, 1933

COURSES
PROFESSIONAL AND POST GRADUATE
2 YEARS OF 8 MONTHS EACH
4 YEARS OF 7 MONTHS EACH
4 YEARS OF 8 MONTHS EACH

TO WHOM IT MAY CONCERN:

I have examined the preliminary sheets of the work on Medical Astrology by Doctor H.L. Cornell, and this work will be a monument to Doctor Cornell, and to Astro-Science.

It is a Work that should be in every Astrologian's Library for study and reference. As soon as this book is off the Press, the First National University of Naturopathy will make it one of the standard Textbooks for the Chair in Astro-Pathological Diagnosis.

We have known Doctor Cornell for many years, and have given him our highest Honors. He has spent the best years of his life in research study along the lines of Medical Astrology, and also used this knowledge to practical advantage in his many years of Practice as a Physician. This Encyclopaedia is the only book of its kind ever attempted in the history of the World, as far as we know, and it gathers together the knowledge along the lines of Medical Astrology in a way that students can get at it, as subjects are all arranged alphabetically.

We trust the book will be well-received, and appreciated by the Astrological and Scientific World, and by Healers of all Schools who are interested in Astrology as an aid in Pathological Diagnosis, Prognosis, and in the etiological factors in knowing more about the Philosophy of Disease, and the Planetary Causes of Disease.

Respectfully,

*Frederick W. Collins, M.D., A.M., Dean*

Frederick W. Collins, M.D.,A.M.,Dean
FIRST NATIONAL UNIVERSITY OF
NATUROPATHY AND ALLIED SCIENCES.

# ABBREVIATIONS AND SYMBOLS USED IN THIS BOOK

**ABBREVIATIONS—**
affl.—afflicted, afflicting.
apply.—applying, apply.
A.P.—(See Vertebrae).
Asc.—Ascendant.
asp.—aspect.
asps.—aspects.
AT.—(See Vertebrae).
AX.—(See Vertebrae).
B.—birth.
Card.—Cardinal.
Chap.—Chapter.
Coc.—Coccyx.
C.P.—(See Vertebrae).
d.—days.
Dec.—Decanate, Declination.
Decan.—Decanate.
decumb.—decumbiture.
decr.—decrease, decreasing.
deg.—degree, degrees.
Desc.—Descendant.
Dir.—Direction, Directed.
E.—East, Equinox.
Eq., Equi.—Equinox.
espec.—especially.
Fem.—Feminine, Female.
Fig.—Figure.
gd.—good.
H.—House.
Horo.—Horoscope.
Hor'y Q.—Horary Questions.
H.P.—(See Vertebrae).
incr.—increasing, increase.
infl.—influenced, influence.
ill-dig.—Ill-dignified.
1001 N.N.—1001 Notable Nativities.
K.P.—(See Vertebrae).

**ABBREVIATIONS—**
Lat.—Latitude.
Long.—Longitude.
L.C.P.—(See Vertebrae).
Li.P.—(See Vertebrae).
L.P.P.—(See Vertebrae).
Lu.P.—(See Vertebrae).
m.—months.
M.C.—The Midheaven.
M.C.P.—(See Vertebrae).
Mut.—Mutable.
N.—North.
N.N.—Notable Nativities.
No.—Number.
occi.—occidental.
ori.—oriental.
Per.—Periodic.
P.P.—(See Vertebrae).
Pr., Prog.—Progressed, Progression.
Q.—Question, Questions.
R.—Retrograde.
Rev.—Revolution.
S.—South.
Sac.—Sacrum.
Sec.—Section.
sepr.—separating.
Sig.—Significator.
Sigs.—Significators.
Spl.P.—(See Vertebrae).
S.P.—(See Vertebrae).
Subs.—Subluxations.
Tr., tr.—Transit.
U.P.P.—(See Vertebrae).
V.—Vertebra, Vertebrae.
W.—West.
well-dig.—well-dignified.
y.—years.

**ASPECTS—**
V—Semi-Sextile—30°.
∠—Semi-Square—45°.
✳—Sextile—60°.
□—Square—90°.
△—Trine—120°.
⬓—Sesquiquadrate—135°.
8—Opposition—180°.
P.—Parallel.
☌—Conjunction.

**PLANETS—**
☉—Sun.
☽—Moon.
♆—Neptune.
♅—Uranus.
♄—Saturn.
♃—Jupiter.
♂—Mars.
♀—Venus.
☿—Mercury.

**SIGNS OF THE ZODIAC—**
♈—Aries.
♉—Taurus.
♊—Gemini.
♋—Cancer.
♌—Leo.
♍—Virgo.
♎—Libra.
♏—Scorpio.
♐—Sagittarius.
♑—Capricorn.
♒—Aquarius.
♓—Pisces.

**OTHER SYMBOLS—**
⊕—Part of Fortune.
℞—Retrograde.
☊—Ascending Node.
Dragon's Head.
☋—Descending Node.
Dragon's Tail.
°—Degrees.
'—Minutes.
"—Seconds.
×—Multiplied By.
+—Plus.

# THE CHART OF BIRTH

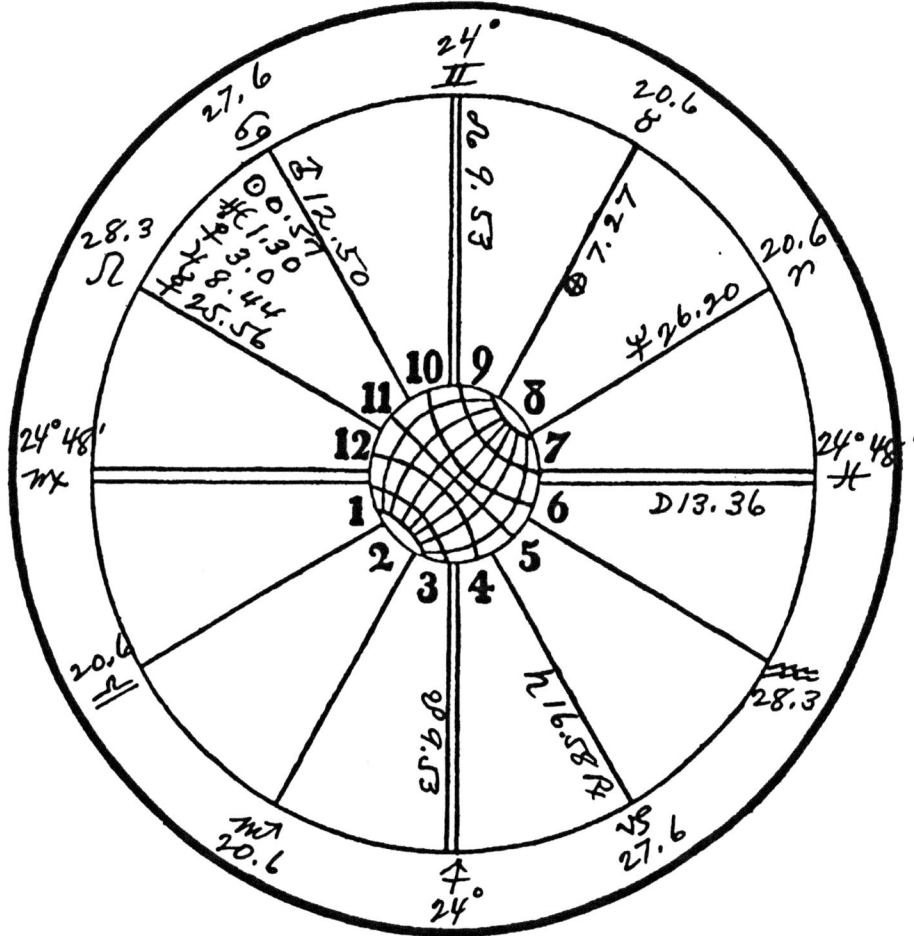

24°
♊

27.6
♋

20.6
♉

28.3
♌

20.6
♈

24° 48'
♍

24° 48'
♓

⊕ 7.27

♅ 12.50
⊙ 0.57
♂ 1.30
♃ 3.0
♄ 8.44
25.56

♇ 26.20

☽ 13.36

28.3
♏

20.6
♎

20.6
♏
20.6

♄ 16.58 ℞

♐
27.6

24°
♐

10  9
11      8
12      7
1      6
2      5
3  4

H. L. CORNELL, A.M., M.D., Ph.D.

Born July 23, 1872, 9:27 A.M.
Hartsville, Bucks County, Pennsylvania
75° W. L., 40° 12' N. Lat.

# FOREWORD

For some years in my study of Astrology as a Physician and Surgeon, and in an effort to get at the Planetary Causes of disease, I searched through the Textbooks of Astrology to find something about the disease I was treating, but my efforts were often in vain. There are many fine things said in the Textbooks along the lines of Medical Astrology, but such statements are often made at random, and in obscure places, and are not indexed. To be sure, there are classified lists of the Planets in Signs, and the diseases they cause, but in making a study of any one disease, it is almost impossible to find in the regular Textbooks and Manuals of Astrology all that has been said about this disease, and its planetary causes, and this knowledge could only be obtained by a systematic search through my entire Astrological Library. Being so inconvenienced myself, and with a desire to get the knowledge along the lines of Medical Astrology into classified shape, about fifteen years ago I conceived the idea of making this Encyclopaedia, and of arranging the Disease Subjects alphabetically, and of gathering up the material on each subject from all the Astrological books of my Library. This has been a momentous and tedious task. To begin with, I opened up a Ledger Account for each disease subject, and began a systematic digest of my entire Library, and in reading, line by line, would post the thoughts into the Ledger under each disease subject as I would come to them. By keeping up this practice for some years I eventually had two large Ledgers filled with material. Then came the task of arranging, classifying, disentangling, and writing up these ledger Articles into readable form, as each Article was posted in as read, and like a jungled mass, and without form. It took me four years to go thru this and finish the first writing entirely in English. Then, in 1928 the idea came to me that I should retype and rearrange the entire book, and type it on an Astronomical Typewriter, and use the Symbols for the Planets, Signs, and Aspects. In this second writing it was necessary to rearrange the subjects, and place many Articles under a different letter. The system of Synonyms and cross references in the book has taken a great deal of time, and to see to it that such references were in harmony. To shorten the manuscript I have used many abbreviations, and a list of these abbreviations you can find in the front of this book.

When this mass of material was straightened out, arranged, classified, and the various influences causing a disease were gotten together and studied, it has been an interesting study to note the fundamental influence and nature of the various Planets, and how these influences were in the minds of the various Writers, from the time of Ptolemy, and on down thru the Centuries until the present time, and with these facts and data before me, it has become an easy matter for me to see what influences were missing, and which have never been listed or tabulated in any book, as far as I have been able to discover, and to fill these in, and to do my part in helping to develop the Science of Medical Astrology, and get the knowledge along this line into such shape that students can get at it quickly, and by merely turning to a subject in the alphabetical arrangement. Also in this Encyclopaedia I have given attention to the Higher and Spiritual side of Astrology, to Esoteric Astrology, and have tried to arouse the readers to an inner consciousness of their Higher Powers, to rule their stars, and not be a slave to the various planetary aspects and influences which operated over them at birth, or may be manifesting themselves along thru life.

The fundamental purpose of this Encyclopaedia is to give the planetary influences which cause the various diseases, afflictions, events, accidents, and injuries of life, and to gather such knowledge under subjects, and arrange them alphabetically. I am not attempting to repeat the Classifications to be found in the various Textbooks of Astrology, and the student is asked to use this volume in connection with his other books. Also this book does not attempt to go into the Elements of Astrology, or to be a Textbook of such Elements, although many Articles do deal with these Elements, and especially as they are related to Medical Astrology, and the Diagnosis of Disease by Astrology. The student, in order to use this Encyclopaedia intelligently, should first be a student of Astrology, and to know the Elements and Fundamentals of Astrology and Astronomy, and be familiar with the Signs and Symbols of Astronomy. Also this book is not intended to be a Treatise on the various Systems of Healing, or Schools of Treatment, but to give the planetary causes and philosophy of disease, and to allow each student to use his own methods of treatment. I honor and respect all Schools of Healing, and recognize that there is good in all, but it would be impossible in a book of this kind to go into the merits of the different Schools. The Theory of Chiropractic is closely related to Astrology, due to the planetary rulerships over the Spine and Vertebrae, and I have attempted to give and list, under various diseases, the Subluxations caused by the planetary influences. It is also my desire to have students in the various Schools of Healing, and when they are studying a certain disease, to consult this Encyclopaedia on the subject in hand, and note the planetary influences which cause such disease, and to understand the philosophy of the case, and not to be satisfied merely with the treatment of the ailment. In Ancient Times all Physicians and Healers were required to know Astrology, and its relation to disease, and to the individual afflicted, as by a study of his Star Map of Birth, and the adverse Directions which might be operating over him, and such applicants for Medical, or Healing Licenses, were not allowed to become full-fledged Physicians until they could pass a satisfactory examination in Astrology. But, for various reasons, the knowledge of Astrology became more or less suppressed during the Middle Ages, but is now being revived again, and coming into its own, and is being more and more recognized as a true and Ancient Science. Physicians and Healers should lay aside their prejudices, and investigate Astrology, prove it by observation, and when they do, I feel sure they will give it its rightful place in their Schools and Colleges of Healing, and in their daily practices among their patients. In my own practice I found Astrology of inestimable value in diagnosing my cases, and to quickly determine the seat of the disease in the patient, how long they have been sick and ailing, and to form a reasonably accurate prognosis.

In this book, the Form and Shape of the body, and the planetary influences along the lines of Form, Shape, Height, Weight, Complexion, Hair, etc., are given. Also there are many Articles along the lines of Conduct, Habits, Morals, Temperament, etc. Also the prominent Fixed Stars, and their influences, are listed. Under each subject the sub-heads are arranged alphabetically for quick reference, and the student can very quickly get at the knowledge he is seeking, on any subject, as far as they are listed and recorded in this book.

One very great difficulty I have encountered in building up this Encyclopaedia has been to determine what subjects should go in, and what should be left out, and especially along the lines of Mental Traits. The Mind and Body are so closely related, and there are so many Mental Traits which are Pathological, and practically amount to a diseased Mind, that I have listed in this volume a great number of the less desirable Mental Traits, and also for a study in contrasts, some of the more desirable ones. During my years of study in the preparation of this volume I have gathered enough material for a separate Encyclopaedia, to be known as "The Encyclopaedia of Psychological Astrology", and hope soon to begin to assemble this book, and leave it to the World as the sister book to this present volume.

In the Fall of 1918, after many years of active Practice in Medical work in this Country, and in India, I gave up the Practice of Medicine, moved my family to Los Angeles, and have lived here ever since, and given my whole time to Astrology, Writing, and in the preparation of Star Maps, Horoscopes, and Astrological Health Readings for people over the World. When this Encyclopaedia is out, circulated, and established, it is my plan to make a World Lecture Tour, and speak before the various Healing Centers and Schools in the U. S. A., and other Nations, and to make an effort to have the various Faculties make Medical Astrology one of the required studies for their students who are aspiring to be Healers. I plan to have this Encyclopaedia in the prominent Public Libraries in the large Cities over the World, and also in the Occult, Metaphysical, Astrological, and Healing Centers, and where students can have access to it. I am giving this book to the World as a labor of love, and trust it will prove of great help to you and be a fitting monument to my life work.

H. L. CORNELL, M.D.

Los Angeles, Calif.
March 21st, 1933.

# INTRODUCTION TO SECOND EDITION

The results which this book will produce on the readers and students will, of course, depend largely upon the attitude of mind and mental advancement in which they approach the subject with which it deals.

Many students approach metaphysical phenomena with ingrained disinclination, to accept facts and conclusions which interfere with their preconceived opinions and dogmatic, youth-instilled beliefs.

Readers of this category will be necessarily incapable of comprehending the message and helpful advice contained in the following pages.

Those who are ready, cosmically speaking, to study this subject with an open, unbiased and unprejudged mind will find, perhaps, that whilst they can accept factors stated, they cannot reconcile themselves to PROGRESS—progress in thought, progress in the application thereof, no matter how sane they may appear to them.

The exposition as portrayed by Dr. Cornell in his treatise of something new, that has been suppressed for the past century, is but the beginning of a NEW ERA in the field of the Healing Arts; whatever conclusions or repercussions may arise therefrom are but a step FORWARD in the RIGHT DIRECTION.

A science whose significance is so far reaching and whose influence on the entire field in the Healing Arts will be revolutionary, to say the least, is bound to have repercussions from the old, obsolete and, by demonstration, impractical methods belonging to the past.

But, we must not overlook the fact, that with all our so-called advancements of standards of living, we still have with us a daily floating hospital population of close to 2,500,000 sick and ailing people in these United States. What is the cause? Too many 'Doctors' or not enough? Maybe not the right kind that know how to CURE disease or to alleviate suffering? Something surely IS wrong! Maybe, after all, the ancients knew more about relieving pain and suffering when they used common sense remedies, such as herbs, teas, poultices, made from various roots, plants and foliage.

Everything in this world was created for a well-defined and special purpose, including the stars, which were the first LINK between Man and the Heavens. The ancients knew well how to interpret the influence of these stars, especially that of the planets, upon ALL things terrestrial, including our health.

One of the most ancient and most reliable writers on this subject, Ptolemy, in his Quadripartite on the influence of the Stars, makes special reference to the stellar influence regarding localities north or south of the equator. Nicholas Culpepper, in his treatise on English Herbs (edition of 1695) allocates not less than 369 herbs to the various planets and their correlation to the Healing Arts. L. D. Broughton, M.D., in his work on this subject (Elements of Astrology) brings out very potent and convincing factors that the stars were made for something other than for professional 'Star-gazers' to look at.

An eminent Viennese medico, Dr. Friedr. Feerhov, as late as 1914, blazed the trail in Europe by publishing an astro-medical treatise, setting forth the close relationship between physical manifestation and metaphysical influence, between chemistry and biochemistry and alchemical allocation of human types.

At that time his 'findings and observations' were ridiculed by whom? By such who "Were down on something on which they were not up on!" It is the same today, albeit in a lesser way. After all, whenever I hear 'people' talking against something they do not know anything about, I am reminded of Shakespeare's lines in Julius Caesar, act I, scene III: "And that which would appear offence in us, His countenance, like richest alchemy, will change to VIRTUE and to WORTHINESS."

All good things take time! Ever since the beginning of the Aquarian age new systems within the healing arts have been proposed and expounded. Yet, the attacks made against all and everyone by the old, intrenched and well organized medical oligarchy (serum trusts and patent medicine vendors) have wrought havoc within the ranks of progressive exponents. Yet, with all the opposition, the 'old' must give way to the 'young' and the same holds good in medicine.

Disease is caused by retention of septic matter within the body; cure can be effected only by elimination of such septic retentions. The homeopathic and naturopathic systems have done more good than all the allopaths together.

I am well aware of the consequences of this statement, but, having graduated from both schools I know whereof I speak. Anyone, who is sceptically inclined, is advised to read: "Devils, Drugs and Doctors." (Howard W. Haggard, M.D., 1929.)

At the present time, there is a revolutionary trend within the ranks of the orthodox practitioners against the dictum of the medical trust. Yet, with all their wrangling they are not able to diminish the present day, ever-increasing 2,500,000 daily floating hospital population in the United States. Something is wrong somewhere. But the guilty parties are too stubborn to admit defeat from within. It will come from without.

The natural methods of healing, when well understood and judiciously applied, bring results. They fail only when suffocated herbs are used; this latter happens quite often lately, more so since the universal use of transparent water-proof wrapping material which excludes all oxygen not only from foods, but also from therapeutics. No wonder cancer has increased by leaps and bounds since the initiation of this oxygen-excluding wrapping material.

But, we are not interested in 'health-destroying' agencies; the point is to introduce something that WILL alleviate human suffering, and Dr. Cornell's book is one link in the long chain of Real Healing.

It might not be amiss to mention that Dr. Cornell, in his later years of life, became a loyal follower of the great genius, Emanuel Swedenborg, who, albeit not having been a licentiate of any orthodox school, laid the foundation of naturopathic principles.

Undoubtedly, Dr. Cornell gleaned many valuable pointers from Swedenborg's doctrines.

Dr. Cornell, whom, unfortunately I met too late and lost too soon, has built himself an everlasting monument; the future generation will honor him alongside the great souls, such as Pasteur, Koch, Lavoisier, Roentgen, Florence Nightingale, Lord Lister, for his contribution to mankind.

## R. I. P.

### HENRY J. GORDON, M. D., A. M., N. D., Ph. D. *h. c.*

Los Angeles, California
Easter, 1939

# AN

# ENCYCLOPAEDIA

## OF

# MEDICAL ASTROLOGY

**ABATEMENT OF DISEASE**—(See Antipathy, Amelioration, Better, Crises, Minimizing, Moderation, Modification, Opposites, Recovery, Recuperation, Remission, Resolution).

**ABDOMEN**—Abdominal Region—Abdominal Organs—Belly—Bowels—Hypogastrium—Navel—Peritoneum—etc. This region is ruled principally by the ♍ sign, and the 6th H. The internal parts of the abdomen, such as the bowels, are under the internal rulership of ♍, and the more external and surface parts are under the external rule of ♍. The muscles of the abdomen are especially under the rule of ♂, and tend to be greatly influenced when ♂ is in ♍ at B. The ♓ sign, opposite to ♍, and also all the common signs, when occupied by planets, or with common signs upon the angles, tend to affect the abdomen. The ☽ and ♀ are also said to rule over the abdominal region. The Belly is ruled by the ☽. The following subjects have to do with the Abdomen, which see in the alphabetical arrangement when not considered here.

**Appendicitis; Ascites**—(See "Abdomen" under Dropsy).

**Belly**—Bellyache—(See Belly).

**Bowels**—Disorders of—(See Bowels).

**Colic; Complaints**—Abdominal Complaints—(See "Diseases", "Prevalent", and the various subjects in this section).

**Constipation; Convulsive Movements**—In the abdominal region—♅ in ♍. (See Colic, Ileac Passion, Spasmodic).

**Cramps; Diarrhoea; Diseases**—Abdominal Diseases—Causes of—Liable to—The ☉ and ☽ acting through the ♍ sign, and especially through the Solar and Mesenteric Plexuses, and the Splanchnic Ganglia, tend to affect the abdominal organs; the ☉ affl. in ♍ or the 6th H.; afflictions to the ☽ or ♀, and especially when these planets are in ♍, ♓, the 6th H., or in any common sign; planets in ♍ and affl.; planets in ♓, and affl.; planets in ♊, ♐, or any common sign, and affl.; ♍ on the cusp of the Asc. or 6th H., afflicted, or containing a malefic; ♍ intercepted in the 6th H., and containing the ☉, ☽, or malefics, and affl.; common signs on the angles at B., and containing the Lights, or malefics, and affl.; rulers of the 6th, 8th, or 12th H. in ♍, and affl.; ♍ upon the Asc. at the Vernal, and with ☿ affl., or with ☿ in ♎ at the

Vernal, lord of the year, and affl., tends to a general prevalence of bowel and abdominal disorders. (For further influences see the various subjects in this section, and the references).

**Distentions**—(See Dropsy, Flatulence, Gas, Swellings, Tumors, Tympanites).

**Dropsy**—Of Abdomen—(See "Abdomen" under Dropsy).

**Dry Bellyache**—(See Belly).

**Enema; Enteritis**—(See "Inflammation" under Bowels).

**Flatulence; Fluxes; Gas in Abdomen**—(See Gas, Colic, Flatulence, Wind).

**Gripings; Hernia; Hypogastrium**—Disorders of—(See Hypogastrium).

**Ileac Passion; Intestines**—(See Bowels).

**Injuries**—To Abdomen—♄ or ♂ affl. in ♍; afflictions in ♍; ♂ affl. in ♍ in 6th H.

**Large Abdomen**—(See "Prominent" in this section).

**Lower Parts**—Of Abdomen—All Diseases In—Signified by the 6th H.

**Meteorism**—Distention by Gas—(See Gas).

**Muscles**—Of Abdomen—Disorders of—Spasm of—(See Muscles).

**Navel**—Disorders of—(See Navel).

**Neuralgia**—In Abdomen—(See Neuralgia).

**Obstructions In**—(See "Obstructions" under Bowels).

**Operations On**—Surgical—(See "Abdominal" under Operations).

**Pain In**—(See "Pain" under Bowels).

**Pancreas; Phthisis**—Of Abdomen—(See Phthisis).

**Prevalent**—Abdominal Diseases Prevalent—(See "Diseases" in this section).

**Prolapsus**—Of Abdomen—(See Prolapsus).

**Prominent Abdomen**—Large—Fullness of—The ☉ in ♋ or ♍, or ♋ or ♍ on the Asc. at B., and espec. in middle life; ♃ in the Asc.; ♋ on the Asc., and often due to over-eating; ♍ on Asc. at B. tends to a prominent abdomen in middle life; ♂ affl. in ♍. (See "Corpulent" under Middle Life. Also see Flatulence).

**Rickets; Ruptures**—(See Groins, Hernia, Rupture).

**Spasmodic Disorders**—(See Colic, Cramps, Gripings, Ileac Passion; "Abdominal" under Muscles).

**Swellings**—☽ affl. in ♍. (See Ascites, Flatulence, Gas, Tumors, Tympanites, Wind).

**Tumors**—(See "Abdomen" under Tumors).

**Tympanites; Umbilicus**—(See Navel).

**Ventral Hernia**—(See Hernia).

**Wind In**—(See "Wind" under Bowels).

**Wounds To**—♂ ♍.

**ABEYANCE**—Of Bodily Energies—Caused by the afflictions of ♄; ♄ affl. the ☉, ☽, Asc. or hyleg at B., and by dir.; ♄ ☌ ☉ or ☽ in 6th H. (See Coma, Energy, Inactive, Lethargy, Saturn, Suppressions; "Weak Body" under Weak).

**ABILITIES**—(See "Great Ability" under Great. See Inability).

**ABLATION**—Of Organs or Functions—(See Removal, Suppression).

**ABNORMAL**—Abnormalities—There are many abnormal conditions of Mind and Body, both congenital and acquired, which would be too numerous to list here. See the subject you have in mind in the alphabetical arrangement. Especially note the following subjects: Appetite, Appetites, Augmented, Births, Congenital, Cravings, Deformities, Desires, Defects, Deviations, Drink, Drug Habit, Dwarfed, Eye Balls, Fat, Food, Functions, Giants, Gluttony, Growth, Growths, Habits, Hermaphrodites, Hypertrophy, Idiocy, Increase, Insanity, Malformations, Mental, Mind, Monsters, Narcotics, Passions, Perverse, Perversions, Precocious, Prenatal, Premature, Sex, Stomach, Tall, Tastes, Thin, Unhealthy, Unnatural, etc.

**ABORTION** — Miscarriage — Premature Expulsion of a Foetus—The ♏ sign rules the womb, and afflictions in this sign, and espec. the malefics ♅ and ♂ in ♏ at B., and affl., tend to cause abortions. The afflictions of ♄ in ♏ also tend to, and to hinder and retard the growth of the foetus. Some women abort habitually at a certain stage of pregnancy, and are unable to carry a child thru to term when the ♏ sign is heavily afflicted by malefics at B. Abortion is more apt to occur at the regular monthly menstrual period under the ☽ influence at such times, working together with other malefic influences, transits and directions. Note the following planetary influences as causes of Abortion: If one of the Lights be in an aphetic place at conception, conjoined to a malefic, or in □ or ☍ to it, or if the ☉ or ☽ be in P. Dec. a malefic, there will be an abortion, the child dies in the womb, or dies soon after birth. Also, under these circumstances, if the Lights are in ☍ to ♄ and ♂ from angles, in exact or wider aspect, or if one or two malefics afflict either the ☉ or ☽ by an exact, or partile aspect, there will be an abortion. If the conditionary Luminary is applying to a malefic, and sepr. from a benefic, the child will be born alive, but live only a few hours, days or months, as there are °, ′, and ″ between the Luminary which is apheta, and the nearest malefic, but if the Luminary is sepr. from a malefic and applying to a benefic, the child will be sickly, but will do well and recover. (See Conception, Embryo, Foetus). The ☉ and ☽ in angles, and espec. in the 1st or 7th, or in the 6th H. in ☌ ♄, ♂, or ♀, liable to an abortion, and to have no children. (See Barren, Pregnancy); an eclipse of the ☉ or ☽ falling in ♏, and espec. when the ♏ sign contained the ☉, ☽, or malefics at B., or when ♏ was on an angle at B., or on the cusp of the 6th, 8th or 12th H.; ☽ in the 4th or 7th H. at B., and affl. by ♂; ♅ in ♏ at B., and affl., tends to cause a spasmodic action of the uterus, and expulsion of the fetus when the directions to H are evil during pregnancy; ♄ influence tends to abortive births, and especially when in ♏ at B., or afflicting the ♏ sign by asp., or planets in ♏; ♄ tends to cause contractions of the womb at inopportune and abnormal times during pregnancy, when in ♏ at B., and affl. by the directions of malefics; ♄ and ♀ in the 7th H, and ♂ elevated above them, tend to spontaneous abortion; ♄ or ♂ in the 5th H., and in □ or ☍ asp. the lord of the 5th; ♄ lord of the 8th, and with a barren sign on Asc., or cusp of the 5th; ♂ in an angle at B., occi. of the ☉, and ori. of the ☽; caused by ♂ when the dominion of death is vested in him; ♂ affl. in ♏; ♂ in the 6th H. in ♒ or ♏, and affl.; ♂ in ♏ and affl. the ☽ or Asc.; ☋ in 5th H. denotes abortion, and in the 1st H. in Hor'y Ques., great danger of it; a malefic in cazimi is a sign of abortion in a Hor'y Ques. (See "Premature Birth" under Premature).

**Cases**—Of Abortion. See Fig. 8J in "Astro-Diagnosis" by Mr. and Mrs. Max Heindel. Case of Death by Hemorrhage from Miscarriage—See "Death from Hemorrhage", No. 168, in 1001 N. N. Also see Cases of Premature Birth under Premature.

**Death from Abortion**—♂ occi. at B. in ♏, and affl. the hyleg by dir.; ♂ afflictions show, and espec. when ♂ is affl. the ♏ sign. Often results from operations on the womb when the ☽ is passing thru ♍, ♎, or ♏ signs. (See Stillborn).

**Death by Miscarriages**—Or at Parturition—The ☽ affl. at the birth of a child tends to death of the mother, or much trouble, and a bad time for the mother after confinement, and espec. if the ☽ is in the 4th or 8th H., and affl.; ♂ affl. the hyleg by dir.; caused by ♂ when the dominion of death is vested in him. (See "Death" under Hemorrhage, Miscarriage, Parturition).

**Premature Birth**—(See Premature).

**Seeks Abortions**—The ☉ ☌ ♅ in ♏; ☽ ☌ ♄ ♏; ♄ ☌ ♂ ♏.

**Subluxations**—Abortions are caused, and contributed to, by subluxations of the vertebrae at PP, the Private Place, the 2nd, 3rd and 4th Lumbar Vertebrae. (See Vertebrae).

**ABOVE THE EARTH**—Planets Above—(See Elevated).

**ABRASIONS**—Excoriations—A ♂ affliction Caused by ♂ in the 1st H. at B., making one more subject to accident or injury; ♄ in the 1st H.; ♄ or ♂ in the 1st or 7th H. at B., or by tr. or dir., and espec. when in ♋, ♑, or ♓; ♄ or ♂ in all signs ascribed to animals or fishes, and the malefics ori. of the ☉, and occi. of the ☽. Sugar of Lead (Lead Acetate) Solution is a good remedy locally to relieve the irritation or inflammation from an excoriation. (See Accidents, Hurts, Injuries, Wounds).

**ABROAD**—Foreign Lands—Benefits or Dangers In—

**Accidents Abroad**—Danger of Accidents, Death, Ill-Health, or Violence Abroad—A malefic planet ruler of the 9th H. at B.; malefics in the 9th H., and affl.; the hyleg in the 9th H., and affl. by the ☌ or evil asps. of malefics; one or more malefics in the 9th H., or in ☌ in the 9th at a Solar Rev., and the hyleg affl. by a train of evil directions; lord of the 9th in the 8th, danger of death Abroad; lord of the 8th in the 9th and in ☌ lord of the Asc.; lord of the 10th in the 9th; the 2nd dec. of ♐ on the Asc., ruled by the ☽; planets ruling the anaretic places being in the cadent houses, and espec. if the ☽ be in one of the anaretic places, or in ☌ or ☍ asp. to them; the ☉ or ☽ affl., and the ☽ or lord of the 1st be near violent fixed stars, or a malefic or violent stars ascending, danger of an untimely death Abroad; the ☽ sepr. from ♂ and applying to the ☉, indicates a violent death in a strange land if Abroad at the time; ♄ in the 12th H. at B., and affl., causes the danger of detention in out-of-the-way places Abroad, by accident; ♄ or ♂ in the 9th H., and affl.; malefics in the 9th H., and affl. the hyleg. (See Sea, Ships, Shipwreck, Travel, War. See "Sickness", and the various paragraphs in this section).

**Assassinated Abroad**—(See Assassination).

**Battle**—Death or Injury in Battle and War Abroad—♂ lord of the 8th, and in the 9th H.; ♂ affl. the significators denotes death in battles Abroad, or by pirates, fire, mutiny, massacre, or lightning. (See War).

**Death Abroad**—(See "Accidents", and the various paragraphs in this section). Case—Death Abroad at 40 years of age—(See "Ellis", No. 830, in 1001 N. N.).

**Detention Abroad**—From an Accident —(See "Accidents" in this section).

**Disaster Abroad**—May Meet With— (See "Accidents", "Sickness", and other paragraphs in this section).

**Distress Abroad**—(See "Sickness" and the various subjects in this section).

**Falls**—Suffers from Abroad — (See Heights).

**Fire—Suffers From**—Death By—(See "Battle" in this section).

**Foreign Travel**—Unfortunate In— Meets with Accident, Death, Falls, Injury, or Sickness In—(See the various paragraphs in this section). Also see Pirates, Sea, Ships, Shipwreck, Travel).

**Health**—Good Health Abroad—Ill-Health Abroad—The benefics in 9th H., and this house free from affliction,

tends to good health Abroad, and may make it advisable for the native to live Abroad, but malefics in the 9th tend to ill-health, and all kinds of misfortune, injury, ill-health, or death Abroad, and the native should remain in the land of birth. (See "Native Land" under Native; the various subjects under Travel).

**Ill-Health Abroad**—See "Accidents", "Health", "Sickness" in this section).

**Journeys Abroad**—Should Take— Should Avoid—(See "Health" in this section. Also see "Abroad" under Journeys; Travel).

**Lightning**—(See "Battle" in this section).

**Massacre**—Death In Abroad — (See "Battle" in this section).

**Mutiny**—Death in Abroad—(See "Battle" in this section).

**Native Land**—Should Remain In— Should Remove—(See "Native Land" under Native; "Place of Birth" under Place).

**Pirates**—(See "Battle" in this section. Also see Pirates).

**Residence Abroad**—(See Residence).

**Sickness Abroad**—Lord of the 6th in the 9th, or lord of the 9th in the 6th, sickness Abroad, or at Sea; lord of the 1st, or the ☽ in the 6th, 8th, or 12th, or if combust, peregrine, or ☌ or evil asp. a malefic, much sickness or distress Abroad; the 9th H., its lord, or the ☉ or ☽ affl., denotes sickness and disaster Abroad; ♄ afflicting the Sigs. of travel, or ♄ in 9th, ruler of 9th, or affl. lord of the 9th, sickness, or chronic ill-health Abroad. (See "Accidents", "Health" in this section).

**Soldiers**—Death or Injury Abroad in War—(See "Battle" in this section. Also see War).

**Suffering**—And Distress Abroad— (See "Accidents", "Sickness", and other paragraphs in this section).

**Travel Abroad**—(See "Health", "Native Land" in this section. Also see Travel).

**Untimely Death Abroad**—(See "Accidents" in this section).

**Violence**—Meets with Violence, or a Violent Death Abroad—The ☽ sepr. from ♂ and applying to the ☉, a violent death in a strange land, or meets with violence; ♂ affl. in 9th H.; ♂ ruler of the 8th, and in the 9th. (See "Accidents", "Battle", in this section. Also see War).

**War**—Death or Injury in Abroad— (See "Battle" in this section. Also see War).

**ABSCESSES**—Imposthumes—A Circumscribed Cavity Containing Pus—A disease of the ☽ and ♃; a disease of the ♋ sign, and caused by afflictions in ♋; due to corrupt blood; ♃ causes abscesses due to blood changes and accumulations of fluid in a part; ♃ in ♈; ♃ affl. in ♉, abscesses of the throat or neck, and over the body due to blood disorders; ♃ in ♏ and affl., and espec. when in 6th H.; caused by afflictions to the ☽ or ♃ at B., or by dir.; ♃ in signs which rule the arms, hands, legs and feet tends to abscesses in these parts; ♄ or ♂ in angles at B., occi. of the ☉, and ori. of the ☽, and ☿ in familiarity with ♂, the frequency and number of abscesses are increased; ♂ and ☿ holding dominion at B., in familiarity with each other, and with ♂ affl. the hyleg, and elevated above the Luminaries; ♀ affl. by malefics; abscesses are denoted by afflictions in or about the 25° of ♌ or ♒, or in the 21° of ♈ or ♎. See the following subjects in the alphabetical arrangement.

**Arms**—Abscesses In—♃ in signs ruling the arms. (See Arms).

**Aural Meatus**—Abscesses In—(See Ears).

**Back**—(See "Abscesses" under Back).

**Bladder**—(See "Abscess" under Bladder).

**Blood**—From Blood Disorders—From Impure Blood—(See "Impure Blood" under Impure).

**Body**—Abscesses Over the Body—♃ affl. in ♉.

**Boils**—(See Boils).

**Bowels**—(See "Abscess" under Bowels).

**Brain**—(See "Abscess" under Brain).

**Breasts**—(See "Abscess" under Breast).

**Carbuncles; Causes of Abscess**—(See the first part of this Article).

**Corrupt Blood**—Abscesses Caused By—(See "Impure Blood" under Impure).

**Ears**—(See "Abscess" under Ears).

**Enteritis**—With Abscess—(See "Inflammation" under Bowels).

**Feet**—Abscess In—♃ affl. in ♓. (See Feet).

**Frequency of**—(See the first part of this Article).

**Frontal Bone**—Abscess In—♆ in ♈, and espec. when affl. by the ☉, ♄, or ♂. (See Frontal).

**Generative Organs**—Abscess In—(See "Abscess" under Secrets).

**Hands**—Abscesses In—(See Hands).

**Impure Blood**—Abscesses Caused By—(See "Impure Blood" under Impure).

**Increased**—(See the first part of this Article).

**Kidneys**—(See "Abscess" under Kidneys).

**Liver**—(See "Abscess" under Liver).

**Loins**—(See "Abscess" under Loins).

**Mastoid; Neck**—Abscess In, and on the back of the Neck—(See Neck).

**Ovaries**—Abscess of—(See Ovaries).

**Pharynx; Phlegmonous** — Phlegmonous Enteritis with Abscess—(See "Inflammation" under Bowels).

**Privy Parts**—(See "Abscess" under Secrets).

**Pus; Pyaemia**—(See Septic).

**Pyonephrosis**—(See "Abscess" under Kidneys).

**Pyorrhoea; Reins; Retropharyngeal**—(See "Abscess" under Pharynx).

**Secrets; Septic; Sores; Stomach; Suppuration; Throat; Ulcers; Urethra; Vulva**—(See "Abscess" under these subjects).

**ABSENT PARTY**—These influences are especially to be noted in Hor'y Questions.

**Cuts To**—or Stabs—(See "Weapons" under Cuts).

**Danger**—Absent Party Has Been in Great Danger—Has Been Ill, But Will Recover—(See "Recovery" in this section).

**Dead**—Absent Party Is Dead—The ☉ and ☽ affl., and lord of the 8th affl. the Sig. also; the ☽ sepr. from the ☌ or evil asp. lord of the 8th, and without the assistance of any benefic ray that could save, he has been deceased for so many days or months as there are degrees between the signs; the Sig. affl., and lately in □ or ☍ asp. a malefic; the Sig. combust in the 8th H., or the ☉ be lord of the 8th; translation of light between the lord of the Asc. and lord of the 8th; lord of the 8th in the Asc., and lord of the Asc. in the 8th; lord of the 8th in the 4th, or lord of the 4th in the 8th, and espec. if the Sig. be affl. by evil asps., and malefic planets in angles, and the benefics cadent; lord of the Quesited's Asc. in the 4th or 8th, may be dead; Sig. of the party in the 12th, in □ or ☍ a malefic, or the ☉ or ☽ unfortunate in like manner; lord of the Asc. in the 4th in □ the ☽, the party is dead, or near great danger; an Infortune translating the light of the lord of the 8th to him is a symbol of death; lord of the 1st, or the ☽ in ☌ lord of the 8th in the 8th or 4th, he is dead, or if in the 6th, he will die; lord of the 1st, or the ☽ in the 8th, combust, or in the 4th, he is dead, or if in their fall or ℞, he is at the point of death; the Sigs. combust or ℞, and ☌ a malefic or lord of the 8th, indicate certain death, and that the absent party is dead. (See the various paragraphs in this section).

**Death**—Is at the Point of Death—(See "Dead" in this section).

**Feverish**—(See "Absent Party" under Fever).

**Good Health**—In Good Health—The ☉ in the 6th H.; the ☽ in good asp. lord of the Asc.; the ☽ in the 8th, or 12th, and not afflicted; ♃, ♀, or ☊ in the Asc.; ♃ or ♀ in good asp. the cusp of the 1st, or 6th; lord of the Asc. free from affl. by lord of the 8th; lord of the Asc. in dignity, and not affl. by ♄, ♂, or lord of the 6th; no malefics in the 6th; a benefic in the Asc., M. C., and the ☉ and ☽ well asp., and the lord of the Asc. in a good house.

**Great Evil**—Some Great Evil Has Overtaken the Absent Party—The Sig. combust in all Hor'y Q. of one absent.

**Mind**—Absent Minded—(See Mind).

**Near Death**—Has Been Near Death—Lord of the Asc. sepr. from lord of the 8th H.; lord of the 1st and 8th in ☌ in the 8th, or in ☍ from the 6th or 8th.

**Not Dead**—Absent Party Is Not Dead—The Sig. of the party strong, in a good house, and sepr. from a benefic.

**Prison**—Lord of the Asc., or ☽, sepr. from lord of the 12th, has been in prison, or great trouble; the Sig. of the party combust.

**Recovery**—(1) No Hope of—☽ Sig. applying to the ☌ or evil asp. lord of the 8th H., or in the 8th, and if no good asps. interfere, absent party will die. (See "Dead" in this section). (2) Will Soon Recover—If the ☽, or lord of the 1st sepr. from lord of the 6th or 8th, and the benefics give a good asp.

**Reported Dead**—But is Alive—If the lord of his Asc. be in the 9th, 10th or 11th houses, ♃ or ♀ lord of the Asc., and either in the Asc., and in no asp. to lord of the 8th.

**Sick**—(1) Has Lately Been Sick—Lord of the Asc. sepr. from the ill-asp. lord of the 6th; the ☽ sepr. from the □ or ☍ or ♄ or ♂. (2) Absent Party is Sick—Lords of the 1st and 8th in ☌ in the 8th, or in ☍ from the 6th or 8th. (See "Absent Party" under Fever).

**Will Die**—(See "Dead", "Recovery" in this section).

**ABSORPTION**—The Absorptive System—Absorbent Vessels—Ruled in general by ♃. The ☽ in ♉, ♊, and ♋ rules and affects the absorbent and lymphatic vessels of the Respiratory System, the throat and lungs, etc. (See Lymph, "Absorbent Vessels" under Moon).

**Chyle**—Abated Absorption of—(See Chyle).

**Tissues**—Absorption of—(See Tissues). (See Assimilation, Nutrition, Phagocytes, "Resolution of Tissues" under Resolution; Resolvent).

**ABUNDANCE**—Abundant—Plenty—Excessive—

**Blood**—Abundance of Blood in a Part—♂ in the sign ruling the part. (See Plethora, "Too Much Blood" under Blood; "Blood" under Head; "Blood Vessels" under Rupture).

**Energy**—(See "Abundance" under Energy).

**Hair**—(See "Abundance" under Hair).

**Health**—(See "Abundance" under Health).

**Heat**—(See "Abundant" under Heat).

**Humours**—(See "Abounding" under Humours; "Humours" under Moist).

**Moist Humours**—Abundance of—(See "Humours" under Moist).

**Superabundance**—(See Excess, Excesses, Increased, Overabundance, Plenty, Superabundance).

**Vitality**—Abundance of—(See "Good" under Vitality).

**ACCELERATION**—The work of ♂. (See Exaggerated, "Accelerated" under Motion; Rapid).

**ACCIDENTS**—Accident—Accidental—Casualties—Unexpected Events, etc.—This is a big subject, and there is perhaps more said along this line in the textbooks of Astrology than upon any other subject. The general planetary causes of accidents, their nature and kind, etc., will be given in the various paragraphs of this Article, and especially under the headings of "Causes", "Danger of", etc. From an Occult standpoint Accidents are not always considered as matters of chance, but may come, and do come, upon scheduled time, according to a prearranged plan of the Higher Powers and Hierarchies, or they may come upon a Nation or individual by a special decree, all which must be considered for the good of the individual, the Nation, or for the advancement and betterment of the Planet as a whole. Some star maps of birth show practical immunity from accidents, or violence, while others contain many influences which would lead to them, or a violent death. Every part and organ of the human body may be subject to a hurt, injury, or accident, according to the planetary positions and configuations at B., and the influences by direction, transit, or progression. Many of the subjects which have to do with Accidents are considered and also listed under the subjects of "Hurts", "Injuries", and these subjects should be studied and referred to along with the study of this Article. See the following subjects in the alphabetical arrangement when not considered here, and especially look for "Accidents", "Hurts", "Injuries", "Wounds", etc., under each subject.

**Abdomen; Aeroplanes; Amusements; Animals; Ankles; Arms; Bathing; Battle**—(See War).

**Beasts; Bites; Blindness; Blows; Bones**—(See Bones, Fractures).

**Breasts; Brother; Bruises; Buildings**—(See "Buildings" under Falls).

**Buried Alive**—(See Burial).

**Burns**—(See Burns, Fire, Heat, Scalds).

**Buttocks; Casualties**—(See "Death", and the various paragraphs in this section).

**Cattle; Causes of Accidents**—General Causes—Ptolemy held that planets oriental at B. indicate accidents, and planets occidental, disease, but this rule does not always hold good, as the opposite is often the case. Many planets in violent signs of the zodiac at B., and espec. in angles, indicate more danger of accidents. Accidents are to be judged from the planets which may happen to be exactly rising or setting at B., and those in configuration or aspect with the ☉ and ☽, or the ascending degree. The afflictions of the malefic planets to the ☉, ☽, Asc., M.C., or hyleg at B., and by dir., and espec. when these places were affl. at B. by malefics, are common causes of accidents. The ♐ sign on the Asc., 6th or 12th H. at B.; ruler of the 8th H. at B. in the 4th H. at a Solar Rev.; Fixed Stars of the nature of ♂ ascending at B. make one more or less liable to accidents along thru life under the evil directions of these stars, or of the malefic fixed stars, to the places of the ☉, ☽, Asc., or Hyleg; the violent fixed stars, as Antares, Betelguese, etc., tend to cause accidents by their afflictions to the planets at B., or by dir. (For further influences see the various subjects in this Article).

**Childbirth**—(See Parturition).

**Childhood**—(See "Accidents" under Childhood).

**Children; Clavicle; Concussions; Contusions**—(See Blows, Bruises, Falls).

**Cranium**—(See Skull).

**Crippled; Crushed; Cuts; Danger of Accidents**—Liable to—Tendency to—In judging of the danger of accidents, note the Asc., the cusp of the 6th H., and whether the malefics ♄ or ♂ afflict the Luminaries at B., or by dir. The following planetary aspects and influences tend to make the native more liable to accidents, be in greater danger of, and to have a more violent map, and with greater danger of death by violence, the result of an accident. The ☉ affl. by ♂ at B., or by dir.; the ☉ or ☽ to the ☌ or ill-asp. ♂ in the zodiac or mundane; the ☉ in fixed signs at B., and coming to the ☌ or ill-asp. ♂ by dir.; the ☉ to the ☌ or ill-asp. ♆, ♄, or ♅ by dir., and espec. when in the card. or fixed signs at B., or when the directions fall in this class of signs; the ☉ or ☽ rising at B., and affl. by the ☌ or ill-asps. of ♂, or other malefics; the ☉ or ☽ in the oriental Quadrants between the Asc. and M.C., or between the Desc. and Nadir, and affl. by the ☌ or ☍ of ♂, produces accidents; the ☉ or ☽ affl. in ori. Quarters; the ☉ ori., and affl. by the malefics at B., is apt under evil directions of the malefics to the ☉ to result in an injury causing death; the prog. ☉ to the □ or ☍ the radical ☽, and the parts of the body subject to injury are ruled by the signs containing the Luminaries; the pr. ☉ or ☽ to the ☌ or ill-asp. ♂ at B.; the ☽ in asp. to ♄ or ♂ by tr. or dir., or passing the ☌ of their place at B.; the same influences and directions that apply to the ☉ will also generally apply to the ☽; the ☽ to the ☌ or ill-asp. ♂ by dir., and ♂ affl. the ☽ at B.; a Lunation, as the New or Full ☽, falling on the place of any malefic at B, and espec. if there are also evil primary directions to the hyleg at the time; the ☽ at a Solar Rev. passing over the place of ♄ or ♂ at B.; the ☽ to the ☌ or P. asp. ☿ by dir., and the ☽ hyleg, and ☿ afflicted at B.; the ☽ to the ☌ P., or ill-asp. ♅ or ♂, and the ☽ hyleg at B.; the ☽ rising at B., and affl. by ♄ or ♂; the ☽ to the ☌ or ill-asp. ♄, ♅, or ♆ by dir., and the accident will be of the nature of the afflicting planet, and espec. if the ☽ be hyleg at B., or affl. by the malefic; the ☽ ☌ ♂ in the M.C. at B., and in evil asp. to Antares; the ☽ in any evil asp. to ♂ at B. predisposes to, and to bring the danger of accident when the ☽ is affl. by the adverse directions of ♂; the pr. ☽ to the ☌ or ill-asp. any of the malefics in the radical map; the ☽ ☌, □, or ☍ ♅, ♄, or ♂ at a Solar Rev.; ♆ passing the place of ♅ at B. by tr.; ♆ coming to the ☌ or ill-asp. ♂ by dir., danger of accident on the water, or shipwreck; ♆ in the 8th H. at B., afflicted, and afflicting the hyleg by dir.; ♆ in the 9th H. at a Solar Rev., and affl. by the lord of the 8th H. (For other ♆ influences tending to accidents, see Drowning, Journeys, Shipwreck, Travel); ♅ in ♏ or ♒ at B., and affl.; ♅ tends to cause accidents espec. by explosions or machinery; ♅ affl. at B., and coming to the evil asps. ♂ or the Asc. by dir., or to the ill-asps. his own place at B.; ♅ exactly rising at B., or within 1 or 2° of the ascending degree, and affl. by a malefic; ♅ ☌ or P. the ☉ at a Solar Rev.; ♅ ☌ ♄ in ♈, and espec. if ♅ be affl. by an evil asp. in the M.C., or in an angle; ♅ ☌ ♂ in angles; ♅ ☌ ☿ in ♊, ♍, ♎ or ♒; ♅ in the Asc., 3rd, 9th H., or M.C. at B., and affl., and the accident is usually in that part of the body ruled by the sign containing ♅ at B.; ♅ ☌ the Asc. by dir.; a tr. of ♅, ♄ or ♂ coming to an evil asp. the places of the pr. ☉ or ☽, and espec. if these places coincide with an evil dir.; ♅ or ♂ in ☌ or ☍ asp. at B., in card. signs, or angles; ♄ to the ☌ or evil asp. the Asc. by dir., and espec. if the Asc. is hyleg; ♄ ascending at B., and afflicted, or affl. the hyleg; ♄ exactly rising on the Asc. at B. tends to serious accidents from time to time; ♄ in the Asc. at B., and ill-asps. of the ☉ or ☽ to ♄ by dir.; transits of ♄ over the places of the pr. ☉ or ☽ or in evil asp. to them, and espec. if these aspects coincide with an evil dir.; ♄ ☌ or ☍ ♂ in angles and card. signs at B., and when affl. by evil directions; ♄ ☌ or evil asp. the ☉ in fixed signs; ♄ ☌ or ill-asp. the ☽, and the planets ori.; ♄ ruler of the Asc. at B., and in ill-asp. the benefics; ♄ in the M.C. at B., afflicted, and elevated above the Luminaries; the Periodic Dir. of ♄ to the radical ♂; ♂ afflictions, transits and progressions affl. the ☉, ☽, Asc., or M.C. at B., and espec. when ♂ afflicted any of these places at B., but not so dangerous when ♂ is in good asp. to them at B.; ♂ □ or ☍ the ☉ at B., and by dir.; ♂ elevated in the East, or in the Asc., and in ☌ or ill-asp. other malefics, or affl. the ☉ or ☽; ♂ ☌, □, or ☍ the Asc.; ♂ to the ☌ or ill-asp. the Asc. by dir. ♂ ☌ ☽ in the M.C. at B., and evilly aspected by Antares; ♂ in the Asc. at B., and affl. by the ill-asps. the ☉ or ☽ by dir.; ♂ ☌ or ill-asp. ♄ in angles or card. signs at B.; ♂ at a Solar Rev. passing the radical place of ♄ or ♅; ♂ ruler of the Asc. and afflicting the benefics at B. or by dir.; ♂ □ or ☍ the ☉ or ☽ at B.; ♂ afflicting the 1st or 10th houses at B., and by dir.; ♂ afflicted in ♈ or ♌; ♂ the ruling planet, or ruler of the Asc.; ♂ pr. in ☌ or ill-asp. the ☉, ☽, Asc., M.C., or any malefic planet; ♂ in the M.C. at B., and elevated above the ☉ and ☽; ♂ rising at B., and again at a Solar Rev.; ☿ affl. at B., and the ☽ to the ill-asp. ☿ by dir.; ☿ affl. by the malefics at B., liable to accidents under the evil directions of the malefics to ☿; the Asc. a fiery sign, and containing a malefic, and afflicted; the Asc. to the ☌ or ill-asp. the malefics by dir., and espec. if the Asc. is hyleg; a planet in the Asc. at B., and affl. by the ☌ or ill-asp. a malefic, and the injury is in the part of the body ruled by the sign ascending, or that occupied by the afflicting planet, and espec. if in a card. sign; ♐ on the Asc., or planets in ♐. (See the various subjects in this Article).

**Dangerous Accidents**—Serious Accidents or Injuries—The ☉ or ☽ to the ☌ or ill-asp. ♂ by dir., and espec. if ♂ affl. the ☉ or ☽ at B.; the ☉ ori. at B., and affl. by the malefics; the ☽ in the 8th H. at B., and affl. by ♅, ♄, or ♂; the ☽ in the obnoxious signs at B., as in ♈, ♉, ♎, ♏, or ♑, and in her Nodes, or in extreme Lat., and the malefics brought up to the Luminaries; ♄ to the ☌ or ill-asp. ♂ by dir.; ♄ exactly rising on the Asc. at B.; ♄ or ♂ ☌ the ☉, ☽, or Asc. by dir.; ♂ in the 8th H. at B., and badly aspected by the ☉ by dir.; transits of ♂ over the places of the ☉ or ☽ at B., or in ☍ to them; the Asc. to the ☌, P., or ill-asp. ♄ by dir., and ♄ ori. at B.; the Asc. to the ☌ or P. asp. ☿ and ☿ affl. at B.; malefics in angles at B., and the ☉ and ☽ in ☌ or ☍, brought up to them. (See Excrescences).

**Death by Accident**—Accidental Death—Casualties—Fatalities—Causes and Indications of an Accidental Death—The ☉ or ☽ affl. by malefics at B., or by dir., and with no assistance from the benefics; the ☉ and ☽ ori., and affl. by malefics, and espec. by ♄ or ♂; the ☉ and ☽ in evil asp. to ♂ at B., or by dir., and ♂ on the Asc. at B., and afflicted; the ☉ or ☽ to the ☌, P., or ill-asp. ♂ by tr. or dir., and espec. when ♂ afflicted the hyleg at B., or was in the 8th H., or in the Asc., or M.C.; the ☉ or ☽ in evil asp. to ♂ at B., or under the directions of ♂ to the ☉, ☽, or Asc.; the ☉ or ☽ to the ☌ or ill-asps. ♂ by dir., and ♂ affl. the ☉ or ☽ at B., or be in the Asc.; the ☉ or ☽ rising at B., and affl. by ♄ or ♂; the ☉, ☽, and other planets, in the Asc. at B. with Regulus; the ☉ or ☽ Sig., and coming to the ☌ or ill-asp. ♂ by dir.; the afflictions of ♆, the ruler of the water and the Sea, tend to accidental death by drowning. (See Drowning); the afflictions of ♅ tend to accidental death by bathing at home, in pools, or at the Sea Shore, and also death by machinery in the employment, by electricity, lightning, explosions, and sudden and unexpected death. (See these subjects); ♅ in the 8th H. at B., and afflicted, or affl. the hyleg; ♄ causes an accidental death by falls, bruises, contusions, fractures, dislocations, crushes, suffocation, fall of buildings, buried alive by landslides, falls from heights or precipices; trampled by mobs, cattle or animals, strangulation, etc. (See these subjects); ♄ ☌ the Asc. by dir. when ♄ is not ruler of the Asc.; ♄ rising at B., and to the ☌ the Asc. by dir.; ♄ and ♂ both affl. the ☉ or ☽ at B., or by dir.; ♄ in the 8th H. at B., and afflicted, or affl. the hyleg at B., or by dir.; directions of ♄ falling in the 8th H., and affl. the hyleg; ♃ Sig. ☌ ♂, and ♂ ill-dignified; ♂ causes accidental death by burns, cuts, bites, stabs, assassination, loss of blood, murder, kicks, injuries, wounds, gun-shot, fury, madness, scalds, in War, by operations, knife-wounds, by iron, sharp instruments, fire-arms, fractures, abortions, miscarriages, childbirth, mob-violence, on railroads, in vehicles, etc. (See these subjects); ♂ in the 8th H. at B., and afflicted, or affl. the hyleg by dir.; evil directions of ♂ falling in the 8th H., and affl. the hyleg; ♂ to the ☌ or ill-asps. the ☉, ☽, Asc., or hyleg by dir; ♂ rising at B., and to the ☌ of the Asc. by dir.; ♂ and ♄ both affl. the ☉ or ☽ at B., or by dir.; ♂ Sig., and ill-dig. at B., and to the ☌ the ☉, ☽, Asc., or hyleg by dir.; ♂ in particular predisposes to accidental death, and espec. by violence, and ♂ in the 8th H. at B. indicates a sudden and violent death, and by some accident. In Hor'y Questions, ♂ in the 8th H., and ruler of the 8th, or affl. the ruler of the 8th, or the cusp of the 8th., or malefic planets in the 8th, indicate an accidental death, and usually by violence of some kind; ☿ when ori., and affl. the hyleg in a train of fatal directions, the accident and the death will be of the nature of the planet with which ☿ is in asp.; many planets in violent signs at B.; a strong 6th H., and the hyleg affl. by malefics; lord of the 8th a malefic, and in the 8th, and affl. by lord of the 6th or 12th, and espec. if the lord of the Asc. and the hyleg be affl. at the same time; the 14° ♍ on the Asc.; the 28° ♐ on the Asc. at B. (For further influences along this line, note carefully each subject in this section and Article).

**Deformities; Directions**—(See Directions, Events).

**Dislocations; Distortions; Drowning; Earthquakes; Electricity; Employment; Escapes**—Narrow and Hair-breadth Escapes from Accidents, Injuries, or an Accidental Death—These are always brought about by the intervention of the benefic planets ♃ and ♀ taking part in the configuration and directions, and espec. if these planets were strong, dignified, well-aspected and placed at B., and in good asp. to the ☉, ☽, Asc., M.C., or the hyleg; ♃ and ♀ ori., in angles, and elevated above the malefics. (See "Victims" in this section. Also see Rescue).

**Events**—(See Directions, Events).

**Excrescences; Explosions; Extraordinary Accidents**—Sudden, Peculiar, and Unusual Accidents—These are caused by the afflictions of ♅, as his influence is sudden, unexpected, and acts in a peculiar, singular, strange, and unusual way. The following aspects and influences, in which ♅ takes part, are said to cause this class of accidents,—♅ affl. at B., and in ☌, P., or evil asp. the ☉, ☽, Asc., M.C., or the hyleg; ♅ in the 8th H. at B., and affl. the hyleg at B., and by dir.; ♅ in the 8th H. at the Solar Ingress of the ☉ into ♈, and affl. the ☽ or planet ascending; the ☉ hyleg, and with ♅ in the 8th H. and Anareta, and the ☉ to the ☌, P., or evil asp. ♅ by dir.; the ☽ to the ☌ or evil asp. ♅ by dir.; ♂ to the ☌ or ill-asp. the radical ♅ by dir., or vice versa. These same influences may also cause a sudden, peculiar, singular, unusual and extraordinary death, as many accidents caused by ♅ prove fatal. (See Extraordinary, Peculiar, Strange, Sudden, Unusual, etc.). Case—Of an Extraordinary Accident—See "Extraordinary", No. 192, in 1001 N.N.

**Extremities; Face; Falls; Fatal Accident**—Case—See "Fatal", No. 346, in 1001 N.N. (See "Death", and the various subjects and paragraphs in this section).

**Father; Feet; Females; Femur; Fire; Fire Arms**—(See Gunshot); **Floods; Foetus; Fractures; Fury; Genitals**—(See "Mens' Genitals" under Genitals).

**Groins**—(See "Injuries" under Groins).

**Gunshot; Hands; Haunches; Head; Heat; Hemorrhage**—(See "Lesions" under Hemorrhage).

**Hips; Horary Questions**—In Hor'y Questions, if the ☽, lord of the Asc., or the Asc., be applying to the ☌, P., or any ill-asp. of the malefics, and espec. to ♄ or ♂, there is danger of an accident just ahead, and espec. if the ☽ or lord of the 1st be in ♉ or ♌, unless great care and caution are used, and dangers avoided. In Hor'y Questions, if the ☽ or lord of the Asc. are separating from the ☌, or ill-asp. of a malefic, and applying to the ☌ or good asp. of a benefic, there is little danger of an accident in the near future, or on a journey contemplated. The Asc. and the ☽ have affinity in denoting the accidents of life, and become the Significators of such events. (See Horary).

**Horses**—(See "Hurts By" under Horses. Also see Bites, Kicks).

**Houses**—(See "Buildings" under Falls).

**Human Hands**—(See "Hand of Man" under Man).

**Hurts**—(See "Violent" in this section. Also see Hurts).

**Husband; Illness**—Illness and Disease from Accidents—Sickness and Illness may result from accidents caused by ♅, where there was great shock to the nervous system, as ♅ by his afflictions tends to greatly weaken the nervous system, and to cause collapse. ♅ strongly afflicting the ☉, ☽, Asc., or hyleg at B., and by dir.

**Injuries**—By Accidents—(See Hurts, Injuries. Also see "Violent", and the various subjects in this Article).

**Intestines**—See "Injuries" under Bowels).

**Inventions**—(See Employment, Machinery).

**Iron; Jaws; Joints; Journeys; Kicks; Killed; Kind of Accidents**—(See "Nature Of" in this section).

**Knees; Knife Wounds**—(See Cuts, Instruments, Stabs).

**Lacerations; Lameness; Landslides**—(See ♄ influences under "Death" in this section. Also see Crushed).

**Left Side of Body**—(See Left).

**Less Liable**—To Accidents—Born under the Airy Signs ♊, ♎, ♒, also known as the whole signs, and with these signs upon the Asc. at B., or with the ☉ well-aspected in these signs. These signs when strong at B., tend to keep the body more intact, and to be free from accidents, injuries, or mutilations.

**Liable to Accidents**—Hurts and Injuries—(See "Danger of" in this section. Also see "Liable to" under Hurts; "Tendency to" under Injuries).

**Lightning; Limbs; Machinery; Madness; Maimed; Males; Mangled; Marriage Partner; Mines; Miscarriage; Mobs; Mother; Murder; Mutilated; Narrow Escapes**—(See "Escapes" in this section).

**Nature of Accidents**—Kind of—The planets each have a specific nature of their own, and tend to produce accidents or injuries after their nature, and to injure the part, or parts of the body, ruled by the Signs or Houses in which they were posited at B., or in which they may be by tr., dir., or progression. The afflictions of ♆ tend to accidents by water, drowning, shipwreck, etc. The accidents of ♅ are sudden, extraordinary, or unusual, such as by lightning, electricity, inventions, machinery, explosions, at bathings, on railroads, and in connection with the employment. Saturn governs accidents by falls, bruises, contusions, crushes, buried alive, fall of buildings, suffocation, etc. Mars rules accidents by cuts, stabs, loss of blood, wounds, burns, scalds, injuries in quarrels, and where violence is present in some form. The ☉, ☽, ♀, and ☿ are passive, and do not usually act as the cause of accidents unless they are afflicted by one or more malefics, or are united with them in common action. (See the Introduction under "Hurts". Also see each of the planets in the alphabetical arrangement as to their special influences).

**Operations**—Danger of Accidental Death From—Caused by ♂. (See "Dangerous" in this section. Also see Operations).

**Painful Accidents**—Caused especially by ♂, and when this planet enters into the configuration, and with loss of blood, violence, etc. (See Pain).

**Paralysis**—Resulting from Accident—(See "Blows", "Injuries", and other subjects under Paralysis).

**Parents; Parts of Body**—Liable to Accident and Injury—These are known by the Sign and House containing the malefics at B., and the malefic afflicting planets by dir. The ☉ or ☽ rising at B., and affl. by the ☌ or ill-asp. ♂, or other malefics, tend to injury in those parts of the body ruled by the sign containing the Lights, or the afflicting planets. The first 10° of a sign show the upper part of an organ afflicted. The middle 10°, the middle part of an organ, or region, and the last 10°, the lower part of the organ, or part. If ♂ be in the 3rd H., it shows injury to the left side of a male, or to the right side of a female. For accidents to the various parts of the body, see the part, or organ, in the alphabetical arrangement. (See Decanates, "Left Side" under Left; Lower, Middle, "Parts of the Body" under Parts; "Right Side" under Right; Upper).

**Parturition; Peculiar**—(See "Extraordinary" in this section).

**Pirates; Pleasure; Poison; Precipices**—(See Heights).

**Precipitate; Predisposes**—To Accidents—(See "Danger" in this section).

**Prevalent; Public; Quadrupeds; Quarrels; Railroads; Rash Acts**—(See Rashness); **Relatives; Reptiles; Ribs; Right Side**—Of Body—(See Right).

**Scalds; Sea; Serious**—(See "Dangerous" in this section).

**Serpents; Ships; Shipwreck; Shocks; Shoulders; Sickness**—(See "Illness" in this section).

**Sister; Skull; Spine; Sports; Stabs; Steel**—(See Iron); **Stings; Storms; Strange; Strangulation; Sudden; Suffocation; Suicide; Sunstroke; Surgical Operations**—(See Operations).

**Sword; Teeth; Tendency To**—(See "Danger" in this section).

**Testes; Thieves** —(See Highwaymen, Robbers, Thieves).

**Thighs; Time of Accidents**—The Asc. and the ☽ have affinity in denoting the accidents of life, and become Significators, and directions to the ☽ and Asc. espec. show the times of possible accidents. Accidents are indicated by directions, and espec. when the directions are formed in the Ori. Quarters of the heavens, as between the 1st and 10th houses, and the 7th and 4th, and affl. the ☉, ☽, Asc., M.C., or hyleg at B. Accidents, injuries, or illnesses usually occur when the ☉ or ☽ are transiting the places of the four malefics at B., and espec. ♄ and ♂, or when ♄ and ♂, and other malefics, are on the places of the radical ☉, ☽, or Asc., or in evil asp. to them, and at these times more care and caution are necessary, espec. if the hyleg was afflicted at the previous New or Full ☽. Fixed stars of the nature of ♂, when ascending at B., make one more liable to accidents at the times when they form evil asps. to the ☉, ☽, Asc., M.C., or hyleg in the radical map by dir. (See Directions, Events, "New Moon" under Moon; Time; "Hurts" under Travel).

**Tornadoes**—(See Wind).

**Trampled; Travel; Treachery; Uncommon**—(See "Extraordinary" in this section).

**Unexpected**—(See Sudden, Unexpected).

**Untimely; Unusual**—(See Extraordinary, Peculiar, Uncommon, Mysterious).

**Vehicles; Victims**—Of Accidents—The victims of accidents, and those who suffer death, or great injury from them, are those who have ♃ and ♀ weak at B., affl. the hyleg, or some vital place in the map, and also at the same time are under evil directions or transits of the malefics to the hyleg, and with no assistance from the benefics in the configurations. (See Escapes. Also see "Escapes" in this section).

**Violent Accidents**—Hurts, Injuries, or Death, by Violence—The ☉ and ☽ are the positive, heat-producing, and electric planets, and afflictions to them by directions, transits, or progressions, are more apt to result in accidents accompanied by hurts, injuries, violence, loss of blood, fractures, wounds, etc. People who are born under the strong influence of ♂, or who have ♂ badly affl. at B., are more subject to violent accidents. Strong ♅, ♄, and ♂ afflictions to the ☉, ☽, Asc., or hyleg at B., and by dir., and with little or no help from the benefics; the ruler of the Asc. a malefic, and evilly aspected by malefics; malefics in the 6th, 8th, or 12th houses at B., and afflicting the ☉, ☽, Asc., or hyleg. (See Hurts, Injuries; "Death" under Violent).

**Volcanoes; Voyages** — (See Abroad, Sea, Ships, Shipwreck, Voyages).

**War; Water; Weapons; Wife; Wild Animals**—(See Wild). **Wind; Women; Wounds.**

**ACCOMMODATION**—The Focus of the Eyes—Defects and Errors of Accommodation are ruled by the ☽, and are considered ☽ diseases. For the various errors, and disorders of Accommodation, see Astigmatism, Eyes, Hyperopia (Far-sighted); Mydriasis, Myopia (Near-sight); Presbyopia (Old Age Vision); Sight, Vision.

**ACCUMULATIVE**—♄ exercises a strong influence for the accumulation of wastes in the body, and the retention of waste matter which should be thrown off, and to accumulate the poisons of the body in the various tissues and organs, which wastes and deposits tend to hardening, suppressions, etc. (See Crystallization, Elimination, Hardening, Obesity, Retention, Saturn, Stoppages, Suppressions, Tumors, Wastes). ♃ tends to accumulate fluids in localized parts of the body, and in the blood vessels, causing Apoplexy, bursting of blood vessels, swellings, tumors, abscesses, etc. (See these subjects). The ☽ also has an accumulating tendency of the fluids to circumscribed parts of the body, when affl. at B., or by dir. (See Congestion, Fluids, Functions, Oedema).

**ACEPHALOCYSTS**—Taenia Echinococcus—The Bladder Worm—A ♀ disease. ♀ affl. in ♏. (See Worms).

**ACHES**—Lingering Pains—Chronic Pains—Continuous, or Throbbing Pains —The ♄ influence is the principal cause of slow, continued, and throbbing aches and pains, while ♂ tends to the more sharp and acute pains of brief duration. See the following subjects in the alphabetical arrangement.

**Backache**—(See Back).

**Bellyache**—(See Belly).

**Body Suffers**—From Aches and Pains —The ☽ to the ☌ or ill-asps. ♄ by dir.; ♄ rising at B., afflicted, or affl. the hyleg at B., or by dir.; ♄ to the ☌ or ill-asp. the ☉ or ☽ by dir.; ♄ tends to retard and stop the functions of the body, cause retention of the wastes and excretions, and the deposit of Uric Acid over the body, which tends to general Malaise and depression. (See Deposits, Excretion, Malaise, Uric Acid, etc.).

**Earache**—(See Ears).

**Feet**—Aches In—(See Feet).

**Headaches; Heavy Aches**—And Pains —All heavy and dull aches and pains are ruled by ♄, and caused by his afflictions to the ☉, ☽, Asc., or hyleg at B., or by dir. (See "Pains" under Dull).

**Hips and Thighs**—(See "Aches" under Hips).

**Legs**—(See "Aches" under Legs).

**Pains and Aches**—(See "Heavy" in this section).

**Parts of Body**—Afflicted by Aches—(See the various subjects in this Article).

**Stomachache**—(See "Ache" under Stomach).

**Thighs**—(See "Hips" in this section).

**Throbbing Aches**—♄ influence. (See Throbbing).

**Toothache**—(See Teeth).

**ACHILLES TENDON**—Contraction of is caused by ♄ affl. in ♒, and often resulting in Club Feet. (See "Club Feet" under Feet).

**ACHONDROPLASIA**—(See Cartilage).

**ACIDS**—Acid—Acidity—Sodium Phosphate, the Salt ruled by the ♎ Sign, is said to be connected with the Acids of the body. Acids are said to be under the rule of the negative Signs of the Zodiac, and the negative planets, and remedies to produce more acidity in the system are ruled by the negative planets, the ☽, ♆, ♄, ♀. A predominance of the planets in the negative signs at B. tends to an over-production of the acids of the body, while the positive signs tend to too much alkalinity. Also the negative planets prevailing at B., and afflicted, tend to acidity, and in those parts of the body ruled by the signs containing them at B., and the afflicting planets. For Acids not listed here look for the subject in the alphabetical arrangement.

**Gastric Acidity**—Acidity in the Stomach—♆, ♄, ♀ or the ☽ in ♈, ♒ or ♑ at B., and afflicted. (See Gastric, Juices, Stomach).

**Hot Acids**—The ♂ influence in and over the body, and over acids in general, corresponds to hot acids, and to burning astringents, pungent odors, etc. (See Pungent).

**Hydrochloric Acid**—(See Hydrochloric, Digestion, Stomach).

**Hydrocyanic Acid**—(See Hydrocyanic).

**Signs**—Acid Signs—(See the first part of this Article).

**Stomach**—Acidity of—(See "Gastric" in this section. Also see "Over-acidity", "Hydrochloric" under Stomach).

**Urine**—Acidity of—The ♏ sign rules the Urine, and the negative planets in ♏, and affl. at B., or by dir., and espec. ♄ in ♏, tend to acid urine. (See Alkaline, Impure, Positive, Negative).

**ACNE**—Inflammation of the Sebaceous Glands from Retained Secretion—A ☉ and ♈ disease; ☉ affl. in ♈; ☉ □ or ☍ ☽ or Asc. at B., or by dir.; ♂ affl. in ♉ tends to Acne Rosacea, or chronic congestion of the skin of the face; afflictions in the cardinal signs, as such signs denote the skin; ♄ affl. in ♈ or ♉, as ♄ tends to retention, and disordered functions of the glands of the skin of the face. Caused by subluxations at M. C. P., the 3rd, 4th and 5th Cervical vertebrae, and by afflictions in ♈ and ♉, the signs which influence these vertebrae. This disease is also contributed to by disturbed kidneys, and Subs at KP, Kidney Place. (See Pimples, Sebaceous, Skin, Vertebrae).

**ACONITE**—A ♄ remedy, and ruled by ♄, and is opposed to ♂ and ♂ diseases. Is antipyretic, diuretic, and a cardiac sedative. Aconitum Napellus is one of the 12 typical Polycrest Remedies, and corresponds to the ♈ sign. (See "Polycrest" under Zodiac).

**ACQUAINTANCES**—The ☽ and ☿ rule Acquaintances.

**Death of**—An Acquaintance—The ☽ to the place of Cor Scorpio by dir. (See Execrated, Friends).

**ACQUIRED DISEASES**—Those which arise after birth. Ruled by the ☽. Indicated by the condition of the ☽ at B., and her evil aspects. The ☽ is functional, while the ☉ is organic and constitutional. The ☽ denotes the acquired diseases and tendencies arising from external causes, as environment, climate, food, habits, clothing, etc. Acute diseases, and those of short duration, are generally acquired, while the chronic and lasting diseases result from organic and inherent weaknesses and defects, and the fundamental inability of an organ, or the constitution, to recover from the evil effects of an acute disease, shock or injury. (See Acute, Chronic, Congenital, Constitution, Consumption, Deformities, Environment, External, Functions, Heredity, Inherent, Organic, Structural, Susceptibility, Tendencies, etc.).

**ACROMEGALY**—(See "Enlargement" under Extremities).

**ACTINIUM**—A metal of H. Commercialized Zinc is obtained from it.

**ACTION**—Mars is the planet of action, of insistent action, and of dynamic energy. All of the planets, however, have their definite and specific modes of action in and over the mind and body, for good or ill, according to the aspects and influences at B., and by their transits, directions, and progressions. (See "Desire Body" under Desire).

**Accelerated Action**—♂ influence. (See Fever, Inflammation, Motion, Quick, Rapid).

**Automatic Action**—(See Automatic).

**Coordinated Action**—(See Coordination).

**Cramped Action**—(See "Action" under Cramps).

**Disturbed Action**—In Mind and Body—(See Disturbed, Disease, Erratic, Exaggerated, Incoordination, Irritable, Irritations, Mental, Mind, Motion, Movement, Rapid, Spasmodic, Slow, Walk, etc.).

**Dull**—(See Dull).

**Erratic Action**—(See Erratic, Incoordination, Jerky, Spasmodic, Tics, Walk).

**Eruptive Action**—(See Eruptions).

**Exaggerated Action**—(See Exaggerated).

**Feeble Action**—(See Feeble, Debility).

**Feverish Action**—(See Fever).

**Full of Action**—(See "Active Body", "Active Mind", under Active; Cardinal, Dynamic, Energy, Quick, Positive).

**Hyperkinetic Action**—(See Hyperkinesia, Muscles).

**Incoordinated**—(See Incoordination).

**Inflammatory**—(See Inflammation).

**Lack of Action**—(See Dull, Feeble, Inactive, Inertia, Languor, Lassitude, Lethargy, Listless, "Weak Body" under Weak, etc.).

**Limp Action**—Uncertain Action—(See Limp).

**Mind—Action Of**—(See the various headings in this section. Also see "Active Mind" under Active; Clogging, Clouded, Dull, Diseases and Disturbances of the Mind under Mental, Mind).

**Perverted Action**—(See Perversions).

**Planets—Action Of**—(See Benefics, Malefics, Planets, and each planet in the alphabetical arrangement).

**Precipitate Action**—(See Precipitate).

**Quick in Action**—(See "Active Body" under Active; Gait, Quick, Walk).

**Rash in Action**—(See Rashness).

**Reflex Action**—(See Reflected).

**Retarded Action**—(See Retarded).

**Slow Action**—(See Clumsiness, Retarded, Slow).

**Spasmodic Action**—(See Spasmodic).

**Tonic Action**—(See Tonic).

**Uncertain Action**—(See Limp).

**Walk**—(See the subjects under Gait, Walk).

**Weak Action**—(See Feeble, "Weak Body" under Weak).

**Weakest Action**—♋ or ♓ on Asc. at B., or many planets in watery signs, and espec. in ♋ or ♓. (For other kinds of action see the subject in the alphabetical arrangement).

**ACTIVE**—Activity—

**Active Body**—Sthenic—Active and Strong Body—Physical Activity Increased—Active Appearance—The fiery signs upon the Asc. at B., and many planets in fiery or airy signs, and rising or elevated at B.; ♐ on Asc. at B., active body, and with great desire for sports, out-door life, and athletics; the 3rd face of ♐ on Asc., an unusually active body; ♊ upon the Asc., strong and active body; cardinal signs upon the angles, or many planets in cardinal signs, and espec. rising or in angles, as the cardinal signs relate to physical activity; ☉ well-asp. in ♐; ☉ or ☽ to the good asps. ♂ by dir., and ♂ in good asp. to these bodies at B.; ☿ strong at B., and well-asp. by ♂; ☿ in ⚹ or △ the Asc., active, and with quick action and movement; ☿ Sig. in ♑, active body, yet feeble and sickly. Many of the influences which tend to give an active body also produce a strong body. (See Brisk, Cardinal, Energy, "Energetic" under Gait; Exertion, Motion, Movement; "Strength" under Muscles; "Activity" under Physical; Quick, Sthenic, "Strong Body" under Strong; "Good" under Vitality; Walk).

**Active Mind**—Active Disposition—Active Nature—☿ is the principal ruler of the mind, and this planet when well-asp. by ♂, or in his own signs, as in ♊ or ♍, or when in the Asc., rising in the East, and well-asp. by the ☽ and ♂, tends to give an active mind; ☿ rising before the ☉; ☿ ☌ or good asp. the ☽, and free from ♄ affliction; ☿ to the good asps. ♂ by dir.; ☿ in ♊, ♍, or ♐, in good asp to ♃, and espec. if in ☌ or P. asp. to ♃; ☿ Sig. in ♑, an active mind, but the body may be feeble thru worry; the ☉ or ☽ ☌ ♂ at B., or by dir.; the ☉ well-asp. in ♐; the ☉ in a fiery sign at B.; the ☽ ☌ or good asp. ♂ or ☿ at B., or by dir.; ♆ in the 3rd H. at B., and well-asp. tends to enhance the mental faculties; ♅ or ♂ in ♊ or ♍, and well-asp.; ♅ in ⚹ to ♃ and ☿, and ☿ in ⚹ or △ to ♂ at the same time; ♄ infl. and affliction tends to restrain the mind, or limit the action of the brain cells, and make the mind less active in manifestation; ♂ in ♈, ♌, or ♑ at B., well-aspected and placed in the map; ♂ rising at B.; ♂ strong at B., rising, and ruler; ♂ ☌ ☿ at B., except when in ♓; ♂ to the good asps. ☿ by dir.; ♂ ☌ the ☉ or ☽ at B.; ♂ in ♊, ♍, or ♐ at B., and well-asp.; fiery signs on the Asc. at B.; the airy signs strong, prominent, and well-occupied and placed at B., and espec. if there be one or more planets in fiery signs; ♏ on the Asc., this being the sign of ♂; lords of the nativity in S. Lat. at B., more active than when in N. Lat. Temperate climates, with alternate heat and cold produce an active mind. (See "Mental Energy" under Energy; "Quickened" under Mental).

**Degree of Activity**—The degree of activity in the mind and body depend largely upon the planetary positions and aspects at B., and by progression, direction, or transit. Planets rising at B., or rising and elevated, dignified, and strongly fortified by sign and aspect, tend to give greater activity of mind and body, while planets setting, below the western horizon, in weak signs, and badly aspected, tend to give less activity. The positions and aspects of the planets at B. may give too much activity, or too little, and there are very few people who are perfectly balanced in mind and body, and who do not tend to extremes in some way.

**Energy**—(See the various paragraphs under Energy).

**Hyperactivity**—(See this subject).

**Mind**—(See "Active Mind", "Over-Active Mind", in this section).

**Muscular Activity**—(See Muscles).

**Over-Active Mind**—Effervescent Mental Activity—Bubbling Over—The ☽ and ♂ influences when combined tend to produce, and to spend their force, by the display of temper, anger, excess of feeling, emotion, and result in the dissipation and dispersion of the brain and nerve force; ♅ in ♈ or ♊, and afflicted, and aspec. if ☿ is aspected by ♂ at the same time; ♂ in ♈; ☿ in ♈ ☌ ♂; ☿ in the 6th H. at B., and affl., and espec. ☿ in ♍ in the 6th, which tends to undermine the health also. (See Effervescent).

**Perverted Activity**—(See "Activity" under Perversions).

**Qualities**—Heat and Cold are active qualities, while dryness and moisture are passive qualities. (See Cold, Dryness, Heat, Moisture).

**Sources of Activity**—The ☉ and ♂ are the greatest sources of activity and energy in our Solar System, both being of a fiery nature, and having great affinity for each other. The Solar Forces are reflected upon us by ♂, to produce greater activity, and if it were not for the strong ♂ force over us there would be very little activity in the world. The ☉ and ♂ when combined in their action at birth, as the ☉ ☌ ♂ in ♈, the exalted sign of the ☉, and the sign of ♂, tend to give great activity, strong vitality, and espec. if ♈ also be on the Asc. (See Dynamic, Mars, Over-Activity, Sun).

**Zest**—(See Zest).

**ACUTE**—Acute Diseases—Acute Fevers—Short Diseases—Acquired Ailments, etc.—Diseases beginning in Summer tend to be acute, and shorter than those which begin in Winter. Acute diseases begin from the surface, and from disturbances of the Peripheral Nerves, and work toward the center, and remedies to combat acute diseases should be those which will act upon these nerves. (See Centrifugal). In chronic diseases, the cause is from within, and working outward, and caused by irritations to the ganglionic centers, and usually brought on by ♄ influence, by chilling of the surface, driving the blood inwards. (See Centripetal). Acute diseases are usually brought on by ♂ in an effort to burn up the surplus of wastes and poisons in the system, in an effort to restore the balance in the body, and to maintain normal health conditions, and are usually accompanied by a fever or inflammation. An acute disease may attack any part of the body, and instead of listing every acute disease in this Article, will ask you to see in the alphabetical arrangement the disease you have in mind if it is not listed here. Note the following general subjects concerning Acute Diseases and conditions.

**Causes**—General Causes of Acute Diseases—The ☉, ♃, and ♂ tend to cause acute diseases, and ♂ the acutest of all; the ☉ hyleg at B., and afflicted, and the ☉ to the ☌ or evil asps. the Asc. or ♂ by dir.; the ☉ affl. in ♌ or ♐ at B., and by transits and directions, as acute fevers are a ☉ disease, as well as diseases of ♃ and ♂; the ☉ to the ☌ or P. Dec. the Ascelli by dir. (See "Sun Diseases" under Sun); the ☽ to the ill-asps. the ☉ or ♂ by dir.; the ☽ □ or ☍ the Asc.; the ☽ in ♊, ♐, or ♓, and affl. by the ☉ or ♂ when taken ill; the ☽ in ♒ when taken ill, affl. by the ☉ or ♂, and the ☽ slow in motion and decreasing in light; ♅ causes sudden and short illnesses of an acute nature, and espec. when in the 6th H. at B., and afflicted. (See "Sudden Illnesses" under Sudden); ♃ causes acute diseases from indiscretions in eating and drink, and by cor-

rupt blood, too much blood, plethora, surfeits, etc. (See "Jupiter Diseases" under Jupiter); ♂ and the ☉ in fiery signs at B., and affl.; ♂ and the ☉ are fiery, electric, positive and heat-producing planets, and are great factors in causing fevers and acute diseases by their afflictions, or afflictions to them; an evil ♂ transit afflicting his place at B., or passing thru the birthsign, or affl. the place of the ☉, ☽, Asc., or hyleg at B. by his ☌ or ill asps.; ♂ to the ☌ or ill-asp. the ☉, ☽, or Asc. by dir.; ♂ occi. at B., and affl. the hyleg by dir.; ♂ in the 8th H. at a Solar Ingress of the ☉ into ♈, and affl. the ☽, or the planet ascending; ♂ in the Asc. at an illness causes the disease to be swift, acute and violent; ♂ in the 8th H. at B., affl. the ☉, ☽, Asc., or hyleg, or in the 8th H. by tr. or dir. at the time of the illness, ruler of the 8th, or affl. the cusp of the 8th, acute and violent sickness, and with danger of death; the Asc. to the ☌ or ill asps. ♂ by dir., and ♂ in a fiery or airy sign at B.; the Asc. to the ill-asps. the ☉ by dir., and the ☉ affl. at B.; fiery signs upon the Asc. at B., or the cusp of the 6th H., and espec. when containing the ☉ and ♂, and afflicted; many planets in fiery signs at B.; afflictions in ♌, the sign of the ☉; a ♌ disease; ♌ on the Asc. at B., or the cusp of 6th H., and containing the ☉ or ♂, and afflicted; afflictions from cardinal signs, and such diseases are usually of short duration, run their course rapidly, and leave no bad after effects unless they run into a chronic disease. (See "Illnesses" under Short).

**Crises in Acute Diseases**—Critical Days In—Course of—The phases and Quarters of the ☽ govern the course and crises in acute diseases, from the time of decumbency, or the taking of the patient to bed. (See "Acute Diseases" under Crises; "Course of Disease" under Course; "Moon" under Motion).

**Danger Of**—Liable to an Acute Disease—The ☉ to the ☌ ♂ by dir., or ♂ to the ☌ ☉. (See "Causes" in this section).

**Death By**—The following influences tend to cause death by an Acute Disease, and an Acute Fever—The ☉ to the ☌ or ill-asp. ♂ by dir.; ♂ afflictions tend to death after a short or sudden illness; ♂ occi. at B., and affl. the hyleg by dir.; ♂ in the 8th H., ruler of the 8th, or affl. the cusp of the 8th at the beginning of an illness; ♂ in the 8th H. at a Solar Ingress of the ☉ into ♈, and affl. the ☽, or planet ascending. See "Arguments for Death" under Death).

**Duration of**—Acute Diseases are of different duration, according to the severity of the disease and the afflictions, the degree of vitality, etc., and some acute diseases will resolve themselves on the 7th day, and others on the 14th, 21st or 28th days. An acute disease can last for 28 days, one complete revolution of the ☽, and if it does not resolve, or prove fatal, on the 28th day, it runs into a chronic form. (See Continuity, Duration, End).

**Ease In**—(See Magnetic).

**Fevers**—Acute Fevers—Causes of—Acute fevers are caused principally by the afflictions of the ☉ and ♂; the afflictions of ♂ to the ☉, Asc., or hyleg; by afflictions in the fiery signs, and such signs on the Asc. (See the influences of the ☉, ♂, the Asc., and fiery signs under "Causes" in this section. Also see Ephemeral, Fever).

**Hot Diseases**—Acute Hot Diseases—The ☽ weak and ill-dig. at B., and to the ☌ Regulus.

**Liable To**—Liable to Acute Disease, or Acute Fevers—(See "Causes" in this section).

**Periods of Acute Disease**—Subject to—Time When Apt to Come—The ☉ affl. at B. makes the native more liable to times of acute disease, and when the ☉ comes to the evil directions the Asc., or to the ☌ or ill-asps. ♂, and also when the Asc. comes to the ill-asps. the ☉ or ♂ by dir. An evil ♂ transit, affl. his place in the radical map, or passing thru the birthsign, or affl. the place of the ☉, ☽ or Asc. at B., may precipitate an acute disease, and cause a fever. (See "Periods of Bad Health" under Health).

**Precipitated**—An Acute Disease, or Acute Fever Precipitated—(See "Periods" in this section).

**Prevalent**—Acute Diseases and Sharp Fevers Prevalent—♄ lord of the year at the Vernal, in ♍, and occi. of the ☉ or ☽ in fiery signs; ♂ having sole dominion of the year at a Solar Eclipse. (See "Prevalent" under Fevers).

**Quick Diseases**—(See Quick).

**Signs**—The Cardinal Signs of the Zodiac are called the Acute Signs, and planets in them at B., and by dir., or at the time of decumbiture, tend to acute, rapid, short, and swift diseases. (See Cardinal).

**Suffering**—Acute Suffering—This is usually caused by the afflictions of ♂, as in injuries, wounds, and violence to the person. (See Injuries, Pain, Wounds, Violence). For the various kinds of Acute Diseases, and the parts of the body affected, see the subject, and the disease or condition you have in mind, in the alphabetical arrangement. Also see such subjects as Abatement, Acquired, Better, Cadent, Diathesis, Feelings, Fierce, Grevious, Hexis, Inflammation, Mild, "Acute" under Mind; Moderation, Pain, Quick, Rapid, Severe, Sharp, Short, Slight, Sudden, Swift, Vehement, Violent, Worse, etc.).

**ADAM'S APPLE**—Thyroid Cartilage—(See Thyroid).

**ADDER**—Stings By, or by some obnoxious creature, and espec. stings to Kings or Rulers—(See Bites, Kings, Rulers, Serpents, Stings, Venomous).

**ADDICTS**—Addicted To—For the various form of Addictions see Drink, Drugs, Drunkenness, Gluttony, Habits, Narcotics, Passion, Pleasure, Sex, Tobacco; "Solitary Vice" under Vice; Women, etc.

**ADDISON'S DISEASE**—(See Adrenals).

**ADDRESS**—(See Appearance, Manner, Speech).

**ADENOIDS**—A Vegetable Growth—Caused by afflictions in ♉ and ♏, and espec. in the 25° of these signs, when affl. by malefics in, or in evil asp. to this degree; ♅ or ♂ in, or affl. the 25° of ♉ or ♏; ♅ and ♂ combinations in ♉ or ♏, and also ♄ in or near the 25° ♏, and afflicted; the ☉ in the 25° ♏ or ♉, and affl. by the ☌, □, or ☍ the malefics; ♄ ☌ ♆ in ♉; ♄ affl. in ♉ or ♏; ♃ ☌ ♂ in ♉ or ♏; ♀ in ♉ or ♏ in the Asc., and afflicted; caused by Subs at LCP and SP. (See Nose, Pharynx, Throat, Tonsils, Vertebrae). Cases—See Figures 3A and 3B in "Astro-Diagnosis", and Fig. 27, in "Message of the Stars", books by Mr. and Mrs. Max Heindel.

**ADENOMA**—A Glandular Tumor—Quite frequent in Scrofula. The Glands are strongly acted upon by ♀, and afflictions to this planet tend to disturbances of the glands, and to swellings and tumors. As a whole, the ☉ and ♃ rule the glands, and afflictions to these bodies may cause Adenoma, and other glandular troubles. (See Glands, Scrofula, Tumors).

**Breast**—Adenoma of—♀ affl. in ♋. (See Breast).

**ADHESIONS**—The union of two surfaces, or parts, and due to the degeneration of the parts, the restraint of the function or blood circulation in the part, the deposit of wastes and mineral substances, and is the work of ♄. The parts most liable to such affliction are those ruled by the sign containing ♄ at B. Adhesions and fusion may also result from extreme heat in a part, causing melting of the tissues, or bones, the work of the ☉ and ♂ in ☌ in a fiery sign, and possibly with other planets also in the same sign, and espec. if the sign also be on the Asc. The fiery sign ♌ rules the spine, and the ☉, ♂, and many planets in ♌, afflicted, and espec. in the 5th H., the house of ♌, may result in adhesions, and ankylosis of the vertebrae, due to melting and excess heat. (See Ankylosis, Coalition, Heat, Mars, Stricture, Sun).

**ADIPOSE**—Fatty—Adipose Tissue—(See Fat).

**Adiposis**—(See Corpulent," Fat Body", "Fatty Degeneration" under Fat).

**Adiposa Dolorosa**—(See Fat).

**ADJUSTMENT**—(See Coordination, Incoordination).

**ADOLESCENCE**—Disorders at time of—(See Puberty).

**ADOPTION**—Of Children—Children Separated from Parents, and Adopted—(See "Death of Parents", "Separated", under Parents). The afflictions of ♆ in, or to the 5th H., often indicate the denial of children, and the necessity for adoption of children. (See Barren, Bastards; "Early Death" under Father, Parents).

**ADRENALS**—Suprarenal Capsules—Ruled by ♃ and the ♎ Sign. The Adrenals are Ductless Glands, and in a general way also come under the rule of ♏. When the mind has been greatly disturbed, and the poise and equilibrium lost for a time, due to the emotional disturbances caused by ♄, ♂, and the ☽, the Adrenal secretion tends to restore calm and quiet to the mind, and also when the heart action is weakened thru worry, melancholy, or sorrow, tends to act as a heart stimulant. Lack of the adrenal secretion tends to depression, dejection, despondency, gloom, and worry. (See Atrabile). During fits of anger, rage, or passion, brought on by ♂, and when the muscles are trembling and tense, the glycogen in the liver is released in larger quantities by the action of ♃, and acts as a soothing, calming influence, and to restore poise. (See Soothing). Thus the Adrenals, thru the saving and benevolent action of ♃, keep the body from being permanently weakened, destroyed, and thrown into disease, ill-health, or premature death, by the adverse action of the malefic planets ♄ and ♂ upon the mind. The Adrenals are said to be connected with the Personality. The Adrenals are quite fully discussed from an Occult and Metaphysical standpoint in the book, "The Message of the Stars", by the Heindels.

**Addison's Disease**—Tuberculosis, or Consumption, of the Suprarenal Capsules—Caused by ♄ affl. in ♎ or ♏.

**Coma**—Influence of Adrenals In—(See Coma).

**Consumption of**—Tuberculosis of—(See "Addison" in this section).

**Diminished Secretion**—Lack of Adrenal Secretion—♃ affl. in ♈ or ♎. (See Fainting).

**Plexus**—The Suprarenal Plexus—(See "Ductless Glands" under Ductless).

**ADULTS**—Adult Life—The ☽, ♀, and ☿ rule the earlier years of life, but when maturity is reached, then the ☉ and the larger, or major planets assume rule. Old age is ruled by ♄. (See Maturity, "Middle Life" under Middle; "Periods of Life" under Periods). There are diseases which are peculiar to adult life, and others to infancy, childhood, youth, middle life, and old age, etc., as the planets bear rule over the different stages of life, and the ruler of such a Period in life when affl. by directions tends to the special diseases, or afflictions, peculiar to that planet. (See Periods).

**Duration of Life**—Of Adults—(See "Long Life" under Life; Maturity, "Death at Middle Life" under Middle Life; Old Age).

**ADYNAMIA**—A Deficiency, or Loss of Vital Power—A ♄ disease. Also caused by Subs of the Atlas and Axis, and by ♄ affl. in ♈ or ♉, the signs which rule these vertebrae. (See Asthenia, Debility, Feeble, Infirm, Sickly, Vital, Vitality, Vertebrae, Weak, etc.).

**AEROPLANES**—Aviation—Death or Injury By—The ♒ sign, and ♅, have special rule over the Air and the Ether, and the evil directions of ♅ to the ☉, ☽, Asc., or Hyleg, tend to accidents in the air, and by machinery used in such service. Also to start an air journey when ♅ is badly afflicting the ☽ and ♂ tends to mishaps, injury,

death, and for a safe journey a propitious planetary time for the start should always be chosen. (See Accidents, Journeys, Railroads, Travel, Vehicles).

**AFFECTIONS**—There are some morbid and pathological deviations, or diseases of the affections and the passional nature. (See Deviations, Love Affairs, Passion, Perversions, Reins, Sex, etc.).

**AFFLICTION**—Afflictions—The 12th H. is known as the house of affliction, sorrow, self-undoing, confinement, restraint, limitation, etc., and planets affl. in this house at B. tend to a greater number of afflictions to mind or body. Also the planets ill-placed at B., and with many □ and ☍ asps. in the map, tend to multiply the afflictions, miseries, sufferings, ill-health, and troubles of life unless self-control, wisdom, discrimination, knowledge, and spiritual attainment enter in, and change, modify, or prevent the calamities of life on the Earth Plane. The planet ♄ is known as the Chastener, the Tester, the special Afflictor among the planets, and his afflictions tend to sorrow, trouble, delays, hindrances, restraints, worry, melancholy, and chronic forms of disease. However, Saturn people are patient under affliction. (See Saturn).

**Bodily Afflictions**—For the various diseases and bodily afflictions, see the subject you have in mind in the alphabetical arrangement.

**Causes of Affliction**—Afflictions in the 12th H., ruler of the 12th, a malefic, and espec. ♄, and in the 12th H.; the ☉ or ☽ ☌ or ill-asp. ♄ at B., and by dir.; the ☉ or ☽ joined to the Whale's Jaw, great affliction, sickness, disgrace, or ruin; ♄ or ♂ in the 12th H. (For further influences see Disgrace, Misfortune, Misery, Reversals, Ruin, Sorrow, Trouble, etc.).

**Many Afflictions**—The ☉ and ☽ in cadent houses at B., in weak signs, and afflicted, and espec. when in the 3rd or 6th H.; the ☽ decr. in light, and sepr. from the ☉ or ♃ at B., and applying to ♄; the ☽ at the Full, or incr., sepr. from ♀ and applying to ♂ in a day geniture; ♄ or ♂ by dir. in ☌ or ill-asp. the ☉, ☽, Asc. or M.C.; ♂ ☌ ☉ at a Solar Rev. All manner of afflictions are ruled by the 12th H. and its influences. (See Miseries).

**Mental Afflictions**—Mental Disorders—(See the various subjects under Mental, Mind. Also see Anguish, Anxiety, Dejection, Dementia, Depression, Despondency, Distress, Epilepsy, Fear, Frenzy, Hallucinations, Hypochondria, Idiocy, Insanity, Mania, Melancholy, Memory, Miserable, Obsessions, Paranoia, Sadness, Sorrow, Worry, etc.).

**Parts of the Body**—The Parts Afflicted, or Diseased—(See "Parts of the Body" under Parts; Upper, Middle, Lower).

**Planets**—Affliction By—(See Malefics, Planets. See each of the planets in the alphabetical arrangement).

**AGARICUS**—A typical drug of the ☽. (See Moon).

**AGED PEOPLE**—(See Old Age).

**AGILE**—Brisk, Nimble, Quick, Active Body—(See "Active Body" under Active; Brisk, Muscles, Nimble, Quick, Sports, etc.).

**AGITATION**—The ☽ affl. by ♄ at B., the mind and body are afflicted with agitation, and espec. with females. (See Excitable, Fretfulness, Nervous, Paralysis Agitans, etc.).

**AGONY OF MIND**—(See Anguish, Anxiety, Distress, Melancholy, Worry).

**AGUE**—Malaria—intermittent Fever—Ague is threatened, and to be long-continued, when earthy signs are in the Asc., or on the 6th H., or the ☽ in an earthly sign at B., or at decumbiture, and also to threaten Consumption. (See Consumption); caused by ♄ when the dominion of death is vested in him; a ♄ disease; ♄ affl. the hyleg or the Asc.; ♄ in the 6th H.; ♄ in ♋ when ♄ is the afflictor in the disease; ♄, ♅, or ♆ in ♋, and affl. the ☉ or ☽; the ☉ or ☽ to the ☌ ♄ by dir.; ♂ too much in evidence at B. (See Intermittent, Malaria).

**Death by Ague**—♄ occi. at B., and affl. the hyleg by dir.; ♄ afflictions tend to; an evil dir. of ♄ to the hyleg when ♄ holds the dominion of death; fixed stars of the nature of ♄ affl. the hyleg.

**Mother**—The Mother afflicted by Ague—The ☽ in the 1st or 10th H., and affl. by ♄. (See Mother).

**Quartan Ague**—Arising from Cold—A disease and affliction of ♄; caused by ♄ when the dominion of death is vested in him; ♄ sole ruler at an eclipse of the ☉; earthy signs on the Asc. and 6th H. at B., or at decumbiture; the ☽ in ♋ ☌ or ill-asp. ♄ (or ☿ if he be of the nature of ♄) at the beginning of an illness, or at decumbiture. If the ☽ be decr., and near the body of ♄, the disease will tend to be long-continued (Hor'y). (See Quartan).

**Tertian Ague**—Tertian Fever—A ♂ disease, and caused by the afflictions of ♂; ♂ sole ruler at an eclipse of the ☉. (See Intermittent, "Low Fevers" under Fevers; Malaria, Miasma, Quartan, Quotidan, Remittent, Semitertian).

**AILING OFTEN**—Is Always Ailing—(See Feeble, "Ill-Health All Thru Life" under Ill-Health; Infirmities, Invalids, "Much Sickness" under Sickness).

**AILMENTS**—Indisposition of Body and Mind—(See Disease, Debility, Deformities, General, Ill-Health, Indisposition, Infirmities, Mental, Mind, Sickly, Sickness, Weak, etc.).

**AIR**—Atmosphere—The Air is ruled by ♅ and ☿. The Ether is ruled by ♅. The condition of the air has much to do with health and disease, and the atmosphere is much acted upon by the planetary influences each day, and so much so that the weather can be predicted a year ahead by making a study of the planetary aspects and influences that will be forming, as is done by the Hicks Almanac People, of St. Louis, Mo. The air may be corrupted and vitiated by the planetary vibrations and aspects, causing disease, epidemics, famine, pestilence, fevers, and under certain planetary influences an epidemic may spread over the World, or parts of the World ruled by the Signs of the Zodiac involved in the planetary configurations for the time. This is the reason why Cholera, a disease native to India, will spread to other shores in certain years. The germs of certain contagious diseases are developed by atmospheric conditions spontaneously in different Countries, and not spread by the transmigration of germs, as commonly supposed. See the following subjects in the alphabetical arrangement when not considered here, which have to do with the air.

**Aeroplanes—Accident or Death By**—(See Aeroplanes).

**Air Cells**—Of the Lungs—(See "Air Cells" under Cells).

**Air Signs**—(See "Signs" in this section).

**Apparitions**—In the Air—(See Phenomena).

**Birds of the Air**—The Body Devoured by Beasts and Birds after Death—Lack of Possible Burial—This is especially so if the malefics at B. are in Signs assigned to beasts and birds, and also when the benefics offer no assistance to the anaretic places, or to the 4th H., which house rules the end of life; ♂ in signs of human form, as in ♊, ♍, 1st half of ♐, or in ♒, or in □ or ☍ the ☉ or ☽. (See "No Burial" under Burial; Fowls, Vultures).

**Breath**—Breathing—(See Breath; "Tidal Air" in this section).

**Caisson Disease**—(See Caisson, Compressed).

**Cells**—Air Cells of Lungs—(See "Air" under Cells).

**Clear Air**—(See "Healthy Air" in this section).

**Cold Air**—(See "Cold" under Weather; also see the Introduction under Cold).

**Compressed Air**—(See Caisson, Compressed, Gases).

**Corrupt Air**—Unhealthy Air—Stagnant Air—Dark Air—Vitiated Air—Foul Air—Impediment in the Air—Malignant Air—Mephitic Air—Pestilential Air—Impure Air—Unwholesome Air, etc.—♄ sole ruler at a Solar Eclipse makes the air turbulent, gloomy, and impure; ♄ ☍ ♂ in Equinoctial signs, and controlling the Luminaries; ♄ in ♊, direct in motion, and angular at the Vernal Equinox; ♄ in ♋, and ori. at the Vernal, makes the air dark and unhealthy; ♄ ☌ ♂ in fiery signs; ♄, ♃, or ♂ in Perihelion. (Planets in perihelion tend to disturb the equilibrium of the gases of our atmosphere); ♄ in the ascendancy, rising in the ascendant, or lord of the year at the Vernal, tends to foul, noxious, stagnant, mephitic air, and conduces to the spread of fevers; ♂ sole ruler at a Solar Eclipse; ♂ in power at the Equinoxes or Solstices, or lord of the year at the Vernal, the atmosphere is parched by hot, blasting, and pestilential winds; ♂ in aphelion; the ☌ of malefic planets in fiery signs; the ascending sign be ♉, and ♀ affl. at a Solar Ingress into ♈; ♊ ascending at a Solar Ingress into ♈, and ☿ be affl., Countries under ♊ will suffer thru corrupt air, by high winds, tending to obstruction of the lungs and bronchial tubes; a malefic planet in power at a Summer Solstice, and affl. the ☉, ☽, or planets in the 6th H., and also a malefic in the 8th H.; the matutine rising of Sirius causes great heat and unwholesome air; coincident with the appearance of Comets, and espec. when they appear in ♋, ♑, or ♒; caused by the ☌ of several superior planets in airy signs, and due to the maximum of planetary influence. (See Cholera, Contagious, Epidemics, Miasma, Noxious, Pestilence, Plague, "Public Health" under Public, Typhus).

**Dark Air**—(See "Corrupt" in this section).

**Dryness of the Air**—(See Drouth, Dryness, Famine, Fountains, "Dry and Hot Air" under Heat; "Hot Winds" under Wind).

**Epidemics**—(See Cholera, Epidemics. See the Introduction to this Article).

**Equilibrium**—Of the Gases of the Air Disturbed—(See "Corrupt Air" in this section. Also see Gases).

**Ether**—The Ether is ruled by ♅. (See Ether).

**Foul Air**—Foul Vapors—(See "Corrupt" in this section; "Foul" under Vapors).

**Fowls**—Of the Air—(See "Birds" in this section. Also see Fowls).

**Gas**—Gases—(See Gas).

**Good Air**—(See "Healthy" in this section).

**Healthy Air**—Good Air—Pure Air—Temperate Air—Pleasant Air—Clear Air—Wholesome Air, etc.—♃ in ♉, ♋, ♎, ♏, ♐, ♑, ♒, and ♓ at the Vernal Equi., and lord of the year; ♃ in an angle at an Equinox or Solstice, and receiving the application of the ☽ at the New ☽, and espec. that nearest the Equinox, tends to temperate, good and wholesome air; ♂ in ♋, direct in motion, and lord of the year at the Vernal.

**Heated and Turbulent Air**—(See Comets; "Hot" under Wind; Weather).

**High Winds**—(See Wind).

**Hot and Dry Air**—Little Rain—Extreme Heat—(See Drought, Famine, Heat, Weather).

**Impediment**—In the Air—(See "Corrupt" in this section).

**Lungs**—Air Cells of—(See "Air Cells" under Cells).

**Malignant Air**—The ☉, ☽ and ♃ conjoined in ♎. (See "Corrupt" in this section).

**Moist Air**—Overmoist Air, and Suffering from—Excess of Rain—Floods—(See "Abundance" under Moisture; Rain).

**Night Air**—(See Miasma).

**Obnoxious Air**—When ♂ is in ♋, in N. Lat., or when rising or setting with Arcturus, Attair, Oculus Taurus, Cauda Delphini, Procyon, Sirius, the bright star in the Crown, Orion, Regulus, Hyades, Antares, or Spica, causes a windy, tempestuous, sultry and obnoxious air, leading to public ill-health. (See "Corrupt" in this section).

**Obscuration**—Of the Air—Comets appearing in ♒. (See Comets).

**Overmoist Air**—(See "Moist" in this section).

**Oxygenation**—(See Oxygen).

**Parched Air**—(See "Corrupt", "Heated", "Hot" in this section; "Extreme Heat" under Heat).

**Pestilential Air**—Pestilential Winds—(See "Corrupt Air" in this section. Also see Epidemics, "Winds" under Pestilence).

**Pleasant Air**—(See "Healthy" in this section).

**Pressure**—Air Pressure—(See Caisson, Compressed, in this section).

**Pure Air**—(See "Healthy" in this section).

**Signs**—The Air Signs—Sweet Signs—Whole Signs—Nervous Signs—The Air signs are ♊, ♎, and ♒, which signs are in △ aspect to each other, and in harmony. The fiery and airy signs are opposed to each other in the Zodiac, as ♈ and ♎, ♊ and ♐, ♌ and ♒. The Air Signs are connected with Gases, Air Cells, Intercellular Spaces, Arteries, Veins, and the Capillaries of the body. The Airy and Earthy signs are the least excitable. They are related to the Intellect, and tend to worry and nervous troubles, and are classed as Nervous Signs. Air is cooperative, self-conscious, and impersonal. The ☉ in an airy sign gives a strong constitution, but of a refined and mental character rather than physical. These signs are next to the fiery signs in degree of vitality. The Air Signs are good for the ☽, and the ☽ is better placed in these signs than in fire signs, and tends to more normal and regular functions and secretions, as the airy signs are moist and warm, and especially ♒. The ☽ in these signs also gives a tendency to worry, anxiety, and mental strain, and liable to Anaemia, Blood, Kidney, and Skin Disorders. The Air signs tend to diseases arising from Corrupt Blood, as Gout, Leprosy, etc. Air Signs on the Asc. and 6th H. at B., or at decumbiture, or the Significators of the disease in an airy sign at the beginning of an illness, show Gout, Cutaneous Diseases, Scrofula, Corrupt Blood, etc. Afflictions in Air Signs tend to broken bones, and also to impure breath. People born under Air Signs, and with many planets in these signs, should sleep and work in well ventilated rooms, as they require more oxygen, and it is also well to live in a high altitude. Collectively the Air Signs rule the Lungs (♊), the Kidneys (♎), and the Blood (♒). They also rule the Breath, the Houses of Kin (Brethren), of Partners, Marriage, and Friends, and also give the Sanguine and Artistic Temperament. (See the subjects mentioned in this paragraph. Also see Air, Altitude, Aquarius, Atmosphere, Blood, Breath, Brethren, Eruptions, Ether, Events, External, Friends, Gases, Gemini, Introspection, Kidneys, Libra, Lungs, "Amiable" under Manners; Marriage, "Operations" under Nature; Orator, Oxygen, Partner, Pestilence, Refined, Residence, Sanguine, "Sweet Signs" under Sweet; Uranus, "Signs" under Whole, etc.).

**Sultry Air**—(See "Obnoxious" in this section).

**Stagnant Air**—(See "Corrupt" in this section).

**Superabundance**—Of Air—Death or Diseases From—Caused by ♃ when the dominion of death is vested in him.

**Temperate Air**—(See "Healthy" in this section).

**Tidal Air**—In the Lungs—(See Tidal).

**Turbulent Air**—(See "High Winds", "Tornadoes", and other subjects under Wind).

**Unhealthy Air**—Unwholesome Air—(See "Corrupt" in this section).

**Vapors**—Foul Vapors—(See Vapors).

**Vitiated Air**—(See "Corrupt" in this section).

**Warm Air**—Warm, Pestilential Air—(See "Corrupt", "Pestilential", in this section).

**Weather; Wholesome Air**—(See "Healthy" in this section).

**Wind.**

For further subjects which relate to the Air, its composition, action, etc., see Altitude, Apparitions, Carbon, Comets, Distentions, Eclipses, Emphysema, Events, Hydrogen, Lightning, Miasma, Nitrogen, "Operations" under Nature; Perigee, Perihelion, "Vital Force" under Vital; "Vocal Cords" under Voice, etc.

**ALBA DOLENS**—Phlegmasia Alba Dolens—(See "Milk Leg" under Legs).

**ALBUMEN**—Albuminuria—Albumen is ruled by the ♋ sign. (See Proteids).

**Albuminuria**—Albumen in the Urine—The work of ♃, and is a ♃ disease; ♃ or ♀ affl. by the □ of ♄; ♃ ☍ ♆; the ☽ affl. in ♋; fixed signs prominent, with many planets in them, and espec. in ♌, ♏, ♒; a fixed sign on the Asc. This disease is especially caused also by Subs at KP, the Kidney Place in the Spine, and by afflictions in ♎. (See Bright's Disease, Kidneys, Urine, Vertebrae).

**ALCOHOL**—Alcoholism—A Toxic Psychosis—Given to Alcoholic Excesses—(See "Softening" under Brain; "Delirium Tremens" under Delirium; Drink, Drunkenness, Intoxication).

**ALDEBARAN**—Bull's North Eye—A star of the nature of ♂, in the 2nd face of ♊. This great star when affl. the ☉, ☽, and the planets of our Solar System, tends to cause extreme suffering to humanity, sickness or death, and when directed to the angles of the horoscope produces periods of terrible stress and nervous strain. For the various influences of this star see Blindness, Blows, Calamities, Cuts, Danger, Death, Disease, Disgrace, Enemies, Face (Injury to); Falls (Death By); Fire, Hanging, Hot Distempers, Ill-Health, Indisposition, Injuries, Military, Peril, Pestilence, Pirates, Putrid Fevers, Rashness, Red Hair, Ruin, Sickness, Sight, Soldiers, Stabs, Stars, Strain, Strangulation, Surgeons, Trouble, Untimely Death, Violence, Violent Death. For Bull's South Eye, see Oculus Taurus, Stars.

**ALEXIPHARMIC** A Medicine Neutralizing a Poison. A Therapeutic Property of ♃. (See Antidotes).

**ALGENIB**—A Violent, unfortunate star of the 2nd magnitude, in the 2nd face of ♈, of the nature of ♂ and ☿. The M.C. directed to tends to imprisonment, and many adversaries. (See Enemies, Forgers, Imprisonment, Libel).

**ALGOL**—Caput Algol—Medusa's Head—Gorgon's Head—A star of the nature of ♄ and ♃, situated in the 5th face of ♉, and considered to be the most evil of all the fixed stars. The M.C. directed to Algol tends to make the native murderous, riotous, turbulent. The ☽ directed to tends to make the native dangerous and violent. Algol when in line of the R.A. of the ☉ or ☽ in a violent nativity tends to make a murderer, and to lead to an untimely end, and a tragic death. Robespierre was an example of this. (See Pearce's Text Book of Astrology, Chap. XIX, page 120). The Algol region of ♉ also tends to Apoplexy, and death by Spasms. (See Apoplexy, "Death" under Fits). In Hor'y Questions, the lord of the Asc. conjoined with Algol gives danger of death by illness or accident. (See Burns, Decapitation; Goiter; Hair, "Death by Sentence" under Judges; Operations).

**ALIMENTARY CANAL**—Alimentary System—Alimentary Tract—The Digestive Tube and Accessory Glands—Alimentation—Ruled by the ☽ and the ♋ Sign, and has to do with nourishment. Planets afflicted in ♋ tend to disorders of Alimentation, and of the Alimentary System. Such disorders are also caused by Subs at SP, the Stomach Place in the Spine. (See Assimilation, Digestion, Duodenum, Food, Indigestion, Nutrition, Oesophagus, Stomach, Vertebrae).

**ALKALINITY**—Alkaline—The positive Signs of the Zodiac, ♈, ♊, ♌, ♎, ♐, and ♒, are alkaline in a physiological way, and also the positive planets, the ☉, ♅, ♃, ♂, are alkaline in their influence. Several positive planets in positive signs, and with positive signs on the angles at B. tend to an excess of alkalinity in the body, an unbalanced body, and to lead to disease or discomfort, increased nervousness, alkaline urine, etc. Remedies under the rule of the negative planets or signs tend to neutralize alkalinity in the system. (See Acids, Electric. Also see "Drugs", "Remedies" under each of the planets ♆, ♄, ♀, ☽, the negative planetary bodies. Also see "Causes of Impure Blood" under Impure; Remedies).

**ALLOPATHY**—(See Antipathy, Hippocrates).

**ALOPECIA**—Loss of the Hair—(See Baldness; "Scanty" under Hair).

**ALPHARD**—A malefic Star. (See Hydra's Heart).

**ALTAIR**—The Eagle—Vulture—A star in 29° ♑, of the nature of ♅. Also listed by Pearce as being of the influence of ♄ and ☿. The ☽ to the place of gives promise of marriage and children. (See Fruitful).

**ALTERATIONS**—Changes—Modification—

**Blood**—(See "Alterations" under Blood).

**Cells**—Alterations In—(See "Alterations" under Cells).

**Disease**—Alteration In—(See Abatement, Amelioration, Better, Crises, Moderation, Modification, Recovery, Recuperation, Worse, etc.).

**Tissues**—Alteration In—(See "Alterations" under Cells. Also see Disintegration, Fruit, Inflammation, Metabolism, Metamorphosis, Putrefaction, Sensations, Tissues).

**ALTERATIVE**—Drugs which alter the processes of nutrition or excretion. Therapeutic properties of the ☽, ♂, and ☿.

**ALTERNATING**—Alternating, or Clonic Spasm—(See "Clonic" under Spasmodic. Also see Intermittent, Remittent, Returning).

**ALTITUDE**—Location—Residence—People born with the ☉, ☽, and many planets in the airy signs, ♊, ♎, or ♒, or with the airy signs upon the Asc. and angles of the map, should live in the higher and mountainous altitudes where the air pressure is lighter, as the airy signs rule largely over the Air and Ether, and espec. the ♒ sign. (See Air, Ether). Also when a cardinal sign is rising at B., the native should live upon a hill, and in a commanding situation, for the best health. People born with the ☉, ☽ and Asc. in the watery signs have better health in the low altitudes, and at Sea level, and to live near water, as rivers, lakes, or the Sea. With a common sign on the Asc. at B., live at Sea level. With a fixed sign on the Asc., live in a valley. Lung diseases are usually found in people who have the ♊ sign strongly afflicted at B., and by dir., and Physicians have found out by experience that such cases are benefited by high altitudes, altho they may not know the reason unless they are students of Astrology. The star map of birth shows what altitudes and locations, and whether At Home, or Abroad, and what Countries are best suited to the native for better health or success in life. (See "Air Signs" under Air; Heights, Location, "Native Land" under Native; "Place of Birth" under Place; Residence, Travel).

**ALUMINUM**—A metal ruled by the ☽. Also said to be ruled by ♃.

**ALZHEIMER'S DISEASE**—(See "Atrophy" under Brain).

**AMATIVE**—Amativeness—Amative Tract.

**Amativeness**—A strong desire to propagate, and is largely a ♉, ♌, 5th and 7th H. influence. Is a strong ♌ characteristic, as ♌ is the sign of children, and the 5th H., the House of children. The ☉ in ♉, or ♉ on the Asc. at B., tend to make the bump of amativeness prominent. Mars in the 5th H. at B., makes one highly sexed, and espec. when in asp. to ♀. The ♉, ♌, and ♑ signs are strongly sex-conscious. (See Amorous, Passion, "Sex-Conscious" under Sex).

**Amative Tract**—Headaches In—♀ affl. in ♉. (See Headaches).

**AMAUROSIS**—Gutta Serena—Partial or Total Blindness—(See Gutta Serena; "Total Blindness" under Blindness).

**AMBER**—A color ruled by ♍. The amber color of the sky is ruled by ♅. Amber,—a yellowish, translucent Resin, is ruled by ♅. (See Colors).

**AMBERGRIS**—A waxy substance found floating in the Indian and Tropical Oceans. A morbid substance originating in the alimentary canal of the Sperm Whale. Ruled by ♆.

**AMBIDEXTROUS**—☿ in a double-bodied sign at B., and espec. in ♓; the double-bodied signs, and espec. ♊ or ♓, upon the Asc. or angles at B., and containing ☿, the ruler of the mind; ♆ affl. ☿ tends to; ♃ in ♊; the planets well-scattered out at B., and about equally divided between the positive and negative signs, which signs rule the right and left side of the body respectively. (See Right, Left).

**AMBITION**—The Ambitions, Hopes, and Desires are ruled by the 11th H. (See Eleventh). The fiery and cardinal signs on angles, espec. the Asc., and many planets in fiery signs at B. tend to give ambition, and an active mind and body; many planets rising and elevated in the East at B., and espec. when also in the positive, and masculine signs. The influences which give ambition also give more power and ability to resist and overcome disease, to hold on and never give up in despair as long as there is life, whereas the negative people, and those lacking in ambition, succumb to disease more easily. (See Negative, Positive, Purposes).

**Of No Ambition**—The ☽ or ♀ ill-dig. at B.; ♂ weak and ill-dig. at B.; many planets setting in the West at B., and espec. when below the western horizon, ill-posited, afflicted, and in signs of little or no dignity, and also with the majority of planets in the negative, or feminine signs of the zodiac, and people born under these conditions tend to succumb to disease more easily, be without hope and courage, to worry and be melancholic, and often to commit suicide. (See Carelessness, Desires, Dull, "Lack of" under Energy; "Hopes Cut Off" under Hope; Idle, Improvident, Inactive, Indifferent, Inertia, Lassitude, Lazy, Lethargy, Listless, Sedentary, etc.).

**AMBUSHES**—Death or Injury By—The ☉ to the place the Bull's South Horn; the ☽ to the ☌ or ill-asp. ♅ by dir.; ♆ when the afflicting planet tends to;

♂ in the 12th H., and affl., denotes violence from enemies in ambush; denoted by the 12th H., and malefic planets afflicted therein at B., and by dir. (See "Secret Enemies" under Enemies; Highwaymen, Plots, Treachery).

**AMELIORATION**—Of Disease, Hurts, or Injuries—The same benefic influences which tend to ameliorate and moderate disease also tend to lessen the evil effects of a hurt or injury. The good asps. of the benefics in the afflicting configuration, the afflicting planet separating from a malefic, and applying to a benefic, tend to ameliorate and modify the disease, and give a more favorable prognosis. The influences favorable for amelioration and alleviation of the evils of disease, hurts, or injury, are quite fully considered under the following subjects. (See Abatement, "Escapes" under Accidents; Alterations, Better, Continuity, Course, Crises, Curable, Curtailed, Ease, Epilepsy, "Amelioration" under Hurts; Improvement, Insanity, Minimizing, Moderation, Modification, "Action" under Morbid; Prognosis, Recovery, Recuperation, Remission, Separation).

**AMENDMENT**—Of Disease—(See Ameliortion).

**AMENORRHEA**—(See Menses).

**AMNESIA**—(See "Amnesia" under Memory).

**AMNIOTIC FLUID**—(See Foetus).

**AMOEBOID MOTION**—(See "Amoeboid" under Cells).

**AMOROUS**—

**Amorous Eyes**—(See "Amorous" under Eyes). (See Amative, Excesses, "Energies Wasted" under Love Affairs; "Health Suffers" under Opposite Sex; "Addicted to Women" under Men; "Loose Morals" under Morals; "Excess" under Passion; Sensuality, etc.).

**Amorous Indulgence**—Disease and Ill-health from Excess of—♂ in the 1st H., and affl. by ♀; ♂ affl. in the 5th H.; ♂ □ or ☍ ♀, the vitality sapped by sex excesses; lord of the 6th or 10th H. in the 5th, and afflicted. (See "Passional Excesses" under Passion; Sex, Venery).

**Amours**—(See this subject under Love Affairs).

**AMPUTATIONS**—(See "Amputations" under Operations).

**AMULETS**—Charms—Talismans—Amulets were worn in Ancient Times against infectious and contagious diseases, and such are in use today. Certain metals and minerals, flowers or herbs, have inherent powers to ward off disease, evils, and mischief of various kinds. Copper is worn by the natives of India, and other Countries, against Cholera. Physicians use copper internally in bowel disorders, and copper is one of the best intestinal remedies for diarrhea, dysentery, etc., and is a remedy taken from the Ancient and Oriental Peoples. In Hungary a copper plate is worn next to the skin to ward off Cholera. A Coral Necklace is worn against Whooping Cough. (See Cholera, Contagions, Copper, Coral, Infections, "Birth Stones" under Stones; Whooping).

**AMUSEMENTS**—Play—Recreations—Sports, etc.—Amusements, Play, Love Affairs, Opposite Sex, Theatres, Women, etc., are ruled by the 5th H., and malefics in this house at B., a malefic ruler of the 5th, lord of the 5th H. in the 6th, 8th or 12th houses, and afflicted, or afflicting the hyleg, tend to make people less fortunate in Amusements and Recreation, and more subject to accidents, injury, or death in such pursuits. Also certain Fixed Stars, and the Nebulae, have an adverse influence in these matters, and espec. to cause injury to the eyes, and blindness from some accident to the eyes while at play. (For further influences along this line see the various paragraphs under Accidents, Blindness, Exercise, Falls, Frivolity, Hunting, Injuries, Pleasure, Recreations, Sports, Theatres, Travel).

**AMYGDALITIS**—(See "Tonsilitis" under Tonsils).

**AMYLOID**—Starch-like—(See Starches, "Amyloid Kidney" under Kidneys).

**ANABOLISM**—(See Constructive, Metabolism).

**ANAEMIA**—A Deficiency of Blood and Red Corpuscles—Impoverished Blood Anaemic—Pale—

**Causes**—General Causes of Anaemia—The ☉ in ♉, ♌, ♒, and affl. by the malefics ♆, ♅, or ♄; afflictions in ♌ at B., the sign which rules the heart, and also in ♒, the sign which bears strong rule over the blood, tend to, and to disturb the equilibrium of the blood; a ♌ and ♒ disease; ♒ on the Asc. at B., and afflicted; the ☉ affl. in ♊ or ♋; afflictions to the ☉ in a male nativity, and to the ☽ and ♀ in a female; the ☽ affl. in airy signs; the water signs and the ☽ influence, as well as the afflictions of ♆, tend to this disease; caused by the atonic action of the ☽; ♆ afflicted, or affl. the ☉, ☽, Asc., or hyleg at B., or by dir.; ♆ afflicting ☿ at B.; ♄ affl. in ♊, ♋, or ♒; a ♄ disease; ♄ in the 6th H., and affl. the ☉, ☽, or ♃; a ♊ disease; many planets afflicted in fixed signs, strongly characteristic of the Lymphatic Temperament; caused by improper oxygenation of the blood, and lung disturbances. (See "Beriberi" under Dropsy; Emaciation, Leukocytes, Malnutrition, "Non-Oxygenation" under Oxygen; Pale, "Blood" under Red; Sickly, Thin, Wasting, Weak. Also note the other paragraphs in this section).

**Cerebral Anaemia**—An ♈ disease; the ☉ or ♄ affl. in ♈ at B. (See Cerebral).

**Chlorosis**—Anaemia in Young Women—(See Chlorosis).

**Pernicious Anaemia**—The ☉ affl. in ♎ or ♒; the ☉ affl. by ♄ in males, or with females the ☽ ☌ or ill-asp. ♄; the 8° ♌ or ♒ containing the ☉, ☽, or malefics at B., and afflictions to this degree.

**Women**—Anaemia In—The ☉ in the sex sign ♏, affl. by ♆, ♅, or ♄, and often attended by profuse menstruation (See "Profuse" under Menses); the ☉ in ♉, ♌, ♏, or ♒, the fixed signs, and affl. by malefics; the ☽, ♏, and affl. by malefics. (See Chlorosis).

**Young Women**—Anaemia In—(See Chlorosis).

**ANAESTHETICS**—Anaesthesia—Remedies and means of producing Insensibility—Typical drugs of ♆, such as Analgesics, Anodynes, Chloroform, Ether, Hypnotics, Narcotics, Opiates, Soporifics. (See these subjects. Also see Insensibility, "Neptune Influence" under Neptune; "Sleeping Potions" under Heart).

**ANALEPTIC**—An agent restoring health and strength. A therapeutic property of ♃ and ♃ remedies. (See Jupiter, Restoratives).

**ANALGESIA** — Analgesics — Producing Insensibility to Pain and Suffering—A ♆ influence, and caused by ♆ afflictions at B., or by dir., or produced by the use of ♆ drugs and remedies, or methods and influences under the rule of ♆. Analgesic drugs are under the rule of ♆. (See references under Anaesthetics. Analgesia is also caused by Subs of the Atlas, the 1st Cervical vertebra. (See Vertebrae).

**ANALYSIS**—Of Tissues—(See "Absorption" under Tissues).

**ANAPHRODISIACS**—Remedies which lessen passion and sexual desire. A therapeutic property of ♆ remedies, such as narcotics, opiates, and sedatives. Also the remedies of ♄ act as sedatives. (See Aphrodisiac, Narcotics, Neptune, "Drugs" and "Remedies" under Saturn; Sedatives, etc.).

**ANARCHISTS**—Anarchy—Dangerous to the Community and Society—Destructive—Riotous—Cranks—Bomb Plotters, etc.—In the star maps of Anarchists the malefics bear sway, as a rule, are strongly fortified, usually in angles, or rising and elevated in the East, and above the Luminaries; the ☉ ☌ or ill-asp. ♅; ♆ affl. in ♈ or ♒; ♆ affl. in ♈, bomb plotters; ♅ □ or ☍ ☿ at B; ♅ ☌ or ill-asp. ♂; ♅ in the 5th H., and espec. when affl. by ♆; ♅ affl. in the 9th H. tends to make red Anarchists and Fanatics; ♅ affl. in ♎; ♅ □ or ☍ ♄; ♃ affl. in ♒; ♂ in the 3rd or 9th H., and strongly afflicting ☿, the ruler of the mind; ♂ ☌ or ill-asp. ♆; ☿ affl. by ♂ and other malefics, and espec. by ♂, the planet of violence. (See Assassins, Dangerous, Destructiveness, Enthusiasm, Fanatical, Fury, Ideals, Ideas, Imprisonment, Notions, Politics, Radicalism, Rashness, Reactionary, Reformers, Revolutionary, Riotous, Sedition, Violent, etc.).

**ANARETA**—The planet which destroys life, and the Anaretic Place is the sign and degree occupied by the Anareta at B. Any of the planets can act as Anareta when the dominion of death is vested in it, and when the planet afflicts the hyleg at B., and by dir., in a train of evil directions, and also occupies an Anaretic Place at B. (See Killing Place). The dominion of death is vested in the planet which occupies an Anaretic Place at B., as in the 4th, 6th, 8th, or 12th Houses, and the planets ruling the signs on the cusps of these houses are the disposers of these places. The strength of the Anareta, and of the Anaretical Places, and the rulers of these places, must be considered in passing judgment as to the duration of life. The Anareta falling in the term of a malefic greatly increases the danger, but if in the term of a benefic, almost any asp. of the benefic would save life. A malefic in the term of ♃ or ♀ would lose much of its anaretic power, and be scarcely able to kill, and a benefic in the terms of a malefic would be rendered equally unable to save. The ☉ may become Anareta when the ☽ or Asc. are hyleg, and the ☽ may become Anareta when the ☉ or Asc. are hyleg. The ☉ or Asc. may become Anareta when the ☽ is hyleg. The ☉, ☽, and ☿, being variable, may become Anareta when in asp. to ♄ or ♂, unless a benefic give testimony, and also the ☽ can operate as Anareta when in evil asp. the malefics. The ☉ can be Anareta when he is in the signs of ♄, and evilly aspected by ♄ and ♂, and acting in a train of evil directions, and cause death. The ☉, ☽, ♃, ♀ and ☿ can act as Anareta in morbid deaths. When acting as Anareta, ♆ disposes to death in a riotous manner, assassination, or a violent death. ♅ as Anareta causes death by violent accidents, explosions, machinery, or by suicide. ♄ when Anareta causes death by falls, bruises, crushes, hurts and concussions. As Anareta ♄ and ♂ are equally destructive whether by day or night in nativities. ♂ when Anareta causes death by burns, scalds, fire, cuts, stabs, explosions, etc., according to the nature of the sign he is in, and aspects to him. Planets in the 8th H. at B. can act as Anareta, and cause death by accidents or injuries when they reach the Descendant, the cusp of the 7th H. by dir. The Part of Fortune, ⊕, can become Anareta when the ☉, ☽, or Asc. are hyleg. A malefic when Anareta, and elevated above the Lights, will tend to a violent death, but if a benefic be elevated above the malefic, it will destroy or modify the anaretic tendency, and also the injurious effects of a malefic, when Anareta, will be greatly lessened if the ☉ and ☽ be elevated above the malefic at B. (See Apheta, "Arguments for Death" under Death; Directions, Hyleg. Also see the subject of "Death" under each of the planets, and note the kinds of death caused by the planets).

**ANASARCA**—General Dropsy—(See "Anasarca" under Dropsy).

**ANATOMICAL CHANGES**—♄ tends to change the body by retention of wastes, deposits, crystallization, decay, slowing up or stopping of functions, etc., and thus change the form and shape of the body, leading to deformities, disease, or death. ♂ changes the anatomy by too much heat in a part, causing fusion of parts, or the burning up of too much tissue. The ☉ also, when acting with ♂, and in a pathological way, will give a surplus of heat to a part, resulting in anatomical changes. The vertebrae of the spine being subjected to much heat thru the afflictions of the ☉ and ♂, tend to melt the bones, and cause the spine to assume many different shapes. (See Ankylosis, Spine, Subluxations, Vertebrae). Each of the planets have a beneficial and a pathological, or disease and disturbing influence, according to their sign positions, aspects to each other, and to the ☉, ☽, Asc., or hyleg at B., and by dir. (See "Action", "Influence", under each of the planets).

**ANCESTRY**—(See Aunts, Birth, Grandparents, Heredity, Inherent, Organic, Parents, Uncles).

**ANDROGYNOUS**—(See Hermaphrodite).

**ANDROMEDA**—Caput Andromeda—A Constellation of the nature of ♃ and ♀ in the 3rd face of ♈. (See Impalement). Zona Andromeda, in the last face of ♈, is of the nature of ♀.

**ANEMIA**—(See Anaemia).

**ANEURYSM**—A Dilatation of an Artery, The ☽ affl. in ♊; the ☽ and ♃ in signs which rule the arms, hands, legs and feet affect the vesicles and glands of these parts causing cysts, ulcers, aneurysms, and varicose veins; the ☽ in ♊, ♋, ♌, ♍, ♐, ♑, ♒, and ♓, in parts ruled by these signs; ♂ in signs which rules the arms, hands, legs and feet tends to aneurysms and inflammatory complaints in these parts; ♂ in ♌; ♂ in ♌ in the 6th H., and afflicted; a ♌ disease, and afflictions in ♌; ♌ on the Asc. at B. Aneurysm of the arch of the Aorta is caused by afflictions in ♌, and by Subs at AP, HP, and Lu.P., and which may be caused by spasmodic gushing of the blood thru the aorta, and espec. when ♅ is in ♌, and affl. by ♄ and ♂. (See Aorta, Arteries, Dilatations, Heart, "Blood Vessels" under Rupture; Varicose, Vesicles, Vessels).

**Hernial Aneurysm**—(See "Aneurysm" under Hernia).

**Varicose Aneurysm**—The simultaneous rupture of an artery and a vein—Caused by the ☽ affl. in ♊. (See Rupture, Varicose).

**ANGER**—Choler—Wrath—Ruled principally by ♂.

**Disease Arising from Anger**—Caused by ♂; ♂ in ♉ or ♏ and □ ♅; ♂ □ or ☍ ♄, and both in angles; many planets in fixed signs at B., and espec. malefics in such signs in angles, and afflicting each other, retains anger; ☽ ☌ ♂ in the Asc. when taken ill, and afflicted with spleen (Hor'y); ♅ ☌, □, ☍ ♂; ♅ in ♉ or ♏ in □ ♂; ♏ on the Asc., and espec. if ♂ be there in ♏. (See Choler, "Choleric Temperament" under Choleric; "Desire Body" under Desire; Dispersions, Effervescent, Enmity, Excitable, Fighting, Folly, Frenzy, Furious, Leukocytes, Madness, Profane, Quarrels, Rashness, Riotous, Temper, Violent, etc.).

**ANGINA**—A sense of suffocation—A ♉ disease; ♄ affl. in ♉ at B.; ♂ affl. in ♉ or ♌. (See Croup, Dyspnoea, Suffocation; "Quinsy" under Tonsils).

**Angina Pectoris**—Pain and oppression about the heart—A sense of suffocating contraction and compression about the lower part of the chest, and associated with heart disturbances—Caused by afflictions in ♌; a ♌ disease; ♂ affl. in ♌; Subs. at HP, the Heart Place, and at Lu.P., 3rd Dorsal.

**Case of Angina**—See "Angina Pectoris", Chap. 13, page 90, in Daath's Medical Astrology.

**False Angina**—Pseudo-Angina—May be caused by ♆, ♅, ♄, or ♂ in the ♉ or ♊ signs, but with lesser affliction if there be favorable asps. from the benefics and to the hyleg. Subs of the Atlas, the 1st Cervical vertebra. (See Heart, Vertebrae).

**ANGLES**—The angles of the star map are the 1st, 4th, 7th and 10th houses, and correspond to ♈, ♋, ♎, and ♑. Planets in angles are very strong and powerful in matters of health and disease, and are stronger than when in succedent or cadent houses, and have more power for good or ill over the life of the native. The malefic planets in the angles at B. become more powerful, and tend to disease, accidents, downfall, misfortune, or calamity to the native periodically along thru life, and when the angles are afflicted by directions, or when planets in angles at B. afflict their own places by dir., or transits. Angles show strength and vitality, and do not hasten death. In diagnosing disease by Astrology, and giving a prognosis, the student should note the influences affecting the angles, and the cardinal signs, as well as the influences of the 6th, 8th and 12th houses. (See Cardinal).

**ANGUISH OF MIND**—Tormented in Mind—Suffering in Mind—The ☉, ☽, or ☿ to the ill-asps. ♄ by tr. or dir.; the ☽ passing over the radical places of ♄, ♂, or ♀ at a Solar Rev., and these planets affl. at B.: the ☽ to the ☌ or P. Dec. the ☉ if the ☽ be hyleg and the ☉ affl. at B.; the ☽ to the □ or ☍ the ☉ by dir.; ♄ ruler of the 12th H., and ♄ in the 1st, 3rd or 9th houses if in these houses at B., and affl. the ☉, ☽, or ☿; anguish of mind is ruled over by the 8th H. conditions; in Hor'y Questions the dispositors of the ☉ and ☽ much afflicted and weak, and the ☽ □ the degree ascending, but with no ill-asp. of ♄ or ♂, the mind is much tormented; ☿ joined to the Anareta causes great anguish and delirium in illness. (See Anxiety, Dejected, Despondent, Depression, Despair, Fears, Hypochondria, "Low Spirits" under Low; Melancholy, Pain, Suffering, Worry, etc.).

**ANGULAR**—

**Angular Body**—(See "Angular" under Body).

**Angular Face**—(See "Angular" under Face).

**Planets Angular**—(See Angles).

**Spine**—Angular Curvature of—(See "Humpback" under Spine).

**ANIDROSIS**—Anhidrosis—Deficiency of Sweat—(See "Lessened" under Sweat).

**ANIMAL**—

**Animal Bodies**—Putrefaction of—(See Putrid).

**Animal Character**—Animal Expression—The Signs ♈, ♉, ♌, ♏, the 2nd half of ♐, and ♑, when on the Asc. at B. tend to give an animal expression, and more of the animal instincts to the human mind, except when ☿, the ruler of the mind, is in the Asc. and configurated with the ☽ and benefics. (See Personality).

**Animal Heat**—(See "Animal" under Heat).

**Animal Instincts**—Animal Propensities—The ☽ rules the animal instincts, and the ☽ strong at B., rising and elevated, or in the Asc., and espec. in an animal sign, tends to make the animal instincts stronger, and to give more of the primitive instincts, rash impulses, animal and passional gratifications, which, unless controlled, lead to disease, suffering, and an earlier death. (See "Atrophy" under Brain). Animal propensities depend almost wholly upon the ☽, her position and aspects, and the ☽ when afflicted tends to drink, debauchery, dissipation and gluttony. (See Desire). ♆ in evil asp. to ♀ gives larger animal propensities, and also ♆ in the 5th H. at B., and afflicted, or affl. ♀ and the ☽. The 5° ♍ on the Asc. at B. is said to make one full of animal spirits. (See "Animal Character" in this section).

**Animal Magnetism**—(See Magnetism).

**Animal Sensations**—(See Sensation).

**Animal Signs**—The Signs which have animals as symbols, as ♈, ♉, ♌, 2nd half of ♐, and ♑. People born with the ☉, ☽, and planets in these signs, or when they are on the Asc., are apt to be more subject to disease, live more in their lower minds until awakened into a higher spiritual life. (See Beasts; "Dogs" under Children; Quadrupeds).

**Animal Tissues**—(See Tissues).

**ANIMALS**—Beasts—Quadrupeds—Man is more or less subject to injuries, sufferings, and vicissitudes by animals acording to the positions of the planets at B., and whether they occupy animal signs or not, and are afflicted therein by ♂, or other malefic planets at B., or by dir.

**Bites by Animals**—(See Bites).

**Cattle**—Hurts and Injuries By—(See Cattle).

**Death by Animals**—Sickness of—♄ ☌ ♂ in animal signs, and chiefly the sickness or death of animals of the nature and form of the sign containing the ☌; the ☽ and planets in Quadrupedal Signs at the birth of an animal, or at the Equinoxes and Solstices, tend to bring disease, suffering and death to animals, and events affecting them. (See "Virus" under Pestilence).

**Devoured By**—The Body Devoured by after Death—(See "Birds of the Air" under Air; "Body Devoured" under Burial).

**Elephants**—Sickness or Death of—(See Elephants).

**Ferocious Animals**—Hurts By—☉ to ☌ ♂ by dir.

**Good or Ill**—Animals Affected for Good or Ill—The Zodiacal Constellations, and those of the ruling Fixed Stars out of the Zodiac, in terrestrial or quadrupedal signs at a Solar Eclipse, the effects fall upon animals of similar form. (See Quadrupeds).

**Great Beasts**—Attacks By—(See Beasts, Cattle, Great, Horses).

**Horses**—(See Horses).

**Hurts by Animals**—Injury or Death By—♂ by dir. to the ☌ or ill-asp. the Asc.; the Asc. to the place of the Ascelli or Capricornus; ill-asps. of ♂ to the ☉, ☽, Asc., or M.C.; the ☽ in earthy signs at B., and to the ☌ or ill-asps. ♂ by dir.; the ☉ affl. in ♐ at B., and by dir. (See Beasts, Bites, Bruises, Cattle, Distortions, Horses, Kicks, Quadrupeds).

**Kicks**—(See Horses, Kicks).

**Large Animals**—Hurts and Injuries By—(See "Great" under Beasts, Cattle; Horses, Quadrupeds).

**Odors From**—(See Odors).

**Quadrupeds**—(See Quadrupeds).

**Reptiles**—(See Reptiles).

**Resembles Animals**—(See "Dogs" under Children; Inhuman; "Animal Forms" under Monsters).

**Sickness of Animals**—(See "Death" in this section).

**Small Animals**—Ruled by the 6th H., and when the native has malefics in this house at B., he tends to be unfortunate with, and have losses of small animals, as with sheep, goats, rabbits, etc. (See Goats, Sheep).

**Sterility In**—(See Mules).

**Venomous Animals**—Bites By—Injuries By—(See Venomous).

**Very Animal Like**—(See "Resembles" in this section. Also see Case, "Female", Chap. 8, page 49, in Daath's Medical Astrology).

**Wild Animals**—Death or Injury By—Attacks By—♄ and ♂ in terrestrial signs, and afil. the ☉ or ☽; ♄ occi., in signs of bestial form, and the ☽ succedent to him, and the death will occur by day, and in public, if ♃ offer testimony and be afflicted at the same time, and such a death may occur in a public combat with wild beasts; ♄ near the Constellation of the Serpent; Comets appearing in ♌. (See Beasts, Wild).

**ANIMATION**—

**Full Of**—(See Active, Energy, Zest).

**Lack Of**—(See Apathy, Dull, Inactive, Inertia, Lassitude, Lethargy, Listless, Malaise, Weak, etc).

**Suspended Animation**—(See "Suppression" under Functions).

**ANISOCORIA**—(See Iris).

**ANKLES**—Shank—Shin Bone—Tibia—Astragalus—The Ankles are under the structural rulership of the ♒ sign, and correspond to the wrists, ruled by the ♌ sign. The ankles are also ruled and influenced by the 11th H. (See Arms, Wrists).

**Affected**—The ankles tend to be affected with the ☉ in ♊, and ♅ in ♐. (See Table 196 in Simmonite's Arcana).

**Afflictions In**—All Diseases and Afflictions In—Signified by the ♒ sign, the 11th and 12th houses, and afflictions therein; ♄ or ♂ in ♒; signified in horary questions by ♂ in ♓.

**Broken Ankles**—Fractures of—The ☽, ♄, or ♂ affl. in ♒; ♒ on the Asc. at B., and containing a malefic, and afflicted by an adverse direction, or a malefic coming to the ☌ or ill-asp. the Asc.

**Cramps In**—♅ in ♒.

**Dropsy**—(See "Swellings" in this section).

**Injuries To**—(See "Broken" in this section).

**Knocking Together**—Caused by ♄ influence strong at B., or ♄ affl. in ♒; ♄ ascending at B. In Horary Questions ♄ as Sig. indicates such a person. (See "Dragging" under Gait).

**Lameness In**—♄, ♂, ☿, or the ☽ affl. in ♒, or ♒ on the Asc. and afflicted. (See Lameness).

**Operations On**—Incisions, and surgical operations upon the ankles should be avoided when the ☽ is passing thru ♒. (See Operations).

**Sprains**—Afflictions in ♑ or ♒; ♄ in ♑ or ♒ and afflicted; ♒ on the Asc. (See Sprains).

**Swollen Ankles**—The ☽ or ♀ affl. in ♒; afflictions in ♒; an ♒ disease; ♃ affl. in ♌ or ♒. (See Swellings).

**Weakness In**—♄ affl. in ♒, weakness in or near the ankles. (See Legs, Lower Extremities, Tibia).

**ANKYLOSIS**—The union or fusion of the bones of a joint, resulting in a stiff joint. Is caused by the ♄ deposits of waste or excess minerals of the system. Also caused by the excess heat of the ☉ and ♂ over the part, resulting in fusion and melting of the bony tissues. (See Adhesions, Anatomical, Joints). Ankylosis can occur between the joints of any part of the body, but is more common between the vertebrae, and in the hip joint, knee joint, elbow, wrists and finger joints. ♄ in the sign ruling the affected joint tends to dry up the fluids of the joint, cause deposits, solidification, hardening, Gout in the joint, etc., resulting in a stiff joint, and ankylosis. The ☉ ☌ ♂ in a sign, both hot and fiery planets, intensifies the heat in the part, and especially if in a fiery sign in the Asc. Thus the ☉ ☌ ♂ in ♌, and with ♌ on the Asc., would tend to fusion and ankylosis of the dorsal vertebrae; ♄ affl. in ♌ or ♒ tends to ankylosis of the spine thru deposits; ♄ in ♑ would tend to a stiff knee joint, from deposits; ♄ affl. in ♋, the sign opposite ♑, would tend to stiff elbow joints; ♄ in ♍, the sign opposite ♓, would tend to ankylosis of the finger joints, etc., due to cold, deposits, whereas ♂ in the same signs would tend to fusion by excess of heat. Improper kidney action, and Subs at KP, also usually enter into ankylosis afflictions, and in addition to adjusting the vertebra, or vertebrae, thru which the nerves pass to the part afflicted, KP, the Kidney Place in the spine, should be adjusted, to aid in elimination, secretion, and proper kidney action. (See Coalition, Crystallization, Deposits, Gout, Hardening, Heat, Stiff, etc.).

**Case**—A case of Ankylosis of the Hip Joint. See "Deformed", No. 689, in 1001 N.N.

**ANODYNE**—A drug relieving pain—A Therapeutic property of ♆. (See Anaesthetics, Analgesia, Narcotics, "Therapeutic Qualities" under Neptune; Sedatives).

**ANOREXIA**—Loss of Appetite—(See Appetite).

**ANOSMIA**—Loss of Smell—(See Smell).

**ANTARES**—Scorpion's Heart—Cor Scorpio—A violent fixed star of the 1st magnitude, situated in the 8° ♐, of the nature of ♃ and ♂. This star has an inimical influence on the eyesight for evil, and when the ☉ or ☽ are with it at B., tends to blindness, weak sight, eye trouble, etc. This star by its conjunctions and evil asps. tends to bring many dangers and evils upon humanity, and is one of the most mentioned stars in the textbooks of Astrology, for his evils. The good asps. of ♆ to Antares tend to give increased Spiritual Sight of a favorable nature, and the evil asps. of ♆ to Antares tend to Involuntary Clairvoyance and Mediumship, Obsessions, Spirit Controls, etc. The adverse influences of Antares when with the ☉ or ☽ at B., or afflicting them by dir., are mentioned under the following subjects, which see in the alphabetical arrangement—Accidents, Acquaintance (Death of); Assassination, Assaults (Violent); Beasts (Attacks by Great Beasts); Blindness, Blows, Burns, Calamities, Cattle, (Attacks By); Conjunctivitis, Dangers, Death (Violent Death); Demoniacal, Disease, Disgrace, Distempers (Hot); Drowning, Enemies, Eyes (Injury To and Eye Trouble); Falls (Danger From); Female Friend (Death Of); Fever (In Whole Body, and Putrid Fevers); Hanging; Hot Distempers; Ill-Health, Imprisonment; Injury (See Eyes, Right Eye, Military Life, Violence); Mediumship (Involuntary); Military Life (Injury In); Mother (Death of); Obsessions; "Over-heated" under Blood; Pestilence (Sickness or Death By); Peril, Pirates, Putrid Fevers; Right Eye (Injury to); Ruin; Scalds; Sickness (Extreme); Sight (Weak Sight and Injuries to); Spirit Controls; Strangulation; Stress (Periods of); Suffering; Suffocation, Treachery; Trouble; Vehicles (Dangers by); Violence; Violent Assaults; Violent Death; Whole Body (Fever In); Wife (Death of).

**ANTENATAL**—(See Conception, Foetus, Gestation, Pregnancy, Prenatal Epoch).

**ANTHELMINTIC**—A remedy expelling Worms. A therapeutic property of ♃.

**ANTHONY'S FIRE**—St. Anthony's Fire—(See Erysipelas).

**ANTHRAX**—(See Carbuncles).

**ANTICACHECTIC**—A therapeutic property of the ☉. (See Cachexia).

**ANTIDOTES**—An agent counteracting the action of a Poison. Each planet rules over certain drugs, herbs, minerals, metals and poisons, and as the planets are arranged in pairs of opposites in their effects, the poisons of one will be counteracted by drugs and remedies of the other. (For further consideration of this subject see Alexipharmic, Antipathy, Cure, Opposites, Poison, Remedies, Treatment).

**ANTIMONY**—A typical drug of ♄. (For use as a remedy, see Leprosy, Voluntary).

**ANTINEPHRITIC**—A remedy for inflammation of the Kidneys. ♀ remedies, and a therapeutic property of ♀. (See "Inflammation" under Kidneys).

**ANTIPATHY**—Contraries—Aversion—Dislike—The planets which rule opposite signs of the zodiac are in antipathy to each other. ♂ rules ♈, and ♀ rules ♎, the opposite sign. Thus ♂ is opposed to ♀, and the remedies of ♀ will oppose those of ♂. Also planets in their exalted signs are opposed to the rulers of the opposite signs. ♃ is exalted in ♋, and in vibratory, or therapeutical value, is opposed to ♄, the ruler of ♑, the sign opposite to ♋. Planets have antipathy to certain signs, which signs are their detriment or fall. ♂, a fiery planet, is weak and disturbing to the health when in ♓, a watery sign; ♄, a cold and dry planet, disturbs the body when in ♌, a fiery sign, as he is in antipathy with ♌, and has his detriment in ♌, and his fall in the fiery sign ♈. Each planet also has its especial therapeutical value, some working in harmony with each other, and some opposing, and in treating disease with medicines these values should be kept in mind. (See Drugs, Praeincipients, Remedies, Signatures, Therapeutic Properties, under each of the planets. Also see Chemical, Herbs, Medicines, Minimizing, Opposites, Remedies, Sympathy, Treatment).

**Disease by Antipathy**—When the afflicting planet causing the disease is opposed, or an enemy to the planet which rules the part of the body diseased or afflicted, the disease is said to arise from antipathy. Thus diseases under ♄ (♑) are treated by ☽ (♋) remedies. Disease under the ☉ (♌) are treated by ♄ (♒) remedies. Hippocrates and Galen taught antipathy and contraries in the treatment of disease. (See Hippocrates). Thus the expression, "Contraria Contrariis Curantur". Allopathy uses Contraries in the treatment of disease. (See Homeopathy). The Astrological selection of remedies has been based upon the antipathy or sympathy between the planetary influences ruling each herb, mineral or remedy. Among the planets ♄ opposes the ☉, ♂, ♀ and the ☽; ♃ opposes ♂; ♂ opposes ♄, ♃, ♀, ☿, and the ☽ in therapeutical ways, but ♂ is friendly with ♀ in helping to arouse the passions and the lower nature, and when the lower vibrations of ♂ and ♀ combine their forces in the unawakened soul, their influences tend to dissipation, debauchery, passional excesses. ♀ opposes ♄ and ♂.

A planet when passing thru its own sign is less apt to cause disease in the part ruled by such sign, but planets when passing thru signs which oppose their own strong signs are apt to produce irritation or disease, as when ♂ (♈) passing thru ♎ (♀) tends to acute inflammation of the kidneys for the time if ♎ was afflicted by ♂, or malefics at B. These rules will be easy to apply if the student will become thoroughly acquainted with the nature of each planet and sign, and then apply his knowledge to each case as it arises. A Table of the Friendships and Enmities of the Planets is given on page 241 in Dr. Broughton's Elements of Astrology. (See Kinetic).

**Enemies**—Antipathy Between People—Malefics in one nativity on the place of the ☉, ☽, or benefics in the other tend to antipathy and discord, and such are apt to dislike and mistrust each other, irritate each other, cause the other to weaken thru worry and discord, antagonism, etc., and to invite disease or an earlier death of the other in their natural unawakened states, and this is also the case when the Asc., or rising signs in the two maps are in □ or ☍ to each other between the two parties, and people who are contemplating marriage should see to it that their star maps blend if they would have the best of health, happiness, and contentment with each other. These rules also apply in the choosing of a Healer, Physician, or even a business associate. People also should avoid each other when the Asc. in the radix of one is on the cusp of the 6th, 8th or 12th house in the other. (For the rules in choosing a Healer, see "Compatibility" under Healers. Also see Enemies, Friends).

**Healers**—The Antipathy or Compatibility of a Healer to the patient—The magnetism of some Healers tends to kill the patient, while the magnetism of others, where the star maps of patient and healer blend, tends to the more quickly restore the patient to health, and thousands of lives would be saved if people knew Astrology, and would spend some time beforehand in deciding upon some one who is to be their permanent advisor and healer before sickness overtakes them. (These rules are further considered under the subjects of Healers, Polarity, Sympathy, and Treatment. Also see Hatred, Husband, Love Affairs, Marriage, Marriage Partner, Wife).

**ANTIPERIODIC**—(See Apiol; "Typical Drugs" under Mercury).

**ANTIPERISTALSIS**—An abnormal movement of the bowels towards the stomach, or of the stomach towards the oesophagus.

**Of the Bowels**—(See "Antiperistalsis" under Bowels).

**Of the Stomach**—(See "Antiperistalsis" under Stomach. Also see Emetics, Nausea, Peristalsis, Vomiting).

**ANTIPHLOGISTIC**—An agent reducing inflammation. A therapeutic property of ♄ remedies, as opposed to ♂, causing inflammations. (See Inflammation, Saturn Remedies).

**ANTIPYRETIC**—A Febrifuge—A Fever-reducing remedy—A therapeutic property of ♄ and ♄ remedies. (See Aconite, Fever, Saturn Remedies).

**ANTISPASMODIC**—A therapeutic property of ♃ remedies. (See Spasmodic).

**ANURIA**—Absence, deficiency, or suppression of Urine. (See Urine).

**ANUS**—Sphincter Ani Muscle—Ruled by ♏. Also under the external rule of ♎.

**Condyloma**—Wart-like Growth on Anus—Caused by afflictions in ♏; ♄ in ♏; Subs at LPP, the 4th and 5th Lumbar vertebrae. (See Warts).

**Diseases of Anus**—Troubles with the Anus—♂ in ♏ or ♐, and afflicted; ♂ in ♐ in 6th H., and afflicted. (See Fundament, Rectum).

**Fissure**—Afflictions in ♏, and Subs at LPP. (See Fissure, Fistula, Vertebrae).

**Fistula**—(See Fistula).

**Hemorrhoids**—(See Hemorrhoids).

**Imperforate Anus**—♄ affl. in ♏. Case —(See "Puzzle Horoscope", No. 273 in 1001 N.N.).

**Inbreathing Thru Anus**—♄ affl. in ♏ tends to a tight and constricted Sphincter Ani muscle, which disturbs the intake of air thru the Rectum, and the air pressure in the bowels, which indirectly disturbs the diaphragm and respiration. In such cases it is necessary at times to forcibly dilate the sphincter ani.

**Piles**—(See Hemorrhoids).

**Sex Relations**—By Rectum and Anus —(See Homosexuality, "Sex Perversions" under Perversions).

**Ulceration Of**—♄ or ♂ affl. in ♏. Caused by Subs at PP and LPP, and also at KP. (See Ulcers, Vertebrae).

**Wart-like Growth**—On Anus—(See "Condyloma" in this section).

**ANXIETY**—Anxiety Neuroses—Anxious Fears—Worry—Fixed Ideas—♆ and ♄ by their afflictions are the principal planets causing anxiety, worries, false fears, obsessions, and to give a sense of impending danger, calamity, ill-health, or reversals. The ♓ sign, and the 12th H. are also important to be considered in this connection, and espec. when occupied by malefic planets. Anxiety and worry are also more common with people born under the Mutable Signs, and who also may have many planets in such signs. Fixed Signs tend to the least worry and anxiety. Cardinal signs are usually too much absorbed in their plans and promotions to realize their dangers. Afflictions to the ☽ also tend to increase fear, apprehension, worry, and anxiety. The 12th H. is the house of tribulation, worry, anxiety, affliction, self-undoing, confinement, imprisonment, distress, trouble, and people born with this house much afflicted tend to have more than their share of what they may call "Ill-Fate". The following are some of the important planetary influences which tend to produce anxiety,—The ☉ ☌ the Asc. by dir., much anxiety; the ☉, ♄, or ♆ affl. in the 12th H.; an eclipse of the ☉ falling on the place of ♄ at B.; the ☉ ill-aspected at B., and to the ☌ or ill-asp. the ☽, ♄, ♃, ♂, ☿, Asc., or M.C. by dir.; the ☉ or ☽ hyleg, and to the ☌ or ill-asp. ♄ by dir.; the ☽ ill-aspected at B., and to the ☌ or ill-asps the ☉, ♄, ♅, or ♂ by dir.; the ☽ affl. in ♑; the ☽ affl. in airy signs; the ☽ to Castor, Cauda Lucida, and Caput Algol, great anxiety; the ☽ to the ☌ Arcturus or Deneb, many cares and anxieties due to the native's own folly; the Prog. ☽ to the □ or ☍ the Asc. or M.C.; the ☽ to the ☌ or ill-asp. ♂ by dir., strange anxieties; the Pr. ☽ to the ☌ or ill-asp. the ☉, ♄, or ♂; ♆ and ♄ afflicted in the houses of mind, the 3rd or 9th houses; ♄ in the 10th H. at a Solar Rev., and elevated above the ☉ and ☽; ♄ to the ☌ or ill-asp. the ☉, ☽, Asc., M.C., or any planet by dir.; ♄ or ♃ to the cusp the 12th H. by dir.; the transits of ♄ over the places of the ☉, ☽, and planets in the radical map, or thru the Asc., M.C., 6th or 12th houses; ☿ affl. at B., weak and ill-dignified; ☿ □ or ☍ ☽, worry, anxiety and mental strain; 2nd Dec. of ♊ on Asc.; 3rd Dec. ♊ on Asc., an anxious and restless life; 3rd Dec. ♒ denotes; Asc. to the □ or ☍ ☽ by dir. (See Anguish, Cares; "Anxiety" under Children; Digestion, Fears; "Irregular" under Functions; Hypochondria, Responsibility, Restless, Sorrow, Stomach, Strange, Worry).

**AORTA**—The main Arterial Trunk—Ruled by the ♌ Sign.

**Aneurysm Of**—(See Aneurysm).

**Aortic Disease**—Planets affl. in ♌, and espec. ♃ or ♀, as ♃ rules the arterial circulation, and ♀ the venous blood; ♅ in ♌, and affl. by ♄ or ♂, tends to spasmodic gushing of the blood thru the aorta; also caused by Subs. at HP, the Heart Place. (See Arteries, Blood, Circulation, Heart, Vertebrae, Vessels).

**Aortic Plexus**—(See Hypogastrium).

**APATHY**—A Want of Passion or Feeling—Indifference—(See Cohabitation, Dull, Feelings, Indifference, Inertia, Lassitude, Lethargy; "Free from Passion" under Passion; Rouse, Weak).

**APHASIA**—Loss of Speech—(See "Aphasia" under Speech).

**APHETA**—Giver of Life—Prorogator—(See Hyleg).

**Aphetic Processes**—(See Nutrition).

**APHONIA**—Loss of Voice due to a peripheral lesion. (See "Aphonia" under Vocal).

**APHRODISIACS**—Remedies which increase passion and sex desire. A therapeutic property of ♂ and ♂ remedies. Cantharides, a ♂ drug, is the principal drug used for this purpose. Also Love Potions, ruled by ♀, are used for this purpose. (See Anaphrodisiac).

**APHTHAE**—An Eruption—Thrush—Roundish pearl-colored flakes or specks on the lips, in the mouth, or in the gastro-intestinal tract—Small, white Ulcerous patches—

**Mouth**—Aphthae In—Thrush—Aphthous Stomatitis—Canker—Sore

Mouth—The ☽ or ♀ affl. in ♉; afflictions in ♋, and due to indigestion; ♂ affl. in ♎. Also occurs in adults as a result of general weakness, and a run down condition of the system; Subs at MCP, SP. (See Debility, Gangrene, "General Ill-Health" under Health; Indigestion, Mouth, Thrush, Ulcers, Vertebrae). Aphthae of the Intestines may occur when there are Subs at KP, and PP, 2nd Lumbar. Aphthae of the Rectum occurs when there are Subs at KP, and LPP, the 4th and 5th Lumbar. Look up these centers under Vertebrae.

**APIOL**—Parsley—Petroselinum—A typical drug of ☿. An Antiperiodic.

**APOLOGETIC ATTITUDE**—(See "Inferiority Complex" under Inferiority).

**APOPLEXY**—Apoplexies—The rupture of a blood vessel, or the oozing of blood into a part without rupture of the blood vessel. Is principally of two kinds, Cerebral and Pulmonary, but may also occur in the Spinal Cord, and also in the Spleen, in the Splenic substance.

**Causes**—The bad aspects of ♃, and high blood pressure, are the principal causes, and may also be the result of gluttony, gormandizing, causing plethora, and too much blood; a ♃ disease; ♃ affl. in ♉, ♌, ♏, or ♒; the ☉ in ♈ and ☌ or any asp. ♂, and afflicted by malefics; the ☉ affl. by ♃; ☉ affl. in ♉; the ☽ hyleg, and to the ☌ or ill-asps. ♄ by dir.; a ☽ disease; the ☽ afflicted at B., or by dir., by ♃ and the malefics; ♅ rising, or afflicting the Asc.; a ♄ disease; ♄ ☌ or ill-asp. the ☽ or ♃ at B., or by dir.; ♂ ☌ or ill-asp. ♃ at B., or by dir; ♂ in ♈ in the 6th H., and afflicted; ☿ at B. in P. Dec. ♄ and ♂, and in □ the ☽ from the 1st or 7th H.: an ♈ and ♉ disease; ♈ or ♉ on the Asc. at B., and afflicted; associated with the 16° and 24° ♉. (See Aneurysm, Plethora, Pressure, Rupture, Vessels).

**Cerebral Apoplexy**—An ♈ disease when the ☉, ☽, ♃, and the malefics are in ♈ at B., and afflicted; the ☉ to the ☌ or ill-asp. ♂ by dir.; the ☉ in ill-asp. ♃ at B., and by dir.; the ☽ hyleg, and to the ☌ or ill-asp. ♄ by dir.; the Prog. ☽ to the □ or ☍ the radical ♃; caused by ♃ when the dominion of death is vested in him; ♃ affl. in ♈; ♃ affl. in ♌ or ♒; ♂ afflicting the hyleg at B.; ☿ □ ☽ from the 1st or 7th houses, and ☿ at the same time afflicted by both ♄ and ♂ by □ or ☍; the Asc. to the place of Regulus. (See Cerebral, "Rush of Blood to Head" under Head).

**Death by Apoplexy**—♃ shows; ♃ much afflicted at B., and affl. the hyleg by dir.; ♃ ☌ ☉ in ♈, and affl. the hyleg; the ☉ affl. at B., and in □ or ☍ the ☽ or Asc., whichever may be hyleg, and the hyleg afflicted at the same time with a train of fatal directions. Case—See "Inquest on Birthday", No. 792 in 1001 N.N.

**Pulmonary Apoplexy**—♃ affl. in ♊ or ♐. (See Hemorrhage, Lungs).

**APOTHECARY**—(See Chemists).

**APPARITIONS**—(See Phenomena, Psychic).

**APPEARANCE**—The Physical and Personal Appearance—The Form and Figure—The Physical Appearance is denoted by the 1st H., and the sign upon the Asc., the Decanate rising, together with the sign occupied by the ruler of the rising sign. (See Decanates). Lilly judges the appearance from the sign ascending on the Asc., and the two signs containing the lord of the Asc., and the sign the ☽ is in, and by mixing these influences judiciously takes the greater number of testimonies. He also takes the sign descending as playing an important part. The appearance is judged by the lord of the Asc., planets in or near the Asc., planets rising, and by the positions of the ☉ and ☽, and their aspects. Planets which aspect the Asc. influence both mind and body, and tend to modify the influence of any sign, or planets in signs. When the latter part of a sign is upon the Asc., and a large part of the next sign in the Asc., and party will partake of both signs, and both will tend to influence the appearance and shape of the body. For example, a person having the latter part of ♐ upon the Asc. may have a handsome forehead, and a fine head of hair, but with ♑ also largely in the Asc. the rest of the face, and the lower part, the chin and jaw, may be very ugly. In the case of Twins, one being born with the last degrees of ♐ on the Asc. may be tall, and largely of the ♐ nature and appearance, while the second twin, born a little later, having ♑ rising, would tend to be shorter, and perhaps more sickly than the first one, and also more ugly and crooked in appearance. The subject of appearance, and the form and stature of the body, are further considered under the following subjects, which see in the alphabetical arrangement,—(1) See subjects naming the parts of the body, as Chin, Dimples, Head, Hair, Eyes, Ears, Face, Lips, Mouth, Neck, Nose, Teeth, Shoulders, etc., and on down to the feet. (2) See such subjects as Active, Animal, Aspect, Attractive, Awkward, Beautiful, Big, Blemishes, Bodily, Body, Broad, Careless, Cheerful, Color, Commanding, Commonplace, Complexion, Constitution, Consumptive, Corpulent, Countenance, Crooked, Defects, Deformities, Distorted, Dress, Dull, Dwarf, Effeminate, Erect, Expression, Extremities, Fair, Fat, Features, Feeble, Fierce, Fiery, Filthy, Flabby, Fleshy Form, Fowls, Fragile, Freckles, Full, Gait, Genteel, Giants, Good, Graceful, Grave, Great, Growth, Handsome, Harmonious, Healthy, Heavy, Height, Idiots, Ill-formed, Impairments, Imperfections, Indifferent, Infirm, Inhuman, Intellectual, Jerky, Lame, Large, Lean, Light, Limbs, Limp, Long, Look, Lumpish, Maimed, Malformed, Manner, Map, Marks, Meagre, Mean, Medium, Melancholic, Members, Middle, Misshaped, Moles, Monsters, Moping, Muscular, Mutilated, Narrow, Natural, Neat, Negro, Nervous, Normal, Obesity, Ordinary, Pale, Parts of the Body, Pensive, Personal, Physical, Pimpled, Pleasant, Plump, Pockmarked, Posture, Prepossessing (see Commanding); Prominent, Protruding, Proud, Puffing, Race, Raw, Red, Rigid, Robust, Ruddy, Rugged, Sad, Savage, Scars, Serious, Shaggy, Shape, Shiny, Short, Sickly, Size, Skeleton, Skin, Slender, Small, Smart, Smiles, Smooth, Soft, Spare, Spotted, Squab, Stature, Stiff, Stooping, Stout, Straight, Strength, Strong, Sturdy, Sunken, Swarthy, Tall, Tan, Temperament, Thick, Thin, Thoughtful, Troubled, Ugly, Uncleanly, Undersized, Undeveloped, Ungainly, Unhealthy, Unrefined, Untidy, Upright, Visage, Vulgar, Walk, Wanton, Weak, Weight, Well, White, Wide, Withered, Wrinkled, Youthful-looking, etc. There are also a class of diseases which affect the appearance, as Anaemia, Emaciation, Enlargements, Jaundice, Sores, Tumors, Ulcers, Wasting, etc. If the subject you have in mind is not listed here, look for it in the alphabetical arrangement, as these subjects mentioned are only suggestive, and to help the student to locate subjects which might be overlooked. The subject of Appearance is largely considered, and with references, under "Body", "Complexion", "Face", "Hair", and "Stature".

**APPENDIX**—Appendix Vermiformis—The Appendix is under the internal rule of the ♏ Sign, and is also influenced by the ♍ Sign. Some Writers say ♅ rules the Appendix. Another modern Writer says it is his opinion that ♆ rules the Appendix, and that disturbances of this organ are closely associated with Psychic, Spiritual, and Astral causes.

**Appendicitis**—Diseases of the Appendix—Inflamed Appendix, etc.—Afflictions in ♍ and ♏, and espec. ♂ affl. in these signs; a ♍ and ♏ disease; the ☉ affl. in ♏; ♅ is a common afflictor in this disease, and with ♅ affl. in ♍ or ♏; ♆ affl. in ♍ or ♏, and espec. with ♆ in the 6th H.; a ♆ disease; ♄ or ♂ in ♍ or ♏, and afflicted; afflictions in or to the 18° ♏; afflictions in the first three degrees, and in the 22° of the common signs; afflictions in or to the 22° of ♌ or ♒; caused by Subs at CP, KP, UPP, and PP. (See Abdomen, Bowels, Vertebrae).

**Death by Appendicitis**—♂ in ♍ or ♏ in the 6th H., affl. the hyleg, and ♂ holding the dominion of death. Case of Death by Appendicitis—See "Perhouse", No. 301, in 1001 N.N.

**Left Side**—Case of the Appendix and Caecum on the Left Side—See "Heart", No. 981, in 1001 N.N.

**Operations**—Do not operate upon, or remove the Appendix when the ☽ is passing thru ♍, ♎, or ♏, as increased inflammation of the surrounding tissues, infections, or death, are apt to result. (See Caecum, "Inflammation" under Bowels).

**APPETITE**—Appetites—The Animal Appetites—Desire for Food—Sexual Appetites—Lust, etc. The ♉ and ♋ Signs have close relationship to the appetite for food, and also the planets ♃ and ♀, and these signs and planets when afflicted tend to abuses in eating. The sexual appetites are dominated largely by the lower vibrations of ♂, ♅, and ♆, and the afflictions of these planets to ♀. The following subjects have to do with Appetite, the Appetites, and the Desires of the physical body, and of the Lower Mind, which subjects see in the alphabetical arrangement when not considered here.

**Abnormal Appetite**—♄, ♃, or ♂ affl. in ♋; afflictions in ♉ and ♋; ♂ affl. in ♉. (See Abnormal, Eating, Excesses, Food, Gluttony, Obesity, etc.).

**Amorous; Animal Appetites**—(See Animal, Eating, Food, Gluttony, Lust, Passion, etc.).

**Anorexia**—(See "Loss of" in this section).

**Bad Appetite**—(See "Loss of" in this section).

**Belly**—Love Their Belly—(See Eating, Epicureans, Feasting, Food, Gluttony).

**Big Appetite**—(See "Excesses" under Eating and Food. Also see Gluttony).

**Blood**—Blood Corrupted from Over-indulgence of Appetites—(See Impure).

**Capricious Appetite**—(See "Appetite" under Peculiar).

**Chaotic**—(See Chaotic, "Sensuous" under Sensuality; Unnatural).

**Conviviality**—(See Feasting).

**Cravings; Death**—From Excesses in Eating—(See Eating).

**Delicate Appetite**—♀ in the 6th H.

**Depraved Appetites**—(See Depraved).

**Desire; Diet**—(See Diet, Eating, Food).

**Drink; Drugs**—(See Narcotics).

**Eating; Epicureans; Excesses; Extravagance; Fantastic Appetites**—(See Peculiar).

**Feasting; Food; Free Living**—(See Free).

**Gluttony; Gormandizing**—(See Gluttony).

**Gratification**—Of Appetites—(See References under Gratification).

**Gustativeness Large**—(See "Abnormal" in this section. Also see Epicureans, Feasting, Gluttony).

**Habits; Hearty Eater**—(See Eating, Gluttony).

**High Living**—(See Free, High, Riotous).

**Hunger**—(See Cravings, Food)

**Illicit Appetites**—(See Chaotic, Drink, Drunkenness, Love Affairs, Lust, Narcotics, Perversions, Sensuous, Sex).

**Illusory Appetites**—(See "Appetites" under Peculiar).

**Immoderate**—(See Drink, Eating, Excesses, Gluttony, Lewd, Lust, Passion, Sensuous, etc.)

**Indisposition**—From Excessive Appetite—(See "Sickness from Over-eating" under Eating).

**Indulgences; Inherent**—Inherent Abnormal Appetite—Goes to Extremes in Eating—(See "Extremes" under Eating).

**Large Appetite**—(See "Gustativeness", and other paragraphs in this section).

**Lascivious; Lewd, Licentious; Longings**—(See Cravings).

**Loss of Appetite**—Anorexia—Bad Appetite—No Appetite—The ☽ in ♋ ☌ or evil asp. ♄, or a malefic; the ☽, ♌, and affl. by ♄ or ♂; ♄ affl. in ♋; ♀ affl. in the 6th H., a delicate appetite; Subs at SP. Orange, the color, ruled by the ☉, tends to sharpen the appetite, and rooms so papered or decorated with orange colors are good for people with little appetite.

**Lower Nature**—(See "Nature" under Lower).

**Lust; Luxuries; Malacia**—(See "Appetite" under Depraved).

**Narcotics; No Appetite**—(See "Loss of" in this section).

**Obesity; Opiates**—(See Narcotics).

**Orange Color**—Sharpens the Appetite—(See "Loss of" in this section).

**Overeating**—Sickness from Overeating—(See "Sickness" under Eating; "Excesses" under Food; Feasting; Gluttony; Impure; Obesity; Plethora, Surfeits, etc).

**Over-Indulgence**—Of the Appetites—(See "Overeating" in this section. Also see Amorous, Excesses, Indulgences, "Passional Excesses", and "Too Much Passion" under Passion; Sex Diseases; Venery, etc).

**Passion**—Excessive Passional Appetites—(See Excesses, Lewd, Lust, Passion, Sex, Venery, etc).

**Peculiar Appetites**—(See Peculiar).

**Perversions; Pleasure; Plethora; Poor Appetite**—(See "Delicate", "Loss of" in this section).

**Prodigal; Ravenous Appetite**—(See "Big Appetite" in this section).

**Riotous Living**—(See Riotous)

**Sensuous Appetites**—(See Lust, Sensuality).

**Sex Excesses**—(See Amorous, Lewd, Lust, "Passional Excesses" under Passion; "Sex Excesses" under Sex; Venery, etc.)

**Sexual Appetites**—Are ruled by ♌, ♏, 5th H., ♂ and ♀. (See Love Affairs, Lust, Passion, Sex, Venery).

**Sharpened Appetite**—(See "Loss of" in this section).

**Sickness**—From Overeating—(See "Sickness" under Eating).

**Surfeits; Sybarites**—(See Epicureans).

**Tastes; Unnatural Appetites**—(See Unnatural).

**Venery; Voracious Appetite**—An Insatiable Appetite—(See Gluttony, Voracious).

**Whimsical Appetite**—(See Peculiar).

**Wine; Women**—(See "Addicted to" under Men. Also see the various paragraphs under Women).

**APPLICATIONS—**

**Stimulant Applications**—A therapeutic property of ♂. In deficiency of circulation in a part, ♂ remedies are demanded to offset the work of ♄. (See "Deficiency" under Circulation. Also see Caustic, Rubefacient, Stimulant, Tonic, Vesicant).

**AQUARIUS**—The Aquarius Sign (♒). The eleventh Sign of the Zodiac, and affiliated with the 11th H. Ruled by ♅ and ♄. This Sign is classed as an airy, diurnal, fixed, fortunate, fruitful (more fruitful than barren), hot, human, masculine, mental, moist, nervous, obeying, rational, sanguine, southern, speaking, strong, sweet (a sweet disposition), vital, western, whole, wintry, etc. The Sign gives a humane and spiritual nature, when well-aspected and occupied, and when on the Asc. at B., tends to give a strong and beautiful body, with good vitality. This Sign has close affinity with the sense of Sight, as ♒ corresponds to the etheric vibrations. It is also closely associated with the blood, its composition, circulation and distribution in the tissues, and afflictions in ♒ tend to great disturbances in the circulation, and to impure blood. The pathological action of ♒ tends to gloom, nervousness, and supersensitiveness, and being a fixed sign, to make disease more enduring, and the mind and habits more fixed and set. The planet ♅ is strong in this sign, and ♒ is considered the most spiritual sign, the Sign of "The Son of Man", symbolized by the Water Pourer, pouring out blessings and alleviation upon Humanity. Some great characters have been born with the ☉ in this sign, such as Abraham Lincoln, Thomas Edison, and others of note, who have proven great Benefactors of Humanity. The Color ruled by ♒ is sky blue.

**AQUARIUS RULES**—Each sign has an external, internal and structural rulership. Externally the ♒ Sign rules the calves and ankles. Internally, rules the circulation, the breath, and the eyesight. Structurally rules the bones of the lower limbs, as the Tibia, Fibula, Astragalus, bones of the Ankles. As a general classification, the ♒ Sign rules the following things, which subjects see in the alphabetical arrangement,—Achilles Tendon; Ankles; Arsenicum Album (see Arsenic); Astragalus; Blood; Breath; Calves; Circulation of the Blood (see Circulation); Color,—Sky Blue; Composition of the Blood; Eyesight (see Sight); Fibula; Heart, by reflex action to ♌; Internal Saphenous Vein; Legs from Knees to Ankles; Lower Limbs; Lymph; Nations (see Nations); Shanks; Shin Bone; Sky Blue Color; Teeth; Tendo Achilles; Tibia; Vein,—Internal Saphenous Vein; Vision (see Sight).

**AQUARIUS DISEASES**—The Diseases and Afflictions of the ♒ Sign—See the following subjects in the alphabetical arrangement,—

**Accidents**—Hurts—Injuries—(See these subjects under Ankles, Calves, Legs).

**Aches**—In the Legs—(See "Aches" under Legs).

**Anaemia; Ankles**—Diseases In—Fractures—Swellings—(See Ankles).

**Atmospheric Pressure**—Disease from working under Increased Air Pressure—(See Caisson).

**Blindness; Blood Disorders**—Blood Poisoning—(See Blood, Impure, "Blood Poisoning" under Poison).

**Bowels**—Wind In—Wind Colic—(See "Wind" under Bowels).

**Broken Ankles**—(See Ankles. Also see Tibia, Fibula, "Fractures" under Legs).

**Bruises**—To Legs—(See "Bruises" under Legs).

**Caisson Disease**—(See Caisson).

**Calves**—Disorders and Hurts to—(See Calves).

**Circulation**—Of the Blood—Disorders of—(See Circulation, Blood, Impure).

**Consumption; Contractions**—In Legs, Ankles and Feet—(See Achilles, Contractions, Cramps, "Club Feet" under Feet; "Contractions" under Legs, Spasmodic).

**Corrupted Blood**—(See Impure).

**Cramps**—In Bowels, Legs or Feet—(See "Cramps" under Bowels, Legs, Feet).

**Crawling Sensations**—Over the Body—Creeping Sensations—(See Paraesthesia).

**Cutaneous Diseases**—(See Skin).

**Disease Threatened**—(See "Threatened" under Disease).

**Disgrace; Dropsy**—Of the Heart, Limbs, Legs, Ankles, and General—(See Dropsy. Also see "Dropsy" under Heart, Legs, Feet, and "Swellings" under Ankles).

**Extraordinary Diseases**—And Accidents—Caused by ♄, a strong ruler of the ♒ sign. (See "Extraordinary" under Accidents, Disease. Also see Peculiar).

**Eye Diseases**—(See Blindness, Eyes, Nebulae, Sight, Urn of Aquarius).

**Foul Blood**—(See Impure).

**Fractures**—Of Legs and Ankles—(See "Broken" in this section).

**Gloom, Gout, Heart Disorders**—Heart Dropsy—Heart Irregularities—Heart Weakness, etc.—(See Heart).

**Hurts**—To Legs and Ankles—(See "Accidents" in this section).

**Hyperaesthesia; Impure Blood**—(See Impure).

**Injuries**—(See Legs, Calves, Ankles).

**Irregularities**—(See "Irregular" under Heart. Also see Spasmodic).

**Lameness**—(See "Lameness" under Legs, Ankles, Feet).

**Legs**—Aches In—Fractures, Infirmities, Swellings—(See Legs).

**Nervous Diseases**—Nervousness—(See Nerves).

**Peculiar Diseases**—(See Extraordinary, Mysterious, Peculiar, Uncommon).

**Rheumatism; Ruin; Sensations**—(See Paraesthesia, Sensations).

**Sickness**—(See Blood Disorders, Disease, Ill-Health, Nervousness, Sickness).

**Sight**—Disorders of—(See Blindness, Eyes, Sight).

**Skin Diseases**—Causes extreme sensitiveness of the skin when the nerves are weakened and impaired. (See Skin).

**Spasmodic Diseases**—(See Spasmodic).

**Sprains**—(See "Sprains" under Legs, Ankles).

**Supersensitiveness**—(See Hyperaesthesia, Sensitive).

**Swellings**—(See "Swelling" under Legs, Ankles, Feet).

**Teeth**—Disorders of—(See Teeth).

**Tendo Achilles**—Disorders of—(See Achilles; "Club Feet" under Feet).

**Ulcers**—(See "Ulcers" under Legs. Also see Varicose).

**Uncommon Diseases**—(See Uncommon, Peculiar, Extraordinary).

**Varicose Veins**—(See Varicose).

**Windy Disorders**—Wind in Bowels—(See Wind). See "Airy Signs" under Air; "Fixed Signs" under Fixed.

**AQUEOUS**—

**Aqueous Humor**—(See Eyes).

**Aqueous Tumor**—(See "Aqueous" under Tumors).

**Aqueous Vapors**—Condensation of—(See Rain).

**ARBOR VITAE**—Of the Cerebellum. Ruled by ♄. (See Cerebellum).

**ARCTURUS**—Bootes—Star in the 5th face of ♎. The ☽ to the place of by dir. favors good health. The Asc. to place of tends to melancholy and timidity. (See Anxiety, Calamities, Melancholy, Suffocation).

**AREOLAR**—(See "Areolar" under Tissues).

**ARGENTUM**—(See Silver).

**ARGO**—A Southern Constellation resembling a ship. Malefic planets passing thru this Constellation tend to shipwreck, calamities at Sea, and much loss of life. (See Shipwreck).

**ARGUMENTATIVE**—(See Religion).

**ARGYLL-ROBERTSON PUPIL**—A failure of the pupil of the eye to respond to light. A symptom of Locomotor Ataxia. (See Locomotor Ataxia; "Mydriasis" under Iris).

**ARIES**—The Aries Sign—(♈). The first Sign of the Zodiac, ruled by ♂, and affiliated with the 1st H. Each year when the ☉ passes into ♈ is known as the Vernal Equinox. (See Equinoxes, Vernal). The ♈ Sign is known as a barren, bitter, cardinal, choleric, commanding, diurnal, dry, eastern, equinoctial, fiery, fortunate, four-footed, hoarse, hot, hurtful, inflammatory, luxuriant, masculine, mental, movable, northern, violent sign, etc. It is the day sign of ♂, the exaltation of the ☉, and the fall of ♄. (See Cardinal; "Fire Signs" under Fire). This sign gives much force, energy, and vitality when upon the Asc. at B. It is known as the

"Cerebral Pole of Paracelsus." The Sympathetic Nervous System begins with this sign, and ends with the other ♂ Sign ♏, which latter sign is known as the "Genital Pole of Paracelsus". (See Scorpio, Sympathetic). The Form of the Body given by ♈ when on the Asc. tends to be dry, spare, moderately sized, strong, red or sandy hair, a piercing eye, and a swarthy or sallow complexion. The Symbol of this sign is the Ram. The Colors ruled by ♈ are white and red, or red and white mixed. For Countries ruled by ♈, see Nations.

**ARIES RULES**—Some parts of the head are ruled by the ♉ and ♏ signs, but the head, taken as a whole, is ruled by the ♈ Sign. Also ♈ exerts an internal, external, and structural rulership over various parts of the head, and these will be mentioned in this section. The head is a very complicated part of the body, due to its many parts and organs, and all of the planets have a special rule over the different parts and organs of the head. The Cerebellum, base of the brain, the chin, lower lip, lower teeth, lower jaw, eustachian tubes, and the inner parts of the ears, are ruled by the ♉ sign. The right ear is ruled by ♄, and the left ear by ♂. The nose and nasal bones are ruled by ♏. The ☉ rules the right eye in a male and the left eye in a female. The ☽ rules the right eye in a female, and the ☉ the left eye in the male. The Pineal Gland, optic nerve, and the conjunctiva, are ruled by ♆. The Pituitary Body, Dura Mater, and the membranes of the brain are ruled by ♅. The skull, teeth, and skin of the head and face are ruled by ♄. The arteries, blood, and blood vessels of the head are ruled by ♃. The nose, forehead, and muscles of the head, are ruled by ♂. The complexion, cheeks, chin and upper lip, are ruled by ♀. The cerebral nerves, mouth, tongue, lower lip, and the hair, are ruled by ☿. Externally ♈ rules the head, face, nose, ears, eyes, and mouth. Internally ♈ rules the brain and nerve centers. Structurally ♈ rules the cranium and facial bones.

**Alphabetical Arrangement**—Of the Rulerships of ♈. See these subjects in the alphabetical arrangement,—Aconite Napellus (see Aconite); Arteries of the Head and Brain (these are especially ruled and affected by ♃ in ♈); Blood Vessels of the Brain; Bones of the Face, Skull, and Cranium, except those of the Ears and Nose; Carotid Arteries (the Internal Carotid); Cerebral Hemispheres—Cerebro-Spinal System—Cerebral Nerves, (which are especially ruled and affected by ☿ in ♈); Cheeks (ruled and affected by ♀ in ♈); Chin (ruled by ♀ in ♈); Colors—White and Red, and White and Red mixed; Complexion (ruled and affected by ♀ in ♈); Conjunctiva of the Eyes (ruled and affected by ♆ in ♈); Cranium; Dura Mater; Ears (ruled by both ♈ and ♉. The right ear is ruled by ♄, and the left ear by ♂); Eastern Parts (see Eastern); Encephalon; Externally ♈ rules the head, face, nose, ears, eyes, mouth; Eyes; Face and Facial Bones, except the bones of the nose, which are ruled by ♏ (the skin of the face is ruled and affected by ♄ in ♈); Forehead (ruled and affected by ♂ in ♈); Hair of the Head and Face, except the hair on the chin, which is ruled by ♉ (☿ in ♈ rules and affects the hair of the head); Head and its Organs, except the Internal Ear and the Nose (♄ in ♈ rules and affects the skin of the head, and ♂ in ♈, the muscles); Internally ♈ rules the brain and nerve centers; Jaw (Upper); Left Ear (ruled by ♂ also); Left Eye (also the ☉ rules the left eye of the female and the ☽ the left eye of the male); Lips (Upper Lip is ruled and affected by ♀ in ♈, and the Lower Lip by ☿ in ♈); Mouth (ruled and affected by ☿ in ♈); Muscles of Head and Face (also ruled and affected by ♂ in ♈); Nations (see Eastern, "Aries" under Nations); Nerves (Cerebral, and which are also ruled and affected by ☿ in ♈); Nose (under the external rule of ♈, and the Nose and Nasal Bones are also ruled by the ♏ sign); Optic Nerve (also ruled and affected by ♆ in ♈); Organs of the Head, except the Internal Ears and Nose; Pineal Gland (also ruled and affected by ♆ in ♈); Pituitary Body (also ruled and affected by ♅ in ♈); Potassium Phosphate (the ♈ Sign Salt); Rams (see Sheep); Red Color (the color of ♂, and also red and white mixed); Right Ear (and also ruled by ♄); Right Eye (☉ rules right eye in males, and the ☽ the right eye in females); Scalp; Sheep; Skin of Head and Face (also ruled and affected by ♄ in ♈); Skull (also ruled and affected by ♄ in ♈); Structurally ♈ rules the Cranium and the Facial Bones; Sympathetic Nervous System (presides to); Teeth (also ♄ in ♈ rules and affects the teeth); Temples; Tongue (also ruled and affected by ☿ in ♈); Upper Lip (and also ruled and affected by ♀ in ♈); White Color (White and Red mixed).

**ARIES DISEASES**—And Afflictions—The pathological action of ♈ tends to excesses, dryness, heat, inflammation, excess of forcefulness and energy. Being a mental sign, afflictions in ♈ tend to produce mental diseases and afflictions, and disorders of the brain. When afflicted at B., ♈ tends to heat and disturb the system, causing inharmony. The first half of the ♈ Sign gives a stronger constitution than the second half, and also greater muscular development. Comets appearing in ♈ tend to bring sorrow to ♈ people, and Countries ruled by ♈. The health tends to be good for the time for ♈ people, and for Countries ruled by ♈, when the ☉ is lord of the year at the Vernal Equinox, and free from affliction, but the health is bad when the ☉ is afflicted at the Vernal, and when malefics are in ♈ at this time. A classified list of the diseases caused by each of the planets in the 12 Signs of the Zodiac can be found in a number of the standard textbooks of Astrology. The following are the diseases and afflictions caused and ruled by the ♈ Sign, which subjects see in the alphabetical arrangement—

**Acne; Alopecia; Anger**—Diseases Arising From—(See Anger).

**Apoplexy; Astigmatism; Baldness; Blindness; Brain**—Disorders of—(See Brain).

**Catarrh; Cerebral Disorders; Coma; Complexion**—Disorders of—(See Complexion, Cosmetics, Face).

**Congestion**—Of Brain—(See Brain).

**Conjunctivitis; Cosmetics**—Disorders from Improper Use of—(See Cosmetics).

**Deafness**—(See Hearing).

**Delirium; Determination of Blood**—To the Head—(See "Rush of Blood" under Head).

**Dreams; Dryness and Heat**—All Diseases Proceeding From—(See Dryness, Heat).

**Ear**—Polypus of—External Diseases of—(See Ears, Polypus).

**Encephalitis**—(See "Inflammation" under Brain).

**Epilepsy; Epistaxis; Eruptions**—On Head, Scalp and Face—(See Acne, Cosmetics, Eruptions, Face, Head, Pimples, Scalp).

**Eye Diseases**—(See Accommodation, Blindness, Eyes, Optic, Retina, Sight).

**Face**—Diseases of—(See Face).

**Fevers; Fits; Giddiness**—(See Fainting, Vertigo).

**Glaucoma; Gumboils**—(See Gums).

**Harelip**—(See Lips).

**Head**—Diseases of—(See Head).

**Headaches; Heat**—Heat Disturbances in the System—Heat and Dryness, and all Diseases From—(See Dryness, Fevers, Heat).

**Humourous Discharges**—From Eyes—(See "Humourous" under Eyes).

**Hydrocephalus; Inflammations; Inharmony**—In the System—Due to Fevers and High Temperatures—(See Fever).

**Injuries**—To Head and Face—(See Face, Head, Skull).

**Insomnia; Kidney Disorders**—(See Kidneys).

**Measles; Megrims**—(See Migraine).

**Memory**—Loss of—(See Memory).

**Mental Disorders**—(See Insanity, Mania, Mental, Mind, etc.).

**Migraine; Mind**—Disorders of—(See Mind).

**Mouth**—Diseases of—(See Mouth).

**Nasal Bones**—(See Nose).

**Neuralgia**—Of Head and Face—(See "Neuralgia" under Face, Head).

**Nightmare**—(See Dreams, Sleep).

**Nose Bleed**—(See "Epistaxis" under Nose).

**Ophthalmia**—(See Conjunctiva).

**Palsy; Paralysis**—Of Face—(See Face).

**Phrenitis**—(See "Inflammation" under Brain; Delirium).

**Pimples; Polypus**—Of Nose, Ear, or Throat—(See Polypus).

**Rashes**—On Face—(See Acne, "Eruptions" under Face; Pimples, etc.).

**Red Face**—(See "Red" under Face).

**Ringworm.**

**Rupture**—Of Blood Vessel in Brain—(See Apoplexy).

**Rush of Blood**—To Head—(See "Blood" under Head).

**Shingles**—(See Herpes).

**Smallpox.**

**Somnambulism**—(See Sleep).

**Sorrow**—To ♈ People—♄ affl. in ♈ at B.; Comets appearing in ♈, and to Countries ruled by ♈; malefics in ♈ in the 12th H. at B. (See Sorrow).

**Spasms**—Of Facial Muscles—(See "Neuralgia", "Spasmodic" under Face; Tics).

**Stomach Disorders**—By reflex action to the ♋ sign from ♈, and the cardinal signs—(See Stomach).

**Swellings**—In Head and Face—(See "Swellings" under Face; "Growths" under Head; Hydrocephalus).

**Teeth**—Decay and Disorders of—(See Teeth).

**Temperature**—High Temperature and Fevers—(See Fever).

**Throat Troubles**—(See "Humours" under Throat).

**Tics**—Of Face—(See Tics).

**Toothache**—(See Teeth).

**Vertigo; Visions.**

**ARISTA**—A star in the 1st face of ♎, said to be fortunate, and when ascending at B. to give good health, renown, happiness, contentment and success. This star is also known as Spica Virgo, and is of the nature of ♂ and ♀.

**ARMPITS**—(See Axillae).

**ARMS**—The arms are ordinarily said to be ruled by ☿, ♊, and the 3rd House. However, there are several divisions to the arms, the upper arms, elbow, forearm, wrists and hands, which correspond to their opposite parts, the thighs, knees, ankles, and feet. Most Authors and Writers assign the one sign ♊ to rulership of all parts of the arms, including the shoulders. The upper arms are under the external rule of ♊. The humerus, opposite to the femur (♐), is under the structural rulership of ♊. (See "Middle Cervical" under Ganglion). The elbow, opposite to the knees (♑), is under the external rulership of ♋. The forearm, consisting of the radius and ulna, opposite to the tibia and fibula (♒), is under the structural rulership of ♌. The wrists, opposite to the ankles (♒), are under the rule of ♌. The hands, opposite to the feet (♓), are under the external rulership of ♍. The nerves of the arms and legs are ruled by ☿; the veins by ♀; the arteries by ♃; the muscles by ♂; the bones and joints of the arms and legs by ♄. The arms, hands, legs and feet should be studied together, as they have many points in common, as opposite signs are complemental and affect each other, and diseases which affect the hands may also affect the feet, or vice versa, etc. The Arm Place in the Spine is the 7th Cervical and 1st Dorsal. (See Vertebrae).

**Brachial Plexus**—(See Brachial).

**Long Arms**—Slender Arms—♅ ascending at B.; ☿ ascending at B., and free from the afflictions of other planets; ♊ gives, or ♊ on the Asc.; the 3rd or 4th faces of ♎ on the Asc. The ☿ influence especially tends to long arms, hands, fingers, legs and feet. ♊ on the Asc., when modified by planets rising, may give long arms, but with short and fleshy hands and feet.

**Short Arms**—The ☽ gives; the ☽ ascending at B.; ♓ influence tends to short and fin-like arms and legs; the 4th and 6th face of ♒ on the Asc.; the ♍ influence tends to brevity of members. (See "Short" under Legs).

**DISEASES OF ARMS**—Diseases, Infirmities and Afflictions to the Arms—See the following subjects in the alphabetical arrangement when not considered here—

**Abscesses In**—(See "Arms" under Abscesses).

**Accidents To**—Cuts, Fractures, Hurts, Injuries, Wounds, etc.—Generally caused by the afflictions of ♄ or ♂, or both, in signs which rule the different parts of the arms, as in ♊, ♋, ♌, or ♍; afflictions in ♊ or ♐; the ☽ in ♊ and afflicted by the ☉ or ♂; ☽ to place of the Pleiades or Praesepe; ♄ ☌ ♂ in the Asc. or M.C., in the latter degrees of ♊ or ♐; ♂ affl. in ♊ or ♐; ♂ affl. in ♐ in the 6th or 12th H.; ♂ ☌ the ☉ or ☽ in ♐ in the 6th or 12th H., and affl. by the benefics; ♂ affl. in ♊, ♍, or ♐, and ☌ or evil asp. the Asc. by dir.; ☿ ill-asp. by ♂; ♊ on the Asc., and affl. by ♂, or with ♂ in ♊ in the Asc., espec. tends to fractures and wounds to the arms; malefics and afflictions in the mutable signs, and with such signs on angles, as all the mutable, or common signs, as ♊, ♍, ♐, ♓, afflict each other, and the parts ruled by such signs. (See "Broken" in this section; "Fractures" under Legs).

**Affected**—The arms tend to be affected by the ☉ ♎; ☽ ♍; ♄ ♈; ♃ ♒; ♂ ♊ or ♑; ♀ ♐; ☿ ♌ or ♏. (See Table 196 in Simmonite's Arcana).

**All Diseases In**—Are signified by the 3rd H., the ♊ Sign, the planet ☿ and its afflictions, and also afflictions in the mutable signs and cadent houses; planets afflicted in ♊, or the opposite sign ♐, tend to the greatest number of diseases and afflictions to the arms, as listed in the textbooks of Astrology. Many of the influences which tend to afflict the arms also afflict the lungs, bowels, hips, thighs and feet, parts ruled by the common signs. Subs at LCP, the 6th and 7th Cervicals, and at AP, the 1st Dorsal, and at HP, the 2nd Dorsal vertebra, tend to various disorders of the arms, hands and shoulders. (See Vertebrae. Also note the various subjects in this section).

**Aneurysm; Ankylosis; Armless Wonder**—Case—(See "Armless Wonder", Case No. 054, in 1001 N.N. Also see "Missing" in this section).

**Armpit—Tenderness In**—(See Axillae).

**Arthritis Deformans**—In the Arms—(See Arthritis, Joints).

**Atrophy of Arms**—Caused by ♄, and with ♄ afflicted in signs which rule the arms; caused by Subs at LCP, the 6th Cervical, and at AP, 1st Dorsal, the Arm Place. (See Atrophy, Vertebrae).

**Axillae**—Tenderness In—(See Axillae).

**Blood In Arms**—Disordered—Impurities of—The ☉ in signs which rule the arms governs the blood in these parts, and tends to blood poisoning and blood impurities. Also ♃ in these signs tends to blood disorders in these parts.

**Bones of Arm**—Enlargement of Radius—Osteitis of Radius—Outgrowth of Bone (Exostosis)—The ♂ influence tends to enlargements, inflammation, and ♂ in the signs which rule the arms. The deposits of ♄ tend to enlarged parts of the bone, and outgrowth, as in ankylosis, while ♂ tends to enlargement thru heat, inflammation, etc. The ♆ influence also tends to enlargements. Also caused by Subs at LCP, the 6th Cervical, and at AP. (See Bones, Enlargement, Inflammation, Radius, Vertebrae).

**Broken Arms**—(See "Accidents in this section). Cases—See "Broken Arm", No. 140, 141, 142, 157, in 1001 N.N. Also see Case mentioned in Daath's Medical Astrology, Chap. 13, page 97. See Fig. 22 in "Message of the Stars" by the Heindels.

**Burns**—Arms Contracted By—Case—See "Extraordinary Accident", No. 192, in 1001 N.N.

**Carpus**—Carpal Bones—(See Wrists).

**Circulation**—The Circulation Obstructed in the Arms and Legs—♅ ☌ ♂ in ♊, and ☍ ♃ in ♐, and also afflicted by □ asps. from ♍ and ♓; ♄ ☌ ♃ in ♊ or ♐, or in ☍ from these signs; the ♄ influence tends to obstructions in the circulation when in ☌ or ill-asps. the rulers of the circulation, ♃ and ♀; ♄ and planets in common signs. (See "Circulation" under Legs. Also see Circulation).

**Clavicle**—Afflictions to—(See Clavicle).

**Clonic Spasm**—(See "Myoclonia" in this section).

**Contractions**—♅ or ♄ in signs which rule the arms. (See Burns, Cramps, in this section. Also see Contractions, Spasmodic).

**Cramps In**—♅ afflicted in ♊, and signs which rule the arms. Caused by Subs at HP, the 2nd Dorsal. (See Cramps, Vertebrae).

**Cuts To**—(See "Accidents" in this section).

**Cysts**—(See Aneurysm).

**Deformities**—Common signs on the Asc., and containing the malefics, and espec. ♅ or ♂, and these planets in ☌ or evil asp. to each other. (See Armless, Arthritis, Missing, in this section. Also see Deformities).

**Diseases Of**—Infirmities In—♊ signifies all diseases and infirmities in the arms, hands and shoulders, and accidents to these parts; afflictions in signs which rule the various parts of the arms, as in ♊, ♋, ♌, ♍, and also with any of these signs on the Asc. at B., and afflicted by malefics; ♄ or ♂ affl. in ♊; ♄ in ♓; the ☉ affl. in ♊, ♎, or ♐; the ☽ affl. in ♊, ♌, ♍, or ♐; ♃ affl. in ♉, ♊, or ♒; ♂ affl. in ♊, ♐, or ♑; ♀ affl. in ♊, ♋, or ♐; ☿ affl. in ♌ or ♏. Also caused by Subs at LCP, the 6th Cervical, and at AP. (See Cardia, Vertebrae).

**Dislocations**—♄ influence; ♄ affl. in ♊, ♋, ♌, or ♍, and in the part ruled by the Sign. (See Dislocations).

**Elbows**—Disorders of—Injuries To—(See Elbows).

**Elephantiasis; Enlargements**—(See "Bones" in this section. Also see Enlargements).

**Eruptions**—♂ affl. in ♊ in the 6th H., and in signs which rule the different parts of the arms; ♀ affl. in signs which rule the arms, due to wrong living. (See Eruptions).

**Erysipelas**—Of the Upper Arm—(See Erysipelas).

**Exostosis**—Abnormal Outgrowth of Bone—(See "Bones" in this section).

**Extremities; Fingers**—Disorders of—(See Fingers).

**Forearm**—Fracture of—Missing—(See Forearm. Also see Armless, Missing, in this section).

**Four Arms**—(See "Four" under Hands).

**Fractures**—(See Accidents, Broken, in this section. Also see Fingers, Fractures, Hands, Humerus, Radius, Ulna, Wrists).

**Frog Child**—Right Forearm Missing—(See Forearm).

**Glands Of**—Ruled by ♆ when this planet is in signs which rule the arms, and ♆ afflicted in these signs tends to disorders of. (See Aneurysm).

**Gout**—(See "Arms" under Gout).

**Hands**—Disorders and Afflictions to—(See Hands).

**Humerus**—Fracture of—(See Humerus).

**Hurts**—(See Accidents, Broken, Fractures, in this section).

**Infirmities**—(See "Diseases" in this section).

**Injuries To**—(See Accidents, Broken, Fractures, in this section).

**Lameness In**—(See Ankylosis; "Arms" under Fractures, Gout, Paralysis. Also see "Broken", "Deformities", and other paragraphs in this section).

**Left Arm**—Fracture of Radius Of—(See Radius).

**Limbs; Lower Arm**—(See Forearm).

**Marks On**—(See Marks).

**Metacarpal Bones**—(See Hands).

**Missing**—Both Arms Missing—(See "Armless", "Forearm", "Frog Child", in this section. Also see Malformations, Members, Missing, Prenatal Epoch).

**Moles on Arms**—Malefics in the 3rd H. (See Moles).

**Motor Nerves**—Afflicted—♅ in signs ruling the arms. (See Motor).

**Movement**—Of the Arms—Inability to Move Arms—♄ afflicted in ♊. Also caused by Subs at LCP, the 6th Cervical, and at AP. (See "Arms" under Gout; "Paralysis" in this section. Also see Vertebrae).

**Muscles**—Of Arms—Disorders of—♄ affl. in ♊. Subs at AP. (See Gout. Movement, Paralysis, Rheumatism, in this section).

**Myoclonia**—Of Upper Arm—♅ afflicted in ♊. (See Myoclonia; "Clonic" under Spasmodic).

**Neuralgia In**—☿ affl. in signs which rule the arms. (See Neuralgia).

**Numbness In**—(See Numbness).

**Osteitis**—(See "Bones" in this section).

**Outgrowth of Bone**—(See "Bones" in this section).

**Paralysis**—♅ and ☿ affl. in signs which rule the arms. (See Motor, Paralysis). Case—(See "Tunison", No. 113, in 1001 N.N.

**Pains In**—♂ affl. in ♊, and signs which rule the arms; the ☉ affl. in ♎; ☽ to the Bull's Horns in 5th face of ♊, of the nature of ♂; ☿ affl. in ♊, nerve pains in the arms and shoulders; ☿ affl. in ♏ tends to flying, or running pains in the arms and shoulders when ☿ is the afflictor in the disease. (See Pains).

**Radius**—Disorders, and Fracture of—(See Radius).

**Rheumatism In**—Muscular Rheumatism—Rheumatic Pains in the Arms or Shoulders—The ☉ in ♎, and ☌ or ill-asp. any of the malefics as Promittors; the ☽ affl. in ♊; ♄ ♊, occi. of the ☽, and ori. of the ☉, and affl. the ☉, ☽, or Asc.; ☿ affl. in ♏. Caused by Subs at LCP and AP. (See "Arms" under Gout; "Disease" under Extremities; Rheumatism, Vertebrae).

**Right Forearm Missing**—(See Forearm).

**Running Pains**—(See "Pains" in this section).

**Scar**—Malefics in 3rd H., a scar or mole on arms. (See Moles, Scars).

**Shoulders**—The shoulders and arms are afflicted by influences in ♊. (See Shoulders).

**Skin Diseases**—Of Arms—(See "Eruptions" in this section. Also see "Arms" under Skin).

**Spasm**—Of Muscles—(See "Myoclonia" in this section).

**Swellings**—(See "Arms" under Swellings).

**Tenderness**—In Armpits—(See Axillae)

**Ulcers**—(See Aneurysm; "Arms" under Ulcers).

**Ulna**—Fracture of—(See Ulna).

**Upper Arm**—Disorders In—Fracture—Afflictions in ♊ tend to disorders of the upper arm; afflictions in ♋ and ♌, in the elbow and middle arm, and afflictions in ♌ and ♍ to the lower arm, as the wrists and hands. (See

"Upper Arm" under Erysipelas; Humerus, Myoclonia).

**Varicose Veins**—In Arms—(See Aneurysm, Varicose).

**Verruca**—(See Warts).

**Vesicles**—(See Aneurysm, Vesicles).

**Wandering Gout**—(See "Arms" under Gout).

**Warts**—(See Warts).

**Wasting**—Of the Arms—(See "Arms" under Wasting).

**Weakness In**—The ☽ affl. in ♊, ♍, or ♐; ♄ affl. in ♊.

**Wounds To**—♂ affl. in signs which rule the arms; ☽ to the place of the Pleiades or Praesepe. (See "Accidents" in this section).

**Wrists**—Fracture and Disorders of—(See Wrists).

**ARMY AND NAVY**—Dangers In—Injuries, Wounds or Death In—(See Maritime, Military, Sailors, Ships, Soldiers, War).

**ARNICA**—A typical drug of ♂. (See "Typical" under Mars; Stimulants).

**ARRESTED**—Stoppage—Hindered—

**Arrested Emotions**—(See Emotions).

**Arrested Functions**—(See "Ablation", "Suppression" under Functions).

**Arrested Growth**—(See Deformities, Dwarf, Growth).

**Arrested Mental Powers**—This condition is also associated with retarded, or arrested physical growth. Also the vitality is generally reduced, and the recuperative powers may be low. (See Backwardness, "Arrested" under Mental; Recuperation, Vitality, "Weak Body" under Weak). Case—See "Never Grew Up", No. 720 in 1001 N.N.

**ARROW HEAD**—Of ♐. Harrow of ♐. (See "Blindness in One Eye" under Blindness. Also see Nebulous).

**ARSENIC**—Arsenicum Album—One of the 12 typical Polycrest Remedies, corresponding to the ♒ sign. A typical drug of ♂. (See Mucous, "Polycrest" under Zodiac).

**ARSON**—Tendency to Commit Arson—(See Incendiarism).

**ARTERIES**—The Arterial System—Ruled by the ☉ and ♃. Also under the internal rulership of the ♐ Sign. The airy signs also have much to do with the blood and circulation, and the ♒ sign especially, with morbid blood conditions. The watery signs also greatly influence the blood. ♃ dominates the arterial blood, and ♀ the venous blood. The ☉ and the ♌ Sign, and the opposite sign ♒, have much to do with the disturbances and morbid conditions of the arteries. ♃ in ♈ especially affects the arteries of the head; ♃ ♉ rules the arteries of the neck and throat; ♃ in ♉, ♊, and ♋ rules and affects the arteries and veins of the respiratory system; ♃ in ♋ rules the arteries of the stomach; ♃ in ♌ rules and affects the arteries and right ventricle of the heart; ♃ in ♍ rules the arteries of the bowels and abdomen, etc. (See Veins). See the following subjects in the alphabetical arrangement when not considered here—

**Aneurysm; Aorta; Arterio-Sclerosis**—Hardening of the Arteries—A destructive process, and the work of ♄ by abnormal mineral deposits carried by the blood, and ruled by ♄. Caused by afflictions in ♌ or ♒; ♄ ☌ or ill-asp. ♃, or ♄ ☌ both ♃ and ♀; ♄ ☌ ♃ in the 6th H.; the ☉ in ♌ or ♒; and ☌ or ill-asp. ♄, or ♄ and ♅; caused by Subs at CP, the 5th Dorsal Vertebra, ruled by ♌, and also by Subs at KP, Kidney Place. (See Crystallization, Hardening, Minerals, Vertebrae). Cases of Hardening of the Arteries—See Figures 13B and 18F in the book, "Astro-Diagnosis" by the Heindels.

**Arteritis**—(See "Inflammation" in this section).

**Blood**—Disorders of the Arterial Blood—(See "Disorders", and other paragraphs under Blood. Also see Circulation).

**Carotid Arteries**—(See Carotid).

**Circulation**—(See "Arterial Circulation" under Circulation).

**Dilatation**—Of Artery—(See Aneurysm; "High Blood Pressure", and "Too Much Blood", under Blood; Plethora; "Vascular Fullness" under Vascular).

**Diseases of Arteries**—The excess of mineral deposits laid down by the pathological action of ♄ tend to diseases of the arteries, hardening, crystallization, etc., and impair their elasticity and powers to accommodate the different volumes of the blood stream. The ☉, the ♌ Sign ruled by the ☉, and its opposite sign ♒, have much to do with the disturbances and morbid conditions of the arteries, and also the afflictions of ♄ to ♃. The good asps. of the ☽ and planets to ♃ at B., and along thru life, tend to healthy arteries, and normal replenishment of the blood flow. (See Aneurysm, Arterio-Sclerosis, and other subjects in this section).

**Expansile Impulse Of**—(See Pulse).

**Fullness Of**—(See "Dilatation" in this section).

**Hardening**—(See "Arterio-Sclerosis" in this section).

**Head**—Rupture of Artery in the Head, or Brain—(See Apoplexy; "Blood" under Head; "Blood Vessels" under Rupture).

**Healthy Arteries**—(See "Diseases" in this section).

**Iliac Arteries**—And Veins—Ruled by ♐. (See Ilium).

**Inflammation**—Of an Artery—Arteritis—♂ ☌ ♃.

**Legs**—Arterial Circulation Obstructed In—(See "Arterial" under Legs).

**Mineral Deposits**—Affecting the Arteries—(See "Arterio-Sclerosis" in this section).

**Morbid Conditions**—Of the Arteries—(See "Diseases" in this section).

**Obstructed Circulation**—In the Arteries—(See "Arterial" under Circulation).

**Poor Circulation**—(See "Obstructed" in this section).

**Rupture**—Of an Artery—(See "Head" in this section).

**ARTHRALGIA**—Pain in a Joint—(See "Arthritis", "Gout", "Pain" under Joints).

**ARTHRITIS**—Inflammation of a Joint—(See Joints).

**ARTICULAR RHEUMATISM**—(See "Rheumatism" under Joints).

**ARTICULATION**—Articulate—The Articulate Signs of the Zodiac are ♊, ♍, ♎, ♐, and ♒, and these signs are said to give clear articulation of words and speech. These are also called Human Signs, with the exception of ♎. The Inarticulate Signs tend to cause defects of speech. (See Dumb, Human, Inarticulate, "Hand of Man" under Man; Speech, Vocal).

**ARTICULATIONS**—(See Joints).

**ARTIFICE**—Cunning—Trickery—Strategy—Treachery—

**Blindness By**—(See "Artifice" and "Total Blindness" under Blindness).

**Injury or Death By**—(See Enemies, Mischief, Plots, Poison, Treachery).

**ARTISTIC TEMPERAMENT**—(See Sanguine).

**ASCELLI**—The Cratch—Praesepe—A Nebulous Cluster in the first decanate of ♌, of the nature of ♂ and the ☽. The Ascelli have special affinity with the Eyes and the Sight, and to cause Blindness when with the ☉ or ☽ at B. Their influence is said to be malefic, and to cause a variety of afflictions when the ☉, ☽, or malefics are near them at B. The Ascelli denote Death by fevers, fire, hanging, beheading, or some violent catastrophe, and often ruin and disgrace, when joined with the ☉ in an angle at B. Their Evils are Wounds, Hurts to the Face, Bad Eyes, Blindness, Imprisonment, Disgrace, and every evil that can befall Humanity, when directed to the ☉, ☽, or Asc. For the influences of the Ascelli, see the following subjects in the alphabetical arrangement,—"Acute Fevers" under Acute; Animals; "Bad Eyes" under Eyes; Beasts (Hurts By—See Animals; Beheaded (see Decapitation); Conjunctivitis; Crime; Defective Sight—(See Sight); Disgrace; Dissipation; Evils; Eye Disorders (see Eyes); Falls; Fevers—Death by, Inflammatory, Violent (see Fever); Gunshot; Hanging; Head—Pains In—(See Head); Honour—Loss of—(See Honour); Imprisonment; Inflammatory Fevers—(See Inflammation); Left Eye—Blindness In (see Blindness, "Left Eye" under Left); Liquids—Death or Injury By—(See Scalds, Shipwreck, "Hot Liquids" under Heat); Murderer (see "Murderous" under Murder); Pains in Head (see Head); Pestilence; Quarrels; Ruin; Scalds; Shipwreck; Sight—Danger to (see Sight, Blindness); Stabs; Violent—Violent Catastrophies, Violent Death, Violent Fevers (see Violent, and these subjects); Wounds. For collateral study see Nebulous, Praesepe, Stars.

**ASCENDANT**—The First House—The Sign rising upon the Eastern horizon at B. Determines largely the physical appearance, description of the body, height, weight, the degree of vitality, etc., and is very important to study in connection with health and disease. (See "First House" under First; "Passive Planets" under Passive; "Rising Sign" under Rising).

**ASCETIC**—(See Self-Denying).

**ASCITES**—Dropsy of the Abdomen—(See "Abdomen" under Dropsy).

**ASH**—Ashes—Waste Products in the System—The product of combustion and decay, and ruled by ♄. All influences which tend to interfere with elimination, excretion and secretion, etc., tend to deposit ash, and clog the system—(See Clogging). The body becomes heavily charged with Ash in such conditions as Impure Blood (see Impure), Gout, Kidney Trouble, Rheumatism, Uraemia, Wasting Diseases, etc. (See these subjects. Also see Elimination, Excretion, Secretion, "Influence of Saturn" under Saturn, Wastes, etc).

**ASPECTS**—Aspect—Appearance—Look.

**Commanding Aspect**—(See Commanding).

**Lowering Aspect**—(See "Downward Look" under Look; Stooping).

**Planetary Aspects**—No Planet is considered evil in itself, but it is their ever changing aspects, and angles they form with each other, that tend to make their influences and vibrations good or evil, positive or negative, contracting or expansive, etc. (See Reaction). The aspects of pathological importance are the ☌, P., □, and ☍. (See Opposition, Parallel, Square). The four Signs of any one Quadruplicity implicate each other pathologically, as by the □ and ☍. The most fortunate aspects that can be formed between the planets for good health and good fortune in life are ♃ ☌, ⚹, or △ ♀. The fortunate aspects between the planets are the ⚹ and △, and also the ☌ and P. between planets which are in harmony with each other. There are other good aspects, divisions of the ⚹ and △, which you can see listed in the Textbooks of Astrology. The evil, sinister, or adverse aspects, are the □ and ☍, and the ☌ and P. when occurring between malefics, or when a malefic afflicts the ☉, ☽, ♃, ♀, ☿, or other malefics, by a ☌ or P. As a rule only the major aspects, benefic and malefic, are listed in this book, and when the good aspects are referred to, it means not only the ⚹, △, but also all the minor good aspects, as the semi-sextile, quintile, etc. When bad aspects are referred to it means also the semi-square, the sesquiquadrate, and all sinister aspects referred to in the textbooks of Astrology. To print all minor aspects, good and bad, would involve the printing of thousands of extra symbol characters, which the Writer deems unnecessary. Many good aspects between the planets at B. tend to give better health, a stronger and better balanced mind, etc., while the evil aspects, and many of them at B. between the planets, tend to give a weaker constitution, more liable to ill-health, and also a more evil, unbalanced disposition and temperament. (See Directions, Dominion, Evil, Good, Kinetic, Opposition, Orbs, Planets, Polarity, Separation, Sextile, Square; "Perverted" under Tonic; Trine, Triplicities, etc.).

**Sad Aspect**—(See Sad).

**Sober Aspect**—(See Commanding)

**Surly Aspect**—♄ in ♌, in partile asp. the Asc. (See Appearance, Countenance, Expression, Face, Features, Look).

**ASPHYXIA**—Asphyxiation—Caused by Non-Oxygenation of the Blood—The ☉ affl. in ♒; ♅ in 6th H.; afflictions to ♃ and ♀, obstructing the arterial and venous circulation; ♄ or ☋ in ♊, or in □ or ☍ to ♊; ☿ affl. in ♊. (See Cyanosis, Drowning, "Non-Oxygenation" under Oxygen; Strangulation, Suffocation, etc).

**Birth**—Danger of Asphyxiation at Birth—Blue Baby—♄ exactly rising at B., on the Asc., or ♄ exactly on the Descendant, or ♄ ☍ the Asc. The ♄ influence also tends to delay birth. The Poet Goethe had ♄ exactly rising at B., which tended to delay his birth, and also nearly caused his death by asphyxiation at his birth. Cases—See Case of Premature Birth, and Asphyxiation soon after birth, Chap. XIV, page 102, in Daath's Medical Astrology. Also see Cases, "Strangled at Birth", No. 922 and 923, in 1001 N.N. (See "Delayed Births" under Children).

**Cutaneous Asphyxiation**—Suppression of the Skin Breathing—Afflictions in ♑, and espec. when also afflicting the hyleg. (See Skin). For further study see Drowning, Hanging, Strangulation, Suffocation.

**ASSASSINATION**—Danger of—Death By—Assassinations are ruled by the 12th H. In violent deaths the afflictions of ♆ dispose to thru treachery; ♅ affl. in ♏; ♂ afflicted, or afflicting in a human sign; ♂ in the 12th H., and affl. the ☉ or ☽; the ☽ with ♄ and Orion's Belt, or ☽ with Antares or Caput Hercules; ♄ ☌ or ill-asp. ♃, and elevated above ♃ at a Solar Ingress or Eclipse, tends to assassination of Great and Noble Men; afflictions in the 12th H., and afflicting the Hyleg; the 24° ♑ on the Asc. at B. Cases of Death By Assassination,—In 1001 N. N. see the following cases and birth data,—"Duke", No. 701; "Russia", No. 738; "Terris", No. 789; "Austria", No. 809; "Italy", No. 840; "Portugal", No. 902. (See Ambushes; "Death By" under Enemies; Kings, Stabs, Treachery; "Death" under Violent).

**Assassinated Abroad**—The ☽ Sig. ☌ ♂, and ♂ well-dignified, and thru a desire for travel and exploration. (See Abroad; "Journey" under Murder).

**ASSASSINS**—An Assassin—The following influences and afflictions tend to produce Assassins,—Caused by the ☉ and ♂ afflicted at B., which are the positive, electric and heat-producing planets; ♆ affl. in ♈; ♄ □ or ☍ ♂, in bad positions and angles; ♄ Sig. □ or ☍ ♂, or vice versa; ♂ and ☿ lords of the employment or 10th H., with ♂ strong or elevated above the Luminaries, and ♂ affl. by the ☽; ♂ Sig. in □ or ☍ ☿; ☿ ill-posited at B., and in □ or ☍ ♂. (See Anarchists, Crime; "Death By" under Enemies; "Patricide" under Father; Homicide; "Murderous" under Murder; Plots, Robbers).

**ASSAULTS**—Batteries—Attacks—Bodily Injury—The Afflictions of the malefics ♄ and ♂ to the ☉, ☽, Asc., or hyleg at B., and espec. with the malefics in the 12th H., or in angles, and elevated above the Lights, make the native more liable to assaults and violent attacks, and many times due to his own folly or rash acts. An Eclipse of the ☉ in ♈ tends to a prevalence of Assaults and Batteries. The planetary influences which lead to assaults cover quite a large and varied field. (See the following subjects in the alphabetical arrangement,—Ambushes, Assassins, Attacks, Blows, Bruises, Cuts, Enemies, Highwaymen; "Hand of Man" under Man; Homicide, Maiming, Mobs, Murder, Pirates, Prisons, Robbers, Ruffians, Stabs, Stones, Sword, Travel, Treachery, Violence, War, Women, Wood, etc).

**ASSIMILATION**—Absorption of Nourishment—Distribution of Food—The Assimilative System—Assimilation is a function of the ♍ Sign. Also ♀ rules the functions of Assimilation, Nutrition and Growth until puberty, and then ♅ takes rule. The assimilation of food is regulated by ♅ thru the Pituitary Body. The ☽ is assimilative in action, as she rules the stomach, and has strong rule over the receiving and preparing of the bodily sustenance. Assimilation is aided and furthered by the good influence and aspects of ♃. (See Absorption, Alimentary, Digestion, Growth, Nutrition, Pituitary).

**Imperfect Assimilation**—Impaired and Poor Assimilation of Food—Disturbed Distribution of—The ☽ in ♋ or ♍ in the 6th H., and afflicted; ♅ ☌ ☽ in ♍; ♄ affl. in ♋, ♍, or ♑; ♄ ☌ ♃, ♀, or the ☽ in ♍, ♃ ☌ ♂ in ♍, disturbed assimilation in the small intestines; ♂ ☌ ☽ in ♍, the ♍ sign afflicted by the □ and ☍ aspects from common signs. (See Anaemia, Diet, Emaciation, Food, "Malnutrition" under Nutrition; Wasting, etc).

**ASTHENIA**—Asthenic—Asthenic Process—Loss of Strength—Adynamia—Asthenia is presided over by ♄ and his afflictions; the ☉ ☌ ♄; ♄ affl. in ♒. Also especially caused by Subs at AT, AX, or CP. The degree of Asthenia, and Low Vitality, will depend largely upon the severity of the afflictions of ♄ to the vital places in the map, as to the ☉, ☽, Asc., and Hyleg, and also the nature of the sign rising, etc. (See Adynamia, Anaemia, "Bad Health" under Health; Emaciation, Feeble, Infirm, Invalids, Pale, Plethora, Sickly, Vitality Low, Wasting, "Weak Body" under Weak; "Weakened" under Strength, etc).

**ASTHENOPIA**—Weak or Painful Vision—(See Sight).

**ASTHMA**—Paroxysmal Dyspnoea with Oppression—Asthmatic Diathesis—Phthisic—Asthma is considered a disease of the ☽, ☿, the ♊ and ♋ Signs, of ♐ by reflex action to ♊, and also of the common signs. Important areas in the disease are the 18° ♊ and ♐, the 4° of ♍ and ♓. Also the last few degrees of ♈ and the first part of ♉. Other causes are,—☉ ☐ or ☍ ☽ in common signs; ☉ affl. in 6th H. in a fixed sign; the ☽ or ☿ affl. in ♊ or ♐; the ☽ hyleg and afflicted in ♊ in a female nativity; ♆ ♊ ☌ ♄ or ☍; ♅ affl. in ♊; ♅, ♄, or ☿ in ♉, ♊, or ♎; ♅ ♋ ☌ ☽, and also affl. by ♆ or ♂, and usually due to spasmodic disturbance of the diaphragm; ♄ afflicted in ♊ or ♋; ♄ afflicted in the 3rd H.; ♄ in ♋, occi., and affl. the ☉, ☽, Asc., or hyleg; ♄ affl. in ♋ when he is the afflictor in the disease; ♄ ☌ or ☍ the ☉ in ♋ or ♑; ♄ ☌ ♃ in ♍ in the 3rd H., and in ☐ to bodies in the 18° ♊ or ♐; ♄ affl. in ♌, and due to heart trouble and deficiency; ♄ ☌ ♃ or ♀, by disturbance of the circulation; ♃ affl. in ♏, and ♏ on cusp of 3rd H.; ♂ affl. in ♊; ♂ in ♊ and affl. by ♃; ♂ affl. in ♉ or ♏; ♀ in ♉ ☌ or ill-asp. ♂; ♊ on the Asc., and afflicted; afflictions in the common signs, and with these signs on angles. Also caused by Subs at LCP, the 6th Cervical; at AP, the 1st Dorsal; at Lu.P, the Lung Place in the Spine, and at HP, the Heart Place. (See Breathing, Bronchial, Circulation, Consumptive, Diaphragm, Dyspnoea, Heart, Lungs, Oxygen, Respiration, Spasmodic, Stomach, Vertebrae, etc.).

**Bronchial Asthma**—See the first part of this Article. Also see "Congestion" under Bronchial).

**Cases of Asthma**—See the following case records, figures, and birth data,—Fig. 17 in "Message of the Stars" by the Heindels. Figures 10A, 20A, 20B, 20C, 20D, 20E, in "Astro-Diagnosis" by the Heindels.

**Death By**—Afflictions in common signs.

**Hay Asthma**—(See "Hay Fever" under Nose).

**Heart Asthma**—♄ affl. in ♌, due to disturbed heart action and deficiency.

**Spasmodic Asthma**—♅ affl. in ♉, ♊, or ♋; ♅ ☌ ☉ in ♊. (See Spasmodic).

**Stomach Asthma**—♅ affl. in ♋, due to stomach trouble and distention; ♅ ☌ ☽ ♋, and also affl. by malefics.

**ASTIGMATISM**—The ☉ or ☽ rising, and both in mutual affliction, and espec. by ♄ or ♂; the ☉ rising in ♈, ♉, ♌, ♑, or ♒, and afflicted; the ☉ rising in ☍ ☽ in 7th H. in ♋ and ♑; the ☽ or ☿ affl. in ♈; many planets in ♋ or ♑ in ☌ or ☍, and with ♋ or ♑ on the Asc. (See Accommodation, Eyes, Sight). Case—See "Diseases to the Eyes", page 87, Chapter 13, in Daath's Medical Astrology.

**ASTRAGALUS**—The Ankle Bone—Under the structural rulership of ♒. (See Ankles).

**ASTRAL BODY**—The Sidereal Body—One of Man's Vehicles, and an exact counterpart of the physical body. The focal point of the Astral Body is in the Spleen. The Astral Body is the seat of the Sensations. The planetary influences work upon man strongly thru his Astral Body, his Aura, his Mind, and his etheric parts, the Etheric Double, and it is thru these channels that disease and sickness gain their entrance to, and hold upon the body and mind. The afflictions of ♆ to the hyleg and mental rulers tend to make man subject to adverse Astral Influences, to obsessions, spirit controls, and death from such causes. In the Astral Body ♃ has direct relation to the Breath and the Blood, and ♂ and ♀ more especially to the sensations and passions, and as all diseases originate in, and have their counterpart in the Astral Body, it would be well for all students to study up on the subjects which have to do with the Astral Plane. The Astral Body is the mould, pattern, or counterpart, upon which the physical body is built, and when the physical body in utero is finished, and conforms to the Astral Model, birth takes place if conditions are normal. (See "Moment of Birth" under Birth; Blood, Breath, Build, "Desire Body" under Desire; Emotions, Liver, Neptune, Obsessions, Physical, Sensations, Sidereal Body, Spirit Controls, "Body" under Vital).

**Astral Entities**—Discarnate Spirits—Elementals, etc.—Are the Forces on the Astral Plane which greatly influence the mind of man, and to obsess, or bring diseases and troubles upon man, if they are of the evil types. (Good books to read along these lines are the Astral Plane books by Mr. Leadbeater, and also "The Message of the Stars", and "Cosmo-Conception" by the Heindels; "Realms of the Living Dead" by Dr. and Mrs Homer Curtiss).

**Astral Shells**—The etheric counterpart of the physical body, which separates at death, usually remains in the vicinity of the corpse, which may be seen as a "Ghost", and disintegrates with the physical body. (See "Silver Cord" under Silver).

**ASTRINGENTS**—Astrictives—Haemostatics—Contracting Agents—A therapeutic property of ♄, and tends to contract organic tissues and stop discharges. Acids are astringent. The influence of ♆ is also said to be astringent and contracting. (See Acids, Collyria, Contractions, Constrictions, Haemostatics, "Drugs", under Saturn).

**ASTROLOGY**—Study of—(See Science).

**ASYLUMS**—Are generally ruled by the 12th H.

**Confinement In**—(See Hospitals, "Asylums" under Insanity. Also see Confinement, Imprisonment, Twelfth House).

**ATAXIA**—An Incoordination of Muscular Action—Caused by afflictions in the ♈, ♉, and ♌ Signs, and by Subs at AT and CP. Locally caused by afflictions in the Sign ruling the part. (See Incoordination, Locomotor Ataxia, "Action" under Muscles).

**ATHETOSIS**—(See "Athetosis" under Fingers, Toes).

**ATHLETICS**—Athletic—A strong and athletic frame is given when the strong signs ♌, ♏, ♐, or ♒ are on the Asc. at B. (See Exercise, Muscles, Sports, "Strong Body" under Strong).

**Pugilist**—See "Sayers", No. 175, in 1001 N.N.

**Wrestler**—Champion Wrestler—Case See "Carkeek", No. 167, in 1001 N.N.

**ATHYMIA**—(See Despondency, Melancholia). Caused especially by Subs at AT, the Atlas, 1st Cervical Vetebra. (See Atlas, Vertebrae).

**ATLAS**—The first Cervical Vertebra, ruled and acted upon by the ♈ and ♉ Signs. (See "First Cervical" under Vertebrae).

**ATMOSPHERE**—Air—(See Air, Aquarius, Breath, Caisson Disease, Carbon, Compressed, Drought, Dry, Electricity, Epidemics, Ether, Famine, Floods, Gases, Heat, Hydrogen, Influenza, Lightning, Miasma, Moisture, Noxious, Oxygen, Pestilence, Pressure, Rain, Storms, Sun Spots, Thunder, Uranus, Vapor, Weather, Wind, etc).

**ATONIC**—Atony—Want of Tone or Power—Debility—The Atonic Planets are ♆, ♄, ♀, and the ☽. The action of planets when below normal is atonic. The minus and negative influences and aspects of the planets are atonic, while their plus and positive aspects tend to be tonic, expanding, beneficial and increasing in their effects over body and mind. (See Anaemia, Chronic, Debility, Emaciation, Feeble, Gout, Infirm, Invalids, Pale, Plethora, Sickly, Strength, Tone, Tonic, Vitality Low, Wasting, "Weak Body" under Weak).

**ATRABILE**—Atrabiliary—Melancholy—Suprarenal Disturbances—(See Adrenals, "Black Bile" under Bile; Depression, Hypochondria, Melancholy, Suprarenals).

**ATROPHY**—Wasting of a Part from Lack of Nutrition—A ♄ disease, and ♄ is the planet of atrophy; denoted by ♀; the hyleg much affl. at B., congenital atrophy. Atrophy may attack any part of the body, the organs, muscles, functions, etc., and principally in the part, parts, or organs ruled or afflicted by ♄ at B., and by dir., and by the sign and house containing ♄. (See Hemiatrophy).

**Death By**—Denoted by ♀ when she is the afflictor in the disease, having the dominion of death, and afflicting the hyleg; also ♄ afflicting the hyleg at B., and by dir., tends to, and espec. when taking part in a train of evil directions.

**Progressive Muscular Atrophy**—(See "Progressive" under Muscles). For the various matters concerning Atrophy, see Diminished, Dry, Emaciation, Growth, Nutrition, Tabes, Wasting, etc. See "Atrophy" under Arms, Brain, Congenital, Eyes, Face, Feet, Functions, Hands, Heart, Legs, Limbs, Liver, Muscles, Spine, etc).

**ATROPIN**—(See Belladonna).

**ATTACHMENTS**—(See Adhesions).

**ATTACKS**—Injury or Violence to the Body—Caused generally by ♂—(See the following subjects,—Animals, Assassination, Assaults, Beasts, Beaten, Bites, Blows, Cannibals, Cattle, Cuts, Enemies, "Hand of Man" under Man; Highwaymen, Hurts, Injuries, Kicks, Kidnapped, Killed, Lynching, Maimed, Mobs, Murder, Mutilated, Pirates, Poison, Quadrupeds, Reptiles, Robbers, Serpents, Stabs, Stings, Stones, Sword, Travel, Treachery, Venomous, Violence, "Wild Animals" under Wild; Wounds, etc).

**ATTENTION**—Inability to fix the mind at Attention—(See "Attention" under Mind).

**ATTENUANT**—Increasing the fluidity of the blood or other secretions—A therapeutic property of the ☽ remedies and herbs. (See Moon; "Moon Herbs" under Herbs).

**ATTRACTIVE**—Attracts—

**Attractive Power**—(See Healers, Magnetic, Sympathy).

**Attractive Stature**—(See Appearance, Beautiful, Complexion, Face, Hair, Handsome, Stature, etc.).

**Attracts Disease**—(See Contagions, Contracts, External, Infections, Magnetic, Negative, Passive, Scorpio, Suggestion, Susceptible, Sympathy, etc.).

**AUDITORY ORGANS**—The Organs of Hearing—Auditory Nerve—(See Ears, Hearing).

**AUGMENTED**—Increased—Enlarged—

**Abundance**—(See the subjects under Abundance).

**Blood Augmented**—In a Part—(See "Blood" under Abundance).

**Cerebral Substance**—Augmented—(See "Medullary Substance" under Medulla).

**Death Rate Augmented**—(See Mortality).

**Disease**—(See "Increase" under Disease).

**Enlarged**—(See the subjects under Enlarged).

**Functions**—(See "Over-functional" under Functions).

**Growth**—(See Giants, "Increase" under Growth).

**Health**—(See "Strengthened" under Health).

**Increased**—(See the subjects under Increase).

**Motion**—(See "Accelerated", "Quick" under Motion).

**Nerve Force**—(See "Augmented" under Vital).

**Sensibility**—(See "Augmented" under Sensibility).

**Strength**—(See "Increased" under Strength, Vitality).

**Vitality**—(See "Augmented", "Increased" under Vitality). Also see such subjects as Abnormal, Appetite, Corpulent, Evil, Excess, Excesses, Height, Hyper, Obesity, Over, Super, Weight, etc., and other subjects which may occur to your mind, which have to do with augmentation and increase in the body.

**AUNTS**—The mother's relatives in a male horoscope are ruled by the 6th H., and in a female nativity by the 12th H. The father's relatives, as his brothers and sisters, your paternal aunts and uncles, are ruled by the 6th H. in a female nativity, and by the

12th H. in a male horoscope. The mother's relations are ruled by ☿, and those of the father by ♄. Relatives in general, on both sides of the house, are ruled by ♅, and his positions and aspects tend to indicate the danger of ill-health or death among them, sudden events in connection with their lives, etc., when ♅ at B., or by dir., afflicts the parts of the native's map which rule these matters.

**Case**—Remarkable Similarity Between Aunt and Niece—See "Remarkable Similarity", No. 343, in 1001 N.N.

**Death of An Aunt**—Ill-Health or Sickness of an Aunt—The ☉ to the ☌, P., or ill-asp. ♅ by dir.; an eclipse falling on the radical ☿ in a child's map; ♄ ruler of the 6th or 12th H. at B., and ♄ to the ☌ or ill-asp. the Asc. by dir., and espec. if the native be very young, and under 7 years of age.

**Death of An Aged Aunt**—Death of a Grandmother, or an Aged Female in the Family—The ☽ hyleg, and to the ☌, P., or ill-asp. ♄ by dir., and espec. if the direction fall in the 8th or 12th H.; the ☽ to the place of Rigel; ♂ to the ☌ or ill-asps. ♄ by dir.

**Maternal Aunts**—Or Uncles—Death of —(See Maternal).

**Paternal Aunts**—Or Uncles—Sickness or Death of—Afflictions to the 6th or 12th H., according to the sex of the native, etc. (See the rules in the first part of this section. Also see Uncles). For collateral study see Family, Father, Grandparents, Maternal, Mother, Old Age, Paternal, Relations, Sixth House, Twelfth House, Uncles.

**AURA**—The Magnetic and Physical Aura are ruled by ♅. The conditions of the mind, body and spirit are reflected in the Aura, and can be seen by a genuine Clairvoyant or Medium. The health and disease conditions of the body and mind affect the Aura, varying its colors, etc. The magnetic aura is strengthened by the ⚹ and △ aspects of ♅ to the Asc. The question of the Aura is a large and important one, and students of Healing should make a study along this line in the Occult and Metaphysical books. (See Astral Body, Desire Body).

**AURAL**—Pertaining to the Ears—Aural Ducts—(See Ears).

**AURICLE**—The External Ear—One of the upper cavities of the Heart. (See Ears, Heart).

**Auricular Disease**—Of the Heart—(See "Auricular" under Heart).

**AURIGA'S RIGHT SHOULDER**—(See Disgrace, Ruin, Violent Death).

**Auriga's Left Shoulder**—Capella—(See Capella).

**AURUM**—(See Gold).

**AUSTERE**—Austere Countenance—Austere Look—Stern—Severe—Characteristic of ♄ people; ♄ in ♌; ♄ Sig. □ or ☍ ♂; ♄ in ♈ or ♊; ♄ well-dig. in ♎, ♑, or ♒; ♄ Sig. ⚹ or △ the ☉; ♄ ruler of the Asc., or horoscope at B., and affl.; the ☉ Sig. in ♐; ♂ Sig. in ♈; ♂ Sig. □ or ☍ ♄; ☿ Sig. in ♍, or ☿ ♍ partile the Asc.; ♌ gives. Austerity is a trait usually accompanied by melancholy, and tends to invite disease unless controlled. (See Countenance, Cruel, Ferocious, Fierce, Fiery, Fulminating, Grave, Morose, "Disposition" under Severe; "High Temper" under Temper).

**AUTOINTOXICATION**—From wrong diet, and accumulation of poisons in the system—☽ ☌ ♅ ♍; ♄ affl. in ♎; ♃ ♋ in 12th H., and afflicted. Case—See Fig. 18D, in the book, "Astro-Diagnosis", by the Heindels. (See Autotoxic, Diet, Excesses, Food, Gluttony, Intoxication, Poisons).

**AUTOMATIC ACTION**—Under rule of the ☽. Tending to form habits by repetition of certain acts, whether for good or evil, for health or disease. Afflictions to the ☽ tend to interfere with the automatic action of the body and cause clumsiness. (See Clumsiness, Habits).

**AUTOMOBILES**—Injury or Death By—(See Vehicles).

**AUTOTOXIC PSYCHOSES**—(See Autointoxication, Diabetes, Psychoses, Toxic, Uremia).

**AUTUMNAL**—The Autumnal Signs are ♎, ♏, and ♐, and Autmnal diseases are more prevalent while the Sun is passing thru these signs, and also Kidney troubles, sex derangements or weaknesses, diseases in the hips or thighs, or accidents to these parts. (See Scurvy). For matters concerning the Autumnal Equinox see Equinox, Ingresses.

**AVALANCHES**—Danger, Injury, or Death By on Voyages, in Travel or Inland Journeys, etc.—Malefics in the 3rd or 9th H., and affl. the ☉, ☽, Asc., or hyleg at B., or by dir.; ♄ in the 3rd H., and affl. the hyleg at B., and by dir. (See Crushed, "Earthquakes" under Earth).

**AVENA**—A typical drug of ☿. (See Mercury).

**AVERSIONS**—Dislikes—Irrational Fears or Aversions—(See Antipathy, "Morbid" under Fears; Hatred, Misanthropic).

**Marriage**—Opposite Sex—Aversion to —(See Deviations; Homosexuality; "Aversions", "Indifferent" under Marriage; Perversions).

**Pleasure**—Averse to—(See Pleasure).

**Study**—Aversion to—(See "Aversion" under Study).

**AVERTED**—Avoided—Prevented—

**Death**—Death In Sickness Averted—Lord of the Asc. in the 8th H., going to combustion, intervened by a good asp. from ♃, ♀, ☿, or the ☽, and in such a case the natural strength, or the proper treatment, will modify or avert the misfortune. The interventions of the benefics, ♃ and ♀, by their good asps. to the hyleg in a train of evil directions tend to avert death, and espec. if the vitality be strong, and the hyleg favorably aspected by the benefics at B., and the patient be young. (See Crises, Curable, Escapes, Moderation, Prevented, Recovery, Recuperation, Resistance, Vitality, etc.).

**Death Not Averted**—(See "Arguments for Death", "Sure Death", "Time" under Death).

**Disease Averted**—(See Averted; Immunity; "Disease" under Prevented).

**AVIATION**—Death or Injury In—(See Aeroplanes).

**AWKWARDNESS**—Gawky—Afflictions in the mutable signs, which signs rule the limbs, and espec. afflictions to ♃ or ☿ in these signs; ♄ affl. in ♉; ♄ rising in the Asc., and espec. if ♑ is also on the Asc.; ♄ and the ♑ sign, when strong and prominent at B., tend to give a heavy and awkward appearance, and ♂ also in the configuration tends to make the native rough and careless; ♃ afflicting ☿. (See Appearance, Clumsiness, Gait, Heaviness, Posture, Stooping, Walk, etc.).

**AWRY GAIT**—(See Gait).

**AXILLAE**—Armpits—Ruled by the ♋ Sign.

**Cancer Of**—♄ affl. in ♋.

**Scirrhus Of**—Of the Breast or Axillae—A hard form of Carcinoma—♄ or ♂ affl. in ♋. (See Carcinoma).

**Sweating Of**—Fetid Perspiration In—♂ affl. in ♋. (See Sweat).

**Tenderness**—In the Armpits—Caused by afflictions in ♉, ♊, ♋, or ♌, and by Subs at LCP, the 6th Cervical, and at AP and HP, the 2nd Dorsal Vertebra. (See Vertebrae).

**AXIS**—(See Vertebrae).

**AZIMENE**—The Azimene Degrees of the Zodiac—Deficient Degrees—Weak or Lame Degrees—If the Asc., or its lord, be in one of these degrees at B., the native tends to be lame, crooked, deformed, or blind. These degrees are as follows: ♈ 0°; ♉ 6, 7, 8, 9 10°; ♊ 0°; ♋ 9, 10, 11, 12, 13, 14, 15°; ♌ 18, 27, 28°; ♍ 0°; ♎ 0°; ♏ 19, 28°; ♐ 1, 7, 8, 18, 19°; ♑ 26, 27, 28, 29°; ♒ 18, 19°; ♓ 0°. (See Blindness, Crooked, Deformed, Incurable, Lameness, Weak).

**AZOTE**—(See Nitrogen).

**AZOTH**—The luminous, brilliant and fiery coloring in the Spinal Canal, seen by Clairvoyants, brighter in some than in others, according to the stage of spiritual development. Ruled by ♆. (See "Spinal Canal" under Spine. Also see Ether).

# B

**BACHELORS**—The planetary influences at B. often tend to delay or deny marriage, or to give little or no sex desires, which conditions often lead to single life in both sexes. Malefics in the 5th or 7th H., ☌ or ill-asp. the ☽ tend to; the ☽ □ or ☍ ☉, and affl. by ♄; ☽ in the sex sign ♏ in ☌ or ill-asp. ♄; ♄ ♏ in ☌ or ill-asp. the ☉, ☽, Asc., or Hyleg, tends to deaden the passions and make the native more indifferent to the opposite sex. (See Celibacy, Deviations, Eunuchs, "Aversion" under Marriage; "Free from Passion" under Passion; Perversions; the various paragraphs under Sex; Spinsters, etc.)

**BACILLUS**—(See Germs).

**BACK**—Rear Part of the Body—The Dorsal Region—The Back is ruled by the ☉, the ♌ Sign, and the 5th H. Under the external rule of ♌. The lower part of the back (Loins), ruled by ♎ and the 7th H. (See Front). See the following subjects in the alphabetical arrangement when not considered here.

**Abscess In**—Imposthumes In—A ♎ disease. (See Abscesses).

**Affected**—The Back tends to be affected when the ☉ is in ♑; the ☽ ♐; ♅ ♊; ☿ ♏. (See Table No. 196 in Simmonite's Arcana). Case Record of the Back Affected—See Case 3, page 89, Chap. 13, in Daath's Medical Astrology.

**Ailments Of**—(See "Diseases" in this section).

**Backache**—Afflictions in ♌ or ♒; the ☉, ☽, or ♀ affl. in ♌; ♄ affl. in ♌. Case—See "Backache", page 90, Chap. 13, in Daath's Medical Astrology.

**Chronic Diseases Of**—The ☉ hyleg, and to the ☌ or ill-asp. ♄ by dir.; ♄ affl. in ♌.

**Diseases Of**—Ailments—All Diseases In—Distempers In—Distempered Back, etc.—Afflictions in ♌ or ♒, and also in any of the fixed signs, or many planets in the Fixed, or Succedent Houses, tend to diseases and ailments of the back; afflictions in ♉, ♌, ♎, ♏, ♒, the fixed signs, and also in the 5th H.; the ☉ affl. in ♌ or ♒, and the fixed signs; the ☉ Sig. in ♑ in horary questions; the ☉ to the ☌ or ill-asps. ♄ by dir.; diseases of the ☉ and ♀; the ☽ Sig. in ♐ (Hor'y); ♄ affl. in ♎; ♀ diseases, and afflictions to ♀; ☿ Sig. in ♏ (Hor'y); ♌, ♏, and ♒ diseases. (See the various paragraphs in this section. Also see Table on page 179, Chapter 29, in Lilly's Astrology).

**Dorsal Region**—(See Dorsal).

**Imposthumes In**—(See "Abscesses" in this section).

**Injuries To**—The ☉ in ♌ and affl. by malefics; ♄ or ♂ in ♌, and affl. the ☉, ☽, Asc., or hyleg.

**Kidneys; Loins; Lower Part**—Of the Back—All Diseases In—Injuries to, or Weaknesses In—♎ diseases and afflictions. (See Loins).

**Lumbago; Moles**—Marks—Scars—Planets below the earth, and in signs which rule the back. (See "Rear Parts" under Marks).

**Muscular Rheumatism**—In Back—♂ affl. in ♌ or ♒. (See Lumbago).

**Pains In**—Backache—Afflictions in ♌, ♎, ♒, and all the fixed signs; the ☉ in ♉, ♌, or ♒, and to the ill-asps. any of the malefics as promittors; the ☉ affl. in ♌ when the ☉ is the afflictor in the disease; ♄ affl. in ♌, ♎, or ♒; ♄ ☌ ♃ or ♀ in ♌, due to weak heart and impaired circulation; ☿ and the ☽ in ♌, and to the ☌ or ill-asp. any of the malefics; ☿ affl. in ♌, ♑, or ♒, and to the ill-asps. the malefics; ☿ affl. in ♌, from colds caught in the feet. (See Backache, Lumbago, Muscular, in this section).

**Reins of the Back**—All Diseases In—(See "Back" under Reins).

**Rheumatism In**—(See "Muscular" in this section).

**Scapula**—(See Shoulders).

**Scars**—(See "Moles" in this section).

**Spine**—(See Spine, Vertebrae).

**Weak Back**—Weakness in the Back—A ☉ disease; the ☉ affl. in ♌ at B., or ♌ on Asc.; the ☉ to the ☌ or ill-asp. ♄ by dir.; the ☉ in 6th H. at B., in a fixed sign, and afflicted; the ☽ affl. in ♎ or ♑, and to the ☌ or ill-asps. the malefics; ☿ affl. in ♐, and to the ☌ or ill-asps. the malefics; a ♌ and ♎ disease, and afflictions in these signs. (See Dorsal, Humpback, Kidneys, Leo, Libra, Loins, Lumbar, Muscles, Reins, Rheumatism, Spine, Vertebrae). Case—Of Weak Back—See Fig. 30 in "Message of the Stars" by Max Heindel.

**BACKWARDNESS**—Slow in Growth and Development—Dull—Bashfulness—Retarded, etc.—The influence of ♄ tends to retard both the mental and physical growth and development; ♄ affl. in 3rd H., or the ☉ and ♄ affl. in ♊ at B., and with ☿ weak, afflicted and ill-posited, tend to backwardness of mental growth; ☿ and the ☽ afflicting each other, and in no asp. to the Asc. at B., and also ☿ ☌ ♄, or afflicted by malefics, mental growth is retarded; the conditions of the 3rd H. and ☿ give clues to backwardness along mental lines. The physical growth tends to be backward when the malefics afflict the hyleg at B., and when there are weak signs on the Asc., and the vitality low. Also caused by derangements of the Thyroid Gland. Precocity is the opposite condition to this and tends to premature development, and to Prodigies, Geniuses, etc. (See Bashful, Blushing, Dull, Genius, Giants, Growth; "Arrested" and "Deficiency" under Mental; Modesty, Precocious, Prodigies, Prudery, Retarded, "Slow" under Motion; Thyroid, etc.).

**Speech**—Backwardness of—(See Speech).

**BACTERIA**—(See Germs, Microbes).

**BAD**—Badly—Ill—Evil—Defective—Imperfect—Unfavorable, etc.—See the following subjects in the alphabetical arrangement—

**Appetite Bad**—(See "Loss Of" under Appetite).

**Blood Bad**—(See Corrupt, Impure).

**Body**—The Body Badly Made, Crooked, etc.—(See Crooked; "Ill-formed" under Ill; Ugly, etc.).

**Breath Bad**—(See Breath).

**Children**—Death Caused by Bad Children—(See "Bad" under Children).

**Color**—A Bad Color—(See "Bad Complexion" under Complexion; Pale, Sickly).

**Complexion Bad**—(See Complexion).

**Conduct Bad**—(See Criminal, Debauchery, Dissipation, Drink, Drunkenness, Evil, Lewd, Morals, Sex, Temper, etc.).

**End**—A Bad End—(See Hanging, Imprisonment, Judges, Murdered, Ruin, Suicide, Untimely Death, etc.).

**Evil**—(See Evil).

**Gait**—A Bad Gait—(See Deformed, Feet, Gait, Lameness, Legs, Walk).

**Habits**—Bad Habits—(See Drink, Eating, Food, Habits, Narcotics, Passion, Pleasures, Sex, etc.).

**Health Bad**—(See Health, Ill-Health, Invalids, Sickly, Weak, etc.).

**Ill**—(See Ill).

**Impure Blood**—(See Impure).

**Legs**—Bad Legs—(See Legs).

**Loose Habits**—Morals—(See Habits, Morals).

**Magnetism**—(See Healers, Incompatibility, Magnetism).

**Men**—Bad Men—(See the various paragraphs under Men).

**Morals**—Bad Morals—(See "Loose" under Morals).

**Perversions; Teeth Bad**—(See Teeth).

**Vitality Bad**—(See Vitality).

**Women**—Bad Women—(See Harlots, Treachery, Women). Any condition of the mind or body which is not normal may be classed as "Bad", and for subjects not listed here, look for it in the alphabetical arrangement.

**BALANCE**—Equilibrium—

**Balance of Movement**—The ♎ Sign gives grace and balance of movement. (See Coordination, Dexterity, Incoordination, "Muscular Action" under Muscular; Rhythm, Walk, "Well-Balanced" under Well).

**Lack of Balance**—The planetary influences and aspects at B., when not well-balanced, as when many planets are out of dignity and in evil aspect to each other, tend to cause the mind and body to be one-sided in their manifestations, and more apt to lead to mental and physical disorders until the Soul becomes awakened, and learns how to rule its stars. These evil, or negative planetary influences at B., and by transits, directions, etc., are sent upon us to try the Soul, and for experience, and no Soul can find peace, soul-growth, or any very great degree of satisfaction in earth life until it learns to conquer the "Monsters of the Zodiac" and keep its poise and balance at all times under the ever-changing planetary aspects and influences. The ♎ sign is called the Sign of "The Balance", or The Scales. (See Equilibrium, Harmony, Libra). Diseases of the Mind and Body are due to an unbalanced condition of mind and body, as a rule, and also due to sin somewhere in the life, now or in the past. The subjects in this book are taken up largely with Diseases, and the unbalanced conditions, and what you have to rule and overcome in life.

**BALANITIS**—Inflammation of the Glans Penis—(See Penis).

**BALDNESS**—Alopecia—Falling Hair—Loss of Hair—Baldness is due to an excess of heat in the system, causing a dryness, lack of proper circulation in the scalp. The fiery signs strong at B., on the Asc., and also well-occupied by planets, tend to baldness, and especially when the scalp fits tightly over the cranium. A loose scalp gives more freedom of circulation and nutrition to the part. The earthy and watery signs tend to give plenty of hair, and to retain it. The airy signs give a heavy head of hair, and tend to grayness rather than baldness. Some people are destined from birth to baldness, which is the normal condition for them, and the teachings in the Occult books are that any relief is only temporary, and massage and tonics may succeed for a time in restoring the hair, but when discontinued the hair falls out again. Some signs and influences at B. give an abundance of hair on the head and body, while others give little, or no hair. (See Beard, and the various paragraphs under Hair). The following planetary influences tend to Baldness—The ☉ in a fiery sign at B., and espec. in ♈; fiery signs upon the Asc.; many planets in a fiery sign, rising, and espec. in the Asc.; the ☉ and ♂, the fiery planets, *in a fire sign*, and espec. in ♈, and in the Asc.; the ☽ ☌ the ☉ or ♂ in ♈, and espec. when in the Asc.; ♄ occi. of the ☉ at B. tends to fewer hairs on the head and body; born under the ☉, as with ♌ on the Asc., soon becomes bald; ♃ ruler of the Asc., and occidental; ♃ in ♐, and espec. with ♐ on Asc., rapid falling out of the hair early in life, and in youth; ♃ Sig. ✱ or △ ♄, and ♄ well-dignified; ♂ in ♑, and in □ to ♀ in ♎; ♑ influence, and with ♑ on the Asc., the sign ruled by ♄; an ♈, ♌, and ♐ disease, and with these signs upon the Asc.

**Case**—Loss of Hair and Eyebrows—See "Aqueous", No. 120, in 1001 N.N. (See "No Hair" under Hair).

**Early in Life**—Bald Early in Life—Premature Baldness—Quickly Bald—The ☉ afflicted at B.; the ☉ rising in fiery signs or fiery signs afflicted on the Asc.; ♄ or ♃ rulers of the Asc., and occi., as when between the 1st and 4th houses, or between the 10th and 7th H.; ♃ and ☿ affl. in ♐; ♂ afflicting ♀, and ♂ elevated above ♀; ♂ in ♊, ♐, or ♒, and afflicting ♀; ♐ on the Asc.; many planets in fiery signs at B., and espec. when rising in the Asc.

**Forehead**—Bald About the Forehead—The ☉ rising at B.; ♃ and ☿ affl. in ♐, and espec. when rising in the Asc.; ♐ on the Asc. (See Forehead. Also see "Temples" in this section).

**Inhibited Growth**—Of Hair—The ☉ or ♄ in the 5° ♈ or ♐; ♄ tends to inhibitions in any part of the body, according to the sign or house he is in, and espec. when affl. the ☉, ☽, Asc., or hyleg. (See Inhibitions).

**Loss of Hair Increased**—The high fevers of the ☉ in ♈, or ♈ on the Asc. and afflicted, tend to cause the hair to fall out rapidly, or cause complete baldness for a time after illness; the ☉ or ♂ in ♈, and espec. with ♈ on Asc., due to too much heat in the head and scalp; ♄, the ruler of ♑, occidental; ♃ in 1st H., and affl. by ♂ or ♀, and espec. with ♃ in ♐; ♂ or ☿ holding dominion at B., and in familiarity with each other, and ♂ affl. the hyleg and elevated above the Luminaries; ♂ Sig. in ♒, without much hair; ♂ in ♑ and □ to ♀ ♎; ♂ ☌ ♀ tends to increased falling of hair; look to the aspects of ♂ and ♀ to the Asc., to each other, and their strength or weakness, exaltation or detriment, etc.; ♀ in 6th H., and affl. by ♂; ☿ ori. at B.; ♈ or ♐ on the Asc. at B.

**Scanty Hair**—Fewer Hairs on Head or Body—♀ Sig. in ♎, scanty, but grows long. (See Beard; "Body", "Disorders", under Hair).

**Temples**—Bald About the Temples—Hair Growing Off the Temples—♐ on Asc. at B.; many influences in fiery signs; ♃ ♐, or ♃ ori. at B.; ♃ ♐ in Asc. (For further study see "Abundance", and the various paragraphs under Hair).

**BALSAMIC**—A therapeutic property of ♃. Produces an agent resembling a balsam.

**BANDITS**—Death or Injury By, and especially during Travel—♄ and ♂ in human signs and controlling the Luminaries. (See Highwaymen, Robbers, "Dangers", under Travel).

**BANISHMENT**—The ☉ directed to all Nebulous Clusters, and to Castor and Pollux, threaten banishment, and which may result in sickness and early death. (See Exile).

**BAPTISM**—The Planetary Baptism—The influences of the planetary vibrations stamped upon you at B., when you breathe in the magnetism of the Universe at your first cry. This is the photograph, the negative of your tendencies, possibilities, the diseases subject to, the picture of your personality, and the nature of the environment you will be apt to encounter in this day of school in earth life, and to gain experience, learn the necessary lessons for Soul-growth, etc. The map of birth is the foundation upon which you are to build a superstructure, and how you build will depend upon your degree of advancement, your spiritual insight and foresight, and your attainments, self-control, poise, balance, etc. (See "Moment of Birth" under Birth, Moment. Also see Fate, "Map of Birth" under Map; Nativity; "Free Will" under Will).

**BARBERS**—The ♂ influence strong at B., ♂ the ruling planet, or ♂ well-asp. in the 10th H., tend to make good Barbers, as well as Chemists, Surgeons, etc., and all who use sharp tools and instruments in their vocation. (See Chemists, Healers, Surgeons).

**Barber's Itch**—Inflammation of the Hair Follicles of the Face and Neck—Sycosis—Caused by afflictions in ♑, as a rule, and with ♂ in ♑ in the Asc., and also by ♂ ♈ in the Asc. or in the 6th H.; caused by Subs at MCP, the 4th Cervical, and also by Subs at KP, afflictions in ♎, as such are usually due to retained poisons, and lack of proper secretion and elimination. (See Itch, Ringworm, Vertebrae).

**BARRENNESS**—Sterility—Unprolific—Impotency—Unfruitful—With animals the propagative faculty is in charge of the Group Spirits presiding over the different classes of animals. The mixture of blood between animals of different species tends to sterility. The Mule is a hybrid and sterile because the horse was bred with the Ass, two different species. This displeases the Group Spirits of Horses and Asses, and sterility is imposed upon the crossed offspring to prevent its further propagation. The Human Family in its evolution is beyond the power of these Group Spirits, and Races can interbreed without the penalty of sterility, as is the case with animals. However, certain Races become sterile sooner or later, and die out when they finish a Cycle in their evolution, and are ready to enter a new Race. Thus the Bushman of Australia are being exterminated thru sterility, and in spite of all the British Government is doing to perpetuate and increase their numbers. The Occult and Inner side of this question is quite fully discussed in the book, "Cosmo-Conception", by Max Heindel. Also see the subject of "Seed Atom" in this same book.

**Barren Signs**—Barren Planets—In Astrology there are certain Signs of the Zodiac known as Barren Signs, as ♈ (rather barren), ♊, ♌, and ♍. The planets classed as Barren are the ☉, H, ♄ and ♂, which signs and planets tend to deny or kill the children when found in the houses of children, as in, or on the cusps, of the 5th or 11th houses of the parents, one or both parents. Also Cauda (☋) is classed as a barren influence, of the nature of Saturn. Both parents must have fruitful maps in order to have children, and also the Seed Atom of an incoming Ego must be implanted in the spermatozoa of the father to produce a normal child, and one with an Ego and Spirit. The Givers of children are the ☽, ♃, and ♀, when in the houses of children and well-aspected, and also the watery signs are classed as fruitful. (See Fruitful). In studying thru a library of Astrological Textbooks, I have recorded and classified the following planetary influences given as reasons for sterility, or the denial of children.

**Causes of Barrenness**—Children Denied—The Map of Husband or Wife Barren—Impotency—Unfruitfulness, etc.—The ☉ and malefics in barren signs, and dominating the houses of children, the 5th and 11th houses, and also the M.C., or Zenith, and the benefics below them; the ☉ and the malefics being the rulers of offspring in the map, and in barren signs, and without the good aspects of ♃ or ♀, and the malefics elevated above the benefics; the ☉ in ♑ and afflicted; the ☉ and ☿ in the 5th H., and afflicted in barren signs; the ☉ in the 5th H. causes barrenness, except he be in a watery sign, and even this doubtful; if the ☉ be joined to ☿, and apply to the ☌, P., or ☍ of both ♄ and ♂, and angular, and espec. in ♈, ♌, ♏, ♑, or ♒, the native will be wholly unfit for generation; the ☉, ♅, ♄ or ♂ in the 5th or 11th houses, and afflicted; the ☉, ♄, and ♂ deny children, or allot but few, espec. when in the 5th or 11th houses and afflicted; the ☉, ♄, ♂, or ☋ in the 5th H., or a barren sign on the cusp of the 5th., and the ☽ in a barren sign, or if the lord of the 1st and 5th be in evil asp. to each other, or with ♄ or ♂, are all causes of barrenness; the ☉ to the ill-asps. ♀ by dir., a barren time; the ☽ in ♈, ♌, or ♑, and in evil asp. to the ☉, ♅, ♄, ♂, or ☋, denotes barrenness; the ☽ sepr. from the ☉, and applying to ♀ in a day geniture; the ☽ in a husband's horoscope, and the ☉ in the wife's, applying to ♅, ♄, or ☋ in the 5th H., there will be no family unless there be powerful testimonies for fruitfulness in both maps, and even if children are born they are subject to early death; the ☽, ♃, and ♀ weak, afflicted and unfortunate at B., and not in fruitful houses or signs, tends to deny children; one or both Lights in an angle, and espec. in the 1st or 7th houses, or in the 6th in ☌ ♄, ♂, and ♀, no children, and if a female is liable to abortion; ♅ tends to deny children, or allot but few; ♅ affl. in the 5th or 11th houses, or afflicting these houses, denial of children; ♄ in 5th H. in ♊, ♎, or ♑ denies children; ♄ in the 11th H., and ♂ in □ asp. to the cusp of 5th H.; ♄ affl. in ♎ or ♏; ♄ ☌ ♀ in the 7th H.; ♄ and ♀ in the western angle and afflicted; ♄ in the 5th or 11th houses, and afflicted; ♄ tends to deny children, or allot but few; ♄ in an angle and afflicting both the ☽ and ♀; ♄ or ☋ in the 5th H., or ♄ or ♂ in evil asp. to the 5th, or its lord, or the Sigs. or Benefics be in barren signs, and if any born they will not live; ♄, a cold and barren planet, in the 11th H. frustrates the hope of children in Hor'y Questions, and espec. if at the same time there are barren signs on the Asc., or cusp of the 5th; ♂ in the 5th or 11th houses, and afflicted; ♂ denies children, or allots but few, when afflicting the houses of children; ♂ in □ or evil asp. the cusp of 5th H., and with ♄ in the 11th H.; ♀ afflicted by the malefics; the atonic action of ♀ tends to sterility; ♀ affl. in ♑; afflictions to ♀; a ♀ disease or affliction; ♀ in a ♄ sign, and affl. by the ☽ and ♄; ☿ and the ☉ in the 5th H., in barren signs and afflicted; a cold and dry body, ruled by ☿ or ♄, tends to make the nature unprolific; ☿ denies offspring when occidental if in a barren sign and configurated with barren planets; ☿ either gives or denies children according to the planets he is configurated with at B.; malefics in the 5th or 11th houses in barren signs; the malefics H, ♄, ♂, and also the ☉ and ☋, when in the houses of children, and afflicted, or in barren signs, tend to deny children, allot but few, or cause their early death; the malefics and the ☉ being the rulers of offspring, and in barren signs, and without the good asps. of the benefics, and the malefics elevated above the benefics; the malefics ori. and angular, and afflicting the ruler of the 5th H., or elevated above such ruler, and also afflicting planets in the 5th, tend to deny children, and espec. when the ruler of the 5th receives no help from the benefics, and with no benefics or givers of children in the 5th H., or in fruitful signs; a malefic in a house of children, and espec. if with the ☉, the native will always be barren; ♈ is rather barren because of ♂; the ♈, ♌, or ♒ signs on the cusp the 5th H., and with no intercepted sign in the 5th, are indications of no offspring; ♊ is called a barren sign because ☿ has no particular sex; ♌ is wholly barren because the ☉ is barren; ♌ or ♒ on the Asc., 5th, or 11th houses tend to deny offspring; the ♌ sign, or the ☉ and ♂ in ♌ on the cusp of the 5th H., the human plant is scorched by excess of passion before it has time to grow; ♍ is rather barren because of its ruler ☿; ♏ is the least fruitful of the watery signs because of its ruler ♂; ♎, ♑ and ♒ are classed as indifferent signs, neither fruitful nor barren; ♑ is rather barren because it is the sign of ♄, and the exaltation of ♂; ♑ on the Asc. at the Vernal Equi., Places and Peoples ruled by ♑ suffer from great sterility; ♒ is more fruitful than barren; the lord of the 11th H. a malefic, and in the 5th H. and afflicted; planets which promise or deny children, when posited together in prolific signs, and in ☌, or afflicting each other, tend to deny children or cause their early death, or very few will be reared; a barren sign on the Asc. or cusp of 5th., and espec. on the cusps of both the 1st and 5th at the same time, as ♊ on Asc., and ♍ on the 5th; barren signs in, or on cusps of 1st and 5th, without their Sigs. being in reception, good asp., or translation, the party will not conceive; a barren sign on the cusp of the 4th H., the house denoting the end of all things, gives little hope of ever having children in Hor'y Questions. Barrenness is also caused by Subs at the Private Place, PP, the 2nd, 3rd, and 4th Lumbar vertebrae. (See Vertebrae). For collateral study, and for further influences along this line, see Abortion, Children, Conception, "Cold and Dry Body" under Dry; Fruitful, Gestation; "Anchorite" under Husband; Impotent, Maimed, Men, Pregnancy, Unprolific, Wife, Women.

**BASAL GANGLIA**—The Ganglia at the base of the Brain—(See "Basal" under Ganglion).

**BASHFULNESS**—Shy—A ♄ influence; ♄ in the 1st H. at B.; ♄ ruler of the Asc. at B., and afflicted; a characteristic of ♄ people; the ♍ influence also tends to make one "Bashful as a Virgin". (See Backwardness, Modesty, Prudery, Reserved, Retiring, Shy).

**BASTARDS**—Illegitimate Birth—Children Born Out of Wedlock—The 5th H. should be especially noted.

**General Causes**—♆ in the 5th H., or afflicting the 5th, or planets in the 5th; ♄ ruler of the 5th H. at B., and by dir. in ☌ or evil asp. the Asc., and espec. if ♄ afflict ♂ and ♀ at B.; the ☋ in the 5th H. is an indication the child may be illegitimate if there is any doubt or question about it.

**Horary Questions**—In Lilly's Astrology Horary Questions are considered along the following lines: (1) Is the Child Legitimate and the Child of the Reputed Father? It is if the following conditions exist in the Horary Map,—The lord of the Asc. and the ☽, signify the Querent, and the sign of the 11th H., and its lord, signify the Issue. If these Sigs are in ⚹ or △ asp. in the hor'y map, and behold each other with reception, or not, the conception is legitimate, and the child of the supposed father. If the Sigs be in □ or ☍ asp., in close or perfect asp., and with reception; lord of the Asc., or ☽ be in the 5th H., or lord of the 5th be in the Asc., and with no evil asp. from the malefics, with one of the benefics in favorable asp. to the cusp of the 5th, or lord of the 5th, then also the child is legitimate. (2) The Child May Not be Legitimate—The Husband has Children by other Women than his Wife—Or the Wife has Children by other Men than her Husband—If none of the foregoing aspects and conditions concur; if ♄, ♂, or ☿ are in ill-asp. to the lord of the 5th, or the cusp of the 5th, there may be suspicion of adultery, or that the child is not the child of the Querent. Also if the lord of the 9th is in the 5th, and espec. if the lord of the 5th afflict the lord of the Asc., the husband may have children by other women, or the wife by other men. (See Adoption. Also see Case No. 688, "Illegitimate Birth" in 1001 N.N.).

**BATHING**—Bathings—The planet ♅ has special rule over bathing, swimming, etc., and his afflictions tend to bring dangers in connection with bathing and the water, and to cause the unexpected. There are times when it is dangerous to go near water, or to bathe in the Ocean, and the many deaths recorded from Sea bathing, and by drowning while bathing, have a close relation to the afflictions of ♅, and also to the afflictions of ♆ for the time. Accidents by water and bathing usually come on scheduled time unless you are forewarned of the dangers, and keep away from large bodies of water, or even be careful in your own bathtub, when these adverse planetary aspects are operating. (See "Dangerous", "Disease" in this section. Also see "Water" under Skin).

**Bath House Keepers**—Good influences for are ♂ and ♀ rulers of the employment and ♅ conjoined with them.

**Cold Baths**—Tabulated statistics show that the ♉ people are averse to taking cold baths.

**Dangerous to Bathe**—Dangerous to Go Near Water—Possible Death at Bathings—Drowned While Bathing—The ☽ to the ☌ or ill-asps. ♅ by dir.; ♆ by transit over the radical place of ♂, and ♂ afflicted at B. in a watery sign; ♆ in the 8th H. in ♓, and affl. by ♂; ♅ affl. in ♋ or ♓, should be warned against bathings in ponds, rivers, or at the Seashore; ♅ in the 8th H., afflicting the hyleg at B., and by dir.; ♂ by periodic direction to the ill-asps. of ♅. Here is the birth data of a case of death while bathing in the Ocean. See "Death by Drowning", Case No. 402, in 1001 N.N.

**Death from Bathing**—(See "Dangerous" in this section).

**Demoniacal Complaints**—From Bathing—(See "Bathing" under Demoniac).

**Disease, Illness or Injury**—From Bathing—The ☉ ruler of the 6th H. at B., and to the ☌ or ill-asp. ♅ by dir.; the ☽ to the ☌ or ill-asp. ♅ by dir. (See "Dangerous" in this section. Also see Cold, Drowning, Exposure, "Perils by Water" under Water).

**Mud Baths**—(See "Mud Baths" under Healers).

**BATTERIES**—(See Assaults, Blows).

**BATTLE**—Death or Injury In—(See Soldiers, War).

**BEAR**—Cynosura—Little Bear—(See Cynosura).

**BEARD**—Whiskers—The Beard is ruled by the ♉ sign, and espec. the chin beard.

**Auburn Color**—Sad Color—Next to Black—Typical of a ☿ person.

**Barber's Itch**—(See Barbers).

**Color Of**—(See the various paragraphs in this section).

**Flaxen Beard**—Sandy Flaxen—Given by ♃ influence.

**Full Beard**—(See "Much" in this section).

**Heavy Beard**—(See "Much" in this section).

**Light Beard**—The Beard Lighter than the Hair of the Head—♃ Sig. of the person; ♃ Sig. in ♑.

**Little Beard**—(See "Thin" in this section).

**Much Beard**—Full—Heavy—Thick—The ☉ gives much hair on the beard; the ☉ rising at B.; the ☽ gives; ♃ in ♐ in partile asp. the Asc.; ♃ in the Asc. (See "Abundance", "Bushy", "Hairy Body", under Hair).

**No Beard**—Often No Beard At All—☿ as Sig. in Hor'y Questions denotes.

**Red Beard**—Reddish—Characteristic of ♂ people; ♂ strong at B., in the Asc., or rising; ♂ in fiery or airy signs, and with fixed stars of his own nature, a deep, sandy red; in Hor'y Questions ♂ Sig. denotes reddish beard and hair, but this is according to the sign, except he be with fixed stars of his own nature. (See "Red Hair" under Hair).

**Sandy Beard**—(See "Flaxen", "Red" in this section).

**Scanty Beard**—(See "Thin" in this section).

**Thick Beard**—(See "Much" in this section).

**Thin Beard**—Little Beard—Scanty—♄ in ♈; ♄ signifies a thin, weak beard, and with the ♄ sign ♑ upon the Asc.; in Hor'y Questions ♄ or ☿ as Sigs. of the party, indicate one of a scanty, thin and spare beard; ♄ ascending at B.; ♄ gives a thin beard when he builds the body; ♃ in ♑, in partile asp. the Asc., the beard is usually thinner and lighter than the hair of the head; ☿ people have thin beards, little beard, and often no beard at all; ☿ strong and rising at B., and free from the rays of other planets, a scanty beard, and little hair on the chin; ♑ influence, and with ♑ on Asc. (See Baldness, Hair).

**BEASTS**—Bestial—Beastly—The Bestial Signs, the Feral Signs, those of animal form, are ♈, ♉, ♌, ♐, ♑. (See "Brutish Signs" under Brutish). See the following subjects, which have to do with Animals, Beasts, Quadrupeds.

**Animals**—Attacks By—Injury or Death By—Death of, etc.—See Animals).

**Attacks By**—(See Animals, Cattle, Horses. Also see the various paragraphs in this section).

**Beastly Form**—If at conception the ☉ and ☽ are in the 6th or 12th houses in four-footed signs, and the malefics angular, the embryo will be of beastly form, but if a benefic give testimony the child will be of human shape, but of savage disposition. If ☿ be in good asp. the ☽ the faculties will be improved, altho the body will be ill-formed. The shape will be much better if the ☉ and ☽ be in signs of human form. (See Dogs, Foetus, Inhuman, Monsters).

**Bestial Signs**—(See the first part of this Article).

**Bites by Beasts**—(See Bites).

**Cattle**—Injury or Death By—(See Cattle).

**Death by Beasts**—♄ ori. in fixed signs, □ or ☍ the ☉ at B., or occi. in fixed signs, in □ or ☍ the ☽, and ♄ in a brutal sign. (See "Hurts", "Wild Animals" under Animals. Also see Cattle, Elephants, Horses, Quadrupeds. Note the various paragraphs in this section).

**Devoured By**—After Death—(See "Birds" under Air).

**Dogs**—The Offspring resembles Dogs, etc.—(See "Dogs" under Children; Inhuman, etc.).

**Elephants**—Death of—Death or Injury By—(See Elephants).

**Embryo**—Of Beastly Form—(See "Beastly" in this section. Also see Inhuman).

**Epidemics Among**—Of Cattle and Sheep—(See Epidemics; "Virus" under Pestilence; Sheep).

**Form**—Offspring of Beastly Form—(See "Beastly" in this section).

**Furious Beasts**—Injury or Death By—The ☽ to the ☌ ♂ by dir. (See "Wild Animals" under Animals).

**Great Beasts**—Death or Injury By—(See Cattle, Elephants, Great, Horses).

**Horses**—Hurts, Injuries, Kicks By—(See Horses).

**Hurts by Beasts**—(See "Injury", and the various paragraphs in this section. See Animals, Cattle, Elephants, Horses, etc.).

**Injury By**—The ☽ to the ☌ ♂ by dir.; the ☽ to the ☌ the Ascelli. (See Animals, Cattle, Elephants, Horses, etc.).

**Kicks**—(See Horses, Kicks).

**Quadrupeds**—Death or Injury By—(See Animals, Cattle, Elephants Horses, Quadrupeds, etc.).

**Reptiles**—Death or Injury By—(See Reptiles).

**Sickness**—The Sickness or Death of Beasts—(See "Death" under Animals; Epidemics, "Virus" under Pestilence; Sheep, etc.).

**Signs**—The Bestial Signs—(See the first part of this section).

**Travel**—Attacks by Beasts During Travel—(See "Wild" under Animals; "Travel" under Cattle; "Dangers" under Travel).

**Venomous Beasts**—Injuries By—(See Venomous).

**Wild Beasts**—Death or Injury By—(See "Wild" under Animals; "Dangers" under Travel; Wild, etc.).

**BEATEN**—(See Assaults, Blows, Iron, Lynching, Mobs; "Beaten in Prison" under Prison; "Assaults" under Stones; Sword, etc.).

**BEAUTIFUL**—Beauty—Elegantly Formed—Handsome, etc.—All Constellations of Human Form, both within and without the Zodiac, tend to give due proportion to the body, and a handsome shape. Also the signs of ♀ give when on the Asc., as ♉ and ♎, or with ♀ in the Asc., or rising and well-aspected. The ♒ sign on the Asc. is notable for the beauty it gives, and many times with white hair in youth, or before middle life. For further influences along this line see the following subjects,—Body, Comely, Commanding, Compact, Complexion, Dimples, Elegant, Eyes, Face, Fair, Fine, Graceful, Hair, Handsome, Harmony, Neat, Refined; "Pure Skin" under Skin; Stature; Well-composed, Well-favored, Well-proportioned, Well-shaped, etc., under "Well".

**BED**—Taking First to Bed in Sickness—(See Decumbiture).

**Bedridden Invalids**—(See Confinement, Hospitals, Invalids).

**Bed Sores**—Caused by the excess heat of the ☉ or ♂ in the sign ruling the part affected, or afflicting such sign and part. (See Sores).

**Bed-Wetting**—(See "Incontinence" under Urine).

**BEES DESTROYED**—♂ in ♐ at the Vernal Equinox, and espec. in Places and Countries ruled by ♐.

**Droning Of**—Humming Of—Said to be ruled by ♆.

**BEGGING**—Murmuring—(See "Exhibition of Maladies" under Exhibition).

**Beggarly**—Lives Beggarly and Carelessly—The ☽ ill-dignified at B.; ♃ Sig. □ or ☍ ♄. (See Poverty, Privation).

**BEHAVIOR**—(See the references under Conduct, Habits, Love Affairs, Marriage, Morals, Passion, Pleasures, Religion, Sex, etc.).

**BEHEADED**—Decapitation—Danger of Death By—The ☉ joined with the Ascelli, Castor, Pollux, Hyades, Pleiades, Praesepe; the ☉ directed to all Nebulous Clusters, and espec. to Castor or Ascelli, threatens decapitation; ♂ afflicted in Imperfect or Mutilated signs; ♂ in the 8th H., or ruler of the 8th, and with Caput Algol; ♂ near Gorgon in the 5th face of ♉, and in ☌ or ☍ the ☉ or ☽, death by, or mutilation of limb; ♂ ori., in mutilated signs, in □ or ☍ the ☉, or ♂ occi. in □ or ☍ the ☽, or with Caput Medusa; malefics in earth signs, and espec. in ♉; the hyleg ☌ Caput Algol in an angle. (See Distortions, Guillotined, Hanging, "Death by Sentence" under Judge; Maimed, Mutilated, etc.).

**BELCHING**—Eructations—Pyrosis—Water Brash—Burning Pains at Stomach, with Eructations—Emission of Gas Thru Mouth—A disease of the ♋ sign; ♄ or ☿ affl. in ♋; ♂ in ♋ or ill-asp. the ☽ tends to eructations and burning pains at the stomach. (See Digestion, Flatulence, Gas, "Gastric Acidity" under Acids; Heartburn, Indigestion; Stomach; "Stomach" under Wind, etc.).

**BELLADONNA**—Atropin—One of the 12 Polycrest Remedies, and corresponding to the ♉ Sign. Also a typical drug of ♄. (See "Polycrest" under Zodiac; "Mydriatics" under Iris).

**BELLATRIX**—Orion's Left Shoulder—A star of the nature of ♂ and ☿ in 19° ♊. The ☉ and ☽ to the place of tend to cause Blindness by Accident. Its influence also tends to Extreme Sickness, Dangers, Blindness, Disgrace, Drowning, Calamity, Disease, Hot Distempers, Putrid Fevers, Ruin, Violent Death, etc. (See these subjects. Also see Orion, Rigel).

**BELLY**—Ventral—Abdomen—The word Belly is frequently used in the textbooks of Astrology, and is merely another word for Abdomen. The most of the subjects concerning the Belly you will find under Abdomen. The Belly is ruled by the ☽ and the ♍ Sign. The inferior part of the Belly, the lower Belly, is ruled by the 6th H.

**Any Disease**—In the Belly—A ♍ disease; afflictions in ♍.

**Bellyache**—Dry Bellyache—The ☽ affl. in ♍ or ♎; ♄ affl. in ♊. (See "Pain" under Bowels).

**Diseases Of**—Disorders—♀ diseases, and afflictions to ♀; ☽ affl. in ♍; afflictions in ♍ or the 6th H.

**Fluxes Of**—☽ diseases, and afflictions to the ☽; the ☽ affl. in ♍.

**Large, Deep Belly**—♃ in the Asc. (See "Prominent" under Abdomen).

**Love Their Belly**—(See Eating, Feasting, Gluttony, etc.).

**Short and Lank Belly**—♄ ascending at B.

**Ventral Hernia**—(See Hernia). See Abdomen, Bowels, Hypogastrium, Intestines, Navel, etc.

**BENDING**—Bent—Flexed—Flexion—Flexible—Flexure—☿ affl. in ♌ warns against bending the body.

**Body Bent Forward**—(See Crooked, "Downward Look" under Look; Legs, Stooping; "Round Shoulders" and "Stoop Shoulders" under Shoulders).

**Flexed Signs**—(See Mutable).

**Womb**—Flexion of (See Flexure, Womb).

**BENEFICS**—The planets ♃ and ♀. These planets in ☌ or good asp. the ☉, ☽, Asc., M.C., or Hyleg at B. tend to benefit and preserve the health, and give greater vitality. The Benefics afflict only by their □ and ☍ aspects. Heat and moisture are given by the benefics, both benevolent influences, and for this reason the Ancients called them Benefic planets. The more angular, oriental and elevated the benefics at B., the more powerful are their effects for good, and to assist in the cure and alleviation of disease. The Benefics may act as Anareta under certain circumstances. (See Anareta). They also exert a protective, preservative, nourishing influence. (See these subjects). The ☉, ☽, and ☊ are also classed as Benefics when giving their good aspects. (See these planets and Dragon's Head. Also see Horas, Malefics).

**BEREAVEMENT**—The general causes of a death in the family, or among relatives or friends, and to bring bereavement, are as follows,—The ☉ or ☽ to the ☌ or ill-asps. ♅, ♄, or ♂ by dir.; the ☉ to the ill-asps. the ☽ by dir.; the ☉, ♅, ♄, or ♂ by their evil directions to the hyleg, and to the vital places in the map; the progressed ☉ to the □ or ☍ ♃ by dir.; the ☽ to the ill-asps. the ☉ by dir., and espec. to females; the ☽ to the ill-asps. ♀ by dir.; ♄ to the ☌ or ill-asp. the ☉, ☽, ♀, ☿, Asc., or M.C. by dir. (For further influences along this line see Acquaintances, Aunts, Brothers, Children, Father, Friends, Grief, Grandparents, Infants, Mother, Parents, Prevalent, Relatives, Sisters, Uncles, etc.).

**BERIBERI**—(See this subject under Dropsy).

**BESIDE ONESELF**—Frenzy—Excessively Excitable—(See Excitable, Frenzy, Fury).

**BETELGEUSE**—(See Orion).

**BETTER**—The Disease is Better—(See "Better" under Disease, Health; Improvement).

**BICORPOREAL SIGNS**—(See Double-Bodied).

**BILE**—Bilious—The Gall—Gall Bladder—Choler—Cholic—The Bile is ruled by ♄, ♂, ☿, and the ♌ and ♏ signs. The Gall Bladder, the reservoir of the Bile, is ruled by ♄, and as a receptacle, by the ☽. The Bile holds dominion from 9 A.M. to 3 P.M. The First Quarter of the ☽, which is hot and dry, acts on the Bile. The Bile is formed by ♄ in the liver, and deposited by ♄ over the body in the form of Uric Acid, causing Gout, Rheumatism, etc. (See Gout, Rheumatism). Mars portends the Gall, and also causes diseases arising from too much choler. The Bilious Signs are ♈, ♌, ♐, the fiery signs. Note the following conditions concerning the Bile, Gall Bladder, Ducts, etc., and diseases connected with them,—

**All Diseases**—Of the Gall—♂ diseases, and due to ♂ afflictions.

**Atrabilarious Attacks**—(See "Black Bile" in this section. Also see Depression, Hypochondria, Melancholy).

**Biliousness**—Liverishness—A disease of the ☉ and ♂, and characteristic of the Bilious, or Choleric Temperament ruled by the ☉, ♂, and the fiery signs; the ☉ ♈, ☌ or ill-asp. any of the malefics as promittors; the ☉ in ill asp. to ♃; the ☉ in ♎ and affl. by ♃; the ☽ ♍ and to the ☌ or ill-asp. any of the malefics as promittors, and tends to great mental depression; ♆, ♅, or ♄ in ♊ or ♏, and affl. the ☉ or ☽; ♂ affl. in ♌; ♂ ♍ ☌ or ill-asp. the ☉; caused by Subs at Li.P., Liver Place, in spine.

**Black Bile**—Blackness of Bile—Atrabilarious Attacks—Depression—Hypochondria—Melancholy, etc.—♄ and ♂ in an angle, occi. of the ☉, and ori. of the ☽, and ☿ in familiarity with ♂; ♂ or ☿ holding dominion at B., and in familiarity with each other, and ♂ affl. the hyleg and elevated above the Luminaries, blackness of bile is increased. (See Adrenals, Atrabile).

**Calculi**—(See "Gall Stones" in this section).

**Choler**—(See Choler).

**Cholera**—Bilious Cholera—(See "Cholera Morbus" under Cholera).

**Choleric Distempers**—And Humours—(See Choleric).

**Cholic**—Biliary Colic—Hepatic Colic—Disturbances of the Bile—Pain in the Liver, Gall Bladder, Gall Ducts—Cramps About the Gall Bladder, etc.—A ☽ and ♍ disease; afflictions in ♍; ♄ in an angle, occi. of the ☉, and ori. of the ☽; ♀ lord of the 1st H., and applying to the □ or ☍ ♄ or a malefic.

**Complaints**—Bilious Complaints—Given by the Bilious, or Choleric Temperament; diseases of the ☉, ♂, and the fiery signs; a ♊ disease; afflictions in ♊ or ♐; ♂ affl. in ♊; ♂ affl. in ♎ in the 6th H. (See "Choleric Temperament" under Choleric).

**Cough**—Bilious Dry Cough—(See Cough).

**Deficiency of Bile**—♄ affl. in the 6th H.

**Diarrhoea**—(See "Bilious" under Diarrhoea).

**Diseases**—And Disorders of the Bile and Gall Bladder—(See the various paragraphs in this section).

**Distempers**—Choleric Distempers and Humours—(See Choleric).

**Disturbances**—Of the Bile—(See the various subjects in this section).

**Ducts**—The Gall Ducts—The Bile Ducts Disordered—Stenosis of—♄ affl. in ♍, and espec. in the 6th H.; ♂ affl. in ♍; caused by Subs at Li.P., and afflictions in the signs acting thru Li.P. (See Vertebrae).

**Fevers**—Bilious Fevers—Burning, Hot, Fiery, Violent Fevers, and which grow worse towards sunrise—(See "High Fevers" under Fevers).

**Flatulency**—Bilious Flatulency—♀ affl. in ♎; ☿ affl. in ♊. (See Flatulence).

**Gall Stones**—Biliary Calculi—Cholelithiasis—Are formed by ♄ in the Gall Bladder, and painful Gallstones are the work of ♄; ♄ ☌ or ill-asp. ♂; ♄ affl. in ♌; a disease of the ☽; afflictions in ♒; ♑ on the Asc., thru worry and brooding; caused by Subs at Li.P. For Birth Data and Cases of Gall Stones, see Figures 10A and 10B in the book, "Astro-Diagnosis" by the Heindels. (See Stone).

**Headache**—(See "Bilious" under Headache).

**Humours**—Choleric Humours—(See Choleric).

**Hypochondria**—(See this subject).

**Jaundice**—(See Jaundice).

**Liver**—(See the various subjects under Liver).

**Liverishness**—(See "Biliousness" in this section).

**Melancholy**—Atrabile—Black Bile—(See "Black Bile" in this section. Also see Atrabile, Melancholy).

**Nausea**—Bilious Nausea—(See Nausea).

**Obstruction**—Of the Bile Passages—♆, ♅, or ♄ in ♊, and affl. the ☉ or ☽.

**Pain**—In the Gall Bladder—(See "Cholic" in this section).

**Stenosis**—Of the Gall Ducts—(See "Ducts" in this section).

**Temperament**—The Bilious Temperament—(See Choleric).

**Treatment**—(See Signature).

**Vomiting**—Bilious Vomiting—(See Nausea, Vomiting).

**BINDING**—Limiting—Restraining—Confining—The influence and action of ♄, and also of the 12th H. (See Chronic, Confinement, Hospitals, Invalids, Limitations, Retraction, "Influence of Saturn" under Saturn; Twelfth House).

**BIOCHEMISTRY**—The Chemistry of Living Tissues. The study of the Chemistry of the human body in its relation to the Zodiac, and the Tissue Salts of the body under the rule of the 12 Signs of the Zodiac. (See "Salts" under Zodiac).

**BIRDS**—(See "Birds of the Air" under Air; Fowls, Vultures).

**Bird Features**—(See Monsters).

**BIRTH**—Births—Born—etc.—(See the following subjects in the alphabetical arrangement,—

**Abnormal Births**—(See Abortion, "Excision" under Foetus; Premature, Stillborn, etc. Note the various subjects in this section).

**Abortion; Accident at Birth**—(See "Accidents" under Infancy).

**Asphyxiation**—At Birth—(See Asphyxia).

**Big at Birth**—Very Big at Birth—See Case, "Short Life", No. 371 in 1001 N.N.

**Birthday**—Anniversary of Birth—The Solar Revolution—The time when the ☉ passes over the same degree of the Zodiac he was in at B. The birthday each year begins your new year, and when the vital forces of the body begin to take on new and greater activity. During the period of 105 days before the birthday the forces of the body are usually at their lowest ebb. In each life the year is divided into seven divisions, or days, corresponding to the days of the week, periods of 52 days each, and the 105 days before the birthday are the Friday and Saturday periods of the year for the native. The Friday Period is the 52 days "On the Cross", and the Saturday Period the 52 days "In the Tomb", and these are usually very difficult and trying periods of the year for the average person unless he is settled, contented, prosperous, and of good health. These Periods and Cycles are discussed in the book called "Periodicity", by Dr. James Buchanan. (See "Solar Revolution" under Solar).

**Birthmarks**—(See Naevus).

**Birth Place**—(See "Place of Birth" under Place).

**Birthrate**—The birthrate is increased when the ☽ is in the 5th H. at a Vernal Equinox, Ingress, or Solstice, and well-aspected by the benefics, and decreased when the ☽ is in the 5th H. at these times, and afflicted by malefics, and with no assistance from the benefics).

**Birthstones**—(See this subject under Stones).

**Blind from Birth**—(See this subject under Blindness).

**Cause of Birth**—From a physical standpoint the immediate cause of birth of the body into the world is due to the influence of ♂ and the ☽. The violent influence of ♂ ushers the child into the world, and normally at the 10th menstrual period, which periods are ruled by the ☽. There exists in Nature a sympathy between parent and child, and children are born at a moment when the constitution of the heavens is such as to produce one with the traits and characteristics of one or both parents. Family resemblances are thus handed down in this way. (See "Moment of Birth" under Calamity; Foetus, Gestation, Heredity, Nativity, Parturition, Prenatal Epoch).

**Child**—Birth of a Child Promised—(See "Birth of a Child" under Children; "Birth of a Female" under Female; "Births" under Male; "Birth of a Son" under Son).

**Childbirth**—(See Parturition).

**Children**—Birth of—(See Fruitfulness. Also see "Child" in this section).

**Congenital**—Existing from Birth—Innate—(See Congenital, Heredity, Innate).

**Crippled**—From Birth—(See Arms, Congenital, Deformed, Distortions, Excrescences, Infancy, Lame, Legs, Maimed, Monsters, Paralysis, etc.).

**Daughter Born**—(See "Birth of a Female" under Female).

**Dead**—Born Dead—(See Stillborn).

**Deafness from Birth**—(See "Born Deaf" under Hearing).

**Death at Birth**—(See "Birth", "Born Almost Dead", under Children).

**Death Soon After Birth**—(See "Born Almost Dead" under Children; "Nurture" under Infancy. Also see Abortion, Foetus).

**Defective Births**—(See "Crippled" in this section. Also see Blind, Congenital, Defects, Distortions, Freaks, Idiots, Monsters, Mute, etc).

**Deformed**—From Birth—(See "Crippled" in this section. Also see Deformed; "Deformed" under Infancy).

**Delayed Birth**—(See "Birth" under Asphyxia).

**Diseases and Infections**—At Birth—(See Infancy).

**Distortions**—From Birth—(See Distortions).

**Eclipses**—At Time of Birth—Danger of Death—(See Eclipses).

**Embryo; Female Births**—(See "Birth of a Female" under Female).

**Foetus; Gestation; Heredity; Illegitimate**—(See Bastard).

**Incomplete**—Born Incomplete—Members or Parts Missing—(See Arms, Congenital, Deformities, Incomplete, Malformations, Missing, Monsters).

**Infancy**—(See the various paragraphs under Infancy).

**Injury at Birth**—(See Parturition).

**Lame from Birth**—(See Lameness).

**Large at Birth**—(See Large).

**Life**—Continuance of Life After Birth—(See "Continuance" under Life).

**Maimed from Birth**—(See Maimed).

**Male Born**—(See "Births" under Male).

**Miscarriage; Moment of Birth**—This is counted from the time of the first cry, the first breath, when the magnetism of the Universe is breathed in. The time and moment of birth are considered fixed unless interfered with by unnatural causes. (See "Causes" in this section. Also see Baptism; Conception; Congenital; "Moment of Birth" under Moment).

**Monsters; Mother**—Death of In Childbirth—(See "Death of the Mother" under Parturition).

**Multiple Births**—(See Twins).

**Normal Birth**—(See Normal).

**Overtime Birth**—(See "Delayed", "Moment" in this section. Also see Prenatal Epoch; "Excision" under Foetus).

**Paralyzed from Birth**—(See Distortions).

**Place of Birth**—(See "Place of Birth" under Place).

**Precocious Births**—(See Precocious).

**Premature Births**—(See Abortion, Miscarriage, Premature).

**Prenatal Epoch; Single Births**—One Only—(See "Single Births" under Children).

**Son Born**—(See Son. Also see "Births" under Male).

**Star Map of Birth**—(See Map. Also see "Moment" in this section).

**Stillborn; Strangled at Birth**—(See Asphyxia).

**Suffocated at Birth**—(See Asphyxia, Suffocation).

**Time of Birth**—(See "Moment" in this section. Also see Baptism, Prenatal Epoch, Time).

**Triplets; Twins.**

**BISEXUAL**—(See Hermaphrodites).

**BITES**—Stings—Are usually caused by the ♂ influence, and the afflictions of the malefics.

**Adder**—Bites or Stings By—♄, ♂, and ♀ conjoined in ♏, Kings are stung by an Adder or some obnoxious creature. (See Adder).

**Animals**—Beasts—Horses—Bites By—The ☽ in an earthy sign, and to the ☌ or ill-asp. ♂ by dir.; ♄ in an animal sign, as in ♈, ♉, ♌, ♐, or ♑; the Asc. to the place of Hydra's Heart. (See "Hurts" under Horses).

**Death By**—The ☽ hyleg, and to the ☌ or ill-asp. ♂ by dir., and the ☽ affl. at B.; ♄ affl. in ♏, danger of death by bites of serpents; ♄ in animal signs, and afflicted, danger of death by bites of animals. (See Serpents, Stings, Venomous).

**Dogs**—Bites By—The ☉ to the ☌ or ill-asp. ♂ by dir., bites by dogs, mad dogs, and death by Hydrophobia. (See Dogs, Hydrophobia).

**Horses**—Bites By—(See "Animals" in this section).

**Insects**—Bites By—(See Stings, Venomous).

**Journeys**—Travel—Bites or Stings During Travel—Malefics in the 3rd or 9th H., in fiery signs, and affl. the ☉ or ☽. (See Venomous).

**Kings**—Ruler—(See "Adder" in this section).

**Mad Dog**—(See "Dogs" in this section).

**Obnoxious Creatures**—Bites By—(See "Adder" in this section. Also see Obnoxious, Venomous).

**Reptiles**—Bites By—(See Reptiles, Serpents, Venomous).

**Serpents**—Snakes—Bites By—(See "Death" in this section. Also see Serpents, Venomous).

**Travel**—Bites During—(See "Journeys" in this section).

**Venomous Creatures**—(See Adder, Death, in this section. Also see Serpents, Venomous).

**Various Kinds**—Of Bites—The ☉ hyleg, and the ☉ to the ☌ or ill-asp. ♂ by dir.; the ☽ to the ☌ or ill-asp. ♂ by dir.; ♄, ♂, and ♀ conjoined in ♏.

**Voyages**—Bites On—(See "Journeys" in this section).

**BITTER**—Acrid—Pungent—

**Bitter Drugs**—Acrid and Pungent Drugs—Are mostly ruled by ♂, as Nux Vomica, Strychnine, Quinine, etc. (See Acids, Pungent, Signature).

**Bitter Signs**—♈, ♌, ♐, said to be bitter, fiery and hot.

**Bitter Temper**—(See Sarcasm; "Nasty" under Temper).

**BLACK**—As a color, is ruled and signified by ♄. Is also denoted by the 6th, 7th and 8th houses. The ♍ sign signifies black spotted with blue; ♎ denotes black or swarthy; ♑ denotes black. Black, ruled by ♄, has a deadening and devitalizing influence, and black clothing should be avoided. (See Color, Colors).

**Black Bile**—(See Bile).

**Black Death**—(See Plague).

**Black Eyebrows**—(See Eyebrows).

**Black Eyelids**—(See Eyelids).

**Black Eyes**—(See "Black" under Eyes).

**Black Figure**—(See "Skin" in this section).

**Black Hair**—(See Hair).

**Blackheads**—(See "Comedo" under Sebaceous).

**Black Jaundice**—(See Jaundice).

**Black Magic**—(See Magical).

**Blackmailers**—(See Libel).

**Black Marks**—On Body—(See Marks).

**Black Skin**—Black Personal Figure—(See "Black" under Skin; "Dark Personal Figure" under Dark; Negro).

**BLADDER**—Vesica—Receptacle of the Urine—Vesical Muscle—All vesicles, or containers, which hold liquids and fluids in the body, are fundamentally ruled and influenced by the ☽ and the ♋ sign. The urinal bladder is under the internal rule of the ♏ sign. Also ♉ has affinity with the bladder. According to the various Authors and Textbooks, the Bladder is ruled by ♄, ♂, the ☽, ♎, ♏, and the 7th and 8th houses. Elimination of the urine thru the bladder is ruled by ♂ and ♏. In infants the bladder is largely ruled and dominated by the action of the ☉ and ☽ working thru the ♎ sign, and gives way to the Renal Diathesis. (See Hypogastrium). Note the following diseases and conditions concerning the Bladder:

**Abscess In**—Impostumes—A ♎ disease, and afflictions in ♎; ♃ affl. in ♏ in the 6th H. (See Abscesses).

**All Diseases In**—Are indicated by the 7th and 8th Houses, by ♎, ♏, and the afflictions of ♂, and are diseases of ♂ and the ☽.

**Atony Of**—♄ affl. in ♏; ♄, ♏, □ or ☍ ♆ or ♂. (See Atonic).

**Bladder Troubles**—(See "Diseases" in this section).

**Bladder Worm**—(See Acephalocyst).

**Catarrh Of**—(See "Cystitis" in this section).

**Cloaca**—(See Cloaca).

**Concretions In**—Gravel or Sand In—(See "Gravel", "Stone" in this section).

**Cystitis**—Inflammation and Catarrh of the Bladder—♂ in ♏ and affl. the hyleg; a ♏ disease, and planets affl. in ♏; ♂ affl. in ♎, and ♎ on the cusp of 8th H.; caused by Subs at PP, and LPP, and also at KP, from irritating urine. (See Catarrh, Urine, Vertebrae).

**Diseases Of**—Bladder Troubles—The ☉ or ☽ in the 6th H., and afflicted; the ☉ and ☽ acting thru the ♏ sign, and give way to the Hepatic Diathesis (See "Basal" under Ganglion); the ☉ or ☽ affl. in ♏; the ☽ in the 6th H., in fixed signs, and afflicted; caused by the ☽ affl. at B.; the ☽ in ♏ or ♒, and to the ☌ or ill-asps. any of the malefics by dir., and espec. if ♂ affl. the ☽ at B., or ♂ occupy the 6th H.; ♂ diseases and afflictions; ♂ ♏ ☌ or ill-asp. the ☉ or ☽; ♂ in 6th H., and affl. the ☉, ☽, or hyleg, and espec. if ♂ be in the fixed signs ♉, ♌, ♏; the ♉ or ♏ signs on the cusp of 6th H., and afflicted; caused by Subs at KP, PP, LPP. (See "All Diseases", and the various paragraphs in this section).

**Gall Bladder**—(See Bile).

**Gravel In**—Sand—(See Gravel, Sand, Stone).

**Hypertrophy Of**—♂ affl. in ♏. (See Hypertrophy).

**Imposthumes**—(See "Abscess" in this section).

**Incontinence**—Of the Urine—(See "Incontinence" under Urine).

**Inflammation Of**—(See "Cystitis" in this section).

**Irritable Bladder**—Constant Desire to Urinate—(See "Strangury", "Micturition" under Urine).

**Micturition**—(See Urine).

**Neck of Bladder**—Vesicae Cervis—Neuralgia of—♂, ♀, or ☿ affl. in ♏. (See "Neck" under Womb).

**Neuralgia**—(See "Neck" in this section).

**Pains In**—Violent Pains In—The ☉ affl. in ♓ when the ☉ is the afflictor in the disease, violent pains; the ☽ in ♒ and with ♏ upon the Asc. when taken ill; ♂ in ♏ when ♂ is the afflictor in the disease; ☿ affl. in ♏.

**Sand**—(See "Gravel" in this section).

**Spasm**—Stricture—♅ affl. in ♎ or ♏. (See Spasmodic).

**Stone**—(See Stone).

**Stricture Of**—(See "Spasm" in this section).

**Tuberculosis Of**—♄ affl. in ♏; Subs at KP and PP. (See Tuberculosis, Vertebrae).

**Ulcers**—A ♎ disease and afflictions in ♎. (See "Abscess" in this section).

**Urine**—Bladder Disorders Thru Disturbed Urine—(See the various subjects under Urine, as **Micturition**, Strangury, etc.

**Violent Pains In**—(See "Pain" in this section).

**Worm**—Bladder Worm—(See Acephalocyst).

**Weakness Of**—The ☽ hyleg in ♏ in a female nativity; ♀ affl. in ♏ in 6th H., or affl. the ☽ or Asc. (For collateral study see Elimination, Excretion, "Impar" under Ganglion; Kidneys, Secretion, Urethra, Urine).

**BLEB**—**Bulla**—(See Blister).

**BLEEDING**—Loss of Blood—(See Discharges, Effusions, Epistaxis, Hemorrhage, "Flooding" under Menses).

**Blood-Letting**—Transfusion—Withdrawing blood from the circulation should not be done in a ♃ hour, or when ♃ is affl. by the ☽, as ♃ rules the blood. (See Blood, Effusions, Jupiter).

**Gums**—(See "Bleeding" under Gums).

**Piles**—(See "Bleeding" under Hemorrhoids).

**BLEMISHES**—Blemished—Bodily Blemishes—External Blemishes—Ptolemy associates the words "Diseases and Blemishes", in giving the causes of Disease. (See "Causes of Disease" under Disease). The Asc. rules over Blemishes and External Complaints. The Asc. affl. by ♂ tends to hurts and blemishes; ♅, ♄, or ♂ on the cusp of the 1st, 6th, or 7th houses, or in exact evil asp. to these degrees, and espec. if the ☉ or ☽ be in ☌ or ☍ in the 1st or 7th houses; ♅, ♄, or ♂ ori. tend to blemishes or hurts; the ☽ is said to give blemishes when she is in Tropical or Equinoctial Signs, as in ♈, ♎, ♋, ♑; malefics ori., and in evil asp. the Lights, but if occi. cause diseases; malefics in angles, occi. of the ☉, and ori. of the ☽, and with no benefic configurations of the benefics to ♄ or ♂, or to the ☉ or ☽, the blemishes become permanent and can never be removed, and espec. if the malefics be fortified and elevated above the benefics. If the benefics in the foregoing configuration are elevated above the malefics, the blemishes will be mitigated, and may entirely disappear or be removed. (See Blotches, Children, Defects, Deformities, Disfigurements, Eruptions, Face, Freckles, Marks, Moles, Monsters, Naevus, Pimples, Parts, Pockmark, Scars, Sores, Teeth, Ulcers, Varicose, etc.).

**Eyes**—Blemish In or Near the Eyes—The ☽ at exactly New or Full ☽ at B., and in evil asp. ♂, a scar or mole; the ☽ impedited by, or evilly aspected by the ☉ at B.; the ☽ impedited by the ☉ in an angle gives a blemish in the eye, but if she be with Nebulous or violent Fixed Stars, in a succedent house, the blemish will be near the eye; the ☽ impedited in succedent houses; the ☽ ☌ or ☍ the ☉ in angles, and the ☉ or ☽ affl. by ♂; the ☽ ☌ or ill-asp. the ☉ at B. (See Cataracts, Defects, Impediments, Marks, and other paragraphs under Eyes).

**Face**—Blemishes On—(See Blemishes under Face).

**BLEPHARITIS**—(See Eyelids).

**BLIGHT**—Blights—Cessation of Growth—Decay—Fading—Withering, etc.—The influence of ♄, and a ♄ disease. (See Decay, Fruit, Growth, Herbs, Vegetation, Withering).

**Eyes**—Blight In the Eye—(See "Blight" under Eyes).

**BLINDNESS**—Loss of Sight in One or Both Eyes—Light Rays are transmitted by ♅, which planet rules the Ether. Thus ♅ indirectly tends to affect the eyes thru the light rays, and cause blindness or eye diseases. (See Ether, Light, Retina, Uranus). The Nebulous Spots in the heavens when found with the ☉ or ☽ at B. also tend to blindness, and many eye disorders and weaknesses. (See Nebulous). In the Hindu System of Astrology the 2nd H. is given rule over the eyes, and afflictions in or to this house tend to impair the sight, or cause blindness. The malefics, when with the ☉ or ☽ at B., or with Nebulous Stars, increase the danger of blindness. Under the heading, "Causes of Blindness" in this section will be given the influences of the ☉, ☽, ☿, and each of the malefics in causing blindness. The Asc., or ruler of the Asc., in one of the Azimene Degrees of the Zodiac at B. also tend to Blindness. (See Azimene). Note the following conditions and influences which have to do with Blindness and its causes, and see these subjects in the alphabetical arrangement when not considered here.

**Accidents**—Blindness By—The ☉ or ☽ joined to Bellatrix at B., or by dir.; the ☽ or Asc. in Nebulous parts at B., or by dir., and affl. by ♂; caused principally by ♂ afflictions to the ☉ or ☽ at B., or ♂ with violent Nebulous stars; a malefic in a Nebulous place and affl. the ☉ or ☽, and espec. if the malefic be elevated above the Lights. There is more hope of relief from the accident when the malefic in a Nebulous place afflicts the ☽ rather than the ☉. (See the various paragraphs in this section. Also see "Accidents" under Eyes).

**Amaurosis**—Partial or Total Blindness By—(See Gutta Serena. Also see "Total Blindness" in this section).

**Amusements**—Sports—Blindness from Injury During—(See the ♂ influences under "Causes" in this section. Also see "Total Blindness" in this section).

**Artifice**—Blindness By—(See the ♂ influences under "Causes" in this section).

**Azimene Degrees**—(See Azimene).

**Birth**—Blind from Birth—(See "Born Blind" in this section).

**Blind Spot of Retina**—(See "Blind Spot" under Eyes; Retina).

**Blows**—Blindness by Blows—(See "Accidents", "Injury", under Eyes; "Eyes" under Sword).

**Born Blind**—Blind from Birth—The actual planetary causes of this condition are not generally shown in the natal map, but in the prenatal conditions, the Lunar Epoch, and Chart of Descent. Afflictions to the ☽ at each Lunar return during pregnancy, corresponding to the monthly period, often show the causes of congenital deformities, afflictions, blindness, and malformations which exist at B. The following conditions have existed in the maps of those born blind,—In males, ♄ on the Asc., or in the M.C., afflicting the ☉, and the ☽ sepr. from the ☉ and applying to ♂; the ☽ near a Nebulous place at B., ☌ or ill-asp. a malefic, and the ☉ also afflicted; the ☽ and ♆ conjoined in the 2nd H., and in □ to ♂ in the 6th (Hindu); ♆ on the Asc., and afflicting ♃, and possibly from some affection of the optic nerve; ♄ in the 2nd H., and affl. the ☉ or ☽ (Hindu). (See Azimene, Congenital,

Prenatal Epoch). Cases of Born Blind—See "Arundel", and "Seventeen Years In Bed", Cases No. 159 and 843 in 1001 N.N. See "Diseases to Eyes", Case No. 4, page 87, Chap. 13, in Daath's Medical Astrology.

**Both Eyes**—Blind In—(See "Total" in this section).

**Bruises**—Blindness By—The ☉ directed to Praesepe, Hyades, Pleiades, Castor, Pollux, or other stars of the nature of ♂ and the ☽ combined, and espec. if Praesepe be in the Asc., or with the ☉ or ☽ in an angle. (See "Total" in this section).

**Burning**—Blindness By—The ☉ in the Asc. or M.C., with ♂ rising before him, and the ☉ ☌ or ☍ the ☽; the ☉ in an angle in the same sign with the ☽, or in ☍, with ♄ and ♂ ori. of the ☉, ascending before him, and ♄ and ♂ occi. of the ☽. (These same influences also apply to injuries to the eyes by blows, strokes, or the sword. (See "Injuries to Eyes" under Eyes).

**Cataracts;**

**Causes of Blindness**—The ☉ or ☽ with the Pleiades, Ascelli, Antares, Praesepe, Deneb, Hyades, Castor, Pollux, or Orion's Belt, at B., or afflicted by these, and other Nebulous stars by dir., tend to blindness, or at least in one eye, or to serious injury to the eyes, and espec. when the Lights are also afflicted by ♂ from an angle; the ☉ ☌ or ☍ the ☽ in any of the Nebulous parts of the Zodiac; the ☉ with the Pleiades at B., and espec. if ♅ afflict; the ☉ or ☽ with stars of the nature of ♂ and the ☽ combined, as with the Pleiades, Praesepe, Hyades, Castor and Pollux, etc.; the ☉ ☌ ☋ in ♐ near the place of Antares; the ☉ or ☽ in the 6th H. in ☌ with Antares or the Ascelli, and in ☍ to any of the malefic planets; the ☉ or ☽ ☌ Nebulous stars, and affl. by malefics; the ☉ to the ☌ or ill-asp. the ☽ by dir., and the ☽ affl. at B.; the ☉ and ☽ in the signs of their fall, and afflicted, as the ☉ in ♎, and the ☽ in ♏; the ☉ or ☽ joined to Bellatrix; the ☉ and ☽ in ☍ from ♌ and ♒; the ☉ and ♂ in ☌ Nebulous stars, and affl. by ♅; the progressed ☉ to the bad asps. ♅; the ☉ or ☽ in the angles of the map, afflicting each other, and also afflicted by Nebulous stars; the ☉ directed to any of the Nebulous clusters threatens blindness; the ☉ and ☽ ascending, and impedited by ♄ or ♂, gives blindness, bad eyes, or scars or marks in them; the ☉ Sig. in ☌ ♄ and ♄ ill-dig; the ☉ Sig. ☍ ☽ if the ☽ be hyleg, and the ☍ close, may be blind; the ☉ to the ☌ ♂ by dir.; the ☉ to the □ or ☍ ♂ or the ☽ by dir.; the ☽ ☌ the Pleiades in the 7th H., and espec. if affl. by ♂; the ☽ to ☌ or ill-asp. ♂ by dir., and ♂ be near the Ascelli, Aldebaran, Bull's Eye, or Cor Scorpio, and affl. by the ☉ or ♄; the ☽ to the place of Praesepe, and other Nebulous stars of the nature of ♂ and the ☽, great defect in sight, and often blindness, espec. when both Lights are with Nebulous stars and affl. by malefics; the ☽ sepr. from the ☉ and applying to ♂ in a day geniture; the ☽ in an angle with the Pleiades, Praesepe, or Antares; the progressed ☽ in ☌ with malefics in ♈, and espec. if the ☉ or ☽ were with Nebulous stars at B., and afflicted; the ☽ affl. at B., and to the ☌ or ill-asps. the ☉ by dir., and espec. if either of the Lights were near Nebulous stars at B.; the ☽ in the western angle, or 7th H., conjoined with the Pleiades, which was the case with Milton, the blind Poet; the ☽ Sig. ☌ the ☉ near the Pleiades, Hyades or Praesepe; the ☽ or Asc. in Nebulous parts, and affl. by ♄; the ☽ directed to the Pleiades, Hyades, Praesepe, or the Twins and Ascelli; the ☽ Sig. ☌ the ☉; the ☽ Sig. □ or ☍ the ☉, and espec. if sepr. from the ☍; the ☽ to the □ or ☍ the ☉ by dir.; ♆ or ♅ joined with Nebulous stars; ♆ ☌ the Ascelli; ♅ in evil asp. the ☉ or ☽ when near the Pleiades, Antares, or the Ascelli, tends to weaken the eyes, or produce blindness; ♄ causes blindness by cold, colds, cataracts, specks, films, Gutta Serena, etc., and if ☿ be with him it will be from mental exertion, reading, study, etc.; ♄ affl. the ☽ or Asc. when the latter are in Nebulous parts; ♂ causes blindness by bruises, fire, wounds, smallpox, lightning, accidents, injuries, strokes, blows, etc., when affl. the ☉ or ☽ in or near Nebulous parts, and if ♂ be with ♀ he causes blindness at some amusement, in sports, at play, by private injury, treachery, or some vile artifice; ☿ causes blindness from eye-strain, mental exertion, and from hard reading or over-study, and espec. when conjoined with the ☉ or ☽ afflicted in Nebulous spots. (For further influences see the various paragraphs in this section, and under "Eyes", "Sight", etc). Cases and Birth Data of Blindness, Acquired Blindness, Going Blind, etc.—In 1001 N.N. see cases No. 099, 159, 684, and 843, under the headings of "Marsten", "Arundel", "Sight Defective", and "Seventeen Years in Bed". See Fig. 32 in book, "Message of the Stars" by the Heindels. See Cases 2 and 4, Chap. 13, "Diseases to Eyes", in Daath's Medical Astrology. (See Heredity).

**Cold**—Blindness from Cold or White Film—The ☉ in an angle ☌ or ☍ the ☽, and ♄ ascending before the ☉.

**Color Blindness**—Afflictions to ♀ by the malefics, and espec. by ♄, and also strong afflictions in the ☍ sign, and espec. to the 16 and 17°, tend to produce color blindness; Subs at AT and MCP, 4th C. (See Color).

**Day Blindness**—Nyctalopia—♆ afflictions to the ☉ or ☽, with vision best at night; ♆ with Nebulous stars, and afflicting the ☉ or ☽.

**Deaf, Dumb and Blind**—(See Hearing, Mutes. See Case, "Arundel", No. 159, in 1001 N.N.).

**Defects**—Blindness From—(See Cataracts, Film, Specks, and the various paragraphs in this section).

**Exercise**—Blindness By—(See "Sports" in this section).

**Explosions**—Blindness By—(See Explosions).

**Eye Strain**—Blindness By—(See "Eyestrain" under Eyes; "Mental Exertion" in this section).

**Film**—Blindness from White Film—(See "Cold" in this section).

**Fire**—By Fire—(See "Burning" in this section).

**Glaucoma**—Blindness By—(See Glaucoma).

**Growths**—Blindness By—The ☽ or Asc. in Nebulous Parts, and affl. by ♄. (See Cataract, Film, Obstructions, Specks, and other paragraphs in this section. Also see "Defects" under Eyes).

**Gunshot**—Blindness By—Caused by ♂, and his afflictions to the ☉ and ☽, and ♂ also with Nebulous Stars. (See Gunshot).

**Gutta Serena**—Blindness By—(See Gutta Serena).

**Hemianopia**—Blindness of One-Half the Visual Field—(See this subject under Sight).

**Injury**—Blindness by Injury, Wounds, etc.—(See Accidents, Artifice, Burning, Bruises, Treachery, Violence, etc., in this section).

**Lame**—Case of Lame, Deaf, Dumb, and Blind—See Case, "Arundel", No. 159, in 1001 N.N.

**Left Eye**—Blindness In—(See "Eyes" under Left). Case—See "Blind", Case No. 629, in 1001 N.N.

**Lightning**—Blindness By—Caused by ♂. (See ♂ influences under "Causes" in this section).

**Measles**—Blindness By—The Pleiades when joined with the ☉ or ☽, when rising, or when directed to the Asc.; the ☉ directed to Praesepe, Hyades, Pleiades, Castor, Pollux, and other stars of the nature of ♂ and the ☽ when combined, and espec. if Praesepe be on the Asc., or with the ☉ or ☽ in an angle; ♂ causes; the ☽ ☌ ♂ with the Pleiades, and ♄ with Regulus. (See "Total" in this section. Also see Measles).

**Mental Exertion**—Blindness From—Caused by ☿ entering into the configurations which otherwise cause blindness. Also caused by ♄ and ☿ afflicting the Lights. (See "Eyestrain" under Eyes; Reading, Study).

**Mutes**—Blind and Deaf—(See Mutes. Also see "Deaf and Dumb" in this section).

**Natural Defects**—Blindness By—(See "Defects" in this section).

**Nearly Blind**—The ☽ Sig. ☌ the ☉, and both near the Hyades, Pleiades, or Praesepe. (See Sight).

**Nyctalopia**—(See "Day Blindness" in this section).

**Obstructing Growths**—Blindness By—(See "Growths" in this section; "Growths' under Eyes).

**One Eye**—Blindness In—Loss of One Eye—The ☉ directed to Praesepe, Hyades, Pleiades, Castor, Pollux, and other stars of the nature of the ☽ and ♂ combined, and espec. if Praesepe be on the Asc., or with the ☉ or ☽ in an angle; the ☽ ☌ ♂, and with the Pleiades; the ☽ in an angle, in the Asc. or Desc., ☌ or ☍ the ☉, and connected with a Nebulous Spot, as the Cloudy Spot of ♋, the Pleiades of ♉, the Sting of Scorpio, the Arrowhead of ♐, the Mane of ♌, or the Urn of ♒; the ☽ in the 1st or 7th H., in exact ☌, □, or ☍ the ☉, and affl. by ♅, ♄, or ♂, or with any Nebulous Spots, such as just mentioned; the ☽ affl. in the 22° ♊; ♄ with Regulus. (See Right, Left, in this section. Also see "One Eye" under Eyes).

**One-Half Vision**—(See "Hemianopia" in this section).

**Optic Nerve**—Inhibition of—(See Optic).

**Over-Study**—Blindness From—(See "Eyestrain" under Eyes; the ♀ influences under "Causes", and "Mental Exertion" in this section).

**Partial Blindness**—(See "Amaurosis" in this section).

**Piles**—Blind Piles—(See Hemorrhoids).

**Private Injury**—Blindness By—Caused by ♂ influence in the configuration. (See "Artifice", "Treachery" in this section).

**Reading and Study**—Blindness By—(See the ☿ influences under "Causes", and also "Mental Exertion", in this section. See "Eyestrain" under Eyes).

**Retina**—Blind Spot of—(See "Blind Spot" in this section).

**Right Eye**—Blind In—(See "Eye" under Right).

**Searing**—Blindness By—(See "Burns" in this section).

**Sight**—(See the various paragraphs under Sight).

**Smallpox**—Blindness From—Caused by ♂ in the configuration with the ☉, ☽, and Nebulous Spots; ♂ afflicted in ♈. (See the ♂ influences under "Causes" in this section. Also see Smallpox).

**Specks**—(See Specks. Also see "Defects" in this section).

**Sports**—Blindness from Injury In—(See "Amusements" under Sports; "Amusements" in this section).

**Strokes**—Blindness By—(See "Blows" in this section. Also see "Eyes" under Sword).

**Study**—Blindness from Over-study and Reading—(See "Reading" in this section).

**Sword**—Blindness by Injuries By—(See "Eyes" under Sword. Also see "Blows" in this section).

**Total Blindness**—Blind in Both Eyes—The ☉ in ♒, affl. by ♄, and espec. ☌ or ☍ ♄, tends to stone blindness; the ☉ directed to Praesepe, Hyades, Pleiades, Castor and Pollux, and other stars of the nature of the ☽ and ♂ combined, and espec. if Praesepe be on the Asc., or with the ☉ or ☽ in an angle, which tends to certain blindness; the ☽ combust and conjoined with the Pleiades and ♄, or ♂ with Regulus, sometimes total blindness ensues; the ☽ in the 1st, 4th or 7th H., in decrease, ☌ or ☍ ♅, ♄, ♂, and the malefics be occi., and at the same time ♅, ♄, or ♂ be in ☌ or ☍ the ☉, ori. of the ☉ and ascend before him, and under these circumstances ♄, ♂, (or ☿ the afflicting planet) tend to total blindness by the diseases or afflictions as set forth under "Causes" in this section; the ☽ ☌ ♂ with the Pleiades, and ♄ with Regulus. (See "Causes", and the various paragraphs in this section. Also see Gutta Serena; "Accidents" under Eyes).

**Treachery**—Blindness By—Caused by the combined influences of ♂ and ♀ entering into the configurations which cause blindness. (See the ♂ influences under "Causes" in this section. Also see Treachery).

**Violence**—Injury—Wounds—Blindness By—The ☽ or Asc. in Nebulous parts, and affl. by ♂. (See Accidents, Blows, and other paragraphs in this section).

**White Film**—Blindness By—(See "Cold" in this section).

**Wounds**—Blindness By—(See Accidents, Injury, Violence, in this section).

**BLISTERS**—Blebs—Bulla—A ♂ disease, and caused by ♂ afflictions, as ♂ is vesicant and tends to produce blebs and blisters; the ☽ to the ☌ or ill-asps. ♂ by dir. (See Dysidrosis, Rubefacient, Serum, Vesicles).

**BLIZZARDS**—Much Loss of Life From—☿ in an angle, and afflicted, at a Vernal Equi., or Winter Solstice. (See Cold, Snow, Storms, Weather, Wind).

**BLOATING**—Flatulence—Gas in Stomach or Bowels—(See Flatulence).

**Bloated Face**—(See Face).

**BLONDES**—(See Complexion, Hair).

**BLOOD**—The Blood—The Sanguineous System—The Blood is ruled by ♃, altho his main activities are confined to the arterial blood. The Blood is also under the internal rule of the ♌ Sign. The Arterial Blood is ruled by ♃, and ♀ rules the Venous Blood. The ♒ sign rules strongly over the blood, its condition and circulation. All the Fixed Signs tend to rule and affect the Blood. The Blood is also ruled and strongly influenced by the Watery Signs. The Blood is one of the manifestations of the Vital Body. (See "Vital Body" under Vital). The ☉ gives oxygen to the blood, and ♂ gives the Iron and Haemoglobin. (See Iron, Haemoglobin). In the Astral Body ♃ has direct relation to the Blood. The activity of ♂ in the blood tends to Hemorrhages, Rupture of Blood Vessels, Hemorrhoids, and Excessive Menses. For the Occult significance of the Blood read what is said about the Blood in the books, "Cosmo-Conception", and "Message of the Stars" by the Heindels. This Article will be arranged in Two Sections, General Considerations, and Disorders of the Blood.

**GENERAL CONSIDERATIONS**—

**Arterial Blood**—(See Arteries).

**Blood Letting**—Transfusion—(See Bleeding).

**Blood-Making**—(See Haematopoiesis).

**Bloodshed**—(See "Shedding of Blood" in Sec. 2 of this Article. Also see War).

**Blood Vessels**—(See Arteries, Capillaries, Veins, Vascular, Vessels).

**Carbon Dioxide**—(See Carbon).

**Centrifugal**—Centripetal—(See these subjects).

**Circulation**—Of the Blood—(See Circulation).

**Coloring Matter**—Of the Blood—The red coloring matter of the blood is ruled by ♂ and the ♏ sign. (See "Haemoglobin", "Iron" in this section).

**Composition**—Of the Blood—Under the rule of ♄ and the ♒ sign.

**Condition**—Of the Blood—Is influenced by all the Fixed Signs.

**Corpuscles**—(See Leukocytes; "Blood" under Red).

**Deposits In**—(See Deposits, Minerals).

**Enrichment**—Of the Blood—The Physiological Action of ♃.

**Fibrin**—Of the Blood—Ruled by ♃, ♂, and the ♓ sign. (See Fiber).

**Haematopoiesis**—Haematosis—Blood-making—(See Haematopoiesis).

**Haemoglobin**—(See Haemoglobin).

**Heat**—Of the Blood—Is maintained by the ☉ and ♂, the iron ruled by ♂, and oxygen ruled by the ☉.

**Inward**—Blood is Driven Inward—(See Centripetal).

**Leukocytes**—White Blood Corpuscles—(See Leukocytes).

**Mineral Deposits**—(See Deposits, Minerals).

**New Moon**—Influence on the Blood—(See "New Moon" under Moon).

**Outward**—The Blood Driven Outward—(See Centrifugal).

**Oxygen**—Oxygenation of the Blood—(See Oxygen).

**Portal Blood**—(See Portal).

**Red Blood**—Red Coloring Matter—Red Corpuscles—(See "Coloring" in this section. Also see "Blood" under Red).

**Rubefacients**—(See this subject).

**Serum**—Of the Blood—Ruled by the ♋ Sign. (See Serum).

**Shedding of Blood**—(See Cuts, Duels, Effusions, Hemorrhage, Injuries, Menses, "Epistaxis" under Nose; Shedding; Stabs, War, Wounds, etc.).

**Transfusion**—Of Blood—(See Bleeding).

**Venous Blood**—(See Veins).

**White Blood Corpuscles**—(See Leukocytes).

**DISORDERS OF THE BLOOD**—See the following subjects in the alphabetical arrangement when not considered here—

**Abscess**—From Blood Disorders—(See "Impure Blood" under Impure).

**Abundance of Blood**—In a Part—♂ in the sign ruling the part. (See Fullness, High Blood Pressure, Plethora, Rush of Blood, Too Much Blood, in this section).

**Accumulation**—Of Blood In a Part or Organ—♃ when afflicted tends to, and to Obesity and Tumors. (See Obesity, Serum, Tumors, in this section).

**Alterations**—In the Red Blood Particles—(See "Blood" under Red).

**Anaemia; Aorta**—Spasmodic Gushing of the Blood Thru—(See Aorta).

**Arms**—Blood Disorders and Impurities In—(See "Blood" under Arms, Hands).

**Arterial Blood**—Disorders of—Poor Circulation of—(See Arteries, Circulation).

**Asphyxia; Autointoxication**—(See this subject. See "Blood Poisoning" in this section).

**Bad Blood**—(See "Corrupt" in this section).

**Bleeding; Blood Affections** — (See "Disordered", and the various paragraphs in this section).

**Blood Letting**—(See Bleeding).

**Blood Poisoning**—(See "Blood Poisoning" under Poison).

**Blood Pressure**—(See "Pressure" in this section).

**Blood Vessels**—Disorders of—(See Arteries, Capillaries, Veins, Vessels).

**Bloodshed**—(See "Shedding" in this section; War, etc.).

**Bloodshot Eyes**—(See Eyes).

**Bloody Flux**—(See Flux).

**Boils**—From Impure Blood—(See Boils).

**Bowels**—Hemorrhage From—(See Bowels, Dysentery, Fluxes, Hemorrhage, Typhoid).

**Brain**—Congestion of Blood In—Hemorrhage of—(See Apoplexy, Brain, Congestion).

**Carbon Dioxide**—Surplus of in Blood—(See Carbon).

**Centrifugal**—And Centripetal Action of the Blood—(See these subjects).

**Cerebral Hemorrhage**—(See Cerebral).

**Changes**—In the Blood Particles—(See "Blood" under Red; Corpuscles; Haemoglobin).

**Circulation**—Of the Blood—Disorders of—(See Circulation).

**Clots**—(See Clots, Embolus, Thrombus).

**Coarse Blood**—(See Impure).

**Cold Blood**—(See Cold).

**Colds**—Due to Chilling of the Surface, and Driving the Blood Inwards—(See Centripetal, Chills, Colds, Congestion).

**Congestion of Blood**—(See Congestion).

**Corpuscles**—(See "Blood" under Red; Corpuscles, Leukocytes).

**Corrupt Blood**—(See "Impure Blood" under Impure).

**Cyanosis; Death**—By Foul Blood—(See "Death" under Impure).

**Debility**—Of the Blood—(See Debility).

**Defective Blood**—(See Anaemia, Haemoglobin, Impure, "Blood" under Red; Leukocytes, Pale, Poor. Also see "Thin Blood" in this section).

**Deficient**—(See "Thin" in this section).

**Deposits**—In the Blood—(See Deposits, Minerals).

**Depraved Blood**—(See Impure).

**Determination**—Of Blood—Rush of—(See "Blood" under Head. Also see Aorta).

**Diluted Blood**—(See "Thin" in this section).

**Discharges of Blood**—(See Cuts, Discharges, Dysentery, Effusions, Epistaxis, Fluxes, Hemorrhage, Injuries, Menses, Stabs, Sword, Typhoid, War, Watery, Wounds, etc. Also see "Shedding" in this section).

**Disordered Blood**—Disorders of—Disturbances of—Caused principally by ♃, and afflictions to ♃, and also afflictions in the ♒ sign; ♃ □ or ☍ the Asc., excess of blood, and ailments from; ♃ in signs which rule the arms, hands, legs and feet, or any part of the body, tends to blood disorders and corrupt blood in these parts; the ☉ in airy signs, and espec. in ♒; the ☽ in airy signs tends to regular and normal secretions, but subject to blood disorders, anaemia, skin and kidney troubles. (See the various paragraphs in this section).

**Disturbances Of**—Ruled by ♒ and are principally ♒ diseases. (See "Disordered", and other paragraphs in this section).

**Driven Inward**—Or Outward—(See Centrifugal, Centripetal).

**Dropsical Blood**—(See Dropsy).

**Ears**—Effusion of Blood From—(See Ears).

**Effusion of Blood**—(See Effusions).

**Embolism**—(See Embolism, Thrombus).

**Epistaxis**—Nose Bleed—(See Nose).

**Eruptions**—From Bad Blood—(See Eruptions).

**Evacuations; Excess of Blood**—Disorders From—♃ □ or ☍ the Asc. (See Plethora, Pressure, Too Much Blood, in this section).

**Excesses**—Blood Disorders From—(See Excesses).

**Excessive Discharges**—Of Blood—(See Effusions, "Flooding" under Menses; Fluxes, Hemorrhage. Also see "Shedding" in this section).

**Expectoration**—Of Blood—(See Haemoptysis).

**Eyes**—Bloodshot Eyes—(See Eyes).

**Feet**—Blood In—(See "Disordered" in this section).

**Feverish Blood**—Hot Blood—Over-Heated Blood—(See "Over-Heated" in this section).

**Fevers**—From Too Much Blood—A disease of ♃. (See Plethora. Also see "Too Much" in this section).

**Flooding**—(See Menses).

**Flow of Blood**—Determination of—Rush of—etc.—(See Aorta, "Blood" under Head; Effusions, "Flooding" under Menses; Fluxes, Hemorrhage, etc. Also see Injuries, Loss of, Shedding, in this section).

**Fluids; Fluxes**—Bloody Discharges In—(See Dysentery, Evacuations, Fluxes).

**Foul Blood**—Death By—(See "Death" under Impure).

**Fullness of Blood**—(See Plethora, Pressure, Too Much Blood, in this section).

**General Debility Of**—(See "Blood" under Debility).

**Good Order**—(See "Pure" in this section).

**Gout**—From Too Much Uric Acid in the Blood—(See Gout, Uric Acid).

**Gross Blood**—(See Gross, Impure, Plethora. Also see "Too Much", "Rich", in this section).

**Gushing**—Of Blood—(See Aorta, "Blood" under Head; Effusions, "Flooding" under Menses; Hemorrhage, etc.).

**Haematemesis**—(See "Blood" under Vomiting).

**Haematoma**—Blood Tumor—(See Haematoma).

**Haematopoiesis**—Blood-Making—Disorders of—(See Haematopoiesis).

**Haemoglobin**—Disorders of—(See Haemoglobin, "Blood" under Red).

**Haemophilia**—Abnormal Tendency to Hemorrhage—(See Hemorrhage).

**Haemoptysis; Hands**—(See "Disordered" in this section).

**Head**—Rush of Blood To—(See "Blood" under Head).

**Heated Blood**—Feverish Blood—(See "Over-Heated" in this section).

**Heavy Blood**—(See Impure).

**Hemorrhage; Hemorrhoids; High Pressure**—(See "Pressure" in this section).

**Hot Blood**—(See "Over-Heated" in this section).

**Humours**—With Bloody Discharges—(See Humours, "Watery Humours" under Watery).

**Hydraemia**—(See "Thin Blood" in this section).

**Ill-Blood**—(See Impure).

**Impoverished Blood**—(See Anaemia; "Thin Blood" in this section; Emaciation, Malnutrition, Pale, Wasting).

**Impure Blood**—Impurities in the Blood—Diseases Arising From—(See Deposits, Impure, Minerals, Sores, Syphilis, Ulcers, etc.).

**Indifferent Blood**—(See "Poor" in this section).

**Indulgence**—Blood Disorders From—(See Gluttony, Impure, Indulgence, Syphilis, Venery, etc.).

**Infiltration**—Of Serum—(See Serum).

**Inflamed Blood**—The ☉ affl. in ♊, ♎, or ♒ when the ☉ is the afflictor in the disease; the Asc. to the ☌ or ill-asp. ♂ by dir., and ♂ in an airy sign. (See Inflammation).

**Injuries**—With Flow of Blood—Caused by ♂, but ♄ causes injuries where blood does not flow, as bruises. (See Injuries).

**Insanity**—From Rush of Blood to the Head—(See Insanity).

**Insufficient Oxygenation**—(See Oxygen).

**Inward**—Blood Driven Inward—(See Centripetal).

**Iron**—In the Blood—(See Haemoglobin, Iron; "Blood" under Red).

**Kidneys**—Hemorrhage of—(See "Hemorrhage" under Kidneys).

**Legs**—Blood In—(See "Disordered" in this section).

**Letting of Blood**—Transfusion—(See Bleeding).

**Leukemia**—(See Leukocytes).

**Loss of Blood**—Bloodshed—Hemorrhage—(See Accidents, Cuts, Effusions, Hemorrhage, Injuries, Menses, "Nose Bleed" under Nose; "Shedding" in this section; Stabs, Sword, War).

**Low Pressure**—(See "Pressure" in this section).

**Melancholic Blood**—(See "Blood" under Melancholy).

**Menses; Mineral Deposits**—In the Blood—(See Deposits, Gout, Minerals, Rheumatism, Saturn, Uric Acid, Wastes, etc.).

**Morbid Blood**—Morbid Changes In—The ♒ sign has much influence over morbid changes in the blood, as incomplete oxygenation, blood poisoning, impure blood, etc. (See Haemoglobin, Impure, Morbid, Oxygen, Pale, Poison; "Blood" under Red; "Sickly Looking" under Sickly; Wasting Diseases, etc.).

**Much Blood**—(See "Abundance", "Too Much" in this section. Also see Impure).

**Non-Oxygenation**—(See Oxygen).

**Nose Bleed**—(See Nose).

**Obesity; Obstructions**—Of the Blood—And From Too Much Blood—(See Clots, Thrombus; "Too Much" in this section).

**Outward**—Blood Driven Outward—(See Centrifugal).

**Over-Heated Blood**—Feverish—Hot—The heat of the blood is maintained by ♂. The ☉ affl. in ♎, and often causing skin eruptions; the ☉ in ♒ ☌ or ill-asp. any of the malefics as promittors; the ☉ ☌ ♂ in ♈, and ♈ on the Asc., the blood may be like a hot, fiery liquid; the ☉ in ♊ or ♎, ☌ or ill-asp. any of the malefics as promittors; the ☉ directed to Cor Scorpio; the ☽ in ♌ or ♎ and affl. by the ☉ or ♂ when taken ill; afflictions in ♐; ♃ affl. in ♌; ♂ in ♌ or ♒ when ♂ is the afflictor in the disease. (See Eruptions, Exercise, Heat).

**Oxygen**—Lack of In Blood—(See Oxygen).

**Part**—Abundance of Blood in a Part—(See "Abundance" in this section).

**Particles**—Changes in the Blood Particles—(See Corpuscles, "Blood" under Red).

**Pernicious Anaemia**—(See Anaemia).

**Plethora**—Fullness of Blood—(See Plethora; "Too Much" in this section).

**Poisoning**—Blood Poisoning—Toxic Blood—Impure Blood—(See Autointoxication, Impure, Poison, Septic, Toxaemia).

**Polluted Blood**—(See "Stagnant" in this section).

**Poor Blood**—Indifferent Blood—Defective Blood—Poor State of the Blood—Watery and Thin—The ☉ in ill-asp. to ♃ at B., or by dir.; the ☉ or ☽ in ♋ or ♓, and in ☌ or ill-asp. any of the malefics as promittors; the ☽ hyleg in ♌ or ♒, and afflicted, and espec. with females; ♆, ♅, or ♄ in ♋, and affl. the ☉ or ☽; ♃ affl. in ♓, poor condition of the blood; ♀ in ♒ and affl. the ☉ or ☽; ♀ in ♒ in the 6th H. (See Anaemia, Impure, Pale, Poison, Septic, Toxic, etc. See "Thin" in this section).

**Pressure**—High Blood Pressure is denoted by ♃ and ♂. The bad asps. of ♃ tend to; ♄ ☌ ♃ or ♀; ♄ in ♌ ☌ ♃; ♄ ☌ ♃ in 6th H. (See "High Pulse" under Pulse; "Too Much" in this section). Low Blood Pressure is caused by ♄ affl. ♃ at B., and by dir. (See "Slow Pulse" under Pulse). ♃ causes complaints due to blood pressure.

**Pure**—The Blood should be kept pure, and in good order, when ♂ is affl. in ♎, and when ♀ is afflicted in ♊, or when ♃ at B., is in ♐, ♑, or ♓, and afflicted, or ♃ affl. the ☉, ☽, Asc. or hyleg from these signs. (See "Remedies" in this section).

**Purpura**—Hemorrhages into the Cutis—(See Purpura).

**Putrefaction**—In the Blood—A disease of ♃; ♃ affl. in ♐; a ♓ disease, and afflictions in ♓. (See Impure, Putrefaction).

**Red Blood**—(See "Coloring" in Sec. 1 of this Article. Also see Arteries, Circulation, Haemoglobin, Iron, "Blood" under Red).

**Remedies**—For Blood Disorders—Purple, the color ruled by ♃ in the Solar Spectrum, and purple rays, are valuable in the treatment of blood and liver disorders. The therapeutic properties of the ☉, ☽, ♅, ♂ and ☿ are classed as being favorable to the relief of blood disorders. (See Alteratives).

**Renal Hemorrhage**—(See "Hemorrhage" under Kidneys).

**Rich Blood**—Too Rich—Gross Blood—♂ □ or ☍ ♃. (See Impure, Too Much, in this section).

**Rubefacients; Rupture**—Of Blood Vessels—(See Apoplexy, Hemorrhage, "Rupture" under Vessels).

**Rush of Blood**—To the Head, or a Part—A ♂ influence. (See "Blood" under Head; "Abundance" in this section).

**Scrofulous Blood**—(See Scrofula).

**Scurvy**—(See Purpura, Scurvy).

**Septicaemia**—(See Septic. Also see "Poisoning" in this section).

**Serum**—Of the Blood—Disorders of—(See Serum).

**Shedding**—Of Blood—A ♂ influence and affliction, as in Accidents, Cuts, Injuries, War, etc. (See Accidents, Cuts, Effusions, Hemorrhage, Menses, Murder, Shedding, Stabs, Sword, War, Wounds, etc.).

**Skin**—Skin Disorders Thru Blood Affections—(See Centrifugal, Eczema, Eruptions, Impure, Purpura, Scrofula, Scurvy, Skin, Syphilis, etc.).

**Sluggish Blood**—(See "Poor", "Sluggish", under Circulation).

**Spitting of Blood**—(See Haemoptysis).

**Stabs**—Loss of Blood From—(See Stabs).

**Stagnant Blood**—Polluted Blood—♄ ☌ ♃ or ♀, the rulers of the circulation; ♃ ☌ ♄, and also affl. by the ☽ and ♀. (See Impure. Also see "Sluggish" under Circulation).

**Sugar**—In the Blood—(See Sugar).

**Surface**—Blood Driven to the Surface—(See Caustic, Centrifugal, Eruptions, Rubefacients).

**Surfeits**—(See "Blood" under Surfeits. Also see "Too Much" in this section).

**Sweat**—Bloody Sweat—(See Sweat).

**Syphilis**—Syphilitic Blood—(See Syphilis).

**Thin Blood**—Hydraemia—Impoverished—Watery—Caused by the predominance of the watery signs at B., and espec. ♋ and ♓, and with these signs on the Asc. (See "Poor" in this section. Also see Anaemia, Dropsy, Emaciated, Pale, Sickly, Vitality Low, Wasting, etc.).

**Thrombus**—Blood Clot—(See Thrombus).

**Too Much Blood**—Gross Blood—Vascular Fullness—High Blood Pressure—The ☽ to the ill-asps. ♃ by dir., the blood is gross and corrupted; the ☽ in ♉ or ♌, and affl. by the ☉ or ♂ when taken ill; the ☽ or ♃ in ♎, affl. by the ☉ or ♂ when taken ill, the patient is grieved with a plenitude of blood, and feverish disorders from too much blood; a ♃ disease when ♃ is afflicted at B., and due to excesses in eating; ♃ affl. in ♎ tends to inflammatory diseases, Piles, etc., from too much blood; ♃ affl. in ♒ tends to flying pains, fevers, many diseases and complications from too much blood; the Asc. to any asp. of ♃ by dir., and with danger of pleurisy; all conditions of vascular fullness are considered ♃ diseases. (See Arteries; "Sluggish" under Circulation; Eruptions; "Blood" under Fevers; Impure, Plethora; "High Pulse" under Pulse; Surfeits, Upper, etc. Also see "Pressure" in this section).

**Toxic Blood**—(See Impure, Poison, Septic, Toxic, Urea, Uric Acid. Also see "Poisoning" in this section).

**Treatment**—Of Blood Disorders—(See "Remedies" in this section).

**Tumors**—Blood Tumors—(See Haematoma).

**Ulcers**—From Bad Blood—(See "Blood" under Ulcers).

**Upper Parts**—(See "Blood" under Upper).

**Uremia; Uric Acid; Urine**—Blood In—(See Urine).

**Veins**—Venous Blood—(See Veins).

**Vessels**—Blood Vessels—(See Vessels).

**Vomiting**—Of Blood—(See Vomiting).

**Watery Blood**—(See "Poor", "Thin" in this section).

**Watery Humours**—With Bloody Discharges—(See Discharges, Dysentery, Fluxes, Humours, Watery).

**Weakest Part**—Blood the Weakest Part—The ☉ affl. in ♐; ☽ hyleg, and affl. in a female nativity.

**White**—White Blood Corpuscles—(See Leukocytes).

**Wind in Blood**—(See Wind).

**Women**—(See "Blood" under Women).

**BLOTCHES**—Blemishes—The ☽ in ♏, and affl. by the ☉ or ♂ when taken ill, due to corrupt blood; the ☽ to the Bull's Horns by dir.; afflictions in ♓; a ♓ disease. (See Acne, Blemishes, Blisters, Eruptions, Pimples, Pustules).

**BLOWS**—Strokes—Concussions—The Hurtful Signs, ♈, ♉, ♎, ♏, or ♑ on the Asc. at B. make the native more liable to Blows, Falls, Wounds, and other Injuries.

**Accidents**—By Blows—(See "Danger" in this section).

**Assaults By**—Battery—(See Assaults).

**Blindness**—By Blows—(See "Accidents", "Injury" under Eyes; "Eyes" under Sword).

**Bruises**—By Blows—(See Assaults, Bruises, Falls).

**Concussions**—(See Concussions).

**Cuts**—From Blows—Caused by ♂. (See Assaults, Cuts, Duels, Hemorrhage, Stabs, Sword, etc.).

**Danger of Blows**—Liable to—Subject to—Accidents or Injuries by Blows—The ☉ or ☽ to the ☌ or ill-asp. ♂ by dir.; ♄ in ♈, ♌, or ♐ in ☌ or ill-asp. the Asc. by dir.; caused by ♄ or ♂, by ♄ ascending, rising or setting at B., and affl. the ☉, ☽, Asc. or hyleg; ♄ in a fiery or airy sign, and to the ill-asps. the Asc. by dir.; the ill-asps. of ♄ or ♂ by dir. to the ☉, ☽, Asc. or M.C.; afflictions in fiery signs dispose to; the Asc. to the ☌ or ill-asps. ♄ or ♂ by dir.; the Whale's Belly joined to the ☉ or ☽. (See Assaults, Bruises, Cuts, Stabs, Sword, etc).

**Death by Blows**—Danger of—Liable to—The ☉ joined with Castor, Pollux, Pleiades, Hyades, Praesepe, or the Ascelli; the ☉ Sig. □ or ☍ ♄, and espec. if either be in the 10th H.; the ☽ with Antares, and ☍ ♄ and Aldebaran, and espec. if in angles; the ☽ Sig. ☌, □, or ☍ ♂; the ☽ directed to Capella, danger of death by blows or stabs; ♄ affl. the hyleg by dir., and holding the dominion of death, and espec. if ♄ be in the 8th H., and afflicted, which influences tend to sudden death by blows; ♄ or ♂ in the M.C., and in □ the Asc., and the ☉ afflicted; ♃ Sig. □ or ☍ ♂; ♂ with Aldebaran, death by blows, falls, stabs, and espec. if in angles, and affl. the ☽; ♂ Sig. □ or ☍ ♄ if either be in the Asc., or ♄ in the M.C.; those born under the hurtful signs, ♈, ♉, ♎, ♏, or ♑, are more liable to. (See Assaults, Cuts, Duels, Murdered, Stabs, Sword).

**Distortions**—By Blows—(See Distortions).

**Duels**—(See Duels, Sword).

**Eyes**—Blows or Strokes to—(See "Accidents", "Hurts", "Injuries" under Eyes).

**Face**—Blows to—(See "Cuts", "Hurts" under Face).

**Falls**—Blows By—(See the various paragraphs under Falls. Also see "Death" in this section).

**Head**—Blows to—(See Head).

**Hurtful Signs**—(See the Introduction to this section).

**Hurts**—Injuries by Blows—(See the various paragraphs in this section).

**Lameness**—From Blows—(See "Blows" under Lameness. Also see Distortions).

**Paralysis**—From Blows—(See Distortions).

**Severe Blows**—(See "Death", Violent" in this section. Also see the Case Record on Page 97, Chap. 13, in Daath's Medical Astrology).

**Skull**—Blows to—(See "Blows" under Head; "Fractures" under Skull).

**Stabs**—(See Cuts, Duels, Stabs, Sword).

**Subject to Blows**—(See "Danger" in this section).

**Sword**—Blows By—(See Sword).

**Violent Blows**—Violent Death by—(See "Death" in this section. Also see "Death" under Violent).

**Wounds**—By Blows—(See the various paragraphs in this section.

**BLUE**—The color ruled by ♀ in the Solar Spectrum. In the Secret Doctrine by H.P.B., Blue is the color assigned to ♃. Blue has a soothing, uplifting, comforting, restful and religious influence over people, and is a good color where brain workers are busy. Blue flowers tend to allay fevers. It has a soothing effect upon melancholic people, Neurasthenics, the Insane, Maniacs, and is also a good color for weak eyes, as to wear blue glasses for a time. (See "Treatment" under Eyes, Insanity, Melancholy, Nerves. Also see Colors).

**Blue Eyes**—(See "Blue" under Eyes).

**Blue Flag**—(See Iridin).

**Blue Marks**—On the Body—(See Marks).

**BLUES**—(See Depression, Despondency, Hypochondria, Melancholy, Vapors, Worry, etc.).

**BLUSHING**—Ruled by the ☽ and ♄. (See Backwardness, Bashful, Flushings, Shame).

**BODY**—Bodily—Frame—Form—Figure Constitution—Physique—Stature, etc.—For the Organs, Parts, and functions of the body, and the various diseases and afflictions, see the subject in the alphabetical arrangement. Only the more abstract subjects, by way of suggestion for study and reference, will be listed in this section. Many subjects concerning the form, shape and appearance of the body are listed under Appearance, Complexion, Face, Form, Height, Shape, Stature, Weight, etc. The physical body is signified by the Asc., the 1st H., and its form, shape, etc., are largely determined by the 1st H., the degree, sign and decanate rising, by planets rising, setting, above or below the horizon, the aspects formed between the planets, the dignity or debility of planets at B., etc. (See Decanates, Physical). The directions, progressed positions of the planets and the Asc., the Transits, Lunations, Eclipses, Solar Revolutions, etc., have much to do with the condition of the body during life, its diseases, its periods of good and bad health, its debilities and weaknesses, etc., and the possible time of death, but subject to modification, according to the degree of knowledge and spiritual advancement of the native. See the following subjects in the alphabetical arrangement when not considered here—

**Able Body**—(See "Strong Body" under Strong).

**Action; Active Body**—(See Active).

**Afflicted**—(1) The Body Alone is Afflicted—When a malefic afflicting the lord of the Asc., or the ☽, and the part afflicted is that ruled by the sign of which the afflicting planet is lord. (2) The Affliction, or Disease, is More in the Body Than in the Mind—Lord of the Asc., and lord of the sign or house containing the ☽, be combust and afflicting the degree ascending, and the degree containing the ☽ be more afflicted than the lords of those signs. (See "Irritations" under Mind). (3) Afflicted in Both Body and Mind—(See "Afflicted in Mind and Body" under Mental). (4) The Affliction, or Disease, is Thru the Whole Body—(See "Disease" under Whole).

**Agile Body**—(See Agile).

**Anatomical; Angular Body**—☿ in ♈; ♈ on the Asc.; the ♈ influence generally gives. (See Lank, Lean, "Raw-Boned" under Bones).

**Animal Propensities**—(See Animal).

**Appearance; Ascendant; Astral Body**—(See Astral).

**Athletic Body**—(See Athletics).

**Awkwardness; Badly Made**—(See Azimene, Crooked, Deformities, "Ill-formed" under Ill; Malformations, Ugly).

**Barren; Beautiful Body**—(See Beautiful).

**Birth; Blemishes; Body Alone Is Afflicted**—(See "Afflicted" in this section).

**Brisk**—In Movement—(See Action, Active, Brisk, Motion, Movement, Quick, etc.).

**Build; Bulky Body**—(See Bulky, Corpulent, Fat, Large, Obesity, etc.).

**Careful**—Of the Body—(See Careful).

**Carriage**—(See Gait, Motion, Movement, Posture, Walk).

**Cavities**—(See Cavities, Receptacles, Viscera).

**Changes In**—(See "Body" under Changes).

**Cleanly; Cleansing; Clogging; Coarse; Cold Body**—(See "Body" under Cold).

**Color Of**—(See Color, Complexion, Face, Hair, Race, "Color" under Skin).

**Comely; Commanding; Commonplace; Compact; Complete; Complexion; Composition Of**—(See the various subjects in this section).

**Condition**—Of the Body—(See Healthy, Sickly, Strong, Vitality, Weak, etc.).

**Confinements**—Of the Body—(See Hospitals, Imprisonment, Insanity, Invalids, Sickness, Twelfth House, etc.).

**Conformity**—Of Members—(See Well-Proportioned).

**Congenital; Conservation**—Of the Bodily and Mental Forces—(See Conservation).

**Constitution; Construction**—Of the Body—Ruled over by the Asc.

**Constructive Forces Of**—(See Constructive).

**Contracted Body**—(See Diminished, Dwarf, Short, Small).

**Control Of**—(See Control).

**Coordination In**—(See Coordination).

**Corpulent; Countenance; Coverings; Cravings; Crippled; Crooked; Dark; Death; Debility; Defects; Defensive Forces Of**—(See Defensive).

**Deficiencies In**—(See Deficient).

**Deformities; Degeneration Of**—(See Degeneration).

**Delicate; Depletions; Description; Desire Body; Destructive Processes**—(See Destructive).

**Deterioration Of**—(See Deterioration).

**Development Of**—(See Development).

**Devoured**—After Death—(See "Birds" under Air).

**Diathesis In**—(See Diathesis).

**Diminished**—(See "Contracted" in this section).

**Directions**—The Effect of Primary Directions Over the Body—(See Directions).

**Dirty Body**—(See Filth, Unclean).

**Disabilities; Disasters To**—(See Disaster).

**Disease; Disfigurements; Displacements; Disproportioned; Distentions; Distortions; Divisions**—Of the Body—(See Divisions).

**Dress; Drooping; Dry Body**—(See Dry).

**Dwarfed; Dying Persons**—(See Dying).

**Eating; Elegant; Elemental Qualities Of**—(See Elemental).

**Endurance; Energy; Enlarged; Entire Body**—(See Whole).

**Environment; Equilibrium; Escapes; Events; Evolution Of**—(See Evolution).

**Excitation; Exercise Of**—(See Exercise, Sports).

**Expansions In**—(See Expansion).

**Exposures; External Influences**—(See External).

**Fading; Fair; Fasting; Fears**—Bodily Fears—(See Fears).

**Feasting; Features; Feeble; Female; Filthy; Fine; First House; Flabby; Fleshy; Fluids; Foetus; Food; Forces Of**—(See Forces).

**Form; Frail; Frame; Freaks**—Of Nature—(See Freaks, Monsters).

**Fruitful; Fuel**—Of the Body—(See Fuel).

**Full-Bodied**—(See Full).

**Functions; Fundament; Gait; Genteel; Gestation; Giants; Gluttony; Good Build**—(See Good).

**Graceful; Gratifications Of**—(See Appetites, Cravings, Gratification, Passion, Sex).

**Great Body**—(See Giants).

**Growth; Habits; Hairy Body**—(See Hair).

**Handsome; Hardening; Harmony In**—(See Harmony).

**Health Of**—(See Health).

**Heat Of**—(See Heat).

**Heavy; Height; Helplessness; Heredity; Hermaphrodites; High Body**—High Forehead—High Nose—(See High, Forehead, Nose, Tall, Giants).

**Hooked Forward**—(See Bending, Stooping).

**Hot Body**—(See Heat).

**Humpback; Hurts; Ill-formed; Ill-health; Impairments; Imperfections; Imprisonment; Inactive; Incomplete; Incomposed; Incurvating; Indifferent; Inefficiency; Inferior; Infirm; Inflated; Inhuman; Injuries; Insufficiencies; Inward Parts; Juvenility; Lank; Large; Lean; Left Side**—(See Left).

**Lengthening; Life**—Of the Body—(See Life).

**Light; Limitations; Limp; Little; Local Parts**—(See Local).

**Locomotion; Long; Look; Loss Of**—(See Loss).

**Lovely; Low Stature**—(See Dwarf, Low, Short, Small).

**Lower Parts**—(See Lower).

**Lubrication; Luminous; Lumpish; Magnetic; Males; Malnutrition; Marks; Meagre; Mean Stature**—(See Mean).

**Medium Stature**—(See Medium).

**Members; Membranes; Metabolism; Mind and Body**—(See Mind).

**Misshaped; Moderate Stature**—(See Moderate).

**Moist Body**—(See Moist).

**Moles; Monsters; Motion; Movement; Moving Parts; Muddling Creature**—(See Ill-formed).

**Mulatto; Narrow; Natural; Neat; Negro; Nimble; Normal; Nutrition; Odors; Oils; Operations; Organic; Organs; Orifices; Parts of the Body**—(See Parts).

**Perfect; Physical; Pleasing; Plump; Portly; Posture; Powerful; Preservation; Processes; Prominent; Propensities; Proper Stature**—(See Proper).

**Protruding; Puffing; Pure; Quality; Quick; Quiet; Quivering; Race; Raw-Boned; Receptacles; Recuperative Powers; Refined; Relaxed; Remote Organs**—(See Remote).

**Reproduction; Reserve Forces**—(See Reserve).

**Resisting Powers**—(See Resistance).

**Restraints Over**—(See Restraint).

**Rhythm; Right Side**—Of the Body—(See Right).

**Rigid; Robust; Rose-Colored**—(See Rosy).

**Rough; Round; Ruddy; Rugged; Sallow; Sanguine; Scaly; Scars; Second Death Of**—(See Twelfth House).

**Sensations; Senses; Sensitive; Servitude; Sex; Shaggy; Shaking; Shallow; Shape; Sharp; Shiny; Shrunken**—(See Shrinkage).

**Sickly; Sickness; Sinking**—Of Parts—(See Sinking).

**Size; Skeleton; Skippish**—In Manner—(See "Nodding" under Head).

**Sleep; Slow; Sluggish; Small; Smooth; Soft; Spare; Speech; Spotted**—(See "Skin Spots" under Spots).

**Squatty; Staggering; Stamina; Stature; Stiff; Stinking; Stooping; Stout; Straight; Strength; Strong; Structural; Strutting; Stupor**—(See Dull, Sleep).

**Sturdy; Suffering; Sunken; Superabundance; Supersensitive; Susceptibilities; Swarthy; Swollen; Symmetry; System; Tall; Temper; Temperament; Temperature; Tendencies; Tender; Tension; Texture; Thick; Thin; Thirst; Tissues; Tone; Torpid; Tough; Treatment; Troubled**—In Mind and Body—(See Mind, Trouble).

**Ugly; Uncleanly; Uncontrolled; Undersized; Undeveloped; Unfruitful; Ungainly; Unhealthy; Unnatural; Unprolific; Unrefined; Unsound; Untidy; Upper Parts**—(See Upper).

**Upright; Vigor; Virile Members**—(See Virile).

**Vital; Vitality; Vitiated; Vulnerable Spots**—(See Vulnerable).

**Waddling; Walk; Wan; Wants; Warm; Wastes; Weak; Wear and Tear**—(See Wear).

**Weariness; Weight; Well-Composed; Well-Favored; Well-Proportioned.**

**Well-Descended**—(See Heredity).

**White; Whole Body**—(See Whole).

**Wide; Wild; Withered; Wretched; Yellow; Youthful; Zones.**

**BOILS**—Risings—A ♓ disease; afflictions in ♓, and due to corrupt blood; ♃ diseases; ♂ in evil asp. the ☉, ☽, Asc., or hyleg; ♂ afflicting ♃; ♂ □ or ☍ ☉; ♂ prog. to the ☌ or ill-asp. ♃, and arising from corrupt blood, evil habits and vices; ♂ affl. in ♐, and espec. in the 6th H.; ♂ in ♐, and affl. the ☽ or Asc.; ♂ affl. in ♊ or ♍, and ☌ or evil asp. the Asc. by dir.; the ☽ affl. in ♑, ♒, or ♓, the Winter Signs; the ☽ in ♒ ☌ or evil asp. ♄ (or to ☿ if he be of the nature of ♄) at decumbiture, or the beginning of the illness; the Asc. □ or ☍ ♂ by dir. if in a fiery sign. Case—See "Cardan", No. 553, in 1001 N.N. (See Abscesses, Carbuncles, "Impure Blood" under Impure; Infections, Pus, Sores, Swellings, Ulcers).

**Buttocks**—Boils On—Afflictions in ♏ or ♐; subs at LPP, the 4th and 5th Lumbars, and at KP. (See Haunches, Vertebrae).

**Face**—Boils On—Afflictions in ♈ or ♉, and espec. ♃ affl. in these signs, due to corrupt blood, excessive eating, bad habits, etc.; Subs at MCP, the 4th Cervical, and at KP. (See Face, Vertebrae).

**Gumboils**—Afflictions in ♈. (See Gums).

**Neck**—Boils On—On Upper Neck, Afflictions in ♈ or ♉, and with Subs at MCP, the 3rd Cervical, and at KP; on the middle part of neck, afflictions in the latter degrees of ♈, and in ♉, and with Subs at MCP, the 4th Cervical, and at KP; ♃ afflicted in ♉.

**BOLD**—A ♂ characteristic; ♂ rising in the Asc. (See "Bold" under Look).

**BONES**—The Framework—The Osseous System—The Skeleton—The Bones, in any and all parts of the body, are ruled by ♄, and also influenced by the ♄ sign ♑. The ☉ or ☽ acting thru the ♑ sign tend to especially affect the Osseous System. The processes of hardening, crystallization, ossification, bone-building, and the deposits of the mineral substances in the bones, are carried on by ♄. An afflicted ♄, or ♄ weak at B., will tend to interfere with the normal workings of these processes, and lead to diseases of the bones and marrow. The influence of ♄ is limitation, confinement, restraint, and the bones under his rulership define the limits of the body. The Osseous structure is also connected with the Earthy Signs. The Articulations, or Joints, are also under the rule of ♄. The bones of the different parts, or zones of the body, are ruled by the Signs which rule those parts, and according to the divisions of the Grand Man. (See Osseous). The principal subjects to be considered in connection with the bones are the size, texture, diseases, dislocations, fractures, and the bones in health, etc. This Article will be arranged in two Sections. (1) General Considerations. (2) Diseases of the Bones.

**GENERAL CONSIDERATIONS—**

**Articulation**—(See Joints).

**Bone Building**—Ruled and denoted by ♄. A ♄ process.

**Bony, Large and Strong**—Given by the ☉.

**Bony, Lean and Muscular**—Born under ♂, and given by ♂.

**Bony and Muscular**—♄ in his nodes, very bony and muscular.

**Bony Body**—The ☉ gives a large, strong, and bony body; ♄ in N. Lat. (See Large, Long, Raw-boned, in this section).

**Brittle Bones**—♄ weak and affl. at B., ♄ in ♌ in many cases.

**Crystallization**—(See this subject).

**Deposits**—Mineral Deposits in the Bones—(See Deposits, Minerals).

**Great Bones**—(See "Large" in this section. Also see Giants).

**Healthy Bones**—♄ well-aspected at B., and not affl. the ☉, ☽, Asc., or hyleg; ♈ gives healthy, lusty, and robust bones.

**Joints**—(See Joints).

**Large Bones**—Given by the ☉, and the ☉ sign ♌; the ⚹ and △ asps. to the ☉ tend to; ☽ ♌ in partile asp. the Asc., tall, large-boned, and strong; ♄ in ♈ or ♌ in partile asp. the Asc.; ♂ in ♈ partile asp. the Asc.; ☿ in ♐ in partile asp. the Asc., well-shaped, but spare and large bones. (See "Bones" under Large).

**Long Bones**—Given espec. by ♊ or ♐ on the Asc.

**Lusty and Robust**—(See "Healthy" in this section).

**Marrow**—♃ and ♀, rulers of the circulation, rule strongly over the marrow, its nourishment and circulation, deposits of fat, etc., and espec. ♃. (See "Marrow" in Sec. 2 of this Article).

**Minerals Of**—Ruled and supplied by ♄. (See Crystallization, Deposits, Hardening, Lime, Minerals).

**Ossification**—The Formation of Bone—Ruled and denoted by ♄. (See "Ossification" in Sec. 2 of this Article).

**Raw-Boned**—Spare Body—Thin—♄ in ♑, in partile asp. the Asc.; ♄ in N. Lat. makes the body more bony; ♄ rising at B.; ♄ Sig. in ♈, ♍, or ♑. ♑ on the Asc. (See Lean, Thin).

**Robust Bones**—(See "Healthy" in this section).

**Skeleton**—(See this subject).

**Small Bones**—(See Diminished, Dwarf, "Short" under Arms, Legs, Limbs; "Small Body" under Small).

**Spine**—(See Spine, Vertebrae).

**Strengthening Of**—♄ in good asp. the Asc., the bodily frame is strengthened.

**Synovial Membranes**—And Fluids—(See Synovial).

**Teeth**—(See Teeth).

**Vertebrae**—(See Vertebrae).

**DISEASES OF THE BONES—**

**Affected**—The Bones are affected—♄ weak and affl. at B. (See "Diseases", "Disorders", and the various paragraphs in this section).

**All Diseases Of**—Caused by ♄ and ♄ afflictions; ♄ weak and affl. at B., and by dir.

**Ankles**—Broken—(See Ankles).

**Ankylosis**—(See this subject).

**Arms**—Broken Arms—(See Arms, Humerus, Radius, Ulna).

**Bow Legs**—(See Legs).

**Break-bone Fever**—(See Dengue).

**Broken Bones**—(See Fractures).

**Caries**—(See Caries).

**Cell Growth**—Increased Cell Growth—(See Rickets).

**Clavicle**—Collar Bone—Fracture of—(See Clavicle).

**Cloaca; Club Feet**—(See Feet).

**Cranial Bones**—(See Skull).

**Death**—From Broken Bones—(See "Death" under Falls, Fractures).

**Deficiency**—Of Mineral Deposits—♄ weak, afflicted, and ill-dignified at B. (See Minerals, Rickets).

**Dengue**—Break-bone Fever—(See Dengue).

**Deposits**—Osseous Deposits—(See Calculi, Crystallization, Deposits, Gravel, Hardening, Minerals, "Influence of ♄" under Saturn; Sand, Stone).

**Dislocations**—Luxations—(See Dislocations).

**Disorders Of**—♄ weak, afflicted, and ill-dignified at B.; ♄ affl. the ☉, ☽, Asc., or hyleg; the afflictions of ♄ are at the bottom of all diseases of the bones, and also of the teeth, which latter are ruled by ♄. (See the various paragraphs in this section).

**Enlargements Of**—(See Ankylosis, Deposits, Enlargements, Minerals, Rickets, etc. Also see "Exostosis", "Inflammation" in this section).

**Exostosis**—An abnormal outgrowth of bone—Exostosis in Arms—(See "Bones" under Arms).

**Femur**—Broken Femur—(See Femur).

**Fractures**—Accidents or Injuries to the Bones—Broken Bones—(See Fractures. For the fractures of the various bones of the body, see the bone, or part, in the alphabetical arrangement).

**Fragile Bones**—(See "Brittle" in this section).

**Hardening**—Hard—(1) The Bones Unusually Hard at Birth—See Case, "Short Life", No. 371 in 1001 N.N. (2) Morbid Hardening of—Morbid Ossification—A ♄ disease; ♄ affl. the Asc. or hyleg; ♄ in the 6th H. (See Hardening).

**Head**—Fractures To—(See Head, Skull).

**Humpback**—(See Spine).

**Inflammation**—In the Bone—Osteitis—Danger of—♂ ☌ ♄, and in the part ruled by the sign containing them. (See "Enlargements" in this section).

**Injuries To**—(See Fractures).

**Knock Knees**—(See Knees).

**Legs**—Fractures of—(See Ankles, Femur, Fibula, Legs, Limbs, Tibia).

**Limbs**—Broken—(See Arms, Legs, in this section).

**Long Bones**—Softening of—(See Rickets).

**Luxations**—(See Dislocations).

**Malformations**—Of the Bones—(See Arms, Deformities, Feet, Legs Malformations, etc. Also see "Misshaped" in this section).

**Marrow**—Disorders of—Inflammation of—(See "Osteomyelitis", "Spine" in this section. Also see Marrow).

**Mineral Deposits**—(See "Deficiency" in this section).

**Misshaped Bones**—(See Ankylosis, Caries, Deformities, "Club Feet" under Feet; "Humpback" under Spine; "Knock Knees" under Knees; "Bow Legs" under Legs; Malformations, Monsters, Rickets).

**Morbid Ossification**—Unnatural Ossification—Caused by ♄ afflictions; ♄ affl. the ☉, ☽, Asc., or hyleg, and espec. when ♄ is in the 6th H.

**Ossification**—Morbid—(See "Morbid" in this section).

**Osteitis**—(See "Inflammation" in this section).

**Osteomyelitis**—Inflammation of the Marrow—Osteomyelitis, or Pus in the bones, resulting from injury, is apt to result in any long bone when the part is afflicted by ♂, and other malefics; ♅ or ♂ ☌ ♄ in the sign ruling the part. (See "Osteomyelitis" under Femur; Marrow). Case—See Fig. 15C, in "Astro-Diagnosis", by the Heindels.

**Pain in the Bones**—A ♄ disease; ♄ in an earthy sign in the Asc., 6th H., or M.C., and affl. the ☉, ☽, Asc., or hyleg; the ☽ in ♉, and affl. by the ☉ or ♂ when taken ill. (See Dengue).

**Periosteitis**—Inflammation of the Periosteum—A ♂ affliction; ♂ in the sign ruling the part; ♂ ☌ ♄. (See "Periosteitis" under Femur).

**Pus in the Bones**—(See "Osteomyelitis" in this section. Also see Cloaca).

**Radius**—Fracture of—(See Radius).

**Rheumatism**—In the Bones—Born under ♄; ♄ ruler of the Asc., and affl. the ☉, ☽, or hyleg; ♄ in asp. to the Asc., and affl. the ☽ or lord of the Asc. (See Rheumatism).

**Rickets**—(See Rickets).

**Softening Of**—(See Rickets).

**Spinal Marrow**—Disorders of—(See "Marrow" under Spine).

**Subluxations**—Of the Vertebrae—(See Subluxations, Vertebrae).

**Teeth**—Decay and Disorders of—(See Teeth).

**Tuberculosis**—Of Bone—Caused by ♄ afflictions in earthy signs, and with ♄ in the Asc., 6th H., or M.C., and affl. the ☉, ☽, Asc., or hyleg (See Tuberculosis).

**Ulcerous Inflammation**—(See Caries, Jaws, Teeth, Ulcers).

**Vertebrae**—(See Vertebrae).

**Wrists**—Fracture of—(See Wrists). For Disorders of the Bones, with Case Records, etc., see Figures 15A, 15B, and 15C, in "Astro-Diagnosis" by the Heindels.

**BOOTES**—Left Shoulder of Bootes—(See Arcturus, Disgrace, Ruin).

**BORBORYGMUS**—(See Bowels).

**BORN**—(See Abortion, Birth, "Excision" under Foetus; Miscarriage, Parturition, Stillborn).

**BOW-LEGGED**—Bandy Leg—(See Legs).

**BOWELS**—Intestines—Intestinal Canal—Enteric—The Bowels are principally under the internal rule of the ♍ Sign. They are also ruled by the ☽, ☿, and the 6th H. The bowels are also influenced and affected by ♓, the sign opposite to ♍, and also by all the common signs. The 6th House is said to rule the intestines, even to the Rectum. The common signs on the 6th H., or on angles, greatly influence the bowels for good or ill, according to the nature of the planets in these signs at B., and by dir., and the aspects formed. The Large and Small Intestines are ruled by ♍. The Colon, Jejunum, Ileum, Ileo-Cecal Valve, and other parts of the Intestinal Tract, and accompanying diseases, are listed alphabetically in this section. The Bowels, as a receptacle, are ruled by the ☽. The Mesentery, or the Peritoneal Attachments of the Small Intestines, are ruled by ♍. The Colon and its different parts are ruled by ♏. (See Colon). The Lower Excretory Bowels, and the Rectum, are ruled by ♏. (See Colon, Rectum). The Intestinal Branches of the Solar Plexus are ruled by ♏. (See this influence under Ductless Glands. See Ductless). The Intestinal Ganglia and Plexuses are ruled by ♂ and the ♏ sign. The ☽ in ♍ rules the glands and functions of the bowels. ☿ in ♍ rules the nerves and nerve fibres. ♄ in ♍ rules the Spleen. ♃ in ♍ rules the Arteries. ♂ in ♍ rules the Muscles. ♀ in ♍ rules the Veins. See the following Diseases and subjects in the alphabetical arrangement when not considered here—

**Abdomen; Abdominal Cramps**—♅ in ♍. (See Colic, Cramps, Flatulence, Gas, Gripings, Wind, etc.).

**Abdominal Phthisis**—(See Phthisis).

**Abscess in Bowels**—♃ affl. in ♍.

**Accidents To**—(See "Injuries" in this section).

**Action of Bowels**—(See the various paragraphs in this section).

**Affected**—The bowels tend to be affected with the ☉ in ♐, ♑; ☽ ♌, ♍, ♎, ♏, ♐; ♅ ♒; ♄ ♉, ♊; ♃ ♈, ♉, ♌; ♂ ♈, ♌, ♍, ♓; ♀ ♓; ☿ ♏, ♒. See Table 196 in Simmonite's Arcana. See "Disordered", and the various paragraphs in this section).

**All Diseases Of**—All Infirmities and Weaknesses of—All Irregularities of —Signified by the 6th H. and the ♍ sign, and planets in them.

**Antiperistalsis**—♃ affl. in ♓; ♄, ♂, or ♅ in ♓, and afflicted, and with the ♍ sign weak at B. and unoccupied. (See "Peristaltic" in this section).

**Anus; Aphthae; Appendicitis**—(See Appendix).

**Arteries Of**—Disordered—♃ affl. in ♍.

**Asiatic Cholera**—(See Cholera).

**Assimilation**—Impaired—(See Assimilation).

**Belly**—Any Disease In—(See Belly).

**Biliousness**—(See Bile).

**Bloody Discharges**—(See Dysentery, Flux, Hemorrhage, Hemorrhoids, Typhoid, Ulcers).

**Borborygmus**—Gas in the Bowels—Croaking and Rumbling—☿ affl. in ♍; a ♍ disease, and afflictions in ♍. (See Flatulence, Gas. Also see "Pains" in this section).

**Bowel Complaints**—(See the various paragraphs in this section. See "Wet Feet" under Feet).

**Caecum**—Disorders of—(See Caecum).

**Cancer Of**—(See "Bowels" under Carcinoma).

**Catarrh Of**—(See "Bowels" under Catarrh).

**Cholera; Cholera Infantum**—(See Cholera).

**Chyle**—Disorders of—(See Chyle).

**Chyme**—(See Chyme).

**Circulation**—Obstructed, Restricted, or Sluggish—♅ ☌ ☽ in ♍, and affl. ♃ and ♀; ♄ affl. in ♍; ♄ ☌ ☽ ♍; ♄ ♍ ☌, □, or ☍ ♃ or ♀, obstructed or sluggish.

**Cold in Bowels**—The ☽ ♍ ☌ or ill-asp. any of the malefics as promittors, and espec. to ♄; ♄ in an angle, occi. of the ☉ and ori. of the ☽; ♄ in ♍. (See Cold).

**Colic**—♅ or ☿ affl. in ♍. Mucus Colic, and Flatulent Colic in Bowels are caused by Subs at KP, and PP, the 2, 3, 4 Lumbars. (See Colic, Flatulence, Gas, Gripings, Wind, etc. See Borborygmus, Cramps, Croaking, Pain, Spasm, in this section).

**Colon**—Disorders of—(See Colon).

**Color**—In the Treatment of Bowel Disorders—(See Yellow).

**Congestion**—In Bowels—♄ ♍. (See Congestion).

**Constipation; Consumption Of**—(See "Abdominal" under Phthisis).

**Costiveness**—(See Costiveness. See "Sluggish" in this section).

**Cramps In**—♅ or ☿ affl. in ♍. (See Colic, Pain, Spasmodic, Wind, in this section).

**Croaking**—Rumbling—(See Borborygmus, Gas, Pain, Wind, in this section).

**Death**—From Bowel Disorder—Common Signs show, and afflictions in them, and espec. when on angles or the 6th H.

**Diarrhoea; Diet**—Bowel Disorders from Wrong Diet—♃ affl. in ♍. (See "Evil Diet" under Diet).

**Digestion**—Disorders of Intestinal Digestion—(See Chyle, Indigestion).

**Diseased Intestines**—The Bowels Affected—Disordered—Afflictions in ♍, ♓, the 6th H., and in the common signs. (See "Disorders", and the various paragraphs in this section).

**Disorders Of**—Disordered—The Bowels Afflicted—Enteric Disorders—Distempers In—Liable to Bowel Disorders —The ☉ affl. in ♍, ♐, ♑, or ♓; the ☉ in ♍, ♑, or ♓, ☌ or ill-asp. any of the malefics as promittors; the ☉ ♍ and affl. by ♃; ☽ diseases and afflictions; born under the ☽; ☽ affl. in ♌, ♍, ♎, ♏, or ♐; ☽ affl. in ♍ or ♐, and espec. affl. the hyleg therefrom; the ☽ hyleg in ♍, and afflicted, and espec. with females; ♆ or ♅ affl. in ♍ in 6th H.; ♄ affl. in ♍ or ♑; ♄ or ☋ in ♍ and afflicted; ♄ in ♍ occi., and affl. the ☉, ☽, or Asc.; ♄ ☌ ♂ in ♍, and espec. in an angle at a Solar Ingress at an Equinox; Signified by ♄ in ♉, ♊, or ♒; ♄ or ♂ in ♍ in the 6th H.; ♄ affl. in the 6th H. in a flexed or mutable sign; ♃ affl. in ♈, ♉, ♌, ♍, or ♓; ♃ in ♊ or ♍ in the 6th H., and afflicted; ♂ affl. in ♈, ♌, ♍, or ♓; ♂ in ♍ ☌ or ill-asp. the ☉; ♂ promittor in ♓, and in ☌ or ill-asp. the ☉; ♂ in ♍ in the 6th H.; ♀ in ♍ and affl. the ☽ or Asc.; ♀ affl. in ♍, ♎, or ♓; ♀ in ♍ in the 6th H., and afflicted; ☿ affl. in ♍, ♎, ♏, ♑, or ♒; ☿ affl. in ♑, due to worry and melancholy; common signs denote, and espec. afflictions in ♍, or with common signs on angles or the 6th H.; ♓ on the Asc.; earthy signs on Asc.; the malefics, or afflicting planets in common signs; a Stellium in ♍ or the 6th H.; ♍ on cusp the 6th H. (See the various paragraphs in this section. Also see Heredity).

**Distempers In**—(See "Disorders" in this section).

**Dropsy**—Of the Glands of—♆ affl. in ♍, dropsy and wasting; ☽ affl. in ♍, as the ☽ rules the glands and functions of the bowels.

**Drugs**—(See "Opiates" in this section).

**Duodenum**—Disorders of—Afflictions in ♍. (See Duodenum).

**Dysentery; Eating**—Bowel Disorders from Improper Eating—♀ affl. in ♍ in 6th H.; ♀ in ♍ and affl. the ☽ or Asc. (See "Diet" in this section. Also see Eating, Food).

**Enema; Enteralgia**—(See "Colic", "Pain" in this section).

**Enteric Fever**—Fever in Bowels—(See "Fever" in this section).

**Enteritis**—(See "Inflammation" in this section).

**Enterocolitis**—Caused by Subs at KP and PP; by afflictions in ♍, ♎, or ♏. (See "Inflammation" in this section. Also see Colon, Vertebrae).

**Enteroptosis**—(See "Prolapse" in this section).

**Entozoons**—Intestinal Parasites—(See Entozoons, Worms).

**Eruptions**—And Lesions in Bowels—(See Typhoid).

**Evacuations**—Bloody—(See Evacuations, Faeces, Flux).

**Faeces**—Disorders of—(See Faeces, Evacuations).

**Feet**—Bowel Complaints from Wet Feet—(See "Bowel Complaints", "Colic" under Feet).

**Fever**—In the Bowels—Enteric Fever—Afflictions in ♍; a ♍ disease; ♄ in ♍, occi., and affl. the ☉, ☽ or Asc.; ♂ affl. in ♍; ♂ in ♒ in the 6th H. (See Typhoid).

**Flatulence**—(See Flatulence. Also see Borborygmus, Colic, Cramps, Wind, in this section).

**Fluxes**—(See Flux).

**Functions**—Of the Bowels—Disordered—☽ affl. in ♍. (See "Irregular", and the various paragraphs in this section).

**Gas In Bowels**—(See Colic, Flatulence, Gas, Tympanites, Wind. Also see Borborygmus, Colic, Cramps, Wind, in this section).

**Gastroenteritis**—Inflammation in Both the Stomach and Bowels—♂ affl. in ♍. (See Gastro).

**Gastro-Intestinal Tunics**—(See "Impar" under Ganglion).

**Glandular Disorders**—☽ affl. in ♍; ♆ affl. in ♍, wasting of the glands of bowels. (See Glands, Wasting).

**Gripings**—(See Colic, Cramps, Pain, Spasmodic, Wind, in this section).

**Hard Faeces**—(See Faeces).

**Hemorrhage Of**—(See Dysentery, "Bloody Flux" under Flux; Typhoid, Ulcers).

**Hemorrhoids**—(See the various paragraphs under Hemorrhoids).

**Hernia**—Ventral Hernia—(See Hernia, Rupture).

**Humours In**—(See "Bowels" under Humours).

**Hypogastrium; Ileum**—Ileo-Caecal Valve—Disorders of—(See Ileum).

**Indigestion**—Intestinal—(See Indigestion).

**Infarctions**—(See "Obstructions" in this section).

**Infections**—Afflictions in ♍. (See Infections).

**Infirmities In**—(See "All Diseases In", and the various paragraphs in this section).

**Inflammation**—Enteritis—Phlegmonous Enteritis—The ☉ in ♍ or ♏, and to the ☌ or ill-asps. ♂ by dir.; the prog. ☽ in ♍ ☌, □, ☍ ♂; the ☽ ♍ ☌ or ill-asp. any of the malefics as promittors; ♂ affl. in ♍ or ♓; ♂ ♍ in 6th H.; ♂ in ♍ ☌ the Asc.; ♂ in watery signs and ☌ or ill-asp. the Asc. by dir.; caused by Subs at KP, UPP, PP, LPP. (See Appendicitis, Caecum; "Enteritis" under Catarrh; Dysentery, Enteritis; "Gastro-Enteritis" under Gastro).

**Inguinal Hernia**—(See Groins, Hernia).

**Injuries**—Accidents To—Afflictions in ♍, and to the ♍ sign, and espec. malefics in ♍, and afflictions in the 6th H. or Asc.

**Intussusception**—A ♅ disease; ♅ in ♍, or afflicted in the 6th H. in ♍.

**Irregular**—Bowel Action Irregular—Irregular Functions—Irregular Peristaltic Action—The ☽, ♄, or ♀ affl. in ♍; ♀ in ♍ in the 6th H., and affl. the ☽ or Asc. (See Constipation, Costiveness, Faeces. Also see "All Diseases", "Peristaltic", "Sluggish", in this section).

**Irritations In**—Intestinal Irritations—♂ in ♍ and affl. the hyleg; ☿ affl. in ♍.

**Jejunum**—Disorders of—(See Jejunum).

**Large Intestines**—Diseases In—Afflictions in ♍ or ♏; caused by Subs from KP to LPP. (See Colon, "Ductless Glands" under Ductless).

**Lesions**—(See Typhoid).

**Looseness In**—(See Cholera, Diarrhoea, Dysentery, Flux, etc.).

**Lower Excretory Bowels**—Colon—Rectum, etc.—Ruled by ♏, and diseases of caused by afflictions in ♏ and by Subs at UPP, PP, LPP.

**Lumpy Faeces**—(See Faeces).

**Melancholy**—Bowel Disorders from—(See Melancholy).

**Mesentery**—Disorders of—(See Mesentery, Peritoneum).

**Mesocolon**—(See Colon).

**Mucus In**—Mucus Colic—The intestinal mucus is ruled by ♓, and also influenced by ♍. Mucus in the bowels is increased and produced by ♀ in ♍, and afflicted, and espec. when ♀ is in 6th H., or affl. the ☽ or Asc.; mucus colic is caused by Subs at PP, the 2, 3, 4 Lumbar vertebrae. (See Mucus).

**Muscles Of**—Disorders of—♂ affl. in ♍.

**Nerves Of**—Nerve Fibres —Disturbances of—☿ affl. in ♍.

**Neuralgia**—Neuralgic Pains—☿ affl. in ♍; Subs at PP, 2nd Lumbar. (See "Pain" in this section).

**Obstructions In**—Infarctions—Hard Faeces—Obstructed Circulation, etc.—♄ affl. in ♍; ♄ ☌ ♃ or ♀ in ♍, sluggish bowels; ♄ ♍ in ☌, □, or ☍ ♃ or ♀; ♄ ☌ ☽ in ♍; ♅ ☌ ☽ in ♍, and also afflicted by the □ or ☍ of ♃ and ♀; the ☉, ☽, ♄, ♂, or ☿ affl. in ♍; ☽ affl. in ♍, and affl. the hyleg therefrom; the ☽ in ♍ ☌ or ill-asp. ♄ (or ☿ if he be of the nature of ♄) at the beginning of an illness, or at decumbiture; the hyleg in ♍ and afflicted, and espec. with females; afflictions in ♍; a ♍ disease. ♄ in ♍ tends to obstructions in the different parts of the Colon, and espec. in the Transverse Colon. (See "Circulation" in this section. Also see Colon, Ileum, Obstructions).

**Omentum**—(See Peritoneum).

**Open**—Bowels should be kept open and regular when ♄ is in ♍ at B.

**Operations**—The bowels, or abdomen, should not be operated upon surgically when the ☽ is passing thru the ♍, ♎, or ♏ signs. Case—Bowels Operated Upon Twice—See Case, "A Luckless Youth", No. 390 in 1001 N.N.

**Opiates**—Bowel Disorders from the Use of Opiates and Drugs—♆ affl. in ♍.

**Pain in Bowels**—Cholera Pains In—Colic—Cramps—Enteralgia—Gripings—Neuralgic Pains—Spasmodic Pains—Wind, etc.—♅ or ☿ affl. in ♍; Subs at UPP, PP, LPP. (See Borborygmus, Colic, Cramps, Neuralgia, Spasmodic, Wind, in this section. Also see Enteralgia, Flatulence, Gas).

**Parasitic Diseases**—(See Entozoons, Parasites, Tapeworm, Worms).

**Peristaltic Action**—Impeded—Sluggish—Weakened—The ♍ sign rules the peristaltic action of the bowels, and afflictions in ♍ tend to disturb this action; the ☽ ☌ ♄ in ♍; ☽ ♍ □ or ☍ ♄; ♄ in ♍; ♀ affl. in ♍. (See Constipation, Costiveness, Expulsion, Faeces, Impediments, Peristaltic, Sluggish).

**Peritoneum**—Disorders of—(See Peritoneum).

**Perityphlitis**—(See Caecum).

**Phthisis Abdominalis**—(See Phthisis).

**Physic**—Cathartics—Purging—(See Physic).

**Piles**—(See Hemorrhoids).

**Prolapse**—Of Bowels—Enteroptosis—♄ influence; ♄ affl. in ♍ or ♏; Subs at PP, LPP. (See "Prolapse" under Womb. Also see Hernia).

**Putrid Matter**—Bowels Filled With—♄ ☌ ♃ or ♂ in ♍, and with the ☉ or ☽ in ♒, and due to over-eating, and fermentation of food. (See Faeces).

**Rectum**—Disorders of—(See Anus, Hemorrhoids, Rectum. Also see "Lower Excretory" in this section).

**Regular**—Bowels Should be Kept Regular—(See "Open" in this section).

**Restricted Circulation**—(See Circulation, Obstructed, in this section).

**Retention**—Of Faeces—(See Constipation, Costiveness, Faeces. Also see "Obstructions" in this section).

**Rumbling**—Croaking—(See Borborygmus" in this section).

**Rupture**—(See Hernia, Rupture).

**Scybala**—(See "Hard" under Faeces).

**Serous Stools**—(See Faeces, Serum).

**Sigmoid Flexure**—(See Colon).

**Sluggish Bowels**—(See Constipation, Costiveness, Faeces. Also see "Circulation", "Peristaltic", in this section).

**Small Intestines**—Ruled by ♍. All diseases in are signified by afflictions in ♍, and in the 6th and 7th houses, and by Subs at UPP and PP. Subs at UPP tend to affect the upper Small Intestines, and at PP and LPP, the lower Small Intestines. (See Assimilation, Caecum, Duodenum, Hypogastrium, Ileum, Jejunum).

**Sores In**—(See "Ulcers" in this section).

**Spasm**—Spasmodic Pains In—Gripings—Cramps—♅ or ♄ affl. in ♍; ♃ affl. in ♉ or ♌; afflictions in ♍; an ♒ disease, and afflictions in ♒. (See Borborygmus, Colic, Cramps, Gas, Pain, Wind, in this section).

**Stools**—(See Faeces).

**Summer Complaint**—(See "Cholera Infantum" under Cholera).

**Suppression**—Of Stools—(See Faeces. Also see "Obstructions" in this section).

**Tapeworm**—(See Tapeworm, Worms).

**Transverse Colon**—(See Colon).

**Treatment**—Of Bowel Disorders—Yellow Color is used in. Copper (Cuprum) is a good medicinal remedy in loose bowels and infections. The bowels should be kept regular and open by proper diet and habits, rather than by the use of physics. (See Physic).

**Tuberculosis Of**—♄ affl. in ♍. (See Phthisis, Tuberculosis).

**Tumors In**—♃, ♂, or ♀ affl. in ♍, and espec. when in the 6th H. and affl. the ☽ or Asc. (See Tumors).

**Tunics**—(See "Impar" under Ganglion).

**Tympanites; Typhoid; Typhlitis**—(See Caecum).

**Ulcers**—(See Duodenum, Dysentery, Ulcers).

**Upper Small Intestines**—(See "Small" in this section).

**Veins Of**—Disorders of—♀ affl. in ♍.

**Ventral Hernia**—(See Hernia).

**Vomiting**—Faecal Vomiting—(See Ileac Passion).

**Wasting**—Of Glands—(See "Glandular" in this section).

**Weakened**—(See "Peristaltic" in this section).

**Weaknesses Of**—(See "All Diseases", and the various paragraphs in this section).

**Wet Feet**—Bowel Disorders From—(See "Colic", "Wet Feet", under Feet).

**Wind Colic**—♅ affl. in ♍. (See "Colic" in this section. Also see Wind).

**Worms**—(See Entozoons, Parasites, Tapeworm, Worms).

**Wrong Diet**—Bowel Disorders From—(See Diet, Eating, in this section).

**Yellow Color**—Favorable in the treatment of Bowel Disorders—(See Yellow).

**Yellow Fever**—With Intestinal Derangements—Caused by afflictions in ♌ and ♍; Subs at CP, SP, and KP. (See "Yellow Fever" under Yellow).

**BOYISHNESS**—(See "Youthfulness" under Youth).

**BOYS**—(See "Births" under Male; "Birth of a Son" under Son).

**BRACHIAL**—The Brachial Plexus—Ruled by ☿. Innervation and nerve force to the lungs and pulmonary apparatus are given by ☿ thru the Brachial Plexus, as well as to the arms, hands and shoulders. (See Arms, "Brachial Plexus" under Plexus).

**BRADYCARDIA**—Abnormally Slow Pulse—(See Pulse).

**BRAIN**—Encephalon—Cerebrum—Cerebellum—The Brain is under the internal rulership of the ♈ Sign. The Cerebellum and Base of the Brain, however, are ruled by ♉. The degree on the Asc. also strongly rules and influences the Brain. Among the planets, ☿ is the strong ruler of the brain, in both sexes. Ptolemy says the ☉ also rules the brain. In males the ☉ is said to rule the brain. The ☉ has special affinity with the brain. The Pons Varolii is ruled by the ☉ and the ♉ sign. The brain substance is ruled by the ☽ and ☿. The Meninges, or Brain Coverings, the Dura Mater, are ruled by the ♋ Sign and ♅. In the foetus the brain development, and specialization of the nerve filaments, are ruled and carried on by ☿. The Cerebral Hemispheres, taken together, are ruled by the ♈ Sign. Separately, the right Cerebral Hemisphere is ruled by ☿, and the left Cerebral Hemisphere by ♂. The Cerebral Ventricles are ruled by ♆. The Cerebro-Spinal Nervous System is ruled by ☿. The Arbor Vitae of the Cerebellum are ruled by ♉. The functions of the brain are ruled by ☿ and the ☽. Brain balance is maintained by the secretions of the Thyroid Gland. The brain is smaller and less in weight at the New Moon, and increases in weight and size until the Full Moon, and then diminishes again. It is largely the relation between the ☉ and ☽ which determines the size and weight of the brain. The nerves of the brain are fed by the rays of the ☉. The planet ♆ has considerable action and influence over the brain and eyes. Brain workers should work in a room predominating in blue colors, as blue is restful, as well as stimulating and invigorating to the brain. The Pineal Gland is ruled by ♆. The Pituitary Body is ruled by ♅ and the ♏ sign. The Medulla Oblongata is ruled by ♉. The Brain and Head correspond to the cardinal signs and the Mental Temperament. (See Cerebellum, Cerebrum, Cerebro-Spinal, Cortex, Medulla, Meninges, Mind, Nerves, Occiput, Pineal, Pituitary).

**DISEASES OF THE BRAIN**—The Brain Afflicted—Brain Disorders, etc.—See the following subjects in the alphabetical arrangement when not considered here—

**Abscess Of**—♅ or other malefics in ♈, or afflicting the ♈ sign; Subs at AT, the Atlas.

**Absence Of**—(See "Malformation" in this section).

**Affected**—The Brain Affected—The ☉ and ☽ acting thru the ♈ sign affect the head and its dependencies, and the Cerebro-Spinal Nervous System, and give way to the Hepatic Diathesis. The ☉ and ☽ acting thru the ♏ sign, by way of the Solar Plexus, and the different plexuses, affect the brain and the medulla. ♅ in ♈ tends especially to affect the brain and its membranes. (See Table 196 in Simmonite's Arcana. Also see the various paragraphs in this section).

**All Diseases Of**—Any Disease of—Diseases of ☿.

**Anaemia**—(See Anaemia, Cerebral).

**Any Disease**—Of the Brain—Encephalopathy—Caused by afflictions in ♈ or ♉; ☿ diseases. Subs at AT, CP and KP.

**Apoplexy**—(See Apoplexy, Cerebral).

**Atrophy Of**—♄ affl. in ♈. Is often found in Alzheimer's Disease, where the primitive or animal instincts prevail. (See "Animal Instincts" under Animal; Atrophy).

**Balance**—The Brain Balance Disturbed—(See Thyroid).

**Basal Ganglia**—(See Basal; "Basal" under Ganglion).

**Blood**—Congestion of in the Brain—Determination, or Rush of to the Head and Brain—(See "Brain" under Congestion; "Blood" under Head).

**Blood Vessel**—In the Brain—Rupture of—(See Apoplexy, Cerebral).

**Brain Disorders**—(See "Disorders", and the various paragraphs in this section).

**Brain Fag**—Caused by ☿ affl. by ♄, and espec. when ☿ is weak by sign or position, combust, or setting in the West at B., or unconnected with the ☽ or Asc. (See Fatigue, Reading, Study).

**Brain Fever**—The ☉ or ♂ affl. in ♈; ☉ ☌ ♄ by dir., in the 1st H., or to the ill-asps. of ♄; ☉ ☌ ♄ in ♎, and also □ ♂; the ☽ in the Asc. and ☌ ♂ at B.; ♂ affl. in ♈ or ♎, and espec. when ♂ is in the 6th H. or Asc.; ♂ □ or ☍ ☿; ♂ ascending, and ♂ afflicting at the Vernal, tend to a prevalence of brain fever in Countries ruled by ♈; ♄ to the ☌ or ill-asps. the ☉ in the Asc. at B.; ☿ affl. in ♈; an ♈ and ♊ disease, and afflictions in these signs. Death from brain fever is more apt to result when there are many afflictions in the cardinal signs, and espec. in ♈, and card. signs on angles, or ♈ afflicted on the cusp of 6th H. Case—See Chap. 13, page 97, in Daath's Medical Astrology.

**Brain Force**—Dispersion of—(See Dispersions).

**Brain Storms**—Violent Brain Storms—☿ affl. by ♂, and espec. when ☿ is affl. by the ☽, and unconnected with the ☽ or Asc.; the ☽ □ or ☍ ☿, and also affl. by ♂. (See Frenzy, Fury, Hysteria, Irrational, Madness, Mania, "Psychic Storms" under Psychic).

**Brain Substance**—(See "Substance" in this section).

**Bulbar Paralysis**—(See Medulla).

**Cerebral Disorders**—(See Anaemia, Apoplexy, Cerebral, Congestion).

**Cerebro-Spinal**—(See Cerebro).

**Clot on Brain**—Death By—♄ afflicted in ♈; ♄ ☌ ♃ or ♀ in ♈. Case—See "Birth and Death", No. 350 in 1001 N.N. (See Clots).

**Concussion**—Of the Brain—From Accidents and Injuries—(See Blows, Concussion, Head, "Fractures" under Skull).

**Condition Of**—Diseases arising from the condition of the Brain—(See such subjects as Anaemia, Apoplexy, Dizziness, Faintings, Headaches, Insanity, Insomnia, Madness, Neuralgia, Swoonings, Syncope, Vertigo, etc. Also see the various subjects in this section).

**Congestions**—In the Brain—Cerebral Congestion—(See Cerebral, Congestion).

**Convulsions**—Due to Brain Disturbances—(See Fits, Spasms).

**Cortical Lesions**—(See Cortex).

**Curable Brain Disorders**—♃ and ♀ rising and elevated, between the 1st and 10th H., while ♄ or ♂ may be in the 7th H., the disease will be curable, altho violent. (See "Incurable" in this section. Also see "Curable Diseases" under Curable).

**Cyst-Like Tumor**—Hydatid—Afflictions in ♈ or ♉; Subs at AT. (See Cysts, Tumors. See "Tumor" in this section).

**Death**—From Brain Disorders—☿ influence; ☿ occi. at B., and affl. the hyleg by dir., and espec. if ☿ be in ♈ and afflicted by malefics. (See Brain Fever, Clots, and other paragraphs in this section. Also see Apoplexy, Cerebral).

**Defects**—Of the Brain—The Brain Defective—The ☉ affl. in ♈ tends to structural defects of the brain; ☿ affl. at B.; ☿ affl. by the ☽ or malefics; ☿ having no relation to the ☽ or Asc., and affl. by malefics. (See Defects).

**Delirium; Demoniac Affections**—(See Demoniac).

**Determination**—Of Blood to the Brain and Head—(See "Blood" in this section).

**Disordered Brain**—Diseased Brain—Disturbed Brain—Distempered Brain—Brain Disorders, etc.—A ☉ disease; the ☉ □ or ☍ the Asc.; the ☉ and ☿ affl. in ♈; the ☉ has affinity with the brain, and the sign position of the ☉, and the aspects to the ☉, largely denote the strength or weakness of the brain; the ☽ and ☿ unconnected with each other or the Asc., and affl. by malefics; the ☽ in the 6th H. and affl. by ☿; the ☽ to the ill-asps. ☿ by dir., and ☿ weak and ill-dignified at B., and espec. when ☿ is in ♈ and affl. by malefics; the ☽ hyleg, affl. in ♈, and espec. with females; the ☽ in fiery signs tends to brain disorders due to haste and excitement, and espec. when affl. in ♈; ♆ affl. in ♈, brain disorders due to the inordinate use of all drugs and opiates; ♆ in ♈, and affl. the ☉, ☽, Asc., or hyleg; ♆ affl. in ♈ in the 6th H.; ♅ affl. in ♈, and espec. to disorders of the meninges; ♄ and ♃ affl. in ♈; ♃ affl. in ♈, by rush of blood to the brain, and oftentimes apoplexy; ♂ affl. in ♈, and espec. ♂ in ♈ in the 6th H.; a ☿ disease; ☿ affl. in the 6th H., and espec. when in ♈; ☿ affl. in ♈, nervous disorders of the brain due to overwork and overstudy; ☿ □ or ☍ the Asc., brain diseases; ☿ afflicted tends to disturb the mind, brain and nerves; ☿ afflicting the hyleg tends to death by brain disorders; an ♈ and ♎ disease, and afflictions in these signs; ♈ on the Asc.; ♈ on the cusp of 6th H. and afflicted; afflictions in ♈ tend to brain exhaustion; the ♌ sign ascending at the Vernal Equi., and the ☉ afflicted, the ♌ people, and those living in Countries ruled by ♌, tend to suffer more from brain disorders, and from disorders brought on by extreme heat, drought, pestilence, and heart disturbances; Subs at AT, AX and CP. (See the various paragraphs in this section. See "Disorders Of The Head" under Head).

**Distempers**—Of the Brain—(See "Disordered" in this section).

**Disturbed Brain**—The ☽ in ♌ and affl. by the ☉ or ♂ when taken ill; ☿ affl. in ♈. (See "Disordered" in this section).

**Dizziness**—Lightness of the Brain—Giddiness—Swimming in the Head—(See Faintings, Vertigo).

**Dropsy**—Of the Brain—(See Hydrocephalus).

**Drugs**—The Brain Affected By, and by Opiates—♆ affl. in ♈. (See Narcotics).

**Dura Mater**—(See Meninges).

**Encephalitis**—Inflammation of the Brain—Phrenitis—(See "Inflammation" in this section).

**Encephalopathy**—(See "Any Disease" in this section).

**Excitement**—Haste, and Brain Disorders From—The ☽ affl. in fiery signs. and espec. when in ♈.

**Exhaustion**—Of the Brain—Afflictions in ♈.

**Fagged Brain**—(See "Brain Fag" in this section).

**Faintings**—(See "Cerebral Anaemia" under Anaemia; Coma, Delirium, Faintings, Fits, Vertigo).

**Fever**—(See "Brain Fever" in this section).

**Functions**—Disordered Brain Functions—☿ diseases.

**Fury**—(See Frenzy, Fury, Insanity, Madness, Mania, etc.).

**Giddiness**—(See Faintings, Vertigo).

**Haste**—And Excitement—(See "Excitement" in this section. Also see Excitable).

**Headaches; Heat**—Excessive Heat In the Brain—Encephalitis—(See "Inflammation" in this section).

**Hemorrhage**—Of the Brain—(See Apoplexy, Cerebral).

**Hernia Of**—(See Hernia).

**Hydatids**—(See "Cyst" in this section).

**Hydrocephalus; Idiocy; Ill Blood In**—♃ affl. in ♈ tends to ill blood in the veins of the head and brain.

**Incurable Brain Disorders**—♄ or ♂ alone ruling the ☽, ☿, or the 1st H.; ♃ and ♀ setting or occi., and ♄ or ♂ be angular and ori., the disease becomes more conspicuous and less liable of a cure. (See Curable, Incurable).

**Inflammation**—Of the Brain—Encephalitis—Phrenitis—Excessive Heat In—An ♈ disease; ♂ affl. in ♈; ☿ ill-dignified at B., and under the severe affliction of the malefics by dir.; ☿ affl., and afflicting the hyleg, tends to produce death by inflammation of the brain; malefics in ♈, and the hyleg much afflicted at B.; ♀ affl. in ♈; Subs at AT. (See "Wild Delirium" under Delirium; Encephalon).

**Injuries to Brain**—(See "Accidents", "Blows", "Cuts", under Head; "Fractures" under Skull).

**Insanity; Insensibility; Insomnia**—(See Sleep).

**Intoxication**—(See "Delirium Tremens" under Delirium; Drink, Drunkenness).

**Leptomeningitis**—(See Meningitis).

**Lesions**—(See Cortical).

**Lightness**—In the Brain—(See "Dizziness" in this section).

**Madness**—(See Frenzy, Fury, Madness, Mania).

**Malformation**—(See Idiocy. Also see Case, "Malformation", No. 921, in 1001 N.N.).

**Medulla**—Disorders of—(See Medulla).

**Membranes**—Distempers of, etc.—♅ affl. in ♈. (See Meninges. Also see "Inflammation" in this section).

**Meninges**—Meningitis, etc.—See Meninges).

**Mental Disorders**—From Brain Diseases and Defects—(See "Defects", and the various paragraphs in this section. Also see Idiocy, Insanity, Mania, Mental, Mind, etc.).

**Microcephalic Head**—(See Idiocy).

**Mind**—Disorders of the Brain Affecting the Mind—Afflictions in ♈, and Subs at AT. (See Mind. Also see the various paragraphs in this section).

**Moisture**—Of the Brain—(See "Brain" under Moisture).

**Motor Functions**—Diseases of the Brain Causing Disorders of—(See "Brain" under Motor).

**Nervous Disorders**—Of the Brain—☿ affl. in ♈.

**Neuralgia**—(See Headaches, Neuralgia).

**No Brain**—Merely a Frontal Mask—Case—See "Malformation", No. 921 in 1001 N.N.

**Obstructions In**—♄ affl. in ♈.

**Opiates**—(See "Drugs" in this section).

**Organic Diseases**—Of the Brain—The ☉ affl. in ♈; Subs at AT. (See Organic).

**Over-Activity**—Of the Brain—♂ in ♈.

**Over-Study**—Brain Disorders From—☿ affl. in ♈. (See "Brain Fag" in this section. Also see Insanity).

**Over-Worked Brain**—Denoted by ☿, and ☿ affl. in ♈; ♂ ☌ ☿ in ♈. (See "Brain Fag" in this section. Also see Reading, Study).

**Paralysis**—Bulbar—(See Medulla).

**Peculiar Brain Diseases**—♅ diseases, ♅ in ♈; ☿ affl. by ♅. (See Peculiar).

**Phrenitis**—(See "Inflammation" in this section. Also see Phrenitic).

**Polioencephalitis**—Inflammation of the Gray Matter of the Cortex—♂ affl. in ♈ or ♉; ☿ in ♈ and affl. by ♂.

**Posterior Portion**—Of the Brain Undeveloped—Case—See "Idiot from Birth", No. 742 in 1001 N.N. Also see Case, "Female", Chap. 8, page 49, in Daath's Medical Astrology.

**Rattle-Brained**—(See "Rapid" under Speech).

**Rupture of Vessels**—In Brain—(See Apoplexy, Cerebral).

**Shocks**—Brain Disorders from Shocks—♅ in ♈. (See Shock).

**Shrinkage**—Of the Brain—♄ affl. in ♈. (See "Atrophy" in this section).

**Softening**—Of the Brain—A ♓ disease, and with many planets in ♓ and afflicted; is often the result of Alcoholism, a ♓ affliction; Subs at AT cause acute softening of the brain. (See Alcoholism, Softening).

**Spasmodic Diseases**—Diseases of the Brain Causing—♅ affl. in ♈; Subs at AT. (See Spasmodic).

**Spinal Cord**—Diseases of the Brain and Spinal Cord—Subs at CP; afflictions in ♈ and ♌. (See Cerebro-Spinal).

**Storms**—(See "Brain Storms" in this section).

**Strengthened**—The Brain Strengthened—♅ ✶ or △ the Asc.

**Structural Defects**—The ☉ affl. in ♈; Subs at AT. (See "Organic", "Substance" in this section).

**Study**—Brain Disorders from Over-Study—☿ affl. in ♈; ☿ affl. in ♈ in 6th H. (See "Brain Fag" in this section).

**Substance**—Disorders of the Substance of the Brain—☉ affl. in ♈; ☿ diseases, and ☿ affl. in ♈; diseases of the ☽; the ☽ affl. in ♈ or ♎, and espec. when in the 6th H.; Subs at AT. (See "Organic", "Structural" in this section. Also see Substance).

**Swimming**—In the Head (See Vertigo).

**Swoonings**—(See Faintings).

**Syncope**—(See Fainting).

**Thrombus**—(See "Clot" in this section).

**Tuberculosis**—Of the Brain—♄ affl. in ♈; Subs at AT.

**Tumor Of**—Hydatid, Cyst-like Tumor—♄ affl. in ♈ tends to unusual deposits in the brain tissues, hardening of the vessels, and tumors; ♃, ♀, or the ☽ affl. in ♈, and often the result of bad living, dissipation, Alcoholism, Too Much Blood, Gluttony, etc. (See "Cyst-like" in this section. Also see Tumors).

**Unconsciousness**—(See Anaesthetics, Apoplexy, Catalepsy, Coma, Delirium, Dreams, Faintings, Insensibility, Sleep, Trance, etc.).

**Vertigo; Vessels of Brain**—Rupture of—(See Apoplexy, Cerebral).

**Violent Brain Storms**—(See "Brain Storms" in this section. Also see Violent).

**Water**—On the Brain—Dropsy of—(See Hydrocephalus).

**Weight**—Of the Brain—(See Introduction to this section).

**BRASH**—Water Brash—Eructations from Stomach—(See Belching).

**BREAK-BONE FEVER**—(See Dengue, Fermentation, Zymotic).

**BREAKDOWN IN HEALTH**—(See "Breakdown" under Health, Mental).

**BREAKING**—

**Of Blood Vessels**—(See Apoplexy, "Blood Vessels" under Vessels; Hemorrhage, Rupture, etc.). See Bursting, Lacerations.

**Of Bones**—(See Fractures).

**BREAKINGS OUT**—(See Acne, Chickenpox, Eruptions, Measles, Pimples, Rashes, Scarlatina, Skin Diseases, Smallpox, Sores, Syphilis, Ulcers, Venereal, etc.).

**BREAST**—Breasts—Mammae—Breast Bone—Pectoral Region—Chest—The Milk, etc.—Are denoted by the 4th H. and the ♋ Sign. Are under the external rule of ♋. Are also ruled by the ☽ and ♀. The Mammary Glands and the Lacteal System are ruled by the ☽ and the ♋ sign. The breasts of women are ruled by the ☽ and ♀. The Milk is ruled by the ☽, ♀, the ♋ sign, and the watery signs in general. The Sternum, or Breast Bone, the flat bone of the breast, is under the structural rulership of ♋. The Nipples, or Paps, are ruled by ♋. (See Chest, Milk). See the following subjects in the alphabetical arrangement when not considered here—

**Ablation**—Suppression of the Mammae—♄ in ♋ or ♑, and espec. when affl. the ☽, the ruler of the breasts, and the ♋ sign; ♄ in ♋ in the 1st or 4th H., and affl. the ☽. (See Removal, Remote, Suppressions).

**Abscess Of**—Imposthumes—Ulcer—A ♋ disease, and afflictions in ♋; ♂ ♋ ☌ or evil asp. ♄, and ♂ affl. the hyleg. (See Abscesses).

**Accidents To**—Injuries or Hurts To—♅, ♄, or ♂ in ♋ or the 4th H., and afflicted; ♋ sign on the Asc., and containing malefics, or otherwise afflicted; afflictions in ♋. (See "Bruises" in this section).

**Adenoma**—Glandular Tumor of the Breast—♀ affl. in ♋. (See Adenoma, Glands, Scrofula).

**Affected**—The Breast tends to be affected with the ☉ in ♏; ♅ ♉; ♄ in ♈, ♉; ♃ ♊, ♒, ♓; ♂ ♊, ♋, ♒; ♀ ♌, ♑; ☿ ♍, ♐. (See Table 196 in Simmonite's Arcana).

**All Diseases**—In the Breast—Signified by the ♋ sign, the 4th H., and afflictions therein.

**Breastbone**—Protrusion of—Chicken-breasted—♋ on the Asc., and affl. by ♄ or ♂; Subs at Lu.P.

**Breast Pang**—(See Angina Pectoris).

**Broad Chest**—Or Breast—♄ lord of the Asc., and ori., as from the Asc. to M.C., or from Desc. to Nadir. (See "Stout" under Chest).

**Bruises In**—♄ ♋. (See "Accidents" in this section).

**Caked Breasts**—♄ affl. in ♋. (See Milk).

**Cancer of the Breast**—(See "Breasts" under Carcinoma).

**Chest; Chicken-Breasted**—(See "Breastbone" in this section).

**Cyst Of**—(See "Breast" under Cyst).

**Defects**—Such as Marks, Moles, Scars, etc.—♋ on the Asc. (See Marks, Moles, Scars).

**Fever In**—♂ affl. in ♋.

**Full, Large Breasts**—The ☉ or ☽ ♋; many planets in ♋; ♋ on the Asc.

**Glands**—Disorders of—(See "Adenoma in this section. Also see Glands, Milk).

**Heat In**—The ☽ in ♈, affl. by the ☉ or ♂ when taken ill; the ☽ ☌ or ill-asp. ♄ in ♌ (or ☿ if he be of the nature of ♄) at the beginning of an illness, or at decumbiture, and they frequently die when the ☽ comes to the ☍ of ♄ if no good asps. prevent it.

**Heaviness**—Of the Breast—The ☽ ☌, □, ☍, or P. ♄ (or ☿ if he be of the nature of ♄) at the beginning of an illness or at decumbiture (Hor'y).

**Humours Falling Into**—The ☽ ♋ ☌ or ill-asp. ♄ (or ☿ if he be of the nature of ♄) at the beginning of an illness or at decumbiture (Hor'y). If the ☽ be decr., and near the body of ♄, the disease may continue for a long time.

**Imperfections In**—A ☽ disease; a ♋ sign disease and affliction, and afflictions in ♋; ♋ on the Asc. (See "Defects" in this section).

**Imposthumes**—(See "Abscess" in this section).

**Inflammation In**—♂ affl. in ♋; ♂ in ♋ in the Asc. or 6th H., and afflicted; the ☽ in ♑ and affl. by the ☉ or ♂ when taken ill. (See Inflammation).

**Injuries To**—(See "Accidents" in this section).

**Lacteals**—(See Milk).

**Large Breasts**—(See "Full" in this section).

**Lungs; Mammary Glands**—Disorders of—Afflictions in ♊, ♋, ♌; Subs at Lu.P. (See Milk).

**Marks**—Moles—Scars—♋ on the Asc. (See "Imperfections" in this section).

**Milk**—Disorders of—(See Milk. Also see "Mammary" in this section).

**Moles**—(See "Marks" in this section).

**Narrow Breast**—(See "Narrow" under Chest).

**Nipples**—Disorders of—(See Nipples).

**Obstructions In**—♄ affl. in ♋. (See Adenoma, Milk).

**Pain In**—♂ affl. in ♋; ♂ in ♋ in the Asc.; the ☽ in ♈, affl. by the ☉ or ♂ when taken ill; ♋ on Asc. at the Vernal, and the ☽ weak and affl. by ♂, or ♂ in ♋. This is espec. true of people who have ♋ on the Asc. at B., and also among people in Countries ruled by ♋. (See "Pain" under Nipples).

**Pang**—(See "Breast Pang" in this section).

**Paps**—(See Nipples).

**Pectoral Disorders**—(See the various paragraphs in this section).

**Peculiar Disorders**—Of the Breasts—♅ affl. in ♋. (See Peculiar).

**Phlegm**—The Breast Affected With Tough Phlegm—(See "Breast" under Phlegm).

**Pigeon-Breasted**—(See "Breastbone" in this section).

**Prominent Breasts**—(See "Full" in this section).

**Protrusion**—(See "Breastbone" in this section).

**Scars**—(See "Defects", "Imperfections", in this section).

**Scirrhus**—A Hard Form of Carcinoma—(See Axillae, Carcinoma).

**Slimy Matter**—Breast Much Affected With—(See "Breast" under Phlegm).

**Thorax; Tough Phlegm**—(See Bronchial; "Breast" under Phlegm).

**Tumors**—Subs at Lu.P., 3rd Dorsal, and at KP. (See "Adenoma" in this section).

**Ulcers**—(See Abscess, Cancer, in this section).

**Weaning**—(See Weaning).

**BREATH**—Breathing—Respiration—Organs of Respiration—Respiratory Tract, etc. The Respiratory Tract consists of the Mouth, Nose, Throat, Larynx; Trachea, or Windpipe; Bronchial Tubes, Lungs, and Diaphragm, etc., all of which have a part in connection with the Breath, Breathing, Inhalation, Exhalation, the taking in of the Air, Oxygen, Oxygenation, and the expulsion of the Carbon and Wastes of the body. The Respiratory Tract and Organs are ruled by the ♉, ♊, and ♋ Signs. The Breath is ruled by ☿, ♃, the Airy Signs in general, and is especially under the internal rulership of ♊, as Breathing is a special function of ♊. Physiologically ☿ rules Respiration. In the Astral Body ♃ has direct relation to the Breath. (See Astral). The Throat, Windpipe, and the Larynx, are ruled by the ♉ sign. The Bronchi, the smaller Bronchial Tubes, and the Upper Lobes of each Lung, are ruled by ♊. The Pleura, the Pleural Cavity, Lower Lobe of the Left Lung, the two Lower Lobes of the right Lung, and the Diaphragm, are ruled by the ♋ sign. Neptune, ♅ and ☿ in ♉, ♊, and ♋ rule and affect the Breath, Breathing, the Respiratory System, Nerves of the Respiratory System, the Air Cells, and the Windpipe. ♅ espec. has strong rule over the Respiratory action and Breathing. The following subjects have to do with the Respiratory Tract, its action, conditions, afflictions, etc., which see in the alphabetical arrangement when not considered here—

**Abnormal Breathing**—Afflictions in ♉, ♊, and ♋; Subs at AP and Lu.P. (See the various paragraphs in this section).

**Absorbent Vessels**—(See Absorption).

**Action**—The ☉, ☽, ♅, or ☿ in the ♉, ♊, or ♋ sign, and afflicted, tend to disturb the respiratory action. (See the various paragraphs in this section).

**Affected**—The Breath and Breathing Affected—Afflictions in ♉, ♊, and ♋, and espec. the malefics in these signs. (See the various paragraphs in this section. See "Middle Cervical" under Ganglion).

**Affections**—Of the Breath—(General)—☿ affl. at B., and in evil asp. the Asc. by dir.; the Asc. to the evil asps. ☿ by dir., and ☿ affl. at B., and espec. if ☿ be affl. by ♄ at B. (See the different paragraphs in this section).

**Air Cells**—Tidal Air—☿ affl. in ♉, ♊, or ♋ tends to disturbances of the air cells in lungs, and respiration. (See "Tidal" in this section).

**Anus**—Inbreathing Thru—(See Anus).

**Asphyxiation; Asthma; Bad Breath**—(See "Foul" in this section).

**Bad Respiration**—Due to Tight Lacing—(See Dress, Lacing).

**Breath**—Breathing—Disorders and Irregularities of—(See the various paragraphs in this section).

**Bronchial Disorders**—(See Bronchial, Lungs).

**Carbonic Acid Wastes**—(See Carbon).

**Chest; Cheyne-Stokes Breathing**—Rhythmical Irregularity of the Breathing—♄ affl. in ♊.

**Complaints**—Respiratory Complains—(See the various paragraphs in this section).

**Consumption; Cough; Croup; Cyanosis; Death**—Disease and Death from Impure and Immoderate Respiration—Caused by ♃ when the dominion of death is vested in him.

**Deep Breathing**—Prevented—(See "Obstructions", "Shallow" in this section).

**Defects**—Of the Respiratory Organs—☿ affl. in ♊. (See Structural, Troubles, and other paragraphs in this section).

**Diaphragm; Difficult Breathing**—(See "Labored" in this section).

**Diseases Of**—The Respiratory Tract—(See "Troubles", and the various paragraphs in this section).

**Disorders**—Of the Breath—Of Breathing, etc.—(See the various paragraphs in this section).

**Dress**—Breathing Interfered With By—(See Dress).

**Dust**—Inhalation of and Disease From—(See "Dust" under Lungs).

**Dyspnoea**—(See "Labored" in this section).

**Exercise**—The Respiratory Organs should have proper exercise when ♀ is in ♊.

**Exhalation**—Expiration—Interferences With—(See "Irregular", "Labored" in this section).

**Fainting; Foul Breath**—Foul Tongue—Bad Breath—Halitosis—Impure Breath—Putrid Breath—Unpleasant Breath—Stinking Breath, etc.—A ☉ disease, and caused by an afflicted ☉; the ☉ affl. by ♄; a ♄ disease; a ☿ disease, and espec. when ☿ is affl. by ♄; ☿ affl. in the 6th H., and espec. by ♄; a 1st H. disease, and espec. when ♄ is there and affl. the ☉, ☿, or the hyleg; the 4th face of ♉ on the Asc., and ♄ there. In Hor'y Questions ♄ as Sig. denotes a person seldom free from bad breath. (See Carbon, Foul, Impure, Indigestion, Gangrene, Mouth; "Foul" under Tongue).

**Goitre**—Interfering with Breathing—(See Goitre).

**Halitosis**—(See "Foul" in this section).

**Hiccough**—Spasmodic Inspiration—(See Hiccough).

**Hurried Respiration**—(See "Rapid" in this section).

**Immoderate Respiration**—(See "Death", "Rapid", and other paragraphs in this section).

**Impure Respiration**—(See "Death", "Foul", in this section).

**Inbreathing**—Thru the Rectum—(See Anus).

**Inspiration**—(See Cheyne-Stokes, Hiccough, Irregular, Labored, and other paragraphs in this section).

**Interference**—With Breathing—Many afflictions in common signs, and espec. in ♊, ♐, and ♓; ♅ ☌ ☽ in ♋, and afflicted by ♆, ♂, and other planets, and due to gas and stomach dilatation. (See Dress, Hiccough, Labored, and the various paragraphs in this section).

**Interrupted Breathing**—(See Hiccough, Interference, Obstructions, and the various paragraphs in this section).

**Irregular Breathing**—(See Cheyne-Stokes, Hiccough, and the various paragraphs in this section).

**Jerky Breathing**—(See Cheyne-Stokes, Hiccough, in this section).

**Labored Inspiration**—Dyspnoea—Difficult Breathing—Wheezing—Caused by afflictions in ♊, to the ♊ sign, or to planets in ♊; the ☉ ☌ ♅ in ♊; the ☉ at B., or by progression, □ or ☍ ♃ or ♀, the rulers of the circulation; the Prog. ☉ □ or ☍ planets in ♊, and espec. when a malefic transits the 6th H. at the same time; ♄ in ♊ ☍ the ☽, by insufficient tidal air; ♄ ♌ and affl. by ♅; ♄ in ♊ or ♐, by interfering with the circulation in the lungs; ♄ in ♋ or ♑, by disturbances of the diaphragm; ♃ ☍ ♀, and espec. in ♊ and ♐; ♀ in ♊ ☍ ♃, and espec. when transits or prog. influences afflict ♀. (See Angina, Asthma, Bronchial, "Convulsive" under Cough; Croup; Cyanosis, Diaphragm, Dyspnoea, Goitre, Heart, Hiccough, Oxygen, Tidal, etc. Also see "Interference", "Obstructions", in this section).

**Lacing**—Tight Lacing—(See Dress).

**Larynx; Lungs; Lymphatic Vessels**—Of the Respiratory System Affected—(See Absorption).

**Membrane**—Deficient Secretion of Mucus On—(See "Respiratory" under Mucous).

**Mouth Breathing**—(See Adenoids, Nose, Polypus, Snoring. Also see "Stertorous" in this section).

**Mucous Membranes**—Of the Respiratory Tract—(See "Respiratory" under Mucous. Also see Phlegm).

**Muscles**—Of Breathing—(See "Speech" in this section).

**Nasal Polypus**—(See Polypus).

**Noisy Breathing**—(See "Snoring", "Stertorous", in this section).

**Non-Oxygenation**—(See Oxygen).

**Nose**—Interference with Breathing—(See Adenoids, Nose, Polypus).

**Obstructions**—To Breathing—Deep Breathing Prevented—Obstructions in the Circulation—The afflictions of ♄ to ♃ and ♀, and also tend to non-oxygenation; ♃ or ♀ affl. in ♊, and espec. when in the 6th H., and which may also be from tight lacing. (See Adenoids, Dress, "Non-Oxygenation" under Oxygen; Nose, Polypus. Also see "Labored", "Rhythmic", "Shallow", in this section).

**Organic Defects**—(See "Lungs" under Structural).

**Oxygen**—Insufficient—(See Oxygen).

**Phthisic; Phthisis; Pleura; Pneumoconiosis**—(See "Dust" under Lungs).

**Polypus; Putrid Breath**—(See "Foul" in this section).

**Rapid Breathing**—Hurried—A ☿ disease, and afflictions to ☿. Also occurs in high fevers, and with high pulse. (See "High Fevers" under Fever; "High Pulse" under Pulse).

**Rectal Breathing**—(See Anus).

**Respiratory Tract**—Disorders of—(See the various paragraphs in this section).

**Rhythmic Breathing**—Interference With—The ☉ in ♊ or ♐, in □ or ☍ the ☽, as the ☽ governs the tidal air; ♅ ☌ ♂ in ♊; ♅ elevated in ♊ or ♋, and afflicted; ♄ ☌ ♅ in ♉ or ♏; ♄ in ♉ or ♏, by afflicting the throat region by growths or obstructions. (See Dress, Hiccough, Oxygen, Tidal. Also see the various paragraphs in this section).

**Shallow Breathing**—Superificial Breathing—♄ in ♊, in ☍ the ☽, lack of tidal air, and the breathing restrained; ♄ in ♊ and affl. by both ♃ and ♀ from common signs; ♄ ♊ ☌ or ill-asp. ♃ and ♀; ♅ ☌ ☽ ♋, due to gas and distended stomach; Subs at Lu.P. and SP. (See Oxygen. Also see Obstructions, Rhythmic, in this section).

**Short Breath**—(See Labored, Rapid, Shallow, in this section).

**Sighs Frequently**—Prolonged Deep Inspiration—The ☽ or ♅ ☌, □, or ☍ ♄ (or ☿ if he be of the nature of ♄), and espec. at the beginning of an illness, or at decumb.; the ☽ ☌ ♄ in ♊; caused by non-oxygenation, and ♄ affl. in ♊. (See Oxygen. Also see "Shallow" in this section).

**Skin Breathing**—Interfered With—(See "Cutaneous" under Asphyxiation).

**Snoring**—Usually caused by the vibrations of a long Uvula, and sleeping on the back; ♅, ♂, or ♀ in ♉ may cause excessive growth of the Uvula. (See "Stertorous" in this section. Also see Uvula).

**Spasmodic Breathing**—♅ affl. in ♉, ♊, or ♋. (See Cheyne-Stokes, Interference, Labored, Rapid, in this section. Also see Asphyxiation, Hiccough, Oxygen).

**Speech**—Improper Breathing in Speaking or Singing—Usually caused by ♄ affl. in ♊ or ♋, causing improper action of the muscles of breathing, and of the Diaphragm, and also causing disturbances of Oxygenation. (See Diaphragm, Oxygen, Speech, Vocal).

**Stertorous Breathing**—Noisy—Snoring—A Sonorous, Resonant, Ringing Sound in Breathing—A ☿ disease; ☿ affl. in ♊. (See "Snoring" in this section).

**Stinking Breath**—(See "Foul" in this section).

**Structural Defects**—The ☉ afflicted in ♉, ♊, or ♋, structural defects in throat, lungs, and respiratory system.

**Suffocation**—(See Asphyxia, Drowning, Hanging, Oxygen, Suffocation, Strangling).

**Suspension**—Temporary Suspension of Breathing—(See Cheyne-Stokes, Interference, Interrupted, Obstructions, Spasmodic, in this section. Also see Catalepsy, Fainting, "Stoppage" under Heart; Trance, etc.).

**Swoonings**—(See Fainting).

**Syncope**—(See Fainting).

**Throat**—Interferences with Breathing from Throat Disorders and Obstructions—(See Goitre, Tonsils. Also see "Swellings", and paragraphs under Throat).

**Tidal Air**—Insufficient—(See Carbon, Oxygen, Tidal. Also see Labored, Rhythmic, Shallow, in this section).

**Tight Lacing**—Interfering with Breathing—(See Dress).

**Tissues Affected**—Wasting of—♆ in ♉, ♊, or ♋.

**Tongue**—Foul Tongue—(See "Foul" in this section).

**Tonsils**—Enlarged, and Interfering with Breathing—(See Tonsils).

**Trachea; Tract**—Disorders of the Respiratory Tract—(See "Troubles", and the various paragraphs in this section).

**Trance**—With Suspended Breathing—(See Catalepsy, Trance).

**Troubles**—Respiratory Troubles—Diseases of the Respiratory Organs and Tract—Are ruled and caused principally by ☿, afflictions to ☿, and afflictions in the ☿ sign ♊; malefics in the 3rd, 6th, 9th, or 12th Houses, and in common signs; ☿ affl. in ♊; the ☽ hyleg in ♊, and espec. with females; the ☽ ♊ ☌ or ill-asp. ♆, ♅, ♄, or ♂ as promittors; ♄ ☌ or ill-asp. the ☽; ♄ affl. in ♊; ♂ promittor in ♓ and in ☌ or ill-asp. the ☉. (See the various paragraphs in this section. Also see Cardia; "Middle Cervical" under Ganglion).

**Unpleasant Breath**—(See "Foul" in this section).

**Uvula**—(See "Snoring" in this section).

**Veins**—(See "Respiratory" under Veins).

**Voice**—Disorders of from Respiratory Troubles—(See Voice. Also see "Mouth Breathing", "Speech", in this section).

**Waste of Tissues**—(See "Tissues" in this section).

**Wheezing**—(See "Labored" in this section).

**Whooping Cough**—(See Whooping).

**Windpipe**—(See Trachea).

**Yogi Breathing Exercises**—One Occult Writer says that holding the breath in deep breathing exercises poisons the system, and creates unusual physic conditions. (See Yogi).

**BREECH**—Breech Presentation—(See Parturition).

**BRETHREN**—Shown and governed by ♊ and the 3rd H., and our relations to them, their sicknesses, prospect of life, death, etc. The term Brethren as used here espec. refers to brothers and sisters. One writer says that the 3rd H. and its lord signify brethren in Hor'y Questions, but not in Nativities, and that Brethren in Nativities are signified by the sign on the M.C., and the sign following, and to these are added the maternal place of ♀ by day, and the ☽ by night. In a predominance of Textbooks the 3rd H. is said to rule brothers, sisters, cousins, neighbors, etc., and our relations to them for good or ill, according to the signs and planets ruling this house at B. The following influences should be noted in the map of birth of the native as regards his relationships to his brethren. The following subjects have to do with Brethren, Relatives, Kindred, etc., which see in the alphabetical arrangement when not considered here—

**Brothers; Death**—Of Brethren—(See "Death" under Brothers, Family, Relatives, Sisters, etc.).

**Elder Born Brethren**—Are represented by the more oriental stars, while the younger brethren are denoted by the more occidental stars.

**Family; Few Brethren**—(See "Few" under Brothers).

**Increase Of**—Many Brethren—Increase of brothers and sisters is indicated by the sign on the M.C. and 11th H., and by ♀ by day, and the ☽ by night. These places favorably aspected by benefics give increase according to the number of planets by which they are aspected, and the number is doubled if the planets be in double-bodied signs. Also the ☉ surrounded by good stars, or well-aspected by many, gives many brethren.

**Length of Life Of**—(See Brothers, Sisters).

**Many Brethren**—(See "Increase" in this section).

**Marriage Partner**—Brethren of—Are ruled by the 9th H. (See "Relatives" under Marriage Partner).

**Relatives**—Conditions Concerning—(See Relations).

**Short-Lived**—Sickly—If both malefics and benefics aspect the M.C., the 11th H., ♀ and the ☽, and the malefics outnumber the benefics.

**Sickness Among**—Lord of the 3rd H. in the 6th, or lord of the 6th in the 3rd, there is much sickness among them.

**Sisters; Younger Brethren**—(See "Elder" in this section). For collateral study see Aunts, Children, Father, Mother, Uncles, etc.

**BREVITY**—Brief—

**Brevity of Members**—(See Ephemeral, Limbs, Members, Short, "Brevity" under Signs of the Zodiac).

**Disease Is Brief**—(See Quick).

**BRIGHT'S DISEASE**—Nephritis—Inflammation of the Kidney—

**Acute Bright's Disease**—Acute Nephritis, and usually attended with Albumen in the Urine—A predominance of afflictions in the fixed signs, and a fixed sign rising; ♂ affl. in ♎; ♀ affl. by ♄, ♃, or ♂; a ♎ disease, and afflictions in ♎; ♎ on the 6th H., and espec. when ♂ is in ♎ in the 6th. (See Albuminuria; "Nephritis" under Kidneys).

**Cases of Bright's Disease**—See Cases on pages 92, 93, and 94, Chap. 13, in Daath's Medical Astrology. (See Kidneys, Urine).

**Chronic Bright's Disease**—♄ affl. in ♎; ♄ in ♎ in the 6th H.; ♄ □ or ☍ ♃ and ♀; ♃ affl. by ♆; the ☉ or ☽ in ♎, and affl. by ♄, and espec. when the ☉ or ☽ are in ♎ in the 6th H., and affl. by ♄. (See "Cirrhosis" under Kidneys).

**BRISK**—Brisk in Movements—(See Action, Active, Energetic, Gait, Manner, Motion, Movement, Quick, Rapid, Smart, Walk, etc.).

**BRITTLE**—(See Fragile, Nails).

**BROAD**—(See "Broad", or "Wide", under Chest, Face, Forehead, Ligaments, Nails, Shoulders, etc.).

**BROKEN**—Fractured—Sundered, etc.

**Broken Bones**—(See Fractures).

**Broken Heart**—Dies of Sorrow and a Broken Heart—♄ and ♑ influence; ♄ affl. ☿ at B., and by dir.; ♄ in the 1st or 10th H., and affl. the ☉, ☽, ☿, and hyleg; ☿ in ♑ and otherwise affl. by ♄; ♑ on the Asc., and espec. the 29°, and ☿ also affl. by the ☽ and ♄; lord of the 1st in the 8th, and the ☽ in evil asp. lord of the 8th by application, and without reception, or if lord of 8th be a malefic and in the 1st. (See Despondency, Melancholy, Sorrow).

**Broken Signs**—Of the Zodiac—♌, ♏, and ♓. Also called imperfect, or mutilated signs, as people born under them tend to be broken, or deformed in some way. (See Crooked, Deformities, Distortions, Imperfect, Mutilated).

**Broken Sleep**—(See Sleep). See Lacerations, Rupture, Vessels.

**BROMIDROSIS**—Fetid Perspiration—Caused by ♂. In the Axillae, ♂ in ♋; in the feet, ♂ in ♓; ♂ in common signs. (See Excrement, Excretion, Sweat).

**BRONCHIAL**—The Bronchials—Bronchial Tubes—Are ruled by ☿, the ♊ sign, and the 3rd H. One writer gives ♏ also as ruler, as the Bronchials are concerned with elimination, which function is largely under the rule of ♏. The Bronchial Tubes are ruled by ♊. The following subjects have to do with the Bronchial Tract and System, which see in the alphabetical arrangement when not considered here—

**Acute Bronchitis**—(See "Bronchitis" in this section).

**Affections**—Bronchial Affections—The ☉ affl. in ♊; the ☽ hyleg in ♊ in a female nativity; ♄ occi. in ♉, and affl. the ☉; ♀ affl. in ♐; a ☿ disease; ☿ affl. in ♊ or ♐; ♊ on the cusp the 6th H. (See the various paragraphs in this section).

**Asthma**—Bronchial Asthma—(See Asthma. Also see "Congestion" in this section).

**Breathing; Bronchiectasis**—(See "Dilatation" in this section).

**Bronchioles**—Disturbance of—♆ ♊, and espec. in the Summer months, and greatly disturbing in Asthma cases from pollen.

**Bronchitis**—Acute—Inflamed Bronchi—The ☉, ☽, ♅, ♄, ♂, or ☿ affl. in ♊ or ♐; the ☉ or ☽ in the 6th H. in fixed signs, and afflicted; ♅ in ♉ or ♊ and affl. the ☉, ☽, Asc., or hyleg; a ♄ disease; ♄ affl. in the 6th H. in a fixed sign; ♄ in ♊, ♐, or ♓; ♄ ☌ ♀ in 3rd H.; ♄ and ♀ afflictions involving the 3rd H. by rulership or occupancy; a ♃ disease; ♃ ♊ and affl. by ♂; ♂ in ♊ in the 3rd H.; ♂ in ♉, ♊, or ♐ at B., and affl. the hyleg at B., or by dir.; ♂ in ♊ or ♐ predisposes to; ♂ in ♊ in the 6th H.; ☿ affl. in ♉, ♊, or ♋; ☿ ☌ or ☍ the malefics, and the hyleg afflicted; the Asc. to the □ or ☍ ☿ and ☿ affl. at B.; a ♊ and ♐ disease; also caused by afflictions in ♉, ♏, and ♓; afflictions in ♓ predispose to quick attacks of from wet feet; caused by planets in ♊ opposed by malefics in ♐; the hyleg much afflicted at B., and espec. by malefics in ♊ and ♐; ♏ on the Asc. at B.; afflictions in the 29° ♋ or ♑; Subs at LCP, AP, and HP. (See "Chronic" in this section).

**Catarrh**—Bronchial Catarrh—The ☽ in ♉, ♊, or ♋ tends to. (See Catarrh).

**Chest; Chronic Bronchitis**—♄ affl. in ♉, ♊, or ♋; ♄ in ♓ and affl. the ☉ or ☽ in ♊; ♄ ☌ ☿ in ♊ in 3rd H.; ☉ ☌ ☽ in ♊, and in □ to ♄ in ♓; Subs at Lu.P. (See Case, "Chronic Bronchitis", Chap. 13, page 91, in Daath's Medical Astrology).

**Colds; Congestion**—Of the Bronchials—And tending to Asthma, and Bronchial Asthma—♃ affl. in ♏, and ♏ on the cusp the 3rd H. (See Asthma. Also see "Bronchioles" in this section).

**Consumption**—Bronchial Consumption—Malefics in ♉ tend to; a ♉ disease; ♄ ♉. (See Consumption).

**Cough**—Bronchial Cough—Afflictions in ♊ or ♐; the ☉, ♂, ♀, or ☿ in ♊ or ♐, and afflicted; the ☉ or ☽ in the 6th H., in fixed signs, and afflicted; ♅ and ♂ in ♏ on the Asc.; ♄ lord of the 3rd H., and afflicting ♀; ♄ afflicted in the 6th H. in fixed signs; afflictions in ♉. (See Cough).

**Death**—From Bronchitis, and Bronchial Trouble—♄ or ♂ in ♊, and affl. the hyleg at B., or by dir.; ♂ occi. at B., and affl. the hyleg at B.; afflictions in fixed signs, and espec. when on the cusp of 3rd, 6th, or 8th H., and affl. the hyleg; lord of the 8th in ♊, and affl. the hyleg at B., and by dir.

**Dilatation**—Of the Bronchial Tubes—Bronchiectasis—Afflictions to ♃ and ♀, causing disturbances in the circulation; ♄ or ♂ in ♊ in ☌ or ill-asp. ♃ or ♀; Subs at AP. (See Dilatations).

**Dyspnoea; Hay Fever**—Hay Asthma—(See Asthma, Nose).

**Hemorrhage**—Broncho-Pulmonary Hemorrhage—♄ or ♂ affl. in ♊; Subs at AP., 1st Dorsal, and at Lu.P. (See Hemorrhage under Lungs).

**Inflammation**—Of Tubes—(See "Bronchitis" in this section. Also see "Inflammation" under Lungs).

**Lungs; Mucous; Obstructions**—Bronchial—♊ ascending at a Solar Ingress into ♈, and with ☿ afflicted, Countries and People under ♊ suffer thru corrupt air, by high winds, and by obstructions of the lungs and bronchial tubes; ♄ affl. in ♊, and espec. when in the 3rd or 6th H.; Subs at LCP, 6th Cervical, at AP and SP. (See Chest, Lungs, Obstructions, Phlegm, Pneumonia).

**Phlegm; Phthisis; Pleura;**

**Pneumonia** — Broncho - Pneumonia — The ☽ hyleg in ♊ or ♋, and affl. by ♄ or ♂; the hyleg afflicted at B., and with malefics in ♊ or the 3rd H.; Subs at LCP, the 6th Cervical, at AP and Lu.P. (See Pneumonia).

**Respiration**—Difficult Bronchial Respiration—Breathing Difficult—♄ affl. in ♊; ♄ ☌ ♃ or ♀ in ♊. (See "Labored" under Breathing).

**Tuberculosis; Tubes**—Dilatation of the Bronchial Tubes—(See "Dilatation" in this section).

**Upper Bronchi**—Superior Bronchi—Disorders In—Afflictions in ♋ and the first degrees of ♊; Subs at LCP., AP., HP.

**Winds**—Bronchitis-Producing Easterly Winds—♄ rising in the Asc., or lord of the year at the Vernal Equinox. (See Air, Epidemics, Wind).

**BRONCHOCELE**—(See Goitre).

**BROODING**—Introspection—Moodiness Moods—Melancholy—The ☉ in ♑ and affl. by ♄; the ☉ hyleg, and to the ☌ or ill-asps. ♄ by dir.; due to ♄ and ♆ afflictions; ♄ prog. to the ☌ or ill-asps. ☿, or vice versa; ♄ to the ill-asps. his own place by dir., or transit; ♄ Sig. □ or ☍ the ☽; ♄ in the Asc., 3rd or 9th H., and affl. ☿; ♂ affl. in ♍. (See Anguish, Anxiety, Dejection, Depression, Despondency, Fears, Gloom, Introspection, Melancholy, Retrospective, Worry, etc.).

**Imaginary Diseases**—Imaginary Troubles—Brooding Over—♄ to the ill-asps. his own place by dir., or tr.; ♂ affl. in ♍; ☿ in the 6th H., and affl. by ♅, ♄, or ♂. (See Hypochondria, Imaginary).

**BROTHERS**—Much that is said here will also apply to sisters. Our brothers and sisters are shown and ruled by the 3rd H., and our relations to them, whether for good or ill. Their sicknesses are also largely denoted by the conditions over the ♊ sign in your map or birth.

**Brothers Indicated**—Stars masculinely constituted indicate brothers. The place of brethren (brothers or sisters) in the native's map is taken from the sign on the cusp the 10th or 11th H., and the maternal places, which are the position of ♀ by day, and the ☽ by night. This refers only to children of the same mother. The signs on the 10th and 11th being maternal, are indicative of the mother and her children, and the same places may, therefore, be allotted to brothers and sisters. (See "Births" under Male. Also see Son).

**Death of a Brother**—An eclipse falling on the radical place of ♂ in the map. Should a hostile configuration be in the Asc., and ♂ there also, or ♂ in any angle, and espec. when in the 10th, then ♂ will tend to destroy or diminish the total number of brothers or sisters. (See Eclipse. Also see "Few", "Fratricide", in this section).

**Delicate Constitution**—The malefics elevated above those which promise, or give brethren; lord of the 8th in the 3rd H., and a malefic and afflicted. (See "Short-lived", "Sickness", under Brethren).

**Elder-Born Brethren**—(See Brethren).

**Few Brothers**—Or Sisters—Few Brethren—The malefics having superiority in power or numbers in the 10th, 11th, or 4th H., and espec. if the ☉ be surrounded by malefics; malefics configurated to the 10th or 11th H., or to the ☽ or ♀, or if they surround the ☉, the number is decreased; both ♄ or ♂ in the 1st or 7th show few brothers or sisters, or their early death, and also the lord of the 10th affl. in the 3rd.

**First-born Brother**—Death or Sickness of—♄ represents the first-born brother, and should the hostile configuration be from the Asc., would tend to his death, or a lingering illness.

(See "Elder-Born" under Brethren. Also see "Near Relatives" under Relations).

**Fratricide**—♂ affl. in ♊ or the 3rd H.

**Health Poor**—Lord of the 6th H. in the 3rd, and afflicted. (See "Near Relatives" under Relations. Also see Sixth House, Third House).

**Hurts**—Accidents or Injuries To—Malefics in the 3rd H. of the native, and afflicted; lords of the 6th, 8th, or 12th H. in the 3rd, and afflicted; lord of the 3rd H. a malefic, and afflicted, and espec. if ♄ or ♂.

**Length of Life**—(See the various paragraphs in this section).

**Long Life**—A benefic in the 3rd, or lord of the 3rd H., well-aspected, and with no malefics in the 3rd; the benefics elevated above the lord of the 3rd H., and in favorable aspect.

**Possibility**—Of Brothers and Sisters—(See "Several" in this section).

**Several Brothers**—The benefics favorably configurated with the 10th or 11th H., or in these houses.

**Short-Lived**—(See "Death of", "Delicate", "Health Poor", in this section).

**Sickness Of**—(See the various paragraphs in this section. Also see "Sickness" under Brethren).

**Younger Brethren**—(See Brethren). For other study, see Daughters, "Birth of a Female" under Female; Family, Relatives, Sisters, etc.).

**BROW**—(See Forehead).

**Eye-Brows**—(See Eye-Brows).

**BROWN**—The Color Brown—Ruled by ♏, and espec. Dark Brown. ♑ rules black, and dark brown. Brown is also ruled by the 7th H.

**Complexion**—Brown Complexion—Brown Skin—☿ ascending at B., and free from the rays of other planets; ☿ ori. at B.; ☿ in ♈ or ♑; ♄ indicates one of an earthy, brown, swarthy, dark, or dusky complexion; ♃ gives when rising and well-aspected; ♀ in ♏; ♈, ♏, and ♑ give. (See Olive, Sunburnt, Tan, under Complexion).

**Eyes**—Brown Eyes—(See "Brown" under Eyes).

**Hair**—Brown Hair—(See "Brown" under Hair).

**Skin**—(See "Complexion" in this section).

**BRUISES**—Contusions—Concussions—The subject of Bruises is largely considered under the subjects of Blows, and Falls.

**Accidents By**—Hurts and Injuries By—Liable To—♄ causes hurts and injuries by bruises, blows and falls; ♄ ascending at B.; ♄ rising or setting at B.; ♄ by transit in ☌ or ill-asp. the ☉, ☽, ♃, or ♀ in the radix; ♄ in ♈, ♌, or ♐, ☌ or ill-asp. the Asc. by dir.; ♄ affl. the ☉ at B., and by dir.; ♄ rising, and affl. the ☉ or ☽ at B.; ♄ ruler of the 4th or 8th H., and to the ill-asps. of ♂; ♄ ☌ ♂ in ♑; the ☉ affl. in ♑; the ☉ and ☽ ori., and affl. by ♄ or ♂; the ☉ directed to the Cratch (Praesepe) in the 6° ♌; ♅ to the ill-asps. his place at B.; ♂ in the 1st H., and affl. by ♅ or ♄; ♂ or ♄ in ♑, and affl. the ☉, ☽, or Asc.; ♑ on the Asc.; the Asc. to the ☌ or ill-asp. ♄ by dir. (See Blows, Concussion, Falls).

**Animals**—Bruises by Large Animals—♄ in the 12th H. (See Animals).

**Blindness**—By Bruises—(See "Bruises" under Blindness).

**Blows**—Bruises By—(See Blows).

**Breasts**—Bruises To—(See "Bruises" under Breast).

**Death by Bruises**—♄ and ♂ denote death by; ♄ rising or setting at B., and affl. the hyleg; ♄ ☌ or evil asp. the Asc. when ♄ is not ruler of the Asc.; the ☉ or ☽ ori., and affl. by ♄ and ♂; ♂ in the 10th H., and □ the Asc., and the ☉ also afflicted. (See "Death" under Blows, Falls).

**Falls**—Bruises By—(See Falls, Fractures, Heights).

**Head**—Bruises To—(See "Bruises" under Head).

**Hips**—Thighs—Bruises To—(See Hips).

**Large Animals**—Bruises and Hurts By—(See "Large Animals" under Animals).

**Legs**—Bruises To—(See Legs).

**Liable to Bruises**—Predisposition To—(See "Accidents" in this section).

**Thighs**—Bruises To—(See "Bruises" under Hips).

**BRUNETTES**—(See "Dark" under Complexion; "Black" and "Dark" under Hair).

**BRUTISH**—Cruel—Unfeeling.

**Brutish Signs**—♌ and the 2nd half of ♐, and those born under them are said to be brutish, savage, and inhuman; ♌ or the 2nd half of ♐ on the Asc. at B., or the ☉ or ☽ in either of them, and the malefics in angles, render the native fierce, cruel and brutish. (See Cruel, "Human Signs" under Human; Madness).

**BRYONIA**—Bryonia Alba—One of the typical Polycrest Remedies corresponding to the ♊ sign. Also a typical drug of ♂. (See Resolvent; "Polycrest" under Zodiac).

**BUBO**—Bubo Inguinal Tumor—A Swelling in the lymphatic gland of the Groin—A ♏ disease, and by reflex action affecting the Parotid Gland ruled by ♉; caused by Subs at PP, the 2, 3, 4 Lumbars, and also at KP. (See Gonorrhea, Groins).

**Bubo Plague**—Bubonic Plague—Afflictions in ♏; a ♏ disease; ♄ ☌ ♃ in the first 6 deg. of the ♈ sign; a ♂ disease and caused by ♂ afflictions; the ☉ affl. in ♌; eclipses of the ☉ or ☽ tend to, and in Nations ruled by the Sign in which they occur. No Plague from an eclipse can affect the whole earth, nor endure more than 4 months or 4 years, according to the nature and duration of the eclipse. Caused by Subs at CP, KP, LPP. (See Eclipse, Plague).

**BUDDING**—Reproduction By—(See Gemmation).

**BUILD**—Of the Body—(See Appearance, Body, Corpulent, Defects, Deformities, Fat, Form, Good, "Ill-Formed" under Ill; "Muscular" under Muscles; Shape, Short, Stature, Strong, Tall, Thin, Weak, etc.).

**Building of the Body**—The body is built along the lines of its Astral Double, and each of the planets have their part in the work, according to the parts they rule. Thus ♄ builds the bones, framework, skeleton, etc. (See Blood, Bones, Cells, Processes, Tissues, etc. See the influence of each of the planets, and also of the Signs of the Zodiac). A good description of the building of the body, from an Occult standpoint, and its evolution from the earliest stages of Humanity on this planet, can be gotten from the various books on Rosicrucianism, Theosophy.

**BUILDINGS**—Houses—Death or Injury by Falls from Buildings, or by the Fall of Buildings—(See Crushed, "Earthquakes" under Earth; "Buildings" under Falls; Incendiarism).

**BULBAR PARALYSIS**—(See Medulla).

**BULKY BODY**—♃ in the Asc. tends to give bulk to the body. (See Corpulent, Fat, Fleshy, Lumpish, Stoutness, etc.).

**Bulky Organs**—Enlarged—Over-developed—(See Enlargements).

**BULLA**—(See Blisters).

**BULLS**—Oxen—Large Cattle—

**Attacks By**—(See Animals, Cattle, Quadrupeds).

**Bull Fighter**—Killed in Bull Fighting—Case—See "Bull Fighter", No. 063 in 1001 N.N.

**Bull's Eyes**—Bull's South Eye—(See Oculus Taurus).

**Bull's North Eye**—(See Aldebaran, "Death by Fire" under Fire; "Good Health" under Health; Pestilence).

**Bull's Horns**—Bull's North Horn—Bull's South Horn—Situated in ♊, and of the nature of ♂. The Bull's N. Horn, when crossing the Asc. of ruling signs of a Country or City, tends to great fires, calamity, and loss of life. This was the case in London in the year 1866, the year of the Great Fire, when this star was passing thru ♊, the Asc. of the City of London. (See Lilly's Astrology, page 5). For the various influences of the Bull's Horns, see Ambushes; "Pains" under Arms; Blotches, Fury, Inflammation, Intoxication, Rashness; "Strangury" under Urine; Violent.

**BUNIONS**—Corns—A ♓ disorder, and afflictions in ♓; ♅, ♄, ♂, ♀, or ☿ affl. in ♓; ♀ ♓ in 6th H., and afflicted; ♀ ♓, and affl. the ☉ or ☽; the ☽ hyleg in a female nativity, and afflicted. (See Crusts; "Skin" under Hardening; Scales).

**BUOYANT**—Vivacious—Hopeful—Cheerful—Full of Life and Activity—♃ influence; ♃ rising in the Asc. or M.C., well-aspected and dignified, and also the ☉ and ♂ in strong positions at B.; fiery signs upon the Asc. at B., and many planets in these signs; cardinal signs on the angles at B.; the majority of the planets at B. rising and elevated in positive signs of the Zodiac. (See "Active Body", "Active Mind", under Active; Cheerfulness; "Abundance of" under Energy; "Excess of" under Force; Hope, Joy, Mirth, Optimism, Positive Nature, Power; "Strong Will" under Will, etc.).

**BURGLARS**—Injury or Death By—(See Highwaymen, Robbers, Thieves).

**BURIAL**—

**Buried Alive**—Danger of Premature Burial—♆ in 8th H., and due to Trance conditions simulating death; ♄ causes death, being buried alive, as by landslides, fall of buildings, etc. (See Avalanches; "Fall of Buildings" under Buildings; Crushed, Trance, etc.).

**No Burial**—The Body Not Interred—No Church or Regular Burial—Several malefics ruling the Anaretic places, or occupying them; ♅, ♄, or ♂ claiming prerogative in the Anaretic Places, and with no assistance from the benefics to the 4th H., or to the Anaretic Places.

**Body Devoured**—The body may be devoured by beasts or birds after death if the malefics are in signs assigned to beasts and birds, and also when the benefics offer no assistance to the Anaretic Places, or to the 4th H., the house which rules the end of life. (See "Birds of Air" under Air; Vultures).

**Buried Under the Earth**—♅ or ♄ in ♈, ♋, ♎, or ♑, in the 4th H., and in ☌, □, or ☍ the ☉ or ♂; ♄ in ☍, ♍, or ♑, ☌, □, or ☍ the Asc. by dir., and ♄ holding the dominion of death, danger of being buried alive under the earth, as by Cave-ins, Avalanches, Landslides, etc. (See "Buried Alive" in this section).

**BURNS**—Burning—Searing—Scalds, etc.—Burns are caused by the ☉ and ♂, the positive, electric, and heat-producing planets. The following subjects are connected with Burns, Burning, Fire, Injuries or Disorders from Intense Heat within or without the body; Scalds, Hot Liquids or Metals, Searing, etc., which see in the alphabetical arrangement when not considered here—

**Accidents by Burns**—(See "Danger", and the various paragraphs in this section).

**Arms**—Burns To—The ☉ or ♂ affl. in ♊, and signs which rule the arms. (See "Burns" under Arms).

**Blindness By**—(See "Burning" under Blindness).

**Burned Alive**—Danger of—The ☉ directed to the Ascelli; the ☽ Sig. ☌ ☉ or ♂; ♂ in fiery signs and ☌ the Asc. by dir.

**Burned at Stake**—(See "Stake" in this section).

**Danger of Burns**—Liable to Burns—Subject To—Accidents By—The ☉ or ☽ hyleg, and to the ☌ or ill-asps. ♂ by dir.; the progressed ☉ or ☽ to the ☌ or ill-asps. ♂; the ☽ ☌ ♂ in the M.C., and evilly aspected by Antares; the ☽ Sig. ☌ the ☉, subject to burns and scalds; ☽ Sig. □ or ☍ ☉, and espec. if ♂ aspect the ☉; caused by ♂ afflictions; ♂ affl. in ♈, ♌, or ♐, the fiery signs; ♂ affl. in the 6th H., and espec. in a cardinal or fiery sign; ♂ affl. in the 4th H., and espec. in a fiery sign, burns due to fire in the home; ♂ affl. in the Asc. or M.C.; ♂ □ or ☍ the ☉ at B., and by dir.; ☿ Sig. ☌ the ☉ and the ☉ ill-dignified; ♈ on the Asc.; fiery signs in the Asc. or 6th H., or the ☽ in a fiery sign at B., threatens burns under the evil directions of ♂ to the ☽, or ♂ in or to the Asc. or 6th H. (See "Danger" under Fire. Also note the various paragraphs in this section).

**Death by Burns**—Burned to Death—Death by Burning or Searing—The ☽ affl. by ♂, and ♂ descending, and if ♂ also be configurated with ☿, it happens from an accident in sports, or by robbers; the ☽ hyleg, and to the ☌ or ill-asp. ♂ by dir.; ♂ in ♉ near Caput Algol, or in ♏ in ☍, and in □ or ☍ to the ☉ or ☽; ♂ ori. at B., and affl. the hyleg by dir., and espec. if ♂ be in a violent sign; ♂ in ♉ or ♏, and affl. the hyleg; ♂ afflicting from fiery signs. Cases—See "Burned to Death", No. 687, and No. 889, in 1001 N.N. (See "Burned Alive" and "Searing" in this section. Also see "Death" under Fire, Scalds; "Hot Liquids" under Heat).

**Electricity; Explosions; Eyes**—Injury to by Burns—(See "Burning" under Blindness; "Accidents" under Eyes).

**Face**—Burns To—♂ affl. in ♈, and espec. in the Asc. Case—Left Side of Face and Neck severely burned—See "Extraordinary Accident", No. 192 in 1001 N.N. (See "Searing" in this section).

**Father**—Burns To—(See "Burns" under Father).

**Fevers**—High, Burning Fevers—(See "High Fevers" under Fever).

**Fire**—Danger or Death By—(See Fire. Also see the various paragraphs in this section).

**Gun Powder Burns**—(See Gunshot).

**Home**—Burns in the Home—Danger of—♂ affl. in the 4th H. in a fiery sign. (See "Fire" under Home).

**Injuries by Burns**—(See "Danger", and the various paragraphs in this section).

**Journeys**—Travel—Voyages—Burns on Journeys or in Travel—Malefics, and espec. ♂, in the 3rd or 9th H., and afflicting the ☉ or ☽ in fiery signs.

**Liable to Burns**—(See "Danger" in this section).

**Lightning; Liquids**—Burns or Death by Hot Liquids—(See "Hot Liquids" under Heat. Also see Scalds).

**Mother**—Burns To—Death By—(See "Burns" under Mother).

**Neck**—Burns To—(See "Face" in this section).

**Pains**—Burning Pains in the Stomach —(See Belching).

**Powder Burns**—(See Gunshot).

**Robbers**—Burned By—(See "Death" in this section).

**Scalds; Searing**—Injury or Death By —♂ in ♉ near Caput Algol, or in ♏ in ☍ aspect, and in □ or ☍ the ☉ or ☽. (See "Burning" under Eyes).

**Sensations**—Burning Sensations—(See Belching, "Heartburn" under Heart; Paraesthesia, Sensations, etc.).

**Sports**—Burned During—(See "Death" in this section).

**Stake**—Burned at the Stake—Case—See "Savonarola", No. 459, in 1001 N.N.

**Stomach**—Burning Pains At—(See Belching).

**Travel**—Burns During—(See "Journeys" in this section).

**Voyages**—Burned During—(See "Journeys" in this section).

**Water**—Burns by Hot Water—(See "Hot Liquids" under Heat. Also see Scalds).

**BURSA**—A small sac between movable parts.

**Bursitis**—In the Knee—♀ affl. in ♑. (See Joints, Synovial).

**BURSTING**—Rending—Tearing—Rupture—Laceration, etc.—

**Blood Vessels**—Bursting of—(See Apoplexy, Cerebral, Hemorrhage, "Blood Vessels" under Vessels).

**Parts**—Bursting and Rending of—(See Hernia, Lacerations, Rupture).

**BUSHY**—(See "Bushy" under Eyebrows, Hair; "Curly" under Hair).

**BUSINESS**—The Trade or Employment—

**Death In**—Accident, Injury or Illness In—(See Cares, Employment, Explosions, Machinery, Occupation, Partner, Ruin, Vocation).

**BUTCHERS**—♂ strong at B., or the ruling planet, tends to make good Butchers, Cutters and Surgeons; the ☉, ☽, or ♂ well-asp. in ♏; ♂ in the Asc. or M.C. in ♏. The ♏ influence should predominate at B. to make good Surgeons, Cutters, or Butchers. (See Surgeons).

**BUTTOCKS**—Nates—Gluteal Region—Rump—Haunches—Ruled by ♎ and the 7th H., and the parts adjoining the Hips, included in the Haunches, are ruled and influenced by ♐.

**Boils On**—(See "Buttocks" under Boils).

**Diseases In**—Afflictions in ♎ and ♐.

**Fistulous Tumors**—A ♐ disease, and afflictions in ♐.

**Heats In**—Humours In—A ♎ disease, and afflictions in ♎; ♂ affl. in ♎ or ♐.

**Hurts To**—Accidents or Wounds To—Afflictions in ♐; ♄ or ♂ affl. in ♐. (See Haunches, Hips, Ilium, Loins).

**BUZZARDS**—Vultures—Fowls of the Air—The Body Devoured By After Death—No Burial—(See "Birds of the Air' 'under Air; "Body Devoured" under Burial; Fowls; "Vultures Eat the Body" under Vultures).

**BUZZING**—

**Buzzing Noises**—In Ears—(See "Buzzing" under Ears).

**Buzzing Sensations**—As in the Spine or Nerves—Usually caused by pressure upon the nerves, or sublaxations of vertebrae, and should be studied locally, and the planetary afflictions noted in the sign ruling the afflicted part. (See Paraesthesia).

**Droning**—Buzzing—(See Humming).

# C

**CACHEXIA**—A Depraved condition of Nutrition—(See Anaemia, Anticachectic, Assimilation, Emaciation, Nutrition, Pale, Sickly, Unhealthy; "Vitality Low" under Vitality; Wasting, Weak, etc.).

**CADAVEROUS**—Pale, Corpse-like, Unhealthy—(See Pale, Unhealthy, White).

**CADENT HOUSES**—As the 3rd, 6th, 9th and 12th H., and correspond to the Mutable Signs. These houses are identified with disease, and tend to give a weak constitution, and espec. when occupied by the ☉, ☽, and many planets at B. The 6th and 12th houses are the more evil of the cadent houses. The 6th H. is more noted for acute diseases, and the 12th H. denotes lingering and chronic diseases. (See Houses, Mutable).

**CAECUM**—Ruled by ♏.

**Inflammation Of**—Typhlitis—Perityphlitis—♂ affl. in ♏. Caused by Subs at PP, the 2nd and 3rd Lumbars. (See Appendix).

**Ileo-Caecal Valve**—(See Ileum).

**CAESARIAN OPERATION**—(See "Excision" under Foetus).

**CAISSON DISEASE**—Symptoms from working under increased air pressure—Compressed Air and Gases are ruled by ♅, which planet strongly rules over the ♒ sign. An ♒ disease; the ☉ affl. in ♒. (See Air, Compressed, Ether, Gases, Pressure).

**CALAMITY**—Catastrophies—Disaster—Misfortune—Tragedies, etc.—

**Great Calamities**—Are heralded by the appearance of Comets, and espec. to People, Individuals, and Countries ruled by the sign thru which the Comet is seen to pass. Great Calamities to the individual, as disgrace, ruin, scandal, breakdown in health, etc., are indicated when one has eminent fixed stars of the nature of ♄ in the angles at B., and with the ☉, or afflicting the angles or the ☉ by dir.; also caused by ♄ afflicting his own place at B. by tr. or dir., or ♄ passing the place of the ☉, Asc., M.C., or hyleg, or severely afflicting these places. ♄ is considered the planet of Calamity to those who are not living right, as he is the Tester, the Chastener, the Judge, to mete out justice, and to punish and correct the evils in the life of the native. (See Comets, Events, Disgrace, Misfortune, Ruin, Trouble, Sorrow).

**Impending Calamity**—Fear of—The ☉ or ☽ to the ☌ or ill-asp. ♄ by dir.; the ☽ to the ☌ or ill-asp. ♂ by dir., and espec. if ♂ afflict the ☽ at B.; the Prog. ☽ to the ☌ or ill-asp. ♄ or ♂ by dir.; ♆ afflicted at B.; ♆ □ or ☍ ♅ at B., and by dir.; ♅ affl. in ♓ or the 12th H. at B., or by dir.; ♄ affl. the ☉ or ☽ at B., and ♄ to the ☌ or ill-asps. the Lights by dir.; the transit of ♄ over the place of the ☉ at B., and espec. if ♄ afflict the ☉ at B., and have no dignity in the sign of transit. (See Anxiety, Fear, Obsessions).

**Many Calamities**—The ☉ to the ☌ or ill-asp. ♄, ♂, or the malefics by dir.; the ☉ Sig., and to the ☌ or ill-asp. ♄ by dir.; the ☉ to the ill-asps. ♅ by dir.; the ☉ ☌, or to the place of Aldebaran, Antares, the Ascelli, Arcturus, Cor Hydra, Fomahaut, Hircus, Markab, Pleiades, or Regulus, and espec. when culminating, tend first to great honors, to be followed by the greatest calamities; the ☽ sepr. from ♄ and applying to the ☉ at B., or by dir.; the ☽ with Antares or Aldebaran in the 1st or 10th H.; the ☽ to the place of Hercules; ♄ to his own ill-asps. by dir.; the M.C. to the place of Algenib, Antares, Bellatrix, Betelgeuse, Procyon, or any star of the nature of ♂ and ☿; Praesepe rising with the ☉ or ☽, and espec. in ☌ in an angle, causes every calamity upon the native. (See Evils, Reverses, Ruin, etc.).

**Moment of Birth**—Calamity From—Malefics with the ☉ or ☽ at B., and affl. the hyleg. This is espec. true of Excrescences, Distortions, Lameness or Paralysis. (See these subjects. Also see "Moment of Birth" under Birth).

**Sea**—Calamities at Sea—(See Maritime, Navigation, Ocean, Sea, Ships, Shipwreck, Waters).

**Serious Calamities**—Or Disasters—Danger of—Lord of the 6th in the 10th H., and afflicted, meets with many downfalls, or serious disasters in life, and espec. if lord of the 6th is a malefic. (See Disasters).

**Strange Calamities**—Or Catastrophies—Subject To—♆ or ♅ in the Asc. or M.C. at B., and affl. the ☉, ☽, or hyleg at B., or by dir.; ♀ Sig. in ♑. (See Extraordinary, Mysterious, Peculiar).

**Sudden Calamity**—The ☉ to the ☌ or ill-asps. ♅ by dir. (See Sudden).

**Threatened**—Calamity or Disaster Threatened—♆ in tr. over the place of ♄ at B.; a total eclipse of the ☉ falling on the place of the ☉ at B. (See Disaster).

**Travel**—Calamities During—(See Journeys, Maritime, Navigation, Railroads, Sea, Ships, Travel, Vehicles, Voyages).

**Violent Calamities**—Death by Violent Catastrophies—☉ to the ☌ ♂ by dir., and ♂ affl. the ☉ at B.; ☉ joined with the Ascelli at B., or by dir. (See Violent).

**Wind**—Calamities By—(See Wind). For collateral study see Affliction, Anguish, Anxiety, Assassination, Catastrophies, Death, Desert, Disaster, Disgrace, Dishonor, Earthquakes, Enemies, Execution, Floods, Famine, Highwaymen, Misfortune, Pirates, Prison, Reputation, Reversals, Ruin, Sickness, Sorrow, Suicide, Sudden, Storms, Thieves, Trouble, Untimely, Volcanoes, etc.

**CALCES**—Calx—Calcium—(See Chalk, Lime). Coral is a form of Calcium, or Lime. (See Coral).

**CALCULATOR**—Lightning Calculator—(See Prodigies).

**CALCULUS**—Stone-like Concretions in the Body—Lithiasis—(See "Gall Stones" under Bile; Concretions, Deposits, Gravel, Minerals, Sand, Stone).

**CALLOUS**—Hard—Indurated—(See Hard).

**CALM**—When a patient is nervous, excitable, and of an angry disposition, he can be more easily calmed in a ♄ hour. (See "Hours" under Planets).

Spiritual Calm—Lack of—(See Spiritual).

**CALOMEL**—A typical drug of ☿. (See Mercury).

**CALORIC**—(See Fever, Heat, Temperature).

**CALVES**—Fleshy part of the leg below the knee. Are under the external rule of ♒. Also ruled by ♄ and the 11th H.

Diseases Of—Afflictions in ♒ or the 11th H.

Hurts To—Accidents or Injuries To—♄ or ♂ afflicted in ♒ or the 11th H.; ♒ on the Asc., and afflicted.

Stiffness Of—♄ affl. in ♒. Subs at PP and LPP tend to the various disorders of the Calves. (See Ankles, Fibula, "Dropsy" under Legs; Tibia, Varicose).

**CALX**—(See Chalk, Lime).

**CAMELS**—Sickness or Death of—(See Cattle).

**CAMP FEVER**—(See Typhus).

**CANALS**—(See Alimentary, "Inguinal Canal" under Groins; "Intestinal Canal" under Bowels; Lachrymal Canal (see Tears); Sinus; Spinal Canal (see Spine); Tubes, etc.).

**CANCER DISEASE**—(See Carcinoma).

**CANCER SIGN**—The 4th sign of the Zodiac, the only sign of the ☽, and affiliated with the 4th H. The Symbol of this sign is the Crab. The ☉ enters ♋ at the Summer Solstice. This sign is classed as a cardinal, cold, commanding, crooked, destructful, feminine, fruitful, moist, mute, negative, phlegmatic, psychic, sensitive, unfortunate, tropical, watery, weak, sign. It is the home sign of the ☽, the exaltation of ♃, and the fall of ♂. It is considered the weakest sign of the Zodiac, along with ♓, for vitality, and espec. when upon the eastern horizon at B., and afflicted, and with the ☉, ☽, or hyleg afflicted with. This sign is considered weak owing to its receptivity to outside influences, and afflictions in ♋ tend to quickly affect the mind and the digestive organs. The ☉ well-aspected in the ♋ sign at B., and rising and elevated, tends to strengthen the constitution, to augment the recuperative powers, give better health, etc., as the ☉ in any sign tends to bring more vital force and power to that sign. The ☉ affl. in ♋ tends to a weakened constitution, and lowered vitality. The ☽ well-aspected in ♋ is strong, and tends to regular functions and good health. Ipecac, an emetic, is classed as the typical Polycrest Remedy corresponding to the ♋ sign.

Cloudy Spot of Cancer—(See Cloudy).

**CANCER RULES**—Externally ♋ rules the Breast, Epigastric Region, and the Elbow. Internally, ♋ rules the Stomach, Digestive Organs, and the Womb. Structurally, ♋ rules the Ribs, Sternum, Elbow Joint. In general ♋ is said to rule Albumen, the Axillae, the Bladder as a receptacle; Blood (Serum of); Brain Coverings; Breastbone (Sternum); Breasts (Mammae); Chymification; Color—Green or Russet; Diaphragm; Digestion, which is a function of the ♋ sign; the Digestive Organs and System; Duct (Thoracic); Elbow Joint and Elbow; Epigastric Region; Ganglia (Semilunar); Green Color; Ipecac; Lacteals; Liver (Upper Lobe); Lung (lower lobe of left lung, and the two lower lobes of right lung); Mammae; Milk; Oesophagus; Pancreas; Pleura and Pleural Cavity; Ribs; Russet Color; Serum (of Blood), Sternum; Stomach, and the Peristaltic action of; Thoracic Duct; Womb. (See these subjects in the alphabetical arrangement).

**CANCER DISEASES**—And Afflictions—The special pathological quality of ♋ is lowered vitality. See the following subjects in the alphabetical arrangement—

Abscesses; Appetite Bad—(See "Bad", "Delicate", "Loss of" under Appetite).

Asthma; Blood—Spitting of—(See Haemoptysis).

Breath—Short Breath—(See "Labored", "Shallow", under Breath).

Cancers—(See Carcinoma).

Catarrh—Of the System—(See Catarrh).

Constitution Weak—(See "Vitality Low" under Vitality; "Weak Body" under Weak. Also see Constitution, Resistance, Recuperation).

Consumptions; Coughs; Diaphragm—Disorders of—(See Diaphragm).

Dipsomania; Dropsy; Flatulence;

Gastric Catarrh—(See "Stomach" under Catarrh).

Haemoptysis; Hiccough;

Imposthumes—(See Abscesses).

Indigestion; Inflamed Lungs—(See "Pulmonitis" under Lungs).

Lungs—Inflamed—Ulcerated—(See "Pulmonitis", "Ulceration", under Lungs).

Sclerosis; Stomach—Disorders of—(See Digestion, Gastric, Indigestion, Stomach, Vomiting).

Vitality Low—(See Vitality).

Weak Constitution—(See Constitution, Recuperation, Resistance, Sickly, Vitality, Weak).

**CANDY**—Misuse of—(See Sugar).

**CANCRUM ORIS**—Gangrene of the Mouth—(See Gangrene).

**CANIS MAJORIS**—☽ to the place of tends to bring pleasure and good health.

**CANKER**—(See Aphthae, Carcinoma, Gangrene, Sores).

**CANNABIS INDICA**—Canabis Sativa—Indian Hemp—A typical plant and drug ruled by ♄.

**CANNIBALS**—Savages—Attacks, Injuries or Death by During Travel—The afflictor to the Sig. of Travel being in the 12th H., and in ♊ or ♍, and espec. if ♂ or ☿ be the afflictor. (See Savage, Travel).

**CANTHARIDES**—A typical drug of ♂, and a strong vesicant. (See Aphrodisiac, Rubefacient, Sinapis, Vesicant).

**CAPELLA**—A Fixed Star in 4th face of ♊, of nature of ♂ and ☿. (See Auriga, Blows, Hircus, Stabs, Vices).

**CAPILLARIES**—Minute Blood Vessels—Tubules—Are ruled by, and associated with the ♊ sign in particular, and also connected with all the airy signs. The influence of ♄ (cold) tends to contract them, driving the blood inward, and causing congestions, colds, etc. The ♂ influence (heat) tends to dilate them, and make the surface circulation in them more free. Morbid dilatation of the capillaries, however, is a ♄ influence, due to deposits, wasting, and a weakened condition of the walls of the vessels. Capillary obstructions are caused by ♄ afflictions, and by the afflictions of ♄ to ♃ and ♀, rulers of the blood and circulation. For various conditions affecting the capillaries, see Acne, Centrifugal, Centripetal, Circulation, Congestion, Constrictions, Dilatation, Erythema, "Red Face" under Face; Lungs, Nose, Obstructions, Oxygen, Veins; "Blood Vessels" under Vessels.

**CAPRICORN**—The Goat—Capricornus—The 10th sign of the Zodiac, and affiliated with the 10th H. The ☉ enters ♑ at the time of the Winter Solstice. The night sign of ♄; the exaltation of ♂; the fall of ♃, and the detriment of the ☽. Is a cardinal, changeable, cold, crooked, domestic, earthy, egotistical, feminine, four-footed, hoarse, hurtful, melancholic, moveable, negative, nocturnal, obeying, southern, tropical, unfortunate, violent, winter sign. Is a rather weak sign as regards vitality, and espec. when upon the eastern horizon at B. However, the ♑ people do not yield readily to disease, but when once sick and diseased they become despondent and melancholic, hold onto it, and often become hypochondriacs. This sign is not strong in vitality during the early years of life, and espec. from birth to the 7th birthday, and there is much infant mortality among those born with the ☉, ☽, and other planets in ♑, and afflicted, or with ♑ upon the Asc. at B. In adult life the diseases produced by ♑ tend to become chronic, being under ♄ rule. It does not contribute much to the beauty of the human form, and espec. when rising, and often tends to ugliness, crookedness of body, deformities, and a thin, angular, awkward and ungainly physique. The ☉ is weak in ♑, but tends to longevity. The ☽ is weak in this sign, in which she is in detriment and debility, and when afflicted in this sign tends to impeded, uncertain and irregular functions, and lowered vitality, due to mental depression, worry, and anxiety. It is a strong business sign, and the ♑ people are usually full of business, promotion, and many of their diseases result from business anxieties, cares, or losses. The accidents of ♑ are broken limbs, bruises, falls, sprains, dislocations, and hurts to the knees and lower limbs. The Symbol of this sign is the Goat. The pathological qualities of ♑ are crystallization, deliberation, dryness, and limitation. Sulphur is a typical remedy of ♑. For an illustration, and birth data, of a person born with 6 planets in ♑ in the 3rd H., see "Pasteur", No. 950, in 1001 N.N.

**CAPRICORN RULES**—Barrenness, Black, Bones, Brown (Swarthy or Dark Brown, and Dark Gray); Cold, Connective Tissue, Cutaneous System, Cuticle, Dryness, Epidermis, Epithelial Tissue, Goats, Hams, Hair of Pubes, Joints, Knees, Knee Cap, Legs, Limitations, Mineral Deposits in the System, Mucous Surfaces (the outer); Nations (see ♑ under Nations); Nucleolation, Patella, Peripheral Nerves (the Sympathetic Peripheral); Pubes and Pili; Resources (the husbanding of the material resources); Restraints, Russet Color, Servitude, Skin (the outer skin, cuticle, or epidermis); Sterility (♄, ruler of ♑ tends to deny or destroy children); Stomach (by reflex action to ♋ from ♑); Sulphur; Swarthy Brown; Sympathetic Nerves (the Peripheral). Externally ♑ rules the Knees and Epidermis. Structurally ♑ rules the Patella, and the bones of the Knee Joint.

**CAPRICORN DISEASES**—And Afflictions—See the following subjects in the alphabetical arrangement when not considered here—The ☉, ☽, planets, and afflictions in or to ♑, or ♑ upon the Asc., the 6th or 12th H., and containing malefics, or otherwise afflicted, tend to produce the following diseases and afflictions—

**Accidents**—The Accidents of ♑—(See the Introduction to this Article).

**Animals**—Hurts By—(See "Hurts" under Animals).

**Antiperistalsis**—Of the Stomach—(See Vomiting).

**Articular Rheumatism**—(See Joints, Rheumatism).

**Anxiety; Bones**—Diseases of—Broken Bones—(See Bones, Femur, Fractures, Knees, Legs, Limbs).

**Bruises; Chest Disorders**—(See Breast, Chest, Lungs).

**Chronic Diseases**—(See Chronic).

**Cold**—All Diseases Arising From—(See Cold).

**Conjunctivitis; Criminal Tendencies**—(See Crime).

**Cutaneous Complaints**—Eruptions—(See Eruptions, Skin).

**Depression**—Depressed—Dejection—Hypochondria—Low Spirits—Melancholy—Despondency—Worry, etc.—(See these subjects).

**Despondency; Digestive Disorders**—(See Digestion, Gastric, Indigestion, Stomach).

**Dislocations; Dry Skin**—Dry and Sallow—(See Dry; "Dry Skin" under Skin).

**Eczema; Eruptions, Erysipelas; Falls; Fever; Fractures**—(See "Bones" in this section).

**Functions**—Impeded Functions—(See "Disorders" under Functions).

**Gastric Disorders**—(See Digestion, Gastric, Indigestion, Stomach).

**Gloom; Gout; Gunshot**—(See "Danger" under Gunshot).

**Hardening; Heat**—Insufficient Heat in the Body—(See "Body" under Cold; "Lack of" under Heat).

**Hypochondria; Hysteria; Impediments**—Impeded Functions—♑ being ruled by ♄ acts in a similar manner to ♄, and the diseases of ♄ and ♑ are much the same, and whatever ♄ does, the ♑ influence will also do, and espec. when this sign is strong at B., on the Asc., or occupied by ♄ and many planets, and afflictions to ♑. (See the list of diseases under "Saturn". Also see Functions, Impediments).

**Impetigo; Indurations**—(See Cirrhosis, Deposits, Hardening, Minerals, Sclerosis, Thickening).

**Infancy**—Low Vitality In—Much Mortality In—(See Childhood, Infancy, Vitality. Also see the Introduction to this Article).

**Injuries**—To the Knees or Legs—(See Knees, Legs).

**Itching; Knees**—Accidents To—Disorders of—Weak Knees—(See Knees).

**Leprosy; Liquids**—Hot Liquids—Danger From—(See Liquids).

**Lower Limbs**—Legs—Diseases of—Injuries To—(See Extremities, Legs, Limbs, Lower).

**Lowered**—Lowering—Lowered Vitality—(See Low, Lowered, Vitality).

**Lungs**—Disorders of—(See Bronchial, Consumption, Phthisis, Pulmonary, Tuberculosis).

**Luxations**—(See Dislocations).

**Melancholy; Mental Depression**—(See Anguish, Anxiety, Depression, Melancholy, Worry, etc.).

**Mucous Diseases**—(See Humours, Mucous, Phlegm).

**Nausea**—(See Nausea, Vomiting).

**Nettle Rash**—(See Urticaria).

**Parasitic Diseases**—(See Parasites).

**Pruritis**—(See Itch).

**Rheumatism**—In Knees or Lower Limbs—(See Gout, Knees, Legs, Rheumatism).

**Scabies**—(See Itch, Scabies).

**Scalds; Sensitive; Skin Diseases**—(See Eruptions, Skin).

**Sprains; Stomach**—Diseases of—Antiperistalsis—Indigestion—(See Digestion, Gastric, Indigestion, Stomach).

**Synovitis**—(See Joints, Synovial).

**Tibia**—Dislocation of Head of—(See Tibia).

**Tissues**—Hardening of—(See Crystallization, Hardening, Tissues).

**Urticaria; Vitality Lowered**—(See Vitality).

**Vomiting; Worry.**

**CAPSICUM**—Red Pepper—Ruled by ♂. (See "Mars Group" under Herbs; Rubefacients).

**CAPSULES**—Suprarenal Capsules—(See Adrenals).

**CAPTIVE**—Captivity—Held in Captivity for Ransom During Travel—Possible Death or Injury In—The 12th H. strongly occupied by malefics at B., or by dir., and afflicted, tends to captivity, exile, or imprisonment, and injury therein, torture or death; the ☽ sepr. from ♃ and applying to the ☉, and espec. if the ☽ be in ♈, ♏, ♑, or ♒; the ☽ decr. in light, sepr. from ♃ and applying to ♄. (See Abroad, Exile, Pirates, Prison, Travel).

**Many Held In Captivity**—An eclipse of the ☽ in ♏.

**CAPUT**—

**Caput Algol**—(See Algol).

**Caput Andromeda**—(See Andromeda).

**Caput Draconis**—(See Dragon's Head).

**Caput Hercules**—Pollux—Of the nature of ♂. (See Assassination, Calamity, Disgrace, Drowning, Fever, Pollux, "Imprisonment" under Prison; Ruin; "Extreme Sickness" under Sickness; Suffocation; "Death" under Violent).

**CARBON**—Carbonic Acid—Carbon Dioxide—Carbon is ruled by ♄, and is a dominant element of the earthy signs ♉, ♍, an ♑. Carbonic acid gas is expelled from the lungs in the breath. The obstructive influences of ♄ tend to retention of the wastes within the system, and the obstruction of the circulation of the blood, and its purifying influences. (See "Operations" under Nature).

**Carbohydrates**—(See Hydrocarbonates).

**Carbonic Acid Poisoning**—A surplus of carbonic acid, and not sufficient cleansing from the blood—Retention of—Lack of Tidal Air—The ☉ affl. in ♒; ♄ or ☋ in ♊, and espec. when afflicting the ☽, tends to make the blood unable to throw off the carbonic acid in sufficient quantities, due to the obstructive power of ♄; ♄ □ ☍ ☽, lack of tidal air; ♄ ☌ ♃ or ♀ tends to obstruct the arterial and venous circulations, and cause carbonic acid to be retained. (See "Non-Oxygenation" under Oxygen; "Tidal Air" under Tidal).

**Elimination Of**—The ♒ sign rules, and has principle charge of, the elimination of carbonic acid gas from the system. Afflictions in, or to the ♒ sign, tend to obstruct and hinder this elimination. (See Air, Elimination, Gases, Malnutrition, Miasma, Nitrogen, Oxygen, "Blood" under Poison; Tidal). See Hydrocarbonates, Sugar.

**CARBUNCLES**—Anthrax—♃ affl. in ♉, the result of plethora and gormandizing; a ♂ disease, and caused by ♂ afflictions; ♂ affl. in ♑; ♂ ♑, occi., lord of the year at the Vernal, tends to a prevalence of boils and carbuncles; Subs at CP and KP. (See Abscesses, Boils, Plethora, Swellings, Tumors, Ulcers, etc.).

**CARCINOMA**—Cancers—Malignant Tumor—Epithelioma—

**Carcinoma** (Cancer) is a ☽ disease, a ♋ sign disease, and caused by afflictions in the ☽ sign ♋; the ☽ affl. at B., and to the evil asps. the Asc. by dir.; the ☽ affl. in ♋, or affl. the hyleg therefrom; the ☽ affl. in ♈, ♉, or ♊; the ☉ in asp. at B. with both ♃ and ♄, or in asp. with one of them in, or from a sign, ruled by the other; caused by the ♄ influence when he enters into the configuration; ♄ ☌ ♃ or ♀; ♄ opposes ♃, and this conflict between entirely different influences tends to set up the disease in weakened constitutions; ♄ affl. in the 6th H. in mutable signs; ♄ affl. in ♋ when he is the afflictor in the disease; ♆ affl. the ☉ tends to produce the disease under evil directions of ♆ to the ☉ or hyleg; sensitive degrees in this disease are the 25° ♍ and ♓, and the ☉, ☽, or malefics in or afflicting these degrees tend to cancer; caused by Subs at CP and KP. (For further influences, and the different forms of cancer, see the various paragraphs in this section).

**Axillae**—Cancer and Scirrhus of—(See Axillae).

**Bowels**—Cancer of—The ☉ or ♄ affl. in ♍; Subs at KP and PP, the 2nd Lumbar.

**Breasts**—Cancer of—A ☽ disease; a ♋ disease, and afflictions in ♋; the ♋ sign on the Asc., and afflicted; ♄ affl. in ♋, afflicting the hyleg, and being the afflictor in the disease; ♄ ♋, occi., and affl. the ☉, ☽, Asc., or hyleg; ♃ ♋, and aspecting ♄, or ♄ ♋ affl. by ♃, and where one or both may be affl. the hyleg. (See Axillae, Breasts).

**Canker**—A Cancerous Sore—(See Canker, Gangrene).

**Death by Cancer**—Afflictions in the cardinal signs dispose to, and espec. in ♋; ♄ ♋ and affl. the hyleg at B., and by dir.; ♄ in a fixed sign at B. and affl. the hyleg by dir.; ♃ causes death by when afflicting the hyleg at B., and by dir., and being the afflictor in the disease; ♀ affl. the hyleg by dir., and ♀ much afflicted at B., and holding the dominion of death. Case—Death by Cancer—See "Food Reformer", No. 264 in 1001 N.N.

**Epithelioma**—A Cancerous growth of the skin—(See Epithelioma).

**Face**—Cancer of—♄ affl. in ♈ or ♉; Subs at MCP, the 5th Cervical. (See Face).

**Fatty Cancer**—Lardaceous—Waxy—Caused by the afflictions of ♃.

**Gangrene**—(See Canker, Gangrene).

**Generative Organs** — Sex Organs—Womb, etc.—♅ or ♄ affl. in ♏, or both in ☌, in ♏ and affl. the hyleg, and espec. when ♄ is the afflictor, or holds the dominion of death; caused by Subs at KP and PP, the 2, 3, and 4th Lumbars. (See Sex, Womb).

**Hard Form Of**—(See "Scirrhus" in this section).

**Head**—Cancer of—Afflictions in ♈ or ♉, and espec. ♄ affl. in these signs; caused by Subs at MCP, the 5th Cervical.

**Lardaceous Form**—(See "Fatty" in this section).

**Liver**—Cancer of—♄ affl. in ♋ or ♍; afflictions in the 5th H.; Subs at Li.P. and KP. (See Liver).

**Oesophagus**—Cancer of—♄ affl. in ♋. (See Oesophagus).

**Operated Upon**—For Cancer—Case—See "Unfortunate Case", No. 351 in 1001 N.N.

**Pancreas**—Cancer of—(See Pancreas).

**Rectum**—Cancer of—(See Rectum).

**Scirrhus**—Hard Form of—Occurs espec. in the Breasts—♄ or ♂ affl. in ♋. (See Axillae).

**Sex Organs** — (See "Generative" in this section).

**Solanoid Form** — Potato-like Formations—Caused by the afflictions of ♃.

**Spleen**—Cancer of—(See Spleen).

**Stomach**—Cancer of—A ☽ disease; a disease of the ♋ sign, and afflictions in ♋; the ☉, ♅, or ♄ affl. in ♋, and also affl. the hyleg; Subs at SP, the 7th Dorsal, and at KP. (See Stomach).

**Treatment Of** — Injections of Potassium are said to cure cancer, as the disease is often due to a lack of this Salt. The Grape Cure is also highly successful. For Cases of cancer cured, see birth data, and Figures 21A and 21B in "Astro-Diagnosis" by the Heindels.

**Waxy Form** — (See "Fatty" in this section).

**Womb**—(See "Generative" in this section). For collateral study see Abscesses, Sores, Tumors, Ulcers.

**CARDIA**—Cardiac—Pertaining to the Heart. Cardia is also an orifice of the stomach. The action of the ☉ and ☽ thru the Sympathetic Nervous System affect the Cardia, the Heart, the upper part of the Stomach, and the Dorsal Vertebrae, and give way to the Cardiac Diathesis. The therapeutic properties of ☉ remedies are cardiac and affect the heart action.

**Cardiac Diathesis**—(See the Introduction to this section).

**Cardiac Diseases**—(See Heart).

**Cardiac Muscle**—(See "Jupiter Group" under Muscles).

**Cardiac Plexus**—The ☉ and ☽ acting thru the deep Cardiac Plexuses affect the Respiratory System and the upper Limbs, and give way to the Cranian Diathesis.

**Cardiac Sedative**—(See Aconite).

**Cardialgia**—Heartburn—Pain in the Heart—(See "Heartburn" under Heart).

**Carditis**—(See Heart).

**CARDINAL SIGNS**—Moveable Signs—Acute Signs—They are ♈, ♋, ♎, and ♑, and have largely to do with physical activity. These signs are ruled by ♂, ☽, ♀ and ♄. These four signs form the cardinal cross, and are all in □ or ☍ asp. to each other, and in affliction. Thus a person born with a majority of planets in the cardinal signs may tend to have a more or less unbalanced condition of mind and body, and with less harmony in the system. The cardinal signs are mental in temperament. An affliction in one cardinal sign tends also to afflict the parts ruled by all the other cardinal signs, and this is also true of all the fixed and common signs, as all Signs of the same group afflict each other. Thus ♄ in ♋ at B. can cause stomach trouble, kidney disorders, eye infirmities, and weak and disordered knees. The cardinal sign ♈ rules the head; ♋, the stomach; ♎, the kidneys, and ♑, the knees. These signs are affiliated with the Angles of the map, the Equinoctial and Tropical Points, the 1st, 4th, 7th and 10th Houses, which are known as the cardinal houses. The cardinal signs on the angles at B. give an active nature, a restless energy, and considerable ability to throw off disease, but diseases caused by them tend to be acute, quick, severe, and to soon run their course. (See "Disease" under Nature). On the angles they also tend to lessen the chances of Insanity, or an unbalanced mind. Afflictions from the cardinal signs are moveable, and not as fixed or stationary, and can be overcome. People born with many planets in these signs, or when they are upon the angles, have more power to throw off disease or trouble, and to start life anew after failure, being hopeful, aggressive and optimistic. They try hard to get well when sick, and to cooperate with the Healer. The intensity of disease is associated with the cardinal signs. (See Severity). The cardinal signs denote the head, stomach, kidneys and skin. Cardinal signs also show death on railways, by fire, fits, scalds, gunshot, lightning, murder, and a notorious death. (See Active, Acute, Angles, Aries, Cancer, Capricorn, Curable, Energy, Functions, Head, Houses, Kidneys, Knees, Libra, Morbid, Skin, Stomach).

**CAREFUL**—The ☽ and ♄ influences make one careful, and give strong instincts of self-preservation and self-protection, and espec. the good asps. of the ☽ and ♄. The fiery signs tend to be lacking in caution, carefulness and prudence.

**Careful of the Body**—A ♍ characteristic. (See Cleanly, Neat).

**Careful in Diet**—(See "Careful" under Diet). See Careless.

**CARELESS** — Carelessness — Negligent —Slovenly—A ♓ influence; many planets in bicorporeal, or double-bodied signs at B.; the ☽ to the ☌ or ill-asp. ♆ by dir., indifferent to life's duties; the ☽ ill-dig. at B., lives carelessly and beggarly, and content in no condition of life, either good or ill; ♃ to the bad asps. of ♂ by dir.; ♂ afflicting ☿; ♀ ill-dig. at B., nothing careful of the things of this life, and tending to dissipation, sickness, or early death.

**Ailments From**—Diseases and Irregularities From—The ☽ affl. by ♀; ♓ on the 6th H., and afflicted, from carelessness in personal cleanliness; ♓ produces ailments thru carelessness and forgetfulness. (See "Of No Ambition" under Ambition; Awkwardness, Cleanly, Excesses, Filth, Folly, Forethought, Forgetful; "Free Living" under Free; "Bad Habits" under Habits; "High Living" under High; Improvident, Imprudent, Indifferent, Indiscretions; "Requirements" under Nature; Neglect, Poverty, Slovenly, Uncleanly, Untidy).

**CARES**—

**Cares Multiplied**—Full of Cares—♄ ☌ or ill-asp. the ☽ at B., or by dir.; the evil directions of ♂ to the ☉, ☽, or Asc.; fixed stars of the nature of ♄ ascending. (See Anxiety, Responsibility, Worry).

**Disease from Cares**—The ☽ ♊ at B., in ☌ or ill-asp. ♄, and when ♄ may be affl. the natal ☽ by dir., the disease has its origin in the mind, and from the multiplicity of business cares, or fatigue from over-study, writings or literary work; the ☽ ♊ and in □ or ☍ ♄ (or ☿ if he be of the nature of ♄) at the beginning of an illness, or at decumbiture. (See Anxiety, "Brain-Fag" under Brain; Fatigue, Reversals, Trouble, Vexations, Worry, etc.).

**CARIES**—Ulcerous Inflammation of Bone—A ♄ disease. (See Bones).

**Nose**—(See "Caries" under Nose).

**Spine**—(See "Caries" under Spine).

**Teeth**—Caries of—Decay of—(See "Carious", "Decay", "Toothache" under Teeth). See Decay, Ulcers.

**CAROTID**—

**Carotid Arteries**—The Internal Carotid Artery is ruled by ♈, and the External Carotid Artery is ruled by the ♉ sign.

**Carotid Plexus**—(See "Ribes" under Ganglion).

**Fullness Of**—Plethora of—Increased Beating of—A ♃ disease. (See Arteries, Circulation, Plethora).

**CARPUS**—Carpal Bones—(See Wrist).

**CARRIAGE**—Of the Body—The Gait, etc.—(See Awkward, Clumsiness, Commanding, Erect, Gait, Locomotion, Motion, Movement, Posture, Quick, Slow, Stooping, Walk, etc. This subject is mostly considered under "Gait", and "Walk").

**CARTILAGE**—Gristle—Ruled by ♄, and also crystallized by ♄. Cartilaginous tissue building is the work of ♄. (See Tendons).

**Achondroplasia**—Lack of Proper Formation of Cartilage, as in Foetal Rickets—A ♄ disease; ♄ ☌ or ill-asp. ♂, or ♂ ☌ or ill-asp. ♄, according to which is the dominating planet. (See Rickets).

**Caries Of**—(See "Caries" under Nose).

**Chondroma**—Cartilaginous Tumor—(Fibro-Cartilaginous Tumor)—♄ ☌ or ill-asp. ♃. (See Fiber).

**Nose**—Caries of Cartilage of—(See "Caries" under Nose).

**CARUNCLE**—A Small Fleshy Growth—Occurs usually on the Conjunctiva, near the inner canthus, and caused by ♄ affl. in ♈; a ♄ influence, and due to suppression of function, or of the nerve supply to the part; ♄ ☌ ♃ or ♀, due to disturbed circulation in the part. Caruncle also occurs on the posterior lip of the meatus urinarius, and caused by ♄ affl. in ♏; Subs at PP. (See Conjunctiva, Growths, Sarcoma).

**CARUS**—Complete Insensibility—The Last Degree of Coma—A ♆ disease. (See Analgesia, Coma, Insensibility, Neptune).

**CASEIN**—The Clotted Proteid of Milk. Ruled by the ☉. (See Milk).

**CASTOR**—A violent star of the 2nd magnitude, in the 18° ♋, of the nature of ♄, ♂ and ♀. Makes one liable to violence, and also portends mischievousness. The ☉ with at B. is indicative of evil, and liable to a violent death. The Knee of Castor and Pollux with the ☉ in an angle at B. tend to much sickness, trouble and disgrace. When directed to the ☉, ☽, or Asc., tends to Bad Eyes, Hurts to the Eyes; Blindness in One or Both Eyes; Hurts to Face; danger from Sharp Instruments; Imprisonment; Violence or a Violent Death; Wounds, and every evil and calamity that can befall humanity. The influence of Castor when with the ☉, ☽, or Asc. at B., or afflicting them by dir., also tends to Beheading, Blows, Cuts, Disgrace, Measles, Much Evil, Rape, Ruin, Stabs, Shipwreck, Shooting, Trouble, and the native also often turns out to be a murderer, or is murdered. Castor and Pollux are called "The Twins". The star Propus is the Left Foot of Castor, and of the nature of ♂. (See Pollux. Also see these various subjects in the alphabetical arrangement).

**CASTRATION**—(See Testes).

**CASUALTIES**—See Accidents, Calamity, Death, Drowning, Earthquakes, Electricity, Fire, Floods, Lightning, Machinery, Murder, Railroads, Ships, Shipwreck, Travel; "Untimely Death" under Untimely; Volcanoes, Water, Weather, Wind, etc.

**CATABOLISM**—A Retrograde Change in the Tissues of the Body—♄ influence. (See Consumption, Crystallization, Decay, Emaciation, Hardening, Softening, Tuberculosis, Wastings).

**CATALEPSY**—A Neurosis caused by ♆; a ♆ disease; ♆ in the 8th H. In this disease there is loss of will and muscular activity, but with no change in the circulation. (See Coma, "Neurosis" under Nerves; Trance).

**CATALYSIS**—A Chemic Reaction or Change—Death—Decay—Dissolution—Degeneration—♄ is the principal Significator of, and by his asps. to the ☉, ☽, Asc., M.C., and hyleg; ♆ also causes catalysm when affl. the hyleg at B., and by dir. (See "Arguments for Death", "Danger of Death", and the various paragraphs under Death; Decay, Degeneration, Dissolution, Saturn).

**CATAMENIA**—(See Menses).

**CATAPHORA**—Lethargy attended by short remissions—A ♆ disease. (See Lethargy).

**CATARACT**—Opacity of the Crystalline Lens—A ☉ disease; the ☉ affl. in the Asc.; the ☉ in the Asc., or M.C. in ☌ or ☍ the ☽, and ♄ rising before the ☉, or evilly configurated with the ☉; the ☽ or Asc. in Nebulous Parts, and affl. by ♄; ♆ ♈ and affl. by ♄; ♄ causes blindness by (See "Total" under Blindness); ♄ ♈; ♄ ☌ ☉ or ☽ in ♈; ♄ ♈ and □ the ☽ in ♋; Subs at MCP, and KP, the 11th Dorsal. (See Blindness, Eyes, Sight). Cases—See Fig. 11B in Astro-Diagnosis by the Heindels. Also see "Diseases in the Eyes", Chap. 13, page 88 in Daath's Medical Astrology.

**CATARRH**—Catarrhs—Defluxions—Fluxions—Rheum—Inflammation of Mucous Membranes, with Watery Discharges, etc.—Fluxions follow a Solar Periodicity. Catarrh is listed as a disease of the ☉, ☽, and ♄; ♄ ☌ the Asc. by dir.; lord of the 1st or 6th H., or the ☽, in watery signs; the watery signs strong and predominating at B., and with afflictions in such signs, predispose to. (See the various paragraphs in this section).

**Bladder**—Catarrh of—Subs at LPP, the 4, 5, and 6th Lumbars tend to acute catarrh of; ♂ affl. in ♏. (See "Cystitis" under Bladder).

**Bowels**—Catarrh of—☽ affl. in ♍; ☽ ♏ ☌ ♅ or ♄; a ♍ disease and afflictions in ♍; ♄ affl. in ♍; ♄ ☌ ♃ in ♍, and affl. by dir. or progression. (See "Enteritis" in this section).

**Bronchial Catarrh**—(See "Catarrh" under Bronchial).

**Colds**—(See Colds).

**Coryza**—(See "Coryza" under Nose).

**Death by Catarrh**—♄ in the 8th H. at a Solar Ingress into ♈, and affl. the ☽ or planet ascending, tends to be very fatal, according to the sign occupied by ♄.

**Defluxions**—(See Defluxion).

**Discharges**—(See "Catarrhal" under Discharges).

**Ears**—Catarrh of—(See Ears).

**Enteritis**—Catarrhal Enteritis—The ☉, ☽, or ♂ affl. in ♍; ♂ ♍ in the 6th H. (See "Inflammation" under Bowels).

**Fever**—Catarrhal Fever—(See Fluxes, Influenza).

**Flux**—Fluxions—(See Flux).

**Gastric Catarrh**—(See "Stomach" in this section).

**Head**—Catarrh In—(See Head).

**Humours**—(See Fluids, Humours).

**Influenza**—Catarrhal Fever—(See Influenza).

**Larynx**—Catarrh of—(See Larynx).

**Leucorrhoea**—Catarrh of Womb—(See Leocorrhoea).

**Liver**—Catarrh of—(See Liver).

**Lungs**—Catarrh of—(See Lungs).

**Mucous**—Mucus—(See Mucous).

**Nasal Catarrh**—Nose—Catarrh of—(See Nose).

**Phlegm**—(See Mucous, Phlegm).

**Pneumonia**—Catarrhal Pneumonia—(See Pneumonia).

**Rheum**—Catarrhal Discharge—(See Rheum).

**Spleen**—Catarrh of—(See Spleen).

**Stomach**—Catarrh of—(See "Catarrh" under Gastric, Stomach).

**Subject to Catarrh**—Liable To—Predisposed To—♄ people are espec. subject to; ♄ in the Asc. at B.; ♄ affl. in ♈ or ♓; a ☉ disease, and caused by an afflicted ☉; a ☽ disease; the ☽ affl. in ♈, or in watery signs; the ☽ in ♋, ☌ or ill-asp. ♄ (or ☿ if he be of the nature of ♄) at the beginning of an illness, and will tend to become chronic, and continue for a long time, if the ☽ be decr., and near the body of ♄ at the time; ♆, H., or ♄ in ♈ or ♓, and affl. the ☉ or ☽; ♋, ♏, or ♓ upon the Asc., and affl. at B., or by dir.; afflictions in ♏. (See the first part of this section).

**Throat**—Catarrh In—(See Throat).

**Watery Discharges**—(See Fluxes, Humours, Rheum, Watery).

**Womb**—Catarrh of—(See Leucorrhea, "Catarrh" under Womb).

**CATASTROPHIES**—Death By—Injury By—Death by a Violent Catastrophe—The ☉ joined with the Ascelli; ♀ in ♑, partile asp. the Asc., often meets with strange and sudden catastrophe. (For further influences see Calamity, Casualties).

**CATHARTIC**—(See Physic).

**CATS**—Sickness or Death of—(See Pets; "Pestilential Virus" under Pestilence).

**Resembles Cats**—(See "Animal Forms" under Monsters).

**CATTLE**—The 6th H. rules Small Cattle, and the 12th H. the Great, or Large Cattle. Many of the planetary conditions which affect Man, in health or disease conditions, also affect the Animal Kingdom. Man is also subject to attacks, injuries, and infirmities received thru Cattle, Horses, Wild Animals, Reptiles, Insects, etc.

**Attacks by Cattle**—Danger of Injury or Death by the Attacks of Bulls, Oxen, and Large Cattle—The ☉ to the cusp the 12th H. by dir.; the ☽ to the place of Cor Scorpio or Ceti by dir.; a malefic ruler of the 12th H. at B., and located in the 12th H. in a Solar Rev.; ♂ in the 12th H., and affl. by ♅ or ♄; Ceti joined with the Luminaries at B.; lord of the 6th H. in the 12th H.; the Whale's Jaw in the M.C. (See Animals, Beasts, Elephants; "Great Cattle" under Great; Quadrupeds).

**Cattle Breeders**—Death of—Presignified by ♄ lord of the year at the Vernal Equi., in ♒, and ℞.

**Death of Cattle**—Loss of Cattle—Loss of Camels—An eclipse of the ☉ or ☽ in a fiery sign; an eclipse of the ☉ in ♉. (See "Death" under Animals; Blizzards; "Virus" under Pestilence; "Cold" under Weather).

**Destruction Among**—♂ in the 6th or 12th H.; an eclipse of the ☽ in the 1st Decan. of ♉.

**Diseases Among**—Much Sickness Among—Lord of the 6th in the 12th, or lord of the 12th in the 6th H. of the native, tends to bad fortune with his cattle, and with small or large animals. (See the various paragraphs in this section).

**Epidemics Among**—(See Events; "Epidemics" under Sheep).

**Great Cattle**—Large Cattle—Attacks By—Disease or Death of—(See "Great Cattle" under Great; "Cattle" under Detriment).

**Hurts By**—Attacks or Injury By—(See "Attacks" in this section).

**Injury to Cattle**—To Camels and Horses—An eclipse of the ☉ in ♐; ♄ or ♂ affl. in the 6th or 12th H. (See "Destruction", and the various paragraphs in this section).

**Large Cattle**—(See "Great" in this section).

**Loss Of**—(See the various paragraphs in this section).

**Much Sickness Among**—(See "Diseases" in this section).

**Resembles Cattle**—(See "Animal" Forms" under Monsters).

**Sickness Among**—(See "Disease", "Epidemics", and the various paragraphs in this section).

**Small Cattle**—Diseases Among—Loss of—Malefics in the 6th H.; Comets appearing in ♈; afflictions and eclipses in ♈ at a Solar Ingress.

**Travel**—Attacks by During Travel—The afflictor to the Sig. of Travel being in the 12th H., and in ♐, and espec. if ♂ or ☿ be the afflictor.

**Veterinary**—Makes a Good Cow Doctor—(See Veterinary). For collateral study see Animals, Beasts, Elephants, "Nature Of" under Events; Horses, Quadrupeds, Sheep, Sixth House, Twelfth House.

**CAUDA**—

**Cauda Draconis**—Moon's South Node—(See Dragon).

**Cauda Leonis**—Cauda Lucida—Deneb—(See Lion's Tail).

**CAUL**—Born With—(See "Caul" under Face).

**CAUSTIC**—Escharotic—♂ influence. A therapeutic property of ♂. (See Applications, Rubefacients, Stimulant, Vesicant).

**CAVERNOUS PLEXUS**—(See "Ribes" under Ganglion).

**CAVITIES**—A Hollow—A Receptacle—There are both normal, and abnormal or disease cavities, in the body. (See Follicles, Receptacles, Sacs, Vesicles).

**Pus Cavities**—(See Cloaca, Pus).

**CECUM**—(See Caecum).

**CELIBACY**—The bad asps. of ♄ to the ☉, ☽, ♀, and ☿ tend to pervert, or destroy passion, and espec. when ♄ is in, or afflicts the 5th and 7th houses, and in fiery signs at B.; ♄ affl. in ♈ tends to apathy, want of feeling and passion. (See Apathy, Bachelors, Barren, "Anchorite" under Husband; "Aversion", "Indifferent", under Marriage; "Free From" under Passion; Perversions, Spinsters).

**CELLS**—Cell—A Small, Protoplasmic Mass, and usually Nucleated.

**Air Cells**—Are connected with the airy signs; ☿ in ♉, ♊ and ♋ rule and affect the air cells of the lungs. (See Air, Breathing, Lungs, Oxygen, Trachea).

**Alterations**—In the Cells and Tissues —The five planets, ♄, ♃, ♂, ♀, ☿, and the 5 Processes which they rule, namely, the Splenic Process, Thoracic Process, Hepatic Process, Renal Process, and the Nervous Influx respectively, have to do with the alteration and metabolism of the cells, and organic changes, and the alterations occur in the zones of the body ruled by the sign in which the respective planets may be located. In alterations the ☉ tends to structural changes; ♄ to stenosis; ♃ to hypertrophy; ♂ to the Sthenic Process; ♀ to Retrogressive Metamorphosis; ☿ the Irritation and Periodicity. (See Alterations, Decay, Degeneration, Metabolism, Metamorphosis, Periodicity, Processes, Stenosis, Sthenic, Structural, Tissues, etc. Also see "Renal Process" under Kidneys; "Hepatic Process" under Liver; "Influx" under Nerves; Spleen, Thorax).

**Amoeboid Motion**—Nebuloid Motion —Under the rule of ♆.

**Asthenic Process**—Presided over by ♄. (See Asthenia).

**Blood Cells**—(See "Corpuscles" under Blood. Also see Haemoglobin, Leukocytes).

**Budding**—(See "Gemmation" in this section).

**Cellular Tissue**—Hypertrophy of— (See Elephantiasis, Hypertrophy).

**Cellular Tissue Building**—(See "Tissue Building" in this section).

**Cellulose**—Ruled by ♃.

**Congestion**—Cellular Congestion— The work of ♀.

**Cytoplastema**—A Plastic Fluid—♆ presides over cell development in this fluid. (See Cytoplastema, Plastic).

**Development**—Cell Development— The physiological action of ♃. Cell development in the plastic fluid, and independent of other cells, is presided over by ♆. (See the Introduction under Jupiter).

**Diseases of the Cells**—The 5 Processes mentioned under "Alterations" in this section have to do with all the diseases to which the cell is liable.

**Division**—♃ rules cell reproduction by division of the cell. (See "Gemmation", "Reproduction", in this section).

**Excitation**—The ☉ and ☽ influences sum up the 5 Processes mentioned herein, and manifest them by cellular excitation, and cellular zymosis. (See Zymosis).

**Filtration**—(See "Substance" in this section).

**Fluids**—The intercellular fluids, and the organic systems thru which they circulate, are ruled by the ☽. (See Fluids, Oedema).

**Gemmation**—Budding—Cell reproduction by is under the rule of ♀. (See Gemmation. Also see "Division", "Reproduction", in this section).

**Haemoglobin**—(See Haemoglobin).

**Hypertrophy**—♃ rules hypertrophy, or the abnormal increase in the size of the cell. (See Hypertrophy).

**Inflammation**—Inflammation of the cell takes place under the action and afflictions of ♄, ♃, and ♂. (See Inflammation).

**Intercellular**—Interstitial—The intercellular spaces are connected with the airy signs. (See "Fluids" in this section. Also see Intercellular; "Air Signs" under Air).

**Irritation Of**—(See "Alterations" in this section).

**Lungs**—Air Cells of—(See "Air Cells" in this section).

**Metabolism**—(See Metabolism. Also see "Alterations" in this section).

**Metamorphosis**—(See Metamorphosis. Also see "Alterations" in this section).

**Molecular Nutrition**—(See Nutrition).

**Nebuloid Motion**—(See "Amoeboid" in this section).

**Nucleus**—Ruled and supported by the ☉ influence. (See Nucleus, Protoplasma).

**Organic Changes**—Structural Changes —Ruled by the ☉. (See "Alterations" in this section. Also see Organic, Structural).

**Periodicity**—Of the Cell—Presided over by the ☽ and ☿. (See Periodicity. Also see "Alterations" in this section).

**Polarity Of**—(See Polarity).

**Protoplasma**—(See Protoplasma).

**Reproduction**—(See "Division", "Gemmation" in this section. Also see Proliferation).

**Reservation**—(See "Substance" in this section).

**Retrogressive Metamorphosis**—(See "Alterations" in this section).

**Salts**—Cell Salts—(See Salts; "Salts" under Zodiac).

**Selection**—(See "Substance" in this section).

**Spaces**—(See "Intercellular" in this section).

**Stenosis**—Narrowing or Constriction of the Cell—Presided over by ♄. (See Stenosis).

**Sthenic Process**—The activity, strength, and excessive force of the cell given by ♂. (See Sthenic).

**Storing**—(See "Substance" in this section).

**Structural Changes**—(See "Organic" in this section).

**Substance**—The storing, filtration, reservation, selection, and transformation of the various cell substances are the work of ♆, ♃, and ♀. (See Defensive).

**Thickening**—The thickening of cell walls is the work of ♄ and a ♄ disease. (See Thickening).

**Tissue Building**—Cellular Tissue Building is the work of ♆, ♃, ♀, and the ☽. (See Tissues).

**Walls of Cells**—Changes In—Division of—Thickening of, etc.—(See the various paragraphs in this section).

**Zymosis**—(See "Excitation" in this section).

**CENTRAL**—

**Central Ganglia**—(See "Vaso-Dilator" under Vaso).

**Central Line of Impulse**—(See Prenatal Epoch).

**CENTRES**—Centers—Nerve Centers—Spinal Centers—Vital Centers—(See Erethism, Ganglion, "Centers" under Nerves; Spine, Vascular, Vital).

**CENTRIFUGAL**—Receding from the center. The ♂ influence over the body tends to drive, or draw, the blood outward towards the surface, causing fevers, inflammation, surface congestions, acute diseases, etc. (See Acute, Centripetal, Rubefacients, "Vaso-Dilator" under Vaso).

**CENTRIPETAL**—Traveling toward the center. The ♄ influence over the body is to drive the blood inward, leaving the surface chilled, and to cause colds, internal congestions, chronic diseases, constrictions, mortifications, etc. (See Chronic, Cold, Constrictions, Derma, Gangrene, Intropulsion, Peripheral, Saturn, "Vaso-Constrictor" under Vaso).

**CEPHALIC**—Affecting the Head. A therapeutic property of ☿ and ☿ remedies. (See Head).

**CEPHEUS**—A Northern Constellation. (See Hanging, Impalement).

**CEREBELLUM**—The Instrument of Coordination. Ruled by the ☽ and the ♉ sign. Is under the internal rulership of ♉. The Arbor Vitae of the Cerebellum are ruled by ♉. The ♎ and ♏ signs, classed as nervous signs, have a special action on the Cerebellum (vegetative life). (See Brain, Cerebral, Cerebrum, Cerebro-Spinal; Coma, Coordination).

**CEREBRAL**—Pertaining to the Brain. The Cerebral Hemispheres are ruled by ♈, and the ♈ sign is called the "Cerebral Pole" by Paracelsus. The right Cerebral Hemisphere is ruled by ☿, and the left one by ♂. The Cerebral Ventricles are ruled by ♆. The Cerebral Nerves are ruled by ☿, and ☿ in ♈. The Cerebro-Spinal System is ruled by ☿. (See Brain, Cerebellum, Cerebro-Spinal, Cerebrum).

**Cerebral Anaemia**—(See Anaemia).

**Cerebral Apoplexy**—(See Apoplexy).

**Cerebral Congestion**—(See Congestion).

**Cerebral Functions**—Derangement of—The ☽ affl. in ♈, and espec. with females.

**Cerebral Hemispheres**—Diseases of—♈ diseases, and afflictions in ♈; ♄ affl. in ♈; ♂ affl. in ♈, afflictions to the left hemisphere; ☿ affl. in ♈, afflictions of the right hemisphere. (See "Hemispheres" under Head).

**Cerebral Hemorrhage**—Rupture of a Blood Vessel of the Brain—The ☉ or ♂ affl. in ♈; ♂ ♈ in the 6th H. and afflicted. (See Apoplexy).

**Cerebral Meningitis**—(See Meninges).

**Cerebral Substance**—Augmented and Diminished—(See Medulla).

**Cerebral Symptoms**—(See Anaemia, Apoplexy, Brain, Coma, Congestion, Delirium, Faintings, Headaches, Vertigo, etc. Also note the various paragraphs in this section).

**Cerebral Syncope**—♄ affl. in ♈. (See Coma, Delirium, Fainting, Fits, Vertigo, etc.).

**CEREBRO-SPINAL**—Relating to the Brain and Spine.

**Cerebro-Spinal Meningitis**—Afflictions in ♈ and ♌; ☉ affl. in ♌, and with ♂ in ♈, or ♂ affl. in ♌, and with ☉ affl. in ♈. (See Meninges, "Spotted Fever" under Spotted).

**Cerebro-Spinal Nervous System**—Ruled by ☿. Also ruled and influenced by the ♈ sign. The ☉ and ☽ acting thru the ♈ sign tend to affect this system. (See "Ribes" under Ganglion). The ☉ Group of Minerals and Herbs have a physiological action on it. The ♂ Group of plants and minerals have a pathological action. The Cerebro-Spinal System being ruled by ♈, is opposed to the Renal System, ruled by the opposite sign ♎. Thus malefics and afflictions in ♎ tend to affect the Cerebro-Spinal System, and afflictions in ♈, the Renal System, or Kidneys. (See Cerebral, Medulla, Pituitary, Spine).

**CEREBRUM**—The chief portion of the Brain. The same influences that tend to affect the Brain will also apply here. (See Brain, Cerebral).

**CERVICAL**—Pertaining to the Neck, or to a Cervix—

**Cervical Ganglion**—The Superior Cervical Ganglion are ruled by the ♉ sign. The ☉ and ☽ acting thru the Cervical Ganglion affect the Eustachian Tubes, Cervical Glands, the Throat, Neck, and their dependencies, and give way to the Renal Diathesis. (See "Cervical" under Ganglion).

**Cervical Nerves**—Owing to the strong relationship existing between the two opposite signs ♉ and ♏, planets in either of these signs, and espec. when afflicted, affect the Cervical Nerves, the Neck, Throat, and the Genito-Urinary System.

**Cervical Vertebrae**—Are under the structural rulership of ♉. Also ♄ when in ♉ espec. rules and affects them, as ♄ rules the bones. (See "Cervical" under Vertebrae).

**CERVIX**—Neck—

**Cervix Vesicae**—Neck of the Bladder—(See "Neck" under Bladder).

**Uterine Cervix**—(See "Cervix" under Womb).

**CESSATIONS**—(See Saturn, Stoppages, Suppressions, etc.).

**CESTODE**—Resembling a Tapeworm—**Stomach**—Cestode of—(See "Worms" under Stomach. Also see Tapeworm, Worms).

**CETI**—Menkar—Whale's Jaw—Lucida Maxilla—A star of the nature of ♄ in the 3rd face of ♉. Tends to cause disease and sickness when with the ☉ and ☽ at B. Dangers from cattle, from great beasts, and ill-fortune, disgrace, etc., are indicated when in the M.C. at B., or by dir. (See Cattle, Disgrace, Falls, Fortune, Menkar, Whale).

**CHALCOLITE**—A mineral ruled by ♅. (See Uranus).

**CHALK**—Calx—Chalk and Lime formations in the body are ruled by ♄.

**Chalk Stones of Gout**—The work of ♄ retaining and crystallizing the waste products of the body. (See Deposits, Gout, Lime, Minerals, Wastes, Whooping Cough).

**Chalky Skin**—Given by ♓. (See Pale, Sickly, Skin, White).

**CHAMOMILLA**—A typical drug of the ☉. One of the 12 Polycrest Remedies corresponding to the ♌ sign. (See "Polycrest" under Zodiac).

**CHANCES**—Endures Many Sudden and Violent Chances in Life—The ☉ or ☽ near the Bull's North Eye at B., or by dir. (See Aldebaran, Dangers, "Narrow Escapes" under Escapes; Foolhardy, Oculus Taurus, Perils, etc.).

**CHANCRE**—(See Syphilis).

**Chancroid**—Soft Chancre—(See Gonorrhea).

**CHANGE**—Changes—Mutations—The principle of the ☽ is change. Also ♅ is the principal planet causing changes, removals, journeys, and furnishes the sudden notions or impulses by his directions and afflictions, which lead to changes, and espec. among people who are drifting in life, who have not yet found their true calling, work or location, and where much inharmony exists in the environment. The ♅ influence espec. tends to many changes in seeking health, or business advancement. The ☿ influences also conduce to changes in life. The ☽ influence tends to changes in the body by acting upon the bodily fluids.

**Better**—Changes For the Better in Life—The ☽ to the ☌, or P. asp. the ☉ if the ☉ be strong and well-aspected by ♃ or ♀ at B. For change for the better or worse in disease, see Crises; "Worse" under Disease; "Better" under Disease and Health; "Improved" under Health.

**Blood Particles**—Changes In—(See "Blood" under Red).

**Body**—Changes In—Changes and mutations in the body are ruled by the ☽, and espec. thru the bodily fluids. (See Fluids, Moon, Mutations).

**Change of Life**—(See "Menopause" under Menses).

**Changeable**—(See Mutable, Signs).

**Comfort**—Changes Which Interfere with Comfort and Health—(See Comfort).

**Disease**—Changes to Some Other Form of Disease—(See Chronic, Complications, Crises, Relapses, Return, Worse).

**Fluids**—(See "Mutation" under Fluids).

**Healers**—Change of Healer Advisable—(See Healers).

**Humoural Changes**—(See this subject under Humours).

**Life**—Change of Life in Women—(See "Menopause" under Menses).

**Location**—Change of Location Advisable—(See Location, "Native Land" under Native; "Place of Birth" under Place; Residence).

**Metabolism**—Cell Changes—(See Cells, Metabolism, Metamorphosis, Processes, Tissues).

**Scenery**—Change of Good for the Health—(See Location, Residence, Travel).

**Sudden Changes**—Subject To—♅ influence and afflictions; ♀ Sig. in ♑. (See Restless, Sudden).

**Worse**—The Disease Changes for the Worse—(See Complications, Crises, "Worse" under Disease; Relapses).

**CHANNELS**—And Vents—Sex Channels—(See "Channels" under Genitals). See Passages.

**CHAOTIC**—Confused—Disordered—Disorganized—

**Acts**—Chaotic and Unnatural Acts—(See Perversions, Unnatural).

**Appetites**—Chaotic, Sensuous, Unnatural—(See Appetites, Food, Gluttony, Morbid, Passion, Perversions, Sensuous, Sex, Unnatural).

**Confusion**—Confusion of Ideas—Of Mind—(See Ideas, Projects. Also see "Mental Chaos" in this section).

**Fancies**—Chaotic Fancies—(See Fancies).

**Mania**—Chaotic Religious Mania—(See Mania, Religion).

**Mental Chaos**—Chaotic Mind—Confusion of Mind—Vague Mental States—Flightiness—Caused by the afflictions of ♆ to ☿, or to the Sigs., the ☉, ☽, or Asc., by dir.; ♆ in the 3rd or 9th H. in ill-asp. to the ☽ or ☿; a ♆ disease and affliction; ♆ affl. in ♊; ♆ ♊ and affl. the ☽ or ☿; ♆ ☌ ☽ or ☿, and affl. by the □ or ☍ ♅; ♆ ♈ ☌ ☽ or ☿, and □ or ☍ ♅; ♆ □ or ☍ ☿; the □ or ☍ asps. of ♆ to the ☉, ☽, ☿, Asc., or hyleg, and espec. under the evil directions of ♆ to these places in the natal map; ☽ ☌ ♆ or ♂ in ♈, and affl. by the □ or ☍ of ♅, ♄, or ♃; the 30° ♍ on the Asc. at B., and afflicted. (See Fears, Flightiness, Hallucinations, Idiocy, Imaginations, Insanity).

**Religion**—Chaotic Religious Mania—(See Mania, Religion).

**Sex Relations**—Chaotic, Irregular and Unlawful—(See "Relations" under Sex).

**Unnatural**—Chaotic and Unnatural Acts—(See Perversions, Sex, Unnatural, Vices). For further study see Clairaudience, Clouded, Concentration, Dreamy, Ideas, Incoordination, Obsessions, Projects, Spirit Controls, Vagaries, Vague, Vain, Weird, etc.

**CHARACTER**—The ☽ represents the personal character, the Personality or lower mind. The Higher Mind, or the Individuality, is denoted by the sign the ☉ is in at B. However, the real and true character of the Ego, its present stage in evolution, is difficult to determine from the star map of birth. It is said that the character of an incoming Ego is more typically shown and represented by the star map for the time of conception, the Prenatal Epoch map, and usually this map will reveal many hidden traits of the character not shown on the map of birth. The map of birth shows tendencies of the temperament, the environment and external conditions and associations which the native will encounter during the present life; shows the nature of the experiences necessary and the lessons to be learned for soul growth, but does not necessarily reveal the character, or the real nature of the Ego, or the Soul. The native may have a good reputation, yet be hypocritical and evil in his inner character, may be unawakened and unspiritualised, and not yet conscious of his inner, higher, and Divine powers. Advanced Egos have more power over disease, while the younger, negative, inexperienced, and more susceptible souls give way to disease more easily and are more bound by earth and materialistic conditions. The student can learn much about the nature and meaning of Character by making a study of the Occult and Metaphysical books, and too much space cannot be given the subject here. All the good manifestations in a person come down from the Higher Mind, the Spirit, while the evils are usually the emanations of the Personality, or Lower Mind. There are no diseases, or disease thoughts in the Higher Mind, and the afflictions, diseases, ailments, traits of temperament, etc., listed in this work are mostly those of the Lower Mind. (See Conduct, Desires, Disease, Dishonesty, Fate, Heredity, Morals, Religion, Responsibility, and the various subjects thruout this Encyclopaedia).

**CHARMS**—Amulets—Talismans— (See Amulets).

**CHART**—

**Chart of Birth**—(See Map, Nativity).

**Chart of Descent** — (See Prenatal Epoch).

**CHARTERING**—Injury or Death By— (See Contests, Duels, "Death" under Quarrels).

**CHEATING**—Fraudulent— A Swindler —Afflictions to ☿, ruler of the mind; ☿ ill-dig. at B.; ☿ Sig. ☌ ♂; ♂ affl. in ♊; ♂ ill-dig. at B., and affl. ☿; ♄ Sig. ☐ or ☍ ☿. (See Deceitful, Dishonest, Forgers, Liars, Pettifogging, Swindlers, Shrewdness, Thieves, etc.).

**Much Cheating Generally**—☿ elevated above, and configurated with ♄ at a Solar Ingress or Eclipse.

**CHEEKS**—Sides of Face—Ruled by ♀ and the ♈ sign. (See Decanates).

**Bloated Cheeks**—(See "Bloated" under Face).

**Dimples In**—(See Dimples).

**Falling In Of**—Hollow Cheeks—♂ Sig. in fiery signs; Subs at MCP, the 3rd Cervical. (See "Sunken" under Face).

**Moles On**—(See Moles).

**Puffy**—Blub-Cheeked—Caused by the ☽ influence, and espec. the ☽ in watery signs. (See "Bloated", "Lumpish", under Face).

**Red Cheeks**—(See "Red" under Face; "Cheeks" under Red).

**CHEERFULNESS**—The ♃ influence makes one jovial, and also the ♀ influence strong at B. tends to mirth and cheerfulness; the ☽ Sig. in ♎, a cheerful face. The ♄ people tend to be lacking in cheerfulness, and to be morose and melancholic. The ♐ sign gives cheer to the nature, which is a ♃ sign, and espec. when ☿ is not affl. by ♄. Cheerfulness is a strong asset for good health and longevity. (See Contentment, Happiness, Joy, "Peace of Mind" under Mind; Optimistic, Sanguine, Smiling, etc.).

**CHEMICAL ACTION**—All of the planetary rays have a special chemical action of their own upon the Mineral, Vegetable and Animal Kingdoms. Some of these rays are agreeable and compatible among themselves, and others incompatible, the same as among chemicals, and a bad mixture of the planetary rays at B., or at any time or period in life, tends to explosions in the temperament, or to ill-health and disease, whereas a good mixture of planetary rays which are agreeable tend to expansion, benefits, good health, peace of mind, etc. For the subjects of planetary affinities and repulsions, see Antipathy, Opposites, Sympathy.

**Chemical Changes**—(See Explosions).

**CHEMISTS**—Chemistry—Apothecary— Druggists—Pharmacists—

**Chemistry of the Body**—There are 12 basic and fundamental chemical elements in the body, and each ruled over by one of the Signs of the Zodiac. These chemical constituents may be well-balanced in the different parts and organs of the body, or very much out of proportion, which latter condition may lead to disease unless rectified. For a further study of this subject see "Salts" under Zodiac. For the general chemical processes in the body see such subjects as Assimilation, Bone Building, Digestion, Elimination, Excretion, Gastric Juices, Haematopoiesis (Blood-Making); Nutrition, etc.

**Make Good Chemists**—The ♂ and ♏ influences are said to bear strong rule over Chemists, and Chemistry, and people born with the ☉, ☽, ♃, ♂, or ☿ in ♏, and well-aspected, or with ♏ on the Asc., usually make good Chemists or Druggists, and are drawn to such study or practice. Other influences are the ☉ or ☿ in the 12th H., and well-aspected; ♂ a strong ruler at B.; ♂ in ♍ or ♏ and well-aspected; ♂ in the 10th H.; ♂ in good asp. to ☿; ♂ and ♀ together rulers of the employment make good Druggists, and espec. if ♅ be joined with them; ♂ in ✶ or △ asp. the ☉ at B.; ♂ ascending in a watery sign; ♂ ruler, and lord of the Asc.; any asp. of ♂ to the ☽ or ☿ inclines to the study of Chemistry, Dentistry, Medicine or Surgery; lord of the Asc. in his own dignities if he apply to ♂ exalted, and in an angle, honours for Chemists, Surgeons or Physicians; the ✶ or △ asps. of ♂ to the ☉, ☽, and planets; ♃ Sig. in ✶ or △ ♂, a good Chemist; ♃ Sig. ☌ ♂; ♀ Sig. ☌ ♂, and ♂ well-dignified; ♀ ruler, and in the 10th H., favors dealings in drugs, poisons, dyes, colors, and perfumes; ♀

and ☿ as joint rulers make good Apothecaries or Physicians; the ☽ Sig. in ☌ ♂, and ♂ well-dig.; the M.C. or Asc. to the ✱ or △ ♂ by dir., success as Chemists; the majority of planets in earthy signs at B.; lord of the employment in ♏ or ♐, and well-asp.; the 6th face of ♐ culminating on the M.C. at B.; the 1st or 4th faces of ♌ culminating. In Hor'y Questions, the Sig. in ♏, denotes a good Chemist, Pharmacist, Surgeon or Healer; the Sig. in fiery signs indicates a good Chemist or Apothecary. Case—Famous Chemist—See "Davy", No. 703, in 1001 N.N. (See Drugs, Dentists, Healers, Herbs, Medicine, Remedies, Surgeons).

**CHESS PLAYERS**—Great Ability At—Geniuses—(See Genius, Mathematical, Prodigies).

**CHEST**—Thorax—Upper Portion of the Body—Trunk—The Chest is ruled by the ♋ sign, and the 3rd H. The chest cavity generally is ruled by ♋. (See "Impar" under Ganglion).

**Afflicted**—The Chest Afflicted—(See "Disorders" in this section).

**Broad Chest**—(See "Broad" under Breast).

**Burning Sensation In**—(See "Heartburn" under Heart).

**Capacious Chest**—Good Lung Capacity—(See "Capacity" under Lungs).

**Colds on Chest**—(See "Colds on Chest" under Lungs).

**Congestions**—Congested and Feverish Chest—♂ affl. in ♊. (See "Congestion" under Bronchial, Lungs).

**Deformities Of**—Afflictions in ♊ or ♋. (See "Breastbone" under Breast. See "Hollow", "Narrow", in this section).

**Disorders Of**—The Chest Afflicted—The Chest Deranged—Liable to Chest Disorders—The ☉ in the 6th H., and affl. in common signs, liable to Consumption, and all kinds of chest disorders, and espec. when affl. by the ☽ or ♄; the ☉ affl. in ♋; the ☽ hyleg in ♊, and espec. in female nativities; ♃ affl. in 6th H. in ♊ or ♍; ♂ in the 6th H. at B., in common signs, and affl. by the ☉ or ☽; ☿ affl. in ♎; ♋ on the Asc.; afflictions in ♋ or ♑; Subs at Lu.P. (See Breast, Bronchial, Consumption, Dress, Lungs, Trunk, Tuberculosis).

**Dropsy Of**—Hydrothorax—Water in the Chest—The ☽ in ♋, and a watery sign on cusp 6th H., and with other planets in watery signs; the ☽ affl. in ♌ or ♒, with people suffering from heart trouble; the ☽ affl. in ♍ or ♓; the ☽ ♓, ☌ or ill-asp. ♄ (or ☿ if he be of the nature of ♄) at the beginning of an illness or at decumb.; ♃ affl. in ♓; Subs at H.P., Lu.P. and K.P., the 11th Dorsal. (See Dropsy).

**Emphysema**—Pleural and of Chest—♅ affl. in ♊; a ♅ disease. (See Emphysema).

**Feverish and Congested**—(See "Congestions" in this section).

**Fluids Of**—(See "Chest" under Fluids).

**Heartburn**—(See "Heartburn" under Heart).

**Hollow Chest**—♄ affl. in ♊. (See "Narrow" in this section. Also see Consumption).

**Hydrothorax**—(See "Dropsy" in this section).

**Intercostal**—Intercostal Bulging—Intercostal Neuralgia—(See Intercostal, Neuralgia).

**Lungs**—(See Lungs).

**Mediastinal Tumors**—(See Tumors).

**Narrow Chest**—Hollow Chest—♄ and ♑ influence; ♑ on the Asc. at B., and afflicted; ♄ affl. in ♊; ♄ ☌ or ill-asp. the ☽. (See "Deformities", "Hollow", in this section).

**Neuralgia**—(See "Intercostal" in this section).

**Pains**—In Chest—♄ affl. in the 6th H., in cardinal signs; ♂ affl. in ♊ or ♋; great pains in the chest are caused when, at the beginning of a disease or at decumb., the ☽ is in ♒, slow in motion, decr. in light, and affl. by the ☉ or ♂. (See "Pain" under Breast).

**Pigeon Shaped**—(See "Breastbone" under Breast).

**Pleura**—(See Pleura).

**Prevalent**—Chest Disorders Prevalent—♂ lord of the year, in ♋, at the Vernal; ☿ in ♋ at the Vernal Equi., lord of the year, and affl. by ♂.

**Ribs**—(See Ribs).

**Short and Wide**—Born under ♃. (See "Wide" in this section).

**Sternum**—(See Breast, Sternum).

**Stout Chest**—Stout and Broad Chest—♄ ori. at B.; ♃ in the Asc. (See "Broad" under Breast. Also see "Short and Wide", "Wide", in this section).

**Sunken Chest**—(See "Hollow", "Narrow" in this section).

**Thorax**—(See Thorax).

**Tightness Of**—♄ affl. in ♊, or affl. the ☉ or ☽; also a ♃ disease. (See Bronchial, Cough, Lungs).

**Tuberculosis**—(See this subject).

**Tumors Of**—(See "Mediastinal" under Tumors).

**Trunk**—(See Trunk)).

**Water In**—The ☽ in ♓, ☌ or ill-asp. ♄ when taken ill, or when compelled to take to bed. (See "Dropsy" in this section).

**Weak Chest**—(See "Weak" under Lungs).

**Wide Chest**—♄ ori. at B.; ♄ in ♌, partile the Asc.; ♄ Sig. in ♌. (See "Broad", "Short and Wide", "Stout", in this section).

**Wounds To**—♂ affl. in ♊, ♋, or ♌, or other malefics and afflictions in these signs. (See "Accidents" under Breast).

**CHEYNE-STOKES BREATHING**—(See "Cheyne-Stokes" under Breathing).

**CHICKEN-POX**—Varicella—A ♂ disease; ♂ affl. in ♑; Subs at MCP., the 4th and 5th Cervicals, and at CP, KP, the 11th Dorsal. (See Infectious Diseases, Scabs, Scarlet Fever, Sloughing, Smallpox, etc.).

**CHILBLAIN**—Cutaneous Inflammation Due to Cold—A ♄ disease, and due to cold; a ♀ and ♓ disease; ☽, ♄, or ♀ affl. in ♓; ♀ ♓ in the 6th H., and afflicted; ♀ ♓ and affl. the ☽ or Asc. (See Cold, Feet).

**CHILDBED FEVER**—(See "Puerperal Fever" under Puerperal. Also see Parturition).

**CHILDBIRTH**—Accouchment—Labor—Confinement—(See Parturition, Puerperal).

**CHILDHOOD**—Early Years of Life—This subject is considered largely under Infancy, and Children, but for convenience of reference. subjects which relate to Childhood in general will be listed and considered in this section. The Period of Childhood is divided into three parts. The first 7 years are under the rule of the ☽; the period from 7 to 14 years under the rule of ☿, and the period from 14 to 21 under ♀ rule. Some Authors divide these periods differently, which divisions are given under "Periods." (See Periods). The Period from 1 to 7 years is also discussed under Infancy. (See Infancy). In the Kabala the period of childhood was dedicated to the ☽. The Vital Body, one of the human vehicles, takes charge of the child at the 7th year, at the 7th birthday, and tends to excessive growth from 7 to 14 years of age. (See "Body" under Vital). At the age of 14 comes Adolescence, and the birth of the Desire Body, another of the human vehicles. (See Desire Body, Puberty). The birth of the Desire Body gives the power of procreation, and also tends to passion. The Mind does not take full control of the body until the 21st birthday, the end of the third seven-year cycle of childhood, and at 21 the child becomes "Of Age" legally. The following influences are listed in this section, which are supplemental to those which appear under "Children", "Infancy", "Youth".

**Accidents in Childhood**—Accidents in the early years of life are caused by the same general influences as given in the Article on "Accidents", only these influences come to a climax sooner after birth. A child having a malefic anywhere from 1 to 15° from the vital points of the map, such as the ☉, ☽, Asc., M.C., Desc., Hyleg, etc., would be liable to an accident, injury, fall, blow, fracture, sickness etc., according to the time it took the afflicting malefic, or planet, to reach the Asc., by direction, or other vital places in the map, and the affliction would be according to the nature of the afflicting planet. The same influences which cause accidents in childhood may also cause death, according to the severity of the afflictions, and a train of evil directions to the hyleg. (See Accidents; "Accidents" under Children, and Infancy; "Children" under Hurts).

**Danger in Early Years**—Weak Body During Early Childhood—Not Strong in Early Years—Much Sickness in Childhood—♑ on the Asc., or the ☉ or ☽ affl. in ♑, the early years weak, and with greater danger of death; ♄ affl. in the Asc.; lord of the 6th H. in the Asc., and affl.; the 19° ♓ on the Asc. (See "Death", "Poor Health", "Vitality", under Infancy. Also note the various paragraphs in this section).

**Death During Childhood**—These influences are much the same as given in the section on "Arguments for Death" under Death, only that they come to a climax earlier in life. If in the 6th year of life a train of evil directions afflict the hyleg, the child will be apt to pass out in that year. Children are more susceptible to planetary afflictions, and to pass out under conditions which an adult might weather thru, as children have not yet learned the laws of mind and spirit, and also the mind does not take more complete possession of the body until the 21st year. Thus an Astrologer can make a study of the star map of a new-born infant, and usually tell whether the child will live thru the first year, or not, by the transits, afflictions, and directions that may culminate over the hyleg in that year, if any. However, it is unethical for Astrologers to predict the time of death, even if they knew, as such would only tend to worry the parents, and the child also if old enough to comprehend the meaning of it. For the planetary influences along this line see "Arguments for Death", "Early Death", "Time of Death", under Death; "Death in Infancy", and other paragraphs under Infancy; "Short Life" under Life; "Death in Early Youth" under Youth. Also note the various paragraphs in this section. Here are a few cases and Birth Data of children dying during childhood, given in 1001 N.N., and dying at ages of 5, 14, 15 and 16 years of age. See "Early Death", No. 428; "Elizabeth" No. 654; "Prince", No. 654; and "France", No. 533, all in 1001 N.N. Also under the heading of "Death" under Infancy, there are about 12 Cases, and Birth Data listed from 1001 N.N., cases of Death in Infancy.

**Early Childhood**—Early Years of Life—Sickness or Death In—(See the various paragraphs under Children, Infancy, and in this Article. Also see "Short Life", under Life; Youth, etc.).

**Enteritis in Childhood**—Inflamed Bowels In—Afflictions in ♍; ♂ affl. in ♍; Subs at UPP. (See "Inflammation" under Bowels).

**Fevers in Childhood**—And Early Youth—♂ coming to the ☌ or ill-asp. the Asc. in early years, tends to chickenpox, fevers, hurts, inflammations, measles, smallpox, wounds, etc. (See Fever).

**Many Diseases**—In Childhood—No asp. between the ☉ and ♂ at B. (See "Danger" in this section).

**Much Sickness**—In Childhood—The Body Weak in Early Years—(See "Danger" in this section; "Much Sickness" under Infancy; "Vitality Low" under Vitality).

**Restricted and Unhappy**—An Unhappy Childhood—The ☉ in ♓ in the 12th H., and affl. by ♄; ♄ ☌ ☉ or ☽ in the Asc. at B. (See Saturn, Twelfth House).

**Rickets**—In Childhood—(See Rickets). For other subjects, diseases or afflictions concerning Childhood and Children, see the various paragraphs under Children, Infancy, and also look in the alphabetical arrangement for the subject you have in mind.

**CHILDREN**—Offspring—Progeny—Issue—The 5th and 11th Houses are the principle rulers of children. The 10th H. is also strongly related to children. According to Ptolemy the 10th and 11th Houses signify children, and planets in them, or configurated with them, but if there are no planets in these houses, or in aspect to them, then take the 4th and 5th Houses. ♃, ♀, and the ☽ are the Givers of Children. ♄ and ♂ tend to deny them, and cause barrenness. ☿ is variable according to stars with which configurated. ☿ ori. tends to give children, but occi. to deny them, and cause barrenness. (See Fifth House, Eleventh House, Tenth House, Fourth House). The subjects of Childhood, Early Years, Infancy, Diseases of Infancy, Death in Infancy, Youth, etc., are considered under the subjects of Childhood, Infancy, Youth. So much has been said in the Textbooks of Astrology on the subject of Children, and I have gathered so much material, that I will arrange this Article in three Sections as follows—

Section One—General Considerations. Section Two—The Diseases of Children. Section Three—Duration of Life, and Death of Children. See the following subjects in the alphabetical arrangement when not considered more fully in this Article.

## — SECTION ONE —

### GENERAL CONSIDERATIONS—

**Adolescence**—(See Puberty).

**Adoption**—(See Adoption, "Early Death or Parents", "Separation from Parents", under Parents).

**Advent of a Child**—(See "Birth of a Child" in this section).

**Amativeness In**—(See Amativeness).

**Anxiety to Parents**—(See "Parents", "Worries", in this section).

**Barren Time**—No Issue—The ☉ to the bad asps. ♀ by dir. (See Barrenness).

**Barrenness**—No Children—(See Barrenness, Husband, Impotence, Wife. Also see "Denial" in this section).

**Bastards; Birth of a Child**—Time of Advent of a Child—Promise of a Child—The ☉ to the ☌ and good asps. ♀ by dir.; the ☉ to the P., and good asp. the ☽ by dir. if the ☽ be strong at B.; the ☉ to the ☌ or P. asp. ☿ by dir., and ☿ strong and well-asp. at B.; the good asps. of the ☉ by dir. to the ☽, Asc., M.C., or to the ⚹ his own place; the ☽ to the good asps. the ☉ by dir. unless the ☉ be greatly affl. at B.; the ☽ or ♀ to the ⚹ or △ the Asc. by dir., and a daughter espec. is promised; the ☽ to the ☌ or good asps. ♃ by dir.; the ☽ to the good asps. ☿ by dir.; the ☽ at a Solar Rev. passing over the place of ♃ at B.; the ☽ to the ☌ or good asps. of ♀ by dir., and espec. if the ☽ was in the 5th H. at B., and children were not denied; ♃ at a Solar Rev. ☌ or P. the place of the ☉ or ☽ at B.; ♃ to the ☌ the ☽ by dir., and espec. if in the 5th H.; ♃ or ♀ to the ⚹ or △ the ☉ or ☽ by dir.; ♃ by Periodic Rev. to the ☌ the place of the ☽ at B.; the good asps. of ♃ by dir. to any of the Moderators, as the ☉, ☽, Asc., or M.C.; the good directions of ♃ to the M.C., or fruitful places, or a giver of children in the map; ♂ ⚹ or △ the Asc. or M.C. by dir.; ♀ in ♉, ♎, the Asc., or 7th H., and the place of ♀ ascending at a Solar Rev., a child that year if married; ♀ ☌ the Asc. by dir.; ♀ to the ☌, ⚹ or △ the M.C. by dir.; the Asc. to the ☌, P., or good asp. ♃ or ♀ by dir.; the Asc. to the ⚹ or △ ☿ by dir.; the M.C. to the ☌, P., ⚹ or △ ♃ or ♀ by dir.; the M.C. to the good asps. the ☽ by dir. (See "Female Births" under Female; "Births" under Male; "Time" under Parturition. Also see "First Born" in this section).

**Birth Delayed**—(See "Delayed in this section).

**Birth of Children Prevented**—(See "Denial" in this section. Also see Barren).

**Birthrate**—(See this subject under Birth).

**Black Sheep**—The Black Sheep in the Fold—The house ruled by a malefic planet, in the order of children given, will tend to be the black sheep among the children, and bring sorrow, trouble, or disgrace upon himself and the parents. (See "Parents", "Worries", in this section).

**Blessing**—Children tend to prove a blessing to the parents—♃ or ♀ well-asp. in the 5th H., and no malefic influences over this house at B. in the maps of the parents.

**Born**—When Will the Child Be Born?—Probable Time of Birth—Birth usually takes place when the ☽ reaches her 10th Lunation from the time of conception. Usually when the ☉ is passing some asp. of the cusp of 5th H.; when the ☉ or ♂ reach a ☌ with lord of the 5th; at the time of the ☌ of lord of the 5th with lord of the Asc. in the 5th; when the lord of the Asc. goes out of one sign into another. These influences tend to precipitate the birth if they exist near the time of regular delivery. Note the distance of lord of the 5th H. from the cusp of the 5th., and give one month to each sign. Judge according to the majority of testimonies. (See "Moment of Birth" under Birth, and Moment; "Time" under Parturition; Premature. Also see "Delayed" in this section).

**Boy Born**—(See "Births" under Male. Also see Son. See "First Born" in this section).

**Brothers Indicated**—(See Brothers).

**Child Promised**—(See "Birth of a Child" in this section).

**Childbirth**—(See Mother, Parturition).

**Childhood**—(See Childhood, Infancy, Youth. Also see the various paragraphs in this section).

**Childless**—(See Barren, Husband, Wife. Also see "Denial" in this section).

**Complexion**—Fair in Youth—(See Youth).

**Conception**—Moment of—Signs of— (See Conception).

**Creative Powers**—Of the Parents— (See Barren, Creative, Fruitful, Husband, Powers, Wife).

**Daughter Born**—(See "Female Births" under Female).

**Decreased**—The Number of Children Decreased—♄ in the 5th H., and affl. The number of children will be increased or diminished according to the nature of the planets in the 5th H., and the asps. to such planets. (See "Increased" in this section).

**Delayed Births**—♄ rising, or on the Asc., and with danger of Asphyxiation. This was the case with Goethe, the Poet. (See "Birth" under Asphyxia). Also what some people would consider a delayed, or overtime birth may be normal according to the laws of the Prenatal Epoch, as in Epochs of the 2nd and 3rd Orders, which show 273 days + x in utero, etc. (See Prenatal Epoch).

**Denial of Children**—The ☉, ♅, ♄ and ♂ tend to deny children, or allot but few, or cause their death when born, and espec. if these bodies are in the 5th H. of the parents at B., and affl. (See Barrenness, Husband, Wife).

**Denoted**—Children Denoted—Promise of—(See Fruitful, Husband, Wife. Also see "Birth of" in this section).

**Desire For Children Strong**—(See Amativeness).

**Directions and Children**—The Primary or Secondary Directions of Childhood and Youth—In case of young children and infants, the first train of evil directions to the hyleg tend to kill, and espec. during the ☽ period from 1 to 7 years of age. Children at an older age may survive evil directions, and even have good health if born with strong vitality, but the evil directions may severely afflict the parents, cause disease, suffering, or the death of a parent. (See "Direction" in Sec. 3 of this Article. Also see "Directions" under Infancy, Parents).

**Disposition Of**—(See Disposition, Savage, Temperament. Also see "Savage" in Sec. 2 of this Article).

**Dogs**—May Resemble Dogs—(See "Dogs" in Sec. 2 of this Article).

**Double Births**—(See Twins).

**Drink**—Parents Given to Drink and Neglect of Children—(See "Drink" under Parents).

**Duration of Life**—(See Sec. 3 of this Article).

**Dwarfs; Early Years**—Conditions Affecting—(See the various paragraphs in this section. Also see Childhood, Infancy, "Short Life" under Life; Youth, etc).

**Eclipses**—Children Born at Time of— (See Eclipses, "New Moon" under Moon).

**Eight Months Children**—Children Born at the 8th month of Pregnancy— A child born at the 8th month is more apt to die because, according to the Science of Numbers, the number 8 is made up of two feminine factors,

4+4=8, the two elements making up 8 both being even, or feminine numbers. (See Climacteric). Children born at the 7th month live, it is said, because the elements making up 7, consisting of 3+4=7, combine an odd and even number, or a masculine and feminine number. (See Cases under Premature). Children born at the 9th month also have a positive and feminine combination, an odd and even number, as 4+5=9, and such combinations give force and vitality, whereas the combination of the two even numbers lack balance and the vital force necessary to sustain the child after delivery. This theory is discussed in books on the Science of Numerals, and is undoubtedly, in my opinion, the true explanation and philosophy of the matter. All Nature is founded upon the laws of Mathematics, Numbers, Vibration, etc., and the Planetary influences also work according to these rules and laws. (See Gestation).

**Eleventh House**—As Related to Children. (See the Introduction to this Article. Also see Eleventh).

**Embryo**—(See Foetus).

**Faithful Children**—(See "Blessing" in this section).

**Family**—A Large Family of Children —(See "Many Children" in this section).

**Father**—Conditions Affecting the Father—(See Father, Parents. Also see "Parents", "Worries", in this section).

**Female**—Barrenness In—(See Barrenness).

**Female Births**—Daughter Born—(See "Female Births" under Female).

**Female Child Promised**—(See "Birth of a Child" in this section. Also see "Female Births" under Female).

**Female Children**—Predominance of— This matter is largely judged from the sex of the horoscope. In female nativities the 5th H. is female, and the 4th H. is male. In male horoscopes the 5th H. is male, and the 4th H. is female. The conditions of these houses will show the predominating sex, and which gives the greater promise of fruitfulness, while the opposite houses show detriments. The majority of planets at B. in the feminine signs also indicate more female births, and the majority in masculine signs, more male births. (See "Female Births" under Female; "Births" under Male; Predetermination. Also see "First Born" in this section).

**Female Horoscope**—First Born Child In—(See "First Born" in this section).

**Female or Male**—During Pregnancy —(See "First Born" in this section. Also see Predetermination).

**Few Children**—But Few Promised— Few or No Children—One or Two Allotted—Small Family—The ☉, ♅, ♄, ♂, and ☋ allot but few, or deny children; the ☉ affl. in ♑; the ☉ in the 5th H. of the marriage partner; the ☉, ♅, ♄, ♂ or ☿ in the 5th H. may give a few, but if afflicted, apt to see their early death; ☿ occi., in a barren sign, and configurated with barren planets; the ♌ sign on the cusp of 5th H.; a barren sign on the Asc. or cusp of 5th H., or the ☽ ruler of the Asc. in such signs; lord of the Asc. in the 5th H., and affl. by ♄, ♂, or ☋. (See Barrenness. Also see "Denial" in this section).

**Fifth House**—This is the principal house of children, and the conditions affecting this house in the maps of the parents indicate much along the lines of children, their fate and destiny, and whether children will be born or denied; whether they will live or die; whether they may prove a blessing to the parents, or a source of worry and anxiety, etc. (See Fifth House).

**First-Born Child**—In a male horoscope the 5th H. denotes the first child, and the possible sex. The 7th H. denotes the second child, and the 9th H. the 3rd child; the 11th H., the 4th child, etc., in a male horoscope. Thus if there are malefics in the 5th H. of the father the first child is apt to be sickly, or die early; if malefics in the 7th H., the second child may die; if in the 9th H., the third child, etc. Benefics in these houses would show which of the children would be more fortunate, honorable, useful, a blessing, etc. In a female nativity the first child is denoted by the 4th H.; the second child by the 6th H.; the third child by the 8th H., etc., and the nature and possible destiny of each, from the mother's standpoint, is to be judged from the nature of the planets in these houses in her map. ♅, ♄, or ♂ in the 5th H. of the father, or in the 4th H. of the mother, indicate accidents, injuries, or sickness, death, etc., of the first child. Malefics in other houses, as stated, indicate hurt, loss of, or detriment to the second or third child. (See "First Born Brother" under Brothers). Cancer, a feminine sign, on the cusp of the 5th H., and with the ☽ or ♀, feminine planets also in ♋ in the 5th H., indicate a daughter in a male nativity. The ♐ sign on cusp of 5th H., and masculine planets in the 5th, would indicate a son as the first child in a male nativity, etc. The 7th H. dominated and influenced by masculine planets, and a masculine sign, indicate that the 2nd child, in a male nativity, would be a boy, etc. These rules, of course, apply to the natural order of conceptions, and where conception has not been interfered with, or prevented in any way. (See "Female Births" under Female; "Births" under Male; Son).

**Foetus**—Embryo—For matters concerning the Embryo and Foetus, see Abortion, Conception, Foetus, Gestation, Miscarriage, Pregnancy, Prenatal Epoch).

**Fortunate Children**—(See "Blessing" in this section).

**Fourth Child**—(See "First Born" in this section).

**Fruitful**—The Parents Fruitful, and a Large Family Indicated—(See Fruitful, Husband, Wife. Also see "Many Children" in this section).

**Geniuses**—(See Geniuses, Prodigies).

**Gestation; Givers of Children**—Gives Children—♃, ♀, and the ☽ are Givers of Children, and espec. when in the 5th H., and in fruitful signs. ☿ either gives or denies children, according to the planet, or planets configurated with at B. (See Fruitful, Moon, Jupiter, Venus).

**Good Health**—Of Children—(See "Long-Lived" in Sec. 2 of this Article. Also see "Long Life" under Life; "Good Vitality" under Vitality).

**Grandchildren**—Indicated when the maps of the parents are fruitful, and when good influences in the houses of children indicate good health and long life for children. (See Fruitful. Also see "Long Life" in Sec. 2 of this Article).

**Grief Through Children**—Malefics in or ruling the 5th H. of a parent. (See "Directions", "Parents", "Worries", in this section. Also see Parents).

**Growth of Children**—(See Corpulent, Diminished, Dwarf, Enlarged, Fat, Growth, Short, Tall, Thin, etc.).

**Guardians; Healthy**—(See "Long Life" under Life; "Children", and "Good" under Resistance; Vitality Good. Also see "Long-Lived" in Sec. 2 of this Article).

**Heredity; Houses of Children**—(See the Introduction to this Article).

**Human Shape**—Not of Human Shape—Resembles Animals—(See Inhuman, Monsters. Also see "Dogs" in Sec. 2 of this Article).

**Ill-Fortune**—Children bring ill-fortune, grief and sorrow to Parents—(See Parents. Also see "Black Sheep", "Grief", "Parents", "Worries", in this section).

**Illegitimate Children**—(See Bastards).

**Imprisonment**—A Parent Imprisoned Thru the Plots of Children—Lord of the 12th H. a malefic, and in the 5th H. (See "Plots" under Prison).

**Increased Number**—Of Children—Several Children—The ☽, ♃, or ♀ in the 5th H., in a fruitful or double-bodied sign, as in ♋, ♏, or ♓, or in ♊ or ♐; the ☽ in the 5th or 11th H. in a fruitful sign. (See Fruitful. Also see "Decreased", "Many", in this section).

**Increased Strength**—(See "Strength" under Infancy; Vitality. Also see "Strength" in this section).

**Infancy**—For the various conditions affecting Infants see Infancy, Childhood, and also note the various paragraphs in this Article).

**Injured**—Children Injured—Parents Injured by Children—(See "Accidents" in Sec. 3 of this Article. See "Parents" in this section; "Injured" under Parents).

**Issue**—No Issue—A Barren Time—(See "Barren Time" in this section).

**Kidnapped; Labor**—Confinement—(See Parturition).

**Lactation**—(See Milk, Nursing).

**Large Family**—(See Fruitful, Husband, Wife. Also see "Increased", "Many", in this section).

**Legitimate**—Is the Child Legitimate? —(See Bastards).

**Lives**—The Child Will Live and be Healthy—(See "Long-Lived" in Sec. 2 of this Article).

**Long-Lived**—(See "Long-Lived" in Sec. 2 of this Article).

**Love and Affection**—Love and Affection of the Parents For—(See "Love and Affection" under Parents).

**Male Children Born**—(See "Births" under Male; Son. Also see "Female Births" in this section).

**Male Nativity**—First Child In—Second Child In, etc.—(See "First Born" in this section).

**Male or Female**—During Pregnancy —(See Predetermination).

**Males**—Two or Three Males Born at One Confinement—(See "Births" under Male; Twins, Triplets).

**Many Children**—A Large Family— The ☽ in ♋, ♏, or ♓, or in the double-bodied signs ♊ or ♐, in the 5th H., and well-asp. by ♃ or ♀; the ☽ in the 5th or 11th H. in a fruitful sign; the ☽ in the 5th H. in other than barren signs, and well-asp. by benefics; the ☽ in ♉, her exalted sign, in the 5th H., and well-asp.; ♃, ♀, or ☽ in 5th H., and the ☽ in good asp. to ♃ or ♀, increases their number; ♃ well-asp. in ♏; ♀ in the 5th H., and well-asp., and espec. in a watery sign; ♋, ♏, ♓, or ♉ upon cusp of 5th H. if the ☽ is well placed and aspected; planets, or ☊ in the 5th H., and well-asp. by ☽ or ♀; rulers of the 1st and 5th H. in fruitful signs, and espec. when ♃ and ♀ are in good asp. to the ☽ or ruler of the 5th; ♋ on the Asc. or 5th H. at B., strong, and with the ☉, ☽, ♃ or ♀ in ♋; lord of the 5th H. in a fruitful sign in the Asc., if not afflicted; ♋ or ♓ on cusp 5th H., and no malefics in the 5th, indicate a large family; cusp of the 5th H., and its lord, strong, or in fruitful signs, or if many planets, and espec. ♃ or ♀ be here, or in translation or reception with its lord, or if lord of the Asc. be there, or ☊, gives many children; lord of the 7th H. in the 5th. (See Fruitful. Also see "Increased" in this section). Cases of Many Children—Had Sixteen Children—See "Anne", No. 518 in 1001 N.N. Had 9 sons and 4 daughters—See "Maximillian", No. 549, in 1001 N.N.

**Matricide**—(See "Patricide" under Father).

**Midwives; Mind**—Children of—(See Creative).

**Misfortune**—Thru Children—(See "Parents", "Worries", in this section).

**Moment of Birth**—(See "Moment" under Birth).

**Moon**—A Female Born at Time of Eclipse of—(See Eclipses).

**Mother**—(For conditions affecting the Mother, see Mother).

**Neglected**—Children Neglected by Parents—(See "Drink" under Parents).

**No Children**—(See Barrenness; "Anchorite" under Husband. Also see "Denial" in this section).

**Number of Children**—(See Decreased, Few, Increased, Many, and the various paragraphs in this section. Also see Barrenness, Fruitful).

**Numerous Children**—(See "Many" in this section).

**Nursing**—(See Breasts, Milk, Nipples, Nursing).

**Obedient Children**—(See "Blessing" in this section).

**One at a Birth**—(See "Single Births" in this section).

**One or Two Allotted**—Few Children— (See "Few", "Worries", in this section).

**Orphans**—(See "Adoption" in this section).

**Overtime Children**—(See "Delayed" in this section).

**Parental Love**—(See "Love" under Parents).

**Parents**—Influences Affecting the Parents Thru the Children—(See Black Sheep, Directions, Imprisonment, Injured, Worries, etc., in this section. Also note the various paragraphs under Father, Mother, Parents).

**Parturition**—Childbirth—(See Parturition).

**Patricide**—(See "Patricide" under Father).

**Perfect**—Some Perfect, and Some Imperfect—(See Beautiful. Also see "Ill-formed", "Imperfect", in Sec. 2 of this Article).

**Periods of Childhood**—(See the Introduction under Childhood).

**Precocious; Predetermination**—Of the Sex During Pregnancy—(See Predetermination).

**Predominance of Sexes**—(See "Female Children" in this section).

**Pregnancy**—Male or Female During —(See Predetermination. Also see "First Born" in this section).

**Pregnant**—The Woman is With Child —The Woman is Not With Child—(See Pregnancy).

**Premature Births**—(See Abortion, Miscarriage, Parturition, Premature, Prenatal Epoch).

**Prenatal Epoch; Prevented**—The Birth of Children Prevented—Denial of Children—(See Barrenness. Also see "Denial" in this section).

**Probability of Children**—Fruitful signs on the cusps of 4th, 5th, 10th or 11th Houses; ♃, ♀, or the ☽ in the 4th, 5th, 10th or 11th Houses, and well-asp. Look first to the 10th and 11th Houses, and if no planets therein, look to the 4th and 5th Houses. If none there look to planets which may be in good asp. to degrees on the cusps of these Houses. (See Fruitful).

**Prodigies; Promise of a Child**—Children Promised—(See "Birth of a Child", and "Increased" in this section. Also see Fruitful).

**Propagation**—Strong Desire For— (See Amativeness).

**Prosperous Children**—(See "Blessing" in this section).

**Puberty; Quadruplets**—(See Quadruplets, Twins, Triplets).

**Religious Veneration**—Children Resemble Animals Held in Religious Veneration—(See "Dogs" in Sec. 2 of this Article).

**Second-Born Child**—(See "First Born" in this section).

**Seven Months Children**—(See "Eight Months Children" in this section).

**Several Children Promised**—(See "Increased", "Many", in this section. Also see Fruitful).

**Sex of Children**—(See "First-Born", "Female Children", "Male Children", in this section. See Predetermination).

**Short-Lived**—(See Sec. 3 of this Article).

**Significators of Children**—♃, ♀, and the ☽. The 5th H. and its lord are Sigs. of children in Hor'y Questions only. (See "Givers" in this section).

**Signs of Children**—(See Fruitful. Also see "Increased", "Many", in this section).

**Single Births**—One Birth Only—Not Twins—Planets which give children placed singly, and unaspected, in the 4th, 5th, 10th or 11th H.; an absence of the givers of children in double-bodied signs, or absence of such signs on the cusps of the 5th or 11th H. (See Twins).

**Sisters Indicated**—(See Sisters).

**Sixteen Children**—Gave Birth To—(See "Many" in this section).

**Small Family**—(See "Few" in this section).

**Son Born**—Son Promised—(See "First Born" in this section. Also see "Births" under Male; Son).

**Sorrow**—Thru Children—(See "Parents", "Worries", in this section).

**Stamina Of**—(See "Long-lived" in Sec. 2 of this Article. Also see Stamina, Tone, Vitality).

**Step Children**—Ruled by the 11th H.

**Strength of Children**—Increased by benefics well-asp. in the 5th or 11th H., and decreased by malefics affl. in these houses. (See "Long-lived" in Sec. 2 of this Article; "Early Death", and other paragraphs in Sec. 3 of this Article. Also see "Long Life" under Life; Resistance, Stamina, Tone, Vitality).

**Strong Children**—(See "Strength" in this section; "Long-lived" in Sec. 2 of this Article).

**Symbols of Children**—(See Fruitful). Also see "Givers" in this section).

**Teething**—(See Teeth).

**Tenth House**—As Related to Children—(See Tenth House).

**Third Child**—(See "First-Born" in this section).

**Three at a Birth**—(See Triplets).

**Time of Advent**—(See "Birth of a Child", "Born", "Delayed", "Premature", in this section. Also see Time).

**Triplets; Trouble to Parents**—(See "Parents", "Worries", in this section. Also see Parents).

**Twins**—Two at a Birth—(See Twins, Triplets).

**Two Children Allotted**—One or Two Allotted—(See "Few" in this section).

**Undertime Children**—(See "Eight Months", "Premature", in this section).

**Unfortunate with Children**—(See "Parents", "Worries", in this section).

**Unhappiness with Children**—(See "Parents", "Worries", in this section).

**Welfare and Health**—Of Children—Ruled by the 5th H. (See Sec. 3 of this Article).

**When Will the Child Be Born?**—(See "Birth of a Child", and "Born", in this section).

**Woman Is With Child**—The Woman Is Not With Child—(See Pregnancy).

**Worries Thru Children**—Malefics in the 5th H., or rulers of the 5th; malefics in the 11th H.; the ☉, ♅, ♄, or ♂, when taken as the Givers of Children in the map, may give one or two if in the houses of children and favorably aspected by the ☽, ♃, or ♀, but those given may cause the parents much trouble, or meet with ruin, disaster, much sickness, or an early death, or prove dissolute; ☿ affl. in the 5th H.; ruler of the 5th H. in the 2nd, 6th, 8th or 12th Houses; lord of the 8th H. in the 5th H. of parent. (See "Parents" in this section).

**Youth**—For conditions concerning Youth, see Childhood, Puberty, Youth, and also note the various paragraphs in this section).

## — SECTION TWO —

**DISEASES OF CHILDREN**—Afflictions to Children—The Health of Children—Children Suffer—Adverse Planetary Influences Affecting Children, etc.—The Welfare and Health of Children are ruled principally by the 5th H. See the following subjects in the alphabetical arrangement when not considered more fully here.

**Abortion; Accidents To**—Hurts or Injuries To—The ☉ or ☽ to the ill-asps. ♅, ♄, or ♂ by dir.; ♅, ♄, or ♂ affl. in ♌ or the 5th H.; ♅, ♄, or ♂ to the cusp the 5th H. by dir; ♅ on, or within 1° of the degree ascending at B.; ♂ in the 5th H. and affl. the ☉ or ☽. These influences may also cause death by accident if the map otherwise indicates a violent death. They also cause hurts, cuts, bruises, wounds, fractures, etc. For accidents at childbirth see Parturition. (See Hurts, Injury, in this section).

**Adolescence**—For disturbances at this period see Puberty.

**Afflicted Children**—Affliction to Children—The ☉ in the 5th H. and affl.; the ☽ in the 5th or 11th H. at B., and to the ☌, P., or ill-asps. ♅ by dir. (For further influences, see the various paragraphs in this section, and also in Sections 1 and 2 of this Article).

**Amativeness; Animal Heat**—Lacking in Animal Heat in Early Years—♑ influence; ♑ on the Asc. at B. (See "Animal" under Heat).

**Asphyxiation**—Danger of at Birth—(See "Birth" under Asphyxia. Also see "Delayed" in Sec. 1 of this Article).

**Bad Children**—♄ or ♂ affl. in the 5th H. at B. (See "Parents", "Worries", in Sec. 1 of this Article).

**Barrenness**—Children Born Barren—(See Barrenness, Impotency).

**Beastly Form**—(See "Beastly Form" under Beasts; Foetus; Inhuman. Also see "Dogs" in this section).

**Bed Wetting**—(See "Incontinence" under Urine).

**Birth**—(1) Delayed Birth—(See "Delayed" in Sec. 1 of this Article). (2) Disease and Infection at Birth Unusual Diseases at Birth—(See "Infections" under Infancy). (3) Injury or Accident to Child at Birth—Injury by Instrumental Delivery—(See "Accidents" under Infancy; "Injury" under Parturition). (4) Birth Prevented—(See "Birth" under Asphyxia; Barrenness, Birth; "Excision" under Foetus; Parturition. Also see "Delayed" in Sec. 1 of this Article).

**Blemishes**—(See Blemishes, Congenital).

**Blind from Birth**—(See "Born Blind" under Blindness).

**Blue Baby**—Nearly Asphyxiated at B. —(See "Birth" under Asphyxia).

**Body**—(1) Not of Human Shape—(See "Beastly Form" in this section). (2) Strong Body—(See Strong, Vitality. Also see "Long-lived" in this section). (3) Weak Body—(See "Low" under Vitality; "Weak Body" under Weak. Also see "Animal Heat", "Sickly", and other paragraphs in this section).

**Born**—But Sickly and Short-lived—(See "Sickly" in this section; "Early Death" in Sec. 3 of this Article).

**Bow Legs**—(See Legs, Limbs).

**Bowel Disorders**—(See Bowels).

**Breech Presentation**—(See "Breech" under Parturition).

**Bronchitis; Caesarian Operation**—(See "Excision" under Foetus).

**Calamity**—From the Moment of Birth —(See "Moment of Birth" under Calamity).

**Cats**—Offspring Resemble—(See "Dogs" in this section).

**Chickenpox; Child Will Suffer**—(See "Afflicted", "Suffers", and the various paragraphs in this section and Article).

**Childbirth**—Accident or Injury at Time of—(See Parturition. Also see "Birth" in this section).

**Childhood**—See the various paragraphs under Childhood, Infancy, and also in this Article).

**Cholera Infantum**—(See Cholera).

**Circumcision; Club Feet**—(See Feet).

**Colic; Congenital Defects**—(See Blemishes, Blind, Congenital, Deaf, Defects, Deformities, Distortions, Idiocy, Missing, Monsters, Mute, etc.).

**Constitution Poor**—(See "Sickly", "Weak", in this section. Also see "Early Death" in Sec. 3 of this Article).

**Convulsions**—(See Convulsions, Fits. Also see "Dentition" under Teeth).

**Cough; Cramps, Cretinism; Crippled** —From Birth—(See "Armless" under Arms; Congenital, Crippled, Deformities, Distortions, Excresences; "Club Feet" under Feet; Lameness, Legs, Limbs, Maimed, Missing, Monsters, Paralysis; "Child" under Walk).

**Croup; Danger to Children**—Danger of Injury—Subject to Many Dangers—♅ or ♂ to the cusp the 5th H. of a parent by dir.; ♅ on, or within 1° of the ascending degree at B.; ♂ affl. in the Asc. of the child at B., or ♂ here afflicting the ☉, ☽, or hyleg. (See "Accidents" in this section, and also under Childhood, Infancy).

**Daughter**—Danger To—(See Daughter).

**Deaf and Dumb**—(See Hearing).

**Defective Births** (See "Defective" under Birth; "Congenital", "Crippled", in this section).

**Deformed**—(See "Deformed" under Infancy; Deformities, Distortions, Inhuman, Lame, Legs, Limbs, Monsters, etc. See "Congenital", "Crippled", and the various paragraphs in this section).

**Delicate**—(See "Sickly" in this section).

**Delivery**—Injury At—(See "Accidents" under Infancy; "Injury" under Parturition).

**Dentition**—Spasms During Teething —(See "Dentition" under Teeth).

**Detriment to Children**—The ☉ in the 5th H. at the Vernal Equinox; malefics affl. in the 5th H. at B., and affl. the 5th H. by dir. (See "Accidents", "Dangers", and the various paragraphs in this Article, and also under Childhood, Infancy).

**Diarrhoea; Diminished Growth**—(See Diminished, Dwarf, Growth).

**Diphtheria; Disease**—Liable To—The Children Diseased—Sickly Children—Diseases at Birth—(See "Sickly", "Unhealthy" in this section; "Many Diseases" under Childhood; "Infections" under Infancy, etc. Also note the various paragraphs in this Article).

**Disposition**—(See Inhuman, Savage, Wild. Also see "Dogs" in this section).

**Distortions; Dogs**—The Offspring Resembles Dogs, Cats, and other creatures held in religious veneration, and used in worship—When the ruler of the last New or Full Moon before birth, and the rulers of the ☉ and ☽ are unconnected with the preceding New or Full ☽, and if in addition to this absence of connection, ♅, ♄, or ♂ be in angles, and the ☉ and ☽ be in a bestial sign, as in ♈, ♉, ♌, ♐, or ♑, then the conception will be normal, and tend to resemble the animal or creature ruled by the sign predominating. If the Luminaries be so unconnected, but with support from the benefics, and be affl. by ♄ and ♂ at the same time, the offspring will then be like Dogs, Cats, or other creatures held in religious veneration. If ♃ and ♀ do not interpose with their good asps., and the ☉ and ☽ are also disconnected, and evilly aspected by ♄ and ♂, then the creature born will be wholly wild, indocile, and of evil nature. Also people born in extreme cold climates, as in the Arctics, tend to have a wild and indocile nature, owing to constant cold. (See "Beastly Form" under Beasts; Foetus, Inhuman; "Animal Forms" under Monsters; Savage, Wild).

**Drunkards**—Children May Become Drunkards—(See Drunkenness).

**Dumb**—Deaf and Dumb—(See "Deaf and Dumb" under Hearing. Also see Mute).

**Dwarf; Dysentery; Early Years**—Influences Affecting Children During—(See the various paragraphs in this Article. Also see Childhood; "Early Years" under Early; "Animal Heat" under Heat; Infancy, Youth, etc.).

**Eclipses**—Children Born at Time of—(See Eclipses).

**Eight Months Children**—Born at 8th month—Sickness or Death of—(See "Eight Months Children" in Sec. 1 of this Article).

**Emaciation; Embryo**—Of Beastly Form—(See "Beastly Form" under Beasts. Also see "Dogs" in this section).

**Enuresis**—(See "Incontinence" under Urine).

**Epilepsy; Eruptions; Evil Children**—Evil in Nature—(See "Parents", "Worries", in Sec. 1 of this Article; "Dogs" in this section; Evil, Parents).

**Excision of Foetus**—(See Foetus).

**Excrescences; Eyes Weak**—(See Blindness, Eyes, Sight).

**Fat Body**—(See Fat).

**Feet**—Disorders and Deformities of—(See Feet).

**Female**—Barrenness In—Disorders of—(See Barren, Females, Impotency).

**Fevers**—In Childhood or Infancy—♂ to the ☌ or ill-asps. the Asc., or to the ill-asps. the ☉, ☽, or hyleg by dir. (See Fever; "Fever" under Infancy).

**Fierce and Savage**—(See "Dogs" in this section; "Beastly Form" under Beasts).

**Fits**—(See Fits; "Dentition" under Teeth; Spasms).

**Foetus**—Disorders of—Excision of—(See Foetus).

**Foolish Children**—(See Foetus, Foolish, Idiocy, Imbecile).

**Frog Child**—(See Frog).

**Gives Children**—But Weakly and Short Lived—The Givers of children, ♃, ♀, or ☽ in barren signs, and the malefics more powerful by strength or number. (See "Sickly", "Short-Lived" "Weak", in this section; "Early Death" in Sec. 3 of this Article).

**Growth**—(See Dwarf, Diminished, Enlarged, Fat, Giants, Growth, Height, Short, Tall, Thin, etc).

**Healthy**—And Long-lived—(See "Long-lived" in this section. Also see Constitution, Health, Strong, Vitality).

**Hearing Affected**—(See Hearing, Mute).

**Heart Affections**—(See Heart).

**Heat**—Lacking in Animal Heat—(See "Animal Heat" under Heat).

**Hermaphrodites; Human Shape**—Not of Human Shape—(See "Dogs", "Inhuman" in this section; "Beastly Form" under Beasts).

**Hurts To**—(See "Accidents" in this section and under Childhood, Infancy; "Children" under Hurts).

**Hydrocephalus; Idiocy; Ill-Formed Body**—(See Ill-formed, Ugly).

**Ill-luck**—To Children—The ☽ in the 5th H. of a parent, and to the ☌ or ill-asp. ♅, ♄, or ♂ by dir.; malefics affl. in 5th H. of parent. (See "Accidents", and the various paragraphs in this section).

**Illegitimate**—(See Bastards).

**Imbecile; Imperfect Shape**—Imperfect Children—If all the configurations are imperfect the child will be imperfect. See "Beastly Form" under Beasts; Defects; Ill-formed, Imperfect, Incomplete, Inhuman, Monsters, etc. See "Crippled", "Dogs", in this section).

**Impotence; Indigestion; Indocile**—(See "Dogs" in this section).

**Infancy—Disorders of**—(See Infancy).

**Infections**—At Birth—Infectious Diseases—(See Contagious, Infections; "Infections" under Infancy).

**Infirmity**—(See "Sickly", "Unhealthy", and the various paragraphs in this section).

**Inhuman Shape**—(See "Beastly Form", "Dogs", in this section. Also see Inhuman, Monsters).

**Injury**—Danger of—Injury at Birth—(See "Accidents", "Birth", "Dangers", in this section. See "Accidents" under Childhood, Infancy).

**Insanity; Instrumental Delivery**—(See "Accidents" under Infancy, Parturition).

**Intestinal Troubles**—(See Abdomen, Bowels, Colic, Cramps, Flatulence, Wind, etc.).

**Kidney Disorders**—(See Kidneys).

**Knock Knees**—(See Knees).

**Lame**—Lame from Birth—(See Congenital, Distortions, Excrescences, Feet, Lameness, Legs, Maimed, Missing, Paralysis, etc.).

**Legitimate**—Is the Child Legitimate?—(See Bastards).

**Liable to Disease**—Liable to Accidents—(See "Accidents", "Dangers", "Sickly", "Unhealthy", in this section. Also see Recuperation, Resistance, Stamina, Tone, Vitality, Weak, etc).

**Lives Thru Sickness**—A fiery sign rising upon the Asc. at B., as ♈, ♌, ♐, as these signs are the strongest for vitality. (See Recuperation, Resistance, Vitality).

**Long-lived**—Healthy and Long-lived Children—The ☉, ☽, ♃ or ♀ in the 5th H. of the parent, and well-asp.; ♃ or ♀ in the 5th or 11th H., well-asp.; lords of the 5th or 11th H. in a fruitful sign, in good houses, well-asp., and free from the affliction of malefics; no malefics in the 5th or 11th houses, or affl. the lords of these houses: lord of the 5th in the 5th H., and espec. if a benefic. (See "Long Life" under Life; "Good" under Vitality).

**Luck**—Good or Bad Luck to a Child—(See "Ill-luck" in this section; "Blessing" in Sec. 1 of this Article).

**Lunatic**—The Child a Lunatic—Born of a Lunatic Mother—(See Insanity. See Case, "Mad Mother", No. 074 in 1001 N.N.).

**Maimed; Males**—For conditions affecting Males, see Males, Son. Also see "First-born", "Female Children", in Sec. 1 of this Article).

**Many Diseases**—(See "Many Diseases" under Childhood. Also see "Sickly" in this section).

**Marasmus**—(See Emaciation).

**Measles; Mentality**—(See "Mind" in this section).

**Mind**—the Mind Afflicted—Weak Mind—(See Imbecile, Idiocy, the various paragraphs under Mental and Mind. Case of Mental Suppression and Childlike Mind — (See Case, "Never Grew Up", No. 720 in 1001 N.N.).

**Miscarriage; Misfortune To** — (See "Accidents", "Luck", and the various paragraphs in this section. Also see Misfortune).

**Moment of Birth**—Calamity From—(See "Moment of Birth" under Calamity, Birth).

**Monsters; Morbid Sex Desires** — At Puberty—(See Puberty).

**Mother**—The Mother as Affected By Children—(See Mother. Also see "Parents", "Worries", in Sec. 1 of this Article).

**Much Sickness Among**—(See "Sickly", "Unhealthy", "Weak", in this section. Also see "Much Sickness" under Sickness).

**Mumps; Mutes** — (See "Deaf and Dumb" under Hearing; Mutes).

**Mutilated**—The Foetus Mutilated—(See Foetus).

**Myxoedema; Nativity Weak** — But Reared—(See "Reared" in this section).

**Nature**—Savage and Fierce—(See "Dogs" in this section).

**Neglected**—By Parents—(See "Drink" under Parents).

**Never Grew Up**—Mental Suppression—(See "Mind" in this section).

**Nursing**—The Child Could Not Nurse and Died—Case—See "Born Incomplete", No. 281 in 1001 N.N. (See Breasts, Milk, Nipples, Weaning).

**Nurture**—Nutrition—Not Susceptible to Nurture—(See "Nurture" under Infancy; Nutrition).

**Obesity**—(See Fat, Fleshy, Obesity).

**Orphans; Pain**—(See Bowels, Colic, Cramps, and the various paragraphs under Pain).

**Paralysis**—From Birth—(See Paralysis).

**Parents**—The Parents as Affected By the Children—(See Parents. Also see "Parents", "Worries", in Sec. 1 of this Article).

**Parturition**—Danger to Child In—(See Birth, Foetus, Parturition).

**Passional Excesses** — Dies Young From—(See "Dissipation" in Sec. 3 of this Article).

**Polypus; Poor Constitution**—(See Constitution. Also see "Sickly", "Weak", in this section, and "Early Death" in Sec. 3 of this Article).

**Prenatal Epoch**—The Prenatal Period—(See Conception, Gestation, Pregnancy, Prenatal).

**Prepuce**—(See Circumcision).

**Puberty**—Dangers At--Disorders of—(See Puberty).

**Puny and Sickly**—(See "Sickly" in this section. Also see Emaciated; "Malnutrition" under Nutrition; Thin. Vitality, Weak).

**Reared with Difficulty**—Sickly, But Will Be Reared—♋, ♑, or ♓ on the Asc. at B.; the ☽ sepr. from a malefic, and applying to the ♂ or good asp. a benefic; malefics in the 5th or 11th H., but well-asp. by ♃ or ♀; ruler of the Asc. in the 6th H., affl. by lord of 8th H., but assisted by the good asps. of ♃ or ♀, or by planets in their dignities. (See "First-Born" in Sec. 1 of this Article; "Sickly" in this section. Also see Recuperation, Resistance, Sickly, Vitality, Weak).

**Recuperative Powers**—(See Recuperation, Resistance, Robust, Stamina, Strong, Tone, Weak, Vitality).

**Resistance**—To Disease—(See Resistance).

**Rickets; Robust**—(See Robust, Stamina, Tone, Vitality. Also see "Longlived" in this section). Children do not tend to be robust in early years when ♑ is on the Asc. at B., and are also lacking in Animal Heat. (See "Animal" under Heat).

**Savage and Fierce**—(See "Dogs" in this section).

**Scarlet Fever;**

**Separated from Parents**—(See Adoption, Family, Orphans, Parents).

**Sex**—Sex Activity at Puberty—(See Puberty).

**Sex of Children**—(See "Female Children", "First-born", "Male Children", in Sec. 1 of this Article. Also see Conception, Predetermination, Pregnancy).

**Shape of the Body**—(See Beautiful, Crooked, Form, Handsome, Ill-formed, Monsters, Stature, Ugly, Well-formed, etc. Also see "Dogs" in this section).

**Short-lived**—(See "Short Life" in Sec. 3 of this Article).

**Sickly Children**—Vitality Low—Weak Constitution—Much Sickness Among—Unhealthy, etc.—The ☉, ♅, ♄, or ♂ in the 5th H. and affl.; the ☉ affl. in the 5th H., and espec. if benefics are not also in the 5th H., or in good asp. the ☉; the ☉, ☽, or ☿ in the 5th H., and affl. by malefics; the ☉ or malefics in the 5th or 11th H., and affl.; the ☽ in 5th H., and affl. by ♄ and ♀, and the latter two planets being in ♂; the ☽ and ♀ afflicting each other at childbirth; the ☽ in the 5th H., and affl. by ♄, and with no good asps. of the benefics, much sickness among; ♆ or ♅ affl. in 5th H. of a parent; ♅, ♄, or ♂ in the fruitful, or prolific signs, in map of parent, but supported by the good asps. of benefics; ♄ in 5th H., and ill-asp. by the ☉ or ☽; ♄ or ♂ to the cusp the 5th H. by dir.; ♄ or ♂ affl. in the 5th H.; ♅ affl. in 5th H. of parent; ruler of Asc. in 6th H., and affl. by lord of 8th, and with no assistance from benefics; lord of 5th H. weak and affl.; lord of the 5th H. in the 6th or 8th, and affl.; lord of the 6th H. in the 5th H., the children are afflicted; lord of the 10th H. a malefic, and in the 5th. (See "Reared", "Short-lived", "Unhealthy", and the various paragraphs in this section. See Constitution; "Ill Health All Thru Life" under Ill-Health; Recuperation, Resistance; "Much Sickness" under Sickness; "Low" under Vitality; "Weak Body" under Weak).

**Sickly, But Will Be Reared**—(See "Reared" in this section).

**Sickness**—Lives Thru Sickness and Thrives—Fiery signs upon the Asc. at B., and the hyleg well-asp.; also Airy signs upon Asc. at B., or ♍, give good vitality and endurance, and to live thru sickness, where others with weak signs on Asc., and the hyleg badly affl., are more apt to succumb. (See Resistance, Stamina, Tone, Vitality. For the influences causing Much Sickness, see "Sickly", "Weak", in this section. Also see "Much Sickness" under Sickness).

**Sickness of Children Generally**—Malefic planets lord of the year at the Vernal, and posited in the 5th or 11th H. (See Childhood, Infancy, Mortality).

**Skin**—Diseases of—(See Eruptions, Skin).

**Slow Growth** — (See Diminished, Dwarf, Growth, Retarded, Slow, Suppressions).

**Smallpox; Some Perfect**—Some Imperfect—(See "Perfect" in Sec. 1 of this Article).

**Spasms**—(See Fits, Spasmodic; "Dentition" under Teeth).

**Stamina; Stature; Sterility In**—Born Barren—(See Barrenness, Impotency).

**Stomach Trouble**—(See Digestion, Indigestion, Nutrition, Stomach).

**Strength**—(1) The Strength Increased —Benefics or the ☽ in the 5th or 11th H. at B., and well-asp.; fiery signs upon the Asc. at B. (2) Strength Decreased—Malefics in the 5th or 11th H. of a parent, and affl.; ♋, ♑, or ♓ upon the Asc. of the child at B. (See Stamina, Recuperation, Resistance, Stamina, Strength, Strong, Vitality, Weak, etc.).

**Strong**—♑ upon Asc. at B., the child is not strong in early years. Fiery signs upon Asc. give strength and greater vitality all thru life. (See "Strength" in this section).

**Suckling Children**—(See "Nursing" in this section).

**Suffers**—The Child Suffers—Health Will Suffer—A weak sign upon the Asc. at B., as ♋, ♑, or ♓, and the ruler of the Asc. or the hyleg affl. (See "Afflicted", and the various paragraphs in this section and Article).

**Suffocation** — (See "Birth" under Asphyxia).

**Summer Complaint**—(See "Cholera Infantum" under Cholera. Also see Bowels, Diarrhoea)

**Suppressions** — Suppressed Growth—Suppressed Mentality — Suppressed Functions, etc.—(See "Growth", "Mind" in this section. Also see Functions, Suppressions).

**Teeth**—Troubles with Dentition—Bad —Teeth—(See Teeth).

**Thin and Puny**—(See "Puny" in this section. Also see Emaciated, Thin, Weak).

**Tonsils**—Disorders of—(See Tonsils).

**Unhealthy Children**—Sickly—Planets which grant children being in barren signs and places, beneath the malefics, or in such signs as ♌ or ♍, may give children, but they will tend to be weakly, unhealthy, and short-lived; the ☉ and Givers of Children in barren and masculine signs, and the malefics elevated above them; ♄ in the 5th H. and affl. (See "Sickly" in this section; "Early Death" in Sec. 3 of this Article; "Low" under Vitality; "Weak Body" under Weak).

**Unusual Diseases**—♅ in the 5th H. and affl. in map of parent. (See Extraordinary; "Infections" under Infancy; Uncommon, Unusual, etc.).

**Virile Members**—Excessive — (See Virile).

**Vitality**—For the various degrees of Vitality, see Vitality. Also see "Vitality" under Infancy; "Long Life", "Short Life", and "No Duration of Life" under Life. See Recuperation, Resistance, Stamina, Strength, Strong, Tone, Weak, etc.).

**Walk**—(See "Child" under Walk).

**Watery Diseases**—♆ in the 5th H. of parent. (See Watery).

**Weak Body**—(See "Weak" under Constitution, Infancy; "Ill-Favored Body" under Ill; "Ill-Health All Thru Life" under Ill-Health; "Much Sickness" under Sickness; "Low" under Recuperation, Resistance, Vitality).

**Whooping Cough**—(See Whooping).

**Wild Nature** — Savage — (See "Dogs" in this section).

**Worms; Wounds To** — (See "Accidents" in this section).

**Youth**—Early Youth—(See Youth). For diseases and afflictions which may not be listed here, look for the subject in the alphabetical arrangement.

— SECTION THREE —

**DEATH OF CHILDREN**—Duration of Life, etc.—

**Accident**—Death By—(See "Accidents" in Sec. 2 of this Article).

**Adult Life**—Not Apt To Live To— (See "Death" under Childhood, Infancy, Youth; "Early Death" under Death. Also see "Early Death", "One May Live To Adult Life", and the various paragraphs in the section).

**All May Die in Infancy** — (See Infancy).

**Birth**—(1) Death at Birth—♅ in ♏ sometimes causes death at birth by injury in delivery. Males born at an eclipse of the ☉, or females at an eclipse of the ☽, or immediately after, often die at birth, or live but a few hours. (See "Accidents" under Infancy; Eclipses). (2) Dies Soon After Birth—(See this subject under Infancy).

**Born Almost Dead**—Lives But a Few Hours or Days—The ☉ or ☽ in angles in ☍ asp., and two or more malefics in □ to the ☉ or ☽, or ♄ ☍ ♂ occupying the other two angles, and in □ to the ☉ and ☽, and the child will live as many hours or days as there are degrees between the Prorogator and the nearest malefic; the ☉ and ☽ in angles in □ asp. malefics, and the Lights receiving no help from the benefics, and also the malefics elevated above the benefics; the ☉ ☍ ☽, and malefics in □ to the ☉ and ☽, being a double ☍, the child will live if, under such an ☍, the ☉ or ☽ are preceded by ♃ and ♀, and the ☉ or ☽ be separating, but the child will be weakly, and be apt to die early, and when the first evil asp. occurs between the Hyleg and Anareta; benefics in the Asc., 5th or 11th H., and affl. by malefics; planets which promise children being under the Western horizon at B. (See "Death Soon After Birth" under Infancy. Also note the various paragraphs in this section).

**Born Dead**—(See Stillborn).

**Buries His Children**—(See "Loss of" in this section).

**Boy Born at Solar Eclipse**—May Die—(See Eclipse).

**Calamity**—From the Moment of Birth—(See Calamity).

**Childbirth**—Death of Child or Mother In—(See "Birth" in this section. Also see Parturition).

**Childhood**—Death In—(See Childhood. Also note the various paragraphs in this section). Does Not Live Beyond Childhood—(See "Early Death", and the various paragraphs in this section. See "Early Death" under Early; "Short Life" under Life).

**Children Born But They Die**—The benefic and malefic planets mixed in the houses of children; the 5th H. affl. in the mother's horoscope, and espec. if also in the Child's map the ☉ or ☽ are afflicted.

**Children Die Young**—(See "Early Death" in this section).

**Danger of Death of a Child**—The ☉ to the ill-asps. the ☽ by dir. in map of parent; the ☽ to the ill-asps. ♄ by dir.; ♅ affl. in the 5th H., and it is usually the first child; ♄ affl. in the 5th or 11th H.; ♄ to the ill-asps. ♀ by dir.; ♂ affl. in the 5th H.; the M.C. to the □ or ☍ ☿, and ☿ affl. at B. (See the various paragraphs in this section).

**Daughter May Die**—When born at time of an eclipse of the ☽. (See Eclipse).

**Days**—Lives Only a Few Hours or Days—(See "Born Almost Dead" in this section).

**Death at Birth**—(See "Birth" in this section).

**Death Immediately After Birth**—Not Susceptible to Nurture—(See "Nurture" under Infancy. Also see "Born Almost Dead" in this section).

**Death of Children**—♄ in the 5th or 11th H.; lord of the 5th peregrine in the 8th H. denotes the death of the child in Hor'y Q.; a child born at the instant of a Full ☽ dies, it is said, at the next New ☽. A child born at the New or Full ☽ rarely lives unless the benefics give a favorable aspect. (See "Loss of", and the various paragraphs in this section).

**Death of Some**—(See "Some May Die" in this section).

**Death Premature**—(See "Premature", "Untimely", in this section. See "Eight Months Children" in Sec. 1 of this Article).

**Death Soon After Birth**—(See "Born Almost Dead" in this section; "Death Soon After Birth", and "Nurture" under Infancy).

**Dentition**—Child May Die from Spasms During—(See "Dentition" under Teeth).

**Destroys the Children**—♄ in the 5th H. in all signs except ♊, ♍, ♎, or ♑, and affl.; ♄ or ♂ ☍ ♃ destroys some; ☿ in the 5th H. in a barren sign and affl. (See "Death of", "Some May Die", and the various paragraphs in this section).

**Die**—Will the Child Live or Die?—(See "Signs of Death" under Infancy).

**Die Before Maturity**—(See Maturity. Also see the various paragraphs in this section, and under Childhood, Infancy, Youth).

**Die in Infancy**—Or Childhood—(See Infancy, Childhood).

**Die in Womb**—(See Stillborn).

**Directions**—Primary Directions, Secondary Directions, Progressions, Transits, New Moons, Lunations, etc., and the Death of Children—Before the age of 3 years, children are killed by the radical positions in their maps. After 3 years of age they are killed by directions. Children with weak and evil maps usually die when the ☽ by transit or direction reaches a malefic, and espec. in the 4th H., the house of the grave and close of life, or in the 6th or 8th H. Much depends upon the vitality, and also the indications in the maps of the parents as to whether the child will live or die. The signs ♒, ♑ or ♓ on the Asc. at B. tend to lower the vitality, and evil directions are more liable to kill in early life. The New ☽ is critical in infancy and tends to much infant mortality, and the Longitude of each succeeding New ☽ after birth should be noted, and the aspects it forms to the radical map. The evil directions of the ☽ should be carefully studied, and also the transits of malefics over the afflicted portions of the radical figure. (See Directions, Eclipses; "New Moon" under Moon; Transits). In the nativities of children, the influences of evil directions which do not disturb the health, fall on the parents, the Guardian, or the Family. (See Family, Guardian, Parents).

**Dissipation**—Children Die Young Thru Dissipation and Passional Excesses—The 9° ♓ on the Asc. at B. (See Debauched, Dissipation).

**Early Death of Children**—Children Die Young—Of Short Life, etc.—The ☉ and givers of children in masculine and barren signs, and malefics elevated above them; the ☉ in evil asp. to the ruler of 5th H., or to ♅ or ♄ in the 5th; the ☉ or ☽ hyleg and ☌ a malefic at B., and with no assistance to the hyleg from the benefics; children given or allotted by the ☉, ♅, ♄, or ♂ are apt to die early; the ☉ and ☽ angular and conjoined with malefics; the ☉, ♅, ♄, or ☿ in the 5th H. and affl.; rulers of the Lights in the 6th or 8th H.; the ☉ affl. by ♄, danger in early years; the ☽ in the husband's horoscope, and the ☉ in the wife's nativity, applying to ♅, ♄, or ☋ in the 5th H.; ♅ affl. the ☉, ☽, or Asc., and elevated above the Luminaries; ♄ affl. in the 5th H., the untimely death of children; ♂ affl. in the 5th H., or affl. the ☉ or ☽ from this house, some die early and suddenly; the malefics in feminine, or prolific signs, even tho supported by benefics at B., the first train of evil directions to the malefics, or to the hyleg after birth, tend to kill; the malefics angular and oriental, affl. the ruler of the 5th H., or planets in the 5th, and with no assistance from benefics to the givers of children; a malefic on the Asc., affl. by lord of the 8th, and the ☽ also affl. by the ☉, ♄, or ♂, the child soon dies; a malefic on the Asc., and affl. by lord of the 8th, and also the ☉ or ☽ affl. at B.; the hyleg at B. severely affl. by ♄, or ♂, and with no good asps. from the benefics; lord of the Asc. in the 5th, and affl. by ♄, ♂, or ☋; lord of the 7th, 11th, or 12th H. a malefic, and in the 5th H. and affl.; the 5th H. affl. in the mother's map, and the ☉ and ☽ both affl. in the child's map; ♎, ♑, or ♓ on the Asc. at B., and the hyleg severely affl. by malefics; malefics in the 5th or 11th H. at B., and affl., or afflicting the hyleg. Unless the hyleg is much afflicted an early death is not necessarily shown. (See "Death" under Infancy, Childhood; "Early Death" under Death; "Short Life" under Life, and also note the various paragraphs in this section. For the early death of Parents, see Adopted, Orphans, Parents).

**Early Life**—The Early Years of Life—Danger of Death In—♑ on the Asc., or the ☉ or ☽ affl. in ♑, tends to make the early years weak, lacking in animal heat, and with greater danger of death, and to give a weak body; lord of the 6th H. in the Asc., and affl., and espec. with ♑ on the Asc.; the 19° ♓ on the Asc. (See Childhood, Infancy; "Short Life" under Life. Also note the various paragraphs in this section). The hyleg must be severely affl. at B., and by dir., to cause death in early life and childhood, and a good asp. from ♃ or ♀ in the configuration will tend to save the life.

**Eclipses**—A male born at an eclipse of the ☉, or a female at an eclipse of the ☽, are in danger of immediate, or early death. (See Eclipses).

**Eighth Month**—Birth At, and Usually Resulting in Death—(See "Eight Months Children" in Sec. 1 of this Article).

**Extraordinary Death**—Of Children—♅ in the 5th H. of a parent, and espec. the mother. (See Extraordinary).

**Father**—Early Death of—(See Father).

**Female Children**—Death of When Born at an Eclipse of the ☽. (See Eclipses).

**Few Live**—But Few Live—(See "All May Die in Infancy", and "But Few Live", under Infancy).

**Fifteen Years of Age**—Death At—Case—See "Elizabeth", Case No. 654 in 1001 N.N.

**Fifth House**—This is the principal house of children in the map of parents, and malefics affl. in this house tend to death of the children, or to bring much sorrow thru them. (See Fifth House).

**Five Years of Age**—Death Before or at This Age—Child Apt to Die at This Age—♅, ♄, or ♂ ruling the places of the ☉ or ☽ at B., and the benefics affl.; ♅, ♄, or ♂ in the 1st H. at B., and the ☉ or ☽ ☌ a malefic in the 6th, 8th, or 12th H.; a malefic exactly midway between the ☉ and ☽, and the rulers of the ☉ and ☽ controlled by a malefic, and with no assistance from benefics in the configuration. (See "Death" under Infancy; "Early Death", in this section).

**Four Years of Age**—Apt to Die at About This Age—The ☽ sepr. from a benefic, and applying to the ☌, P., or ill-asp. a malefic, the child will hardly attain more than 4 years.

**Fourteen Years of Age**—Possible Death At—Case—See "France", No. 533 in 1001 N.N.

**Fourth Child**—Possible Death of—Malefics in the 10th H. of the mother, or in the 11th H. of the father. (See "First Born" in Sec. 1 of this Article).

**Great Mortality Among**—(See "Mortality" in this section).

**Healthy and Long-lived**—(See "Long-lived" in Sec. 2 of this Article).

**Hours**—Lives But a Few Hours or Days—(See "Born Almost Dead" in this section; "Nurture" under Infancy).

**Immediately Dies After Birth**—(See "Death Immediately" in this section).

**Infancy**—Death In—All May Die In Infancy—Some Die In Infancy—(See the various paragraphs under Infancy).

**Injury at Birth**—Possible Death From—(See "Accidents" under Infancy, Parturition).

**Kill**—Evil Directions More Liable to Kill—(See "Directions" in this section).

**Life Prolonged**—In weak nativities, and where the vitality is low, life may be prolonged if ♃ or ♀ are in the Asc. at B., and not severely afflicted, and also at the same time in favorable asp. to the hyleg, or if the lord of the Asc. is free from affliction and well-placed, and these influences may save the life of the child, or considerably prolong life, even tho a train of evil directions may be operating. (See Recuperation, Resistance, Vitality).

**Live**—Will Live and Be Healthy—(See "Long-lived" in this section). Will the Child Live or Die?—(See "Signs of Death" under Infancy).

**Lives But Short Time**—A Few Hours or Days—(See "Born Almost Dead" in this section; "Nurture" under Infancy).

**Long Life**—Healthy and Long-lived—(See "Long-lived" in Sec. 2 of this Article. Also see "Long Life" under Life).

**Loss of Children**—Loses Many Children—Buries His Children—The ☉ in the 5th H. and affl., and espec. unless ♃, ♀, or the ☽ be also in the 5th, or in good asp. to the ☉; the ☉ to the ill-asps. the ☽ by dir.; the ☽ in the 5th H., and affl. by ♄, ♂, or ♀; the ☽ in the 10th or 4th H., and affl. by malefics; the ☽ in the 5th H., and affl. by any planet in the 8th or 12th H.; the ☽ to the ill-asps. ☿ by dir., and the ☽ or ☿ affl. by a malefic at B.; ♅, ♄, ♂, or ☋ in the 5th H., and espec. in ♌ or ♍; ♅, ♄, ♂, or the ☉ in the 5th or 11th H., and affl.; ♄ in the 5th H., and affl., and espec. ill-aspected by the ☽; ♄ affl. in the 11th H.; ♄ affl. by ♃ threatens loss of offspring; if children are promised, yet if ♄ or ♂ be in the 5th H., and espec. in ♌ or ♍, loses many children; ♂ in the 5th H., and affl. by the ☉, ☽, ♅ or ♄; ♂ affl. in ♌ or ♍ in the 5th H.; ☿ affl. at B., and the ☽ to the ill-asps. ☿ by dir.; ☿ in the 5th H., and affl. by malefics; malefics in the 5th or 11th H.; ruler of the 5th H. in ☌ ruler of the 8th H., or affl. by malefics; lord of the 8th H. in the 5th H. (See "Death", "Destroys", and other paragraphs in this section).

**Majority Will Die**—Most Will Die In Early Years—Malefics in the 5th or 11th H., and affl.; lord of the 5th H. in the 6th or 8th H. and affl.; lord of the 5th in the 8th, and affl. by lord of the 8th; lord of the Asc. in the 6th, and affl. by lord of the 8th, and with no assistance from benefics. (See "All May Die in Infancy" under Infancy).

**May Have Children But They Die**—(See "Children Born But They Die" in this section).

**Middle Life**—Dies Young, or Before Middle Life—(See "Early Death" under Early; "Dies Before Middle Life" under Middle Life; "Short Life" under Life. Also see "Early Death" in this section).

**Miscarriage**—Death By—(See Abortion, Miscarriage, Parturition, Premature).

**Moment of Birth**—Calamity From—Death At—(See Calamity. Also see "Birth" in this section).

**Moon**—Death of Females Born at Eclipse of—(See Eclipses; "New" and "Full Moon" under Moon).

**Mortality Great**—Among Children and Young People—Comets appearing in ♊; ♂ in ♉ and ℞, occi., and lord of the year at the Vernal Equi., and many die from Scarlatina and Smallpox. (See "Directions" in this section, Mortality, Scarlet Fever, Prenatal Epoch, Smallpox).

**Most of Those Born Will Die**—(See "Majority" in this section).

**Mother**—Death of Mother—(See Mother).

**Mysterious Death**—♆ or ♅ in the 5th H. of parent, and espec. of the mother.

**New Moon**—Full Moon—Death of Female Infants Born at Time of an Eclipse—(See Eclipses; "New" and "Full Moon" under Moon. Also see "Directions" in this section).

**No Duration of Life**—(See "Born Almost Dead", and "Birth" in this section; "Death in Infancy" and "Nurture" under Infancy; Eclipses).

**Nurse**—Child Could Not Nurse and Died—Case—See "Born Incomplete" No. 281 in 1001 N.N.

**Nurture**—Not Susceptible to Nurture—Death Soon After Birth—(See "Nurture" under Infancy).

**Old Age**—Children Live To—(See Old Age).

**One May Live to Adult Life**—Malefics in, ruling, or aspecting the 5th or 11th H., other testimonies promising children, and with ♃ or ♀ ⚹ or △ the 10th H., or in good asp. to the ruler of the 5th or 11th. (See "Adult Life" in this section).

**One or More May Die Young**—The ☉, ♃, ♀ or the ☽ in the 5th H., and ill-asp. by ♄ or ♂.

**Parents**—Death of—Death of Caused by Children—(See Adoption, Father, Mother, Orphans, Parents. Also see "Parents", "Worries", in Sec. 1 of this Article).

**Passional Excesses**—Dies Young From—(See Dissipation, "Dies Before Middle Life" under Middle Life; "Passional Excesses" under Passion; Venery).

**Premature Death**—(See Premature, Sudden, Untimely; "Early Death" under Early; "Short Life" under Life; "Death" under Infancy, Childhood. See "Sudden" in this section).

**Probable Death of Those Born**—♅ ☌ or bad asp. ♄ in the 5th H., and affl. the ☉, a sure indication of the death of some; malefics in the 5th or 11th H.; ruler of the 5th H. in the 6th, 8th, or 12th H., and affl. by malefics; lord of the 8th a malefic, in the 5th, and affl.; the benefic and malefic planets mixed at B. in fruitful houses. (See "Danger", "Destroys", "Loss of", "Some May Die", and the various paragraphs in this section).

**Prolonged**—(See "Life Prolonged" in this section).

**Radical Planets and Death** — (See "Directions" in this section).

**Reared With Difficulty**—(See "Reared With Difficulty" in Sec. 2 of this Article).

**Scarlatina**—Many Children Die of, and of Smallpox—(See "Mortality Great" in this section).

**Second Child Will Die**—(See "First-Born" in Sec. 1 of this Article).

**Short Life**—Short-Lived and Sickly—Barren signs on cusp the 1st or 5th H., and other testimonies favorable, and the evil ray of a malefic fall in the place; ♄ or ☋ in the 5th H., or ♄ or ♂ in evil asp. to the 5th and its lord, and other testimonies give children; ♂ affl. in the 5th H., if any children; the Sigs. or Benefics in barren signs, if any children they are short-lived (Hor'y). (See "Early Death", and other paragraphs in this section. See "Short Life" under Life; "Death" under Infancy, Childhood, Youth).

**Short Time**—Lives But a Short Time—Dies Within a Few Hours or Days—(See "Born Almost Dead", "Death Immediately", and other paragraphs in this section).

**Shorter Will Be the Life**—(See "Shorter" under Infancy).

**Sickly, But Will Be Reared**—(See "Reared" in Sec. 2 of this Article).

**Sickness**—Lives Thru and Thrives—(See "Long-Lived", "Sickness", in Sec. 2 of this Article).

**Signs of Death**—Of Children—(See "Signs of Death" under Infancy; "Arguments for Death" under Death).

**Smallpox**—Many Die of—(See "Mortality" in this section).

**Solar Eclipse**—Death of Males Born At—(See Eclipses).

**Some May Die**—The ☽ in the 10th or 4th H., and affl. by malefics; ♄ or ♂ in the 5th H., and affl. the ☉ or ☽; ♄ or ♂ ☍ ♃ destroys some; ♃, ♀, or the ☽ in the 5th or 11th H., and affl. by malefics; ♀ ☍ ♃ or ♂ tends to destroy some; malefics in fruitful signs in the 5th or 11th H. (See "Probable Death" in this section; "Some Die" under Infancy).

**Son Born May Die**—If Born at Time of Solar Eclipse—Male May Die if First-Born—(See Eclipses; "First-Born" in Sec. 1 of this Article).

**Spasms**—Death By—Death By During Dentition—(See Fits; "Dentition" under Teething).

**Stillborn**—(See Stillborn).

**Sudden Death Of**—♅ affl. in ♌ or 5th H. of the parent; ♂ in the 5th H., and affl. the ☉ or ☽. (See "Extraordinary" in this section. Also see "Sudden Death" under Death).

**Sun**—Males Die Born at Eclipse of—(See Eclipses).

**Teething**—Death During—(See "Dentition" under Teeth).

**Third Child**—Possible Death of—(See "First-Born" in Sec. 1 of this Article).

**Three Years of Life**—Possible Death Before the Third Year—Death After the Third Year—(See "Directions" in this section).

**Time of Death**—(See "Directions", "Early Death", and the various paragraphs in this section. See "Death" under Childhood, Infancy, Youth. See "Time" under Death).

**Two Months**—Death at Two Months of Age—Case—See "Born in a Flood", No. 227 in 1001 N.N. Various Cases and Birth Data of Death in Infancy are given under Infancy.

**Undertime Children** — Possible Death of—(See "Eight Months Children" in Sec. 1 of this Article).

**Violent Death**—Danger of—Lord of the 8th H. a malefic, and in the 5th H., and affl. (See Violent).

**Vitality**—For the various degrees of Vitality, see Constitution; "Animal Heat" under Heat; Recuperation, Resistance, Stamina, Strength, Strong, Tone, Vitality, Weak, etc. See "Vitality" under Infancy.

**Weak Body**—Weak Nativities and Death—(See "Directions" in this section. Also see "Weak Body" under Weak).

**Will the Child Live?**—Or Die?—(See "Signs of Death" under Infancy).

**Womb**—Dies in the Womb—(See Abortion, Miscarriage, Stillborn).

**Young**—Dies Young—(See "Early Death", and the various paragraphs in this section. See "Death" under Childhood, Infancy; "Short Life" under Life).

**Youth**—Dies in Early Youth—(See Youth).

**CHILL**—Chill and Cold—Chills—Cold—This subject is largely considered under COLD. (See Cold). Chill is a ♄ influence and affliction. Chill of the surface is due to cold, and ♄ influence, and drives the blood inwards, causing internal congestions, colds, and diseases resulting therefrom. The part of the body most liable to be affected by chills and cold is denoted by the sign and house of ♄ at B., and varies in severity according to the malignancy of the vibration, and the strength of the aspect in any particular case. ♄ in ♑ tends to chills and cold, and people born under this influence should wear warm clothing, and woolen underwear, if necessary, as wool helps to counteract the ♄ influence, and keep the temperature of the surface even.

**Death by Chill and Cold**—Denoted by ♄. (See "Death" under Cold).

**Disorders Arising from Chill**—And Cold—The ☽ in ♓ tends to chills and colds which fly to the lungs; denoted by the ☽ when the ☽ afflicts the ☉ or Asc. at B., or by dir.; women tend to suffer with fever from chills and colds under the asp. of the ☽ to the ☌ the ☉ by dir.; ♆, ♅, or ♄ in ♓, and affl. the ☉ or ☽; ♄ affl. in ♈, ♉, ♋, or ♑; ♄ ☌, P, □ or ☍ the Asc.; the ♑ sign on the Asc., or on cusp of 6th H., predisposes to chill and colds; Subs at CP, and KP, violent shaking from chill or chills. Chills also accompany Acute Fevers, Nervous Conditions, Prostration and Weakness, due to the strong afflictions of ♄. (For Irregularities of the System Arising from Chills and Cold, see "Acute Fevers" under Acute; Centripetal, Chilblain; "Epidemics" under Cholera; Chronic; "Diseases Arising from Cold", and "Cold Diseases" under Cold; Colds; "Deafness" under Hearing; "Chills" under Nerves; Saturn Diseases).

**Functions**—The Functions Suppressed By Cold—The ☽ affl. by ♄. (See Functions).

**Internal Diseases**—Arising From Chill and Cold—♄ ☌, P, □ or ☍ the ☉, internal disorders arising from chill, cold, neglect and privation. (See Congestion; "Congestions" under Internal). For further influences see the various paragraphs under Cold.

**CHIN**—The Mentum—Lower Jaw—The Chin is ruled by ♀ and the ♉ sign. Also ♀ when in ♈ rules and affects the Chin. (See Appearance, Face).

**Beard**—The chin beard is ruled by ♉. When ☿ is ascending at B., and free from the rays of other planets, there is little hair, or beard, on the chin. (See Beard).

**Dimple in Chin**—(See "Chin" under Dimples).

**Face**—The Face Narrows Down to the Chin—(See "Falling In" under Cheeks; Decanates; "Thin Face" under Face).

**Jaws**—(See "Lower Jaw" under Jaws).

**Long Chin**—Long, Narrow, Pointed, Protruding—♆ rising in the Asc., a pointed chin; ☿ gives a narrow chin, and with ☿ rising and free from the rays of other planets; ♑ on the Asc. at B., narrow, and often protruding like that of the Goat, which animal is the symbol of the ♑ sign.

**Marks**—Moles—Scars on Chin—Planets in ♉, and espec. ♄ or ♂ in ♉; the 2° ♉ on the Asc., a mark near the left side of the chin. (See Marks).

**Narrow Chin**—(See "Long" in this section. Also see Decanates).

**Pointed Chin**—Protruding—(See "Long" in this section).

**Receding Chin**—♍ on the Asc. at B.

**Scar On**—(See "Marks" in this section).

**Short Chin**—The ☉ influence denotes; the ☉ in ♉; the ☉ as Sig. of the person in Hor'y Questions.

**Thin Chin**—☿ ascending at B., and free from the rays of other planets (See Beard, Cheeks, Face, Hair, Jaws, Lips).

**CHIROPRACTORS**—(See Healers, Sublaxations, Vertebrae).

**CHLOASMA**—(See "Pigmentation" under Skin).

**CHLORIDE OF POTASSIUM**—(See Potassium).

**Sodium Chloride**—(See Sodium).

**CHLOROFORM**—A typical drug of ♆. (See Anaesthetics, Neptune).

**CHLOROSIS**—Green Sickness—A form of Anaemia common in young women, and attended with menstrual disturbances, and a greenish color of the skin. A ☽ and ♋ sign disease; ♄ affl. in ♋; attended with Subs at SP, KP 11th Dorsal), and at PP. (See Anaemia, Menses).

**CHOKING**—(See Asphyxia, Cough, Drowning, Hanging, Phlegm, Strangulation, Suffocation, Throat, etc.).

**CHOLAGOGUE**—A Remedy That Promotes the Flow of Bile—Podophyllin, ruled by ☿, and also the Mercurials, are types of this group. (See Bile, Mercury, Physic, Podophyllin).

**CHOLER**—Bile—The Gall—A Bilious Complaint—Cholic—etc. Anger is also spoken of sometimes as Choler. ♂ causes diseases arising from too much choler.

**Choleric Temperament**—The Bilious Temperament—(See Choleric). For further influences about Choler, see Anger, Bile, Cholera; "High Temper" under Temper, etc.).

**Diseases Arising from Choler**—Caused by the fiery signs; lords of the 1st, 6th, or the ☽ in fiery signs. (See Anger, Choleric).

**CHOLERA**—Asiatic Cholera—A disease characterized by diarrhoea, vomiting, cramps and pains in the bowels, and prostration. This is principally a ♍, ♏, and ♂ disease. Workers in copper mines are usually free from Cholera. The Hindus wear a copper amulet to ward off Cholera. Copper is a ♀ remedy, opposed to ♂, and a good remedy and antidote for Cholera. In Hungary a copper plate is worn next to the skin against Cholera.

**Asiatic Cholera**—A Malignant Form of Cholera—A ♍ disease, and afflictions in ♍; ♂ affl. in ♍. (See "Causes" in this section).

**Causes of Cholera**—Afflictions in ♍; a ♍ disease; the ☽ affl. in ♍, or affl. the hyleg therefrom; ♂ in ♍ in the 6th H., and affl.; ♂ in ♍, and having the sole dominion at a Solar Eclipse; ♅ in ♍ in the 8th H. at a Solar Ingress of the ☉ into ♈, and affl. the ☽ or planet ascending; ☿ affl. in ♒; the ☉ to the ☌ or ill-asp. ♂ by dir.; violent ♅ or ♂ afflictions involving the ♍ and ♏ signs; Subs at CP, SP, KP, Li.P. and PP. (See the paragraphs in this section).

**Cholera Infantum**—Infectious Diarrhoea—Summer Cholera—Summer Complaint—♂ or the ☽ affl. in ♍ at B., and espec. when in the 6th H. (See "Death" in this section. Also see Diarrhoea).

**Cholera Morbus**—Sporadic Cholera—Bilious Cholera—English Cholera—An acute catarrhal inflammation of the mucous membrane of both the stomach and intestines. Caused by ♂ affl. in ♋ or ♍, in the 6th H., and affl. by a ♂ direction. The symptoms of this disease are much the same as in Asiatic Cholera, but the Bacillus of Koch is absent.

**Cholera Pains**—(See "Cramps" in this section).

**Cholera Prevalent**—Occurs at times of a Solar Eclipse, and the ☉ or ☽ affl. by ♅, ♄, or ♂; ♅ in the 8th H. at times of great conjunctions, as ♄ ☌ ♂; ☿ affl. in ♍ at the Vernal Equi., and lord of the year, so afflicts Peoples and Places under ♍. (See "Epidemics" in this section).

**Cholerine**—A Mild Form of Cholera—A ♍ disease, and afflictions in ♍, but with the other configurations less violent in their effects. Caused by Subs, and other influences, as given under "Causes" in this section).

**Cramps**—Cholera Cramps and Pains in the Bowels—The ☉ to the ☌ or ill-asps. ♂ by dir.; the ☽ in ♈, ♍, or ♑, and affl. by the ☉ or ♂ when taken ill; ♂ affl. in ♍ in the 6th H. (See Cramps).

**Death from Cholera**—The ☽ affl. in ♍, or affl. the hyleg therefrom; ♅ in ♍ in the 8th H. at a Solar Ingress of the ☉ into ♈, and affl. the ☽, or planet ascending; ♂ in ♍, and having the sole dominion at a Solar Eclipse. Case of Death by Infantile Cholera—See "Short Life", No. 371 in 1001 N.N.

**Diarrhoea**—(See Diarrhoea).

**Epidemics**—Cholera Epidemics usually occur when one of the major planets is in perihelion (nearest the ☉) in its orbit. Its spread is due to vitiated atmospheric conditions. It spreads faster than human means of travel, and one Epidemic may quickly encircle the Globe when ♄ or ♃ are in perihelion, and in other years, when no planets are in perihelion, it usually remains in or near its birthplace, which is India. Its germination is dependent upon atmospheric conditions caused by planetary influences, and is not local, or due to insanitation, as commonly believed. The orbit of ♃ is 12 years, and every 12 years he is in perihelion, and Cholera has broken out in India every 12 years for Centuries, and under the influence of ♃ in perihelion. These same influences also tend to cause Floods, Volcanic Eruptions, Earthquakes, which surface changes tend to decomposition and fermentation of vegetation, to vitiate the atmosphere, and produce Chills, Fever, Typhoid, and to lower the vitality of the inhabitants. Cholera also occurs epidemically when ♂ is in perigee, and at the same time in ☍ the ☉, which is once every 15 years. (See Air).

**Immunity To**—(See Immunity).

**Infantile Cholera**—Death By—(See "Death" in this section).

**Sporadic Cholera** — (See "Cholera Morbus" in this section). See Epidemics, Pestilence, Plague).

**Summer Cholera**—Summer Complaint —(See "Cholera Infantum" in this section).

**CHOLERIC**—Related to the Choler, or Bile. ♈, ♌, and ♐ are classed as the Choleric Signs.

**Choleric Distemper**—The ☽ to the ☌ or ill-asp. ♂ by dir.; ♃ affl. in ♐, and arising from putrefaction of the blood; a ♂ disease.

**Choleric Humours**—A ♂ disease; ♂ affl. in ♌ or ♍; the ☽ to the ☌ or ill-asp. ♂ by dir. (See Humours).

**Choleric Passion**—The ☽ in ♐, and affl. by the ☉ or ♂ when taken ill.

**Choleric Temperament**—Bilious Temperament—A Hot and Dry Temperament—Hot and Dry Body—Ruled by the ☉, ♂, and the Fiery Signs, and is a temperament of action. Tends to make one hasty, fiery, irascible, excitable, feverish, easily angered, and subject to bilious and inflammatory affections. Produced principally by ♂, and ♂ affl. in the fiery signs at B.; ♂ in ill-asp. the ☉ at B., and by dir.; the ☉ ☌ ♂ at B.; the ☽ to the ☌ or ill-asp.

♂ by dir.; the sign ascending, or its lord, in fiery signs; ♄ in ♐ in partile asp. the Asc., rather choleric. (See Anger, Bile, Cholic, Excitable, Fevers, Imprudent, Impulsiveness, Temperament).

**CHOLIC**—Pertaining to the Bile. May also refer to Cramps, or Painful Affections About the Gall Bladder, or Bilious Attacks. (See Bile, Cholic, Cramps).

**CHOLOLITHIASIS**—(See "Gall Stones" under Bile).

**CHONDROMA** — A Cartilaginous Tumor—(See Cartilage).

**CHOREA**—(See Saint Vitus Dance).

**CHOROID**—The Second, or Vascular Tunic of the Eye.

**Choroiditis**—Inflammation of the Choroid—A ☉ disease; the ☉ affl. in ♈. (See Eyes).

**CHRONIC DISEASES** — Long, Tedious, Protracted, Slow, Lingering, Deep-Seated, Permanent, Enduring, Sub-Acute, Morbid Diseases, etc., and attended usually with a Decline, Low Fever, Wasting, Decay Emaciation, Crystallization, Hardening, or a Consumption in some part of the body. All Cold, Lingering, and Chronic Diseases are produced by ♄, and espec. when ♄ is in the 6th H. at B., and affl. the hyleg or Asc. Chronic Diseases usually begin in Winter, from cold and chilling of the skin, or surface, driving the blood inwards, and causing internal congestions, the result of ♄ influence, as ♄ rules Cold. (See Centripetal, Chill, Cold, Congestions). In Greek Mythology ♄ is called "Kronos", from which our word "Chronic" is taken. The 12th H. and ♄ have general rule over Chronic Diseases, and those which tend to become morbid. While Permanent Diseases proceed from ♄, their course is regulated by the motion of the ☉, and it is very essential to watch the aspects to, or afflictions to the ☉, to give a prognosis, or forecast, concerning the probable outcome of a chronic disease. The course of Acute Diseases is ruled by the ☽. (See "Crises" under Acute). Chronic Diseases begin their action in the Ganglionic Centers, and all remedies indicated in chronic diseases must begin their action in these centers. (See Ganglion). Diseases indicated by the radical map tend to become chronic, or sub-acute, and espec. when afflicting planets are in the Occidental Quarters, between the Nadir and Asc., and between the Midheaven and Descendant at B., and are usually organic, constitutional, hereditary, or structural diseases. Acquired Diseases, and those of shorter duration, are the result of Directions, rather than from the indications of the map of birth. An Acute Disease which reaches the 28th day, or the Fourth Quarter of the ☽ from the time the disease began, will either resolve itself, or go into the chronic form. Thus any acute disease may become chronic, and run on indefinitely, eventually become cured, or end in death, according to the amount of vitality, resistance, recuperating power, etc. It would consume too much time and space to list all the names of diseases in this section, which may be chronic, and will ask you to look in the alphabetical arrangement for the special disease you have in mind. The more general subjects concerning chronic diseases will be taken up in this section.

**Causes of Chronic Diseases**—The SUN affl. in ♍, as ♍ courts diseases, as a rule, and tends to hold onto it longer (See Virgo); the ☉ hyleg, and to the ☌ or ill-asp. ♄ by dir.; the ☉ in the 12th H. at the Vernal Equi., lord of the year, and espec. if the ☉ is in the 6th, 8th or 12th H. at B., or the ☉ or ♄ in the 12th H. at a Solar Rev.; the ☉ affl. in the 6th or 12th H.; the ☉ occi. at B., and affl. by ♄; the ☉ or ♄ in the 6th H., or either in the 6th in □ or ☍ to each other, denotes heavy affliction; the ☉ in ♋ and affl. by ♄; the ☉ affl. in ♑; the ☉ in the 6th H. unless well-aspected; the ☉, ☽, and many planets in fixed signs at B.; the ☉ and ♄ in P. asp. by Progression; the progressed ☉ to the ☌ or ill-asp. the radical ♄; the ☉ ill-asp. by the ☽ at B., and espec. when ♄ also afflicts the ☉, ☽, Asc., or hyleg in the radix; evil Solar directions to Promittors tend to cause ill-health for a period of four years, two years before the completion of the asp., and two years after, and bad Lunar asps. coinciding with adverse Solar asps. will intensify the evil. In female nativities the ☉ causes chronic troubles when affl. the hyleg. The MOON to the ☌ or ill-asp. ♄ by dir., and the ☽ hyleg at B., and affl., tends to all lingering diseases, according to the nature of ♄ and the sign he occupies; the ☽ in the 6th H. at B., and affl. by malefics; the ☽ affl. in earthy signs tends to Agues, Consumptions, and other Melancholic Diseases; the ☽ to the ☌ or ill-asp. ♆ by dir., wasting chronic diseases; the ☽ decr. at B., sepr. from ♃, and applying to ♄, frequent chronic ailments; the ☽ affl. in the 6th H. in an earthy sign; the ☽ in a fixed sign at B., and affl., and applying to ♄ in a Solar Rev.; the ☽ hyleg in ♑ in a female nativity, and affl.; NEPTUNE in the 1st, 6th, 8th or 12th houses at B., and affl.; ♆ afflictions tend espec. to wasting diseases. (See Wasting); URANUS in □ or ☍ ♄, and in parts or organs afflicted according to the Signs in at B.; ♅ ☌ ♄ in the 6th H., heavy and prolonged sickness; SATURN in the 12th H. at B., or in ♓, the 12th H. Sign, and affl. and with danger of being confined as an invalid in some Hospital, or Institution; ♄ affl. in the 6th H., chronic and deep-seated; ♄ ☌, □, or ☍ the ☉, Asc., or hyleg at B., and by dir.; ♄ denotes death by chronic diseases when affl. the hyleg at B., and by dir., and holding the dominion of death; ♄ occi. at B. and affl. the hyleg by dir.; ♄ in the 6th H., and affl. the Asc. or hyleg; ♄ on the M.C. at B., in a common sign, and affl. the ☉ or ☽ by □ or ☍ asp.; ♄ ☌, P, □, or ☍ the ☉, ☽, Asc., or hyleg at B., or by dir., or to the ill-asps. these places in the radix by progression; ♄ affl. in any sign or house tends to chronic ailments and afflictions in the part ruled by such sign or house; ♄ the sole ruler of a Solar Eclipse (see Eclipses); caused by the afflictions of ♄ to the hyleg and sensitive places of the map, when the dominion of death is vested in him; ♄ exactly rising or setting at B.; ♄ in the 12th H. at a Solar Rev., and affl.; born under the strong influence of ♄, and ♄ ill-dig., and badly aspected at B.; ♄ in the 8th H. at B., or by dir., and affl. the hyleg; ♄ lord of the 6th, ℞, slow of motion, and at the same time in a fixed sign at B., tends to slow and tedious diseases, and poor powers of recuperation; ♄ lord of the Asc., ℞, and slow motion; JUPITER to the ill-asp. ♄ by dir., and espec. if ♄ rule the 1st, 6th, 8th, or 12th H. at B.; VENUS to the ☌ or ill-asp. ♄ by dir., and espec. when ♀ holds the dominion of death and affl. the hyleg at B., and the influence of ♀ in such cases is to cause a consumption or a wasting chronic disease; ASCENDANT to the ☌ or ill-asp. ♄ by dir., and ♄ occi. at B.; the Asc. affl. by the ☌ or ill-asp. ♄ at B., and by dir.; lord of the Asc. in the 6th H., and affl. by lord of the 6th; ruler of the Asc. in the 12th H., and affl.; fixed signs on all four of the angles at B.; many afflictions from fixed signs; the Sig. in a fixed sign (see "Fixed Signs" under Fixed); ♍ on the cusp of 6th H.; earthy signs on the Asc., or cusp of 6th H., and with many planets in such signs; malefics in occi. Quarters of the map of birth indicate long and tedious sicknesses when taken ill; lord of the 6th H. a malefic, and in the 6th H.; lord of the 6th H. slow of motion, and ℞ in a fixed sign; the afflicting planet stationary, ℞, or slow of motion at B., or by dir. (See the various paragraphs and references in this section).

**Cold Chronic Diseases**—(See "Chronic" under Cold).

**Crises in Chronic Diseases**—(See "Chronic Diseases" under Crises).

**Dangerous Chronic Maladies**—The Asc. to the ☌ or ill-asps. ♄ by dir., and ♄ occi. at B.; ♄ affl. the hyleg by dir., and also accompanied by a train of evil directions to the hyleg, or to the ☉, ☽, Asc., or M.C.

**Death by Chronic Diseases**—♄ occi. at B., and affl. the hyleg by dir.; ♄ in the 8th H., ruler of the 8th, or affl. the lord of the 8th, or cusp of the 8th H.; in female horoscopes the ☉ causes death by long, chronic, severe, and painful illnesses when affl. the hyleg at B., and by dir. (See "Arguments for Death", "Death More Certain", under Death; Fatal, Incurable, Lingering, Malignant, Morbid, Tedious, etc.).

**Fevers**—(See "Chronic" under Fevers).

**Long Chronic Distempers**—Fixed signs on the cusp the 6th H., or in the Moon's place; lord of the 6th a malefic, and in the 6th; lord of the Asc., or 6th H., or the ☽, be in ☌, □, or ☍ ♄ or ♂, the disease will be lasting. (See the various paragraphs and influences in this section. Also see "Fixed Signs" under Fixed; "Long Siege of Ill-Health" under Ill-Health; "Tedious Diseases" under Tedious).

**Signs of a Long Disease**—(See "Long" in this section). For further study, see Aches, Agues, Cold, Consumptions, Curable, Crystallization, Decay, Debility, Emaciation, Hardening, Hurts, Invalids; "Low Fevers" under Fever; Malignant, Morbid, Tuberculosis, Wastings, etc. Also see the various Organs and Parts of the Body, and also the subjects of Assimilation, Declines, Digestion, Elimination, Environment, Excretion, Functions, Fluids, Incurable, Inflammation; "Melancholic Diseases" under Melancholy; Nutrition, Organic Diseases; "Low" under Resistance; Saturn, Suppressions, Structural; "Low" under Vitality; Wastings; "Weak Body" under Weak).

**CHRYSOLITE** — A Mineral ruled by the ☉.

**CHYLE**—The Milky Fluid of Intestinal Digestion. The ♍ sign and ♄ are concerned with chylification, or chylopoiesis, the preparation, absorption and assimilation of the Chyle. As a fluid, the ☽ also rules the Chyle. Also the physiological action of the ☽ and ♀ produce Chylification, Chylopoiesis, Chyle formation, and its absorption. The afflictions of ♄ tend to have a pathological action on the Chyle. (See Chyme, Digestion).

**Abated Absorption**—Of the Chyle—A ♍ disease; the ☉, ☽, or ♄ affl. in ♍; ♍ on the Asc. and afflicted. (See "Intestinal" under Indigestion).

**Chyluria**—(See "Milky Urine" under Urine).

**CHYME**—Ruled by the ♋ sign. (See Digestion, Food).

**CIGARETTES**—Smoking of — Craving for—(See Narcotics, Tobacco).

**CINCHONA**—Peruvian Bark—A typical drug of ♂. Quinine, a principal alkaloid. (See Bitter).

**CINNIBAR**—Occurs in brilliant red crystals, and is ruled by ♂.

**CIRCULATION**—Circulation of the Blood, and Other Fluids of the Body—The Arterial Circulation—The Venous Circulation—Circulation of the Fluids of the Body—Circulation of the Nerve Force, etc. The Circulation of the blood is under the internal rule of ♒. The ♌ and ♎ signs also are concerned with distillation and the circulation. Also ruled by Posterior Lobe of the Pituitary Body.

**Arterial Circulation** — Ruled by ♃. Poor Arterial Circulation—Obstructed — Restricted — Impeded — Sluggish — Spasmodic—Good Circulation of, etc.— The afflictions of ♄ to ♃; ♄ ☌, P, □ or ☍ ♃; ♄ ☌ the ☉ and planets in ♌, the heart sign; ♄ ☌ the ☽ in ♌; ♄ affl. in ♌ or ♒; ♄ in the 6th H., and afflicting ♃; ♄ ☌ the ☉ or ☽ in ♌ or ♒, etc., tend to Poor, Restricted, Obstructed, and Sluggish Arterial Circulation, and of the Circulation in general. The afflictions of ♄ to ♃ tend to increase the mineral deposits in the walls of the arteries and blood vessels, restricting circulation, and causing hardening of the arteries. Also the afflictions of ♄ to ♃ tend to over-eating, gluttony, resulting in too much blood, and Plethora, causing sluggish circulation.

Spasmodic disturbances of the Arterial Circulation are caused by the afflictions of ♅ to ♃. The good asps. of the ☽, and other planets, to ♃ at B., and by direction, favor good circulation, normal blood pressure, and to keep the blood properly replenished and in a healthy condition, as well as the arterial walls. (See Arteries, Blood, Cyanosis, Degeneration, Vessels. Also see "Good", "Poor", in this section).

**Bad Circulation**—(See "Poor", and the various paragraphs in this section).

**Blood**—Circulation of the Blood—Upon the action of the heart, and its force or weakness, depends the condition of the circulation of the blood. Therefore, the Circulatory System in general is ruled by the ☉ and the ♌ sign. The ♒ sign, in ☍ to ♌, and complementary to ♌, also has much to do with the circulation of the blood. ♄, the ruler of ♒, and ruler of the peripheral nerves, presides over the circulation and distribution of the blood in the tissues, and the surface of the body, and for this reason the pathological action of ♄, and the influences of Cold, tend to disturb the peripheral circulation, drive the blood inward, and cause internal congestion, colds, etc. (See Centripetal). Afflictions in, or to the ♒ sign, tend to disturb the blood circulation, causing corrupt and impure blood, morbid conditions of the blood, blood poisoning, and incomplete oxygenation. The Blood is of two kinds, the Arterial and Venous. (See "Arterial", "Venous", in this section. Also see "Blood Poisoning" under Poison; "Impure Blood" under Impure; "Blood" under Morbid; Oxygen). The Circulation of the Blood is assisted by the ☉, and impeded by ♄. In a physiological way, the Herbs and Plants ruled by the ☉, affect the heart and circulation in a beneficial way, strengthen and help to restore its action to normal. Gold, the mineral ruled by the ☉, is also a remedy, used in conditions of disturbed circulation and heart disorders. The drugs and remedies of ♄, such as Aconite, tend to slow up the circulation and heart action. The drugs and remedies of ♂ accelerate the heart action and circulation, such as Strychnine, and act as tonics.

**Blood Vessels**—(See Vessels).

**Bowels**—Circulation of Obstructed—(See "Circulation" under Bowels).

**Capillary Circulation**—(See Capillaries).

**Changes in Blood Circulation**—♃ affl. in ♎ or ♒.

**Clots**—Circulation Impeded By—(See Clots).

**Congestion of Blood**—In a Part—(See Congestion).

**Cyanosis**—(See Cyanosis).

**Deficiency of Circulation**—In a Part —A ♄ disease; caused by parts or organs ruled by the Sign or House in which ♄ is found at B., or by progression or direction. Is counteracted by ♂ remedies internally, as by Strychnine, or locally by a rubefacient, as by Cantharides.

**Disorders**—Of the Circulation—See the various paragraphs in this section. Cases and Birth Data of Disorders of the Circulation—See Figures 11A, 11B, 11D, 11E, 11F, 11G, 11H, in the book, "Astro-Diagnosis", by the Heindels.

**Disturbed Circulation**—The ☽ affl. in ♌; ♅, ♄, or ♂ ☌ or ill-asp. ♃ or ♀; ♄ in ♌ tends to obstruct and disturb the circulation thru the heart; ♄ or ♃ affl. in ♒, the circulation disturbed by the blood becoming too thick, impure, or by too much blood. (See the various paragraphs in this section. Also see "Too Much Blood" under Blood; Dropsy, Fainting, Heart, Impure).

**Ears**—(See "Circulation" under Ears).

**Females**—Irregular Circulation In—The ☽ to the ill-asps. ♃. (See Menses).

**Fluids of Body**—Circulation of Disturbed—♄ ☌ or ill-asp. the ☽. (See "Ailments of" under Fluids; Pituitary).

**Good Circulation**—Of the Blood—The ☉, ♃, or ♀ in the ♌ or ♒ signs, and free from affl.; ♂ in any asp. to the ☉ or ☽; airy signs and good ♃ influence; given by the Sanguine Disposition, or Temperament, and espec. when the ♌ and ♒ signs are free from the affliction of the malefics. (See "Sanguine Temperament" under Sanguine).

**Head**—Rush of Blood To—(See "Blood" under Head).

**Heart**—(See "Circulation" under Heart).

**Hemorrhages**—(See Hemorrhage, Menses; "Nose Bleed" under Nose).

**Impeded Circulation**—♄ influence and affliction; ♄ affl. in ♌ or ♒. (See "Poor", and the various other paragraphs in this section).

**Infarct**—(See Clots, Thrombus).

**Interferred With**—♆ or ♄ ☌ ♃ and ♀; ♆ and the ☽ □ or ☍ ♃ and ♀. (See the various paragraphs in this section).

**Intestines**—Circulation Restricted In—(See "Circulation" under Bowels).

**Irregular Circulation**—Mostly in Females—(See "Females" in this section).

**Kidneys**—(See "Renal" in this section).

**Letting of Blood**—(See Bleeding).

**Lower Limbs**—Circulation In Obstructed—(See "Circulation" under Arms, Legs).

**Nerve Force**—The Vital Fluid—Circulation of—(See "Fluid" under Vital).

**Neuralgia**—(See "Circulation" under Neuralgia).

**Obstructions**—In the Circulation—♄ affl. in ♌ tends to obstruct the passage of the blood thru the heart; ♄ in ♊, obstructions and poor circulation in the lungs; ♄ or ☋ in any sign tends to poor circulation at times, according to the sign they are in, and the parts ruled by such sign; ♃ affl. in ♎ tends to obstruct the circulation. (See the various paragraphs in this section. See "Too Much Blood" under Blood).

**Peripheral Circulation**—(See "Blood" in this section).

**Poor Circulation**—Of the Blood—Impeded—Defective—Disordered—Disturbed—Weak—Sluggish, etc.—The ☉ affl. in ♌ or ♒, defective circulation; the ☉ ☌ ♄ or ☋, and in □ or ☍ ♃ or ♀; the ☽ □ or ☍ ♃ or ♀; the ☽ hyleg in ♌ or ♒ with females, and affl.; ☽ ☌ ♄ in ♌ or ♒; a ♄ disease; ♄ in evil asp. the ☉ from common signs; ♄ ☌, □, ☍ ♃ or ♀; ♄ or ♃ in ♍ and □ the ☉ or ♅ in ♊; ♄ in the 6th H. and affl. ♃ or ♀; ♄ affl. in ♌ or ♒; ♄ in the Asc. in ♌; a ♃ disease; ♃ affl. in ♌ or ♒; ♃ or ♀ in the Asc., and affl.; ♃ □ or ☍ the ☉; ♃ affl. in ♑; born under ♃; ♂ □ or ☍ ♃ or ♀; caused by an afflicted ♀; ♑ or ♒ on the 6th H.; ♒ on cusp the 6th H. tends to diseases arising from bad circulation. (See "Arterial", "Impeded", "Venous", and the various paragraphs in this section).

**Pressure**—High Blood Pressure—(See "Pressure" under Blood).

**Pulmonary Circulation**—(See "Blood" under Lungs; Pulmonary. Also see "Obstructions" in this section).

**Renal Circulation**—(See "Circulation" under Kidneys).

**Restricted Circulation**—(See "Arterial", "Impeded", "Poor", and the various paragraphs in this section. See Case, 11E in "Astro-Diagnosis" by the Heindels).

**Serous Circulation**—Interferences With—♄ affl. in ♎ or ♏; afflictions to the ☽; Subs at KP, the 12th Dorsal. (See Dropsy, Serum).

**Sluggish Circulation**—♄ influence; ♄ ☌ or ill-asp. ♃ or ♀. (See "Poor" in this section. See "Too Much Blood" under Blood, Tumors).

**Spasmodic Circulation**—♅ ☌, □, ☍ ♃ and ♀. (See Spasmodic).

**Stomach**—Circulation In Impeded—(See "Circulation" under Stomach).

**Thrombus; Veins**—(See Veins).

**Venous Circulation**—Ruled by ♀. For Disorders of the Venous Blood and Circulation see Veins.

**Vital Fluid**—Circulation of—(See "Fluid" under Vital).

**Weak Circulation**—(See "Poor" in this section. Also see Pulse; "Weak Heart" under Heart). See Aquarius.

**CIRCUMCISION**—Male children who have ♄ in ♏ at B. should, as a rule, be circumcised, as ♄ in this sign tends to contraction of the prepuce, with its attendant sex irritations and disorders. (See Penis).

**CIRRHOSIS**—Thickening of the connective tissue of an organ. Occurs mostly in the liver or kidneys, and is a ♄ disease and affliction. (See Connective Tissue, Density, Fiber, Hardening; "Cirrhosis" under Kidneys, Liver; "Local Parts" under Local; Sclerosis).

**CLAIRAUDIENCE**—Hears voices, which may be of an undesirable character. Caused by ♆ rising and elevated in the East at B., and affl. the ☽ or ☿; ♆ affl. in the 12th H., or in the M.C.; the progressed ☽ to the ☌ or ill-asp. ♆ in the radix, and espec. if ♆ be affl. at B. (See Chaotic, Clairvoyance, Hearing, Mediumship, Obsessions, Prophetic, Spirit Controls, Weird, etc.).

**CLAIRVOYANCE**—Clear Sight—Insight —Divination—Crystal Gazing—Mediumship—Given by ♆ and the watery signs. There are two kinds of Clairvoyance, the genuine, or trained Clairvoyance, which can be called into action at will, and the Involuntary form of Clairvoyance which comes upon people at any time, without an act of the will, and leads to obsessions, or undesirable mediumship.

**Involuntary Clairvoyance**—♆ ruler of the horoscope, and afflicted; due to the pathological action of ♆; ♆ affl. in the 6th or 12th H. at B.; ♆ □ or ☍ ♅ at B.; the evil directions of ♆ to the ☉, ☽, ☿, or the Asc. tend to intensify the evil, and espec. if the radical map shows such an affliction. (See Antares, Clairaudience, Fears, Hallucinations, Illusions, Imagination, Insanity, Mediumship, Obsessions, Pituitary, Prophetic, Psychic, Spirit Controls, etc. Case— See "Clairvoyant", No. 322 in 1001 N.N.

**CLAP**—The popular term for Gonorrhoea. (See Gonorrhoea).

**CLAUSTROPHOBIA**—A morbid dread of an inclosed place, or a morbid fear of crowds, or being tightly confined in a large crowd, or jam of people. A ♅ disease and affliction, and also associated with an evil asp. of ♄ to ☿; ☿ in a sign of ♄ and affl. by ♅; ♅ □ or ☍ ♄. Also caused by the pathological action of ♆, and with ♆ afflicting ☿ at B. (See "Morbid Fears" under Fears; Neurasthenia, Obsessions).

**CLAVICLE**—The Collar Bone. Under the structural rulership of ♊. (See Arms, Shoulders).

**Disease or Injury Of**—♄ or ♂ affl. in ♊; Subs at LCP, the 6th Cervical; at AP, the 1st Dorsal.

**Fracture Of**—♂ affl. in ♊. Cases of Fracture—See "Saturn in the Tenth", No. 831 in 1001 N.N. Twice Broken— Case—See "A Luckless Youth", No. 390 in 1001 N.N.

**Swelling**—About the Clavicle—The ☽ affl. in ♊; planets affl. in ♊; Subs at LCP and AP. (See "Disease" in this section).

**CLEANLINESS**—Cleanly—The ♍ influence strong at B.; ♀ in ☌ or good asp. the ☽; good asps. between ♀, ☿, and the ☽. (See Careless, Dress, Filthy, Habits, Neat, Sanitation, Uncleanly, Untidy).

**CLEANSING OF THE BODY**—♂ cleanses the body of wastes and filth, and when the system becomes clogged thru excesses, dissipation, or gluttony, brings fevers and inflammation to quickly burn up the wastes, and thus save life. The ☽ also is cleansing and fluidic, and acts thru the fluids of the body in carrying off wastes. (See Combustion, Deposits, Destructive, Elimination, Enemas, Excretion, Fever, Inflammation; "Lease" under Life; Physic, Poisons, Retention, Wastes).

**CLEAR**—

**Clear Complexion**—Clear Skin—(See Complexion, Skin).

**Clear Eyes**—(See Eyes).

**Clear Intellect**—(See Intellect).

**Clear Voice**—(See Voice).

**CLEFT**—Cleft in the Spine—(See "Spina Bifida", and "Diseases of the Spine" under Spine. Also see Fissure, Palate).

**CLERGYMEN**—Ministers—Priests—

**Anxiety To**—Sadness To—An eclipse of the ☽ in ♓. (See Religion).

**Ill-Health Of**—♄, or other malefics, afflicting ♃ at B.; malefics in the 9th H.; planets in the 9th, and affl. by lords of the 6th, 8th, or 12th H.; lord of the 6th in the 9th, or lord of the 9th in the 6th; lord of the 6th as Sig. in Hor'y Questions.

**CLIMACTERIC YEARS**—Critical Years of Life—Every 7th and 9th year of life are called Climacterical because the ☽ then repeats her □ and △ aspects to her positions at B. by progression. The □ asps. of the ☽ to her radical place are the 7th, 14th, 21st, 28th, 35th, 42nd, 49th, 56th, 63rd years, etc., and are considered unfortunate and critical years, while her △ asps. fall in the 9th, 18th, 27th, 36th years, etc., and are more fortunate years in life. The ☉ hyleg, and to the □ or ☍ ♂ by dir. is a very evil, and often a fatal influence, when falling due in a climacteric year, or under any other fatal direction or Lunation. (See Directions). Also it takes ♄ a little more than 28 years to make one circuit in his orbit, and his first □ asp. to his radical place comes about the 7th year; his ☍ at the 14th year; his □ again at about the 21st year, and his ☌ with his radical place about the 28th or 29th years of life, which tends to make these times very critical years in life every seven years, and subject the native to ill-health, reversals, self-undoing, or a downfall, etc.

**Grand Climacteric**—Double Climacterical Years—The 49th and 63rd years, being 7×7, and 7×9, and the statistics of Undertakers show that the years of greatest mortality among adults are the 49th and 63rd years. In the 49th and 63rd years of life, the native usually continues to live if the ☽ at B. is well-aspected, and the directions for the year are good, but if not, death is more apt to come, especially if there is worry, anxiety and unsettledness. A fundamental rule is that the number 7 when multiplied by an odd number, as by 1, 3, 5, 7, 9, indicate the more evil and critical years in life, the climacterical years, while multiplied by an even number, as by 2, 4, 6, 8, give the more fortunate years, or years of less danger to life under evil directions. The even numbers are feminine, and the odd numbers masculine, and a masculine and feminine number when combined by addition or multiplication, according to the Science of Numbers, give greater strength and resistance to the body, whereas two masculine, or two feminine numbers combined tend to lowered vitality. (See "Eight Months Children" in Sec. 1 under Children). There are other years in life which may become critical, due to the aspects and directions, and yet not be called Climacteric. (See Crises, Critical, Cycles, Enneatical, Periodic, Periods).

CLIMATE—In considering the physical constitution and its welfare, the ☽ and her positions and aspects at B., becomes the Significator of affections which proceed from external causes, as climate, clothing, food, environment, etc. Climate is very important to good health. The different Climates, Countries, and parts of the Earth, are ruled by the different Signs of the Zodiac, and Planets, and in deciding upon the location, kind of climate, etc., for any individual, it is necessary and important to make a detailed study of the Star Map of Birth. Climates which would kill some people are beneficial for others. Some constitutions require a high altitude for good health, and others the Sea Level, or a low altitude, all which is shown and indicated by the Map of Birth. Many people suffer ill-health because they are in the wrong location and climate. Chronic diseases are often developed by people removing from their native climate, as to the Tropics, if born in a Northern Latitude, and then find a cure again by returning to their own Country. This subject of climate, location, etc., is further considered under Abroad, Altitude, Cold, Endemic, Environment, Exposure, External, Heat, Location, Nations; "Native Land" under Native; "Place of Birth" under Place; Races, Residence, Travel, Weather, etc.).

CLITORIS—The Glans Clitoris—Ruled by ♏.

CLOACA—A Cavity Containing Pus—An Opening in a Diseased Bone—A Common Outlet to the Recum and Bladder—A ♄ disease and affliction. In the Rectum and Bladder, ♄ affl. in ♏. In the Bones, ♄ affl. in an earthy sign, and principally in ♑. (See Abscesses, Malformations, Pus, Rectum, Urethra).

CLOGGING—Hindrances, Impediments, Stoppage, etc.

Clogging of the Mind—♓ on the Asc., physical condition often tends to clog the mental action. (See Dull, Languid, Lassitude, Lethargy, Listless, Stupidity, etc.).

Clogging of the System—The work of ♄ impeding and obstructing elimination; ♄ affl. in ♎, due to retention of wastes, poisons and toxins; the work of ♃ and ♀ thru excesses, gormandizing, and bad habits. (See Ash, Crystallization, Cleansing, Deposits, Elimination, Excretion, Hardening, Hearing, Impeded, Impediments, "Impure Blood" under Impure; Obstructions; "Poor Circulation" under Circulation; Retentions, Stoppages, Suppressions, Wastes).

CLONIC—(See "Clonic" under Spasmodic; Epilepsy, Muscles. Also see Myoclonus).

CLOSE OF LIFE—The 4th H. rules and denotes the conditions at the close of life, and is to be judged by the rulership of this house, and the nature of the planets in this house. Also the manner of death in old age is partly indicated by the 8th H. conditions, and planets in the 8th. (See Old Age).

CLOSURES—(See Imperforate, Orifices).

CLOTHING—(See Acquired, Cleanly, Climate, Colds, Comforts, Dress, Habits, Linen, Uncleanly, Wet).

CLOTS—Blood Clots—Coagulations in the Body—Congelation—Infarct—Thrombus—A ♄ influence. (See Congelation, Haemostatics, Infarct, Obstructions, Thrombus, Vessels). Case —Died from Blood Clot on the Brain —See "Birth and Death", No. 350 in 1001 N.N.

CLOUDED—Clouding—Cloudy—

Clouded Mind—(See "Clouded" under Mind).

Clouded Sight—(See Blindness, Cataract, Nebulous, Sight).

Clouding of Consciousness—(See Chaotic).

Cloudy Complexion—(See Complexion).

Cloudy Spot of Cancer—(See "One Eye" under Blindness. Also see Nebulous).

Cloudy Urine—(See Urine).

CLOUDS—The Clouds are ruled by ♃. The influence of ♃ in his configurations with the different planets tends to free the moisture of the clouds in superabundance, causing excessive rains and floods, which endanger human life, and cause sickness and suffering. (See Floods, Lightning, Rain, Storms, Wind).

CLUMSINESS — Awkwardness — Afflictions to the ☽ at B.: ♀ to the ill-asps. ☿ by dir. (See Automatic, Awkwardness, Gait, Motion, Movement, Walk).

CLYSTER—Clystering—Injections—(See Enema).

COAGULATION—Clotting—♄ influence. (See Clots).

COALITION—Fusions—Union of Parts —Bringing Together—In a beneficial way, as causing harmony and rhythm in the mind and body, and eliminating discordant elements, coalition is the work of ♀. In a pathological way ♄ tends to coalition, union of parts, etc., thru deposits, hardening, crystallization, etc. The influences of the ☉ ☌ ♂ also tend to fusion of parts thru excessive heat. (See Adhesions, Anatomical, Ankylosis, Crystallization, Deposits, Fusions, Hardening, Harmony, Rhythm, etc.).

COARSE—Rough—Unrefined—

Body—Coarse Body—♏ on the Asc. (See Rough, Unrefined).

Features—(See "Coarse" under Features).

Hair—(See "Coarse" under Hair).

Legs—(See "Coarse" under Legs).

Manners—Coarse Manners—(See Gross, Obscene, Manners, Rough, Sensual, Unrefined).

Skin—Coarse and Rough—(See "Rough" under Skin).

Voice—(See "Coarse" under Voice).

Women—Coarse Women—(See Deviations, Effeminate, "Tomboyishness" under Females; "Coarse" under Voice).

COCAINISM—(See "Drug Habit" under Narcotics. Also see "Neptune Group" under Herbs).

**COCCYX**—The Os Coccyx is under the structural rulership of the ♏ sign. The Coccygeal Region of the Spine, the Coccygeal Vertebrae, are ruled by the ♐ sign. (See Vertebrae).

**Coccydynia**—Pain in the Coccyx—♄ or ♂ affl. in ♏ or ♐; Subs at LPP, and of the Sacrum and Coccygeal Vertebrae. (See Sacrum).

**COCTION**—The Coction Process—Digestion—Combustion—(See Combustion, Digestion).

**COFFEE**—(See "Neptune Group" under Herbs).

**COHABITATION**—Coition—

**Little or No Desire For**—The ☉ or ☽ in ♏ ☌ or ill-asp. ♄; the ☉ by progression making no asp. to planets for a long period of time; the ☽ void of course, and in the last degrees of a sign, and making no asp. to planets; ♄ influence tends to produce apathy, and espec. when in ♈, and lack of passion and feeling. (See Apathy, Bachelors, Celibacy; "Aversion" under Marriage; "Free from Passion" under Passion; "Married Women" under Sex; Spinsters).

**Passional Excesses**—(See Intercourse, Passion, Sex, Venery, etc.).

**COHESION**—Lack of Cohesion of Parts—A ♆ disease and affliction.

**COLD**—Chill—Saturn rules and produces Cold, and excess of cold in the body, or in the atmosphere. Cold is noxious and destructive, and all matter is dissipated by coldness and dryness. Cold and Dry are malevolent influences and tend to decay. Cold is affiliated with moisture, and heat with dryness. Cold is a negative quality, and also passive, and predominates in the left side of the body. (See Left). The watery signs, ♋, ♏, and ♓ are cold in nature. The therapeutic action of ♄, and ♄ remedies, are cooling and refrigerating, and such remedies are used to combat the high fevers given by ♂. Hydrogen, ruled by ♄, has affinity with Cold. Statistics show that about 50% of all our diseases come from cold, chill, exposure to cold, and the chilling of the skin, or surface of the body, by improper clothing, thus driving the blood inwards and causing functional disorders, internal congestions, colds, etc. (See Centripetal, Colds, Congestion, Ganglion). Cold, Lingering, and Chronic Diseases are produced by ♄. The parts of the body, or organs more liable to be afflicted with cold, colds, or chill, are those ruled by the Sign or House containing ♄ at B., and espec. when ♄ is in an earthy or watery sign, affl. the ☉, ☽, Asc., or hyleg, and when this class of Signs may also be on the Asc., or cusp of the 6th H., or the ☉, ☽, and a majority of planets in such Signs at B., tending fundamentally to give a cold body or constitution. Cold tends to contractions and obstructions in the body. There are diseases and bodily conditions which arise from Cold alone. Others from a combination of Cold and Moisture, and others from a combination of Cold and Dry causes. The following diseases and afflictions have to do with Cold, Cold and Moisture, and with the ♄ influence. Also the diseases listed under Saturn are mostly Cold Diseases, and caused by Cold at their beginnings. (See "Cold", "Diseases of Saturn", under Saturn. Also see Chill, Dry, Moisture).

**Ague**—(See "Quartan Ague" under Ague).

**Augmented Cold**—Cold Augmented In the Body—(See "Body" in this section).

**Blindness from Cold**—(See "Cold" under Blindness).

**Blood**—Cold Blood—The ☉ or ☽ in ♓ and affl. by ♄; the ☽ affl. in ♍; the ♓ influence tends to cold blood, and ♓ on the Asc. at B.

**Body**—Cold Body or Constitution—Cold Augmented In the Body—The System Affected Generally with Cold—The ☉ affl. by the ☽ at B.; the ☉ or ☽ ☌ or ill-asp. ♄ at B., and by dir.; the ☉ afflicting the Asc. at B., or by dir.; the ☽ in a watery sign at B., and espec. if the Asc. is also a water sign; the ☽ from her 3rd Quarter to the New ☽ makes the constitution more cold; ♄ in an angle, occi. of the ☉, and ori. of the ☽, and espec. if ♄ be in familiarity with ☿; ♄ or ☿ holding dominion at B., and these planets being in familiarity; ♄ ☌ or ill-asp. the ☉, ☽, Asc., or hyleg at B., or by dir.; the Asc. affl. by the ☉, ☽, or ♄; earthy or watery signs in the Asc. at B., or on the cusp of 6th H., and the ☉, ☽, or ♄ also in this class of signs at the same time. Those born in the Arctic Regions and in cold climates tend to have a cold constitution. (See "Animal Heat" under Heat. Also see "Temperament" in this section).

**Bowels**—Cold in the Bowels—(See "Cold" under Bowels).

**Chilblain**—(See Chilblain).

**Chill**—Chills—(See Chill).

**Chronic Diseases**—From Cold—♄ ☌ or ill-asp. the ☉, ☽, Asc., or hyleg at B., or by dir., and espec. the ☽ affl. by ♄. (See Chronic).

**Climate**—Cold Climate—Suffering From—(See "Cold" under Weather; also see Blizzards, Snow, Winter).

**Cold Baths**—(See Bathing).

**Cold Body**—(See "Body" in this section).

**Cold and Chill**—(See Chill. Also note the various paragraphs in this section).

**Cold and Dry**—(See "Cold and Dry Body", "Cold and Dry Diseases" under Dry).

**Cold and Heat**—(See "Cold and Heat" under Heat).

**Cold and Moist**—(See "Cold and Moist" paragraphs under Moisture).

**Cold Temperament**—(See "Body", "Temperament", in this section).

**Cold Water**—(See Cravings).

**Cold Weather**—(See "Climate" in this section).

**Colds**—Catching Cold—(See Colds).

**Constitution Cold**—(See "Body" in this section).

**Contractions**—Due to Cold—(See Contractions).

**Crystallization**—The Result of Cold—(See Crystallization, Hardening, Petrifaction, Stone).

**Dampness and Cold**—Diseases and Fevers Arising From—Caused by ♄ and ♅. (See "Cold and Moist" under Humours, Moisture; "Humours" under Watery).

**Death**—By Cold, and Cold Diseases—Denoted by ♄ and the ☽, and by fixed stars of the nature of ♄; the evil directions of ♄ to the hyleg, and espec. when holding the dominion of death; when the ☉ or Asc. are hyleg, the ☽ by her evil asps. and directions to the ☉ or Asc. tends to cause death by cold and chronic diseases. (See "Arguments for Death" under Death; "Cold, Phlegmatic Diseases" under Phlegm).

**Defluxions**—Cold Defluxions—♄ diseases. (See Defluxions, Fluxions).

**Diseases Arising from Cold**—Cold Diseases—Irregularities of the System Thru Cold and Chill—All Illnesses Arising from Cold—The ♄ influence is the principal cause of all Cold diseases, and his afflictions to the vital places of the map, the ☉, ☽, Asc. or hyleg. Also watery signs on the Asc., or on cusp of the 6th H. predispose to cold diseases. Note the following influences which cause diseases arising from Cold,—The SUN affl. by the ☽, the system is generally affected with cold; the ☉, ☽, and many planets in watery signs at B.; the ☉ in ♑ at B., or ♑ upon the Asc., as ♑ is the coldest of the earthy signs; the ☉ or ☽ ☌ or ill-asp. ♄ at B., and by dir.; the ☉ affl. the Asc. at B., and by dir.; MOON ruler of the Asc. in an earthy or watery sign, and affl. by ♄, diseases of a cold nature, and people so born rarely suffer from hot or burning fevers; the ☽ in a watery sign at B., and a watery sign upon the Asc. or cusp of 6th H.; the ☽ ☌ or ill-asp. ♄ or ☿ at B., and by dir., or at the beginning of an illness if ☿ be of the nature of ♄; the ☽ to the ill-asps. the Asc. or hyleg by dir.; URANUS afflictions to the ☉, ☽, Asc. or hyleg, diseases arising from sudden exposure to cold, as at bathings; SATURN to the ☌ or ill-asps. the Asc. by dir.; ♄ in the 6th H., and affl. the Asc. or hyleg; ♄ the sole ruler at a Solar Eclipse, a prevalence of colds, and diseases arising from cold; ♄ having the dominion of death in the map of birth; the ASCENDANT affl. by the ☉ or ☽; the Asc. ☌ or ill-asp. ♄ at B., or by dir.; the Asc. an earthy or watery sign, and the ☽ at the same time in one of these signs; earthy or watery signs on the cusp the 6th H., and espec. if one of these signs be also on the Asc., or containing the ☽, and the ☽ affl. by ♄. (See the various paragraphs in this section. Also see Chill, Concretions).

**Distempers**—Cold Distempers—Cold and Moist Distempers—♓ diseases. (See "Cold and Moist" under Humours, Moisture).

**Dry and Cold**—(See "Cold and Dry" under Dry).

**Excessive Cold**—(See "Climate" in this section).

**Exposure to Cold**—Diseases Arising From—(See Exposure, External; "Cold" under Weather).

**Externally Cold**—With Internal Heats—(See "Internal Heats" under Heat).

**Extremely Cold Weather**—General Suffering From—(See "Cold" under Weather).

**Extremes of Heat and Cold**—Body Suffers From—(See "Cold and Heat" under Heat).

**Extremities**—Cold Extremities—(See "Cold" under Extremities, Hands, Legs, Feet).

**Feet**—Cold Feet—Cold Taken In—(See Feet).

**Frost**—Ruled by ♄. (See Frost).

**Hands**—Cold Hands—(See Hands).

**Head**—The Head Disordered by Cold—Cold In the Head—(See "Colds" under Head).

**Health Suffers**—From Cold—(See the various paragraphs in this section).

**Heat and Cold**—(See "Cold and Heat" under Heat).

**Hips**—Cold and Chill In—♄ ♐. (See Hips).

**Humours**—Cold Humours—Cold and Moist Humours—(See "Cold" under Humours).

**Ice**—Ruled by ♄. (See Hail, Snow).

**Indigestion**—From Cold, or Taking Cold—(See "Cold" under Indigestion).

**Irregularities**—Of the System from Cold and Chill—(See "Diseases", and the various paragraphs in this section. See "Irregular" under Functions).

**Knees**—Cold In—(See Knees).

**Legs**—Cold In—(See Legs).

**Liver**—Cold and Dry—(See Liver).

**Lumbar Region**—Cold and Chill In—(See Lumbar).

**Lungs**—Cold In—(See "Colds on Chest" under Lungs).

**Manner**—(See "Coldness" under Manner).

**Moist and Cold**—(See "Cold and Moist" under Moisture).

**Nose**—Cold In—(See Nose).

**Organs**—Cold Organs—(See Organs).

**Phlegmatic**—Cold, Phlegmatic Diseases—(See Phlegm).

**Quartan Ague**—Arising from Cold—(See Ague).

**Rheumatic**—Cold, Rheumatic Diseases—(See Rheumatism).

**Rigor Mortis**—The Rigidity After Death—Ruled and produced by ♄. (See Death).

**Rigors**—Coldness—Stiffness—(See Rigid, Rigors, Stiffness).

**Skin**—Cold Skin—(See "Cold" under Skin).

**Snow**—Ruled by ♄. (See Snow).

**Stiffness from Cold**—(See Rigors; "Cold Weather" under Weather).

**Stomach**—Cold Stomach—The Stomach Afflicted With Cold Humours—(See "Raw Humours" under Indigestion).

**Stone**—(See Concretions).

**Superabundance**—Of Cold In the System—Disease or Death Produced By—Caused by ♄, and when ♄ holds the dominion of death in the map of birth; ♑ on the Asc. at B. (See "Animal Heat" under Heat).

**Susceptible to Cold**—The Body Susceptible to Cold—(See "Body" in this section).

**System**—The System Affected Generally with Cold—(See "Body" in this section).

**Taking Cold**—Diseases Arising Therefrom—(See "Causes of Colds" under Colds).

**Temperament**—Indisposed by Cold Temperament—Fixed Stars of the nature of ♄ and ♂ ascending at B.; ♄ in the Asc. at B., in ♑, and ♑ upon the Asc.; ♓ upon the Asc., or cusp of 6th H.; an earthy sign upon the Asc., and with the ☽ in ♓. (See "Body" in this section).

**Thighs**—Cold In—♄ ♐. (See Thighs).

**Toes**—Coldness of—(See Toes).

**Watery and Cold Diseases**—(See "Cold and Moist" under Humours, Moisture).

**Weather**—Cold Weather—(See "Cold" under Weather).

**COLDS**—Saturn causes and rules Colds, which arise principally from Cold, and chilling of the surface of the body, driving the blood inwards, and causing internal congestions. (See Centripetal, Congestions, Constrictions). People who have ♄ weak at B., and not afflicting the ☉, ☽, Asc., or hyleg, and when the watery sign element also is not prominent, do not suffer much from Colds. People who have ♄ in an earthy or watery sign at B., and affl. the ☉, ☽, Asc., or hyleg, and when this class of Signs may also be upon the Asc., or cusp of the 6th H., should guard against Colds. Saturn people catch cold easily from wet feet, drafts, or from the slightest wetting. It is said that Colds are caused by Sidereal influences, and disturbed atmospheric conditions, as taking cold in a room, and against which no precautions seem to be available or successful. For the general influences causing Colds, see "Causes" in this section. Also the following diseases and afflictions are associated with Colds and Cold, or are the direct result of them.

**Blindness from Colds**—Caused by ♄; ♄ affl. in ♈. (See "Causes" and "Cold" under Blindness).

**Body**—Cold Taken from Over-Exertion of the Body or Mind—(See "Colds" under Exercise; "Over-Exertion" under Exertion).

**Bowels**—Colds In—(See "Cold" under Bowels).

**Bronchitis**—(See Bronchial; "Cold on Lungs" under Lungs).

**Catarrh**—(See the various paragraphs under Catarrh).

**Catches Cold Easily**—(See "Causes" in this section).

**Causes of Colds**—Liable to Colds—Tendency to Colds—Catches Cold Easily—Susceptible to Colds—Suffers from Colds—The ☉ or ☽ to the ☌ or ill-asps. ♄ by dir., and espec. if ♄ be strong at B., and affl. the Lights, or the ☉ or ☽ be hyleg; the ☉ or ☽ ☌ or ill-asp. ♄ at B., and espec. when occupying watery signs, or an earthy or watery sign upon the Asc. or cusp the 6th H.; the ☉ affl. in ♑; the ☉ affl. by the ☽ at B., or by dir.; the ☽ affl. in ♓, colds which fly to the lungs; the ☽ in bad asp. to the ☉ at B., and by dir.; denoted by the ☽ when the ☽ afflicts the ☉ or Asc.; the ☽ to the ill-asps. ♅ or ♆ by dir.; ♄ ☌ or ill-asp. the ☉, ☽, Asc., or hyleg at B., or affl. these places by dir.; ♄ to the ☌ or ill-asp. the ☽ if the ☽ be hyleg, or ruler of the 6th or 8th H.; ♄ by transit ☌ or ill-asp. the ☉, ☽, ♃, or ♀ in the radical map; ♄ ruler of the 6th H. at B., and the M.C. to the ☌ or ill-asp. ♄; ♄ in ♋, ♏, ♑, or ♒ warns of cold and chills to the system; ♄ in ♈, and espec. colds in the head; ♄ ☌ or ill-asp. the ☉ in common signs; ♄ in the 1st H.; ♄ in any sign or house tends to colds and chills in the parts of the body ruled by the sign containing ♄ at B.; ♄ in ♓, colds in and thru the feet; ☿ affl. in ♋ or ♌, and espec. when ☿ partakes of the nature of ♄; afflictions in ♓, and are ♓ diseases; afflictions in common signs; many planets in watery signs, or a water sign upon the Asc. or cusp of 6th H.; afflictions in ♋; ♑ on cusp the 6th H.; the Asc. to the ☌ or ill-asp. ♄ by dir. (See the various paragraphs in this section).

**Chest**—Colds On—(See "Bronchitis" in this section).

**Chills and Colds**—(See Chill).

**Clothing**—Colds from Wet Clothing or Linen—(See "Cold Taken" under Feet; "Colds" under Moisture; "Linen" under Wet).

**Coryza**—(See "Coryza" under Nose).

**Cough from Colds**—(See Cough).

**Damp Places**—Colds from Living In—(See "Colds" under Moisture).

**Death from Colds**—Or Coughs—(See "Death" under Cough).

**Delirium**—From Colds and Coughs—(See "Death" under Cough).

**Exercise**—Colds from Over-Exercise and Over-Exertion of the Body—(See "Colds" under Exercise).

**Feet**—Colds from Wet Feet—(See "Cold" under Feet).

**Hay Fever**—Rose Cold—(See "Hay Fever" under Nose).

**Head**—Colds In—(See "Colds" under Head; "Coryza" under Nose).

**Hips and Thighs**—Cold and Colds In—♄ ♐.

**Indigestion**—From Taking Cold—(See "Cold" under Indigestion).

**Influenza**—(See Influenza).

**Knees**—Cold In—(See Knees).

**La Grippe**—(See Influenza, La Grippe).

**Lameness**—From Colds—♄ affl. in signs which rule the legs, knees and feet, as in ♐, ♑, ♒ or ♓. (See "Cold" under Legs, Knees, Feet. See Lameness).

**Legs**—Cold and Colds In—(See Extremities, Legs, Limbs).

**Liable to Colds**—(See "Causes" in this section).

**Linen**—Cold from Wet Linen—(See "Clothing" in this section).

**Lungs**—Colds On—(See "Bronchitis" in this section).

**Mind**—Colds Taken from Over-Exertion of Mind and Body—(See "Colds" under Exercise).

**Moist Places**—Colds Taken from Living in Damp and Moist Places—(See "Colds" under Moisture).

**Mother**—Death of the Mother from Extreme Colds—(See "Cold", "Death", under Mother).

**Mucus**—Mucous Discharges—(See Defluxions, Discharges, Humours, Mucous, Phlegm, Rheum, Watery, etc.).

**Over-Exertion**—Colds Taken By—(See "Colds" under Exercise).

**Phlegm**—Discharges of—(See Phlegm).

**Places**—Damp Places—Colds from Living In—(See "Colds" under Moisture).

**Pneumonia**—Colds Resulting In—(See Pneumonia).

**Prevalence of Colds**—♄ sole ruler at a Solar Eclipse. (See "Diseases" under Cold).

**Rheum**—Catarrhal and Watery Discharges—(See Rheum).

**Rhinitis**—(See "Coryza", "Rhinitis" under Nose).

**Rose Cold**—(See "Hay Fever" under Nose).

**Severe Colds**—Death From—(See "Death" under Cough).

**Sneezing**—(See Nose).

**Suffers from Colds**—(See "Causes" In this section).

**Susceptible to Colds**—(See "Causes" in this section).

**Taking Cold**—Takes Cold Easily—Diseases Arising From—(See "Causes" in this section. Also see "Diseases Arising From" under Cold; External).

**Tendency to Colds**—(See "Causes" in this section).

**Thighs**—Colds In—♄ ♐. (See Hips, Thighs).

**Wet Feet**—Colds From—(See "Cold" under Feet).

**COLIC**—Spasmodic Pain in the Abdomen—Cholic—

**Biliary Colic**—(See "Cholic" under Bile).

**Bowels**—Colic In—(See "Colic" under Bowels).

**Causes of Colic**—A ♍ disease, and afflictions in ♍; ♍ on the Asc., or cusp of 6th H.; the ☉ affl. in ♍; a ☽ disease; the ☽ affl. in ♍, or affl. the hyleg therefrom; the ☽ hyleg, and to the ☌ or ill-asp. ♄ by dir.; the ☽ in ♈ or ♍, and affl. by the ☉ or ♂ when taken ill; the ☽ hyleg, and to the ill-asps. the ☉ by dir.; the ☽ weak and affl. at B., and ☌ Asc. by dir.; the ☽ ☌ ♂ in ♍ in the Asc. when taken ill; the ☽ decr. in light, sepr. from ♄, and applying to ☿; the ☽ hyleg in ♍, and afflicted, and espec. in a female nativity; caused by fixed stars of the nature of the ☽; a ♄ disease; caused by ♄ when he is strong at B., and espec. when the dominion of illness or death is vested in him; ♄ in an angle, occi. of the ☉, and ori. of the ☽; ♄ affl. in ♍, and espec. in the 6th H.; ♃ affl. in ♌ or ♍; ♂ in ♍ in the Asc. or 6th H., and afflicted; ☿ affl. in ♍ or ♓; ☿ in ♍, and to the ☌ or ill-asp. ♆, ♅, ♄, or ♂; ☿ affl. in ♎, due to worry and anxiety; Asc. to the □ or ☍ ♄ by dir.; afflictions in ♓.

**Cramps**—(See Cramps).

**Enteralgia**—(See Enteralgia; "Pain" under Bowels).

**Erratic Movements**—(See "Movements" under Erratic. Also see Spasmodic).

**Feet**—Colic Taken Thru the Feet—(See "Colic" under Feet).

**Flatulence**—(See Flatulence).

**Gas**—In Bowels—(See "Gas" under Bowels).

**Hepatic Colic**—(See "Cholic" under Bile).

**Incoordination**—In Abdomen and Bowel Tract—The ☉ or ♅ affl. in ♍. (See Incoordination).

**Kidney**—Colic In—Nephritic Colic—Renal Colic—(See "Colic" under Kidneys).

**Lead Colic**—Saturnine Colic—Painter's Colic—A ♄ disease; ♄ affl. in ♍; ☽ ☌ ♄ in ♎. (See Lead).

**Nephritic Colic**—(See "Colic" under Kidneys).

**Pain**—(See "Cramps", "Pain", under Bowels).

**Painter's Colic**—(See "Lead" in this Section).

**Prevalent**—Colic Prevalent—♄ or ♂ holding power at a Summer Solstice, and in ♍, and affl. planets in the 6th or 8th H.

**Renal Colic**—(See "Colic" under Kidneys).

**Saturnine Colic**—(See "Lead" in this section).

**Stomach Colic**—(See "Colic" under Stomach).

**Ureters**—Colic of—(See "Colic" under Kidneys).

**Wind Colic**—(See "Bowels" under Wind. Also see "Cramps", "Pain", under Bowels).

**COLLAPSE**—Complete Collapse—Failure of the Vital Powers—Nervous Collapse—Prostration—

**Danger of Collapse**—♆ in a prominent and powerful position in the map of birth, and affl. by the ☽ or ☿, tends to make some people nervous, excitable, neurotic, and subject to paroxysms of nervous excitation, which are often followed with complete collapse; ☋ on the Asc. at B., danger of collapse. (See "Worse" under Crises; Excitable, Exhaustion, Feeble, Neurasthenia, Prostration, Vitality Low; "Weak Body" under Weak).

**Muscular Collapse**—Case—See "Seventeen Years in Bed", No. 843 in 1001 N.N.

**Sudden Collapse**—The ☉ affl. in ♉, and espec. when the ☉ is hyleg, and affl. by the ☌ or ill-asp. ♄ by dir. (See "Illness" under Accidents).

**COLLAR BONE**—(See Clavicle).

**COLLES FRACTURE**—(See "Fracture" under Wrists).

**COLLIQUATIVE**—Profuse—Excessive—(See Excessive; "Night Sweats" under Phthisis; Profuse; "Excessive" under Sweat).

**COLLYRIA**—Collyrium—A medicinal lotion for the eyes. Sugar of Lead, a ♄ remedy, a principal ingredient in, for its astrictive property. (See Astringent, Lead, Ointments).

**COLOCYNTH**—A typical drug of the ☽. (See "Typical" under Moon).

**COLON**—The superior part of the large intestine. The Colon, and its different sections, the Descending Colon, the Transverse Colon, the Sigmoid Flexure, and the Mesocolon, are ruled by ♂ and the ♏ sign.

**Colitis**—Inflammation of the Colon—♂ affl. in ♏; Subs at PP, the 2nd Lumbar Vertebra.

**Enterocolitis**—Inflammation of the Intestines and the Colon—Malefics in both ♍ and ♏; Subs at KP, and PP, the 2nd Lumbar.

**Inflamed Colon**—(See "Colitis" in this section).

**Obstructions**—In the Colon—♄ affl. in ♍ tends to obstructions in the Transverse Colon.

**Sigmoid Flexure**—Disorders of—(See Sigmoid).

**COLOR**—

**Bad Color**—Bad Complexion—(See "Bad Complexion" under Complexion; Pale; Sickly, White).

**Blindness**—Color Blindness—(See "Color" under Blindness).

**Blood**—Red Coloring Matter of—Ruled by ♂ and the ♏ sign. (See Haemoglobin; "Blood" under Red).

**Clothing**—Color of—(See Colors, Dress).

**Complexion**—Color of—(See "Bad Color" in this section).

**Good Color**—(See "Good" under Complexion).

**Hair**—(See "Color" under Hair).

**Reddish Color**—(See "Red" under Complexion).

**Sense of Color**—Is ruled by ♀. Also the 16° and 17° ♉, a sign of ♀, are said to strongly rule this sense.

**Skin**—Color of—(See Complexion, Pigment, Races, Skin). See the next Article on Colors.

**COLORS**—Colors, according to Astrology, are symptoms of the nature of the Stars. Fixed Stars of the color of ♂ are of the nature of ♂; those of the color of ♃, of the nature of ♃, etc. The ☉, ☽, and planets, each have a color under their rule. The colors in the Solar Spectrum are ruled by the ☉, ☽, and the five planets, excepting ♅ and ♆. For the rulership of the various colors, see "Planets", "Signs", and the various paragraphs in this section.

**Clothing**—Dress—Colors of Clothing in Horary Questions are said to be according to the mixture of the planets, and the Signs and Terms they are in, as follows—The ☉, saffron or sandy color; the ☉ and ☽, light yellow or green; the ☉ and ♄, dark yellow, or bronze color; the ☉ and ♃, very deep, shining red; the ☉ and ♂, deep shining red; the ☉ and ♀, olive; the ☉ and ☿, light gray; the ☽, light mixed colors, white, cream-colored, or pale green; the ☽ and ♄, deep gray or russet; the ☽ and ♃, bright green; the ☽ and ♂, light red; the ☽ and ♀, light blue, or bluish white; the ☽ and ☿, buff or fawn color; ♄, black; ♄ and ♃, dark black green; ♄ and ♂, dark brown; ♄ and ♀, whitish gray; ♄ and ☿, dark gray or blue; ♃, green, spotted, or ash colored; ♃, red mixed with green; ♃ and ♀, blue and yellow, or greenish gray; ♃ and ☿, spotted green; ♃ and ♂, tawny, with light spots; ♂, red; ♂ and ♀, light red or crimson; ♂ and ☿, red tawny; ♀, white or bluish; ♀ and ☿, purple or light mixture; ☿, gray or dove color; ♉, red mixed with citron; ♊, red and white mixed. When a planet is in the house of another planet, judge of him as mixed with that planet. Thus, ♄ in ♌, the house of the ☉, denotes the dress to be either dark yellow, or bronze color, etc. (See Mixed).

**Complexion**—For the various colors of the complexion, see Complexion, Face. Also see the remarks under "Signs" in this section.

**Dress**—Colors of—(See "Clothing" in this section).

**Houses**—Colors of—(See Houses).

**Light Colors and White**—Are ruled by the 1st H.

**Mixed Colors**—Ruled by ♅ and the ☽. (See "Clothing" in this section. Also see the ♅ influences under "Planets" in this section).

**Planets and Color**—Planetary Colors—In the Secret Doctrine by H. P. B., the colors in the Solar Spectrum are assigned to the planets as follows,—The ☉, Orange; the ☽, Violet; ♄, Green; ♃, Blue, or Purple; ♂, Red; ♀, Indigo; ☿, Yellow. Astrological Authorities seem to differ some from this classification, and in the following notes, I am using the assignments as given in the textbooks of Astrology. The ☉ rules orange in the Solar Spectrum. Orange is the color of the Pranic life forces in the blood. The ☉ rules yellow, or golden, inclined to purple, has an active power, and gives radical heat. The ☽ rules green in the Solar Spectrum. The ☽ rules white, or white spotted, or a light mixed color. The ☽ has a passive power, and is the sign of radical moisture. One Author ascribes violet to the ☽. In the Solar Spectrum ♄ rules Indigo. ♄ signifies black, and black being ruled by ♄, has a deadening and devitalizing influence, and black clothing should be avoided. ♄ rules lead color, and is a sign of intemperate coldness and dryness. One Author ascribes green to ♄. In the Solar Spectrum ♃ rules violet. ♃ opposes ♄ in nature, which makes the Violet Ray helpful in treating chronic and morbid conditions, and violet is considered a beneficent color. One Author ascribes purple to ♃. Also ♃ is listed as ruling blue, and red mixed with green. The blue and yellow of ♃ and ♀ are signs of heat and moisture united. Heat is predominant in ♃, and moisture with ♀. ♂ rules red in the Solar Spectrum. ♂ rules fiery red, the result of intemperate heat and dryness. Red being ruled by ♂ is a tonic color. Red and orange are the predominant masculine colors. Yellow in the Solar Spectrum is ruled by ♀. One Author ascribes blue and indigo to ♀. White and purple are also ascribed to ♀. In the Solar Spectrum blue is the color of ☿. Yellow is also ascribed to ☿. Azure and light blue are also ascribed to ☿. Mixed colors, checks and plaids are ruled and given by ♅. Lavender, and a smoky gray or blue, are ascribed to ♆. Color Therapy has its value by using the ray or color of one planet to oppose that of another, and the diseases caused by each. (See Antipathy, Opposites, Polarity, Sympathy, Vibration). For each of the colors of the Solar Spectrum, ruled by the planets, such as Blue, Green, Indigo, Orange, Red, Violet, and Yellow, see these subjects in the alphabetical arrangement. Also see Black, White.

**Race Horses**—Color, or Combined Colors of a Winning Horse—When two horses, or more, are to race, if a Horary figure is set up, the sign or planet signifying their color, which is strongest, or posited in the best house, shows which horse will win. (See the book, "The Silver Key" by Sepharial).

**Sense of Color**—(See this subject under Color in the section before this one).

**Signs of the Zodiac**—Colors Ruled By—The Colors ruled by the Signs are given under each Sign. (See "Colors" under Aries, Taurus, Gemini, etc. Also the colors ruled by each planet are given under the planets. (See "Color" under Sun, Moon, Saturn, etc.). The Colors are said to be an indication of the color of the complexion of any person signified by these signs and planets, or by the combination of sign and planet, and in Hor'y Questions to also indicate the color of their dress. (See "Clothing", "Complexion", "Skin", and the various paragraphs in this section).

**Skin**—For the various colors of the skin, or discoloration, normal and abnormal, see such subjects as Black, Blemishes, Brown, Complexion, Dark, Discolorations, Face, Freckles, Jaundice, Marks, Moles, Naevus, Negro, Pigment, Races, Red, Skin, White, Yellow, etc.

**Solar Spectrum**—(See "Planets and Color" in this section).

**Therapy**—Color Therapy—(See "Planets" in this section).

**Vibration**—Each Color has its special rate of vibration, and these vibrations are in tune and harmony with the rate of vibration of the planet, sign, or combination of planet and sign, which rule the various colors, singly, or in mixed combinations. It is on the basis of the rate of vibration of the different colors that they can be used with success in the treatment of disease, the same as the planetary herbs or minerals are used. Thus the violet rays of ♃ oppose the vibrations given off by ♄, and assist in alleviating the symptoms produced by ♄ in chronic diseases. (See "Planets" in this section. Also see Polarity, Vibration).

**Vocation and Colors**—♀ ruler, and in the 10th H. favors dealing in Dyes, Colors, Perfumes, etc.

**Zodiac Colors**—(See "Signs" in this section). For odd colors, and the various shades of colors, look in the alphabetical arrangement for the subject you have in mind. Also many of the odd colors and mixtures are mentioned in this section under the headings of "Clothing", "Planets".

**COLUMNS**—Motor Columns of the Spine—(See "Spinal Cord" under Motor; "Lesions" under Spine).

**COMA**—Stupor—An Abnormally Deep Sleep—Comatic—Comatose—♆ is comatic, and Coma is due principally to ♆ afflictions; ♆ □ or ☍ ♅; ♆ in the 8th H., affl. the hyleg, tends to Coma, ending in death. Produced by ♆ when the Psychic Powers are in a state of hyperactivity, and the bodily energies are held in abeyance. Coma is also caused by afflictions in ♈ or ♎, and is an ♈ and ♎ disease; ♃ affl. in ♎ tends to; Subs at AT, Lu.P. and KP.

**Carus**—The last degree of Coma. A ♆ disease. (See Carus).

**Uremic Coma**—The connection of ♏ with ♈, both ♂ signs, the former influencing the Kidneys and Suprarenal Capsules, and the latter the Cerebellum, in pathological conditions tends to Uremic Coma in kidney troubles, and also to disturbed sleep. Also caused by Subs at AT, and KP, the 11th D. (See Catalepsy, Delirium, Epilepsy, Fainting, Hysteria, Insensibility, Sleep, Stupor, Trance, Uremia).

**COMBUSTION**—Coction Process—One of the four fundamental and essential operations of Nature. (See "Operations" under Nature). A ☉ and ♂ influence; a physical action of the ☉; ♂ tends to the combustion of the wastes of the body by his fevers and inflammations. (See "Combustion" under Tissues. Also see Cleansing, Digestion, Fevers, Inflammation, Mars, Oxygen, Sun).

**COMEDO**—Blackheads—(See "Comedo" under Sebaceous).

**COMELY**—Beautiful Body—Graceful—Handsome—The ☉ in ♐ in partile asp. the Asc.; the ☉ configurated with lord of the Asc., more comely, and the habit better; the ☉ as Sig. in Hor'y Questions, a fair and comely person is denoted; the ☽ in ♊, partile the Asc., a tall, comely, and well-made person; the ⚹ or △ asps. of the ☽; ♃ in ♌, in partile asp. the Asc., rather comely; ♀ ☍ partile the Asc., comely, but with a mean stature; ♀ Sig. ⚹ or △ ♄, comely, but rather pale; the ⚹ or △ asps. of ♀ to the ☉, ☽, and planets. (See Beautiful, Face, Fair, Graceful, Hair, Handsome).

**COMETS**—From Ancient Times the appearances of Comets have had a special significance of calamity or disease in some form. They tend to affect the Regions and Places ruled by the Sign, or parts of the Zodiac, in which they appear, and in the direction of their trains, and those Parts suffer most toward which its tail points. Coincident with their appearance have occurred Famine, Pestilence, Drought, Floods, Fires, Bloodshed, War, Slaughter, Fevers, Epidemics, Endemic Diseases, Calamities, Earthquakes, Tidal Waves, The Plague; Death of Rulers, Nobles, Kings and Prominent People; the death of Children; affections of the Eyes; loss of Cattle; the death of Fish in the Rivers and Seas; Attacks upon Man by Wild Animals; Dissentions and Quarrels; the Locust Pest; Robberies, Increase of Crime, Poverty, unusual Sadness among Peoples; Treachery, Wind, Storms, Rain, Hurricanes, Dangers to Women; Derangement of the System; a prevalence of Urinary and Sex Disorders; Obscuration of the Air; Dangers in Navigation; Hot Seasons in Countries ruled by the Sign in which they appear; Troubles in Religion, and to bring every kind of evil upon Mankind. Comets appearing in the Airy Signs tend to Disturbances in the Air, as Corrupt Air, etc. In the earthy signs, Famine, Drought, Loss of Crops, Rottenness of Seeds, Pestilence, etc. Fevers are prevalent when Comets appear in ♍. In the fiery signs, Fevers, Fires, Wars, Quarrels, Hot Weather, etc. In the watery signs, Floods, Destruction of Fish, Perils, Dangers on the Seas, Tidal Waves, Disturbances of the Fluids of the Body, etc. Halley's Comet is the best known of the Comets, and the different appearances of this Comet along thru the Ages have been attended with Plague, Spotted Fever, Pestilence, Volcanic Eruptions, and great calamities of some kind, and espec. in the years when there were great conjunctions between the major planets, or many major planets in cardinal signs. Halley's Comet appeared in 1909 and 1910, and the death of King Edward, of England, followed within 12 days of its appearance. Also Revolution broke out in Portugal in 1910, and King Manuel fled to England. A good Chapter on Comets, and their influences over disease and afflictions to Humanity, is to be found in Pearce's Textbook of Astrology. (See Eclipses, Events. Also see the subjects mentioned in this Article).

**COMFITS**—Confections—Sweet Things—Over-indulgence In—♀ in ♎. (See Food, Sugar, Sweets).

**COMFORTS**—The 6th H. denotes the comforts of life, as food, clothing, servants, etc. ♆ affl. in the 6th H. tends to loss of physical comforts. ♅ affl. in the 6th H. tends to many sudden changes, and a mental restlessness, which interferes with health and comfort. ♃ in the 8th H., and not seriously afflicted, indicates an easy and natural death, and "In comfort and order". ♀ in good asp. the ☽, the comfort and general health of the native are enhanced. (See Contentment, Dress, Food, Happiness, Luxuries; "Peace of Mind" under Mind; Poverty).

**COMMANDING**—Commanding Appearance—Commanding Aspect—Prepossessing Appearance—Given by the ⚹ and △ asps. of the ☉, ☽, and ♀; the ☉ rising in ♌; ♂ rising in ♎, tall and commanding; ☿ Sig. ☌ ♀, prepossessing; ♌, ♎, or ♒ on the Asc., and many planets rising and elevated, and espec. in fiery or airy signs; ♌ on the Asc., tall and commanding; born under ♃, sober and commanding; one strong planet rising and elevated in the East, in good asp. the Asc., generally gives distinction of appearance. (See Appearance, Form, Giants, Portly; "Positive Form" under Positive; Stature, Tall, etc.).

**Commanding Signs**—The Northern Signs, ♈, ♉, ♊, ♋, ♌, ♍. (See Northern). The six Southern Signs are called Obeying Signs.

**COMMON**—

**Common People**—The Public—The Common People, and the Laboring Classes, are ruled by the 6th H. Injury by the Common People is denoted when ♃ is in □ or ☍ asp. the ☽ at B., and by dir. (See Crushed, Hanging, Humanity, Lynching, Mankind, Mobs, Poor, Public, Riots, Tumults).

**Common Sense**—Lacking In—(See Erratic, Judgment, Notions).

**Common Signs**—(See "Mutable Signs" under Mutable).

**COMMONPLACE APPEARANCE**—Many planets setting in the West at B., and out of dignity by Sign or House; a lack of aspects to the rising degree. (See Appearance, Stature).

**COMPACT BODY**—♃ ♉, partile the Asc., strong and compact; ♃ ♊ partile Asc., a decent-made, compact body; ♃ ♏ partile Asc., compact and corpulent; ♃ ♒ partile Asc., compact and of middle stature; ♂ ♉ partile Asc., compact, short and corpulent; ♂ ♐ partile Asc., compact, fleshy, tall and well-made; earthy signs on the Asc., or many planets in earthy signs at B., give compact forms of body, but with less physical power; ♉ on the Asc., usually compact, well-formed, or beautiful, with ♀ as ruler; ♍ on Asc., compact, neat, well-proportioned, and well-made. (See Beautiful, Corpulent, Neat, Well-Made, Well-Proportioned).

**Compactness**—(See Density).

**COMPANIONS**—Associations—Company—Friends—Social Relations—(See Environment, External, Family, Friends, Husband, Love Affairs, Low, Marriage, Men, Morals, Pleasant, Pleasures, Social Relations, Wife, Women, etc.).

**COMPATIBILITY**—(See Antipathy, "Chemical Action" under Chemical; Healers, Magnetism, Opposites, Polarity, Repulsion, Sympathy, Vibration).

**COMPLAINING**—Complaining of Their Maladies—(See Exhibition, Murmuring). The ♉ and ♍ people tend to complain much about their diseases, and to hold onto them. (See Taurus, Virgo).

**Does Not Complain**—Endures Disease Without Complaining—Lord of the 5th H. in the 6th H.

**COMPLAINTS**—(See Diseases, Disorders, Distempers, Humours, Ill-Health, Infirmities, Sickness, etc. Also see in the alphabetical arrangement the complaint, or disease you have in mind).

**COMPLETE**—

**Collapse**—Complete Collapse—(See Collapse).

**Complete and Elegant Form**—(See Beautiful, Form, Handsome, Stature, Well-Made, Well-Proportioned).

**COMPLEX**—(See "Inferiority Complex" under Inferior; "A Murderer" under Murder.

**COMPLEXION**—The Complexion is said to be ruled by ♀, and to be especially affected by ♀ in ♈. Venus has to do with the skin of the face, and disorders of the face and complexion by the indiscriminate use of Cosmetics. Many subjects which have to do with the Complexion are considered and listed under Eyes, Face, Hair. In a general way the Complexion may be divided into four classes, such as Dark, Light, Pale and Ruddy. The fiery signs, and the ☉ and ♂ strong at B. tend to give a red and ruddy complexion. The earthy signs give a more dull, muddy, and obscure complexion. The airy signs, a clear and rather delicate complexion. The watery signs, and espec. ♋ and ♓, give a pale and more sickly complexion when upon the Asc. at B., and due largely to a weakened and lessened vitality from birth. The following subjects have to do with the Complexion, which see in the alphabetical arrangement when not considered here.

**Bad Complexion**—Pale—Poor—Sickly Bad Color—♋ or ♓ upon the Asc. at B.; the ☽ in ♉ or ♑ in partile asp. the Asc.; ♂ in ♑ or ♓, partile the Asc.; ☿ in ♋ or ♍ in partile asp. the Asc.; ☿ ruler of the Asc., and occi. (See Evil, Pale, Poor, Sickly, in this section).

**Beautiful Complexion**—Beautiful, Sanguine—(See Clear, Fair, Good, Ruddy, Sanguine, in this section. Also see Beautiful, Fair, Handsome).

**Birthmarks**—(See Naevus).

**Blemishes; Blond Complexion**—(See "Light" in this section. Also see "Light Hair" under Hair).

**Blotches; Bronzed**—(See "Tan" in this section).

**Brown; Brunettes**—(See "Dark" in this section. Also see "Black", "Dark", under Eyes, Hair).

**Cheeks; Chestnut Complexion**—♐ influence. (See "Chestnut" under Hair).

**Clear Complexion**—Given by the airy signs, and espec. by ♒ on the Asc.; ♄ ♎ or ♐, in partile asp. the Asc., tolerably clear; ♄ or ☿ in ♒, partile the Asc.; ♀ ♉ partile the Asc., ruddy, but not clear; ♀ ♌, partile the Asc. (See "Good" in this section).

**Cloudy**—(See Dull, Obscure, Sunburnt, in this section).

**Colors**—Of the Complexion—(See "Complexion" under Colors. Also see the various paragraphs in this section).

**Cosmetics**—Bad Effects of Upon the Complexion—(See Cosmetics).

**Cruel Complexion**—(See Cruel).

**Dark Complexion**—Brunettes—Made principally by ♄ and the ☽; ♄ occi. at B.; ♄ ascending; ♄ ♊, dark sanguine; denoted by ♄ as Sig. of the party in Hor'y Questions; ♄ lord of the Asc., and occi., as between the M.C. and Desc., or between the Nadir and Asc.; ♄ in the Asc. at B.; ♄ Sig. in ♊, ♍, or ♑ in Hor'y Questions; ♄ in ♉; ♄ makes the complexion paler or darker; the ☉ or ☽ in ♑, ♒, or ♓, or any of these signs upon the Asc.; The ☉ ♉, partile the Asc.; the ☽ makes the complexion darker when ruling the half sign rising at B.; the ☽ Sig. in ♋, ♍, or ♏; the ☽ in ♏ partile the Asc.; ♃ in ♓, partile the Asc., but with light brown hair; ♀ ♍ partile the Asc.; ☿ ♑ partile the Asc.; ☿ ori. at B., and espec. when ☿ is of the nature of ♄; ♍ on Asc., dark ruddy; ♏, ♑, ♒, ♓ on the Asc. (See "Black" and "Dark" under Hair; "Dark" under Eyes; "Dark Figure" under Dark. Also see Dull, Dusky, Swarthy, in this section).

**Defect In**—☿ ori. at B. (See Blemishes, Face, Freckles, Marks, Moles, Naevus, Pimples, Scars, etc.).

**Delicate Complexion**—Delicate and Clear—The airy signs give, and espec. when ♒ is on Asc. (See Clear, Fair, Fine, White, in this section).

**Dull Complexion**—Cloudy—Dun—Muddy—Not Clear—The ☉ Sig. in ♏, cloudy, dull, dun, or sunburnt; ♄ rising in the Asc., hard and dull; ♃ Sig. in ♏, or ♃ ♏ partile the Asc., dull and muddy; ☿ Sig. in ♈, ♌, or ♍. (See Sunburnt, Swarthy, in this section).

**Dun Complexion**—(See Dull, Smoky, Sunburnt, in this section).

**Dusky**—Somewhat Dark—Obscure—Swarthy—The ☽ ♋, partile asp. the Asc., pale and dusky; ♏ gives; ♃ ♊ partile the Asc., dusky and sanguine; ♀ ♏ partile the Asc.; ☿ in ♈ or ♑ partile Asc. (See Dark, Obscure, Swarthy, in this section).

**Evil Complexion**—♀ Sig. □ or ☍ ♄. (See Bad, Pale, Poor, Sickly, in this section).

**Eyes**—(See the various Colors of the Eyes under Eyes).

**Face**—(See "Cosmetics", "Lotions", and the various paragraphs under Face).

**Fair Complexion**—The ☉ and ☽ ascending, and not afflicted, make the native fair, but the ☉ never causes beauty altho he may give a good complexion; the ☉ ♈, partile Asc., good but not fair; the ☉ ♒ partile Asc.; the ☽ and ♋ give a fair, pale complexion; ♃ ruler of the Asc., and ori., but moderately fair when occi.; ♃ ♍ partile Asc., fair but not ruddy; ♃ in ♎ or ♒ partile Asc.; ♂ ♉ partile Asc., ruddy but never fair; ♀ ♊ partile Asc., rather fair; ♀ ♐ partile Asc., fair sanguine; ♀ ♒ partile Asc., and with light brown or flaxen hair; ♀ ruler of the Asc., and ori.; ☿ ruler of the Asc., and occi., but color not as good; ♊ on Asc., fair, tall and straight. (See "Fair", "Round Face", under Face; "Light Hair" under Hair; "Blue Eyes" under Eyes; also in this section see Clear, Delicate, Good, Light).

**Fine Complexion**—Pure—The ☽ ♎ partile Asc., fine, red and white complexion; ♃ Sig. in Hor'y Questions. ♎ on the Asc., fine in youth. (See Clear, Fair, Good, in this section).

**Florid**—(See "Ruddy" in this section).

**Freckles; Ghastly Look**—(See Pale).

**Good Complexion**—Good Color—Fine—Clear—The ☉ rising at B., and not affl.; the ☉ Sig. in ♈, good altho not very clear; the ☉ ruling the rising sign at B.; the ☉ ♍ partile Asc.; the ☉ or ☽ Sigs. in ♒; the ☉ ♓, well-aspected and partile Asc.; the ☽ in ♊; the ☽ Sig. in ♉ or ♍, tolerably clear; the ☽ in ♎, fine sanguine; the ☽ Sig. in ♒; ♄ Sig. in ♎, tolerably good and clear; ♄ Sig. in ♒; ♃ or ♀ ori., the skin is clear; also ♃ occi. tends to a pure and lovely complexion, but not as fair as when ori., and ruler of the Asc.; ♃ rising in the Asc.; ♃ Sig. in ♎ or ♒; ♂ Sig. in ♒, fair and clear; ♂ rising and ori. of the ☉, clear; ♀ ruler of the Asc., and ori.; ♀ in ♈, partile the Asc., good; ♀ in ♌ or ♒, clear; ♀ in ♐, clear and sanguine; ♀ in ♓, moderately good; ♀ Sig. in ♊ or ♎; ☿ in ♊ partile the Asc.; ☿ Sig. in ♐ or ♒; ♎ or ♒ on the Asc.; Northern Signs, and also ♐ and ♓, are said to give a good color; ♓ also is a mixture, and being a Winter sign, produces a bad color according to its position and aspects; ♈, the house of ♂, and a Northern sign, its color is both good and bad; ♓ on the Asc., if the ☉ be rising in ♓, gives a good complexion, and in females ♓ gives a clear, lucid, and very white skin; the Quadrant from the Asc. to the Nadir tends to produce a good complexion; Temperate climates, with alternate hot and cold Seasons, produce a good complexion; characteristic of those born in cold climates, and in the Arctic Regions. (See Clear, Fair, Light, Red, Ruddy, Sanguine, in this section).

**Hair**—The Colors of Hair and the Complexion—(See Hair).

**Handsome Complexion**—(See Beautiful, Handsome. See "Good" in this section).

**Hard and Dull**—(See "Dull" in this section).

**High-Colored**—(See Ruddy).

**Honey-Colored**—♃ or ☿ ori. at B.

**Ill Complexion**—(See Pale, Sickly. See "Bad" in this section).

**Indifferent**—The ☉ Sig. in ♓; ☿ in ♍; ♋, ♌, or ♍ on the Asc., signs of the Summer Quarter, or the ☉ or ☽ in these signs.

**Jaundiced Look**—(See Jaundice).

**Lead-Colored**—(See Lead).

**Lean and Sallow**—☿ occi. at B. (See Sallow).

**Light Complexion**—Blondes—Fair—The ☉ makes the complexion lighter and fairer when ruling the sign, or part of the sign rising on the Asc. at B.; the ☉ Sig. of the person in Hor'y Questions; ♃ a strong Sig. of the person; ♃ or ♂ as Sigs. in ♒; ♀ strong at B., or ruler; ♀ in ♊; ♀ in the Asc. (See "Blue Eyes" under Eyes; "Light Hair" under Hair; "Degrees" under Light).

**Lovely**—(See Beautiful, Good, in this section).

**Lucid**—(See Clear, Good, in this section).

**Middle Life**—Complexion In—(See "Middle Life" under Pimples).

**Middling Complexion**—☿ as Sig. of the party in Hor'y Questions.

**Moderately Good**—♀ in ♓. (See "Good" in this section).

**Muddy**—Obscure—(See Dull, Dark, Dusky, Olive, Sunburnt, Swarthy, Tan, in this section).

**Mulatto**—(See "Yellow" in this section).

**Obscure**—(See "Muddy" in this section).

**Oily**—Shiny—(See "Oily" under Face).

**Old Age**—Complexion In—(See "Pimples", "Ruddy", under Old Age).

**Olive**—☿ ascending at B., and free from the rays of other planets.

**Ordinary**—The Quadrant from the Summer Tropic to the Autumnal Equinox tends to give an ordinary complexion.

**Pale Complexion**—(See Pale, Sickly. See "Bad", "Poor", in this section).

**Pasty Complexion**—♏ on the Asc.

**Pimpled Face**—(See Pimples).

**Poor Complexion**—Bad—Evil—Sickly—Pale—The ☉ in ♋; the ☽ in ♑ or ♉; the ☽ Sig. in ♑; ♂ in ♑; ♂ Sig. in ♋, ♑, or ♓; ♀ Sig. □ or ☍ ♄, an evil complexion, and not very handsome; ☿ in ♋ or ♍; ♍ seldom gives a good complexion. (See Pale, Sickly. See "Bad", "White", in this section).

**Pure**—(See Clear, Fine, Good, in this section).

**Red Complexion**—Rosy—Reddish Color—Ruddy—The fiery signs, and the ☉ and ♂ strong at B.; ☽ ♎ partile Asc., fine, red and white; ♃ Sig. in Hor'y Questions, red and white mixed; ♂ or ☿ ruler of the Asc., and occi.; ♂ gives, and when born under ♂, red rather than ruddy. (See "Red" under Beard, Eyes, Face, Hair, Lips. See "Ruddy" in this section).

**Rosy**—(See "Red" in this section).

**Ruddy Complexion**—Florid—Rosy—A Healthy Glow—Tinged with a Reddish Hue—(See "Complexion" under Ruddy. Also see "Red" in this section).

**Sad Brown**—A ☿ person, neither black nor white, but between. (See "Sad" under Hair).

**Saffron**—The ☉ gives a Saffron and Yellow Complexion. (See Orange. See "Yellow" in this section).

**Sallow**—An Unhealthy, Yellowish Color—♄ influence; ♄ ♑ partile the Asc.; ♈ on Asc., sallow or swarthy; ☿ occi. at B., lean and sallow. (See Bad, Jaundiced, Pale, Poor, Sickly, Swarthy, Yellow, in this section).

**Sanguine**—(See "Complexion" under Sanguine).

**Shiny**—(See "Oily" in this section).

**Sickly Complexion**—Given by the watery signs, and espec. by ♋ or ♓ on Asc. (See Bad, Poor, Sallow, in this section. See Pale, Sickly, Unhealthy, Vitality Low).

**Smoky**—(See Smoky. Also see Dark, Dull, Dun, Muddy, Swarthy, in this section).

**Soft Complexion**—♀ rising in the Asc.

**Sunburnt Complexion**—The ☉ gives; the ☉ Sig. in ♏, dun or sunburnt; the ☉ ♏ partile Asc., cloudy, sunburnt; the ☉ Sig. in ♐, olive brown, or sunburnt; ♂ Sig. in ♌; ♂ ♌ partile Asc.; characteristic of ♂; in Hor'y Questions, a person denoted by ♂; ☿ ori. as regards the ☉ except when ☿ is in ♊; ☿ Sig. in ♉ or ♌; ☿ ♉, partile Asc., swarthy, sunburnt; ♐ gives. (See Dull, Olive, Smoky, Swarthy, Tan, in this section).

**Swarthy Complexion**—Dark—Cloudy—Muddy—Tawny—Tan—Obscure—Dusky—Smoky, etc. The ☉ Sig. in ♉; in Hor'y Questions, the ☉ Sig. of the party, sometimes swarthy or bronzed; the ☽ makes the complexion darker when ruling the half sign rising at B.; the ☽ Sig. in ♋ or ♏; the ☽ in ♍, dark ruddy; the ☽ ♏; ♄ ascending at B.; ♄ signifies one of a swarthy or lead color; ♄ makes the complexion paler or darker; in Hor'y Questions ♄ as Sig. indicates one of a dark or swarthy complexion; in Hor'y Questions, ♄ as Sig. in ♊, ♍, or ♑; ♄ in ♉, ♊, or ♏; ♄ ♊, dark sanguine; ♄ ♍ partile Asc.; ♄ ori., and lord of the Asc., as between the Asc. and M.C., etc.; denoted by ♄; ♃ ♉ partile Asc.; ♃ Sig. in ♉ or ♊; ♃ Sig. in ♓, obscure; ♂ Sig. in ♈, ♉, ♍ or ♑; ♂ ♈, swarthy; ♂ ♉ or ♏; ♂ ♍, dark ruddy; ♂ rising at B., dark reddish; ♂ ♈ partile the Asc., but if ♂ be ori. the native will be tall and less swarthy; ♂ ♍ or ♏ partile Asc.; ♀ Sig. in ♍ or ♏, dusky; ♀ ♍, dark sanguine; ☿ ori. at B., swarthy brown; ♑ rules swarthy brown; ☿ in ♈, ♉, ♊, ♌, or ♏; ☿ Sig. in ♉, ♌, ♏, or ♑; ☿ ♉ partile Asc., swarthy, sunburnt; ☿ ♌ or ♏ partile Asc.; ♈ on the Asc., swarthy or sallow; ☿ ruler of the Asc., and ori.; ♉ on the Asc.; ♉ gives a large, swarthy, shining face; ♊ gives; ♊ on the Asc., dark, sanguine; ♍, ♏, ♑ give; the Quarter from the Winter Tropic to the Vernal Equinox gives a dark complexion. (See Black, Brown, Brunettes, Dark, Dull, Dusky, Lead, Muddy, Obscure, Olive, Sad, Sunburnt, in this section. Also see "Smoky Degrees" under Smoky).

**Tan**—Bronzed—Tawny—Brownish Yellow—Sunburnt, etc. The ☽ Sig. in ♐, bronzed; a raw-tanned, leathery appearance is characteristic of ♂ people; ☿ occi. at B., tawny visage. (See Brown, Dull, Olive, Smoky, Sunburnt, Swarthy, in this section).

**Tawny**—(See "Tan" in this section).

**Thin, Pale and Sickly**—Thin, Sickly Visage—(See Pale, Sickly, Thin).

**Tolerably Clear**—(See "Clear" in this section).

**Unhealthy Complexion**—Unwholesome—Sallow—(See Bad, Poor, Sallow, in this section. See Jaundice, Pale, Sickly, White, Yellow).

**Unwholesome**—(See "Unhealthy" in this section).

**White Complexion**—(See "Complexion" under White).

**Women**—Complexion In—(See Cosmetics, Dark, Light, in this section).

**Yellow Complexion**—(See "Saffron" in this section. See Yellow).

**Youth**—Ruddy Complexion in Youth—(See "Complexion" under Youth).

**COMPLICATIONS**—Complication of Diseases—The planets in the Signs show the zones of the body afflicted, but the aspects, and the influences of the planets themselves, have to be considered in complications. (See "Complications" under Disease). Ruling over the human body are three Crosses, known as the Cardinal, Fixed and Mutable Crosses in the star map of birth. The Fixed Signs ♉ and ♏, being opposites, and also the ♌ and ♒ Signs being opposites, and all four of these signs being in □ or ☍ asp. to each other, the fixed signs when occupied by many planets, and espec. malefics, tend to diseases or complications in parts or organs ruled by all four of these Signs. Thus a disease starting in the throat, ruled by ♉, may affect the Heart, Sex Organs, Lower Limbs, or the Circulation of the Blood, all of which are ruled by the fixed signs. Evil Directions, or Transits, coming into a Fixed Sign during the course of a disease may tend to involve and complicate, or extend the first disease to other parts of the body ruled over by a fixed sign. Also during the course of a disease, if the ☉, in the case of a male, comes to an evil asp. a malefic, or some evil direction be formed to the ☉, there is apt to be a relapse, or a complication of diseases, according to the signs occupied by the ☉ and the afflicting planet. The same with the ☽ in the case of a female. In males, afflictions to the ☉ rule the course of the disease, and to the ☽ in females. (See Chronic, Crises, Continuity, Course, Curable, Duration, Incurable, Moderation, Opposites, Prognosis, Prolonged, Relapses, Remote, Return, Sympathy, Tedious, Various, etc.).

**Many Complications**—The ☉ to the ill-asp. his own place at B., and by dir.; ♄ in the 6th H., and affl.

**Many Diseases**—Many Diseases Afflict the Body—The ☉ to the ill-asps. his own place by dir., and the ☉ affl. by malefics at B.; no asp. between the ☉ and ♂ at B., and espec. in childhood; ♃ affl. in ♒, due to the blood being corrupted by too much blood. (See

Impure; "Much Sickness" under Sickness; "Too Much Blood" under Blood).

**Shifting of the Disease**—Changes to Some Other Form of Disease—The Sig. of the disease being in a double-bodied sign; the afflictor in the disease changing signs, or passing from one house into another, and the disease will either shift to some other form, become chronic if it has been acute, or resolve itself. The strong affinity which exists between opposite signs of the Zodiac also tends to complications, and a change in the disease. Thus stomach disorders, rulder ordinarily by the ♋ sign, may have skin complications and eruptions, and espec. if there are also afflictions in ♑. (See Crises, Opposites, Praeincipients, Remote, Scope, Sympathy, Various, etc. Also note the different paragraphs in this Article).

**COMPREHENSION**—Is ruled by ☿.

**Dull**—The Comprehension Dull—(See Dull, Intellect, the various paragraphs under "Mental", "Mind"; Perception, Understanding, etc.).

**Good**—The Comprehension Good—(See "Active Mind" under Active; "Good Judgment" under Judgment; "Activity" under Mental; "Sound Mind", and other paragraphs under Mind; Perception; Reason, Understanding).

**COMPRESSED**—Compression—

**Compressed Air**—Ruled by ♅. (See Air, Caisson, Ether, Gases, Uranus).

**Compressed Gases** — (See Caisson, Gases).

**Organs**—Compression of—Compression of organs, or parts, is denoted by ♄; ♄ ☌ or ill-asp. ♅.

**Spinal Cord**—Compression of—♄ affl. in ♌ or ♒ especially, or ♄ affl. in the sign ruling the part compressed or pinched. (See Contractions, Depressions, Saturn, Spine, Subluxations, Vertebrae).

**COMPULSIONS**—Morbid Compulsions—(See "Compulsions" under Morbid).

**CONCEALMENT** — Of Disease — (See "Concealment" under Disease).

**CONCEITED**—(See Pretender).

**CONCENTRATION**—Of Mind—

**Good Powers Of**—Good asps. of ♄ to the ☉, ☽, or ☿; ♄ in ♎, ♑, or ♒, and well-dignified; many planets in fixed signs at B., or with fixed signs upon the angles; ♅ gives the ability to work a long time upon one subject; ☿ in a fixed sign at B., and in good-asp. to the ☽ or Asc.

**Inability to Concentrate**—A Wandering Mind—♆ affl. in ♊; ☿ Sig. □ or ☍ ☽, never applies very closely to any subject; many planets in common signs at B., and such signs upon the angles; ☿ in a weak sign at B., and affl. by the ☽, ♄, and ♃; ☿ in no asp. to the ☽ or Asc. (See "Mental Chaos" under Chaotic; Confusion, Dreamy, Visionary).

**CONCEPTION**—The Fecundation of the Ovum—Conception is under the rule of the ☽.

**Abnormal Conceptions**—Inhuman in Shape—Deformed, or Afflicted in Vari-

ous Ways During Pregnancy and At Birth — (See Congenital; "Beastly Form" under Beasts; "Dogs" under Children; Deformities, Foetus, Inhuman, Monsters, etc.).

**Conception Has Taken Place**—Conception Has Not Taken Place—(See "Woman Is With Child", "Woman Is Not With Child", under Pregnancy).

**How Long Conceived?**—(See "How Long Pregnant?" under Pregnancy).

**Moment of Conception**—A Star Map of the Heavens for the moment of conception is very important to study in helping to know the character and temperament of a person, and also to diagnose diseases which are not especially shown or indicated in the map of birth. The Moment of Conception is known as "The Epoch", and is determined by the rules of the Prenatal Epoch. The moment of birth and the moment of conception have a fixed relation, and when the moment of birth is known approximately, the moment of conception can be determined by the laws of Astronomy, as the degree on the Asc. or Descendant at B. is said to be the Longitude of the ☽ at conception. The moment of conception may occur some days, or a week after coition, and is ruled by the motion of the ☽ in the individual case. (See "Moment of Birth" under Birth; Prenatal Epoch). The Occult Side of Conception, the connection of the Ego with conception, etc., is discussed under the headings of "Conception", "The Ego", "The Seed Atom", etc. in the book entitled "Cosmo-Conception" by the Heindels.

**Party Has Just Conceived**—If the dispositor of the ☽, and the lord of the hour be angular, or ♂ in the 7th H. (Hor'y).

**Party Will Not Conceive**—(See Barrenness).

**Predetermination**—Of the Sex at Conception—(See "Sex of Children" under Children; Predetermination).

**Pregnancy**—(See Pregnancy).

**Prenatal Epoch**—(See this subject).

**Quadruplets Conceived**—(See Quadruplets).

**Sex of the Conception**—(See "Predetermination" in this section).

**Single Conceptions** — (See "Single Births" under Children).

**Signs of Conception**—(See Fruitfulness; "Signs of Children" under Children).

**Signs of No Conception**—(See Barrenness, Pregnancy).

**There Is No Conception**—(See Barrenness; "Woman Is Not With Child" under Pregnancy).

**Time of Conception**—It is said if the lord of the 5th H. be in the 1st, it will be in the first year of married life; if in the 2nd H., in the 2nd year; in the 10th H., in the 3rd year; in the 7th H., in the 4th year; in the 4th H., in the 5th year, and so on, in accordance with the preeminence of the houses. Others measure the time by the application of the lord of the Asc., or the

☽, to the lord of the 5th, or to ♃ or ♀, reckoning by degrees according to the nature of the sign the applying planet is in. (See "First-Born Child" under Children).

**Triplets Conceived**—(See Triplets).

**Twins Are Conceived**—(See Twins, Triplets. Also see "Single Births" under Children). For further study see Barren, Birth, Children, Fecundation, Female, Fruitful, Gestation, Heredity, Mother, Pregnancy, Prenatal Epoch, Wife, Women.

**CONCRETIONS**—A Calculus—An Osseous Deposit—Stone—Concretions are the work of ♄, by crystallization, and mineral deposits which should be eliminated. They are formed by mineral deposits carried by the blood, and are ruled by ♄. They are connected with the earthy signs. They are also the result of Cold. ♄ influence, and are associated usually with Cold Diseases. (See Chalk, Cold, Crystallization, Deposits, Elimination; "Gall Stones" under Bile; Gravel, Growths, Hardening, Lime, Minerals, Osseous, Sand, Stone, Suppressions, etc.).

**CONCUSSION**—A Shaking—Shock—Bruises—Hurts by Concussion, etc.—

**Brain**—Concussion of—(See "Blows", "Accidents", under Head; "Fractures" under Skull). Case of Concussion of Brain—See Case, "Concussion of Brain", No. 890, in 1001 N.N.

**Hurts by Concussion**—♄ causes concussions and contusions where blood does not flow; ♄ ☌, P, or ill-asp. the Asc. at B., and by dir.; also caused by the afflictions of ♅ or ♂ to the ☉, ☽, Asc., or hyleg. (See Blows, Bruises, Buildings, Crushed, Explosions, Falls, Fractures, Hurts, Injuries, Kicks; "Assaults by Stones" under Stones; Violence; "Storms" under Wind; Wounds).

**CONDEMNED TO DEATH**—(See "Death by Sentence" under Judges).

**CONDENSATION** — One of the four Operations of Nature. To make more dense, to harden. A ♄ influence, and the work of ♄. (See Concretions, Crystallization, Clots, Density, Hardening, Nitrogen; "Operations" under Nature; "Saturn Influence" under Saturn).

**CONDUCT**—Behavior—Deportment—Actions—The conduct of the individual has much to do with health and disease, of both mind and body. Therefore, a number of subjects relating to conduct, habits, morals, etc., have been considered in this work. The ☽, her sign, position, afflictions, good aspects, etc., have much to do with the conduct and habits of the native. Many of the subjects along this line you will find listed alphabetically at the end of the Article on the Mind, both good and bad traits. However, a few prominent and suggestive subjects will be listed here. For subjects not listed here, or under Mind, look in the alphabetical arrangement for what you have in mind. See the following subjects,—Anger, Amorous, Bad, Careless, Cheating, Cleanly, Companions, Criminal, Cruel, Dangerous, Debased, Debauched, Deceitful, Depraved, Disgrace, Dis-

honest, Disorderly, Dissipated, Dissolute, Drink, Drunkenness, Effeminate, Erratic, Erring, Evil, Excesses, Females, Filthy, Folly, Foolhardy, Foul Minded, Fierce, Forgers, Furious, Gambling, Gentle, Gluttony, Good, Habits, Harlots, Honest, Husband, Immoral (see Morals); Improvident, Imprudent, Indecent, Intemperate, Intoxication, Knavish, Lascivious, Lewd, Liars, Libelers, Licentious; "Loose Morals" under Morals; Love Affairs; "Low and Base" under Low; Lustful, Luxurious, Madness, Manners, Marriage, Mean, Men, Mild, Morals, Murderous, Neat, Newsmonger, Noble, Obscene, Obstinate, Passion, Perverse, Perversions, Pettifogging, Prison, Prodigal, Profligate, Quarrelsome, Rashness, Recklessness, Religion, Responsibility, Riotous, Robbers, Rough, Saucy, Savage, Scandal, Sensuous, Sex, Shameless, Shrewd, Social Relations, Strange, Swindler, Temper, Thieves, Ungovernable, Unruly, Vagabond, Venery, Vices, Vicious, Violent, Wanton, Wench, Wife, Women, etc. The references and paragraphs under these subjects will lead you to others along the lines of conduct throughout the book.

**CONDYLOMA**—(See Anus, Warts).

**CONFECTIONS**—Sweets—Given To Excess of in Eating—(See Sugar, Sweets).

**CONFINEMENT**—In the sense of limitations, restraints and restrictions over your liberty of action, it is principally a 12th H. influence, and the nature of the confinement is indicated by the planets therein, and the sign upon the cusp. Also ♄ tends to bind, hinder, confine and restrict, and espec. when ♄ or ☋ are in the 12th H., and affl. the ☉ or ☽.

**Asylum**—Insane Asylum—Confinement In—(See "Asylums" under Insanity).

**Bed**—Long Confined to Bed—(See "Sick Bed" in this section).

**Captivity**—Held In—(See Captive).

**Chronic Diseases**—Confined By—(See Chronic, Infirmities, Invalids, Lameness, Paralysis, etc.).

**Deformities** — Malformations — Confinement By—(See Deformities, Malformations, Monsters, etc.).

**Exile**—(See Exile).

**Hospitals** — Confinement In — (See Hospitals).

**Invalids**—Confined Upon Sick Bed—(See Invalids. Also see "Sick Bed" in this section).

**Limitations**—Upon the Body—(See Limitations).

**Parturition**—The Period of Confinement—(See Parturition).

**Prison**—Confined In—(See "Imprisonment" under Prisons).

**Restraints**—Over Mind and Body—(See Restraint).

**Sick Bed**—Long Confinement Upon—The ☉ ☌ ♄ or ☽ in 12th H.; many afflictions in the 12th H.; ♄ in 12th H., and affl. the hyleg therefrom. Case—See "Seventeen Years In Bed", No.

843 in 1001 N.N. Case—See Fig. 25 in "Message of the Stars" by the Heindels. (See Chronic, Invalids, Lingering, Long Diseases, Prolonged, Tedious). See "Saturn Influence" under Saturn; Twelfth House.

**CONFORMITY OF MEMBERS** — (See "Well-Proportioned" under Well).

**CONFUSION—**

**Ideas**—Confusion of—(See Chaotic, Dreamy, Ideas, Projects).

**Mind**—Confusion of—(See "Mental Chaos" under Chaotic; "Inability" under Concentration; Dreamy, Fears, Flightiness).

**CONGELATION**—Clotting—Thickening—A Concretion—One of the four Operations of Nature, and ruled by ♄. (See Cirrhosis, Clots; "Operations" under Nature; Nitrogen).

**CONGENITAL**—Existing from Birth—Innate—The derivation, causes, and explanations of congenital afflictions, defects and deformities are shown in the figure of the Prenatal Epoch, in the aspects and afflictions to the ☽ in the Chart of Descent, and are reflected in the horoscope thru the interchange of the two factors the ☽ and the Asc. at the Epoch and at birth. The horoscope influences begin with the moment of birth, and continue in power until the death of the body. The ☉, ☽, Asc., or Hyleg much afflicted by malefics at B. will account for most of the diseases and afflictions which develop after birth, or known as Acquired Ailments. Deep-seated, organic, structural, and innate ailments, can usually be located in the map of the heavens for the time of conception, or in figures erected for the time of the return of the ☽ to her place each month during gestation. This subject is further discussed under Prenatal Epoch. The list of congenital defects is a large one, and a few of them are here suggested for study, and if the subject, or disease, is not mentioned here, look for it in the alphabetical arrangement. See the following subjects,—Acquired, Atrophy, Birth, Blemishes, Blind, Constitutional, Crippled, Cyclops, Deaf, Defects, Deformities, Distortions, Dumb, Excrescences, Heredity, Hermaphrodites, Idiots, Imbecility, Imperfections, Inhuman, Infancy, Lameness, Limbs, Maimed, Malformations, Marks, Members, Mind, Monsters, Mutes, Naevus, New Moon, Organic, Organs, Paralysis, Pressure, Prenatal Epoch, Savage, Structural, Triplets, etc.

**CONGESTION**—Congestions—Hyperaemia of a Part—A ♄ disease and condition, and often caused by Cold and Chill, and also by the deposits of the waste materials of the body, causing stoppages, retention, crystallization, hardening, suppression of function, etc.; ♄ ☌ or ☍ Asc. Also a ♃ disease, as ♃ tends to congestion, surfeit, overfunctional activity of the part of the body ruled by the sign he is in at B., by dir., or by transit. The afflictions and bad asps. of ♃ to the ☉, ☽, ♀, Asc., or the hyleg, tend to, and principally from over-eating, gluttony, etc. Also

the ill-asps. of the ☽ to ♃ by tr., progression, or dir., tend to congestion of the part of the body ruled by the sign in which ♃ was posited at B. (See Centripetal, Chill, Circulation, Cold, Complications, Constrictions, Consumption, Deposits, Eating, Erythema, Functions, Gangrene, Gluttony, Hardening, Hyperaemia, Mortification, Plethora, Retention, Stoppages, Suppressions, Surfeits, Wastes, etc.).

**Bowels** — Congestion In — (See Bowels).

**Brain**—Congestion of the Blood in the Brain—Cerebral Congestion—Encephalic Congestion—The ☉ affl. in ♈; an ♈ disease; the ☉ ☌ ♄ or ☋ in ♈, and in ☐ asp. to ♃ or ♀; ♄ ☌ or ill-asp. the ☽, and espec. if neither be in ♈; ♃ affl. in ♈ or ♎; ♂ in ♈, affl. the hyleg at B., or ♂ in the 6th H., and afflicted. (See Accumulative, Brain, Cerebral; "Blood" under Head).

**Bronchial Congestion** — (See Asthma, Bronchial; "Congestion" under Lungs).

**Cellular Congestion**—(See Cells).

**Cerebral Congestion**—(See "Brain" in this section).

**Ears**—Congestion In—(See "Venous Circulation" under Ears).

**Encephalic**—(See "Brain" in this section).

**External Congestions** — (See External).

**Eyes**—Congestion of Muscles of—(See "Crystallization" under Eyes).

**Face**—(See "Congestion" under Face).

**Inflammation**—Congestive Inflammation—(See "Congestive" under Inflammation).

**Internal Congestions**—(See "Congestive" under Internal).

**Intropulsive Congestion** — (See Centripetal, Intropulsion).

**Kidneys**—Congestion In—(See Kidneys).

**Lungs**—Congestion In—(See "Bronchial" in this section).

**Stomach**—Congestion In—(See Stomach).

**Vascular** — (See "Vascular Fullness" under Vascular).

**CONIUM**—Hemlock—A typical drug of ♄.

**CONJUNCTION ASPECT** — (See Aspects).

**CONJUNCTIVA**—The Mucous Membrane of the Eye—Ruled by the ♈ Sign. Also especially ruled and influenced by ♆ when this planet is in ♈.

**Caruncle**—(See Caruncle).

**Conjunctivitis**—Inflammation of the Conjunctiva—Opthalmia—Sore Eyes—Ulcer—Eyes Red and Inflamed—The ☉ affl. in ♈; the ☉ affl. in fiery signs, and ☌, ☐, or ☍ the Asc. by dir.; the ☉ affl. the ☽ or Asc.; the ☉ or ☽ hyleg, and the ☉ to the ☐ or ☍ the ☽ by dir.; the ☉ to the ☐ or ☍ ♂ by dir., bloodshot and inflamed; the ☉ to the place of Cor Scorpio; a ☉ disease; the ☽ affl. in ♈; the ☽ in ♐ and affl. by the ☉ or ♂ when taken ill (Hor'y); the ☽ to the place of the Pleiades or Praesepe; ♆ in ♈, and affl. the ☽, Hyleg, or Asc.;

♆ in ♈ in the 6th H.; ♂ in ♈, lord of the year at the Vernal Equi., and affl. by ♄, much conjunctivitis prevalent; ☿ lord of the year at the Vernal, and ☌ ♂, much inflammation of the eyes generally; a ♂ disease; a ♌ disease, and afflictions in ♌; the Asc. to the place of the Ascelli or Capricornus; Fixed Stars of the nature of ♂ and the ☽ ascending at B.; Subs at MCP, the 4th Cervical, and at KP. Green, the color of ♄, is good for inflamed eyes, and to wear green glasses, or work in a green room, have green lamp shades, etc. Case—An Infant—Inflammation of eyes sets in a day or two after birth — See "Sight Defective", No. 684, in 1001 N.N. (See "Eye Trouble", "Inflamed", under Eyes; "Conjunctivitis" under Infancy; "Defective Sight" under Sight).

**Trachoma**—(See "Granulated" under Eyelids).

**CONNECTIVE TISSUE**—The Binding Tissue of the Body—Interstitial—Areolar Tissue—Cellular Tissue—Dominated largely by ♄ and the ♑ sign.

**Anasarca**—(See "Anasarca" under Dropsy).

**Cells**—(See "Cellular Tissue", "Thickening", "Walls", under Cells).

**Cirrhosis**—Thickening—(See Cirrhosis).

**Fiber**—Connecting Fiber—(See Fiber).

**Hardening**—Induration—(See Hardening, Hypertrophy, Sclerosis).

**Induration**—(See Hardening).

**Over-Growth**—Of Connective Tissue—Of Organs—The work of ♄, and mineral deposits.

**Parenchyma**—Soft Cellular and Connective Tissue—The Functioning of—(See Parenchyma).

**Sarcoma**—A Connective Tissue Tumor—(See Sarcoma).

**Sclerosis**—(See Hardening, Sclerosis).

**Soft**—Soft Connective Tissue—(See Parenchyma).

**Thickening**—(See Cirrhosis).

**Tissues**—(See the various paragraphs under Tissues).

**CONSCIOUSNESS**—Conscious Life—The ☉, his position, and aspects at B., are the essential factors in our conscious life. (See Ego).

**Clouding of Consciousness**—(See "Confusion", "Mental Chaos", under Chaotic; "Clouded" under Mind).

**Unconsciousness**—(See Anaesthetics, Catalepsy, Coma, Delirium, Dreams, Epilepsy, Faintings, Fits, Insanity, Insensibility, Madness, Sleep, Subconscious, Trance, etc.).

**CONSERVATION**—Conservation of the Mental and Bodily forces is the work of ♃ and ♀, the benefic planets. ♃ exerts a conservative and preservative influence over the body. The conserving, transforming and storing functions of the body are under the influence of ♃, ♀, and ♆. (See "Substance" under Cells; "Conservation" under Energy; Nutrition, Preservation).

**CONSIDERABLE**—Considerable Diseases Ensue—See Disease; "Ill-Health All Thru Life", "Signs of Ill-Health", under Ill-Health; "Much Sickness" under Sickness; "Vitality Low" under Vitality; "Weak Body" under Weak).

**CONSISTENCY**—The Degree of Density or Hardness—

**Adipose Tissue**—The Consistency of Increased—(See Fat). See Condensation, Crystallization, Hardening.

**CONSOLIDATION**—Consolidating—The consolidating influences in the body are the work of ♄, as in crystallization, condensation, hardening, etc. ♄ ⚹ or △ the ☉ tends to strengthen and consolidate the constitution. Consolidation in Pneumonia is ruled by ♄. (See Concretions, Condensation, Consistency, Crystallization, Deposits, Hardening, Minerals, Pneumonia, Retention, Stone, Suppression, Wastes).

**CONSPICUOUS DISEASES**—The ☽ or ☿ unconnected with each other or the Asc., but the benefics ♃ and ♀ conciliated and posited in Eastern Parts, and in angles, and the malefics in Western Parts, under these conditions the disease may be highly conspicuous, but susceptible of a cure. (See Curable, Exhibition, Incurable).

**Conspicuous Marks**—(See Marks, Moles).

**Conspicuous Mental Diseases**—♄ and ♂ angular and ori., and ♃ and ♀ setting and occi. (See Demoniac, Epilepsy, Frenzy, Fretfulness, Fury, Idiocy, Imbecility, Incurable, Insanity, Madness, Mania, etc.).

**CONSTANCY**—Constant—Fixed—Durable—Prolonged—

**Cough**—Constant Cough—(See "Constant" under Cough).

**Disease**—The constancy and duration of the effects of disease are aggravated and prolonged by the afflicting planet being stationary in position at B., or at the beginning of an illness. Also many planets in fixed signs at B., and at the beginning of, or duration of a disease, and espec. the afflicting planet, or planets, tends to make the disease more constant. (See Chronic, Continuity, Crises, Direct, Duration, Fever; "Fixed Signs" under Fixed; Persevering, Prolonged, Retrograde, Stationary, Tedious, etc.).

**CONSTELLATIONS**—(See Stars).

**CONSTIPATION**—A Sluggish Action of the Bowels—The ☉ affl. in ♍ or ♑; the ☽ hyleg in ♍ or ♑ in females; ♆, ♅, or ♄ in ♍, and affl. the ☉ or ☽; a ♄ disease; born under ♄; ♄ in ♉, ♍, ♏, or ♑; ♄ in the Asc., and ♏ rising; ♄ in some asp. to the Asc., or in ill-asp. to the ☽ or lord of the Asc.; ♄ or ☋ in ♍ or ♏ and afflicted; ♄ and ♂ in ♏, by bringing piles, tending to neglect of stools, and resulting in constipation; ♄ affl. in ♏, and tending to an obstructed rectal region; ♂ in ♍, ☌ or ill-asp. the ☉; ♂, ruler of the rectum, affl. by ♄; ♀ in ♑ and affl. the ☽ or Asc.; ♀ in ♑ in the 6th H., and affl.; ☿ affl. in ♑, due to worry and melancholic tendencies; a ♉ disease, by reflex to ♏; a ♍ disease, and ♍ on the

Asc.; afflictions in ♍; ♍ or ♎ on the 6th H.; Subs at KP, Li.P. and PP, (2L). Cases — See Figures 7, 8, and 27 in "Message of the Stars", by the Heindels. (See Faeces).

**Headaches of Constipation**—♄ affl. in ♍ or ♏; Subs at PP (2L). (See Headaches).

**Nervous Constipation**—☽ in ♍ ☌ ♄ and ☿; ♄ ☌ ☿ ♍. (See "Requirements" under Nature).

**CONSTITUTION** — Constitutional — Organic Constitution—The Physical Constitution—Constitutional Diseases, etc. —Planets in the East at B. affect the physical constitution. The 1st H., or the Asc., rule the constitution, the peculiarities and construction of the physical body. (See the Introduction under Body). In a female nativity the asps. to the ☽ determine the strength of the constitution, and the asps. and position of the ☉ in a male horoscope. In general, however, the strength of the constitution in both sexes is denoted by the ☉ at B., his asps. and power, as the ☉ is the central source of power, and the ☽, and other planets, reflect the Sun's rays, power and influence, for good or evil for the time, according to the aspects. In judging the constitution, the ☉, ☽, Asc., and Hyleg, and their conditions, must be carefully noted. (See "Strength" in this section). Many subjects concerning the physical constitution are considered under the Articles on Appearance, Body, Complexion, Defects, Form, Height, Organs, Stature, Weight, etc. The physical body, (the constitution), is subject to two classes of diseases, those which are congenital, innate, hereditary, organic and structural, and secondly, acquired and the more temporary ailments. (See Acquired, Acute, Chronic, Congenital, Diathesis, Organic, Prenatal, Structural, etc.). The Constitutional, or Conditional Signs, are the Cardinal, Fixed and Mutable classifications, and the Constitutional Temperament is determined by the groupings of the planets in the Constitutional Signs. (See Temperament). Note the following subjects, conditions, benefits, afflictions, diseases, etc., which have to do with the Constitution. For the diseases of the Constitution, and subjects which may not be listed here, see "Diseases", and also look for the subject in the alphabetical arrangement.

**Cold Constitution** — (See "Body" under Cold).

**Cold and Dry**—(See "Cold and Dry Body" under Dry).

**Cold and Moist**—(See "Cold and Moist Body" under Moisture).

**Consolidation Of**—(See Consolidation).

**Constitutional Diseases**—Organic Diseases—Structural Diseases—Innate —Hereditary—Inherent, etc.—These are diseases indicated by the radical map, and prenatal conditions, are more inherent, and in contrast to Acquired Diseases. The latter class of diseases are of shorter duration, more often acute, while Constitutional diseases tend to become chronic, and

sometimes incurable. Constitutional Diseases are ruled by the ☉, and the ☉ much affl. at B. brings the danger of serious and severe constitutional, deep-seated, and organic diseases. The ☉ affl. by the ☽ at B. tends to weaken the constitution, and make one more liable to some form of Constitutional Disease. Also the sign ♄ is in tends to weaken the part of the body ruled by such sign, and to make the part, or organ ruled by the sign, more subject to inherent disease, and espec. if ♄ be severely afflicted, or weak in the sign, and also the map show weak vitality in general, and poor health conditions. The following are a few of the more serious Constitutional Diseases, which have to do with Constitutional Disorders and Defects, their cause, etc., which subjects see in the alphabetical arrangement, — Anaemia, Asthma, Atrophy, Cancer, Chronic, Congenital, Consumption, Crystallization, Decay, Defects, Deformities, Distortions, Emaciation, Epilepsy, Excrescences, Hardening, Heredity, Incurable, Insanity, Latent, Leprosy, Leukaemia, Malnutrition (see Nutrition), Organic, Palsy, Paralysis, Phthisis, Prenatal, Rickets, Sclerosis, Scrofula, Stone, Structural, Suppressions, Tuberculosis, Wastings, etc. The lists of diseases given under Chronic, the Sun, and Saturn, also suggest diseases which tend to be constitutional, inherent, and organic. Also see "New Moon", "First Quarter", "Full", "Last Quarter", under Moon; "Solar-Lunar" under Solar.

**Constitutional Hurts**—(See "Hurts" in this section).

**Defects** — Constitutional Defects — (See Defects).

**Diathesis; Dry Constitution** — (See "Dry Body" under Dry).

**Dry and Cold**—(See "Cold and Dry Body" under Dry).

**Dry and Hot**—(See "Dry and Hot Body" under Dry).

**Dull Constitution**—Dull and Effeminate—♋ gives; ♋ on the Asc. (See Dull, Effeminate).

**Effeminate in Constitution**—(See Effeminate).

**Endurance**—Of the Constitution— (See Endurance, Recuperation, Resistance, Solid, Strong, Vitality, Good).

**Feeble Constitution**—(See Feeble, Infirm, Weak, etc.).

**Female Constitution** — The Strength or Weakness of—(See "Constitution" under Female).

**Fine Constitution**—(See "Good" in this section).

**Frail Constitution** — (See "Weak" in this section).

**Full** — The Constitution is at Full when the ☉ at B. is between the middle of the 1st H., on around by the Mid-heaven, and on down to the middle of the 6th H., and in a Hylegiacal Place. (See Hyleg).

**Functions**—When there is no asp. between the ☉ and ☽ at B. constitutional defects do not disturb the functional activities, and also functional derangements do not act detrimentally upon the vitality. (See Defects, Functions).

**Good Constitution**—Fine Constitution —Advantageous Stature—Strong Constitution—Healthy Body—Vitality Strong—The Quadrant from the Asc. to the Nadir tends to produce, and espec. the 1st H. strong at B., and a fiery sign upon the Asc.; the ☉ in the Asc., or M.C., and well-asp.; the ☉ in ♐ unless the hyleg be affl. at B.; the ☉ strong and dignified at B.; the ☉, ☽, and Asc. well-asp. by benefics, and free from evil asps. of malefics; the ☽ strong at B., and free from affl.; ♄ ori.; ♄ moderately fortified in the 1st H., and in good asp. to the ☉, ☽, ♃, or ♀; ♃ ascending at B., and in good asp. to the ☉ and ☽; ♃ in the 1st H., or having the same or opposite Dec. with the Asc.; ♃ ⚹ or △ the ☉ at B., and if the ☽ and Asc. be free from affl.; ♃ or ♀ in the Asc. at B., and well-asp.; ♂ ascending at B.; ♂ ☌, ⚹ or △ the ☉; ♀ ascending at B., well-placed and aspected; ♈, ♌, ♍, ♎, ♏, or ♐ on the Asc.; given by the fixed signs when on the angles at B., and well-fortified and occupied; the ♒ influence when strong, or on the Asc., gives a healthy appearance. (See "Good Health" under Health; "Great Physical Powers" under Physical; Recuperation, Resistance, Robust, Ruddy, Stamina; "Body" under Strong; Tone, Vitality Good).

**Harmonious Constitution**—(See "Good Health" under Health; Harmony. See "Good Constitution" in this section).

**Hot Constitution** — (See "Hot Bodily Temperament" under Heat, Temperament).

**Hot and Dry** — (See Choleric; "Hot and Dry" under Heat; "Dry and Hot" under Temperament).

**Hot and Moist**—(See "Hot and Moist" under Moisture, Temperament).

**Hurts**—Constitutional Hurts—These may be in the form of disease, wounds, or injuries to the body. Planets in the 8th H. at B. tend to, and at the time they set in ☌ with the Desc. by oblique descension. (See Accidents, Hurts, Injuries, Wounds).

**Increased Strength**—Of the Constitution—(See "Strengthened" in this section).

**Internal Diseases**—(See Internal).

**Moist Constitution**—(See "Bodily Temperament" under Moist).

**Moist and Cold**—(See "Cold and Moist Body" under Moist).

**Moist and Hot**—(See "Hot and Moist Body" under Moist).

**Not Very Strong**—(See Debility, Feeble, Infirm, Sickly, Vitality Low; "Weak Body" under Weak).

**Organic Diseases**—(See Internal, Organic, Structural).

**Positive Constitution**—(See Positive).

**Powerful Constitution**—Given by the ☉ in a fiery sign, and espec. when the ☉ is in a fiery sign in the Asc. (See "Strong" in this section).

**Robust Constitution** — Ruddy — (See Robust, Ruddy).

**Sensitive Constitution** — (See Sensitive).

**Sickly**—(See Delicate; "Ill-Health All Thru Life" under Ill-Health; Pale; "Much Sickness" under Sickness; Sickly, Vitality Low, Weak, etc.).

**Signs**—The Constitutional Signs— (See the Introduction to this Article).

**Solid Constitution**—(See Solid).

**Sound Constitution**—(See "Good", "Powerful", "Strong", in this section).

**Stamina**—(See Stamina, Tone; "Vital Force" under Vital; Vitality, etc.).

**Strength**—Of the Constitution—The strength and vital forces of the Constitution depend upon the position of the ☉ at B., and must be judged by the influence of the ☉, no matter in what part of the horoscope he may be in, in either a male or female nativity. (See the Introduction to this section).

**Strengthened**—The Strength of the Constitution Increased — The ☉ well-asp. by the ☽ at B.; the ☉ in a fiery sign; the ☉ ☌, or good asp. ♃; the ☉ well-asp. by ♂; the ☽ in ♉, ♋, ♍, or ♓; ♆ in ⚹ or △ asp. the ☉ benefits the constitution psychically rather than in a physical way; ♄ ⚹ or △ the ☉ tends to strengthen and consolidate the constitution. (See "Increased" under Vitality).

**Strong Constitution**—(See "Body" under Strong. Also see "Good", "Powerful", in this section).

**Strongest Constitution**—The ☉ gives the strongest constitution when in the 1st, 10th, or 7th H.; the next strongest when in the 9th or 11th H., and weaker when in the 8th or 12th H. (See "Strongest Body" under Strong).

**Vital Force**—(See Vital).

**Vitality**—(See Vitality).

**Weak Constitution**—(See Feeble, Invalids, Majority, Retrograde, Sickly; "Much Sickness" under Sickness; "Low" under Vitality; "Weak Body" under Weak).

**Weak Parts** — Of the Body — (See "Weak Parts" under Parts).

**Weakened Constitution**—(See Depletion, Lack of, Lessened, Weakened, under Vitality).

**Weaker Constitution**—The ☉ below the horizon at B., and not in a hylegiacal place, tends to give a weaker constitution. (See "Weaker" under Weak).

**Weakest Constitution**—The ☉ in the watery signs ♋ or ♓, and afflicted by malefics or the ☽; ♋ or ♓ on the Asc. at B. (See "Weakest" under Weak).

**Weakness**—Constitutional Weakness —See the various paragraphs in this section. See Vitality Low; "Weak Body" under Weak. Case—A Case of Constitutional Weakness—See "Loss of Hair", No. 121, in 1001 N.N.

**CONSTRICTIONS** — Stenosis — Contractions — Constrictive — Constrictor Nerves—The Blood Vessels of the surface and extremities are constricted by cold, the work of ♄, driving the blood inwards, causing internal congestions, colds, etc. The influence of ♄ is to narrow, bind, and constrict, and to cause stenosis of vessels, or parts. ♄, the ruler of ♑ and ♒, has a special pathological action over the cutaneous capillary vaso-constrictor nerves, and by cold to cause them to contract, throwing the blood inwards. Constrictions also are caused by the contracting influence of ♅, and espec. of the spasmodic variety. Constrictions may occur in any narrowed channel of the body, as in the Blood Vessels, Bowels, Capillaries, Ducts, Nose, Heart, Pylorus, Throat, Ureters, Urethra, and caused by ♅ or ♄ afflictions, and with these planets in the sign ruling the afflicted part. See these parts in the alphabetical arrangement, or any other part or organ you may have in mind, and remember that ♄ especially tends to constrict, hamper, restrain, and suppress any part or organ ruled by the sign containing ♄ at B. ♆ is also referred to by some Authors as causing constrictions. (See Astringents, Capillaries, Centripetal, Cold, Colds, Congestions, Contractions, Cramps, Hernia, Spasmodic, Stenosis, Strictures; "Vaso-Constrictor" under Vaso; Vessels).

**CONSTRUCTIVE** — Constructive Energies—Constructive Metabolism—Anabolism — Constructive Processes—Constructive Functions—The ☉ and ♂ are constructive in the body. The principle of the ☉ is constructiveness, and the constructive energies in the body are directly under the influence and rule of the ☉. The ☽ rules the constructive functions, and the general health. In subsidiary ways ♄ and ♂ have a part in the constructive work going in the body. Bone building is carried on by mineral deposits formed by ♄. Mars has a constructive influence by burning up wastes and refuse in the body by fevers and inflammations. (See Action, Blood, Bones, Destructive, Energy, Fevers, Functions, Granulations, Haemoglobin, Inflammation, Iron, Mars, Metabolism, Muscles, Nerves, Sun, Tissues, Vital).

**Constructive Mind**—(See Inventive).

**CONSUMPTION** —Consumptions—A Consumption — Consumptive — A Consuming Disease—A Wasting Disease—Tuberculosis—Phthisic — Phthisis, etc. —Consumption is a ♄ disease, appears in many parts of the body, and is a consuming, or wasting of that part, and is not limited to the lungs. Note the following Consumptive conditions.

**A Consumption**—♄ ☌ or evil asp. the Asc. by dir.; ♃ affl. in ♍; the Asc. to the ☌ or ill-asp. ♄ by dir., and ♄ occi. at B.

**Abdominal Phthisis**—(See Phthisis).

**Acquired Consumption** — This affection, and also congestion of the lungs, are often caused by the afflicted bodies being in the ♒ sign.

**Acute Phthisis**—(See Phthisis).

**Adrenals**—Consumption of—(See Adrenals).

**Appearance**—Consumptive Appearance—The 4th face of ♊, the 2nd face of ♋ or ♌ on the Asc. at B. (See Complexion, Face, Pale, Sickly, White).

**Asthma**—(See Asthma).

**Bones**—Tuberculosis of—(See Bones).

**Bowels**—Consumption In—(See "Abdominal" under Phthisis).

**Bronchial Consumption**—(See Bronchial).

**Chest** — Consumption In — (See "Disorders" under Chest).

**Cold In Feet**—Consumption From—(See "Cold Taken In" under Feet).

**Colliquative Sweats**—Of Phthisis—(See "Night Sweats" under Phthisis).

**Consumptions**—General—Prevalent—♄ or ☿ (when ☿ partakes of the nature of ♄) sole rulers of a Solar Eclipse; a ♉ disease.

**Consumptive**—Liable to Consumption —Danger of—Tendency to—Predisposed to some form of Consumption, Tuberculosis, and a Wasting Disease—The ☉ affl. in common signs in the 6th or 12th H.; the ☉ in ♓ in the 6th or 12th H., and affl. by ♄ and malefics; the ☉ hyleg and affl. by ♄ in an angle, and espec. with ♄ in the Asc.; the ☉ and ☿ in the 6th H., in a common sign, and afflicted, and with ♍ rising; the ☉ or ☽ in the 6th H. in a common sign, and affl. by ♄; a ☽ disease; ☽ to the ☌ ♄ by dir.; prog. ☽ ☌ ♄ in ♊, galloping consumption; ♆ in ♉, ♊, or ♋; ♄ denotes death by; ♄ ☌ the Asc. by dir.; ♄ in ♉, ♊, ♋, or ♓; ♄ afflictions to the hyleg; ♄ on the M.C. in □ or ☍ the ☉, and espec. if ♄ is in a common sign; ♄ ☌ or ill-asp. the ☉ at B., and by dir., and espec. in common signs; ♄ affl. in the 6th H. in a common sign; ♂ affl. in ♉, ♊, or ♋; ♀ Sig. ☌ the ☉, and the ☉ ill-dig.; lords of the 1st or 6th H., or the ☽, in earthy signs, and affl.; a ♉, ♊, and ♋ disease, and afflictions in these signs; many planets in common signs; a common sign on the Asc., and espec. ♓; common signs on the cusp of 6th H.; malefics in ♊, ♐, or ♓, and espec. consumption in the lungs; afflictions from malefics in common signs, and espec. when the malefic is in the common sign division of the common sign in which placed; Subs at Lu.P. (See Lungs, Navamsa, Phthisis, Tuberculosis; "Body" under Wasting). Cases of Consumption — See "Bankruptcy", No. 093; "Consumption", No. 070, No. 348, No. 678; "Spendthrift", No. 262, all in 1001 N.N.

**Danger of Consumption**—(See "Consumptive" in this section. Also see "Pulmonary" under Phthisis).

**Death by Consumption** — ♄ denotes death by; the hyleg affl. by ♄; denoted by fixed stars of the nature of ♄ or ☿; ♄ in a common sign, the afflictor in the disease, afflicting the hyleg, and holding the dominion of death; ☿ affl. in 8th H. (See "Death" under Phthisis). Cases of Death By—See the cases under "Consumptive" in this section. Also see Chap. 14, page 104 in Daath's Medical Astrology.

**Diseases Proceeding From**—Diseases Which Proceed from Consumption—(See the various paragraphs in this section. Also see Atrophy, Emaciation, Wasting, etc.).

**Feet**—Consumption from Colds Taken in the Feet—(See "Cold Taken In Feet" under Feet).

**Galloping Consumption**—(See "Consumptive" in this section).

**Hectic Fever of Phthisis**—(See Phthisis).

**Inward Parts**—Consumption of (See "Consumption" under Reins).

**Knees**—Consumptive Pains In—(See Knees).

**Laryngeal Consumption**—(See Larynx).

**Liable To**—(See "Consumptive" in this section).

**Lingering Consumption**—Long Continued—Earthy signs in the Asc. or 6th H., or the ☽ in an earthy sign at B., or at decumbiture; ♄ the afflictor in the disease; ♄ in the 6th or 8th H., in a common sign, and affl. the hyleg. (See Ague, Chronic, Lingering; "Diseases" under Long; Prolonged, Slow, Tedious).

**Lungs**—Consumption of—Tuberculosis of—(See "Pulmonary "under Phthisis; Tuberculosis).

**Lupus**—A Tubercular Skin Disease—(See Lupus).

**Mother**—The Mother Afflicted with Consumption—Death By—(See "Consumption" under Mother).

**Night Sweats Of**—(See "Night Sweats" under Phthisis).

**Pains**—Consumptive Pains in Knees or Thighs—(See Knees, Thighs).

**Phthisis**—(See Phthisis).

**Pulmonary Consumption**—(See "Pulmonary" under Phthisis).

**Reins—Consumption of**—(See Reins).

**Scrofula**—Tubercular Tendency In—(See Scrofula).

**Skin**—Tubercular Skin Disease—(See Lupus).

**Suprarenal Capsules**—Consumption, or Tuberculosis of—(See Adrenals).

**Symptoms of Consumption**—Symptoms of Spleen—The ☽ in ♊, □ or ☍ ♄ (or ☿ if he be of the nature of ♄) at the beginning of an illness, or at decumbiture (Hor'y). (See "Consumptive" in this section).

**Tendency To**—(See "Consumptive" in this section).

**Thighs**—Consumptive Pains In—(See Thighs).

**Tuberculosis**—(See Tuberculosis).

**Various Forms of Consumption**—Caused by the afflictions of ♄ at B., and by dir.; the Asc. ☌ or ill-asp. ♄ by dir., and ♄ occi. at B.; earthy signs on the Asc. or 6th H. at B., or at decumbiture, or the Sigs. of the disease in such signs.

**Wasting Away**—Or Consumption—(See Emaciation, Hardening, Tabes, Wasting, etc. Also note the various paragraphs in this section).

**CONTAGIOUS DISEASES**—Contagions—The Process of Transfer of Specific Diseases—Infectious Diseases—Communicable Diseases—The ☉ affl. in ♏ or ♓; the ☉ to the ☌ ☋ by dir.; the ☽ people become easy subjects to contagious and infectious diseases and fevers; ♅ affl. in the Asc. at B. makes the native more subject to contagious diseases; caused and ruled by ♂ afflictions; a ♂ and ♏ disease; ♂ Sig. ☌ the ☉. The ♏ sign, having an excess of magnetic power, tends to attract disease, and espec. contagious and infectious complaints, and the ♏ people fall easy victims to epidemics. (See "Corrupt Air" under Air; Amulets, Cholera, Epidemics, Eruptions, External, Infectious, Influenza, Magnetic, Measles, Pestilence, Plague, Pox, Scarlet Fever, Smallpox, Venereal, Vesicles, etc.). For Contagious Diseases not listed here, see the subject in the alphabetical arrangement.

**Death By**—Death By a Contagious or Infectious Fever—The planetary influences causing contagious and infectious diseases are much the same, and death by these diseases and fevers is espec. caused by the severe afflictions of ♂ to the hyleg at B., and by dir. (See Infectious, Mars, Perihelion, Scorpio, etc.).

**CONTENTMENT**—Contented—Content of Mind—Health of Mind—Peace of Mind—The ☉ well-asp. at B., and espec. by the ☽ and ♂, and the ☉ to the good asps. the Asc. by dir.; the ☉ or ☽ to the ☌ or good asps. ♃ by dir.; the ☉ directed to Arista; the ☽ well-asp. at B., and to the ☌ or good asp. ♃, ♀, or the Asc. by dir.; the ☽ to the ☌ ☊ by dir.; ♃ at a Solar Rev. passing the place of the radical ☽, and the ☽ well-asp. at B., or ♃ passing over the radical ♄ if ♄ be in one of his strong signs and well-asp. at B.; the Asc. meeting the good directions of the benefics; the Asc. to the place of Crater or ⊕ by dir.; good asps. to ♀ and the ♎ sign; Arista ascending at B. The benefic asps. and influences at B., and by dir. tend to bring peace and contentment. (See Cheerfulness, Comforts, Discontentment, Fortune, Happiness; "Good Health" under Health; Hope, Jovial, Joy, "Peace of Mind" under Mind; Optimistic, Prosperity, Restlessness, etc.).

**CONTESTS**—Killed or Injured in Some Contest—The ☉ Sig. to the □ or ☍ ♂; the 26° ♊ on the Asc. at B. is said to bring such a fate. (See Disputes, Duels, Feuds, Fighting, Gunshot, Instruments, Quarrels, Sword, War, etc.).

**CONTINUITY**—Continuous—Continued—The Continuity of Disease is associated with the Fixed Signs. The afflicting planet stationary tends to continuity, duration of effects, and constancy of the disease. Direct motion of the afflicting planet favors continuity of the disease. A planet ℞ tends to disorganization of the disease when the afflictor, and to solution of continuity. (See Amelioration, "Better" under Disease; Chronic, Constancy, Course, Crises, Direct, Duration, Fixed Signs (see Fixed); Incurable, Interrupted, Invalids, Lingering, Long Diseases (see Long); Moderation, Prolonged, Relapse, Resolution, Retrograde, Sequence, Return, Tedious, Worse, etc.).

**Continued Fever**—See "Constant", "Low", under Fever; Flux).

**Continued Sickness**—The Disease Prolonged—The afflicting planets in fixed signs; the ☌ of the rulers of the 1st and 6th houses unless free from affliction. Continuous fevers grow worse towards sunset. (See the references in the first part of this section).

**Disease Will Continue**—The Disease Will Continue Until, etc.—The lord of the 1st H. in the 6th, and the lord of the 6th in the 1st H., the disease will continue until one of them quits the sign he is in, and then if he meets the □ or ☍ of ♄, ♂, or lords of the 4th or 8th, it is a symbol of death. (See Duration).

**Life**—Continuity of After Birth—(See "Continuance" under Life).

**Muscles**—Continued Contraction of—(See Contraction, Muscles, Tetanus; "Tonic" under Spasmodic).

**Pains and Aches**—Continuous—(See the various paragraphs under Aches, Headaches, Neuralgia, Pains).

**Solution of Continuity**—(See the Introduction to this section).

**Spasms**—Spasmodic Action—Continuous—(See "Muscles" in this section).

**CONTORTIONS**—Contorted—Twistings—A ♅ disease. The organ of Coordination is under the rule of ♉, and reflex afflictions in ♉ from ♏, the exalted sign of ♅, tend to contortions and twistings of parts.

**Awry Gait**—A Twisted Walk—(See "Awry" under Gait).

**Rigid Parts**—Contortions of—(See Rigid).

**Wry Neck**—Torticollis—(See Neck). See Congenital, Contractions, Coordination, Deformities, Distortions, Erratic, Face, Features, Genitals, Lameness, Muscles, Paralysis, Spasmodic, Spine, Subluxations, Trunk, Twistings).

**CONTRACTIONS**—Contracted—Contracting—♄ is contracting in his influence, and also the influence of Cold, and Astringent Drugs, which he rules. Cold Diseases, ruled by ♄, are accompanied by contractions. ♆ is contractive and astringent. ♅ tends to spasmodic contractions by his afflictions to the Center of Coordination ruled by ♉; ♅ in the 6th H. tends to contractions, spasmodic and erratic diseases; the ☽ affl. by ♅; ♄ influence; ♄ ☌ or ill-asp. ♅. Parts of the body ruled by the signs containing the malefics, ♆, ♅, and ♄ at B., or parts afflicted by the asps. of these malefics, are subject to contractions, and the list of diseases associated with contractions would be too long to list here. Look in the alphabetical arrangement for the subject you have in mind. Also see the following subjects,—Astringent, Capillaries, Clonic, Cold, Colic, Compressed, Constrictions, Contortions, Convulsions, Coordination, Cramps, Deformities, Depressions, Distortions, Dwarfed, Epilepsy; "Movements" under Erratic; Exaggerated, Expansion; "Crossed Eyes" under Eyes; "Club Feet" under Feet; Fits, Gripings; "Orifice" under Heart; Hyperkinesia, Imperforate, Incoordination, Inertia, Irregular, Jerky, Legs, Limbs, Muscles; "Wry Neck" under Neck; Opisthotonos; "Spasmodic" under Pain; Retraction, Rigidity, Saint Vitus Dance; "Spasms" under Spasmodic, Tonic; Spine, Stature, Stenosis, Stiffness; "Pylorus" under Stomach; Strictures, Tetanus, Tics, Torsion, Torticollis, Tremors, Twistings, Windpipe; "Hour Glass" under Womb; "Wry Neck" under Neck, etc.

**CONTRACTS**—

**Contracts Disease Easily**—☽ people; born under the strong influence of the ☽, or with the ☽ much afflicted at B. by the ☉ and malefics, and with little assistance to the ☽ from the benefics. (See Attracts, Contagious, Magnetic, Resistance; "Low" under Vitality).

**Injury Thru Contracts**—Death Thru Contests, Quarrels, etc. (See Contests, Duels).

**CONTRARIES**—(See Antipathy, Hippocrates).

**CONTROL**—

**Mind**—Lack of Control Over—(See Anger; "Brain Storms" under Brain; Chaotic, Coma, Confusion, Delirium, Demoniac, Fears, Furious, Fury, Hypochondria, Idiocy, Insanity, Intemperate, Madness, Mania, Melancholy, Mental, Mind, Obsessions; "Self-Control" under Self; Spirit Controls, Suicide, Temper, Uncontrolled, Vicious, Violent, Worry, etc.).

**Muscles**—Lack of Control Over—(See Erratic, Incoordination, Involuntary, Jerky Muscles, Paralysis, Spasmodic, Tics, Twitchings, Uncontrolled, etc.).

**Self-Control**—(See this subject under Self).

**Spirit Controls**—(See this subject).

**Voice**—(See "Control" under Voice).

**CONTROVERSIES**—Death or Injury By—(See Contests, Duels, Fighting, Quarrels, etc.).

**CONTUSIONS**—(See Assaults, Attacks, Blows, Bruises, Falls, Fractures, Kicks, etc.).

**CONVALESCENCE**—Recovery from Disease—(See Abatement, Amelioration; "Better" under Disease; Continuity, Crises, Improvement, Moderation, Recovery, Resolution, etc.).

**CONVERTIBLE DISEASES**—(See Curable).

**CONVICTS**—Danger of Injury By, or Death at Hands of Fellow Prisoners—(See Prisons).

**CONVULSIONS**—A Spasm or Fit—Spasmodic Jerking—In Convulsions the trouble lies between the fixed and common signs, and also the fixed and common Navamsas are in full evidence. (See Navamsa). The Nervous System is ruled by the common signs, and espec. ♊ and ♐. Convulsions are a secondary complaint, and result from some other cause or complaint. They may be Epileptic in origin. Convulsions are an ♈ and ♌ disease; a ☿ disease; ♅ is also spasmodic and convulsive, and his afflictions to ☿ or the hyleg, tend to convulsions; ♅ affl. by ♆; ♅, ♄, ☿ and the ☽ in fixed signs and afflicted; the ☽ to the ☌ or ill-asp.

♂ by dir., in children, and may result in death; the ☽ and ☿ affl. by ♅ and ♄; a majority of planets in fixed signs; caused by Subs at AT, AX, CP, KP (11D), and at PP. Cases of Convulsions, Birth Data, etc., are considered on pages 85 and 86, Chap. 13, in Daath's Medical Astrology. Cases of Death by Convulsions, see "Convulsions", No. 155, and "Short Life", No. 371, in 1001 N.N. (For further influences see Coma, Contractions, Coordination; "Dentition" under Teeth; Delirium, Eclampsia, Epilepsy, Erratic, Faintings, Fits, Hysteria, Incoordination, Infancy, Involuntary; "Spasms" under Spasmodic; Uremia, etc.).

**Death by Convulsions**—(See the first part of this Article. Also see "Death" under Fits).

**Movements**—Convulsive Movements—(See Contractions, Cough, Cramps, Erratic, Incoordination, Jerky, Movements, Muscles, Saint Vitus Dance, Spasmodic, Tics, Twitchings, etc.).

**Puerperal Convulsions**—At Delivery—(See "Convulsions" under Parturition).

**Uremic Convulsions**—(See Uremia).

**COOLING**—Refrigerant—A therapeutic property of ♄. (See Cold, Refrigerant, Saturn).

**Cooling Medicines**—Cooling Remedies—(See Ice; "Cooling" under Medicines; Snow).

**COORDINATION**—Harmonious Action—The instrument of coordinated action is under the rule of the ♉ sign. The Cerebellum is the organ of Coordination. (See Cerebellum).

**Coordinated Action**—Harmonious Action in the Body—(See Balance, Dexterity, Equilibrium, Harmony; "Good Health" under Health; "Clear Intellect" under Intellect; "Judgment Good" under Judgment; "Good Mind" and "Peace of Mind" under Mind; Perception, Reason, Rhythm, Understanding).

**Disorders of Coordination**—(See such subjects as Action, Anxiety, Ataxia, Contortions, Convulsions, Cramps, Disease, Distortions, Epilepsy, Erratic, Fits, Gait, Hiccough, Hysteria, Ill-Health, Incoordination, Insanity, Involuntary, Jerkings, Lameness, Melancholia, Motion, Movement, Muscles, Nausea, Paralysis, Saint Vitus Dance, Spasmodic, Speech, Taurus, Tetanus, Tics, Tremors, Twitchings, Unbalanced, Walk, Winking, Worry, etc.).

**COPIOUS**—Excessive—

**Discharges**—Copious or Excessive Discharges—(See Blood, Bowels, Catarrh, Cholera, Defluxions, Diarrhoea, Discharges, Dysentery, Ears, Excess, Excessive, Eyes, Faeces, Fluids, Fluxes, Head, Humours, Leucorrhoea, Menses, Nose, Rheum, Sweat, Urine, etc.).

**COPPER**—Cuprum—Ruled by ♀. A typical drug of ♀. Copper is correllated with ♀ and the color Indigo. (See Amulets, Cholera, Therapeutics).

**COPROLALIA**—The insane use of obscene words. (See "Obscene" under Speech).

**COR HYDRA**—(See Hydra's Heart).

**Cor Leonis**—(See Regulus).

**Cor Scorpio**—(See Antares).

**CORAL**—(See Amulets, Lime, Whooping Cough).

**CORD**—Cords—

**Silver Cord**—(See Silver).

**Spermatic Cord**—(See Spermatic).

**Spinal Cord**—(See Spine).

**Umbilical Cord**—(See Navel).

**Vocal Cords**—(See Vocal).

**CORDIALS**—An Aromatic Spiritous Stimulant—Ruled by ♀. (See Stimulants, Tonics; "Professions" under Venus; Wines).

**CORIUM**—The deep layer of the Cutis. (See Derma, Skin).

**CORN**—

**Corn Destroyed**—(See Drought, Fruit, Famine; "Corn" under Scarcity; Vegetation, Wheat).

**CORNEA**—(See "Cornea" under Eyes).

**CORNIFICATION**—Making Hard or Horny—♄ influence. (See Bunions; "Skin" under Hardening; Horny, Scales).

**CORNS**—Bunions—(See Bunions; "Skin" under Hardening; Scales).

**CORONARY**—Coronary Plexuses—(See "Middle Cervical" under Ganglion).

**CORPSE**—

**Devoured After Death**—(See "Birds of the Air" under Air; "Body Devoured" under Burial; Vultures).

**Dissolution Of**—(See Cremation, Decay, Disintegration, Dissolution, Matter).

**Rigor Mortis**—(See Rigors, Morgues).

**CORPULENT**—Corpulency—Largeness of the Body—Obesity—Adiposis—The ☉, ☽, and many planets in watery signs, or with such signs upon the Asc. at B.; the ☉ ♒ partile Asc., middle stature, corpulent, and well-made; the ☽ gives a smooth, corpulent and phlegmatic body; the ☽ when ori. gives a body more corpulent, tall and smooth; the ☽ ♉, partile Asc., strong, corpulent and well-set; the ☽ ♒ partile Asc., corpulent, middle-sized, but well-formed; ♄ in N. Lat. makes the body more corpulent, strong and bony; ♄ ♒ partile the Asc.; ♃ influence; born under ♃ if ♃ is ori.; ♂ ♉, partile the Asc., corpulent, short and compact; ♂ ♍ partile Asc., corpulent, well-set and middle sized; ♂ ♒ partile Asc., corpulent, well-set and tall, or middle-sized; ♀ ♏ partile Asc., short, corpulent and well-set; ♀ ♒, handsome, well-made and rather corpulent; ☿ ♉ partile Asc., corpulent, well-set, and middle stature; ♏ on the Asc., corpulent, strong, robust, middle-sized; ♒ on the Asc., sometimes corpulent. (See Bulky, Fat, Fleshy, Full, Large, Mean, Middle Life, Muscles, Obesity, Phlegmatic, Plump, Portly, Puffing, Robust, Short, Stout, Strong, Tall, Thick, Well-Set).

**CORPUSCLES**—Blood Corpuscles—(See Anaemia, Haemoglobin, Iron, Leukocytes; "Blood" under Red).

**CORRESPONDENCES**—Law of Signatures—(See Antipathy, Harmony, Signature, Sympathy).

**CORROSION**—To Eat Away, and Destroy—The general influence of ♄ on the tissues by his evil aspects and afflictions is to eat away, waste, and destroy, or cause decay. ♅ has an especially corrosive influence on the Nervous System, tending to Lesions and Paralysis. ☿ affl. by ♅ also tends to corrosion of the nerves. (See Decay, Destructive, Lesions, Paralysis, Saturn, Uranus, Wasting, etc.).

**CORRUPT**—Corruptive—Corruption—Corruptive Disorders are ♄ and ☽ diseases as a rule.

**Corrupt Air**—(See Air).

**Corrupt Blood**—(See Carbon; "Morbid", "Poor", "Thin", "Too Much Blood", under Blood; Foul, Impure; "Non-Oxygenation" under Oxygen; Ulcers).

**Corrupt Breath**—(See "Foul" under Breath).

**Corruption of Fruit**—Sickness from Eating—(See Fruit).

**Corrupt Humours**—Corruptive Disorders—(See Decay, Humours, Impure, Mortification, Pus, Putrefaction).

**Corruption of Waters**—Corruption of Moisture—(See Fish, Moisture, Rivers, Waters).

**CORTICAL**—Cortex—The external gray layer of the brain. Is ruled by ♈.

**Cortical Lesions**—(See Lesions; "Aphasia" under Speech).

**Cortical Substance**—Of the Kidneys—(See Kidneys).

**CORYZA**—Catarrhal Inflammation of the Nose—(See "Coryza" under Nose).

**COSMETICS**—Remedies for Beautifying the Skin—Lotions—Hair Tonics—Toilet Articles, etc.—

**Indiscreet Use Of**—Injurious Use of—Venus has to do with the complexion and skin of the face, and disorders from unwise use of Cosmetics. ♀ in ♈, eruptions due to injudicious use of cosmetics; ♀ affl. in ♈ in the 6th H.; ♀ affl. in ♑ tends to misuse of skin and hair lotions, and to mar the beauty of the complexion; ♆ affl. in ♑ tends to indiscreet use of cosmetics and lotions; ♎ people are more adversely affected by their use, as ♎ is the exalted sign of ♄, and tends to skin diseases. (See Barbers, Complexion, Eruptions, Face, Lotions, Pimples, Skin, etc.).

**COSTAL**—Pertaining to the Ribs—(See Intercostal, Ribs).

**COSTIVENESS**—Hardness and Retention of the Faeces—(See "Sluggish" under Bowels; Constipation; "Hardening" under Faeces; "Requirements" under Nature; Retention).

**COUGH**—Tussis—Coughs—A Sudden, Forced Expiratory Noise—Caused by afflictions in ♉, ♊, ♋, ♏, ♐, and ♓, and afflictions in the common signs. The planets tending to cause coughs are the ☽, ♄, ♅, ♂, and ☿. Afflictions in ♉ and ♏, supplemental signs, cause coughs originating more in the throat, as ♏ suffers almost as much from coughs and throat troubles as ♉. Afflictions in ♊, ♐, or ♓ tend to lung coughs. ♅ causes convulsive and spasmodic coughs when affl. in ♊. The coughs arising from weakness, lingering and chronic diseases, as from Consumption or Tuberculosis, are caused by ♄, and espec. when ♄ is in ♊ or ♓, and afflicted. Afflictions in ♋ tend to stomach coughs, and also all coughs and colds in general. Coughs are caused by ♄ when he has strong rule (and by ☿ when he is of the nature of ♄), and the dominion of death is vested in them; ♄ in an angle, occi. of the ☉, and ori. of the ☽; ♄ to the ☌ or ill-asps. the ☽ if the ☽ is hyleg, or ruler of the 6th or 8th H. at B.; ♄ ☌ the Asc. by dir.; ♄ ☌ ♂ in ♉ or ♊; ♄ ☌ ♅ or ♆ in ♊; the ☉ to the ☌ ♄ or ☿ by dir.; the ☽ hyleg, and to the ☌ or ill-asps. the ☉ or ♄ by dir.; the ☽ decr. in light, sepr. from ♄ and applying to ☿; the ☽ in ♋ and affl. by the ☉ or ♂; the ☽ to the bad asps. the ☉; the ☽ in ♋ at B., and the transit of ♄ over the place of the radical ☽, and espec. if the native is of weak constitution; the ☽ in ♋ or ♎, ☌ or ill-asp. ♄ (or ☿ if he be of the nature of ♄) at the beginning of an illness, there is cough, and if the ☽ be decr., and near the place of ♄, the cough will tend to be of long duration; ♂ affl. in ♊; ♂ ☌ ☋ in ♊; a ☿ disease; ☿ affl. in ♊ or ♐; ☿ affl. at B., and evilly aspecting the Asc. by dir.; ☿ sole ruler at an eclipse; the Asc. to the ill-asps. ♄ by dir.; the Asc. to the ill-asps. ☿ by dir., and ☿ affl. by ♄ at B.; malefics in ♊, and afflicting ♃ and ♀, rulers of the circulation, and interfering with proper oxygenation of the blood; watery signs on the Asc. and 6th H. at B., or at decumbiture, and the Sigs. in water signs at the beginning of an illness. (See the various pararaphs in this section).

**Bilious Dry Cough**—♂ affl. in ♋. (See Bile).

**Bronchial Cough**—(See "Cough" under Bronchial). Also caused by Subs at AP, L.C.P. (6th C.), and at SP.

**Constant Cough**—Seldom Free from a Cough—♅ ☌ ♄ in ♉, and affl. the ☉, ☽, or Asc.; denoted by ♄; ♄ strong at B., and affl. the hyleg, seldom free from a cough; ♄ in ♉ or ♊; in Hor'y Questions ♄ Sig. of the party. (See Constant).

**Convulsive Coughing**—Paroxysms of—♅ in ♊, from the lungs; ♅ in ♋, from stomach disorders. Also convulsive, or spasmodic coughing, results when ♅ is affl. in ♍, ♐, or ♓, due to reflex action and irritations to the bronchial tract ruled by ♊. (See Spasmodic, Violent, Whooping, in this section).

**Death from Coughs**—Death from Severe Colds—♄ affl. the hyleg by dir., and ♄ holding the dominion of death; ☿ affl. the hyleg by dir., and ☿ affl. by ♄ at B., and ☿ holding the dominion of death; ☿ in the 8th H. at B., and in ☌ or ill-asp. ♄, and ♄ affl. the hyleg by dir., and ♄ holding the dominion of death, and also much delirium may attend; afflictions in the common signs. (See Colds).

**Dry Coughs**—The ☽ to the ☌, □, or ☍ ♄ or ☿ by dir., and espec. if ☿ be of the nature of ♄; ♄ ☌ or ill-asp. ☿, due to deficient secretion of mucus on the respiratory membranes; ♂ affl. in ♋; a ☿ disease, and afflictions to ☿ at B. (See "Bilious", "Dry Hard Cough", in this section. Also see Dry).

**Dry Hard Cough**—♅ affl. in ♊, dry, hard lung cough; ♅ affl. in ♋, dry, hard stomach cough; ♂ ♋ ☌ or ill-asp. the ☉, dry, hard stomach cough.

**Frequent Short Cough**—Hacking Cough—♅ affl. in ♊.

**Hacking Cough**—(See "Frequent", "Throat", in this section).

**Hiccough**—(See Hiccough).

**Long Duration**—(See the first part of this section).

**Lung Cough**—♅ ♊ tends to a hard, spasmodic, dry lung cough; ♄ ♊, coughs from lingering or chronic lung trouble; ♂ ♊, due to acute colds on the chest; Subs at Lu.P. (See Bronchial, Consumption, Lungs, Mucus, Phlegm, Phthisis, Tuberculosis).

**Paroxysms**—Of Coughing—(See "Convulsive" in this section).

**Pertussis**—(See "Convulsive", "Whooping", in this section).

**Rotten Coughs**—A ☽ disease, and afflictions to the ☽ at B., and by dir.; the ☽ ♓ ☌ or ill-asp. ♄ (or ☿ if he be of the nature of ♄) at the beginning of an illness; a ♋ sign disease and afflictions in ♋. (See Rotten).

**Seldom Free from Cough**—(See "Constant" in this section).

**Short and Frequent**—♅ affl. in ♊.

**Spasmodic Cough**—♅ affl. in ♊, from the lungs. (See "Convulsive" in this section. Also see Spasmodic).

**Stomach Cough**—♅ affl. in ♋ tends to a hard, dry, spasmodic and convulsive stomach cough, and from stomach disorders; ♂ ♋ ☌ or ill-asp. the ☉; a ♋ sign disease, and afflictions in ♋; Subs at SP.

**Throat Cough**—♅, ♄, or ♂ affl. in ♉; a ♉ disease; ♅ affl. in ♉, a hacking, tickling, spasmodic throat cough; Subs at LCP, and SP (7D). (See Mucus, Phlegm, Throat).

**Violent Cough**—The ☽ ♓, and affl. by the ☉ or ♂ when taken ill; ♂ configurated with influences which tend to cause cough make the cough more severe and violent.

**Whooping Cough**—(See Whooping).

**COUNTENANCE**—Face—Expression—Look—Features—Visage, etc.—This subject is largely considered under such subjects as Appearance, Aspect, Complexion, Expression, Eyes, Face, Features, Look, etc. In this section, however, some subjects which have to do with the countenance will be considered and listed alphabetically. Disease, Conduct, Habits, Ill-Health, Pain, Suffering, etc., tend to change the countenance, and it would take considerable space and time to list here every subject related to countenance. Therefore, if the subject is not listed here, or under the subjects mentioned, look in the alphabetical arrangement for the subject you have in mind. See the following subjects,—Anaemic, Animal, Appearance, Aspect, Austere, Beautiful, Blemishes, Bold, Cheeks, Cheerful, Chin, Commanding, Complexion, Contented, Cruel, Debauched, Dimples, Dissipated, Downward Look (see Look); Effeminate, Expression, Eyes, Face, Fair, Features, Fierce, Fiery, Glances, Gloomy, Good, Grave, Handsome, Harmless, Humane, Indifferent, Intellectual, Intemperate, Jaundiced, Kind, Lean, Long, Look, Lowering, Lumpish, Lustful, Mouth, Nose, Open, Oval, Pale, Peaceful, Pensive, Piercing, Pleasant, Pimpled, Pockmarked, Red, Refined, Robust, Round, Ruddy, Sad, Savage, Scarred, Scurvy, Sensual, Serious, Severe, Sharp, Sickly, Slender, Smiling, Smooth, Solid, Sympathetic, Sober, Stern (see Austere); Strong, Surly (see Aspect); Teeth, Thin, Thoughtful (see Grave); Unhealthy, Violent, Visage, Voluptuous (see Amorous, Sensuous); White, Wicked, Wide, Wrinkled, Youthful, etc.

**COUNTER-IRRITANTS**—Ruled by ♂. (See Caustics, Rubefacients, Vesicant).

**COUNTRIES RULED BY SIGNS**—Nations—The different Countries, Nations, Cities, and Parts of our Globe, have been assigned to the rulership of the different Planets and Signs of the Zodiac. A list of these rulerships can be found in Lilly's Astrology, and other textbooks. In travel, and espec. for health, it is very important for people to avoid Countries ruled by the Signs in which they have the malefic planets at B., unless such planets have dignity and power in the sign, and are well-aspected. Under the subject of "Nations", the rulership of the different Countries and prominent Cities is given. Also see Location; "Native Land" under Native; "Place of Birth" under Place; Residence, Travel, etc.).

**COURAGE**—(See Bold, Mars, Positive, Resolute, Servitude).

**COURSE OF DISEASE**—As no two people are born exactly alike, and have varying inherent, natal and prenatal qualities, there can be almost a limitless number of ways in which a disease may manifest itself, and the course it will pursue. In making a prognosis as to the course any particular disease will pursue, you should make a detailed study of the map of birth, the prenatal epoch map, and also the map of the heavens for the time of decumbiture, the beginning of the illness, or when the patient takes to his bed, and interpret it according to the Laws of the Science. The transits, directions, and progressed influences now working over the native should be studied. The nature of the signs and houses containing the afflicting planet, or planets, should be considered, and the afflicting planet, and the times when such planet, or planets, will change signs or pass into the next house, etc. (See Continuity). Disease tends to take its course when the ☉, ♀, or ☿ are in the 8th H. at B., as there is less resistance by the mind under these conditions. Also in negative people illness is more apt to take its own course and time, as such people give up easily, and lack will-power, resistance, grit and determination.

**Danger In Course Of**—The lord of the Asc. in evil asp. the ☽; the malefics affl. the hyleg at B., and by dir., and espec. when the hyleg is affl. by a train of adverse directions, and without the favorable intervention of the benefics ♃ and ♀. (See "Certain", "Sure", under Death; Fatal; "High" under Fever; "Dangerous" under Ill-Health; Malignant; "Disease" under Severe; "Violent" under Sickness; Vehement, Worse).

**Irregular Course**—☿ diseases. (See Irregular).

**Peculiar Course**—(See Peculiar).

**Various Course**—☿ diseases. (See Erratic, Irregular, Peculiar, Various). For further study along this line see the following subjects,—Acute, Alteration, Amelioration; "Better" under Disease; Changes, Chronic, Complications, Constancy, Continuity, Convalescence, Crises, Critical, Curable, Curtailed, Cycles, Dangerous, Death, Direct, Disease, Disturbances, Duration, Ease, Elimination, Erratic, Extraordinary Fever, Grievous, Ill-Health, Improvement, Incurable, Intermittent, Lingering, Long, Mild, Moderation, Modification, Negative, Painful, Peculiar, Periodic, Periodicity, Periods, Pernicious, Positive, Prognosis, Prolonged, Quick, Recovery, Recuperation, Recurrent, Relapses, Remission, Remittent, Resistance, Resolution, Retrograde, Return, Severe, Sharp, Shifting, Short, Shortened, Sickness, Slight, Slow, Solution, Stamina, Stationary, Susceptibility, Swift, Symptoms, Tedious, Termination, Variable, Various, Vitality, Wasting, Worse, etc.

**COURSES**—(See Menses).

**Bad Courses**—(See "Conduct" under Evil; Debauched, Dissipation, Drink, Drunkenness, Men, Morals, Passion, Sex, Women, etc.).

**COUSINS**—Ruled by the 3rd House. (See Relations, Third House).

**COVERINGS**—

**Of the Bowels**—(See Peritoneum).

**Of the Brain**—(See Brain, Meninges).

**Of the Lungs**—(See Pleura).

Also see Membranes, Mucous Membranes, Respiratory, Serous, Skin, Spine, etc.

**COWPER'S GLANDS**—Ruled by ♏. (See Urethra).

**COXALGIA**—Pain In the Hip Joint—(See Hips).

**CRAMPS**—Gripings—Spasmodic Muscular Contraction with Pain—Cramps are partly caused by lack of coordination, and afflictions to the Organ of Coordination ruled by ♉. The principal planet causing cramps and incoordination is ♅, and in the part ruled by the sign containing ♅ at B. ♅ and ☿, when associated together, also tend to cause cramps, and in the parts ruled by the signs containing them. Also ♄ by his binding and restricting influences tends to cause cramps in that part of the body, or organ, ruled by the sign he is in at B., and espec. in the limbs when in signs ruling the limbs, and afflicted, or in configuration with ♅. Also ♃ may cause cramps indirectly, due to gorging, excesses, gluttony, indigestion, etc. Cramps are also considered a ☉ disease, and espec. when the ☉ is configurated with ♅. (See Uranus). The following subjects have to do with Cramps in the various parts and organs of the body, and the causes of Cramps, which see in the alphabetical arrangement when not considered here—

**Abdominal Cramps**—♅ or ☿ affl. in ♍. (See "Cramps" under Bowels).

**Action**—Cramped Action—♆ and ♅ when afflicted tend to. (See Action, Movement).

**Ankles**—Cramps In—♅ ♒.

**Arms**—Cramps In—♅ and ☿ in signs which rule the Arms, Shoulders, Hands, Legs and Feet tend to cramps in these parts. (See "Cramps" under Arms).

**Borborygmus**—(See Bowels).

**Bowels**—Cramps In—♅ affl. in ♍. (See "Cramps", "Gas", "Pain", under Bowels).

**Cholera**—(See "Cramps" under Cholera).

**Cholic**—(See "Cholic" under Bile).

**Colic; Constrictions; Contractions; Coordination; Curable Cramps**—Curable when affecting the Limbs—Malefics angular, occi. of the ☽, and in the last degrees of ♊ or ♐, if the benefics are with the malefics, or ori., or angular, and cast any ray to the Lights, they will be curable, but incurable if the benefics are weak and give no assistance. (See Curable, Incurable).

**Erratic Movements**—(See Erratic).

**Exaggerated Action**—(See Exaggerated).

**Exalted**—Exalted Excito-Motory Function—Cramps From—(See Exaltation).

**Extremities**—(See "Arms", "Curable", in this section).

**Eyelids**—(See "Winking" under Eyelids).

**Feet**—(See "Arms", "Curable", in this section; "Cramps" under Feet).

**Flatulence; Gas; Gripings; Hands**—(See "Arms", "Curable", in this section; "Cramp" under Hands).

**Heart**—(See "Cramp" under Heart).

**Hips**—Cramps In Hips and Thighs—(See "Cramps" under Hips).

**Incoordination; Incurable**—(See "Curable" in this section).

**Indigestion**—Cramps From—(See "Cramps" under Indigestion).

**Intermittent Cramp**—(See Intermittent).

**Intestines**—(See "Bowels" in this section).

**Knees**—(See "Cramps" under Knees).

**Legs**—(See "Arms", "Curable", in this section; "Cramps" under Legs).

**Limbs**—(See "Arms", "Curable", in this section).

**Motor Nerves**—(See Motor).

**Muscles**—(See Contractions, Intermittent; "Cramps" under Muscles).

**Neck**—(See "Cramps" under Neck).

**Nerves**—(See "Cramps" under Nerves).

**Pain; Paralysis; Saint Vitus Dance; Shoulders**—(See "Arms" in this section; "Cramp" under Shoulders).

**Spasmodic; Stomach**—(See "Cramp" under Stomach).

**Tetanus; Thighs**—(See "Cramp" under Thighs).

**Toes**—(See "Feet" in this section; "Cramps" under Toes).

**Tympanites; Wind**—(See "Bowels" under Wind).

**Winking**—(See Eyelids).

**Writer's Cramp**—(See Hands).

**CRANIUM**—Cranial—Cranian—The Skull—The Head—The Bony Case of the Brain—For considerations concerning the bony structure of the Cranium, see Skull.

**Cranian Diathesis**—The ☉ and ☽ acting thru the ♊ and ♍ signs affect the Respiratory System, the Upper Limbs, the Abdominal Organs, and the Lower Part of the Stomach, and give way to the Cranian Diathesis. The elemental qualities of this Diathesis are Cold and Dry. (See "Middle Cervical" under Ganglion).

**Cranio-Abdominal Diathesis**—(See "Fifth Thoracic" under Ganglion).

**Cranial Nerves**—Ruled by ♈.

**Depressions**—In the Cranium, or Skull—(See "Depressions" under Skull).

**Fractures**—(See Skull).

**Malformations**—(See Skull). See the various paragraphs under Brain, Head.

**CRATCH**—The Cratch—(See Ascelli, Praesepe).

**CRATER**—A Constellation of the nature of ♃ and ♀, in the 5th face of ♍, and said to be fortunate. The Asc. to the place of tends to bring good health, happiness and contentment.

**CRAVINGS**—Longings—Hunger—Desires—

**Cold Water**—A Craving For In Illness—The ☽ in ♉ and affl. by the ☉ or ♂ when taken ill (Hor'y). (See "Craving" under Liquids; Thirsty).

**Drink**—Craving for Drink and Liquors—(See Dipsomania, Drink, Drunkenness, Intemperance, Intoxication, Liquors, Wines, etc.).

**Drugs**—Craving For—(See Narcotics).

**Food**—Abnormal Cravings Along Food Lines—(See "Cravings", "Eccentric", "Peculiar", under Food).

**Liquids**—Craving For—(See Drink; "Craving" under Liquids; Thirst).

**Sex Cravings**—(See Amorous, Lascivious, Lewd, Licentious, Lust; "Loose Morals" under Morals; Men, Nymphomania, Passion, Pituitary, Sensuous, Sex, Unsavory, Women, etc.).

**Wine**—A Foolish Craving for Wine—(See Wine). See Appetites, Desires, Eating, Epicureans, Gluttony, Habits, Luxuries, Perversions, Pleasures, Unnatural, etc.

**CRAWLING SENSATIONS**—(See Hyperaesthesia, Sensations).

**CRAZY**—(See Dementia, Demoniac, Fury, Insanity, Madness; "Unbalanced", "Unsound", under Mind).

**CREATIVE**—

**Creative Force**—Sex Force—(See "Creative Force" under Sex).

**Creative Powers**—Are associated with the ☉ and the 5th H., the house related to the ☉ and the ♌ sign. The 5th H. denotes the offspring, whether physical, or the creations and children of the mind. (See Children, Fifth House).

**CREEPING SENSATIONS**—Crawling Sensations—(See Hyperaesthesia, Sensations).

**CREMATION**—(See "Silver Cord" under Silver).

**CRETINISM**—Deficient Development of the Organism, and Accompanied by Idiocy, and also often with Goiter. Caused by degeneration of the Thyroid Gland, ruled by ☿, and by afflictions to ☿. (See Diminished, Dwarfed, Goiter, Idiocy, Myxoedema, Thyroid).

**CREVICE**—A Small Fissure—

**Spine**—Crevice In—(See "Spina Bifida" under Spine). See Fissures.

**CRIMINAL TENDENCIES**—Criminals—Crime—Inclined to Criminal Acts—Due to ♂ afflictions to the ☉, ☽, ♄, ☿, the Asc., M.C., and ♂ in ♏ at B.; ♂ in ♉, ♋, or ♎, and affl. by the □ or ☍ of planets; ♂ Prog. ☌, P, □ or ☍ ♄ or ♃, or vice versa; ♂ in the 7th H. at a Solstice tends to make criminals active for the following Quarter, and lead to many robberies, much violence and murder; ♆ by tr. ☌ to ☽ or ☿ at B. of ♆ also be affl. in the radical map; ♅ ☌ ♂ in ♈; ♄ Sig. to the ill-asp. ♂ by dir., and espec. if ♄ or ♂ be in the 1st, 3rd, 9th or 10th H. at B.; ☿ ruler of the horoscope and affl. by malefics; Asc. to the place of the Ascelli or Capricornus. (See Anarchists, Assassins, Cheating, Deceitful, Destructiveness, Evil, Execution, Forgers, Gamblers, Highwaymen, Incendiarism, Intercourse, Liars, Mischief; "A Murderer" under Murder; Outrages, Pirates, Prison, Robbers, Swindlers, Thieves, Violent, Wicked, etc.).

**Much Crime Prevalent**—♂ in ♋, ℞ at the Vernal, lord of the year; Comets appearing in ♑. (See Assassination, Assaults, Comets, Murders, Outrages, Robberies, Slaughter, Violence, etc.).

**CRIPPLED**—Disabled—Partial or Total Loss of Use of Limbs—

**Crippled by Accident**—The Prog. ☉ or ☽ to the ☌, □, ☍, or P. ♂ by dir.; ♄ to the ☌ or ill-asp. ♂ by dir., danger of being crippled for life by accident or injury. The malefics ♄ and ♂ in the signs ruling the arms, legs, knees and feet bring great danger of accidents and injuries in these parts, in loss of members, disease, fracture, ankylosis, deposits, etc., by which the members, or parts, are temporarily or permanently crippled. (See Accidents, Arms, Birth, Congenital, Contortions, Contractions, Deformities, Distortions, Falls, Feet, Fractures, Gait, Hands, Incoordination, Infancy, Injury, Joints, Lameness, Legs, Limbs, Maimed, Members, Monsters, Muscles, Mutilated, Paralysis, Parturition, Rheumatism, Rigid, Spine, Walk, etc.).

**Crippled from Birth**—(See "Crippled" under Birth; Congenital).

**CRISES IN DISEASE**—Turning Point in Disease—A Paroxysm or Increase in the Disease—Crises are brought about by the changes of the ☽, by transits, by Prog. ☽ aspects, or a New ☽, and by directions. Judgment should not be based upon any one affliction, but all are to be considered. In making a judgment about crises, for the better or worse, the fundamental vitality should be considered, the indications of the radical map. The time of death usually comes at a crisis time, but should not be predicted openly, or to a sick person, even though certain death is indicated by the planetary influences, configurations and directions. The map of birth shows the days when crises are due, and when the transits or progressed planets will affect the radical planets by aspect.

**Acute Diseases**—Crises In—The 7th, 14th, 21st, and 28th days from the time the patient is taken sick are crises days of the disease, being based upon the Four Quarters of the ☽. (See Critical). The ☽ makes on revolution in her orbit in about 28 days, and the 7th, 14th, 21st days, and her return to her place at the time of the New Moon, correspond to her Quarters, adverse aspects, and crises times in the disease. The First, Second, and Third Quarters of the ☽, from the time the illness began, are crises days in acute diseases and fevers. If the patient lives thru these crises, and until the ☽ returns to her place, the disease will dissolve itself, or run into a chronic form. A person taken sick with a fever exactly at the New ☽ would have the crises days on the exact Quarters of the ☽ as given in the Calendar. In Acute diseases and fevers, the crises days are the dangerous ones. The most serious crisis day in an acute disease is on the 14th day, as a rule, when the ☽ arrives at the ☍ asp. to her place at the beginning of the illness, and this crisis day is called "The Criticus Primus", the one of prime importance. More patients die on the 14th day of a serious fever than on the other crises days, and if they do not die on the 14th day their chances for recovery and moderation of the disease are usually good. The patient is usually worse on the 7th and 21st days of the disease, but these crises are considered of minor importance as compared to the 14th day crisis. Improvements in the disease are due on the 9th, 10th, 18th, and 19th days of the disease, as these aspects correspond to the △ aspects of the ☽, her good aspects from the day

the illness began. (See Acute, Climacteric, Enneatical).

**Better**—Crisis a Turn for the Better— The Crisis Favorable—The ☽ in good asp. a benefic when she is 45, 90, or 135° from her place at the beginning of the illness; the ☽ on a crisis day in ✳ or △ asp. the lords of the Asc., 9th, 10th or 11th Houses, gives an interval of ease and relief; lord of the Asc. on a crisis day in good asp. the ☉ if the ☉ does not have the power of dominion over the disease. (See Amelioration; "Solution" under Continuity; "Better" and "Ease" under Disease; Enneatical, Moderation, Modification, Recovery, Recuperation, Remission, Resistance, etc.).

**Chronic Diseases**—Crises In—In Chronic Diseases the crises are Solar, and based upon the movements of, or aspects to the ☉, rather than to the ☽. Chronic disease follows the motion of the ☉, and acquires a crisis after the 40th day, and judgment, or prognosis, can be made when the ☉ arrives to the □ his own place in the map. Then there is a turn for the better if the ☉ is well-asp. by the benefics, but worse if configurated with malefics. The ☉ to the ✳ or △ his own place indicates improvement, but to the □ or ☍, a change for the worse. As ♄ is the author of chronic diseases, a serious crisis usually comes, with a turn for the worse, or death, when ♄ by direction comes to the ☌ or ill-asp. the ☉, ☽, Asc., or Hyleg, and also when accompanied by a train of evil directions to the hyleg, and when there is little or no assistance, or favorable intervention, from the benefics. Crises days, crises periods, and the critical times in life in health matters can thus be somewhat predicted, and possible forecasts of the outcome made, by looking ahead in the planetary tables, and by calculating the times when evil aspects and directions form and culminate, tending to make the patient worse, and when the favorable aspects come, making moderation, convalesence, and cure possible. (See Chronic).

**Eye Diseases**—Crises In—(See "Crises" under Eyes).

**Fevers**—Crises In—(See "Acute Diseases" in this section. See Fever).

**Indicative Crises**—(See Indicative).

**Worse**—The Crisis a Turn for the Worse—The ☽ at 45, 90, or 135° from her place at the beginning of an illness, and in evil asp. a malefic, or lords of the 6th or 8th H.; the ☽ at crisis day ☌ or ill-asp. a planet which afflicted the lord of the Asc. at decumbiture; the ☽ at a crisis day ☌ or ill-asp. lord of the 6th, or planets in the 6th H., the disease runs high and relief measures do little good. (See "Acute", "Chronic", in this section. See "Increase", "Worse", under Disease; "High Fevers" under Fevers). For collateral study see Accidents, Acute, Amelioration, Better, Childhood, Chronic, Convalescence, Critical, Course, Curable, Dangerous, Death, Directions, Duration, Ease, Fatal, Fever, Improvement, Increase, Incurable, Infancy, Mild, Moderation, Modification; "New Moon", "Quarters", under Moon; "Moon" under Motion; Paroxysms, Pestilence, Quick Diseases, Recovery, Relapses, Remission, Resolution, Severe, Solution, Stamina, Termination, Tone, Vitality, Worse, etc.).

**CRITICAL**—Pertaining To a Crisis—

**Critical Days**—The critical days in acute diseases and fevers are the crises days. (See "Acute", "Fevers", under Crises). For critical days and times in Chronic diseases, see "Chronic" under Crises. Every individual meets with many critical days in life, due to transits, progressions, or directions over the radical map, and the ☽ aspects, which may precipitate an accident, injury, fever, disputes, quarrels, misfortune, reversal in business, sorrow, worry, etc., and it would take considerable time to study out beforehand all the critical days and crises each person is apt to meet during life. The person who becomes advanced, spiritualized, with balance, equilibrium, poise, self-control, wisdom, knowledge, discretion, discrimination, foresight, intuition well developed, etc., one who has found his right calling and place in the world, and who can keep quiet, work, persist and endure in his work, can usually pass thru the critical days of life unharmed, can pilot his ship of life safely thru the troubled waters of earth existence, and be a master of his destiny. The critical days and times in life, the evil planetary aspects from day to day, etc., are more apt to overtake, weaken, discourage, or ruin the one who is drifting along thru life, like a ship without control or a pilot, and who lacks knowledge of the scheme of things, the laws of the Universe, the philosophy of life and destiny, etc. The study of Astrology is one of the very important Guides in life, and to learn from it, and by a study of your own star map of birth, what the Will of the Higher Powers is for your life. (See Fate; "Free Will" under Will).

**Critical Degrees**—(See "Sensitive Degrees" under Zodiac. Also see Azimene, Degrees).

**Critical Disposition**—(See Scolding, Virgo).

**Critical Epochs In Life**—Are under the rule of the ☽. (See Climacteric, Periods, Years).

**Critical Illnesses**—(See Dangerous, Fatal, Fierce, Grievous; "High Fevers" under Fever; Heavy, Incurable, Malignant, Morbid, Mortal, Rapid, Serious, Severe, Sharp, Swift, Vehement, Violent, Virulent, Wastings etc.).

**Critical Periods**—In Life—(See Climacteric, Periods, Years; "Critical Epochs" in this section).

**Critical Years**—(See Climacteric, Periods, Years).

**Hypercritical**—(See Petulant).

**CRITICUS PRIMUS**—The 14th day of a fever, the second crisis. (See "Acute Diseases" under Crises).

**CROOKED**—Not Straight—Irregular—Ill-Shaped—Incurvating—Imperfect—Bent, etc.—

**Crooked Body**—Denoted by ♄, and the ♄ sign ♑ on the Asc.; ☽ Sig. ☐ or ☍ ♄; the ☐ and ☍ aspects of the ☽ tend to a badly made and ugly body; ♄ ♋ partile asp. the Asc.; ♂ ♋ partile Asc., crooked, short, and ill-made; ☿ ♑ partile the Asc., often crooked; ♉, ♑, and ♓ give. For further influences see "Ill-Formed" under Ill. Also see Azimene, Bent, Broken, Contortions, Defects, Deformed, Distortions, Feet, Incurvating, Knees, Legs, Malformations, Paralysis, Spine, Stooped, Ugly.

**Crooked Knees**—(See Knees).

**Crooked Legs**—(See the various paragraphs under Legs. Also see "Knock Knees" under Knees).

**Crooked Shoulders**—(See Shoulders).

**Crooked Signs**—♉, ♋, ♑, and ♓. The ☽ or Asc. in one of these signs at B., and affl. by malefics, the native tends to be crooked or imperfect. (See Azimene, Broken, Distortions; "Ill-Formed" under Ill; Imperfect, Mutilated).

**Crooked Teeth**—(See Teeth).

**CROPS**—Destruction of—(See Corn, Drought, Famine, Fruit, Scarcity, Vegetation, Wheat).

**CROSSED EYES**—Squint—(See "Strabismus." under Eyes).

**Crosses**—(See Complications).

**CROTON OIL**—A typical drug of ♅. (See "Typical Drugs" under Uranus).

**CROUP**—A ♉ disease, and afflictions in ♉; the ☽ hyleg in ♉, and afflicted, and espec. with females; ♄ or ☿ affl. in ♉; ♄ ♉ and affl., membranous deposits in croup; many planets in fixed signs, and espec. in ♉ or ♏; Subs at LCP (6th C), and SP (7th D). Case—See No. 1, Chap. 13, page 86 in Daath's Medical Astrology. (See Angina, Diphtheria, Dyspnoea, Larynx, Pneumonia, Trachea).

**Croupous Pneumonia**—(See Pneumonia).

**CRUCIFIXION**—Death By—(See Impalement).

**CRUEL**—Harsh—Severe—Pitiless—Inflicting Mental or Physical Pain—Unfeeling—Without Mercy—Brutish—The ☽ Sig. ☐ or ☍ ♂; the ☽ at full, or incr. in light in a nocturnal geniture, sepr. from ♀ and applying to ♂, tends to cruel persons in great power, but subject to many dangers; ♂ and ☿ lords of the employment, and if ♂ be stronger than ☿, the native will be more violent and wickedly inclined, and engage in cruel practices; ♂ affl. in ♈; ♂ Sig. in ☐ or ☍ ♄, and vice versa; ☿ Sig. ☐ or ☍ ♂; the ♉ influences, when afflicted, or containing ♂, tend to make one abusive and unfeeling; the brutish signs ♌, and the 2nd half of ♐, when on the Asc., or afflicted, tend to make the native cruel and brutish; the 22° and 28° of ♏ on the Asc.; the 2° and 6° ♑ on the Asc. (See Assassins, Beastly, Brutish, Destructiveness, Fierce, Inhuman, Irrational, Masochism, Merciless, Murderous, Prison, Profane, Pity, Raving, Savage, Violent, etc.).

**Cruel Complexion**—Cruel Countenance—♂ Sig. □ or ☍ ♂, and vice versa.

**Death from Cruelty**—Death from Cruel Treatment—Case—See "Popejoy", No. 771, in 1001 N.N.

**Surgeons**—(See "Unfeeling" under Surgeons).

**CRUSHED**—Mashed—Pressed—

**Accidents By**—Injury or Death By, or by Being Buried Alive—Caused by ♄; ♄ in an earthy sign, and to the ill-asp. the Asc. by dir., and ♄ holding the dominion of death; ♄ in ♉, ♍, or ♑, ☌ or ill-asp. the Asc. by dir.; ♄ affl. the hyleg by dir., or when in the M.C., or close to the Asc. at B.; ♄ the afflicting planet, and in a violent sign, and affl. the hyleg by dir.; the ☉ hyleg, and to the ☌ or ill-asp. ♄ by dir.; ♅ or ♄ in ♈, ♋, ♎, or ♑, in the 4th H., and ☌ or ill-asp. the ☉ or ♂. (See Avalanches; Burial, Earthquakes; "Buildings" under Falls; Mobs; "Death" under Suffocation; Trampled). Cases—Death by Being Crushed—See "Crushed", No. 686, and "Pressed to Death", No. 626, in 1001 N.N.

**CRUSTS**—A Dried Mass of Exudate on the Skin—(See Corns, Decay, Excretion, Exudate, Favus, Gangrene, Hardening, Scabs, Scales, Skin, Sloughing, Sores; "Crusts under Tissues; Wastes).

**CRYING**—Shedding of Tears over Sorrows or Troubles—(See "Crying" under Tears).

**CRYSTAL GAZING**—(See Clairvoyance, Mediumship, Psychic).

**CRYSTALLIZATION**—The Formation of Crystals—Hardening—The work of ♄, the ☽, and the ♑ sign. A principle of ♄. Renal Stones and Gravel are crystallizations, carried on by ♄ by virtue of his exaltation in ♎, the kidney sign. Also ♄ crystallizes Gall Stones, furnishes the mineral deposits which harden the Bones. Hardness, density, strength, and resistance in the tendons and cartilages are given by ♄. All crystallization is the effect of the electric action of the planets, whether in the body or in the mineral world. Rock, Coal, Lead, etc. are the crystallizations of ♄ in Nature. Up to a certain point the crystallizing work of ♄ in the body is normal, but ♄ also has his pathological action in the body by causing too much crystallization by his afflictions, and causing disease, such as Stone, Hardening of the Arteries, hard Tumors containing mineral deposits, such as Goiter, and also by crystallizing the Nerves and Muscles. After middle age the body begins to crystallize more rapidly, and when at last it is so hardened as to lose its elasticity, death comes to the body, and the separation of its vehicles. The action of the ☽ is also crystallizing, and the ☽ is a hard, crystal body, incapable of sustaining animal life or vegetation. Crystallization is also the result of Cold, and Cold Diseases tend to abnormal and pathological crystallization. Cauda (☋), the Dragon's Tail, also exerts a ♄ influence along this line. ♄ in any sign tends to more rapid crystallization in the part, or organ, ruled by the sign he is in, and espec. after middle life, but it may be earlier in life if ♄ is badly afflicted, and also the afflictor in the disease, holding the dominion of death, etc. Thus ♄ in ♊ tends to crystallization in the lungs; ♄ in ♎, to crystallizations in the kidneys; ♄ ☌ ♃, to crystallization and hardening of the arteries, etc. (See Arteries, Bile, Bones, Cold, Concretions, Condensation, Congestion, Consolidation, Density, Deposits, Elimination, Eyes, Fiber, Goiter, Gout, Gravel, Hardening, Lameness, Lime, Minerals, Muscles, Nerves, Obstructions, Optic Nerve, Osseous, Retention, Rheumatism, Rigidity, Sand, Saturn, Stone, Suppressions, Tumors, etc.). For crystallizations in the various organs and parts of the body, and as associated with the various diseases, if not mentioned in the preceding list, see the subject in the alphabetical arrangement.

**CULPEPPER**—"Culpepper's Herbal" is a large book giving the planetary rulership of Herbs, and is a good book for students to have, as it is quite exhaustive along the lines of Herbs, their use in the treatment of disease, and the best times to gather them to get their best medicinal values. (See Herbs).

**CUPRUM**—(See Copper).

**CURABLE**—Cure—Cured—Cure of Disease—

**Curable Diseases**—Convertible Diseases—A disease is more curable when the afflictions are in the cardinal or common signs, as the influences of these signs are more flexible and amenable to treatment and a cure, but when in the fixed signs tend to be incurable, or greatly prolonged. However, if a disease is allowed to run its course, no matter from what kind of signs the afflictions may be, the disease may become chronic, and espec. if the mind and temperament are too weak to throw off the trouble, as is the case with many negative people. (See Negative). Disease is more curable if the benefics are with the malefics, or ori., angular, and cast any ray to the Lights, but if the benefics do not lend any assistance, or are weak, the disease tends to be incurable. The absence of malefics with the ☉ and ☽ in angles, and the benefics giving a good aspect, tends to hope of a cure, and the alleviation of the disease. Also if the 6th H. is free from afflictions there is more hope of a cure. (For further influences as to when a disease is curable, or incurable, see in the alphabetical arrangement the disease subject you have in mind, such as "Curable" under Cramps, Epilepsy, Fits, Insanity, etc.).

**Curable Mental Disease**—(See Conspicuous; "Curable", and "Incurable" under Brain).

**Cure of Disease**—Afflictions from the fixed signs are difficult to remedy. From the common signs are more amenable to treatment. From cardinal signs are more acute and transient, and may be quickly broken or cured. (See "Curable" in this section. Also see Native Land. Prognosis; "Cure of the Sick" under Sick; Treatment).

**Cured But Has Relapse**—(See Relapse).

**Difficult to Cure**—(See Chronic, Grievous, Incurable; "Sure Death" under Death). For collateral study see Antipathy, Cardinal, Complications, Constancy, Continuity, Course, Crises, Death, Duration, Environment, Fatal, Fixed Signs, Healers, Incurable, Influenced, Lingering, Malignant Medicines, Moderation, Majority, Mutable, Native Land, Nature, Negative, Opposites, Polarity, Positive, Praeincipients, Prolonged, Recovery, Relapse, Remedies, Return, Short Diseases (see Short), Subluxations, Sure Death (see Death), Sympathy, Tedious, Treatment, Vehement, Vertebrae, Violent, etc.

**CURIOUS**—

**Curious Death**—(See Extraordinary).

**Curious Diseases**—(See Mysterious, Strange).

**Curious Forebodings**—(See Forebodings).

**Curious Studies**—(See Occult).

**CURSED**—Cursed by the Multitude—(See Execrated).

**CURTAILED**—Shortened—Modified—

**Disease**—The Disease Is Curtailed—(See Amelioration, Course; "Better" under Disease; Duration, Modification, Recovery, Recuperation, Resolution, Short, Solution, etc.).

**CURVATURE**—Of the Spine—Kyphosis—(See Curvature, Humpback, Pott's Curvature, Tubercular, under Spine).

**CUTANEOUS**—Pertaining to the Skin. (See Skin).

**Cutaneous Asphyxia**—(See "Cutaneous" under Asphyxia).

**Cutaneous Diseases**—(See Eruptions, Skin).

**Cutaneous Inflammation**—(See "Inflammation" under Skin).

**Cutaneous Spots**—(See Moles).

**CUTICLE**—The Epidermis or Scarf Skin—Ruled by ♄. (See "Epidermis" under Skin).

**CUTIS**—The Derma—Corium—The True Skin—(See Derma, Skin).

**Hemorrhages Into**—(See Purpura).

**CUTS**—Incised Wounds—Knife Wounds—Stabs—Injuries by Sharp Instruments, the Sword, etc.—♂ afflictions predispose to, as ♂ is the instigator of quarrels, disputes and violence. The ☉ and ♂ both tend to incised wounds and injuries, as they are the positive, electric, and caloric-producing planets. ♂ in the Asc. at B., liable to; ♂ in the 8th H. at B., and affl. the ☉, ☽, or hyleg; ♂ □ or ☍ the ☉; ♂ by dir. ☌ or evil asp. the ☉, ☽, Asc., or M.C.; ♂ ruler at B., ruler of the Asc.; people born under the strong influence of ♂; the ☉ or ☽ ori., and affl. by ♂; the ☉ or ☽ in fire signs; the ☉ affl. by ♂; the ☉ or ☽ to the ☌ or ill-asp. ♂ by dir.; the Prog. ☉ or ☽ to the ☌, □, or ☍ ♂; the Asc. to the ☌ or evil asp. ♂ dir., and espec. if ♂ is in a fiery sign; the Asc. to the place of the Pleiades, Hyades, or Castor; Fixed Stars of the nature of ♂ ascending at B. (See the various paragraphs in this section).

**Absent Party**—Cuts or Stabs To—(See "Weapons" in this section).

**Arms, Hands, Shoulders**—Slight Cuts To—♂ in ♊; ☿ in ill-asp. to ♂. (See "Accidents" under Arms; "Cuts" under Hands).

**Danger of Cuts**—Liable To—Predisposed To—(See the first part of this section).

**Death by Cuts**—By Stabs, Daggers, Wounds, Sword, Sharp Instruments, etc.—♂ with Aldebaran, and ♂ in □ or ☍ the ☉, and ♂ just setting at B.; ♂ the afflicting planet in a violent sign, and affl. the hyleg; the ☽ to the ☌ or ill-asp. ♂ by dir. (See "Death" under Duels, Stabs, Sword).

**Face**—Cuts To—(See "Cuts" under Face).

**Hands**—Cuts To—(See "Arms" in this section).

**Hips and Thighs**—Cuts To—(See Hips).

**Instruments**—Cuts by Sharp Instruments—(See Instruments. Also note the various paragraphs in this section).

**Lameness from Cuts**—Or Stabs—♂ in ♐, on the Asc., from accidents to the hips or thighs; ♂ in ♑, ♒, or ♓, from cuts to lower limbs, knees, or feet. (See Distortions).

**Murdered**—By Cuts or Stabs—(See Assassinated, Murdered, Stabs).

**Operations**—Rules for Time of, and Making Incisions—(See Operations).

**Paralysis**—From Cuts—Or Stabs—(See Distortions).

**Severe Cuts**—The ☉ or ☽ ori., and affl. by ♂. (See Severe).

**Shoulders**—Cuts To—(See "Arms" in this section).

**Slight Cuts**—To Arms or Hands—(See "Arms" in this section).

**Surgery**—(See Operations).

**Sword**—Cuts By—(See Duels, Sword, War).

**Throat**—Cuts His Own Throat—Suicide By—(See "Cuts" under Throat).

**Travel**—Journeys—Voyages—Cuts or Stabs During—♂ in the 3rd or 9th H. at B., and affl. the ☉ or ☽ at B., or by dir.

**Violent Death**—By Cuts—(See "Death" in this section. Also see Violent).

**Voyages**—Cuts On—(See "Travel" in this section).

**Weapons**—Cuts by Sharp Weapons—♂ in the 8th H. at B., or by dir., and affl. the ☉, ☽, Asc., or Hyleg; ♂ in the 8th H. in a Hor'y Map, and affl. the ☉, ☽, or Asc., indicates the absent party may be wounded by cuts or stabs. (See Instruments, Iron, Sword). For collateral study see Accidents, Assassination; "Shedding" under Blood; Blows, Contests, Enemies, Falls, Hurts, Injuries, Iron, Lacerations, Mobs, Murdered; "Death" under Quarrels; Riots,

Robbers, Stabs; "Flying Stones" under Stones; Suicide, Sword, Violence, War, Wounds, etc.

**CYANOSIS**—Blue Discoloration of the Skin and Nails—Nonoxygenation of the Blood—Afflictions in ♌ or ♒; ♄ affl. in ♌; many planets in fixed signs. (See Asphyxia, Breathing, Circulation, Nails, Oxygen. Case—See "Male", Chap. 8, page 48, in Daath's Medical Astrology.

**CYCLES**—(See Climacteric, Crises, Critical, Periodic, Periodicity, Periods, Years). Good books on the Law of Cycles are "Periodicity", by Dr. James Buchanan, and the book, "The Law of Cycles", published by the Aryan Theosophical Press, Point Loma, Calif.

**CYCLOPS**—A Monster with Eyes Fused Into One. The following influences have been noted to exist in the natal maps of these cases,—The ☉ and ☽ in the 6th or 12th H., and affl. by ♅, ♄, and ♂; ♅, ♄, and ♂ in the 5th, 6th, or 12th H., or afflicting these houses, or the cusp of Asc.; ♅, ♄, and ♂ in fixed signs in ☌ or ☍ asp.; ♉, ♏, or ♑ on the Asc.; many planets in ♍ in the 6th or 12th H., and afflicted. Case—See "Male", Chap. 8, page 48 in Daath's Medical Astrology. (See Congenital, Deformities, Monsters, Prenatal Epoch).

**CYNOSURA**—A Northern Constellation —Ursa Minor—The Little Bear—Is

mentioned in Wilson's Dictionary several times as having an evil influence. (See "Much Evil" under Evil; "Much Sickness" under Sickness; Thieves).

**CYSTITIS**—(See "Cystitis" under Bladder).

**CYSTS**—A Membranous Sac containing Fluid.

**Arms**—Cysts in the Arms, Hands, Legs and Feet—(See Aneurysm, Vesicles).

**Brain**—(See "Cyst" under Brain).

**Breast**—Cyst of—♀ affl. in ♋; ♀ in ♋ in the 6th H., and afflicted; ♀ afflicting the ☽ or Asc. (See Breast).

**Disorders**—Disorders Attended with Cysts—♀ diseases.

**Hollow**—Cystic and Hollow Tumor Formations—♀ diseases.

**Hydatid Cysts**—Caused by ♃ affl. in ♓. (See "Cyst" under Brain).

**Sebaceous Cysts**—(See Fat, Wen).

**Steatoma**—(See Wen).

**Tongue**—Cystic Tumor under the Tongue—Ranula—(See "Cystic Tumor" under Tongue).

**Wen**—A Sebaceous Cyst—(See Wen).

**CYTOPLASTEMA**—The Cytoplastema— To ♆ belongs cell development in a plastic fluid, the Cytoplasm, and independent of other cells. (See "Cytoplastema" under Cells; Plastic).

# D

**DAMPNESS**—(See Exposure, Moisture, Vapors, Water, Wet).

**DANCING**—Dancing Spasm—(See "Saltatory" under Spasmodic; "Dancing" under Sports).

**DANGER**—Dangers—Perils—The malefic planets strong at B., and affl. the ☉, ☽, Asc., or hyleg, predispose to unusual dangers all thru life, and espec. when the Asc. is afflicted by evil directions; the ☽ Sig. □ or ☍ ♂, passes thru innumerable dangers; the ☽ incr. in light, sepr. from ♃ and applying to ♂ in a nocturnal nativity; the ☽ with Antares or Aldebaran in the Asc. or M.C.; ♃ ruler of the 1st H., and to the ill-asps. ♄ by dir.; ♂ ☌ ☋; Comets appearing in ♏ tend to great perils generally. (For further influences see the various paragraphs in this section). For the dangers and afflictions which accompany the various diseases, and when the disease may become dangerous, and for the dangers which any organ, or part of the body may be subject to, see in the alphabetical arrangement the subject you have in mind. Also note the alphabetical list at the end of this Article, which deals with sources of danger, the kinds of danger, and the classes of people especially subject to dangers and perils in their various phases. Death of the body is the ultimate result of all dangers, and for the various kinds and causes of death, and the dangers contributing to death, see the various

paragraphs under Death, Disease, and also in this section. Here are a few of the more abstract subjects concerning danger—

**Beset with Dangers**—♆ affl. in the 12th H.

**Dreams of Danger**—(See Dreams).

**Fond of Danger**—People born under strong ♂ influence, as with ♂ in the Asc. or M.C., or ♂ rising in one of his own signs in ☌ with the ☉, ☽, or Asc., or ♂ rising and ruler of the Asc., etc., such tend to be fond of danger, risks, and exposures.

**Great Dangers**—(See "Many" in this section).

**Great Perils Generally**—Comets appearing in ♏.

**Has Endured Many Dangers**—(See Escapes, Foolhardy).

**Many Dangers**—Subject To—The ☉ Sig. ☌ ♂ and ♂ ill-dig.; the ☉ or ☽ to the place of Antares; the ☽ to the □ or ☍ the ☉ by dir., great dangers; the ☽ with Antares or Aldebaran in the 1st or 10th H.; ♂ Sig. □ or ☍ ♄, meets with much danger and suffering, or a violent death, and espec. if ♄ be stronger than ♂ (see "Short Life" under Life; "Death" under Violent); Antares, Aldebaran, Regulus, Deneb, Frons Scorpio, or the Shoulders of Orion, when directed to the ☉, ☽, or Asc., bring danger, violence, trouble, or sickness. (See Perils, Precarious, Sickness, Trouble).

**Near Some Danger**—♄, ♂, or ☋ in the Asc. or 7th H., peregrine, R, or in detriment, some danger or misfortune near according to the quality of the Significators, and of the houses those planets are lords of which afflict the ☽ (Hor'y). (See Imminent: "Some Misfortune Near" under Misfortune).

**Premonition of Danger**—Fear of—(See Calamity; "Danger" under Fear).

**Rushes Into Danger**—Born under ♂. (See "Fond of" in this section).

**Secret Dangers** (See Ambushes; "Secret Enemies" under Enemies; "Poison Death" under Poison; Treachery).

**Sudden Dangers**—(See "Danger" under Sudden).

**Unknown Danger**—Fear of—(See "Danger" under Fear). For further influences along the lines of Danger, see the following subjects,—Abroad, Accidents, Acquaintance, Aeroplanes, Air, Animals, Assassins, Aunts, Bathings, Beasts, Bloodshed (see Blood); Blows, Brethren, Brothers, Bruises, Buildings, Buried Alive (see Burial); Burns, Calamity, Cattle, Childhood, Children, Cold, Criminals, Crushed, Cuts, Dampness, Dangerous, Daughter, Desert, Directions, Disaster, Disease, Disgrace, Drink, Drowning, Duels, Earth, Earthquakes, Eclipse, Electricity, Employment, Enemies, Escapes, Events, Execution, Explosions, Exposures, External, Extraordinary, Falls, Father, Females, Fire, Fire Arms, Floods, Food, Foreign Lands, Friends, Great Men (see Great); Gunshot, Hanging, Heat, Heights, Highwaymen, Homicide, Honor, Husband, Impalement, Imprisonment, Infancy, Injuries, Insects, Instruments, Intoxication, Journeys, Kings, Life, Lightning, Liquids, Machinery, Males, Members, Men, Middle Life, Military, Mischief, Misfortune, Moisture, Monarchs, Mother, Murder, Navigation, Nobles, Old Age, Operations, Parents, Peculiar, Perils, Periods (Danger Periods); Pirates, Plots, Poison, Presidents, Princes, Quadrupeds, Quarrels, Railroads, Rain, Relatives, Reptiles, Reputation, Rescues, Reversals, Robbers, Ruin, Rulers, Sailors, Scalds, Scandal, Sea, Seduction, Sharp Instruments (see Instruments); Ships, Shipwreck, Short Journeys (see Journeys); Sister, Sons, Stabs, Storms, Suffocation, Suicide, Surgeons, Sword, Thieves, Travel, Treachery, Uncles, Vehicles, Venomous, Volcanoes, Voyages, War, Water, Weapons, Weather, Wife, Wind, Women, Wounds, Young, Youth, etc. (For subjects not listed here look for them in the alphabetical arrangement).

**DANGEROUS**—Fierce—Savage—Vicious—Violent, etc.

**Accidents**—(See "Dangerous" under Accidents).

**Chronic Diseases**—(See "Dangerous" under Chronic).

**Community and Society**—Dangerous To—(See Anarchists).

**Dangerous Accidents**—(See Accidents).

**Destructiveness**—Dangerous Destructiveness—(See Anarchists, Destructiveness).

**Disease Not Dangerous**—Lord of the Asc. strong, angular, and not afflicted, the disease is not dangerous. (See Course, Crises; "Better" under Disease).

**Disposition**—Dangerous—(See Beastly, Cruel, Fierce, Savage, Temper).

**Fevers**—Dangerous Fevers—(See "Dangerous" under Fevers).

**Illness**—Dangerous Illness—(See "High Fever" under Fever; Fierce, Grievous, Rapid, Severe, Sharp, Vehement, Violent, etc.).

**Internal Disease** Dangerous—(See "Women" under Internal).

**Lunatics**—(See "Dangerous" under Insanity).

**Operations**—Surgical—(See "Dangerous" under Operations).

**Periods**—Dangerous Periods in Life—(See Climacteric, Crises, Critical; "Menopause" under Menses; Parturition, Periods, Puberty, Years, etc.).

**Sickness**—Dangerous Sickness—(See "Illness" in this section).

**DARK**—Darkened—

**Air**—Dark Air—(See "Corrupt" under Air).

**Black**—(See Black).

**Brunettes**—(See "Dark" under Complexion; "Black" and "Dark" under Hair).

**Brown**—Dark Brown—(See "Dark" under Hair).

**Complexion**—Dark Complexion—(See "Dark" under Complexion).

**Darkened Desires**—(See "Darkened" under Mind).

**Degrees**—The Dark Degrees of the Zodiac—(See "Dark Degrees" under Zodiac).

**Eyes**—Dark Eyes—(See "Dark" under Eyes).

**Figure**—Dark Personal Figure—♄ indicates a person of a black, earthy, or brown complexion; ♄ occi. at B. Predominant in people born under Southern Parallels, and who have the ☉ continually in their Zenith, and are scorched by his rays. (See Black, Negro).

**Hair**—(See "Black", "Dark", under Hair).

**Marks**—Dark Marks on Body—(See "Dark" under Marks).

**Mind Darkened**—(See Mind).

**Races**—Dark Races—(See "Figure" in this section).

**DARKNESS**—Governed by ♄.

**Fear of the Dark**—Fear in Solitude—♆ affl. the ☽ or ☿; ♆ afflicted in one of the houses of mind, as in the 3rd or 9th H., and also in the 8th H., more liable to obsessions and morbid fears. (See Claustrophobia; "Morbid", "Solitude" under Fears). Case—See "Strange Case", No. 379 in 1001 N.N.

**DAUGHTER—**

**A Daughter Born**—A Daughter Promised—(See "Birth of a Female" under Female; "First-born Child" under Children).

**Danger to a Daughter**—Ill-Health of—Damage To—The M.C. to the ill-asps. the ☽ or ♀ by dir.; the ☽ to the place of Hercules by dir., damage to.

**Death To**—Danger of—(See Eclipse; "Death" under Females, Women).

**Ill-Health Of**—(See "Danger" in this section. See "Ill-health" under Females; "Women" under Misfortune).

**DAY**—Diurnal—The Daytime—Day Nativities, etc. The Daytime is electric, and ruled by the ☉, and the influence of the ☉ by day is to restore the vitality, and destroy morbid germs. (See Magnetic). The day is more vitalizing than the night. The ☽ rules the night. (See Elevated, Magnetic, Night).

**Blindness**—(See "Day Blindness" under Blindness).

**Day Dreamer**—(See Dreamy).

**Day of Death**—(See "Day", "Hour", "Time", under Death).

**Death by Day**—(See "Wild Animals" under Animals).

**Disease by Day**—The Disease Is Better or Worse by Day—♄ or ♂ by Day in Disease—♂ is more malignant by day as the ☉ adds to his heat and dryness. ♄ is less malignant by day as the ☉ moderates his coldness. Thus ♄ is less malignant in day nativities, and ♂ more so. However, as Anareta, ♄ and ♂ are equally destructive whether by day or night. (See Epilepsy, Fits, Insanity, Night).

**Insanity by Day**—When Caused in a Day Nativity—(See the ♄ and ♂ influences under Insanity).

**Pain**—The Pain Less by Day—(See "Pain" under Night).

**Parents**—(See "Day" under Parents).

**Patient Better by Day**—Better by Day—Worse at Night—(See Magnetic; "Diseases", "Pain", "Worse" under Night).

**Signs**—Diurnal Signs—(See "Nocturnal Signs" under Night).

**DAYS—**

**Critical Days**—(See Crises, Critical).

**Days of the Week**—(See Week).

**Hour of the Day**—Best Hour to Give Medicines—(See "Hours" under Planets).

**Treatment**—Best Days and Times For in Individual Cases—(See "Days of the Week" under Week).

**DEAD—Deadly—**

**Absent Party is Dead**—(See "Dead" under Absent).

**Corpse**—(See Corpse).

**Deadly Diseases**—(See "Fatal Illness" under Fatal).

**Fugitive is Dead**—(See Fugitive).

**Tissue**—Crusts of Dead Tissue. (See Crusts, Gangrene, Hardening, Scales; "Crusts" under Tissues).

**Womb**—Dead in the Womb—(See Stillborn).

**DEAFNESS**—(See "Deafness", and the various paragraphs under Hearing).

**Deaf and Dumb**—(See "Deaf and Dumb" under Hearing. Also see Mute.

**DEATH**— Dissolution—The Terminus Vitae. The 8th H. is known as the House of Death, and the death dealing forces act the strongest thru this house. The 4th, 8th and 12th Houses are called the Terminal Houses, and have to do with the close and end of life, and the death of the physical body. (See Fourth, Eighth, Twelfth, Terminal). The ♏ Sign, affiliated with the 8th H., is said to give the death sting, and the malefic planets, ♄ and ♂ to cut the Silver Cord. (See "Silver Cord" under Silver). The general influence of ♄ especially is to bring death of the body by his afflictions to the Hyleg. ♄ is called the Planet of Death. He is The Tester, Father Time, and it is his business to ultimately separate the Soul from its earthly vehicle, and set the Soul free. ♄ is the principal Significator of death by disease, and ♂ by accident or violence. The Benefics do not of themselves cause death, and even their evil aspects will often avert death when they fall in a train of evil directions. However, the Benefics, when holding the dominion of death, do largely contribute to the causes leading to death. (See Saturn, Mars, Jupiter and Venus Influences. Also see Scorpio). The New Moon implies decay, disintegration, and death, and the preparation for a new cycle, and is the low ebb of the physical forces. (See "New Moon" under Moon). The Killing Place is called the Anareta, and death depends upon the one, or more, killing planets which occupy an Anaretic Place at B. (See Anareta). The ☐ aspect by direction from the Killing Planet to the hyleg is known as the Killing Arc. The Diseases and Afflictions which tend to cause, produce, contribute to, and be the immediate cause of death of the physical body, are legion in number, and too numerous to list here. For Death by the various diseases, see the disease subject in the alphabetical arrangement. For death by Accidents, Bruises, Blows, Hurts, Injuries, Violence, Wounds, etc., see the various headings under these subjects. Only the more abstract subjects concerning death will be listed and considered here, such as Arguments for, Causes, Kinds, Manner, Quality, etc., and also a number of subjects listed for your attention, which you might overlook. See "Death" under the following subjects in the alphabetical arrangement when not more fully considered here, which subjects have to do with death, causes of death, the manner, time or place of death, death to others, death by others, etc.—

**Abortion; Abroad; Absent Party**—(See Absent).

**Accidents**—Accidental Death—(See Accidents).

**Acquaintance; Adversary**—Death By—Death of—(See Enemies).

**Aeroplanes; Aged People**—(See Old Age).

**Air**—(See Air, Gases).

**Ambushes; Amputations**—(See Operations).

**Anareta**—The Killing Planet—(See Anareta. Also see "Arguments" in this section).

**Animals**—Death By—Death of—(See Animals, Beasts).

**Arguments for Death**—Danger of Death—Death Threatened—The Causes of Death—The Life in Danger, etc.— The influences in this paragraph are given in the following order,—☉, ☽, ♆, ♅, ♄, ♃, ♂, ♀, ☿, ☋, Asc., M.C., 4th H., 6th H., 8th H., 12th H., Fixed Stars, Eclipses, Hyleg, Anareta, Directions. SUN—The ☉ by his ill-aspects to the ☽ or Asc. acts like ♂, and assists in causing death; the ☉ to the □ his own place by dir., almost certain and sure death; the ☉ and hyleg both badly afflicted at same time increases the danger; the ☉ hyleg ☌ ♅ as Anareta in the 8th H., and the ☉ to the ☌ or ill-asp. ♅ by dir.; ☉ to the place of Aldebaran; the ☉ hyleg, and to the ☌ or ill-asp. ♄ or ♂ by dir., and espec. if ♄ or ♂ rule the 6th, 8th, or 12th H., and either of them be Anareta; the ☉ to the evil asps. the ☽ if the direction falls in the 8th H., or the ☉ or ☽ rule the 8th, and are radically afflicted by ♄ or ♂ ruler of the 8th; evil directions of the ☉ to the ☽ or Asc. when they are hyleg; the ☉ to the P. asp. ♄ in the Zodiac by direct or converse motion; an eclipse of the ☉ falling in the same degree held by the ☉ at B., and with the ☉ strongly afflicted at B., or by dir., and the hyleg also affl. by malefics; the ☉ lord of the 8th H. at B., and affl., and the ☉ to the evil asps. the Asc. by dir.; adverse asps. of the ☉ to ♄, ♂, ♅ or ♆ by dir., and espec. among the aged and those frail of constitution; the ill-asps. of several malefic promittors to the ☉ tend to double or treble the danger to life, cause breakdown in health, disaster, or death; the ☉ in the 6th or 8th H. at B., and to the ☌ or ill-asp. ♄ by dir.; the ☉ and ☽ both affl. by ♄ in an angle; the ☉ in the 4th H. with ♄ or the ☽ in the 4th H. with ♂; the ☉, the Light of Time, ☌ or ill-asp. ♄ lord of the 6th, in fixed signs when taken ill; the ☉ in the 8th H., or with the lord of the 7th by dir. at the time of the illness; in female horoscopes the ☉ causes death by severe illnesses and feverish disorders. (See "Death" under Sun). MOON—The ☽ hyleg and affl., and to the cusp the 8th H. by dir.; the ☽ hyleg, and in evil asp. to ♄, ♂, or ☿ threatens death; the ☽ weak and affl. at B., and ☌ the cusp the 4th H. by dir.; ☽ to the □ or ☍ ♄ or ♂ by dir., and espec. if the ☽ be hyleg; prog. ☽ ☌ ♄ in 8th H., and ♄ affl. the hyleg at B.; the ☽ sepr. from the ☉ and applying to ☿ in a night nativity; the ☽ at Full, or increasing in a night nativity, sepr. from ♀ and applying to ♂ (Hor'y); the ☽ at a Solar Rev. passing the place of ♂ at B., and the ☽ affl. at the Rev.; the ☽ to the □ or ☍ ☿ if the ☽ be hyleg, and ☿ affl. at B.; the ☽ applying to the ☍ ♂ in the 8th H., and when in exact ☍; the ☽ hyleg, and to the ☌ the ☉ by dir., and the ☉ and ☽ affl. at B.; the ☽ affl. at B., and to the ☌, P, or ill-asp. the Asc. by dir.; the ☽ hyleg, and to the ☌ or ill-asp. ♄ by dir., and espec. if the direction fall in the 6th or 12th H.; the ☽ hyleg, and to the ☌ or ill-asp. ♂ by dir.; the ☽ to the ☌ or P. Dec. the ☉ if the ☽ be hyleg and the ☉ affl. at B.; the ☽ to the ☌ or P. Dec. Aldebaran, Antares, or Regulus, if the ☽ be hyleg; the ☽ Sig., applying to the ☌ the ☉, is in danger of death, and espec. if it happen in the 8th H., or the ☉ be lord of the 8th, but if sepr., the danger is not as great; the ☽ hyleg, and directed to the ☌ a malefic, and both with the same Lat.; the ☽ hyleg and affl. by ♄ from an angle by dir.; the ☽ near the cusp of the Asc. by dir., and in □ to ♂ in the 4th H.; the ☽ in the 8th H. by dir., and combust; the ☽ lady of the 6th H., and combust in the 1st or 4th H., and espec. if lord of the 8th be affl.; the ☽ hyleg and applying to the ☌ ☉, but not so evil when in ♈, ♎, or ♌; the ☽ in the 4th H. in asp. to ♄ in the 6th, and applying to the □ the ☉; ☽ affl. by a malefic in 1st H., the house of life; the ☽ sepr. from lord of the Asc., in signs of long ascension, and transferring her light to lords of the 4th or 8th; the ☽ leaving the ☍ ☉ and applying swiftly to the □ or ☍ ♂, threatens a fatal end; the ☽ and lord of the Asc. in ☌ lord of the 8th, and without the interposing good asps. of ♃ or ♀; ☽ affl., and applying to a planet in the 8th; ☽ ♈ when taken ill, and espec. if the ☽ leave the ☌ ♂ and go to the ☌ or ill-asp. ♄, or if the ☽ decr. in light, or be slow of motion; the prog. ☽ to the □ or ☍ her radical place, and espec. if affl. at B. by the ☌, □, or ☍ malefics. (See "Death" under Moon). NEPTUNE—♆ in evil asp. the hyleg, or Giver of Life, helps to destroy life. (See "Buried Alive" under Burial; "Death" under Neptune). URANUS—♅ does not kill of himself, but assists by his evil asps., and when affl. the hyleg; ♅ passing the place of ♂ at B. by transit, if affl. the ☉ at same time; ♅, ♄, or ♂ in the 1st or 7th H. in ☍ each other, or in mutual reception, or with the ☉ or ☽, death will be more certain; ♅ by Periodic Rev. to the evil asps. the hyleg; ♅ in the 8th H., and Anareta, the ☉ hyleg, and the ☉ to the ☌ or ill-asp. ♅; adverse asps. of ♅ to the ☉ by dir., and espec. among the aged and those of frail constitution; ♅ affl. the hyleg by dir. (See "Death" under Uranus). SATURN—♄ ☌, □, or ☍ the radical ☉ by dir.; ♄ affl. the hyleg at B., and by dir., and ♄ holding the dominion of death; ♄ in the 8th H. at B., and near the place of violent fixed stars. (See "Death" under Saturn. Also in this paragraph see the ☉, ☽, ♅, Asc., 6th, 8th and 12th H. influences). JUPITER—(See the Introduction to this Article, and the Moon influences in this paragraph. See the Introduction and "Death" under Jupiter). MARS—♂ in the Asc. at decumb., and the ☉ and ☽ and their dispositors affl.; ♂ by dir. to the ☌ or ill-asp. the Asc., and espec. if ♂ is Anareta. (See "Death" under Mars. Also see the influences of the

⊙, ☽, ♅, and Asc. in this paragraph). VENUS—(See "Death" under Venus. Also see the Moon influences in this paragraph). MERCURY—(See "Death" under Mercury. Also see the Moon influences in this paragraph). CAUDA—☋—The Dragon's Tail—Exerts much the same influence as ♄, and when the Sig. of death is very evil. (See Dragon). ASCENDANT—Lord of the Asc. in the 6th H., and lord of the 6th in the Asc., and one of them in changing signs meets the evil asps. of malefics, or lords of the 4th and 8th, and they slow in motion, and it be from signs in □ or ☍ to each other, the sick one usually dies (Hor'y); the Asc. to the cusp of the 4th H. by dir.; the Asc. to the □ ♄, and ♄ affl. the hyleg at same time; the Asc. to the ☌ ♄, or ♄ ☌ Asc. by primary dir.; very few deaths occur without some unusual and severe afflictions to the Asc. at B., or that which holds the Asc. by dir. at death; the Asc. affl. by ♄ by dir.; lord of the Asc. affl. by a malefic, or in ☍ the ⊙, or in ☌, □, or ☍ lord of the 8th, or in the 8th, combust or ℞, threatens death, and espec. if the Lights be afflicted; the Asc. affl. by the malefics, or having violent fixed stars near its cusp, and the nearer the cusp the greater the danger; the Asc. to the □ or ☍ ♄ or ♂ by dir.; lord of the Asc., or sign ascending, affl. by lord of the 8th, or a planet in the 8th, tends to be fatal, and death approaching; lord of the Asc. affl., and in the 8th, and the ☽ also weak and in no dignity; lord of the Asc. ☌ lord of the 4th, 6th, 8th, or 12th; lord of the Asc. combust in the Asc.; lord of the Asc. in the 4th, 6th, 8th, or 12th, and affl. by malefics; lord of the Asc. affl. by lords of the 6th or 12th, and lord of the Asc. in ♌ or ♒; lord of the Asc. conjoined with Antares, Caput Algol, Aldebaran, or with violent fixed stars; lord of the Asc. in the 8th, or with lord of the 8th, or lord of the 8th in the Asc. (See "First House" under First. Also see the ⊙, ☽, ♄, ♂, 6th, 8th, and 12th H. influences in this paragraph). MIDHEAVEN—M. C.—The M.C. affl. by the ☌ or ill-asp. ♄ by dir. (See "Tenth House" under Tenth). FOURTH HOUSE—The 4th H. is a Terminal House, and indicative of death and the end of life when severely afflicted during an illness, or at B.; lord of the 4th in the 6th, 8th, or 12th; lord of the 4th in ☍ the Asc. (See Terminal; "Fourth House" under Fourth. Also see the ⊙, ☽, Asc., 6th, 8th and 12th H. influences in this paragraph). SIXTH HOUSE—The 6th H. has no affinity with the Asc., and signifies loss of life. The ☽ lady of the 6th, and combust in the 1st or 4th, and espec. if lord of the 8th be affl.; the lord of the 4th in the 6th, and affl. (See "Sixth House" under Sixth. Also see the various influences of the ⊙, ☽, and all the planets and houses mentioned in this paragraph). EIGHTH HOUSE—Known as the House of Death, and espec. indicates the Manner, Kind, and Quality of death. A malefic passing thru the 8th, and affl. the place of the ⊙ or ☽ at B., or the place of the prog. ⊙ or ☽; the 8th H. has no affinity with the Asc.,

and signifies loss of life; lord of the 8th angular, and lord of the Asc. cadent, and espec. if lord of the 8th be a malefic; neither of the Fortunes will save life if the lords of the 8th and 6th are in evil asp. to each other; lord of the 8th crossing the cusp of the Asc. by transit; the ☽ transferring the light of lord of the 8th to the lord of the Asc.; lord of the 8th in the Asc., and in ill-asp. to lord of the Asc. under the earth, or if lord of the 8th and lord of the Asc. be in ☌ in the 4th; lord of the 8th in the 10th, and lord of the Asc. in the 4th, 6th, 8th, or 12th, and affl. by malefics; lord of the 8th in ☌ or ill-asp. the ☽; lord of the 8th in the 8th; malefic planets in the 8th, and affl. the hyleg; the ☽ applying to the □ or ☍ asp. the lord of the 8th, or the Sig. to the evil asps. the lord of the 8th; the Sig. applying to the ✶ the lord of the 8th, in signs of long ascension, have the same effect as the □ asp.; lord of the Asc. in the 8th, or with lord of the 8th. (See "Eighth House" under Eighth. Also see the various planetary and house influences in this paragraph). TWELFTH HOUSE — This house has no affinity with the Asc., and indicates death and loss of life. (See "Twelfth House" under Twelfth. Also see the various planetary and house influences in this paragraph). FIXED STARS—The fixed star Antares is productive of death when afflicting, or joined to the hyleg at B. (See Aldebaran, Algol, Antares, Regulus; "Fixed Stars" under Fixed; Stars. Also see the Moon influences in this paragraph). ECLIPSES —(See Eclipses. See the Eclipse influence under the Sun influences in this paragraph). HYLEG—Life is not destroyed unless the hyleg be severely afflicted, however evil the directions may be, altho the health may suffer greatly by the directions. (See the mention of the various afflictions to the hyleg under the ⊙, ☽, ♆, ♅, ♄ influences in this paragraph. Also see Hyleg). ANARETA—The △ asps. of the Anareta to the hyleg, in signs of short ascension, or the □ asps. in signs of long ascension, according to Ptolemy, will kill or threaten death; the Anareta ☌ or evil asp. the hyleg by dir. (See Anareta. Also see the mention of the Anareta among the ⊙, ♅ and Directions influences in this paragraph). DIRECTIONS—A train of evil directions afflicting the hyleg and the vital points of the map are necessary to produce death. The hyleg must be affl. by the ☌, P, □ or ☍ asp. of the killing, or Anaretical stars, and these also must be afflicted of themselves to cause death. To produce death there must be a combination of several evil directions to the hyleg, and without the aid or intervention of the Benefics to the Anaretic Places, or to the 4th H. One evil direction to the hyleg, however powerful, rarely destroys life. The hyleg evilly aspected at B., but supported by the Benefics, brings great danger of death under a train of evil directions to the hyleg, but with possibility of escape and mitigating influences, and espec. if the benefics give a good asp. to the hyleg at the time of the evil directions. (See Directions; "Danger to Life" under Life. Also see "Certain", "Symbols", in this section). Each of the Houses and Signs of the Zodiac also bear rule over certain diseases, and to contribute to death by these diseases, or afflictions, and for these influences see each of the Houses, and the Signs, in the alphabetical arrangement, in addition to the 4th, 6th, 8th, and 12th H. influences already given in this paragraph.

**Asphyxiation; Assassination;**

**Assaults; Aunt; Automobiles**—See Vehicles).

**Averted**—Death Averted—(See "Death" under Averted. Also note the influences of the Benefics under "Arguments" in this section).

**Bad End**—(See Beheaded, Execution, Hanging, Judges, Lynched, Suicide, Untimely, etc.).

**Bathings; Battle**—(See War).

**Beasts**—Death By—(See Animals, Beasts).

**Beheaded; Bereavement; Birth**—Death at Birth, or Soon After Birth—(See Abortion, Birth, Parturition).

**Bites; Blasts of Wind**—(See Wind).

**Blizzards; Blows; Born Alive**—Dies Soon After Birth—(See "Birth" in this section).

**Broken Heart**—Dies of—(See Broken).

**Bruises; Buildings**—By Fall of, or Falls from—(See "Buildings" under Falls).

**Burglars**—(See Robbers, Thieves).

**Burial; Burns**—Burned at Stake—(See Burns).

**Calamity; Casualties; Catalysis;**

**Cattle; Causes His Own Death**—♀ ruler of the 8th H., or ♀ in this house and afflicted, and usually caused by dissipation, debauchery, indiscretions, or quarrels in love affairs; the 2nd dec. of ♏ on the Asc.; lords of the 1st and 8th being the same planet, as when ♎ is on the Asc., and ♉ on the 8th, or when ♈ is on the Asc., and ♏ on cusp the 8th, and the death is usually the result of intemperance, dissipation, etc., when ♀ rules, or by contests, duels, quarrels, rashness, suicide, violence, etc., when ♂ rules the two cusps or houses. (See these subjects).

**Causes of Death**—(See "Arguments", and the various paragraphs in this section).

**Certain Death**—Death More Certain—Death Inevitable—Sure Death, etc.—The ☉ to the □ his own place by dir.; the ☽ and lords of the 1st and 8th in the 6th; the ☽ or lord of the Asc. apply by evil asp. to lord of the 8th, and the latter a malefic; Antares or Caput Algol ascending tends to be fatal; lord of the 1st in the 8th, and lord of the 8th in the 1st, renders death inevitable; the Anareta in the 4th H., death is certain; lords of the 4th and 6th, or lords of the 8th and 6th, in reception or in evil asp. each other denotes death. (See "Arguments", "Fatal", "Symbols", in this section; "Small Hope of Life" under Life; "Many Sicknesses" under Sickness).

**Chartering; Childbirth**—Death In—(See Parturition, Puerperal).

**Childhood; Children**—Death of—Death of Parent Caused by Bad Children—(See "Death", "Parents", "Worries", under Children).

**Church**—No Church or Regular Burial—(See Burial).

**Condemned to Death**—(See Judge).

**Contempt for Death**—No Fear of Death—♂ strong ruler of the horoscope. (See "Fear" in this section).

**Corpse; Cremation**—(See "Silver Cord" under Silver).

**Crucifixion**—(See Impalement).

**Cruel Treatment**—Death By—(See Cruel).

**Crushed; Curious Death**—(See Extraordinary).

**Cuts; Danger of Death**—(See "Arguments", "Certain", in this section; "Danger" under Life).

**Daughter; Day of Death**—Is apt to be on a day when the ☽ is in a sign afflicting the Asc., the M.C., or the afflicting planet. (See "Hour", "Time", in this section).

**Daytime Death**—Death by Day—(See "Wild Animals" under Animals).

**Dead**—(See Dead).

**Death More Certain**—(See "Certain" in this section).

**Death Not Indicated**—Is not indicated unless the hyleg is afflicted by a train of evil directions, and by the very evil asp. of the Anareta to the hyleg by dir. Also the good asps. of the benefics to the hyleg in a train of evil directions, and also a benefic supporting the Anareta, tend to spare life. (See "Spared" under Life).

**Death Rate High**—(See Mortality).

**Death to Be Feared**—(See "Arguments", "Certain", in this section).

**Death Will Ensue**—(See "Certain" in this seetion).

**Debauchery**—(See Debauchery, Dissipation. Also see "Causes His Own Death" in this section).

**Decapitation**—(See Beheaded).

**Denotes Death**—The 3rd Dec. of ♍ denotes death and dissolution, decay, weakness, infirmity and old age. (See "Arguments", "Certain", "Symbols", in this section).

**Depopulation**—(See Mortality).

**Desert**—Lost In—Death In—(See Desert).

**Desire for Death**—The ☉ to the □ his own place by dir., gives a desire to depart from earth life.

**Devoured**—Body Devoured After Death—(See Burial).

**Disease**—The Disease Which Is the Immediate Cause of Death—(See Immediate. Also see "Quality" in this section).

**Disintegration; Dissipation**—(See "Debauchery" in this section).

**Dissolution**—(See "Denotes Death" in this section).

**Dominion of Death**—Is vested in the Anareta, the planet causing death. (See Anareta).

**Dreadful Death** — (See "Burned at Stake" under Burns; Execution, Fire, Hanging, Ignoble, Impalement, Judges, Lynched, Murdered, Poison, Prison, Treachery, etc.).

**Drink; Drought; Drowning;**

**Drug Habit**—(See Narcotics).

**Drunkenness; Duels; Dying Persons** —(See Dying).

**Early Death**—(See Early).

**Earthquakes**—(See Earth).

**Easy Death**—Gentle, and with Little Suffering—Peaceful Ending to Life— ♃ in the 4th H.; ♃ in the 8th H., and well-asp., and usually after a long life; ♃ and ♀ in the 8th H. indicate a quiet end, and without pain or distress; ♃ and ♀ in the 8th, rulers of the 8th, or in good asp. to cusp the 8th, and with no malefics in the 8th; ♄ lord of the 4th, usually an easy departure, and expiring without a struggle; a benefic acting as Anareta, or afflicting the hyleg, if the Anareta be not near violent fixed stars; lord of the 11th in the 8th H. (See Comforts; "Natural Death" under Natural).

**Eating** — Death from Excess in Eating—(See Eating).

**Eighth House**—(See the Eighth House influences under "Arguments" in this section).

**Elderly People** — Death of — (See Adults, Grandparents, Old Age).

**Electricity; Embryo** — (See Embryo, Foetus).

**Employment**—(See Employment, Explosions, Machinery).

**Enemy**—Death of — Death By — (See Enemies).

**Enmity; Epidemics; Epilepsy;**

**Escapes**—Narrow Escapes from Death —(See Escapes).

**Events; Excesses; Execution** — (See Execution, Judge, Law).

**Exercise**—(See Exercise, Sports).

**Explosions; External Causes**—As by Accident, Air, Blows, Bruises, Cuts, Earthquakes, Epidemics, Fire, Heat, Hurts, Injuries, Railroads, Robbers, Travel, Water, Wounds, etc. See the various paragraphs in this section.

**Extraordinary; Falls; Family**—Death In—(See Family, Relatives).

**Famine; Fatal; Fatality; Father;**

**Fear of Death**—Fears His Own Death —No Fear of Death—(See "Death" under Fear).

**Female Friend**—Death of — (See Friends).

**Female Relative** — Death of — (See Aunt, Grandparents, Mother, Relatives, Sister, Wife).

**Female Treachery**—Death By — (See Treachery).

**Females**—Death of—(See "Death" under Female; Women. Also see Aunt, Mother, Sister, Wife,, etc.).

**Fiancee; Fire; Fistula; Floods;**

**Fluxes; Flying Stones**—(See "Flying" under Stone).

**Foetus; Folly; Foreign Lands**—Foreign War — (See Abroad, Foreign, War).

**Foretold Own Death** — (See "Foretold", Case No. 979, in 1001 N.N.).

**Fourth House** — (See Fourth, Terminal).

**Fractures; Frenzy; Friends; Fury;**

**Gases; Grandparents; Great** — Death of the Great—(See Great).

**Guillotine; Gunshot; Habits; Hand of Man**—Death By—(See Hand of Man, Human, Man).

**Hanging; Happy Death** — (See "Desire", "Easy", in this section).

**Heat; Heights; Highwaymen; Home** —Dies In His Own Home—Lord of the 8th in the 4th H.

**Homicide; Honour**—Death In Affairs of—(See Duels, Honour).

**Horses**—Death By—Death of — (See Horses).

**Hospital**—Death In—(See Hospital).

**Hot**—Hot Diseases—Hot Water—Hot Weather — Death By — (See Heat, Liquids, Scalds, Water, Weather).

**Hour of Death** — Wilson says that when the ☉ is Anareta in a train of evil directions, and affl. the hyleg, and the hour of death is imminent, that death, or an important crisis, usually occurs at about the hours of 2 A.M., or 2 P.M. when the ☉ is 1/3 of his semi-arc either beyond the N. or S. angles. The hour of ♄ is also called the hour of death. (See "Hours" under Planets).

**House of Death**—(See Eighth House influences under "Arguments" in this section).

**Houses**—Buildings—Death By Fall of —(See "Buildings" under Falls).

**Human Means** — Death By — (See "Hand of Man" in this section. Also note the various subjects in this Article).

**Hurts; Husband; Ignoble Death** — Ignominious—♄ ruler of the horoscope and affl. by malefics; ♄ in the 10th H., afflicted, and affl. the hyleg. (See Execution, Judges, Law, etc.).

**Immediate Cause** — Of Death — (See "Disease" in this section. Also see Accidents, Injury, and the various paragraphs in this section).

**Imminent**—Death Imminent—Not Imminent—(See "Arguments", "Certain", in this section. See Moderation, Recovery; "Spared" under Life).

**Impalement; Imprudence;**

**Incised Wounds**—(See Cuts).

**Incurable; Indicated**—Death Indicated —(See "Arguments", "Certain", in this section).

**Indiscretions; Indulgences; Inevitable** —(See "Certain" in this section).

**Infancy; Injuries; Instruments;**

**Intemperance; Internal Causes**—(See Congenital, Heredity, Organic, Structural).

Intoxication; Iron; Irregularities;

Journeys; Judge — By Sentence of — (See Judge).

Justice — By Hand of — (See Judge, Law).

Kicks — (See Horses, Kicks).

Killed; Killing Planet — (See Anareta, Killing. Also see Anareta influences under "Arguments" in this section).

Kinds of Death — (See the various subjects in this Article).

Kings; Law; Lethargy; Life — Danger To — Life Spared — (See Life. Also see "Arguments", and the various paragraphs in this section).

Lightning; Limb — By Mutilation of — (See Beheaded, Mutilation).

Lingering Death — Slow Death — Tedious Death — The ☉ or ☽ ☌ ♄ in the 12th H.; caused by ♄ afflictions to the hyleg; ♄ affl. in the 6th, 8th or 12th H., and espec. when affl. the hyleg; ♅ in the 8th H., and affl. the hyleg. (See Chronic, Continuity; "Fixed Signs" under Fixed; Invalids; "Long Diseases" under Long; Prolonged, Tedious, etc.).

Loved Ones — Death of — (See Family, Loved Ones, Relatives).

Lynching; Machinery; Madness;

Males — Male In Family — (See Family, Males).

Man — Death by Hand of — (See "Hand of Man", "Human", in this section).

Manner of Death — (See "Quality", and the various paragraphs in this section).

Many Deaths — (See Mortality).

Marriage Partner — (See "Death" under Husband; Marriage Partner, Wife).

Melancholy; Men — Much Mortality Among — (See "Death of Men" under Men).

Middle Life — Death At — Death Before Middle Life — (See Middle Life).

Mines; Miscarriage; Miserable Death — The ☽ Sig. □ or ☍ ♄, usually dies a miserable death; ♃ Sig. ☌ ♄, and espec. if ♂ afflict ♃ and ☿ at the same time; ♄ Sig., ill-dignified, and ☌ the ☉ or ♂; lord of the 12th in the 8th, and after great misfortunes. (See Miserable, Misfortune).

Mobs; Moisture — (See Floods, Moisture, Rain, Water, etc.).

Monarchs; Morbid Deaths — (See Anareta).

Morgues; Mortal Illness — (See "Certain" in this section; "Fatal Illness" under Fatal).

Mortality; Mother; Multitude — (See Mobs).

Murdered; Mutilated;

Mysterious Death — Mysterious and Sudden — Caused by ♆ or ♅; the evil asps. of ♆ or ♅ to the hyleg at B., and by dir.; ♆ affl. in the 8th H.; ♆ the afflicting planet; ♅ affl. in the 8th H., or affl. the hyleg, tends to a strange and mysterious death, and in an uncommon and extraordinary manner. (See Extraordinary, Notorious, Peculiar, Remarkable, Strange, Trance, Untimely, in this section).

Narcotics; Narrow Escapes — (See Escapes).

Natural Death — (See Natural).

Nature of the Death — (See Quality, and the various paragraphs in this section).

Nobles; Not Indicated — (See "Death Not Indicated" in this section).

Notorious Death — Cardinal signs signify, as by murder, lightning, scalds, gunshot, fire, or on railroads, etc. Also see such subjects as Execution, Hanging, Judges, Law; "Public Death" under Public.

Obscure Death — (See Obscure).

Obstructions; Occurs — (See "Hour", "Time", in this section).

Officers; Old Age — (See Old).

Operations; Own Death — Causes His Own Death — Fears His Own Death — (See "Causes", "Fear", in this section).

Ordinary Deaths — (See "Desire", "Easy", "Home", "Natural", in this section).

Painful Death — (See "Death" under Pain. For Death Without Pain, see "Easy", "Natural", in this section).

Parents; Parturition; Passion — Thru Passional Excesses — (See Amorous, Passion, Sex, Venery).

Patricide — (See Father).

Peaceful Death — (See "Desire", "Easy", "Natural", "Old Age", in this section).

Peculiar Death — (See Extraordinary. See "Mysterious" in this section).

Pestilence; Phrenzy — (See Frenzy, Phrenitic).

Pirates; Place of Death — (See Place).

Plague; Planets and Death — (See Anareta. See "Death" under each of the Planets).

Pleasures; Plots; Poison; Police — (See Officers).

Precipices — Falls From — (See Falls, Heights).

Premature Death — (See Accidents, Burial, Execution, Extraordinary, Judges, Law, Mysterious, Officers, Remarkable, Sudden, Trance, Untimely, and the various paragraphs in this section).

Presidents; Pressed — (See Crushed, Trampled).

Princes; Prison; Property — Death from Loss of — (See Property).

Public Death — Public Mortality — (See Public, Mortality).

Putrefaction; Quadrupeds; Quality of Death — Manner — Nature — Species — Any planet being in the Anaretic Place, or a planet having dignity therein, will show the quality of death, but if no planet is in this place, then the first planet which comes to the Anaretic Place by body or aspect will show it. The Manner and Quality of death are shown from that planet which follows the Anareta by ☌, or aspect, to the place of the hyleg, but if none follow it is taken from that which last preceded. Thus ♃ or ♀ can show the nature of the death altho they do not cause it. The Quality of the Death is indicated by the nature of the least prominent, or least powerful directions in a train of directions to the hyleg, and by the nature of the sign, or signs, containing them. (See "Immediate Cause of Death" under Immediate; "Death" under Nature; Species. Also note the various paragraphs in this section).

**Quarrels; Quick Death**—(See Quick).

**Quiet Death**—(See "Peaceful" in this section).

**Railroads; Recreations; Relatives;**

**Religion**—Death on Account of—(See "Persecution" under Religion).

**Remarkable Death**—Singular—Sudden—Unusual—Extraordinary—♅ as the afflicting planet tends to death in some remarkable, sudden, violent, tragical, and extraordinary manner; ♄ and ♂ both in evil asp. to the ☉ and ☽, or even only one, and at the same time the Asc. be afflicted; the malefics in ☌ or ☍, and lords of the Anaretic Places, and if one or more malefics attack the ☉ or ☽. (See Extraordinary, Peculiar, Sudden, Tragical, Untimely, Unusual, Violent, in this section).

**Remedy**—Incapable of—(See "Hurts" under Remedy; Incurable).

**Reptiles; Rescue Work**—(See Rescue).

**Respiration**—(See "Death" under Breathing).

**Riots; Robbers; Rulers; Ruptures; Sad Death**—Death from Sadness—(See Sad).

**Sailors**—(See Maritime).

**Saved**—The Life Will Be Saved—Will Not Be Saved—(See "Certain Death" in this section. See "Spared" under Life).

**Scalds; Sea; Searing**—(See "Searing" under Burns).

**Second Death**—(See the Introduction under Twelfth House).

**Secret Enemies**—(See "Secret Enemies" under Secret).

**Sentence of Law**—(See Judge).

**Serpents; Sharp Instruments**—Sharp Diseases—(See Cuts, Duels, Instruments, Sharp, Sword).

**Sheep**—Death of—(See Sheep).

**Ships; Shipwreck; Shock;**

**Short Journeys**—(See Journeys, Railroads, Travel).

**Short Life**—(See Life).

**Silver Cord**—(See Silver).

**Signs of Death**—(See "Symbols" in this section).

**Signs of Zodiac**—(See each of the Signs, as Aries, Taurus, etc.).

**Simulated**—(See Trance).

**Singular Death**—(See Extraordinary, Mysterious, Remarkable, in this section).

**Sister; Sixth House**—(See Sixth).

**Slaughter; Sleep**—Death During Sleep—(See Sleep).

**Slow Death**—(See "Lingering" in this section).

**Son; Spared**—(See "Spared" under Life).

**Species of Death**—(See "Quality" in this section).

**Spiritual Causes**—Of Death—(See Astral; "Death" under Neptune; Spiritual).

**Sports; Stabs; Starvation; Steel and Iron**—(See Iron).

**Stillborn; Stings; Stones**—(See "Flying Stones" under Stones).

**Storms; Strange Death**—Death from Strange Causes—♆ the afflicting planet. (See "Mysterious" in this section).

**Strangers**—Death in the Presence of—The ☽ in the 8th H.

**Strangulation; Strokes**—(See Assaults, Attacks, Blows, Stabs, Sword, Violence, etc.).

**Sudden Death**—(See Sudden).

**Suffocation; Suicide; Sure Death**—(See "Certain" in this section).

**Surgical Operations**—(See Operations).

**Sword; Symbols of Death**—Signs of Death—Arguments for Death, etc.—The ☉ in ☌, P, or ☍ by application acts as a powerful Anareta, and denotes death; if the lord of the 1st be in the 6th, and lord of the 6th in the 1st, when they leave the sign or signs they are in, and meet with the □ or ☍ asps. of ♄, ♂, or lords of the 4th or 8th, death may follow; lord of the 1st in the 4th or 8th, if he be afflicted; lord of the Asc., or the ☽ combust, but with hopes of recovery if the ☽ or lord of the Asc. dispose of the ☉; lords of the 4th or 6th, or lords of the 8th and 6th, in reception, denotes death; lord of the 1st and 8th being the same planet; in sickness lord of the 6th ☌ the Anareta, and espec. if the ☌ is in the 4th H., the house denoting the grave. (Hor'y); a malefic lord of the fatal 4th, and posited in the 6th, or 8th; lord of the disease, or of the 6th H., and lord of the 4th in mutual reception, indicate that the disease will end in death; lord of the Asc. also lord of the 8th, and espec. if ℞ and afflicted (Hor'y); the afflictors in the disease in the terms of the lords of the 4th, 6th, 8th or 12th H. (Hor'y); lord of the 4th disposing of the Anareta, or being posited in or near the cusp of the 6th H. (See Arguments, Anareta, Certain, Denotes, Quality, and the various paragraphs in this section. Also see "Signs of Death" under Infancy).

**Tedious Death**—(See "Lingering" in this section).

**Theatres; Thieves; Threatened**—Death Threatened—Threatened With Death Many Times—(See "Arguments", and the various paragraphs in this section. See "Danger to Life" under Life; "Narrow Escapes" under Escapes).

**Thunder Storms**—(See Thunder).

**Time of Death**—(See Time. See "Day of Death", "Hour", in this section).

**Tornadoes**—(See Wind).

**Tortured to Death**—(See Banishment, Beaten, Captivity, Cruel, Exile, Lynched, Pirates, Robbers, Prison; "Stake" under Burns, etc.).

**Tragical Death**—♅ in 8th H., and affl. the hyleg; the M.C. to the place of the Pleiades, or Pollux, tends to a tragic death by women. Caput Algol disposes to a tragic death when angular at B., and affl. the hyleg. See Algol, Beheaded; "Death" under Sudden; Enemies, Execution, Extraordinary, Hanging, Judge, Poison; "Public Death" under Public; Treachery, Untimely, etc.)

**Trampled**—(See Crushed, Trampled).

**Trance; Travel**—(See Journeys, Railroads, Travel, Vehicles, Voyages).

**Trodden**—(See Trampled).

**Twelfth House**—(See Twelfth).

**Uncle; Uncommon**—(See Mysterious, Peculiar, Remarkable, Strange, Tragical, in this section).

**Unexpected**—(See Accidents; "Death" under Sudden).

**Untimely Death**—(See Untimely. Also note the various paragraphs in this section).

**Unusual**—(See Extraordinary, Mysterious, Peculiar, Remarkable, Strange, Tragical, and the various paragraphs in this section).

**Vehicles; Venomous Creatures**—(See Adder, Bites, Reptiles, Serpents, Stings, Venomous, etc.).

**Vexation; Violent Death**—(See Violent).

**Viscera**—By Obstruction of—(See Obstructions, Viscera).

**Voyages; War; Wasting Away**—(See Wasting).

**Water; Weak**—Death of the Weak and Frail—(See "Death" under Weak).

**Weapons; Weather; Wife;**

**Wild Beasts**—(See Wild).

**Wind; Womb**—Death In—(See Stillborn).

**Women**—Death By—Death of—(See Women).

**Wounds; Wrath; Young**—Dies Young—Death of Young Men—Death of Young People—(See Young).

**Youth**—Dies In Youth—(See "Early Death" under Early; Youth).

**DEBASED IN MIND**—The ☉ conciliated with the ruler of the mind, and cadent and occidentally posited. (See Debauched, Degenerate, Dissipated, Drunkenness, Depraved; "Immoral" and "Loose Morals" under Morals; Perversions, Shameless, Wanton, etc.).

**DEBAUCHERY**—Debauched—Afflictions in the watery signs ♋, ♏, and ♓ tend to more of debauchery, dissipation, drunkenness, and depravity, and espec. when the malefics ♄ and ♂ are also in these signs, and afflicting the ☉, ☽, Asc., or hyleg; the malefics in the 5th H., and affl. the Asc. by dir.; the ☉ to the ☌ ♀ by dir., and ♀ peregrine or afflicted at B.; the ☉ to the □ the ☽ or ♀ by dir.; the ☉ to the ☌ ☽ by dir., and the ☽ badly affl. at B.; the ☽ to the Left Hand of Ophiucus, debauchery and infamy; ♃ Sig. □ or ☍ ♀, a countenance indicative of intemperance and debauchery; in Hor'y Questions ♂ as Sig. denotes one drunken and debauched; ♀ ☌ the Asc. by dir.; ♀ ruler of the horoscope, and affl. by malefics; Asc. to the □ or ☍ ☽ by dir.; lord of the 8th in the 5th H.

**Death from Debauchery**—Lord of the 8th in the 5th, and with drinking, intoxication, etc.

**Debility from Debauchery**—A Debauched Look—The ☉ Sig. in ♓; the ☉ Sig. □ or ☍ ♃; the ☽ Sig. in ♑; ♄ ruler of the 5th H. at B., in ♏, and ♄ in ☌ or evil asp. the Asc. by dir., and espec. if ♏ be in the 5th H. at B.; ♄ or ♃ Sig in □ or ☍ ♀; ♂ Sig. in ♉, ♋, or ♓, and affl.; ♂ to the ill-asps. the ☽ or ♀ by dir.; ♀ ruler of the horoscope, and affl. by malefics; ♀ ill-dignified at B.; ♀ affl. at B., and to the ☌ or ill-asps. the Asc. or ♂ by dir.; ♀ or ☿ in watery signs, and affl. by ♆, ♅, ♃, or ♂; ♀ and ☿ in bad familiarity, in weak signs, and ill-posited; ☿ Sig. in ♉; ☊ on the cusp of 5th H. at B., and afflicted. (See "Causes Own Death" under Death; Debased, Dissipated, Dissolute, Depraved, Drink, Drunkenness, Folly; "Free Living "under Free;"High Living" under High; Infamous, Intemperance, Intoxication, Pale, Profligate, Prodigal; "Riotous Living" under Riotous, etc.).

**DEBILITY**—Debilitated—Weakness—Denoted by ♄; a ♄ disease; ♄ ascending at B., and affl. the ☉, ☽, Asc., or hyleg; denoted by the ☽ when the ☽ afflicts the ☉, Asc., or hyleg; the ☽ affl. in ♑, or ♑ upon the Asc., and espec. in the early years of life; afflictions in ♎, and a ♎ disease; watery signs on the Asc. at B., and espec. ♋ or ♓, and afflicted. (See Feeble, Infirm, Ill-Health; "Weak Body" under Weak).

**Atony**—Want of Tone and Power—(See Atony, Stamina, Tone, Vitality Low, Weak).

**Blood**—Debility of—♀ affl. in ♒ warns against. (See Blood; "Impure Blood" under Impure).

**Body**—Debility of—The ☉ or ☽ hyleg, and to the ☌ or ill-asp. ♄ by dir.; the ☉ to the ill-asps. ♃ by dir.; the ☽ affl. in ♍, or affl. the hyleg therefrom; ♄ ascending at B.; ♄ to the ill-asps. his own place at B. by dir.; ♄ afflictions are responsible for debility and morbid conditions; characteristic of the Lymphatic Temperament. (See Feeble; "Bad Health" under Health; Infirm, Ill-Health, Lassitude; "Weakened" under Strength; "Low" under Vitality; "Weak Body" under Weak).

**Chronic Debility**—The ☉ hyleg, and to the ☌ or ill-asps. ♄ by dir.; the ☉ or ☽ in the 6th H. at B., and affl. by malefics. (See Chronic, Lingering, Prolonged, Tedious).

**Countenance**—Debilitated Look—(See Anaemia, Emaciated, Pale, Sickly).

**Debauchery**—Debility By—(See Debauchery, Dissipation, Dissolute, Drink, Intemperance, etc.).

**General Debility**—The ☉ afflicting the ☽; the ☽ hyleg in ♒ in a female nativity; the ☽ affl. by ♄, and espec. with females, or the ☉ affl. by ♄ in males; the ☽ affl. by ♄ tends to long, lingering and chronic complaints arising from general debility; ♆ □ or ☍ the

Asc.; ♄ in the 6th H. and affl. the hyleg; a ♀ disease, and afflictions to ♀. (See Feeble; "General Ill-Health" under Ill-Health; "Debility" under Nerves; Sickly; "Weakened" under Strength; "Weak Body" under Weak; Vitality Low, etc.).

**Health**—Debility of—(See "Bad Health" under Health; Ill-Health).

**Heart**—Debility of—(See "Weak Heart" under Heart).

**Look**—Debilitated Look—(See Emaciated, Pale, Sickly, White, etc.).

**Males**—Debility of—(See "Ill-Health" under Males; Impotency).

**Men**—Debility of—(See "Debility" under Men).

**Mental Debility**—A Diseased Mind—(See Demoniac, Insanity, Idiocy, Imbecility, Madness, Mania; "Diseased Mind" and "Weak Mind" under Mind).

**Morbid Debility**—Caused by ♄.

**Nervous Debility**—(See "Debility" under Nerves).

**Physical Debility**—(See "Body" in this section. Also see Disease, Ill-Health, Physical, Sickness, etc.).

**Sickness**—Debility Greater in Sickness—The ☽ ☌ or ill-asp. ♄ or ♂, or the place of either in the radical map, and ♄ the stronger afflicting planet at the beginning of the illness. (See Recuperation, Resistance, Recovery, Vitality, etc.).

**Strength**—Strength of the Body Rendered Weaker—(See "Weakened" under Strength).

**Weakness**—Weak Body—(See Endurance, Feeble, Infirm; "Ill-Health All Thru Life" under Ill-Health; Invalids; Vitality Low; "Weak Body" under Weak).

**Women**—Debility of—(See Females, Women). For other study see Consumptions, Dull, Lethargy, Nutrition, Wastings, etc.

**DECANATES**—The division of a Sign into three parts of 10° each. The first ten degrees are of the nature of the Sign itself; the second 10° of the nature of the next sign of the same element; the 3rd part, of the nature of the third sign of the same element. Thus the first ten degrees of ♈ are of the nature of ♈; the second ten degrees of the nature of ♌, and the last ten degrees of the nature of ♐. (See Chap. 4 in Sepharial's Manual of Astrology, on the relation of the decanates and planets, and the diseases and qualities given by each of the 36 decanates). The Decanate rising on the Asc. has a distinct influence over the height, weight, bodily development, personal appearance, facial characteristics, and also determines the natural temperament. The first Dec. of cardinal signs is mental; the second Dec. is mental-vital, and the third Dec. is mental-motive. The first Dec. of Fixed Signs on the Asc. is vital; the second Dec. is vital-motive; the 3rd Dec. is vital-mental. The first Dec. of mutable signs on the Asc. is motive; the 2nd Dec. is motive-mental; the 3rd Dec. is motive-vital. The Bodily Tem-

perament given by the Asc. may thus be either mental, motive, or vital, or a combination of two of these, as mental-vital, mental-motive, etc. These Decanates on the Asc. also have much to do with the shape of the face. The mental type is shaped like a pear, and the head narrows down to the chin, and is wide at the temples. The vital type is widest about the cheeks, and with an oval or round face. The motive type has the head and face flatter at the sides, and the square-shaped head. Each of these types are also subject to three variations or combinations, according to the Dec. rising, such as vital, vital-motive, and vital-mental, etc. Planets rising, and the position of the ruler of the Asc., also produce other variations. Also the personal appearance is much affected by the ☽, and her sign and position. Also it is said the height of a person is partly determined by the Moon's Nodes, but this cannot always be relied upon. (See Navamsa). (See Appearance, Ascendant, Body, Face, Height, Stature, Temperament, Weight, etc.).

**DECAPITATION**—Danger of Death By —(See Beheaded).

**DECAY**—Putrefactive Changes—Decomposition—Governed by ♄ and the ☽. Cold and Dryness tend to decay, dissipation and decomposition of matter, and are malevolent influences. Organic and vegetable decay are under the rule of the ☽. (See Blight, Catalysis, Cold, Corrosion, Death, Decrepitude, Degeneration, Dissolution, Dryness, Excretions, Gangrene, Granulations, Moisture, Mortification, Moonlight, Necrosis, Noxious, Putrefaction, Rotten, etc.).

**Death by Decay**—♃ causes death by a decayed system, and due to corrupt blood, surfeits, and brought on by excesses of various kinds. (See Excesses, Impure, Jupiter, Plethora, Surfeits, etc.).

**Decayed System**—(See "Death" in this section).

**Old Age**—The 3rd Decanate of ♍ denotes old age, decay, infirmity, weakness and dissolution. (See Infirm, Old Age, Shrinkage, Wasting, Withering, Wrinkles, etc.).

**Organic Decay**—Ruled by the ☽. (See Moon, Organic).

**Premature Decay**—(See "Fluid" under Vital).

**Teeth**—(See "Decay" under Teeth).

**Tissues**—Decay of—(See "Decay" under Tissues. Also see Corrosion, Degeneration, Emaciation, Gangrene, Mortification, Putrefaction, Urea, Wasting, etc.).

**Vegetable Matter**—Decay of—(See Vegetation).

**DECEITFUL** — Deceptive—Duplicity—False Pretenses—Deception—Largely a ♄ influence; ♄ or ♂ Sig. in □ or ☍ ☿, or ☿ Sig. in □ or ☍ these planets; ♄ Sig. in ♋ or ♓; the ☉ or ♃ Sig. ☌ ♄; ♂ Sig. in ♓; ♂ or ☿ ill-dig. at B.; ♀ or ☿ Sig. in ♋; ☿ Sig. ☌ the ☉; ☿ Sig. □ or ☍ the ☽; characteristic of the negative signs; many planets in bicorporeal signs; a ♏ influence when this sign is badly afflicted; characteristic of bad ♏ and ♑ maps when under strong ♆ afflictions; deceptions are also ruled by ♆. (See Cheating, Dishonest, Dual, Evil, Forgers, Gambling, Hypocritical, Liars, Mischief, Mockery, Pettifogging, Shrewd, Swindlers, Thieves, Treachery, etc.).

**Deceitful Relatives**—Injured By—The ☽ Sig. □ or ☍ ♃; lord of the 10th in the 12th; lord of the 10th a malefic, and in the 11th H., and afflicted. (See Enemies, Plots, Treachery).

**DECLINATION**—(See Latitude, Nodes).

**DECLINES**—(See Chronic, Consumptions, Emaciation; "Malnutrition" under Nutrition; Wasting Diseases, etc.).

**DECOMPOSITION**—(See Decay, Degeneration, Putrefaction, Disintegration).

**DECREASE**—Decrease of—Decreased—(See Diminished, Lack of).

**Birth Rate Decreased**—(See "Birthrate" under Birth).

**Death Rate Decreased**—(See "Death Rate" under Mortality).

**Moon**—Decrease of—(See "Decrease" under Moon).

**Motility**—Decreased Motility—(See Motion, Motor, Movement, Neuroses, Paralysis, Retarded, Slow, etc.).

**The Disease Will Decrease**—(See "Decrease" under Recovery).

**DECREPITUDE**—Senile Feebleness—♄ is the planet of, and of decay. (See "Senility" under Old Age. Also see Decay, Feeble, Infirm, Weak).

**DECUMBITURE**—This means "Lying Down", the beginning of an illness, or when the patient first takes to his bed in the illness. A Horary map made up for this time gives very valuable indications as to the nature and prognosis of the disease, and when studied along with the map of birth. The ☽ and Asc. are always taken as hyleg at decumbiture in Horary Questions. The afflicting planet, or planets, in cardinal signs at decumb. show a more rapid disease, and soon over. The afflicting planet in a fixed sign shows continuity, a prolonged or tedious disease, etc. (See Acute, Cardinal, Chronic, Continuity, Crises, Duration, Fixed Signs under Fixed; Mutable, Particular, Prolonged, Short Illnesses under Short, Praeincipients, Prognosis, Symptoms, Tedious, etc.).

**DEEP**—

**Deep Cardiac Plexus**—(See Cardiac).

**Deep Forehead**—(See Forehead).

**Deep Lines**—(See Wrinkles).

**Deep Mind**—(See Mind).

**Deep-Pitted**—Pitted or Deep Degrees of the Zodiac—(See Pitted).

**Deep-Seated Diseases**—(See Chronic, Heredity, Organic, Structural).

**Deep-Set Eyes**—(See Eyeballs).

**Deep Vexation**—Sickness From—(See Vexation).

**Deep Voice**—(See Voice).

**Deep Yellow**—(See Yellow).

**DEFECATION**—Evacuations—(See Evacuation, Faeces).

**DEFECTS**—Defective—Imperfections—Absence of a Part or Organ, etc.—Defects may occur in any part or organ of the body, and may be congenital, from birth, or acquired. For the various Defects of Parts of the Body, Organs, Functions, etc., see the Part, Organ, or Function in the alphabetical arrangement. The ☉ in the different Signs, if afflicted, tends to cause organic and structural defects in the part or organ ruled by such sign. Also the malefics ♄ and ♂ in the various signs at B. tend to defects, marks, deformities, and afflictions to the part, or organs ruled by the sign containing them. The planet ♄ especially causes defects in the personal appearance when he is in the Asc. at B., or rising, and afflicting the ☉, ☽, or Asc. at B. The Prenatal Influences, and the planetary afflictions during Gestation, also account for many of the bodily, physical and mental defects, which defects exist from birth, and are conspicuous thruout the life. Heredity also accounts for many defects, and which are handed down from parent to child from generation to generation, such as Birthmarks, Marks, Moles, Deformities, Insanity, etc. For the Defects which arise from disease, such as Blindness, Deafness, Lameness, Paralysis, Stiff Joints, and a multitude of subjects, look for the disease and the subject in the alphabetical arrangement if not listed here. The following subjects are suggestive along the lines of Defects, which see in the alphabetical arrangement,—Abnormalities, Accommodation, Acquired, Appearance, Arms, Atrophy, Azimene, Baldness, Barrenness, Beastly Form (see Beasts); Breathing, Births, Blemishes, Blind, Blood, Blotches, Body, Brain, Breasts, Broken, Build, Chest, Children, Circulation, Cloaca, Complexion, Congenital, Constitutional, Contortions, Contractions, Crippled, Crooked, Cyclops, Deaf, Deaf and Dumb (see Hearing, Mutes); Deficient, Deformities, Digestion, Diminished, Disabilities, Displacements, Disfigurements, Distortions, Dumb, Dwarfed, Ears, Enlargements, Eunuchs, Excrescences, Eyes, Eyesight (see Sight); Face, Faulty, Feet, Foetus, Freaks, Freckles, Gait, Growth, Hair, Hands, Heart, Heredity, Hermaphrodites, Idiocy, Ill-formed, Imbecility, Imperfections, Inefficient, Inhuman, Insanity, Insufficient, Irregularities, Joints, Judgment, Knees, Lameness, Left Eye (see Left); Legs, Limbs, Locomotion, Lungs, Maimed, Malformations, Marks, Matrix (see Womb); Members, Memory, Mental, Mind, Missing, Moles, Monsters, Mutes, Mutilated, Naevus, Natural, Nerves, Ocular, Organic, Organs, Paralysis, Personal Appearances (see Appearance); Physical, Posture, Prenatal, Pressure, Rectum, Respiratory Organs (see Breathing); Right Eye (see Right); Rigidity, Savage, Scars, Sex Organs, Sight, Skin, Speech, Spine, Stature, Stooped, Structural, Teeth, Throat, Tongue, Vision, Walk, etc.

**DEFENSIVE FORCES**—Of the Body—Are under the especial rule of ♃, and assisted by ♀ and ♆. (See Cells, Phagocytes, Preservation, Recovery, Recuperation, Resistance, Tissues, Vital, Vitality).

**DEFICIENT** — Deficiency — Deficiencies —Are ruled over strongly by ♄, as ♄ tends to slow up the functions, retard, suppress bodily activities, and espec. when he is badly afflicted at B., or afflicting the vital centers, as the ☉, ☽, Asc., or hyleg. The influence of ♆ when conjoined with ♄, and affl. the rulers of the circulation, ♃ and ♀, also tends to increase the afflictions of ♄ along this line. (See Obstructions, Retardation, Stoppages, Suppressions).

**Blood**—Deficiency of Red Blood Corpuscles—(See "Blood" under Red).

**Circulation**—Deficiency of Circulation In a Part—(See "Deficiency" under Circulation).

**Degrees**—Deficient Degrees of the Zodiac—(See Azimene).

**Devoid Of**—(See Void).

**Fluids**—Of the Body—Deficiency of—(See Fluids).

**Functions**—(See "Suppression" under Functions).

**Insufficiencies**—(See Insufficient).

**Lack Of**—(See Lack).

**Loss Of**—(See Loss).

**Lymph**—Deficiency In—(See Lymph).

**Mentally Deficient** — (See "Deficient" under Mental).

**Mineral Salts**—Deficiency of in Blood —(See "Blood" under Minerals).

**Mucus**—Deficiency of on Respiratory Membranes—(See "Respiratory" under Mucus).

**Organism**—Deficient Development of —(See Diminished; "Deficient", "Undersized", under Organs).

**Red Blood Corpuscles**—Deficiency of —(See "Blood" under Red).

**Secretions** — Deficient — (See Fluids, Glands, Secretions, Suppressions).

**Stomach Juices** — Deficiency of — (See Digestion; "Ailments" under Fluids; Gastric, Juices, Stomach).

**Void Of**—(See Void). For Deficiencies in any part of the body, of any organ, function, etc., and which may not be listed here, see the subject in the alphabetical arrangement. Also see Defects, Diminished, Imperfections, Inefficiency, Irregularities, Suppressions).

**DEFLUXIONS** — Catarrh—A Downward Flow of Humours—Defluxions are diseases of the ☉, ☽, and ♄. (See Catarrh, Fluxion, Humours, Mucus, Phlegm; "Watery Humours" under Watery).

**Cold Defluxions**—♄ diseases.

**Head**—Defluxions of Rheum From—☽ affl. in ♈. (See Catarrh; "Rheum" under Head).

**Rheum**—Defluxions of—(See Rheum).

**DEFORMITIES**— Deformed — Imperfect in Body—Disablements—These may be congenital or acquired. The congenital deformities are usually the result of prenatal afflictions during gestation, assisted by strong afflictions of the malefics at birth, or with what are known as the Broken, Imperfect, or Mutilated Signs on the Asc., strong, or occupied by malefics. (See Broken, Distortions, Mutilated, Prenatal).

The following subjects have to do with deformities in the various parts, and organs of the body, and also with mental deformities, defects, and deficiencies, which subjects see in the alphabetical arrangement—

**Abdomen; Accidents; Acquired;**

**Action; Anatomical Changes**—(See Anatomical).

**Animals; Amputations** — (See Operations).

**Ankles; Ankylosis; Antenatal** — (See Prenatal).

**Anus**—Imperforate Anus—(See Anus).

**Appearance; Arms**—Armless Wonder —(See Arms).

**Arthritis Deformans**—(See Joints).

**Atrophy; Azimene Degrees**—The Lame Degrees of the Zodiac—(See Azimene).

**Beastly Form**—(See Beasts).

**Birth**—Deformed from Birth—(See Congenital, Infancy, Prenatal).

**Blind from Birth**—Born Blind—(See Blindness).

**Body Deformed**—Deformed in Body and Mind—Body Incomplete—(See "Armless" under Arms; "Deformed" under Mind; Hands, Incomplete, Legs, Members, Missing, Organs, etc. Also note the various paragraphs in this section).

**Bow Legs**—(See Legs).

**Breast**—Chicken-Breasted, Pigeon-Breasted—(See Breast).

**Broken** — Broken Bones — Broken Limbs—Broken Signs—(See Broken).

**Causes of Deformities**—The planetary influences at B. attributed to deformities are as follows,—The ☉ and ☽ affl. in the 6th and 12th H. at B.; ♆ afflictions and diseases; deformities are largely ruled and controlled by ♆; ♅, ♄, and ♂ closely associated, in ☌ or ☍ in fixed signs; ♅, ♄, or ♂ in the 5th, 6th or 12th H., or afflicting these houses or cusps by aspect, or affl. the Asc.; ♄ and ♂ joined anywhere in the map, and espec. in angles, or in their own nodes, or in the Lunar Nodes; ♀ Sig. □ or ☍ ♄; many planets in ♍ in the 6th or 12th H.; ♉, ♎, ♏, ♑, ♓, or the last part of ♈ and ♌, when on the Asc. at B., or occupied by malefics, are said to cause deformity; people born under the broken signs, ♌, ♏, and ♓, tend to be deformed in some way. (For further influences see the various paragraphs in this Article).

**Channels** — (See "Channels" under Genitals. Also see Cloaca).

**Chest; Chicken-Breasted** — (See Breast).

**Children** — (See "Deformed" under Birth, Children).

**Chronic Deformans**—(See "Ankylosis", "Arthritis", "Rheumatism", under Joints).

**Cloaca; Club Feet**—(See Feet).

**Congenital**— (See Birth, Congenital, Heredity, Prenatal).

**Constitution**—(See Constitution, Defects. Also note the various paragraphs in this section).

**Contortions; Contractions; Crippled; Crooked; Crossed Eyes**—(See Eyes).

**Curvature; Cyclops; Deafness; Deaf and Dumb**—(See Mute).

**Defects; Deficiencies; Depressions; Diminished; Disabilities;**

**Disfigurements; Dislocations;**

**Displacements; Distortions; Dogs**— Resembles Dogs, Animals, etc. — (See "Dogs" under Children).

**Dwarfed; Enlargements; Eunuchs;**

**Excessive Members** — (See Hands; "Two Heads" under Head; "United Twins" under Twins; Virile).

**Excrescences; Exophthalmos** — (See Eyeballs).

**Eyes**—Blindness—Crossed Eyes— Focussed into One — Protrusion of — (See Blindness, Cyclops, Exophthalmos, Eyeballs, Eyes, Goggle).

**Face; Feet; Fingers; Form;**

**Fractures; Freaks; Frog Child**—(See Frog).

**Gait; Generative Organs; Giants;**

**Goiter; Gout; Growth; Hair**—Little Hair—No Hair or Teeth—(See Baldness, Hair).

**Hands**—No Hands or Arms Below the Elbows — Four Hands — (See "Frog Child" under Frog; Hands).

**Harelip; Head** — (See "Deformities" under Head. Also see Excrescences, Idiocy, Skull).

**Heart**—Heart on Right Side—(See Heart).

**Hermaphrodite; Hips; Hollow;**

**Humpback**—(See Spine).

**Hydrocephalus; Idiots; Ill-Formed;**

**Impediments; Imperfections;**

**Imperforations; Incomplete;**

**Infirmities; Inhibitions; Inhuman;**

**Injuries; Joints; Knees**—(See "Knock Knees" under Knees).

**Lameness**—Lame Degrees of the Zodiac—(See Azimene, Lameness).

**Legs**—Various Deformities of—(See Feet, Knees, Hips, Legs, Thighs).

**Limbs; Limitations; Limping; Local Parts**—(See Local).

**Locomotion; Maimed; Malformations;**

**Members; Mind and Body**—Deformed In—(See "Body" in this section).

**Mineral Deposits**—(See Deposits, Minerals, Urea, Uric Acid).

**Missing Members**—(See Arms, Hands, Legs, Members, Missing).

**Monsters; Motion; Movement;**

**Mutilated; Narrow; Neck; Operations;**

**Opisthotonos; Organs; Paralysis;**

**Pigeon-Breasted**—(See Breast).

**Prenatal; Protruding; Rectum;**

**Rheumatism**—Chronic Deformans— (See Joints, Rheumatism).

**Rickets; Sex Organs**— (See Genitals, Sex, Womb).

**Shape; Shoulders; Siamese Twins**— (See "United" under Twins).

**Skull; Slightly Deformed**—(See Slight).

**Spasmodic; Spine; Sternum; Stiff;**

**Stooped; Strabismus**—(See Eyes).

**Teeth**—Crooked Teeth—No Teeth or Hair—(See Teeth).

**Thorax; Toes; Treachery; Triplets;**

**Twelfth House**—(See Twelfth).

**Twins; Urethra**—(See Cloaca, Urethra).

**Virile; Walk; Womb; Wry Neck**—(See Neck). Case of Deformity—Birth Data, etc.—(See "Deformed", No. 689, in 1001 N.N.).

**DEGENERATE**—Degeneracy—Base—A Low Fellow—Degraded in Character— A Vagabond—♄ Sig. □ or ☍ ☿; ♂ Sig. □ or ☍ ☽, a fit companion for the lowest and most unprincipled of mankind. (See Debased, Low, Unnatural, Vile).

**DEGENERATION**—Deterioration in the structure of a tissue or organ—Degeneration of Parts of the Body is the work principally of ♄ and ♃. Jupiter helps in degeneration by giving Fatty Tumors and Growths, increase of Adipose Tissue, and by disturbances of the Arterial Circulation over which he rules. Degeneration thru Excesses and Surfeits is generally the work of ♃, ♂, and ♀. (See Catalysis, Death, Decay, Destructive, Decomposition, Emaciation, Fat, Fatigue, Growths, Hardening, Tumors, Wasting, etc.).

**Fatty Degeneration**—Of the Heart, Liver, Muscles—(See "Fatty Degeneration" under Fat, Heart, Liver, Muscles).

**Fibrous Degeneration**—(See Fiber).

**Progressive Degeneration** — (See Progressive, Tabes, Wasting).

**Tissues**—Degeneration of—(See Tissues).

**DEGLUTITION**—Swallowing—The ☽ rules the swallow.

**Difficulty In Swallowing**—Inability to Swallow — Dysphagia — ☿ affl. in ♉, thru loss of nervous control; Subs at SP, the 7th D. (See "Control", "Obstructions", "Swellings", under Throat. Also see Glass).

**DEGREE**—Degrees—

**Disease**—Degree of Disturbance In— (See Disturbances).

**Physical Strength** — Degree of, and Degree of Vitality—Is largely determined by the Rising Sign and the Asc., its aspects and conditions, in both sexes. (See Physical, Strength, Vitality).

**Response Against Disease**—The Degree and Response by the System against Disease, Exposure, Injury, Wounds, etc.—(See Endurance, Immunity, Recuperation, Resistance, Stamina, Strength, Tone, Vitality).

**Vitality**—Degree of—(See "Physical Strength" in this section. Also see Vitality).

**Zodiac**—Degrees of the Zodiac—Each degree of the Zodiac has a different meaning and expression, and in matters of health, mind, temperament, appearance, etc., the degree rising upon the Eastern horizon at B., or the degree upon the M.C., and also the degrees occupied by planets at B., have a special significance. The meanings of these degrees are well set forth and explained in the little booklet called "The Degrees of the Zodiac Symbolised", by Charubel. The Degrees of the Zodiac which have special influence over the body and mind, in matters of health, disease, deformities, form and shape of the body, complexion, the constitution, etc., are given under the following subjects. See Azimene, Critical (see "Sensitive Degrees" under Sensitive); Dark, Deep (see Pitted); Deficient (see Azimene); Fair (see Light); Feminine, Fortunate, Lame (see Azimene); Light, Masculine, Mutilated, Pitted, Predetermination, Sensitive, Smoky, Violent, Void, Weak (see Azimene). See Signs, Zodiac.

**DEJECTED**—Dejection—Despondent—Cast Down—Low Spirits, etc.—The ☉ or ☽ to the ill-asps. ♄ by dir; the ☽ Sig. to the ☌ the ☉ or ♄; ♄ Sig. ☐ or ☍ the ☽; ♄ to the ill-asps. his own place by dir. or tr.; ♄ Sig. ☐ or ☍ ♂, generally lives a most dejected life; ♄ affl. in ♋ or ♓; ♃ Sig. ☐ or ☍ ♄; void of strong ♂ influence and aspects at B.; ☿ Sig. in ♑; ☿ ♑ partile asp. the Asc.; lord of the 8th H. in the Asc.; the 2° ♌ on the Asc. (See Anguish, Anxiety, Brooding, Depressed, Despair, Despondency, Fears, Gloomy, Hypochondria, Introspection, Low Spirits (see Low); Melancholia, Miserable, Moods, Morose, Peace, Repining, Peevish, Sad, Unhappy, Worry, Wretched).

**DELAYS**—Delayed—

**Birth Delayed**—(See "Delayed Births" under Children).

**Disease Delayed**—Long Illnesses—(See Chronic, Continuity, Course, Crises, Duration, Long, Prolonged, Relapse, Slow, Tedious, Worse, etc.).

**Growth Delayed**—(See "Arrested", "Retarded", under Growth; Retarded).

**Mental Development** — Delayed Mental Growth — (See "Arrested" under Mental).

**Puberty Delayed** — (See Puberty). Saturn is the planet of delays, whether in physical ailments or conditions, mental, or in the daily affairs of life. (See Saturn influences under Saturn).

**DELICATE**—Delicacy—Frail—Tender—Weak—

**Delicate Appetite**—(See Appetite).

**Delicate Body**—(See Constitution, Pale, Sickly, Vitality Low, Weak, White).

**Delicate Children**—Sickly Children—(See "Sickly" under Children).

**Delicate Complexion** — (See Complexion).

**Delicate Health**—(See "Bad Health" under Health; "Signs of Ill-Health" under Ill-Health; "Weak Body" under Weak).

**Delicate Skin**—(See Skin).

**DELIRIUM**—The ☽ to the ill-asps. ☿ by dir., and ☿ affl. by malefics at B., danger of delirium and madness; the ☽ ☍ ☿ at decumb., and ☋ or a malefic in the Asc. (Hor'y); ♂ in ♈ and affl. ☿ at B., or by dir.; a ☿ disease; ☿ affl. at B., and the ☽ to the ill-asps. ☿ by dir.; ☿ joined to the Anareta causes delirium in disease; ☿ afflicting the ☽ during the course of an acute disease, and espec. if ☿ be in ♈ at B., and afflicted. (See Anguish, Coma, Epilepsy, Fainting, Hysteria, Madness,, Mania).

**Colds and Coughs**—Delirium With—(See "Death" under Cough).

**Delirium Tremens**—Delirium from Alcoholic Poisoning—A Toxic Psychoses—Afflictions in ♓, from drink or drugs; ♆ affl. in a watery sign; ♆ in ♓, and espec. in the 6th or 12th H. (See Drink, Narcotics, Pineal Gland).

**Typhus**—Delirium of—Typhomania—(See Typhus).

**Wild Delirium**—A Phrenitic Man—Phrenitic Delirium—An ♈ disease, malefics in ♈, and the hyleg much affl. at B.; ♂ or ☿ affl. in ♈; ☿ ill-dig. at B.; Subs at AT. (See "Inflammation" under Brain; Coma, Convulsions, Demoniac, Dreams, Epilepsy, Fears, Fits, Frenzy, Fury, Insanity, Madness. Mania; "Brain" under Moisture; Obsessions, Pineal Gland, Spirit Controls. Also see "Delirium Tremens" in this section).

**DELIVERY**—Childbirth—(See Birth, Foetus, Parturition, Puerperal).

**DELUGES** — Floods — Great Suffering From, and Loss of Life—(See Clouds, Floods, Rain).

**DELUSIONS**—A ♆ disease; ♆ in ♈; ♆ in ♈ in the 6th H., and affl.; ♆ in ♈, and affl. the ☉, ☽, Asc., or hyleg; also a ♄ disease and affliction; Subs at Atlas. (See Fears, Hallucinations, Hearing, Hysteria, Ideals, Ideas, Illusions, Imagination, Insanity, Judgment, Madness, Mania, Mental Disorders, Notions, Obsessions, Paranoia, Persecution, Spirit Controls, etc.).

**Delusive**—(See Deceitful, Dual, Hypocritical, Liars, Mockery).

**DEMENTIA**—A Profound Mental Incapacity—A Toxic Psychoses—The influences causing Dementia are much the same as those causing Fears, Idiocy, Imbecility, Insanity, Weak Mind, etc. (See these subjects).

**Dementia Praecox**—A form of Dementia occurring at the time of puberty, and thru disturbanes at this period. (See "Trouble" under Puberty).

**DEMONIAC** — Demoniacal Affections—One supposed to be possessed with a Demon, or Evil Spirit—Imagines Himself to Be Possessed With a Demon—♆ in ♈ and affl. the ☽, Asc., or hyleg; ♆ in ♈ in the 6th H.; ♆ affl. in ♏; ♆ affl. in the 12th H.; ♆ ☍ Antares; ♆ adding his evil asps. to those of ♄ and ♂, and affl. the ☽, ☿, Asc., or hyleg; ☿ and the ☽ unconnected with each other or the Asc., and with ♄ and ♂ in angles ruling the scheme, and with ♂ the strong ruler by day, or ♄ by night, and espec. if the malefics be in ♋, ♍, or ♓; ♄ ruling the ☽ at the time of a New ☽, when the ☽ is coming to the ☌ ☉, but the ☽ ruled by ♂ when the ☽ is at Full, and espec. when it may happen in ♐ or ♓, then under these conditions if the malefics be in the Eastern Parts and in angles, and the benefics in the West, the demoniacs become furious, unmanageable, wounding themselves and uttering mysterious sayings; ♄ and ♂ in angles, elevated above ♅, ☿, and the ☽, and if ♅, ☿, and the ☽ be unconnected with each other by good asps., and affl. by ♄ or ♂, and with no assistance from ♃ or ♀, tend to demoniacal affections, and also to epilepsy; ♄ and ♂ in angles ori., and with ♃ and ♀ setting and occi., the demoniac utters mysterious sayings, becomes furious, or wounds himself; the ☽ ☌ ☉, and governed by ♄, or the ☽ ☍ the ☉ governed by ♂, and espec. when in ♎, ♐, or ♓; lords of the 1st or 6th in ♈ and affl. by ♅; Subs at AT and AX usually exist in these cases. (See "Delirium Tremens", "Wild", under Delirium; Epilepsy, Fears, Fury, Hallucinations, Imaginations, Insanity, Madness, Mania; "Brain" under Moisture; Narcotics, Obsessions, Pineal Gland, Spirit Controls).

**Bathing**—Demoniacal complaints as a result of bathing are caused by ♅, and espec. when the ruler of the 1st, or 6th H. is in ♈ and affl. by ♅. (See Bathing).

**DEMULCENT**—A mucilaginous substance allaying irritation. A therapeutic property of ♀. (See Venus).

**DENEB** — Cauda Leonis — Lion's Tail. (See Lion's Tail).

**DENGUE** — Break-Bone Fever—Sometimes called Rheumatic Fever. A zymotic disease, with pain in the bones, swollen joints, fever, and an eruption which resembles measles. A ♂ disease; ♂ affl. the Asc. at B., and by dir. Many of the influences which cause Measles will also apply to this disease. Also ♄ usually is configurated in the afflictions, affecting the bones and joints. (See "Pain" under Bones; Eruptions, Joints, Measles; "Fever" under Rheumatism; Zymosis).

**DENSITY**—Compactness—The work of ♄. (See Cirrhosis, Condensation, Consistency, Consolidation, Crystallization, Fiber; "Density" under Fluids; Hardening).

**DENTAL**—Dentist—Dentition—Pertaining to the Teeth—

**Decay of Teeth** — Disorders of — (See Teeth).

**Dentition** — Teething—Convulsions at Time of—Difficult Dentition, etc.—(See "Dentition" under Teeth).

**Dentist**—Makes a Good Dentist—♂ in good asp. to ♅; ♂ in the 10th H., and well-asp. by the ☉, ☽, or ♅. The influences given under Chemists and Surgeons also apply here, as ♂, and the ♂ influence, is usually predominant in the maps of those who succeed in Surgery of any kind, and the use of tools and sharp instruments. (See Butchers, Chemists, Healers, Operations, Surgeons).

**DENTS**—A Dent in the Body, Mark, or Scar Indicated—(See Marks, Scars).

**DENUDES**—Denuding — Depletion—Weakening—♄ denudes, depletes, and weakens the physical constitution, while ♂ intensifies and accelerates its action. (See Depletion, Saturn Influence under Saturn).

**DEPLETION**—The work of ♄ and ♆; the ☉, ☽, Asc., or hyleg affl. by ♄ or ♆ at B., and by dir. Any part, organ, or function of the body tends to be weakened and depleted when ♄ is in the sign at B. ruling such part or function, and espec. when ♄ is afflicted, or afflicting the vital parts of the map. The bodily forces are also depleted when the watery signs ♋ or ♓ are on the Asc. at B., and the constitution rendered more watery and phlegmatic. (See Constitution, Eclipses; "Quarters of the Moon" under Moon; "Moonlight" under Sleep; Strength; Vitality, Weak).

**Constitution Depleted**—The Tissues Depleted—The ☉ affl. in the 6th H., the constitution and vitality are depleted. (See "Lessened", "Wasted" under Vitality. Also see the first part of this section).

**Energy Depleted**—(See "Depletion" under Energy. Also note the various paragraphs in this section).

**Functions Depleted**—The ☽ affl. by ♄ at B., and by dir. (See "Suppression" under Functions).

**Heart Action**—♄ affl. in ♌ tends to weak and depleted heart action. (See "Weak Heart" under Heart).

**Nerve Fluids**—Depletion of—♅ □ or ☍ Asc. (See Fluids, Nerves).

**Vital Fluids**—Depletion of—♆ □ or ☍ Asc. (See "Fluid" under Vital).

**Vitality**—Depletion of—(See "Constitution" in this section). See Atrophy, Collapse, Decay, Debility, Dissipation, Emaciation, Enervation, Exhaustion, Feeble, Neurasthenia, Weak.

**DEPOPULATION**—(See Mortality).

**DEPORTMENT**—Behavior—(See Conduct, Morals, etc.).

**DEPOSITS**—Sediments—Collections of Morbid Particles In the Body—Mineral Deposits—Deposit of Wastes in the Tissues, Organs, and various Parts of the Body—The various mineral deposits of the body are precipitated by ♄. Some are constructive, and help to form the bones and the normal harder structures. Others are poisonous and destructive and tend to cause disease, hardening of the arteries, articulations, joints, organs, tissues and parts, membranes, and to cause gout, rheumatism, contortions, cirrhosis, deafness, deformities, gravel, stone, sand, concretions, lameness, retentions, suppressions, tuberculosis, sclerosis, arterio-sclerosis, gall stones, congestions, disturbed functions and elimination, excretion, secretion, etc. The influence of Cold, which is ruled by ♄, also tends to abnormal and morbid deposits and precipitations over the body. See these subjects. Especially note the subjects of Cold, Concretions, Crystallization, Gravel, Growths, Hardening, Lime, Leokocytes, Minerals, Osseous, Pressure, Sand, Saturn Influence, Stone, Tumors, Urea, Uric Acid, Wastes, etc.).

**DEPRAVED**—Depravity—Total Depravity—Dycrasia—Depraved Tastes, Desires, and Habits—Turpitude—etc.— The ☉ conciliated with the ruler of the mind, and being cadent and occidentally posited; ♆ affl. in the 5th or 7th H.; ♆ ♓ in the 5th H., and afflicted, depraved habits and dissolute vices; ♄ ☌ or ill-asp. ♀; ♄ in ♋ or ♓ and affl.; ♄ to the ill-asps. ♂ by dir.; ♂ Sig. □ or ☍ ♀; ♀ ill-dig. at B.; ♀ to the ☌ ♂ by dir.; ♀, ☌, □, or ☍ the malefics, and ♀ ruler of the horoscope; ♀ affl. at B., and to the ☌ or ill-asps. the Asc. by dir.; the 3rd Deg. of ♎ on Asc., drunkenness, licentiousness, etc. (See Appetites, Debauched, Desires, Dissolute, Drink, Drunkenness, Habits, Harlots, Indecent, Infamous, Lascivious, Leprosy, Lewd, Licentious, Low, Lust, Morals, Obscene, Passion, Perversions, Shameless, Sottishness, Tastes, Turpitude, Vices, etc.).

**Depraved Blood**—(See Impure).

**DEPRESSANTS**—An agent reducing functional activity—(See Anaphrodisiac, Narcotics, Palliatives, Sedatives, Tobacco, etc.).

**DEPRESSED**—Depressions—Depressed in Mind—Depressions in the Body—
  **Body**—Depressions In—Caused by ♄. (See Contractions, Dents, Hollow).

  **Compressions**—(See Compressions).

  **Diseases**—Diseases Arising from a Depressed Mind—♄ affl. in the 6th H., or affl. the hyleg or Asc. (See Aches, Functions, Melancholy).

  **Extreme Depression**—Of Mind—Morbid Anxiety Concerning the Health—(See Hypochondria).

  **Mental Depression** — Cast Down — Atrabilarious Attacks—Melancholy—A ♄ disease and influence, and of the ♄ sign ♑, which sign produces a depressing and lowering tendency; the transit of ♄ as promittor over the place of the radical ☽ or ☿, depressed and melancholic, and espec. when ♄ is ℞ or Stationary; ♄ in the Asc., 3rd, or 6th H., and affl. ☿ or the ☽ at B., or by dir.; ♄ affl. in ♍; ♄ to the ☌ or ill-asps. his own place by tr. or dir.; ♄, ♅, or ♆ in ♏ and affl. the ☉ or ☽; ♄ in the 6th H., or affl. the ☉ or ☽; ♄ to the ☌ or ill-asp. the ☽ or ♀; the ☉ or ☽ hyleg and to the ☌ or ill-asp. ♄ by dir.; the ☉ in ♑ and affl. by ♄ or ♃; the ☽ to the ☌ or ill-asp. ♄ by tr. or dir.; the ☽ or ☿ affl. in ♑; the ☽ in ♍ and ☌ or ill-asp. ♄, ♅, ♆, or ♂ promittors, depressed thru biliousness or nervous debility; ♆ afflictions to the ☉, ☽, Asc. or hyleg tend to cause illnesses of a depressive nature; ♃ affl. in ♈ or ♎; the 2° ♌ on the Asc., depressed and nerveless. Lack of the Adrenal secretion tends to depression. (See Adrenals, Anxiety, Atrobile; "Biliousness" and "Black Bile" under Bile; Dejected, Despair, Despondent, Emotions; "Morbid Fears" under Fears; Gloom, Grief, Hypochondria; "Low Spirits" under Low; Melancholy, Moods, Morose, Peace, Peevish, Sadness, Sorrow, Suicide, Worry, etc.).

  **Nervous Depression**—(See "Debility", "Depressed", "Neurasthenia", under Nerves).

  **Skull**—Depressions In—(See Skull).

  **Spinal Cord**—The Cord Compressed—(See Compressions, Subluxations).

**DEPRESSOR**—Depressor Nerves—Are influenced strongly by ♆.

  **Heart**—Depressor Nerves of—(See "Depressor" under Heart). See Inhibition).

**DERANGED**—Derangements—Disordered—Discomposed—The malefics ♄ and ♂ are the principal factors in causing physiological derangements. Mental derangements are due more to the influence of ☿ and the ☽, afflictions to them, and their relations to each other and the Asc. (See "Derangement" under Mental). Any part of the body, as well as the different parts or qualities of the mind, are subject to derangement under the various planetary afflictions at B., and by dir., and for these disorders, and the influences causing them, see the subject, and the disease, disorder, or weakness, in the alphabetical arrangement. The word "Deranged" is used very little in Astrological Literature, but has been used in connection with the following subjects.

  **Deranged Blood**—Caused by afflictions to ♃ and ♀, the rulers of the blood. (See the various paragraphs under Blood, Circulation).

  **Mental Derangement**—(See "Derangement" under Mental).

  **Physiological Derangements**—Bodily Disorders—(See Disease, Disorders, Distempers, Fevers, Functions, Glands, Heaviness, Humours, Ill-Health, Imperfections, Indispositions, Infirmities, Irregularities, Irritations, Lethargy, Morbid, Sickness, etc. Also see each organ and part of the body, functions, etc., for the various derangements of such parts).

  **Stomach Deranged**—(See Digestion, Indigestion, Stomach).

  **System Deranged**—(See "Disordered System" under System. Also see Body, Constitution, Disease, Ill-Health, Nerves, Sickness, etc.).

**DERMA**—The Cutis—The Corium—The True Skin—The Derma comes under the same rulership as the Skin in general. (See Skin). The Derma is contracted by ♄ and Cold, driving the blood inwards, causing internal congestions, colds, etc., and is relaxed by the heat of ♂, which influences tend to draw the blood to the surface again. (See Centrifugal, Centripetal, Cold, Colds, Congestions, Corium, Cutis, Eruptions, Purpura, Rubefacient, Skin).

**DESCENDANT**—The 7th H., the Cusp of the 7th, the Western Angle, etc.— This is one of the vital and sensitive places of the map of birth, and espec. the degree on the Western horizon at B. Planets when reaching this degree after birth by direction or progression tend to cause diseases, accidents, or death, according to the nature of the planets and influences. (See Physical; "Seventh House" under Seventh).

**DESCENDING COLON**—Ruled by ♂ and ♏. (See Colon).

**DESCENT**—The Chart of Descent—(See Prenatal Epoch).

**DESCRIPTION**—Description of the Body—Planets in the Rising Sign modify the description of the body. (See Appearance, Ascendant; "First House" under First; Form, Height, Shape, Stature).

**DESERT**—The Desert—Desert Places—Ruled by ♄.

**Lost in the Desert**—Sickness or Death In—The afflictors to the Significators of travel being in the 12th H. at B., or by dir., and usually in one of the watery signs; malefics in the 12th H. at B.; ♄ or ♂ controlling the Luminaries, in ♋, ♏, or ♓, and espec. when in the 12th H. at B., or by dir., and affl. the hyleg; ♄ and ♂ governing the Lights, being in watery signs, and espec. when in ☍ the ☉ and ☽ during the period of travel. These same influences also apply to being lost in, starvation in, death or sickness in desolate, inaccessible, or wilderness places. (See "Dangers" under Travel).

**DESIRE**—Desires—Desire Body—The Desires, Hopes and Ambitions are ruled by the 11th H. The principle of ♀ is desire. Venus ill-dig. at B. leads to wrong desires, illicit affections, increase of passion, excess of amorous indulgences, etc. When ♀ is well-asp. at B., and by dir., the desires are of a higher, purer, and more spiritual nature. (See Character). There are many subjects affiliated with Desire and Desires which tend to cause ill-health and disease when illicit and perverted desires are given too much liberty, and especially along the lines of food, eating, drink, pleasure, passion, sex, etc., and for subjects which may not be included in this section, look for it in the alphabetical arrangement. (See Eleventh House).

**Abnormal Desires**—(See Abnormal, Appetites, Cravings, Depraved, Drink, Eating, Excesses, Food, Gluttony, Lascivious, Passion, Perversions, Sex, Unnatural, etc.).

**Cravings**—(See Cravings).

**Darkened Desires**—(See "Darkened" under Mind).

**Death**—Desire For—(See "Desire" under Death; Suicide).

**Depraved Desires**—(See Depraved).

**Desire Body**—This is one of Man's finer Vehicles and made of Desire Stuff. Our emotions, feelings and passions originate in this body. The Desire Body being the seat of the passions and emotions is a strong factor in causing disease and sickness. The Desire Body, also known as the Animal Soul, is ruled by the ☽ and ♂, and is also influenced by ♄, ♃, and ☿. The impulses of ♂ stir the Desire Body into action. The Animal Soul has its seat in the Liver, and the Liver is the great central vortex of the Desire Body. (See Liver). The Desire Body urges us on to Action. (See Action). Desires, and the Desire Body, are affiliated with the watery signs. The Astral Body is the seat of the Desires. (See Astral, Childhood, Emotions, Feelings, Impulses, Iron, Sensations).

**Failure of Desires**—The ☉ □ or ☍ ♄ at B., and by dir. (See Ambition, Hopes).

**Faulty Desires**—(See "Abnormal" in this section).

**Insistent Desire**—♂ influence.

**Low Desires**—(See Depraved, Debauched, Dissipated, Drunken, Intemperate, Low, Morals, Passion, Perversions, etc.).

**No Desire**—Free from Passional Desire—(See Celibacy).

**Perverted Desires**—(See Perverse, Perversions).

**Sex Desires**—(See Amorous, Passion, Sex).

**Spiritual Desires**—(See Spiritual).

**Unnatural Desires**—(See Chaotic, Perversions, Unnatural).

**Violent Desires**—(See "Desires" under Violent).

**Wrong Desires**—(See the first part of this section). See Affections, Illicit, Love Affairs, Pleasures, Recreations.

**DESPAIR**—Hopelessness—Despondency—Discouragement—Desperation, etc.—♄ influence; ♄ in the 11th H., the house of hopes and wishes; ☿ affl. by ♄; ☿ affl. in ♑; ☿ in ♑ ☌ or ill-asp. ♄ tends to produce death thru despair, and abandonment of hope. (See Anxiety, Anguish, Dejected, Depressed, Despondent, Distress, Gloom, Hope, Melancholy, Peevish, Suicide, Worry).

**DESPONDENCY**—Mental Depression—Dejection—Athymia—Melancholy, etc. —The ☉ or ☽ to the ☌ or ill-asps. ♄ by dir.; the Prog. ☽ to the ☌ or ill-asps. ♄; ♄ affl. in the 3rd or 9th Houses, the houses of mind; lord of the 6th H. in the 11th H., often despondent and gloomy, and with little hope, and espec. if the lord of the 11th afflict the lord of the Asc.; lord of the 8th in the Asc.; Subs at AT. (See Anxiety, Brooding, Dejected, Depressed, Despair, Discontentment, Gloom, Grave, Hopes, Melancholy, Moods, Peace, Peevish, Worry, etc., and the references under these subjects).

**DESQUAMATION**—Scaling of the Cuticle—(See Scales, Skin).

**DESTINY**—(See Character, Events, External, Fate; "Periods" under Health; "Free Will" under Will).

**DESTROYERS OF LIFE**—(See Anareta).

**Destroys the Children**—(See "Death of Children" under Children).

**Life Destroyed**—(See "Certain Death" under Death; Fatal; "Life Destroyed" under Life).

**DESTRUCTIVE**—Destructiveness—Pernicious—Ruinous—Noxious—Cold and Dry are destructive and noxious forces in Nature, and espec. when in excess. Cold is ruled by ♄, and excess of dryness by ♂. (See Cold, Dry). Heat and Moisture, on the other hand, are prolific and nutritive, when not in excess, and are ruled by the benefic planets ♃ and ♀. (See Heat, Moisture).

**Destructive Processes**—In the Body—Are the work principally of ♄ and ♂, and also of the ☉ when he is in □ or ☍ asp. to the malefics, and espec. to ♄ and ♂. Saturn is destructive by retention of wastes, deposits, hardening, corrosion, stagnation of functions, suppressions, impeded elimination, concretions, retention of Urea, obstructions, atrophy, crystallization, etc., and by causing fears, worry, pessimism, etc. Mars is destructive for the time by causing high and violent fevers to burn up the wastes of the system, and by causing accidents and violence. Scorpio, one of the signs of ♂, is concerned in both the destructive and reproductive processes. Thus ♄ and ♂ are both constructive and destructive according to their different aspects and influences. Destructive energy is under the rule of ♂. (See Anaemia, Atrophy, Cells, Constructive, Corrosion, Crystallization, Decay, Degeneration, Deposits, Destructiveness, Deterioration, Emaciation, Hardening, Impediments, Mars, Metabolism, Noxious, Obstructions, Pernicious, Processes, Retention, Saturn, Stagnation, Stone, Suppressions, Tissues, Wastes).

**DESTRUCTIVENESS** — Pernicious — Ruinous—Tending to Destroy—Mental Destructiveness—A ♂ disease and affliction; afflictions to ♂ at B., and by dir.; ♂ and ♅ prominent at B., and afflicted, tend to wanton and dangerous destructiveness; the ☽ □ or ☍ ♂ at B., and by dir.; the 3rd Decanate ♌ on the Asc. In a good horoscope these same forces manifest themselves in Reforms, and in the destruction of evil, sin, wickedness and vice wherever they may be found. (See Anarchists, Criminal, Cruel, Dangerous, Destructive, Fierce, Furious, Murderous, Pernicious, Rashness, Reformers, Religion, Revolutionary, Riotous, Savage, Temper, Violent, etc.).

**DETERIORATION**—To Reduce, Degenerate, Impair, Make Worse, etc.—The work of ♄.

**Emotional Deterioration** — (See "Arrested" under Emotions).

**Mental**—(See Idiocy, Imbecile, Insanity, Intellect, Mental, Mind, etc.').

**Physical**—(See Atrophy, Consumptions, Death, Decay, Degeneration, Destructive, Disease, Emaciation, Wasting, etc.).

**DETERMINED** — Mental Resolution — (See Positive, Resolute; "Strong" under Will).

**DETERMINATION**—Directed to a Part or Organ—

**Blood**—Determination of Blood to a Part—♂ influence. (See "Determination", "Rush of Blood", under Blood).

**To the Head**—Determination of Blood to the Head—Rush of to the Head—Flow of Blood to the Head — (See "Blood" under Head).

**DETRIMENT**—Injury—Loss—Impairment—

**Cattle**—Detriment to Large Cattle—The 12th H. in the map of the owner rules his cattle, and ♄ or ♂ affl. in this house indicate the death of, diseases among, injury and detriment to his large cattle. (See "Diseases Among", "Small Cattle", under Cattle).

**Children**—Detriment To—(See "Detriment" under Children).

**Detriment to Everything**—The ☉, ♄, ♃, and ♂ conjoined in ♋; the ☽, ♀, and ☿ conjoined in ♋.

**Planets in Detriment**—Planets are in detriment, and weaker in influence, and afflicting, when in the signs opposite to the signs they rule. Thus the ☉ rules ♌, and is in detriment in ♒. Planets in detriment, being weaker and less fortunate, tend to invite disease and affliction to the parts of the body ruled by the sign they are in at B., and to increase the inherent debility of that part, and espec. when such planet is very evilly aspected. (See Opposites). For detriment to Men, Women, Children, Brother, Sister, Father, Mother, Aunts, Uncles, Grandparents, Family, Relatives, Kings, Nobles, Monarchs, Rulers, Presidents, etc., see these subjects in the alphabetical arrangement. Also see Accidents, Afflictions, Blows, Bruises, Disease, Disgrace, Evils, Falls, Hurts, Ill-Health, Injuries, Mental, Mind, Miseries, Misfortune, Ruin, Suffering, Trouble, Wounds, etc. For subjects not mentioned here look for them in the alphabetical arrangement.

**DEVELOPMENT**—Progression Toward Maturity—

**Bodily Development**—(See Body, Decanates, Growth, etc.).

**Early Development**—(See Precocious, Premature).

**Late Development** — (See Backwardness).

**Mental Development**—(See Dull, Geniuses, Imbecile, Intellect, Mental, Mind, Perception, Prodigies, Understanding).

**Organic Development** — (See "First Quarter" under Moon; Organic).

**Over-Developed Organs** — (See Organs).

**Perfect Physical Development**—(See Harmony).

**Tissues**—Development of — (See Tissues). See other subjects, such as Diminished, Dwarf, Enlarged, Giants, Height, Ill-Formed, Inhuman, Monsters, Organs, Undersized, Undeveloped, Weight, etc.).

**DEVIATIONS**—Abnormalities—

**Faculties**—Deviation of the Passive or Sensitive Faculties — Deviation in these faculties is discernible chiefly in the excess or deficiency of the masculine or feminine genders, and lack of the proper balance and conformation agreeable to its own nature. Thus in a male horoscope many planets in feminine signs tend to make men effeminate, and in a female nativity many planets in masculine signs tend to make women more coarse and masculine, and to deviate from the usual limits of nature. (See Abnormal, Aversions, Bachelors, Celibacy, Effeminate, Fears, Perversions, Sex, Spinsters).

**Mental Deviations**—Morbid Mental Deviations—(See "Morbid" under Mind; Unsavory).

**DEVITALIZATION**—A ♄ disease and affliction. (See Consumption, Emaciation, Feeble; "Lessened", "Low", under Vitality; Wastings; "Weak Body" under Weak).

**DEVOID OF**—Void of—(See Deficient, Diminished, Insufficient, Lack, Loss, Void, etc.).

**DEVOURED**—The Body Devoured After Death—(See "Body Devoured" under Burial).

**DEXTERITY**—Quickness of Mind and Body Right-Handedness Due largely to the influence of ☿ and the ♊ sign; the good asps. of ♂ to ☿. (See Action, Balance, Coordination, Graceful, Harmony, Quick; "Right Side" under Right).

**DIABETES**—An Auto-Toxic Psychoses—Diabetes Insipidus—An Excessive Flow of Urine—Diabetes Mellitus—A ♎ disease, and afflictions in ♎, ♈, or ♏; the ☉, ♃, ♂ or ♀ affl. in ♎; is also a ♃, ♂, or ♀ disease; ♃ affl. in ♈ or ♎; ♃ affl. in ♎ tends to the sugar variety, Mellitus, as waste of sugar is the work of ♃; ♃ and ♀ in ♎ and affl. the ☽ or Asc.; a ♂ disease; ♂ in ♎ and affl. the hyleg; ♂ in ♏; caused by afflictions to ♀; a ♀ disease; ♀ affl. in ♎; ♀ or ♃ in ♎ in the 6th H., and afflicted; ♀ to the ☌ or ill-asps. ♂; the ☽ in ♏, ☌ or ill-asp. ♄ (or ☿ if he be of the nature of ♄) at the beginning of an illness, or at decumb. (Hor'y); ♎ on the Asc. or 6th H. at B., and containing malefics; Subs at KP (11D) in the Insipidius form; Subs at KP (11D), and at Li.P. in the Mellitus, Sugar form. (See Kidneys, Sugar; "Polyuria" under Urine).

**Cases of Diabetes**—See Figures 7G and 7H in the book, "Astro-Diagnosis" by the Heindels.

**Death from Diabetes**—♀ affl. the hyleg by dir., and ♀ much affl. at B., and ♀ holding the dominion of death; common signs show, and with common signs on the angles, or many afflictions at B. in such signs. (See Mutable).

**DIAGNOSIS**—The Diagnosis of Disease—Judgment of the Disease—In judging and diagnosing disease by Astrology look to the 6th H., planets in the 6th, lord of the 6th, the position of lord of the 6th, and its aspects; the rising sign; lord of the Asc., and its aspects, and the aspects to the ☉ and ☽. (For further influences see Acute, Chronic, Continuity, Course, Crises, Curable, Death, Duration, Fatal, Incurable; "Judgment of the Disease" under Judgment; "Long Diseases" under Long; Prognostication, Prognosis, Prolonged; "Short Diseases" under Short; "Sixth House" under Sixth; Tedious, etc. Also note the various paragraphs and subjects under Disease, Extraordinary, Health, Ill-Health, Recovery, Recuperation, Remedy, Resistance, Sickness, Treatment, Vitality, etc.).

**Locating the Disease**—The planets in the different Signs at B., and also the signs on the Asc., 6th, 8th, and 12th Houses, show what parts of the body are afflicted. The Signs containing the malefics usually show what parts of the body are most afflicted from birth, and the directions, transits, and progressed influences after birth show when the afflicted organ is more apt to become diseased, and the duration of the affliction. (For further influences along this line see each of the planets, signs, and houses in the alphabetical arrangement, and note the parts of the body, or organs, they rule. Also see Left, Lower, Majority, Malformations, Middle, Organs, Parts, Prenatal, Right, Sympathy, Symptoms, Upper, etc.).

**DIAPHORETICS**—An Agent Producing Perspiration—(See Sudorific).

**DIAPHRAGM**—Midriff—Phren—Phrenic—Ruled by the ♋ and ♍ Signs.

**Affected**—(See "Diseased", and the various paragraphs in this section).

**Breathing**—Diaphragmatic Breathing—Disorders of—Afflictions in ♋; Subs at SP (8 D). (See Breathing).

**Convulsive Movements**—Spasmodic Disturbances of—♅ in ♍. (See Asthma, Erratic, Spasmodic).

**Diaphragmatic Plexus**—The ☉ and ☽ acting thru the ♋ sign, and thru this plexus, tend to affect the diaphragm, the stomach, the digestive organs, and give way to the Cranio-Abdominal Diathesis. (See "Fifth Thoracic" under Ganglion).

**Diseased**—♄ afflicted in ♊ or ♋; ♂ in ♉, ♊, or ♋ rules and affects the diaphragm and intercostal muscles. Also affected by Subs at LSP (8 D).

**Erratic Action Of**—And Tending to Cause Hiccough—♅ afflicted in ♋ or ♍. (See Asthma; "Labored" under Breathing; Hiccough; "Convulsive" in this section).

**Hernia Of**—♂ influence; ♂ afflicted in ♍; Subs at SP (8D).

**Hiccough**—(See "Erratic" in this section).

**Inflammation Of**—A ♋ disease; ♂ afflicted in ♋.

**Paralysis Of**—Paresis—Phrenasthenia—A ♄ disease; ♄ affl. in ♍; ♄ ☌ ☉ in ♍; Subs at SP (8D). (See Paralysis).

**Rhythm Of**—Rhythmic Action of Disturbed—♅ afflicted in ♋, and also tends to Asthma. (See Asthma, Rhythm).

**Spasmodic Disturbance Of**—(See "Convulsive" in this section).

**DIARRHOEA**—Looseness of the Bowels—Morbidly Frequent Evacuations of the Bowels—Profuse Watery Discharges—A ☽, ♂, and ♍ disease, and caused principally by afflictions in ♍; caused by the ☉, ☽, ♂, ♀, and ☿ affl. in ♍, and espec. when these planets in ♍ afflict the hyleg at the same time; the ☉ to the ☌ or ill-asp. ♂ by dir.; the ☽ in ♓ and affl. by the ☉ or ♂ when taken ill (Hor'y); ♃ affl. in ♍; ♂ affl. in ♍ or ♓; ♂ in ♍ in the 6th H.; malefics in ♍ at B., and the hyleg much afflicted. (See "Treatment" under Bowels; Cholera, Dysentery, Evacuations, Faeces, Flux, Physic). Case of Diarrhoea—Birth Data, etc.—See "Diarrhoea", Chap. 13, page 90 in Daath's Medical Astrology).

**Bilious Diarrhoea**—♂ affl. in ♊; ♂ to the ☌ or ill-asps. ☿. (See Bile).

**Chronic Diarrhoea**—The ☉, ☽, and other planets in ♍ and affl. by ♄; ♄ in ♍, and espec. when in the 6th H., and affl. the hyleg; Subs at KP (11D), and at PP (2, 3, 4L). Case—See Chap. 13, page 90, in Daath's Medical Astrology.

**Diarrhoea Prevalent**—☿ in ♍ at the Vernal Equi., lord of the year, and afflicted, and espec. among People and Places ruled by ♍.

**Infectious Diarrhoea**—(See "Cholera Infantum" under Cholera).

**DIASTASE**—(See Pancreas).

**DIASTOLE**—The Lunar Diastole—(See "Diastole", "Full Moon", under Moon).

**DIATHESIS**—A Constitutional Predisposition to Disease—The Transient Disposition in Disease—Indicated by Directions. (See Directions). The Hexis, or Permanent Habit in disease, is indicated by the radix. If the Hexis and Diathesis agree, the disease is more certain and pronounced, and of the nature produced by the strong afflicting planets at B., or by dir. (See "Disease" under Severity). For the different forms of Diathesis see Asthma, Cardiac, Cells; "Cranio-Abdominal" under Cranian; Ganglion, Hemorrhage, Hepatic, Heredity, Hexis, Metabolism, Metamorphosis, Praeincipients, Processes, Renal, Splenic, Thoracic, etc. The different forms of Diathesis, and the planetary influences working with them, are given in the different paragraphs under Ganglion).

**DIET**—Dietetics—Eating—Food, etc. The matter of Diet is considered mostly under the subjects of Eating and Food. The ♍ Sign rules strongly over matters of Diet, Food, etc. (See Virgo). The following subjects have to do with Diet, Habits of Diet and Eating, and Ill-Health from Indiscretions, or Wrong Diet, which see in the alphabetical arrangement when not considered here—

**Ailments Due to Diet**—Ailments from Wrong or Bad Diet—♃ causes complaints from High Living and injudicious dieting; the ☉ □ or ☍ ♃, ailments from indiscretions in diet; ♃ in bad asp. the ☽, impeded functions thru injudicious diet; ♃ in ♌, ailments due to diet; ♃ or ♀ affl. in ♍, disorders due to wrong and bad diet; the ☉, ☽, ♄, or ♀ affl. in ♋, or ♋ upon the Asc., diseases from wrong diet; ♀ affl. in ♋, complaints, complications, surfeits, vomiting, from wrong diet; ♀ affl. in ♍; ♋ and ♍ diseases; ♄ affl. in ♋ tends to Scurvy due to deficient, wrong and improper diet. (See "Too Much Blood" under Blood; Digestion; "Impure Blood" under Impure; Indigestion, Indiscretions, Plethora, Scurvy, Surfeits, Vomiting, etc.).

**Appetite; Appetites; Assimilation;**

**Bad Diet**—Illness From—(See "Ailments", "Evil", in this section).

**Careful in Diet**—♀ in the 6th H., and well-aspected; the 3rd Dec. of ♍ on the Asc., ruled by ☿. (See "Fastidious" in this section. Also see "Eccentric" under Food).

**Deficient Diet**—(See "Ailments" in this section. Also see Scurvy).

**Dietetics**—Favorable for the Study of—The ☉ or ☽ well-asp. in ♍; planets in ♍ in the Asc. or 6th H.; ♍ influence; ♍ on the Asc. (See Hygiene).

**Digestion; Drink; Eating;**

**Epicureans; Evil Diet**—Wrong Diet—Indiscretions in Diet—Improper Diet—Errors of Diet, etc.—Diseases and Surfeits Proceeding From—The ☉ affl. by ♃ or ♀; the ☽ in the 6th H., and in ill-asp. to ♀; ♃ affl. in ♉, ♋, or ♑; a ♃ disease, as most of the ♃ diseases arise from indiscretions in diet; a ♀ disease; an afflicted ♀; ♀ in ♍ and affl. the ☽ or Asc.; ♀ affl. in ♍ in the 6th H.; ♀ affl. in ♋; the Asc. to the ill-asps. the ☽ or ♀ by dir., and the ☽ or ♀ affl. at B.; ☿ affl. in ♋. (See "Ailments", "Excesses", in this section. Also see Gluttony, Indiscretions, Scurvy).

**Excesses in Diet**—Diseases and Surfeits Arising From—The ☉ affl. by ♃ or ♀; the ☽ in ♎ and affl. by the ☉ or ♂ when taken ill (Hor'y); the ☽ in ♎, and in ☌ or ill-asp. ♄ (or ☿ if he be of the nature of ♄) at the beginning of the illness, or at decumb., disease arising from surfeit of wine (Hor'y); ♃ affl. in the 6th H.; ♂ affl. in ♋ or ♓; ♀ in ♎ when ♀ is the afflictor; the Asc. to the ☌ or any asp. ♀ by dir., and ♀ affl. at B. (See "Ailments", "Evil", in this section. Also see Autointoxication, Drink, Eating, Excesses, Feasting, Food, Gluttony, Obesity, Plethora, Surfeits, Toxaemia, Wine, etc.).

**Extravagant in Diet**—♂ in the 6th H. (See Extravagance; "Rich", "Sugar", "Sweets", under Food; Luxuries).

**Fastidious in Diet**—Particular—Careful—Is the result of positions and influences involving the 6th H., ☿, and the ♍ sign. The ♋ people are also very particular about their food and diet. Also a ♆ trait, and espec. with ♆ in ♊ in close asp. with ☿. Aspects between ♅ and ☿, espec. if ☿ signs are involved. (See "Careful" in this section).

**Fasting**—People of the Sanguine Temperament benefit by fasting. (See Sanguine).

**Feasting; Feeding; Food;**

**Functions Impeded**—By Wrong Diet—(See "Ailments" in this section).

**Gluttony; Gormandizing; Habits;**

**High Living**—(See "High Living" under High).

**Hygiene**—Hygiene and Diet Specialist—(See Hygiene. Also see "Diatetics" in this section).

**Improper Diet**—(See "Ailments", "Evil", "Excesses", and the various paragraphs in this section).

**Indiscretions**—In Diet—(See "Ailments", "Evil", in this section).

**Injudicious Dieting**—(See "Ailments", "Evil", in this section).

**Intemperate in Diet**—(See "Excesses" in this section. Also see Intemperance; "Officer" under Military).

**Luxuries; Nutrition;**

**Particular About Diet**—(See "Fastidious" in this section).

**Rich Diet**—(See "Rich Foods" under Food).

**Surfeits from Diet**—(See "Ailments", "Evil", "Excesses", in this section. Also see Surfeits).

**Vomiting**—From Wrong Diet—(See "Ailments" in this section. Also see Nausea, Vomiting).

**Wrong Diet**—Illness from—(See "Ailments", "Evil", "Excesses", in this section).

**DIFFICULT**—Difficulty—

**Breathing Difficult**—(See "Laboured" under Breathing).

**Difficult to Cure**—(See Chronic, Fatal, Grievous, Incurable, Invalids, Long Diseases, Malignant, Morbid, Slow Diseases, Tedious, Wastings, etc.).

**Feminine Functions**—Difficult and Slow—(See "Difficult" under Menses).

**Food**—Difficulty in Retaining Food—(See Food).

**Micturition Difficult**—(See Urine).

**Swallowing Difficult**—(See Deglutition). See such subjects as Constipation, Deafness, Hearing, Retardation, Sight, Slow, Speech, Suppressions, Walk, etc. Look in the alphabetical arrangement for other subjects which you may have in mind along this line).

**DIFFICULTIES**—See such subjects as Accidents, Disaster, Disease, Disgrace, Dishonour, Hurts, Ill-Health, Injuries, Miseries, Reverses, Ruin, Sickness, Sorrow, Trouble, Worry, Wounds, etc., and other subjects you may have in mind. The influences of ♄, and also the 12th H., are to place difficulties, delays, hindrances, obstacles, etc., in our path, and to meet with self-undoing, prolonged sickness and affliction, unless we can qualify, resist, overcome, and become Masters of our Destiny.

**DIFFUSIVENESS**—A Scattering—

**Energy**—Diffusiveness of—(See Dispersions, Dissipation, Energy, Scattering, Vacillating).

**DIGESTION**—Coction—Digestive Organs—Digestive System—Digestive Canal—Digestive Tract—Alimentation—The Conversion of Food into Chyle and Chyme, etc.—Digestion is a function of the ♋ sign, and the Digestive Organs and System are under the internal rule of ♋. (See "Fifth Thoracic" under Ganglion). Digestion is also ruled and influenced by ♃ and the 4th H. The Coction Process in the body is ruled by ♂. The following subjects have to do with Digestion, the Digestive System, and their activities, which see in the alphabetical arrangement when not considered here—

**Absorption; Acids**—The Stomach Acids—(See Acids, Fluids, Gastric, Hydrochloric, Juices).

**Activity**—Digestive activity is ruled by ♃ and the ☽.

**Alimentation**—(See Alimentary).

**Anxiety**—Digestive Disorders from Anxiety and Worry—♄ in ♋ or ♑, and affl. the ☉ or ☽; ☿ affl. in ♋; ♑ on the Asc. (See Anxiety, Worry).

**Appetite; Assimilation; Belching;**

**Bowels**—Intestinal Indigestion—(See "Digestion" under Bowels).

**Chronic Indigestion**—(See Indigestion).

**Chyle; Chyme; Cold**—(See "Cold" under Indigestion).

**Defect**—Some Defect in the Digestive Organs—Born under ♃.

**Diet; Digestive Disorders**—Digestive Troubles—The ☉, ☽, or ♃ in ♋, and affl. by malefics; the ☉ or ☽ affl. in ♋; the ☉ or ☽ in the 6th H., in card. signs, and affl.; the ☉ to the ☌ or P. the ☽ by dir.; the ☉ or ☽ in ♋, and to the ☌ or ill-asp. the malefics; the ☉ to the ill-asps. ♃; the ☉ in ♉, due to rich foods; the ☉ in ♋ and affl. by ♃; the ☉ or ☽ affl. in ♑; the ☽ affl. in ♍; the ☽ affl. at B., and to the evil asps. the Asc.; the ☽ □ or ☍ ♃ or ♀; the ☽ in the 6th H., and affl. by ♃; the ☽ applying to ♂, or conjoined with him in a day geniture; ♆ or ♅ affl. in ♋ or ♑; ♄ in ♋ or ♑; ♄ ☌ ☽, and espec. with females; ♃ affl. in ♋ or ♑; ♃ □ or ☍ ☽; ♂ affl. in ♋ or ♑; ♂ □ or ☍ ☽; ♂ affl. in 4th H., and espec. by the □ or ☍ asps.; ♀ affl. in ♑; caused by ♀ when the dominion of death is vested in her; ☿ affl. in ♋. Other influences affecting the digestion are given in the various paragraphs of this section, and also under Belching, Chyle, Dyspepsia, Gastric, Indigestion, Stomach, etc. Cases of Digestive Disorders, Birth Data, etc.—See Fig. 17, 18, in the book, "Message of the Stars" by the Heindels.

**Dyspepsia; Eating; Emaciation;**

**Eructations**—(See Belching).

**Fermentation**—In the Stomach—(See "Fermentation" under Stomach).

**Flatulence; Fluids**—Of the Stomach—Digestive Juices—Disturbances of—Lacking—♄ affl. in ♋. (See Acids, Fluids, Gastric, Juices).

**Food; Functions**—The Digestive Functions Disturbed—Afflictions to ♃, as ♃ rules the digestive functions; ♃ affl. in ♋ or ♑; the ☉ or ☽ affl. in ♋ or ♑, the digestive functions are weakened, causing functional derangements of the Digestive System; the ☽ hyleg in ♋, and afflicted, and espec. with females; ♄, ♅, or ♆ in ♊ and affl. the ☉ or ☽. (See Functions; "Functions" under Stomach).

**Gas in Stomach**—(See Gas).

**Gastric Juices**—Gastric Troubles—(See Gastric, Stomach. Also note the various paragraphs in this section).

**Gluttony; Good Digestive Powers**—♂ well-asp. in the 4th H.

**Hindered**—Digestion Hindered—Obstructed—♄ affl. in ♋ or ♑.

**Humours**—Raw Humours in Stomach—See Indigestion).

**Illness from Indigestion**—(See Indigestion).

**Impaired Digestion**—Imperfect—(See Dyspepsia, Indigestion).

**Impurities of the System**—Digestive Disorders Arising From—The ☉ affl. in ♓. (See Impurities, Wastes).

**Inability to Digest Food**—♆ in ♋ and affl. by ♅ and ♄; ♆ ♋ in ☍ ♅ ♑, and both affl. by the ▢ of ♄, the food is often undigested and appears in the stools in pieces; ♄ in ♋, and affl. by the ☌, ▢, or ☍ of ♆ and ♅. (See "Chronic Indigestion" under Indigestion).

**Indigestion**—(See the various paragraphs under Indigestion).

**Intestinal Indigestion**—(See "Digestion" under Bowels).

**Irregularities**—Of Digestion—♍ on the Asc. (See "Digestive Disorders", and the various paragraphs in this section).

**Juices**—Lack of Digestive Juices—(See "Fluids" in this section).

**Malnutrition**—(See Assimilation, Nutrition).

**Metabolism**—Metabolism of the Digestive Tract Disturbed—The Prog. ☽ in ♋ or ♍, and ☌, ▢, or ☍ the place of malefics at B. (See Metabolism).

**Nausea; Nervous Indigestion**—(See Indigestion).

**Nourishment**—(See Nutrition).

**Obstruction**—Digestion Obstructed—(See "Hindered" in this section).

**Organs of Digestion**—Are ruled by the ☽, ♃, the ♋ and ♍ signs, including the Stomach, Duodenum, and Intestinal Digestion. These Organs are weakened by the ☉ affl. in ♋, ♍, or ♑.

**Poor Digestion**—(See "Digestive Disorders" in this section. Also see Dyspepsia, Indigestion).

**Powers**—The Digestive Powers—(See "Disorders", "Good", "Promoted", "Weak", and the various paragraphs in this section).

**Promoted**—The Digestive Powers Promoted and Strengthened—The ☽ well-asp. in ♋. (See "Good" in this section).

**Raw Humours**—In Stomach—(See Indigestion).

**Stimulated**—Pineapple is a good digestive stimulant. Also ♂ remedies, such as Nux Vomica in small doses before meals. (See Stimulants).

**Stomach Disorders**—(See Indigestion, Stomach).

**Stopped**—Digestion Stopped—The work of ♄ impeding the action of the Pneumogastric Nerve; signified by ♄ in ♈ when ♄ is the afflictor in the disease; ♄ in ♈, ♉, or ♋; afflictions in ♋; a ♋ and ♍ disease, and espec. with ♄ affl. in these signs; the ☽ in ♋, ♍, ♎, or ♑, and ☌ or ill-asp. ♄. (See Stoppages).

**Undigested Humours**—(See "Raw Humours" under Indigestion).

**Vomiting; Wastings; Weak Digestion**—Weak Stomach—Afflictions in ♋; a ♋ and ☽ disease; ♋ on the Asc.; the ☉, ☽, ♄, or ♂ affl. in ♋; the ☉ in the 6th H. and in a card. sign, and affl.; cardinal signs show; the ☽ in ♋, ☌ or evil asp. a malefic; ♄ affl. in the 6th H. in a card. sign; ♄, ♅, or ♆ in ♊ or ♋; and

affl. the ☉ or ☽; watery signs on the Asc. or 6th H., and the ☽ in a water sign at B., or at decumb. (See "Disorders", and the various paragraphs in this section. Also see Dyspepsia, Indigestion).

**Weakened**—(See "Functions", "Organs", and the various paragraphs in this section).

**Weakest**—The digestion is weakest when the ☉ is affl. in ♋ or ♑, and these signs on cusp the 6th H.

**Women**—Digestive Disorders In—The ☽ hyleg in ♋, and afflicted; ♄ ☌ the ☽; ♃ ▢ or ☍ the ☽.

**Worry**—Digestive Disorders Thru Worry and Anxiety—(See "Anxiety" in this section).

**DILATATIONS**—Dilation—Dilated—Dilatation of a Vessel or Organ—See the following subjects—

**Aneurysm; Arteries**—Dilatation of—(See Aneurysm; "Dilatation" under Arteries).

**Blood Vessels**—Dilatation of—(See Aneurysm, Capillaries; "Dilatation" under Arteries; "Vaso-Dilator" under Vaso; Vessels).

**Bronchial Tubes**—(See "Dilatation" under Bronchial).

**Cerebral**—(See Apoplexy; "Vaso-Dilator" under Vaso).

**Face**—Dilatation of the Capillaries of the Face—Morbid Red Face—(See "Red Face" under Face).

**Heart**—Cardiac Dilatation—(See Aneurysm; "Dilatation" under Heart).

**Oesophagus**—Dilatation of—(See Oesophagus).

**Pupils of Eyes**—Dilated—(See "Mydriasis" under Iris).

**Scrotal Veins**—Dilatation of—(See "Varicocele" under Scrotum).

**Stomach**—Dilatation of—(See "Dilatation" under Stomach).

**Varicocele; Varicose Veins**—Dilated Veins—(See Varicose).

**Vaso-Dilator Action**—(See Vaso).

**Veins Dilated**—(See Varicose). See Distentions, Flatulence, Gas, Swellings, Tympanites, Wind, etc.

**DILUTED**—Dilutions—

**Diluted Blood**—(See "Thin Blood" under Blood).

**Diluted Fluids**—Of the Body—The ☽ influence tends to dilution of the fluids of the body. (See Fluids, Watery).

**DIM**—Dimmed—Weakened—Faded, etc.

**Dim Eyes**—(See Eyes).

**Dim Sight**—(See Sight).

**Energies Dimmed**—(See "Depletion" under Energy). See Clouded, Depletion, Diminished, Dull, Faded, Feeble, Weakened, etc.).

**DIMINISHED**—Diminishments—Diminutive—Decreased—Lessened—Reduced, etc. The evil aspects between the ☉ and ☽ at B., the afflictions of ♄ to the vital centers of the map, weak signs upon the Asc., the ☉ or ☽ affl. in the 6th H., etc., tend to greatly diminish the bodily powers, the strength and vitality, the secretions, lower the functional powers, the powers of resistance to disease, etc., all which tend to disease, chronic infirmities, or an earlier death. A few subjects along this line will be listed here, but for those not listed, look for the subject in the alphabetical arrangement.

**Adrenal Secretion Diminished**—(See Adrenals).

**Body Diminished**—(See "Body" under Large; Cretinism, Dwarf, Growth, Idiocy, Organs; "Short Stature" under Short; Undersized, etc.).

**Cerebral Substance**—Diminished—(See "Medullary Substance" under Medulla).

**Death Rate**—Diminished—(See Mortality).

**Pituitary Secretion**—Diminished—(See Pituitary).

**Secretions Diminished**—(See Secretions).

**Sensibility Diminished**—(See Sensibility). For other subjects along this line see Abatement, Amelioration, Apathy, Atrophy, Brevity, Condensation, Constrictions, Contractions, Curtailed, Decreased, Deficient, Depleted, Dropsy, Elimination, Emaciation, Energies, Functions, Hectic, Impairments, Insufficient, Lack of, Lessened, Little, Loss of, Lowered, Moderation, Motion, Movement, Organs, Recuperative Powers, Reduced, Resistance, Retardations, Short, Shrinkage, Slow, Small, Stature, Strength, Suppressions, Undersized, Vital Powers, Vitality, Void of, Weakened, Worse, etc.).

**DIMPLES**—

**In Cheeks**—Born under ♀, dimples in cheeks or chin; ♀ in the Asc., dimples in one or both cheeks; ♀ in ♎, partile the Asc., beautiful dimples; ♀ in ♓, a round, dimpled face; ♀ rising and elevated at B., in one of her own signs, or in ☌ with the ☉; ♀ Sig. of the person in Hor'y Questions.

**In Chin**—♀ strong at B.; ♀ Sig. in ♓; ♀ in ♓, in partile asp. the Asc.; ♀ in the Asc. (See Cheeks, Chin, Face).

**DIPHTHERIA**—A ♉ disease; associated with the fixed signs, and espec. ♉ and ♏, and the 3° of these signs; the ☉ affl. by ♅, ♄, ♂, or ♀; the ☉, ☽, and afflicting bodies in the 12th H.; the ☉ afflicted in ♉; the ☽ affl. by ♄ or ♂; the ☽ in a common sign and affl. by ♆; afflictions in the 12th H.; Subs at LCP (6C), and at SP (7C). Scarlet Fever is a predisposing cause. (See Croup, Epidemics, Exudations, Fauces, Fever, Immunity, Pharynx, Scarlet Fever, Throat). Cases of Diphtheria, Death By, etc.—See "Diphtheria", No. 163, in 1001 N.N. Also see Cases in Chap. 13, in Daath's Medical Astrology.

**DIPLEGIA**—Double Symmetric Paralysis—(See Paralysis).

**DIPLOPIA**—Double Vision—(See Sight).

**DIPSOMANIA**—An Uncontrollable Desire for Intoxicating and Spirituous Liquors—Vehement Thirst—A disease of the watery signs; ♋, ♏, or ♓ on the Asc. at B., and afflicted; ♆ affl. in ♋; ♆ in ♋ in the 6th H., and affl. the ☉, ☽, Asc., or hyleg; ♄, ♂, or ☿ affl. in ♋; Subs at AT, SP (7D), and at KP. (See Drink, Drunkenness, Intoxication). Case—See "Dipsomaniac", No. 287, in 1001 N.N.

**DIRECT MOTION**—Of Planets—The disease tends to be more continuous and intense under the direct motion of the planets when such a planet is the afflictor in the disease. (See Continuity, Disturbances, Intensity, Interrupted, Retrograde, Sequence, Stationary).

**DIRECTIONS**—Primary and Secondary Directions—Effects of Upon the Health, Mind, and Affairs of the Native—Diseases caused by Directions tend to be functional and temporary unless neglected and allowed to progress into morbid conditions. Diathesis and the Transient Disposition in disease are indicated by Directions, while the Radix denotes the Hexis, or Permanent Habit in Disease, Structural, Organic and Constitutional Diseases. (See Diathesis). The Time and Type of the disease are shown by Directions, but only such as are foreshadowed by the radical map. (See Events, Progression, Secondary; "Spared" under Life). Mars a strong afflictor at B., and by dir., tends to Acute and Swift Diseases, Accidents, Injuries, Death by Wounds and Violence, while ♄ the afflictor tends to Chronic Ailments, and so on with the nature of each planet. The directional strength of planets depends upon their aspect, mundane position, and their position in the Zodiac. Directions of the planets are more evil in disease when they occur during the different periods of life ruled by the planets. Thus a ♄ direction is more evil during the ♄ period of life, etc. (See Periods. Also see "Directions" under Saturn, and each of the planets). Also evil Directions to the Hyleg in the Climacterical Years of life are more dangerous in health matters. (See Climacteric).

**Childhood**—Directions In—During Childhood and Youth the effects of Directions are said to be transferred to the Parents or Guardian. (See "Directions" in Sec. 1 under Children).

**Death**—Directions and Death—It takes a train of evil Directions to the Hyleg to cause death. (See Anareta, Benefics; "Directions" in Sec. 3 under Children; "Arguments for Death", "Quality", under Death; Epidemics, Hyleg; "Death" under Immediate; Malefics).

**Evil Directions**—(1) First Train of Evil Directions Destroys—(See Crises; "Directions Kill" under Infancy; "Directions" in Sec. 3 under Children; "Resistance Weak" under Resistance; "Vitality Low" under Vitality; "Weak Body" under Weak). (2) Good Powers to Overcome Evil Directions—(See "Abundance of Health" under Health; Immunity, Recuperation, Resistance, Vitality Good, etc.).

**Females and Directions**—When the ☽ is weak, ill-dig., and badly aspected at B., the constitutional powers are often so reduced as to be unable to withstand the shock of subsequent evil directions, and with females in infancy, under such conditions, the first train of evil directions tends to kill.

**Mind Afflicted by Directions**—The ☉ to the bad asps. ☿; the ☽ to the bad asps. the ☉ or ♄; the M.C. to the ☌ or P. asp. the ☽. (See Drink; "Diseases", "Irritations", under Mental).

**Overcoming Directions**—(See "Evil Directions" in this section).

**Primary Directions**—If the nativity is weak, and the constitution broken by disease or age, a primary direction will kill if the planets at B. are unfortunate, and without the assistance of benefics, or an attending good Secondary Direction. In a stronger constitution a train of evil primary directions is necessary to kill, and espec. in childhood, youth, or middle life. (See Primary, Transits).

**Secondary Directions**—(See Secondary).

**Succumbs Easily**—To Directions—(See "Evil Directions" in this section. Also see Feeble; "Ill-Health All Thru Life" under Ill-Health; Incurable; "Life Destroyed" under Life; Sickly; "Much Sickness" under Sickness; "Weakened" under Strength; "Low" under Vitality; "Weak Body" under Weak).

**Train of Directions**—(See "Death", "Evil Directions", "Females", "Primary", in this section. Also see "Life Destroyed" under Life; "New Moon" under Moon).

**Youth and Directions**—(See "Childhood", "Primary", in this section).

**DIRTY**—(See Careless, Filthy, Habits, Unclean, Untidy, etc.).

**DISABILITIES**—Disablements—

**Bodily Disabilities**—Caused mostly by ♄. Caused by retention of wastes, mineral deposits, concretions, crystallization, hardening, deposits of Urea and Uric Acid, resulting in rigidity, stiffness, lowered functions, deformities, infirmities, total disability, etc., all which are the work of ♄, and assisted by the afflictions of the ☽. (See Accidents, Body, Congenital, Crippled, Defects, Deformities, Form, Imperfections, Infirmities, Injuries, Lameness, Limitations, Maimed, Malformations, Monsters, Paralysis, Stature, etc.).

**Mental Disabilities**—Are ☿ diseases, and afflictions to ☿; ☿ afflicted, and in no good relation to the ☽ or Asc. (See Coma, Delirium, Epilepsy, Faintings, Fury, Insanity, Intellect, Judgment, Madness, Mania, Mental; "Weak Mind" under Mind; Perception, Understanding, etc.).

**DISAGREEABLE**—Unpleasant—Offensive—

**Disagreeable Breath**—(See "Foul" under Breath).

**Disagreeable Temper**—(See Anger, Cruel, Conduct, Manners, Savage; "High Temper" under Temper; Vicious, etc.).

**DISASTER**—Calamity—Catastrophies—

**Disaster Threatened**—A total Eclipse of the ☉ falling on the place of the ☉ at B.; ♆ passing over the place of the radical ♄ by tr.; the ill-asps. of several malefic Promittors to the ☉. (See Calamity, Disgrace, Dishonour, Misfortune, Reversals, Ruin, Treachery).

**Fear Of**—Fear of Impending Disaster—(See "Impending Calamity" under Calamity; Fears).

**Meets with Disaster**—Lord of the 6th H. in the 10th H., and afflicted, danger of meeting with serious disaster, downfall, dishonour, etc. (See Abroad, Accidents, Death, Dangers, Downfall; "His Own Worst Enemy" under Enemies; Imprisonment (see Prison); Self-Undoing, etc.).

**DISCERNMENT**—(See Comprehension, Intellect, Judgment; "Quickened" under Mental; Mind, Perception, Reason, Understanding, Shrewdness, etc.).

**DISCHARGES**—A Morbid Secretion—An Evacuation—Astringents, which are remedies of ♄, tend to stop discharges by their powers of constriction. (See Astringents). The natural discharges from the body are such as Breath, Tears, Milk, Sweat, Faeces, Urine, Mucus, Saliva, Menses, Oils of the Skin. (See these subjects). Discharges occur from the orifices of the body, organs, and membranes, as from the Eyes, Ears, Nose, Mouth, Throat, Lungs, Breasts, Navel, Rectum, Skin, Urethra, Vagina, etc., and may be natural, or morbid in disease conditions.

**Bloody Discharges**—(See "Discharges" under Blood; Dysentery; "Bloody Flux" under Flux; Hemorrhage, Menses; "Nose Bleed" under Nose).

**Catarrhal Discharges**—(See Catarrh, Colds, Defluxions, Fluxes, Humours, Mucus, Nose, Phlegm, Rheum; "Watery Humours" under Watery, etc.).

**Involuntary Discharges**—(See Emissions, Faeces, Incoordination, Involuntary, Menses, Nose Bleed, Semen; "Incontinence" under Urine; Vital Fluids, Urine, etc.).

**Offensive Discharges**—Purulent—Putrid—Morbid—Pus—Foul, etc. Caused by ♄, ♂, and the ☽. (See Abscesses, Carcinoma, Catarrh, Decay, Eruptions, Evacuations, Excretions, Exudations, Fistula, Foul, Gangrene, Hemorrhoids, Menses, Morbid, Offensive, Pus, Putrid, Rotten, Sores, Sweat, Syphilis, Ulcers, Venereal, etc.).

**Profuse Discharges**—(See Catarrh, Diarrhoea, Dysentery, Effusions, Flow, Fluxes, Hemorrhage, Menses, Nose Bleed, Profuse, etc.).

**Unnatural Discharges**—A ♏ disease, and afflictions in ♏; a ♀ disease. (See Gonorrhoea, Leocorrhoea, Salivation, and Diseases of the Bowels, Skin, and Fluids of the Body).

**Watery Discharges**—(See Catarrhs, Diarrhoea, Fluxes, Humours, Rheum, Serous, Watery). For other subjects not mentioned here look for the subject in the alphabetical arrangement.

**DISCOLORATIONS**—(See Abscesses, Blemishes, Blotches, Blows, Bruises, Burns, Carcinoma, Cataract, Complexion, Cuts, Cyanosis, Defects, Epithelioma, Eruptions, Erythromelalgia, Excrescences, Eyes, Face, Freckles, Growths, Hemorrhages, Hyperaemia,

Imperfections, Marks, Moles, Naevus, Nails, Nose, Pimples, Purpura, Scars, Skin, Smallpox, Sores, Swellings, Syphilis, Teeth, Ulcers, Varicose, etc.).

**DISCOMFORT**—Lack of Ease—A Feeling of Discomfort or Uneasiness, as in Disease or Plethora—♂ affl. the ☽, the functions are painful and excessive, causing discomfort; ♀ □ or ☍ ☽, the functions are painful and irregular, causing discomfort, and usually due to loose living. The various diseases and afflictions of the mind and body tend to a feeling of discomfort, and for the influences causing such, see in the alphabetical arrangement the subject you have in mind. Also see such subjects as Affliction, Anxiety, Despondency, Disease, Flatulence, Gas, Ill-Health, Malaise, Melancholy, Miseries, Nervousness, Pain, Plethora, Restlessness, Sickness, Suffering, Trouble, Worry, Worse, etc.

**DISCOMPOSED**—Disturbed—Derangements—Irritations, etc.—

**Discomposed Body**—(See Deformed, Deranged, Disease, Disturbances, Ill-formed, Irritations, etc.).

**Discomposed Mind**—(See the various paragraphs under Mental, Mind. Also see Anxiety, Dejected, Depressed, Despondent, Discontentment, Fears, Hypochondria, Insanity; "Low Spirits" under Low; Melancholy, Morbid, Worry).

**DISCONTENTMENT**—Dissatisfied—Restlessness—Uneasiness—Lack of Happiness or Peace of Mind—The ☉ or ☽ to the ☌ or ill-asps. ♄ by dir.; ♆ □ or ☍ ♅; ♄ in ♑ at B., and affl. the ☉, ☽, or ☿; ♄ Sig. in ♑; ♀ affl. at B., or by dir.; ☿ Sig. in ♑; ♑ on the Asc. at B., and with ♄ as ruler; the Asc. meeting the evil directions of planets; ♊ on the Asc.; the Asc. to the place of Deneb; the 3rd Dec. of ♒ denotes. (For further influences along this line see Anxiety, Changes, Complaining, Contentment, Despondency, Erratic, Fears, Fretful, Happiness; "Low Spirits" under Low; Melancholy, Murmuring; "No Peace of Mind" under Mind; Patience, Peevish, Repining, Residence, Restlessness, Unhappy, Worry, etc.).

**DISCORD**—(See Contests, Duels, Emotions, Enemies; "Discord" under Mind; Quarrels).

**DISCRIMINATION**—Lack of—(See "Bad Judgment" under Judgment; Erratic).

**DISCUTIENT**—An Agent Removing a Swelling or Effusion—A therapeutic property of ♂ remedies. (See Resolvent).

**DISEASE**—Diseases—Ailments—Complaints—Distempers—Disordered System—Maladies—Ill-Health—Pathological Disorders—Sickness, etc.

The following influences tend to cause disease,—The ☉, ☽, and planets in the Occidental Quarters at birth show disease, and in the Oriental Quarters indicate Acute Pains and Accidents. (See "Causes" under Accidents). Malefics occidental, and affl. the ☉ and ☽, cause diseases, and when oriental cause Blemishes (see Blemishes). Disease is indicated by the planetary positions and aspects to the ☉, ☽, Asc. and Hyleg, and their positions in the 6th, 8th, or 12th Houses. Ptolemy says disease and blemishes belong to the 6th and 7th Houses, and to the Asc. Malefics when ori. to the ☉, and occi. to the ☽, cause diseases. The diseases caused by each planet are said to arise from the planet whose aspect or body first arrives at the Anaretic Place. If there be no such aspect, that planet causes the disease which last separated by body or aspect from the Anaretic Place. (See Anareta). Planets ℞, or in Perigee, tend to cause disease and distempers. Disease is caused by planets afflicting the ☉, ☽, or Asc., if they be malefics, or if the malefics and the ☉ and ☽ have the same Declination. No aspect of ♃ or ♀ alone causes disease, but only as configurated with malefics. Some say most diseases owe their origin to the ☽, and they are at least governed by the aspects and periods of the ☽ for some time if they are acute diseases, and even chronic diseases are much affected by the ☽ at her Quadratures and Semi-Quadratures. At the New and Full ☽ the ☽ influence is not so manifest, except with Lunatics, whose fluids are more violently disturbed at the New and Full ☽. Common Signs and cadent houses are closely identified with disease, and are weaker constitutionally. The 3rd and 9th houses, both cadent, are especially connected with the Mind and Mental Disorders, and ♃ and ♀ in these houses at B. will help to overcome disease thru a good state of the mind. The 6th House and the ♍ Sign are important in the consideration of disease. In these Spirit, Mind and Matter meet, as ☿, the ruler of the mind, is also the ruler of the 6th H. It is thru the Vital Principle that disease acts upon the mind, and diseases of the mind upon the body. The power and degree of morbid action show a falling off as the planets pass from cardinal to common signs. The intensity of disease is associated with the cardinal signs, and its remission with the mutable signs. (For further influences along this line, see Health, Ill-Health; "Organic" under Functions; Sickness. Also note the various paragraphs in this section. For the various diseases to which mind and body are liable, look for the subject in the alphabetical arrangement, as only the more abstract subjects concerning disease, the causes of disease, the classification of diseases, the nature and quality of the disease; the time, duration, and possible outcome of the disease, and subjects closely affiliated with disease, will be listed in this section. See the following subjects in the alphabetical arrangement when not considered here—

**Abatement; Accidents; Acquired; Acts**—Disease from Rash Acts—(See Rashness).

**Acute; Ailing**—Is Always Ailing—(See Ailing).

**Ailments; Air**—Diseases from Corrupt Air, Compressed Air—(See Air).

**Alteration**—In the Disease—(See Alteration).

**Amelioration; Amendment; Anareta; Anger**—Diseases Arising From—(See Anger).

**Animals**—Diseased—Death of—(See Animals).

**Antidotes; Antipathy; Aquarius Sign**—Diseases Ruled By—(See Aquarius).

**Aries Sign**—Diseases Ruled By—(See Aries).

**Attracts Disease**—(See Attracts).

**Autumnal Diseases**—(See Autumnal).

**Bad Blood**—Diseases From—(See Blood, Impure).

**Bad End**—To the Disease—(See End, Termination).

**Bathing**—Disease or Death From—(See Bathing).

**Beginning**—Of the Disease—(See Directions. Also see "Event", "Time", in this section).

**Benefics**—The Benefics and Disease—(See Anareta, Benefics, Jupiter, Venus).

**Better**—Disease Turns for Better—(See Amelioration, Continuity, Course, Crises, Moderation, Modification; "Action" under Morbid; Polarity, Recovery).

**Bites; Blemishes; Blood**—Diseases from Blood Disorders—(See Blood, Impure).

**Body**—(1) Diseased Body—The ☉ Sig. □ or ☍ ♄, and ♄ be in the Asc., diseased body, and short-lived unless a good asp. of ♃ intervene, which may save after a severe illness if ♃ be angular. (2) Body Alone is Affected—(See 'Afflicted" under Body). (3) The Disease is More in the Body than in the Mind—(See "Afflicted" under Body). (4) The Disease is in Both Body and Mind—(See "Afflicted in Body and Mind" under Mind). (5) The Disease is Thru the Whole Body—(See "Disease" under Whole).

**Brief**—The Disease is Brief—(See Quick).

**Brings Disease Upon Himself**—Causes His Own Illnesses—Mars people; ♂ ruler, and strong at B.; the ill-asps. of ♀ by dir. to the ☽, ♂, Asc., or M.C., and brought on by free living; ☽ in 6th H., affl. by ♀, thru disorderly conduct; ♏ on the Asc. at B., and thru anger, folly, peevishness, rash acts, etc. (See Debauchery, Dissipation, Drink, Excesses, Extravagance, Folly; "Free Living" under Free; Gluttony; "High Living" under High; "His Own Worst Enemy" under Enemies; "Loose Living" under Loose; Plethora, Rashness, Surfeits).

**Brooding Over Disease**—(See Brooding, Hypochondria, Imaginary).

**Business Cares**—Diseases Caused By—(See Business, Cares).

**Cadent Houses**—And Disease—(See Cadent).

**Cancer Sign**—Diseases of—(See Cancer).

**Capricorn Sign**—Diseases of—(See Capricorn).

**Cardinal Signs**—And Disease—(See Cardinal).

**Cares**—Diseases From—(See Cares).

**Causes**—(1) Causes of Disease—(See the Introduction to this Article). (2) Causes His Own Illnesses—(See "Brings Disease" in this section).

**Certain**—The Disease is More Certain and Pronounced—When evil Directions agree with the radical afflictions; when the Diathesis agrees with the Hexis, or permanent habit in disease, the disease is more certain and pronounced. Thus if the Directions agree with strong ♂ affliction at B., the disease will tend to be acute, a fever, an inflammation, or perhaps bring a surgical operation, and so on with the nature of each planet. (See Diathesis, Severity).

**Changes**—(1) The Disease Changed—(See "Complications" in this section). (2) The Disease Changes for the Better or Worse—(See "Better", "Worse" in this section). (3) Changes to Some Other Disease—Or a Relapse—(See Chronic, Complications, Crises, Relapse, Return, Worse).

**Childhood**—Children—Diseases of—(See Childhood, Children, Infancy).

**Choler**—Diseases Arising from Too Much Choler—(See Choler).

**Chronic; Clothing; Cold; Colds;**

**Common Signs**—And Disease—(See Mutable).

**Complaining; Complaints**—(See the various paragraphs in this section).

**Complications**—In Disease—Planets in the Signs show the Zones of the body afflicted, but complications, as when inflammation and congestion attack an organ at the same time, or where Plethora accompanies a nervous condition, the aspects and influences of the planets themselves must be considered, and the nature of each planet involved in the disease condition. Each planet imparts a special type of disease to an organ, but the disease may become disguised, modified, or changed by cross aspects from other planets. (See Complications, Zones).

**Concealment**—Of Disease—♃ in the Asc. or M.C., in a strong sign, well-aspected and elevated above the malefics; the influence of wealth, rank, or command given by ♃ well placed at B.; ☿ well configurated with ♃ gives the addition of skillful Healers, the proper treatment and remedies. (See Exhibition).

**Congestions; Considerable Diseases Ensue**—(See "Many Diseases" under Childhood; Complications; "Ill-Health All Thru Life". "Signs of Ill-Health", under Ill-Health; Increase; "Much Sickness"—under Sickness. Also see "Many" in this section).

**Conspicuous; Constancy;**

**Constitutional; Contagious;**

**Continuity; Contracts Disease Easily**—(See Contracts).

**Convalescence; Convertible**—(See Curable).

**Corrupt Diseases**—(See Corrupt, Foul, Impure, Pus, Putrid, Rotten, etc.).

**Course of Disease**—(See Course).

**Courts Disease**—(See Virgo).

**Crises; Curable**—Cure of—(See Curable).

**Curious Diseases**—(See Mysterious, Strange).

**Curtailed; Dampness**—Diseases From —(See Moisture, Vapors, Water, Wet).

**Danger**—Danger in Course of—Danger of Disease—(See Course. See "Threatened", and the various paragraphs in this section).

**Dangerous**—The Disease is Dangerous—The Disease is Not Dangerous— (See Dangerous).

**Day**—The Disease is Better or Worse by Day—(See Day, Night).

**Death**—The Disease Ends in Death— The Disease Which is the Immediate Cause of Death—(See "Certain", "Immediate", under Death).

**Debauchery**—Disease From—(See Debauchery).

**Debility; Decay; Decrease**—The Disease Will Decrease—(See "Decrease" under Recovery).

**Decrepitude; Deep-Seated** — (See Deep).

**Degeneration; Degree**—The Degree of Disturbance in Disease—(See Disturbed).

**Delayed**—(See Chronic; "Long Siege" under Ill-Health; Lingering, Prolonged, Tedious).

**Delirium; Derangements;**

**Destructive Diseases**—(See Destructive).

**Deteriorations; Detriment;**

**Deviations; Diagnosis; Diathesis; Diet** —Diseases from Wrong Diet—(See Diet).

**Difficult to Cure**—(See Cure, Difficult).

**Direct Motion**—Of the Planets in Disease—(See Direct).

**Directions and Disease**—(See Directions).

**Disabilities; Discomfort**—In Disease —(See Anguish, Malaise, Pain, Plethora, Suffering).

**Diseased Body**—(See "Body" in this section).

**Disguised**—(See "Complications" in this section).

**Disorderly Conduct**—Disease Brought On By—(See "Brings Disease" in this section).

**Disorders**—(See Disorders. Also note the various paragraphs in this section).

**Dispersions; Disposition**—The Transient Disposition in Disease—(See Diathesis, Directions).

**Dissipation**—Disease By—(See Debauchery, Dissipation, Drink, Excesses, Habits, etc.).

**Dissipation of Forces**—(See Dispersions).

**Distempers; Distressful Diseases**— (See Anguish; "High Fevers" under Fevers; "Diseases" under Pain; Suffering, etc. Also look in the alphabetical arrangement for the subject you have in mind).

**Disturbance**—The Degree of Disturbance in Disease—(See Disturbed).

**Dorsal Diseases**—(See Dorsal).

**Dreadful Diseases** — (See Dreadful, Terrible).

**Dress**—As a Cause of Disease—(See Clothing, Colds, Dress, Exposure; "Wet Feet" under Feet; Linen, Moisture).

**Drink**- Diseases from Excesses In— (See Drink, Drunkenness, Intoxication).

**Drought** — Diseases From — (See Drought, Dryness, Famine, Pestilence).

**Dryness**—Dry and Hot Diseases—Diseases Concomitant with Dryness—Dry and Cold Diseases—(See Dryness).

**Duration** — Of Disease — (See Constancy, Continuity, Course, Duration).

**Ease**—Intervals of Ease—(See Ease).

**Eating**—Disease from Improper Eating—(See Diet, Eating, Food).

**Effects Of**—Duration of the Effects of Disease—(See Constancy, Duration).

**End of the Disease** — (See Curable; "Certain Death" under Death; End, Fatal, Incurable, Recovery, Resolution, Termination, etc.).

**Endemic; Endurance** — Endurance Against Disease—(See Endurance, Immunity, Recuperation, Resistance, Vitality, etc.).

**Endures Disease Cheerfully**—(See Complaining, Endures).

**Enemas and Disease**—(See Enema).

**Enlarged Scope**—Of the Disease—(See Enlarged).

**Entire Body Disordered**—(See Whole).

**Environment**—And Disease—(See Environment, External).

**Epidemics; Erratic Course** — (See Course, Erratic, Irregular, Various).

**Escape**—The Sick Will Hardly Escape —(See Escape).

**Event** — The Event, or Time of Disease—When Due, etc.—(See Events. Also see "Time" in this section).

**Every Species of Disease**—Causes of —(See South Scale, Species).

**Evil End To**—(See "End" in this section).

**Excesses**—Diseases From—(See Excesses).

**Excrescences; Exercise**—Disease from Over-Exercise and Fatigue—(See Exercise, Fatigue).

**Exhibition of Maladies**—(See Exhibition).

**Exopathic**—(See External).

**Exposure**—Diseases Arising From— (See Exposure).

**External Causes**—Of Disease—(See External).

**Extraordinary Diseases** — (See Extraordinary).

**Extravagance**—Health Undermined By—(See Extravagance; "Undermined" under Health).

**Falling Off** — Of the Disease — (See Amelioration; "Action" under Morbid; Moderation, Recovery).

**Famine**—Disease, Suffering or Death From—(See Famine).

**Fatal; Fatigue; Fear of Disease**—(See Fear, Taurus).

**Female Diseases**—(See Female).

**Fierce Maladies**—(See Fierce).

**Fixed Signs** — And Disease — (See Fixed).

**Fluidic System**—Diseases of—(See Fluids).

**Folly**—Diseases From—(See Folly).

**Food and Disease**—(See Diet, Digestion, Eating, Food, Stomach).

**Force of the Disease**—(See Force).

**Foul Vapors**—Disease From—(See Vapors).

**Frame**—The Whole Frame Is Disordered—(See Whole).

**Free Living** — Disease From — (See Free).

**Frequent Attacks**—Of Disease—(See "Ill-Health All Thru Life" under Life; "Much Sickness" under Sickness).

**Full Moon and Disease**—(See "Causes" in this section; "Full Moon" under Moon).

**Fulminating**—Sudden Severity of Disease—(See Fulminating).

**Functional Diseases**—(See Directions, Functions).

**Gemini Diseases**—(See Gemini).

**General Ailments**—(See General).

**Gives Up Easily**—To Disease—Does Little for Himself—Drifts with the Tide of the Disease—The ☉ affl. in ♉ or ♍; ♄ in ♍ in the 6th, 8th, or 12th H.; ♄ ruler of the Asc., in ♍, and in the 6th, 8th, or 12th H.; ♄ affl. in ♉ in the 6th H.; ♅ and ♍ influence; common signs on the angles; many planets in feminine signs. (See Brooding, Hypochondria, Majority, Negative, Taurus, Virgo).

**Gluttony**—Diseases From—(See Gluttony).

**Good End to Disease**—(See Curable, End, Recovery, Resolution).

**Grievous Diseases** — (See Grievous, Severe, Vehement).

**Habit**—The Permanent Habit in Disease — (See Diathesis, Directions, Hexis).

**Hard to Cure**—(See Chronic, Cure, Difficult, Grievous, Incurable).

**Healers; Health Bad** — (See Health, Ill-Health, Invalids, Sickness, etc.).

**Heat**—Diseases from Excessive Heat —(See "Excessive" under Heat).

**Heaviness** — All Over the Body — Heavy and Sad Sickness—(See Heaviness, Whole).

**Hemorrhages; Heredity; Hexis** — The Permanent Habit in Disease—(See Diathesis, Directions, Hexis).

**High**—The Disease Runs High—(See "Worse" under Crises; High; "Diseases" under Pain).

**High Living**—Diseases From—(See High).

**Hot Diseases**—Hot and Dry Diseases —(See Fevers; "Dry and Hot", "Hot Diseases", under Heat).

**Houses** — Diseases Ruled by the Houses—(See Angles, Ascendant, Descendant, Houses, Midheaven, Nadir, Terminal, etc.).

**Humours; Hygiene;**

**Hyleg and Disease**—(See Hyleg).

**Identified with Disease**—The Common Signs and Cadent Houses are identified with disease. (See Cadent, Mutable).

**Ill-Health** — (See the various paragraphs under Ill-Health).

**Illusory Diseases**—(See Delusions, Hallucinations, Illusions, Imaginary, Insanity).

**Imaginary Diseases** — (See Brooding, Hypochondria, Imaginary, Psychic).

**Immunity; Impairments;**

**Impediments; Imperfections;**

**Important**—The Disease is Not Important—(See Mild, Slight).

**Improvement; Imprudence**—Diseases From—(See Folly, Imprudence, Indiscretions, Rashness, etc.).

**Incipient**—(See Praeincipient).

**Increase**—In the Disease—The Disease Will Increase—(See Crises, Increase, Worse).

**Increased Resistance**—To Disease — (See Resistance).

**Incurable; Indicated**—Disease Indicated—(See "Causes", "Threatened", in this section).

**Indicators**—Of Disease—(See "Significators" in this section).

**Indiscretions**—Diseases From—(See Indiscretions).

**Indispositions; Indulgences; Infancy** —Diseases of—(See Infancy).

**Infectious; Infirmities; Inflammations;**

**Inherent Tendencies**—In Disease— (See Constitutional, Diathesis, Heredity, Inherent, Organic, Structural).

**Innate**—Inborn—Inherited Diseases— (See Heredity, Innate).

**Intemperance** — Diseases Arising From—(See Debauchery, Dissipation, Drink, Drunkenness, Excesses, Intemperance, Intoxication, etc.).

**Intensity**—Of the Disease—Severity of—(See Cardinal; "Direct Motion of Planets" under Direct; Fulminating, Increase, Intensity, Severity).

**Internal Diseases**—Internal Ease in Disease—(See Ease, Internal).

**Interrupted Sequence**—In Disease— (See Interrupted, Sequence).

**Intervals of Ease**—(See Ease).

**Irregular Maladies**—Irregularities— (See Irregular).

**Irritations; Journeys**—Diseases On— (See Journeys, Travel).

**Judgment** — Of the Disease — (See Diagnosis, Judgment, Majority, Modification, Prognosis).

**Jupiter Diseases**—(See Jupiter).

**Kings**—Diseases To—(See Kings).

**Latent Diseases**—(See Constitutional, Diathesis, Hereditary, Hexis, Latent, Organic, Structural, etc.).

**Left Side of Body**—Diseases In—(See Left).

**Length of the Disease**—(See Course, Crises, Duration, Long, Prolonged, Short, etc.).

**Leo Diseases**—(See Leo).

**Less Liable**—To Disease—(See "Good Health" under Health; Immunity, Recuperation, Resistance, Strong, Vitality Good, etc.).

**Less Power**—To Throw Off Disease—(See Inability; "Resistance Low" under Resistance; "Slow Recuperation", under Recuperation; "Vitality Low" under Vitality; "Weak Body" under Weak, etc.).

**Lethargy; Liable to Disease**—(See "Causes", "Less Power", "Threatened", in this section. Also see "Bad Health", "Periods of Bad Health", under Health).

**Libra Diseases**—(See Libra).

**Linen**—Diseases from Wet Linen—(See Linen. See "Dress" in this section).

**Lingering Diseases**—(See Chronic, Lingering, Long, Prolonged, Slow, Tedious, Wasting, etc.).

**Lives Thru Disease**—Lives Thru Serious Diseases—(See Serious).

**Locating the Disease** — (See Diagnosis).

**Long Diseases**—Signs of a Long Disease—Will the Illness be Long?—(See Chronic, Consumptions, Lingering, Long, Prolonged, Slow, Tedious, Wastings).

**Lower Parts**—Of the Body—Diseases In—(See Abdomen, Extremities, Feet, Knees, Legs, Limbs, Lower, etc.).

**Lunar Diseases**—(See Moon).

**Lust**—Diseases from Inordinate Lust—(See Lust).

**Luxuries**—Health Undermined By—(See Extravagance; Food; "High Living" under High; Luxuries).

**Magnetism**—And Disease—(See Magnetic).

**Makes Effort**—To Throw Off Disease—(See "Throwing Off Disease" in this section).

**Malaise**—Discomfort in Disease—(See Malaise).

**Malefics**—And Disease—(See Anareta, Malefics, Mars, Neptune, Saturn, Uranus).

**Malignant; Many Diseases** — Many Complications—(See Complications; "Many Diseases" under Childhood, Impure; "Ill-Health All Thru Life" under Ill-Health; "Much Sickness" under Sickness; Various).

**Mars Diseases**—(See Mars).

**Meat**—Diseases from Ill-Digested Meat—(See Indigestion, Meat).

**Medicines**—Medicines Do Little Good —(See Grievous, Incurable, Medicines, Remedy, Treatment).

**Melancholy**—Disease Arising From—(See Melancholy).

**Members**—Members Affected by Disease—(See Members, Organic, Organs, Parts, Structural).

**Men**—Diseases of—(See Men).

**Mental Diseases** — (See Mental, Mind, Psychic).

**Mercury Diseases**—(See Mercury).

**Middle Life**—Diseases of—(See Middle Life).

**Mild**—(See Mild, Minor, Slight).

**Mind**—Diseases of—The Disease is Chiefly in the Mind—The Disease is in the Mind Only—The Disease is in Both Mind and Body—The Mind is Centered Upon Disease—(See "Afflicted in Body and Mind", "Disease", under Mind. Note the various paragraphs under Mental, Mind).

**Minimizing**—Of the Disease — (See Amelioration, Mild, Minimizing, Moderation, Recovery, Slight).

**Minor Diseases** — (See Colds, Mild, Minimizing, Minor, Slight).

**Moderation**—Of Disease—(See Moderation).

**Modification**—Of Disease—(See Modification; "Complications" in this section).

**Moist Diseases**—Moist Humours—Diseases Arising from Moisture—(See Moisture, Vapors, Water, Wet).

**Moon Diseases**—(See Moon).

**Morals**—Diseases Arising from Loose Morals—(See Excesses, Morals, Passion, Sex, Venereal).

**Morbid Diseases**—Morbid Action in Disease—(See Morbid).

**Mortal Illness** — (See "Arguments", "Certain", under Death).

**Motional Strength**—Of Planets in Disease—The Motion of the Planets, and Disease—(See Motion).

**Much Sickness**—(See "Much Sickness" under Sickness).

**Murmuring**—And Complaining About Their Disease—(See Complaining, Exhibition, Grief, Murmuring).

**Mutable Signs**—Common Signs and Disease—(See Mutable).

**Mysterious Diseases**—(See Mysterious).

**Nature of the Disease**—(See "Disease" under Nature).

**Neglect**—As a Cause of Disease—(See Neglect, Privation).

**Neptune Diseases**—(See Neptune).

**Nervous Diseases**—(See Nerves).

**Neutralizing**—Of the Disease—(See Minimizing).

**New Moon**—The New Moon and Disease—(See "New Moon" under Moon. Also see "Causes" in this section).

**Night Diseases**—Night Diseases More Prevalent—The Disease Worse at Night—(See Day, Night).

**Noisome Diseases**—(See Frenzy, Fury, Insanity, Madness, Mania, Noisy).

**Noxious Complaints**—(See Noxious).

**Nutrition**—Nourishment—Diseases from Disturbances of—(See Assimilation, Digestion, Food, Indigestion, Nutrition).

**Obscure Diseases**—(See Mysterious, Obscure, Peculiar, Psychic, Strange, Uncommon).

**Obstructions; Offensive; Old Age** — Diseases of—(See Old Age).

**Old Maladies Return**—(See Return).

**Organic Diseases**—(See Organic).

**Origin**—Of the Disease—(See "Beginning", "Causes", in this section).

**Outcome**—Of the Disease—(See Better, Death, End, Force, Minimizing, Termination, Worse, in this section. Also see such subjects as Amelioration, Crises, Moderation, Modification, Prognosis, Recovery, Recuperation, etc.).

**Outrageous** — Outrageous Diseases — Outraging Nature's Laws, and Diseases Caused By—(See "Nature's Laws" under Laws; Perversions, Scandalous, Sex, Venery).

**Overcoming Disease**—(1) Has Good Power to Overcome Disease—(See Immunity; "Good" under Resistance). (2) Has Little Power to Overcome Disease—(See "Ill-Health All Thru Life" under Ill-Health; "Low" under Recuperation, Resistance, Vitality; Sickly; "Much Sickness" under Sickness; "Weak Body" under Weak). (3) Makes an Effort to Overcome Disease—Fixed Signs on the Angles, and ♂ well-aspected at B. (See "Fixed Signs" under Fixed; Majority, Positive, Recuperation, Resistance, Stamina, Tone, Vitality, Will, etc. See "Throwing Off Disease" in this section).

**Over-Exercise**—Diseases from Over-Exercise and Over-Exertion of Mind and Body — (See "Brain Fag" under Brain; Exercise, Exertion, Fatigue, Reading, Sports, Study).

**Own Illnesses**—(See "Brings Disease Upon Himself" in this section).

**Painful Diseases**—Distressful—Poignant—Sharp—(See "Diseases" under Pain).

**Pandemic; Particular Disease**—The Course Any Particular Disease May Follow—(See Course, Prognosis, Various).

**Parts of the Body**—Parts Liable to Disease—(See Blemishes, Diagnosis, Members, Parts).

**Passion**—Diseases from Passional Excesses — (See Excesses, Passion, Sex, Vehement, Venery).

**Pathological Action**—Of Planets in Disease—(See Pathological, Planets. Also see "Pathological Action" under each of the Planets).

**Patient**—(1) Patient Causes the Disease — (See "Brings Disease" in this section). (2) Patient Will Die—(See "Certain Death" under Death). (3) Patient Will Recover—(See Recovery). (4) Patient In Disease—(See Patience).

**Peculiar Diseases**—(See Peculiar).

**Peevishness**—Diseases From—(See Peevish; "Brings Disease" in this section).

**Periodical Diseases**—(See Periodical).

**Periods**—Of Disease and Ill-Health—(See "Periods of Bad Health" under Health; "Long Siege" under Ill-Health; Periodical, Return).

**Permanent Habit**—In Disease—The Hexis—(See Diathesis, Directions. Also see "Certain" in this section).

**Pernicious Diseases**—(See Pernicious).

**Pestilence; Phlegmatic Diseases** — (See Phlegm).

**Pisces Diseases**—(See Pisces).

**Plague; Planets and Disease**—(See Anareta, Benefics, Directions, Malefics, Pathological, Planets. Also see each of the planets in the alphabetical arrangement).

**Plethora; Poignant Maladies** — (See Fierce, Painful, Poignant, Quick, Sharp, Swift, Vehement, Violent).

**Poison**—Disease and Ill-Health from —(See Deposits, Drugs, Intoxicants, Medicines, Narcotics, Poison, Septic, Stimulants, Toxic, Uric Acid, Wastes).

**Poverty**—Disease from Poverty, Privation and Neglect—(See Neglect, Poverty, Privation).

**Power**—The Power of the Disease—Has Power to Throw Off Disease—Has Little Power to Overcome Disease —(See "Intensity", "Overcoming", "Severity", in this section).

**Praeincipients; Predisposition;**

**Prenatal; Pretended; Prevention**—Of Disease—(See Hygiene, Prevention, Sanitation).

**Private Diseases**—(See Private).

**Privation**—Diseases From—(See Neglect, Privation).

**Profit and Support**—By Exhibition of Diseases—(See Exhibition).

**Prognosis; Progress; Progression;**

**Progressive; Prolonged; Promissor;**

**Promittor; Pronounced**—(See "Certain" in this section).

**Proof Against Disease**—(See Immunity, Resistance, Vitality).

**Protracted; Psychic; Pus-Forming**—(See Pus).

**Putrid; Quality**—Of the Disease—Nature of—(See "Disease" under Nature; Quality, Species, Type).

**Quarters of the Moon**—And Disease—(See Moon).

**Quick Diseases**—Quick Termination to Disease—(See Acute, Brief, End, Ephemeral; "High" under Fever; Fierce, Pernicious, Quick, Recovery, Sharp, Short, Swift, Termination, Vehement, Violent, etc.).

**Rapid; Rashness**—Diseases From—(See Anger, Folly, Imprudence, Rashness, etc. Also see "Brings Disease Upon Himself" in this section).

**Ravings in Disease**—(See Raving).

**Reading and Study**—Diseases from Overstudy, etc. — (See "Reading and Study" under Blindness; "Brain Fag" under Brain; Fatigue, Reading, Study).

**Recovery; Recuperation;**

**Recurrent Diseases**—(See Periodical, Recurrent, Remittent, Returning).

**Refreshment**—Disease from Lack of—(See Famine, Neglect, Poverty, Privation, Rest, Sleep, Starvation, Thirst).

**Relapses; Relatives**—Illnesses of—(See Family, Relatives).

**Religion**—Diseases Caused By—(See Religion).

**Remission**—Of Disease—(See Remission).

**Remittent; Remove**—The Disease Will Remove Shortly—(See "Decrease" under Recovery).

**Resistance**—To Disease—(See Resistance).

**Resolution**—Of Disease—(See Resolution).

**Response**—The Degree of Response Against Disease—(See "Response" under Degree).

**Rest**—Has No Rest in Disease—(See Rest).

**Retrograde Planets**—And Disease—(See Retrograde).

**Return of Disease**—Old Maladies Return—(See Periodical, Returning).

**Rich Food**—Diseases From—(See Diet, Extravagance, Food; "Impure Blood" under Impure; Luxuries, Plethora, Surfeits, etc.).

**Right Side of Body**—Diseases In—(See Right).

**Sagittarius Diseases**—(See Sagittarius).

**Sanitation; Saturn Diseases**—(See Saturn).

**Scandalous Diseases**—(See Scandalous).

**Scope of the Disease**—The Scope Enlarged—(See Enlarged).

**Scorpio Diseases**—(See Scorpio).

**Seat of the Disease**—In Hor'y Questions the seat of the disease can be judged and taken from the sign in which the ☽ is posited, or from the sign on the cusp of 6th H. (See Diagnosis, Judgment, Members, Organs, Parts, etc.).

**Self-Motivated Acts**—Diseases From—(See Rashness).

**Sensuality**—Diseases From—(See Amorous, Excesses, Passion, Sensuality, Sex, etc.).

**Sequence**—In Disease—Interrupted Sequence—(See Sequence).

**Serious Diseases**—(See Serious).

**Severe Diseases**—The Severity of the Disease—(See "Intensity" in this section; Fulminating, Severe).

**Sex Excesses**—Diseases From—(See Amorous, Excesses, Passion, Sex, Venery, etc.).

**Sharp Diseases**—(See Sharp).

**Shifting**—Of the Disease—(See Chronic, Complications, Course, Crises, Relapse, Remote, Return, Sympathy).

**Short Diseases**—(See Acute, Curtailed, Quick, Sharp, Short, Swift, Violent).

**Sick**—The Sick—(See Sick).

**Sickly; Sickness; Significators**—Of Disease—Indicators of Disease—Diseases come from, and are indicated by the 6th H., and planets therein, signs on cusp of 6th, lord of the 6th. In chronic and lingering diseases ♄ is the Significator. In acute diseases, accidents, violence, etc., ♂ is the Sig., and so on with each of the planets, according to their influence and nature. (See "Indicators of Health" under Health).

**Signs of Zodiac**—Diseases Ruled By—(See Aries, Taurus, Signs, etc.).

**Sixth House**—And Disease—(See Sixth).

**Sleep**—Diseases from Lack of—(See Debauchery, Dissipation, Neglect, Privation, Refreshment, Rest; "Insomnia" under Sleep).

**Slight Disorders**—(See Colds, Mild, Minor, Slight).

**Slow Diseases**—(See Chronic, Consumptions, Lingering, Prolonged, Slow, Tedious, Wastings, etc.).

**Solution**—Of Continuity In Disease—(See Continuity, Solution).

**Spasmodic; Species**—Causes Every Species of Disease—(See South Scale, Species).

**Sports**—Diseases Caused By—(See Exercise, Sports).

**State of Mind**—Diseases Caused By—(See Anguish, Anxiety, Dejected, Depression, Despondency, Grief, Imagination, Insanity, Melancholy, Mental, Mind, Negative, Psychic, Sadness, Sorrow, Trouble, Worry, etc.).

**Stationary Planets**—And Disease—(See Stationary).

**Strange Diseases**—(See Strange).

**Strong**—(1) Strong Disposition to Disease—The ☽ P ♄ at B., and by dir., and espec. if the ☽ be hyleg, shows a strong tendency to disease and premature dissolution except some benefic intervene. (See "Ill-Health All Thru Life" under Ill-Health; Invalids, Sickly; "Much Sickness" under Sickness; "Low" under Vitality; "Weak Body" under Weak, etc.). (2) Strong Drink—Diseases from Excess of—(See "Delirium Tremens" under Delirium; Drink, Drunkenness, Intoxication, etc.).

**Structural; Stubborn Diseases**—(See Chronic, Constitutional, Consumptions, Cure, Difficult, Hereditary, Incurable, Invalids, Long, Malignant, Medicines, Obstinate, Organic, Prolonged, Remedy, Slow, Structural, Tedious, Treatment, Wastings, etc.).

**Study and Reading**—Diseases from Over-Study, etc.—(See "Reading" in this section).

**Succumbs Easily**—To Disease—(See "Low" under Recuperation, Resistance, Vitality; Succumbs; "Weak Body" under Weak). For influences which show strong resistance to disease, and where the patient does not succumb easily, see Immunity; "Good" under Resistance, Vitality; Robust; "Body" under Strong).

**Sudden Diseases**—Sudden Attacks of—Sudden Distempers—Sudden Severity of Disease—(See Fulminating, Sudden, Unexpected).

**Suffers Much**—In Disease—(See Anguish, Pain, Suffering).

**Summer Diseases**—(See Summer).

**Sun Diseases**—(See Solar, Sun).

**Support**—Seeks Profit and Support by Exhibition of Disease—(See Exhibition).

**Suppurative Diseases**—(See Abscesses, Pus).

**Surfeits; Susceptibility**—To Disease—(See Constitutional, Diathesis, Heredity, Organic, Praeincipients, Predisposed, Susceptibility, Vitality Low; "Weak Body" under Weak).

**Swellings; Swift Diseases** — (See Swift).

**Sympathy**—Sympathy and Antipathy—Sympathetic Diseases— (See Antidotes, Antipathy, Attracts, Complications, Opposites, Remote, Removal, Sympathy, etc.).

**Symptoms**—In Disease—(See Diagnosis, Prognosis, Symptoms).

**System Disordered**—See Constitution, Disorders, Ill-Health, Infirmities, Sickness, System. Also note the various paragraphs in this section).

**Taurus Diseases**—(See Taurus).

**Tedious Diseases**—(See Chronic, Lingering, Long, Prolonged, Slow, Tedious).

**Temporary Diseases** — (See Acute, Colds, Indisposition, Mild, Slight, Temporary, etc.).

**Tendency to Disease**—(See Attracts, Diathesis, Feeble, Infirm, Predisposition; "Low" under Resistance, Vitality; "Weak Body" under Weak. Also see "Causes", "Susceptibility", "Threatened", in this section).

**Termination**—Of the Disease—(See End, Prognosis, Termination).

**Terrible Diseases**—Dreadful Diseases—(See Terrible).

**Threatened with Disease**—Liable To—Strong Disposition to Disease—The ☉ or ☽ to the ☌, P, □ or ☍ ♄ or ♂, or other malefics, by dir. in the Zodiac, or Mundane; the ☉ directed to Aldebaran, Regulus, Antares, Deneb, Betelguese, Bellatrix, or Frons Scorpio; the ☽ ☌, P, or ill-asp. ♄ at B., and by dir., and espec. if the ☽ be hyleg; the ☽ directed to the Back, Neck, or Wing of the Lion; to South Scale, Right Leg of Ophiucus; Deneb, Goat's Back, or Left Shoulder or Right Arm of Aquaries, and in those parts of the body signified by the sign in which those stars are posited; the ☽ at a Lunation on the place of the malefics at B., and espec. of ♄ and ♂; the Pr. ☽ to the evil asps. of her own place at B. if affl. by malefics at B.; the Asc. to the □ or ☍ the ☉ or ♄ by dir. (See "Causes", "Liable To", "Tendency To", in this section. Also see "Danger of Sickness" under Sickness).

**Thrives and Lives**—Thru Serious Diseases—(See Serious).

**Throwing Off Disease**—(1) Has Power to Throw Off Disease Easily and Quickly—(See Immunity; "Rapid" under Recuperation; "Good" under Resistance; "Body" under Strong; "Good" under Vitality). (2) Has Little Power to Throw Off Disease—(See "Overcoming" in this section). (3) Makes Effort to Throw Off Disease—(See "Overcoming" in this section).

**Time of the Disease**—Time When Disease is Apt to Come—The Event of the Disease—The ☽ sepr. from the ☍ of the ☉, the next planet she applies to decides the event of the disease. (See Directions, Eclipses, Equinoxes, Events, Ingresses, Lunations; "New Moon" under Moon; Progression; "Solar Revolution" under Solar; Solstices, Time, Transits, Vernal, etc.).

**Transient**—(1) Transient Disposition in Disease—(See Diathesis, Directions). (2) Transient Diseases — (See Acute, Colds, Mild, Minor, Slight).

**Transits**—And Disease—(See Transits; "Time Of" in this section).

**Treatment**—Of Disease—(See Antidotes, Antipathy, Colors, Cure, Diet, Drugs, Healers, Herbs, Hygiene, Medicines, Opposites, Prevention, Remedies, Sanitation, Sympathy, Treatment, etc.).

**Twelfth House**—And Disease—(See Twelfth).

**Two Diseases**—At the Same Time—The ☉ affl. in ♊, and arising from congestion or inflamed blood. (See Complications, Gemini, Remote, Removal, Sympathy, etc. Also see "Many Diseases" in this section).

**Type**—Of the Disease—(See "Disease" under Nature; Quality, Type).

**Uncleanliness**—Diseases From—(See Carelessness, Cleanliness, Filth, Habits, Uncleanly).

**Uncommon; Understand**—The Disease is Difficult to Understand—♆ and ♅ diseases. (See Difficult, Extraordinary, Mysterious, Neptune, Obscure, Peculiar, Psychic, Strange, Uranus).

**Unexpected Diseases**—(See Sudden).

**Unusual**—(See Extraordinary, Uncommon).

**Upper Parts**—Of the Body—Diseases In—(See Upper).

**Uranus Diseases**—(See Uranus).

**Vague Diseases** — (See Mysterious, Obscure, Psychic, Strange, Vague).

**Vapors**—Diseases from Foul Vapors—(See Vapors).

**Variable; Various; Vascular;**

**Vehement; Venereal; Venomous;**

**Venus Diseases**—(See Venus).

**Vessels; Vexation**—Diseases Caused By—(See Vexation).

**Vibration and Disease**—(See Vibration).

**Vicarious; Violent; Virgo Diseases**—(See Virgo).

**Virulent; Viscera; Vision**—Disorders of—(See Sight).

**Vital**—Vital Force—Vital Principle—As Related to Disease—(See Vital).

**Vitality**—Disorders of—(See Vitality).

**Voyages**—Diseases On—(See Voyages).

**Vulnerable Parts**—Disorders of—(See Vulnerable).

**Wandering Diseases**—(See Flying, Wandering).

**Wards Off Disease**—(See "Overcoming", "Throwing Off", in this section).

**Wasting Diseases**—(See Wasting).

**Water**—Diseases Arising From—(See Moisture, Water, Wet).

**Watery Diseases**—(See Watery).

**Weakness**—Diseases Arising From—(See Weak).

**Weather**—Diseases Caused by the Weather—(See Weather).

**Weird Diseases**—(See Weird).

**What Is The Disease?**—(See Diagnosis, Judgment, Nature, Parts, Vulnerable).

**Whole Body**—The Disease Is Thru the Whole Body—(See Whole).

**Wind**—Windy Disorders—(See Wind).

**Winter Diseases**—(See Winter).

**Withering Diseases**—(See Withering).

**Women**—Diseases of—(See Female, Women).

**Worse**—The Disease Becomes Worse —(See Complications, Crises, Day, High, Increase, Night, Relapses, Worse, etc.).

**Youth**—Diseases of—(See Young, Youth).

**Zones**—Diseases of the Different Zones of the Body—(See Aries, Taurus, Gemini, etc.; "First House" under First; "Second House" under Second, etc.; Members, Organs, Parts, Signs, Zodiac, Zones).

**Zymotic Diseases**—(See Zymotic). For Diseases, Afflictions, and Conditions not listed here, look for the subject in the alphabetical arrangement.

**DISFIGUREMENTS**—Blemishes—Defects—Caused by the pathological deposits of ♄, as in the joints, causing swollen, enlarged, and stiff joints. Mars causes disfigurements by cuts, blows, scars, violence, wounds, amputations, etc. All the Constellations not of human form tend to disfigure the body and model it after their own forms, whether they be fowls or animals. (See "Beastly Form" under Beasts; Birthmarks (Naevus), Blemishes, Blotches, Contortions, Crooked, Cyclops, Defects, Deformities, Discolorations, Distortions, Dogs, Eyes, Face, Fowls, Freckles, Frog, Head, Ill-formed, Imperfections, Inhuman, Joints, Lameness, Marks, Members, Moles, Monsters, Naevus, Nose, Paralysis, Pimples, Scars, Smallpox, Sores, Teeth, Ulcers, etc.).

**DISGRACE**—Dishonour—Disrepute—Loss of Honour and Reputation—Scandal—Disease and Sickness resulting therefrom due to worry, grief, sorrow, disfranchisement, isolation, reversals, ruin, etc.—

**Causes of Disgrace**—Planetary Causes —These influences tend especially to affect those who are drifting along in life, unawakened, unspiritualized, living in sin or wickedness, etc., and such influences need not affect the more advanced Souls, and who are living lives of wisdom, honor, discrimination, self-control, etc. Much has been said in the Astrological Textbooks along this line, and these influences usually contribute to, and go hand in hand with disease and its planetary causes. Note the following influences,—The ☉ Sig. □ or ☍ ♄; the ☉ by Periodic Rev. to the ill-asps. ♅; the ☉ to the □ ♀ by dir.; the ☉ conjoined with Hercules, Antares, Hyades, Regulus, Aldebaran, or any eminent star of the nature of ♂; the ☉ to the ☌ or P. the Ascelli by dir.; the ☉ with South Scale and Knee of Ophiucus; the ☉ directed to Deneb, and all others of the nature of ♅; the ☉ or ☽ joined with the Whale's Jaw; the ☉ directed to stars in the Lion, the South Scale, the Knee and Right Leg of Ophiucus, the Goat's Back, Left Shoulder and Right Arm of Aquaries, causes disgrace, sickness, ruin, and every evil; the ☉ ☌ a malefic in the M.C.; the ☽ to Ceti; the ☽ decr., sepr. from ♂ and apply. to ♀, disgrace thru wantonness; the ☽ decr. in a day geniture, sepr. from ♀ and apply. to ♄, brings disgrace and ruin upon himself; the ☽ directed to Deneb, public disgrace, ultimate disgrace and ruin; the ☽ directed to the Pleiades, Hyades, Praesepe, or the Twins; the ☽ directed to the Back, Neck, or Wing of the Lion; South Scale, Right Leg of Ophiucus; Deneb, Goat's Back, or to the Left Shoulder and Right Arm of Aquaries, ruin and disgrace; the ☽ to Cor. Hydra; the ☽ weak and ill-dig. at B., and to the ☌ the M.C.; the ☽ to the Left Shoulder of Bootes; the ☽ to the □ or ☍ ♂, disgrace thru women; the ☽ combust by application is fatal to position in life (Hor'y); ♄ in an angle with the ☉ or ☽, and with no good asps. from benefics; ♄ to the ☌ or ill-asp. the ☉ or ☽ by dir.; ♄ Sig. □ or ☍ the ☉ or ☽; ♄ to the place of ☋ by dir.; ♄ is the Sig. of disgrace and ruin in Hor'y Questions; ♄ affl. in the 10th H., danger of disgrace and downfall; ♅ affl. in the 10th H.; ♃ Sig. □ or ☍ ♄; ♂ in det., and ☍ the Asc.; ♀ weak at B., and affl. by ♂, much scandal and disgrace; ♀ to the ☌ ♂ or ☋ by dir., disgrace by lewd courses; ☿ affl. by malefics at B., and to the ☌ the M.C. by dir., scandal and disgrace; the Asc. to the □ or ☍ ♄ or the ☽ by dir.; the M.C. to the ☌ or ill-asps. ♄ or ♂ by dir.; the M.C. to the ill-asps. the ☉, sudden disgrace; the M.C. to the ill-asps. ♀, disgrace thru women; M.C. to the place of Cauda at B.; M.C. directed to Algol, Hydra's Heart, Ascelli, Castor, Pollux, Hyades, Praesepe, Shoulders of Orion, Markab, Auriga's Right Shoulder; M.C. to the □ or ☍ ☿ by dir., disgrace thru false reports; Part of Fortune (⊕) to the ill-asps. ♀ by dir., disgrace thru females; the 12th H. is the house of disgrace and misfortune, and with malefics and afflictions in this house at B., and in or to this house by dir.; lord of the 12th in the 1st H.; lord of the 12th in the 10th, sad disgrace; lord of the 10th a malefic, and in the 10th; lord of the 11th, a malefic, and in the 11th and affl.; lord of the 6th in the 10th, sickness from disgrace or shame; lord of the 10th in the 12th; lord of the 10th a malefic, and espec. if posited in the 1st or 10th; lords of the 1st and 10th sepr. from each other by asp., or the ☽ sepr. from lord of the 10th, and apply to no benefic, but apply to malefics, tends to bring disgrace, downfall, and loss of position, and the same if lord of the 1st be ℞ or combust (Hor'y); lord of the 1st or the ☽, □ or ☍ lord of the 10th, or the ☉, and if at the same time they separate from benefics and apply to malefics without reception or translation (Hor'y); malefics in the 1st or 10th H., and affl.; malefics in the 10th H. at a Solar Rev.; a malefic ☌ the ☉ in the M.C.; the 3° ♋ on the Asc. at B.; fixed stars of the nature of ♄ ascending at B.; fixed stars of the nature of ♄ and ♂ culminating at B.; fixed stars of the nature of ♂ and the ☽ culminating at B., such as the Pleiades, and other nebulous stars of this nature; all eminent fixed stars of the nature of ♄ in an angle with the ☉ at B.; Cauda (☋) in the 8th H. in a Hor'y Map; the Pleiades, Castor, Pollux, Hyades, Aselli, or Praesepe directed to the Asc. or Lights; the Pleiades rising, or with the ☉ or ☽, or directed to the Asc.; the Pleiades rising, and ☌ the ☉ or ☽ in an angle. (See in the alphabetical arrangement each of the Fixed Stars and Constellations mentioned in this Article. Also see such subjects as Banishment, Conduct, Dishonest, Downfall, Evil, Execrated, Executed, Exile, Fortune, Grief, Habits, Harlots, Honour, Infamous, Judge, Law, Lewd, Love Affairs, Misfortune, Morals, Prison, Reputation, Reversals, Ruin, Scandal, Self-Undoing, Sentence of Law (see Judge); Shame, Sorrow, Trouble, etc.).

**Harlots**—Suffers Disgrace Thru Harlots—(See Harlots).

**High Position**—Rises to a High Position in Life, but Soon Falls Into Disgrace—♄ Sig. □ or ☍ ☉ or ☽; ♄ in the Midheaven at B., in a weak sign, afflicted, or affl. the ☉ or ☽.

**Lewd Courses**—Disgrace By—(See Lewd).

**Perpetual Disgrace**—Perpetual Trouble and Disgrace—♄ on the Meridian, or coming to the Meridian at B.

**Wantonness**—Disgrace By—(See Lewd, Wanton).

**Women**—(1) Women Fall into Disgrace—The ☽ to the ill-asps. ♅, ♄, or ♂ by dir., and espec. if the ☽ be affl. by these planets at B.; ♂ ☌ or ill-asp. the ☽ or ♀; ♀ to the ☌ or ill-asp. ♅ by dir. if ♅ afflict ♀ at B.; malefics in the 7th H. at a Solar Rev. (2) Disgrace Thru Women—The ☽ to the □ or ☍ ♂ by dir.; the M.C. or ⊕ to the ill-asps. ♀ by dir. (See Men, Women).

**DISHONESTY**—Dishonorable—Cheating—Crafty—Cunning—Artful—Sly—Fraudulent—Liars—Subtle—False Pretenses—Dual—Duplicity—Wily—Shrewd—Insincere—Unfair—Unprincipled—Unscrupulous—Hypocritical—Thieving—Swindling—Underhanded, etc. Dishonesty is a disease of the Mind, and for this reason these influences are inserted here. Such influences, however, can be overcome. There are usually some good influences in every map of birth, or in the character, which tend to make a person honest, kind, balanced, good, and upright, and also some evil influences which tend to the opposite unless they are controlled and transcended. Wilson has observed that those who have a copious flow of Humours from the head are remarkable for Shallowness of Intellect, and for Dishonesty. The following influences tend to Dishonesty, and to the traits of mind listed in the first part of this Article.

**Causes of Dishonesty**—The Planetary Causes at Birth and by Direction—The Prenatal Causes, the Epochal Map, the map for the time of Conception, also show the character, and contributary fundamental causes. The ☉ Sig. ☌ ♄; the ☉ Sig. □ or ☍ ♂; the ☉ Sig. ☌ ♃, and ♃ ill-dig. and ill-aspected, espec. false and hypocritical in religion; the ☽ Sig. □ or ☍ ☿, a low cunning used for dishonest purposes, but if ♃ be in △ asp. to ☿ the evil will be lessened; the ☽ to the ☌ or ill-asp. ♂, and ♂ affl. by ☿, or in a sign or house of ☿; the ☽ Sig. in ♊, crafty and subtle to excess; ♆ and ♓ are prominent and afflicted in most cases of deception; ♆ affl. the ☉, ☽, and ☿; ♅ influences and afflictions tend to make one dishonest and deceitful in love affairs, and espec. ♅ ☌ or ill-asp. ♀; ♄ Sig. □ or ☍ ☿, schemes to deceive his most intimate friends; ♄ and ♂ afflicting ☿; ♄ Sig. □ or ☍ ♀; ♄ ☌ or ill-asp. ♀ or ☿; ♄ in the 9th H., apt to be deceitful and hypocritical in religious matters; ♄ Sig. in ♊, ♋, ♍, ♏, or ♓; ♄ affl. in ♏; ♄ Sig. ☌ ☿, subtle and crafty; ♃ Sig. ☌ ♄, mean and deceitful; ♃ Sig. in ♏, subtle and crafty, and to be very warily dealt with; ♃, ♀, ☿, and the ☽ strongly afflicted, and espec. in mutable signs, should guard against being deceitful and dishonest in money matters; ♂ ☌ ☿ and affl. by ♄, and also ♄ affl. the ☉ and ☽ at the same time; the evil asps. between the ☽, ♂, and ☿ incline the native to dishonesty; ♂ Sig. in ♑; ♂ Sig. in ♓, sly and artful if in the terms of ☿; ♂ Sig. ☌ ♄, sly and cowardly; ♂ ill-dig. at B., and affl. ☿; ♂ Sig. □ or ☍ ♄, ☿, or the ☽; ♂ ruler at B., and affl. by ♄, ☿, or the ☽; ♂ represents subtle men, and ♄ tends to dishonesty from malicious motives; ♂ in bad asp. to ♄; ♂ affl. in ♊, ♍, ♑ or ♓; ♀ Sig. ☌, □, or ☍ ♄; ♀ Sig. in ♋; ♀ Sig. □ or ☍ ♄ or ♂, full of mischief; ☿ Sig. in ♋; ☿ Sig. in ♊, cunning; ☿ ill-dig. at B.; ☿ Sig. □ or ☍ the ☽, not very sincere in their professions of friendship, and also unscrupulous in their methods by which they attain their ends; ☿ Sig. □ or ☍ ♄ or ♂; ☿ Sig. ☌ ♄, calculating and covetous; ☿ affl. in the 12th H., active in schemes, plots and intrigues; ☿ Sig. ☌ ♂; ☿ when ill-dig., and afflicted by malefics, is the author of tricks and deception; ☿ Sig. in ♈, and affl. by ♄ and ♂, often a mere knave; ☿ Sig. in ♊, and affl. by malefics and the ☽; ☿ in the Asc. in □ or ☍ ♄ or ♂, and with no good asps. to the benefics; ☿ elevated above and evilly configurated with ♄ or ♂; the Asc. to the place of Hircus, apt to defraud others; the ♏ influence in its lower vibrations, uncontrolled, not spiritualized, and as deceitful as the Scorpion; ♑ influence tends to make one subtle and witty, but capricious like the Goat; the negative, or feminine signs, prominent at birth, evilly aspected and occupied by malefics, tend to give a more deceitful and dishonest nature fundamentally; violent afflictions in common signs unless ♃ is strong and well-aspected; the bicorporeal signs strong at B., and many planets in them, tend to duplicity, hypocrisy, etc., and espec. the double-bodied signs of ♃. (For collateral study and further influences along these lines see Artifice, Character, Cheating, Criminal, Deceitful, Dual-Minded, Enemies, Evil, Gambling, Hypocritical, Kleptomaniac, Knavish, Liars, Libellers, Malevolent, Mischief, Perjury, Pettifogging, Plots, Prisoners, Principles, Religion, Responsibility, Robbers, Shrewdness, Thieves, Treachery, Wicked, etc.).

**DISHONOUR**—Dishonourable—(See Disgrace, Dishonest, Honour, Reverses, Ruin, Reputation, etc.).

**DISINTEGRATION**—The New ☽ implies disintegration. (See Death, Decay; "New Moon" under Moon).

**DISLIKES**—(See Antipathy, Aversions, Food, Likes).

**DISLOCATIONS**—Luxations—Displacements—A Displacement of Organs or Articular Surfaces—Caused by ♄ afflictions; ♄ coming to the cusp of the Asc. by a direction in the Zodiac causes; afflictions in ♐ or ♑; a ♑ disorder; ♑ on the Asc. Bones and Organs in the parts of the body ruled by the sign containing ♄ at B. are espec. subject to displacement and dislocation, or the trouble brought on by the afflictions of ♄ by dir. to the part so afflicted at B. The afflictions of ♅ also cause violent dislocations, and espec. when configurated with ♄ or ♂ at the time. Mars also tends to cause dislocations by his violent nature, as by injury in accidents, etc. Mechanical Displacements, espec. of organs, are both ♄ and ♀ disorders. Organs are often displaced due to the weakening effect of ♄ afflictions to ligaments and supports.

**Displacements**—(See Displacements).

**Femur**—Dislocation of—(See Femur).

**Heart**—The Heart on the Right Side—Case—(See "Right Side" under Heart).

**Hip Joint**—Dislocation of—(See "Joint" under Hip).

**Kidneys**—(See "Floating" under Kidneys).

**Joints**—(See Joints).

**Neck**—(See "Dislocations" under Neck).

**Organs Displaced**—(See Displacements, Organs. Also see the Introduction, "Heart", "Kidneys", in this Article).

**Partial Dislocation**—(See Subluxations).

**Shoulder**—Dislocation of—♄ affl. in ♊. (See Shoulders).

**Subluxations**—A Partial Dislocation—(See Subluxations, Vertebrae).

**Tibia**—(See Tibia).

**Vertebrae**—Subluxations of—(See Subluxations, Vetebrae).

**Wrist**—Dislocated Wrist—(See Wrist).

**DISORDERLY**—

**Disorderly Conduct**—The ☉ to the bad asps. ♀ by dir., and ♀ ill-dig. at B. (See Conduct, Debauchery, Drink, Drunkenness, Intoxication, Quarrels).

**Illness**—Brought On by Disorderly Conduct—(See "Brings Disease Upon Himself" under Disease).

**DISORDERS**—Disordered—Ailments—Diseases—Derangements—Faulty—Ill-Health—Complaints—Sickness, etc.—This subject has been largely considered in the sections on Disease, Health, Ill-Health, Sickness, etc. The following subjects have been especially mentioned in the textbooks of Astrology as "Disordered", which subjects for convenience of reference are listed here.

**Disordered Blood**—(See "Disordered", "Impure", "Poor", "Thin", under Blood).

**Disordered Mind**—(See the various paragraphs under Imagination, Intellect, Mental, Mind, Perception, Understanding, etc.).

**Disordered Stomach**—(See "Disordered" under Stomach).

**Disordered System**—(See "Disordered" under System). For the various disorders of the Organs, Functions, and Parts of the Body, see in the alphabetical arrangement the subject you have in mind.

**General Disorders**—(See General).

**DISORGANIZED**—Disorganization—Disorganizing—The ♅ influence is disorganizing, and espec. the lower vibrations of this planet. The influence of ♄ is disorganizing and depleting. Also the influence of ♆ tends to be disorganizing and chaotic in influence over the mind until the native becomes awakened and spiritualized, and learns how to rule his stars. (See Chaotic, Interrupted).

**DISORIENTATION**—(See Identity).

**DISPERSIONS**—Dispersals—Dissipation of Forces and Energies—

**Forces**—Dispersion and Dissipation of Forces—♂ and the ☽ combinations (fire and water) tend to, and to angry feelings, effervescent mental activity, and dissipation of brain force. (See "Over-Active Mind" under Active; Anger, Diffusiveness, Dissipation, Effervescent, Scattering).

**Functional Energy**—Dissipation of—♆ diseases and afflictions. (See Energy, Functions).

**Violent Dispersals**—♂ with ♄, and both the afflictors in the disease at the same time. (See "Compound" under Fractures; Violent).

**DISPLACEMENTS**—

**Mechanical Displacements**—♀ diseases; ♀ afflicted, or afflictions to ♀ by the malefics. (See Dislocations).

**Organs Displaced**—♄ influence, due to weakening of ligaments and supports. (See Dislocations, Organs; "Falling" under Womb).

**DISPOSITION**—The Temper—Temperament, etc.—This work is not primarily a treatise on the Disposition, but the Disposition and Disease are so intimately bound up and interdependent that many traits of Temperament have been listed and considered. The subjects are too numerous to list here.

Look in the alphabetical arrangement for the subject you have in mind. Especially see the subjects of Conduct, Decanates, Habits, Manners, Mental, Mind, Temper, Temperament, etc. Also see each of the Signs, as Aries, Taurus, etc. See each of the Planets, as Sun, Moon, Mars, etc. There are a number of classified lists of the traits of Temperament given in the various Textbooks of Astrology, such as given by each of the Signs, Planets, etc.

**Transient Disposition**—In Disease—(See Diathesis, Directions).

**DISPROPORTIONED**—

**Body**—Disproportioned Body—(See Corpulent, Crooked, Fat, Fleshy, Ill-shaped, Short; "Tall and Thin" under Thin; Ugly, etc.).

**Cold**—Disproportioned Cold, Heat, Dryness and Moisture—Extremes of—Lack of—Diseases Resulting From—(See Air, Atmosphere, Cold, Diminished, Drought, Dryness, Epidemics, Famine, Floods, Heat, Increased, Moisture, Pestilence, Rain, Summer, Superabundance, Weather, Winds, Winter).

**DISPUTES**—Controversies—Contests—Dissentions, etc.—Danger of Injury or Death From—(See Chartering, Contests, Cuts, Duels, Enemies, Feuds, Gunshot, Misunderstandings, Poisoning, Quarrels, Treachery, Sword, War).

**DISRUPTION**—Disruptive Agencies—♅ and ♂ influence. (See Bursting, Explosions, Lacerations, Rupture, Perversions, Vessels, etc.).

**DISSATISFIED**—(See Anxiety, Despondent, Discontentment, Fears, Melancholy, Restless, Unhappy, Worry, etc.).

**DISSIPATED**—Scattered—(See Cold, Decay, Dispersions, Dry, Energy, Scattering, Strength, etc.).

**DISSIPATION**—Dissipated—Liable to Dissipated Conduct—The Energy and Strength Dissipated—Disease and Ill-Health Arising From—The ☉ Sig. to the ☌ ♀; the ☉ to the □ or ☍ ♀ by dir., and ♀ affl. at B.; the ☉ to the □ or ☍ ♃; the ☉ directed to the Ascelli; the ☉ to the ill-asps. the cusp of the 2nd H., or ruler of the 2nd; the ☽ affl. at B., cadent, in ♏ or ♑, and with no good asps of ♃ or ♀; the ☽ to the ☌ Procyon; the ☽ decr. in light, and carried to, or conjoined with ♀, and ♂ behold ♀; the ☽ decr. in light, sepr. from ♄ and apply. to ♀; the ☽ in ♏ or ♓ at B., and ♀ passing the radical ☽ or ♂ at a Solar Rev.; ♄ Sig. □ or ☍ ♀; ♃ Sig. □ or ☍ the ☉ or ♀; ♃ Sig. □ or ☍ the ☉ or ♀; ♃ Sig. ☌ ♂, and ♂ ill-dig. and affl.; ♂ affl. in the 4th H., and espec. in ♋ or ♓, and affl. by the □ or ☍ of planets; ♂ in ♋ or ♓ in the 12th H., and affl.; ♂ □ or ☍ ♀; ♂ in the 5th H. in ♋, ♏, or ♓, and affl. by the ☽ or ♀; ♂ affl. in the 11th H., thru the influence of friends; ♂ at a Solar Rev. passing over the radical ☽; ♂ Sig. ✱ or △ the ☽; ♀ ☌ the Asc. by dir., and ill-health following; ♀ in the Asc., and affl. by ♄ or ♂; ♀ rising and affl.; ♀ to the □ or ☍ the M.C.; ♀ lady of the year at the Vernal, and affl. and weak, tends to a prevalence of dissipation; ♀ affl. in the 5th H., ill-health by; ♀ ill-dig. at B., much given to dissipation; ♀ Sig. □ or ☍ ♄, altho not suspected; M.C. to the □ or ☍ ♀. (See Conduct; "Brings Disease Upon Himself" under Disease; "Causes His Own Death" under Death; Debased, Debauched, Depraved, Dispersals, Dissolute, Drink, Drunkenness; "Early Death" under Early; Eating, Energy Dissipated (see Energy); Excesses, Feasting, Folly, Food, Free Living (see Free); Gluttony, Habits, Harlots, High Living (see High); Infamous, Intemperance, Intoxication, Lewd, Loose, Low and Base (see Low); Lustful, Men, Middle Life—Death At—(see Middle Life); Morals, Narcotics, Opposite Sex (see Opposite); Own Worst Enemy (see Enemies); Passion, Perverted, Prodigal, Profligate, Redundant, Sex, Shameless, Taverns, Venery, Vices, Vile, Wanton, Wine, Women).

**Energy Dissipated**—The Strength and Energy Dissipated—Dissipation of Energy—The ☉ in ♌ in the Asc., in ✱ or △ ♂, great energy, but tendency to dissipate it; ♂ in ♌ in the Asc., and ☉ ruler of the Asc., and afflicted; ♂ in ♌ in the Asc., and affl. by ♃ or ♀. (See Dispersions, Dissipated, Effervescent, Energy; "Energy" under Functions; Irresponsible; "Activity" under Perversions; Roaming, Scattering; "Weakened" under Strength; Unreliable, Vacillating; "Lessened" under Vitality).

**DISSOLUTE**—Dissolute Habits—Dissolute Living—Caused by an afflicted ♀; ♀ to the ill-asps. the Asc., M.C., or the ☽ by dir.; the ☽ affl. in ♏ in female nativities; the ☽ ascending at B., weak, and ill-dig.; ♄ to the ill-asps. ♂ or ♀ by dir.; ♆ in ♓ in the 5th H., and affl., dissolute vices and depraved habits; ♆ affl. in the Asc. in male nativities tends to dissolute habits. (See Debauched, Depraved, Dissipation, Drink, Drunkenness, Infamous, Loose, Morals, Prodigal, Profligate, Riotous, Tumors, Vices, etc.).

**DISSOLUTION**—Death—The Process of Dissolving—Catalysis—(See Catalysis; "Denotes Death" under Death; Decay, Disintegration, Putrefaction, Resolution, etc.).

**Dissolution of Tissues**—The Dissolving of Bodily Tissue—The pathological action of the ☽, and afflictions to the ☽. The 3rd Dec. of ♍ denotes death, dissolution, decay, infirmity, and old age. (See Death, Decay, Disturbances, Infirmity, Old Age, Resolvent, Resolution, Solution, Tissues, etc.).

**DISSPIRITED**—(See Anxiety, Brooding, Dejected, Depressed, Despondent, Discontentment, Fears, Gloom, Hope, Hypochondria, Irritable; "Low Spirits" under Low; Melancholia, Repining, Restless, Worry, etc.).

**DISTEMPERS**—Distemperatures—Diseases—Ailments—Indispositions, etc. The word Distemper in Modern Therapeutics is applied more to Animals than to diseases of Man. However, the word Distemper appears very frequently in Astrological Literature, and for convenience of reference the various forms of Distempers have been gathered, listed and classified in this section. Also see the Article on Disease.

**Back**—The Back Distempered—(See "Diseases" under Back).

**Bodily**—The Distemper is Bodily—The Disease is More in the Body Than in the Mind—(See "Afflicted" under Body).

**Bowels**—The Bowels Distempered—(See "Disorders" under Bowels).

**Brain**—Distempers of the Membranes of the Brain—(See "Disordered" under Brain; Meninges).

**Choleric Distempers**—(See Choleric).

**Chronic**—Long Chronic Distempers—(See Chronic).

**Cold Distempers**—$\mathcal{H}$ diseases. (See Cold).

**Cold and Moist Distempers**—(See "Cold and Moist" under Humours, Moisture).

**Disease**—The Disease Changes into Some Other Form of Distemper—(See "Changes" under Disease).

**Dry**—Dry and Melancholic Distempers—(See "Melancholy" under Dry).

**Fancies Distempered**—(See Fancies).

**Feet Distempered**—(See "Distempers" under Feet).

**Feverish Distempers**—(See Fever).

**General Distempers**—The Distemper General Over the Body—(See "General" under Whole).

**Genitals**—Distempers In—(See "Diseases" under Genitals; "Distempers" under Secrets).

**Gluttony**—Distempers Proceeding From—(See Gluttony, Intemperance, Plethora, Surfeits).

**Head**—Distempers In—(See "Disorders" under Head).

**Heart**—The Heart Distempered—(See "Heart Trouble" under Heart).

**Hot Distempers**—Hot and Moist Distempers—(See Fever; "Hot Diseases" under Heat; "Hot and Moist" under Heat, Moisture).

**Inflammatory Distempers**—Liable To —(See "Causes" under Inflammation).

**Intemperance**—Distempers From—(See "Diseases" under Intemperance).

**Intestines**—Distempers In—(See "Disorders" under Bowels).

**Kidneys Distempered** — (See "Diseased" under Kidneys).

**Liable to Distempers**—Planets in Perigee, and also when ℞, tend to cause diseases and distempers. (See "Causes" under Disease; Perigee, Retrograde).

**Long Distempers**—Long Chronic Distempers—(See Chronic).

**Mad and Sudden Distempers**—(See "Sudden" under Head).

**Melancholic Distempers**—Melancholic and Dry Distempers—(See "Melancholy" under Dry; "Diseases" under Melancholy).

**Meninges of Brain**—Distempers of—(See "Brain" in this section).

**Mental**—Mind—The Distemper is More in the Mind Than in the Body—(See "Afflicted" under Body; Cares; "Diseased Mind" under Mind; "Disease" under Psychic).

**Moist Distempers**—Cold and Moist Distempers—(See "Cold and Moist" under Humours; Moisture).

**Morbid Distempers**—(See "Diseases" under Morbid).

**Neck**—Chronic Distempers About the Neck—(See "Chronic" under Neck).

**Putrid Distempers**—(See Putrid).

**Reins**—Distempers In—(See "Disorders" under Reins).

**Secret Parts**—Distempers In—(See "Diseases" under Genitals; "Distempers" under Secrets).

**Sudden Distempers**—Mad and Sudden—(See "Sudden" under Head; "Diseases" under Sudden).

**Throat**—Chronic Distempers In—(See "Chronic" under Throat).

**Toes**—Distempers In—(See "Distempers" under Feet, Toes).

**Veneral Distempers**—(See Venereal).

**DISTENTIONS**—Distention—A $\delta$ and $\mathcal{4}$ disease. The Distentions of Plethora are caused by $\mathcal{4}$, and resulting from Gluttony, and the Blood Vessels being too full. (See Gluttony, Plethora, Surfeits; "Too Much Blood" under Blood; "Vascular Fullness" under Vascular; Vessels).

**Distended Abdomen**—(See "Distentions", "Prominent", under Abdomen).

**Distended Body**—The Body Inflated—(See Bloating, Flatulence, Gas, Inflation, Swellings, Tympanies).

**Distended Stomach**—(See Digestion, Emphysema, Flatulence, Gas, Indigestion; "Distended" and "Wind" under Stomach; Tympanites, etc.).

**Distended Vessels**—(See Aneurysm, Arteries; "Too Much Blood" under Blood; Capillaries, Dilatations, Varicose, Vascular, Vessels, etc.).

**DISTILLATION**—Distillatory—Sublimation—The Distillatory Processes of the Kidneys are ruled by $\female$ and the $\triangleq$ sign. Leo and $\triangleq$ are concerned with distillation and circulation, and $\triangleq$ espec. with distillation in the kidneys, and filtration. (See Kidneys, Nutrition).

**Distillation of Rheum**—(See Rheum).

**Distilled Water**—(See "Mineral Waters" under Healers; "Water" under Skin). See Filtration, Sublimation.

**DISTORTIONS**—Twisted Out of Natural or Regular Shape—

**Causes Of**—Many planets in Imperfect or Mutilated Signs at B., or with such a sign upon the Asc., as $\Omega$, $\mathfrak{m}$, or $\mathcal{H}$ (some Authors include $\simeq$ and $\mathcal{V}$), are apt to produce distortions of body and limbs; malefics in angles, and the $\odot$ or $\mathcal{D}$ in $\delta$, or brought up to them; the $\odot$ or $\mathcal{D}$ $\delta$ or $\delta$ $\hbar$, in angles, and espec. if the $\mathcal{D}$ be in her nodes, or in extreme Lat., or in hurtful signs, and $\mathcal{P}$, $\delta$, $\simeq$, $\mathfrak{m}$, or $\mathcal{V}$,—under these conditions if the $\odot$ or $\mathcal{D}$ be in $\delta$ with $\hbar$ or $\delta$, the defect will be from birth, but if $\hbar$ or $\delta$ be in $\delta$ to the $\odot$ or $\mathcal{D}$, or $\hbar$ or $\delta$ in the M.C. in $\square$ the $\odot$ or $\mathcal{D}$, it will be from Cuts, Blows, Stabs, Falls from Heights, Injury by Robbers, Quadrupeds, by Shipwreck, and in Accidents;

the ☽ in obnoxious signs, as ♈, ♉, ♋, ♏, or ♑, in her nodes, or in extreme Lat., and the malefics brought up to the Luminaries, the body is afflicted with Excrescences, Distortions, Lameness, or Paralysis. The calamity takes place from the moment of birth if the malefics be with the ☉ or ☽, but if the malefics be in the 10th H., and elevated above the Lights, or in ☍ to each other, then the trouble arises from Falls from Heights, Attacks by Robbers or Quadrupeds, or by some dangerous Accident, Cut, Stab, etc. (See Excrescences).

**Features Distorted**—(See Features).

**Gait**—Awry Gait from Distortions—(See "Awry" under Gait).

**Limbs Distorted**—(See Limbs. Also see "Causes" in this section).

**Teeth Distorted**—(See Teeth).

**Views Distorted**—(See Chaotic, Confusion, Eccentric, Erratic, Ideals, Ideas, Judgment, Notions, etc.). See Accidents, Animals, Birth, Calamity, Congenital, Contortions, Contractions, Crippled, Cuts, Defects, Deformities, Dwarf, Excrescences, Face, Falls, Feet, Fingers, Gait, Hands, Heights, Imperfections, Infirmities, Injuries, Lameness, Legs, Limbs, Maimed, Malformations, Monsters, Mutilated, Neck, Paralysis, Quadrupeds, Robbers, Shipwreck, Spasmodic, Spine, Stabs, Twistings, Walk, etc. For Distortions of the various organs or parts of the body not listed here, look for the subject in the alphabetical arrangement.

**DISTRACTION**—Distracted of Mind—(See Anguish, Anxiety, Dejected, Depressed, Despondent, Distress, Grief, Hypochondria; "Low Spirits" under Low; Melancholy, Miserable, Sadness, Sorrow, Trouble, Worry, etc.).

**DISTRESS**—Distressful—Suffering—

**Abroad**—Distress and Suffering Abroad—(See "Distress" under Abroad).

**Death**—Death Without Distress—(See "Easy Death" under Death).

**Dreams**—Distressful Dreams—(See Dreams).

**Every Kind**—Of Distress—Ruled and Denoted by the 12th H. (See Twelfth).

**Maladies**—Distressful Maladies—(See Fierce, Grievous, Heavy, High, Painful, Severe, Sharp, Vehement, Violent).

**Mind**—Distress of Mind—The 2nd Decan. ♐ on the Asc. (See Anguish, Disgrace, Dishonour, Distraction, Reputation, Reversals, Ruin, Trouble, etc. Other references are given under Anguish. For other kinds of Distress, see in the alphabetical arrangement the subject you have in mind.

**DISTURBED**—Disturbances—

**Brain**—The Brain Disturbed—(See "Disturbed" under Brain).

**Circulation**—Circulation of the Blood Disturbed—(See Arteries, Blood, Circulation, Congestions, Determination, Heart, Impure, Pulse, Rush, Veins).

**Degree of Disturbance**—In Disease—This is greater when the tempo of the movements of the planets is slower in forming or separating from aspects, as when the planets are ℞, Stationary, Slow of Motion, etc. The rate of progression of the planets varies from day to day, and in disease the daily motion, or rate of movement of the planets, should be studied in helping to form a judgment. Planets rapid and direct in motion, and at their normal daily rate, tend to more rapid dissolution of disease. (See Direct; "Planets" under Motion; Retrograde, Stationary).

**Mind Disturbed**—(See Anguish, Anxiety, Insanity; "Irritations" under Mental; "Diseased Mind" under Mind; Worry, etc.).

**Sleep Disturbed**—(See Refreshment, Rest; "Insomnia" under Sleep).

**System Disturbed**—(See Constitution, Disease, Derangements, Disorders, Ill-Health, Infirmities, Sickness; "Disordered" under System).

**DISUNION**—Of Cells—(See "Division" under Cells; Death, Decay, Disintegration, Dissolution, etc.).

**DIURESIS**—Excessive Secretion of Urine—(See Diabetes; "Excess", "Polyuria", under Urine).

**DIURETICS**—A Medicine Increasing the Flow of Urine—A Therapeutic Property of ♀ and ♀ remedies, and also of ♄. (See Aconite, Urine, Venus).

**DIURNAL**—(See Day).

**Diurnal Signs**—And Houses—(See "Nocturnal Signs" under Night).

**DIVINATION**—(See Clairvoyance, Magic, Mediumship, Necromancy).

**DIVISION**—Divisions—

**Divisions of the Body**—The 12 parts, or divisions of the body, as ruled by the 12 Signs of the Zodiac. (See each of the Signs as Aries, Taurus, etc. Also see Signs, Vertebrae, Zodiac).

**Division of Cell**—(See "Division" under Cell).

**Divisions of Life**—The Periods of Life from Infancy to Old Age, and their planetary rulerships. (See Periods).

**DIZZINESS**—Giddiness—Light-Headedness—Vertigo—A ☉ disease; an ♈ disease; ♄ ☌ ♃ or ♀ in ♈; ♄ ☌ ♃ in the Asc.; ♃ affl. in ♈; ☿ affl. in ♐; Subs at AT, Li.P, and SP. (See Fainting, Vertigo).

**DOCTORS**—Influences which tend to make good Physicians and Healers of the various Schools. (See Healers, Surgeons).

**DOGS**—Dog Bites—Mad Dogs—Resembles Dogs, etc. Domestic Pets are ruled by ♃. (See Pets).

**Death of Dogs**—(See "Virus" under Pestilence).

**Dog Bites**—Death, Injury, or Disease From, and from Mad Dog Bites—The ☉ to the ☌ ♂ by dir. makes one liable to dog bites whether the dog is healthy or mad; caused by ♂ afflictions. (See "Dogs" under Bites; Hydrophobia).

**Dog Days**—Named originally after Sirius, the Dog Star, and the ☌ of the ☉ with Sirius in July. However, they are now made to depend upon the Summer Solstice, and to have no connection with Sirius, as in Ancient Times. Dog Days begin on July 3rd, or 12 days after the Summer Solstice, and end August 14th. (See Hydrophobia).

**Mad Dog Bites**—(See Hydrophobia. Also see "Dog Bites" in this section).

**Resembles Dogs**—(See "Dogs" under Children).

**Sickness of Dogs**—(See Hydrophobia; "Virus" under Pestilence).

**DOLEFUL**—(See Grief, Imagination, Melancholy, Mournful, Sadness).

**DOLENS**—Phlegmasia Alba Dolens—(See "Milk Leg" under Legs).

**Dolens**—Grief—(See Grief).

**DOMINION**—

**Dominion of Death** This is vested in the planet which occupies an Anaretic Place at B. (See Anareta; the Introduction, and "Quality" under Death).

**Dominion of the Planets**—(See Planets, and each of the planets in the alphabetical arrangement, as Saturn, Sun, Moon, Mars, etc. Also see Angles, Aspects, Benefics, Cadent, Directions, Elevated, Feminine, Majority, Malefics, Masculine, Occidental, Oriental, Negative, Positive, Rising, Setting, etc.).

**DORSA LEONIS**—Lion's Tail—(See Lion, Melancholy, Stars).

**DORSAL**—Pertaining to the Back—

**Nerves**—The Dorsal Nerves—The Upper Dorsal Nerves are ruled by ♊; the Middle Dorsal Nerves are ruled by ♌, and the Lower Dorsal Nerves are ruled by ♍.

**Spine**—The Dorsal Region of the Back and Spine—Ruled by the ☉ and the ♌ Sign. This part of the Spine is afflicted, or becomes diseased, with ♄ affl. in ♌, or the ☉ afflicted, and known as ☉ diseases. (See Back, Spine).

**Tabes Dorsalis**—(See Tabes).

**Vertebrae**—The Dorsal Vertebrae—(See "Dorsal" under Vertebrae).

**DOUBLE-BODIED SIGNS**—Bicorporeal Signs—These Signs are ♊, ♐, and ♓. These Signs are formed, or symbolized, by two distinct animals, or contain two distinct animals. These signs when upon the Asc., 5th, or 11th H. at B., and espec. when rising upon the Asc., or containing the ☉, ☽, and many planets, tend to Twins, and multiple births. They also tend to a dual mind, and scattering of the mental and physical energies. (See Castor, Dual, Gemini, Mutable, Pisces, Pollux, Sagittarius, Twins).

**DOUBTS**—The ☽ Sig. ☌ ♄, likely to doubt and deliberate too long in the moment of action; the ☽ Sig. ⚹ or △ ♄, does nothing with much thought or deliberation, doubting, and with some fear of consequences; ☿ affl. by ♄; the 29° ♊ on Asc., is full of doubt, misgivings, fears, suspicions, and is pessimistic; the 21° ♐ on Asc. Neptune is also called the Planet of Doubt and Fear. (See Anguish, Anxiety, Fears, Forebodings, Hallucinations, Imaginations, Imprudent, Jealousy; "No Peace of Mind" under Mind; Mistrustful, Neptune, Obsessions, Pessimistic, Premonitions; "Excess Of" under Prudence; Recluse, Reserved, Scepticism, Suspicious, Thinking, Worry, etc.).

**DOWN**—

**Downcast**—(See Dejected, Depressed, Despondent, Hope; "Low Spirits" under Low; Melancholy; "No Peace" under Mind; Sadness, Worry, etc.).

**Downcast Look**—Downward Look—(See "Downward" under Look).

**Downfall**—Sudden Downfall—♂ Sig. ☌ ☉. (See Disgrace, Fortune, Honour, Reputation, Reverses, Ruin, Scandal, Trouble, etc.).

**Downward Flow**—Of Humours—(See Defluxion).

**DRAGON'S HEAD**—(☊)—Caput Draconis—The ☽'s North Node—Is said to be of the nature of the ☉, and fortunate in health, and other matters, when conjoined with the Asc., M.C., or in ☌, ⚹, or △ the planets. Wilson in his Dictionary says that ☊ is equal to ♃ and ♀ in benign influence. The house, or sign, of ☊ is said to be ♉.

**Dragon's Tail**—(☋)—Cauda Draconis—The ☽'s South Node—Is of the nature of ♄ and ♂, corresponds to ♄, and ♎, the exalted sign of ♄, and tends to suppression and obstruction of the bodily functions, the same as with ♄, only in a lesser degree. When in ☌ with a planet it has a ♄ influence, and tends to crystallize, harden, and obstruct. In ☌ with malefics it tends to double and treble their evil. According to the Ancients it is classed as malefic in influence. Its sign, or house, is said to be ♏. Is very evil when the Sig. of Death. (See Nodes, Saturn).

**DRAUGHTS**—Drafts—Catching Cold By—(See Colds, Tuberculosis).

**DREADFUL**—Terrible—

**Dreadful Death**—(See "Dreadful" under Death).

**Dreadful Diseases**—The ☉ directed to all Nebulous Clusters, and to Castor and Pollux, threatens dreadful diseases. (See Portentous, Terrible).

**DREADS**—Fears—(See Darkness, Dreams, Fears, Obsessions, Premonitions; "Terrors" under Strange).

**DREAMS**—Visions—Dreamy—Dreams are ruled and presided over by ♆ and the 9th H. Dream Consciousness is ruled by the 9th H. Dreams and Nightmare occur mostly about 48 hours before the ☽'s Perigee, and when the ☽ is about an hour high. The Hebrew letter Lamed (L) is connected with Dreams, Sleep, and the ♎ Sign. Dreams are also caused by the ☽ in the 9th H., and aspected by ♆; ♆ ⚹ or △ the ☽, ♅, or ♃; ♆ affl. in ♐, dreams of danger; ♆ ⚹ or △ the ☽, prophetic dreams; ♆ ☌ or in transit over the radical ☽ or ☿; ♆ in the 9th H., strange dreams; ♆ in ♈ □ or ☍ ☽, nightmare; ♅ ⚹ or △ ♆, of a prophetical and inspirational nature; ♅ in ♐; ♅ in the 8th H. predisposes to dreams and visions; ♃ affl. in ♈, strange dreams, ♂ in the 9th H., distressful dreams. Case of Strange Dreams and Premonitions—See "Dreams", No. 312, in 1001 N.N. (See

Astral, Clairvoyance, Coma, Delirium, Fears, Forebodings, Hallucinations, Premonitions, Prophetic, Psychic, Sleep; "Terrors" under Strange; Trance, Visions, etc.).

**Dreamy Mind**—Dreamy Manner—A Day Dreamer—Absent-Minded—Visionary—Inability to Concentrate—Mental Fantasies—♎, ♒, and ♓, and with many planets in these signs, and ♂ obscurely placed, indulge much in day dreams. (See Absent-Minded, Chaotic, Concentration, Confusion, Delusions, Erratic, Fancies, Fears, Flightiness, Hallucinations, Ideals, Illusions, Imagination, Obsessions, Phantasies, Psychic, Recluse, Secretive, Spirit Controls, Vagaries, Vague, Visionary, Weird, etc.).

**Wet Dreams**—(See Semen).

**DREAMY**—(See "Dreamy" under Dreams).

**DRESS**—Clothing—Linen—Food and Clothing are ruled by the 6th H. and the ♍ sign. Venus also rules strongly over Dress, Adornment, and the indiscretions of dress.

**Adornment**—Fond of Personal Adornment, Fine Clothes and Jewelry—(See Pretender).

**Bad Respiration**—Due to Indiscretions in Dress, Tight Lacing, etc.—(See "Indiscretions" in this section. Also see Lacing).

**Colors of Dress**—(See "Clothing" under Colors. Also see Black).

**Extravagance**—In Dress and Food—♂ in the 6th H. (See Extravagance, Luxuries).

**Indiscretions**—In Dress, Illness and Disturbances From—Injudicious Dressing—♀ affl. in ♉, ♊, or ♋ tends to bad respiration due to injudicious dressing and tight lacing; ♀ in ♊ in the 6th H., and afflicted, or affl. the ☽ or Asc., tends to bad respiration from tight lacing; with ♃ or ♀ in ♊, indiscretions in dress should be avoided, as they are harmful to the health; ♀ in ♌ in the 6th H., and afflicted, or afflicting the ☽ or Asc., tends to palpitation of the heart thru indiscretions in dress, or tight lacing; malefics in ♊ also tend to harmful effects upon the chest, lungs and breathing from tight lacing. (See "Obstructions" under Breathing; Exposure, External, Indiscretions, Lacing).

**Neat in Dress**—(See Neat).

**Peculiar Tastes**—In Dress—♆ in the 6th H. (See Eccentric, Fancies, Food, Habits, Ideas, Notions, Peculiar, Tastes, etc.).

**Pretentious**—In Dress—(See Pretender).

**Throat Disorders**—From Improper Dress—(See "Dress" under Throat).

**Tight Lacing**—(See "Indiscretions" in this section).

**Untidy**—(See Untidy).

**Wet Clothing**—Colds and Illness From—(See "Clothing" under Colds; "Cold Taken" under Feet).

**DRIBBLING**—(See "Salivation" under Saliva; "Incontinence" under Urine).

**DRINK**—Drinking—Tendency to Drink—Danger of Excesses In—Fond of Intoxicating Drink, etc.—The watery signs ♋, ♏, and ♓, when strong and predominating the map of birth, and the ☉, ☽, Asc., or many planets in such signs at B., and affl., tend to strong drink, and dissipation therefrom; especially a ♓ disease and affliction, and with the ☉ or ☽ affl. in ♓, and many planets in watery signs also; the ☽ ill-dig. at B., given to drink; the ☽ or ☿ affl. by ♆; the ☽ to the ⚹ or △ ♂ if ♂ be weak and ill-dig. at B.; the ☽ in ♉ in the 5th H., and affl.; ♆ ☌, □, or ☍ the ☽; ♆ ☌ ♀ in ♉, and affl. by the ☽; ♆ and ♂ in ♉, and with the ☽ in a water sign; ♅ ☌ ☽ in ♋, and affl. by the □ or ☍ of ♂ causes strong drink; ♃ Sig. □ or ☍ ☉; ♃ or ♀ affl. in ♋; ♂ affl. in ♉, ♋, or ♓; ♂ in ♋, □, or ☍ ♆, fond of liquids and drink; the aspects of ♂ cause when ♂ is ill-dig.; ☿ in ♓ partile asp. the Asc.; Subs at SP and KP tend to, and to create a morbid condition due to excessive use of alcohol. Cases of Given to Drink, Birth Data, etc.—See "Spendthrift", No. 262, in 1001 N.N. Also see Fig. 14 in "Message of the Stars" by the Heindels. (For further influences see the various paragraphs in this Article, and the references given).

**Alcoholic Excesses**—♓ on the Asc., and tending to habitual drunkenness. (See "Excess" in this section. Also see Drunkenness, Intoxication).

**Ale Houses**—Saloons—Taverns—A Frequenter of—Brawling in Saloons—(See Taverns).

**Bacchus**—Partial to the Joys of Bacchus—The 19° ♐ on the Asc. (Charubel).

**Brain**—Softening Of Due to Alcoholism—(See "Softening" under Brain).

**Brawling in Saloons**—(See Drunkenness, Taverns).

**Children**—The Children May Become Drunkards—(See "Children" under Drunkards).

**Craving for Drink**—(See "Fond Of", and the various paragraphs in this Article).

**Death from Drink**—(See "Death" under Eating, Intoxication).

**Delirium Tremens**—(See Delirium).

**Dipsomania**—An Uncontrollable Desire for Drink—(See Dipsomania).

**Disease**—Disease and Ill-Health from Too Much Strong Drink—(See "Strong Drink" in this section).

**Drunkenness**—(See Drunkenness).

**Excess in Drink**—The ☉ and ☽ badly affl., and espec. in or from fire and water signs; a weak polarity between the ☉ and ☽; the ☉ affl. in ♉, excess in eating and drinking; the ☽ affl. by ♀, and the ☽ or ♀ in a water sign at B.; the ☽ in a water sign, and to the ☌ or ill-asp. ♂ by dir.; ♆ affl. in ♋; ♆ in ♋ in the 6th H., and affl.; ♆ in ♋ and affl. the ☉, ☽, Asc., or hyleg; ♆ in the 5th H., in a water sign, and affl.; ♄ ☌ or ill-asp. ♀ or ☿, and espec. in water signs; ♃ in the Asc. in a water sign, and affl.; ♃ affl. in ♉, over-indulgence in drinking and eating, and suffering from; ♃ □ a malefic; ♂ in the Asc. in a water sign, and affl.; afflictions in or to the 11° of cardinal signs, or to the 9° or 25° of fixed signs; the 19° ♐ on the Asc.; ♉ influence and afflictions in; ♓ on the Asc. (See Debauchery, Delirium Tremens, Dissipation, Dissolute, Drunkenness, Excesses; "Sugar" under Food; Intemperance, Intoxication, Sottishness. Also see the various paragraphs in this section).

**Fits of Drink**—And Sensuality—♂ ☌ or ill-asp. the ☽ or ♀ by dir., and ♂ affl. these planets at B.

**Fond of Drink**—Craving for Drink—The ☉ to the ☌, or any asp. ♀ in a water sign, and ♀ afflicted; the ☉ to the ☌, or any asp. ♀ by dir., and ♀ affl. at B.; the ☉ to the ill-asps. the ☽ by dir., and in water signs; the ☉ affl. in a watery sign; the ☉ in a water sign ☌ ♀, and affl.; the ☉, ☽, and ☿ in ♓; the ☉ ☌ ☽ in 12th H.; the ☽ to the ☌ or ill-asp. ♂ by dir., if the nativity shows a tendency to drink; the ☽ in ♋ or ♓ and affl. by the ☉ or ♂; the ☽ weak and affl. at B., and espec. in water signs; the ☽ to the ⚹ or △ ♂ by dir., and ♂ affl. at B., and both in water signs; ♆ ♓ in the 5th H.; ♆ ♋ in the 6th H., and affl.; ♅ affl. in ♏; ♄ ♏ at B., and affl. the Asc. by dir.; ♄ ☌ or ill-asp. ♀ in water signs; ♃, ♓, □ or ☍ ♂; ♃ in the 1st H. in ♓; and affl.; ♂ in ♓; ♂ ♓, ☌ ☽ or ♃; ♂ ♓, □ or ☍ ♃; ♂ ♉, ♋, or ♎, and affl. by the □ or ☍ of planets; ♂ affl. in the 12th H. in ♋ or ♓; ♂ evilly posited, and afflicting ♀; ♂ in the sign or house of the ☽, and affl.; in Hor'y Questions, ♂ Sig. of the person; ♂ ruler at B., and affl., and espec. in water signs; ♂ Sig. in ♉; ♀ ill-dig. at B.; ♀ or ☿ affl. in ♓; ♀ in the Asc. or M.C., or in water signs, and affl.; ♀ Sig. ☌ ♂; ☿ affl. in ♋ or ♓; watery signs on the Asc., and espec. ♓, and afflicted; a ♋, ♏, and ♓ disease. (See the Introduction, "Excess", and the various paragraphs in this section).

**Given to Drinking**—(See "Fond Of" in this section).

**Habits**—A Habitual Drunkard—(See Drunkenness).

**Husband**—The Husband Given to Drink—The Marriage Partner Drinks—(See "Drink" under Husband, Marriage Partner, Wife).

**Intoxication**—Intemperance—(See these subjects).

**Liquids**—Craving for Liquors—Spirituous Liquors—The ☽ in water signs; the ☽ affl. in ♓. (See Intoxication, Liquids, Wine. Also note the various paragraphs in this section).

**Marriage Partner**—Given to Drink—(See "Husband" in this section).

**Meals**—Drink With—(See Food).

**Moderate Drinker**—The ♊ influence strong at B., and mixed in with the evils which cause Intemperance.

**Over-Indulgence in Drink**—(See "Excess" in this section. Also see "Delirium Tremens" under Delirium; Drunkenness, Intoxication).

**Parents**—The Parents Drink and Neglect the Children—(See "Drink" under Parents).

**Period of Drinking**—A Period of Drinking caused by evil Directions—The Prog. ☉ □ or ☍ the radical ☽, and espec. if both are in water signs at B.; the ☉ to the bad asps. ♀ or the ☽ by dir.; the ☽ to the ☌ or ill-asps. ♂ by dir., if the nativity shows a tendency to drink; the ☽ to the ⚹ or △ ♂ by dir. if ♂ be weak and affl. at B., and the radical ☽ be in a watery sign; ♄ ♏ ☌ or evil asp. the Asc. by dir.; ♃ in ♓ at B., and affl., and to the ☌ or ill-asp. ♂ by dir., and ♂ also in a water sign at B., and afflicting ♃, ♀, or the ☽; ♂ to the ☌ or ill-asp. ♀ or the ☽ by dir., and espec. if these planets be in watery signs at B. and afflicted. (See Directions).

**Protracted Drinking**—(See "Habitual" under Drunkenness; "Period Of" in this section).

**Saloons**—Frequenter of—Brawling In—(See Taverns).

**Softening of Brain**—(See Brain).

**Sottishness**—A Sot—A Toper—Habitual Drunkard—(See "Habitual" under Drunkenness; Harlots, Sottishness, Taverns).

**Spirituous Liquors**—An Uncontrollable Desire For—(See Dipsomania).

**Stimulants**—Addicted to the Use of—(See Dipsomania, Drunkenness, Intoxication, Narcotics, Stimulants, Sugar, Wine, etc. Also note the various paragraphs in this section).

**Stomach Disordered**—By Drink—The ☽ in ♋ and afflicted by the ☉ or ♂ when taken ill.

**Strong Desire**—For Intoxicating Liquors—(See Dipsomania, Drunkenness, Intoxication; "Fond Of" in this section).

**Strong Drink**—Strong Coffee—Addicted To—Disease From—♆ in ♋ or ♍ in the 6th H., and affl.; ♆ in ♋ and affl. the ☉, ☽, Asc., or hyleg; ♄ ☌ ♀ in ♋; the ☽ ♓ and affl. by the ☉ or ♂ when taken ill; ♂ affl. in ♉ or ♋; ☿ affl. in ♓, in some cases; ♓ on the Asc., and with other afflictions tending to drink. (See "Softening" under Brain; Delirium Tremens, Demoniac, Intoxication, Thirst).

**Surfeits**—From Too Much Drink—(See "Surfeits" under Diet; Eating, Food, Surfeits; "Excess", "Strong Drink" in this section).

**Temperate**—In Drink—(See "Moderate" in this section).

**Tendency to Drink**—(See the various paragraphs in this section).

**Thirst**—For Drink—(See "Fond Of" in this section; "Drinks" under Thirst).

**Too Much Drink**—(See "Excess" in this section).

**Too Strong Drink**—Uses Too Strong Liquors and Intoxicants—♆ affl. in ♍, and espec. in 6th H. (See Delirium Tremens, Intoxication; "Strong" in this section).

**Toper**—(See "Habitual" under Drunkenness).

**Uncontrollable Desire**—For Strong Drink—(See Dipsomania; "Strong Drink" in this section).

**Vicious Drinking**—♂ affl. in ♉, ♊, ♋, ♍, ♒, or ♓, and espec. when affl. the ☉, ☽, or ♀, and with the latter in water signs.

**Wife**—The Wife Given to Drink—(See "Husband" in this section).

**Will Power**—Lack of Will to Curb Appetite for Drink—♓ on the Asc. at B., and afflicted. (See Dipsomania; "Habitual" under Drunkenness).

**Wine**—Addicted To—(See Wine).

**Women Crave Drink**—♄ ☌ or ill-asp. the ☽ at B., and by dir. (See the various paragraphs under Women). For further study along this line see Conduct, Cravings, Debauchery, Disorderly, Dull; "Free Living" under Free; Habits; "High Living" under High; Improvident; "Loose Morals" under Morals; "Low Public Houses" under Low; Madness, Morals, Pineal Gland, Pleasures, Prodigal, Profligate, Ravings, Sensuality, Temperance, Vagabonds, Vices, etc.

**DROOPING**—Limp Body—Bodily Action Uncertain—(See Limp, Ptosis, Relaxed, Stooping).

**DROPSY**—Dropsies—Dropsical Humours—Hydropical Diseases—Anasarca—Oedema—Effusion of Fluids into the Tissues—etc. Dropsy is principally a disease of the ☽, the ♋ sign, and is also closely related to the watery signs, and afflictions in them. Saturn causes Dropsy by stoppages, obstructions, retentions, suppressions, and by interfering with the bodily functions. Jupiter and ♀ afflictions cause Dropsies by surfeits, over-indulgences, etc., and ♆ causes them thru excesses of various kinds, and dissipation. The Common Signs, and afflictions in them, also show Dropsy. Dropsical swellings change for the better or worse at the changes of the ☽. (See "Full Moon" under Moon). Dropsy follows the course of the ☉ when chronic, and is worse when the ☉ reaches the □, or ill-asp. his place at B. by transit, and especially when in aspect with the malefics, and diminishes when the ☉ is in good asp. his own place, or in good asp. to the benefics. Dropsy occurs in various parts of the body, from the brain to the feet, and according to the planetary afflictions at B., and by direction. The following paragraphs have to do with Dropsy, its nature, and the parts of the body so afflicted.

**Abdomen**—Dropsy in the Abdominal Region and Bowels—Dropsy of the Abdomen—Dropsy of the Peritoneum—Ascites—The ☽ affl. in ♍ or ♓; ♆ affl. in ♍; ♄ in ♍ or ♓; ♃ affl. in ♓; ♓ on the Asc.; Subs at KP (11D) and PP. (See Abdomen; "Dropsy" under Bowels).

**Anasarca**—General Dropsy—♃ affl. in ♋; afflictions in ♎ and ♑, due to the close association of these signs in ruling the kidneys and the connective tissues; Subs at KP (11D), and at UPP (1 and 2L). (See Puffing).

**Ankles**—(See "Swollen" under Ankles).

**Ascites**—Dropsy of the Abdomen—(See "Abdomen" in this section).

**Beriberi**—A Disease accompanied by Acute and Anaemic Dropsy, with great Weakness, Dyspnoea, and Paraplegia—Caused by many afflictions in watery signs, and espec. ♓, and with ♓ on the Asc., and afflicted; a ♄ disease; ♄ affl. in ♓ in the Asc., 6th, or 12th houses; afflictions in the common signs; afflictions in ♐, ♑, ♒, and ♓, the signs which rule the lower limbs; Subs at KP, UPP and PP. (See Anaemia, Dyspnoea; "Paralysis" under Legs).

**Blood**—The ☽ hyleg in ♓, dropsical condition of the blood in women (see "Blood" under Women); ♃ affl. in ♏, dropsy arising from blood discharged with watery humours; ♃ affl. in ♓, dropsy from thin and watery blood. (See "Thin Blood" under Blood).

**Bowels**—Dropsy In—(See "Dropsy" under Bowels; "Abdomen" in this section).

**Brain**—Dropsy of—(See Hydrocephalus).

**Cancer Sign**—An eclipse of the ☉ in the 3rd Dec. of ♋ tends to hydropical diseases among Peoples of Africa, Armenia, and Regions under ♋. (See "Cancer" under Nations).

**Cardiac Dropsy**—(See "Dropsy" under Heart).

**Cases of Dropsy**—Birth Data, Map, etc.—(See Fig. 33 in "Message of the Stars" by the Heindels).

**Chest**—Dropsy In—(See "Dropsy" under Chest).

**Chronic Dropsy**—(See the Introduction to this section).

**Circulation**—The Circulation and Dropsy—Serum Collections—(See "Poor", "Weak", under Circulation; Serum).

**Danger of Dropsy**—Liable To—Tendency To—Dropsical Complaints—The ☉ affl. in ♋, ♏, ♒, or ♓, and espec. when in ☌ or evil asp. the Asc.; the ☉ in ♓ and affl. by ♃; the ☉ affl. in ♋; a ☽ disease; the ☽ affl. in ♋, ♏, ♒, or ♓ (♒ rules strongly over the circulation of the blood, and dropsy results from disturbance of the circulation by afflictions in ♒); the ☽ to the ☌ ♄ by dir.; denoted by the ☽ when the ☽ afflicts the ☉ or Asc.; the ☽ hyleg, and to the ☌ or evil asp. ♄ by dir.; the ☽ sepr. from ♄ and apply to the ☉; the ☽ decr. in light and sepr. from ♄ and apply. to ☿; the ☽, or lords of the 1st or 6th H. in water signs; the ☽ affl. in ♋, ♏, or ♓, and affl. the hyleg therefrom; the ☽ in ♓ and affl. by the ☉ or ♂ when taken ill; the ☽ affl. at B., and to the ill-asps. the Asc. or hyleg by dir.; the ☽ hyleg in a watery sign, and affl., and espec. in female nativities; the ☽ in ♏, ☌ or ill-asp. ♄ by dir. (or ☿ if he be of the nature of ♄) at the beginning of an illness, or at decumb.; the ☽ in ♓ and in ☌, □, or ☍ ♄; ♆ affl. in ♎; a ♄ disease, and caused by ♄ afflictions; ♄ in ♋, ♏, or ♓, ☌ or evil asp. the Asc. by dir.; ♄ in ♓, occi., and affl. the ☉, ☽, or Asc.; ♃ affl. in ♋, ♏, ♑, ♒, or ♓; ♃ in ♋ or ♏ in the 6th H., and affl.; ♂ affl. in ♓ sometimes causes dropsical affections; a ♀ disease; ♀ affl. in ♊; a disease of the watery signs ♋, ♏, and ♓, and with ♋ or ♓ on the Asc.; an ♒ disease; ♒ on the Asc., and affl.; ♒ or ♓ ascending at the Vernal Equi., tend to a prevalence of dropsy among people ruled by these signs, or in Countries ruled by them; Subs at KP and Local. (See "Aquarius", "Pisces", under Nations. Also see the various paragraphs in this section).

**Death By**—♄ denotes death by dropsy; caused by ♄ directions when he afflicts the hyleg and holds the dominion of death; afflictions in common signs show, and espec. ♄ in a common sign and affl. the hyleg, and ♄ in the 8th H. at B., and by dir.

**Diminished**—The Dropsy Is Diminished—(See the Introduction to this section).

**Effusions**—Serous Effusions—(See Effusions, Osmosis, Serum).

**Eyeballs**—Dropsy of—(See Eyeballs).

**Fallopian Tubes**—Dropsy of—Hydrosalpinx—(See Fallopian).

**Feet**—Dropsy In—(See "Dropsy" under Ankles, Feet, Legs).

**Fluids**—(See the various paragraphs under Fluids).

**General Dropsy**—Anasarca—(See "Anasarca" in this section).

**Heart Dropsy**—(See "Dropsy" under Heart).

**Humours**—Dropsical Humours—The ☉ in ♓, and affl. by ♃; the ☽ in ♏, ☌ or ill-asp. ♄ (or ☿ if he be of the nature of ♄) at the beginning of an illness or at decumb.; a ♋ disease, and afflictions in ♋, or ♋ on the Asc. (See "Danger Of", and other paragraphs in this section).

**Hydrocephalus**—(See this subject).

**Hydronephrosis**—Renal Dropsy from Obstruction—(See "Dropsy" under Kidneys).

**Hydrosalpinx**—Water in the Fallopian Tube—Dropsy of—(See Fallopian).

**Hydrothorax**—(See "Dropsy" under Chest).

**Increased**—The Dropsy Increased—(See the Introduction to this section).

**Kidneys**—Dropsy of—Renal Dropsy—Hydronephrosis—(See Kidneys).

**Limbs**—Dropsy of Lower Limbs—(See Ankles, Feet, Legs).

**Liver**—Dropsy of—(See Liver).

**Mucus-Like Dropsy**—(See Exudations, Mucus, Myxoedema).

**Obstructions**—♄ causes Dropsy by obstruction of the circulation and functions. (See Obstructions. Also see the Introduction to this section).

**Oedema**—(See Oedema, Serum).

**Osmosis**—Exosmosis—Oozings—(See Osmosis).

**Ovaries**—Dropsy of—(See Ovaries).

**Peritoneum**—Dropsy of—Ascites—(See "Abdomen" in this section).

**Prevalence Of**—(See "Danger" in this section).

**Renal Dropsy**—(See "Dropsy" under Kidneys).

**Serum**—Dropsical Effusions of—(See Serum).

**Sleeping Dropsy**—(See "Sleeping Sickness" under Sleep).

**Swellings**—Dropsical Swellings—(See the Introduction, and the various paragraphs in this section. Also see Incurable, Swellings).

**Thorax**—Dropsy In—Hydrothorax—(See "Dropsy" under Chest).

**Transudations**—(See Osmosis).

**Watery Diseases**—(See Swellings, Watery. Also note the various paragraphs in this section).

**Worse**—The Dropsy Is Worse—(See "Increased" in this section).

**DROUGHT**—Hot and Dry Air—Intemperate Heat—Famine and Suffering From—

**Causes Of**—General Causes—Eclipses of the ☉ or ☽ in earthy signs, and espec. when the shadow falls over the Regions under the Signs involved; the ☉ eclipsed in the 1st Dec. of ♈, drought and intemperate heat; eclipses of the ☉ in fiery signs, and espec. in those Regions under the rule of the Sign in which they occur; an eclipse of the ☽ in the 2nd Dec. of ♏, dry air; ♄ ☌ ♂ in fiery signs; ♂ in power, and lord of the year at the Vernal Equinox; Comets affect the places ruled by the Signs in which they appear; Comets appearing in the Eastern Quarters of the heavens. (See Air, Atmosphere; "Cold and Dry" under Dry; Corn; "Cold and Dry", "Diseases", "Dryness of the Air", under Dryness; Epidemics, Famine, Fountains, Fruits, Grain, Heat, Pestilence, Scarcity, Vegetation, Wheat, Weather, Winds, etc.).

**Disease**—Disease, Death, or Suffering from Drought—Eclipses of the ☉ or ☽ in earthy signs, and affecting those People and Places ruled over by the Signs under which they occur; ♄ near the cusp of the 4th H., and in S. Lat. at the Vernal Ingress; ♂ sole ruler at an eclipse of the ☉; ♈ ascending at a Solar or Vernal Ingress, and ♂ be afflicted, Countries and Peoples ruled by ♈ suffer from extreme heat and drought; ♌ ascending at the Vernal, and the ☉ afflicted, ♌ People and Countries under ♌ suffer thru extreme heat, drought, warm pestilential air, and diseases of the heart and brain; ♑ ascending at the Vernal, and ♄ afflicted, Places and People under ♑ suffer, and have a very dry Season.

**DROWNING**—Death by Water—Death by Drowning—Danger of—The ☉ to the ☌ or ill-asp. ♄ or ♂ from water signs; when the ☉ or Asc. are hyleg, the ☽ by her evil directions to them assists in causing death by drowning, and espec. when in ♋, ♏, or ♓ by dir., and the ☽ holds the dominion of death; the ☉ or ☽ affl. in the 1st Dec. of ♉, ♌, ♏, or ♒, the 2nd Dec. of ♍, or when the malefics afflict the ☉ or ☽ from these decanates, dispose to drowning; the ☽ in a watery sign at B., afflicted by ♄, and afflicting the hyleg by dir., or taking part in a fatal train of directions; the ☽ lady of the 8th H. at B., and to the evil asp. the

Asc. by dir., and the ☽ in a water sign at B.; the ☽ ☌ or ill-asp. ♅ at B., and by dir., dangerous to go near water; the ☽ in a water sign, and to the ☌, P., □ or ☍ ♂ by dir., and ♂ in a water sign at B.; the ☽ with Cor. Hydra, and ☌ or ill-asp. ♄ or ♂, and ♂ in an angle; the ☽ with Antares or ♄; the ☽ affl. in the 8th H.; caused by the □ and ☍ aspects of the ☽; the ☽ weak and afflicted at B., and ☌ the Asc. by dir.; the ☽ with ♄ and Orion's Belt, or with Antares or Caput Hercules; caused by fixed stars of the nature of the ☽; death by is denoted by the ☽; ♆ the afflicting planet; ♆ affl. in ♏, accidental drowning, or suicide by, and especially if in the 8th H.; ♆ affl. in the 8th H. at B., or afflicting the hyleg therefrom; ♆ in the 8th H. in a water sign, afflicting the hyleg at B., and by dir.; ♆ ☌ the hyleg at B., and with ♆ afflicted in a water sign; ♅ or ♄ in ♋, ♍, ♏, or ♓, and affl. the ☽; ♅ afflicting the hyleg, and concurring with other testimonies for drowning; ♄ in a watery sign and affl. the Asc. or hyleg by dir.; ♄ ♍ and affl. the ☽ hyleg; ♄ in a watery sign, or in ♍, ori. of, and □ or ☍ the ☉ at B., or occi. and □ or ☍ the ☽ at B., and if near Argo, by shipwreck; ♄ ☌ the Asc. by dir., danger of if the sign be watery, or a violent fixed star near the place; ♄ in ♋, ♍, ♏, or ♓, and configurated with the ☽; ♄ in a water sign and ☌ or ill-asp. the Asc. by dir., and espec. if the Asc. be hyleg; ♄ in the Asc. when starting on a voyage, or a fiery sign on the Asc., which usually puts a watery sign on cusp of the 8th H.; ♄ affl. in the 5th H., and ♄ also affl. the hyleg; ♄ ☌ or ill-asp. the ☉ in fixed signs; ♄ espec. tends to, and to suffocation in any form; ♂ affl. in water signs, and ☌ or evil asp. the Asc. by dir.; ♂ in the 9th H. in a water sign, and affl. the ☉ or ☽ at B., and by dir.; ♂ affl. in the 9th H. on a voyage, if in a water sign; Asc. to the ☌ or evil asp. ♂ by dir., and ♂ in a water sign; Asc. to the □ or ☍ the ☽ by dir.; the 25° ♌ on the Asc.; the 1st Dec. ♓ on the Asc., ruled by ♄; a water sign ascending, with ♆ there, and ♆ affl. the hyleg; Asc. to the ☌ or ill-asp. ♄ by dir., and both ♄ and the Asc. in water signs; lord of the 8th in 9th H.; water signs dispose to; planets in ♋, ♏, or ♓, and affl. the ☽; Cor. Hydra joined to ♂, or in evil asp. the ☉ or ☽; the fixed star Hydra's Heart joined to ♂ at B.; Scheat Pegasi produces danger from drowning; malefics in the 9th H. in fire signs, and affl. the ☉ or ☽ on voyages; fixed signs, and many afflictions from them, show danger of drowning; malefics in the 3rd or 9th H. in water signs, and affl. the ☉ or ☽, danger of drowning during travel, or on a journey; planets in ♋, ♏, or ♓ during travel, and afflicting the Sigs. of travel, danger of drowning while traveling. Cases—Of Death by Drowning—See "Death by Drowning", No. 100, No. 402; "Conder", No. 315; "A Luckless Youth", No. 390; "Medici", No. 468; "Died in Harness", No. 802, all in 1001 N.N. (For further influences along this line see Abroad, Bathing, Journeys, Liquids, Maritime, Moon, Navigation, Neptune, Scalds, Sea, Ships,

Shipwreck, Suffocation, Strangulation, Travel, Voyages; "Death", "Perils", "Tidal Waves", under Water).

**DROWSINESS**—Sleepiness—Stupor— (See "Drowsiness" under Sleep).

**DRUGGISTS**—Make Good Druggists— Good Influences For—(See Chemists).

**DRUGS**—Medicines—Drugs as Remedies—The Harmful Effects of Drugs, etc.—

**Brain**—The Brain Affected by Drugs and Opiates—(See "Drugs" under Brain).

**Drug Habit**—Doping—Drug Taking— (See Heart, Narcotics, Poisons).

**Remedies**—Drugs as Remedies—The Therapeutic Properties of Drugs—The Action of Drugs—The Various Classes of Drugs, Herbs, Metals, Minerals, Plants, etc.—See Acids, Alexipharmic, Alkaline, Alterative, Anaesthetics, Analeptics, Analgesics, Anaphrodisiac, Anodyne Anthelmintic, Anticachectic, Antidotes, Antinephritics, Antiperiodic, Antipathy, Antiphlogistic, Antipyretic, Antispasmodic, Aphrodisiac, Astringents, Attenuants, Balsamic, Bitter, Cardiac, Cathartic, Caustic, Cephalic, Cholagogue, Collyria, Cooling, Cosmetics, Demulcent, Depressants, Diaphoretics, Emetic, Emollient, Escharotic, Febrifuge, Healers, Herbs, Hypnotic Drugs (see Narcotics); Liniments, Lotions, Medicines, Metals, Minerals, Narcotics, Nervine (see Nerves); Ointments, Opiates, Opposites, Planets and Drugs (see "Drugs", "Typical Drugs", under each of the Planets); Plants, Polarity, Poisons, Refrigerants, Remedies, Resolvent, Roots, Rubefacient, Sedatives, Seeds, Soothing, Soporifics, Stimulants, Styptics, Sudorifics, Therapeutics, Tonics, Treatment, Vesicants, etc. Also look for the various Drugs, Medicines, Metals, Minerals, Plants, and Remedies, in the alphabetical arrangement.

**DRUNKENNESS**—Inebriation—Intoxication, etc.—Many of the influences given and listed under "Drink" will also apply here. The influences of the water signs, and afflictions in them, tend to drink, and afflictions in the ♓ sign, and the ♓ sign upon the Asc. at B., to drunkenness, inebriety, and intoxication. The ☽ rules drunkards.

**Children May Become Drunkards**—♄ affl. in the 5th H. in a parent's map, and espec. if ♄ be in a watery sign.

**Dipsomania**—An Uncontrollable Desire for Drink—(See Dipsomania).

**Drink**—(See Drink).

**Drunkenness**—Tendency to Drunkenness—The ☉ or ☽ affl. in ♓; the ☉ and ♀ affl. in a watery sign, and the ☉ to the ill-asps. ♀ by dir.; the Prog. ☉ □ or ☍ the ☽, and espec. if either be in watery signs; the ☉ and ♂ in water signs at B., or by dir., and espec. if the ☉ or ☽ are affl. by ♄ or ♂ at B.; the ☉ in ♏, or ♏ on the Asc., and afflicted; the ☽ ill-dig. at B.; the ☽ affl. in ♓; ♃ in ♓, □ or ☍ ♂; ♃ affl. in 1st H. in ♓; ♂ ☌ the ☽ in ♓; ♂ □ or ☍ the ☽, and espec. if ♂, the ☽, or Asc. are in ♓; ♂ Sig. in ♋ or ♓; ♂ in ♓, □ or ☍ ♃; ♂ in ♉, ♋, or ♎, and affl. by the

□ or ☍ of planets; ♂ affl. in the 12th H. in ♋ or ♓; ♂ evilly aspected and badly placed in the map; ♂ evilly posited and afflicting ♀; ♂ to the ☌ or ill-asp. ♀ by dir.; ♂ in the sign or house of the ☽, and afflicted; in Hor'y Questions ♂ Sig. of the person; ♂ in the Asc. in water signs, and afflicted; ♀ ill-dig. at B.; ♀ affl. in ♓; ♀ Sig. ☌ ♂; ☿ affl. in ♋ or ♓; a ♋ and ♓ disease, and with these signs affl. on the Asc. at B.; the 3° ♎ on the Asc. (For further influences along this line see the various paragraphs in this section. Also see the various paragraphs and references in the Article on Drink).

**Father**—The Father May Become a Drunkard—Ruler of the 10th or 4th H. □ or ☍ ♀ or ♂, and espec. in ♓ or water signs, or ♀ in ♉, the sign ruling the palate, throat, appetite, etc. (See "Drink" under Parents).

**Habitual Drunkards**—A Sot or Toper—The ☉ or ☽ affl. in ♓; ♂ Sig. in ♋ or ♓; ♓ on the Asc., and afflicted. (See Sottishness, Taverns).

**Husband a Drunkard**—Cases—See "Marriage", No. 295, and No. 833, in 1001 N.N. (See "Drink" under Husband).

**Incurable Drunkard**—♆ in the 1st H. in ♓, and afflicted.

**Inveterate Drunkard**—♂ □ or ☍ ☽, and espec. if ♂, the ☽, or Asc. are in ♓.

**Is Yet Drunk**—Frequently Shows the Person Is Yet Drunk—The ☽ in ♓, and affl. by the ☉ or ♂ when taken ill (Hor'y).

**Marriage Partner**—A Drunkard—May Become a Drunkard—♂ in ♋, ♏, or ♓ in the 7th H., and afflicted. (See "Drink" under Husband, Wife).

**DRY**—Dryness—Dried—Hot and Dry—Dry Body—Dry Diseases, etc.—Dryness is noxious and destructive, and tends to diseases accompanied by friction, and by irritation of both mind and body. Dryness is associated with the earthy signs ♉, ♍, and ♑, and when acting alone is considered passive and feminine. When associated with heat, as acting thru the fiery signs, ♈, ♌, and ♐, the combination of hot and dry becomes more positive. The fiery and earthy signs contribute the heat and dryness, while the airy and watery signs are cold and moist. Dryness and Moisture are considered passive qualities. (See Moisture). The Nocturnal Signs ♉, ♋, ♍, ♏, ♑, and ♓, excel in dryness and moisture. Excess of dryness is caused by ♂. Moderate dryness is produced by the ☉, ♄, and ♂. The ☉ produces dryness due to his heat; ♂ by his hot and fiery nature; ♄ by being remote from the ☉. When masculine, ☿ produces dryness, and moisture when femininely constituted, and as ☿ is variable, produces both dryness and moisture, according to his distance from the Earth and ☽. The ☉, ♅, ♄, ♂, and ☿ tend to dryness of the body and to dry diseases. ♅ exerts a dry influence. ♅ and ♄ are cold and dry, and ☿ so when configurated with them. ♄ causes dryness when occi., and ♂ causes dryness only when occi., and when ori. causes heat and dryness. Dry and Cold are malevolent influences and tend to decay. (See Decay). The elementary qualities Dry and Hot are positive, while Dry and Cold are negative. The Dry and Cold of the left side of the body are more feeble than the Hot and Dry of the right side. (See Left, Right). The elementary qualities Dry and Moist alternate, so that the 12 divisions of the body, as ruled by the 12 Signs, are once dry and once moist, positive and negative in rotation. The following subjects have to do with Dryness, which see in the alphabetical arrangement when not considered here.

**Air**—A Dry Air—Unusual Dryness of the Air—Eclipses of the ☽ in the 1st Dec. ♈, or in 2nd and 3rd Dec. ♏; ♂ in an angle at the Equinoxes or Solstices, and espec. in ♈, ♋, ♌, and with N. Lat.; ♂ in ♌ at the Winter Solstice, a dry Winter; Comets appearing in the Eastern Quarters of the heavens. (See "Dry Air" under Air; Drought, Heat).

**All Diseases**—Proceeding from Dryness and Heat—♈ diseases. (See Fever; "Dry and Hot Diseases" under Heat; Parched).

**Bellyache**—Dry Bellyache—(See Belly).

**Body**—Dry Body—Dry Constitution—Dry Bodily Temperament—The ☉, ☽, Asc., and many planets in earthy signs at B.; the ☽ from the Full to the 3rd Quarter makes the constitution more dry; the ☽ in ♌ when taken ill, and affl. by the ☉ or ♂, the body is dry and parched (Hor'y); ♂ ori. or occi.; ♂ descending; ♂ or ☿ ruler of the Asc., and occi.; ♀ occi. as regards the ☉ except when ☿ is in ♊; ♈ gives excess of heat and dryness in the body, produces a lean and dry body, and espec. when on the Asc.; born under ♈ or ♑; ♑ on the Asc., or strong at B.; ♈ on the Asc. at B. gives a dry, spare, strong, and moderate sized body. (See "Hot and Dry", "Increased Dryness", in this section).

**Cold and Dry Body**—Dry and Cold Constitution—Given by the earthy signs, which are cold and dry, and earthy signs on the Asc. at B.; ♄ occi.; ♄ in the Asc. at B., and in power; a cold and dry body ruled by ♄ or ☿ tend to make the nature unprolific, as cold and dry combinations are negative; the Quadrant from the Autumnal Equi. to the Winter Solstice tends to produce a cold and dry body. (See Barren; "Cranian Diathesis" under Cranium; Nervous Temperament, Noxious).

**Cold and Dry Diseases**—These are diseases of ♅ and ♄, and also of ☿ when ☿ is configurated with them; diseases of the earthy signs, and espec. of ♑. (See Diseases under Mercury, Saturn, Uranus).

**Cold and Dry Signs**—The earthy signs, ♉, ♍, and ♑.

**Cough**—Bilious Dry Cough—(See Cough).

**Crusts**—Dry Crusts—Dried Exudate—(See Crusts).

**Death**—(See "Dry Habit" in this section).

**Destruction**—From Dryness—(See "Fountains" in this section).

**Diseases Concomicant with Dryness**—Diseases Which Arise from Superabundant or Disproportionate Dryness—In general, ♂ sole ruler at an eclipse of the ☉; caused by ☿ when the dominion of death is vested in this planet. (See "Dry Diseases", "Dry and Hot Diseases", in this section; "Dry and Hot Diseases", "Excessive Heat", under Heat).

**Disproportionate Dryness**—Diseases Arising From—(See "Diseases Concomitant" in this section; Drought, Famine).

**Drought**—(See Drought, Famine, Heat, etc. Also see "Fountains" in this section).

**Dry Body**—(See "Body" in this section).

**Dry Diseases**—♄ and ♈ diseases. (See "Diseases Concomitant", "Dry and Hot Diseases", in this section).

**Dry Habit**—☿ produces death from diseases which proceed from a dry habit. (See Habit).

**Dry and Hot Body**—(See "Hot and Dry Body" in this section).

**Dry and Hot Diseases**—(See "Dry and Hot Diseases" under Heat; Fevers, Parched).

**Emaciated and Dry**—The Body Dry and Emaciated—(See Emaciation).

**Excess of Dryness**—In the Body—(See "Body", "Increased", "Superabundance", in this section).

**Eyelids**—Dryness of—(See Eyelids).

**Faeces**—Dryness of—(See Constipation; "Hardening" under Faeces).

**Fauces**—Dry Fauces—(See Fauces).

**Fluids**—Drying Up of—♄ diseases and afflictions. (See Fluids, Saturn, Suppressions).

**Fountains Dry Up**—The Drying Up of Fountains, Rivers, Springs, etc.—♂ in power, and lord of the year at Equinoxes or Solstices, tends to an atmosphere parched by hot, dry, pestilential, blasting winds, accompanied by drought, lightnings, fires emitted from the sky, hurricanes, attended with shipwrecks, the failing of rivers, and the drying up of springs. (See Drought, Famine, Fountains, Weather, etc.).

**Habit**—Dry Habit—(See "Dry Habit" in this section).

**Hair**—(See "Dry" under Hair).

**Head**—Hot and Dry Head—(See "Feverish", "Hot Diseases In", "Hot and Dry", under Head).

**Heat and Dryness**—All Diseases Proceeding From—The ☉ and ♂ are hot and dry, and their diseases tend to be hot and dry; the ☉ and ♂ in asp. to each other, as ☉ ✶ or △ ♂; the ☽ during her First Quarter is hot and dry, and during this time her afflictions tend to increased heat and dryness in the body; ♂ ruler of the Asc., and ori.; ♈ diseases; fiery signs on the Asc. at B., and espec. ♈; many planets in fiery and earthy signs. (See "Hot and Dry Diseases" in this section).

**Hot and Dry Air**—(See "Hot and Dry" under Air; "Air" in this section).

**Hot and Dry Body**—Hot and Dry Bodily Temperament—Hot and Dry Constitution—(See "Choleric Temperament" under Choleric; "Hot and Dry Body" under Heat. Also see "Body", "Heat and Dryness", in this section).

**Hot and Dry Diseases**—(See Fevers; "Dry and Hot", "Fevers", "Hot Diseases", under Heat; Parched; "Heat and Dryness" in this section).

**Hot and Dry Plants**—The ☉ and ♂ Groups. (See these Groups under Herbs).

**Humours**—Dry Humours—Humours of the Body Generally More Dry—♂ occi. at B. (See Humours).

**Increased Dryness**—Of the Body—Dryness of the Body Augmented—The malefics ♄ and ♂ in angles, and ♂ in familiarity with ☿, and the malefics occi. of the ☉, and ori. of the ☽; ☿ or ♂ holding dominion at B., and in familiarity with each other. (See Augmented).

**Irritations and Dryness**—(See Irritations).

**Lean and Dry Body**—♈ gives, and ♈ on Asc. (See Lean; "Body" in this section).

**Liver**—Dry and Cold Liver—(See "Cold and Dry" under Liver).

**Melancholy**—Dry and Melancholy Distempers—(See "Dry and Melancholic" under Melancholy).

**Mischief**—From Dryness—(See "Fountains", and the various paragraphs in this section).

**Parched and Dry Body**—Parched, Dry, and Hot Diseases—(See "Body", "Hot and Dry Body", "Hot and Dry Diseases", in this section; "High Fever" under Fever; "Dry and Hot Diseases" under Heat; Parched).

**Plants**—Dry and Hot Group of Plants—(See "Hot and Dry Plants" in this section).

**Rivers**—The Drying Up of Rivers, Springs and Fountains—(See "Fountains" in this section).

**Scales**—Dry Scale Formations—(See Psoriasis, Scales; "Dry Skin" under Skin).

**Signs**—The Dry Signs—The Earthy Signs, ♉, ♍, ♑, are cold and dry. The fiery signs ♈, ♌, ♐, are hot and dry.

**Skin**—Dry Skin—(See "Dry Skin" under Skin).

**Sloughing**—Dry Sloughing—(See Sloughing).

**Spare and Dry Body**—(See "Body", "Lean", in this section).

**Strong and Dry Body**—♈ gives. (See "Body" in this section).

**Superabundance of Dryness**—Disease and Suffering From—Excess of Dryness In the Body—Dry and Hot Weather—(See "Body"; "Diseases Concomitant", "Excess", "Fountains", "Increased", and the various paragraphs in this section; Drought, Famine; "Extreme Heat" under Heat).

**Temperament**—Dry Bodily Temperament—(See "Body", "Hot and Dry Body", in this section; Temperament).

**Tetter**—Dry Tetter—(See Tetter).

**Throat**—Dry and Feverish Throat—(See "Dry" under Throat).

**Tissues**—Drying Up of—♄ diseases and afflictions. (See Atrophy, Tissues).

**Winter**—A Dry Winter—(See Winter).

**Withering; Wrinkles.**

**DUAL-MINDED**—Duplicity—The Bicorporeal Signs strong at B., or many planets in them, and espec. in ♊, the sign of The Twins; ♄ and ♂ afflicting ☿; ♀ Sig. in ♋; the ☽ □ or ☍ ☿. (See Deceitful, Dishonest, Double-Bodied, Gemini).

**Dual Personality**—(See Memory).

**Dual-Sexed**—(See Hermaphrodite).

**DUCTLESS GLANDS**—Organs Without Ducts—Endocrine Glands—These Glands are seven in number, and are ruled by the ♏ sign and ♂, taken as a whole. The Ductless Glands are the Pituitary Body, ruled by ♅; the Pineal Gland, ruled by ♆; the Thyroid Gland, ruled by ☿; the Thymus Gland, ruled by ♀; the Spleen, ruled by the ☉; the two Adrenals, ruled by ♃. (See these subjects in the alphabetical arrangement). The substance produced by these Glands is called Endocrine. The ☉ and ☽ acting thru the ♏ sign, and thru the Intestinal and Lumbar branches of the Solar Plexus, thru the Renal, Supra-Renal, Hepatic, Spermatic and Hemorrhoidal Plexuses, affect the Medulla, the Brain, the Pituitary Gland, the Basal Ganglia, the Ductless Glands, the Bladder, Genito-Urinary System, Uterus, Rectum, Anus, Large Intestines, and give way to the Hepatic Diathesis. (See "Basal Ganglia" under Ganglion; "Pathological Action" under Mars; "Petrification" under Stone). The effects of the Ductless Glands today are said to be mostly mental and spiritual. The Occult significance of these Glands is written up in the Chapter on Ductless Glands in the book, "Message of the Stars" by the Heindels.

**Disorders Of**—General Derangement of the Ductless Glands—♆ diseases and afflictions; ♆ afflicted at B.; ♆ □ or ☍ ♅. Cases of Disorders of—See Figures 17A, 17B, 17C, 17D, in the book "Astro-Diagnosis" by the Heindels. (See "Sugar" under Food).

**DUCTS**—A Tube Conveying a Liquid—

**Bile Ducts**—Gall Ducts—(See "Ducts" under Bile).

**Nasal Duct**—The Tear Duct—(See Tears).

**Sebaceous Ducts**—(See Sebaceous).

**Thoracic Duct**—(See Thorax). For other Ducts in various parts of the body, look in the alphabetical arrangement for the subject you have in mind.

**DUELS**—Affairs of Honour—Contests—Quarrels—Chartering—

**Death in Duels**—The 7th H. rules and concerns duels, and malefics in this house, and affl. the ☉, ☽, Asc., or hyleg make it dangerous to engage in them; the ☉ Sig. ☌ ♂, death in, or terribly wounded; ♂ just setting in □ or ☍ the ☉ or ☽, and ♃ bearing testimony to ♂; ♂ to the ☌ ☋; ♂ Sig. and affl. the ☽, or the ☽ Sig. ☌ ♂, given to duels, and with danger of death thru them; lord of the Asc. in the 8th H. at the time; the 26° ♊, or the 20° ♏ on the Asc. at B. (See "Death" under Cuts; Gunshot, Quarrels, Sword. Also see Chartering, Contests, Cuts; "Causes His Own Death" under Death; Disputes, Enemies, Feuds, Fighting, Folly, Instruments, Quarrels, Rashness, Stabs, Wounds, etc.).

**Injury in Duels**—The ☉ Sig. □ or ☍ ♂; ♂ in fiery signs, and ☌ or ill-asp. the Asc. by dir.; ♂ Sig. □ or ☍ the ☉; to engage in a duel when the ☽, ♄, and ♂ are joined together, or in evil aspect, tends to dangerous injury, and great effusion of blood; the 26° ♊ on the Asc.

**DULL**—Dullness—Dulling—Dull Mind—Lack of Animation—Hebetude—Apathy—Vapid, etc.—

**Aches**—Dull and Heavy Aches or Pains—(See "Heavy" under Aches).

**Appearance**—Dull Appearance—♓ on the Asc. at B.; the ☽ Sig. of the party in Hor'y Questions. (See Appearance).

**Apprehension Dull**—(See "Mind", "Understanding", in this section).

**Complexion Dull**—(See "Dull" under Complexion).

**Comprehension Dull**—(See "Mind" in this section; "Weak" under Understanding).

**Constitution**—The Constitution Dull and Effeminate—(See "Dull" under Constitution; Effeminate).

**Disposition Dull**—(See "Mind" in this section; Apathy, Lassitude, Lethargy).

**Effeminate and Dull**—(See Effeminate; "Dull" under Constitution).

**Eyes Dull**—Heavy, Languid and Sleepy Eyes—(See "Dullness" under Eyes; "Drowsiness" under Sleep).

**Genius**—The Genius is Dull—(See Genius).

**Hebetude**—Dulling of the Senses and the Intellect—(See "Mind" in this section; "Dulling" under Senses).

**Husband**—The Husband is Dull and Timid—(See "Dull" under Husband).

**Intellect Dull**—(See "Mind" in this section; Intellect; "Smoky Degrees" under Smoky).

**Lassitude**—(See Lassitude).

**Lethargy**—(See Lethargy).

**Mind**—Dull Mind—Dull Disposition—Hebetude—Dull Intellect—Comprehension Dull—Heavy Mind—Dull Capacity, etc.—Tropical and hot climates produce; no asp. to the ☉ or ♂ at B.; the ☽ and ☿ in no asp. with each other or with the Asc.; the ☽ Sig. in ♓; the ☽ Sig. of the person, and the ☽ affl., and ill-dig. at B.; the ☽ sepr. from ☿ and apply to the ☉; the Prog. ☽ to the ☌ or ill-asp. ♆ if ♆ be affl. at B.; the ☽ Sig. in ♑; the ☽ to the ill-asps. ☿ by dir.; ♄ in ♈, apathy and want of passion or feeling; ♄ ☌ ☿, heavy and morose; ♄ affl. ☿ at B.; ♄ in ♋; ♄ ☌ the Asc. by dir.; ♃ affl. and ill-dig. at B.; ♃ Sig. in ♑; ♂ Sig. in water signs, and espec. in ♓; no asp. between ♂

and ☿; no asp. between ♂ and the ☉ at B.; ♀ Sig. in ♋, dull and idle disposition; ♀ in ♏, inert; ♀ affl. in ♈; ♀ ruler of the mind and badly aspected and placed; ☿ ☌ the ☉, and combust; ☿ rising in ♋ or ♓; ☿ ☌ or ill-asp ♄; the cross asps. of ♂ or the ☽ to ☿ beget stupidity; the periodic directions of ♄′ to ☿; ☿ Sig. ☌ ♄; ☿ affl. by ♄ at B., a dull wit; ☿ to the ☌ the ☉ by dir.; ☿ in ♉, an inert disposition; the ♋ influence tends to make dull, and timid as the Crab; ♓ on the Asc., the physical condition often tends to clog the mental action; the Asc. to the ☌ or ill-asps. ♄ by dir. (See Action, Apathy, Backwardness; "Brain Fag" under Brain; Chaotic, Clogging, Diminished, Energy, Faculties, Fatigue, Feelings, Heaviness, Hyperaesthesia, Idle, Inactive, Indifferent, Inertia, Intellect, Labour, Languid, Lassitude, Lethargy, Listless, Melancholy, Morose, Motion, Movement, Perception, Rouse, Senses, Sensibility, Slow, Sluggish, Smoky, Stupid, Study, Timidity, Understanding, Weariness; "Weak Mind" under Mind).

**Pains**—Dull Pains and Aches—(See "Heavy" under Aches; "Dull Pains" under Head; Headaches, Neuralgia).

**Senses** — The Senses Dulled—Hebetude—(See "Mind" in this section; Senses).

**Timid and Dull**—♋ influence. (See Timid).

**Understanding Dulled**—(See "Mind" in this section; Judgment, Understanding).

**Unfeeling and Dull**—♉ influence.

**Wit—A Dull Wit**—☿ affl. by ♄ at B.

**DUMB**—Dumbness—Mute—Without the Power of Speech—Caused by afflictions in the Dumb, or Mute Signs, ♋, ♏, or ♓ at B., or these signs greatly afflicted at conception, or during gestation. These signs are also called Reptilian Signs, as they rule creatures which make no audible sound. The Mute Signs tend to cause impediments of speech, and espec. when ☿ is also afflicted at the same time. Other Causes of Dumbness are,—A ☿ disease, as ☿ rules the speech; caused by the □ and ☍ asps. of ☿; ☿ in a mute, or dumb sign, and affl. by ♄; afflictions to ☿ at B.; ☿ in ♉ in the 12th H., as ♉ rules the vocal organs and ears; ☿ in ♉ in the 12th H. and ☌ ♆, □ ♃, which are the aspects of a case of record; if at conception the ☉ or ☽ be in the 6th or 12th H., and ☿ with one of them in the 12th H., the child will be dumb, altho of good abilities; a mute sign on the Asc., and ☿ be afflicted, or if ☿ be afflicted by a malefic posited in a dumb sign, the native will be dumb, or have a great impediment in his speech; afflictions in the ♋ sign, a mute sign, and slow of voice; afflictions in the mute signs, as these signs are typical of creatures, animals, or insects which make no audible sound. (See Inarticulate; "Impediment", and the various paragraphs under Speech; Voice).

**Deaf and Dumb**—(See this subject under Hearing).

**Deaf, Dumb and Blind**—(See Hearing, Mutes).

**Deaf, Dumb and Idiot**—(See Idiots, Hearing). For further study see Foetus, Mercury, Prenatal Epoch, Speech, Twelfth House).

**DUN COMPLEXION** — (See "Dull", "Swarthy", under Complexion; "Smoky Degrees" under Smoky).

**DUODENUM**—The First Part of the Small Intestines—Ruled by the ♍ sign. (See "Small Intestines" under Bowels; "Organs of Digestion" under Digestion; Pylorus).

**Inflammation**—Of the Duodenum—Duodenitis—♂ affl. in ♍; Subs at SP (8D), and at Spl.P (9D). (See "Inflammation" under Bowels).

**Ulcer**—Of the Duodenum—♂ affl. in ♍ or ♓; Subs at SP (8D), and at Spl.P. (9D). (See Ulcers).

**DURA MATER**—The Outer Membrane of the Brain and Spinal Cord—Ruled by ♅, and is much affected when ♅ is in ♈. (See Brain, Meninges, Spine).

**DURATION**—

**Duration of Disease**—The Length of the Disease—This may be judged by the nature of the Signs in which the afflicting planets are found, and which cause the illness. The afflictions in cardinal signs show the disease to be very severe, but soon over. Afflictions in fixed signs show long, chronic, stubborn, tedious diseases, and with slow recovery. In common signs, difficult to cure, or incurable, due to the passive and indifferent state of the patient's mind, and amenability to adverse suggestions. For the influences along this line see the following subjects in the alphabetical arrangement—Acute, Alterations, Amelioration, Cardinal, Changes, Chronic, Convalescence, Constancy, Course, Crises, Curable, Death, Decrease; "Better" under Disease; End, External, Fatal, Fever; "Fixed Signs" under Fixed; Force, Increase, Incurable, Invalids, Lingering, Long, Moderation, Modification; "Moon" under Motion; "Mutable Signs" under Mutable; Prolonged, Quick, Recovery, Recuperation, Relapses, Remission, Remote, Resolution, Return, Short, Slow, Tedious, Termination, Violent, Worse, etc.

**Duration of Fever**—(See "Duration" under Fever).

**Duration of Life** — (See "Duration" under Life. Also see the various paragraphs under Death).

**DUSKY COMPLEXION**—(See "Dusky" under Complexion).

**DUST**—Pneumoconiosis—A Disease of the Lung from Inhalation of Dust—(See "Pneumoconiosis" under Lungs).

**DUTY**—

**Faithful to Duty**—(See Honest, Reliable, Trustworthy).

**Indifferent to Duty**—(See Careless, Dull).

**DWARF**—Dwarfed—Diminutive Body—Midgets—Arrested Physical or Mental Growth—Due to afflictions at B., or during the prenatal period, to ☿, the ruler of the Thyroid Gland. Degeneration of this Gland tends to Cretinism, and to stop and arrest the growth of the mind and body. Also caused by disturbances of the Pituitary Body, which is ruled by ♅ and the ♉ Sign, and by lack of the Pituitary secretion. An earthy sign on the Asc., and two or three planets in the Asc., tend to make Dwarfs and people under the usual stature, and espec. if ♄ is also in the Asc. At the birth of Dwarfs, the ♉, ♏, or ♑ Signs are usually rising, and also there is usually an affliction between ♄ and ♂, or between ♅ and ♂. The ☌ of the malefic planets ♅, ♄, and ♂, or their ☍ aspects, in fixed signs, tend to; the ☉ and ☽ in the 6th or 12th H., and affl. by ♅, ♄, or ♂; the malefics ♅, ♄, or ♂ in, or afflicting, the 5th, 6th, or 12th H., the cusps of these houses, or the cusp of the Asc., or if they be in ♍; ♄ □ ♆; ♃ in ♋, principally in the 6th H., and below the horizon, and with ♓ on the Asc., and the ☽ in ♓; many planets in ♍ in the 6th or 12th H.; ♉, ♏, or ♑ on the Asc.; ♑ on the Asc., and containing ♄, ♀, and ☿ in ☌; the lord of the Asc., and the ☽ in the last degree of a sign, and without Latitude.

**Cases of Dwarfs**—Birth Data, etc.—See "Dwarf", No. 064, 622, 669, and also "Wilder", The Dwarf Humorist, No. 916, all in 1001 N.N. Also see the Cases on page 49, Chap. 8, in Daath's Medical Astrology, cases of a Dwarf Hunchback, and an Adult Dwarf with the Mind of a Child. There is also the case of the Dwarf, Darius Alden, born Aug. 14, 1842, and died Sept. 22, 1926, height 3 feet, 6 inches. No further birth data available on this case. (For further influences along this line see Arrested, Contracted, Cretinism, Decreased, Deformities, Diminished, Distortions, Growth, Idiocy, Imbecility; "Body" under Large; Malformations, Monstrosities, Myxoedema, Pituitary Body, Prenatal Epoch; "Short Body" under Short; "Small Body" under Small; "Hunchback" under Spine; Thyroid, Undersized, Undeveloped, etc).

**DYES**—(See Chemists; "Vocation" under Colors).

**DYING PERSONS**—Persons About to Die—The ruling places at a Solar Eclipse situated in the West tend to affect persons about to die, for good or ill, according to the signs, houses, and aspects, and espec. people born under the signs taking part in the influence. (See Death, Eighth House).

**DYNAMIC**—Sthenic—Active—Strong—Mars is called the planet of Dynamic Energy, and of Action. The ☉ is also dynamic. The ☉ and ♂ when both strong in the map of birth tend to give great vitality, force, and energy. Mars weak at B., and in no asp. to the ☉, tends to lower the vitality and energy, and to give less of the dynamic force of this planet, and tending to lassitude. Dynamic power is principally given by the Solar Forces being reflected upon us by the ♂ influence, and dynamic energy is the most salient characteristic of ♂. (See Action, Active, Endurance, Energy, Force, Lassitude, Mars, Motion, Movement, Sthenic, Strength, Vitality, etc.).

**DYSENTERY**—Inflammation and Ulceration of the Intestinal Mucous Membrane, and with Bloody Evacuations—Bloody Flux—A ♍ disease; ♍ on the Asc.; ♍ on the 6th H.; the ☉, ☽, or ♂ affl. in ♍, and espec. when in the 6th H.; the ☉ to the ill-asps. ♂ by dir.; the ☽ affl. in ♍, or affl. the hyleg therefrom, and espec. with females; the ☽ in ♋, and affl. by the ☉ or ♂; the ☽ in an earthy sign, and to the ☌ or ill-asp. ♂ by dir., and the ☽ hyleg; ♄ in an angle, occi. of the ☉, and ori. of the ☽; ♂ ☌ the ☉ at B., and espec. in the 6th H.; ♂ in ♑ in the 6th H., or affl. the ☽ or Asc.; ♂ in ♍ in the 6th H.; caused by ♀ when the dominion of death is vested in her, and espec. ♀ in ♍ in the 6th H., and affl. the hyleg; Subs at CP, KP (11D), and PP (2, 3, 4L); Subs at PP tend to Chronic Dysentery. (See "Inflammation" under Bowels; Diarrhoea; "Bloody Flux" under Flux).

**DYSIDROSIS**—Dyshidrosis—Pompholyx—A rare disease, with Bullas and impaired perspiration of the Hands and Feet—Caused by ♂; ♂ affl. in ♍ or ♓. (See Blisters, Hyperidrosis; "Anidrosis" under Sweat).

**DYSMENORRHOEA**—Painful Menstruation—(See "Painful" under Menses).

**DYSPEPSIA**—Impaired or Imperfect Digestion—Indigestion—Afflictions in ♋ tend to Dyspepsia of all kinds; a ♋ disease; a ♍ disease, and afflictions in ♍; ♍ on the Asc.; ♋ or ♍ on the Asc., and afflicted; the ☉, ☽, ♄, ♃, or ♂ affl. in ♋; the ☉ affl. in ♍; the ☽ afflicted; the ☽ and ♀ in ♋, and affl. by ♄; the ☽ affl. in ♋, or afflicting the hyleg therefrom; ♄ in ♋ or ♑; ♄ in ♋ and affl. the ☽, tends to chronic dyspepsia; ♂ in ♋ on cusp of 4th H.; ♂ in ♋ or ♑; ☿ affl. in the 6th H., arising from excessive mental or nervous action; the Asc. to the place of ☋ by dir.: Subs at SP. (See Digestion, Hydrochloric, Indigestion, Stomach). Cases of Dyspepsia—See "Stone in Kidney", and "Dyspepsia", pages 89 and 92, in Daath's Medical Astrology.

**Chronic Dyspepsia**—♄ in ♋, and afflicting the ☽.

**Nervous Dyspepsia**—♅ or ☿ affl. in the 6th H., and espec. when in ♋ or ♍; Subs at SP (7D).

**DYSPHAGIA**—Inability to Swallow—(See Deglutition).

**DYSPHASIA**—Disconnected Speech—(See "Dysphasia" under Speech).

**DYSPHONIA**—Difficulty in Phonation—(See "Dysphonia" under Larynx; "Aphonia" under Voice).

**DYSPNOEA**—Difficult or Laboured Breathing—Paroxysms in Breathing—Caused by afflictions in ♊; Subs at LCP (6C), AP (1D), LHP (3D), and Lu.P. Subs at Lu.P (3D) tend to painful and rapid Dyspnoea. (See Angina, Asthma; "Laboured Breathing" under Breathing; Croup, Diaphragm; "Beriberi" under Dropsy; Gas, Heart, Stomach, etc.).

**DYSTROPHIA**—Imperfect or Faulty Nourishment—Defective Nutrition—(See Nutrition).

**DYSURIA**—Difficult or Painful Micturition—(See "Strangury" under Urine).

# E

**EAGLE FEATURES**—(See "Eagle" under Features).

**EARLY**—

**Early Death**—Short Life—The Life Shortened—The ☉ affl. in the 8th H.; the ☉ and ☽ in common signs, and affl. by malefics, and espec. when in ♓; the ☉, ☽, and ☿ conjoined in a sign of low vitality, and affl. by malefics; the ☽ apply. to the ☌ the ☉; the ☽ sepr. from ♄ and apply. to ♂ if the ☽ be hyleg; ♅ in the 8th H. at B., and death is apt to occur at the subsequent evil asps. of the ☉ to ♅, and cause early death if within orb of the asp. at B.; ♂ affl. in ♏, from sex excesses and loss of vitality; lord of the 10th H. in the 5th, thru feasting and dissipation; the ☌ of the rulers of the 1st and 6th H., or of the 1st and 8th, unless free from affliction; a strong 6th H., but with the hyleg badly afflicted; many planets near cusps of angles, and espec. the malefics; many planets in signs of low vitality, as in ♋, ♑, and ♓, and afflicted, and espec. with these signs on cusp of the Asc. at B.; when planets are near the cusps of angles, death is apt to take place when the afflicting planet reaches the cusp; if planets afflicting the hyleg be in the 4th, 6th, 8th, or 12th H., early death is indicated under the evil directions of these planets to the hyleg if there are no good counteracting aspects. Cases of Early Death—(See "Early Death", No. 428, in 1001 N.N. Also see the Cases and Birth Data in Daath's Medical Astrology, Chap. 14. (For further influences see Accidents. Anareta, Birth, Childhood, Children, Death, Directions, Escapes, Father, Husband, Hyleg, Infancy, Life, Maturity, Middle Life, Mother, Parents, Relations; "Short Life" under Life; Sudden Death (see Sudden); Untimely, Wife, Youth, etc.).

**Early Years of Life**—Danger In the Early Years—Hurts In—Accidents In—Sickness In—Disorders of—♑ on the Asc., or the ☉ and ☽ in ♑, tend to make the early years weak, and with greater danger of death, and to give a weak body; the native does not tend to be strong in the early years when the lord of the 6th H. is in the Asc., and afflicted, or when ♑ is on cusp of the Asc.; the 19° ♓ on the Asc.; the ☽ affl. in ♑; ♄ in the Asc. at B. tends to falls, bruises, or fractures when ♄ by dir. reaches the rising degree at B.; ♂ in the Asc., accidents, hurts, injuries, etc., when ♂ reaches the ascending degree by dir (See "Early in Life" under Baldness; Childhood, Children; "Animal Heat" under Heat; "Early Life" under Hurts; Infancy, Youth).

**EARS**—Organs of Hearing—Auditory Organs—Aural, etc.—The Ears in general, the Ossicles, Nerves, and all parts of the Ears, are ruled by the ♉ sign, the external rulership of ♉, and are also influenced by the ♈ Sign. The Ears have special affinity with ☿ and the ♉ Sign. The 12th H. also tends to affect the Ears for good or ill, as this house is closely connected with the Senses, and limitations upon them, and in cases of Deafness, ☿ and the 12th H. are usually badly afflicted, or with ☿ and other planets afflicted in the 12th H. The right ear is said to be ruled by ♄, and the left ear by ♂. In the Hindu System the 3rd H. is assigned to rulership of the ears, and in our System of Astrology, the 1st H. rules and affects the ears. The Auditory Organs are also ruled by ♄ in general, and espec. the right ear, and an afflicted ♄ in ♈ or ♉, in the 12th H. at B. tends to greatly hamper the functions of the ears. The Aural Ducts are ruled by ♀. The Eustachian Tubes leading to the ears from the nasal cavity are ruled by ♀ and ♉. The following subjects have to do with the Diseases and Afflictions of the Ears, and of parts adjacent.

**Abscesses In**—Accompanied by afflictions in the 3° ♈ or ♎. (See Mastoid. Also see "Discharges", "Meatus", in this section).

**All Diseases In**—Signified by the 1st H., and planets therein.

**Auditory Nerve**—Clogging of—(See "Auditory Nerve" under Hearing).

**Aural, Diseases**—(See "Disordered", and the various paragraphs in this section).

**Aural Ducts**—Ruled by ♀, and an afflicted ♀ tends to disorders of.

**Auricles**—The External Ear—Are large and great when ♄ is in the Asc. at B., or affl. the Asc., and protruding when ♂ afflicts the Asc.

**Blood Effusion**—From the Ear—A ♂ disease and affliction; ♂ affl. in ♉; Subs at AT. (See Effusions).

**Bony Parts**—The Ossicles—The Small Bones of the Ear—Hardening of—Disorders of—Due to mineral deposits by ♄, checking vibration and causing deafness. The bones grow denser when ☿ is afflicted in any part of the map, or in the 12th H.; Subs at AT and AX. (See Hardening; "Deafness" under Hearing).

**Buzzing**—In the Ears—Caused usually by ♄, and the obstructions or catarrhal conditions caused by ♄, and by diseases in the Eustachian Tubes; Subs at AT. (See Buzzing, Catarrh, Eustachian. Also see Catarrh, Circulation, Clogging, Obstructions, Ringing, in this section).

**Catarrh Of**—♄ affl. in ♉; Subs at AT. (See "Buzzing" in this section).

**Circulation**—Sluggish Circulation In—The Circulation Obstructed—Obstruction of the Venous Blood in the Ears—Congestion in the Ears, etc.—The ☉ ☌ ☿ in the 12th H., and ☿ combust, lack of nerve force and vital fluid to the ears; ♄ ☌ ♀ in ♉ in the 12th H.; ☿ and other planets combust in the 12th H. (See "Poor Circulation" under Circulation; Congestion; "Obstruction" under Veins).

**Clogging**—Of the Auditory Nerve—(See "Auditory Nerve" under Hearing).

**Congestion**—Congested Circulation In—(See "Circulation" in this section).

**Deafness**—(See "Deafness" under Hearing).

**Defects**—In the Ears—♄ in ♒.

**Discharges**—From Ear—Perforated Drum—♄, ♂, or the ☽ affl. in ♉; Subs at AT. (See Abscesses, Meatus, in this section).

**Disordered Ears**—Diseased—Afflicted—Afflictions in ♈, ♉, and the 1st or 12th H.; Subs at AT and AX. (See "Ear Trouble", and the various paragraphs in this section).

**Drum**—The Ear Drum—Tympanum—Disorders of—Perforated Drum—Inflammation of—Tympanitis, etc.—♄ or ♂ affl. in ♉; Subs at AT and MCP tend to inflammation of, and espec. with ♂ in ♉, or ♂ affl. in ♉ in the 12th H.

**Ducts**—(See "Aural Ducts" in this section).

**Earache**—Pain In Ear—The Prog. ☽ ☌ a malefic in ♈; ♄ or ♂ affl. in ♈ or ♉; Subs at AT.

**Ear Trouble**—Cases—See Figures 1A, 1B, 1C, in the book "Astro-Diagnosis", and also Fig. 7, 8, 30, 31, in "Message of the Stars", books by the Heindels. (See "Disordered" and the various paragraphs in this section).

**Effusion of Blood**—(See "Blood" in this section).

**Endolymph**—Lack of—♄ in ♉, and espec. when ☌ ♃ or ♀, rulers of the circulation of the blood in the ears.

**Eustachian Tubes**—Disorders of—(See Eustachian).

**External Ear**—Auricles—The Outer Ear—(See "Auricles" in this section).

**Great Ears**—(See "Auricles" in this section).

**Hardening**—Of the Bony Parts—(See "Bony Parts" in this section).

**Hearing**—(See Hearing).

**Inflammation**—In the Ears—General and Prevalent—♂ in ♊, and lord of the year at the Vernal Equinox. (See "Drum" in this section).

**Injuries To**—♄ or ♂ affl. in ♈ or ♉.

**Large Ears**—(See "Auricles" in this section).

**Left Ear**—Pain and Disease In—The left ear in both sexes is ruled by ♂, and Pain, Impediments, Injuries, Hurts, Accidents To, Deafness, etc., in this ear are caused by ♂ afflictions; ♂ afflicted in ♈ or ♉; ♂ or ☿ in the 12th H., and afflicted, or ♂ ☌ ☿ in the 12th H., or ☿ in the 12th, and afflicted by ♂; afflictions in the 12th H. (See Left).

**Mastoid Abscesses**—(See Mastoid).

**Meatus**—Aural Meatus—External Auditory Canal—Abscess of—Inflammation of—♄, ♂, or ☽ in ♉, and afflicted; Subs at AT and KP. (See "Abscess", "Discharges", in this section).

**Nerve**—(See "Auditory Nerve" under Hearing).

**Nerve Force**—Lack of to Ears—(See "Circulation" in this section; "Deafness", under Hearing).

**Nodes**—Nodules—Tubercles In—Tophus—A ♄ disease; ♄ affl. in ♉; Subs at MCP (4C), and at KP. (See Tubercles).

**Obstructions**—Congestion—(See "Circulation" in this section).

**Ossicles**—(See "Bony Parts" in this section).

**Outer Ear**—(See "Auricles" in this section).

**Pain In**—(See Earache, Left Ear, in this section).

**Perforated Drum**—(See "Drum" in in this section).

**Polypus**—(See "Ear" under Polypus).

**Protruding Ears**—(See "Auricles" in this section).

**Pustules In**—A Small Purulent Papule—♂ in ♊ and lord of the year at the Vernal.

**Right Ear**—Ruled by ♄. Also strongly influenced by ♃, and with ♃ in ♈. Disease, injury, and pain in the right ear are espec. ♄ afflictions; born under ♄, or with ♄ affl. in ♈, tends to congestions, blood disturbances, and interference with the circulation in this ear. (See "Circulation", "Left", in this section. Also see Right).

**Ringing in Ears**—Tinnitus Aurium—♄ affl. in ♉; Subs at AX and MCP. (See "Buzzing", "Catarrh", in this section).

**Throbbing**—Pulsating—Beating—♅ or ♂ affl. in ♉; Subs at AT. (See Palpitation).

**Tinnitus Aurium**—(See "Ringing" in this section).

**Tophus**—(See "Nodes" in this section).

**Tubercles**—(See "Nodes" in this section).

**Tympanitis**—Inflammation of Drum—(See "Drum" in this section).

**Upper Ears**—Disorders of—Afflictions in ♈ or ♉; ♄ and ♂ in ♈ or ♉; Subs at AT.

**Venous Blood**—Obstructed Circulation of—(See "Circulation" in this section).

**Vital Fluid**—Lack of In Ears—(See "Circulation" in this section).

**Weak Ears**—Weak Hearing—(See "Weak" under Hearing).

**Wounds To**—(See "Injuries" in this section).

**EARTH**—The Earth and Mundane Conditions—Telluric Influences. In Geocentric Astrology the Earth is taken as a center in the Solar System, and all Astrological positions are Geocentric, as they relate wholly to the Earth, the life and conditions on the Earth. (See Geocentric).

**Barrenness of**—Failure of Crops, etc.—An eclipse of the ☽ in the 2nd Dec. of ♉; eclipses in earthy signs. (See Drought, Famine, Scarcity, Starvation, etc.).

**Bloodshed**—Bloodshed and Loss of Life from War and Strife Increased Over the Earth—(See "Shedding" under Blood; Shedding, War).

**Buried Alive**—Under the Earth—(See Burial).

**Corn Destroyed**—(See Corn, Scarcity).

**Earthquakes**—♉ and ♏ are considered the earthquake signs, and also all the fixed signs when well-occupied with planets tend to cause them. Also caused by the earthy signs. They occur when planets are in violent signs, and also at the time of, or soon after an eclipse. They are also coincident with the appearance of Comets. Caused by eclipses of the ☉ in ♒ or ♓; an eclipse of ☉ in 2nd Dec. of ♒ or ♓; the ☉ to the ☌ ♄ in an earthy sign during travel brings danger of injury or death in an earthquake; the ☉ and ☽ in fixed signs, and also with heavy afflictions from several major planets in fixed signs at the same time; an eclipse of the ☽ in ♏; ♅, ♄, ♃, and ♂ in ♉ and ♏, and with other planets in fixed signs; ♄ and ♂ in terrestrial signs, and afflicting the Lights; ♄ ☌ ♂ in ♉, ♊, ♌, or ♏, in the 4th H., and on the lower Meridian; ♄ in the 4th H., and affl. the hyleg, subject to injuries or death in an earthquake; ♃ in ♉ or ♏ in ☌, P., or ☍ ♀ or ☿; several planets on or near the Equator; eclipses in the 1st Dec. of ♏; many aspects between the planets exist at the time of; great Comets in their perihelion, and within the orbits of ♅ and ♄; the 19° ♑ on the Asc., subject to earthquake casualties. (See Avalanches, Calamity, Casualties, Catastrophies; "Epidemics" under Cholera; "Danger" under Travel; Volcanoes, etc.).

**Earthy Matter**—Deficiency of In the Bones—(See "Deficiency" under Bones; Deposits, Minerals).

**Earthy Signs**—Of the Zodiac—The Earthy Signs are ♉, ♍, and ♑, and are cold and dry Signs. Taken collectively they rule the neck, throat, bowels, bones, knees, skin, the flesh, the carbon in the body, and are connected with the mineral salts of the body, the osseous structures, and the concretions. They give the Nervous and Melancholic Temperament. When on the Asc. they tend to give a compact body, but with less vitality and physical power than is given by the Airy or Fiery Signs. ♑ on the Asc. tends to give low vitality, an ill-shaped body, and a melancholic temperament, being the sign of ♄. The ♉ and ♍ Signs tend to strengthen the general health when containing the ☉ and benefics, and not seriously afflicted. The earthy signs are more free from fevers than other signs. Significators in, or earthy signs on the Asc. and 6th H. tend to all chronic, long and tedious diseases, Ague, Intermittent Fevers, and such as proceed from Consumptions or Melancholy. They dispose to falls, fluxes, hanging, and death by beheading. The action of the ☽ is different in all three of the earthy signs. The ☽ well-asp. in ♉ tends to good health, regular functions, and methodical habits. The ☽ in ♍ tends to bowel disturbances and irregularities, irregular intestinal functions, and digestive disorders. The ☽ is very weak in ♑, and tends to irregular functions, and which may be impeded and uncertain. Despondency and melancholy easily result, which tends to lower the vitality and

weaken the functional activities. The airy and earthy signs are the least excitable. (See in the alphabetical arrangement the various subjects mentioned in this paragraph). For other subjects which have to do with the Earth, Human Affairs, the Peoples of the Earth, etc., see the following subjects,—Air, Animals, Calamities, Catastrophies, Cold, Crime, Epidemics, Events, Famine, Fig Trees, Fire, Fish, Floods, Frost, Fruits, Grains, Heat, Herbs, Mankind, Materials, Metals, Minerals, Miseries, Mortality, Murderers, Nations; "Operations" under Nature; Ocean, Pandemics, Perils, Pestilence, Plague, Prevalent, Public, Rain, Rationalism, Reptiles, Rivers, Sadness Everywhere (see Sadness); Scarcity, Seas, Seasons, Seeds, Serpents, Slaughter, Snow, Summer, Tides, Trouble, Vegetation, Vines, Volcanoes, War, Water, Weather, Wheat, Winter, etc.

**EARTHQUAKES**—(See this subject under Earth).

**EASE**—Interval of Ease In Acute Diseases—Takes place on the crisis days if the ☽ forms a good asp. to a benefic at the time, or if the ☽ be in good asp. to the lords of the 1st, 9th, 10th or 11th Houses. (See Amelioration; "Better" under Disease; Course, Crises, Intermittent, Interrupted, Magnetic, Moderation, Modification, Recovery, Remission, Remittent,). etc.

**Fond of Ease**—♉ influence. (See Dull, Idle, Inactive, Indifferent, Inertia, Lassitude, Lethargy, Listless, Sedentery).

**Lack of Ease**—(See Discomfort, Malaise).

**EASTERN PARTS**—Eastern Countries —Ruled by ♈. The fiery signs are classed as Eastern Signs.

**East Winds**—Ruled by ♄.

**Much Mortality In**—(See "Eastern" under Mortality).

**Nobles**—Death of In Eastern Parts— (See Nobles).

**EASY**—

**Easy Death**—(See "Easy Death" under Death).

**Easy-Going**—(See "Fond of Ease" under Ease).

**EATING**—Eater—

**Abnormal Eater**—(See "Excesses", "Great", "Immoderate", in this section. Also see Gluttony).

**Appetite**—(See Appetite).

**Bowel Disorders**—(See "Eating" under Bowels).

**Chewing**—(See "Fast Eater" in this section; Mastication).

**Death**—Death from Excess in Eating or Drinking—♀ much affl. at B., and affl. the hyleg in a train of evil directions. (See Drink, Intoxication).

**Diet**—(See Diet).

**Drink**—(See Drink).

**Epicureans**—(See this subject).

**Eruptions**—(See "Arms" under Eruptions).

**Excesses in Eating**—Overindulgence in Diet—Love Their Belly—Abnormal

Appetite—Immoderate Eater—Sickness from Overeating—A Great Eater, etc. —Characteristic of ♉ people; the ☉ affl. in ♉, or ♉ on the Asc., and afflicted; the ♉ sign strong at B.; the ☉ affl. by ♃ or ♀; the ☉ ☌ ♅ in ♋ in the 12th H., and in □ or ☍ ♆, tendency to overeat; the ☉ in ♉, and affl. by ♃; ☉ or ☽ in ♋, ✱ or △ ♀; the ☽ or ♅ □ ♃ or ♀; the ☽ to the ill-asps. ♃ or ♀ by dir.; ♄ ☌ ♀ in ♋; ♄ in ♋, ℞ and □ or ☍ ♂; ♄ affl. in ♋; ♄ ill-dig. at B.; ♄ Sig. of the party in Hor'y Questions; a ♃ disease and affliction; ♃ in ♉, □ or ☍ the ☉; ♃ affl. in ♉, ♋, or ♑; ♃ affl. in ♋ in the 12th H.; ♃ affl. in the 1st or 6th H.; ♃ affl. by the ☽; ♃ or ♀ affl. in ♉; ♃ affl. in ♋, and ♋ on the Asc.; ♃ affl. in ♍, warns against overeating; ♃ affl. in ♉, ♋, or ♍ in the 6th or 12th H.; ♃ ☌ ♂ in ♋ or ♑; ♃ or ♂ affl. in ♋; ♃ in asp. or relation to planets or signs which rule the appetite; ♂ affl. in ♋; ♂ Sig. □ or ☍ ♃ or ♀; ♂ ♋, □ or ☍ ♆, ♃ or ♀; ♂ affl. in ♉; ♂ ♉, □ or ☍ ♆, ♅, ♃, or ♀; ♀ in ♉, ♋, or ♏, and affl. by ♃, ♄, ♂, or the ☽, tend to overindulgence of the appetite and indisposition therefrom; ♀ Sig. in ♑; ♀ in ♋, and affl. by the □ or ☍ ♂; ☿ affl. in ♉; ♀ affl. in ♎; ♀ in ♋ and affl. by the ☽; ♀ affl. in the 5th H.; ☿ in ♌ or ♓ warns against overeating and indiscretions in diet; the Asc. to the ill-asps. ♀ by dir., and ♀ affl. at B.; ♓ on the Asc. or 6th H. at B., and the ☉, ☽, or other planets in ♓, and afflicted; afflictions in ♏ tend to overeating, excesses in drink, food, etc., and disease from; ♉, ♋, ♍, ♑, or ♓ on the Asc., and afflicted. (For further influences along this line see "Abnormal" under Appetite; Carbuncles, Cravings, Diet, Digestion, Drink, Epicureans, Excesses, Extravagance, Feasting, Food, Gastric, Gluttony, Habits; "High Living" under High; "Impure Blood" under Impure; Indigestion, Indulgence; "Enlarged Liver" under Liver; Noxious Growths, Obesity, Overindulgence, Plethora, Stomach, Surfeits, Toxaemia, etc.).

**Fast Eater**—Bolts the Food—Eats Hurriedly—The ☽ or ♃ in ♋, ☌ ♂; ♅ ☌ ☽ in ♋, and affl. by the □ or ☍ ♂; fast eating should be avoided when ♅ is in ♍ and afflicted; ♄ in ♋, and □ ♂; ♂ ☌ ☽ in ♋; ruler of the Asc. ☌ ♂.

**Feasting**—(See Feasting).

**Feeding**—(See Feeding).

**Food**—(See Diet, Food).

**Gluttony**—Gormandizing—(See Gluttony).

**Great Eater**—Goes to Extremes In Eating—(See "Excesses" in this section; "Fondness" under Food).

**Hearty Eater**—Characteristic of ♉ people; ♉ on Asc., or ☉ in ♉; ♃ in ♉, □ or ☍ ☉; ♃ affl. in ♋ in 12th H. (See "Excesses" in this section).

**Hurriedly**—Eats Hurriedly—(See "Fast Eater" in this section).

**Immoderate Eater**—Abnormal Eater —(See "Excesses", "Hearty", in this section).

**Indiscretions**—In Eating—Due to an afflicted ♃ or ♀; ♃ affl. in ♉ or ♋; ♀ affl. in ♋. (See "Ailments", "Evil Diet", under Diet; Feasting, Gluttony, Indiscretions, Obesity, Overindulgence, Plethora, Surfeits. Also see "Excesses" in this section).

**Lives to Eat**—(See Epicurean).

**Moderate**—In Eating and Drinking—♊ influence—(See "Moderate" under Drink).

**Over-Eating**—Tendency To—Sickness From—(See "Excesses", "Indiscretions", "Sickness", in this section).

**Sickness**—From Overeating—♃ affl. in ♉; ♃ in ♋ on the Asc., and afflicted; ♀ affl. in ♎; the ♉ sign strong at B. (See "Excesses", "Indiscretions", in this section).

**Surfeits**—From Excess In Eating—See "Evil Diet", "Excesses", under Diet; Obesity, Puffing, Surfeits. Also see "Excesses" in this section).

**Swallowing Difficult**—(See Deglutition).

**Wrong Tendencies**—In Eating or Feeding—Should be avoided when ♂ or ♀ are affl. in ♍, or in the 6th H. (For further influences along this line see Assimilation, Digestion, Gastric, Indigestion, Intemperance, Nutrition; "Hot Stomach" under Stomach; Tumors, Wasting, etc.).

**ECCENTRIC**—Eccentrics—Odd—Peculiar—Queer—Freakishness—Misunderstood By the Common People—Caused principally by the ♅ influence; ♅ ascending at B., or with the chief Significator in the nativity; ♅ in the Asc., or 1st H.; ♅ in the 10th H.; ♅ in any asp. to ☿, and espec. in □ or ☍ asp.; ♅ □ or ☍ ♄; ♅ affl. in ♊, ♐, ♑, ♒, or ♓; the ☽ to the ☌ or ill-asp. ♅ by dir.; the ☽ and ☿ unconnected with each other or the Asc., and with ♄ and ♂ angular and ori., the benefics setting and ori., and with ♅ and ♀ also partaking in the scheme. (See "Fastidious" under Diet; Dress, Erratic, Fancies, Ideals, Ideas, Imagination, Independent, Judgment, Misunderstood, Notions, Occult, Peculiar, Persecution, Tastes, etc.).

**ECLAMPSIA**—An Epileptic Seizure—(See Convulsions, Epilepsy; "Puerperal Fever" under Puerperal; Spasms).

**ECLECTICS**—The Medical School of—(See Healers).

**ECLIPSES**—Eclipses affect those individuals whose maps of birth have configurations similar to those at the time of the eclipse, and who may also be living under the shadow of the eclipse, or if it is visible to them. At a Solar Eclipse the Solar activity is depleted and low. At the New Moon, if an Eclipse of the ☽, the Lunar activity is more depleted than that of the ☉. Eclipses are portends which should not be overlooked. (See Lunations). The effect of an Eclipse of the ☉ endures a year for every hour the ☉ is eclipsed, and a month for every hour the ☽ is eclipsed. An Eclipse of the ☉ especially falling on the places of malefics in the radical map tend to renew and increase the original strength of such malefic, whether it relate to trouble, sickness, or death. No effect of an Eclipse can be very good even tho falling on the place of a benefic, but the evil effects ascribed to them are very probable. The lord of an Eclipse being in a human sign, its evil effects will fall upon Mankind. (See "Human Signs" under Human). They are more important, and more serious in their effects if they happen on the birthday, and take part in the Solar Revolution. A male born at an Eclipse of the ☉ may never breathe, or expire soon after birth, and so with a female born at an Eclipse of the ☽. (For Cases and Birth Data of death of Males born at time of a Solar Eclipse, see "Austria", No. 152, and "Short Life", No. 775, in 1001 N.N.). An Eclipse of the ☉ threatens some male member of the family with sickness, hurt, or death, and an Eclipse of the ☽ some female member. An Eclipse falling on the ☽ in a child's map denotes hurt to the mother; falling on the ☉, hurt to the father; on the place of ♃, hurt to an uncle; on the place of ♂, to a brother; on the place of ♀, hurt to a sister; on the place of ☿, to an aunt. (For the further mention of Eclipses, and the diseases and afflictions they cause, see Air, Bubo, Calamity, Cattle, Childbirth, Cholera, Cough, Death, Disaster, Drought, Earthquakes (see Earth); Endemic, Epidemics, Events, Fainting, Famine, Fever, Floods, Fruit, Functions, Influenza, Mankind, Middle Life, Miseries; "Full Moon", "Metonic Cycle", "New Moon", under Moon; Mortality, Murder, Old Age; "Virus" under Pestilence; Pirates, Plague, Public, Rain, Revolutionary, Rottenness, Scarlet Fever, Sedition, Shipwreck, Storms, Trouble, Volcanoes, War, Weather, Wind).

**ECSTASY**—Religious Ecstasy—(See "Beside One's Self" under Excitable; "Ecstasy" under Religion).

**ECZEMA**—Inflammation of the Skin, with Lymph Exudation—Weeping Eczema—A ♑ disease; afflictions in ♎ and ♑, or with these signs on Asc.; ♄ or ♃ affl. in ♑; ♃ affl. in the 6th H. in ♑; ♃ in ♑, from sluggish circulation; ♃ in signs which rules the arms, hands, legs and feet tends to in these parts; ♂ in ♒ and affl. the hyleg; ♀ in ♈ or ♎, and affl. the ☽ or Asc.; ♀ affl. in ♈ or ♎ in the 6th H.; the ☽ or ♀ afflicted, weeping Eczema; the ☽ hyleg in ♍, and espec. with females.

**Head and Face**—Eczema of—♀ affl. in ♈; ♀ in ♈ or ♎ in the 6th H., and afflicted; ♀ in ♎ and affl. the ☽ or Asc.; Subs at KP, and Local. (See Exudations, Herpes, Ringworm, Skin Diseases, Tetter).

**Salt Rheum**—Chronic Eczema—♄ affl. in ♑. (See Rheum).

**EDEMA**—Oedema—(See Dropsy, Oedema, Serum, Swellings).

**EDGED TOOLS**—Sharp Tools—Injuries By—(See Cuts, Duels, Instruments, Stabs, Sword).

**EDUCATION**—(See "Active Mind" under Active; Dull, Genius, Intellect, Knowledge, Learning, Mental, Mind, Perception, Reading, Science, Study, Understanding, etc.).

**EFFECTS**—

**Directions**—Effects of—(See Directions).

**Disease**—The Constancy and Duration of the Effects of Disease—(See Constancy).

**EFFEMINATE**—The Luminaries in female signs, configurated together with ♂ and ♀ tend to make men effeminate, lustful, salacious, wanton, and to deviate from the limits of nature, and to make women masculine, and espec. if ♂ and ♀ be also in feminine signs; the ☉ and ☽ both in masculine signs, configurated together, and with ♂ and ♀, females will be salacious, of a masculine turn, and men will be effeminate; the ☉ Sig. ☌ ♀, soft and effeminate; ♆ in the Asc. with males; the bad asps. of ♆ to the Sigs. tend to, as to the ☉, ☽, Asc., M.C., or to ♀ or ☿; ☿ in ♓, partile the Asc., very foppish and effeminate; airy signs on the Asc., and people born under them, tend to be effeminate; the 3rd decanate of ♈ on the Asc., ruled by ♀; the ♋ and ♎ influences tend to, and with many planets in these signs, and when the positive planets, as the ☉, ♅, and ♂ are in positive, or masculine signs. (See Soft).

**Appearance**—Effeminate In Appearance—♂ Sig. in ♎. (See "Feminine Degrees" under Female).

**Constitution**—Effeminate In Constitution and Disposition—The ☉ Sig. ☌ ♀; the ☉ or ☿ Sig. in ♓; ♋ gives, and with ♋ on Asc.; the 6th face ♑ on Asc., and to have a weak and vacillating nature; the ♓ influence tends to, and with ♓ on the Asc.; the 4th face ♐ on Asc. (See "Dull" under Constitution).

**Men**—Men Effeminate—The Voice Effeminate In Men—Due to degeneracy, sex excesses, and afflictions to ♉ and ♏. A high and effeminate tenor voice is often produced by castration, affecting the ♉ and ♏ signs which rule the voice and larynx, and many tenor singers in Italy are eunuchs. (See the first part of this section. Also see Deviations; "Castration" under Testes; "Coarse Voice" under Voice).

**Signs**—Effeminate Signs—♓ is the only one so called.

**Women**—Masculine Women—(See the first part of this section. Also see Deviations; "Fixed Signs" under Fixed; "Degrees" under Male; "Coarse Voice" under Voice).

**EFFERVESCENT**—Bubbling Over—Effervescent Mental Activity—Over-Active Mind—♂ and the ☽ influences combined, being fire and water, tend to displays of feeling, anger, and the dissipation and dispersal of brain force, and eruptive conditions. (See "Over-Active Mind" under Active; Anger, Dispersals, Hyperactivity, Impulses, Riotous, Temper, Violent).

**EFFLORESCENCE**—Redness of the Skin—Rashes—Exanthem—(See Eruptions, Exanthema, Rashes, Red, Roseola, Rubefacient, Skin).

**EFFUSIONS**—Extravasation of Fluid Into the Body Tissues or Cavities—

**Blood**—Effusion of Blood Prevalent—

A ♂ affliction; ♂ in ♌ at the Vernal Equi., and lord of the year, and chiefly in places ruled by ♌ (see "Leo Rules" under Nations); ♂ in ♍ at the Vernal, and lord of the year, and espec. in Northern Parts, and in places subject to ♍. (See "Shedding" under Blood; "Virgo Rules" under Nations; "Northern Parts" under Northern; "War and Bloodshed" under War).

**Ears**—Effusion of Blood From—(See "Blood Effusion" under Ears).

**Menstrual Effusions**—(See "Profuse", "Vicarious", under Menses).

**Profluvial Effusions**—A Flowing Out—Discharges Which Leave the Body—A ☽ disease and affliction. (See Discharges, Hemorrhage, Humours, Menses, Watery, etc.).

**Serous Effusions**—(See Serous).

**Tissues**—Effusions Into—(See Dropsy, Hemorrhage, Oedema, Osmosis, Tissues). For further influences along this line see "Loss of Blood" under Blood; Catarrhs, Discutient, Evacuations, Expectoration, Fluids, Fluxes, Haemoptysis, Kicks, Rheum, Serum.

**Treatment for Effusion**—(See Resolvent).

**EGO**—

**Egotistical**—The influences of the fire, earth, and water signs are instinctively egotistical, while the airy signs are self-conscious. The □ and ☍ aspects to ♃ tend to. In Hor'y Questions ♄ Sig. in ♎. (See Pretender).

**Exaggerated Ego**—Egoism—Ego Mania—♂ associated with ☿, and usually by the ☌ or ☍; ♂ ☌, □, or ☍ ☿, in angles, or in the 3rd or 9th H.; ☿ and the ☽, the mental rulers, both afflicted, or afflicting each other. (See Character, Genius, Giants, Judgment, Opinions, Religion, Saint Vitus Dance, Selfishness, Self-Righteousness, Soul, etc.). Case—See Chap. 13, Daath's Medical Astrology.

**EIGHTH HOUSE**—The house of ♏, ruled by ♂, and called the House of Death, and denotes the time and manner of death. It is classed as one of the evil houses, along with the 4th, 6th, and 12th Houses. It is a Terminal House, and forms one of the angles of the Terminal Triangle. (See Terminal). This being a terminal house, it indicates the end of physical life, the sundering of soul and body, the transition from the physical to the spiritual. It concerns disease, death, the nature, kind and quality of death. The different planets in this house at B. indicate the kind and nature of death, according to the nature of the planet. It is one of the Anaretical places of the map. (See Anareta). Benefics here at B. tend to an easy and natural death, and ♃ in this house tends to long life, and a natural death. Malefics in this house tend to a more sudden, accidental, or violent death. Neptune and the ☽ in this house tend to death by drowning; ♅ here, a sudden death, as by an explosion; ♂ here, a violent death, as by accident, injury; ☿ here, death by consumption. This house also rules Fear, Anguish, the Bladder, the Privy Parts, Poisons, and Poison Death. It is a feminine house, and denotes the Genitals and Sex Organs. Its Colors are gray and black. (See the subjects mentioned in this paragraph. Also see "Eighth House" under Death).

**Diseases Ruled By**—Hemorrhoids, Rectal Diseases, Stone, Strangury, Diseases of the Bladder, Genitals, Generative, Reproductive and Sex Organs. (See these subjects. Also see "Scorpio Diseases" under Scorpio).

**ELASTIC FIBER**—(See Fiber).

**ELATION**—(See "Emotional Exaltation" under Emotions).

**ELBOWS**—In the arms, the elbows correspond to the knees in the legs. The knees are ruled by ♑, and the elbows by ♋, the opposite sign. The Elbow is under the external rulership of the ♋ sign, and the Elbow Joint is under the structural rulership of ♋. In a general way also the ♊ sign is said to rule the arms, hands, and shoulders. (See Arms).

**Ankylosis Of**—Dislocation of—Fracture of—Disorders of, etc.—♄ or ♂ affl. in ♋. (See Ankylosis, Dislocations, Forearm, Fractures, Hands, Joints).

**ELDERLY PEOPLE**—Aged People—(See Adults, Grandparents, Maturity, Middle Life, Old Age).

**ELECTRIC**—The positive or electric Planets are the ☉, ♅, ♃, and ♂, and are alkaline in action. (See Alkaline). ♅ espec. is electric, and rules electricity. The electric planets produce heat in the body, and are expansive, and when well placed at B. conduce to a positive, confident and forceful state of mind, and correspond to the warmth and expansion of the physical functions. (See Day, Electricity, Environment, Magnetic, Positive, Tonic).

**Electric Pains**—Caused by ♅; ☿ in ♈, and affl. by ♅, electric pains in the head. (See Pain).

**Electro Signs**—Positive and Negative—See "Electro" under Signs).

**ELECTRICITY**—This is the force of the ☉ reflected thru ♅. It is ruled by ♅, and ♅ rules the Ether thru which electricity travels. (See Ether; "Operations" under Nature).

**Accidents By**—♅ setting in ☍ to the Luminaries; ♅ afflicting the Asc. (See Lightning, Machinery).

**Death By**—Or by Electric Apparatus—♅ ☌ or ill-asp. the ☉; ♅ affl. the ☉ at B., or by dir.; ♅ affl. the hyleg by dir.

**Electrocution**—Death In the Electric Chair by Sentence of Law—In these cases ♅ is espec. strong, and usually afflicts the ☉, ☽, Asc., M.C., or hyleg at B., or by dir., which predisposes to such a death if convicted of murder. (See Judge).

**Healing by Electricity**—People who have ♅ strong at B., as in the Asc., or M.C., and well-aspecting the ☉, are usually susceptible to the healing influence of electricity when it is applied in the right manner, and with the proper current. (See Healing, Magnetism).

**Pains**—Electrical Pains—(See "Electric Pains" under Electric).

**Shock by Electricity**—Caused by ♅ influence and afflictions. (See "Electricity" under Shock).

**ELEGANT**—

**Elegant Body**—Elegantly Formed—(See Beautiful, Handsome).

**Elegant Mind**—Refined Mind—☿ Sig. ☌ ♃; ☿ Sig. ☌ or good asp. ♀; ♀ Sig. ☌ or good asp. ☿. (See "Activity", "Quickened", under Mental; "Good Mind" under Mind).

**Elegant Proportions**—Of Body—♃ Sig. ☌ ☿ and ☿ well-dig., angular, and free from affliction; ♀ Sig. ☌ ☿, and both well-dignified; ♀ as Sig. in Hor'y Questions; born under ♀; given by the ⚹ and △ asps. of ♀ or ☿ if well-dignified; ♎ on Asc. (See Beautiful, Handsome, Well-Proportioned).

**Tall and Elegant**—Tall and Handsome Body—The ☉ Sig. in ♐; ♃ in ♎, partile asp. the Asc.; ☿ ♎, partile the Asc., but not thin; born under ♀ and ♀ ori.; ♎ on the Asc. (See Tall).

**ELEMENTAL QUALITIES**—Of the Body—(See Cold, Dry, Heat, Moisture, and note the various combinations, such as Cold and Dry, Cold and Moist, Dry and Hot, Moist and Hot, etc. Also see "Bodily Temperaments" under Temperament).

**ELEMENTS**—Exposure to the Elements, resulting in Ill-Health—Exposure in Travel, Causing Sickness, etc.—(See Exposure, External; "Weather" under Travel; "Wet" under Journeys).

**Elemental Signs**—The Elemental, or Temperamental Signs, are the Fire, Air, Earth, and Water Signs. (See "Air Signs" under Air; "Earthy Signs" under Earth; "Fire Signs" under Fire; "Signs" under Water).

**The Elements**—Fire, Air, Earth, Water—(See these subjects).

**ELEPHANTIASIS**—Chronic Oedema In the Skin—Hypertrophy of Cellular Tissue—Afflictions in ♉ or ♏, and due to disturbances of coordination; Subs at AT, KP, and Local. (See Enlargements, Hypertrophy, Oedema, Skin).

**In Arms**—And Hands—Afflictions in ♉; Subs at MCP (5C), LCP (6C), AP, and CP.

**In Skin**—Afflictions in ♉; Subs at AT, AX, CP, KP, Local. (See Hypertrophy, Oedema).

**ELEPHANTS**—Large Beasts—The 12th H. conditions show profit or loss thru, sickness or death of, etc.

**Injuries By**—Hurts or Death By—Malefics in the 12th H. (See Animals, Beasts, Cattle, Horses, Quadrupeds).

**ELEVATED PLANETS**—Above the Earth, or Horizon, In a Nativity—The ☉ is more powerful in a day nativity, being elevated above the Earth, and in a night nativity the ☽ is more powerful when elevated, in which case the ☉ rules by day and the ☽ by night. The ☽ to be in her power should be above the Earth by night, and below the Earth by day. The planet nearest the midheaven, the M.C., at B. is the most elevated planet, and powerful in matters of health and disease. The ☽ elevated above the Earth in a nocturnal map tends to more regular and normal functions, and to weakened functions when elevated in a day nativity. A malefic elevated above the Lights denotes sickness, misfortune, death, and if the malefic is Anareta, a violent death. If a malefic be elevated above a benefic, such benefic cannot save, but if the benefic be elevated above the malefic, it will destroy or modify its anaretic tendency, and if also both the ☉ and ☽ be elevated above the malefics, it greatly lessens the injurious effects of the malefics. (See Anareta, Majority, Power, Rising, Setting).

**ELEVENTH HOUSE**—This House is affiliated with ♒, the 11th Sign. It is a masculine house. It rules the Legs, Calves, Ankles. Also rules Friends, Children, Stepchildren, the Hopes, Wishes and Desires. Its Colors are Saffron and Deep Yellow. This House is called "The Good Daemon" by Ptolemy. In matters of children, and as to the indications of fruitfulness or barrenness, this house is closely associated with the 5th H., as the 5th and 11th are opposite and supplemental houses, and when the 5th H. conditions tend to deny children, they are often promised if the Benefics, or the ☽, be in the 11th H., and well-aspected. The 11th H. signifies all diseases in the legs from the knees to the ankles, and in the shin bone, shank, etc. When in this house at B., ♄ brings despair, false friends, and death of children; ♂ here brings false friends, ruin, and wicked children. (See Children, Fifth House, Friends, Fruitful, Hopes, Wishes, and other subjects mentioned in this paragraph).

**ELIMINATION**—Excretion—The Eliminative Organs—The Organs of Elimination and Excretion are ruled by the ♏ Sign. Elimination of Urine thru the Bladder and Urethra is ruled by ♏; elimination thru the Kidneys by ♄ and his exalted sign ♎; thru the Skin, by ♄, which planet rules the Skin. (See Cleansing, Excretion, Faeces, Fever, Inflammation, Poisons, Secretions, Sweat, Uric Acid, Urine, Wastes, etc.).

**Carbonic Acid Gas**—Elimination of—(See Carbon).

**Disorders**—Of Elimination—Caused by ♄ and his afflictions.

**Faulty Elimination**—Afflictions in ♏ cause faulty elimination of the kidney secretions, and the retention of calcareous and poisonous matter, tending to Stone, Sand, Gravel, Disease, Tumors, Toxaemia, etc.

**Hindered**—Retarded—Impeded—Stopped—Obstructed—Faulty, etc.—Due to the obstructing and retarding influence of ♄; ♄ affl. in ♉, ♏, or ♎; ♄ to the ill-asps. his own place by tr. or dir.; afflictions in ♏, and espec. ♄ affl. in this sign; ☋ in ♏. (See Accumulative, Fluids, Functions, Impeded, Obstructions, Retarded, Stoppages, Suppressions, Tumors, etc.).

**Impeded**—(See "Hindered" in this section).

**Kidneys**—(See "Faulty" in this section).

**Obstructed**—(See "Hindered" in this section).

**Poisons**—(See "Elimination" under Poisons).

**Rectal Elimination**—Obstructed—(See Constipation, Expulsion, Faeces, Rectum).

**Retarded**—(See "Hindered" in this section).

**Skin**—Elimination Obstructed In—(See the first part of this section).

**Stopped**—(See "Hindered" in this section).

**Sweat**—Perspiration—(See "Lessened" under Sweat).

**Urine**—The Elimination of Urine Retarded—(See "Elimination" under Urine).

**Wastes**—Elimination of—(See Wastes).

**Water**—Elimination of from the System—(See "Elimination" under Water).

**EMACIATION**—Loss of Flesh—Leanness—Tabefactions—Atrophy—Wasting—Marasmus—Thin Body, etc.—A ♄ disease; ♄ in an angle, occi. of the ☉ and ori. of the ☽; ♄ in ♓ occi., and affl. the ☉, ☽, or Asc., and the hyleg much afflicted at B. (See Assimilation, Atrophy, Decay, Degeneration, Destructive, Diminished, Flesh, Hardening, Lean, Marasmus, Tabes; "Body" under Thin; Tuberculosis, Wasting).

**Body Dry and Emaciated**—The ☉ in ♌ or ♒, ☌, P, □ or ☍ ♅ or ♄; ♄ ☌ ☉ or ☽ in the 6th H.; ♄ in ♑ in the Asc., and afflicted. (See Dry).

**Consumption**—Emaciation With a Consumption—Caused by ♀ when the dominion of death is vested in her. (See Consumption, Wasting).

**Progressive Emaciation**—Gradual and Progressive—(See Malnutrition, Tabes).

**Skeleton**—A Living Skeleton—(See Skeleton).

**EMBALMING**—(See "Silver Cord" under Silver; Undertakers).

**EMBOLISM**—The Obstruction of a Blood Vessel by a Blood Clot or Embolus—(See Clots, Infarcts, Obstructions, Thrombus).

**EMBRYO**—A Fecundated Germ Up To the Fourth Month—The Foetus—(See Foetus. Also see Abortion, Conception, Gestation, Miscarriage, Pregnancy, Prenatal Epoch).

**Embryonic Tumor**—Embryonic Connective Tissue Tumor—(See Sarcoma).

**EMERALD**—A Mineral under the rule of the ☽.

**EMETICS**—Emesis—An Agent Causing Emesis, or Vomiting—A Therapeutic Property of ♀ and the ☽. The best time to give an Emetic is when the ☽ and lord of the Asc. are above the horizon, and the ☽ in one of the ruminant, or cud-chewing signs, as in ♈, ♉, or ♑. In using a drug to produce Emesis, Apomorphine and Ipecac are standard in use among Physicians. (See Antiperistalsis, Ipecac, Medicines, Nausea, Ruminant, Vomiting).

**EMISSIONS**—Ejections—Ejaculations—They are greatest at the Full ☽. (See "Full Moon" under Moon).

**Loss of Seed**—Involuntary Losses of Semen—Wet Dreams—(See "Emissions" under Semen).

**Vital Fluids**—Emission of—Depletion of—(See "Fluid" under Vital). Also see Discharges, Effusions, Epistaxis, Evacuations, Hemorrhage, Haemoptysis; "Nose Bleed" under Nose.

**EMOLLIENT**—An Agent which softens and relaxes the tissues to which applied, as Hot Fomentations, Poultices, Oils, Resolvents, etc. A Therapeutic Property of ♃ and ♃ Remedies. (See Jupiter).

**EMOTIONS**—The Feelings—The Emotions arise in the Desire Body. (See "Desire Body" under Desire). In a general way ♂ is king and ruler of the emotional nature. The ☉ rules the emotional nature in women, which makes them more liable to Hysteria. Venus has to do with all complaints which arise from disturbances of the emotions. When ♆ is strong in the map of birth people are easily swayed by their emotions, and become subject to Hysteria, Crying Spells, Psychic Storms, Fainting and Trance conditions, and espec. when ♆ is afflicted, or affl. the ☉, ☽, ☿, or the Asc. The emotions are made prominent by a predominance of the watery signs and elements in the map of birth, and many planets in water signs. Also the Fixed Signs relate to feeling and emotion. The Astral Body is the seat of the emotions and desires, which are principally connected with the watery signs. (See Astral Body, Desires, Excitable, Fainting, Feelings, Hysteria, Impulses, Psychic, Sensation, Sensational, Trance; "Signs" under Water).

**Arrested Emotions**—Emotional Deterioration—Lack of Emotion—Weak Emotional Nature—♄ strong at B., as in the Asc., or M.C., and affl. the ☉, ☽, ☿, or Asc.; many planets in air or earth signs at B., and with an airy or earthy sign on the Asc., as these signs tend to depress and restrain the emotions, while the fiery and watery signs stimulate them.

**Depressed Emotions**—(See "Arrested" in this section).

**Discord**—(See "Mind" in this section).

**Disorders Of**—♆ strong in the map, but severely afflicted by malefics, or ♆ affl. the ☉, ☽, ☿, Asc., or hyleg; ♂ affl. by ♆, ♅, or ♄. (See Anger, Anxiety, Dejection, Dementia, Depression, Desires, Ecstasy, Equilibrium, Exaltation, Excitable, Fear, Frenzy, Fury, Hypochondria, Hysteria, Insanity, Madness, Mania, Melancholy, Passion, Perversions, Worry, etc. Also note the various paragraphs in this section).

**Disturbances Of**—Complaints Arising From—Due principally to ♀ influence, and afflictions to ♀; also caused by ♆ and ♂ influences. (See the various paragraphs in this section).

**Emotionalism**—The ☽ influence tends to; the ☉ or ☽ in ♓; the ☽ ☌ ♅ in a fire or water sign; many planets in fire or water signs; ♀ affl. in ♏; the 25° ♌ on the Asc. (See Romance).

**Exaltation** — Emotional Exaltation—Elation — Devotional — Religious Awakening—Caused by the afflictions of ♆ and ♂; ♀ progressed in ⚹ or △ ♄ in the radical map, or vice versa. (See Ecstasy, Religion).

**Instability**—Of the Emotions—Afflictions in fiery signs. (See Moods).

**Intensified Emotions** — Over-Emotional—The ☉, ☽, and many planets in the watery signs; ♆ affl. in ♎; ♆ ⚹ or △ ♂. (See Passion).

**Lack of Emotion**—(See "Arrested" in this section).

**Mind and Emotions**—Inner Discord Between—Afflictions to ♀ or ♎, or afflictions in or to any of the airy signs, causes inharmony and maladjustment, and often resulting in a quarrelsome nature. (See Irritations, Quarrelsome).

**Perversion**—Emotional Perversions—(See "Desire Body" under Desire; Perversions).

**Psychic**—Psychic and Emotional Disturbances—(See Psychic).

**Quarrelsome**—(See "Mind" in this section; Quarrelsome).

**Restrained**—(See "Arrested" in this section).

**Sensations**—(See Astral Body; "Desire Body" under Desire; Sensations).

**Spasmodic Emotions**—♅ in ♌ in the Asc., and in ☍ ♂ in the 7th H.; ♅ influence; ♅ ☌ ☽ in the Asc. or 10th H. (See Spasmodic).

**Stimulated Emotions** — (See "Arrested" in this section).

**Swayed by Emotion**—♆ strong at B. (See the Introduction to this Article).

**Uncontrolled Emotions**—♅ in ☌ or evil asp. the ☉; ♆ □ or ☍ ♃.

**Weak**—The Emotions Weak—(See "Arrested" in this section).

**EMPHYSEMA**—A Distention of the Tissues with Air, or Other Gases—A ♅ disease and affliction. (See Air, Distentions, Flatulence, Gases, Uranus).

**Chest**—Emphysema of—(See Chest).

**Pleural Emphysema**—(See Pleura).

**EMPLOYMENT**—The Business—The Vocation—(See Business, Occupation, Vocation).

**Accidents**—In the Employment—The ☉ ruler of the 9th or 10th H. at B., and to the ☌ or ill-asp. ♅ by dir.; ♅ in the 6th H.; ♅ affl. the ☉ at B., and to the ☌ or ill-asp. the Asc. by dir.; ♂ affl. in the 6th H. (See Machinery, Mangled, Occupation).

**Death**—Danger of Death by Machinery in the Employment—(See Machinery). Danger of death in the trade or Employment occurs under the evil directions of ♅ to the hyleg, or Giver of Life; ♅ afflicted at B., and to the ☌ or ill-asps. the Asc. by dir., and espec. if the Asc. be hyleg at B.; the ☽ to the ☌ or ill-asps. ♅ by dir. (See Accidents, Air, Burns, Electricity, Explosions, Fire, Heat, Injuries, Liquids, Mines, Railroads, Residence, Sea, Scalds, Ships, Travel, Vehicles, Voyages, Water, etc.).

**EMPTY**—Empty and Void of Knowledge—(See "Void Of" under Learning; "Void Degrees" under Void).

**EMUNCTORY DUCTS**—And Organs—(See Excretion).

**ENCEPHALON**—Encephalic—The Brain—Pertaining to the Brain—

**Encephalic Ailments**—Afflictions in ♈ or ♎. (See "Disordered" under Brain).

**Encephalitis**—(See "Inflammation" under Brain). Encephalitis, with great Lethargy, accompanies Influenza, and Sleeping Sickness. (See Influenza; "Sleeping Sickness" under Sleep).

**Encephalocele**—Hernia of the Brain—(See "Brain" under Hernia).

**Encephalopathy**—(See "Any Disease" under Brain).

**Lethargic Encephalitis**—(See "Encephalitis" in this section).

**ENCYSTED**—Enclosed in a Cyst—

**Tumors**—Encysted Sebaceous Tumors—(See Wen).

**END**—

**Bad End**—Bad End to Life—(See the various paragraphs under Death; Debauchery, Disgrace, Dissipation, Executed, Hanging, Judge, Murdered, Old Age, Prison, Reputation, Suicide; "Untimely Death" under Untimely, etc.).

**End of the Disease**—Termination of the Disease—Signified by the 4th H. conditions and its influences, and the planets in this house at B., and by dir. Also the 8th and 12th H. conditions should be noted. (See Acute, Chronic; "Certain Death" under Death; Fatal, Incurable, Quick, Recovery, Slow, Tedious, Termination, etc.).

**Evil End to the Disease**—Malefics in the 6th H., and affl. the hyleg. (See Sixth House).

**The Disease Will Soon End**—Benefics in the 6th H., and in good asp. the hyleg; the ☽ sepr. from a malefic and apply. to the good asp. a benefic soon after decumbiture, and espec. in acute ailments. (See Acute, Mild, Quick; "Short Diseases" under Short; Slight).

**The End of Life**—(See the various paragraphs under Death; "Early Death" under Early; "Death" under Childhood, Children, Fourth House, Infancy; "Long Life", "Short Life", under Life; Old Age, Middle Life, Youth. Also see "Bad End" in this section).

**ENDEMIC DISEASES**—Those Peculiar to a Nation or People—Afflictions in ♐; the ☉ to the ☌ ☋ by dir. Also caused by afflictions in the Sign ruling the Country, afflictions to the lord of such Sign, and espec. at the time of Eclipses, being lord of the year at the Vernal Equinox, and afflicted. Caused by the appearance of Comets in the ruling sign of a Country. (See Cholera, Comets, Eclipses, Epidemics, Leprosy, Nations, Pandemic, Pellagra, Perihelion, Pestilence, Plague, Races).

**ENDOCARDIUM**—The Lining Membrane of the Heart—(See "Endocarditis" under Heart).

**ENDOCRINE GLANDS**—(See Ductless).

**ENDOLYMPH**—(See "Endolymph" under Ears).

**ENDOSMOSIS**—(See Osmosis).

**ENDURANCE**—Endures—

**Endures Sickness**—Without Complaining—(See Complaining).

**Much Physical Endurance**—Good Powers of Endurance Against Disease—Can Stand Much Wear and Tear—A ♄ influence, and also of the Fixed Signs. These influences also give more moral endurance. (See "Endurance" under Morals). The ♉ and ♏ signs espec. have much endurance. The feminine signs have more perseverance and patience than the masculine signs. The ☽ influence tends to give a weaker body, and also ♀ does not have much endurance as a planet. The masculine signs, and also ♅ and ♂, tend to sudden and forceful efforts, but do not have as much endurance. Other influences and aspects which tend to greater physical endurance are,—The ☉ in ♌, or ♌ on the Asc.; the ☉ in an earthy sign, much endurance in the constitution, and can stand wear and tear; the less the ☉ is afflicted at B. the greater is the endurance; the ☉ or ☽ may be afflicted, but if they are above the malefics the endurance is greater; the body of ☽ persons is usually weak; ♄ people have great powers of endurance; ♄ ✱ or △ ☉, endures against disease, and with strength and consolidation of constitution; ♄ ✱ or △ the Asc., much physical endurance; ♃ in the Asc. at B., and in good asp. the ☉ and ☽; ♃ in the 6th H. at B., and not afflicted; ♂ in the 1st H., even tho afflicted; ♂ ✱ or △ ♄, ♃, or the ☽; ♂ well-aspected at B.; ♂ in good asp. the ☉ at B.; ♉ or ♌ on the Asc.; the 2° ♍ on the Asc. (See "Active Body" under Active; Consolidation; Constitution (see "Good", "Endurance", "Powerful", under Constitution); Dynamic, Energy; "Fixed Signs" under Fixed; Forces; "Abundance" under Health; Immunity, Patience, Perseverance, Physical, Powerful, Prolonged, Protective, Recuperation, Resistance, Robust, Ruddy, Solid, Stamina, Strength, Strong, Tone, Vital, Vitality, etc.).

**ENEMA**—Clystering—A Rectal Injection of Food or Medicine. The abdominal organs, and the abdomen, ruled by ♍, are usually the beginning of most of the disturbances of the organic functions, and of diseases, and therefore purging, giving enemas, or clystering, are said to be a good beginning in the healing of many diseases, and espec. where medicines and physical and material means are used. (See Cure, Healers, Medicines, Physic, Treatment).

**ENEMIES**—Adversaries—Open Enemies—Secret Enemies—Open Enemies are ruled by the 7th H., and Secret Enemies by the 12th H., and its conditions. In the Hindu System of Astrology the 6th H. rules Enemies. The enemies of the native are usually those born with the ☉ and ☽ in the signs containing the malefics in the map of birth, and espec. of ♄ and ♂, which causes the malefics in one map to be on the places of the Lights in the other, an evil exchange. Various Chapters are given in the Textbooks of Astrology, and the rules concerning Enemies, and this Article is intended more to give the evil and dangerous influences which an enemy may have over the health and life of the native. (See Antipathy, Opposites, Sympathy).

**Ambushes**—Violence, Death, or Injury from an Enemy in Ambush—(See Ambushes, Feuds, Treachery. Also see "Murdered", "Secret Enemies", in this section).

**Asylum**—Confined Unjustly in an Insane Asylum or Prison by an Enemy—(See "Danger of Imprisonment" under Imprisonment; "Asylum" under Insanity. Also see "Plots", "Treachery", in this section).

**Blindness**—Is Blinded by the Artifice or Treachery of an Enemy—(See Artifice; "Treachery" under Blindness).

**Dangerous Enemy**—The native proves a dangerous enemy, and is strong in enmity—♄ ruler of the Asc., or the horoscope, and affl. by ♂, and is very hostile when enraged. (See Anger, Enmity, Hatred).

**Death by An Enemy**—Danger of—Injury By—♅ ☌ ♂ in the 7th or 12th H., and espec. at the times when these planets form evil directions to each other, or to their places in the radical map. (See Ambushes, Injury, Murdered, Plots, Poison, Secret, Treachery, in this section).

**Disgrace**—By the Work of an Enemy, and by False Reports—The M.C. to the □ or ☍ ☿ by dir. (See Disgrace).

**Enemies Do Not Live Long**—Lord of the 7th H. in the 2nd; lord of the 12th in the 8th H., lives to see the death of his enemies.

**Fear of Enemies**—Dread of—♆ in the 12th H.; ☿ elevated above, and configurated with ♂ at a Solar Ingress or Eclipse, tends to a general prevalence of fear of enemies. (See Fear).

**His Own Worst Enemy**—The ☉ affl. in ♓, and generally by extravagance, indulgence and feasting; the ☽ Sig. in ♓; the ☽ decr. in a day geniture, sepr. from ♀ and applying to ♄; ♃ Sig. in ♊ and near Aldebaran, inimical to himself; the Martialist, or ♂ person, tends to bring wounds and diseases upon himself by rushing into danger and excesses; ♀ to the ☌ ♂ or ☋ by dir.; ☿ Sig. in ♐, rash in many things to his own injury; lord of the 12th also lord of the Asc. (See Debauched; "Brings Disease Upon Himself" under Disease; Disgrace, Dissipated, Drink, Excesses, Extravagance, Feasting, Folly, Foolhardy, Gluttony, Habits, Indulgence, Narcotics, Rashness, Reputation, Recklessness, Ruin, Scandal, Unfortunate, Vices, etc.).

**Injured by An Enemy**—Danger of, or Death By—Malefics in the 7th H., by open enemies, or by secret enemies if in the 12th H.; lords of the 7th or 12th in evil houses, as in the 4th, 6th, 8th or 12th, and affl. the lord of the Asc.; the ☽ affl. at B., and to the ☌ the cusp of 12th H. (See Ambushes, Death, Murdered, and the various paragraphs in this section).

**Magistrates**—Enemies Among—(See Judges).

**Many Adversaries**—Has Many Enemies—The ☉ to the cusp the 12th H. by dir.; born with the ☉, ☽, or ☿ much afflicted at B.; the ☽ to Cor Scorpio; ♃ by Periodic Rev. to the ☌ or ill-asp. ♄, and ♄ ill-aspected at B.; many planets in the 7th or 12th H. at B., and malefics among them; the M.C. to the place of Algenib. (See Antares, Algenib. Also see "Secret" in this section).

**Murdered by Enemy**—♂ Sig. □ or ☍ ☉ if the ☉ is lord of the 7th or 12th H. (See Ambushes, Death, in this section).

**Open Enemies**—Ruled by the 7th H. Danger of being injured or killed by them when there are malefics in the 7th H., and under the evil directions of such malefic to the hyleg, or when the malefic, or malefics, afflict the 7th H., and their own place by dir. (See Seventh House).

**Own Worst Enemy**—(See "His Own" in this section).

**Plots**—Death or Injury by the Plots of Enemies—(See Ambushes, Plots; "Enemy" under Poison; Revenge, Treachery. Also see Death, Injured, Murdered, in this section).

**Poisoned by Enemies**—(See "Enemy" under Poison).

**Prison**—Confined Unjustly in Prison by an Enemy, and False Charges—(See "Asylum" under Insanity; "Plots" under Prison).

**Relatives**—Enemies Among—(See Relatives).

**Secret Enemies**—Private and Secret Enemies are ruled and indicated by the 12th H. conditions. The Signs of the Zodiac containing the malefics at B. show the types and locations of the native's worst enemies. The 8th H. shows the influences working over, and the fate of secret enemies. Note the following paragraphs about Secret Enemies,—(a) Death or Injury by Secret Foes—Denoted by the 12th H.; ruler of the 12th H. afflicting the Significator; lord of the 7th H. a malefic, and in the 12th H., and afflicted; lord of the 8th H. a malefic, in the 8th, and affl. by lord of the 6th or 12th, and espec. if the lord of the Asc., or the hyleg, be also afflicted; lord of the 8th in the 12th, and affl. the lord of the Asc., and no benefics in the 12th; the ☽ to the cusp 12th H. by dir.; the ☽ to the ☌ or ill-asp. ♂ by dir.; the ☽ in the 12th H. at the Vernal Equi., lady of the year, and afflicted, and with no good asp. of ♃ or ♀; ♆ the afflicting planet denotes death by the treachery of secret enemies; ♆ affl. in the 1st H.; ♅ ☌ ♂ in the 7th or 12th H.; ♄ or ♂ to the cusp of 12th H. by dir.; ♄ in ♏, ☌ or evil asp. the Asc. by dir.; the 20° ♍ on the Asc. at B., and affl. by malefics. (See Ambushes, Assassination; "Tragical Death" under Death; "Deceitful Relatives" under Deceitful; "False Friends" under Friends; "Murdered" under Murder; "Secret Poisoning" under Poison; Revenge, Treachery; "Twelfth House" under Twelfth; "Violent Death" under Violent). (b) Injured by Secret Enemy—The ☽ affl. at B., and to cusp the 12th H. by dir.; malefics in the 12th H.; lord of the 12th a malefic, and espec. ♄ or ♂. (c) Secret Enemy Dying—Near Death—Lord of the 12th H. be with lord of the 4th or 8th H., or in those houses (Hor'y). (d) Sickness of—Secret Diseases of—Afflicted with Some Secret Malady—Lord of the 12th H. in the 6th H., or joined to lord of the 6th.

**Treachery**—Death or Injury by the Treachery of Enemies—(See Plots; "Enemy" under Poison; Treachery).

**Violence**—Suffers Violence from Enemies—(See Ambushes, Plots, Poison, Prison, Treachery. Also see the various paragraphs in this section).

**ENERGY**—Energies—Energetic—Mars is espec. the planet of dynamic energy. The energy of the system is scattered, used up and dissipated by ♂ during muscular activity. Aspects to the ☉ and ♂ tend to give energy and zest, and even the bad aspects of ♂ are better to give energy than no aspects at all. In the wide sense energy is the manifestation of ♅ and ♂, acting thru the signs and houses occupied, and the planets in aspect. A new lease on the bodily energy is given by ♂ when he brings fevers and inflammations to burn the impurities from the system. The following subjects have to do with the Energies, which see in the alphabetical arrangement when not considered here—

**Abeyance**—Of the Bodily Energies—(See Abeyance).

**Abundance of Energy**—Great Energy—The ☉ in ♌ in the Asc.; the ☉ ⚹ or △ ♂; the ☉ or ☽ ☌ ♂; the ☽ hyleg and in ⚹ or △ ♃; the Prog. ☽ ⚹ or △ the radical ♂ if ♂ be well-asp. at B.; the ☽, P, ⚹, or △ ☿; ♆ well-aspected in ♏; ♅ well-asp. in ♈; ♅ or ♄ ⚹ or △ ♂; ♃ well-asp. at B., and ♃ to the good asps. ♂ by dir.; ♂ in the Asc., and well-aspected, and espec. in one of his strong signs; ♂ ⚹ or △ the ☉ or Asc; ♂ in ♌, ♏, or ♑, and well-aspected; ♂ □ or ☍ the ☉, as the evil asps. of ♂ tend to give energy and activity as well as his good aspects, but with more danger of excesses, and misuse of the energies; ♂ Prog. to the ⚹ or △ the radical ♃, and vice versa; ♀ ⚹ or △ ♂. (See Abundance, Action, Active, Buoyant, Dynamic, Endurance, Exertion, Immunity; "Force" under Life, Powerful, Resistance, Robust, Stamina, Strength, Strong, Vitality, etc. Also see "Great" in this section).

**Action**—(See the various paragraphs under Action).

**Active Body**—Active Mind—(See Active).

**Apathy; Brain Storms**—(See this subject under Brain).

**Conservation of Energy**—♄ when in ♌, and not afflicted, tends to conserve the energies of the body, and maintain good health. (See Conservation, Preservation).

**Constructive Energy**—(See Constructive).

**Debility; Depletion;**

**Destruction of Energy**—(See Destructive).

**Diffusiveness of Energy**—♂ in a mutable sign. (See Diffusiveness).

**Dispersions; Dissipation Of**—(See "Energy" under Dissipated).

**Dull**—(See Dull, Idle, Inactive, Inertia, Lassitude, Lethargy, Listless, etc.).

**Dynamic; Endurance; Ennui; Excess; Excesses; Excitation; Exercise; Explosive; Fatigue; Feeble; Fevers**—Fevers and Inflammation as Related to the Energies—(See Constructive, Destructive, Fevers, Inflammation).

**Fiery Signs**—Are the Most Energetic and Vital Signs. (See "Fire Signs" under Fire).

**Functional Energies**—(See "Dissipation of" under Functions).

**Gait**—(See "Energetic" under Gait).

**Great Energy**—A Time of Great Energy and Activity—The ☉ to the ✶ or △ ♃ by dir.; the Prog. ☉ or ☽ to the ✶ or △ ♂; ♂ Prog. in ✶ or △ the radical ♃, and vice versa. (See Activity. Also see "Abundance" in this section).

**Hyperactivity; Idle;**

**Increase of Energy**—(See "Abundance", "Great", in this section. Also see "Increased" under Vitality).

**Indifferent; Inefficiency; Inertia;**

**Inflammation**—(See "Fevers" in this section).

**Lack of Energy**—Lack of Enterprise—The ☽ ☍ ♂; afflictions to ♀, and the ill-asps. of ♀ tend to loss of stimulus, and general relaxation; the 2nd and 4th faces of ♉ on the Asc. (See "Of No Ambition" under Ambition; Dull; "Resignation" under Fate; Idle, Indifferent, Inefficiency, Inertia, Labor, Lassitude, Lazy, Lethargy, Listless, Relaxation, Retrograde; "Low", "Weak", under Vitality; "Weak Body" under Weak).

**Lassitude; Lethargy; Listless; Mars**—(See "Mars Influence" under Mars).

**Mental Energy**—Mental Activity—The ☉ or ☽ ☌ ♂; the ☉ well-asp. in ♐; the ☽ ☌, ✶, or △ ☿; ♅ ✶ ♃ or ♀, and with ☿ in ✶ or △ ♂; ♂ rising at B.; ♂ in fiery signs, or in ♏ or ♑, and espec. when rising; ♂ to the good asps. ☿ by dir.; ♀ Sig. in ♍, an active mind; ☿ well-asp. in ♊, ♍, or ♒; ☿ in ♑, an active mind, yet feeble or sickly body; ♏ or ♐ on the Asc.; Temperate climates, with alternate heat and cold, tend to produce an active and energetic mind and nature; produced by fiery and airy signs; lords of the nativity in Southern Signs give energy and activity. (See "Active Mind" under Active; "Activity", "Quickened", under Mental; "Strong Mind" under Mind; "Scattered" in this section. Also for the opposite influences which tend to a dull and inactive mind, see "Mind" under Dull).

**Motion; Movement; Muscular Energy**—Muscular Activity—Ruled by ♂. (See "Activity" under Muscles).

**Natural Energies**—Natural Abilities—(See Natural).

**Nervous Energy**—Is upheld, given, and ruled by ☿, and depressed or suppressed by ♄. (See Nerves).

**New Lease on Energy**—(See the Introduction to this Article).

**Opposite Sex**—Energies Wasted On—(See "Health Suffers" under Opposite Sex).

**Pleasure**—Energies Wasted In—(See "Energies" under Pleasure).

**Power; Quick; Resistance;**

**Restless Energy**—Cardinal signs on the angles, and many planets in cardinal signs. (See Cardinal, Restless).

**Robust; Ruddy, Scattered Energy**—The bodily energy is scattered by ♂ during muscular activity. The mental energies are more quickly scattered by afflictions to ☿. (See Active, Dispersions; "Energy" under Dissipation. Also see "Diffusiveness", and the various paragraphs in this section).

**Sex Energies**—Dissipation of—(See Amorous, Lascivious, Lewd, Licentious, Lust, Passion, Sex, Venery, etc.).

**Slow; Spasmodic Energies**—(See Spasmodic).

**Sports; Stamina; Strength; Strong;**

**Superabundance**—(See "Abundance" in this section; Excess, Excesses, Superabundance).

**Time of Great Energy**—(See "Great Energy" in this section).

**Tone; Vital Energy**—The ☉ and ♂ represent the vital energy. The ☉ gives the vital heat, or the vital energy to the body. Also connected with the ♓ sign, and Iron Phosphate, the ♓ Salt. (See "Energy", "Heat", under Vital).

**Vital Powers Weak**—(See "Weak" under Vital).

**Vitality**—The Vitality Strong—Weak—(See Vitality).

**Void of Energy**—(See "Lack Of" in this section).

**Walk**—(See "Energetic" under Gait).

**Wasted Energies**—(See Debauchery, Dissipation, Excesses, Exercise, Love Affairs, Opposite Sex, Passion, Sex, Venery, etc.).

**Weak Body**—(See "Weak Body" under Weak).

**Weariness; Zest.**

**ENERVATION**—Enervating—Weakening—♄ affl. the ☉, ☽, Asc., or hyleg at B., and by dir.; ♃ in evil asp. to ♀, and ♃ weak and ill-dig. in the map; ♂ weak at B., and forming no asp. to the ☉, or vice versa. (See Debility, Decreased, Decrepitude, Depletion, Diminished, Feeble, Neurasthenia, Resistance Low, Vitality Low, Weak, Weakening).

**ENGLISH CHOLERA**—(See "Cholera Morbus" under Cholera).

**ENGORGEMENT**—(See "High Pressure" under Blood; Diet, Distentions, Food, Gluttony, Plethora, Surfeits; "Vascular Fullness" under Vascular; Vessels, etc.).

**ENHANCED**—The Health Good and Enhanced—(See "Enhanced"; "Good", under Health).

**ENJOYMENT**—Given to Pleasure and Enjoyment—(See Pleasure).

**ENLARGED**—Enlargements—Over-size—Swollen—The following subjects have to do with Enlargements, Abnormally Large Parts, Overgrowth, etc., which see in the alphabetical arrangement when not considered here.

**Abdomen**—(See "Prominent" under Abdomen).

**Abnormalities; Acromegaly**—(See "Enlargement" under Arms, Extremities, Face, Feet, Hands).

**Arms**—(See "Enlargement" under Arms, Extremities).

**Body**—Enlarged Body—The ♌, ♍, or ♐ signs when upon the Asc. at B., or strong in their influences, tend to enlarge the body. (See Corpulent, Excessive, Fat, Fleshy, Giants, Growth, Large, Tall, etc.).

**Bones**—(See "Large", "Long", under Bones).

**Cells**—(See "Hypertrophy" under Cells).

**Chest**—(See "Dropsy" under Chest).

**Corpulent; Deformities; Deposits;**

**Development; Dilatations;**

**Distentions; Dropsy; Elephantiasis;**

**Engorgement; Excessive; Expansion;**

**Extremities; Face**—(See "Enlargement" under Face).

**Fat; Feet**—(See "Enlargement", "Swollen", under Feet).

**Flatulence; Fleshy; Fullness; Gas;**

**Giants; Glands; Great; Groins;**

**Growth; Growths; Hands**—(See "Enlarged" under Hands).

**Head**—(See "Tumor" under Brain; "Enlarged" under Head; Hydrocephalus).

**Heart**—(See "Enlarged" under Heart).

**Hernia; Hydrocele; Hydrocephalus**—(See "Dropsy" under Brain).

**Hydrothorax**—(See "Dropsy" under Chest).

**Hypertrophy; Increased;**

**Inflammations; Joints**—(See "Stiff Joints" under Joints).

**Large; Limbs; Liver**—(See "Enlarged" under Liver).

**Mineral Deposits**—Enlargements From—(See Deposits, Joints, Minerals, Wastes).

**Morbid Enlargements**—(See Abscesses, Morbid, Swellings, Tumors, Ulcers).

**Neck**—(See Goiter; "Swellings" under Neck).

**Oedema; Organs**—♂ tends to enlargement of organs, and also ♃ by the formation of fat, adipose tissue, tumors, and growths. Enlargement of parts, or organs, as in hypertrophy and excessive growths, is due to the tonic, or plus action of ♂. (See Hypertrophy; "Over-Developed" under Organs; "Tonic Action" under Mars; "Planets" under Tonic).

**Overgrowth; Prostate Gland**—(See Prostate).

**Rickets; Ruptures; Scope**—Enlarged Scope of the Disease—The two heat-producing planets, the ☉ and ♂, when combining their influences, tend to both febrile and inflammatory conditions. (See Fever, Inflammation).

**Stomach**—(See "Dilatation" under Stomach).

**Swellings; Tall; Testes;**

**Thyroid Enlargement**—(See Goiter, Thyroid).

**Tissues; Tonic Action**—(See "Organs" in this section).

**Tonsils; Tumors; Tympanites; Uvula;**

**Varicocele; Varicose; Veins; Vessels;**

**Virile.** For subjects which may not be mentioned here, look for them in the alphabetical arrangement.

**ENMITY**—Hatred—Malice—

**Against the Native**—♆ in the 1st H.; the ☽ to the ☌ or ill-asp. ♂ by dir. tends to enmity against the Native.

**Death Thru Enmity**—Death from Plots—♆ affl. in the 1st H. (See Enemies, Feuds, Plots; "Death by Poison" under Poison; Treachery, etc.).

**Strong In Enmity**—♄ ruler of the Asc., or horoscope, at B., and affl. by ♂. (See Anger, Contests, Duels, Feuds, Hatred, Jealousy, Malice, Murderous, Plots, Poison, Revenge, Temper, Treacherous, Vicious, Violent, etc.).

**ENNEATICAL**—A Climax in Disease. The 9th day of a disease or illness. Also the 9th year of life is called an Enneatical Year. The word means "Nine", and refers to the 9th of any series. The 9th day of the ☽, being the trine aspect after the New ☽, or the 9th day of a fever, are crisis days, but rather favorable, and indicate relief, ease, and more favorable conditions. In Geometry, a figure with nine faces or surfaces. (See Climacterical, Crises, Critical, Periods, Years).

**ENNUI**—Vapors—Mental Weariness—Lack of Interest in Life—(See Apathy, Dejected, Depressed, Despondency, Dull, Hypochondria, Lassitude, Lethargy, Listless; "Low Spirits" under Low; Melancholy, Weariness, Worry).

**ENOPHTHALMOS**—(See Eyeballs).

**ENRICHMENT**—Of the Blood—(See "Enrichment" under Blood).

**ENSNARING**—Enticing—♆ influence—(See Illaqueative).

**ENTERALGIA**—Pain In the Bowels—Neuralgia In—A ♍ disease, and afflictions in ♍; the ☽ affl. in ♍, great pain and disorder in the bowels; the ☽ in ♈ or ♓, and affl. by the ☉ or ♂ when taken ill (Hor'y); the ☽ in ♎, ☌ or ill-asp. ♄ (or ☿ if he be of the nature of ♄) when taken ill (Hor'y); ♆, ♄, or ♅ in ♍, and affl. the ☉ or ☽. (See Colic, Cramps, Gripings, Pain, under Bowels; Cholera, Dysentery,• Flatulence).

**ENTERIC FEVER**—(See "Fever" under Bowels; Typhoid).

**ENTERITIS**—(See "Inflammation" under Bowels; "Enteritis" under Catarrh, Childhood, Phlegmon).

**ENTEROCOLITIS**—(See Bowels).

**ENTEROPTOSIS**—(See "Prolapse" under Bowels).

**ENTHUSIASM**—

**Enthusiasts**—♂ or ☿ □ or ☍ ♄; the 2nd Dec. of ♑ on the Asc., red hot enthusiasm.

**Sudden Enthusiasms**—The ♐ influence strong at B.

**Temperaments**—(See Choleric, Sanguine).

**The Fury of Enthusiasm**—The ☽ and ☿ unconnected with each other or the Asc., and with the malefics in the Eastern Parts and in angles, and the benefics in the West, and also with ♀ and ♂ taking part in the scheme; a ♂ disease and affliction; also connected with ♅ afflictions; many planets in fiery signs at B. (See Anarchists, Emotions, Frenzy, Fury, Madness, Mania, Religion, etc.).

**ENTIRE BODY**—(See Whole).

**ENTOZOONS**—Intestinal Parasites—They are more active and burstling at the Full ☽. (See "Full Moon" under Moon; Parasites, Worms).

**ENURESIS**—(See "Incontinence" under Urine).

**ENVIRONMENT** — Surroundings—The nature of the individual environment, and hereditary tendencies, are indicated by the Sign ruling the Place or Country of birth. If the sign is positive or masculine, it denotes an electro-positive environment. If the sign is negative, an electro-negative environment. In long and chronic diseases the environment of the birthplace, or of the Native Country, is often a curative agent, and espec. if there are benefics with the ☉ at B., or in the 4th H. (See Abroad, Climate, Curable, Disorientation, Employment, External, Family, Friends, Habits, Heredity, Home, Incurable, Identity, Location, Marriage, Native Land (see Native); Negative, Orientation, Parents, Place of Birth (see Place); Positive, Relations, Residence, Social Life (see Social); Susceptible, Travel, Treatment, Utopianism).

**Much Affected By**—Much Influenced By—♅ or the ♋ sign on the Asc.; the 4th face of ♋ on the Asc.; the 6th face of ♓ on the Asc.; mutable signs on the angles at B., and also many planets in feminine and negative signs. (See External, Influenced, Mutable, Negative, Suggestion, Susceptible).

**EPHEMERAL FEVERS**—Brief Fevers—Fevers Which Last for Only a Day—♀ in a fiery sign and afflicted at a decumbiture; Subs at CP and KP. (See Acute, Indiscretions, Mild, Minor, Slight).

**Ephemeral Skin Eruption**—(See Urticaria).

**EPICUREANS**—Sybarites—Given to Luxury, Pleasure, Feasting, etc.—The ☉ Sig. in ♍, convivial and fond of feasting; the ☽ affl. in ♓, given to the pleasures of the table; ♆ afflictions to ♀ or ☿, or to the Sigs., the ☉, ☽, Asc., or M.C. at B., or by dir., a Sybarite, a luxurious person; ♃ in □ or ☍ the ☉; the 2nd Dec. ♉ on the Asc., ruled by the ☽, fond of dainty foods and good living; the 16° ♑ on the Asc., lives to eat; the 22° ♓ on the Asc. (See Appetite, Diet, Drink, Eating, Extravagance, Feasting, Food, Gluttony; "High Living" under High; Intemperance, Luxuries, Pleasures, Prodigal).

**EPIDEMICS**—A Prevailing Disease, and Common to Many People—

**Causes**—Epidemics are caused by the major planets in perihelion, and espec. ♄ and ♃, and also by ♂ in perigee. The greatest epidemics have occurred when ♃ is perihelion, and ♂ perigee at the same time. People born under the ♏ sign are very susceptible to epidemics, and to infectious and contagious diseases, due to the magnetic nature of this sign, and they fall easy victims. When in perihelion, the planets ♆ and ♅ have also been observed to cause epidemics of various kinds. They also occur at the time of the appearance of Comets, and are coincident with Earthquakes and Earth disturbances. Fatal Epidemics can be due to general causes, as great Eclipses, and may not show fatal Directions in the cases of every individual affected. The influences of the Equinoxes and Solstices also have their effects, such as ♃ in ♊, and lord of the year at the Vernal Equi., and ♄ therein conjoined with ♂, or ♄ ☌ ♂ therein, and with ♃ ℞, and ♀ combust; ♄, ♃, and ♂ conjoined in ♉; ♄ in ♏, ℞, occi., and ruler of the year at the Vernal Ingress; ♃ ☌ or ☍ ♅; ♂ supreme at the Equinoxes and Solstices; a ♌ disease; afflictions in ♌, and with several superior planets in ☌ in ♌; coincident with the appearance of Comets, and espec. in ♒. (For the various kinds of Epidemics, their nature, and causes, see Air, Atmosphere, Cattle, Cholera, Comets, Contagions, Diphtheria; "Earthquakes" under Earth; Eclipses, Equinoxes, External, Fruit, Horses, Infections, Influenza, Ingresses, Measles, Moisture, Pandemics, Perigee, Perihelion, Pestilence, Plague, Putrefaction, Rottenness, Scarlet Fever, Scorpio, Sheep, Smallpox, Solstices, Sun Spots (see Spots); Susceptibility, Typhoid, Typhus, Vegetation, Vernal, Virus, Yellow Fever).

**Epidemic Fevers**—The ☉ affl. in ♊; the ☉ to the ☌ ☋ by dir.; ♄, ♂, and ☿ conjoined in ♑; ♂ supreme at the Equinoxes and Solstices. (See "Low Fevers" under Fever; "Fevers" under Pestilence).

**Fatal Epidemics**—(See the Introduction to this section).

**Great Epidemics**—(See "Severe" in this section).

**Heat**—Epidemics Thru Excess of Heat—Eclipses of the ☉ or ☽ in fiery signs. (See Famine; "Fire Signs" under Fire; Heat).

**Immunity To**—(See Immunity).

**Low Fevers**—Epidemic of—(See "Low Fevers" under Fever).

**Mild Epidemics**—Only two of the superior planets in ☌ or ☍. (See Mild).

**Moisture**—Epidemics Arising from Too Much Moisture—Caused by ♀. (See Floods; "Superabundance" under Moisture; Rain).

**Pandemics**—Wide Spread Epidemics—(See Pandemics).

**Severe Epidemics**—Great Epidemics—Three or four of the superior planets in ☌ or ☍. The great epidemics correspond to the periodicity of the ☌ and ☍ of the superior planets.

**Wide Spread Epidemics** — (See "Severe" in this section).

**EPIDERMIS**—The Outer Layer of the Skin—The Cuticle—Scarf Skin—Ruled by ♄. Also under the external rule of ♑. (See Excoriations, Scales, Skin).

**EPIGASTRIUM** — Epigastric Region—The Region Over the Stomach—Under the external rule of the ♋ sign.

**Disorders In** — (See "Heartburn" under Heart).

**EPILEPSY** — Eclampsia — By Ancient Writers this was classed as a mental disease, and was called the "Holy Disease", as they considered the patient in a fit, or paroxysm of the disease, to be under the influence of a Supernatural Power. Most Astrologers consider it a mental disease, as many of the same planetary influences which cause Insanity also cause this disease. Some Writers, and also Modern Medical Authorities, class it as a Nervous Disease, with loss of consciousness, and with tonic and clonic convulsions. The major attacks of Epilepsy are called "Grand Mal", and the milder forms, "Petit Mal". Eclampsia is a milder form without loss of consciousness. Some Writers say that Epilepsy is due to an abnormality of one of the Ductless Glands, the Pineal Gland, which Gland is ruled by ♆, and as ♆ rules the Spiritual Faculties, Epilepsy, no doubt, has a spiritual, as well as a mental or psychic cause, and may also be due to some obsession, or Spirit Control. (See Neptune, Obsessions, Spirit Controls). The Planetary Causes of Epilepsy are as follows — The ☉ above the horizon (daylight horoscope), with ☿ and the ☽ unconnected with each other or the Asc., and with ♄ and ♂ in angles ruling the scheme, ♄ by day and ♂ by night. (Note—♄ ruling the scheme by night and ♂ by day, tends to Insanity (see Insanity); the ☽ rules diseases which return after a time, such as Epilepsy; the ☽, ☿, and the Asc. unconnected with each other, and affl. by ♄ and ♂ from angles, and with no assistance from the benefics, tend to Epilepsy and Falling Fits, and espec. if ♄ be so posited by day, and ♂ by night; the ☽ in ♋, ☌, or ill-asp. any of the malefics as promittors; the ☽ decr., and sepr. from ♂ and apply. to ♄; a ☽ disease; the ☽ affl. in ♋, and affl. the hyleg therefrom; patients tend to be worse at the Full ☽; ♆ afflicted; ♅ in the 6th H., and affl. ☿ or the hyleg; ♅ ☌ or ill-asp. the ☉ at B., and by dir.; ♄ in an angle, occi. of the ☉, and ori. of the ☽, and ☿ in familiarity with ♂; ♄ or ♂ in the Asc. or M.C. in ♊ or ♐; a ♄ disease, and ♄ denotes death by; ♄ and ♂ ruling ♃ and ☿, and at the same time the ☽, ☿, H. and the Asc. be unconnected with each other; ♄ and ♂ angular, occi. of the ☉, and ori. of the ☽, and ☿ in familiarity with ♂; the combined influence of ♄ and ♂; ♄ and ♂ in angles, elevated above H, ☿, or the ☽, and if H, ☿, and the ☽ be unconnected with each other by good asps., and be affl. by ♄ or ♂, and with no assistance from ♃ or ♀; ♂ and ☿ holding dominion at B., and in familiarity with each other, and ♂ affl. the hyleg, and elevated above the Luminaries, the Epilepsy is increased; ☿ affl. at B., and to the ☌ or ill-asps. the ☽ or hyleg by dir., or by Periodic Revolution; ☿ in the 8th H., and affl. at a Solar Ingress of the ☉ into ♈, and ☿ affl. the ☽ or planet ascending (see Madness); ☿ denotes death by; ☿ and the ☽ unconnected with each other or the Asc., and ♄ and ♂ in angles ruling the scheme, ♄ by day, and ♂ by night,—under these conditions if the malefics be in Eastern Parts and angles, and the benefics in the West, the epileptic person will be subject to constant fits, danger of death, and the epilepsy becomes conspicuous; ☿ and ♃ cooperating in the scheme contribute to epilepsy, and ☿ espec. when the dominion of death is vested in him and he is of the nature of ♄; an ♈ disease; Subs at AT, CP, KP and PP. Epilepsy also is strongly associated with the ♏ sign and sex, highly sexed people, and espec. with females. (For further influences along this line see Coma, Convulsions, Consciousness, Day, Delirium, Demoniac, Deranged, Fainting, Fits, Idiocy, Insanity, Insensibility, Madness, Mania, Night, Obsessions, Pineal Gland, Spasms, Spirit Controls, etc.). Case of Epilepsy—See "Epilepsy", No. 668, in 1001 N.N.

**Ameliorated** — (See "Curable" in this section).

**Causes of Epilepsy** — (See the first part of this Article).

**Conspicuous**—(See the ☿ influences in the first part of this section).

**Constant Epileptic Fits**—(See the ☿ influences in the first part of this section).

**Curable** — Ameliorated — Mitigated — Epilepsy will tend to be mitigated, or curable, if the benefics are elevated at B. above the malefics which produce it, and espec. under favorable directions to the ☽ or ☿. The more oriental and angular the benefics may be, the more powerful will their effects be for good, and espec. if the malefics are setting in the West, and out of power and dignity. The opposite to these conditions would tend to make the Epilepsy incurable ordinarily, and without the proper treatment. (See Amelioration, Curable, Incurable, Modification, Recovery).

**Death by Epilepsy**—Danger of—♅ in the 8th H., and affl. ☿ and the hyleg, and with the malefics ♄ and ♂ elevated in the East, and above the Luminaries at B., or in angles; ♄ occi. at B., and affl. the hyleg by dir., and holding the dominion of death; ☿ affl. the hyleg, or giver of life, by dir.; ☿ affl. by ♄ or ♂ at B., and affl. the hyleg by dir., and also holding the dominion of death. (See the ☿ influences in the first part of this Article, and also the paragraph on "Curable").

**Increased**—The Epilepsy Is Increased—(See the ♂ influences in the first part of this Article).

**Incurable**—(See "Curable" in this section).

**Mitigated** (See "Curable" in this section).

**Worse**—Epileptic patients tend to be worse at the Full ☽. (See "Worse" under Disease; "Full Moon" under Moon).

**EPIPHORA**—Watery Eyes—Overflow of Tears—(See Tears).

**EPISTAXIS**—Nose Bleed—Hemorrhage from the Nose—(See "Epistaxis" under Nose).

**EPITHELIOMA**—A Cancerous Growth of the Skin—An Affection of the Epithelium—♂ affl. in ♉; also a ♑ disease, as the Epithelial tissues, or the Epithelium, are connected with ♑. (See Carcinoma; "Epithelioma" under Nose; Skin).

**EPOCH**—(See "Critical Epochs" under Critical; Prenatal Epoch).

**EPULIS**—(See "Cystic Tumor" under Tongue).

**EQUATOR**—(See Nadir).

**EQUILIBRIUM**—Poise—Balance—Ruled by the ♎ sign, the sign of "The Balance".

**Disturbed**—The Equilibrium and Balance of the Body Disturbed—Lack of Balance Between Mind and Body—Incoordination—♄ in ♉; many planets, or a Stellium, in ♉, afflicting the organ of coordination, and resulting in inability to walk without swaying, or pitching forward. (See Balance, Coordination, Gait, Harmony, Incoordination, Libra, Miscarriage, Rhythm, Spasmodic, Walk).

**Loss of Equilibrium**—Caused by the ♌ sign and influence, as this is a fiery and hot sign, heats the system when strong at B., or occupied by the ☉, ♂, and many planets, thus causing loss of equilibrium. (See "Animal Heat", "Heats the System", under Heat).

**EQUINOXES**—Equinoctial—These are the points in the Zodiac when the ☉ enters the Signs ♈ and ♎, which are Equinoctial Signs, and the planetary aspects and configurations at these times are very important in the consideration of disease and health, as they are very sensitive points in the Zodiac. The ☉ enters ♈ at the Vernal Equinox, as he crosses the Equator on his Northward journey from out of the Tomb of Winter, and in the Fall of the year, at the Fall, or Autumnal Equinox, the ☉ enters ♎, and begins his Southward journey. The influences which afflict the ☉ at his Ingress into ♈ or ♎ tend at times to cause Drought, Epidemics, and other evils. (See "Corrupt Air" under Air; Drought, Dry, Earthquakes, Eclipses, Epidemics, Hail, Ingresses; "Nil" under Mars; Minor Disorders, Mortality, Pestilence, Solstices, Tropical, Vernal, Weather).

**ERECT**—Erect In Posture—Upright—Erect and Straight—Tall and Straight—The ☉ in ♎; the ☽ Sig. in ♊; ♃ in the Asc.; ♃ in ♐; ♃ Sig. in ♎ or ♐; born under ♃; ♀ Sig. in ♊ or ♎; ♀ oriental; ☿ ascending at B., and free from the rays of other planets; ☿ strong at B., as rising, or in the Asc. (See Straight, Tall, Upright).

**ERECTIONS**—Painful Erections—Priapism—(See "Chordee", "Erections", "Priapism", under Penis).

**ERETHISM**—Abnormal Increase of Nervous Irritability—A ♂ disease and affliction; ♂ afflicting ☿; ♂ ☌ or ill-asp. ☿ tends to increased irritability and vascular excitement of the nerve centers. (See "Centers", "Neuritis", under Nerves).

**ERGOPHOBIA**—Fear of Work—(See Work).

**EROSIONS**—(See "Ulceration" under Teeth; Ulcers).

**EROTIC**—Pertaining To Sexual Passion—

**Erotic Disturbances**—(See Amorous, Passion; "Sex Desires" under Sex).

**Erotic Mania**—(See "Erotic" under Mania).

**ERRATIC**—Irregular—Changeable—

**Conduct**—Erratic Conduct—(See Conduct).

**Course of Disease**—Erratic Course—(See Course, Irregular, Peculiar, Various).

**Judgment Erratic**—(See Judgment).

**Mind**—Erratic Mind—♅ is the principal planet which, by his afflictions, gives erratic states of mind and blind impulses; ♅ ruler of the horoscope, and afflicted; ♅ in the 1st H.; ♅ in the 3rd or 9th H., and afflicted, or affl. ☿; ♅ □ or ☍ ☽; ♅ ☌ or ill-asp. ♂; ♅ by transit ☌ ♂, ☿, or the ☽; the ☉ ☌ ☿ combust in ♓, the ☉ □ or ☍ the ☽ or ♄; the Prog. ☉ or ☽ ☌ or ill-asp. ♅; the ☽ in the Uranian sign ♒ at B., and afflicted; the ☽ □ or ☍ ☿ at B.; the ☽ ☌ ♆ or ♂ in ♈, and in □ to ♅, ♄, or ♃; ♄ ☌ or ill-asp. ☿; ♃ in ♊, □ ♅ or ♂ in ♍; ♃ affl. in ♒; ☿ ruler of the horoscope, and affl. by malefics; many planets in the signs of ☿, as in ♊ or ♍, and affl. by the □ asps. of other planets; ☿ and ♀ progressed to the ☌ or ill-asp. ♅ at B., or vice versa; ☿, the mental ruler, prog. to the ☌ or ill-asp. ♅ or ♂ at B. (See Chaotic, Deviations, Dreamy, Eccentric, Emotions, Folly, Foolhardy, Habits, Ideals, Impulses, Judgment, Perversions, Peculiar, Rashness, Reckless, Religion, Riotous, Unbalanced).

**Movements**—Erratic Movements—Motor Neuroses—Caused by ♅ influence, by reflex action in ♉, and afflictions to planets in ♉ where the organ of coordinated action is located; a ♉ disease; a ♅ disease; ♅ in the 6th H. (See Action, Antiperistalsis, Clonic, Colic, Contortions, Contractions, Convulsions, Coordination, Cramps, Distortions, Fits, Hiccough, Incoordination, Involuntary, Irregular, Jerkings, Motion, Movement, Organs, Saint Vitus Dance, Spasms, Tics, Tremors, Twitchings, Vomiting).

**Organs**—Erratic Action of Organs—Caused by ♅ afflictions. (See the various Organs of the Body in the alphabetical arrangement. Also see "Movements", "Organs", in this section).

**Personality** — Erratic Personality — (See Personality).

**Sex Life**—Erratic In—(See Amourous, Excesses, Passion, Scandal, Sex, Venery, etc.).

**ERRING**—Intractable—Unruly—Willfully Wrong and Erring—Refractory —♄ affl. in ♊. (See Conduct, Cruel, Erratic, Errors, Evil, Judgment, Obstinate, Perverse, Rashness, Temper, Unruly, Vicious, Violent, Wicked, etc.).

**ERRORS—Diet**—Errors of—(See Diet, Eating, Feasting, Food, Gluttony, Habits, Indiscretions, Intemperance).

**Mind and Judgment**—Errors of—(See Eccentric, Erratic, Erring, Judgment, Mind, Perception, Understanding, etc.).

**ERUCTATIONS**—(See Belching).

**ERUPTIONS**—A Breaking Out—A Rash —Eruptive Diseases—Exanthema—Efflorescence, etc. Eruptive diseases, and also contagious and infectious diseases, are caused principally by the ♂ influence, and by ♂ and the ☽ combinations. They are also a ♏ disease, the sign ruled by ♂; the ☽ to the ☌ ♂ by dir.; ♄ in any sign tends to draw to, and deposit wastes in the part, or parts, ruled by the sign he is in, and cause eruptions; ♃ afflicted by ♂; ♂ also tends to draw an excess of heat and blood to the part ruled by the sign he is in, and cause eruptions, abscesses, ulcers, and sores; the afflictions of ♂ tend to hot, fiery and burning eruptions; ♂ ☌ the Asc. by dir., eruptions of all kinds; ♀ in ♈ tends to eruptions on the face due to the wrong use of cosmetics; ♀ in signs which rule the arms, hands, legs, and feet tends to skin eruptions of these parts; the Asc. to the □ or ☍ ♂ by dir., if in fiery signs, pestilential eruptions; the Asc. to the □ or ☍ ♂ by dir., if in airy signs, violent eruptions; ♑ diseases, and cutaneous; Subs at KP and Local.

**All Kinds Of**—♂ ☌ the Asc. by dir.

**Arms**—Face—Hands—Legs—Feet—Eruptions In—♀ affl. in signs which rule these parts, and due to wrong habits of living and eating. (See "Eruptions" under these subjects).

**Blood**—Eruptions from Bad Blood—(See "Fevers" in this section).

**Cosmetics**—Eruptions Caused By—(See Cosmetics; "Lotions" under Face).

**Cutaneous Eruptions**—Skin Eruptions —♑ diseases. (See the various subjects under Skin).

**Death By**—(See "Eruptive Fevers" in this section).

**Eating**—(See "Arms" in this section).

**Eruptive Fevers**—Exanthematous Fevers—The ☉ or ☽ hyleg, and the ☉ to the □ or ☍ the ☽ by dir.; the ☉ affl. in ♎, from overheated blood; ♂ affl. the ☉, ☽, Asc., or his own place by dir. or tr.; ♂ ☌ or ill-asp. the ☽ at B., or by dir.; ♂ in the Asc. at B., and affl. the hyleg; ♂ occi., and affl. the hyleg by dir., brings danger of death by an eruptive fever; afflictions in ♌ or ♒, due to disordered blood; Subs at CP, KP, Local. (See "Corrupt" under Blood; Impure).

**Face**—(See Acne, Cosmetics; "Lotions" under Face; Pimples).

**Feet**—(See "Eruptions" under Feet).

**Fevers**—(See "Eruptive Fevers" in this section).

**Generative Organs**—(See "Eruptions" under Generation).

**Hands**—(See "Eruptions" under Hands).

**Hot Eruptions**—Heat Rashes—♂ the afflictor in the disease; Subs at CP and KP.

**Impure Blood**—Eruptions Caused By —(See Impure. Also see "Eruptive Fevers" in this section).

**Legs**—(See "Eruptions" under Legs).

**Pestilential Eruptions**—The Asc. to the □ or ☍ ♂ by dir., if in fiery signs. (See Pestilence).

**Violent Eruptions**—The Asc. to the □ or ☍ ♂ by dir., if in airy signs. (See "Eruptive Fevers" in this section). For further influences along the lines of Eruptions, see the following subjects in the alphabetical arrangement, —Abscesses, Acne, Aphthae, Bites, Blemishes, Blood, Blotches, Boils, Breakings Out, Carbuncles, Carcinoma, Chancre, Chancroid, Chickenpox, Contagions, Cosmetics, Dengue, Diphtheria, Eczema, Efflorescence, Epidemics, Epithelioma, Erysipelas, Exanthema, Favus, Herpes, Hives, (see Urticaria); Infections, Itch, Ivy, Lupus, Measles, Ointments, Pimples, Pox, Pruritus, Psoriasis, Purpura, Pus, Rashes, Ringworm, Roseola, Rubefacients, Sarcoma, Scabies, Scarlet Fever, Scrofula, Scurvy, Shingles, Smallpox, Sores, Stomatitis, St. Anthony's Fire (see Erysipelas); Stings, Swellings, Syphilis, Tetter; Sore Throat (see Throat); Thrush (see Apthae; Tinea, Ulcers, Urticaria, Varicella (see Chickenpox); Variola (see Smallpox); Vesicles, Zoster (see Herpes, Shingles); Zymotic. Eruptions may occur on any part of the body, and may be both external and internal, and for parts, or organs, which may not have been mentioned in this Article, look for the Part, or Subject, in the alphabetical arrangement.

**ERYSIPELAS**—St. Anthony's Fire—A ♑ disease, and afflictions in ♑; ♄ or ♂ in ♑; ♄ or ♂ in an angle, occi. of the ☉, and ori. of the ☽, and ☿ in familiarity with ♂; a ♂ disease; ♂ in ♈, ♉, ♑, or ♒; ♂ denotes death by; ♂ in ♉ or ♒ in the 6th H., and afflicted; ♂ in ♒ and affl. the ☽ or Asc., erysipelas in the lower parts; the hyleg much affl. a B. by ♂; caused by ♂ when the dominion of death is vested in him; ♂ or ☿ holding dominion at B., and in familiarity with each other, with ♂ affl. the hyleg, and elevated above the Luminaries, erysipelas is increased; cardinal signs show, and espec. afflictions in ♑; fiery signs on the Asc. or 6th H.; Subs at HP (2D), KP (11D), Local.

**Arm**—Upper Arm—Erysipelas In—♂ affl. in ♉ and the 1st face of the ♊ sign; Subs at LCP (6C), AP, KP. (See Arms).

**Death By**—Caused by ♂ when the dominion of death is vested in him.

**Extremities**—Lower Extremities—Legs—Calves—Erysipelas In—♂ in ♒ in the 6th H., and afflicted; ♂ in ♒, and affl. the ☽ or Asc.; Subs at PP, LPP. (See Calves, Legs).

**Face**—Erysipelas of—♂ affl. in ♈ or ♉, and espec. when in the 1st H.; Subs at MCP (3C), AP (7C), KP.

**Head**—(See "Face" in this section).

**Increased**—The Erysipelas Increased—(See the opening paragraph in this section).

**Legs**—(See "Extremities" in this section).

**ERYTHEMA**—Erythematous—A Superficial Blush or Redness of the Skin—A Morbid Redness—Dilated Capillaries—Usually caused by ♄ afflictions. Also may be caused by ♃ or ♀, due to congestion of blood, plethora, surfeits, etc. (See Capillaries, Congestion, Dilatation, Pellagra; "Red" under Face; Red, etc.).

**ERYTHROMELALGIA**—A Painful Affliction of the Extremeties, with Purplish Discoloration of the Parts—(See this subject under Feet).

**ESCAPE**—Escapes—

**Accidents**—Narrow Escapes From—(See "Escapes" under Accidents).

**Death**—Narrow Escapes From—Configurations which otherwise indicate early or untimely death are modified, and narrow escapes intervene if ♃ or ♀ form good asps. by ⚹ or △ to the afflicted planet, or lord of the 8th; the malefics attacking one or both Luminaries, and with the ⚹ or △ of ♃ or ♀ intervening; the ☉ affl. in the 8th H., has many narrow escapes, and is often threatened with death; ♅ ☌ ♄ in ♈, and espec. if ♅ is in the M.C., and afflicted; ♅ ☌ ☿ in ♊, ♍, ♎, or ♒, and afflicted. (See Averted).

**Prison or Bondage**—Escapes From—(See "Escapes" under Prison).

**Sick**—The Sick Will Hardly Escape—The ☉ and ☽ with malefics, or in ☌ with them, at the beginning of an illness. (See "Arguments", "Certain Death", under Death"; "Fatal Illness" under Fatal; "Death" under Fever; "Diseases" under Grievous; "Life Destroyed", "Small Hope", under Life; "Doubtful" under Recovery; "Disease" under Severe).

**Travel**—Narrow Escapes from Accident or Death In Travel—(See "Escapes" under Travel).

**Vital Fluids**—Escape of—(See "Fluid" under Vital).

**ESCHAROTIC**—(See Caustic).

**Eschar**—A Dry Slough—A Crust of Dead Tissue—♂ disorders, and caused by ♂. (See Crusts; "Tissue" under Dead; Sloughings).

**ESOPHAGUS**—(See Oesophagus).

**ETHER**—The Ether—Ethers—Ruled by ♅ and the ♒ sign. Light is transmitted by the Ether, and thru ♅ tends to adversely affect the eyes and the sight when affl. the ☉ or ☽ at B., and cause eye diseases or blindness. Electricity, which travels thru the Ether, tends to shock and injury under ♅ afflictions. It is said the Spinal Canal is filled with Ether during life, which is called the "Spinal Spirit Fire", which becomes condensed, and a fluid, when exposed to the air. (See Air, Azoth, Blindness, Electricity, Eyes, Gases; "Light Rays" under Light; Matter, Retina, Shock, Sight; "Spinal Canal" under Spine; Uranus).

**Etheric Fluid**—(See "Fluid" under Vital).

**Etheric Parts of Man**—(See Astral).

**The Drug Ether**—A typical drug of ♅. Is also classed as a drug of Neptune because of its sleep-inducing and anaesthetic effect. (See Anaesthetics).

**ETHIOPIAN**—(See "Black Skin" under Black; "Figure" under Dark; Negro).

**EUNUCHS**—♀ in an angle, configurated with ☿, and with ♄ and ♂ elevated above her, or ☍ to ♀, tends to produce Eunuchs or Hermaphrodites, or one devoid of the natural channels and vents; ♄ and ♀ in the 4th H., and afflicted. (See "Channels and Vents" under Genitals; Effeminate, Hermaphrodites; "Castration" under Testes; Virile).

**EUPATORIUM**—A typical drug of ♃. (See Jupiter).

**EUSTACHIAN TUBES**—Ruled by ♀ and the ♉ sign, and are espec. affected by the ☉ or ☽ acting thru this sign, and with afflictions in or to ♉. Also ☿ when in ♉ greatly affects the tubes, and causes disorders of when afflicted, or afflicted in the 12th H., and which may lead to deafness and ear troubles. These Tubes are affected by Subs at AT, AX, and MCP (4C). (See Catarrh; "Cervical Ganglion" under Cervical; "Deafness" under Hearing; "Diseases" under Neck; Nose).

**EVACUATIONS**—Defacation—Evacuations of various kinds from the body tend to be more free and profuse at the time of the Full Moon when the fluids of the body are at high tide, as those thru the nose, bowels, the urine, perspiration, etc. (See Faeces).

**Bloody Evacuations**—Are generally considered ♂ diseases and afflictions. (See "Bloody Discharges" under Discharges; Dysentery, Effusions, Faeces, Fistula; "Bloody Flux" under Flux; Haemoptysis, Hemorrhage, Menses; "Epistaxis" under Nose; Rectum, Sweat, Typhoid, Urine, etc.).

**Morbidly Frequent**—(See Diarrhoea).

**EVENTS**—Accidents, Calamity, Sickness, etc., are events, and are usually precipitated by the aspects and movements of the ☽, and also by progressed influences, transits, and directions over the map. The ☽ tends to bring events to pass, as she is the time marker in Human Affairs and World Conditions, and on the dial of destiny corresponds to the minute hand, while the movements of the ☉ represent the hour hand. The aspects of the ☽, Lunations, New Moons, and Eclipses, indicate the times when directions and progressed influences will culminate into action.

Events, and the time of sickness, accidents, etc., are shown by the aspects of progressed planets, transits and directions, as they affect the radical map, and thus in this way "Coming Events Cast Their Shadows Before." Obstructions and impediments can be placed in the way of the planetary influences, thus greatly diminishing their force, or preventing them altogether. Events can be altered and modified by foreknowledge of their nature, and by the use of wisdom, self-control, discretion, discrimination, will-power, spiritual attainment, mastery of the lower nature, and by ruling one's stars, conquering the Monsters of the Zodiac, etc. For this reason the Ancients instituted remedies, preventatives, preservatives, and propitiations. The time of death, injuries, accidents, and dangers, is shown by the arcs of directions to the Sig. for the event.

**Accidents**—The Event of—(See "Time" under Accidents. Also see the first part of this Article).

**Calamity**—The Event of—(See Calamity, Disgrace, Misfortune, Reversals, Ruin, Trouble, etc.).

**Coming Events**—Are indicated by aspects applying, and past events are shown by aspects separating.

**Danger**—Near Some Danger—Danger Is At Hand—(See Danger).

**Death**—The Event of Death—Time of —(See "Time of" under Death).

**Directions and Death**—(See Anareta; "Arguments for" under Death; Directions).

**Disease**—The Event of—(See "Time of" under Disease).

**Evil Events**—(See "Good and Evil" in this section).

**Good and Evil Events**—Good events are indicated by the ☽ forming favorable aspects to the Benefics, and evil events by the afflictions of the Malefics to the ☽. The ☽ ☍ ☉ by dir., and at 'the same time in □ to a malefic, indicates a very evil time in the life, illness, accidents, afflictions, reversals, and possible death, and under such a configuration a remarkably evil event usually takes place. (See "Time" under Evil).

**Great Events**—Are coincident with the appearance of Comets. (See Comets).

**Ill-Health**—The Event of—(See "Periods of Bad Health" under Health; "Long Siege of" under Ill-Health).

**Injury**—Event of—(See "Time of" under Accidents).

**Modification of Events**—(See the Introduction to this Article; Destiny, Fate, Prevention; "Free Will" under Will).

**Nature of the Events**—The ☽ in signs of human form tends to events affecting Mankind; in air signs, the Air; in earth signs, the Earth and its fruits; in water signs, the Waters and Seas; in quadrupedal or animal signs, cattle, horses, sheep, and all four-footed Beasts. (See "Air Signs" under Air;

Animals, Beasts, Cattle; "Earth Signs" under Earth; Floods, Fruits, Horses; "Human Form" under Human; Mankind, Nature, Public, Quadrupeds, Scarcity, Seas, Sheep, Ships; "Signs" under Water; Weather).

**Past Events**—(See "Coming Events" in this section).

**Prevention of Events**—(See the Introduction to this section. Also see Prevention).

**Sickness**—The Event of—(See "Ill-Health" in this section; "Time of" under Disease).

**Strange Events**—Sudden Events—Unexpected Events—The ☉ to the ill-asps. ♅ by dir.; the ☽ to the place of ♅ at B. by dir. or tr. tends to sudden ill; ♅ stationary near the place of the ☉ or ☽ at B., or in evil asp. to either; ♅ ascending at B.; the asps. of ♅ to the ☉, ☽, Asc., M.C. by dir.; the evil asps. of ♂ to the ☉, ☽, Asc., or M.C. also tend to sudden events, and generally of an evil or violent nature, as accidents or injuries. (See Extraordinary, Mysterious, Neptune, Peculiar, Strange, Sudden, Unexpected, Untimely, Uranus).

**Sudden Events**—(See "Strange" in this section).

**Time of Events**—(See the various paragraphs in this section. Also see Time).

**Unexpected Events**—(See "Strange" in this section). Life is but one succession of events from the cradle to the grave, and for subjects not mentioned here, look for the subject in the alphabetical arrangement. Especially note the following subjects,— Abroad, Accidents, Afflictions, Bereavement, Birth, Blows, Bruises, Catastrophies, Character, Climacteric, Comets, Cuts, Cycles, Danger, Death, Destiny, Directions, Disease, Disgrace, Disturbances, Drought; Earthquakes (see Earth); Eclipses, Evils, Falls, Famine, Fate, Fire, Fortune; Free Will (see Will); Hurts, Imminent, Injuries, Journeys, Judges, Lunations, Malice, Mankind, Mischief, Miseries, Misfortune; New Moon (see Moon); Murder, Periods, Prison, Prognosis, Progression, Public, Railroads, Reversals, Ruin, Scandal, Seas; Secondary Directions (see Secondary); Ships, Shipwreck, Sickness, Sorrow, Stabs, Suicide, Travel, Treachery, Trouble, Vehicles, Violence, Volcanoes, Water, Weather, Wounds, etc.

**EVIL**—Evils—Evilly—

**Absent Party**—Some Great Evil Has Overtaken the Absent Party—(See "Great Evil" under Absent Party).

**Complexion**—Evil Complexion—(See Bad, Evil, Poor, Sickly, under Complexion).

**Conduct**—Evil Conduct—Disgraceful Actions—Bad Courses—Wild Conduct —The ☉ to the ill-asps. ♀ by dir.; the ☉ Sig. □ or ☍ ♃; the ☽ Sig. in ♓, not inclined to action unless of the worst kind; the ☽ in bad asp. to ♅ does not improve the moral nature; ♄ or ♂ Sig. □ or ☍ ♀; ♂ at a Solar Rev. passing the place of the radical ☽ or ♀; ♀

Sig. in ♏, and ♀ affl. by ♄ or ♂, disgraceful actions, and with very evil propensities if ♃ or the ☉ do not assist by their good asps.; the Asc. to the ill-asps. ♀ by dir., and ♀ affl. by ♄ or ♂ at B. (See Conduct, Criminal, Cruel, Debauched, Depraved, Disgrace, Dishonest, Drink, Drunkenness, Gambling, Lewd, Licentious, Mischief; "Loose Morals" under Morals; Murderous, Perverted, Profane, Riotous, Thieving, Unnatural, Vices, Violent, Wicked, etc.).

**Deeds**—Delights In the Most Evil Deeds—(See "Conduct" in this section).

**Directions**—Evil Directions—(See Directions).

**Disease**—Evil End to the Disease—(See Death; "End" under Disease; "Evil End" under End; Fatal).

**Drink**—Evils From—(See Drink, Drunkenness, Intoxication).

**Events**—Evil Events—(See Events).

**Every Evil**—(1) Every Evil Upon Humanity—Many Evils Upon Humanity—The appearance of Comets tends to bring many evils upon Mankind, and to cause a deranged system; the Pleiades rising, or with the ☉ or ☽, or directed to the Asc., every evil that can befall Humanity; Eclipses of the ☽ in the 3rd Dec. of ♐; ♄, ♃, ♂, and the ☽ conjoined in ♌; ♏ ascending at the Vernal, and ♄ ☌ ♂ therein, and with ♃ ℞, and ♀ combust; the Ascelli conjoined with the ☉ or ☽. (See Ascelli, Calamity, Castor, Comets, Eclipses; "Public Grief" under Grief; Humanity, Mankind, Mischief, Miseries, Nebulous, Pleiades, Public; "Much Sadness" under Sadness, Sorrow, etc.). (2) Every Evil Upon the Native—♄ affl. in the 12th H. denotes every evil that can befall the native except death; the ☉ directed to the Jaw of the Whale, South Scale, Cynosura, or the Twins, tends to much evil for the native; the ☽ to the □ or ☍ ♂ by dir., every evil; the ☽ directed to the Whale's Jaw, Knees of Castor and Pollux, Belly of the Twins, or Cynosura, many evils; the M.C. to the □ or ☍ ♂ by dir., many evils; lord of the 9th H. weak, ℞, or combust, denotes great evils upon the native; the Pleiades rising, or with the ☉ or ☽, or directed to the Asc. (See Ascelli, Calamity, Castor, Cynosura, Disgrace, Honour, Pleiades, Pollux, Reverses, Ruin, Trouble, Twelfth House, Whale's Jaw).

**Evilly Disposed**—Evil Propensities—Evil Tendencies—The ☽ Sig. in ♓; ♂ Sig. ☌ or ill-asp. ♄ or ☋, and espec. in angles, the disposition is very evil, and the person often fierce and violent; ♀ Sig. in ♏, and affl. by ♄ and ♂, and no good asps. from the ☉ or ♃, very evil propensities. (See "Conduct", "Qualities", in this section).

**Excesses**—Evils From—(See Excesses).

**Habits**—(See "Evil" under Habits).

**Indicative of Evil**—The ☉ with the Pleiades, Hyades, Praesepe, the Ascelli, Castor or Pollux. (See "Every Evil" in this section).

**Influences**—Evil Influences—Evil Aspects—The evil aspects and influences in a map, as related to the health of the body and mind, are increased when augmented by the ill-asps. of the malefics, and diminished by the good asps. of the ☉, ♃, or ♀. (See Aspects, Benefics, Malefics).

**Manners**—Evil Manners—The ☽ sepr. from the ☉ and apply. to ☿ in a day geniture. (See Manners).

**Many Evils Upon Humanity**—(See "Every Evil" in this section).

**Much Evil**—Upon the Native, and Upon Humanity—(See "Every Evil" in this section).

**Nobles and Grandees**—Evil To—(See Nobles).

**Qualities of Mind**—Evil Qualities—An Evil Nature—Caused by the evil asps. of ♂ to the Sigs., the ☉, ☽, ☿, or Asc. (See "Conduct", "Evilly Disposed", in this section. Also see Malevolent).

**Serious Evils In Life**—The ☽ to the ill-asps. ♄ by dir. (See Saturn).

**Sudden Evils**—The ☉ to the ill-asps. ♅ or ♂ by dir.; ♅ weak and ill-dig. at B., or by tr. or dir. (See Sudden).

**Tendencies**—Evil Tendencies—(See "Evilly Disposed" in this section).

**Thoughts**—The Mind Disturbed by Evil Thoughts—(See "Conduct" in this section; "Unclean" under Mind).

**Time**—An Evil Time for the Native—The ☉ to the ill-asps. the ☽, ♄, ♃, ♅, or ♂ by dir.; the ☽ to the ill-asps. the ☉ by dir. (See Accidents, Affliction, Calamity, Climacteric, Dangers, Directions, Disease, Disgrace; "Good and Evil Events" under Events; "Periods of Bad Health" under Health; Honour, Ill-Health, Imprisonment (see Prison); Injury, Judges, Misery, Misfortune, Periodic, Reverses, Ruin, Scandal, Sickness, Sorrow, Suffering, Trouble; "Time" under Accidents and Disease; Unexpected, Worry, Wounds).

**EVOLUTION**—The Occult teaches that Man's Mind and Body have evolved gradually thru many stages before coming to their present efficiency. Man's early bodies were bisexed, hermaphrodites, and the separation of the sexes began in the Lemurian Epoch, and Adam and Eve are considered types of the first of the separated sexes. There are still remnants of hermaphrodites in the World to-day. Also in the early stages of the Earth, when it was hot and fiery, people could not stand upon the Earth, and their bodies were like gas bags, capable of living and floating in the air. They also had a third eye in the back of their heads so they could see approaching dangers from all sides. This eye has now been drawn inward, and is the Pineal Gland. When language was needed, and a voice, the larynx and vocal cords, ruled by the ♉ sign, were taken from ♏, the sex sign, and this is the reason why the voice and the sex organs are so closely related, and why the voice in males changes at puberty. Man's body is still far from being perfect, and is still evolving and improving, and in future Ages will be a much better, and more highly spiritualized body than now. This subject of the Evolution of Man and his Vehicles, is a big one, and only a few things can be mentioned here. If you are interested in the whole story of the Evolution of Man, and of the Earth in its various Epochs, read the books, "Cosmo-Conception", by Max Heindel, and also the book, "The Key To The Universe", by Dr. and Mrs. Homer Curtiss. These books also explain the two stories of Creation in the Bible. (See Build, Character, Larynx, Pineal Gland, Puberty; "Separation of" under Sex).

**EVOLVED TYPES**—(See Genius, Prodigies).

**EXAGGERATED**—Exaggeration—

**Exaggerated Action**—♅ influence, as in Cramps, Hernia, Ruptures, Shock, Spasms, etc. (See these subjects). The plus, or tonic action of ♂, also tends to exaggerated action of mind and body.

**Exaggerated Ego**—(See Ego).

**Exaggerated Hysteria**—(See Hysteria).

**Exaggerated Sex Desires**—(See Passion).

**EXALTATION**—

**Emotional Exaltation**—(See Ecstasy, Emotions, Religion).

**Functions**—Exalted Excito-Motory Function—With Pains and Cramps From—♂ ☌ or ill-asp. ♅. (See Cramps, Excitable, Motor, Pain).

**Mind and Body Exalted**—The good asps. of ♂ to the ☉, ☽, ☿, Asc., and the hyleg. (See Mental, Mind).

**Planets**—Exaltation of—Planets in their exalted signs have more power for good or evil in health matters, and espec. when aspecting the hyleg. Planets in their detriment, or fall, have less power for good, and also tend to be more unfortunate over the life, health, mind, and affairs of the native. (See the Tables of Exaltations, Detriment, Fall, etc., in the Textbooks of Astrology).

**EXAMINATIONS**—Fails In—Poor In Study—Loses Interest In Studies—The ☉ to the ☌ ☿ by dir., or vice versa; ☿ combust, setting in the West at B., and affl. by the ☽, and also ☿ in no good asp. to the Asc.; the ☽ to the ill-asps. ☿ by dir., loses interest in studies for the time. (See Forgetful, Learning; "Shallow" under Mentality; Reading, Study).

**EXANTHEMA** — Exanthematous—(See Efflorescence, Eruptions, Rashes).

**Fevers**—Exanthematous Fevers—(See "Eruptive Fevers" under Eruptions).

**Throat**—Exanthematous Sore Throat —(See "Exanthematous" under Throat).

**EXCELLENT**—

**Abilities**—Excellent Abilities—(See "Active Mind" under Active; Elegant, Examinations, Genius, Learning; "Quickened" under Mentality; "Good Mind" under Mind; Prodigies, Reading, Study).

**Disposition**—Excellent Disposition—Even Temper—The ☉ Sig. ⚹ or △ ♃. (See Disposition, Generous, Mild, Temper, Temperament).

**Health**—Excellent Health—(See "Abundance", "Good", under Health; Immunity, Recuperation, Resistance, Robust, Ruddy, Stamina, Strength, Strong, Tone, Vitality, etc.).

**Qualities**—Excellent Mental Qualities —Good Abilities—(See "Abilities", "Disposition", in this section).

**EXCESS**—Excessive—Excessively—Colliquative—Copious—Overflowing—Immoderate—Profuse—Redundant—♂ is excessive. ♃ is overflowing. ♀ is redundant and overflowing in quality. (See Abundance, Colliquative, Copious, Increase, Jupiter, Mars, Plenty, Profuse, Redundant, Venus).

**Acidity**—Excessive Acidity—(See Acids).

**Albumin**—Excess of In Urine—(See Albumen).

**Alkalinity**—Excess of In System—(See Alkaline).

**Animal Heat**—In the Body—Excess of—(See "Animal Heat" under Heat).

**Atmospheric Pressure** — Excessive — Disease From—(See Atmosphere, Caisson, Compressed, Gases, Pressure).

**Blood**—Excess of—(See "Too Much Blood", "Pressure", under Blood; Plethora; "Fullness" under Vascular).

**Cold**—Excess of—Caused by ♄. (See Cold; "Lack of Animal Heat" under Heat; Saturn; "Cold" under Weather).

**Colliquative Sweats**—Excessive Sweats of Phthisis—(See "Night Sweats" under Phthisis).

**Corpulence**—Excess of—(See Corpulence, Fat, Obesity).

**Discharges**—Excessive—(See Discharges).

**Dryness**—Excess of—(See Drought; "Excess" under Dryness; Famine, Fountains, Scarcity).

**Fat**—Excess of—(See Fat, Obesity).

**Fever**—Excessive—(See "High Fever" under Fever).

**Fluids**—Excess of—(See Puffing).

**Force**—Excess of—(See "Excess" under Force).

**Functions**—(See Discomfort; "Excessive" under Functions).

**Growth**—Excessive—(See Enlarged, Giants, Growth, Large).

**Heat**—Excess of In the Body—Excessive Heat—(See "Excessive Bodily Heat", "Extreme Heat", "Overabundance", "Warm Weather", under Heat).

**Menses**—Excessive and Copious—(See Menses).

**Mental Action**—Excessive—(See "Over-active Mind" under Active).

**Nervous Action**—Excessive—☿ affl. in the 6th H. (See Erethism, Excitable; "Neurotic" under Nerves).

**Neurotic Action**—Excessive—(See "Highly Neurotic" under Nerves).

**Passion**—Excess of—(See "Passional Excesses" under Passion).

**Phlegm**—Excess of—(See Phlegm).

**Phthisis**—Excessive Sweats of—(See "Night Sweats" under Phthisis).

**Pleasure**—Excessive Pleasure, and Diseases From—(See Pleasure).

**Saliva**—Excess of—(See Saliva).

**Sensibility** — Excessive Sensibility— (See Hyperaesthesia).

**Sugar**—Excess of In Urine—(See Diabetes).

**Sweat** — Excess of — (See "Night Sweats" under Phthisis; Sweat).

**Urates**—Excess of—(See Urates).

**Urea**—(See "Excess" under Urea).

**Uric Acid**—Excess of—(See Deposits, Lithemia, Uric).

**Urine** — Excess of — (See Diabetes; "Excess", "Polyuria", under Urine).

**Virile Members** — Excessive — (See Virile).

**Vitality**—Excess of—(See "Excess" under Vitality).

**Voluntary Power**—Excess of — (See Voluntary). For further study see Abnormalities, Colds, Concretions, Deposits, Diarrhoea, Dropsies, Dysentery, Effusions, Enlarged, Expanded, Excesses, Expectoration, Excitable, Extreme, Evacuations, Flow, Fluids, Fluxes, Full, Gas, Growths,, Hemorrhage, Hermaphrodite, Humours, Hydrocephalus, Hyper (the various subjects beginning with "Hyper"); Juices, Malformations, Moisture, Monsters; "Coryza" under Nose; Over (the various subjects beginning with "Over"); Plethora, Prudence, Pseudo, Rain, Rheum, Secretions, Super (the various subjects beginning with "Super"); Surfeits, Swellings, Tears, Tumors, Wastes, Water, Wind, etc.

**EXCESSES**—Overindulgences—Extravagance—Luxuries — Indiscretions — Carelessness—Inordinate—Free Living —etc.—♂ is excessive in nature, and his afflictions tend to excesses, and espec. along passional lines. They are also the outcome of ♃ or ♀ afflictions, or afflictions to the ☉, ☽, and Asc. Jupiter is overflowing in action. Many maps of birth are unbalanced, full of adverse aspects, and when the lower mind is ruling and dominating, tend to many extremes, excesses, and perversions. The subject of Excesses is a large one, and would be too lengthy to list every known excess in this Article. The following subjects and references are a partial list, and suggestive, and for subjects not listed or mentioned here, look in the alphabetical arrangement for the subject you have in mind.

**Acoholic Excesses** — (See Alcohol, Drink, etc.).

**Amorous Indulgence**—Excess of— (See Amourous).

**Appetites**—Goes to Excesses to Gratify—(See Appetites).

**Blood Disorders**—Thru Excesses— (See "Diseases" in this section).

**Death**—Thru Excesses—(See "Causes His Own Death", and the various paragraphs under Death).

**Degeneration**—Thru Excesses—(See Degeneration).

**Diet**—Food—Ailments from Excesses and Indiscretions in—(See Diet, Eating, Food, Gluttony, etc.).

**Diseases**—Proceeding from Excesses —The ☉ affl. by ♀; the ☽ in water signs, to the ♂ or ill-asp. ♂ by dir.; the ☽ in ♓, and affl. by the ☉ or ♂ when taken ill (Hor'y); ♃ diseases; ♃ affl. in the Asc., or 6th H.; ♃ affl. in ♒, blood disorders thru excesses; ♂ affl. in ♓; ♀ diseases; ♀ affl. in ♏; ♀ affl. by ♂; ♀ affl. in the Asc. or 6th H.; the Asc. affl. by ♃ or ♀; the Asc. to the ill-asps. ♀ by dir., and ♀ affl. at B.; ♌ on cusp of 6th H.; the 11° □ on the Asc.; the 1st Dec. ♏ on the Asc., which is ruled by ♂. (See "Corrupt" under Blood; Carelessness, Cramps; "Causes His Own Death" under Death; Debauchery; "Brings Disease Upon Himself" under Disease; Dissipation, Eating, Extravagances, Gout, High Living (see High); Indigestion, Indiscretions, Indulgence, Obesity, Plethora, Rheumatism, Sex Diseases (see Passion, Sex); Sickness, Surfeits, Vitality Lessened, etc.). The afflictions arising from excesses, irregularities, indulgence of the animal appetites, etc., are legion, and tend to bring disease, death, and suffering upon humanity. Look for further subjects in the alphabetical arrangement.

**Drink**—Excesses In—(See Delirium Tremens, Drink, Drunkenness, Intoxication, etc.).

**Drugs**—Excesses In Drug Taking, Narcotics, etc.—(See Narcotics).

**Early Death**—Thru Excesses and Dissipation—(See "Early Death" under Early).

**Eating**—Excesses and Indiscretions In—(See Diet, Eating).

**Exercise** — Excesses In—Disorders Arising From (See Exercise, Sports).

**Fevers** — From Excesses — (See "Slight" under Fevers).

**Food**—Excesses In—(See Diet, Eating, Indiscretions).

**Genitals**—Diseases of Thru Sex Excesses — (See "Diseases" under Genitals).

**Indulging In Excesses**—Prone To— The prog. ☉ or ☽ to the ♂ or ill-asp. ♂; the ☽ in ♋ or ♓, and affl. by the ☉ or ♂; the ☽ to the ill-asps. ♃, ♀, or ♂ by dir.; ♂ Sig. □ or ☍ ♀; characteristic of ♂ people; ♂ affl. in ♓; ♀ weak and affl. at B.; ♀ affl. in ♏; ♀ Sig. □ or ☍ ♂; ♀ lady of the year at the Vernal Equi., and espec. when ♀ is ruler, and affl. at B.; the Asc. to the ill-asps. ♀ by dir., and ♀ affl. at B.; ♌ on the cusp of 6th H.; 1st Dec. ♏ on the Asc., which is ruled by ♂; 11° □ or 6° ♋ on the Asc. (See "Noises" under Head. Also note the various paragraphs in this section).

**Love Affairs**—Excesses In—(See Amorous; "Free Love" under Free; Intercourse, Love Affairs, Opposite Sex; "Passional Excesses" under Passion; "Clandestine" under Sex; Venery).

**Passional Excesses** — (See Amorous; "Passional Excesses" under Passion; Venery, etc.).

**Sex Excesses**—(See "Love Affairs", "Passional Excesses", in this section; "Early Death" under Early; "Dies Before Middle Life" under Middle Life).

**Sickness**—From Excesses—(See "Diseases" in this section).

**Slight Disorders**—Thru Excesses—(See Indiscretions, Mild, Slight).

**Stomach Disorders**—Thru Excesses—The ☽ in ♋ and affl. by the ☉ or ♂ when taken ill (Hor'y). (See Drink, Eating, Indigestion; "Riotous Living" under Riotous; Stomach).

**Study**—And Reading—Disorders from Excesses In—(See "Brain Fag" under Brain; "Eyestrain" under Eyes; Blindness, Reading, Study). For further study along the lines of Excesses, see the following subjects, and also various other subjects which occur to your mind, and which may not be listed or mentioned in this Article,—Abnormalities, Anger; "Animal Instincts" under Animal; Bad; "Lack of Balance" under Balance; Beastly; "High Pressure", "Too Much Blood", under Blood; Carelessness, Cohabitation, Conduct, Criminal, Debased, Decay, Degenerate, Depraved, Deviations, Disgrace, Dissolute, Dress, Dropsy, Energies, Epicureans, Evils, Extravagance, Feasting, Folly, Free Living (see Free); Frenzy, Fury, Gluttony, Gratification, Habits, Harlots, Heart, Headaches, Ill-Health, Improvident, Impure, Indecent, Indiscretions, Infamous, Infirmities, Inordinate, Insanity, Intemperate, Irregularities, Lascivious, Lewd, Licentious, Lust, Luxuries, Madness, Mania, Men, Morals, Noises, Nymphomania; "Over-Indulgence" under Over; Perversions, Pleasures, Prodigal, Rashness, Recklessness, Scandal; "Self-Indulgent", "Self-Undoing", under Self; Sensuality; "Sex Relations" under Sex; Shameless; "High Temper" under Temper; Tumors, Vices, Vicious, Vile, Violent, Vital Forces (see Vital); Wanton, Wasting, Wicked, Women, etc.

**EXCISION**—Of the Foetus—(See "Excision" under Foetus).

**EXCITABLE**—Excitement—Excitation

**Beside Oneself**—Caused by the afflictions of ♆. Excitement, religious or otherwise, and where Frenzy is apt to accompany. Mostly manifested in emotional religious experiences, which are ruled by ♆, the ruler of the Spiritual Faculties. (See Ecstasy, Emotions, Frenzy, Hysteria, Neptune, Religion).

**Body and Mind**—Excitation of—♂ influence. (See the different paragraphs in this section).

**Cellular Excitation**—(See "Excitation" under Cells).

**Excitable**—High Nervous Tension—High Strung—The ☉ or ☽ in fiery signs, ☌, □, or ☍ ♂; ♆ in a prominent position at B., and affl. the ☽ or ☿, tends to paroxysms of nervous excitation; ♆ affl. in the 3rd or 9th H., or ♆ rising; ♅ or ♂ affl. ☿ tend to high nervous tension, nervous excitability, and an excited manner in speaking; ♃ affl. in ♍; ♂ in ♈, highly excitable; ♂ ☌, □, or ☍ ☿; ☿ influence is excitable,

nervous, quivering, and tends to ceaseless motion; ☿ ill-dig. at B., frantic and excessively excitable, and espec. when affl. by ♂; ♈, ♌, and ♐ are the most excitable signs, and the earthy and airy signs the least; along emotional and sensational lines, the watery signs are excitable; characteristic of the Choleric, or Bilious Temperament, which is ruled by the ☉, ♂, and the fiery signs. (See Choleric; "High Strung" under High; "Neurasthenia" and "Highly Neurotic" under Nerves. Also see "Nerves" in this section).

**Exhaustion**—Nervous Exhaustion from Too Much Excitement—☿ ☌, □, ☍ ♂ at B., or by dir.; Subs at AT, AX, CP (5D), and PP. (See Exhaustion, Fatigue; "Neurasthenia" under Nerves).

**Function**—Exalted Excito-Motory Function—(See "Functions" under Exaltation).

**Hasty and Excitable**—The ☉, ☽, and many planets in fiery signs; the ☉ or ☽ ☌ ♂; ♂ in the Asc., or M.C., and affl. the ☉ or ☽; fiery signs upon the Asc. (See "Excitable" in this section. Also see Rashness, Recklessness).

**High Strung**—(See "Excitable" in this section).

**Ill-Health**—From Over-Excitement—The ☉ affl. in ♈. (See the various paragraphs and references in this section).

**Involuntary**—Involuntary Muscular Excitement—(See "Involuntary" under Muscles).

**Mental Excitement**—A ☿ disturbance; caused by ♂ afflictions to the ☉, ☽, or ☿, or ♂ in the Asc. or M.C., and in one of his strong signs; malefics in the 1st H. at a Solar Rev. (See the various paragraphs in this section. Also see Anger, Choleric; "High Temper" under Temper).

**Mind**—Excitation of Body and Mind—Excitable Mind—♂ influence. (See "Excitable", "Mental", in this section).

**Muscles**—Involuntary Excitement of —(See "Involuntary" under Muscles).

**Nature**—Disposition—An Excitable Nature—(See "Excitable" in this section).

**Nerves**—Nerve Centers—Nervous Excitation—Paroxysms of Nervous Excitement—Neurotic Excitement, etc.— ♆ in a prominent position, or affl. the ☽ or ☿, tends to paroxysms of nervous excitation, and which is often followed by complete collapse; ♆ a strong influence at B., and afflicted; also a ♅ disease; ☿ affl. by ♅ or ♂; ☿ afflicted tends to nervous diseases arising from excitement. (See "Excitable" in this section. Also see Collapse, Erethism; "Centers", "Highly Neurotic", "Neurasthenia", "Prostration", under Nerves).

**Over-Excitement**—Ill-Health From—(See "Ill-Health" in this section).

**Paroxysms**—Of Nervous Excitation—(See "Excitable" in this section).

**Reflected Excitement**—A ☿ disease. (See Reflected).

**Religious Excitement**—Religious Frenzy—♆ tends to produce, and ♆ afflicted, as by ♅ or ♂, as ♆ rules the Spiritual Faculties, and tends to Religious Frenzy, Ecstasy, etc. (See "Beside Oneself", "Excitable", in this section. Also see Emotions, Frenzy; "Religious Mania" under Mania; "Ecstasy" under Religion). For further study along these lines see Action; "Over-Active Mind" under Active; "Brain Storms" under Brain; Demoniac, Dispersions, Effervescent, Erratic, Exaggerated, Exaltation, Explosive, Fierce, Foolhardy, Fury, Hasty, Impulses, Insanity, Irritable, Jealousy, Jerky, Madness, Mania, Motion; "Nerves" under Motor; Murderous; "Strain" under Nerves; "Psychic Storms" under Psychic; Quarrelsome, Quivering, Savage, Sensational, Spasmodic, Temper, Tension, Trembling, Uncontrolled, Vicious, Violent, Wild.

**EXCORIATIONS**—An Abrasion of the Epidermis—(See Abrasions).

**EXCREMENT**—(See Excretion).

**EXCRESCENCES**—An Abnormal Outgrowth on the Body—Malefics in angles, and the ☉ or ☽ in ☌ or ☍, or brought up to them; the ☽ in obnoxious signs, as ♈, ♉, ♋, ♏, or ♑, in her nodes, or in extreme Lat., and the malefics brought up to the Luminaries, then the body is afflicted with excrescences, lameness, or paralysis. The calamity takes place from the moment of birth if the malefics be with the ☉ or ☽, but if the malefics be in the 10th H., and elevated above the Luminaries, or in ☍ to each other, then the trouble arises from falls from heights, attacks by robbers or quadrupeds, or by some dangerous accident. (See Distortions).

**Head**—Excrescences of—♈ or ♎ on the Asc., and the ☽ therein and afflicted; cardinal signs on the angles; many planets in cardinal signs, and espec. in ♈ or ♎. (See "Excrescences", "Malformation", under Head. Also see "Skull" in this section).

**Moment of Birth**—Excrescences From—(See the first part of this section).

**Skull**—And Head—Soft, Watery, Hemispherical Excrescences on the Skull and Head—Case—See "Short Life", No. 778, in 1001 N.N. This case is also commented upon in Daath's Medical Astrology, Chap. 14, page 104. (See "Head" in this section. Also see Skull). For further study see "Moment of Birth" under Calamity; Fungus, Growths, Tubercles, Warts, Wens).

**EXCRETION**—Excretory System—Organs of Excretion—Emunctory Ducts and Organs—Excrement, etc.—Excretion is a function of the ♏ sign. The internal Excretory System is under the internal rulership of ♏. The Excretory Processes of the body are ruled by ♏ in general. Excretion in and from the kidneys is ruled by ♏. The lower excretory bowels are ruled by ♏. The Excrementitious Fluids, such as the Menses, Sweat, Urine, etc., are ruled by ♏. Also ♏ rules the principal excretory orifices, as the Nose, Rectum, Urethra, Vagina, etc. The Ears, and excretions from, are ruled by ♉. The Skin as an organ of excretion is ruled by ♑. The Faeces are ruled by ♄ and ♏.

**Discharges**—The Excretory Discharges—(See Discharges, Expulsion, Faeces, Menses, Sweat, Urine, etc.).

**Disorders**—Of the Excretory System—The malefics, or afflicting planets, in the fixed signs, and espec. in ♉ or ♏; the ☉ affl. in ♏ tends to disorders of a violent or inflammatory nature; afflictions in ♏, or ♏ on the Asc., and afflicted; ♉ on the Asc., by reflex action; ♉, ♌, or ♏ on cusp the 6th H.

**Drugs**—Alteratives—Drugs which Alter the Process of Excretion—(See Alterative).

**Fluids**—Excrementitious Fluids—Ruled by ♏, such as the Menses, Sweat, Urine, Wastes, etc. (See these subjects).

**Obstructions Of**—The afflictions of ♄ tend to obstruct the excretions, and to make it more difficult for waste food products to pass the kidneys, colon, skin and other avenues of outlet, thus accumulating obstructions in the organs of excretion. The avenues of escape being gradually checked, the poisons and wastes of the body are shut in, leading to stone, decay, decrepitude and death. (See Aches, Bowels, Concretions, Decay, Deposits, Elimination, Fluids, Functions, Gravel, Kidneys, Minerals, Obstructions, Sand, Secretions, Skin, Stone, Uric Acid (see Uric); Wastes, etc.).

**Sensitive Excretory Organs**—♏ on the Asc.

**Strain**—♅ in ♏ warns against overstraining the Excretory System.

**EXECRATED**—Cursed by the Multitude—♃ Sig. □ or ☍ the ☽; the 19° ♏ on the Asc. at B., lives a cursed life, a terror and pest to Society, acquaintances, or relatives. (See Acquaintances, Execution, Friends, Hatred, Infamous, Public, Relations, Society, etc.).

**EXECUTION**—Death By—(See Beheaded; "Stake" under Burns; "Electrocution" under Electricity; Guillotine, Hanging, Ignoble, Impalement, Judges, Lynched, Mobs, Murder; "Public Death" under Public; "Flying Stones" under Stones; Tragical, etc.). Cases of Execution—See "Savonarola", No. 459; "Pressed to Death", No. 626; "Princess", No. 697; "Horsford", No. 764, all in 1001 N.N.

**EXERCISE**—Exercises—Pastimes—Athletics—Recreations—Sports, etc.—The ♐ sign bears strong rule over Exercise, Sports, Athletics, Out-door Life, Horseback Riding, Games, Fishing, Hunting, etc.

**Blindness**—Injury During Sports or Exercise, Resulting In Blindness—(See "Sports" under Blindness).

**Blood Overheated**—Thru Sports and Violent Exercise—♃ affl. in ♐.

**Colds**—Cold taken after Over-Exertion, or Over-Exercise of Mind and Body—The ☽ in ♐, ☌ or ill-asp. ♄ (or ☿ if he be of the nature of ♄) at the time. (See Colds).

**Death**—From Accidents in Sports, or after Violent Exercise—(See "Death" under Sports; "Early Death" under Early. Also see Case, "Early Death", No. 428, in 1001 N.N.).

**Eyes**—Injury to the Eyes During Exercise, Athletics, or Sports—Afflictions in ♐; the ☉ in an angle, ☌ or ☍ the ☽, and also ♂ configurated with ☿; the ☉ directed to Praesepe, Hyades, Pleiades, Castor, Pollux, and other stars of the nature of ♂ and the ☽ combined, and espec. if Praesepe be on the Asc., or with the ☉ or ☽ in an angle; the ☽ ☌ ♂ with the Pleiades, and ♄ with Regulus. (See "Amusements", "Sports", under Blindness; "Accidents" under Eyes).

**Falls**—(See "Sports" under Falls).

**Fatigue**—Fatigue or Disease from Over-Exercise—(See "Inordinate" in this section; "Exercise" under Fatigue).

**Fond of Exercise**—Partial to Exercise and Recreations—♃ Sig. in ♎ or ♐. (See Amusements, Pleasures, Recreations, Sports).

**Injuries**—During Exercise or Sports, and in Riding, Hunting, etc.—Afflictions in ♐. (See Hunting, Riding; "Injuries" under Sports).

**Inordinate Exercise**—Over-Exercise—Violent Exercise—Fatigue, Disease or Ill-Health From—The ☽ in ♐ at the time, and also at B., and affl. by the ☉ or ♂, or by ♄ (or ☿ if he be of the nature of ♄); ♄ in ♐ at B., or by dir., warns against over-strain and over-exertion of the body in sports; ♄ in the heart sign ♌, and also in the opposite sign ♒, tends to make physical strain harmful. (See "Over-Exertion" under Exertion; Strain).

**Intemperate**—In Exercise and Sports—♐ diseases, and afflictions in ♐. (See "Inordinate" in this section; "Over-Exertion" under Exertion; Intemperate, Indiscretions; "Intemperate" under Sports).

**Lack of Exercise**—Sedentary Habits—Inclined to Take Little or No Exercise—Caused by ♄ influence; ♄ ruler at B.; characteristic of ♄ people; the ☽ also rules sedentary habits, and espec. when ♂ is weak at B. and not favorably aspecting the ☉ or ☽; ♃ □ or ☍ the ☉ at B., and by dir.; ♀ weak and affl. at B. (See Obesity, Sedentary, Tumors).

**Mind**—Over-Exercise of the Mind, and with Fatigue or Illness From—(See "Over-Active Mind" under Active; "Reading and Study" under Blindness; "Brain-Fag" under Brain; Fatigue, Reading, Study).

**Out-Door Exercise**—Fond of—(See "Out-Door" under Sports).

**Over-Exercise**—(See "Inordinate" in this section).

**Over-Heated Blood**—(See "Blood" in this section).

**Sedentary Habits**—(See "Lack of Exercise" in this section).

**Sports**—Over-Exercise In—Indiscretions In—(See "Inordinate", "Intemperate", in this section. Also see the various paragraphs under Sports).

**Travel**—Over-Exercise In, and Fatigue or Sickness—(See "Fatigue" in this section; "Sickness" under Travel).

**Walking**—A Fondness For—(See Pedestrianism).

**Wrestling**—A Champion Wrestler—Case—(See Athletics).

**EXERTION**—Mars is called the planet of dynamic energy, and of exertion. (See Action, Active, Energy; "Mars Influence" under Mars). The ☉ is also much of the nature of ♂ as regards exertion. The ☉ and many planets in fiery signs, or these signs upon the Asc., tend to greater activity and exertion, and apt to go to extremes. The watery signs tend to inaction, and espec. ♓, and less of exertion of body and mind. (See "Active Body", "Active Mind", under Active; Dull, Inactive, Inertia, Motion, Quick).

**Blindness**—From Mental Exertion—From Over-Study, Reading, Eyestrain, etc.—(See "Mental Exertion", "Over-Study", "Reading and Study", "Total", under Blindness; "Eyestrain" under Eyes).

**Over-Exertion**—Illness from Over-Exertion of Mind and Body—From Too Much Toil of Mind and Body—The ☽ in ♐, ☌, P, □ or ☍ ♄ (or ☿ if he be of the nature of ♄) at the beginning of an illness, or at decumb. (Hor'y). (See "Disease" under Cares; "Colds", "Inordinate", under Exercise; "Mind" under Fatigue).

**Sickly**—Too Sickly To Make Much Exertion—♀ Sig. ☌ ☉. (See Decrepitude, Dull, Feeble, Infirm, Invalids, Lassitude, Lethargy, Listless, Sickly, Vitality Low; "Weak Body" under Weak, etc.).

**EXHAUSTION**—Great Loss of Vital Power—The same influences which tend to low vitality, weak recuperative powers, low resistance to disease, etc., tend to exhaustion, fatigue, feebleness, debility, decrepitude, infirmity, ill-health, sickly body, weak body, etc. (See these subjects).

**Brain**—Exhaustion of—(See "Exhaustion" under Brain).

**Coughing**—Exhausting Paroxysms of—(See "Convulsive" under Cough).

**Heart**—Exhaustion of—(See "Exhaustion", "Weak", under Heart).

**Nervous Exhaustion**—(See "Exhaustion" under Excitement; "Exhaustion", "Neurasthenia", "Prostration", under Nerves. Also see Breakdown, Collapse, Debility, Depletion, Feeble, Prostration, Weak).

**Vital Powers**—Exhaustion of—(See "Depletion", "Loss Of", "Waste Of", under Vital; "Lessened", "Lowered", "Wasted", "Weakened", under Vitality).

**EXHIBITION**—Exhibitionism—

**Maladies**—Public Exhibition of—Begging—Complaining of—Murmuring—♄ evilly configurated with the benefics at B.; ♄ angular, ori., and elevated above the benefics, and entering into the configuration which produces the disease, hurt, or infirmity; ☿ entering into the configuration, they will exhibit for support, and beg from door to door; many planets in bicorporeal signs tend to complaining, murmuring, lamentations, repining, etc.; the ☽ Sig. □ or ☍ ♄, or vice versa. (See Complaining, Conspicuous, Incurable, Lamentation, Murmuring, Repining).

**Sex Organs**—Exhibition of—Exhibitionism—Public Exposure of the Sex Organs—(See Harlots, Immodest, Infamous, Lewd; "Licentious" under Men; Nakedness, Notoriety, Obscene, Perversions, Shameless).

**EXILE**—Banishment—Ruled by the 12th H.; malefics in the 12th; the ☽ sepr. from ♃ and applying to the ☉, and espec. if the ☽ be in ♈, ♏, ♑, or ♒, may become an exile; also ruled by ♆. (See Banishment, Captive, Prison, Twelfth House).

**EXOPATHIC**—(See External).

**EXOPHTHALMIC GOITER**—Exophthalmos—(See "Goggle Eyes" under Eyeballs; Goiter).

**EXOSMOSIS**—Under the rule of ♀. (See Osmosis).

**EXOSTOSIS**—An Abnormal Outgrowth of Bone—(See "Bones of Arm" under Arms).

**EXPANSION**—Increase in Size or Volume—The ☉, ♃, and ♂ exert an expansive influence over the body, while ♆, ♅, and ♄ are contractive.

**Bodily Tissues**—Expansion of—Produced by the positive and electric planets, the ☉, ♃, and ♂.

**Chest Expansion**—Capacious Chest—(See "Capacity" under Lungs). See Contraction, Dropsies, Enlargement, Flatulence, Functions, Gas, Growth, Growths, Hypertrophy, Prominent, Swellings, Tumors, Tympanites, Veins, Vessels, etc.

**EXPECTATION OF LIFE**—(See the various paragraphs under Death; "Duration" under Life).

**EXPECTORATION**—Spitting—Hawking—Coughing—

**Blood**—Expectoration of—(See Haemoptysis).

**Mucus**—Phlegm—Great Expectoration of—(See Mucus, Phlegm).

**EXPENSE**—Expensive Habits—Prodigal of Expense—(See Dress, Extravagant, Food, Habits, High Living (see High); Prodigal; "Riotous Living" under Riotous).

**Expensive Food**—Love of Rich and Expensive Food, and with Disease Resulting From—Fond of Dainty Foods—(See "Dainty", "Rich", under Food. Also see Diet, Epicureans, Feasting, Indigestion, Indiscretions, Luxuries, Plethora, Surfeits).

**EXPIRATION**—Expelling of the Breath—Death—Termination—(See "Exhalation" under Breath; "Close of Life" under Close; Death, End, Fourth House, Terminal, Termination, Time).

**EXPLOSIONS**—Explosives—Explosive—♅ rules Explosives, and the chemical changes in them. (See Chemical). ♅ and ♂ are explosive in nature.

**Accidents By**—♅ causes accidents by explosions, and thru machinery.

**Anger**—Explosive Anger—♅ ☌, □, or ☍ ♂. (See Anger).

**Blindness**—By Explosions—Caused by ♂; the ☽ in the 1st, 4th, or 7th H.,

decr. in light, and affl. by ♂, and espec. if the ☽ be near Nebulous Stars. (See Blindness).

**Causes of Explosions**—Danger of—Injury or Death Resulting From—Caused principally by ♅, and due to nitrogen, a highly explosive and unstable base with ♅ characteristics; ♅ to the P., □, or ☍ the ☉ or ☽ by dir.; ♅ affl. in the 8th H. indicates sudden death from an explosion, and espec. when affl. the hyleg; ♅ affl. the hyleg by dir.; ♅ or ♃ affl. by ♂; ♅ affl. in ♏; the Prog. ☉ or ☽ to the □ or ☍ ♂ or ♅; ♂ disposes to, and is explosive; ♂ Prog. to the ☌ or ill-asp. ♅, or vice versa; the Asc. affl. by ♅ at B., and by dir.; the Asc. to the ☌ or ill-asp. ♅ by dir.; the M.C. to the ☌ ♅ by dir., or vice versa. (See Chemical, Ether, Gases, Machinery, Mars, Nitrogen, Uranus).

**Death By**—♅ affl. in ♏ or the 8th H. at B., and by dir.; ♅ in the 8th H. at B., and affl. the hyleg by dir., and other testimonies concurring for a violent death; ♅ or ♂ affl. the hyleg by dir.; ♂ disposes to.

**Killed**—By An Explosion—Case—See "Died In Harness", No. 800, in 1001 N.N.

**Manner**—Explosive Manner—♅ and ♂ afflictions, and espec. in ill-asp. to the ☽ or ☿; afflictions in fixed signs, and espec. to the ☽ or ☿ in a fixed sign. (See "Explosive" under Manner).

**Ships**—Explosions On—♅ and ♂ ascending, and affl. the ☉, ☽, or Asc. when the ship sails, or these places in the ship's map. (See Ships, Shipwreck).

**EXPOSURE**—Exposure to Cold, Dampness, and the Elements—

**Cold and Dampness**—Diseases and Illness from Sudden Exposure To—Caused by ♅ afflictions to the hyleg, or to the ☉, ☽, or Asc. by dir.; ♄ in ♈, complaints due to cold and exposure; ♄ in ♉, all disorders arising from exposure and cold. (See Bathing, Climate; "Exposure" under Cold, Moisture, Weather; "Clothing" under Colds; Elements, External; "Cold Taken" under Feet; "Cold and Moisture" under Moisture; "Linen" under Wet).

**Fond of Exposures**—(See "Fond Of" under Danger).

**The Elements**—Illness Thru Exposure To—♄ in the 6th H., and affl. the hyleg. (See Elements).

**Travel**—Journeys—The Health Suffers from Exposure In Travel—♄ in the 3rd or 9th H., and affl. the ☉, ☽, Asc., or hyleg. (See "Wet" under Journeys; "Exposure" under Travel).

**EXPRESSION**—The Predominating Facial Expression—The Countenance—The Look—Gestures—Speech—Voice Expression—Expression of the Eyes, etc.—This subject is largely considered under the subjects of Appearance, Aspect, Countenance, Eyes, Face, Features, Gesticulation, Glances, Look, Speech, Voice, etc. Also note the following subjects and references.

**Difficult Expression**—A Very Marked Expression, and One Difficult to Gauge—♅ rising in the Asc.

**Full of Expression**—The Countenance Full of Expression and Vivacity—The ☽ Sig. in ♎; ♂ in ♎. (See Smiles).

**Impulsive Expression**—Hasty Impulses—Ill-Health By—The ☉ affl. in ♈. (See Impulses).

**Marked Expression**— (See "Difficult" in this section).

**Much Expression**—♃ Sig. in ♐.

**Pleasing Expression**— (See "Face" under Pleasant).

**Sad Expression**—♄ in ♋. (See Gloom, Melancholy, Sad).

**Sex Expression**— Freedom of — (See "Freedom" under Sex). For further influences along this line see Amorous, Animal, Austere, Bold, Cheerful, Commanding, Cruel, Effeminate, Fierce, Fiery, Grave, Harmless, Idiotic, Indifferent, Intellectual, Intemperate, Kind, Lips, Lustful, Melancholic, Mouth, Negative, Nose, Peaceful, Pensive, Piercing, Pleasant, Positive, Refined, Resolute, Savage, Sensual, Serious, Severe, Sharp, Sickly, Smiles, Sorrowful, Stern, Sympathetic, Thoughtful, Troubled, Wanton, Wicked.

**EXPULSION**—Expulsive—The ☽ represents the expulsive and natural forces over the body. (See "Influence of Moon" under Moon; "Natural Forces" under Natural).

**Wastes**—Expulsion of—Ruled by the ☽. (See Elimination, Emetics, Excretion, Faeces, Peristalsis, Urine, Vomiting, Wastes).

**EXTERNAL** — Externally — Exterior — Exopathic — Exoteric — Outside Influences Over the Mind and Body—Environment — Climate — Location — Associations, etc.—The Asc. denotes the part of the body more liable to affliction from external causes. The sign on the Asc. at B. rules a part, or organ, externally, internally, and structurally. The fiery and airy signs on the Asc. give stronger physical bodies, and less liable to external disorders. The earthy and watery signs rising make the native more liable, receptive, and susceptible to outside influences, and give a weaker constitution. The watery signs espec. give too much receptivity to outside influences, and make the native more liable to infectious and contagious diseases. The ♏ sign gives greater magnetic and attractive powers, and makes one more liable to attract diseases, or impure magnetism, from the outside. The ♋ sign on the Asc. at B. gives much receptivity to external conditions. When the 4th face of ♑ is on the Asc. at B., the native is much affected by others. Acquired tendencies are denoted by the ☽, and diseases and afflictions which come from external causes, such as climate, habits, clothing, food, etc. Man in his pilgrimage upon the Earth Plane is constantly battling with external conditions, the elements, the forces about him, which he must conquer, use for his own purposes and development, or be overcome by them, and nearly every subject in this Work has some reference to Man's external conditions, his relation to them, and their effects upon

him. There are causes from within affecting man, called innate, inherited, organic and structural disorders of the body, and also mental afflictions, etc. Look in the alphabetical arrangement for the subject you have in mind if it is not listed or mentioned here. Also see the following subjects,— Abroad, Accidents, Acquired, Air, Attracts, Blows, Climate, Clothing, Cold, Colds, Confinement, Contagious, Dangers, Death, Disease, Earth, Elements, Enemies, Environment, Epidemics, Family, Fate, Fire, Food, Friends, Habits, Hurts, Imprisonment (see Prison); Infections, Injuries, Journeys, Location, Magnetism, Marriage, Men, Native Land (see Native); Negative, Passive, Place of Birth (see Place); Positive, Public, Quarrels, Receptivity, Resistance, Residence, Sensation, Social Relations (see Social); Susceptible, Tendencies, Travel, Water, Women, Wounds, etc.

**Blemishes**—External Blemishes—(See Blemishes).

**Cold**—Externally Cold, and With Internal Heats— (See Constrictions; "Internal Heats" under Heat).

**Complaints** — External — (See "Disorders" in this section).

**Congestions** — External Congestion— (See Centrifugal, Centripetal, Cold, Colds, Congestion, Constrictions; "Internal Heats" under Heat; Rubefacients, Skin Diseases).

**Disorders**—External Disorders— Those originating outside the mind or body, and which do not originate in the mind or body—(See the first part of this section, and the references. Also the paragraphs in this Article).

**Generative Organs**—The External Generative Organs—(See "External" under Genitals).

**Heat**— External Heat—Much External and Internal Heat—(See "External" under Heat).

**Hemorrhages** — External Hemorrhages—(See "External" under Hemorrhage).

**Humoural Secretions**— (See "External" under Humours).

**Signs of Zodiac**—External and Internal Rulership of the Signs Over the Various Parts and Organs of the Body —(See "External" under Signs of the Zodiac. Also see each of the Signs in the alphabetical arrangement).

**Stomach**— External Lining of — (See Stomach).

**Urinary Organs**—External Urinary Organs—(See Urine).

**EXTRAORDINARY**—Unusual—Uncommon—Remarkable—Strange—Singular —Curious—Mysterious—Tragical— Violent—Psychic—Sudden—(See these subjects).

**Accidents**—(See "Extraordinary" under Accidents).

**Death** — Extraordinary or Unusual Death — Peculiar Death — Singular Death—Curious Death—♅ tends to cause, and in some uncommon and extraordinary manner, and a death which creates great public concern and interest; the afflictions of ♅ to the hyleg by dir; ♅ does not kill of himself, but assists in destroying life by his evil asps., and when they concur in afflicting the hyleg, the death is usually sudden, singular, and of an extraordinary nature; ♅ conjoined with ♄ or ♂ at B. in the 8th H.; ♅ or ♆ in the 8th H. at B.; ♅ in the 8th H., a sudden, peculiar, extraordinary, and often a violent death; ♆ affl. in the 8th H., or affl. the hyleg, a curious death. (See "Mysterious", "Remarkable", "Tragical", under Death; Execution, Strange; "Death" under Sudden; Untimely).

**Diseases** — Extraordinary, Remarkable, Strange and Uncommon Diseases—Caused by ♅, as this planet gives remarkable features to the sickness; ♅ afflicted in the 6th H., or affl. the hyleg from this house, gives diseases which tend to baffle the skill of Medical Men and Healers; also the Uranian sign ♒ on the Asc. (See Diagnosis, Incurable, Mysterious; "Diseases" under Peculiar; Praecipients, Strange, Uncommon).

**Ideas**—Extraordinary Ideas—Extraordinary Pursuits and Objects—(See Ideas; "Unusual" under Mental; Vocation).

**EXTRAVAGANCE**—Luxuries—Health Undermined By—The ☉ affl. in ♓; the ☉ or ☽ to the ill-asps. ♃ or ♀ by dir.; the ☉ affl. by ♄; the ☽ affl. in ♏ or ♓ at B.; ♄ Sig. ✶ or △ ♀; ♃ to the bad asps. ♂ or ♀ by dir.; bad combinations of the ♃ and ♂ influences, or of the signs which they rule; ♃ affl. in ♉; suffers thru extravagance in eating and drink; ♂ affl. in the 6th H.; ♀ affl. at B., and to the ☌ or ill-asps. the Asc. by dir., or the Asc. to the ☌ or ill-asps. ♀; the ♌, ♎, and 5th H. influences, when containing afflictions, also tend to extravagance, prodigality, and to make the native a spendthrift. (See Conduct, Debauched, Depraved, Diet, Dissolute, Dress, Drink, Eating, Epicureans, Excesses, Expense, Feasting, Food; "Free Living" under Free; Gluttony, Habits; "High Living" under High; Imprudence, Indiscretions, Indulgence, Intemperate, Loose, Luxuries, Pleasure, Plethora, Prodigal, Riches, Riotous Living (see Riotous); Self-Indulgent, Self-Undoing, Surfeits, etc.).

**EXTRAVASATIONS**—(See Effusions).

**EXTREMES**—Extreme—Extremely—

**Childbirth**—Extreme Danger In—(See Parturition).

**Cold**—Extremes of Cold In the Body—Suffers from Extremes of Cold and Heat—(See "Cold and Heat" under Heat).

**Disease**—Extreme Danger In—(See "Illness" under Dangerous).

**Fevers** — Extreme and Dangerous Fevers—(See "High Fevers" under High).

**Heat**—Extreme Heat—Extremes of Heat In the Body—(See "Cold and Heat", "Excessive", "Extreme Heat", under Heat).

**Mental Extremes** — (See Anarchists,

Anger, Cruel, Excitable, Exertion, Fanatical, Frenzy, Fury, Ideals, Ideas, Madness, Mania, Quarrelsome; "High Temper" under Temper; Vicious, Violent, etc.).

**Mouth**—Extreme Heat In the Mouth and Throat — (See "Heat" under Throat).

**Nervousness** — Extremely Nervous — (See "Highly Neurotic" under Nerves).

**Sickness**—Extreme Sickness—(See Dangerous, Escape, Fatal, Fierce, Grievous; "High Fevers" under High; Severe, Sharp, Vehement, Violent).

**Temperature**—Rapid Extremes of—(See Fever; "Rapid Extremes" under Temperature).

**Thirst**—Extreme Thirst—(See Thirst).

**Throat** — Extreme Heat In — (See "Heat" under Throat).

**EXTREMITIES**—Extremities of the Body—Are ruled by the common signs.

**Accidents To**—Accidents, Diseases, Hurts, Infirmities, Injuries, Leprosy, or Wounds To—♄ or ♂ angular in the 1st or 7th H., and in the latter degrees of ♊, ♐, or ♓, and ori. of the ☉, and occi. of the ☽. (See "Accidents", "Hurts", "Injuries", under Arms, Feet, Hands, Legs, Limbs).

**Acromegaly** — (See "Enlargement" in this section).

**Adiposa Dolorosa**—(See Fat).

**Arms**—Disorders of—(See Arms).

**Atrophy**—(See Atrophy).

**Blood Vessels**—Constriction of the Blood Vessels of the Extremities—(See Constrictions).

**Clonic Spasm**—(See "Myoclonia" in this section).

**Coldness Of**—♄ in ♊ or ♓; ☿ affl. in ♓. (See "Extremities" under Cold; Constrictions).

**Cramps In**—(See Cramps).

**Diseases In**—Humours—Accidents—Leprosy—Gout—and other Infirmities in the Extremities, and espec. in the Hands and Feet—(See "Accidents" in this section. Also see Gout, Humours, Leprosy, Rheumatism).

**Enlargements**—Acromegaly—The ☉ and ♂ cause enlargements by drawing heat to the part; ♃ by the deposit of fat; ♄ by deposits and thickening of cell walls, and ♆ by cell development; Subs at AT and CP. (See "Bones of Arm" under Arms; Cells; "Acromegaly" under Enlargements; "Over-Growth" under Growth, etc.).

**Erysipelas Of**—(See Erysipelas).

**Erythromelalgia**—(See this subject).

**Fat** — (See "Adiposa Dolorosa" under Fat).

**Feet**—Disorders of—(See Feet).

**Fingers**—(See Fingers).

**Fractures**—(See Fractures).

**Gout In**—Gout In Arms, Hands, Legs, Feet—(See Gout).

**Hands**—Disorders of—(See Hands).

**Head**—Disorders of—(See Head).

**Humours In**—(See "Accidents" in this section. Also see Humours).

**Infirmities In**—(See "Accidents" in this section. Also see Arms, Feet, Hands, Legs, Limbs).

**Injuries To**—(See "Accidents" in this section).

**Legs**—Disorders of—(See Ankles, Calves, Feet, Knees, Legs, Limbs, Thighs).

**Leprosy In**—(See "Diseases" in this section).

**Limbs**—Disorders of—(See Limbs).

**Long and Slender**—☿ ascending at B., and free from the rays of other planets. (See "Long" under Arms, Feet, Hands, Legs).

**Lower Extremities**—Disorders In—(See Feet, Legs, Lower).

**Muscles**—Disorders of—(See "Muscles" under Arms; "Atrophy" under Muscles; "Myoclonia" in this section).

**Myoclonia**—Myoclonus—Paramyoclonus Multiplex—(See Myoclonia).

**Pain In**—(See "Pain" under Arms; Feet, Hands, Legs, Limbs).

**Paramyoclonus Multiplex**—(See Myoclonia).

**Rheumatism In**—(See "Accidents" in this section. Also see Gout, Rheumatism; "Rheumatism" under Arms, Hands, Legs, Feet).

**Short**—(See "Short" under Limbs).

**Slender**—See "Long" in this section).

**Spasm**—Clonic Spasm—Twitching In—(See Myoclonia, Spasmodic Diseases).

**Swellings In**—(See "Swellings" under Arms, Hands, Legs; "Dropsy" under Feet; Swellings).

**Toes**—Disorders of—(See Feet, Toes).

**Twitchings In**—(See Myoclonia, Twitching).

**Upper Extremities**—(See Arms, Hands, Head, Upper).

**Wounds To**—(See "Accidents" in this section).

**EXTROVERSION**—(See Introversion, Introspection).

**EXUDATIONS**—A Morbid Oozing Out of Fluids—

**Dried Exudations**—(See Crusts).

**Fibrinous Exudations**—(See Fiber).

**Lymph Exudations**—(See Eczema, Lymph).

**Membranous Exudations**—Morbid Discharges—On Mucous Surfaces, as in the Throat, Tonsils, or Pharynx—(See Diphtheria. Also see Discharges, Excretion, Fluids, Morbid, Mucous, Osmosis, Pharynx, Throat, Tonsils).

**EYEBALLS**—For Rulership of see Eyes. The various parts of the Eyeballs are considered under Eyes.

**Abnormal Protrusion Of**—Goggle Eyes—Exophthalmos—Exophthalmic Goiter—The ☉ and ☽ both in cardinal or fixed signs, or in angles; ♀ affl. in ♉ tends to the Goiter variety; the ♌ influence, or the combined ♌ and ♓ influences; ♌ gives large goggle eyes. (See "Full", "Large", under Eyes; "Exophthalmic" under Goiter).

**Clonic Spasm Of**—Hippus—Tremulous Contracture of the Eyeballs—♅ affl. in ♈; Subs at MCP (4C) and SP. (See Clonic, Contractions; "Iris" under Eyes; Spasmodic Diseases, Tremors. Also see "Nystagmus" in this section).

**Contracture Of**—(See "Clonic" in this section).

**Dropsy Of**—The ☽ or ♄ affl. in ♈; Subs at KP (7D), and SP. (See Dropsy).

**Exophthalmos**—(See "Abnormal Protrusion" in this section).

**Goggle Eyes**—(See "Abnormal" in this section).

**Hippus**—(See "Clonic" in this section).

**Nystagmus**—Oscillatory Movement of the Eyeballs—Quivering—A ♅ disease and affliction; afflictions in ♉, causing incoordination; a spasmodic disease, and caused by ♅ affl. in ♈ or ♉; Subs at MCP and SP (7D). (See Incoordination, Spasmodic).

**Oscillation Of**—(See "Nystagmus" in this section).

**Protrusion Of**—(See "Abnormal Protrusion" in this section).

**Quivering Of**—(See "Nystagmus" in this section).

**Retraction Of**—♄ influence; ♄ affl. in ♈; Subs at MCP (4C), and SP. (See Retraction).

**Sunken Eyeballs**—Sunken Eyes—Deep-Set—Hollow Eyes—♄ ascending at B.; ♄ in ♌ in partile asp. the Asc.; ♄ Sig. in ♌ (Hor'y); ☿ occi. of the ☉ except when ☿ is in ♊.

**Tremulous**—(See "Clonic", "Nystagmus", in this section).

**EYEBROWS**—The Hair, Skin, and Tissue Above the Eye—

**Beetle Brows**—Hanging—Overhanging—Lowering—Projecting—Denoted by ♄; ♄ ruler at B.; ♄ or ☋ in the Asc.; the ♄ sign ♑ on the Asc.; the Sig. in a ♄ sign, or ☌ ♄ (Hor'y); ♂ in ♈.

**Black Eyebrows**—♈ on the Asc.

**Bushy Eyebrows**—Full Eyebrows—♈ on the Asc., and espec. when the ☉ is also in ♈. (See "Bushy" under Hair).

**Dark**—♈ or ♊ on the Asc.

**Dark and Full**—♈ on Asc.

**Full**—Bushy—Dark and Full—♈ on Asc.

**No Eyebrows**—Or Hair—Case—See "Aqueous", No. 120, in 1001 N.N. (See "No Hair" under Hair).

**Wide Apart**—Large Space Between—♃ strong at B. tends to give a large space between the eyebrows. (See Eyes).

**EYELIDS**—Eyelashes—

**Black Eyelids**—Black Lashes—Black, Yet Lovely and Graceful—The ♀ influence strong at B. signifies; ♀ Sig. of the person in Hor'y Questions. (See "Black Eyes" under Eyes; "Black Hair" under Hair).

**Blepharitis**—Inflammation of the Edges of the Eyelids—Thick and Inflamed Edges—Falling Out of the Lashes—Inversion of the Lashes—♄ or ♂ affl. in ♈; ♂ ☌ the ☉ or ☽ in ♈;

Subs at MCP, and KP (11D). (See Conjunctivitis; "Eyestrain" under Eyes; "Danger to Sight" under Sight).

**Drooping Lids**—(See "Ptosis" in this section).

**Dryness Of**—♄ affl. in ♈; Subs at MCP and KP (11D).

**Edges**—Inflamed and Thick Edges—(See "Blepharitis" in this section).

**Epiphora**—(See "Moisture" in this section).

**Excessive Moisture Of**—(See "Moisture" in this section).

**Falling Lashes**—(See "Blepharitis" in this section).

**Glands Of**—(See Racemose).

**Granulated Lids**—Trachoma—A Form of Conjunctivitis—♄ affl. in ♈; ♄ ☌ ☉ or ☽ in ♈; Subs at MCP and KP (11D). (See Conjunctivitis. Also "Blepharitis" in this section).

**Inflammation Of**—(See "Blepharitis" in this section).

**Inversion**—Of Lashes—(See "Trichiasis" in this section).

**Lashes**—(See "Black", "Blepharitis", "Trichiasis", in this section).

**Moisture**—Excessive Moisture of—Watery Eyes—Epiphora—(See "Watery Eyes" under Tears).

**Prolapsus**—Of Lid—(See "Ptosis" in this section).

**Ptosis**—Prolapsus of Eyelid—Drooping Lid—♅ or ♄ in ♈, and espec. when affl. the ☉ or ☽ at B., and by dir.; Subs at MCP (4C), and KP (11D). (See Drooping, Prolapse).

**Saint Vitus Dance**—(See Saint).

**Swelling Of**—(See "Blepharitis", "Granulated", in this section).

**Thick Edges**—(See "Blepharitis" in this section).

**Trichiasis**—Inversion of the Eyelashes—Usually the result of Conjunctivitis, Eye Strain, and Granulations, which go with these conditions. (See "Blepharitis" in this section).

**Warts On**—Verruca—(See "Eyelid" under Warts).

**Winking**—Spasmodic and Involuntary—A ♅ influence, due to a spasmodic incoordination; ♅ affl. in ♈ or ♉. (See Incoordination, Spasmodic Diseases). See Eyes.

**EYES**—The Organs of Vision—Ocular—The Eyes are under the external rulership of the ♈ sign. The Eyes are also ruled by the ☉, ☽, ♆, ♅, and the ♒ sign, as ♅ and ♒ rule the Ether, thru which Light is transmitted. It is recognized that ♆ has some action on the Eyes and Brain. The Eyes have affinity with the ☉, ☽, ♅, and the ♈ and ♒ signs, and also with the Pleiades, Antares, and the Ascelli. (See "Eyes" under Mercury). In our System of Astrology the 1st H. rules and affects the eyes. In the Hindu System, the 2nd H. rules the Eyes, and afflictions in the 2nd H. tend to seriously afflict the eyes, or cause blindness. The ☉ is concerned with the structural defects of the eyes, while the ☽ rules the Lachrymal Apparatus, its diseases, and also errors of Accommodation, defective powers of adaptation, as Hyperopia, Myopia, Presbyopia, etc. The ☉ or ☽ at B. affl. by ♅ tends to eye trouble or blindness, and espec. if the ☉ or ☽ be near Nebulous Stars, as the Pleiades, Antares, or the Ascelli. The ☉ rules the right eye of a man, and the left eye of a woman. The ☽ rules the right eye of a woman, and the left eye of a man. Due to the large mass of material to be arranged and classified, and the many subdivisions, many subjects concerning the Eyes are handled elsewhere in the alphabetical arrangement, such as Accommodation, Blindness, Eyeballs, Sight, etc. Also much is said concerning the Eyes under such subjects as Antares, Aquarius, Ascelli, Castor, Ether, Hyades, Light, Moon, Navamsa, Nebulous, Neptune, Pleiades, Pollux, Sight, Sun, Uranus, etc. This article has been arranged in two sections. Section One considers the general conditions about the Eyes, as color, form, expression, characteristics, etc. Section Two, the Diseases and Afflictions to the Eyes, the Sight, etc. See the following subjects of both Sections in the alphabetical arrangement when not considered more fully here in this Article.

**— SECTION ONE —**

**GENERAL CHARACTERISTICS—**

Description of the Eyes—

**Amorous Eyes**—Full of Amorous Enticements—♀ ascending and in power at B. (See Amorous).

**Aqueous Humor**—(See Sec. 2 of this Article).

**Beautiful Eyes**—Handsome—Fascinating—Lovely—♃ in ♊, in partile asp. the Asc., full, handsome; ♃ Sig. in ♊; ♀ ascending, or in configuration with the degree ascending; ♎ on the Asc., or the ☉ and ♀ in ♎, give beautiful eyes. (See Beautiful, Handsome).

**Big Eyes**—(See "Goggle" under Eyeballs. Also see "Large" in this section).

**Black Eyes**—♄ lord of the Asc., and occi., as between the M.C. and Desc., or between the Nadir and Asc.; ♄ ascending, small, black, and deeply set; ♄ denotes small, black, leering eyes; ♀ strong at B. sometimes gives black eyes; ♀ Sig. in ♉, generally black and very expressive; ♀ in the Asc., dark hazel or black; born under ♀, sparkling black eyes; a ☿ person generally has black or gray eyes, but when ☿ ascends at B., and is free from the rays of other planets, the eyes are neither gray nor black; ☿ Sig. of the person in Hor'y Questions; ☿ in ♎, black or gray. (See "Dark Complexion" under Complexion; "Black Hair" under Hair).

**Blind Spot**—Of Retina—(See "Blind Spot" under Retina).

**Blue Eyes**—♃ ☌ or ☍ ♀ in any part of the map tends to give; ♃ gives soft blue eyes; indicated by ♀; ♀ ruler of the Asc., and ori., fine blue eyes; the ⚹ and △ asps. of ♀ give fine blue eyes; the ♀ signs ♉ or ♎ on the Asc.; ♎ on the Asc., beautiful and handsome blue eyes; ☿ in ♎; the ☉ and ♀ in ♎, and espec. in the Asc., and with ♎ rising, beautiful blue eyes; ♋ on Asc., small bluish or gray; ♐ on Asc., fine, clear blue or gray. (See "Light" under Complexion).

**Bright Eyes** — Sharp — Piercing—Sparkling—Red—Fiery—Quick—Darting—Penetrating—Characteristic of ♂ people; ♂ rising at B.; ♂ strong at B., and ruler; ♂ Sig. in ♐; the ♂ sign ♈ on the Asc.; ♂ in ♈ or ♏; ♂ in the Asc. or M.C. at B.; the ☉ gives when strong at B.; ♃ Sig. in ♈; ♀ in the Asc.; ♀ in ♐; given by the ✱ and △ asps. of ♀; ☿ occi. at B.; ♊ gives a sharp, piercing and penetrating eye, and with quick sight.

**Brown Eyes**—The ☉ or ☽ in ♊; ♃ rising in the Asc.; ♀ Sig. in ♊; indicated by ☿; ♊ on the Asc. (See Brown. Also see "Brown Hair", "Dark Brown", under Hair).

**Choroid**—(See Choroid).

**Clear and Fine**—When strongly occupied, given by the Quadrant between the Nadir and Asc., and its opposite; ♐ on Asc., clear and fine; ♃ in ♐, a fine, clear, good eye. (See "Fine", "Good", in this section).

**Dark Eyes**—♄ gives; ♄ occi. at B.; ♄ in the Asc.; ♊ gives; ♊ or ♓ on the Asc. (See Dark. In this section see "Black", "Hazel").

**Darting**—(See "Bright" in this section).

**Deep-Set**—Sunken—Hollow—(See "Sunken" under Eyeballs).

**Downward Look**—(See Look).

**Dull Eyes**—Heavy—Languid—Sleepy—Weary Look—The ☽ in ♈, □ or ☍ ♄ (or ☿ if he be of the nature of ♄), a weariness and dullness of the eyes; the ☽ Sig. in ♓, sleepy eyes; the ♓ influences tends to; ♓ on the Asc.; given by the Lymphatic or Phlegmatic Temperament, which is largely ruled by ♓; ♄ Sig. of the person in Hor'y Questions; ♄ in ♋ in partile asp. the Asc., languid, dull, and heavy. (See Dull; "Temperament" under Phlegmatic).

**Earth**—The Eyes Always Upon the Earth—(See "Downward Look" under Look).

**Expressive and Full**—The ☉ Sig. in ♎; ♃ Sig. in ♊; ♀ Sig. in ♉, very expressive. (See "Black", "Bright", "Full", in this section).

**Eyeballs**—(See Eyeballs).

**Eyebrows**—(See Eyebrows).

**Eye Lashes**—(See Eyelids).

**Eye Lids**—(See Eye Lids).

**Fair Eyes**—☿ strong at B. in the Asc., or rising. (See "Fair" under Complexion).

**Fascinating Eyes**—(See "Beautiful" in this section).

**Ferocious and Fiery**—Sharp—♂ as Sig. in Hor'y Questions; given by ♂; born under ♂. (See Fiery, Sharp, Yellow, in this section).

**Fiery**—Red and Fiery—♃ Sig. in ♌, full and fiery; ♂ ruler, and strong at B., fiery and ferocious; ☿ occi. at B., red and fiery.

**Fine Eyes**—Clear—Good—♃ in ♐, partile asp. the Asc.; ♐ on Asc., fine and clear; ♊ gives fine eyes in a woman. (See Beautiful, Blue, Clear, Good, in this section).

**Full Eyes**—The ☉ Sig. in ♎; the ☉ in ♎, partile asp. the Asc.; the ☽, ♀, or ☿ Sigs. in ♌; ♃ Sig. in ♊, full and expressive; ♃ in ♊, partile the Asc., full and handsome; ♃ in ♌, partile the Asc.; ♃ in ♎, partile the Asc., a full eye; denoted by ♃ as Sig. in Hor'y Questions; born under ♃; ♃ Sig. in ♌, full and fiery; born under ♃, and with ♃ ori., eyes more full; born under ♃ gives full gray eyes; ♀ Sig. in ♌ full and prominent; ♀ ♌ partile the Asc.; ♀ as Sig. in Hor'y Questions denotes full or large eyes; ☿ ♌ partile the Asc.; ♌ gives full round eyes; ♓ on Asc. gives full, prominent, and sleepy eyes. (See Large, Prominent, Round, in this section. Also see Expression; "Goggle Eyes" under Eyeballs).

**Glances**—Of the Eyes—(See Expression, Look. Also note the various paragraphs in this section).

**Goggle Eyes**—Protruding Eyes—(See "Goggle" under Eyeballs. Also see Full, Large, Prominent, in this section).

**Good Eyes**—A Good Eye—Fine and Clear—Perfect and Quick Sight—♊ gives a good, piercing hazel eye, and of perfect and quick sight; ♊, ♑, or ♒ on the Asc.; ♌ gives a good eye, and with quick sight. (See Bright, Clear, Fine, Quick, Sharp, in this section).

**Gray Eyes**—The ☽ gives; the ☽ ascending at B.; the ☽ indicates greenish gray eyes; the ☽ sign ♋ gives, and with ♋ on Asc.; the ♋ sign on the Asc. tends to give small gray eyes; indicated by the ☉ and ☿; ♄ gives a greenish gray eye; ♃ ascending, large, gray eyes; born under ♃ gives full gray eyes; ♂ ascending at B.; ♀ Sig. in ♋, small gray; the ✱ and △ asps. of ♀ to the ☉, ☽, and planets; ☿ in ♎, gray or black; ☿ as Sig. in Hor'y Questions indicates one with gray or black eyes; a ☿ person generally has gray or black eyes, but when ☿ ascends at B., and is free from the rays of other planets, the eyes are neither gray nor black; ☿ ori. of the ☉ except when ☿ is in ♊; ♐ on Asc., fine, clear, blue, or gray eyes. (See Gray).

**Great Eyes**—Great and Large—Full—Prominent—(See "Goggle" under Eyeballs; "Full", "Large", "Prominent", in this section).

**Greenish**—The ☉ indicates greenish gray eyes; ♄ indicates greenish, or greenish gray; ♀ Sig. in ♋, small, greenish or gray. (See Green).

**Handsome Eyes**—(See "Beautiful" in this section).

**Hazel Eyes**—Dark Brown—♊ or ♒ give, and with these signs on the Asc.; ♊ gives a good, piercing, hazel eye; ♂ rising at B.; ♂ gives sharp, piercing hazel; ♀ in the Asc., dark hazel or black; ♀ Sig. in ♊, hazel or brown; born under ♀, sparkling dark hazel; ♊ gives, and with a very quick and penetrative sight; ♊ on the Asc., dark hazel. (See "Brown", "Dark", in this section).

**Heavy and Dull**—Languid—(See "Dull" in this section).

**Hollow Eyes**—Deep-Set—Sunken—(See "Sunken" under Eyeballs).

**Iris**—(See Sec. 2 of this Article).

**Keen Eyes**—♆ or ☿ rising in the Asc. (See Bright, Clear, Good, Piercing, Quick, Sharp, in this section).

**Lachrymal Apparatus**—(See Tears).

**Languid Eyes**—(See "Dull" in this section).

**Large Eyes**—Great—Prominent—Full—The Quadrant from the Summer Tropic to the Autumnal Equi., and its opposite Quadrate, tend to produce; the ☉ rising at B.; the ☉ Sig. in ♈; the ☉ Sig. in ♌, large, staring eyes; the ☉ Sig. in ♎, full, large eyes; the ☉ in ♍; the ☉ gives large goggle eyes; the ☉ indicates large eyes, and often gray; the ☉ in ♌, partile the Asc.; the ☽ Sig. in ♌; the ☽ in ♌, partile the Asc.; ♄ Sig. in ♓; ♄ in ♓ partile the Asc., large head and eyes; ♄ lord of the Asc., and ori., as from the Asc. to M.C., and its opposite Quarter, gives great eyes; ♃ in the Asc., large gray eyes; ♃ in ♌, prominent eyes; ♃ in ♎, large; ♃ oriental; ♃ ruler of the Asc., and ori.; ♃ in ♊, full, handsome eyes; ♃ strong at B.; ♃ as Sig. in Hor'y Questions; ♂ Sig. in ♌; ♂ ♌ partile the Asc., great eyes; ♀ well-dig. at B. signifies a full, large, goggle eye; ♀ denotes full and large eyes in Hor'y Questions; ♀ Sig. in ♌; ☿ Sig. in ♌, large, prominent eyes; the ♉ and ♌ signs give, and with these signs on the Asc.; ♌ gives large goggle eyes. (See Full, Goggle, Prominent, in this section).

**Larger**—One Eye Larger Than the Other—The ☽ causes; the ☽ eye, the left eye in a man, and the right eye in a woman, is apt to be larger, and with more vitreous, and a greater cavity.

**Leering Eyes**—Malicious—♄ Sig. in ♑; in Hor'y Questions, ♄ Sig. of the party, small leering eyes; when ♄ forms the body he gives small, black, leering eyes. (See Malicious).

**Left Eye**—In a male, ruled by the ☽, and the ☽ in ♈. In a female, ruled by the ☉, and the ☉ in ♈. (See "Eyes" under Left).

**Little Eyes**—(See "Small" in this section).

**Look**—Glances—(See "Glances" in this section).

**Lovely Eyes**—(See "Beautiful" in this section; "Lovely" under Complexion).

**Lowering Look**—(See "Downward Look" under Look).

**Malicious Eyes**—(See "Leering" in this section).

**Muscles Of**—(See "Muscles" in Sec. 2 of this Article).

**Nerves Of**—(See "Optic Nerve" under Optic. Also see "Nerves" in Sec. 2 of this Article).

**One Eye Larger**—(See "Larger" in this section).

**Optic Nerve**—(See "Optic Nerve" under Optic. Also see "Nerves" in Sec. 2 of this Article).

**Penetrating Eyes**—♊ gives a penetrating, sharp, and piercing eye; given by ♂; born under ♂; the ✶ and △ asps. of ♀ give a bright and penetrating eye. (See Bright, Ferocious, Fiery, Keen, Piercing, Quick, Sharp, Sparkling, in this section).

**Perfect**—Perfect and Quick Sight—(See "Good Eyes" in this section; "Good Sight" under Sight).

**Piercing Eyes**—The ☉ gives; ♃ in ♈ partile the Asc., quick and piercing; ♂ gives sharp and piercing; ♈ on Asc.; ♈ gives piercing, round, and prominent eyes; ♊ gives a sharp, piercing, and penetrating eye; ♊ gives a good, piercing hazel eye. (See Bright, Fiery, Good, Hazel, Keen, Large, Penetrating, Quick, Sharp, Staring, in this section).

**Prominent Eyes**—♈ gives prominent, round, piercing eyes; ♉ on the Asc.; ♌ on the Asc., prominent and round; ♓ on Asc., prominent, round and piercing; ♃ in ♌; ♀ Sig. in ♌, full and prominent; ☿ Sig. in ♌, large and prominent. (See Full, Large, in this section; "Goggle Eyes" under Eyeballs).

**Protruding Eyes**—(See "Goggle Eyes" under Eyeballs; "Exophthalmic" under Goiter).

**Pupils**—Inequality of—(See Iris, Pupils, in Sec. 2 of this Article).

**Quality Of**—♄ ori. at B., the quality is ordinary; the ♊ and ♌ signs tend to give good quality to the eyes, and with quick slight. (See Bright, Fine, Good, Perfect, in this section. Also see "Bad Eyes" in Sec. 2 of this Article).

**Quick Eye**—Quick Look—Quick Sight—♊ and ♌ espec. give a quick and penetrating eye, and with quick sight; ♃ ♈ partile Asc., quick and piercing; ♂ ♐ partile Asc., a very quick eye; ☿ occi. at B. (See Bright, Good, Hazel, Keen, Penetrating, Piercing, Sharp, in this section. Also see "Good Sight", "Quick Sight", under Sight).

**Red Cast**—Red and Fiery—♂ strong at B., and rising; ☿ occi. of the ☉, except when ☿ is in ♊. (See Bright, Fiery, in this section. Also see "Eyes" under Red).

**Retina**—Rulership of—Disorders of—(See Retina).

**Right Eye**—Ruled by the ☉ in a male, and by the ☽ in the female. (See "Eyes" under Right).

**Rolling Eyes**—Rolling and Wandering—♀ strong at B., or ruler.

**Round Eyes**—♈ gives round, prominent and piercing eyes; ♌ on the Asc. gives round, full, prominent eyes. (See Full, Large, Piercing, Prominent, in this section).

**Sharp Eyes**—Sharp Sight—Sharp Look—Piercing—Penetrating—Quick—Darting—Bright—Sparkling—Keen, etc.—Characteristic of ♂ people; ♂ rising in the Asc. at B.; ♂ Sig. of the person in Hor'y Questions; the ♂ sign ♈ on the Asc. gives sharp eyes and sharp sight; ♂ gives a sharp, piercing hazel eye; the ☉ gives a sharp eye when strong at B., well-aspected, and not afflicted by malefics or Nebulous

Stars; ♃ or ♂ Sig. in ♈; ♊ gives a sharp, piercing and penetrating eye, and often with a wanton look. (See Bright, Ferocious, Fiery, Good, Keen, Penetrating, Piercing, Quick, Yellow, in this section. Also see "Quick Sight" under Sight).

**Sight**—(See Good, Quick, Sharp, in this section. Also see Sight).

**Sleepy Eyes**—Languid—Heavy—Dull—♓ influence; ♓ on Asc. gives full, prominent, sleepy eyes. (See "Dull" in this section. Also see "Drowsiness" under Sleep).

**Small Eyes**—Little Eyes—Indicated by ♄; ♄ in ♑ partile the Asc.; ♄ strong at B.; ♄ Sig. of the party in Hor'y Questions denotes small, black, leering eyes; when ♄ forms the body he gives small, black, leering eyes; ♄ ascending, small, black, and deeply set; ♂ ruler of the Asc., and occi.; ♀ Sig. in ♋, small greenish or gray; ♋ on the Asc. tends to small gray or bluish; ☿ ruler of the Asc., and ori.; ☿ in ♋ partile the Asc.; ☿ Sig. in ♋ in Hor'y Questions; ☿ ori. of the ☉ except when ☿ is in ♊.

**Soft Eyes**—♃ gives soft blue eyes.

**Sparkling Eyes**—Characteristic of ♂ people; born under ♂; ♀ in the Asc.; born under ♀, sparkling black, or sparkling dark hazel eyes; ♀ in ♐; ☿ occi. at B.; ♎ on the Asc. (See Bright, Fiery, Penetrating, Piercing, Sharp, in this section).

**Staring Eyes**—The ☉ Sig. in ♌, large, staring eyes; ♌ gives. (See "Large" in this section).

**Steadfast Eye**—♀ in the Asc., strong and dignified at B.

**Sunken Eyes**—Deep-Set—Hollow—(See "Sunken" under Eyeballs).

**Tears**—Given to Shedding Tears—Sheds Tears Easily—Watery Eyes—(See Tears).

**Third Eye**—(See Pineal).

**Tunics**—(See Choroid).

**Visage**—(See Countenance, Face).

**Vision**—(See Sight).

**Vitreous Humor**—(See "Larger" in this section. Also see "Muscae Volitantes" in Sec. 2 of this Article).

**Wandering Eyes**—(See "Rolling" in this section).

**Wanton Look**—♊ gives. (See Wanton. Also see "Sharp" in this section).

**Winking**—(See "Winking" under Eyelids).

**Women**—Fine Eyes In—♊ gives. (See "Fine" in this section).

**Yellowish Eyes**—A Yellow Tinge—Characteristic of ♂ people; ♂ as Sig. in Hor'y Questions denotes sharp, ferocious eyes, and rather yellow. (See Yellow).

## —SECTION TWO—

**DISEASES OF THE EYES**—Afflictions to the Eyes—Ocular Disorders—

**Accidents to Eyes**—Hurts or Injuries To—Blows or Strokes To—Blindness from Injury to Eyes—The ☉ or ☽ in ♈, ♉, ♋, ♌, ♑, or ♒, and affl. by malefics or Nebulous Stars; afflictions to the ☉ or ☽ by the malefics or Nebulous Stars; the ☉ with the Pleiades, Praesepe, Antares, or Deneb.; both of the Lights are generally afflicted, and with one of them rising and affl. by malefics or Nebulous places; the ☉ to the P. asp. Antares by dir.; afflictions to the ☽ at B., and by dir.; the ☽ affl. by the ☉, and the ☽ affl. at the same time by malefics, or near Nebulous Stars, such as the Pleiades; the ☽ to the bad asps. the ☉ by dir., and falling near Nebulous Stars; the ☽ in an angle with the Pleiades, Praesepe, or Antares; the ☽ directed to the Pleiades, Hyades, Praesepe, or the Twins; the ☽ ☌ or ill-asp. ♄ or ♂ at B., and the ☽ on the radical place of ♄ or ♂ at a Solar Rev.; the ☽ ☌ or ill-asp. ♂ in the ♌ sign, and ♂ aspected by the ☉ or ♄ near the place of the Bull's Eye; the ☽ in the Western Angle conjoined with the Pleiades; the Prog. ☽ ☌ ♄ or ♂ in ♈ or the Asc.; Fixed Stars of the nature of ♂ and the ☽ ascending at B.; the Asc. to the Pleiades, Hyades or Castor. Mars causes injuries to the eyes by burns, blows, strokes, explosions, wounds, gunshot, lightning, smallpox, the sword, etc., which may result in blindness, and espec. when affl. the ☉ or ☽, and the Lights near Nebulous Stars and in angles. (See these subjects. See "Accidents", "Burning", "Explosions", and these various subjects under Blindness; "Eyes" under Exercise. Also see "Hurts", "Injuries", "Robbers", "Sports", in this section).

**Accommodation**—Disorders of the Focus of the Eyes, as Far-Sighted, Near-Sighted, etc.—(See Accommodation, Sight).

**Affected**—The ☉, ☽, and planets in ♈ tend espec. to affect the eyes. Also according to the influences listed in Table 196 in Simmonite's Arcana, the eyes are affected with ♃ in ♎ or ♑; ♂ in ♈; and ☿ in ♋. (See the Introduction to this Article. Also see the various paragraphs in this section).

**Affections**—Eye Affections—(See "Bad Eyes", "Eye Trouble", and the various paragraphs in this section).

**Afflicted**—In the Eyes—(See "Eye Trouble" and the various paragraphs in this section).

**All Diseases Of**—All Infirmities In—Signified by the 1st H. Also diseases of the ☉ and ☽.

**Amaurosis**—Partial or Total Blindness—(See Gutta Serena).

**Anisocoria**—Inequality of the Pupils—(See Iris, Pupils).

**Aqueous Humor**—Is ruled by ♈ and the ☉ in ♈. Stomach Disorders and Indigestion tend to affect the humor, as by floating specks, blurring the field of vision, etc. (See "Muscae Volitantes" in this section).

**Argyll-Robertson Pupil**—(See Argyll).

**Assaults**—Injury to Eyes By—(See "Treachery" under Blindness; "Eyes" under Robbers, Sword).

**Asthenopia**—Weak or Painful Vision—(See "Painful", "Weak", under Sight).

**Astigmatism**—(See Astigmatism).

**Atrophy**—Of the Optic Nerve—Of the Muscles—(See Muscles, Nerves, Optic, in this section. Also see Atrophy).

**Bad Eyes**—Ailing Eyes—The ☉ and ☽ ascending and impedited by ♄ or ♂; the ☉ with the Pleiades or Praesepe; the ☽ Sig. ☌ ☉, in exact ☌, or applying to it; the ☽ to the ☌ ☉ or ♄ by dir.; the ☽ to the □ or ☍ ☉ or by dir.; the Pleiades when rising, and when directed to the ☉, ☽, or Asc., or when with the Lights at B.; the Ascelli, Castor, Pollux, Hyades, Pleiades, or Praesepe, directed to the Asc. or Luminaries. (See "Eye Trouble", "Injuries", "Weak Eyes", and the various paragraphs in this section).

**Blemishes**—Blemish On or Near One or Both Eyes—(See "Eyes" under Blemishes).

**Blights In**—The ☉ ☌ the Asc. by dir. (See Blights).

**Blindness**—(See the various paragraphs under Blindness, Sight).

**Bloodshot Eyes**—(See Conjunctivitis. Also see "Inflamed" in this section).

**Blows To**—(See Accidents, Left, Right, in this section. Also see "Accidents" under Blindness; Blows; "Eyes" under Left, Right).

**Both Eyes**—Injury To—The ☉ in an angle in the same sign with the ☽, or in ☍, and with ♄ and ♂ ori. to the ☉ and ascending before him, and ♄ and ♂ ori. of the ☽; the ☽ in an angle and decr. in light, and ♄ or ♂ matutine, and ascending in succession to the ☽. (See "Accidents" under Blindness. Also see Accidents, Injuries, in this section). For Blindness in Both Eyes, see "Total Blindness" under Blindness.

**Burns To**—Burning—(See "Burning" under Blindness. Also see "Accidents" in this section).

**Cases of Eye Trouble**—See Cases 1, 2, 3, 4, Chap. 13, pages 86 and 87, in Daath's Medical Astrology. See Figs. 2A, 2B, 2C, 2D, 2E, 2G, 2H, in the book, "Astro-Diagnosis" by the Heindels. See Figs. 3, 4, 5, 24, 30, 31, 32, and 34, in "Message of the Stars" by the Heindels.

**Cataracts**—(See Cataract).

**Choroiditis**—(See Choroid).

**Circles Under Eyes**—Dark Circles Under—♄ in the 1st H.

**Clonic Spasm**—Of Iris—Hippus—(See Clonic, Iris; "Clonic Spasm" under Spasmodic).

**Color Blind**—(See Blindness).

**Congestion**—Of the Muscles of—(See "Crystallization" in this section).

**Conjunctivitis**—Bloodshot—Ophthalmia—(See Conjunctivitis).

**Cornea**—Inflamed Cornea—Keratitis —Diseases of—A ☉ disease; the ☉ affl. in ♈; Subs at MCP (3rd, 4C), and at SP (7D). (See "Ulcer" in this section).

**Crises**—In Eye Diseases—Occur when the Prog. ☉ or ☽ pass the place of nebulous stars, and at the same time afflicted by a malefic; the ☉ or ☽ affl. at B. by malefics or nebulous stars, and passing the place of malefics by

dir.; the prog. ☉ or ☽ coming to the □ or ☍ their radical places, and affl. at B. by malefics, or near nebulous stars; the prog. ☽ ☌ malefics in ♈ tends to cause a crisis for the worse if the ☉ or ☽ are with nebulous stars at B., and affl. by malefics; malefics with nebulous stars, and affl. the ☉ or ☽ by dir., and worse when the malefics are R, due to passing the nebulous twice. (See Blindness, Crises, Worse).

**Crossed Eyes**—(See "Strabismus" in this section).

**Crystalline Lens**—Defects and Disorders of—Opacity of—(See Accommodation, Cataract).

**Crystallization**—Of the Muscles and Nerves of the Eyes—Congestion—(See Congestion, Crystallization; "Crystallization" under Sight).

**Cyclops**—Eyes Focussed Into One—(See Cyclops).

**Danger To**—The ☉ directed to Praesepe; malefics ☌ the ☉ or ☽ in ♈; the ☉ or ☽ ☌ nebulous stars at B., and to the evil asps. nebulous places by dir. (See Accidents, Blows, Injuries, in this section. Also see Blindness, Sight).

**Dark Circles**—Under the Eyes—(See "Circles" in this section).

**Decay**—Of the Optic Nerve—Inhibition of—(See "Decay" under Optic).

**Defects In Eyes**—Ocular Defects— Natural and Structural Defects—(a) Natural Defects—The ☽ rules defects of accommodation and of the powers of adaptation; the ☽ Sig. ☌ ☉, and espec. if near the Pleiades, Hyades, or Praesepe, and apt to be nearly blind; the ☽ or Asc. with nebulous, and affl. by ♄, tends to Cataracts, Glaucoma, Obstructing Growths, and Natural Defects. (See Accommodation, Blindness, Cataracts, Defects, Glaucoma, Growths, Natural, Obstructions, Sight. Also note the various paragraphs in this section). (b) Structural Defects—Ruled by the ☉; the ☉ affl. in ♈, and espec. when in the Asc. (See Structural).

**Dilated Pupils**—(See Iris, Mydriasis, Pupils).

**Dim Eyes**—The ☉ in earthy signs and ☌ the Asc. by dir.; the ☉ to the ☌ ♂ by dir. (See "Dim Sight" under Sight).

**Discharges From**—Humorous Discharge From—♀ affl. in ♈. (See Discharges, Humours).

**Diseased**—In the Eyes—(See "Eye Trouble", and the various paragraphs in this section).

**Diseases Of**—The Eyes—(See the various paragraphs in this section. Also see Blindness, Eyeballs, Eyelids, Sight).

**Disordered Eyes**—(See "Eye Trouble", and the various paragraphs in this section).

**Double Vision**—(See "Diplopia" under Sight).

**Dropsy**—Of the Eyeballs—(See Eyeballs).

**Dullness Of**—Weariness of—Heavy—Languid—Sleepy—(See "Dull Eyes" in Sec. 1 of this Article).

**Epiphora**—(See "Watery Eyes" under Tears).

**Exercise**—Injury to the Eyes During—(See "Accidents" in this section; "Eyes" under Exercise).

**Exophthalmos**—(See "Abnormal Protrusion" under Eyeballs. Also see "Large", "Prominent", in Sec. 1 of this Article).

**Explosions**—(See "Blindness" under Explosions. Also see "Accidents" in this section).

**Eyeballs**—Disorders of—(See Eyeballs).

**Eyebrows**—No Eyebrows—(See Eyebrows).

**Eye Lashes**—Turning In of—(See "Trichiasis" under Eyelids).

**Eyelids**—Disorders of—(See Eyelids).

**Eyesight**—Disorders of—(See Accommodation, Blindness, Sight. Also note the various paragraphs in this section).

**Eyestrain**—Over-Worked Eyes—Errors of Accommodation In—The eyes are weaker and easily strained when the ☉ comes to the ☌, or evil directions, of nebulous stars, as Praesepe, Hyades, Castor, Pollux, and at the same time affl. by malefics; the ☽ affl. in ♈; ☿ tends to blindness from eyestrain and hard reading or study. (See "Reading and Study" under Blindness; Reading, Study).

**Eye Trouble**—The Eyes Afflicted—Diseased Eyes—Disordered Eyes—The Eyes Suffer—Infirmities In the Eyes—The ☉ or ☽ affl. in ♈; the ☉ or ☽ affl. at B., and by dir.; the ☉ and ☽ in □ or ☍ each other and in angles; the ☉ affl. by the ☽; the ☉ or ☽ affl. in ♉ near the Pleiades; the ☉ or ☽ in ♌ with the Ascelli; the ☉ affl. in ♒; the ☉ and ☽ are usually in mutual affliction, one of them usually rising, and affl. by ♄ or ♂, and in this respect the worst signs for the Lights are ♈, ♉, ♋, ♌ and ♒; the ☉ to the ☌ or P. asp. the ☽ by dir., and the ☽ ill-aspected; the ☉ or ☽ to the ☌ or ill-asps. ♄ by dir.; the ☉ or ☽ in transit over the place of ♆, and ♆ a promittor, and the ☉ or ☽ affl. at B.; the ☉ or ☽ affl. by ♅, ♄, or ♂, and in orb of the Pleiades, the Ascelli, or Antares, or when ♄ or ♂ are in nebulous parts, and affl. the ☉ or ☽; the ☉ in the 8° ♐ with Antares, and affl. by one or more of the malefics; the ☉ or ☽ ☌ Antares, and in □ or ☍ ♂; the ☉ ☌ ☽ or ☋ near nebulous stars; the ☉ or ☽ with nebulous stars at B., as Antares, the Ascelli, or the Pleiades, and affl. by a malefic; the ☉ affl. at B., and the ☉ by dir. to the evil asp. the Asc.; the ☉ hyleg at B., and to the ☌ or ill-asp. ♄ by dir.; the ☉ directed to the Pleiades, Hyades, Castor or Pollux; the ☽ to the ☌ or ill-asp. the ☉ or ♄ by dir., and the ☉ or ☽ affl. at B., and espec. when falling near nebulous stars; the ☽ in the Western angle and conjoined with the Pleiades; the ☽ affl. in ♌, ♑, or ♒; the ☽ hyleg in ♈ or ♒, and afflicted, and espec. with females; the ☽ in ♈ or ♉, and affl. by ♆; the ☽ ♈, ☍ ♂ in ♎, and ♂ elevated above the ☽; the ☽ with the Pleiades in ♉, and affl. by any of the malefics; the ☽ with the Ascelli in ♌; the ☽ apply. to ♂, or conjoined with him in a day geniture; the ☽ to the bad asps. the ☉, and the aspect fall near nebulous stars; the ☽ passing over the place of the ☉ at B. at a Solar Rev., and espec. if the ☉ or ☽ be affl. by nebulous stars; the ☽ afflicted, according to sign, house, and nature of the afflicting planet; the ☽ Sig. □ or ☍ the ☉, and espec. if the ☉ be affl. by ♂, or either the ☉ or ☽ are with nebulous stars; ♆ affl. in ♈ or ♉; ♆ in ♉ in the 6th H.; ♆ in ♉ and affl. the ☉, ☽, Asc., or hyleg; ♅ in ♌ and ☌ the Ascelli, and □ or ☍ the ☽; ♅ afflicting the ☉ or ☽; ♄ in ♒; ♄ to the ☌ or ill-asps. the ☉ or ☽ by dir., and probably from taking cold; ♃ Sig. in ♎ in Hor'y Questions; ♂ in ♈ and affl. the Lights; ♂ affl. in ♒, as ♒ rules the Ether; ☿ affl. in ♋ or ♎; malefics, or a malefic, with nebulous stars, and affl. the ☉ or ☽, and espec. when the malefic is ℞, and passing over the nebulous stars, back and forth several times by direct, ℞, and redirect motion; the Asc. to the ☌ or ill-asp. the ☉ by dir., and the ☉ affl. at B.; ♌ diseases; ♒ on the Asc.; ♈ or ♒ on the cusp of the 6th H. (See "Affected", "Bad Eyes", "Cases", and the various paragraphs in this section. Also see Aquarius, Ether; "Light Rays" under Light; Nebulous; "Influence of Uranus" under Uranus).

**Failing Eyes**—The ☉ affl. at B., and by dir. (See Affected, Defects, Dim, Weak, and other paragraphs in this section. Also see "Nearly Blind" under Blindness; Sight).

**Far-Sighted**—(See "Hyperopia" under Sight).

**Father**—Injury to Eyes of—(See "Eyes" under Father).

**Film**—White Film Over the Eyes—Blindness From—(See "Cold" under Blindness).

**Floating Specks**—(See "Muscae Volitantes" in this section).

**Fused Into One**—The Eyes Fused Into One Eye—(See Cyclops).

**Glaucoma**—A Disease characterized by increased intraocular tension—(See Glaucoma).

**Goggle Eyes**—(See "Goggle" under Eyeballs).

**Growths**—Obstructing Growths—The ☽ or Asc. in nebulous parts and affl. by ♄. (See "Growths" under Blindness; Cataracts; "Film", in this section).

**Gunshot**—Eyes Injured By—Blindness By—(See "Blindness" under Gunshot).

**Gutta Serena**—Amaurosis—Partial or Total Blindness—(See Gutta Serena; "Total Blindness" under Blindness).

**Focus**—Disorders of—(See Accommodation).

**Headaches**—Ocular Headaches—(See "Ocular" under Headaches).

**Hemianopia**—Blindness of One-Half of the Visual Field—(See "Hemianopia" under Sight).

**Hippus**—Clonic Spasm of the Iris—(See "Clonic" in this section).

**Hot Diseases** — In the Eyes — Hot Humours In — The Asc. to the ☉ the ☉ by dir;. ♂ affl. in ♈. (See Heat).

**Humorous Discharges** — (See "Discharges" in this section).

**Hurts To** — The ☉ and ☽ both impedited by ♄ or ♂ in any part of the figure. (See Accidents, Blows, Injuries, in this section).

**Hyperopia** — Hypermetropia — Far-sighted — (See "Hyperopia" under Sight).

**Hypertrophy** — Of the Muscles — ♂ affl. in ♈; Subs at SP (7D) tend to both Hypertrophy and Atrophy. (See Atrophy, Hypertrophy).

**Impediments** — In One or Both Eyes — (See "One Eye" under Blindness; Impediments; "Eye" under Left, Right).

**Infancy** — Eyes Affected In — (See "Born Blind" under Blindness).

**Infirmities In** — (See "Eye Trouble", and the various paragraphs in this section).

**Inflamed Eyes** — Inflammation in the Eyes — Sore Eyes — Caused by an afflicted ☉; the ☉ affl. in ♈; the ☉ to the ill-asps. the ☽ by dir., and the ☽ affl. at B.; the ☉ affl. by ♄; the ☉ or ☽ in ♈ and affl. by ♂; the ☉ and ☽ in ♊ asp. from ♈ and ♎, and affl. by malefics or nebulous stars; ♂ affl. in ♈; a ♌ disease and afflictions in ♌. and espec. when the ☉ or ☽ are near the Ascelli; fixed stars of the nature of ♂ and the ☽ ascending at B. (See Conjunctivitis; "Blepharitis", under Eyelids. Also see "Eyestrain", "Ulcer", in this section).

**Inhibition** — Of the Optic Nerve — (See "Decay" under Optic).

**Injury to Eyes** — Accidents — Hurts — Wounds To — (See Acicdents, Assaults, Blows, Both Eyes, Burns, Danger, Exercise, Explosions, Father, Gunshot, Hurts, Left, Loss of, Mother, One Eye, Right, Robbers, Scars, Sports, Sword, and the various paragraphs in this section).

**Iris** — Pupils — Disorders of — Clonic Spasm of — Hippus — Iritis — Dilated Pupils — Mydriasis — Inequality of Pupils — Iridoplegia — Paralysis of, etc. — (See Iris).

**Jerky Eyes** — Oscillating — (See "Nystagmus" under Eyeballs).

**Keratitis** — Inflamed Cornea — (See "Cornea" in this section).

**Lachrymal Apparatus** — Disorders of — (See Tears).

**Left Eye** — Disorders of — Hurts To — Sight Affected In — (See "Eye" under Left. Also see "Left Eye" in Sec. 1 of this Article).

**Lens** — (See "Crystalline" in this section).

**Light** — Failure of the Pupil to Respond to Light — (See "Light" under Iris).

**Lightning** — Blindness By — (See "Lightning" under Blindness; Lightning).

**Loss of Eyes** — Loss of Sight In One or Both Eyes — (See "Both Eyes", "One

Eye", in this section. Also see "Total Blindness" under Blindness; "Loss Of" under Sight).

**Males** — Men — Men Suffer In Their Eyes — ♂ in ♏ at the Vernal E., and lord of the year. (See "Eyes" under Men).

**Marks** — Scars — Marks or Scars In the Eyes — The ☉ or ☽ ascending and impedited by ♄ or ♂; the ☉ or ☽ Sig. ♂ ♂ and ill-dig.; the ☽ Sig. ♂ ☉ or apply. to the ♂. (See "Marks", "Scars", under Face; Marks, Scars).

**Mother** — Injury to the Eyes of the Mother — (See "Eyes" under Mother).

**Motor Paralysis** — Oculo Motor Paralysis — (See "Paralysis" in this section. Also see Motor, Paralysis).

**Muscae Volitantes** — Floating Spots In the Visual Field — Threads — Specks — Dots and Semi-Transparent Threads and Spots Before the Eyes from Stomach Trouble and other Indisposition — ♄ the afflicting planet; ♀ in ♈. (See "Specks" in this section).

**Muscles of Eyes** — (a) Atrophy of — ♄ affl. in ♈; Subs at SP (7D). (See Atrophy). (b) Crystallization of — Congestion of — (See "Crystallization" in this section). (c) Hypertrophy of — (See "Hypertrophy" in this section). (d) Paralysis of — Ophthalmoplegia — (See "Paralysis" in this section). (e) Squint — (See "Strabismus" in this section).

**Mydriasis** — Abnormal Dilatation of the Pupil — (See "Mydriasis" under Iris).

**Myopia** — Near-Sighted — (See "Myopia" under Sight).

**Near-Sighted** — (See "Myopia" under Sight).

**Nerves** — Optic Nerve — Crystallization of — (See "Crystallization", "Optic", in this section).

**Nystagmus** — Oscillation of Eyeballs — (See "Nystagmus" under Eyeballs).

**Obstructions In** — Obstructive Growths — Obstruction to the Flow of Tears — ♄ influence and afflictions; ♄ in ♈; the ☽ or Asc. in nebulous parts and affl. by ♄. (See Growths, Obstructions, Tears).

**Ocular** — Ocular Headaches — Oculo Motor Paralysis — (See "Ocular" under Headaches; "Paralysis" in this section).

**Old Age Vision** — (See "Presbyopia" under Sight).

**One Eye** — (a) Blemish In or Near — (See "Eyes" under Blemishes). (b) Blindness In — Loss of — The ☽ in the 1st or 7th H. in exact ♂, □, or ☍ ☉, or if the ☽ be angular and ♂ ♄ or ♂, or with nebulous stars; the ☽ with Orion's Belt. Wilson has observed that those who have lost one eye, or who may have scars in or near the eyes, are extremely irascible and vicious. (See "One Eye" under Blindness). (c) Impediment In — (See "Impediments" in this section. (d) One Eye Larger — (See "Larger" in Sec. 1 of this Article).

**One-Half Vision** — (See "Hemianopia" under Sight).

**Operations** — The eyes should not be tampered with when the ☽ is in ♈ or

♒, or when the ☽ is in an earthy sign, or in ☌, □, ☍ the ☉, or passing the place of nebulous stars, as the Pleiades in ♉. The ☽ should be well-placed, incr. in light, and free from the affl. of the ☉, malefics, or nebulous stars. (See Operations).

**Ophthalmia**—Conjunctivitis—Inflamed or Bloodshot Eyes—(See Conjunctivitis. Also see "Inflamed" in this section).

**Ophthalmoplegia**—(See "Paralysis" in this section).

**Optic Nerve**—Atrophy of—Decay of—Crystallization—Inhibition—(See Optic).

**Oscillation**—Of the Eyeballs—(See "Nystagmus" under Eyeballs).

**Overworked Eyes**—(See "Eyestrain" in this section).

**Pain In**—The ☉ to the place of ☋ by dir.; the ☽ hyleg, and to the ☌ or ill-asp. ♄ by dir.

**Paralysis**—(a) Of the Iris—Iridoplegia—(See Iris). (b) Of the Muscles—Ophthalmoplegia—The ☉ rising in ♈ and affl. by ♄; ♆, ♅, or ♄ affl. in ♈; Subs at MCP and SP. (See Paralysis). (c) Oculo Motor Paralysis—♅ or ♂ affl. in ♈; Subs at SP (7D). (See Motor, Paralysis).

**Partial Blindness**—Amaurosis—(See "Amaurosis" under Blindness; Gutta Serena).

**Presbyopia**—Old Age Vision—(See "Presbyopia" under Sight).

**Prevalent**—Eye Diseases Prevalent—The ☉ in the 6th H. and affl. at the Vernal E., and lord of the year; ♂ in ♍, lord of the year at the Vernal, and espec. in places subject to ♍; ♀ or the ☽ lady of the year at the Vernal, weak and afflicted; Comets appearing in ♌.

**Prominent Eyes**—Protrusion of the Eyeballs—(See "Prominent", "Protruding", in Sec. 1 of this Article).

**Pupils**—Of the Eyes—Dilatation of—Mydriasis—Inequality of—(See Iris).

**Reading and Study**—Eyes Suffer From—(See "Eyestrain" in this section; Reading, Study).

**Red and Inflamed**—(See Conjunctivitis. Also see "Inflamed" in this section).

**Retina**—Disorders of—(See "Optic Nerve" under Optic; Retina; "Hemianopia" under Sight).

**Rheum In**—♂ in ♈ or ♏. (See Rheum).

**Right Eye**—Blindness In—Blows To—Hurts To—(See "Eye" under Right. Also see "Right Eye" in Sec. 1 of this Article).

**Robbers**—Injury to Eyes by Assaults of—The ☉ in an angle, and ☌ or ☍ ☽, and the ☉ configurated with ☿. (See Robbers).

**Scars**—In the Eyes—(See "Marks" in this section; "Eyes" under Blemishes; Left, Right, Marks, Scars).

**Short-Sighted**—(See "Myopia" under Sight).

**Sight**—Vision—Disorders of—(See Accommodation, Blindness, Sight. Also note the various paragraphs in this section).

**Smallpox**—Blindness By—(See "Smallpox" under Blindness).

**Sore Eyes**—(See "Inflamed" in this section).

**Spasm**—Clonic Spasm of the Iris—Hippus—(See Iris).

**Specks**—Over the Eyes—(a) Blindness From—(See "Defects" under Blindness; Specks). (b) Floating Specks in the Visual Field—(See "Muscae Volitantes" in this section).

**Sports**—Injuries to the Eyes During Exercise or Sports—Blindness By—(See Amusements; "Sports" under Blindness; "Eyes" under Exercise; "Amusements" under Sports).

**Spots**—Floating Spots Before the Eyes—(See "Muscae Volitantes" in this section).

**Squint**—Crossed Eyes—(See "Strabismus" in this section).

**Strabismus**—Squint—Crossed Eyes—Incoordination of the Eye Muscles—♄ ☌ ☽, and the ☽ near nebulous stars; ☿ occi.; ☿ ruler of the Asc., and occi.; Subs at MCP and SP (7D). (See Incoordination. Case—See "Diseases to the Eyes", "Chap. 13, page 88, Daath's Medical Astrology.

**Strain**—Of the Eyes—(See "Eyestrain" in this section).

**Strokes To**—(See "Accidents" in this section; "Strokes" under Blindness; "Eyes" under Sword).

**Structural Defects**—In the Eyes—(See "Defects" in this section).

**Study and Reading**—Eye Disorders From—(See "Eyestrain" in this section).

**Suffering**—In the Eyes—(See "Eye Trouble", and the various paragraphs in this section. Also see Blindness, Sight).

**Sword**—Injuries and Cuts to the Eyes By the Sword—Blindness By—(See "Strokes" under Blindness; "Eyes" under Sword; "Accidents" in this section).

**Tampering**—With the Eyes—(See "Operations" in this section).

**Tears**—Lachrymal Apparatus—Disorders of—(See Tears).

**Tension**—The Intraocular Tension Increased—(See Glaucoma).

**Threads**—Floating Threads and Spots In the Visual Field—(See "Muscae Volitantes" in this section).

**Total Blindness**—(See "Total Blindness" under Blindness; "Both Eyes" in this section).

**Tract**—The Optic Tract—Disorders of—(See Optic. Also note the various paragraphs in this section).

**Treachery**—Blindness or Injury to Eyes By—(See "Treachery" under Blindness; Treachery).

**Treatment**—Of the Eyes—Blue, the color of ♀, is soothing to the eyes. Green, ruled by ♄, tends to relieve inflamed eyes. Sugar of Lead, ruled by ♄, is also used as a collyria in inflamed eyes. (See "Operations" in this section. Also see Blue, Green, Lead).

**Trichiasis**—Inversion of the Eyelashes—(See Eyelids).

**Tunics**—Inflammation of the Second Tunic of the Eye—(See "Choroiditis" under Choroid).

**Ulcer**—Of the Conjunctiva or Cornea—Afflictions in ♈; ♄ or ♂ in ♈. (See Conjunctivitis, Ulcers. Also see Cornea, Inflamed, in this section).

**Vision**—Disorders of—(See Accommodation, Blindness, Sight. Also note the various paragraphs in this section).

**Vitreous Humor**—(See "Vitreous" in Sec. 1 of this Article; "Muscae V.", "Tension", in this section).

**Watery Eyes**—Epiphora—Overflow of Tears—Discharges—(See Tears. Also see "Discharges" in this section).

**Weak Eyes**—Weakness In the Eyes—Eyes Out of Order—The ☉ or ☽ affl. in ♈; the ☉ or ☽ ☌ nebulous stars, and in □ or ☍ malefics; the ☉ to the ☌ or P. asp. the ☽ by dir., and the ☽ affl. at B.; the ☉ affl. in ♎; the ☉ or ☽ to the ☌ ♄ by dir.; the ☉ or ☽ affl. at B., and by dir.; the ☽ combust and sepr. from the ☌; the ☽ Sig. □ or ☍ the ☉; the ☽ affl. in ♑; ♄ in ♈; ♄ posited between the 24° and 30° of ♒; ♂ in ♋ and affl. by the ☉ or ☽; the M.C. to the place of the Pleiades or Pollux; in Hor'y Questions, the Sig. with the ☽, and ♄ in ♈. (See "Bad Eyes", "Eye Trouble", and the various paragraphs in this section).

**Weak Sight**—(See Blindness, Sight).

**Weariness Of**—(See "Dull Eyes" in Sec. 1 of this Article).

**White Film**—(See "Film" in this section).

**Winking**—(See Eyelids)

**Wounds To**—(See "Accidents" in this section).

**EYESIGHT**—(See Accommodation; Blindness, Eyes, Sight).

**EYESTRAIN**—(See "Eyestrain" under Eyes).

# F

**FACE**—The Visage—Countenance—Look—Expression—Aspect—Features—Complexion—etc. This Article will have to do with the description, form, shape, and diseases of the Face. For other subjects which have to do with the Face and its subdivisions, see Appearance, Aspect, Beard, Cheeks, Chin, Complexion, Cosmetics, Countenance, Dimples, Ears, Expression, Eyeballs, Eyebrows, Eyelids, Eyes, Features, Forehead, Hair, Head, Jaws, Lips, Look, Mouth, Nose, Profile, Teeth, Temples, etc. The 1st H. represents the Head and Face of Man. The Face is ruled by ♂, and is also under the external rulership of the ♈ sign. The facial bones are under the structural rulership of ♈. The skin of the Face, and the complexion, are ruled by ♀. The form, shape and characteristics of the face are largely determined by the decanate rising on the Asc. (See Decanates). This Article will be divided into two Sections. Sec. 1 will deal with General Characteristics, Description, Form and Shape of the Face, and Sec. 2, the Diseases and Afflictions to the Face. See the following subjects in the alphabetical arrangement when not considered here.

## — SECTION ONE —

**GENERAL CONSIDERATIONS**—General Characteristics—Form and Shape—Description—Countenance — Expression—Look—Complexion, etc.—

**Amorous** — (See "Amorous Eyes" under Eyes).

**Angular**—♄ rising in the Asc. (See "Angular Body" under Body).

**Animal Expression**—(See Animal).

**Appearance; Aspect; Austere;**

**Beard; Beautiful Face**—Lovely Face—Fair Face—Given by ♀; ♀ in the Asc., well-dig., or ♀ ruler of the Asc.; ♀ well-dig. at B., a good, fair, and round visage; ♀ rising in ♉ or ♎, and with one of these signs on the Asc.; ♀ Sig. in ♐, fair, oval face; in Hor'y Questions, ♀ Sig. of the person, fair, round face; ♉, ♎, or ♒ on the Asc.; ♎ gives a round, lovely, and very beautiful face; the ♒ sign gives more beauty of face and form than any other sign except ♎. (See Beautiful, Complexion, Dimples, Handsome. Also see Comely, Fair, Handsome, Lovely, in this section).

**Big Face**—♄ in ♒ in partile asp. the Asc. (See Fat, Fleshy, Full, Large, Lumpish, Plump, Square, in this section).

**Bloated**—The ☽ Sig. in ♓, pale and bloated. (See Pale. Also see "Bulging", "Lumpish", "Puffy", in this section).

**Blushing; Bold Face**—Resolute—♂ in ♈ or ♏; ♂ in the Asc. or M.C. at B.

**Bones Of**—The 14 bones of the face are under the external rulership of ♈. For Disorders of, see "Bones" in Sec. 2 of this Article.

**Broad** — ♏ influence; ♏ on the Asc., broad and square; Martialists have; ♂ strong at B., and ♂ ruler; ♂ Sig. in ♏, broad and plain; ♂ Sig. in ♉ or ♏; ♂ in ♉ or ♏ in partile asp. the Asc.; the ☉ in ♉ or ♏, in partile the Asc.; the ☉ Sig. in ♉, large and broad; the ☉ Sig. in ♏; ♀ Sig. in ♏. (See Full, Large, Round, Wide, in this section).

**Brow**—Lowering Brow—(See Forehead).

**Bulging**—♓ on the Asc., bulging and large. (See Bloated, Large, Lumpish, in this section).

**Caul**—The Fetal Membranes Covering the Head After Birth—Usually a ♄ influence; ♄ rising in the Asc.; ♄ rising and elevated, and in one of his own signs; ♄ well-asp. in ♑ or ♏. Case—See "Born With a Caul", No. 929, in 1001 N.N.

**Characteristics**—Of the Face—Are largely determined by the decanate rising.

**Cheeks; Cheerful Face** — Cheerful Countenance—The ☽ Sig. in ♎. (See Cheerfulness. Also see Pleasant, Smiling, in this section).

**Chin; Coarse Features** — (See Features).

**Color** — Of the Face — (See Color, Complexion, Pigment, Races, Skin).

**Comely**—And Fair—In Hor'y Questions the ☉ as Sig. denotes such a person. (See Comely. Also see "Fair" in this section).

**Commanding; Complexion; Cosmetics** —The Evil Effects of—(See Cosmetics).

**Countenance; Cruel; Dark** — See "Dark" under Complexion).

**Debauched Look**—♂ Sig. in ♓. (See Debauched).

**Delicate**—And Pale Face—(See "Delicate", "Pale", under Complexion).

**Dimples; Dissipated Look**—(See Debauched, Dissipation).

**Downward Look** — (See "Downward" under Look).

**Drawn Face**—Sad Expression—♄ in ♋. (See Gloom, Grave, Grief, Melancholy, Sadness. Also see "Drawn" in Sec. 2 of this Article).

**Eagle Face**—Eagle Features—♏ gives. (See "Eagle" under Features).

**Ears; Effeminate; Evil Complexion**— (See "Bad", "Evil", under Complexion).

**Expression; Eyeballs; Eyebrows; Eyelashes**—(See Eyelids).

**Eyelids; Eyes; Fair**—Denoted by ♀; born under ♀. (See Beautiful, Good, Lovely, Round, in this section. Also see "Fair" under Complexion).

**Fat Face** — (See Bloated, Bulging, Large, Lumpish, in this section).

**Features; Females**—Face In—♀ in the Asc., in ♉ or ♎, the face very beautiful; ♓ on Asc., plump face in females; ♑ on Asc., usually ugly and not good looking. (See Beautiful, Fair, Lovely, Plump, and the various paragraphs in this section).

**Fierce Countenance**—(See Fierce).

**Fiery Countenance**—(See "Fiery" under Eyes; "Fiery").

**Fleshy Face**—♓ gives. (See Fleshy. Also see Bloated, Bulging, Full, Large, Long, Lumpish, Plump, in this section).

**Forehead; Form and Shape** — The form, shape, and characteristics of the face are determined largely by the decanate rising on the Asc. (See Appearance, Decanates, Features, Form, Shape. Also note the various paragraphs in this section).

**Freckles; Full Face**—The ☉ in ♌ or ♒, full, round face; the ☉ Sig. of the person in Hor'y Questions; the ☉ Sig. in ♌, ♒, or ♓, round, full face; the ☽ ascending; the ☽ strong at B.; the ☽ in ♋, or the ☽ Sig. in ♋, full, round face; the ☽ Sig. in ♌, ♏, or ♓; the ☽ Sig. in ♏, full and fleshy face; the ☽ Sig. in ♓, full and bloated; ♄ in ♈, or ♄ Sig. in ♈; ♃ strong at B.; ♃ as Sig. of the person in Hor'y Questions; ♃ Sig. in ♏, full and fleshy; ♂ as Sig. in Hor'y Questions, full, red or sun-

burnt; born under ♂, usually a full face; ♀ Sig. in ♓, full and round; ♀ in ♈, ♉, or ♒; ☿ Sig. in ♒; ♉ gives, and with ♉ on Asc.; ♋ gives round, full face, and with ♋ on Asc.; ♍ on the Asc.; ♏, ♐, ♒, and ♓ give; ♐ on Asc. tends to a long, full face; ♓ gives a good, large and full face; ♓ on Asc., full, and usually bloated or bulging. (See Bloated, Broad, Bulging, Fleshy, Large, Oval, Plump, Round, in this section).

**Ghastly Look** — (See Pale, Sickly, White).

**Glances** — (See Expression, Eyes, Look).

**Gloomy Face**—(See Gloom).

**Good Face**—♀ well-dig. at B., a good, fair and round face; ♓ gives a good, large face. (See Beautiful, Fair, Full, Handsome, Round, in this section).

**Grave Countenance**—(See Grave).

**Hair; Handsome Face**—(See "Beautiful" under Eyes; Handsome; "Beautiful", in this section).

**Harmless Looking**—(See Harmless).

**Head; Honest Face**—(See Honest).

**Humane Face** — (See Humane, Kind, Sympathetic).

**Idiotic**—(See Idiot).

**Indifferent; Intellectual Look** — (See Intellect).

**Intemperate Aspect** — (See Intemperate).

**Inviting Face** — (See "Beautiful" in this section, and under Eyes).

**Jaundiced Look**—(See Jaundice).

**Jaws; Kind Face**—♃ ruler, or strong at B. (See Kind, Humane, Sympathetic).

**Large Face**—The ☉ Sig. in ♉, large and broad; ♄ Sig. in ♒; ♄ ♒ partile asp. Asc.; ☿ in ♒; ♓ on Asc., large, bloated, bulging, pale, fleshy. (See Big, Bloated, Broad, Bulging, Fat, Fleshy, Full, Lumpish, Plump, Round, Square, in this section. Also see "Large" under Ears, Eyes, Lips, Mouth, Nose).

**Lean Face** — Thin—♑ gives a lean, long and slender face; ♑ on Asc.; ♄ gives. (See Long, Slender, Thin, in this section; "Lean Body" under Lean; "Thin Body" under Thin).

**Left Side** — Of Face — (a) Case — Burned—Burns To—(See "Face" under Burns). (b) Marks, Moles, or Warts On—(See "Marks" in this section).

**Lightness**—Of Feature—(See Features).

**Lips; Long Face**—♄ Sig. in ♑; ♄ influence strong at B.; ♄ in the Asc.; ♄ in ♍; ♃ rising at B.; ☿ strong at B., long and narrow; a ☿ person; ☿ Sig. in ♍, long visage; in Hor'y Questions ☿ Sig. of the person; ♈ gives, and espec. when on the Asc.; ♈ gives a long and meagre; ♈ on Asc., long face and neck; ♐ gives long visage, a long, full, and handsome face; ♐ on Asc.; ♑ on Asc., a long, lean, slender, thin face, and generally ugly; ♒ gives; ♒ on the Asc., a long and rather fleshy face. (See Full, Lean, Narrow, Oval, Slender, Thin, Ugly, in this section).

**Look; Lotions**—Face Lotions—(See Cosmetics).

**Lovely Face**—♎ gives a round, lovely face, with great beauty, and with a lovely expression; ♎ on Asc.; ♐ gives. (See "Beautiful" in this section).

**Lowering Aspect**—(See "Downward Look" under Look; Stooping).

**Lumpish Face**—Unpleasant and Lumpish—♄ ascending at B.; ♀ Sig. in ♏, nothing very pleasant in the countenance. (See "Bloated" in this section).

**Lustful Face**—(See Lascivious, Lewd, Lust, Wanton).

**Meagre Face**—Small—Thin—♈ gives a long, meagre face; ♑ gives; the ☽ Sig. in ♑. (See Lean, Small, Thin, in this section).

**Melancholic Face**—(See "Appearance" under Melancholy).

**Misshaped**—♄ and ♑ influence; ♄ in the Asc., or ruler of Asc.; ♑ on Asc. (See "Distortions" under Features; "Not Handsome" under Handsome; "Ill-Formed" under Ill; "Lumpish", "Ugly", in this section).

**Mouth; Narrow Face**—☿ strong at B., a narrow, long face; ☿ ascending at B., and free from the rays of other planets; ☿ gives a thin, sharp, narrow face. The Mental Type has a pear-shaped head, with wide temples, and narrows down to the chin. (See Decanates. Also see Lean, Long, Meagre, Sharp, Slender, Thin, in this section).

**Nose; Oily**—Shiny—♃ Sig. in ♉; ♉ gives a swarthy, shiny face. (See "Glossy" under Hair; Oils).

**Open Countenance**—♐ on Asc. gives an open and handsome face and countenance. (See Honest, Humane, Kind, Sincere, Sympathetic).

**Oval Face**—The ☉ Sig. in ♎, ♐, or ♑, or in these signs in partile asp. the Asc.; the ☉ rising in the Asc.; the ☽ Sig. in ♍, ♐, or ♑, or in partile asp. the Asc. from these signs; ♄ Sig. in ♊ or ♎, or in these signs in partile the Asc.; ♃ Sig. in ♈, ♋, ♎, ♐, or ♑, or in these signs in partile the Asc.; born under ♃; ♃ in the Asc., or ruling the Asc.; ♃ gives when rising at B.; ♃ in ♎, oval and handsome; ♂ Sig. in ♌, ♎, or ♐, or in these signs in partile asp. the Asc.; ♀ Sig. in ♍, ♎, or ♐, or in these signs in partile the Asc.; ♀ Sig. in ♐, a fair and oval; ☿ Sig. in ♈, ♍, or ♐, or partile the Asc. from these signs; ♀ in ♍, oval or thin; ♌ on the Asc., oval and ruddy; ♍ on Asc., but ♍ usually tends to a face more round than oval; ♐ on Asc., long, oval face. The Vital type of Temperament tends to an oval or round face. (See Decanates. Also see Beautiful, Pyriform, Round, in this section).

**Pale Face**—♓ on the Asc. tends to a pale, large, and fleshy face. (See Delicate, Pale, Sickly; "Low" under Vitality).

**Peaceful; Pear-Shaped**—(See Pyriform in this section).

**Pensive; Piercing Look**—(See "Penetrating", "Piercing", under Eyes).

**Plain Face**—♄ in ♏; ♂ Sig. in ♏, broad and plain; ♑ on the Asc.

**Pleasant**—Pleasing—The ☽ Sig. in ♎; the ☽ Sig. of the person in Hor'y Questions; ♃ rising in the Asc. (See Pleasant).

**Plump Face**—♓ on the Asc. gives a plump face in females; ♓ influence. (See Bloated, Bulging, Fleshy, Full, Round, in this section. Also see Plumpness).

**Poor Complexion**—(See "Bad", "Pale", "Poor", under Complexion).

**Profile**—The Outline and Contour of the Face—Side View of the Face—The profile of the face is largely determined by the sign on the Asc. at B. Aries on the Asc. tends to a profile resembling the Ram; ♑ on the Asc., resembling the Goat, etc. When there is an animal sign on the Asc. at B., the native is apt to have features similar to such animal. (See "Animal Signs" under Animals; "Beastly Form" under Beasts; Cheeks; "Dogs" under Children; Chin, Face, Features, Forehead, Fowls, Lips, Mouth, Nose, etc.).

**Puffy Cheeks**—(See "Puffy" under Cheeks; Puffing. Also see "Bloated", "Full", in this section).

**Pyriform**—Pear-Shaped Face—Narrow—☿ gives. (See Narrow, Oval, in this section).

**Ram Face**—Resembles the Ram—♈ on the Asc. (See "Profile" in this section; "Animal Signs" under Animals).

**Red Face**—The ☽ as Sig. indicates a face more white than red; ♃ Sig. in ♈ tends to a peculiar redness, and pimples; ♂ gives a general redness all over the face, but not a rosy hue; ♂ as Sig. in Hor'y Questions gives a full, red, or sunburnt face. (See Freckles, Pimples, Ruddy. Also see "Morbid Red Face" in Sec. 2 of this Article).

**Refined Face**—♀ Sig. ☌ or good asp. ☿; ☿ Sig. ☌ ♃, or ☿ Sig. ☌ or good asp. ♀; ☿ rising at B., and free from the rays of other planets; ♎ on the Asc. (See Elegant, Intellectual, Refined).

**Resolute**—(See "Bold" in this section).

**Right Side**—Of the Face—(See "Face" under Right, Left. Also see Marks, Moles, Scars, Warts, in Sec. 2 of this Article).

**Rosy**—♃ in the Asc. at B., and ♃ in ♈ or ♎, the face and complexion are rosy and handsome. (See "Red Complexion" under Complexion).

**Round Face**—The ☉ in ♌, ♒, or ♓, partile the Asc., or as Sig. in these signs, a round and full face; the ☉ strong at B. generally gives; denoted by the ☉ in Hor'y Questions; the ☽ gives a good, fair and round visage; the ☽ rising in the Asc; the ☽ in ♈, ♋, ♌, or ♓, in partile the Asc., or as Sig. in these signs, round and full; the ☽ Sig. in Hor'y Questions; some say ♂ gives, but it is seldom the case; Born under ♀, and ♀ well-dig. at B., a good, fair, round, smooth and beautiful face; ♀ Sig. in Hor'y Questions; ♀ in ♋, ♌, or ♓, in partile asp. the Asc., or Sig. in these signs; ♀ Sig. in ♋, round, pale, sickly or white; ♀ Sig. in ♓, round, full, fair, and dimpled; ♋ gives round and full, but usually with short or small features; ♋ on Asc., round, full, white or pale; ♉, ♌, ♎, ♒, or ♓ on Asc. The Vital Temperament gives a round or oval face. (See Beautiful, Bloated, Fair, Fat, Fleshy, Full, Large, Lumpish, Oval, Plump, in this section).

**Ruddy Face**—Given by the ☉ and ♂; ♌ gives an oval, ruddy face. (See "Red" in this section; "Red Complexion" under Complexion; Red, Robust, Ruddy, Sanguine; "Good" under Vitality).

**Sad Face**—Sorrowful Face—Pensive Aspect—♄ in ♋, or Sig. in ♋; ♀ affl. in ♈, or Sig. in ♈. (See Anxiety, Gloomy, Grave, Melancholic, Pensive, Sadness, Serious, Worry, etc.).

**Savage Face**—Given by ♂; ♂ affl. in the Asc. or M.C. (See Cruel, Fierce, Savage, Vicious).

**Sensual Face**—(See Amorous, Lewd, Lascivious, Licentious, Lust, Passion, Sensuous, Wanton, etc.).

**Serious**—(See "Sad" in this section).

**Severe**—(See Austere, Cruel, Fierce, Severe).

**Shape Of**—Shape and Form—(See "Form" in this section).

**Sharp Face**—Sharp Features—☿ gives; ☿ Sig. in ♋, sharp and thin. (See Narrow, Thin, in this section).

**Shiny**—(See "Oily" in this section).

**Short**—♋ gives; ♋ on the Asc., a short, small, round face.

**Sickly**—See Delicate, Emaciation, Pale, Sickly. Also see Delicate, Pale, Thin, in this section).

**Sincere Face**—(See "Open" in this section; Generous, Honest, Humane, Kind, Sympathetic).

**Skin Of**—♀ has to do with the skin of the face, and the complexion, and disorders of the face from the indiscreet use of Cosmetics. (See Complexion, Cosmetics. For Skin Disorders of the Face see Sec. 2 of this Article).

**Slender Face**—♑ gives a long, lean, and slender visage; ♑ on Asc. (See Lean, Long, Narrow, Thin, in this section).

**Small Face**—♋ gives a small, short, round face; ♋ on Asc.; ♀ strong at B. gives a round, but not large face; the ☽ Sig. in ♑ indicates one of small features. (See Round, Short, in this section. Also see Features).

**Smiling Face**—Pleasing Smiles—A Cheerful Countenance—♀ in the Asc., or ruler of the Asc., well-dig. and aspected; ♀ Sig. of the person in Hor'y Questions. (See Cheerful, Pleasant, in this section; Cheerfulness, Jovial, Pleasant, Smiling).

**Smooth**—♂ Sig. in ♈ or ♍, ruddy and smooth if ♂ be ori.; born under ♀, and ♀ well-dig. at B., a good, fair, round, smooth, and beautiful face. (See Ruddy, Smooth).

**Sober Face**—Born under ♃, a sober and commanding aspect. (See Sober).

**Solid Countenance**—♄ Sig. in ♍ in Hor'y Questions. (See Solid).

**Sorrowful**—(See "Sad" in this section).

**Square**—♏ influence; ♏ on Asc., square and broad. (See "Broad" in this section).

**Stern**—(See Austere).

**Strong Face**—(See Bold, Commanding, Positive; "Ruddy", in this section).

**Sunburnt**—In Hor'y Questions, ♂ as Sig. denotes a full, red, and sunburnt face. (See "Sunburnt" under Complexion).

**Sunken Cheeks**—Sunken Face—(See "Falling In" under Cheeks; "Sunken" in Sec. 2 of this Article).

**Surly Aspect**—♄ in ♌, in partile asp. the Asc. (See Cruel, Fierce).

**Swarthy**—♉ gives a swarthy and shiny face. (See "Swarthy" under Complexion).

**Sympathetic**—(See "Kind" in this section).

**Tawny**—(See "Tan" under Complexion).

**Teeth; Thin Face**—Lean—Meagre—Narrow—Long—The ☽ Sig. in ♑; the ☽ ♑, partile asp. the Asc., thin face and body; ♄ gives a lean, thin face and features; ♄ in the Asc., or ♑ on Asc., thin, and not very good looking; ♄ ascending at B.; ♄ in ♋, pale and thin; ♄ in ♍, long and thin; ♄ ☌ the Sig. of the party in Hor'y Questions; ♃ in ♑, partile the Asc., or Sig. in ♑; ♂ Sig. in ♑, or ♂ in ♑ in partile the Asc.; ♀ in ♑ in partile the Asc., or Sig. in ♑, thin, lean, pale and sickly face; ☿ gives, and ☿ Sig. of the party; ☿ gives a thin, narrow, pointed, sharp face and feature; ☿ in ♋, ♍, ♑, or ♓, in partile the Asc.; ☿ Sig. in ♋, thin and sharp features; ☿ in ♍, thin or oval; ☿ Sig. in ♑; ♈ gives, and ♈ on Asc., long, meagre and thin face; ♑ on the Asc., long, lean, thin, slender face; the Sig. of the person in ♑, or ☌ ♄. In the Mental Temperament the head is broad and wide above, and narrows down to the chin, and with a thin face. (See Lean, Long, Meagre, Narrow, Slender, in this section; "Thin Body" under Thin).

**Thoughtful Face**—♄ and ☿ give. (See Grave, Intellectual, Serious; "Sad" in this section).

**Troubled**—(See Anxiety, Cares, Fears; "No Peace of Mind" under Mind; Miserable, Sadness, Trouble, Worry).

**Ugly Face**—♑ gives a long, thin and ugly face; ♑ on Asc.; Sig. of the party in ♑ or ☌ ♄. (See "Not Handsome" under Handsome; Ugly).

**Unattractive**—(See "Ugly" in this section).

**Unhealthy Aspect**—Bad Complexion—(See Bad, Evil, Pale, Poor, Sallow, Sickly, White, under Complexion).

**Unpleasant**—(See Bloated, Lumpish, Ugly, in this section).

**Violent Countenance**—♂ influence; ♂ affl. in the Asc. or M.C. at B., and by dir. (See Fierce, Savage, Vicious, Violent).

**Visage**—(See the various paragraphs in this section. Also see Complexion, Countenance, Expression, Eyes, Features, Look, etc.).

**Vivacity**—Full of—(See "Full of" under Expression).

**Voluptuous**—The ☽ Sig. in ♎; ♂ affl. in ♈; the 17° ♏ on the Asc. (See "Sensuous" under Sensuality).

**Wan Face**—(See Pale, Sickly).

**Wanton Look**—♊ gives. (See Wanton).

**Well-Favored**—♍ and ♎ give. (See Beautiful, Fair, Handsome, Lovely, in this section).

**White Face**—The ☽ Sig. in Hor'y Questions, the face is more white than red; ♋ on the Asc., usually white and pale. (See "Good" under Complexion; Pale, Sickly, White).

**Wicked Look**—(See Criminal, Cruel, Deceitful, Dishonest, Evil, Fierce, Malicious, Vicious, Wicked).

**Wide Face**—The Vital Type of Temperament gives a wide face. A ♂ and ♏ influence. (See Decanates, Wide. Also see Broad, Square, in this section).

**Wrinkles; Yellow Face**—(See "Complexion", "Skin", under Yellow; "Yellow" in Sec. 2 of this Article).

**Young Face**—Youthful Looking—(See "Youthfulness" under Youth).

## — SECTION TWO —

**DISEASES OF THE FACE**—Afflictions to the Face—Blemishes—Marks, etc.—See the following subjects in the alphabetical arrangement when not considered here.

**Abnormalities Of**—Caused by the malefics in ♈, or the ☉ and ☽ affl. in ♈ at B. Also caused by the various afflictions during the prenatal period. (See the various paragraphs in this section. Especially note the following subjects in this section, and in the alphabetical arrangement,—Birthmarks (Naevus), Blemishes, Congenital, Contortions, Contractions, Cyclops, Defects, Deformed, Disfigured, Distortions; "Dogs" under Children; Enlarged, Features, Idiots, Ill-Formed, Imperfections, Inhuman, Malformations, Marks, Misshaped, Moles, Monsters, Naevus, Prenatal, Structural, Warts, etc.).

**Accidents To**—(See Blows, Burns, Cuts, Hurts, Scars, in this section).

**Acne, Acromegaly**—(See "Enlarged" in this section).

**Affected**—The face is affected when ♅ is in ♓. (See Table 196 in Simmonite's Arcana. Also note the various paragraphs in this section).

**Afflictions To**—(See the various paragraphs in this Article).

**All Diseases In**—Signified by the 1st H., and afflictions in ♈. (See "Diseases" in this section).

**Atrophy**—Facial Hemiatrophy—♄ affl. in ♈; Subs at AT, MCP, and KP. (See Atrophy).

**Barber's Itch**—Sycosis—(See Barbers).

**Birth Marks**—(See "Naevus" in this section).

**Blackheads**—(See "Comedo" under Sebaceous).

**Blemishes**—The ☉ Sig. ☌ ♄, and ♄ ill-dig.; ♄, ♂, or ☋ ascending, but in a nativity ☋ has no effect unless ☌ ☽; ♂ in ♍ in partile asp. the Asc.; malefics affl. in ♈, or the ☉ or ☽ affl. in ♈. (See Acne, Barber's Itch, Birthmarks, Blemishes, Blotches, Burns, Carcinoma, Contortions, Contractions, Cosmetics, Cuts, Defects, Deformed, Disfigurements, Eruptions; "Blemishes" under Eyes; Freckles, Growths, Harelip, Marks, Moles, Pimples, Pitted, Pockmark, Scars, Smallpox, Sores, Ulcers, Warts, Wrinkles, etc.).

**Bloated Face**—(See "Bloated" in Sec. One of this Article).

**Blotches**—Afflictions in ♈; the ☉ or ☽ in ♈, and affl. by ♄ or ♂. (See Blotches. Also note the various paragraphs in this section).

**Blows To**—(See Cuts, Hurts, in this section. Also see "Blows" under Eyes, Head).

**Blushing; Boils**—(See "Face" under Boils).

**Bones**—Bones of the Face Affected—♄ affl. in ♈; Subs at MCP. (See Bones).

**Burns**—Scars—To the Face—(See "Face" under Burns).

**Cancer On**—Carninoma—(See "Face" under Carcinoma).

**Capillaries**—Dilatation of—Congestion of—(See Acne, Capillaries; "Red Face" in this section).

**Cheeks**—Disorders of—(See Cheeks).

**Comedo**—Blackheads—(See "Comedo" under Sebaceous).

**Congenital Defects**—Of the Face—(See "Abnormalities" in this section).

**Congestion**—(See Acne, Congestion; "Red Face" in this section).

**Contortions**—Twistings—Distortions—♅ affl. in ♈ or ♉; ♄ affl. in ♈; Subs at MCP. (See Contortions, Deformities; "Distortions" under Features; Incoordination, Spasmodic, Twistings).

**Contractions**—♆, ♅, or ♄ affl. in ♈; afflictions in ♈ or ♉. (See Contractions, Deformities, Distortions).

**Cosmetics**—Bad Effects of—(See Cosmetics. Also see "Lotions" in this section).

**Cuts To**—♂ on the Asc., cuts or hurts to the face and head; ♂ in the 1st H.; ♂ in ♈. (See Hurts, Injuries, Marks, Scars, in this section; "Cuts" under Head).

**Cyclops**—A Monster with Eyes Fused into One—(See Cyclops).

**Defects**—♄ or ♂ in the 1st H. at B.; ♄ in ♋; ☿ ori. at B.; afflictions during the prenatal period. (See Blemishes, Defects, Marks, Moles, Scars, in this section).

**Deformed**—Disfigured Face—Afflictions in ♈; the ☉ affl. in ♋; the ☉ Sig. in ♋, or in ♋ in partile asp. the Asc.; ♅ ☌ ♄ in ♈. (See "Disfigured", and other paragraphs in this section. Also see Deformities).

**Delicate Looking**—(See "Delicate" under Complexion; Delicate, Pale, Sickly).

**Dilated Capillaries**—(See Acne, Capillaries; "Red Face", in this section).

**Diplegia**—Double Symmetric Paralysis In—(See "Paralysis" in this section; Paralysis).

**Diseases In** — The ☉ affl. at B., and the ☉ to the evil asps. the Asc. by dir.; afflictions in ♈; ♈ on the cusp of 6th H., or intercepted in the 6th; malefics in ♈; ♈ diseases; Subs at AT, MCP (4C), and SP. (See the various paragraphs in this section).

**Disfigured** — Evil asps. to the Asc., with malefics just setting, and with no good asps. to counteract. (See Disfigurements; Abnormalities, Blemishes, Defects, Deformities, Hurts, Marks, Moles, Naevus, Pockmark, Scars, in this section).

**Distorted** — (See "Distorted" under Features. Also note the various paragraphs in this section).

**Eczema Of**—(See Eczema).

**Enlarged Face**—Acromegaly—♃ or ♂ affl. in ♈; ♄ affl. in ♈, by deposits; Subs at AT and CP. (See Enlargements).

**Eruptions** — Rashes—Pimples—The ☽ affl. in ♈, ♉, or ♊; ♂ or ♀ affl. in ♈; Subs at MCP (4C), CP, and KP (11D). (See Acne, Cosmetics, Eruptions, Measles, Pimples, Smallpox, etc.).

**Erysipelas** — (See "Face" under Erysipelas).

**Eyes; Father**—Hurts to Face of—(See "Face" under Father).

**Features**—Contortions of—Distortions—(See Features. Also note the various paragraphs in this section).

**Flushings; Forehead; Freckles;**

**Ghastly Look**—(See Pale, Sickly).

**Growths On** — (See Cancer, Moles, Warts, in this section; Growths).

**Harelip**—(See Lips).

**Hemiatrophy**—(See "Atrophy" in this section).

**Herpes**—(See "Face" under Herpes).

**Hurts**—Accidents—Injuries—Wounds —Blows—Burns—Cuts, etc.—Afflictions in ♈; the ☉ to the ☌ ♂ by dir.; the ☽ to the ☌ or ill-asps. ♂ by dir., and the ☽ hyleg; the ☽ in the Asc., close to, or ☌ ♂, liable to a blow, cut, accident or injury to face which may require a surgical operation to relieve and remedy; the ☽ to the place of the Pleiades or Praesepe; ♂ in ♈, in the Asc. and rising; the 1st Dec. of ♈ on the Asc., ruled by ♂; the 1st face of ♊ on the Asc., and containing the ☽ with ♄ and ♂. This face contains Aldebaran, of the nature of ♂; the Pleiades rising, or with the ☉ or ☽ at B., or directed to the Asc.; the Pleiades, Hyades, Ascelli, Castor, Pollux, or Praesepe, when directed to the Asc. or Lights. (See "Cuts" in this section. Also see "Hurts" under Eyes, Head).

**Idiots; Ill-Formed**—(See "Misshaped" in this section).

**Imperfections** — (See Blemishes, Defects, Marks, Scars, and the various paragraphs in this section).

**Inhuman; Injuries To** — (See Blows, Burns, Cuts, Hurts, and the various paragraphs in this section).

**Irritations To** — (See Cosmetics, Lotions, in this section).

**Itch**—Barber's Itch—(See Barbers).

**Jaundiced Look**—(See Jaundice. Also see "Yellow" in this section).

**Left Side** — Of the Face — Marks, Moles, or Warts On—A feminine sign on the Asc., and a feminine planet in the Asc. A masculine sign on the Asc., and a masculine planet in the Asc., tend to affect the right side of the face similarly. (See "Face" under Burns; Left; "Location" under Moles; Marks, Moles, Right, Warts, in this section).

**Lotions**—Face Lotions—Irritations By—Cosmetics—The ♎ people are easily affected by, as ♎, the exalted sign of ♄, tends to skin diseases; ♀ affl. in ♈, and espec. when in the 6th H., tends to injury by face and hair lotions; ♀ affl. in ♑ tends to misuse of skin and hair lotions. (See Cosmetics).

**Lumpish Face**—(See "Lumpish in Sec. 1 of this Article).

**Malformations; Marks**—Moles—Scars —The ☉ in ♌, in partile asp. the Asc., sometimes a scar or mark on the face; the ☉ affl. in ♌; the ☉ Sig. in ♌; the ☉ in ♈, in ☌ or near ☋; the ☽ Sig., □ or ☍ ☉; the ☉ Sig. ☌ ♄ and ♄ ill-dig. at B.; the ☽ Sig. □ or ☍ ☉, or sepr. from the ☍; the ☽ Sig. ☌ ☉, or apply. to the exact ☌; the ☽ Sig. ☌ ♂, and ♂ ill-dig.; ♄ in the Asc.; ♂ Sig. of the person; ♂ ruler of the Asc., and in ☌, □, or ☍ the Sig. of the person; characteristic of ♂ people; ♂ rising in ♈; ♂ rising in the Asc., a mole or mark on the face; ♂ affl. in the 1st H.; ♂ in ♉ or ♍, partile the Asc.; ♀ in ♈, partile the Asc.; ♀ Sig. in ♈; afflictions in ♈; ♈ on the Asc.; the 2nd face of ♈ ascending; the 6th face of ♉ on the Asc.; the 1st face of ♐ on Asc.; the 4th face of ♒ on Asc.; a malefic planet a little above, or a little below the Asc. tends to a mark, mole or scar high up on the face, and when the malefic is lower down in the Asc., the mark is near the middle of the face, and when very low in the Asc., the mark is on the lower part of the face, or on the neck. There is usually a mark or mole on the right side of the face when there is a masculine sign on the Asc., and a masculine planet in the Asc., and similar conditions on the left side of the face when a feminine sign and planet ascend. (See Blemishes, Cuts, Disfigured, Hurts, Pockmark, Scars, and the various paragraphs in this section; Left, Lower, Marks, Middle, Moles, Naevus, Right, Scars, Upper, Warts).

**Misfortunes**—To the Face—(See Accidents, Blows, Burns, Cuts, Hurts, Injuries, Marks, Scars, and the various paragraphs in this section).

**Misshaped**—(See "Beastly Form" under Beasts; "Dogs" under Children; Contortions, Cyclops, Deformities, Ill-

Formed, Malformations, Monsters, etc. See Contortions, Contractions, Deformed, Distortions, and the various paragraphs in this section. Also see "Misshaped" in Sec. 1 of this Article).

**Moles**—(See "Marks" in this section).

**Morbid Red Face**—(See Congestion, Red Face, in this section).

**Mother**—Injury to Face of—(See "Face" under Mother).

**Mouth; Naevus**—Birthmarks—♂ rising in ♈. (See Naevus).

**Nerves**—Paralysis of—Facial Paralysis—♅ affl. in ♈. (See Neuralgia, Paralysis, in this section).

**Neuralgia**—Of the Facial Nerves—Spasmodic—Tic Dourouleux—Facial Paroxysms—An ♈ disease; ♅, ♂, or ☿ affl. in ♈; ♂ affl. in ♈ or ♎; a ♎ disease; Subs at MCP. (See "Neuralgia" under Head; Neuralgia, Spasmodic, Tics).

**Nose**—Morbid Red Nose—(See "Red Face" in this section).

**Oily Face**—(See "Oily" in Sec. 1 of this Article).

**Pale Face**—Wan—Delicate—White—Sickly—(See "Bad", "Poor", under Complexion; Delicate, Pale, Sickly, White; Bloated, Pale, Sickly, in Sec. 1 of this Article).

**Palsy Of**—♅ affl. in ♈; Subs at MCP (4C). (See "Paralysis" in this section. Also see Palsy, Paralysis).

**Paralysis**—Facial Paralysis—Diplegia—♅ affl. in ♈; ♂ in ♈, ☍ the Asc., and affl. by ♅ or ♄; ♂ in the Asc., or ☍ Asc., and also in □ or ☍ ☽; Subs at AT, AX, MCP (4C). Case—See Fig. 13C in "Astro-Diagnosis" by the Heindels. (See Atrophy, Diplegia, Palsy, in this section; Paralysis).

**Paroxysms**—Tics—Twitchings—(See Neuralgia, Spasmodic, Tics, Twitchings, in this section; Paroxysms, Spasmodic, Tics, Twitchings).

**Pimples**—(See Pimples; "Eruptions" in this section).

**Pockmarked**—Pitted Face—(See Pitted Degrees" under Pitted; "Face" under Smallpox).

**Poor Complexion**—(See Bad, Poor, under Complexion; Delicate, Pale, Sickly, in this section).

**Psoriasis**—(See "Face" under Psoriasis; Herpes, Scaly, Tetter, in this section).

**Puffy Cheeks**—(See "Puffy" in Sec. 1 of this Article).

**Rashes**—(See "Eruptions" in this section).

**Red**—Morbid Red Face—Congestion—Dilated Capillaries—Abnormal Redness—Red Nose—A ♄ disease; ♄ in ♈; ♃ Sig. in ♈ tends to a peculiar redness and pimples; ♎ on the Asc.; Subs at MCP (3, 4C), HP, and KP. (See Acne, Capillaries, Congestions, Dilatations, Erythema, Pimples; "Red" in Sec. 1 of this Article).

**Right Side**—Of the Face—(See "Face" under Left, Right; "Left Side", "Marks", in this section).

**Saint Vitus Dance**—Chorea—(See Saint).

**Scaly Face**—(See "Psoriasis" in this section; Scales).

**Scars—Marks—Moles**—The ☉ in ♌, partile asp. the Asc.; the ☉ Sig. in ♌; the ☉ or ☽ Sig., and ☌ ♂, and ♂ ill-dig.; the ☽ Sig. ☌ ☉, or apply. to the exact ☌; ♄ or ♂ in the Asc., a scar or mole on the face; ♂ in the 1st H., wounds or scars on the face or head; ♂ in ♈ in the Asc.; characteristic of ♂ people; born under ♂; ♂ in ♍, partile the Asc.; ♂ as Sig. in Hor'y Questions denotes; ♀ in ♈, partile the Asc. (See "Marks" in this section).

**Scurvy; Scars**—(See "Burns" in this section).

**Shape**—Of the Face—Abnormalities In Shape—(See Abnormalities, Bloated, Contortions, Contractions, Cyclops, Deformed, Distortions, Enlarged, Features, Idiot, Inhuman, Misshaped, and the various paragraphs in this section. Also see Sec. 1 of this Article).

**Shiny Face**—(See "Oily" in Sec. 1 of this Article).

**Sickly Looking**—(See Pale, Sickly; Pale, Thin, in this section).

**Skin**—Of the Face—Disorders of—Especially under the rule of ♄, ♂, and ♀. Disorders from wrong use of Cosmetics and Lotions are under ♀. Dry, scaly skin, and such disorders, under ♄. Eruptions and rashes under ♂. (See Complexion, Cosmetics, Eruptions, Pimples, Skin. Also note the various paragraphs in this Article, as Birthmarks, Blemishes, Capillaries, Congestion, Defects, Diseases, Eczema, Eruptions, Freckles, Herpes, Marks, Oily, Red, Scars, etc.).

**Smallpox**—In the Face—Pockmarked—(See "Face" under Smallpox).

**Sores On**—Fixed stars of the nature of ♂ ascending at B.; ♂ affl. in ♈. (See Sores; Blotches, Boils, Cancer, Eruptions, Ulcer, in this section).

**Spasmodic Diseases**—Of the Face—Facial Spasm—Tics—Twitchings—Contractions—♅ affl. in ♈; Subs at AX and LCP. (See Contortions, Contractions, Distortions, Spasmodic, Saint Vitus Dance, Tics, Twitchings; Contortions, Contractions, Neuralgia, Palsy, Paralysis, Paroxysms, in this section).

**Strokes To**—Violent Strokes—(See "Blows" in this section. For Paralytic Strokes, see "Paralysis" in this section).

**Sunken Face**—In Illness—The ☽ in ♑, and affl. by the ☉ or ♂ when taken ill (Hor'y). (See "Falling In Of" under Cheeks).

**Swellings**—In the Face—Swollen Face—An ♈ disease; ♃ affl. in ♓, due to dropsical conditions. (See Dropsy, Swellings; "Bloated" in Sec. 1 of this Article; Boils, Enlargement, Eruptions, in this section).

**Tetter**—Eczema—Herpes—Ringworm—Tetter—Afflictions in ♈, ♎, or ♑; Subs at MCP (4C), and KP. (See "Head and Face" under Eczema; "Face" under Herpes; Psoriasis, Ringworm, Scales, Skin, Tetter).

**Tics**—Tic Douloureux—Spasmodic Facial Neuralgia—(See Tics; Neuralgia, Spasmodic, in this section).

**Tissues**—Of the Face Affected—Afflictions in ♈; Subs at MCP (4C). (See the various paragraphs in this section; Tissues).

**Twistings**—(See "Contortions" in this section; Twitchings).

**Twitchings**—(See "Spasmodic" in this section; Saint Vitus, Spasmodic, Tics, Twitchings).

**Ulcers**—Sores—Suppuration—Afflictions in ♈; ♄ or ♂ affl. in ♈; ♂ in ♈ in the Asc., and afflicted; Subs at MCP and KP. (See Ulcers; "Sores" in this section).

**Unhealthy Aspect**—(See "Pale" in this section; "Poor" under Complexion; Delicate, Emaciated, Low, Pale, Sickly, Unhealthy, Vitality, Weak Body, White).

**Visage**—Sickly, Pale and Thin Visage —(See Pale, Sickly, in this section; Thin, Visage, in Sec. 1 of this Article).

**Wan Face**—(See "Pale" in this section).

**Warts On**—Verruca—(See Blemishes, Left Side, Marks, in this section). Also caused by Subs at MCP (4C).

**White Face**—(See Pale, Sickly; "Complexion" under White; "White" in Sec. 1 of this Article).

**Wounds To**—(See Accidents, Blows, Cuts, Hurts, Injuries, in this section).

**Wrinkles; Yellow Face**—In Illness—The ☽ in ♑, and affl. by the ☉ or ♂ when taken ill (Hor'y). (See "Jaundiced Look" under Jaundice; "Complexion" under Yellow).

**FACULTIES**—Specific Powers of the Mind and Body—The Faculties are ruled by the ☽ and ☿. The ☽ rules over the bodily or sensual faculties, and ☿ more specifically over the mental faculties. (See the various paragraphs under Intellect, Mental, Mind, Perception, Reason, Senses, Understanding, etc.).

**Arrested**—Arrested Faculties—(See Inhibitions; "Arrested" under Mental; Retardation, Suppressions).

**Disease**—Disease-Resisting Faculties —(See the various paragraphs under Recuperation, Resistance, Stamina, Strength, Tone, Vitality).

**Disordered**—(See Idiocy, Imbecility, Insanity, Judgment, Memory; "Faculties" under Mental; "Weak Mind" under Mind; Perception, Reason. Also note the various paragraphs in this section).

**Dull**—The Faculties Dull—(See Dull).

**Emotion**—(See Emotions).

**Endangered**—Signs of Danger to the Mental Faculties—(See "Faculties" under Mental).

**Impaired**—(See Feeble, Idiocy; "Mental" under Impaired; Insanity; "Weak Mind" under Mind, etc.).

**Improved**—(See "Beastly Form under Beasts; "Quickened" under Mental).

**Inhibition Of**—(See Inhibition, Retarded, Suppressed).

**Intellectual Faculties**—(See Intellect, Mental, Mind, Perception, Reason, Understanding, etc.).

**Instincts**—The Instinctual Faculties —(See Instincts).

**Intuition; Inward Faculties**—The Inward Faculties Prejudiced—Disordered —(See Phantasies).

**Irrational Faculties**—The Sensitive Faculties—Ruled by the ☽. (See Deviations, Irrational, Sensitive).

**Judgment**—(See Judgment).

**Loss of Faculties**—Danger of—The 17° ♊ on the Asc., which is a degree of impotence. (See Impotent, Loss).

**Memory; Mental Faculties**—☿ is the chief ruler of the Mental Faculties. In judging of the mental faculties great care is necessary to note what aspects ☿ makes with other planets, for on this chiefly depends the disposition of the native. (See Intellect, Mental; "Judging the Mind" under Mind).

**Moral Faculties**—(See Morals).

**Natural Faculties**—Are ruled by the ☽. (See Natural).

**Passive Faculties**—The Sensitive Faculties—Irrational Faculties—Deviation of—These Faculties are ruled by the Moon. (See Deviations, Irrational, Passive, Sensitive).

**Perception; Physical Faculties**—Are ruled chiefly by the ☉. (See Physical).

**Quickened**—(See "Quickened" under Mental).

**Rational**—Reasoning Faculties—Ruled by ☿. (See Rational, Reason).

**Reason; Religious Faculties**—(See Excitable, Neptune, Pineal Gland, Religion, Spiritual).

**Retarded**—The Faculties Retarded—(See Decreased, Diminished, Dwarf, Hardening, Impairments, Retarded, Suppressions, etc.).

**Retentive Faculties**—(See Retentive).

**Senses**—The Faculties of Sight, Hearing, Smell, Taste, Touch, Feeling, Color, etc. (See these subjects. Also see Senses).

**Sensitive Faculties**—(See Irrational, Passive, in this section).

**Sensual Faculties**—Ruled by the ☽. (See Sensual).

**Sentient Faculties**—Feeling—Ruled by the ☽, ☿, and Asc. (See Sentient).

**Spiritual Faculties**—(See "Religious" in this section).

**Strengthened**—(See "Quickened" under Mental).

**Understanding; Unusual**—Unusual Mental Faculties—(See "Unusual" under Mental. Also see Genius, Prodigies).

**Weakened**—(See Derangement, Faculties, Shallow, Weak, Weakened, under Mental).

**FADING**—Loss of Freshness and Color —Growing Weaker—Loss of Strength, Energy and Vitality, etc.—♄ is the planet of fading, decay, death and depletion. (See Blight, Decay, Declines, Decrease, Decrepitude, Depleted, Diminished, Dimmed, Dull, Feeble, Infirm,

Languishing, Loss Of, Old Age, Pale, Sickly, Vitality (Loss of); Weak, Withering, Wrinkles, etc.).

**FAECES**—Excrement—Dung—Discharge of the Bowels—Evacuations—Defaecation—Waste—Ruled by ♄. Also ruled by the ♏ sign, which sign has charge largely of elimination of organic waste materials, as thru the Urine, the Faeces, and thru the Nose. The following paragraphs have to do with the Faeces, which see in the alphabetical arrangement when not more fully considered here—

**Abnormal Stools**—Afflictions in ♍; Subs at LPP (4, 5L). (See the various paragraphs in this section).

**Bloody Evacuations**—Bloody Flux—(See Dysentery; "Bloody Flux" under Flux; Typhoid).

**Bowels**—(See the various paragraphs under Bowels).

**Cholera; Colon; Constipation**—Sluggish Action—(See Constipation).

**Costiveness**—Hardness and Retention of Faeces—(See Costiveness; "Hardening" in this section).

**Diarrhoea; Discharges; Dryness**—Of the Faeces—(See Constipation, Hardening, in this section).

**Dysentery; Effusions; Elimination;**

**Evacuations; Excretion; Expulsion;**

**Flux; Food**—Undigested Food In—Pieces of Food In the Stools—(See "Intestinal" under Indigestion).

**Hardening**—Of the Faeces—Lumpy—Scybalum—Dryness of—Retention—The work of ♄; a ♄ disease, as ♄ is a scybalous agency; ♄ affl. in ♍, and espec. when ♄ is the afflictor in the disease. (See "Sluggish" under Bowels; Constipation, Costiveness, Hardening).

**Hemorrhages**—(See "Bowels" under Hemorrhage).

**Impeded**—(See "Bowel Action" under Impeded).

**Involuntary**—Involuntary Faecal Discharges—♂ weak at B. (See Involuntary).

**Lumpy Faeces**—(See "Hardening" in this section).

**Mucus In**—(See "Bowels" under Mucus).

**Peristalsis**—(See "Peristaltic" under Bowels).

**Pieces of Food**—In the Stools—(See "Food" in this section).

**Piles**—(See Hemorrhoids).

**Putrid Matter**—In Faeces—(See "Putrid" under Bowels).

**Rectum; Retention**—(See Constipation, Costiveness, Hernia, Retention; "Hardening", "Suppression", in this section).

**Sanguineous**—(See "Bloody" in this section).

**Scybalum**—Hardening—Lumpy—(See "Hardening" in this section).

**Serous Stools**—The ☽ affl. in ♍; Subs at KP, and PP (2L). (See Serum).

**Sluggish Bowels**—(See "Sluggish" under Bowels; "Hardening" in this section).

**Suppression Of**—The work of ♄ impeding the action of the terminal branches of the Pneumogastric Nerve, and by generating the emotions of fear and worry. (See Hardening, Retention, in this section; Pneumogastric Nerve, Saturn, Suppressions).

**Typhoid**—Bowel Lesions and Hemorrhage In—(See Typhoid).

**Undigested Food**—In the Stools—(See "Food" in this section).

**Vomiting**—Faecal Vomiting—Occurs in Ileac Passion. (See Ileac).

**Wastes; Watery Stools**—(See "Cholera Infantum" under Cholera; Diarrhoea, Dysentery).

**FAG**—Brain Fag—(See "Brain Fag" under Brain; Fatigue, Reading, Study, Weariness).

**FAILURE**—

**Business Failure**—Tending to Ill-Health and Worry—(See Reverses).

**Health**—Failure of—(See "Bad Health", "Periods of Bad Health", under Health; Ill-Health, Infirmities, Sickness, etc.).

**Heart Failure**—(See "Failure", "Heart Trouble", under Heart).

**FAINT**—Weak—

**Faint Pulse**—Faintings At the Heart—(See Feeble; "Faintings", "Weak", under Heart; Pulse, Weak).

**FAINTING**—Faintings—Swoonings—Falling Sickness—Syncope—Insensibility—Loss of Consciousness, etc.—Syncope, or Fainting, may be Cerebral, from Heart weakness and disturbances, disturbed Circulation of the Blood, Corrupt Blood, and also accompanies such conditions as Coma, Delirium, Fits, Epilepsy, etc. The following subjects have to do with Faintings, and loss of Consciousness, which see in the alphabetical arrangement when not considered here.

**Causes of Faintings**—General Causes—Afflictions in ♌ or ♒, and the fixed signs; the ☉ in ♌ or ♒, and to the ☌ or ill-asp. ♂ by dir., tends to syncope if the heart is weak; a ☉ disease; the ☉ affl. in ♈, ♉, or ♐; the ☉ affl. in ♐; the ☉ in ♐, and to the ☌ or ill-asp. any of the malefics as promittors, liable to swoonings; the ☽ in ♌ and affl. by the ☉ or ♂ when taken ill; the ☽ affl. in ♌ or ♒; the ☽ ☌ or ill-asp. ♄ in ♌ (or ☿ if he be of the nature of ♄) at the beginning of an illness (Hor'y); the ☽ hyleg in ♒, and affl., and espec. with females; the ☽ in ♏ in ☌ or ill-asp. any of the malefics as promittors, tends to swoonings after over-exertion; some people faint and remain insensible at an Eclipse of the ☽, as long as the eclipse lasts, and espec. if the ☽ be hyleg and affl. at B.; caused by afflictions to ♆, and by the afflictions of ♆ to the hyleg, or to bring on Trance conditions; ♅ affl. in ♌ or ♒, and affl. the hyleg, may cause sudden swoonings due to heart failure or disturbed circulation of the blood; ♄ afflictions tend to; ♄ affl. in ♈, ♌, or ♒; ♄ in the 6th H. at B. in fixed signs, and affl. by the ☉ or ☽; ♄ □ or ☍ ♃, due to disturbed Adrenal secretions;

♃ affl. in ♈; ♂ affl. in ♌ or ♒; ♂ in ♌ in the 6th H.; ♀ in ♌, and affl. the ☽ or Asc.; ♀ affl. in ♌ in the 6th H.; ☿ affl. in ♌; ♌ on the Asc. (See the various paragraphs in this section. Also see Adrenal, Eclipse, Heart, Neptune, Trance).

**Cerebral Syncope**—(See Cerebral).

**Coma; Consciousness**—Loss of—(See Consciousness).

**Death by Syncope**—♆ in the 8th H., and affl. the hyleg; ♄ afflictions tend to; ♂ affl. in ♌ in the 6th H.

**Delirium; Dizziness; Epilepsy;**

**Falling Fits**—Falling Sickness—Swooning Fits—Swoonings—A disease of the ☽, and afflictions to the ☽; the ☽ in ♊ or ♐, injury by falling sickness, and the malefics in angles, and occi. of the ☽; the ☽ affl. in ♋; is a periodic disease caused by the ☽; the ☽ affl. in ♌ or ♒, and affl. by the ☉ or ♂ when taken ill, and the ☽ slow in motion and decreasing in light; the ☽ affl. in ♍; the ☽, ☿, and the Asc. unconnected with each other, and affl. by ♄ or ♂ from angles, and with no assistance from the benefics; ♄ or ♂ angular, in the 1st or 7th H., in ♊ or ♐, ori. of the ☉ and occi. of the ☽; caused by ☿ when the dominion of death is vested in him; an ♈ disease and afflictions in ♈. (See Epilepsy, Fits, Periodic; "Sudden" in this section).

**Hysteria; Insensibility;**

**Sudden Swoonings**—The ☉ gives; a ☉ disease; ♅ affl. in ♌ or ♒, and also affl. the hyleg from these signs, and due to heart failure or disturbed circulation of the blood. (See "Falling Fits" in this section).

**Swoonings**—(See "Falling Fits" in this section).

**Trance; Vertigo.**

**FAIR**—Comely—Beautiful—Light Hue—Pleasing to the Eye or Mind—

**Fair Complexion**—(See "Fair" under Complexion).

**Fair Eyes**—(See "Fair" under Eyes).

**Fair Face**—(See "Fair" under Face).

**Fair Hair**—(See "Light" under Hair).

**Fair Proportions**—The ☉ in ♒, or ♒ on the Asc. (See Beautiful, Comely, Handsome; "Well-Formed" and "Well-Proportioned" under Well).

**Fair Stature**—The ☉ or ☽ give when strong at B.; the ☉ in ♒; ♌ or ♒ on the Asc. (See Beautiful, Comely, Stature).

**Fair and Tall**—♊ on the Asc. (See Tall).

**FAITH HEALING**—(See "Faith" under Healers).

**FALL EQUINOX**—(See Equinoxes).

**FALLING**—Falling In—Falling Out—

**Cheeks**—Falling In of—(See Cheeks).

**Fits**—(See "Falling Fits" under Fainting).

**Hair**—Falling Out of—(See Baldness; "Scanty" under Hair).

**Sickness**—Falling Sickness—(See "Falling Fits" under Fainting).

**Womb**—Falling of—Prolapsus of—(See "Falling" under Womb).

**FALLOPIAN TUBES**—Oviducts—Salpinx—Ruled by the ♎ sign. The Womb and Ovaries are ruled by ♏, and afflictions in ♏ tend to affect the Tubes indirectly, and by sympathetic action.

**Disorders Of**—Inflammation of—Salpingitis—Malefics and afflictions in ♎; Subs at KP and PP (2, 3, 4L).

**Dropsy Of**—Hydrosalpinx—The ☽ affl. in ♎; Subs at KP and PP (2, 3, 4L). (See Dropsy, Ovaries, Womb).

**FALLS**—Falls are caused principally by ♄ and his afflictions, and hurts, bruises or injuries by falls.

**Accidents By**—Also Cuts, Hurts, or Injuries By, or by Animals, and in Sports—The ☉ in ♐ and affl. by malefics. (See the various paragraphs in this section).

**Animals**—Hurts By—Falls From—The ☉ affl. in ♐. (See "Hurts" under Animals; "Falls" under Horses).

**Bruises**—And Hurts by Falls—♅ in the 12th H., and by falls from horses; ♄ rising and affl. the ☉ or ☽ at B.; ♄ in the 8th H. in Hor'y Questions. (See "Falls" under Bruises).

**Buildings**—Houses—Falls From—Accidents, Injury or Death by the Fall of—The ☉ hyleg, and to the ☌ or ill-asp. ♄ by dir.; ♅ or ♄ in ♈, ♋, ♎, or ♑, and in ☌ or evil asp. the ☉ or ♂; ♅ or ♄ in quadrupedal or tropical signs, and in ☌ or ill-asp. the ☉ or ♂; ♄ rising and affl. the ☉ or ☽ at B.; ♄ in cardinal signs, and espec. when in angles; ♄ in the 10th, and in ☍ the ☉; ♄ in a quadrupedal or tropical sign, and the ☉ ☌ or ☍ ♂; ♄ ☌ ♂ in ♉, ♊, ♌, or ♏, in the 4th H., and on the lower meridian. (See Buildings, Crushed; "Earthquakes" under Earth; Quadrupedal, Tropical).

**Cuts By**—(See "Accidents" in this section; Cuts).

**Danger Of**—Liable to Falls—General Causes of—The ☉ in the ♄ sign ♑, and affl. by ♄ or ♂; the ☉ or ☽ affl. by ♄ or ♂; the ☉ or ☽ to the ☌ or ill-asp. ♄ or ♂ by dir.; the ☉ directed to the Cratch; the ☉ or ☽ affl. by ♄ ascending, and espec. if ♄ be in ♊, ♐, or ♒; the ☉ or ☽ ori., and affl. by ♄ or ♂; the ☉ or ♄ affl. in ♐; the ☉ Sig., and ☌ or ill-asp. ♄, and espec. if either be in the 10th H.; the ☽ affl. in ♊ or ♐, and the malefics angular and occi. of the ☽; the ☽ affl. at B., and to the ☌ or ill-asps. ♄, ♂, ☋, or to the place of Ceti; the ☽ to the place of Cor Scorpio; the ☽ in earthy signs, and to the ☌ or ill-asps. ♄ or ♂ by dir.; ♆ by tr. over the place of the radical ♄, and espec. if ♄ is in ♎; ♅ in the 1st H. and affl. the hyleg; ♅ to the ill-asps. his place at B.; ♄ ascending at B.; ♄ rising or setting at B.; ♄ in bad asp. the ☉; ♄ ☌ or ill-asp. the ☽, and ori.; ♄ ☌ or ill-asp. the Asc. at B., or by dir.; ♄ ☌, P, □ or ☍ the ☉ from card. signs, and ♂ with ♄, makes the effect more certain and violent; ♄ in the Asc. or M.C., and the ☉ afflicted; denoted and caused by fixed stars of the nature of ♄; ♄ in a fiery or airy sign, and to the ill-asp. the Asc. by dir.; ♄ ☌ or ill-asp. the ☉ in fixed signs; ♄ ☌ or ill-asp. ♂, and espec. when either be ori.; ♄ by tr. in ☌ or ill-asp. the ☉, ☽, ♃ or ♀; ♄ in the M.C., or angular, holding dominion, and elevated above the Lights, and affl. the hyleg; ♄ in ♈, ♌, or ♐, and ☌ or ill-asp. the Asc. by dir.; ♄ ruler of the 4th or 8th H. at B., and to the ☌ or ill-asp. ♂; the ♄ sign ♑ on the Asc.; ♂ in the 1st H., and affl. by ♅ or ♄; ♂ affl. in ♊ or ♍, and ☌ or evil asp. the Asc. by dir.; ♂ in airy signs, ☌ or ill-asp. the Asc. by dir.; ♂ by periodic rev. to the evil asps. ♅; ♂ affl. in ♑; ♂ with Aldebaran, and espec. if in an angle and affl. the ☽; ♂ in the 7th H. in □ or ☍ ☉, and in a four-footed sign; ♂ Sig. □ or ☍ ♄, if either be in the Asc., or ♄ in the M.C.; afflictions in ♐, or ♐ on the Asc., and afflicted; born under the Hurtful Signs ♈, ♉, ♋, ♏, or ♑; the Asc. to the ☌ or ill-asp. ♄ by dir., and ♄ ori. at B.; the Asc. to the ☌, □, or ☍ ♂ by dir.; the M.C. to the ☌ or ill-asp. ♄ by dir.; malefics in the M.C., elevated above the Luminaries, and espec. when ♄ holds dominion; earthy signs dispose to when afflicted and containing malefics; Whale's Belly when conjoined to the ☉ or ☽. (See the various paragraphs in this section. Also see Accidents, Blows, Hurts, Injuries).

**Death by Falls**—Violent Death By—The ☉ hyleg, and to the ☌ or ill-asps. ♄ by dir.; the ☉ Sig. ☌ ♄, and even tho ♄ be well-dig.; the ☉ Sig. □ or ☍ ♄, and espec. if either be in the 10th H.; the □ or ☍ asps. of the ☉, ☽, ♄, or ♂; the ☽ hyleg, and affl., and to the ☌ ☋ by dir.; the ☽ with Antares, and in ☍ to ♄ and Aldebaran, and espec. if in angles; ♄ ☌ or evil asp. the Asc. by dir., and when he is not ruler of the 1st H.; ♄ the afflicting planet; ♄ ☌, □, or ☍ ☉ from cardinal signs, and ♂ with ♄; ♄ in the M.C. in □ the Asc., and the ☉ afflicted; ♄ the afflicting planet in a violent sign, and affl. the ☉ or ☽; caused by fixed stars of the nature of ♄ when with the ☉ or ☽, or affl. the hyleg; ♂ in ♈, ♉, ♌, ♐, or ♑, and ☍ the Asc.; ♂ in quadrupedal signs, and in □ or ☍ the ☉, and ♂ just setting at B.; ♂ denotes death by falls; ♂ Sig. □ or ☍ ♄ if either be in the Asc., or ♄ in the M.C.; ♂ in the 7th H., □ or ☍ the ☉ or ☽, and in a four-footed sign, denotes death by falls or broken bones. (See Buildings, Heights, and the various paragraphs in this section).

**Distortions**—By Falls—Lameness or Paralysis—By Falls from Heights—(See Distortions; "Limbs", in this section).

**Fractures**—From Falls—(See "Falls" under Fractures).

**Heights**—High Places—Precipices—Falls From, and Resulting in Injury or Death—(See Distortions, Heights; "Travel", in this section).

**Horses**—Falls From—(See Horses).

**Houses**—Injury or Death by the Fall of—(See "Buildings" in this section).

**Hurts by Falls**—(See Accidents, Injuries, and the various paragraphs in this section).

**Infancy**—(See "Fall" under Infancy).

**Injuries By**—♄ on the Asc., or affl. the Asc. by □ or ☍ aspects. (See "Accidents" and the various paragraphs in this section).

**Lameness From**—And Distortions—(See Distortions, Excrescences, Lameness).

**Limbs**—The Limbs Broken by Falls—Distorted by Falls—(See Distortions, Fractures, Legs, Limbs).

**Paralysis From**—(See Distortions).

**Precipices**—Falls From—(See Distortions, Heights).

**Sports**—Falls During Sports, Exercise, Amusement or Recreation—The ☉ affl. in ♐. (See Amusements, Exercise, Recreation, Sports).

**Travel**—Voyages—Inland or Foreign Travel—Falls During, Causing Injury or Death—Malefics in the 3rd or 9th H. at B., and affl. the ☉, ☽, Asc., or Hyleg; the afflictor to the Sigs. of Travel being in the 12th H., and in a fixed sign. (See Heights, Journeys; "Accidents", "Hurts", under Travel).

**Vehicles**—Falls From—(See "Falls" under Vehicles).

**Voyages**—Falls During—Death or Injury By—(See "Travel" in this section. Also see "Accidents" under Abroad; "Injuries" under Travel).

**FALSE**—Pseudo—

**False Angina**—(See Angina).

**False Fears**—(See "Morbid" under Fears).

**False Friends**—Injury By—(See "False" under Friends).

**False Imaginations**—(See "False" under Imagination).

**False Ischuria**—Spurious Ischuria—(See Ischuria).

**False Membranes**—(See Croup, Diphtheria, Pseudo).

**FAMILY**—The Family. The following subjects have to do with the Family, Members of the Family, and the Conditions Affecting them. See these subjects in the alphabetical arrangement when not considered here.

**Aged Female**—Death of Aged Female In the Family—(See "Death of An Aged Aunt" under Aunts).

**Aged Person**—Death of In the Family—(See Grandparents; "Long Life" under Life; Old Age).

**Aunts; Bereavement; Births;**

**Brothers; Burial; Childhood;**

**Children; Daughter;**

**Death In the Family**—A Family Loss—Afflictions to the ☉ by dir. tend to male deaths, and to the ☽ or ♀, female deaths in the family; the ☉ or ☽ to the ☌ or ill-asps. ♅ or ♄ by dir., and espec. if the ☉ or ☽ were in the 8th H. at B.; the ☽ at a Solar Rev. passing the place of ♅ at B.; ♅ ☌ or P. Dec. the ☉ at a Solar Rev.; ♅ by tr. over the radical ☽, or ☌ the ☽ at a Solar Rev.; ♅ passing over his own place at B. by tr., or affl. the ☉ or ☽ by dir.; ♅ by Periodic Rev. in evil asp. the hyleg; ♅ has special rule over the death of relatives; ♄ by tr. over the radical ♅ and ♅ affl. at B.; ♂ to cusp 8th H. by dir.; the M.C. to the ☌ or ill-asp. ♄ by dir.; the M.C. to the ☌, □, or ☍ ♅ by dir., a sudden death in the family. (See Bereavement; "Death" under Aunts, Brothers, Children, Daughter, Father, Grandparents, Husband, Infancy, Mother, Parents, Sister, Son, etc.; "Family" under Fire; Relatives. Also note the various paragraphs in this section).

**Environment; Father; Female; Fire; Grandparents; Heredity; Home;**

**Husband; Large Family**—(See "Many Children" under Children; Fruitfulness).

**Likenesses**—Family Likenesses are caused by having the same rising sign with different members of the family, and with several planets in similar signs, or in the same aspect to the rising degree. (See Heredity).

**Loved Ones**—Death of—(See Loved; "Death", in this section).

**Male**—Death of In the Family—(See "Death" under Male).

**Marriage; Mother; Neglect of Family**—♅ to the ☌ or ill-asp. ♄ by dir. in the map of a parent, and liable to imprisonment. (See "Father" under Drunkenness; "Drink" under Parents).

**Orphans; Parents; Relatives;**

**Separated**—From Parents—(See Parents).

**Servants; Sickness**—In the Family—Malefics in the 4th H. at a Solar Rev. (See "Ill-Health", "Sickness", under Children, Daughter, Father, Husband, Parents, Sister, Son, Wife, etc.).

**Sisters; Small Family**—(See Barren; "Few Children" under Children).

**Sons; Sudden Death In**—The M.C. to the ☌, □, or ☍ ♅ by dir. (See "Death" in this section).

**Uncles; Wife; Youth.**

**FAMINE**—Want of Food—Starvation—Scarcity of Crops—Suffering or Death From—♄ or ♂ sole ruler at a Solar Eclipse; ♄ lord of the year, in ♈ at the Vernal Equinox; ♄ ruler of the Asc., cadent, and the ☉ □ or ☍ ☽ at the Vernal, affects people of all Countries ruled by ♄; ♄ and ♂ in Equinoctial Signs, in ☍ to and controlling the Luminaries; ♄ in ♉ in an angle, direct in motion, and affl. by ♂ and the ☽ at the Vernal E.; ♄, ♃, and ♂ conjoined in signs of their fall; an Eclipse of the ☉ in Airy Signs; a Solar Eclipse in 2nd Dec. of ♍, and espec. among Peoples and Countries ruled by ♍; an Eclipse of ☉ in the 2nd Dec. of ♍, ♎, or ♒, or in the 3rd Dec. of ♉ or ♑; an Eclipse of the ☉ or ☽ in earth signs, and in places ruled by such signs; the ☌ of several superior planets in airy signs; coincident with the appearance of Comets; Comets in ♊ or ♑; malefics in the 9th H. in earthy signs, and affl. the ☉ or ☽, famine and privation on a voyage. (See Calamity, Comets, Corn, Drought, Dryness, Eclipses, Epidemics, Floods, Food, Fountains, Fruits, Grain, Heat, Pestilence, Scarcity, Starvation, Thirst, Travel, Vegetation, Voyages, Weather, Wheat, Winds).

**FAMOUS PEOPLE**—Death of a Famous or Illustrious Person, as a Ruler, King, Queen, President, etc.—An Eclipse of the ☉ or ☽ in ♊, ♌, ♎, or ♓; an Eclipse of the ☽ in the 3rd Dec. of ♊, the 1st Dec. ♌, or the 3rd Dec. of ♎. (See "Great Men" under Great; Kings, Nobles, Presidents, Queens, Renown, Rulers).

**FANATICAL**—Intemperate or Irrational Zeal—(See Anarchists, Crazy, Destructiveness, Insanity, Intemperate, Irrational; "Unbalanced" under Mind; Rashness, Reactionary, Reformers, Religion, Revolutionary; "Impoverished" under Riches; Violent, etc.).

**FANCIES**—The Fancy—Fantasies—Phantasies—Fantastic—Imaginations—Vagaries.

**All Evils In the Fancy**—All Imperfections of the Fancy—A ☿ and ♊ disease, and afflictions to ☿, or afflictions in ♊. (See Mental, Mind).

**Appetites**—Fantastic Appetites—(See "Appetites" under Peculiar).

**Chaotic Fancies**—And Notions—♆ in ♊. (See Chaotic, Confusion, Notions).

**Distempered Fancies**—Strange Tastes and Fancies—Chaotic Fancies—A ♊ disease, and afflictions in ♊; the ☽ to the ☌ ☋; ♆ affl. in ♊, the 3rd or 9th H.; ♄ to the ☌ or ill-asp. ♀, the fancy perplexed; a ☿ disease, and afflictions to ☿; ☿ weak and ill-dig. at B., and in no relation to the ☽ or Asc. (See Chaotic, Confusion, Eccentric, Ideas, Notions, Peculiar, Strange, Tastes, etc. Also note the various paragraphs and references in this section).

**Dreamy Fancies**—(See Chaotic, Confusion; "Dreamy Mind" under Dreams).

**Fears**—Fanciful Fears—(See "Fanciful" under Fears).

**Foolish Fancies**—Foolish and Precipitate—The ☉ ill-dig. at B.; the ☽ □ or ☍ ☿; ♃ Sig. □ or ☍ ☽; ☿ affl. at B., and in □ or ☍ the ☽ or Asc.; fixed stars of the nature of ♂ and ☿ ascending at B.; the 7° ♑ ascending at B., carried away with foolish whims and fancies. (See "Bad" under Judgment).

**Ingenious Fancy**—(See Genius).

**Mental Fantasies**—(See "Dreamy Mind" under Dreams).

**Notions**—Fanciful and Chaotic Notions—(See Ideals, Notions).

**Novelties**—Fond of—(See Novelties).

**Peculiar Fancies**—(See Eccentric, Misunderstood, Peculiar, Strange).

**Perplexed**—The Fancy Perplexed—(See "Distempered" in this section).

**Precipitate Fancies**—(See "Foolish" in this section).

**Prejudiced**—The Phantasies Prejudiced—A ♄ disease and affliction; ☿ weak, unfortunate, and afflicted at B. (See Chaotic, Confusion, Delusions, Erratic, Fears, Hallucinations, Illusions, Imaginations; "Shallow" under Mind; Prejudiced).

**Riotous Fancies**—(See "Turbulent" in this section).

**Strange Fancies**—(See "Peculiar" in this section).

**Tastes**—Fanciful Tastes—(See Desires; "Fastidious" under Diet; "Peculiar" under Dress; Habits, Tastes. Also see "Distempered" in this section).

**Turbulent Fancies**—Riotous Fancies—♂ affl. in the 9th H., and espec. when also afflicting ☿. (See Riotous, Turbulent).

**Vagaries**—Full of, and of Wild Fancies—(See Vagaries).

**Wild Fancies**—♅ affl. by ♀. (See Vagaries). For further influences along this line see Fanatical, Flightiness, Genius, Ideas, Insanity, Intuitions, Mental, Mind, Ninth House, Obsessions, Opinions, Premonitions, Psychic, Reformers, Religion, Revolutionary; "Slights" under Sensitive; Third House, Vague, Visionary, Weird, etc.).

**FANTASIES** — Phantasies — (See Fancies).

**FAR-SIGHTEDNESS**—(See "Hyperopia" under Sight).

**FASTING**—People born under the Sanguine Temperament benefit by Fasting. This Temperament is Moist, and is ruled by ♃ and the Airy Signs. (See Sanguine).

**FAT**—The Yellowish Oily Substance of Adipose Tissue—Fatty—Lardaceous—Waxy—Suet—Adipose Tissue—Sebaceous, etc.—Fat is formed by ♃, and also ♃ largely regulates its disposition. The liver is excited to increased secretion of fat by ♃. The fatty constituents in Milk are added by ♃. Fat acts thru ♃ and ♐ influence, and frequently thru ♊, its opposite sign, and acts upon the lungs. The consistency of adipose tissue, its density and hardness, is increased in disease conditions when ♂ is with ♃ at B., or afflicting ♃ by dir. (See Consistency, Density, Hardening, Jupiter, Liver).

**A Little Fat**—The Body Somewhat Fat—Not Much Fat—♄ in his first station at B.; ♃ in watery signs.

**Adiposa Dolorosa**—Characterized by Nodular Formations—A ♄ disease; ♃ affl. by ♄; ♂ with ♃ at B., or affl. ♃ by dir.; Subs at KP. (See Tubercles).

**Adiposis**—(See Corpulent; "Fatty Degeneration" in this section).

**Body**—Fat Body—The ☽ Sig. in ♓; the ☽ in a water sign; the ☽ in ♓ in partile asp. the Asc., plump or fat, and with a mean, short stature; the ☽ in her incr. gives a full, tall, fat, plump body; ♄ in his 2nd station at B.; ♄ occi. of the ☉, and with great Lat.; ♃ Sig. in water signs, a fat body, but rather comely (Hor'y); ☿ Sig. in ♎; the first parts of ♈, ♉, or ♌ ascending make the body more fat, or the latter parts of ♊ or ♏; water signs on the Asc.; the Sig. of the party in a water sign; the Sig. of the party in N. Lat. in Hor'y Questions; the 2nd face of ♌ on the Asc., grows fat with age; the 4th or 5th face of ♑ on Asc.; the 6th face of ♓ on the Asc. (See Bulky, Corpulent, Fleshy, Large Body (see Large); Lumpish; "Corpulent" under Middle Life; Obesity, Puffing, Stoutness). Case—Birth Data of Fat Man—The birth data of Tom Ton, the fattest man on record, is as follows,—Born March 29, 1896, 5:30 A.M., Florence, Ariz. Weight, 750 lbs. Died on May 27th, 1926, at weight of 900 lbs., having gained 150 lbs in 10 days soon before his death.

**Cancer**—Fatty and Waxy Carcinoma—Lardaceous—(See "Fatty" under Carcinoma).

**Consistency**—Of Fat—(See the Introduction to this Article).

**Corpulent**—(See Corpulent; "Body", in this section).

**Cysts**—Sebaceous Cysts—Wens—Steatoma—(See Cysts, Sebaceous, Steatoma, Wen).

**Degeneration**—Fatty Degeneration—A ♃ disease. (See Degeneration; "Degeneration" under Heart, Liver, Muscles).

**Density**—Of Fat—(See the Introduction to this Article).

**Distribution**—Of Fat—(See Introduction to this Article).

**Face**—Fat Face—(See "Fat Face" under Face).

**Fat Body**—(See "Body" in this section).

**Fat and Plump**—(See "Body" in this section. Also see Corpulent, Fleshy, Plumpness).

**Fat and Short**—(See "Short and Fleshy" under Fleshy; "Mean Stature" under Mean; Short, Stoutness).

**Fat and Tall**—♃ in water signs. (See Tall).

**Fatty Degeneration**—(See "Degeneration" in this section).

**Fleshy Body**—(See Fleshy).

**Fluids**—The fatty consistency of fluids is ruled by ♃. (See Fluids, Milk).

**Foods**—Disorders from Fatty Foods—♃ in ♏. (See Diet, Food).

**Formation of Fat**—Fat is formed by ♃. (See the Introduction to this Article).

**Hardness**—The Hardness of Fat Increased—(See Introduction to this Article).

**Heart**—Fatty Degeneration of—(See "Fatty" under Heart).

**Lardaceous Cancer**—(See "Fatty" under Carcinoma).

**Lipoma**—Fatty Tumor—(See Lipoma).

**Liver**—Fatty Degeneration of—(See "Fatty" under Liver).

**Marrow**—(See Marrow).

**Muscles**—Fatty Degeneration of—(See Muscles).

**Not Much Fat**—(See "A Little Fat" in this section).

**Obesity**—Fat Body—Corpulence—(See Corpulent, Fleshy, Obesity, Stoutness; "Body", in this section).

**Plump and Fat**—(See Plump; "Body", in this section).

**Sarcoma**—Adiposa Sarcoma—(See Sarcoma).

**Sebaceous Cysts**—(See Cysts, Wen).

**Secretion of Fat**—Ruled over by ♃. (See the Introduction to this Article; Liver).

**Short and Fat** — (See "Short and Fleshy" under Fleshy; Short).

**Steatoma**—An Encysted Sebaceous Tumor—(See Wen).

**Tall and Fat**—Tall, Fat, Plump and Full Body—Given by the ☽ in her increase; ♃ in watery signs. (See "Body" in this section; Tall).

**Tumors**—Fatty Tumors—♂ ☌ or ill-asp. ♃; caused by the afflictions of ♃. (See "Fatty" under Carcinoma; Caruncle, Lipoma, Sarcoma, Sebaceous, Wen).

**Waxy**—(See Ambergris; "Fatty" under Carcinoma; Waxy).

**Wen**—A Sebaceous Cyst—(See Wen).

**FATAL**—Deadly—

**Accidents**—Fatal Accidents—Fatalities — (See "Death by Accident", "Fatal", under Accidents).

**Deadly Diseases**—An Eclipse of the ☽ in the 3rd Dec. of ♍ brings deadly diseases.

**Disease**—The Disease May Prove Fatal—(See "Symbols of Death" under Death; "The Sick Will Hardly Escape" under Escape; "Doubtful Recovery", "Little Hope of Recovery", under Recovery).

**Fatal Illness**—Mortal Illness—Deadly Diseases—The ☉ hyleg. and to the ☌, □, or ☍ ♄ by dir. (See "Certain Death" under Death; "Death" under Fevers; Incurable, Malignant, Pernicious; "Impossible" under Recovery).

**Fatal Imprisonment** — (See "Death" under Prison).

**Fatalism**—(See Scepticism).

**FATE**—Destiny—

**A Bad Fate**—A Fatality Hangs Over the Native from Birth—♄ in the 10th H. at B., and espec. when ill-aspected, in a weak sign, and affl. the ☉, ☽, or hyleg. (See "Malice of Fortune" under Fortune; Miseries, Misfortunes, Unfortunate).

**Fate and Free Will**—(See "Free Will" under Will).

**Good Fate**—(See Comforts, Contentment; "Fortunate In Life" under Fortune; "Good Health" under Health; Heredity; "Peace of Mind" under Mind; Riches, etc.).

**Melancholic Fate**—Many cross or □ aspects to a planet, or planets ascending; the 20° ♍ on the Asc. at B. (See Melancholy, Miseries, Reverses, Sadness, Self-Undoing, Sorrow, Trouble).

**Resigned to Fate**—Mars obscurely placed, and afflicted, tends to take the courage out of people, and to offer less resistance to obstacles. On the other hand, a prominent ♂, or ♂ affl. by ♅, many planets in positive and masculine signs at B., tend to give more fight to the nature, and to go to extreme measures to avoid defeat. The good influences of ♀ give resignation and contentment. Also ♄ in good asp. to ♂ gives a better understanding of Divine Things, and to be resigned to fate, environment, circumstances, etc., with more grace and contentment, realizing the Divinity within themselves, and by contacting the Higher Mind. (See Bold, Character, Cheerfulness, Contentment, Destiny, Energy, Environment, External, Individuality, Optimism, Positive, Resignation, Spiritual, etc.).

**Ripe Fate**—This is one which the Occult Writers say cannot be avoided, and that the planetary influences and directions will act with certainty regardless of the will, conduct, or decisions, due to matured Karmic conditions. (See Character, Directions, Events, Prognosis; "Free Will" under Will).

**Suffering and Fate** — (See "Periods" under Health; Suffering).

**The Ways of Fate** — (See the two verses of Poetry at the end of the Article on "Ships").

**FATHER**—The Father—Paternal—The ☉ and ♄ are allotted to the person of the father. In the European System of Astrology, the 4th H. governs the father, and the 10th H. the mother. In finer detail, some Writers say the 10th H. governs the father in a male nativity, and the 4th H. the father in a female geniture. In the Hindu System of Astrology, the 10th H. governs the father, and the 4th H. the mother. In afflictions to the father, the ☉ should be principally observed by day, and ♄ by night. A planet in the 4th H. is Sig. of the father in Hor'y Questions. The ☉ and ♄ are masculine, and rule espec. over the male members of the family. The ☽ and ♀ are feminine, and rule the mother and female members of the family, as sisters, daughters, aunts, grandmother. Conditions concerning the parents are to be noted in the child's map, and espec. in the map of the first-born, and the influences in the following paragraphs and subjects concerning the afflictions to, suffering, wounds, death, etc., of the father, are to be noted in the map of the child. The maps of birth of any of the children are also permissible for such study, but may not be as typical as the map of the first-born. In day maps, the ☉ and ♀ are the chief Sigs. and representatives of the father and mother, and ♄ and the ☽ in night maps, as the ☉ espec. rules by day, and the ☽ by night. (See Day, Night).

**Accidents To**—Hurts, Injuries or Wounds To—The ☉ or ♄ in the 4th, 5th, 7th, or 8th H., and afflicted; ♅ or ♂ in the 4th or 10th H., and afflicted, may be killed by an accident; ♅ or ♂ to the cusp the 4th or 10th H. by dir.; ♄ or ♂ affl. the ☉ in a child's map; ♂ to the cusp the 9th H.; ♂ affl. in the 4th or 10th H.; the Asc. to the ill-asps. the ☉ by dir., and the ☉ affl. at B. by a malefic; an eclipse falling on the ☉ in a child's map; planets cadent and affl. the ☉ or ♄. (See Danger, Death, Detriment, in this section).

**Afflictions To**—The ☉ to the ☌ ♄ by dir., or ♄ to the ☌ the ☉ by dir. (See the various paragraphs in this Article).

**Aunts**—The Sisters and Brothers of the Father—Sickness or Death of— (See "Paternal" under Aunts, Uncles).

**Brothers Of**—(See "Aunts" in this section).

**Burns To**—♂ □ or ☍ ♄ from angles or succedent houses. (See Burns).

**Contractions**—Of the Muscles of the Limbs—(See "Muscles" in this section).

**Danger to the Father**—The Father Threatened—The ☉ affl. at B., and the ☉ to the evil asp. the Asc. by dir., and espec. if the ☉ be lord of the 11th H.; the ☉ in an angle near the cusp, and in □ or ☍ ♄ at a Solar Rev., or in the 8th H.; the ☉ to the ☌ or ill-asps. ♄ or ♂ by dir.; the ☉ in Rapt P. ♄; ♅ to the cusp 4th H. by dir.; ♅ by tr. passing over the radical ♄; ♄, ♂, or ♅ to the cusp 4th H. by dir.; afflictions to ♄ or the ☉ in the child's map; ♄ to the ill-asps. the ☉ by dir.; ♄ in the 10th H. in a masc. nativity, or in the 4th H. in a female, and affl. by the ☉ or ☽; ♂ affl. in the 4th H.; ruler of the 4th H. at B. a malefic, and in the radical 11th or 4th H. at a Solar Rev.; the Asc. to the □ or ☍ ☉ by dir. (See Parents, Death, Detriment, Infirmities, and the various paragraphs in this section).

**Death of the Father**—Danger of—The ☉ affl. at B., and the ☉ to the □ or ☍ the Asc. by dir., and espec. if the ☉ be lord of the 11th H. at B.; the ☉ to the □ or ☍ ♅ by dir., and espec. by the □, if the ☉ be ruler of the 4th, or in the 4th H. at B.; the ☉ hyleg, and to the ☌, □, or ☍ ♄ by dir., and espec. if the ☉ be lord of the 4th H.; afflictions to the ☉ or ♄ in the map of the child, and espec. of the first-born; the ☉ prog. to the ☍ ♄; ♄ to the ☌ or ill-asps. the ☉ by dir.; ♄ ruler of the 4th H. at B., or in the 4th, and to the ☌ or ill-asps. the Asc. by dir.; ♄ or ♂ affl. in the 4th or 10th H.; ♄ in the 10th H. in a male nativity, or in the 4th H. in a female, and affl. by the ☉ or ☽; ♄ at a Solar Rev. ☌ or P. Dec. the radical ☉, and if the ☉ be hyleg, the death of the father in a female nativity is indicated; ♄ by evil dir. to the cusp of 4th H., or to a malefic in the 4th H. at B.; ♄ or ♆ to the ☌ or ☍ the radical ☉ by tr., or at a Solar Rev.; ♂ □ or ☍ ♄ from angles or succedents; ♂ elevated above the ☉ at B., or in evil asp. the ☉, and affl. the ☉ by dir.; the Asc. to the ill-asps. the ☉ by dir., and the ☉ affl. by malefics at B.; the M.C. to the ☌ or ill-asps. the place of the radical ♂ may kill or afflict a parent; the M.C. to the ☌ ☋. (See Early Death, Sudden Death, Short Life, in this section; "Death" under Parents).

**Detriment To**—Misfortune To—The ☉ □ ♄ in the map of the first-born until the next child is born; malefics in the 4th H. of a child until the next child is born with a more favorable map; malefics in the 4th or 10th H. at a Solar Rev.; ☋ in the 4th H. at B., and affl. by evil directions of the Asc. (See Accidents, Afflictions, Danger, Infirmities, and the various paragraphs in this section).

**Diseased**—The Father Much Diseased —♂ □ or ☍ ♄ from angles or succedent houses, the father tends to be much diseased, and to be liable to fevers, burns, wounds, sickness, death, and injuries to the eyes and eyesight.

**Diseases To**—(See Diseased, Infirmities, Much Sickness, Violent, and the various paragraphs in this section).

**Drunkard**—The Father May Become a Drunkard—(See "Father", "Husband", under Drunkenness; "Drink" under Parents).

**Early Death Of**—Dies Young—Short Life for the Father—The ☉ and ♄ affl. at B. in the child's map; short life of the father is espec. indicated by the ☉ or ♄ being in the 1st or 10th H. at B., and afflicted; the ☉ and ♄ affl. in cardinal houses, as the 1st or 10th, or in their succedent houses, the 2nd and 11th, and ♂ be elevated above, or rising before the ☉ and ♄; ♄ affl. in the 4th H.; the ☉ and ♄ affl. in cadent houses, and with many planets in such houses; ♄ in the 1st or 10th H. and in □ or ☍ ☉; ♅ in the 4th H., and near the lower meridian; ♂ in the 4th H. in a female nativity, or ♂ in the 10th H. in a male geniture, and affl.; the 11° ♎ on Asc., the early death of the father, or the father unknown to the child. (See Adoption; "Early Death" under Early; Orphans, Parents; "Separated From" under Parents; Death, Short Life, Sudden Death, in this section).

**Eyes**—Eyesight—Eyes and Face—Disorders of—Injury To—♂ in evil asp. the ☉ at B., and elevated above the ☉; ♂ □ or ☍ ☉ from angles or succedents. In the case of the mother, ♂ affl. the ☽ in the same manner, or ♄ and ♂ both affl. the ☽. (See "Eyes" under Mother).

**Face**—Disorders of—Injury To—(See "Eyes" in this section).

**Father-In-Law**—In a male nativity, denoted by the 10th H., and in a woman's nativity by the 4th H., and afflictions in these houses tend to affect them according to their nature.

**Fevers**—To the Father—(See "Infirmities" in this section).

**Godfathers**—Ruled by ♃. Afflictions or suffering to them is caused by afflictions to ♃ in the map of the child at B., and by dir., and espec. if ♃ is weak, ill-aspected, and badly placed at B. Godmothers are ruled by ♀, and corresponding afflictions to ♀ would result in detriment to them. (See Guardians).

**Good Health**—To the Father—(See "Long Life" in this section).

**Health**—Of the Father—Good Health —Bad Health—(See Infirmities, Long Life, Much Sickness, in this section).

**Humours In**—Suffers from Watery Humours—♄ affl. the ☉ at B. (See Humours; "Humours" under Watery).

**Hurts To**—(See "Accidents" in this section).

**Husband**—(See Husband).

**Infirmities**—The Father Full of Infirmities—Suffers Fevers and Inflammations—The ☉ and ♄ affl. in cadent houses; the ☉ affl. by ♄ or ♂; the ☉ and ♄ in the 4th, 5th, 7th, or 8th H., and affl.; the ☉ to the cusp the 6th H. by dir.; the ☉ to the ☌ or ill-asps. ♄ by dir.; the ☉ in the 10th H., and affl. by ♄ or ♂; an eclipse falling on the radical ☉ in a child's map; the ☉ to the ☌ or P. Dec. Regulus by dir.; ♆ or ♄ passing the place of the radical ☉ by tr., or in ☌ the ☉ at a Solar Rev.; ♄ in the 4th H., and affl.; ♄ debilitated and in □ or ☍ ☉; ♄ in the 10th H. in a male nativity. or in the 4th H. in a female, and affl. by the ☉ or ☽; ♄ ascending at B., and the ☉ to the ☌ or ill-asps. ♄ by dir.; ♄ to the ☌ or ill-asps. the ☉ by dir.; ♂ elevated above, or rising before the ☉ and ♄; ♂ □ or ☍ ♄ from angles or succedents, fevers to; ♂ at a Solar Rev. passing the place of the radical ☉ or ♄; the Asc. to the ill-asps. the ☉ by dir., and the ☉ affl. at B. (See Afflictions, Diseased, Early Death, Much Sickness, Violent, and the various paragraphs in this section).

**Inflammatory Attacks**—(See the ♂ influences under "Infirmities" in this section).

**Injuries To**—(See "Accidents" in this section).

**Killed**—By An Accident—♅ or ♂ in the 4th or 10th H., and afflicted, danger of. (See "Accidents" in this section).

**Limbs and Muscles**—Contractions In—Pains In—(See "Muscles" in this section).

**Long Life**—For the Father—Good Health—Good asps. to the ☉ and ♄ at B., and these planets strong and dignified in the map of the child; ♄ ⚹ or △ the ☉, and ♄ strongly dignified; ♃ and ♀ favorably configurated with the ☉ or ♄; the M.C. favorably aspected by the ☉; ♃ or ♀ in the 4th or 10th H., and in good asp. to the ☉ and ♄, and these houses free from the afflictions of malefics; if ♃ or ♀ have any configuration with the ☉ or ♄, or ♄ in good asp. the ☉, or joined to the ☉ in an angle, or beholding him from angles; lord of the 4th in the 4th, and well-asp., or lord of the 10th in the 10th H., according to the sex of the native, the father lives to an old age. (See "Long Life" under Life).

**Misfortune To**—(See "Detriment" in this section).

**Mother**—(See the various paragraphs under Mother).

**Much Sickness**—The Father Suffers Many Illnesses—Afflictions and much sickness for the father are espec. indicated by the ☉ or ♄ in the 4th or 7th H.; the ☉ hyleg at B., and to the ☌ or ill-asps. ♄ by dir.; the ☉ and ♄ in cardinal or succedent houses, and ♂ elevated above, or rising before them; ♄ in the 4th H. of the child, and afflicted; lord of the 6th H. in the 4th, and afflicted. (See Afflictions, Early Death, Infirmities, Sickly, in this section).

**Muscles and Limbs**—Pains and Contractions In—♂ in evil asp. to ♄, and elevated above ♄. (See Contractions, Limbs, Muscles, Pain).

**Old Age**—Lives To—(See "Long Life" in this section).

**Pain**—In Muscles and Limbs—(See "Muscles" in this section).

**Parents**—(See the various paragraphs under Parents).

**Paternal Aunts**—And Uncles—(See "Aunts" in this section).

**Patricide**—Or Matricide—A Parricide—☿ ill-posited, and in □ or ☍ ♂.

**Relatives Of**—The father's Relatives are ruled by ♃, and the mother's Relatives by ☿. (See Aunts, Maternal, Mother, Paternal, Relatives, Uncles).

**Short Life**—For the Father—The father usually does not live to old age when the lord of the 4th or 10th H. is in the 8th or 12th H. in the map of the child, according to the sex of the child. (See "Early Death" in this section).

**Sickly**—The Father Sickly—Weakly—Vitality Low—(See Early Death, Infirmities, Much Sickness, in this section).

**Sickness To**—The Father Sickly—Weakly—Vitality Low—The ☉ to the ☌ ♄ by dir.; ♄ in the 4th or 7th H., and in □ or ☍ ☉. (See Afflictions, Diseased, Early Death, Infirmities, Much Sickness, Violent, in this section).

**Sisters Of**—Diseases and Afflictions To—(See "Paternal" under Aunts).

**Sudden Death Of**—♂ elevated above the ☉ at B., or in evil asp. the ☉, and affl. the ☉ by dir., danger of sudden death of the father; ♂ □ or ☍ the ☉ from angles or succedents; ♂ or ♅ in the 4th or 10th H. (See Death, Early Death, in this section).

**Suffers**—Father May Suffer—(See Detriment, Diseased, Infirmities, Much Sickness, and the various paragraphs in this section).

**Threatened**—The Father Is Threatened—(See "Danger" in this section).

**Uncles**—Paternal Uncles—(See "Paternal" under Aunts, Uncles).

**Unknown**—The Father Unknown to the Child—(See "Early Death" in this section).

**Violent Diseases To**—The ☉ to the □ or ☍ ♂ by dir.; the ☉ to the place of Cor Leonis, violent to both the native and the father, altho not fatal. (See the ♂ influences under "Infirmities" in this section).

**Vitality Low**—(See "Sickly" in this section).

**Watery Humours In**—(See "Humours" in this section).

**Weak**—Weakly—(See "Sickly" in this section).

**Wife's Father**—Afflicted—(See "Father" under Wife).

**Wounds To**—(See "Accidents" in this section).

**Young**—Dies Young—(See "Early Death" in this section).

**FATIGUE**—Tired—Weariness—Exhaustion of Strength—Languor from Excessive Toxic Materials and Tissue Disintegration—Fatigue is generally caused by the afflictions of ♄ (or ☿ if he be of the nature of ♄), and espec. with brain workers. There is also the fatigue from diseases, toxic accumulations, deposit of wastes and minerals, caused by ♄ afflictions. Physical fatigue may result from over-work, over-exercise, over-study, too much excitement, due usually to a strong ♂ influence at B., and a positive nature. Also fatigue may result from long journeys and tedious travel, confinement and lack of exercise, which is usually the result of low vitality, and the afflictions of ♄ to the 3rd or 9th H. during travel.

**Brain Fag**—(See "Brain Fag" under Brain; Reading, Study).

**Exercise**—Fatigue and Disease from Over-Exercise—(See "Inordinate", "Intemperate", under Exercise; "Over-Exertion" under Exertion; Sports, Study, Weariness).

**Mind**—Mental Fatigue from Over-Study, or from General Weakness—The ☽ in ♊, □ or ☍ ♄ (or ☿ if he be of the nature of ♄) at the beginning of an illness, or from long mental strain. (See Anxiety; "Brain Fag" under Brain; Cares, Exertion, Reading, Rest, Study; "Weak Body" under Weak; Worry).

**Sports**—Fatigue From—(See "Exercise" in this section).

**Travel**—Fatigue or Sickness During Travel—(See "Sickness" under Travel). (See Apathy, Dull, Feeble, Heaviness, Inactive, Inertia, Languid, Lassitude, Lethargy, Listless, Sluggish, Toxaemia.

**FATTY**—Fatty Cancer—Fatty Degeneration—(See Fat).

**FAUCES**—The Throat from the Mouth to the Pharynx—Dryness of—Dry Throat—A ♄ disease; ♄ in ♉; ♂ affl. in ♉ tends to feverish dry fauces and throat. (See Diphtheria, Mouth, Pharynx, Throat, Tonsils).

**FAULTY**—Defective—Deranged—Imperfect—Disordered—The Faulty Action of Functions, Organs, Parts, etc.—Faulty Elimination—Faulty Secretion—(See Defects, Derangements, Disordered, Elimination, Functions, Hardening, Imperfect, Organs, Retarded, Secretions, Stoppages, Suppressions, etc. Also see in the alphabetical arrangement the subject you have in mind).

**Fault-Finding**—(See Petulant, Scolding, Virgo).

**FAVORABLE**—Beneficial—Helpful—Propitious—

**Crises**—Favorable Crises In Disease—(See "Better" under Crises).

**Prognosis**—The Prognosis Favorable—(See "Better" under Crises; Curable; "Disease Will Soon End" under End; Prognosis, Recovery, Termination).

**Years**—Favorable Years and Periods of Life—(See Cycles; "Good Health" under Health; Periods. Also note the various paragraphs under Fortunate, Good).

**FAVORED**—

**Favored Body**—(See Beautiful, Comely; "Good Constitution" under Constitution; Fair, Fine; "Good Health", and "Signs of Good Health" under Health; Robust, Ruddy; "Well-Favored", "Well-Shaped", under Well).

**Favored Mind**—(See Genius, Intellect; "Quickened" under Mentality; "Sound Mind" under Mind).

**FAVUS**—A Contagious Parasitic Disease of the Skin with Crusts—

**Favus of the Scalp**—Porrigo (Scald-Head)—♂ affl. in ♈. (See Crusts, Parasites).

**FEAR**—Fears—Fearful—Phobias—Dread—Awe—Mental Aversions—Doubts—Anxieties—The Mind Fearful—Anguish of Mind—Veneration—The Mind Disturbed by Fear, Obsessions, Worry, Delusions, Superstitions, Hallucinations, etc.—All these subjects have to do with Fear in its different manifestations. See these subjects in the alphabetical arrangement. Fears, Anguish of Mind, Anxieties, etc., are ruled principally by the 8th and 12th H., and also by ♄ and ♆. Spiritual and religious fears are ruled over largely by ♆, while ♄ rules the fears arising from physical, wordly, material, business and earthly conditions. Other influences are noted in this section. The general Causes of Fears are listed under "Fears" in this section. See the following subjects in the alphabetical arrangement when not considered here—

**Anguish**—Of Mind—(See Anguish; "Fears", and the various paragraphs in this section).

**Anxious Fears**—Morbid Fears—(See Anxiety; "Morbid" in this section).

**Astral Influences**—Fears Caused By—♆ influences. (See Fears, Insanity, Obsessions, Spirit Controls, in this section).

**Aversions**—Irrational Fears—Phobias—(See Aversions, Antipathy; "Morbid" in this section).

**Beside Oneself**—(See this subject under Excitable).

**Bodily Conditions**—The Health—The Physical Welfare—Business, Worldly and Material Conditions—Fears Arising From—Ruled by ♄, and caused by ♄ afflictions over the mind at B., and by dir., and the afflictions of ♄ to ☿ or the hyleg. (See Hypochondria, Morbid, in this section).

**Brooding; Business Fears**—(See Cares; "Bodily" in this section).

**Calamity**—Fear of An Impending Calamity—(See "Impending Calamity" under Calamity).

**Cares; Causes of Fears**—(See "Fears", and the various paragraphs in this section).

**Chaotic Mind**—(See "Mental Chaos" under Chaotic; Fears, Morbid, Vain, in this section).

**Claustrophobia**—A Morbid Dread of An Inclosed Space—(See Claustrophobia).

**Comprehension; Confined Spaces**—Fear of—(See Claustrophobia).

**Crowds**—Fear of Being Jammed In a Crowd—(See Claustrophobia).

**Danger**—Fear of An Unknown Danger—♆ in the 12th H. (See "Impending Calamity" under Calamity; "Fear" under Darkness).

**Darkness**—Fear of the Dark—Fear In Solitude—(See Darkness; "Solitude" in this section).

**Death**—(1) Death To Be Feared—Death More Certain—(See "Arguments", "Certain Death", under Death). (2) Fears His Own Death—Fear of Death—The ☉ or ☽ to the cusp the 8th H. by dir.; denoted by ♄, and ♄ to the ☌ or ill-asps. the ☉ by dir. (3) Less Fear of Death—If the fatal asp. or ☌ fall in the term of ♃ or ♀, or in exact ⚹ or △ to ♃ or ♀. (4) No Fear of Death—♂ a strong ruler of the horoscope; ♂ rising in the Asc. or M.C. in ♈ or ♏, well-aspected and fortified. (5) Poison Death—Fear of—(See the influences in the paragraph "Death by Poison" under Poison).

**Dejected; Delirium**—(See "Delirium Tremens", "Wild Delirium", under Delirium).

**Delusions; Dementia; Demoniac;**

**Depressed; Despondent; Deviations;**

**Disaster**—Fear of Impending Disaster—(See Calamity).

**Discontentment; Disease**—Fear of—Dread of—♆ affl. in the 6th H.; a ♄ characteristic; a ♉ trait; earthy signs on the Asc. (See "Earth Signs" under Earth; Hypochondria, Imaginary Diseases, Neptune, Obsessions, Saturn, Taurus).

**Dissatisfied; Doubts**—(See "Fears" in this section. Also see Anxiety, Brooding, Doubts, Hallucinations, Imaginations, Obsessions, Premonitions, Worry, etc.).

**Dreams**—(See "Dreamy Mind" under Dreams).

**Eighth House**—Influences of—(See Eighth).

**Emotions**—(See "Disorders" under Emotions).

**Enemies**—Fear and Dread of—Fear of Enemies Prevalent—(See "Fear" under Enemies).

**Ergophobia**—Fear of Work—(See Dull, Idle, Indolent, Indifferent, Labor, Lazy, Work, etc.).

**False Fears**—(See "Morbid" in this section).

**Fanciful Fears**—The ☽ affl. in the 12th H. (See Fancies, Vagaries).

**Fearful**—Fearful Imaginations—Fearful and Peevish—(See "Fearful" under Imagination; Fears, Peevish, in this section).

**Fearless**—Bold—Courageous—♂ a strong ruler at B.; ♂ rising in the Asc.

**Fears**—Signs of Fear—General Causes of Fear—Caused by ♆, ♅, ♄, the 8th and 12th H. influences. The afflictions of ♆ tend to a chaotic mind, false fears, and Astral disturbances. Fears by the suppression of the bodily functions are caused by ♄. Fear and anguish of mind are ruled over and indicated by the 8th H. conditions. The ☉ or ☽ hyleg, and to the ☌ or ill-asp. ♄ by dir.; the ☉ weak at B., and affl. by ♄; the ☉ or ♃ as Sigs., and to the ☌ or ill-asp. ♄ by dir.; the ☽ to the ☌ or ill-asp. ♆ or ♄ by dir.; the ☽ P ♄, fearful and peevish; ♆ in ♈ ☌ ☽ or ☿, and in □ or ☍ ♅; ♆ affl. in the 3rd or 9th H.; the tr. of ♆ thru the 1st, 3rd or 9th H. if in these houses at B.; ♆ in 1st H. at B.; ♆ affl. in ♐; ♆ □ or ☍ ♅; ♆ in evil asp. ☿; ♄ Sig. in ♑; born under strong ♄ influence; the directions of ♄ to the ☉, ☽, Asc. or M.C.; ♄ in the Asc., and affl. by □ and ☍ asps.; ♄ rules the Pneumogastric Nerve, and by restricting the action of this nerve tends to cause fears and worries; ♄ ☌ or ill-asps. the prog. ☉, ☽, or ☿; ♄ ℞ and in tr. over the place of ☿; ♄ ☌ the Asc. by dir.; ♃ affl. in ♒; ☿ affl. in ♈ or ♓; ☿ affl. by ♄; ☋ in the Asc.; malefic planets in the 8th H. are signs of fear and death; the Asc. to the ☌ or ill-asps. ♄ by dir.; the 21° ♐ on the Asc. (See "Morbid", and the various paragraphs in this section).

**Forebodings; Fright; Functions**—Fear Caused by the Suppression of—Caused by ♄ afflictions. (See Functions, Suppressions; "Fears" in this section).

**Gloom; Hallucinations; Hanging**—Haunted by Visions of Hanging—(See Hanging).

**Hauntings; Health**—Morbid and Anxious Fears Concerning—(See Hypochondria).

**Horrors**—Nervous Horrors—(See Horrors).

**Hydrophobia**—Fear of Water—(See Hydrophobia).

**Hypochondria**—Morbid Fears About the Health—(See Hypochondria).

**Imaginations**—Fearful Imaginations—(See Imagination).

**Impending Disaster**—Fear of—(See Calamity).

**Imprisonment**—Fear of—(See Prisons).

**Inclosed Spaces**—Fear of—(See Claustrophobia).

**Insanity; Introspection;**

**Irrational Fears**—(See "Morbid" in this section).

**Low Spirits**—(See Low).

**Madness; Mania; Melancholy;**

**Mental Disturbances**—Thru Fears—(See the various paragraphs in this section; Mental, Mind).

**Mind Darkened**—Thru Fear—♄ or ☋ in the Asc., in ☌ the ☉, ☽, or ☿.

**Moods; Morbid Fears**—False Fears—Anxious Fears—Aversions—Phobias—Irrational Fears—The ☉ or ☽ to the ☌ or ill-asps. ♄ by dir.; the ☉, ☽, Asc., or hyleg affl. by ♄ or ♆; ♆ affl. the hyleg, and espec. with ♆ in the 6th or 8th H.; ♆ □ or ☍ ♅; ♄ influence strong at B.; ♄ Sig. in ♑; ♄ ☌ the ☉, ☽, or ☿; ♄ ☌ ♃ or ♀ in the 12th H.; ♄ ℞ and in tr. over the radical ☿; the prog. ☽ to the ☌, □, or ☍ ♄; ♃ to the cusp the 12th H. by dir.; malefics in ♊ or the 3rd H., and affl. the hyleg or ☿; watery signs strong and predominating at B., and espec. ♏. Case—See Fig. 25 in Message Of The Stars" by the Heindels. (See Fears, Solitude, in this section; Anxiety, Darkness, Hypochondria, Imaginations, Melancholy; "Neurasthenia" under Nerves; Worry).

**Nervous Fears**—♆ affl. in the 6th H.; ♄ in the Asc. and affl. by cross aspects; ♀ Sig. to the ☌ or ill-asps. ♄ by dir. (See "Neurasthenia" under Nerves).

**Obsessions** — Obsessed with Fears — The Asc. to the ☌, □, or ☍ ♄ by dir. (See Obsessions).

**Own Death**—Fears His Own Death—(See "Death" in this section).

**Peevish and Fearful**—(See Peevish).

**Perceptions; Perversions; Phantasies;**

**Phobias**—(See "Morbid Fears" in this section).

**Physical Conditions**—Fears Arising From—(See "Bodily" in this section).

**Pneumogastric Nerve**—Fears Arising from Restriction of—♄ influence. (See "Fears" in this section; Pneumogastric).

**Poison Death**—Fear of Death by Poison—(See "Death" under Poison).

**Poverty**—Fear of—(See Poverty).

**Premonitions**—Presentiments—(See Forebodings, Premonitions, Psychic).

**Prophetic; Psychic Disorders** — Psychoses—(See Psychic).

**Reason**—Disorders of—(See Reason).

**Religious Fears**—Ruled by ♆. (See "Fears" under Religion).

**Reverential Fear** — (See Religion, Veneration).

**Sciatica**—Fear of—(See Sciatic).

**Signs of Fear** — (See "Fears" in this section).

**Solitude**—Fear and Dread of—The ☽ in ♊, and affl. by ♆; the ☉ or ☽ in the 12th H., and affl. by ♄ or ♆; ☿ affl. by ♄, ♅, or ♆; afflictions which combine the influences of the 3rd H., ♊, ☿, and the watery element. Case—Dread of Solitude—See "Strange Case", No. 379, in 1001 N.N. (See Darkness, Fright, Solitude).

**Spirit Controls**—(See this subject).

**Spiritual Fears**—Ruled by ♆; ♆ affl. in 9th H. (See Religion, Spirit, Spiritual, Veneration).

**Strange Fears** — Strange Terrors—(See "Terrors", "Visions", under Strange).

**Superstitions; Suppressions**—Restrictions—(See Fears, Functions, Pneumogastric, in this section).

**Terrors** — Strange Terrors — (See "Strange" in this section).

**Thinking** — (See Chaotic, Confusion, Clairaudience, Erratic, Judgment, Mental; "Clouded" under Mind; Peculiar, Religion, Thinking, Weird, etc. Note the various paragraphs in this section).

**Twelfth House** — Influences of — (See Twelfth).

**Understanding; Unknown Danger**—Fear of—(See "Danger" in this section).

**Vagaries; Vain Fears**—Vain Imaginations—Caused by ♆ and ♄; ♆ afflictions tend to vain fears and a chaotic mind; ♆ in evil asp. to ☿; ♆ □ or ☍ ♅ or ☿; afflictions in watery signs, and espec. where the influence of ♆ is involved. (See Chaotic, Clairvoyance, Forebodings, Imaginations, Mediumship, Melancholy, Obsessions, Premonitions, Spirit Controls, Vain, etc.).

**Veneration; Visions; Want**—Fear of Coming To Want and Poverty—(See Poverty).

**Water**—Fear of—(See Hydrophobia).

**Weird; Work**—Fear of—(See "Ergophobia" in this section).

**Worldly Conditions**—Fears Arising From—(See "Bodily" in this section).

**Worry.**

**FEASTING—**

**Health Injured By** — Fond of Feasting—The ☉ affl. by ♃ or ♀; the ☉ Sig. in ♍, fond of feasting; lords of the 6th or 10th H. in the 5th H.

**Ruins Himself By**—The ☉ Sig. in ♓; ♀ Sig. in ♎, love their belly; the 1° ♍ on the Asc.; ♓ on the Asc. (See Appetite, Cravings, Diet, Drink; "Early Death" under Early; Eating; "His Own Worst Enemy" under Enemies; Epicureans, Excesses, Extravagance, Feeding, Food; "Free Living" under Free; Gluttony, Habits; "High Living" under High; Indigestion, Indulgence, Intemperate, Luxuries; "Dies Before Middle Life" under Middle Life; Over-Indulgence, Pleasures, Plethora; "Riotous Living" under Riotous; Surfeits).

**FEATURES**—The Different Parts of the Face—The aspects and position of ☿ at B. sometimes express and determine the features. Many of the descriptions and paragraphs under Cheeks, Chin, Complexion, Countenance, Decanates, Ears, Eyes, Eyebrows, Expression, Head, Jaws, Mouth, Nose, Profile, Teeth, etc., will also apply here. See these subjects.

**Bird Features**—(See Fowls).

**Coarse Features** — The ♏ influence tends to coarse features, skin, and body. (See Coarse, Rough). Case—See "Female", page 49, Chap. 8, in Daath's Medical Astrology.

**Contortions Of**—♅ affl. in ♈. (See Contortions; "Contortions" under Face. Also see "Distortions" in this section).

**Deformed**—The Features Deformed—(See Deformities; "Abnormalities", "Disfigured", "Deformed". under Face; "Distortions" in this section).

**Distorted Features**—The ☉ and ☽ in the 6th H. and heavily afflicted; ♅ affl. in ♈ or ♉; ☿ affl. by both ♄ and ♂, and which may be accompanied by some mental weakness; malefics in ♈; malefics in the 5th H., and espec. in ♈; ♈ or ♑ on the Asc. and containing malefics; earthy signs on the Asc.; many planets in fixed signs. Distortions of the face, features, and body are also caused by prenatal afflictions during pregnancy. (See Contortions, Coordination, Cyclops, Deformities, Face; "Wry Neck" under Neck; Prenatal). Case — See "Male", Chap. 8, page 48, in Daath's Medical Astrology.

**Eagle Features** — Given by ♏. (See Scorpio).

**Lightness of Feature**—♂ Sig. in fiery signs indicates.

**Not Very Attractive**—The ☉ in ♉; ♑ influence; ♑ on Asc. (See "Thin", "Ugly", under Face).

**Regular**—All the Features Regular— ♎ on the Asc.

**Sharp Features**—(See "Sharp" under Face).

**Small Features**—(See "Small" under Face).

**Thin Features**—(See "Thin" under Face).

**Tightness of Feature**—Given by ♂; ♂ rising and strong at B.

**FEBRIFUGE**—An Agent that Lessens Fever—♄ herbs and remedies. ♂ is the principal cause of fevers, and the remedies of ♄ counteract. (See Aconite, Antipathy, Antipyretic, Fever, Opposites; "Remedies" under Saturn).

**FEBRILE**—Febrile Indisposition—(See "Over-Heated Blood" under Blood; Fever).

**FECUNDATION**—Fertilization—Impregnation—Conception—Is principally the work of the ☽. Also ♀ rules fecundation. (See Conception, Fertile, Fruitful, Gemmation, Moon, Ovaries, Ovum, Reproduction, Semen).

**FEEBLE**—Adynamic—Weak—Loss of Vital Power—Decrepitude—Asthenic— etc.—The Asthenic Process is presided over by ♄, and tends to feebleness and weakness of the constitution by his afflictions, and by retention, inhibition, suppressing the functions, etc.

**Action**—Feeble Action To the Body— The ☉ to the ☍ or ill-asp ♄ by dir., and the ☉ hyleg at B. In Hor'y Questions the Querent is weak and feeble if the Sig. is going out of one sign into another. (See "Body" in this section).

**Body**—Feeble Body—Feeble Constitution—Weak Body—The afflictions of ♄ to the hyleg at B., and by dir. tend to feebleness of body; ♀ Sig. in ♋ or ♑, feeble and sickly; the watery signs ♋ or ♓ on the Asc. at B. (For the various influences along this line see Adynamia, Asthenia, Consumptions, Debility, Decrepitude, Emaciation; "Bad Health" under Health; Imbecility, Infirm, Invalids; "Senility" under Old Age; "Low" under Recuperation, Resistance, Stamina, Tone, Vitality; Sickly; "Loss Of" under Strength, Vital; "Not Strong" under Strong; "Weak Body" under Weak).

**Digestion**—Feeble Digestive Powers —(See "Weak" under Digestion).

**Health**—Feeble Health—(See "Bad Health" under Health; "Ill-Health All Thru Life" under Ill-Health; Pale, Sickly; "Much Sickness" under Sickness. See the references under "Body" in this section.

**Left Side**—(See "Feeble" under Left).

**Mind**—Feeble Mind—(See Idiocy, Imbecility; "Weak Mentality" under Mental).

**Pulse**—Feeble Pulse—(See "Faint", "Weak", under Pulse).

**FEEDING**—Wrong tendencies in feeding, and improper feeding, should be guarded against when ♂ or ♀ are in ♍. (See Diet, Eating, Food).

**FEELING**—Sensation—The Sense of Touch—(See Sensation, Sensibility, Touch).

**Feeling**—The Emotions—(See Emotions, Feelings).

**Insensibility**—(See this subject).

**FEELINGS**—The Emotions—The Power of Feeling—The Sentiments, etc.—

**Acute Feelings**—Common signs on the angles, or many planets in such signs.

**Intellect**—Feeling and Intellect—Preponderance of Feeling Over Intellect— Indicated by many planets in fiery and fixed signs, and none in airy signs. (See Anger, Desires, Emotions, Excitable, Hatred, Impulses, Intellect, Jealousy, Reins, Romance, Temper).

**Sentient Faculties**—(See "Sentient" under Faculties; Sentient).

**Uncanny Feelings**—(See Weird).

**Want of Feeling**—(See Apathy).

**FEET**—The Feet are under the external rulership of the ♓ sign. They are also ruled by ☿ and the 12th H. The ♓ sign rules from the ankles downward to the extremities of the toes. The Plantar Nerves are ruled by ♓. The bones of the feet and toes are under the structural rulership of ♓. The Os Calcis, the Heel Bone, is ruled by ♓. This Article will be arranged into two Sections. Section One—Description of the Feet. Section Two—Diseases and Afflictions.

**— SECTION ONE —**

**DESCRIPTION OF THE FEET—**

**Fleshy and Short**—The ☽ gives; ♊ often gives. These influences also apply to the Hands.

**Ill-Made**—Irregular—(See Club Feet, Deformities, Ill-Made, Malformations, in Sec. 2 of this Article).

**Left Foot**—(See "Marks" in this section).

**Long Feet**—Slender Feet (and Hands) ♃ indicates long legs and feet; ♃ in the Asc. at B.; ☿ in ♊; ☿ ascending at B., and free from the rays of other planets; the first face of ♍ on the Asc.

**Marks**—Moles On—(1) On Right Foot —Born under ♃ and ♃ ori. (See "Right Foot" in Sec. 2 of this Article). (2) On Left Foot—Marks, Moles, or a Scar On —The ☉, ☽, or malefics in ♓; ♓ on the Asc.; a masculine planet in ♓ in the male, and a feminine planet in ♓ in a female nativity. (See Left, Moles, Right, Scars). (3) On One or Both Feet—A Mark, Mole or Scar on One or Both Feet—The ☉, ♄, or ♂ in ♓; ♓ on the Asc., and espec. if ♅, ♄, or ♂ be in ♓, or afflicting a planet in ♓.

**Moles**—(See "Marks" in this section).

**One or Both Feet**—Marks, Moles or Scars On—(See "Marks" in this section).

**Right Foot**—Mole or Mark On—(See "Marks" in this section).

**Scars On**—(See "Marks" in this section; Scars).

**Short Feet**—♊ signifies long arms, but many times short hands and feet, and fleshy. (See "Short Hands" under Hands).

**Short and Fleshy**—(See "Fleshy" in this section; "Fleshy and Short" under Hands).

**Slender and Long**—(See "Long" in this section).

**Strike Together**—In Walking—♄ ascending at B. (See "Dragging" under Gait).

**Thick Feet**—The ☽ gives thick hands and feet. (See "Broad and Thick" under Hands).

**Turned In**—♓ on the Asc.

**Uncomely**—♃ in the Asc.

## — SECTION TWO —

**DISEASES AND AFFLICTIONS**—To the Feet—

**Abscess In**—(See "Feet" under Abscess).

**Accidents To**—Hurts, Injuries, and Wounds To—All hurts to the feet are signified by the 12th H., and afflictions in ♓, or afflicting a planet in ♓, and with ♓ on the Asc.; ♄ or ♂ in the 1st or 7th H., and in the latter degrees of ♊, ♐, or ♓, and ori. of the ☉ and occi. of the ☽; ♂ affl. in ♋ or ♓; ♂ in the 9th H. in common signs, and afflicting ☿; ♓ on the Asc., and containing malefics. (See "Accidents" under Extremities. Also see "Injuries" in this section).

**Aches In**—The ☽ in ♍, ☌ or ill-asp. ♄ (or ☿ if he be of the nature of ♄) at the beginning of an illness or at decumb. (Hor'y). (See Aches; "Pains" in this section).

**Achilles Tendon**—(See Achilles; "Club Feet" in this section).

**Acromegaly**—(See "Enlargement" in this section; "Enlargement" under Extremities).

**Affected**—The feet are affected when the ☉ is in ♋; the ☽ ♓; ♅ or ♄ in ♑; ♃ in ♏ or ♒; ♂ ♋ or ♎; ♀ ♈ or ♍; ☿ ♉ or ♌. (See Table 196 in Simmonite's Arcana).

**Afflicted**—(See the various paragraphs in this section).

**All Diseases In**—All Infirmities In—Signified by the 12th H; ♓ diseases and afflictions in ♓; the 18° ♑ on the Asc., infirmities in the legs and feet. (See "All Diseases" under Legs; "Distempers", "Humours", in this section).

**Aneurysm**—(See Aneuysm).

**Ankles**—(See Ankles).

**Arches Fallen**—(See "Splay Foot" in this section).

**Atrophy Of**—Claw Feet—A ♄ affliction; ♄ affl. in ♓; Subs at LPP (4, 5L). (See Atrophy; "Wasting" in this section).

**Blisters**—Bullas—♂ affl. in ♓. (See Blisters).

**Blood In**—Stagnation of Blood In—♄ in ♍ or ♓. (See "Feet" under Blood).

**Bones Of**—Disorders of—♄ affl. in ♓; Subs at LPP. (See Bones).

**Bowel Complaints**—From Wet, Cold and Damp Feet—A ♓ disease and afflictions in ♓. (See "Cold Taken", "Colic", in this section).

**Bromidrosis**—Fetid Perspiration In Feet—♂ in ♓; ♂ in common signs. (See Bromidrosis; "Perspiring", in this section).

**Bruises To**—♄ affl. in ♓. (See Bruises).

**Bunions**—Corns—(See Bunions).

**Chilblain**—(See Chilblain).

**Chronic Ailments In**—♄ affl. in ♓. (See Chronic).

**Claw Feet**—Atrophy of—(See "Atrophy" in this section).

**Club Feet**—Talipes Varus—Contraction—Inversion—♄ affl. in ♒, from contraction of the Tendon Achilles; ♄ or ♂ affl. in ♓; the ♏ influence tends to; caused by prenatal afflictions. Subs at LPP. Cases—See "Cripple", No. 190 and 191 in 1001 N.N. Also Placidus records a case of Club Feet where ♂ was in ♓ in mundane □ ☽, and with ♄ ☍ ☽ from ♐, while the ☽ was in the western angle in her south node. (See Deformities, Ill-Made, Malformations, in this section. Also see Achilles).

**Cold Feet**—The feet are naturally moist and cold with ♄ in ♓, and with ♓ upon the Asc.; ☿ in ♓, and espec. when ☿ partakes of the nature of ♄; afflictions in ♓; Subs at AP, CP, KP, LPP. Due to the close connection of the feet (♓) with the brain and cerebellum (♈), the afflictions of ♄ in ♓ in the Asc., and with ♓ upon the Asc., tend to wakefulness by cold feet, and to Insomnia. (See "Cold Taken" in this section; Cold; "Insomnia" under Sleep).

**Cold Taken**—In the Feet—Colds Due To Damp and Wet Feet—Afflictions in ♓; ♓ on the Asc.; the ☽ affl. in ♓, or affl. the hyleg therefrom; the ☽ in ♓, ☌ or ill-asp. any of the malefics as promittors; the ☽ in ♓, ☌, □ or ☍ ♄ (or ☿ if he be of the nature of ♄) at the beginning of an illness or at decumb.; the ☽ affl. in ♓, the body tends to become disordered thru colds taken in the feet; ♄ or ♂ in ♓; ♄, ♆, or ♅, in ♓, and affl. the ☉ or ☽, tend to consumption from colds taken in the feet; ☿ affl. in ♌ tends to pains in the back from colds caught in the feet; ☿ affl. in ♓. (See "Bowel Complaints", "Colic", "Dry", in this section; Back, Cold, Colds, Consumption, Linen, Pneumonia).

**Colic Taken**—Thru the Feet—A ♓ disease, and afflictions in ♓; ♄ affl. in ♓. (See Bowels, Colic).

**Consumption**—Taken from Colds Caught In the Feet—(See "Cold Taken" in this section).

**Contractions**—(See "Club Feet", "Cramps", in this section).

**Corns**—(See Bunions, Scales).

**Corrupt Humours**—In the Feet—(See "Humours" in this section).

**Cramps In**—♅ affl. in ♒ or ♓, cramps in the feet and toes; ♅ affl. in ♓ tends to cramps, paralysis, muscular spasms, and affections of the motor nerves of the feet; ♄ in ♓, liable to cramps in the feet and toes; ♄ or ♂ angular in the 1st or 7th H., in ♊, ♐, or ♓, ori. of the ☉, and occi. of the ☽, and ♄ or ♂ in the latter degrees of these signs; ☿ affl. in ♓; Subs at KP, LPP (4, 5L). (See Cramps).

**Crippled In**—(See "Club Feet" in this section).

**Damp Feet**—Colds From—(See "Cold Taken" in this section).

**Deformities In**—Afflictions and malefics in ♓; malefics in ♓ in the 12th H.; ♓ on the Asc. (See Atrophy, Club Feet, Ill-Made, Malformations, Splay Foot, in this section).

**Disability In**—♄ or ♂ affl. in ♓. (See Atrophy, Club Feet, Deformities, Splay Foot, and the various paragraphs in this section).

**Discoloration**—(See "Erythromelalgia" in this section).

**Diseases In**—(See All Diseases, Distempers, Dropsy, Humours, Weakness, and the various paragraphs in this section).

**Distempers In**—The Feet Diseased—Trouble With the Feet—The ☉ affl. in ♋, ♍, or ♓; the ☽ affl. in ♊ or ♓; ♄ affl. in ♓; signified by ♄ in ♍, ♐, ♑, or ♓; ♃ in ♏, ♒; ♂ in ♋, ♎, ♐, or ♓; ♂ promittor in ♓, and ☌ or ill-asp. the ☉; ♀ in ♈ or ♍; ☿ in ♉ or ♌; ♓ on the Asc.; Subs at KP, PP, LPP. (See Toes. Also see the various paragraphs in this section).

**Dragging**—The Feet—(See "Dragging" under Gait).

**Draws and Writes**—With the Feet—Case—See "Armless Wonder", No. 054 in 1001 N.N.

**Dropsy In**—Oedema—Swollen Feet—Swellings In—The ☽ affl. in ♓; the ☽ ♓, ☌, □, or ☍ ♄; the ☽ ♓, □ or ☍ ♆; the ☉ affl. in ♋; ♃ affl. in ♓; ♂ in ♓; afflictions in ♒ or ♓; an ♒ and ♓ disease; the connection of ♓ with the ♌ sign, and from disturbed heart action and circulation, tends to oedema in the feet; Subs at KP and LPP. (See Dropsy; "Feet" under Gout; Swellings).

**Dry**—Should keep the feet dry when ♄ or ☿ are in ♓ at B., to avoid taking colds thru the feet. (See "Cold Taken" in this section).

**Dysidrosis**—Bullas In the Feet—(See Blisters, Dysidrosis).

**Enlargement**—Acromegaly—The ☉, ♄, ♆, ♃, or ♂ affl. in ♓. (See "Enlargements" under Extremities).

**Eruptions On**—☿ affl. in ♓, and due to wrong habits of living. (See Eruptions; "Eruptions" under Arms, Legs).

**Erysipelas In**—(See "Extremities" under Erysipelas).

**Erythromelalgia**—Pain, Swelling and Purplish Discoloration of the Parts—Redness and Swelling On the Bottom of the Feet—The ☽ in ♓ and affl. by ♄ or ♂; Subs at KP and LPP. (See Neuralgia, Pain, Plantar, Swelling, in this section).

**Extremities**—Disorders In—Accidents To—(See Extremities. Also note the various paragraphs in this section).

**Fallen Arches**—Flat Feet—(See "Splay Foot" in this section).

**Fat Feet**—Excessive Fat In the Feet—♃ affl. in ♓; ♂ ☌ ♃ in ♓; Subs at KP. (See "Adiposa Dolorosa" under Fat).

**Feet First**—Born Feet First—Case—(See "Feet First" under Parturition).

**Fetid Perspiration**—(See Bromidrosis, Odors, in this section).

**Flat Foot**—(See "Splay Foot" in this section).

**Foot and Mouth Disease**—A contagious disease of animals, with the formation of vesicles in the mouth and on the feet—An eclipse of the ☉ in ♍ or ♓, and with ☿ badly afflicted by malefics at the same time; an eclipse of the ☉ in ♉ or ♎, and with malefics in ♓; eclipses in ♓, and with ☿ in the configuration, and afflicted; ♂ in ♓ and lord of the year at the Vernal Equi., and configurated with and afflicting ☿, as ☿ rules the mouth; malefics in ♓ at the Equinoxes or Solstices. This disease may also attack man, and espec. in those who have the ☉, ☽, ☿, and malefics in ♓ at B., or ☿ in ill-asp. to such planets in ♓ at B., and by dir., and when eclipses of the ☉ fall in ♓ on the places of malefics in ♓, and also if ☿ enter into the configuration. In Man, the Chiropractors also find Subs at MCP, CP, SP, and KP to exist at the time of the attacks. (See Vesicles).

**Gait**—Disorders of—(See Gait, Walk).

**Glands Of**—Affected—Ruled and affected by ♆ when this planet is in ♓. (See the Introduction under Aneurysm).

**Gout In**—Podagra—Wandering Gout—(See "Feet" under Gout).

**Granulations**—In the Joints—(See "Joints" in this section).

**Growths**—(See "Lump" in this section).

**Hands**—(See the various paragraphs under Hands).

**Heat**—In the Feet—♂ in ♓. (See Heat).

**Heel Bone**—The Os Calcis—(See Lump, Os Calcis, in this section).

**Humours In**—Corrupt Humours In—The ☽ hyleg in ♓ in a female nativity, moist humours; ♂ affl. in ♓, corrupt humours in; afflictions in ♓, cold and moist humours in; a Stellium in ♓ or the 12th H. (See "Lameness" in this section).

**Hurts To**—(See Accidents, Bruises, Injuries, in this section).

**Hyperidrosis**—Excessive Sweating In the Feet—♂ in ♓. (See Dysidrosis, Hyperidrosis, Sweat; Bromidrosis, Perspiring, in this section).

**Ill-Made Feet**—Irregular—Deformed—Ill-Formed—Malformations—♄ ascending at B.; ♂ in the 9th H. in common signs, and afflicting ☿; ♏ or ♓ on the Asc., or malefics in these signs. (See Club Feet, Deformities, in this section).

**Infirmities In**—♄ or ♂ affl. in ♓. (See All Diseases, Distempers, Humours, Lameness, Weakness, in this section).

**Inflammation In**—Heat In—Fever In—♂ affl. in ♓.

**Injuries To**—(See Accidents, Loss Of, Right Foot, in this section). Cases of Injury—See "Foot", No. 106, and "Puzzle Horoscopes", No. 665 and No. 672, in 1001 N.N.

**Insomnia**—From Cold Feet—(See "Cold Feet" in this section).

**Inverted**—Turned Inwards (See "Club Feet" in this section).

**Inward**—Turned Inward—(See "Club Feet" in this section).

**Irregular**—(See "Ill-Made" in this section).

**Joints**—Granulations In—♄ affl. in ♓.

**Lameness In**—A ♓ disease; afflictions in ♓; ♓ on the Asc.; a ☽ disease; the ☽ affl. in ♓; ♄, ♂, or ♀ affl. in ♓; ♄, ♂, and many planets in the 12th H.; ♂ in ♓, by corrupt humours settled there when ♂ is the afflictor in the disease. (See Club Feet, Deformities, Gout, Splay Foot, and the various paragraphs in this section).

**Left Foot**—Mark, Mole, or Scar On—(See "Marks" in Sec. 1 of this Article. Also see Left).

**Legs**—(See the various paragraphs under Extremities, Legs, Limbs).

**Leprosy In**—(See Leprosy).

**Limbs**—Disorders In—(See Extremities, Legs, Limbs).

**Loss of Foot**—Or Feet—♂ affl. in ♓, danger of; ♂ in ♓ at B., and afflicted, and to the cusp the 12th H. by dir. Case—Loss of Foot—See "Puzzle Horoscopes", No. 665, in 1001 N.N.

**Lower Limbs**—Disorders In—Accidents To, etc.—(See Extremities, Legs; "Lower" under Limbs; Lower. Also note the various paragraphs in this section).

**Lump**—A Lump Growing On the Back of Each Heel—♄ affl. in ♓, due to deposits; ♓ on the Asc. or 12th H., and containing malefics; many afflictions in common signs. Case—See "Unfortunate Case", No. 351, in 1001 N.N. (See Growths, Tumors).

**Malformations**—♄ ascending at B. (See Claw, Club Feet, Deformities, Ill-Made, Splay, in this section).

**Marks**—(See "Marks" in Sec. 1 of this Article).

**Missing**—(See "Frog Child" under Forearm).

**Moist and Cold**—(See "Cold Feet" in this section).

**Moist Humours In**—(See "Humours" in this section).

**Moles**—(See "Marks" in Sec. 1 of this Article).

**Motor Nerves**—Affected—(See "Cramps" in this section).

**Muscular Spasms**—(See "Cramps" in this section).

**Nerves**—Motor Nerves Affected—(See "Cramps" in this section).

**Neuralgic Pains**—Plantar Neuralgia—☿ affl. in ♓; Subs at LPP (4, 5L). (See Cramps, Pains, in this section).

**Odors In**—Unpleasant Odors—The ☽ or ♂ affl. in ♓. (See Bromidrosis, Hyperidrosis, Perspiring, in this section).

**Oedema**—(See "Dropsy" in this section).

**Operations On**—Surgical—Should not be made when the ☽ is in ♓, or when the ☽ is afflicted, if the ☽ was in ♓, or a common sign at B. (See Operations).

**Os Calcis**—Disorders of—♄ affl. in ♓. (See "Lump" in this section).

**Pains In**—A ♓ disease, and afflictions in ♓; the ☽ in ♓ and affl. by ♄ or ♂; the ☽ affl. in ♉ or ♓, or affl. the hyleg therefrom; ♅, ♄, or ♂ affl. in ♓; ♂ affl. in the 12th H.; ☿ affl. in ♉ or ♓. (See Aches, Cramps, Erythromelalgia, Neuralgic, in this section; "Pain" under Extremities, Legs, Limbs).

**Paralysis**—(See "Cramps" in this section). Case—See "Tunison", No. 113, in 1001 N.N.

**Perspiring Feet**—Fetid—Odors—Sweating of—Afflictions in ♓; the ☉, ♃, ♅, or ♂ affl. in ♓; the ☽ hyleg in a female nativity, and afflicted. (See Bromidrosis, Dysidrosis, Humours, Hyperidrosis, Odors, in this section).

**Plantar Region**—Bottom of the Foot—Sole—Affections of—(See Erythromelalgia, Heel, Neuralgic, Pains, in this section).

**Podagra**—(See "Gout" in this section).

**Pompholyx**—Bullas—Blisters—(See Dysidrosis).

**Purplish Discoloration**—(See "Erythromelalgia" in this section).

**Redness**—On Bottom of Feet—(See "Erythromelalgia" in this section).

**Rheumatism In**—♄ in ♊ or ♓. (See "Rheumatism" under Extremities; "Feet" under Gout; Rheumatism).

**Right Foot**—(1) Mark, Mole, or Scar On—Born under ♃, and ♃ ori., a mole; ♓ on the Asc., and espec. if the ☉, ♅, ♄, or ♂ be in ♓, tends to a mole on one or both feet; ♂ in ♓ tends to a scar or mark on either foot by injury. (See "Marks" in Sec. 1 of this Article). (2) Right Foot Repeatedly Injured—Case—See "Foot", No. 106, in 1001 N.N.

**Scars**—(See "Right Foot" in this section).

**Shuffling Gait**—The Feet Drag or Strike Together—♄ ascending at B. (See "Dragging" under Gait).

**Sole of Foot**—(See "Plantar" in this section).

**Spade-Like**—A Condition in Myxoedema—(See Myxoedema).

**Spasms In**—(See "Cramps" in this section).

**Splay Foot**—Flat Feet—Fallen Arches—♄ affl. in ♓; ♄ and ♂ ☌ the ☽ in ♓; the 3rd Face of ♒ on the Asc.; Subs at LPP.

**Stagnated Blood**—In the Feet—(See "Blood" in this section).

**Standing**—On the Feet—☿ affl. in ♎ warns against standing on the feet too long at a time.

**Strike Together**—When Walking—(See "Shuffling" in this section).

**Sweating Of**—(See "Perspiring" in this section).

**Swelling Of**—Swollen Feet—Swellings On—(See Blisters, Blood, Bunions, Bruises, Corns, Dropsy, Glands, Gout, Inflammation, Joints, Lameness, Vesicles, in this section).

**Talipes Varus**—(See "Club Feet" in this section).

**Tender Feet**—Afflictions in ♓; the ☽, ♄, ♀, or ☿ affl. in ♓; ♀ in ♓ and afflicting the ☽ or Asc.; ♀ in ♓ in the 6th H., and afflicted; ♓ on the Asc.

**Tendo Achilles**—(See "Club Feet" in this section).

**Tissues**—Wasting of—♆ affl. in ♓. (See "Wasting" under Tissues).

**Toes**—Disorders of—(See Toes).

**Trouble**—In the Feet—(See "Diseases", and the various paragraphs in this section).

**Twistings**—Contortions—Torsalgia—♅ affl. in ♓. (See Contortions; "Cramps" in this section).

**Ulcers On**—Afflictions in ♓; the ☽ affl. in ♓; ♄ in ♓, occi., and affl. the ☉, ☽, or Asc. (See Ulcers).

**Unpleasant Odors**—(See "Odors" in this section).

**Varicose Veins**—The ☽ affl. in ♓. (See Varicose, Vesicles).

**Vesicles On**—(See "Foot and Mouth" in this section).

**Wakefulness**—From Cold Feet—(See "Cold Feet" in this section).

**Walk**—Irregularities In, Due to Afflicted Feet—(See the various paragraphs under Gait, Walk).

**Wandering Gout**—(See "Feet", "Wandering Gout", under Gout).

**Wasting**—Of Tissues of—(See "Tissues" in this section).

**Weakness In**—A ☽ disease; a ♓ disease, and afflictions in ♓; ♄ in ♓, and espec. ♄ in the 6th or 12th H.; ☿ affl. in ♓; ♓ on the Asc., and espec. if ♅, ♄, or ♂ be in ♓, or in ill-asp. to a planet in ♓; ♓ ascending at the Vernal Equi., Peoples and Countries ruled by ♓ suffer grievous infirmities in the head, feet, and with Gout and Dropsy. (See "Diseases In" in this section).

**Wet Feet**—Colds Taken By—Colic—Bowel Complaints By—(See Bowel Complaints, Cold Taken, Colic, in this section).

**Wounds To**—(See Accidents, Hurts, Injuries, in this section).

**Writes and Draws**—With the Feet—No Arms—(See "Draws and Writes" in this section).

**FELONS**—(See "Felons" under Fingers).

**FEMALE**—Females—Feminine—Women—Girls—Female Children, etc.—The ☽ has great influence in the horoscopes of females, and also ♀, and the ☽ and ♀ are said to rule females, the ☽ especially by night, and ♀ by day. In this Article matters which have to do with Females of all ages, from birth to death, will be listed, and subjects which have especially to do with adult females will be found in the Article on Women in the "W" section. Study both Articles together. See the following subjects in the alphabetical arrangement when not considered here.

**Abortion; Accidents To**—Hurts—Injuries—Wounds—The ☽ or ♀ to the ☌ or ill-asps. ♂ by dir., and espec. if ♂ afflict the ☽ or ♀ at B.; malefics to the ☌ or ill-asp. the ☽ or ♀. (See the various paragraphs under Accidents, Hurts, Injuries, Women, Wounds).

**Active Mind**—And Body—♂ in good asp. to the ☽ at B., and by dir. (See "Active Body", "Active Mind", under Active).

**Adolescence**—(See Puberty).

**Aged Female**—Death of—(See Aunts, Grandparents, Old Age).

**Anaemia**—(See Anaemia, Chlorosis).

**Astray**—Young Females Liable To Be Led Astray—(See Seduction).

**Aunts; Bad Health**—(See Health, Ill-Health, in this section).

**Barrenness; Beautiful**—(See Beautiful, Comely, Complexion, Eyes, Face).

**Bereavement; Birth of a Female**—A Daughter Born—A Daughter Promised—In female horoscopes, the 5th H. is female, and the 4th H. is male, and the conditions of these houses will show the predominating sex, and which gives the greater promise of fruitfulness, and the opposite houses show detriment, etc. More girls than boys are shown when there are many planets in feminine signs. The wife's Significators being stronger than those of the husband in the figure indicate female births, and more girls than boys. Female births are indicated when the sign on the cusp of 5th H. is female, and if the lords of the Asc. and 5th H. be in female signs, and the ☽ also in a female sign. Other indications are,—The ☉ to the ⚹ or △ ♀; if the ☉, ☽, or Asc., or planets in asp. with them, be in feminine signs, or if they are feminine by being occi., the child conceived will be a female if such conditions exist at conception; the ☽ well-aspected at B., and to the ⚹ or △ the Asc. by dir.; the ☽ to the ☌ or good asps. ♀ by dir., and espec. if ♀ is in the 5th H. at B., and children are not denied; ♀ in the 5th H. at B., and espec. when in a watery sign, indicates daughters; ♀ to the ☌ or good asps. the Asc. by dir., and espec. if ♀ be ruler of the 5th H. at B.; the Asc. or M.C. to the ☌ or good asps. ♀ by dir.; the M.C. to the good asps. the ☽ if the ☽ was well-placed at B. for fruitfulness; many planets in female signs and houses, and with the sign on the Asc. and 5th H. a female sign. (For further influences along this line see "Birth of a Child", "Female Births", "First-Born", "Sex of Children", "Single Births", "Time of Birth", all under the subject of Children. Also see Birth, Conception, Daughter; "Male Births" under Male; Predetermination; "Sisters Indicated" under Sisters; "Time of Birth" under Time; Triplets, Twins, etc.).

**Births To**—(See Birth, Children, Conception, Fruitful, Mother, Parents, Parturition, Wife; "Birth of a Female" in this section).

**Blind**—In Left Eye—Accidents To—(See "Eyes" under Left, Right; "Left Eye" under Blindness, Eyes).

**Blondes**—(See "Blond" under Complexion).

**Blood**—The Circulation of Irregular—The Blood Corrupted—Dropsical Blood —(See "Blood" under Women).

**Body and Mind**—Much Activity of—(See "Active Mind" in this section).

**Breasts In**—(See Breasts).

**Brunettes** — (See "Dark" under Complexion).

**Cerebral Functions** — Disorders of — (See Cerebral).

**Cervix**—Disorders of—(See "Cervix" under Womb).

**Chaste**—Virtuous—The ☽ and ♀ free from the afflictions of malefics. (See Virtue, Unchaste).

**Childbirth** — (See Parturition, Puerperal).

**Childhood**—Disorders of Females In —Accidents In—Death In—(See Infancy, Childhood; "Early Years" under Early).

**Children**—Children Given—Children Denied—Trouble and Sorrow Thru—Death of, etc.—(See Barrenness, Children, Fruitfulness, Maternity, Mother, Parents, Wife, etc.).

**Chills and Fever**—(See Chills).

**Chlorosis**—Anaemia In Young Women —(See Anaemia, Chlorosis).

**Chronic Diseases** — Suffer From — Death By — (See "Death" under Chronic).

**Circulation Irregular** — (See "Blood" in this section; "Females" under Circulation).

**Clitoris; Coarse**—Coarse Body—Coarse Voice—(See Coarse).

**Cohabitation; Cold**—Suffers from Cold and Chills—(See Chills).

**Complaints** — Female Complaints—☽ diseases, and the ☽ afflicted; the ☽ affl. in ♏; ♏ diseases and afflictions in ♏. (See the various paragraphs in this section, and under Women).

**Complexion; Conceived**—A Female Conceived—(See "Birth of a Female" in this section).

**Conception; Conduct** — (See Conduct; "Conduct" under Women).

**Constitution**—The Strength or Weakness of the Female Constitution—The ☽ and ♀ strong, well-placed, well-aspected, and in good asp. to each other, strengthen the female constitution and favor good health, but when the ☽ is in bad asp. to ♀, the health is a continual source of trouble, and especially if ♄ and ♂ also afflict the ☽ and ♀, and take part in the configuration. (See Constitution, Strength, Vitality; "Health", "Ill-Health", in this section).

**Corrupt Blood In** — (See Impure; "Blood" under Women).

**Courses** — The Female Courses—(See Menses).

**Danger To**—(See Accidents, Blind, Childbirth, Death, Disgrace, Ill-Health, Seduction, and the various paragraphs in this section and under Women).

**Daughter Born** — Promised — (See "Birth of a Female" in this section).

**Death of Females**—Of Women—The ☽ hyleg, and affl. by ♄ at B., and by dir.; the ☽ and ♀ much affl. at B., and by dir., and the ☽ also without the good asp. of ♀ in the radical map. A female child born at an eclipse of the ☽, and under its shadow, is apt to die immediately, or soon after birth. In female horoscopes, the ☉ causes death by long, severe and painful diseases when afflicting the hyleg. (See Eclipses. Also see "Death" under Aunts. Childhood, Children, Chronic, Fevers, Fiancee, Friends, Grandparents, Infancy, Mortality, Mother, Relatives, Sister, Wife, Women).

**Death by Females**—(See Poison, Treachery; "Death by Women" under Women).

**Debilitated**—(See Constitution, Ill-Health, and the various paragraphs in this section; Debility).

**Degrees of Zodiac**—The Feminine Degrees of the Zodiac—♈, 9, 22; ♉, 5, 17, 24; ♊, 5, 22, 30; ♋, 8, 12, 27; ♌, 8, 23; ♍, 8, 20; ♎, 15, 27; ♏, 14, 25; ♐, 5, 24; ♑, 10; ♒, 15, 25, 30; ♓, 20, 28. The Asc., or its lord, in any of these degrees at B., the native is more effeminate in action or appearance, even though a male. (See Effeminate, Predetermination).

**Deranged System**—(See Constitution, Functions, Health, Ill-Health, and the various paragraphs in this section).

**Detriment to Females**—To Women—(See "Detriment" under Women).

**Digestive Disorders** — (See "Women" under Digestion).

**Directions**—The Effects of Evil Directions—When the malefics afflict the ☽ and ♀ at B., and by dir., and either the ☽ or ♀ are hyleg, there is great danger of serious illness, or death to females so born, and when under a train of such evil directions. (See "Arguments for Death" under Death; "Females and Directions" under Directions).

**Disappointments**—To Females—To Women—The ☽ to the ill-asps. ♀ by dir.; ♄ to the ☌ or ill-asps. the ☽ or ♀ by dir.

**Diseases**—Female Diseases—All feminine complaints come under the rule of the ☽. The ☽ rules the female functions, and afflictions to the ☽ tend especially to upset and derange the female constitution. Also an afflicted Venus tends to female disorders, illnesses, or death. (See Health, Ill-Health, and the various paragraphs in this section; Functions, Menses, Moon, Venus, Women).

**Disgrace To** — Disgrace By—(See "Women" under Disgrace).

**Dissolute Habits** — The ☽ affl. in ♏. (See Dissolute).

**Drink** — Given to Drink — (See "Women" under Drink).

**Dropsical Blood**—(See "Blood" under Dropsy, Women).

**Effeminate; Eminent Female**—Death of—(See "Eminent" under Women).

**Emotions In**—(See Emotions).

**Evil**—Sudden Evil For—The ☽ or ♀ to the ☌ ♅ by dir. (See Evil).

**External Influences** — Susceptible To —The ☽ hyleg in ♏ or ♓. (See Environment, External, Negative, Susceptible).

**Eyes** — (See "Blind" in this section; "Eye Trouble", "Women", under Eyes; "Eyes" under Left, Right).

**Face In**—(See "Females" under Face).

**Faintings** — Syncope — Swoonings — (See Fainting).

**Father**—Death of—Detriment To— (See Death, Detriment, under Father).

**Female Births**—(See "Birth of a Female" in this section).

**Female Child Promised**—(See "Birth of a Female" in this section).

**Female Complaints** — (See Functions, Leucorrhoea, Menses, Ovaries, Womb; the various paragraphs in this section and under Women).

**Feminine Degrees** — Of the Zodiac — Feminine Signs of the Zodiac — (See Degrees, Signs, in this section).

**Fevers In**—Subject to Fevers—Danger of—Death By—(See "Death", "Females", under Fever).

**Fiancee; First Child** — The First Born To—Sex of—And also of the 2nd and 3rd Child—(See "First-Born" under Children, First; Predetermination).

**Flooding**—(See Menses).

**Fluids** — Of the System — (See "Ailments" under Fluids).

**Foetus; Fond of Females** — (See "Addicted To" under Men).

**Freedom** — Unwomanly Freedom — (See "Free Love" under Free; "Unwomanly" under Morals).

**Friend**—Death of a Female Friend— (See "Female Friend" under Friends).

**Fruitful; Functions In** — Disturbed— Difficult—Slow—The female functions are ruled by the ☽, and the ☽ affl. at B., and by dir., or the ☽ in incongenial signs, as in the fiery signs at B., tend to; the ☽ ☌ or ill-asp. ♄ at B., and by dir., tends to suppressed, slow, difficult, and retarded functions in females. The special functions in females are largely under the rule of the ☽, and the ☽ in the Asc. at B. has much effect upon the female constitution, according to the aspects to the ☽. After puberty, in female nativities, the regulation of the health, the regularity of the system, and the function of maternity, depend upon the ☽ and ♀. (See Functions, Maternity, Menses, Regularity; Constitution, Diseases, Health, Ill-Health, in this section).

**Generative System** — Weakness of — (See "Weakness" under Generation).

**Genitals; Gestation;**

**Good Constitution** — Good Health— (See Constitution, Health, in this section; Immunity, Vitality).

**Grandmother**—(See Grandparents).

**Great Women**—Death of—(See Famous; "Great Women" under Great; Queens).

**Grief**—To Females—By Females—The ☽ or ♀ to the ☌ or ill-asps. ♄ by dir., grief, sorrow, and trouble to females, and women. (See Grief; "Grief" under Men; "Women" under Misfortune; Sorrow, Trouble).

**Habits**—(See Dissolute, Drink, and the various paragraphs in this section; Conduct; Habits).

**Hair; Harlots; Hatred Of**—(See "Females" under Hate).

**Headaches** — (See "Women" under Headaches).

**Health**—(1) Bad Health—The ☽ and ♀ weak at B., in evil asp. to each other, and also affl. by malefics at B., and by dir. (See Constitution, Diseases, Ill-Health, and the various paragraphs in this section). (2) Better Health—The Health Better—Stronger —When the ☽ is above the horizon in a night nativity, or below in a day geniture, well-aspected, and espec. with the ☽ in ♋ or ♓, as these signs are watery, plastic, and more agreeable to the lunar nature. (See Day; "Better" under Health; Night). (3) Good Health—Good and Strong Constitution—The Health Strengthened— The ☽ strong at B., and well-asp.; the ☽ above the horizon at B., and well-asp.; the ☽ on the Meridian, elevated above the malefics, and well-asp.; the ☽ to the good asps. the ☉, ♃, or ♀ by dir.; the ☽ and ♀ well-placed, in good asp. to each other, and not seriously afflicted by malefics; ♄ in good asp. to the ☽; ♃ in ☌ or good asp. the ☽; ♂ in good asp. to the ☽ or ♀. (See "Constitution" in this section; "Good Health" under Health). (4) Weaker— The Health Weaker—The ☽ below the horizon in a night nativity, and afflicted. (See Constitution, Diseases, Functions, Ill-Health, and the various paragraphs in this section; "Weak Body" under Weak).

**Hermaphrodites; Hips and Thighs**— (See "Weakness" under Hips).

**Houses**—The Female Houses—(See "Odd and Even" under Houses).

**Humours** — Moist Humours In the Feet—(See "Humours" under Feet; Humours).

**Hurts To** — (See "Accidents" in this section; "Children" under Hurts).

**Husband; Hyleg**—The ☽ or ♀ are the natural hylegs in a female nativity. (See Hyleg).

**Hysteria**—(See Emotions, Hysteria).

**Ill-Health**—For Females—For Women —Disordered System—The ☉ to the ☌ ☽ by dir., and espec. if it occur in the 6th H.; the ☽ affl. by the ☉, ♄, or ♂ at B., or by dir.; the ☽ in the 6th or 12th H. at B., in a weak sign, and affl. by the ☉ or malefics; the ☽ to the ☌ or ill-asps. the ☉, ♄, or ♂ by dir.; the ☽ to the ill-asps. ♃ or ♀ by dir.; the Prog. ☽ to the ☌ or ill-asps. the ☉, ♄, or ♂; the ☽ ☌ ♄ in the 1st H., and in ♑ or ♏; the ☽ below the horizon in a night nativity, and afflicted, the health and functions are weakened; the ☽ to the ill-asps. her own place by dir.; the ☽ affl. in ♏, and generally from dissolute habits; ♄ or ♂ ☌ or ill-asps. the ☽ at B., and by dir.; ♀ affl. the ☽ at B., and by dir. (See Constitution, Diseases, Functions, Health, and the various paragraphs in this section and under Women).

**Impotent; Impurities**—Of the System—The ☽ affl. in ♏ tends to impurities in a female system. (See Impurities).

**Infamous** — (See Infamous, Scandalous).

**Infancy** — Sickness or Death of Females In — (See "Female" under Infancy).

**Inflammations In**—(See "Females" under Inflammation).

**Injuries To**—Injuries By—(See "Accidents" in this section; "Injured" under Men).

**Internal Complaints**—(See "Women" under Internal).

**Irregularities**—Of the Functions—Of the System — The ☽ affl. in ♏. (See "Functions" in this section).

**Left Eye**—Left Ovary—Left Side of Body—(See Left, Ovaries; "Eyes" in this section).

**Length of Life** — The ☽ is hyleg in female nativities, or should be taken as such when possible, and the length of life may be determined according to her strength, weakness, aspects, sign and position, etc. (See "Duration of Life" under Life; "Long" in this section).

**Leucorrhoea; Libidinous**—Violently Libidinous—(See Lewd, Lust, Virile).

**Life**—Length of Life—(See "Length of Life" in this section).

**Liver Disordered**—(See "Women" under Liver).

**Long**—(1) Long Diseases—Death By—(See Chronic, Death, in this section). (2) Long Life—For Females—The ☽ well-placed by sign and house, well-aspected by the ☉, ♃, and ♀, elevated above the malefics, and espec. free from the afflictions of ♄ and ♂. (See "Long Life" under Life; "Short Life" in this section).

**Love Affairs**—(See Love).

**Lower Order**—Of Females—Of Women—(See Harlots, Shameless; Unchaste" in this section).

**Lust In**—Lustful—Unbridled Lust—(See Impotent, Lascivious, Lewd, Lust, Nymphomania; "Women" under Passion; Virile).

**Male Child Promised** — (See "Births" under Male).

**Marriage** — Early Marriage — Late Marriage—No Marriage—Not Inclined to Marry—Marriage Partner—(See Marriage, Marriage Partner; "Free from Passion" under Passion; Spinsters).

**Masculine**—Females with Predominating Masculine Traits—(See Deviations, Effeminate; "Coarse" under Voice).

**Maternity**—(See Maternity; "Functions" in this section).

**Matrix**—(See Womb).

**Menopause; Menses; Midwives; Milk;**

**Mind and Body**—Much Activity of—(See "Active Mind" in this section).

**Minor Disorders**—(See Colds, Leucorrhoea, Menses, Mild, Minor, Slight).

**Miscarriage; Misfortune To**—(See "Women" under Misfortune).

**Modesty; Moist Humours**—(See "Humours" in this section).

**Moon** — The ☽ and Females — (See Moon. Also note the Introduction, and the various paragraphs in this section).

**Mortality Among**—Much Mortality—The ☉, ☽, and ♃ conjoined in ♎; the ☽ or ♀ lady of the year at the Vernal Equi., weak and afflicted; ♂ in ♍ at the Vernal, and lord of the year. (See "Death" in this section; Mortality).

**Mother; Murders** — Many Murders of Females—(See "Women" under Murders).

**Natural Functions** — In Females — Ruled by the ☽. (See "Functions" in this section; Menses).

**Nervous Disorders** — (See Emotions, Hysteria; "Disordered" under Nerves).

**Nurses; Nymphomania; Obesity;**

**One Female Child**—At a Birth—Two Females At a Birth—Three Females At a Birth—(See "Birth of a Female" in this section; Twins, Triplets).

**Opposite Sex**—Dealings With—(See Opposite).

**Ovaries; Painful Diseases**—Much Suffering or Death By—(See "Females" under Fever; "Painful" under Menses; Pain).

**Parents**—Death of—Afflictions To—The ☽ to the ☌ or ill-asps. ♄ by dir. (See Father, Mother, Parents).

**Parturition; Passion In**—Passion in Females is ruled by ♀, and ♀ much affl. by the malefics tends to disordered and perverted passions. (See "Lust" in this section).

**Peace of Mind**—(See "Peace of Mind" under Mind).

**Periods In**—Periodic Illness—(See Menses).

**Planets**—The Feminine Planets—The ☽ and ♀.

**Poisoned** — By the Treachery of Females — (See "Women" under Poison; Treachery).

**Pregnancy; Private Diseases In**—(See Genitals, Gonorrhoea, Private; "Diseases" under Sex; Womb).

**Property**—Wastes His Property and Substance On Bad Women — (See "Health Suffers" under Opposite Sex; "Bad Women" under Women).

**Prostitutes**—(See Harlots).

**Puberty** — (See Puberty; "Functions" in this section).

**Puerperal Fever** — (See Puerperal, Parturition).

**Quarrels** — With Females — With Women—The M.C. to the □ or ☍ the ☽ or ♀ by dir. (See Quarrels).

**Rape; Regularity**—Of the Health and Functions — (See "Females" under Regularity; "Functions" in this section).

**Relative**—Death of a Female Relative—Female Relatives are ruled by ♀. (See "Female Relatives" under Relatives).

**Reproductive Organs**—Disorders of—(See Generation, Genitals, Genito-Urinary, Ovaries, Regeneration, Reproduction, Sex, Womb, etc.).

**Right Eye**—Accidents To—Blindness In—Disorders of—(See "Eyes" in this section; "Eyes" under Right).

**Right Ovary**—(See Ovaries).

**Robust**—(See Constitution, Health, in this section; Robust, Ruddy, Strong, Vitality).

**Ruined**—By Females—By Women—Ruins Himself Among—(See "Ruined by Women" under Love Affairs).

**Salacious**—(See Effeminate, Lust).

**Scandalous**—(See Infamous, Scandalous).

**Seduction; Severe Illnesses**—(See "Death" in this section; Dangerous; "Females" under Fever; Pernicious, Severe, Sharp, Vehement, Violent).

**Sex Gratification In**—Sex Excesses—The ☽ affl. in ♏; ♂ ☌ or ill-asp. ♀. (See Amorous, Cohabitation, Effeminate, Excesses, Lewd, Licentious, Lust, Nymphomania, Passion; "Secret Bad Habits" under Secret; Sex, Shameless; "Solitary" under Vice; Wanton, etc.).

**Shameless; Short Life**—The ☽ weak and ill-dig. at B., badly aspected by the ☉ and the malefics, and with the malefics elevated above the ☽ at B. (See "Early Death" under Early; "Death" under Infancy, Childhood, Children, Youth; "Short Life" under Life; Vitality Low; "Weak Body" under Weak; Constitution, Death, Diseases, Health, Sickness, in this section).

**Sickness**—Caused by Women—Much Sickness Among Women—(See Constitution, Diseases, Functions, Ill-Health, in this section; "Health Injured" under Men; "Much Sickness" under Sickness).

**Signs**—The Feminine Signs of the Zodiac—The Even Signs, as 2nd, 4th, 6th, etc. The Feminine Signs are ♉, ♋, ♍, ♏, ♑, ♓. These signs are considered weaker than the masculine, or odd signs, and are also called negative signs. (See "Negative Signs" under Negative).

**Single Women**—Not Inclined to Marry—(See Celibacy; "Aversion" under Marriage; "Free from Passion" under Passion; Spinsters).

**Sisters; Skin**—In females the ♓ sign gives a clear, lucid skin, but very white. The ♍ sign gives soft, delicate, tender and beautiful skin. (See Complexion, Face, Skin).

**Son Born To**—(See "Births" under Male).

**Sorrow To**—(See "Women" under Misfortune; Sorrow, Trouble).

**Spinsters**—(See "Single Women" in this section).

**Sports**—Indiscretions In—(See "Indiscretions" under Sports).

**Sterility**—(See Barrenness; "Unfruitful" under Wife).

**Stomach Disorders**—Digestive Disorders—(See "Women" under Digestion).

**Sudden Evils**—(See "Evil" in this section).

**Swoonings**—(See Fainting).

**Syncope**—(See Fainting).

**System**—The System Disordered—(See Impurities, Irregularities, in this section; "Disordered System" under System).

**Tomboyishness**—Caused by the positive, or masculine signs, being prominent, and with the ☉, ☽, ♆, ♅, ♃, and ♀ being obscurely placed. (See "Women" under Coarse; "Masculine" in this section).

**Tragical Death**—By Women—(See Tragical).

**Treachery**—Death or Injury By Female Treachery—(See "Injured" under Men; "Women" under Poison; "Female" under Treachery).

**Triplets**—Three Females Born—(See Triplets).

**Trouble**—For Females—By Females—(See "Women" under Misfortune; Tragical, Treachery, in this section).

**Twins; Two Females Born**—(See Twins).

**Ulcers**—(See "Vulva", "Womb", under Ulcers).

**Unbridled Lust**—(See Nymphomania; "Unbridled Passion" under Passion; "Lust" in this section).

**Unchaste**—Danger of—♂ affl. in the 7th H. with females; ♀ ☌ ♂ in ♏; ♄ ☌ ♀ in ♏. (See Chaste, Lust, Unbridled Lust, in this section).

**Unmarried Women**—(See "Single" in this section).

**Vagina; Venus**—Venus Figure—Venus and Females—(See Beautiful; "Brunettes" under Hair; Venus. Also note the Introduction to this Article).

**Vexations**—(1) By Females—By Women—The ☽ in tr. over ☋ at B., or to place of by dir.; the ☽ Sig. □ or ☍ ♀; ♀ by Periodic Rev. to the ill-asps. the radical ☉. (See "Women" under Men; "Female Treachery" under Treachery; Vexations. Also see Treachery, Trouble, in this section). (2) To Females—To Women—(See "Women" under Misfortune; Sorrows, Trouble, Vexations).

**Virgin**—Virginity—Chaste—(See "Chaste" in this section; Apathy, Aversions; "Free from Passion" under Passion; Spinsters).

**Virile; Virtuous**—(See Chaste, Virgin, in this section).

**Vital Spirit In**—(See "Spirit" under Vital).

**Vitality In**—(See Constitution, Health, in this section; "Good Health" under Health; Immunity, Resistance; "Little Sickness" under Sickness; Stamina, Strength, Strong, Tone, Vitality, etc.).

**Voice**—(See Coarse, Effeminate; Gifted, Melodious, Musical, under Voice).

**Vulva; Weak Constitution**—(See "Constitution" in this section; "Weak Constitution" under Constitution; "Low" under Vitality; "Weak Body" under Weak).

**Whites**—(See Leucorrhoea).

**Widows; Wife; Woman with Child**—Is Not with Child—(See "Woman" under Pregnancy).

**Womanish**—(See Effeminate).

**Womanly**—(See "Chaste" in this section; Modesty).

**Womb; Young Women**—(See Chlorosis, Love Affairs, Marriage, Puberty, Young, Youth. Also note the various paragraphs in this section).

**Zodiac**—Feminine Degrees of — (See "Degrees" in this section).

**FEMUR**—The Thigh Bone—Is under the structural rulership of ♐.

**Accidents To**—Injuries—Broken—Fracture, etc.—The ☽ affl. in ♐; ♄ in ♐ in the Asc.; ♂ affl. in ♐ or ♐; ♂ in ♐ and affl. the hyleg; ♂ in ♐ or ♑ in the Asc., and afflicted; ♐ on the Asc.; ♐ on or in the 6th H., and afflicted; ♐ on the Asc., 6th, or 12th H.; ♐ ruler of the 6th H., and affl. by the progressions or transits of a malefic, and espec. by ♄ or ♂; ♐ ruler of the 12th H., and containing malefics, or a malefic affl. the cusp of the 12th at B., and by dir. Cases—See Fig. 15A in Astro-Diagnosis, and Fig. 6 in Message of the Stars, both books by the Heindels. (See "Accidents" under Arms; Bones, Fractures; "Fractures" under Hips; Legs).

**Dislocation**—Of the Femur—♂ affl. in ♐. (See Dislocations; "Joint" under Hips; Thighs).

**Inflammation**—Osteitis—(See "Inflammation" under Bones; "Marrow" in this section).

**Marrow Of**—Inflammation of—♂ affl. in ♐. (See "Osteomyelitis" under Bones; Marrow).

**Osteitis**—(See "Inflammation" under Bones).

**Osteomyelitis**—Inflammation of the Marrow — (See "Osteomyelitis" under Bones).

**Periosteitis**—Of Femur—♂ affl. in ♐; Subs at PP, the 2, 3, 4 Lumbars. (See "Periosteitis" under Bones).

**FERAL**—(See Beasts, Brutish, Savage, Wild).

**FERMENTATION**—Zymosis—The Process of Fermentation—

**Bowels**—Fermentation of Food In—(See "Putrid" under Bowels).

**Stomach**—(See "Fermentation" under Stomach). This subject is considered further under Zymosis. (See "Hot and Moist Body" under Moisture; Zymosis).

**FEROCIOUS**—

**Animals**—Hurts by Ferocious Animals—(See "Ferocious", "Wild", under Animals).

**Eyes**—(See "Ferocious" under Eyes).

**FERRUM**—(See Iron).

**FERTILE**—Fruitful—Capable of Reproduction—The ☽ and ♀ are fertile. (See Conception, Fecundation, Fruitful, Prolific, Pregnancy).

**Fertilization**—The ☽ is the planet of, and of impregnation. (See Conception, Fecundation, Pregnancy).

**FESTERING DISEASES** — Denoted by ♄. (See Pus).

**FESTINATION**—The Peculiar Walk of Paralysis Agitans—(See "Festination" under Walk).

**FETID**—Giving Out Offensive Odors—Fetid Odors are generally the work of ♄ and the ☽. The influences of ♀ also cause fetid conditions, and usually resulting from over-indulgences, excesses, gluttony, venereal diseases, etc. Read the Articles on the Moon, Saturn, and Venus. Also see such subjects as Abscesses, Axillae, Breath, Carcinoma, Catarrh, Corrupt Air (see Air); Corruption, Decay, Decomposition, Discharges, Exudations, Faeces, Feet (see "Fetid" under Feet); Foul, Gangrene, Gases, Halitosis (see "Foul" under Breath); Humours (see "Corrupt" under Humours); Impure, Menses, Moisture, Morbid, Mortification, Necrosis, Noxious, Odors, Offensive, Pools (see "Stagnant" under Pools); Pus, Putrid, Putrefaction, Rottenness, Sores, Sordes, Sweat, Ulcers, Vapors, Vegetation, Venereal, etc.

**FEUDS**—Deadly Feuds and Grievous Dissentions Generally, and with Danger To Life—Eclipses of the ☉ in ♐. (See Ambushes, Contests, Disputes, Duels, Enemies, Enmity, Fighting, Gunshot, Hatred, Quarrels, Revenge, Treachery, etc.).

**FEVER**—Fevers—Febrile Indisposition—Hot Complaints—Pyrexia—Feverish Distempers—The ☉ and ♂, the hot, fiery, and electric bodies of our Solar System, tend to cause fevers and the combustion of tissue. Mars lights the fire of fever to burn out the poisons and impurities of the system. Fevers and Inflammation usually go together, as both are ruled by ♂, and both are processes of elimination and protection to the body to burn up excess wastes, and to rid the body of its cinders and ashes. Fevers are characteristic of the Bilious, or Choleric Temperament. (See Choleric). The ♈ people, a sign ruled by ♂, have great power to resist high fevers that would ordinarily prove fatal to others. Some people are more liable to fevers and hot diseases than others, according to the predominance of the fiery influences, the ☉, ♂, and the fiery signs at B., while other classes of people, as those born with the earthy and watery elements strong at B., are less liable to fevers, and espec. high, burning, or pernicious fevers. The motion of the ☽ regulates fevers. The general causes of fever, and also the various kinds and varieties of fever, etc., will be listed in the following subjects. For the main planetary influences tending to cause fever, see the paragraph, "Liable to Fever" in this section.

**Abatement Of**—(See Remission).

**Absent Party**—An Absent Party Has Recently Been Inclined To a Feverish State—The ☽ sepr. from the ☌, □, or 8 ♄ in a Hor'y Figure. (See Absent).

**Acute Fevers**—(See Acute).

**Ague**—Malaria—Intermittent Fever—(See Ague, Intermittent, Malaria).

**Air**—The Spread of Fevers Due to Noxious Air—(See "Corrupt Air" under Air; Contagions, Epidemics, Pestilence).

**All Feverish Disorders**—♂ affl. in ♈.

**All Kinds of Fever**—♂ diseases; caused by ♂ and his afflictions to the ☉, ☽, Asc., or hyleg at B., and by dir.

**Antipyretics**—A Fever-Reducing Remedy—A Febrifuge—(See Antipyretic, Febrifuge).

**Approaching**—A Fever Is Approaching—The ☽ ☌, □, or ☍ ♄ (or ☿ if he be of the nature of ♄) at the beginning of an illness or at decumb. (Hor'y).

**Better**—(See "Curtailed" in this section).

**Bilious Fevers**—(See "Fevers" under Bilious; "High" in this section).

**Blood**—Fevers Proceeding from Too Much Blood—Hot and Feverish Blood —(See "Fevers", "Over-Heated", and "Too Much Blood" under Blood; Sanguinary).

**Bowels**—Fevers In—Enteric Fever—(See "Fever" under Bowels; Typhoid).

**Brain Fever**—(See Brain).

**Breakbone Fever**—(See Dengue).

**Breasts**—Fever In—Milk Fever—(See "Fever" under Breasts).

**Brief Fevers**—Ephemeral—Lasting For a Day—(See Ephemeral).

**Burning Fevers**—High—Bilious—Violent—Sharp—Severe — Fierce— (See "High Fevers" in this section; Pestilence).

**Camp Fever**—(See Typhus).

**Catarrhal Fever**—(See Catarrh, Fluxes, Influenza).

**Causes of Fever**—(See "Liable to Fever", the Introduction, and the various paragraphs in this section).

**Cerebral Fevers**—Cerebro-Spinal Fevers—(See Brain, Cerebral, Cerebro-Spinal, Meninges).

**Childbed Fever**—Puerperal Fever—(See Puerperal).

**Childhood**—Fevers In—(See "Fevers" under Childhood, Children, Infancy).

**Chills and Fever**—(See Chills, Malaria).

**Cholera**—(See "Epidemics" under Cholera).

**Chronic Fevers**—Lingering—Constant —Continuous—Low Fevers—Are caused by ♄ afflictions and evil directions to the hyleg, as in Consumption, Phthisis, and Wasting Diseases. They usually get worse towards sunset, and during the night. (See Chronic, Complications, Consumptions, Grievous, Lingering, Wasting; Constant, Low, in this section).

**Cleansing**—Of the Body by Fevers—The work of ♂. (See Cleansing, Combustion, Elimination, Inflammation. Also note the Introduction to this Article).

**Cold and Dampness**—Fevers Arising From—Caused by ♅ and ♄. (See "Dampness and Cold" under Cold; "Cold and Dampness" under Exposure; 'Cold and Moist" under Moisture).

**Combustion**—A Purifying Agency Thru Fevers—(See Combustion, Cleansing, Inflammation; "Cleansing" in this section).

**Constant Fever**—Continuous—Low—Chronic—The ☽ in ♈ or ♉, and affl. by the ☉, ♄, or ♂ when taken ill (Hor'y); the ☽ ☌ or ill-asp. ♄ (or ☿ if he be of the nature of ♄) at the beginning of an illness or at decumb. (Hor'y); caused by ♄, and also by ♂, when the dominion of death is vested in them. (See Chronic, Duration, Low, in this section; Continuity, Duration; the Introduction under Flux).

**Contagious Fevers**—(See Contagious, Infectious).

**Continuance**—Of Fever—(See Continuity, Course, Crises, Duration; Chronic, Constant, Duration, Ephemeral, Low, Slight, in this section).

**Continuous Fevers**—Continuing—Synocha—(See Chronic, Constant, Fluxes, Habitual, Hectic, Low, in this section).

**Corrupt Air**—Fevers Arising From—(See "Air" in this section).

**Crises In**—Critical Days In—(See Crises, Critical).

**Critical Days In**—(See Crises, Critical).

**Curtailed Fevers**—Better—Moderated —Shortened—Aspects of the afflicting planet sepr. from the ☉, ☽, Asc., or hyleg, tend to curtail and shorten the fever; the afflicting planet changing signs, or the ☽ coming to a favorable asp. her place at the beginning of the fever. (See Abatement, Amelioration, Better, Crises, Duration, Hectic, Moderation, Recovery, Remission; "Duration" in this section).

**Daily Return Of**—(See "Remittent" in this section).

**Dampness and Cold**—Fevers Arising From—(See "Cold and Dampness" in this section).

**Danger**—(1) Danger by Fevers—(See Death, High, in this section). (2) Danger of—(See "Liable To", and the various paragraphs in this section).

**Dangerous Fevers**—(See Death, High, in this section).

**Death from Fever**—Fatal Fevers—Dangerous—The ☉ affl. at B., and in □ or ☍ the ☽ or Asc., whichever may be hyleg, and the hyleg affl. by a train of evil directions; the ☉ or ☽ Sig., and ☌ ♂ by dir., and affl. by ♂ at B.; an afflicted ☉ causes death by fevers and severe illnesses in a female horoscope; the ☉ to the place of Praesepe; the ☉ joined with the Ascelli; the ☽ ☌ ♂ in the Asc. at B. tends eventually under evil directions of ♂ to death by some feverish complaint; the ☽ to the ☌ or ill-asp. ♂ by dir., the fever is often fatal, and espec. if ♂ affl. the ☽ and hyleg at B.; ♂ Sig. ☌, □, or ☍ ☉ by dir.; ♂ denotes death by; ♂ affl. the hyleg by dir., and holding the dominion of death; in Hor'y Q. ♂ ruler of the 8th H., or in the 8th, or affl. the cusp of 8th; the Asc. to the place of the Pleiades, Hyades, Castor or Pollux. (See "Arguments for Death", "Certain Death", under Death; Fatal; "High" in this section).

**Dengue**—Breakbone Fever—Rheumatic Fever—(See Dengue; "Fever" under Rheumatism).

**Diathesis**—And Fevers—(See Diathesis).

**Directions**—And Fevers—(See Directions).

**Distempers** Liable to Feverish Distempers—(See "Liable To" in this section; Distempers).

**Dreadful Fevers**—(See High, Portentious, in this section).

**Dry and Hot Diseases**—(See Dryness; "Dry and Hot" under Heat; Parched).

**Duration of Fever**—Continuity of—A fever beginning under a lunar sign partakes of the nature of that sign, and tends to run until the ☽ reaches a sign of opposite elementary qualities. A fever beginning when the ☽ is in ♈, a hot and dry sign, and just after the New ☽, will continue and not be naturally modified until the 1st Quarter of the ☽, when the ☽ reaches the ♋ sign, and meets with opposite qualities, cold and moist. Thus a fever is either terminated, ameliorated, or aggravated, according to the elementary qualities of the Sign and Lunar Quarter ruling at the beginning of the fever, and the qualities of the signs thru which the ☽ passes on successive days, whether of the same or opposing nature. Many of the same conditions which relate to the Duration of Disease, Crises Days, Critical Days, etc., will also apply here. (See Chronic, Continuance, Curtailed, Crises, Ephemeral, Habitual, Long, Low, Prognosis, and the various paragraphs in this section).

**Ease**—Intervals of Ease—(See Ease; "Fever" under Intermittent; Remittent).

**Elimination**—(See "Cleansing" in this section).

**Energy**—Fever As Related To the Energies—(See "Fever" under Energy; "Cleansing" in this section).

**Enlarged Scope**—Fever and Inflammation Combined—(See "Scope" under Enlarged).

**Enteric Fever**—(See "Fever" under Bowels; Typhoid).

**Entire Body**—Feverish Action Over the Whole Body—The ☉ directed to Cor Scorpio. (See Whole).

**Ephemeral Fevers**—Brief—One Day Fevers—(See Ephemeral).

**Epidemic Fevers**—(See "Corrupt", "Obnoxious", under Air; Cholera, Epidemics, Noxious, Pestilence).

**Eruptive Fevers** — Exanthematous — (See Eruptive).

**Exanthematous Fevers**—(See "Eruptive Fevers" under Eruptions).

**Excesses**—Indiscretions—Fevers From—(See "Slight" in this section).

**Excessively High**—Hyperpyrexia— Burning—Violent—(See "High" in this section).

**Extremes**—Rapid Extremes of Temperature—♂ with ♄, and both the afflictors at the same time.

**Eyes**—Hot Diseases In—(See "Hot Diseases" under Eyes).

**Fatal**—(See "Death" in this section).

**Father**—Fevers To—(See "Fevers" under Father).

**Febrifuge**—(See "Antipyretic" in this section).

**Females**—Danger of Fever, Severe and Painful Diseases To, or Death by Fever—The ☉ or ♂ to the ☌ ☽ by dir., and espec. if it take place in the 6th H.; an afflicted ☉ causes death by fevers and severe illnesses in a female horoscope; the ☉ to the ☌ the ☽ by dir.; the ☽ to the ☌ the ☉ or ♂ by dir.; the Asc. to the place of Markab. (See "Death", "Ill-Health", under Females).

**Fever and Inflammation**—(See "Enlarged Scope" in this section).

**Feverish Conditions**—Danger of—Is Liable To—(See "Liable to Fever", "Patient Is Feverish", and the various paragraphs in this section).

**Feverishness**—Causes of—(See "Liable To", and the various paragraphs in this section).

**Fierce Fevers**—High—Burning— Sharp—Severe—(See "High", "Pernicious", in this section).

**Free from Fevers**—Immunity—The earthy signs ♉, ♍, and ♑ are cold signs, and in themselves free from fevers, and people born with an earthy sign on the Asc., and with the ☉, ☽, and many planets in earth signs at B., are more immune to, and free from fevers. (See Immunity).

**Frequent Attacks**—Of Fever—The ☉ or ♂ in ♈, and ♈ on the Asc.; ♂ too much in evidence at B.; ♂ in a fiery sign in the 6th H., and affl. the hyleg; cardinal signs on the 6th H. at B. (See "Liable To" in this section).

**Gastric Fever**—(See "Fever" under Gastric, Stomach).

**Generally**—Tends to Fevers Generally —Subject to Fevers of Various Kinds —Diseases of the ☉; the ☉ hyleg at B., and affl. by ♂, tends to fevers generally; the ☉ in a fiery sign in the 6th H., and affl. by ♂.

**Germs and Fever**—(See Germs, Miasma; "Virus" under Pestilence).

**Glandular Fever**—(See Glands).

**Habit**—The Habit In Disease—(See Diathesis).

**Habitual Fever**—Hectic—Chronic— Continuous—(See Chronic, Continuous, Hectic, Low, in this section).

**Hay Fever**—(See Hay).

**Head** — Hot Humours In—Feverish Head—(See Feverish, Hot Diseases, Humours, under Head).

**Heart and Lungs** — Fevers from Obstructions Near the Heart or Lungs— (See "Fever" under Heart).

**Hectic Fever**—Habitual—Protracted —Constant — Continuous — Chronic — The Protracted Fever of Phthisis—The Hectic Fever associated with Phthisis follows the motion of the ☉ and tends to be worse when the ☉ is in □ or evil asp. his own place by Tr. or Dir., and to diminish when the ☉ is in ⚹, △, and good asp. his own place; the ☉ configurated with malefics when □ his own place tends to make the fever worse, and better when configurated with benefics; the ☽ to the □ or ☍ ♄ by dir.; ♄ in fiery signs at a decumb., and when the ☉ is weak and affl.; a ♂ disease when ♂ is afflicted and associated with ♄; ♀ Sig. ☌ ☉, and the ☉ ill-dig. at B., and affl. by ♂; fiery signs on the Asc. or 6th H. at B. This condition is combatted by a ♄ remedy, a preparation of Lead, known as "Tincture Saturnina". (See Chronic, Constant, Continuous, Low, in this section; "Fire Signs" under Fire; Phthisis).

**Hexis**—The Hexis and Fever—The Permanent Habit In Disease—(See Diathesis).

**High Fevers**—Burning—Hot—Dangerous—Bilious—Fierce—Hyperpyrexia—Mischievous—Severe—Sharp—Violent—Pernicious—Raging Fevers—High Temperatures—Vehement—Swift—Quick—The Disease Runs High—Rapid, etc.—The ☉ to the ☌ or ill-asp. ♂ by dir.; the ☉ or ♂ in ♈ at B., or ♈ on the Asc., fevers rise higher than with other classes of patients; the ☉ or ☽ joined with the Ascelli, or the ☉ or ☽ directed to the Ascelli; the ☉ directed to all Nebulous Clusters, and to Castor and Pollux, threatens violent fevers; the ☉ affl. in ♌ at decumb., mischievous fevers; the ☉ to the place of Praesepe, dangerous fever; the ☽ in a fiery sign, and ☌ or ill-asp. ♂ by dir.; the ☽ to the ☌ the Pleiades, Praesepe, or the Ascelli; the ☽ in ♐ and affl. by the ☉ or ♂ when taken ill (Hor'y); the ☽ ☌, P, □, or ☍ ♄ or ♂, or ☌ the radical place of these planets at the beginning of an illness or fever, and espec. if ♂ be the stronger afflicted planet (Hor'y); an eclipse of the ☽ in ♏ tends to high fevers generally; an eclipse of the ☽ in the 2nd or 3rd Dec. of ♏ tends to high and burning fevers; ♂ too much in evidence at B. tends to high temperatures; ♂ with ♄, and both the afflictors at the same time, tend to rapid extremes of temperature; ♂ in a fiery sign at decumb. tends to fevers of a high, burning, pernicious, vehement character, and espec. if ♂ be in the 6th H., or under the Sun's beams at decumb., and affl. the Sig. of the disease; ♂ causes pestilential burning fevers; in Hor'y Q., ♂ Sig. ☌ ☉ indicates that a high and burning fever may be present; ♂ Sig. ☌ or ☍ ☉; ♂ ☌ the Asc. by dir.; a ♌ disease, and afflictions in ♌; Subs at CP and KP. (See Bilious, Crises, Death, Frequent, Liable To, Malignant, Pernicious, Portentious, Swift, Violent, in this section; Acute, Bile, Epidemics, Eruptions, Fatal, Fierce, Grievous, Heat, Malignant, Mischievous, Pain, Parched, Pestilence, Pulse, Rapid, Septic, Severe, Sharp, Swift, Vehement, Violent, Virulent, etc.).

**High Living**—Fevers Arising From—(See "High Living" under High; "Fevers" under Indiscretions; "Slight" in this section).

**Highest**—Fevers are highest at the Full Moon.

**Hot Complaints**—Subject To—(See "Liable To" in this section; "Hot Diseases" under Heat).

**Hot and Burning Fevers**—(See "High" in this section).

**Hot and Dry Diseases**—(See "Dry and Hot" in this section).

**Hot Flashes**—(See Flushings).

**Hot Humours**—(See "Humours" under Heat).

**Hyperpyrexia**—Excessively High Temperature—(See "High" in this section).

**Immunity from Fever**—(See "Free From" in this section).

**Increased**—The Fever Is Increased and Aggravated—The Fever Is Worse—(See Chronic, Duration, Enlarged Scope, Extremes, Hectic, High, Susceptibility, in this section; "Worse" under Crises; Increase).

**Indiscretions**—Fevers Arising From—(See "Diseases" under Excesses; "High Living" under High; "Fevers" under Indiscretions).

**Indisposition**—(See "Febrile" under Indisposition).

**Infancy**—(See "Fevers" under Infancy).

**Infectious Fevers**—(See Contagions, Infections).

**Inflammation and Fever**—(See "Enlarged Scope" in this section).

**Inflammatory Fevers**—(See "Fever" under Inflammation).

**Influenza**—A Catarrhal Fever—(See Catarrh, Influenza).

**Intermittent Fever**—Occurring at Intervals—(See Ague, Ease, Malaria, Quartan, Quotidian, Relapsing, Remission, Remittent, Semi-Tertian, Tertian).

**Intestines**—Fever In—(See "Fever" under Bowels; Typhoid).

**Irregular Fevers**—Remittent—Irregular Course—(See Course, Erratic, Intermittent, Irregular, Mixed, Peculiar, Remittent, Symptoms, Variable, Various).

**Journeys**—Voyages—Fevers On—(See "Fever" under Voyages).

**Kinds of Fever**—(See the various paragraphs in this section).

**Liable to Fevers**—Tendency To—Danger of—Causes of—Fever Threatened—Subject to Feverish Distempers—Suffers from Hot Complaints—May Have Frequent Attacks of Fever—Not Immune to Fevers, etc.—The aspects and influences which indicate that fever is actually present are given in the paragraph "Patient Is Feverish" in this Article. The following influences make one liable to fevers, and feverish conditions—A SUN disease; the ☉ affl. in fiery signs, and espec. affl. by ♂; the afflictions of the ☉ are very productive of fevers, and espec. when ♂ is in the 1st H., and affl. by the ☉; the ☉ affl. in ♈, ♌, ♐ or ♑; the ☉ in ♐ and affl. by ♂ or ♃; the ☉ or ♂ affl. in the Asc.; the ☉ affl. in ♈, due to excess of heat; the ☉ or ♂ in ♈, and ♈ on the Asc.; the ☉ ☌ ♂ in ♈ and ♈ on the Asc., the blood is like a hot, fiery liquid; the ☉ or ☽ ☌, □, or ☍ ♂; the ☉ affl. in ♌ or ♎; the ☉ in a fiery sign at B., affl. by ♂, and the ☉ in ☌, P, □ or ☍ the Asc. by dir.; the ☉ affl. at B., and the ☉ to the evil asp. the Asc. by dir.; the ☉ to the ☌ or ill-asp. ♂, and ♂ ruler of the 6th H.; the ☉ or ☽ Sig. in ☌ ♂; the ☉ Sig. □ or ☍ ♂;

the ☉ to the □ or ☍ ☽ by dir.; the ☉ to the place of ☋; the ☉ in a fire sign at B., affl. by ♂, and to the ☌ or ill-asp. the Asc. by dir.; the ☉ to the ill-asps. the ☽ by dir., and the ☽ hyleg at B., and affl.; the ☉ in ♈, ♌, or ♐, in ☌ or ill-asp. any of the malefics as promittors; the ☉ affl. by ♀, and thru excesses or indiscretions; denoted by the ☉ when the ☉ afflicts the ☽ or Asc.; the ☉ with the Ascelli at B., and to the place of the Ascelli by dir.; the ☉ joined with, or to the place of Antares, Praesepe, or Caput Hercules; the MOON to the ☌ or ill-asp. the ☉ or ♂ by dir.; the ☽ hyleg, and to the ☌ or ill-asp. ♄ or ♂ by dir.; the ☽ to the ☌, P, or ill-asps. the ☉ by dir. if the ☽ be hyleg, and the ☉ affl. at B.; the ☽ in ♐ in ☌ or ill-asp. ♄ (or ☿ if he be of the nature of ♄) at the beginning of an illness or at decumb. (Hor'y); the ☽ hyleg and to the ☌ or ill-asp. ♄ by dir., low fevers; the ☽ in ♌ and affl. by the ☉ or ♂ when taken ill, the body is dry, hot and parched (Hor'y); the ☽ in ♎ and affl. by the ☉ or ♂ when taken ill, tends to fever from too much blood (Hor'y); the ☽ ☌ or ill-asp. ♄ or ♂, or the radical places of these planets, at the beginning of an illness or fever, and espec. if ♂ be the stronger afflicting planet, tends to high, burning fever; the ☽ in fiery signs, and to the ☌ or ill-asps. ♂ by dir.; the ☽ hyleg, and to the ☌ or ill-asps. the ☉ by dir., and the ☉ affl. at B.; the ☽ affl. in ♋ at B., and the tr. of ♂ over the radical ☽, and espec. in people with a weak constitution; the ☽ affl. in an airy sign at B., and a tr. of ♂ over the radical place of the ☽, or the ☽ to the ☌ or ill-asp. ♂ by dir.; the ☽ in ♈, ♉, or ♐, and affl. by the ☉ or ♂ when taken ill (Hor'y); the ☽ to the ☌ or ill-asp. ♂ by dir., and ♂ affl. the ☽ at B., a fever which may endanger the life; the ☽ Sig. ☌ ♂ (Hor'y); the ☽ to the ☌ the Pleiades or Praesepe; SATURN occi., and affl. the hyleg by dir., tends to low fevers; ♄ causes fevers arising from cold or dampness; JUPITER affl. in ♌; ♃ affl. in ♎, from too much blood; ♃ affl. in ♐; MARS in fiery signs and affl. the ☉, ☽, Asc., or hyleg; ♂ affl. in the 1st H.; ♂ in ♈ and affl. the hyleg; ♂ to the ☌ or ill-asp. the Asc. by dir.; ♂ in ♌, □ or ☍ ☉; ♂ □ or ☍ the ☉ or ☽ at B., and by dir.; ♂ affl. in ♈, ♌, ♐, or ♒; ♂ affl. in the 4th, 6th, or 8th H., and espec. when affl. the hyleg; ♂ prog. in ☌ the Asc. or M.C.; ♂ sole ruler at an eclipse of the ☉ tends to much fever everywhere; ♂ affl. in ♊ or ♍, and with ♂ in ☌ or ill-asp. the Asc. by dir.; ♂ in a fiery sign at B., and to the ☌ or ill-asp. the Asc. by dir.; ♂ to the ☌ or ill-asp. ♅ by dir.; ♂ afflicting the ☽ by dir.; ♂ to the ill-asps. his own place by dir., or to the ☉ or ☽; ♂ causes dangerous fevers when the dominion of death is vested in him, and he afflicts the hyleg at B., and by dir.; ♂ in ♐, ☌ or ill-asp. the ☉; ♂ in a fiery sign at decumb.; ♂ in a fiery sign in the 6th H., and under the Sun's beams at decumb. (Hor'y); ♂ and ♄ both the afflictors in the disease, and affl. the hyleg; ♂ in the 6th H. in ☌ the ☉; ♂ and the ☉ both being the afflictors at the same time tend to both fever and inflammation, and to enlarge the scope of the disease; ♂ ☌ the ☉ at B. tends to fevers under the evil directions to the ☉ or ♂; ♂ promittor in ♒ and in ☌ or ill-asp. the ☉, has feverish distempers; the tr. of ♂ over the radical ☉ or ☽, or in ☍ to them; ♂ too much in evidence at B. tends to frequent attacks of fever; the evil directions of ♂ to the hyleg if ♂ is strongly affl. at B.; ♂ in ♐ in the 6th H., and affl.; ♂ in ♐ and affl. the ☽ or Asc.; ♂ affl. the hyleg at B., and by dir., and in a train of evil directions, denotes the danger of death by a high, pernicious, and violent fever, or by an accident; MERCURY Sig. ☌ ☉, and the ☉ ill-dig. at B.; the ASCENDANT a fiery sign; the Asc. to the place of the Pleiades, the Ascelli, or Capricornus; the Asc. to the place of Markab, and espec, to females; the Asc. affl. by ♂ at B., and by dir.; ♐ ascending at the Vernal Equi., and ♃ afflicted, afflicts Peoples with fevers who are born under ♐, and in Countries ruled by this sign, and likewise with People and Countries ruled by ♈ or ♌ when these signs are upon the Asc. at the Vernal, and their rulers, the ☉ and ♂, afflicted; ECLIPSES of the ☽ in ♏, or in fiery signs, tend to high and burning fevers, and espec. among People and Countries ruled by these signs, and with greater intensity if the central line of the eclipse is over them, and they come under its shadow; cardinal signs on the 6th H. at B. tend to frequent fevers; also cardinal signs in general show fevers; fiery signs upon the Asc. at B., people born under a fiery sign, or having the ☽ or lord of the Asc. in a fiery sign, are very subject to fevers and illnesses of a hot and dry nature; fire signs on the 6th H. at B.; many planets in fire signs at B.; fixed stars of the nature of the ☉ and ♂ ascending at B.; the Ascelli directed to the ☉, ☽, or Asc. (See "Patient Is Feverish", "Suffers from a Fever", in this section. Also note the various subjects and paragraphs in this Article).

**Life Endangered** — By Fever — (See Chronic, Constant, Dangerous, Hectic, High, Low, in this section).

**Lingering Fevers**—(See Chronic, Constant, Habitual, Hectic, Low, in this section).

**Liver**—(See "Fever" under Liver).

**Lives Thru Fevers**—The ♈ people, as a rule, live thru fevers where others succumb, as ♂, the ruler of ♈, gives them greater power to resist high fevers. (See Aries).

**Long Fevers**—(See Chronic, Constant, Continuous, Hectic, Low, in this section).

**Low Fevers** — Low and Persistent — Weakening—Apt to Prove Fatal If Not Checked, and the Vitality Raised—The ☽ hyleg, and to the ☌ or ill-asp. ♄ by dir.; ♄ occi. and affl. the hyleg by dir.; ♃ in perihelion, an epidemic of low fevers, and many deaths. (See Ague, Chronic Diseases, Consumptions, Perihelion, Phthisis, Tuberculosis, Wastings; Chronic, Constant, Continuous, Hectic, in this section).

**Lungs**—Lung Fever—Fever from Obstructions Near the Lungs and Heart—(See "Fever" under Heart; "Lung Fever" under Lungs; Pneumonia).

**Malaria Fever**—(See Ague, Intermittent, Malaria).

**Malignant Fevers**—(See Malignant).

**Malta Fever**—Mediterranean Fever—The fiery signs ♈, ♌, or ♐ ascending at the Vernal Equi., and with the ruler of the sign ascending afflicted, tend to this fever, as these signs rule the Peoples and Countries surrounding the Mediterranean, as England, France, Spain, and Italy. Also this fever is attended with Subs at CP and KP. (See Nations).

**Melancholic Fevers** — (See "Fevers" under Melancholy).

**Miasma** — (See "Corrupt Air" under Air; Germs, Miasma, Noxious).

**Mild Fevers**—(See Colds, Ephemeral. Also see Indiscretions, Slight, in this section).

**Milk Fever**—Fever In the Breasts—(See "Fever" under Breasts).

**Mischievous Fevers**—The ☉ affl. in ♌ at decumb. (See "High" in this section).

**Mixed Fevers**—☿ in a fiery sign at decumb. (See Variable, Various).

**Moderation** — Of Fever — (See "Curtailed" in this section).

**Moisture**—Fevers Arising From—(See "Cold and Dampness" in this section).

**Mother** — Fever to the Mother—(See "Slow Fevers" under Mother).

**Mountain Fever**—Rocky Mountain Fever—(See Mountain).

**Nature**—Of the Fever—Quality of—(See "Disease" under Nature; Type).

**Neck** — Glandular Fever In — (See "Neck" under Glands; "Mumps" under Parotid).

**Non-Contagious** — Simple—Those Arising from High Living, Excesses, Indiscretions, etc.—(See High Living, Indiscretions, Slight, in this section).

**Noxious Air**—Fevers Arising From—(See "Corrupt", "Obnoxious", under Air; Cholera, Epidemics, Miasma, Noxious, Pestilence).

**Obstructions**—Fevers Arising from Obstructions Near the Heart, Lungs, or Liver—(See "Fever" under Heart, Liver).

**Ominous Fevers** — (See "Portentous" in this section).

**One Day Fevers**—Brief—(See Ephemeral).

**Parched Body** — The Body Parched and Dry—(See "Dry Body", "Dry and Hot Body", "Dry and Hot Diseases", under Dry; "Dry and Hot Diseases" under Heat; Parched).

**Parents** — Fever Attacks the Parents —(See "Fever" under Father, Mother).

**Patient Is Feverish**—There Is Fever —The ☉ Sig. to the ☌ or ill-asp. ♂ by dir.; the ☽ in ♐ and affl. by the ☉ or ♂ when taken ill; the ☽ or ♃ in ♎, and affl. by the ☉ or ♂ when taken ill, and caused by too much blood (Hor'y). (See "Liable to Fever", "Suffers from a Fever", in this section).

**Periodic Fevers**—Returning At Regular Intervals — (See Intermittent, Malaria).

**Periods of Fever**—Periods and Times When Fever Is Apt To Come—(See "Periods" under Acute; "Periods" and "Time of the Disease", under Disease; Directions, Events; "Periods of Bad Health" under Health).

**Pernicious Fevers**—Fevers of a Vehement, Venomous Nature—♂ in the 6th H. at a decumb., or under the Sun's beams, and affl. the Sig. of the disease. (Hor'y). (See "High Fevers" in this section; "Destructive Processes" under Destructive).

**Pestilential Fevers** — (See "Corrupt Air" under Air; Cholera, Epidemics; "Fevers" under Pestilence, Plague).

**Phthisis**—The Hectic Fever of—(See "Hectic" in this section).

**Pneumonia**—Lung Fever—(See Pneumonia; "Lungs" in this section).

**Portentous Fevers** — Dreadful — Ominous—The ☽ conjoined with ♄, ♃, ♂, ♀, or ☿ in fiery signs at decumb., and when the ☉ is weak and afflicted also. (See High, Pernicious, in this section).

**Precipitated**—An Acute Fever Is Precipitated — (See "Precipitated" under Acute).

**Prevalence of Fevers**—♂ sole ruler at an eclipse of the ☉, much fever everywhere; ♂ in ♋ and lord of the year at the Vernal Equinox; an eclipse of the ☽ in the 1st Dec. of ♈; ☿ in ♊ in ☌ ♂ at the Vernal, and lord of the year; Comets appearing in ♍. (See "High" in this section; "Prevalent" under Acute).

**Prognosis In Fevers** — Depends upon the motion of the ☽ thru the Signs, and the aspects and planets which may interfere with the course of the disease. (See Prognosis; Chronic, Curtailed, Death, High, Low, Mild, and the various paragraphs in this section).

**Protracted Fevers** — (See Chronic, Constant, Continuous, Hectic, Low, in this section).

**Puerperal Fever** — Childbed Fever — (See Puerperal).

**Putrid Fevers**—(See "Fevers" under Putrid).

**Quality** — Of the Fever — (See "Nature", and the various paragraphs in this section).

**Quartan Ague**— (See Ague, Intermittent, Quartan).

**Quarternaries**—(See Quartan).

**Quotidian** — Intermittent — A Daily Paroxysm—(See Intermittent, Malaria, Quotidian).

**Rapid Extremes**—Of Temperature — (See "Extremes" in this section).

**Relapsing Fevers**—The Sig. of the disease in a double-bodied sign at decumb.; Subs at CP and KP. (See Course; "Worse" under Crises; Relapses; Chronic, Constant, Continuous, Increased, Intermittent, Irregular, Remittent, Worse, in this section).

**Remedies** — (See "Treatment" in this section).

**Remission Of**—(See Remission).

**Remittent Fevers** — Abating and Returning—Intervals of Ease—(See Ease, Intermittent, Irregular, Malaria, Quotidian, in this section; Remittent).

**Resists Fever**—♈ people. (See "Lives Thru Fevers" in this section).

**Returning Fever** — (See Intermittent, Remittent, in this section).

**Rheumatic Fever** — (See Dengue; "Fever" under Rheumatism).

**Rocky Mountain Fever** — (See Mountain).

**Runs High**—The Fever Runs High—Hyperpyrexia — Burning Fever — (See "High" in this section).

**Sanguinary Fevers** — (See Sanguinary; "Blood" in this section).

**Scarlet Fever**—(See Scarlet).

**Semi-Tertian Fevers**—(See Ague, Intermittent, Quartan, Semi-Tertian).

**Septic Fevers**—(See Septic).

**Sharp Fevers**—Fierce—High—Burning—(See "High" in this section).

**Short Fevers** — (See Acute, Brief, Slight, in this section).

**Shortened** — The Fever Shortened — (See "Curtailed" in this section).

**Simple Fevers** — (See "Non-Contagious" in this section).

**Slight Fevers**—Small Fevers—Brief—Mild— Non-Contagious — Ephemeral — The ☉ affl. by ♀, thru Excesses or Indiscretions; the ☽ ☌ ♂ in the Asc., and ♄ ruler of the 6th H. when taken ill (Hor'y); the ☽ in ♍ and affl. by the ☉ or ♂ when taken ill (Hor'y); the ☽ in ♊, □ or ☍ ♄ (or ☿ if he be of the nature of ♄) at the beginning of an illness, or at decumb. (Hor'y). (See Colds, Ephemeral, Indiscretions, Indisposition, Mild, Minor, Slight).

**Slow Fevers**—(See Chronic, Constant, Hectic, Low, Mother, in this section; Slow, Tedious).

**Small Fevers**—(See "Slight" in this section).

**Spotted Fever**—(See Spotted).

**Spread of Fever**—(See "Corrupt Air" under Air; Cholera, Contagious, Epidemics, Infectious, Miasma, Noxious, Pestilence, Plague, etc.).

**Stomach** — Fever In — (See "Fever" under Stomach).

**Subnormal Temperature** — (See "Subnormal" under Temperature).

**Sudden Fever** — Denoted and caused by fixed stars of the nature of ♂.

**Suffers from a Fever** — Suffers Hot Complaints—Is Feverish—The ☽ in ♐, and affl. by the ☉ or ♂ when taken ill (Hor'y); the ☽ in ♐, ☌ or ill-asp. ♄ (or ☿ if he be of the nature of ♄) when taken ill (Hor'y); ♂ in a fiery sign when ♂ is the afflictor in the disease; ♂ ruler of the 8th H., or in the 8th, or affl. the cusp of 8th, danger of fever in Hor'y Q.; ♂ in fiery signs and to the ☌ or ill-asps. the Asc. by dir. (See "Liable To", "Patient Is Feverish", in this section).

**Surfeits**—Fevers Arising From—(See "Fever" under Heart; Surfeits).

**Susceptibility**—To Fever Increased—

The ☉ ☌ or ill-asp. ♂ at B., and by dir.

**Swift Fevers** — (See "High" in this section; "Swift Diseases" under Swift).

**Synocha** — (See "Continuous" in this section).

**Temperature** — High — Increase of — Low—Subnormal—etc.—(See Temperature; High, Increased, Low, and the various paragraphs in this section).

**Tendency**—To Fevers — (See "Liable To" in this section).

**Tertian Fevers**—(See "Tertian" under Ague; Intermittent).

**There Is Fever** — (See "Patient Is Feverish", "Suffers from a Fever", in this section).

**Thighs**—Fever and Hot Diseases In—(See "Hot Humours" under Hips; "Feverish" under Thighs).

**Threatened** — Fever Is Threatened — (See "Liable To" in this section).

**Too Much Blood** — Fevers Arising From—(See "Blood", "Patient Is Feverish", in this section).

**Travel**—(See "Fevers" under Travel).

**Treatment of Fevers**—The drugs and remedies of ♄ combat fevers, as Aconite, Tincture Saturnina. Lead, etc. Blue color, and blue flowers, ruled by ♃, tend to allay fevers. Also cold, ruled by ♄, as by cold applications, ice, snow, etc., combat the fever. (See Aconite, Antipathy, Cold, Lead; "Drugs" "Herbs", "Remedies", under Saturn; Treatment; "Hectic" in this section).

**Typhoid Fever**—(See Typhoid).

**Typhus Fever**—(See Typhus).

**Variable Fevers**—Irregular — (See "Irregular" in this section).

**Various Kinds of Fever**—Subject To —Various Course In Fevers—(See Generally, Irregular, in this section).

**Vehement Fevers** — (See High, Pernicious, in this section; Vehement).

**Violent Fevers** — High — Dangerous— The ☉ directed to all Nebulous Clusters, and to Castor, Pollux, or the Ascelli; the ☽ to the Ascelli, Pleiades, or Praesepe; the Asc. to the □ or ☍ ♂ by dir.; the Ascelli directed to the ☉, ☽, or Asc. (See High, Pernicious, in this section; "High Pulse" under Pulse; Vehement, Violent).

**Virus**—The Pestilential Virus—(See "Virus" under Pestilence).

**Vitiated Air** — Fevers Spread By — (See "Corrupt Air" under Air; Contagions, Epidemics, Miasma, Noxious, Pestilence).

**Voyages** — Fevers On — (See "Fevers" under Voyages).

**Whole Body**—The Fever Is Thru the Whole Body — (See "Entire Body" in this section).

**Women**—Fevers To—Death by Fevers — (See "Females" in this section; Chills; "Death" under Women).

**Worse** — The Fever Turns for the Worse — (See Chronic, Flux, Hectic, Increased, Prognosis, in this section; Worse).

**Yellow Fever**—(See Yellow).

**Youth** — Fevers In Childhood and Youth — (See "Fevers" under Childhood).

**Zymotic Fevers** — Fevers from Fermentation — (See Dengue, Fermentation, Zymosis).

**FIANCE**—Fiancee—

**Death Of** — An Ancient Aphorism in Hor'y Q. is if the ☽ be in the first 12 degrees of ♑ when engagement is made, the fiance, or fiancee, usually dies before the marriage, or within six months after marriage. (See "Death" under Husband, Marriage Partner, Wife).

**Sickness Of**—(See "Ill-Health" under Husband, Marriage Partner, Wife). The same rules usually apply to the Fiance, or Fiancee, as to Husband or Wife, for when Engagement results, the parties come under the 7th H. influences of each other's maps, the same as if marriage has taken place, and if marriage is delayed, any evil directions coming to a climax in either map, as related to death, sickness, or accident to either party, usually take place when the event is scheduled unless forewarned, and care is taken to forestall it.

**FIBER** — Fibre — Fibrous — Fibrinous — Fibrosis — Fibrin — Fibro — The Fibro-Ligamentous System—Elastic Fiber—Fibroid—Fibroma—etc.—The building of Fibrous Tissue is the work of ♂, and takes part in the building of the Tendons, Sinews, Ligaments, etc. Elastic Fiber is connected with the ♋ sign, and Calcium Fluoride, the ♋ sign Tissue Salt. The Fibrin of the Blood is ruled by ♃, ♂, and the ♓ sign. The Fibro-Ligamentous System is under the rule of the ♍ and ♓ signs, and the ☉ and ☽ acting thru the ♓ sign affect the Fibro-Ligamentous System, and give way to the Thoracic Diathesis. Also by acting thru ♍, Fibro-Ligamentous affections are caused, and accompanied by Gout in the feet (Podagra). Fibrous tissue is crystallized and hardened by ♄. The density of connecting fiber is increased when ♂ is with ♃. The Nerve Fibers, ruled by ♆, are also under the internal rulership of the ♊ sign. The anterior lobe of the Pituitary Body, ruled by ♅, also influences the nerve fibers. The nerve fibers of the bowels are ruled over, and influenced by ☿, and espec. when ☿ is in ♍.

**Degeneration**—Fibrous Degeneration —♂ influence at B., overlaid and intermixed with other planets, as ♆, ♅, or ♄.

**Exudation**—Fibrinous Exudation—♂ ☌ or ill-asp. ♃.

**Fibroma**—Fibroid Tumor—♂ ☌ or ill-asp. ♀ or ☿. (See "Fibroid" under Womb).

**Fibrosis**—♄ influence; ♄ in ♊ tends to the development of fibrous tissue in the lungs, and likewise in other organs according to the sign position of ♄ at B.

**Filaments**—(See Filaments).

**Hardening**—Crystallization of Fibrous Tissue—The work of ♄.

**Laxity**—Of Fiber—A ♀ disease. (See Relaxation).

**Nerve Fibroma**—(See Neuroma).

**Phthisis** — Fibroid Phthisis In Lungs —(See "Pulmonary" under Phthisis).

**Tonic Fibers** — Over-Braced Tonic Fibers—A ♂ disease. (See Tonic).

**Tumors**—Fibro-Cartilaginous Tumor —(See "Chondroma" under Cartilage; "Fibroid" in this section and under Womb). See Connective, Ligaments, Muscles, Sinews, Tendons, Tissues).

**FIBULA**—The Small Outer Bone of the Leg—Is under the structural rulership of the ♒ sign, and is opposite to, and corresponds to the Ulna in the arm, ruled by ♌. The Fibula is also ruled by the 11th H.

**Disorders Of** — Afflictions in ♒; Subs at LPP, the 4, 5L.

**Fracture Of**—♂ affl. in ♒. (See "Fracture" under Legs). See Arms, Radius, Ulna.

**FIERCE**—Ferocious—Savage—Cruel—Violent—A ♂ characteristic. (See Anger; "Dogs" under Children; Cruel, Evil, Ferocious, Savage, Wild).

**Fierce Fevers** — (See "High" under Fevers).

**Fierce Maladies** — Caused by ♂ afflictions at B., and by dir., to the ☉, ☽, Asc., or hyleg; also caused by the ☉. (See Acute, Dangerous; "High" under Fever; Fulminating, Grievous, Painful, Pernicious, Poignant, Quick, Rapid, Serious, Sharp, Sudden, Swift, Vehement, Violent).

**FIERY**—Characteristic of the ☉ and ♂.

**Diseases**—Hot and Fiery Diseases—Caused by ♂. (See Fever, Heat).

**Eyes**—The Eyes Red and Fiery—(See "Fiery" under Eyes).

**Fiery Signs** — Of the Zodiac — (See "Fire Signs" under Fire).

**Fiery Temperament**—(See Choleric).

**Hair** — Fiery Red Hair — (See "Red Hair" under Hair).

**FIFTH HOUSE**—This is a masculine house, and is closely affiliated with the ☉, the ♌ and ♒ signs, and the 11th H. It is principally the house of children, the creative powers, and along with its opposite house, the 11th H., denotes the state and welfare of children. Fruitful signs and planets here denote many children, and barren signs and planets here tend to deny children, give but few, or cause their early death. The ☽ and the benefics here, well-aspected, denote healthy, strong, fortunate, and long-lived children. The malefics ♄ and ♂ here denote evil, sickly children, or misfortune to or by them. This is also the house of women, the state of woman with child, and parturition. This house rules the back, heart, sides, hind part of the shoulders, the liver, stomach; the appetites, and espec. along pleasurable and sexual lines; love affairs, courtship, the legitimate or illegitimate relations of the sexes before marriage; pleasures, amusements, places of amusement, theatres, music halls, taverns, games, recreations, and the accidents or injuries which may accompany such matters; rules matters of speculation in finance for gain or loss. Its Colors are black, white, mixed black and white, sanguine, and honey color. This house is also said to rule the Soul. (See Amorous, Amusements, Aquarius, Barrenness, Bastards, Children; "Creative Powers" under Creative; Eleventh House; "Free Love" under Free; Fruitful, Leo, Licentiousness, Love Affairs, Parturition, Passion, Pleasures, Recreations, Soul, Theatres, etc., and other subjects mentioned in this section).

**FIG TREES**—Fig Trees Corrupted—Eclipses of the ☉ or ☽ in ♈. (See Corruption, Fruit, Trees).

**FIGHTING**—Quarrels—Contests—Accidents, Injuries, or Death Thru—♄ to an ill-asp. ♂ by dir., and espec. if ♄ or ♂ be in the 1st, 7th, or 10th H. at B.; ♂ to the ill-asps. the ☉, ☽, ♀, or Asc. by dir.; lord of the 6th in the 7th, sickness from fighting. (See Anger, Contests, Cuts, Duels, Feuds, Mobs; "Murderous" under Murder; Quarrels, Rashness, Recklessness, Stabs, Sword, Vicious, Violence, Weapons, Women).

**FIGURE**—The Body—The Form, etc.—(See Appearance, Beautiful, Body, Build, Complexion, Crooked, Dark, Form, Handsome, Height, Ill-Formed, Light, Malformed, Misshaped, Size, Stature, Ugly, Weight, Well-Formed, etc., and note the references given under these subjects).

**Figure of the Heavens**—The Map of Birth—(See Map).

**FILAMENTS**—Thread-like Structures—The filaments making up the muscles are largely ruled and developed by ♂. The nerve filaments are under the rule of ☿. The development of the nerve filaments of the foetus is carried on by ☿. (See Fibers, Foetus, Muscles, Nerves).

**FILM**—Blindness by White Film—(See "Film" under Blindness).

**FILTH**—Filthy—

**Body**—Filthy and Unclean Body—♄ ☌ ♀; ♄ and ♂ in the Asc., and in □ the ☽ and ♀; the afflictions of ♄ tend to, due to deposit of, and retention of wastes; ♀ ☌ ☽ in ♎, and in □ ♂ in ♋. (See Cleansing, Deposits, Elimination, Excretions, Leprosy, Retentions, Uncleanly, Wastes).

**Habits**—Filthy In Talk and Behavior—Filthy In Habits and Deeds—♄ ☌ or ill-asp. ♀; the 17° ♑ on the Asc. (See Carelessness, Conduct; "Bad Habits" under Habits; Obscene, Profane, Uncleanly, Untidy, Vices).

**Mind**—Filthy Mind—Foul Minded—A ♄ characteristic; ♄ ☌ ♀. (See Immodest, Knavish, Morals, Obscene, Profane, Shameless, Vices, Wanton, Wicked).

**FILTRATION**—The Process of Straining or Filtering—

**Cell Substances**—Filtration of—(See "Substance" under Cells).

**Kidneys**—Filtration In—The ♎ sign rules filtration and distillation in the kidneys. (See Distillation).

**Urine**—Filtration of—Sublimation of—(See Distillation, Sublimation; "Filtration" under Urine).

**FINANCE**—(See Money, Poverty, Property, Prosperity, Riches, Wealth, etc.).

**FINE**—Excellent—Beautiful—Elegant, Clear, Handsome, etc.—

**Body**—Fine, Tall, Upright and Well-Made Body—♃ in ♐ in partile asp. the Asc. (See Tall, Upright, Well-Made).

**Complexion**—Fine Complexion—(See "Fine" under Complexion).

**Constitution**—Fine Constitution—(See "Good Constitution" under Constitution).

**Eyes**—Fine Eyes—Fine Blue Eyes—Fine and Clear—(See "Fine" under Eyes).

**Forehead**—Fine Forehead—(See Forehead).

**Stature**—Fine Stature—Finely Built—♃ ruler of the Asc., and ori. (See Beautiful, Commanding, Handsome, Well-Formed, Well-Proportioned; "Body" in this section).

**FINGERS**—The Fingers are ruled by ♊, ♍, and the 3rd H. The feet and toes are ruled by ♓, and the fingers, being the counterpart of the toes, are naturally ruled by ♍, the sign opposite to ♓. Subs at AP, the Arm Place in the Spine, tend to disorders, afflictions, infirmities, distortions, etc., of the fingers, due to lack of proper nerve supply to the fingers. Many influences which affect the Fingers are given under the subject of Hands. (See Hands. Also for comparisons, see Feet, Toes).

**Ankylosis In**—♄ affl. in ♊ or ♍, due to deposits, drying up of the joints, and solidification. Also caused by ♂ in ♊, or ☉ ☌ ♂ in ♊, due to excess heat and fusion of the joints. (See Ankylosis).

**Athetosis**—Incoordination—Inability to keep the fingers or toes in one position for very long at a time. ♅ affl. in ♊ or ♍; Subs at AT and AP. (See "Athetosis" under Toes).

**Broad Fingers**—Broad, Thick and Short—♉ influence; ♉ on Asc., or the ☉ and many planets in ♉. (See Clubbed, Short, in this section).

**Clubbed Fingers**—Club Hands—♄ affl. in ♊ or ♍; Subs at AP, HP (2D), and KP. (See "Club Feet" under Feet).

**Cold Fingers**—(See "Raynaud" in this section).

**Conical**—Long and Slender—♍ on the Asc. (See "Long" in this section).

**Cramps In**—(See "Cramps" under Hands).

**Diseases Of**—Disorders of—Afflictions in ♊ or ♍; Subs at AT, AP, HP (2D), and KP. (See "Diseases" under Hands).

**Distorted Fingers**—♄ affl. in ♊ or ♍; Subs at AP (1D). (See Distortions; "Deformities" under Hands).

**Felons**—Inflammation About the Nails—♂ affl. in ♊; Subs at LCP (2D), AP (1D), HP (2D), KP. (See "Whitlows" in this section).

**Fractures Of**—♄ or ♂ affl. in ♊. (See "Fractures" under Hands).

**Gout In**—(See "Hands" under Gout).

**Hands**—Note the various paragraphs under "Hands", as such influences also tend to affect the Fingers. Also see Feet, Toes).

**Horny Growths**—Instead of Nails—♆ in ♊. (See Horny).

**Humours In**—The ☽ in ♑ and affl. by the ☉ or ♂ when taken ill (Hor'y).

**Incoordination In**—(See "Athetosis" in this section).

**Joints**—Inflamed—Swollen—Ankylosis of—(See "Ankylosis" in this section).

**Long Fingers**—(See "Long" under Hands).

**Nails**—Description of—Disorders of—(See Nails; "Felons", "Horny", in this section).

**Numbness**—(See "Raynaud" in this section).

**Panaris**—(See "Whitlows" in this section).

**Phlegmonous Suppuration**—(See "Whitlows" in this section).

**Pointed Fingers**—(See "Conical" in this section).

**Raynaud's Disease**—Coldness and Whiteness of the Nose, Fingers and Toes—Numbness—A Waxy Pallor of the Fingers and Toes—A ♄ disease; ♄ affl. in ♊, ♍, or ♓; afflictions in ♊ or ♎; Subs at AP (1D), and KP.

**Slender Fingers**—Long and Slender—☿ gives. (See "Long" under Hands).

**Spasm Of**—(See "Tetanus" in this section).

**Suppuration**—About the Nails—(See "Whitlows" in this section).

**Tetanus**—A Tetanic Spasm Affecting the Fingers and Toes—(See "Fingers" under Tetanus).

**Thumb**—The Thumb Nearly Cut Off—See Case, Chap. 13, page 97, in Daath's Medical Astrology.

**Toes**—(See the various paragraphs under Toes).

**Waxy Pallor Of**—(See "Raynaud" in this section).

**White and Cold**—(See "Raynaud" in this section).

**Whitlows**—Panaris—(See "Whitlows" under Toes).

**Writer's Cramp**—(See "Cramps" under Hands).

**FIRE**—Fires—Fire is governed by ♂. (See Combustion; "Operations" under Nature).

**Abroad**—Suffers Injury or Death by Fire Abroad—(See "Fire" under Abroad).

**Accidents by Fire**—Injury By—Wounds By—The ☉ to the ☌ or ill-asps. ♂ by dir.; the ☉ to the place of the Ascelli or Praesepe; the ☽ □ or ☍ ♂ at B., and by dir.; ♂ elevated above, and affl. the Luminaries; the ill-asps. of ♂ by dir. to any of the Moderators, the ☉, ☽, Asc. or M.C.; the Asc. to the ☌ or ill-asp. ♂ by dir., and ♂ in a fiery sign at B.; malefics in the M.C., and ♂ holding dominion; ♈ on the Asc. (See "Death", "Injury", and the various paragraphs in this section).

**Blindness By**—By Burning—(See "Burning" under Blindness).

**Burns**—Burning—Searing Burns—Scalds—(See Burns; "Hot Liquids" under Heat; Scalds).

**Danger by Fire**—Prejudice by Fire—The ☉ hyleg, and to the ☌ or ill-asp. ♂ by dir., and espec. if ♂ be in a fiery sign at B.; the Prog. ☉ or ☽ to the ☌ or ill-asps. ♂, and the ☉ or ☽ hyleg at B.; the ☉ to the ☌ or P. Dec. the Ascelli by dir.; the ☽ at a Solar Rev. passing over the place of ♂ at B.; the ☽ to the ☌ or ill-asps. ♂ by dir.; ♄ in ♌ or ♐, ☌ or ill-asp. the Asc. by dir.; ♂ affl. in the 1st H.; ♂ to the ill-asps. his own place by dir.; the ♂ sign ♈ on the Asc. at B.; ♂ by Periodic Rev. to the ☌ or ill-asps. ♅; ♂ holding dominion, and elevated above the Lights, and affl. the hyleg; ♂ Sig. ☌ the ☉; the Asc. to the ☌ ☉, and the ☉ ☌ ♂; the Asc. to the place of the Ascelli or Capricornus; afflictions in ♐; fiery signs on the Asc. (See Accidents, Burns, Death, Injury, and the various paragraphs in this section).

**Death by Fire**—Danger of—The ☉ or ☽ to the ☌ or ill-asps. ♂ by dir., and espec. if ♂ be near the Ascelli, and affl. by ♄; the ☉ setting in ♌, near the Ascelli, afflicted by malefics, and the ☽ at the same time be affl. by ♂ and ♂ descending; the ☉ joined with the Ascelli; the ☉ in ♌ if other testimonies concur; the ☽ in ♌, and to the ☌ or ill-asps. ♂, with ♂ affl. by the ☉ or ♄, and ♂ near the place of the Bull's Eye; the ☽ to the ☌ or ill-asps. ♂ by dir., and espec. if ♂ be in ♌ near the Ascelli, and ill-asp. by the ☉ or ♄; the ☽ Sig. □ or ☍ ♂; the ☽ Sig. □ or ☍ ☉, and espec. if ♂ aspect the ☉; when the ☽ or Asc. are hyleg, the ☉ by his evil directions to them will assist to cause death by fire, as the ☉ acts like ♂ in this instance, and espec. when in ♌, and when other testimonies concur; ♂ in a fiery sign and in ☍ the Asc. at B., and by dir., and espec. if near the Ascelli; ♂ affl. the hyleg by dir., and holding the dominion of death, and espec. when the radix indicates a violent death; ♂ Sig. ☌, □, or ☍ ☉; ♂ ori. in ♉ or ♏, □ or ☍ ☉, or ♂ occi. in ♉ or ♏ in □ or ☍ ☽; ♂ causes death by; ♂ in the 7th H., □ or ☍ ☉ or ☽, except he be in a four-footed sign. (See "Fire" under Abroad; "Death" under Burns; "Hot Liquids" under Heat; Incendiarism, Scalds; "Family" in this section).

**Electricity**—Injury or Death By—(See Electricity, Lightning, Shock).

**Family**—Loses His Family and Property In a Fire—Case—See "Leland", No. 813, in 1001 N.N. (See Home).

**Fire Arms**—Death or Injury By—(See Guns).

**Fire and Energy**—Are given to the Vitality by ♂. (See Energy).

**Fire Signs**—The Fiery Signs of the Zodiac—These signs are ♈, ♌, and ♐. They rule the head and face by ♈; the heart and back by ♌, and the hips and thighs by ♐. They give the Bilious, or Choleric Temperament. People born under these signs require more sunlight. The ☉ and ♂, the fiery planets, are closely affiliated with the Fire Signs. These signs are connected with the vital heat of the body, oxygen, and also rule the Spirit, and are known to give increased physical strength and vitality when rising on the Asc. They are the strongest signs for vitality when upon the Asc. at B., or the ☉ in them, but are not good signs for the ☽, as they are not in harmony with the nature of the ☽, as the ☽ is cold and watery by nature. The ☉ in a fire sign gives a strong constitution and vitality, with much Prana, or internal force, and great power to resist disease, but with the danger of excess of force. The ☽ in a fire sign tends to a hasty and excitable nature, and to impeded, retarded, prevented, slow and difficult functions, and espec. with females. The ☽ in ♈ tends to brain disorders; in ♌, palpitation of the heart, and in ♐, nervous debility due to too much haste and excitement in the life. When strong on the Asc. at B., or with many planets in them, these signs tend to fever, hot diseases, inflammation, diseases arising from choler; hectic fevers, eruptions, erysipelas, adhesions, fusions, and to cause injury or death by cuts, stabs, blows, gunshot wounds, fire, burns, lightning, etc. (See Aries, Choleric, Fevers, Imagination, Impulsive, Inflammation, Leo, Majority; "Operations" under Nature; Sagittarius, and the various subjects mentioned in this Article).

**Fires**—Conflagrations—Are governed by ♂, and happen to the individual when he is under ♂ afflictions and directions, and to a community when the ☽ is afflicted by ♂ or ♅. (For other causes of Fires see Family, Forest Fires, Great Fires, Home, Ships, Theatre, and the various paragraphs in this section).

**Fires of Life**—(See "Fires" under Life).

**Forest Fires**—An eclipse of the ☽ in ♈.

**Great Fires**—Injury and Loss of Life By—Eclipses of the ☉ or ☽ in fire signs, and occurring in regions under the rule of these signs, and which are under the shadow of the eclipse; ♄ lord of the year at the Vernal Equi., in ♒, and occi.; ♂ lord of the year at the Vernal, and in a fiery sign; Comets appearing in the ruling sign of a Country tend to great fires in such places. (For information concerning the causes of the great London Fire of 1866, see "Bull's Horns" under Bulls).

**Heat**—(See the various paragraphs under Burns, Heat).

**Home**—Accidents, Injury, or Death by Fire In the Home—(See Home).

**Hurts by Fire**—Wounds, Injury, or Accidents by Fire—(See Accidents, Injuries, in this section).

**Incendiarism**—Pyromania—(See Incendiarism).

**Injury by Fire**—Prejudice by Fire or Heat—The ☉ setting in ♌, and afflicted by malefics, and espec. if the ☉ be near the Ascelli; the ☉ or ☽ to the ♂ or ill-asps. ♂ by dir., and espec. when in fiery signs; the ☉ to the Ascelli or Praesepe; ♂ holding dominion at B., elevated above the Lights, and affl. the hyleg; the ☽ passing the place of the radical ♂ at a Solar Rev.; ♂ Sig. ♂ the ☉ at B., or by dir.; ♂ afflicted in fiery signs and ♂ or ill-asp. the Asc. by dir.; in Hor'y Q., ♂ in the Asc., and a malefic planet with the lord of the 1st H.; the ill-asps. of ♂ by dir. to the ☉, ☽, Asc., or M.C.; afflictions in ♐; the 5° ♎ on the Asc. (See Accidents, Danger, Death, and the various paragraphs in this section).

**Journeys**—Fire On Short or Inland Journeys—Danger of Injury By—Malefics in the 3rd H., in a fiery sign, and affl. the ☉ or ☽. On Voyages these same conditions would prevail over the 9th H., the house of Foreign Travel. (See "Ships" in this section).

**Killed**—In a Fire—(See Death, Family, Music Hall, Theatres, in this section).

**Life**—The Fires of Life—(See "Fires" under Life).

**Lightning**—Death or Injury By—(See Lightning).

**Liquids**—Hot Liquids—Injuries By—(See "Hot Liquids" under Heat; Scalds).

**Music Hall**—Killed in a Fire In—Case —See "Lafayette", No. 812, in 1001 N.N. (See "Theater" in this section).

**Prejudice by Fire**—(See Danger, Injury, in this section).

**Property Loss**—By Fire—♂ affl. in the 4th H.; ♂ ♂ ♄ in the 10th or 4th H. (See "Family" in this section).

**Pyromania**—(See Incendiarism).

**Scalds**—(See "Hot Liquids" under Heat; Scalds).

**Sea**—Fire At Sea—(See "Ships" in this section; "Voyages" under Lightning).

**Searing**—(See "Burning" under Blindness; "Searing" under Burns).

**Ships**—Danger of Injury by Fire on Ships At Sea—Malefics in the 9th H. in fiery signs, and espec. ♂, and affl. the ☉ or ☽. There is danger of fire at Sea when a ship sails when ♂ is in the Asc., and affl. the ☽. (See Ships).

**Short Journeys**—Fire On, and Danger By—(See "Journeys" in this section).

**Signs**—The Fiery Signs of the Zodiac —(See "Fire Signs" in this section).

**Spinal Spirit Fire**—(See Azoth, Ether; "Canal" under Spine).

**Theater Fire**—188 Lives Lost In—See "Exeter", No. 717, in 1001 N.N. (See "Music Hall" in this section).

**Violent Death**—By Fire—(See "Death", and the various paragraphs in this section; "Death" under Violent).

**Voyages**—Dangers by Fire On—(See "Ships" in this section).

**Wounds By**—(See Accidents, Blindness, Burns, Injuries, and the various paragraphs in this section).

**FIRST**—

**First-Born Child**—(See "First-Born" under Children).

**First House**—The Ascendant—The Rising Sign—This is a masculine house, and corresponds to the ♈ Sign. This house is a vital center, or part, of the horoscope, and contains the dominant features of the Life that are to be expressed and worked out. The three vital centers of the map are the ☉, ☽, and Asc. This house signifies the nature, life and health of the native, and relates to all questions of life, health, external complaints, appearance, stature, shape, size, color, body blemishes, and also sickness and accidents. It becomes the Sig. in Hor'y Q. in all cases where the life and health are considered. It rules the form, constitution, the bodily temperament, the bodily stamina, animal heat, the health, the personality, general characteristics, and indicates the construction and peculiarities of the physical body; rules the head, eyes, and face. It signifies all matters which affect the physical body, the mind, sickness, travel, health, change of residence, birth or death of children, and the fortunes of the native in general, and has significance of the Life of Man. The physical appearance, description of the body, the strength and vitality of the body, the height, weight, color of the eyes and hair, etc., are largely determined by the sign and degree rising on the cusp of this house, or the Ascendant. The position of the ruler of the Asc., and planets rising, tend to modify the personal appearance. (See Decanates). The 1st H. rules light colors and white. The 1st H. shows the organic elements, the physiological factors, and the physical characteristics which determine the amount of organic resistance, and the strength of the body. It also shows the degree of receptivity to diseases, and which may affect the part of the body ruled by the sign rising. The Asc. denotes, according to the sign rising, the part of the body more liable to affliction from external causes, and is the Indicator of Disease. (See the Ascendant influences in the paragraph, "Arguments for Death" under Death). The benefics, ♃ and ♀, in the 1st H. at B. indicate a good constitution, and much vitality. The malefics in the Asc. at B. denote scars, marks, moles, and defects of the head and face. The 1st H. and its conditions at B., and by dir., signify all diseases in the head, face, eyes, ears, nose, mouth, and foul breath. This house is closely related to the Feelings, Sensations, the Emotions, the Passions, the Manners, the Disposition, the quality of the Mind, etc., according to the nature of the sign rising, signs intercepted in, or partly ruling the Asc. The planet ruling the sign on the Asc. at B. is considered the principal Ruling Planet of the horoscope. (For the nature and meaning of the different kinds of signs on the Asc. at B., see Fire, Air, Earth, Water Signs, under these subjects. Also see Cardinal, Fixed, Mutable, External; "Zodiac" under Degrees). The actual degree rising on the Asc. at B. is to be considered as though it were a planet in forming judgment of the native as to his mind, body, strength, diseases subject to, etc., and all aspects to this degree are to be noted. The degree on the Asc. governs the brain, the body, and according to the sign rising gives a predisposition to certain afflictions and diseases of the body. Planets in the Asc., together with the planet ruling the rising sign, rule the physical body, and the sign and house position of the ruler of the Asc., the aspects to it, and the condition of its disposer, should be considered. The Asc. under certain conditions may become Hyleg. In a nocturnal horoscope the Asc. becomes hyleg if the ☽ is incr., with both the ☉ and ☽ below the horizon and not in a hylegiacal place. In a diurnal horoscope the Asc. may become hyleg if the ☉ or ☽ are not in a hylegiacal place. The Asc. may become Anareta when the ☽ is hyleg. In Mundane Astrology the 1st H., or the Asc., rules the Public Health generally. (See Anareta, Ascendant, Hyleg).

**First Quarter**—Of the ☽—(See "First Quarter" under Moon).

**First Year**—Of Life—(See Infancy).

**FISH**—Fishes—Fishes are ruled by the ♓ sign, which is known as the sign of "The Fishes."

**Death of Fish**—In the Seas and Rivers—Death of Living Creatures In the Waters—Afflictions in ♋, and espec. in the rivers, as ♋ rules rivers; afflictions in ♓ tend to destroy life in the Seas; ♄ in ♋ or ♓, ℞, lord of the year at the Vernal Equi., and affl. by ♂; ♃ in ♓, lord of the year at the Vernal, and affl. by ♄ or ♂; ♂ in ♓ and lord of the year at the Vernal; ♂ in ♌, occi., and lord of the year at the Vernal; Eclipses of the ☉ or ☽ in ♍ or ♓; an Eclipse of the ☉ in the 2nd Dec. of ♓; Comets appearing in ♋ or ♓. (See "Virus" under Pestilence).

**Fishing**—Fond of—(See Sports).

**FISSURE**—A Groove or Cleft—

**Anus**—Fissure of—(See Anus).

**Lip**—Harelip—A Congenital Fissure of the Lip—(See Harelip).

**Palate**—Cleft Palate—(See Palate).

**Rectum**—Fissure of—(See "Fissure" under Anus).

**Spine**—Cleft In—(See "Spina Bifida" under Spine). See Cleft, Crevice, Excrescences, Fistula, Hemorrhoids.

**FISTULA**—Fistulous Tumor—Fistula Near the Anus—A ♄, ♂, and ♀ disease; a ♉, ♏, ♐ disease; caused by afflictions in ♏ or ♐; caused by afflictions in ♉ by reflex action, and with ♉ or ♏ on the Asc.; the ☉ affl. in ♏ or ♐; the ☉ in ♐, ☌ or ill-asp. any of the malefics as promittors; the ☽ in ♏, ☌ or ill-asp. ♄ (or ☿ if he be of the nature of ♄) at the beginning of an illness or at decumb.; ♄ or ♂ in the Asc. or M.C., in ♋, ♑, or ♓, and in signs ascribed to animals or fishes; ♄ in ♏, occi., and affl. the ☉, ☽, or Asc.; ♃ affl. in ♏; a ♂ disease; ♂ in an angle, occi. of the ☉ and ori. of the ☽; ♂ in ♏ and affl. the ☽ or Asc.; ♂ in ♏ in the 6th H.; ♂ influence overlaid and intermixed with other planets, and espec. with the malefics; a ♀ disease, and afflictions to ♀; caused by ♀ when the dominion of death is vested in her; the malefics angular in ♋, ♏, or ♓, or in signs ascribed to animals or fishes; the Asc. to the □ or ☍ ♄ by dir.; Subs at PP, LPP. (See Anus, Discharges, Hemorrhoids, Rectum).

**Buttocks**—Fistulous Tumors In—(See Buttocks).

**Death from Fistula**—♀ affl. the hyleg by dir.; ♀ badly affl. at B., and holding the dominion of death.

**Thighs**—Fistulous Tumors In—A ♐ disease, and afflictions in ♐. (See Thighs, Tumors).

**FITS**—Convulsions—Convulsive Fits or Spasms—A Sudden Paroxysm—

**Causes**—Liable To—Tendency To—Fits, or Convulsions are a disease of ♅, ☿, the ☽, and of the ♈, ♋, and ♌ signs; the ☉ or ☽ hyleg, ☌ or ill-asp. ♄ or ♂, and the hyleg much affl. at B.; the ☽ hyleg in ♈ or ♌, and afflicted, and espec. in females; the ☽ to the ☌ or ill-asps. ♂ by dir., and espec. in children, and may result in death; the ☽ and ☿ receiving the evil rays from ♅ or ♄; the ☽ affl. in ♈, ♋, or ♌, and affl. the hyleg therefrom; afflictions to the ☽ at B., and espec. by ♅, ♄, or ♂; the ☽ and ☿ ☌ each other, or ☌ the Asc., and evilly aspected by ♄ or ♂ from angles, and espec. ♄ by day, or ♂ by night, liable to fits, but if ♂ by day, and ♄ by night, they are apt to be frantic or melancholic; ♄ angular, holding dominion, elevated above the Luminaries, and affl. the hyleg; ♄ or ♂ affl. the ☉ or ☿ in common signs; a ☿ disease; ☿ much affl. at B., and by dir.; ☿ affl. in ♌; ☿ affl. by ♄ or ♅; ☿ in a common sign and affl. by ♄ or ♂; malefics in the M.C., elevated above the Lights, and ♄ holding dominion; a preponderance of planets in fixed signs. (See Convulsions. Also note the various paragraphs in this section).

**Children**—Fits In—(See Causes, Dentition, Spasms, in this section).

**Convulsions**—(See Convulsions; "Causes" in this section).

**Convulsive Movements**—(See "Movements" under Convulsions).

**Curable Fits**—If ♃ or ♀ be ori., or in angles, and have any configuration with the ☽ at B., the disease is curable; if the ☽ is with ♃ the disease can be cured by medicine; if the ☽ is with ♀ it will cure itself; if the benefics are cadent or occi., and the malefics ori., they will be incurable. (See Curable; "Curable" under Epilepsy; Incurable).

**Death by Fits**—By Convulsions—By Spasms—♃ affl. the hyleg by dir., and ♃ much affl. at B.; ♂ in ♉ near Caput Algol, or in ♏ in ☍ to Algol, and at the same time in □ or ☍ the ☉ or ☽; cardinal signs show death by fits; mutable signs show death by spasms. (See "Causes" in this section; "Death" under Epilepsy).

**Dentition**—Fits During—(See "Dentition" under Teeth).

**Drink**—Fits of Drink and Sensuality—(See "Fits" under Drink; Sensuality).

**Epilepsy**—Eclampsia—Constant Fits In—(See "Constant" under Epilepsy).

**Falling Fits**—Falling Sickness—Fainting—(See "Falling Fits" under Fainting).

**Females**—Women—Fits In—(See Fainting, Hysteria).

**Frantic**—(See "Causes" in this section; Frantic).

**Fury**—Alternate Fits of Fury and Melancholy—(See "Fits" under Fury; Madness, Mania, Raving).

**Hysterical Fits**—(See Hysteria).

**Incurable Fits**—(See "Curable" in this section).

**Liable to Fits**—(See "Causes" in this section).

**Long Standing**—Fits of Long Standing—A ☽ disease and affliction; the ☽ hyleg and affl. by malefics.

**Mania**—Fits of—(See "Fits" under Mania).

**Melancholic Fits**—The combined influence of ♄ and ♂ induces to alternate fits of melancholy and fury. (See Fury, Melancholy; "Causes" in this section).

**Nervous Affections**—Fits of—Are more frequent toward the New and Full Moon. (See Nerves; "Full Moon", "New Moon", under Moon).

**Obsessions**—Fits of—(See "Fits" under Obsessions).

**Sensuality**—Fits of—(See "Drink" in this section).

**Spasms**—(See Convulsions, Epilepsy; "Spasms" under Spasmodic; "Dentition" under Teeth; Causes, Death, in this section).

**Strong Fits**—The ☽ in ♌ and affl. by the ☉ or ♂ when taken ill (Hor'y).

**Swooning Fits**—(See Fainting). See Contractions, Delirium, Eclampsia, Erratic, Insanity, Paroxysms.

**FIXED**—

**Fixed Habits**—Fixed Opinions—Not Given to Changes—Many planets in Fixed Signs at B.; fixed signs on the angles; ♄ a strong ruler at B.; good asps. of ♄ to the ☉, ☽, and ☿. (See Habits, Opinions).

**Fixed Ideas**—(See "Anxiety Neuroses" under Anxiety; Ideals, Ideas, Judgment, Monomania, Notions, Opinions).

**Fixed Signs**—The Strong Signs—Constitutional Signs—Foundation Signs—The Earthquake or Seismic Signs—The four Fixed Signs are ♉, ♌, ♏, and ♒, and are ruled by ♀, the ☉, ♂, and ♄ respectively. These four signs form the Fixed Cross, and are all in □ or ☍ asp. to each other, and planets in any one of them tend to affect all the other parts under the rule of the fixed signs. The Fixed Signs correspond to the Succedent Houses. Fundamentally these signs rule the vital parts, as the throat, heart, blood, and the generative system, and all parts or organs under their rule, such as the vocal organs, nose, neck, trunk, sex organs, urinary organs, bladder, excretory system, rectum, urethra, the legs below the knees, as the calves and ankles. The fixed signs give general strength of constitution, endurance, patience of mind, and are thus called the Strong, or Foundation Signs. They are more robust than the cardinal and common signs. They tend to arouse the Desire Nature, and to give stamina and persistence in action. They relate to Feeling and Emotion; are Vital in Temperament, and correspond to the Heart and Life. The Fixed Signs are also called "The Vicious Circle" because of their fixed and unyielding nature. Fixed Sign people are strongly bound by their habits, and are difficult to change or influence, and when a disease gets a firm hold upon them they usually die of it, but tend to cooperate with the Healer, and try to get well. Afflictions from fixed signs tend to cause deep-seated, lingering, tedious, chronic, and permanent diseases, and more difficult to cure or remedy. Many planets in fixed signs at B. tend to give greater resistance to disease, but to prolong disease, and give less power to throw off disease when it once gets a deep hold on the system. A list of the diseases ruled and given by the fixed signs is given under these signs, and for which see "Diseases Ruled By" under Taurus, Leo, Scorpio, Aquarius. Their principle diseases are those of the throat, heart, blood, sex organs, and lower limbs, as in the calves and ankles. (See "Disease" under Nature). The ♒ sign espec. rules the blood, and afflictions in ♒ tend to blood disorders, impure blood, disturbed circulation, etc. These signs also rule strongly over bronchitis, spinal complaints, suffocation, diseases of the back, diphtheria, stone, gravel, bladder troubles, disorders of the excretory system, etc. The throat (♉), and the sex organs (♏) are closely related by opposite signs, and the removal of any part of the sex organs tends to affect the voice, and in women tends to a masculine voice, and in men to an effeminate voice. Removal of the tonsils in childhood tends to make the puberty period more disturbed, and also later childhood and parturition more difficult and painful. Afflictions in these signs at B. tend to hereditary and organic diseases. Saturn in a fixed sign at B., or at the beginning of a disease, tends to be a sore afflictor. On the angles, and espec. on the Asc., they tend to lessen the chances of Insanity, and make the native better able to resist trouble, and protect the mind under stress, but when once disturbed in mind or health, the fixed signs on the angles make equipoise more difficult. The Fixed Signs show death by drowning, suffocation, strangling, hanging; by blood disorders, throat and heart trouble, disorders of the Generative System, the Excretory and Urinary Systems. Afflictions in fixed signs make punishment by Law, or sentence of a Judge, more durable, and espec. when the radical map denotes the danger of imprisonment. Much can be said about the fixed signs, and their influences are much referred to throughout this Work. Here are two cases of individuals who had a Stellium of planets in the Fixed Signs at B. See "Male", Chap. 8, page 48, and "Female", page 49, in Daath's Medical Astrology. One was a Monster, and the other a Dwarf and Imbecile. For further study along this line see Ankles, Back, Blood, Bronchitis, Calves, Chronic, Circulation, Constancy, Constitution, Continuity, Decanates, Deep-Seated, Diphtheria, Drowning, Duration; "Earthquakes" under Earth; Emotions, Endurance, Excretion, Feelings, Generation, Gravel, Habits, Hanging; "Fixity" under Head; Healers, Heart, Heredity, Imprisonment (see Prison); Incurable, Insanity, Invalids, Judges, Lingering, Long; "Monomania" under Mania; Neck; "Negative Signs" under Negative; Nose, Organic, Patience, Perseverance, Prejudice, Prison, Puberty; "Changes" under Residence; Sex Organs, Slow, Spine, Stone, Strangulation, Structural, Suffocation, Suicide, Tedious, Throat, Tonsils, Trunk, Voice, Wastings, etc.

**Fixed Stars** — Constellations — (See Stars).

**FLABBY**—Soft—Flaccid—Relaxed—A ☽ influence and disease. A weak ♂ at B. tends to flaccidity of the muscles; ♓ on the Asc.; ♓ gives flabby skin. (See Collapse, Consumptions, Emaciation, Laxity, Muscles, Puffing, Relaxation, Soft, Tissues, Wasting).

**FLANKS**—The Iliac Region—Ruled by ♏. All diseases in the Flanks are signified by the 7th H., and caused by afflictions in 7th H., and also in ♏. (See Iliac, Sides).

**FLAT**—Flatter—Flattened—

**Face**—The Face Flatter at the Sides —(See Decanates).

**Feet**—Flat Feet—(See "Splay Foot" under Feet).

**Head**—The Head Flatter On the Sides, and Square-Shaped—(See Decanates).

**FLATULENCE** — Gas In the Digestive Canal — Wind — Borborygmus — Colic — Gas — Bloating — Distentions — Inflations—Tympanies, etc.—

**Bilious Flatulency**—(See Bilious).

**Bloating**—(See "Stomach" under Gas; "Distended" under Stomach; "Bowels" under Wind).

**Bowels** — Flatulence In — Colic — Rumbling — (See "Borborygmus", "Colic" under Bowels; "Bowels" under Wind).

**Colic**—Flatulent Colic—(See "Colic" under Bowels).

**General Flatulence**—A ☽, ♃, ☿, ♊, ♋, ♏, and ♒ affliction; ♃ tends to general flatulence thru Plethora, from overeating, etc., and by wind in the blood when ♃ is afflicted in ♉; ☿ affl. in the airy signs ♊ or ♒ tends to general flatulence by wind in the blood, veins, etc. (See Bloating, Distentions, Gas, Inflation, Puffing; "Puffy Body" under Swellings; Tympanies; "Windiness" under Veins; "Blood" under Wind).

**Inflated Body**—(See Inflation).

**Stomach** — Flatulence In — Gas In — Bloating — ♄ in ♋. (See Belching; "Stomach" under Gas; Gripings, Indigestion, Inflation; "Distended", "Wind", under Stomach; Tympanites, Wind).

**FLESH**—The Flesh—Ruled by ♀. Also ruled and influenced by the earthy signs. (See "Earthy Signs" under Earth).

**Loss of Flesh**—(See Anaemia, Emaciation, Malnutrition, Thin, Wasting, Weight).

**Much Flesh**—Corpulent—(See Corpulent, Fleshy).

**FLESHY**—Corpulent—Stout—(See Corpulent; "Body" under Fat; Obesity, Portly, Stoutness).

**Face** — Fleshy Face — (See "Fleshy" under Face).

**Feet**—Fleshy Hands and Feet—(See "Fleshy" under Hands, Feet).

**Fleshy Body** — The ☉ in ♉ or ♓, in partile asp. the Asc., short and fleshy; the ☉ in ♏, partile the Asc., square and fleshy; the ☉ ☌ ♀ in ♓, fleshy after middle life; the ☉ strong at B., and dignified, fleshy, strong, tall, and of large frame; the ☽ Sig. of the party, short and fleshy; the ☽ in ♈, partile the Asc., middle sized, but rather plump and fleshy; the ☽ in ♋, partile the Asc., fleshy, middle sized, and well-proportioned; the ☽ in ♋, Sig. of the party, and in no asp. to the ☉ or ♂, indicates a short and fleshy person in Hor'y Q.; the ☽ in ♏, partile the Asc., a fleshy, short, thick, and ill-made body; ♄ in S. Lat. tends to a fleshy, smooth body, but in N. Lat. to one more hairy, lean, and raw-boned; ♃ in ♋, partile the Asc., fleshy but disproportioned; ♃ in ♏ or ♓, partile the Asc., middle-sized, full, and fleshy; ♂ in ♓, partile the Asc., fleshy, mean and short body; ♂ Sig. in ♓, short and fleshy; ♀ in ♉, partile the Asc., fleshy but well-made; ♀ in ♓, partile the Asc., middle-sized, but rather plump and fleshy; ☿ in ♒, partile the Asc., middle-sized and fleshy; the first half of ♈ when on the Asc. gives more flesh; ♉ on the Asc., or the ☉ in ♉, short, stocky and fleshy; born under ♉ or ♓, fleshy after middle life; ♋ on the Asc., short and fleshy; the first parts of ♋ or ♑ ascending make the body more fleshy than the latter parts; ♏ on the Asc., fleshy and thick body; the latter part of ♐ on the Asc. tends to a fleshy body; ♓ on the Asc., a pale, sickly, short and fleshy body; water signs on the Asc. (See Bulky, Corpulent, Fat, Full, Phlegmatic, Plump, Puffing, Squat, Stout; "Fleshy" under Swellings; Thick).

**Growths**—A Small Fleshy Growth—(See Caruncle, Growths. See "Tumor" in this section).

**Hands**—Fleshy Hands and Feet—(See "Fleshy" under Hands, Feet).

**Tumors**—Fleshy Tumors—(See Caruncle, Sarcoma).

**FLEXED**—Flexible—Flexion—Flexure—Pliable—

**Flexed Signs** — (See "Mutable Signs" under Mutable).

**Flexible Mind**—A Plastic Mind—More Easily Influenced — Changeable — (See Changes, Environment, External, Influenced, Mutable, Negative; "Many Changes" under Residence; Restless, Susceptible, Unstable, Vacillating).

**Flexion**—Bending—The flexion, bending, falling, or prolapsus of organs is a ♄ influence, and due to a weakening of the part. (See Bending; "Flexion" under Womb).

**Hepatic Flexure**—(See Liver).

**Sigmoid Flexure**—(See Sigmoid).

**Splenic Flexure**—(See Spleen).

**FLIGHTINESS** Flightiness of the Mind —Flight of Ideas—Flighty—A ♆, ♅, ♂, and ☿ disease; ♆ or ♅ afflicting ☿; ♅ affl. in ♓; ♃ or ♂ affl. in ♈, and due to a rush of blood to the head. (See "Mental Chaos" under Chaotic; Concentration, Confusion; "Dreamy Mind" under Dreams; "Blood" under Head; Ideas, Imagination; "Absent Minded" under Mind; Obsessions, Scattering, Vacillating, Weird, etc.).

**FLOODING** — Flooding Hemorrhage — (See "Flooding", "Hemophilia", under Hemorrhage; "Flooding" under Menses; "Epistaxis" under Nose; "Hemorrhage" under Womb).

**FLOODS**—Inundations—Violent Rains —Deluges—Great Suffering or Loss of Life From—An eclipse of the ☉ or ☽ in watery signs, and espec. in places ruled by such signs; the ♏ sign ascending at the Vernal E., floods and afflictions by venomous creatures. (See "Epidemics" under Cholera; Clouds, Famine, Moisture, Rain, Storms, Tempests, Thunder, Venomous, Waters, Weather; "Storms" under Wind).

**FLOW**—

**Flow of Blood**—♂ has to do with all injuries attended by a flow of blood. (See "Flow of Blood" under Blood).

**Head**—Flow, or Rush of Blood to the Head — (See Determination; "Blood" under Head; Rush).

**Humours** — Flow of Humours — (See Discharges, Defluxions, Fluxions; "Flow" under Humours).

**Overflowing**—(See Flooding, Overflowing).

**FLOWERS**—(See Herbs, Plants, Vegetation).

**FLUIDS** — The Fluidic System — The Liquid Secretions or Excretions of the Body — Humours — The Fluids of the system are ruled by ♆, the ☽, and the watery signs. The ☽ exerts a strong fluidic influence over fluids in the system, or anywhere in Nature, as over the Tides, Rivers, Water, etc. The ☽ is fluidic and cleansing, and tends to mutations and changes in the body by acting thru the fluids. The ☽ rules or dominates all fluids, yet her real dominion is over the neutral solution, the basic or bland humor which forms the medium thru which certain substances can act and react, and put into the forms necessary for the various functions of the body. Thus in milk the ☽ rules the basic fluid, but other ingredients are developed in milk by the action of the ☉, ♃, and ♄. (See Milk). The ☽ rules the base of any fluid, and not fluids as a whole, in specialized forms, resulting from the action of other influences, agents or reagents. The watery signs are especially connected with fluids. For the different fluids ruled by the watery signs see Cancer, Scorpio, Pisces. Also the fluids of the body are ruled over and controlled by the posterior lobe of the Pituitary Body, ruled by ♅, and espec. the circulation of the fluids in the kidneys. The following subjects have to do with the various fluids, juices, secretions, and excretions of the body, which see in the alphabetical arrangement when not considered here—

**Abdomen**—Fluids of—(See Abdomen, Bowels).

**Accumulations In**—The afflictions of ♃ cause accumulations in the fluids themselves. (See Accumulative).

**Acids**—(See Acids).

**Ailments Of**—Disorders and Disturbances of the Fluids of the Body—Irregularities of—Disturbed Circulation of—Fluidic Derangements—The ☉ affl. in the watery signs ♋, ♏, or ♓ tends to disorders of the fluidic system; the ☽ affl. by ♆; the ☽ hyleg in ♋, ♏, or ♓, and afflicted, and espec. in females; afflictions to the ☽; ☽ diseases; ♆ in ♓, and affl. the hyleg or Asc.; ♆ in ♓ in the 6th H.; ♄ tends to impede the circulation of the fluids; ♄ angular at B., holding dominion, and elevated above the Lights; ♄ or ☿ holding dominion at B., and in familiarity with each other, tend to disturbances of the fluids in the chest, stomach, and throat; ♄ in an angle, occi. of the ☉, and ori. of the ☽, and ♄ also be in familiarity with ☿; ♂ ☌ ♃ tends to increase the density of fluids in the body; ♓ on cusp the 6th H. (Note the various paragraphs in this Article).

**Amniotic Fluid**—(See Foetus).

**Aqueous**—(See "Aqueous Humor" under Eyes; "Aqueous Vapors" under Rain; "Aqueous" under Tumors).

**Arterial Blood**—(See Arteries, Blood, Circulation).

**Bile**—Gall—(See Bile).

**Blood**—(See Arteries, Blood, Circulation, Veins).

**Bowels**—Fluids of—(See the various paragraphs under Abdomen, Bowels).

**Brain**—Fluids and Secretions of—(See Brain, Cerebral, Meninges, Pineal, Pituitary, etc.).

**Brashes**—(See Brash).

**Breasts**—Fluids of—(See Breasts, Milk).

**Bronchial Fluids**—(See Bronchial, Coughs, Lungs, Mucus).

**Capillaries; Catarrhs; Cavities;**

**Cell Fluids**—(See Cells).

**Changes In**—(See "Mutation" in this section).

**Chest**—Fluids of—(See Bronchial, Chest, Lungs, Thorax; "Ailments" in this section).

**Chyle; Chyme; Circulation**—Of the Blood—Of the Fluids—Disorders of—(See Arteries, Blood, Circulation, Veins; "Ailments" in this section).

**Collection of Fluids**—In the System—(See Accumulative, Cavities, Congestion, Cysts, Humours, Receptacles, Serum, Swellings, Watery; "Accumulations" in this section).

**Complaints**—Fluidic Complaints—(See "Ailments", and the various paragraphs in this section).

**Congestion**—Of Fluids—(See Congestion).

**Coryza**—(See Nose).

**Coughs; Crusts**—Dried Exudate—(See Crusts).

**Cysts; Deficiency Of**—Lack of—Caused by ♄ afflictions. (See Deficient, Retarded, Stoppages, Suppressions).

**Defluxions; Density Increased**—(See "Ailments" in this section).

**Depletion Of**—Caused by ♄. (See Depletion, Diminished, Suppressed; Nerve, Vital, in this section).

**Derangements Of**—(See "Ailments" in this section; Deranged).

**Digestive Fluids**—(See Acids, Digestion, Gastric, Juices, Stomach).

**Dilution Of**—(See Diluted).

**Discharges; Disorders Of**—(See "Ailments", and the various paragraphs in this section).

**Disturbances Of**—(See "Ailments", and the various paragraphs in this section).

**Dropsies; Drying Up**—Of the Fluids—Caused by ♄, and are ♄ diseases. (See "Fluids" under Dryness).

**Ebb and Tide**—Of Fluids—(See "Full Moon", "New Moon", under Moon).

**Effusions; Elimination; Emissions;**

**Epistaxis**—(See Nose).

**Evacuations; Excessive**—Excessive Secretion of—Excess of—(See the various paragraphs under Excess).

**Excrementitious Fluids**—(See Excrement).

**Excretions; Exosmosis**—(See Osmosis).

**Expectorations; Exudations; Faeces;**

**Fat**—(See "Fluids" under Fat).

**Females**—Fluids In—(See "Ailments" in this section; Females, Menses).

**Fermentation Of**—(See Fermentation, Zymosis).

**Flow Of**—(See Flow).

**Fluxions; Fullness Of**—(See "Full Moon", "New Moon", under Moon).

**Functions**—(See the various paragraphs under Functions).

**Gastric Fluids**—(See Digestion, Gastric, Stomach).

**Glands; Glycogen; Hemorrhages;**

**High Blood Pressure**—(See "Pressure" under Blood).

**High Tide**—Of Fluids—(See "Full Moon" under Moon).

**Hindered**—The Fluids Hindered—♄ diseases and afflictions. (See Hindered, Retarded, Stoppages, Suppressions).

**Hot Fluids**—(See "Hot Liquids" under Heat).

**Humours; Hydro; Hyperaemia;**

**Impeded**—(See Circulation, Impeded, Retarded, Secretions, Suppressions; "Ailments" in this section).

**Increased**—(See "Excessive" in this section).

**Intercellular Fluids** — (See "Fluids" under Cells).

**Irregularities Of**—(See "Ailments" in this section; Irregular).

**Joints**—Fluids of—(See Synovial).

**Juices; Kidneys** — Fluids of — (See Kidneys, Pituitary Body, Urine).

**Lachrymal; Lack Of**—(See Deficient, Depletion, Diminished, Lack; "Drying Up", and the various paragraphs in this section).

**Lacteals**—(See Milk).

**Leucorrhoea; Liquids; Liver** — Fluids and Secretions of—(See Liver).

**Loss Of**—(See "Lack" in this section).

**Lymph; Membranes** — Fluids and Secretions of—(See Membranes).

**Menses; Milk; Moon**—The Moon and Fluids — (See the various paragraphs under Moon).

**Morbid Fluids**—Morbid Oozing—(See Exudations, Morbid, Osmosis).

**Mouth; Muscae Volitantes** — Floating Specks—(See "Muscae" under Eyes).

**Mucus; Mutation Of**—The physiological action of the ☽. (See "Physiological Action" under Moon).

**Nerve Fluids** — (See "Nerve Fluids" under Depletion; "Fluids" under Nerves).

**Nose** — Fluids of — (See the various paragraphs under Nose).

**Obesity; Obstructions Of**—Caused by ♄. (See Deposits, Obstructions, Secretions, Stoppages, Suppressions; "White Fluids" in this section).

**Oedema; Oils; Oozing** — (See Exudations, Osmosis).

**Osmosis; Pancreas**—Diastase of—(See Pancreas).

**Peritoneum** — Serum of — (See Peritoneum).

**Perspiration**—(See Sweat).

**Phlegm**—(See Mucus, Phlegm).

**Plastic Fluids**—(See Plastic).

**Plenitude** — Fluidic Plenitude — (See "Full Moon" under Moon).

**Plethora; Puffing; Pus; Receptacles;**

**Restricted**—The Fluids Restricted—(See Depletion, Retarded, Restricted, Suppressions; "Ailments", "Lack Of", in this section).

**Retarded; Retention;**

**Revitalization Of**—(See "First Quarter" under Moon).

**Rush Of**—Flow of—Determination of—(See Determination, Flow, Rush).

**Saliva; Secretions; Semen; Serum;**

**Sexual Fluids** — Normal or Abnormal Fluids from the Sex Organs—(See Discharges, Genitals, Generation, Leucorrhoea, Menses, Semen, Sex, Vagina, Womb, etc.).

**Skin**—Fluids of—Fluids from or Thru—(See Exudations, Glands, Oils, Skin, Sweat, etc.).

**Snuffling** — (See "Snaffling" under Nose).

**Spinal Fluids** — Ruled by ♆. (See Spine).

**Spitting; Sputum; Stomach**—Disturbances of Fluids of — (See "Ailments" in this section; Digestion, Gastric, Indigestion; "Fluids" under Stomach).

**Stoppages; Suppressions; Sweat;**

**Swellings**—(See Accumulative, Cysts, Dropsies, Puffing, Swellings, Tumors).

**Synovial Fluid** — Joints — (See Joints, Synovial).

**Tears**—Lachrymal Fluid—(See Tears).

**Thorax** — Chest — Fluids of — (See Chest, Lungs, Thorax; "Ailments" in this section).

**Throat** — Fluids of — (See Diphtheria, Fauces; "Restricted" under Throat; Tonsils; "Ailments" in this Article).

**Tide and Ebb Of**—(See "Full Moon", "New Moon", under Moon).

**Transudations**—Oozing—(See Exudations, Osmosis).

**Tumors**—Watery Tumors—(See Blisters, Cysts, Swellings; "Aqueous" under Tumors; Watery).

**Urine; Vagina**—Secretions and Fluids of—(See Vagina).

**Veins**—Venous Blood—(See Veins).

**Vital Fluid**—Depletion of—(See "Depletion", and the various paragraphs under Vital).

**Vitreous Humor**—(See "Vitreous" under Eyes).

**Vomiting; Water** — Water Brash — Watery Humours, etc.—(See Belching, Humours, Watery. Also note the various paragraphs in this section).

**White Fluids** — Of the Body — Body Oil—(See "Fluids" under White).

**Womb** — Fluids of, or From — (See Menses. Also note the various paragraphs under Womb).

**FLUOR ALBUS**—Whites—(See Leucorrhoea).

**FLUORIDE OF LIME**—Calcium Fluoride—This is one of the 12 Tissue, or fundamental Salts of the Body, and is ruled by the ♋ Sign. (See Lime, Salts; "Salts" under Zodiac).

**FLUSHINGS** — Heated Flushings — Hot Flashes—☉ diseases; ☉ ☌ ♂; ☉ ☌ ♂ in ♈, ♌, or ♐, and espec. when in the Asc. (See Blushing, Fevers, Heat).

**FLUX**—Fluxes—Fluxion—A Flowing—Fluxions, Catarrhal, and Continuous Fevers follow a Solar Periodicity, grow worse towards sunset. (See Periodicity; "Solar Periodicity" under Solar; "Magnetic", "Sunrise", "Sunset", under Sun).

**A Flux**—Suffers from a Flux— Liable To — A Flux Threatened — The ☉ in water signs at B., and to the ☌ or ill-asp. ♂ by dir.; the ☽ to the □ or ☍ ☉ by dir., a flux is threatened; the ☽ hyleg, and to the ill-asps. the ☉ by dir.; the ☽ in ♑, and affl. by the ☉ or ♂ when taken ill (Hor'y); ♄ causes when he has dominion, and afflicts the hyleg; a ♄ disease; ♂ in water signs, and to the ill-asps. the Asc. by dir.; ♀ affl. in ♍ or ♓; ☿ affl. in ♒. (See Catarrh).

**Belly** — Fluxes of the Belly — In Bowels, Abdomen—(See "Fluxes" under Belly).

**Bloody Flux**—Dysentery—The ☉ or ♂ in ♍ when the afflictors in the disease; the ☉ or ☽ affl. in ♍, and to the ☌ or ill-asp. ♂ by dir.; the ☉ to ☌ ♂ by dir., and in watery signs; ♂ affl. in ♍; ♂ affl. in water signs, and to the ☌ or ill-asp. the Asc. by dir.; ♂ ☌ Asc. by dir. if ♂ in a watery sign; a ♂ disease, and caused by ♂ afflictions; the Asc. to the □ or ☍ ♄ by dir. Bloody and sanguineous evacuations are worse at the Full ☽. (See Dysentery).

**Bowels** — Fluxes of — (See "Fluxes" under Belly, Bowels; Cholera, Diarrhoea, Dysentery, Typhoid).

**Death by Fluxes**—Caused by ♄ when he is the afflictor, holds dominion, and the dominion of death is vested in him; ♄ affl. the hyleg at B., and by dir., denotes death by; the ☉ to the place of Praesepe.

**Hemorrhoids**—Too Much Flux of the Hemorrhoids—(See Hemorrhoids).

**Prevalent**— Fluxes Prevalent—Planets in ♍ or the 6th H., and affl. at a Summer Solstice.

**Rheum** — Watery or Catarrhal Discharges—(See Rheum).

**Violent Fluxes** — ♂ affl. in watery signs, and to the ☌ or ill-asp. the Asc. by dir.; the Asc. to the □ or ☍ ♂ by dir., in water signs.

**Watery Flux** — (See Catarrh, Defluxions, Rheum, Watery).

**FLYING**—

**Flying Fowl**—Body Devoured by After Death—Destruction of—Resembles Fowls—(See Fowls).

**Flying Gout**—(See Gout).

**Flying Humours**—(See Humours).

**Flying Pains**—Running Pains—Afflictions in ♒; ♃ affl. in ♒, flying pains due to corruption of blood, and over-abundance of blood in the system; ☿ affl. in ♒, running pains in different parts of the body; ☿ affl. in ♏ when ☿ is the afflictor in the disease, running pains in the arms and shoulders. (See "Too Much Blood" under Blood; Running, Wandering).

**Flying Stones**—Injuries or Death By —(See "Assaults" under Stone).

**FOCUS**—Of the Eyes—Defects of—(See Accommodation, Sight).

**FOETUS** — Embryo — From conception, the following order of the influence of the planets is recognized. (1) The Physical Plasm is formed under ♄. (2) It becomes enveloped by the Amniotic Fluid under ♃. (3) The Limbs are developed under ♂ influence. (4) The ☉ produces Quickening. (5) Sex distinction is effected by ♀. (6) Brain development and specialization of the nerve filaments are done by ☿. The Embryo is the fecundated germ up to the 4th month. The Foetus is the product of conception after the 4th month of gestation. The following subjects have to do with the Foetus, the condition and development of the child, mentally and physically, during pregnancy, or its delivery.

**Abortion Of**—(See Abortion, Miscarriage).

**Accidents To** — Injuries To — (See "Mutilation" in this section).

**Beastly Form**—(See "Beastly Form" under Beasts).

**Birth Of** — Normal Birth of — Occurs under ♃, but the child is ushered into the world under the signature of ♂. (See Birth, Normal, Parturition).

**Born Alive**—Lives Only a Few Hours —Dies Soon After Birth—(See Abortion; "Death Soon After Birth" under Birth; "Born Almost Dead" under Children; Infancy).

**Caul Over Face**—(See "Caul" under Face).

**Childbirth**—(See Parturition).

**Conception** — (See the various paragraphs under Conception).

**Death at Birth**—(See "Death at Birth" under Birth, Children).

**Death In Womb**—(See Abortion, Stillborn).

**Death Soon After Birth**—(See "Born Alive" in this section).

**Defective Births** — (See "Defective" under Birth).

**Dumb**—Born Dumb—(See Dumb).

**Excision of Foetus**—Caesarian Operation Indicated—The ☉ or ☽ to the ☌ or ill-asp. ♂ by dir.; ♂ in ♏ at B., occi., and affl. the hyleg by dir.; ♂ in an angle, occi. of the ☉, and ori. of the ☽. (See "Mutilation" in this section).

**Faculties Improved** — (See "Beastly Form" under Beasts; Quickened" under Mental).

**Foolish**—Born Foolish—(See Foolish, Idiocy, Imbecile).

**Gestation** — (See Gestation, Pregnancy).

**Hermaphrodite**—(See this subject).

**Human Shape**—Is of Human Shape—(See Human).

**Ill-Formed**—(See "Beastly Form" under Beasts; Deformities; "Ill-Formed" under Ill; Inhuman, Monsters).

**Infancy**—(See the various paragraphs under Infancy).

**Inhuman** — Inhuman In Shape — (See "Beastly Form" under Beasts; Inhuman).

**Lateral Position** — Is assumed under ☽ influence.

**Lives Only Few Hours** — After Birth —(See "Born Alive" in this section).

**Monsters**—(See Monsters).

**Mortification Of**—♂ in an angle, occi. of the ☉, and ori. of the ☽.

**Mutilation Of**—The Foetus Extracted In Mangled Parts—♀ in an angle, and espec. in the Western angle, and ♄ be in ☌, or in configuration with her, or in mutual reception, and ♂ elevated above ♀, or ♂ in ☍ with ♀,—these influences tend to impotence in the male, abortions in the female, stillbirth, mangling of the child at B., or extraction in mangled parts.

**Nourishment**—The Embryo, or Foetus Not Nourished—The ☉ or ☽, as Giver of Life, in an angle, and in ☌ a malefic. (See Nutrition).

**Parturition** — (See the various paragraphs under Parturition).

**Pregnancy** — (See Conception, Gestation, Pregnancy).

**Premature Birth** — (See Abortion; "Seven Months Children" under Children; Miscarriage, Premature).

**Quickening**—(See Quickening).

**Rickets**—Foetal Rickets—(See Rickets).

**Savage** — (See "Beastly Form" under Beasts; "Animal Forms" under Monsters; Savage, Wild).

**Shape**—(See Human, Ill-Formed, Inhuman, in this section).

**Sickly** — The Child Will Be Sickly — (See the Introduction under Abortion; Sickly).

**Stillborn**—(See Abortion, Stillborn).

**Version** — Of the Foetus In Utero — (See "Version" under Womb).

**FOLLICLES** — Follicular — A Small Secretory Cavity or Sac—

**Hair Follicles** — Disorders of — (See "Barber's Itch" under Barbers, "Disorders" under Hair).

**Tonsilitis**—Follicular Tonsilitis—(See Tonsils).

**FOLLY**—Foolish Conduct—

**Disease and Sickness From** — Death From—Injury From—The ☽ affl. in ♏; ♏ on the Asc. at B., and espec. with ♂ therein, diseases arising from folly or anger. (See Anger, Conduct, Dissipation; "His Own Worst Enemy" under Enemies; Excesses, Foolhardy, Foolish, Forethought, Hasty, Impulsive, Indiscretions, Judgment, Morals, Passion, Rashness, Recklessness, Self-Undoing, Temper, Violent; "Death" under Wounds).

**Misery From** — Misery and Sickness From—Lord of the 12th H. in the 1st H. (See Misery, Twelfth House).

**Moral Folly**—Is due to the perverted and atonic action of ♀. (See "Loose Morals" under Morals).

**FOMAHAUT**—A star of the 1st magnitude, in the 2° ♓, of the nature of ♀ and ☿. Is said to cause bites by venomous creatures when joined with the ☉ or ♂. Also said to bring Calamity. (See Calamity, Reptiles, Stings, Venomous).

**FOMENTATIONS**—Hot Fomentations—(See Emollient).

**FONTANELLES**—(See this subject under Head).

**FOOD** — Diet — Nourishment — Nutrition — Eating — Provisions, etc. — Food is ruled by ☿, the ♍ sign, and the 6th H. In a general way ☿ represents food stuff. The subject of Food is also largely considered under Assimilation, Diet, Digestion, Drink, Eating, Nutrition, etc. The following subjects have to do with Food, which see in the alphabetical arrangement when not considered here—

**Abnormal Eater**—(See "Excesses" under Eating).

**Acquired Diseases** — And Food — (See Acquired).

**Albumen** — Albumin — (See Albumen, Proteids).

**Appetite; Assimilation;**

**Autointoxication; Belching;**

**Bolts the Food** — (See "Fast Eater" under Eating).

**Bowels**—Decomposition of Food In—(See "Putrid Matter" under Bowels).

**Careful In Diet**—Fastidious—(See "Careful" under Diet; "Eccentric" in this section).

**Chewing of Food**—Insufficient Mastication — Bolts the Food — (See "Fast Eater" under Eating).

**Chyle; Chyme; Coffee**—Craves Strong Coffee and Strong Drink—(See "Strong Drink" under Drink).

**Comfits; Comforts**—Of Life—As Food, Clothing, etc.—(See Comforts).

**Condiments**—Spiced, and Highly Seasoned Foods—Craving For—Such foods are ruled by ♂; desire for given by ♂ affl. in ♉ or ♋; ♂ in ♋ in the 1st, 5th, 6th H., and in evil asp. to ♃ or ♀; ♃ ☌ ♂ in ♋ or ♑; ♃ ☌ ♅ in the 1st or 6th H. Spices are ruled by ♀. (See "Good Things", "Rich Food", in this section).

**Cooked Foods**—Dr. Duz, in his book, "Astral Medicine", says that the organism needs cooked foods, as the fire in cooking them "Strikes off the noxious principles contained in raw substances, but thru the fragrancy it produces by their cooking, stimulates the gastric juice and anticipates the digestion." He also advocates the eating of meat. (See Meat).

**Corn**—Scarcity of—(See Scarcity).

**Cravings**—Abnormal Cravings Along Food Lines—♅ ☌ ☽, or ♅ □ or ☍ ♃ or ♀. (See Cravings, Drink. Also note the various paragraphs in this section).

**Crops**—Destruction of—(See Crops).

**Dainty Foods** — Fondness For — Fond of Good Living Generally—A ♉ influence; the 2nd Dec. of ♉ on the Asc., ruled by the ☽; ♃ affl. in ♉; ♃ or ♂ affl. in ♋. (See "Good Things", "Rich Foods", "Sweets", in this section).

**Decay Of** — Corruption of — Putrefaction of—(See "Putrid" under Bowels; Corruption, Decay, Fruit, Rotten, Vegetation).

**Decomposition Of** — In Stomach or Bowels—(See "Putrid" under Bowels; "Fermentation" under Stomach).

**Deglutition** — Swallowing Difficult — (See Deglutition).

**Desert**—Lost In the Desert—Without Food—(See Desert).

**Diet** — (See the various paragraphs under Diet).

**Digestion; Dislikes**—Has Strong Likes and Dislikes As To Food—♅ or ♄ affl. in ♋.

**Dissipation** — In Food and Drink — Principally ♉ and ♋ influence, and afflictions in these signs; ♂ affl. in ♉ or ♋; ♂ ☍ in □ ♅, ♃, or ♀; ♓ on Asc. (See Drink, Drunkenness, Eating, Excessess, Gluttony, Intoxication, etc.).

**Distribution** — Of Food—Assimilation of — Disturbed Distribution — (See Assimilation).

**Dress and Food**—Extravagant In—♂ in the 6th H. (See Dress, Extravagance, Luxuries; "Rich Food", and the various paragraphs in this section).

**Drink**—(See the various paragraphs under Drink).

**Drinking with Meals** — Excessive Drinking With—♅ ☌ ☽ in ♋, and in □ or ☍ ♂. (See Drink).

**Drought**—Dryness and Shortage of Food—(See Drought, Famine).

**Eating**—(See the various paragraphs under Eating).

**Eccentric**—Eccentric and Peculiar About Food—Fastidious—The ☉ ⚹ or △ ♅; ♆ in the 6th H.; ♆ or ♅ in ♍. (See Eccentric, Peculiar, Tastes; "Fastidious" in this section).

**Emaciation**—(See Assimilation, Emaciation; "Malnutrition" under Nutrition; Wastings).

**Enema**—Of Food—Rectal Feeding—(See Enema).

**Epicureans; Errors In Diet**—(See "Evil Diet" under Diet).

**Evil Diet**—Errors In Diet—Indiscretions In—Wrong Diet—(See "Evil Diet" under Diet).

**Excesses In**—Diseases and Surfeits Arising From—(See "Abnormal" under Appetite; "Excesses" under Diet; Eating, Feasting, Gluttony, Plethora, Surfeits).

**Expensive Foods**—(See Dainty, Rich, in this section).

**External**—Diseases Arising from External Causes, as Food, Clothing, Climate, etc.—(See External).

**Extravagant**—In Food—(See "Dress and Food", "Excesses", "Rich", in this section).

**Famine; Fast Eater**—(See "Fast Eater" under Eating).

**Fastidious**—In Diet—Careful—Particular—(See "Careful", "Fastidious", under Diet; "Eccentric" in this section).

**Fatty Food**—Disorders By—(See "Foods" under Fat).

**Feasting; Feeding; Fermentation**—(See "Decomposition" in this section; Fermentation, Zymosis).

**Fondness**—For Foods Increased—In Hor'y Q. ♄ signifies a person who is a great eater; ♆ in fixed signs, rising, or in the 3rd or 9th H., and afflicted, tends to; ♃ affl. in ♉. (See "Excesses" in this section; "Excesses", "Great Eater", under Eating).

**Fruit**—Cannot Eat Fruit or Vegetables—(See Case, "Cannot Eat Fruit" under Fruit).

**Gluttony; Good Food**—Good Things To Eat—Fond of Good Food—Rich Food—Dainty Foods, etc.—The ☉ or ☽ in ♋, and espec. if ⚹ or △ ♀; ♃ ☌ ♂ in ♋ or ♑; ♂ in ♋, ⚹ or △ ♃ or ♀. (See Condiments, Rich, Sweets, in this section; Epicureans, Feasting).

**Gormandizing; Grains**—(See Corn, Grain, Scarcity, Wheat, etc.).

**Gustativeness; Habits**—Concerning Food—(See Careful, Eccentric, Fastidious, Impulsive, Unnatural, and the various paragraphs in this section).

**Hard To Please**—As to Food—♅ ☌ ☽ in ♋; ♅ in ♋, in □ or ☍ ♆; ♄ affl. in ♋. (See Eccentric, Peculiar, in this section).

**Health Foods**—Has Success In the Preparation of—♂ well-asp. in ♍.

**High Living**—(See High).

**Highly Seasoned Foods**—Fond of—(See "Condiments" in this section).

**Hygiene; Immoderate Eater**—(See Excesses, Hearty, Immoderate, Over-Eating, under Eating).

**Improper Foods**—Given To—(See "Evil Diet" under Diet).

**Impulsive Habits**—Concerning Food—Unnatural Habits—♅ ☌ ☽ in ♋, and affl. by the □ of ♆ or ♂. (See Habits, Unnatural, in this section).

**Indigestible Food**—Desire For—♆ affl. in ♋ in the 6th H. (See Indigestion).

**Indigestion; Indiscretions**—In Diet—(See "Indiscretions" under Diet, Eating; Indiscretions).

**Intemperate**—In Eating—(See "Excesses" in this section).

**Intoxication; Irregularities**—In Food—Denoted by ☿, his positions and aspects.

**Large Quantities**—Desires Food In Large Quantities—Gluttony—♃ in asp. or relation to signs or planets which rule the appetite; ♃ ☍ ☽; ♀ in the 5th H. (See "Excesses" in this section; "Abnormal" under Appetite; Gluttony).

**Likes and Dislikes**—As to Food—(See "Dislikes" in this section).

**Liquids with Food**—Should Be Avoided—When ♅ is in ♓ at B. too much liquid with the food and meals should be avoided. (See "Drinking" in this section).

**Liquids and Sweets**—Strong Craving For With Meals—♂ in ♋, □ or ☍ ♆; ♀ in ♋, and affl. by the ☽. (See Drinking, Sweets, in this section).

**Liquors**—(See Drink, Liquids, Liquors. Also see "Drinking", "Liquids", in this section).

**Luxuries**—Craves Luxuries In Food—(See Dainty, Extravagant, Good Food, Rich, Sweets, in this section; Extravagance, Luxuries).

**Malnutrition**—(See Nutrition).

**Mastication**—(See "Chewing" in this section).

**Meat**—Meat Eating—Undigested Meat and Illness From—(See "Raw Humours" under Indigestion; Meat; "Cooked Foods", "Signs", in this section).

**Minces the Food**—Peculiar In Choice of—(See Fastidious, Peculiar, in this section).

**Moderate In Eating**—(See "Moderate" under Eating).

**Nausea; Nut Butters**—(See "Specialties" under Healers).

**Nutrition; Obesity; Over-Eating**—Over-Indulgence In Food—(See "Excesses", "Hearty", "Indiscretions", under Eating; "Fondness" in this section).

**Particular**—About Food—(See Careful, Eccentric, Fastidious, Peculiar, in this section).

**Pastries**—Starches—Sweets—Fond of —(See Dainty, Rich, Starches, Sweets, in this section).

**Peculiar** — About Food—Peculiar Tastes—Minces Food—♆ affl. in ♋; ♆ in ♋ in the 6th H.: ♄ in ♋, minces the food. (See Careful, Eccentric, Fastidious, Tastes, in this section).

**Perverted Tastes** — (See "Tastes" in this section).

**Please**—Hard To Please—(See Careful, Eccentric, Fastidious, Hard To Please, Peculiar, in this section).

**Plethora; Proteids**—Eats Excess of— ♄ affl. in ♋. (See Albumen, Starches, Sugar, Sweets, in this section; Proteids).

**Provisions** — Scarcity of — (See Drought, Famine, Scarcity, Starvation).

**Putrid**—Putrid and Decomposed Food In Bowels—(See "Decomposition" in this section).

**Raw Foods**—(See "Cooked Foods" in this section).

**Raw Humours**—(See "Raw Humours" under Indigestion).

**Rectal Feeding**—(See Enema).

**Retention**—Of Food Difficult—Difficulty In Retaining Food—The ☉ and ♂ in ♋, and affl. at B., and by dir.; the Solar-Martial action in ♋. (See Nausea, Vomiting).

**Rich Food**—Fond of—Expensive Food —Dainty Foods—Disease and Surfeits Arising From—The ☉ affl. by ♃ or ♀, and tending to Surfeits; the ☉ affl. in ♉; the ☉ ☐ or ☍ ♃; ♃ affl. in ♉, ♋, or ♏; ♃ ☌ ♂ in ♋ or ♑; ♃ or ♀ in the 5th H.; ♂ in ♋ in the 1st, 5th, or 6th H. (See Epicureans, Extravagance, Feasting, "Enlarged Liver" under Liver; Luxuries, Plethora, Surfeits; Condiments, Dainty, Excesses, Good Things, Starches, Sugar, Sweets, in this section).

**Riotous Living**—(See Riotous).

**Rottenness**—Of Food—(See "Putrid" under Bowels; "Corruption" under Fruit; Rottenness; Decay, Decomposition, in this section).

**Scarcity**—Of Food—(See Desert, Drought, Famine, Scarcity, Starvation; "Food" under Travel).

**Scurvy**—Due to Deficient and Improper Food—(See Scurvy).

**Seasoned**—Highly Seasoned Food—Fond of—(See "Condiments" in this section).

**Signs of Zodiac**—The Food Adapted to People Born Under Each Sign—Diet and the Horoscope—(1) ♈—Brain foods, wheat, cereals; fish, but little meat; no stimulants or heating foods. (2) ♉—Avoid heating, fattening, starchy foods, and malt liquors; use stimulants moderately; plenty of lemon drinks. Be moderate in diet, as this sign tends to over-eating, gout, rheumatism, surfeits, plethora, etc. (3) ♊—A mental sign—brain food, fruit, milk, meat once a day; nerve foods. Avoid eating, or a meal, before retiring. (4) ♋—Avoid stimulants, malt liquors, pastry, and all food which tends to ferment or heat in the stomach; fish and cereals are recommended, and little meat. Drink plenty of cold water upon arising in morning, and at bedtime. (5) ♌—A vegetable diet is best, and to avoid meats, and all heating, fattening, stimulating foods. Food which builds blood and red corpuscles is required. Study vegetable foods which contain iron. (6) ♍—Chew food well, and eat at regular intervals. Use plain, well-cooked food, and avoid foods which tend to bind or heat the bowels. Eat fruits, milk, vegetables, and foods which tend to regulate the bowels. Avoid over-eating. (7) ♎—Use a light diet; milk, game, fish, poultry, eggs, cereals, cold water upon arising and at bed time. Avoid sugars, starches, malt, intoxicants. (8) ♏—Avoid all fattening, heating, and intoxicating foods and drinks, malts, meat. Use milk, cereals, fruits, vegetables, and blood-forming diet. (9) ♐—Stimulants and intoxicants should be avoided. A moderate amount of animal food is permissible. Nerve and blood-building food should be taken, a light meal at noon, a more substantial meal at sunset, and with light exercise in the evening. (10) ♑—This is a cold sign, and meat diet, and more heat-producing food, are required, and food to enrich the blood and build red corpuscles. Malts are permissible, and foods which stimulate the bodily functions. (11) ♒—A brain and nerve building diet is required, and foods which stimulate the circulation of the blood. Milk and cereals should be used, and a meat diet at one meal of the day. (12) ♓—Intoxicants should be avoided, and a temperate life lived, as many foods do not agree with this sign, and tend to indigestion, a phlegmatic and watery body. A fish diet is helpful, animal meats once a day, and the liberal use of milk, cereals, wheat products, vegetables, fruits, etc. (See "Salts" under Zodiac).

**Spiced Foods**—Fond of—(See "Condiments" in this section).

**Starches**—Tendency to Excess of In Food—The ☉ or ☽ in ♋, or ♋ on Asc.; ♄ in ♋ or ♑; ♄ ☌ ♃ or ♀ in ♋; ♀ affl. by the ☽. (See Dainty, Rich, Sweets, in this section; Starches).

**Starvation**—Lack of Food—(See "Scarcity" in this section).

**Stomach Disorders**—From Improper Food or Indiscretions—(See Digestion, Fermentation, Indigestion, Indiscretions, Stomach; "Decomposition" in this section).

**Strange Foods**—Desire For—(See "Unnatural" in this section).

**Strong Drink**—Strong Coffee—Desire For—(See "Strong Drink" under Drink).

**Sugar**—Heavy Sugar Eaters—Abnormal Desire For—The ☽ ☌ ♀ in a common sign; ♆ affl. at B.; ♄ in ♋ or ♑; ♀ afflicted in ♎; ♀ conjoined with the ☽ in any part of the map; ♀ ☐ ☽. Sugar in excess, and excess of drink and stimulants, excites the Ductless Glands. (See Sugar; "Sugar" under Urine; "Sweets" in this section).

**Surfeits; Swallowing**—(See Deglutition).

**Sweets**—Sugar—Comfits—Pastries—Fond of—Uses to Excess—Sweets and

Sugars are ruled by ♀, and asps. to ♀ tend to increase desire for; ♀ in ♋, in ⚹ ☽, strong desire for; ♀ afflicted in ♎; ♀ □ ☽, abnormal desire for; ♀ ☌ ☽ in a common sign; ♆ affl. at B. tends to a large consumption of sugar; ♄ in ♋, eats excess of sweets, sugar, proteids, pastries, and espec. if ♀ is involved in the configuration; ♄ in ♋ or ♑, fond of pastries and sugar; ♄ ☌ ♃ or ♀ in ♋, fond of pastries, sweets, starches; ♄ affl. in ♋, overloads the system with proteids, starches and sugars; ♂ in ♋, □ or ☍ ♆, a craving for sweets and liquids with meals. (See Dainty, Good Food, Proteids, Rich Food, Starches, Sugar, in this section).

**Tastes**—Abnormal Tastes and Appetites with Food—Perverted Tastes—Peculiar Tastes—♄ affl. in ♋; ♄ ☌ ♀ in ♋; ♆ in the 6th H.; ♂ in ♋; ♂ in ♋, □ or ☍ ♆; ♀ in ♋, and affl. by the ☽. (See Eccentric, Hard To Please, Peculiar, Unnatural, in this section; Tastes).

**Thirst; Travel**—Lack of Food In—(See Desert; "Privations" under Seas; "Food" under Travel).

**Undigested Food**—In Stomach or Bowels—(See "Putrid" under Bowels; Digestion; "Raw Humours" under Indigestion).

**Unhealthful Foods**—Love of—♄ in ♋ or ♑.

**Unnatural Foods**—Desire For—♆ affl. in ♋; ♄ ☌ ♀ in ♋, and affl. by the ☽ or ♅; ♄ in ♋ or ♑. (See Dainty, Impulsive Habits, Rich, Starches, Sugar, Sweets, Tastes, in this section; "Evil Diet" under Diet).

**Vegetables**—Fruit—Cannot Eat—(See "Cannot Eat" under Fruit; Vegetables).

**Vitamines**—Unable to Extract the Vitamines from the Food—♄ ℞ in ♋, and □ or ☍ ♂.

**Vomiting; Want**—In Want of Food and Water—(See "Scarcity" in this section).

**Wheat; Wine; Wrong Diet**—(See "Evil Diet" under Diet; Excesses; Indiscretions, Luxuries; Dainty, Rich, Starches, Sugars, Sweets, in this section).

**FOOLHARDY**—Reckless—Heedless of Danger—Caused by ♂ afflictions; ♂ affl. in the 1st H.; ♂ □ or ☍ ☉; ♂ ☌, □, or ☍ ☽; ♂ affl. in ♌; due to the □ or ☍ ♂ to planets; ♂ prog. ☌ or ill-asp. ♄, and vice versa; the ☉ ☌ ♂ in ♈, and ♈ on the Asc.; the ☉ to the ☌ or ill-asp. ♂ by dir.; the prog. ☉ or ☽ to the ☌ or ill-asp. ♂; ♅ by tr. ☌ the radical ♂, ☽, or ☿; ☿ ☌ or evil asp. ♂ at B., and by dir.; fixed stars of the nature of ♂ and ☿ ascending at B.; in Hor'y Q., ♄ Sig. in ♏. (See Bold, Chances, Dangers, Own Worst Enemy (see Enemies); Escapes, Excitable, Folly, Forethought, Hasty, Imprudent, Impulsive, Perils, Precipitate, Quarrels, Rashness, Recklessness, etc.).

**FOOLS**—Foolish—The ☽ in ♑, full of light, and conjoined with ♂; the ☽ in ♑, void of light, and conjoined with ♄; ♀ ☌ ♄, and with ♂ ☍ the ☽, a fool, yet thinks he is a Philosopher.

**Foolish Fancies**—(See "Foolish" under Fancies).

**Foolish Mind**—The Child Born Foolish—An Imbecile, or Idiot—If at conception the ☉ and ☽ be in the 6th or 12th H., and a malefic with them, the child conceived will tend to be foolish, but if a fortune be with them, the intellect will be saved, but the child formed a hermaphrodite. (See "Beastly Form" under Beasts; Idiocy, Imbecile; "Weak Mind" under Mind; "Void of Reason" under Reason; Savage).

**FORCE**—Forces—Forceful—

**Bodily Forces**—Organic Force—Physical Strength—Are ruled over by the Asc. (See Ascendant, Body, Organic, Physical, Strength).

**Creative Force**—Sex Force—(See Creative; "Force" under Sex).

**Disease**—Force of the Disease—The horoscope as a whole should be studied in judging of the force, or outcome of the disease, and not any one aspect or influence, as the good asps. from the ☉, ☽, ♃, or ♀, will tend to modify the disease in a fortunate map. If the radical map is generally weak, the disease would tend to be more severe. (See Better, Duration, Worse, and the various paragraphs under Disease).

**Dispersion**—Dissipation of Force—(See Dispersion, Dissipation).

**Dynamic Force**—(See Dynamic).

**Electric Force**—(See Electric, Electricity).

**Endurance**—(See Endurance).

**Energy**—(See Energy).

**Excess of Force**—Danger of—The ☉ in a fiery sign; ☉ ☌ ♂ in ♈ or ♌, and espec. in the Asc. or M.C.; ♈ or ♌ on the Asc. (See Active, Energy, Strength, Vitality Good, etc.).

**Expulsive Forces**—Of the Body—(See Expulsion).

**Internal Force**—Prana—Vital Power—(See "Fire Signs" under Fire; "Force" under Vital).

**Kinetic Force**—(See Kinetic).

**Life Force**—Life Forces—Of the Body—Are ruled by the ☉, and the ☉ is the chief source and regulator of the life forces. Also ♂ aids in giving force, activity, and energy. Orange, the color of the ☉, and red, the color of ♂, are the colors assigned to the life force. (See Life, Mars, Sun, Vital).

**Manner**—Forceful Manner—(See Active, Energetic, Quick).

**Mind**—Mind Force—Forceful State of the Mind—(See "Active Mind" under Active; Electric; "Quickened", "Strong Mind", under Mind; Positive).

**Natural Forces**—Of the Body—(See Natural).

**Negative**—(See Negative, Passive).

**Nerve Force**—Vital Force—The Nerve Force Augmented—(See "Nerve Force" under Nerves; "Augmented", "Force", under Vital).

**Organic Force**—Of the Body—Ruled by the ☉ and the Asc. The sign on the Asc., rules the body and physical strength. (See Organic, Structural).

**Physical Forces**—Physical Strength—(See Motion, Muscles, Physical, Stamina, Strength, Tone, Vitality, etc.).

**Positive Forces**—Of Mind and Body—(See Active, Action, Energy, Electric, Positive, etc.).

**Prana**—Vital Force—(See Prana; "Force" under Vital).

**Sex Force**—Creative Force—(See Creative, Generation, Reproduction; "Force" under Sex).

**Solar Forces**—(See Solar, Sun).

**Strength; Strong; Vital Force**—Prana—(See Prana; "Force" under Vital).

**Vitality; Weak Body**—The Forces Weak, Hindered and Impaired—Weak Mind—(See Feeble, Imbecile, Infirm; "Weak" under Mind; Sickly, Vitality Low; "Weak Body" under Weak).

**Will Power**—The Force of the Will—(See Will).

**FOREARM**—Is ruled by the ♌ sign, being opposite to the calves ruled by ♒. Is also ruled by ♊.

**Fractures Of**—(See Arms, Radius, Ulna, Wrists).

**Frog Child**—(See "Missing" in this section).

**Missing**—One or Both Forearms Missing—Born Incomplete—The Frog Child—Caused by Prenatal afflictions. Cases—See "Armless Wonder", No. 054; "Imperfectly Formed", Case No. 267; "Born Incomplete", Case No. 281, all in 1001 N.N. The Case of the Frog Child, with right forearm missing from the elbow down, and with both legs missing below the knees, is illustrated and written up in the book, "The Prenatal Epoch", by Mr. Bailey, on page 157 of Chap. 27. (See the various paragraphs under Arms, Elbows, Hands, Shoulders, Wrists, etc.).

**FOREBODINGS**—Premonitions—Omens—Presentiments—

**Gloomy Forebodings**—♄ affl. in the 3rd or 9th H. (See Gloom).

**Vague Forebodings**—Curious Forebodings—♆ affl. in the 3rd or 9th H.; ♆ affl. in ♐. (See Chaotic, Dreams, Fears, Portentous, Premonitions, Prophetic, Visions, Weird).

**FOREHEAD**—The Brow—Ruled by the ♈ sign, and espec. affected by ♂ in ♈.

**Accidents To**—♂ affl. in ♈. (See Injury, Scars, in this section).

**Baldness**—About the Forehead and Temples—(See "Forehead" under Baldness).

**Broad Forehead**—The ☉ indicates a broad and high forehead; ♉ gives, and ♉ on the Asc., a broad forehead; ♄ gives a broad forehead.

**Deep Forehead**—Tall, Deep, and Straight—☿ gives; ☿ ascending at B., and free from the rays of other planets.

**Disorders Of**—Afflictions in ♈; Subs at AT or AX.

**Fine Forehead**—♂ in ♐.

**Hair**—Has Light Brown Hair Near the Temples and Forehead—Born under ♃, and ♃ occi. (See "Light Brown" under Hair; Baldness, High, in this section).

**Handsome Forehead**—The latter part of ♐ on the Asc. (See Handsome; "Fine" in this section).

**High Forehead**—The ☉ rising at B.; the ☉ gives a broad and high forehead; born under ♃; ♃ in the Asc. at B.; ☿ in ♍; ☿ strong at B., and rising; a ☿ person; in Hor'y Q., ☿ Sig. of the person.

**Injuries To**—♄ or ♂ affl. in ♈; ♈ on the Asc. at B., and containing malefics. Case—The Forehead Split Open In An Accident—See "Strange Accident", No. 832, in 1001 N.N. (See "Accidents", "Injuries", under Head).

**Large Forehead**—Prominent—♄ in ♎ in partile asp. the Asc. (See Broad, Deep, High, in this section).

**Lowering Brow**—The ☽ ascending at Birth.

**Round and Large**—The ☉ gives.

**Scar—On Forehead**—♂ affl. in ♈. Case—See "Spinal Curvature", No. 838, in 1001 N.N. (See Marks, Scars).

**Temples; Ulceration**—On Forehead—♄ or ♂ affl. in ♈; Subs at AT and KP. (See Ulcers).

**Upper Forehead**—Disorders of—Afflictions in the 1st Dec. of ♈; Subs at AT. (See Navamsa).

**FOREIGN LANDS**—Abroad—

**Death Abroad**—(See "Death Abroad" under Abroad).

**Foreign War**—Death or Injury In—Malefics in the 9th H., and affl. the hyleg. (See "Battle" under Abroad; War).

**Ill-Health Abroad**—Sickness In a Foreign Land—Lord of the 9th in the 6th H. (See "Accidents", "Sickness", under Abroad).

**Residence**—In a Foreign Land—Fortunate or Unfortunate—(See Abroad, Banishment, Environment, Nations, Native Land (see Native); Place of Birth (see Place); Residence, Sea, Ships, Shipwreck, Travel, Voyages).

**FOREST FIRES**—Causes of—Death or Injury By—(See "Forest" under Fires).

**FORETHOUGHT**—Foresight—Forecast—

**Lack Of**—Danger By—Death, Injury, Sorrow, Trouble, etc., from Lack of—The ☉ ☌ ☿ in ♓, and at the same time in □ or ☍ ♅ or ♂, lack of reason and forethought, and haste and impulse predominate; the ☽ strong at B., in the Asc. or M.C., or ruler; the ☽ angular at B., or in ♉ or ♋, little forecast, and providing only for the present; the ☽ ill-dig. at B., of no forecast; ♂ influence; ♂ Sig. ⚹ or △ ♀, improvident and thoughtless; ♐ influence; ☿ rising before the ☉ gives forethought, but rising after the ☉, lack of it. (See Excitable, Foolhardy, Hasty, Improvident, Imprudent, Impulsive, Judgment; "Brightened" under Mind; Precipitate, Rashness, Reason, Recklessness, etc.).

**Painful Complaints**—And Irregularities, due to Rashness and Lack of Forethought—The ☽ affl. by ♂ at B., and by dir., tr., or progression; ♂ affl. the ☽, ☿, or Asc. at B., and by dir. (See Carelessness; "Own Worst Enemy" under Enemies; Folly, Imprudence, Rashness, Recklessness, etc.).

**FORETOLD** — Foretelling — Prognostication — (See "Foretold His Own Death" under Death; Prognosis, Prognostication, Prophetic, etc.).

**FORGERS** — Given to Forgery — Tendency To—Commits Forgery—The ☽ to the ill-asps. ☿ by dir., and ☿ affl. at B.; ♅, ♄, ♃, or ♂ to the ill-asps. ☿ by dir.; ♂ and ☿ together lords of the employment; ☿ affl. by ♅, ♄, or ♂ by dir.; ☿ in the Asc., □ or ☍ ♄ or ♂, and with no good asps. from ♃ or ♀; the M.C. to the place of Algenib, and with danger of imprisonment. (See Cheating, Deceitful, Dishonest, Gambling, Liars, Swindlers, Thieves, etc.).

**FORGETFUL**—(See Carelessness; "Forgetful" under Memory).

**FORM** — Shape and Description of the Body—The Form of the Body is to be judged principally from three factors,—(1) The Sign rising, the degree on the Asc., and the position of the ☽ at B. (2) Planets which exactly aspect the degree rising on the Asc., or when rising or near the Asc. (3) The position and aspects of the ruler of the Asc. The Form of the body proceeds from the Asc., the 1st H., planets in the Asc.; from the ☉ and ☽, and the asps. to the ☽. Ptolemy says the Asc. has the greatest power in forming the body, and next after the Asc., the ☽. (See Relaxation). Many modifications of form arise from the various positions of the majority of the planets, whether rising, elevated, setting, or below the horizon. Many planets in one sign tend to give the predominating characteristics of that sign, both in mind and body. Family Likenesses are caused by having the same sign rising with different members of the family. (See "Likenesses" under Family).

**Significators of Form**—They are the sign on the cusp of the Asc., or 1st H., or a sign intercepted in this house; their lords; planets in the Asc., or in any way aspecting the Asc.; fixed stars near the cusp of the Asc., and to these some add the Luminaries and the stars that aspect them,—all these are Sigs. of both mind and body. For further consideration of Form and Shape, see Appearance; "Beastly Form" under Beasts; Body, Build; "Dogs" under Children; Congenital, Crooked, Constitution, Defects, Deformities, Distortions, Figure, Height, Ill-Shaped, Inhuman, Monsters, Posture, Shape, Stature, Weight, Well, etc.).

**FORTUNE**—The Fortune of the Native —Fortunate—Unfortunate—Malice of Fortune, etc.—

**Children** — Fortunate Children — Unfortunate—Misfortune To—(See "Fortunate", "Unfortunate", under Children).

**Degrees** — The Fortunate Degrees of the Zodiac — The Degrees Increasing Fortune—♈ 19; ♉ 3, 15, 27; ♊ 11; ♋ 1, 2, 3, 4, 15; ♌ 2, 5, 7, 19; ♍ 3, 14, 20; ♎ 3, 15, 21; ♏ 7, 18, 20; ♐ 13, 20; ♑ 12, 13, 14, 20; ♒ 7, 16, 17, 20; ♓ 13, 10. If ♃ be in one of these degrees at B., or if on the cusp of the 2nd H., or lord of the 2nd be in such a degree, riches and great honors are apt to come to the native. (See "Zodiac" under Degrees).

**Evil**—The Fortune Too Evil to Allow the Native to Succeed—♂ Sig. □ or ☍ the ☉. (See Evil, Fate, Misery, Misfortune, Reverses, Ruin, Sorrow, Trouble, etc.).

**Fortunate**—Very Fortunate In Life—Has Good Fortune—A Fortunate Person—The ☉, ☽, ♃, and ♀ above the earth at B., and well-asp.; the ☽ Sig. ☌ ♃; the ☽ well-asp. in ♉, fairly fortunate; the ☽ well-asp. in ♋ or ♐; the ☽ sepr. from the ☉ and apply. to ♃; the ☽ sepr. from the ☉ and apply. to ♀ in a day geniture; the ☽ decr., sepr. from ♂ and apply. to ♀; the ☽ sepr. from ♂ and apply. to ♃; ♃ Sig. ✶ or △ the ☉; ♃ Sig. ☌ or good asp. the ☽; ♃ rising at B., well-asp. and dignified; ♃ Sig. ☌ ♀; ♂ Sig. in ♑; ♀ Sig. in ♉, ♐, ♒, or ♓; ☿ Sig. ✶ or △ ♃. These influences also tend largely to good health. (See "Good Constitution" under Constitution; Fate, Happiness; "Good Health" under Health; Poverty, Riches, etc.).

**Ill-Fortune** — Meets with Much Ill-Fortune—(See Business, Cares, Children, Directions, Dishonour, Disgrace, Enemies, Events, Exile, Family, Fate, Grief, Health, Honour, Ill-Health, Imprisonment (see Prison); Injuries, Marriage, Marriage Partner, Mischief, Miseries, Misfortune, Murdered, Poverty, Relatives, Reputation, Reverses, Ruin, Scandal, Sickness, Sorrow, Suicide, Treachery, Trouble, Twelfth House, Unfortunate, etc.).

**Malice of Fortune**—Ill-Fortune—Misfortune—The ☽ to the place of Ceti, or the Hydra's Heart; the ☽ incr. in a night nativity, sepr. from ☿ and apply. to ♄, if malefic planets afflict them; ♄ in the 10th or 4th H., and affl. the ☉ or ☽, malice of fortune is almost certain, downfalls, reversals, ill-health, etc., and espec. under evil ♄ transits or directions to the hyleg, or to his place in the radical map; ♂ Sig. in □ or ☍ the ☉; ♂ Sig. ☌ ☉, sudden failures and downfalls; ♀ Sig. □ or ☍ ☽. (See "Evil", "Ill-Fortune", in this section).

**Misfortune**—(See "Ill-Fortune", "Malice of Fortune", in this section).

**Moderately Fortunate** — In Life — Not Very Fortunate—♄ Sig. ☌ ☽; ♂ Sig. ☌ ♀; ♀ Sig. in ♓; ☿ Sig. in ♐. (See the various paragraphs in this section. See Unfortunate).

**Part of Fortune**—(See Part).

**Signs of Zodiac**—The Fortunate Signs of the Zodiac are the positive, odd, and masculine, as ♈, ♊, ♌, ♎, ♐, and ♒. These Signs when rising at B., upon the Asc., and espec. when occupied by a benefic, and free from malefics, tend to make the native very fortunate in life.

**Unfortunate** — In Life — (See Unfortunate; "Ill-Fortune", "Malice", in this section).

**FORWARD**—The Body Bent Forward—(See Bending; "Downward" under Look; Stooping).

**FOSSAE** — Fossa — A Depression, Furrow, or Sinus—(See Depression, Frontal, Nose).

**FOUL** — Loathsome — Offensive — Unpleasant — Fetid — Foul Odors — Foul Diseases, etc.—See the following subjects in the alphabetical arrangement when not considered here—Foul Odors and Diseases are generally the work of ♄ and the ☽. Also ♀ tends to fetid and foul conditions in the body, resulting from excesses, dissipation, etc. (See Fetid).

**Air**—Foul Air—(See "Corrupt" under Air).

**Axillae**—Fetid Perspiration of — (See Axillae).

**Blood** — Foul Blood — (See "Impure Blood" under Impure).

**Breath**—(See "Foul" under Breath).

**Cancer** — Carcinoma — (See Carcinoma).

**Catarrhs**—(See Catarrh, Nose).

**Corrupt; Decay**—Decomposition—(See Decay).

**Discharges; Excretions; Exudations;**

**Faeces; Feet**—Foul Odors From—(See "Odors" under Feet).

**Fetid; Gangrene; Gases; Humours**—(See "Corrupt", "Offending", under Humours).

**Impure; Menses; Mind**—A Foul Mind —(See Obscenity).

**Moisture**—(See "Putrefaction" under Moisture).

**Morbid; Noxious; Odors; Offensive;**

**Perspiration**—(See Sweat).

**Pools**—Stagnant Pools—(See Pools).

**Pus; Putrid** — Putrefaction—(See Putrid).

**Rottenness; Sores; Stagnant** — (See Pools).

**Stomach**—(See "Foul" under Stomach).

**Sweat**—(See "Fetid" under Sweat).

**Tongue**—A Foul Tongue—(See "Foul" under Breath, Tongue).

**Ulcers**—(See Gangrene; "Putrifying" under Ulcers).

**Vapors**—(See "Foul" under Vapors).

**Vegetation; Venereal Diseases** — (See "Ulcers" under Venereal).

**FOUNTAINS**—Springs—Drying Up of—Comets appearing in ♈ or ♎; an eclipse of the ☉ in the 2nd Dec. of ♋. (See Drought; "Fountains" under Dryness; Famine).

**FOUR-FOOTED ANIMALS** — Injury, Hurts, or Death By — (See Animals, Beasts, Bites, Cattle, Elephants, Events, Horses, Kicks, Quadrupeds, etc.).

**Signs**—The Four-Footed Signs of the Zodiac — Quadrupedal Signs—Animal Signs—♈, ♉, ♌, ♐, ♑. Those born with such signs on the Asc. at B. have many of the qualities of such animals, and especially if the ☉ or ☽ be in the 6th or 12th H. at conception, or the malefics in angles. (See "Animal Signs" under Animal; Quadrupeds).

**FOURTH HOUSE** — This is a terminal house, a part of the terminal triangle, and denotes old age, the grave, decay, death, rest, the end of life, and the various conditions which affect the close of life, as its diseases, worries, the environment, wealth, poverty, etc. The nature of the death, or the end of life, will be according to the planets in this house, and the sign on the cusp denotes the part, or organ, wherein the complaint lies. The lords of the 4th and 8th H. are Significators of death. This is a feminine House, denotes the breasts and lungs, and is affiliated with the ♋ sign, and is cardinal in quality. This house is the weakest of the angles, and is also an Anaretical Place. The vital powers are at their weakest when the ☉ at B. is on the cusp of this house. This house rules the breasts, the milk, lungs, stomach; inheritance, the birthplace, place of residence, the home and domestic life generally; the mother in a male nativity and the father in a female horoscope; the mother-in-law in a male nativity, and the father-in-law in a female. In Hindu Astrology, this house rules the mother, and the 10th H. the father. Benefics in this house at B. indicate that the native should not leave his native land, but remain at his birthplace all thru his life, if possible, for good health, good fortune, and a happy and peaceful ending to life. The parents usually die before the native if he has ♄ in this house at B. Mars here gives short life to the father or mother, according to the sex of the horoscope. Malefic planets in the 4th H. indicate disease, worry, and distress in old age, and also hurt, sickness, and affliction to the father or mother. This house signifies all diseases in the lungs, breast, and stomach; the end of the disease, and diseases of the ☽ and the ♋ sign. Red is the Color ruled by this house. (See Anareta, Angles, Breast, Cancer; "Fourth House" under Death; End, Environment, Father, Heredity, Home, Inheritance, Lungs, Moon, Mother, Nadir; "Native Land" under Native; Old Age, Place of Birth (see Place); Red, Residence, Stomach, Terminal, etc.).

**FOWLS**—Of the Air—Birds—Vultures—

**Body Devoured By** — After Death — (See "Birds of Air" under Air; "Body Devoured" under Burial; Vultures).

**Death Of** — Destruction of — Eclipses of the ☉ or ☽ in ♊ or ♐, espec. of such as are eaten by man, and which are brought to death by human means for edible purposes; Comets appearing in ♊; ♄ in ♊, angular, direct in motion at the Vernal Ingress. (See "Virus" under Pestilence).

**Parrot Fever**—(See Psittacosis).

**Resembles Fowls** — (See Disfigurements; "Eagle Features" under Features; "Animal Forms" under Monsters).

**FRACTURES**—Broken Bones—

**Compound Fracture** — ♂ with ♄, and both the afflictors at the same time. (See "Violent" under Dispersions; "Scope" under Enlarged).

**Death By**—Caused by ♄ or ♂ when the dominion of death is vested in them; ♄ coming to the cusp. the Asc., causes a fracture, dislocation, and possible death from fracture if affl. the hyleg at the same time; ♂ in ♈, ♉, ♌, ♐, or ♑, and in ☍ the Asc. by dir.; ♂ in the 7th H., □ or ☍ the ☉, and ♂ in a four-footed, or quadrupedal sign, and with ♂ just setting at B. (See Blows, Concussions, Falls, Heights, Quadrupedal).

**Falls**—Fractures By—♂ by Periodic Rev. to the ☌, □, or ☍ ♅, and espec. if ♂ is in the 4th, 6th, or 8th H. (See Falls).

**General Causes**—Afflictions in ♐, and in ♊ by reflex action; ♐ on the Asc., 6th, or 12th H.; afflictions to planets in ♐ cause more broken bones than any other sign influence; afflictions in ♑; afflictions in airy signs dispose to; the ☽ affl. in ♐; the ☽ to the ☌ or ill-asps. ♂ by dir.; ♅ afflictions show fractures, and espec. his evil asps. to the Sigs., the ☉, ☽, Asc., or M.C.; ♄ afflictions give broken bones; ♄ ascending at B.; ♄ to the ☌ or ill-asps. ♂ by dir., and espec. if either be ori.; ♄ by tr. in ☌, □, or ☍ the ☉, ☽, ♃ or ♀ in the radix; ♄, ♅, or ♂ affl. in any sign at B., and by dir., may result in a fracture in the part, or parts, ruled by such sign at B.; ♃ affl. in ♊; ♂ affl. in ♐; ♂ in ♐ in the 6th or 12th H.; ♂ in the 1st H., and affl. by ♃; ♂ to the ☌ or ill-asp. ♄ by dir. (For Fracture of the various bones of the body see "Fracture" under such subjects as Ankles, Arms, Bones, Clavicle, Colles Fracture (see Wrists); Elbow, Face (see "Hurts" under Face); Feet (see "Accidents" under Feet); Femur, Fibula, Fingers, Forearm, Hands, Head, Hips, Humerus, Jaws, Knees, Legs, Limbs, Radius, Ribs, Scapula (see Shoulders); Shoulder, Skull, Thighs, Tibia, Ulna, Vertebrae, Wrists, etc. Also see Dislocations, Joints).

**Simple Fracture**—♅, ♄, or ♂ acting alone as the afflictor, and not in combination.

**FRAGILE**—Brittle—

**Appearance**—Fragile Appearance—♃ affl. in ♋. (See Pale, Sickly).

**Bones**—Brittle and Fragile Bones—(See "Brittle" under Bones).

**Hair**—Dry and Brittle Hair—(See "Dry" under Hair).

**FRAIL**—Frail Body—Frail Constitution—(See "Sickly", "Weak", under Constitution).

**Frail People**—Death of the Frail Among the Aged—(See "Aged People" under Old Age).

**FRAME**—The Body—The Skeleton—

**Athletic Frame**—(See Athletics).

**Whole Frame Disordered**—(See Whole). For the various conditions and descriptions of the Frame see such subjects as Appearance, Body, Constitution, Delicate, Disease, Feeble, Form, Health, Height, Large, Long, Middle Sized, Shape, Short, Skeleton, Small, Stature, Strength, Strong, Stout, Weak, Weight, Wiry, etc.

**FRANTIC**—Frenzied—Excessive Excitement—(See Anger, Excitable; "Causes" under Fits; Frenzy, Fury, Madness, Mania, Raving; "High Temper" under Temper; Wild, etc.).

**FRATRICIDE**—(See "Fratricide" under Brothers).

**FREAKS**—Freaks of Nature—Mental and Bodily Freaks—Influences and Illustrations along this line with the planetary causes, etc., are given under the following subjects,—Anarchists; "Beastly Form" under Beasts; "Born Blind" under Blind; Congenital, Crazy, Cyclops, Deaf and Dumb (see Deaf, Dumb); Defects, Deformities, Demoniac, Dogs—Resembles Dogs—(see "Dogs" under Children); Dwarfs, Eccentric, Effeminate, Fanatical, Fowls—Resembles Fowls—(see Fowls); Frog Child (see Forearm); Giants, Geniuses, Glass, Growth, Hermaphrodite, Idiots, Inhuman, Insanity, Malformations, Mathematical, Monsters, Murderers, Peculiar, Perversions, Pituitary, Precocious, Prenatal Epoch (see Prenatal); Prodigies, Religion (see "Fanatical" under Religion); Savage, Twins (see "Siamese Twins" under Twins); Wild.

**FRECKLES**—Lentigo—Circumscribed Spots On the Skin—Freckles are due principally to a predominance of Iron in the skin (Iron ruled by ♂), and ♂ prominent at B.; ♂ in the Asc., or rising, or a ♂ influence or sign on the Asc.; ♂ rising in ♈ tends to give a face full of freckles, and fiery red hair; the ☉ in ♏; the ☽ in ♋, ♏, or ♓; the ☽ Sig. in watery signs in Hor'y Q.; ♀ Sig. in ♌ or ♎, or in these signs in partile asp. the Asc.; the 4th Face of ♈ on the Asc.; the 5th face of ♍, the 3rd face of ♎, the 1st and 4th faces of ♐ or ♑, or the 4th or 6th faces of ♓ on the Asc. Case—Red Hair and Freckled Face—See "Red Hair", No. 330 in 1001 N.N. (See Blemishes, Complexion, Defects; "Red Face" under Face; "Red Hair" under Hair; Marks, Moles).

**FREE**—

**Free Living**—Loose Living—Diseases From—The ☽ to the ill-asps. ♀ by dir.; afflictions to ♀; ♀ in bad asp. to the ☉; the ill-asps. of ♀ by dir. to the Asc. or M.C.; ♀ by Periodic Rev. to the ill-asps. the ☉; the Asc. to the ☌ or ill-asps. ♀ by dir., and ♀ affl. at B.; ♌ on cusp the 6th H. (See Debauched, Depraved, Dissipated, Dissolute, Drink, Eating, Excesses, Feasting; "High Living" under High; Indulgence, Intemperate, Loose; "Loose Morals" under Morals; Passion, Perversions; "Riotous Living" under Riotous; Sex, Vices).

**Free Love**—Entanglements—Liaisons—Inordinate Affection—Clandestine Love Affairs—Committed To—The ☉ ☌, □, or ☍ ♅ at B.; the ☉, ☽, or ♀ to the ill-asps. ♅ by dir., and espec. if affl. by ♅ at B.; principally a ♅ affliction when under the lower vibrations of ♅; ♅ affl. in ♌, ♏, or the 5th H.; ♅ affl. the ☉, ☽, or ♀; ♀ by Periodic Rev. in ill-asp. the ☉. (See "Free Living" in this section; "Unwomanly Freedom" under Morals; Nymphomania, Perverse; "Clandestine" under Sex).

**Free from Passion**—(See Apathy, Aversions, Bachelor, Celibacy, Deviations; "Free from Passion" under Passion; Perversions, etc.).

**Free Will**—(See "Free Will" under Will).

**FRENZY**—Phrenzy—Violent Mania—Frantic—Beside Oneself—Excessively Excitable—

**Causes of Frenzy**—Due to religious, and other excitement, caused by ♆ and ♂ afflictions; ♆ affl. in the 12th H.; the ☉ Sig. □ or ☍ ♂: a ♂ disease, and with ♂ the afflicting planet; ♂ Sig. ☌ ☉, and with danger of the life being cut short by; ♂ Sig. □ or ☍ ☉; ☿ ill-dig. at B., and espec. when also affl. by ♆ or ♂. (See Anger; "Brain Storms" under Brain; Demoniac, Emotions, Enthusiasm; "Beside Oneself" under Excitable; Frantic, Fury, Hysteria, Impulsive, Insanity, Madness, Mania, Raving, Wild).

**Death By**—♂ the afflicting planet and holding the dominion of death; ☿ badly afflicted, and affl. the hyleg by dir., denotes death by Frenzy.

**Delirium**—Phrenitic Delirium—A Phrenitic Man—(See "Wild Delirium" under Delirium).

**Religious Frenzy**—Caused by ♆; ♆ affl. in the 9th H. (See "Religious Excitement" under Excitement).

**FREQUENT**—

**Abscesses Frequent**—(See "Frequent" under Abscesses).

**Chronic Ailments**—Frequent Chronic Ailments—The ☽ decr. at B., sepr. from ♃, and apply. to ♄. (See the ☽ influences under "Causes" under Chronic Diseases).

**Fever**—Frequent Attacks of—(See "Frequent Attacks" under Fever).

**Headaches Frequent**—(See "Women" under Headaches).

**Ill-Health**—Frequent Ill-Health—(See "Ill-Health All Thru Life" under Ill-Health; "Much Sickness" under Sickness).

**Perspiration**—Frequent Perspiration—(See "Frequent" under Sweat).

**FRESH**—Fresh Coloured and Handsome—Given by the ⚹ or △ asps. of ♂ to the ☉, ☽, or Asc. (See "Good" under Complexion; Handsome; "Complexion" under Ruddy).

**FRETFULNESS**—Peevishness—Discontentment—Worry, etc.—♄ people fret and mope; ♄ affl. in ♈; ♄ Sig. □ or ☍ ☽; ♄ in ♏, conspicuous fretfulness; ♂ to the cusp the 3rd H. by dir.; the 3rd Dec. of ♒ on the Asc., ruled by the ☽. (See Anguish, Anxiety, Dejected, Depressed, Despondent, Discontentment, Fears, Irritable, Low Spirits (see Low); Melancholy, Moping, Morose, No Peace of Mind (see "Peace" under Mind); Patience, Peevish, Petulant, Repining, Restless, Scolding, Worry, etc.).

**FRICTION**—Fremitus—Rubbing—Irritation—Diseases Accompanied By—(See "Dry Cough" under Cough; the various paragraphs under Dry; "Respiratory" under Mucous; "Inflammation" under Pleura).

**FRIDAY**—Ruled by ♀. (See Week).

**FRIENDS**—Ruled by the 11th H. Benefics here, and well-asp., give good and helpful friends. Malefics here tend to false friends, and injury by them. Lord of the 12th in the 11th H. tends to pretended friends, and private enemies.

**Acquaintance**—Death of—(See Acquaintances).

**Danger**—To a Friend—Ruler of the 11th H. affl. in the 6th H. at a Solar Revolution.

**Death**—Of a Friend or Friends—The ☉ or ☽ ☌ ♅, ♄, or ♂, or the ☌ of two malefics in the radical or revolutionary 11th H., indicate a friend lost by death or misfortune; ♄ to the ☌ or ill-asp. the ☉, death of a near friend; the 24° ♏ on the Asc. at B., sorrow thru the death of friends; malefics in the 8th H. at a Solar Rev.; the tr. of malefics thru the 8th H., and espec. if they were in the 8th, afflicting the 8th, or lord of the 8th H. at B. (See "Female Friend", "Short Life", in this section).

**Dissipated**—Thru the Influence of Friends—♂ affl. in the 11th H. (See Dissipation).

**Execrated**—By Friends—(See Execrated).

**False Friends**—Injured By—The ☽ Sig. □ or ☍ ♃; lord of the 10th in the 12th H.; lord of the 10th a malefic, and affl. in the 11th H. (See Antipathy, Deceitful, Dishonest, Fortune, Libel, Mischief, Misfortune, Plots, Poison, Reputation, Ruin, Scandal, Treachery, Trouble, etc.).

**Female Friend**—Death of—The ☽ to the place of Cor Scorpio. (See Antares).

**Few Friends**—Unpopular—The ☉ ill-asp. by the ☽ and ♀ at B.; the ☽ in evil asp. to the ☉ or ♀; malefics in the 11th H. at B., a malefic ruler of this house, and no benefics in the 11th. (See Antipathy, Enemies, Home).

**Many Friends**—The ☉ well-asp. by the ☽ and ♀ at B.; the ☽ ⚹ or △ ♃, sincere in friendships; ♃ or ♀ ruler of the 11th H., or in the 11th, and with no malefics in this house, or ruler of the 11th; ♃ or ♀ ruler of the horoscope, and well-asp., and espec. when placed in the 11th H.; the malefics obscure in the map, and not badly aspecting the Significators; the ♒ sign when well-occupied and aspected, and strong at B., and with other good aspects, tends to many friends, as ♒ is related to the 11th H., and is known as the Sign of Friends. (See "Amiable", "Courteous", under Manners; Popular, Sympathy).

**Short Life**—Of Friends—Near and intimate friends are apt to die before middle life when the lord of the 8th H. is in the 11th H., and afflicted, unless the hyleg be strong, or the Asc. well-asp. by lord of the 1st H. (For further influences see Companions, Compatibility, Enemies, Family, Healers, Home, Incompatibility, Love Affairs, Marriage, Men, Parents, Relatives, Residence, Social Relations, Vagabond, etc.).

**Sickness**—On Account of Friends—Lord of the 6th in the 11th H.

**FRIGHT**—Easily Frightened—The ☽ strong at B., well placed and dignified. (See Darkness, Fears, Nervousness, Sensitives, Shocks).

**Shocks by Fright**—♅ ☌ ☽ in ♈.

**FRIGID**—(See Chill, Cold, Frost, Ice, Rigid, Rigors, Saturn, Snow, Winter).

**FRIVOLITY**—Diseases and Ailments From—(See Amusements, Carelessness, Debauchery, Dissipation, Dissolute, Drink, Eating, Excesses, Feasting, Folly, Free Living (see Free); Hasty, High Living (see High); Love Affairs, Men; "Shallow" under Mind; Opposite Sex (see Opposite); Passion, Rashness, Recklessness, Sex, Sports, Women, etc.).

**FROG CHILD**—Forearm Missing, and Both Legs Missing Below the Knees—(See Forearm).

**FRONS SCORPIO**—Fixed Star in ♐. (See Danger, Disease, Putrid, Sickness, Trouble, Violence).

**FRONT**—Front Part of the Body—Planets above the earth at B. tend to affect the front part of the body, and when below the horizon, the back or hinder parts. (See Back, Lower, Middle, Upper).

**Marks or Moles**—On Front Part of Body—(See Marks).

**FRONTAL**—

**Frontal Bones**—Frontal Sinuses—Abscess In—(See "Frontal" under Abscesses).

**Frontal Headaches**—(See "Frontal" under Headaches).

**FROST**—Ruled by ♄.

**Abundance Of**—♅ in an angle at the Winter Solstice; ♄ ☌ ☉ in ♈, ♑, ♒, or ♓. (See Cold, Ice, Saturn, Snow, Winter).

**FRUIT**—Fruits of the Earth—

**Alterations In Fruit**—Eclipses of the ☉ or ☽ in ♈; the ☽ and planets in earthy signs at Ingresses tend to bring events affecting the fruits of the Earth for good or evil, according to the asps. to the Lord of the Year or Quarter.

**Cannot Eat Fruit**—Case—See "Can't Eat Fruit", No. 365, in 1001 N.N. (See Diet, Eating, Food).

**Corruption of Fruit**—Causing Sickness If Eaten When Gathered—Eclipses of the ☉ or ☽ in ♋, corruption of fruit when gathered; an eclipse of the ☉ in the 2nd Dec. of ♈. (See Comets, Eclipses, Figs, Rottenness, Vegetation, Vines).

**Scarcity**—Of Fruit—Eclipses of the ☉ or ☽ in earthy signs; an eclipse of the ☽ in ♉; ♄ ☌ ♃ in fire, air, and earthy signs; Comets appearing in ♉, ♋, ♎, or ♏. (See Blight, Corn, Drought, Earth, Events (see "Nature Of" under Events); Famine, Figs, Grains, Herbs; Pestilential Virus (see "Virus" under Pestilence); Scarcity, Trees, Weather, Wheat, etc.).

**FRUITFUL**—Fruitfulness—Prolific—Fertile—Children Promised—♃, ♀, and the ☽ are the Givers of Children. The watery signs ♋, ♏, and ♓, are called the fruitful signs. Also ♉, the exalted sign of the ☽, is a very fruitful sign. Other signs are less fruitful, and ♈, ♊, ♌, and ♍ are classed as unfruitful and barren signs. The 5th and 11th H., being opposite houses, are the principal houses of children, and fruitful influences in these houses at B. promise children. The 11th H. is the 5th H. of the marriage partner by turning the map upside down, and the same conditions apply to the 11th H. as to the 5th H. when the map is reversed. The ☽ and ♀ are especially fruitful in the matter of giving children, and the ♋ sign influence tends to make women more fruitful and prolific. The horoscope of both husband and wife should be studied in judging of the matter of children, fruitfulness, and promise of children. If both are fruitful, children will result. If one is fruitful, and the other barren, children will be denied. Thus a woman denied children by her first marriage, if the husband is barren, impotent and sterile, may have them in a second marriage, if both are fruitful. The ☽ is the planet of fecundation. Heat and moisture in the body in abundance tend to make one prolific, while a cold and dry body, ruled by ♄ or ☿, tends to barrenness. When ☿ is ori. in fruitful, or seminal signs, and configurated with fruitful planets, as ♃, ♀, or the ☽, he gives offspring, but when in barren signs, and with barren planets, he denies them. The malefics also may give children when in prolific, or fruitful signs, and supported by benefics, but the children are apt to be sickly and short-lived. (See "Probability of Children", "Sickly Children", under Children). For the general influences which tend to give children, promise of children, and many children, see "Signs of Children" in this section.

**Brothers Promised**—Brothers and Sisters Promised—(See Brothers, Sisters).

**Children Born**—But They Die—(See "Death of Children" under Children).

**Creative Powers**—(See Creative, Generation, Reproduction; "Sex Powers" under Sex).

**Females Fruitful**—(See Probability, Signs, Symbols, in this section. Also see "Fruitful" under Wife).

**Fruitful Signs**—Of the Zodiac—♋, ♏, and ♓, the watery signs. Of these signs ♏ is the least fruitful because of its ruler ♂. The ♋ sign is fruitful because of the ☽. The ♓ sign is fruitful because of ♃, and ♓ is considered the most fruitful of all the signs. The ♉ and ♎ signs are considered rather fruitful because of their ruler ♀. The ♐ sign is rather fruitful because of its ruler ♃. The ♒ sign is considered more fruitful than barren.

**Generative Powers Strong**—(See Creative, Generation; "Sex Powers" under Sex. Also see "Signs of Children" in this section).

**Husband Fruitful**—(See "Fruitful" under Husband).

**Large Family**—(See "Many Children" under Children).

**Male**—Fruitfulness In the Male—(See "Fruitful" under Husband; "Signs of Children" in this section).

**Many Children**—(See "Many Children" under Children).

**Mind**—Fruitful Mind—(See Genius, Inventive).

**Moderately Fruitful**—The ☽ in ♉, ♎, ♏, or ♒.

**Multiple Births**—(See Double-Bodied, Multiple, Triplets, Twins).

**Probability**—Of Children—♃, ♀, or the ☽ in the 4th, 5th, 10th, or 11th H., and well-asp., and espec. if there are fruitful signs on the cusps of these houses. Look first to the 10th and 11th H., and if no planets therein look to the 4th and 5th H. If none there look to planets which may be in good asp. to degrees on the cusps of these houses. (See Eleventh, Fifth, Fourth, Tenth House. Also see "Signs", "Symbols", in this section).

**Signs of Children**—Symbols of Children—Signs of Conception—Children Promised—A Fruitful Marriage—Strong Powers of Generation—These influences should exist in the maps of both husband and wife to give promise of children—The ☽ in the 5th or 11th H. in a fruitful sign, and well-asp.; the ☽ in ♉ in the 5th H.; the ☽, ♃, or ♀ in the 5th H., in a fruitful or double-bodied sign, as in ♋, ♏, ♓, or in ♊ or ♐; the ☽ in the 11th H. in a fruitful sign; if the ☽ apply to the lord of the Asc., or lord of the 5th H. by good asp. from the 10th H., or by evil asp. if with mutual reception; the ☽ in the 5th H. in other than barren signs, and well-asp. by benefics; the ☽ essentially fortified and in reception with any planet in an angle; the ☽ in the 7th H., and beholding the lord of the 7th in the 11th, or the ☽ in the 11th and beholding the lord of the 7th H. in the 7th; the ☽, Asc., or lord of the Asc. in a fruitful sign; the ☽ to the place of Altair gives promise of marriage and children (see Altair); the ☽ in ♋ tends to make a female very prolific, and the ☽ sign ♋ on the Asc. or cusp of 5th H.; ♃ and ♀ in the 5th H., and in no ways afflicted; ♃ or ♀ in the Asc. or 11th H., there will be children, but not speedily; ♃ in the 1st, 5th, or 11th H., and in no asp. to ♄ or ♂, and the malefics be slow in motion, or ℞; ♃ in ♋ or ♏, well-asp., and espec. when in the 5th or 11th H.; ♃ and ♀, and a well-asp. ☉, ☽, or ☿, indicate children; ♃ or ♀ in the Asc., or with lord of the 5th in angles; ♃ in good asp. to the ☽, the body is fruitful and the health good; ♃ and ♀ in fruitful signs, and aspecting the houses of children, angular or succedent, and more ori. than the malefics, children will be stronger and more numerous; ♀ in the 5th H., and well-asp.; ♀ well-asp. in ♉ or ♎; the Asc. a fruitful sign; fruitful signs on the Asc., 5th, 10th, or 11th H.; lord of the Asc., or the ☽, in good asp. with the lord of the 5th, and lord of the 5th strong, or in a fruitful sign; lord of the Asc. in the 5th or 7th; benefics in the Asc., or with lord of the 5th in angles; lord of the Asc. in a good house, and beholding the cusp of the Asc. by good asp.; lord of the Asc. in mutual reception with a planet by house, sign, term, triplicity, or exaltation, with a planet which has the same reception exactly, if each be in the other's house; lord of the Asc., or the ☽, joined to lord of the 5th; lord of the Asc. or the ☽ be in the 5th, and free from affliction by malefics, ☋, or lords of the 6th, 8th, or 12th H.; a fixed sign ascending with ♃ or ♀ therein, or if the lord of the 5th be strong in the Asc. or 10th H.; a planet, or planets, in the 5th H. in good asp. with the lord of the 5th; lord of the 5th in the Asc., or lord of the Asc. in the 5th; the 5th H. and its lord as Sigs. in Hor'y Q. indicate that there are children in the family inquired of; lord of the 5th in the Asc. or 7th H.; lord of the 7th in the 5th, or the ☽ with him; the sign on the 5th, or its lord, in a fruitful sign denote fruitfulness and children; lord of the 5th in the 1st, or lord of the 1st or the ☽ in the 5th, if lords of the 1st and 5th be in ☌; a fruitful sign on the cusp of the 1st or 5th, or their lords, or the ☽, be in a fruitful sign, or if a benefic be in the 1st, 3rd, 5th, 9th, or 11th H.; translation of light between the lords of the 1st and 5th, and particularly if made by the ☽, is a good symptom of children; lord of the 1st angular, with reception, denotes children; the fruitful signs ♋, ♏, or ♓ on the Asc. or 5th H. (See Barrenness, Increased, Many, Probability, under Children; Conception, Fecundation, Fertile, Generation; "Fruitful" under Husband, Marriage, Maternity, Mother, Pregnancy, Reproduction, Seminal, Wife; "Probability", "Symbols", in this section).

**Symbols of Children**—The ☽, Asc., lord of the Asc., or lord of the 5th H., being strong and well-aspected in a fruitful sign, and with fruitful signs on the 5th or 11th H. (See Probability, Signs Of, in this section).

**Triplets**—Quadruplets—(See Multiple, Twins).

**Twins; Wife Fruitful**—(See "Fruitful" under Wife).

**Woman Is With Child**—(See "Woman" under Pregnancy).

**FRUITION**—The Full ☽ is typical of fruition, fullness, plenitude of fluids, etc. (See "Full Moon" under Moon).

**FUEL**—Of the Body—(See Glycogen, Jupiter, Liver).

**FUGITIVE**—Fugitive from Justice—The Fugitive Is Dead—In Hor'y Q. if the ☽ or lord of the 7th be in the 8th, or apply to its lord by evil asp., or to the evil asp. of an infortune in the 4th H., or if the dispositor of the ☽ be in the 8th, he is dead. (See Judges, Law, Prison).

**FULL**—Fullness—

**Abdomen**—Fullness of—(See "Distentions", "Prominent", under Abdomen).

**Arteries**—(See "Fullness" under Arteries).

**Blood**—Fullness of—(See "Fullness" under Arteries; "Too Much Blood" under Blood).

**Body**—Full Body—The ☽ in her increase, full and tall; ♄ Sig. in ♒; ♃ Sig. in ♍, a reasonably full stature; ☿ Sig. in ♌, full and large body; ☿ Sig. in ♏, full and well-set; ♉ gives a full, short, well-set body; ♌ gives a full, tall, portly, and commanding stature. (See Corpulent, Fat, Fleshy, Large, Portly, Stout, Tall, etc.).

**Breasts**—Full Breasts—(See "Full" under Breasts).

**Chest**—Full Chest—(See Capacious, Stout, Wide, under Chest; "Capacity" under Lungs).

**Constitution** — The Constitution At Full—(See "Full" under Constitution).

**Engorgement**—(See "Fullness" under Arteries; Engorgement, Gluttony; "Vascular Fullness" under Vascular).

**Eyebrows**—(See "Full" under Eyebrows).

**Eyes**—Full Eyes—(See "Full" under Eyes).

**Face**—(See "Full" under Face).

**Fat and Full Body**—(See "Body" under Fat).

**Fleshy and Full Body**—(See "Fleshy Body" under Fleshy).

**Fluids**—Fullness of—(See "Fullness" under Fluids; "Full Moon" under Moon).

**Full Habit**—(See Habit).

**Full Moon**—(See "Full Moon" under Moon).

**Full-Sized Person**—(See "Body" under Large).

**High Blood Pressure**—Full Arteries —(See "Fullness" under Arteries; "Pressure" under Blood).

**Lips**—Full Lips—(See Lips).

**Moon**—(See "Full Moon" under Moon).

**Neck**—(See "Thick" under Neck).

**Plenitude** — Fullness — (See "Full Moon" under Moon; Plethora, Plenitude).

**Short**—Short and Full Stature—(See "Body" in this section).

**Stature**—Full-Sized Stature — (See "Body" under Large).

**Stomach**—Fullness At—(See "Stomach" under Gas).

**System**—Fullness of—☉ diseases. (See System).

**Tall and Full Body**—(See "Body" in this section; Tall).

**Vascular Fullness**—(See Arteries, Blood, in this section; Vascular).

**Vital Power At Full**—(See "Hylegiacal Places" under Hyleg; "Full" under Vital; "Good" under Vitality).

**FULMINATING**—The Sudden Severity of Disease—Intensity of the Disease— ♂ action, and a physical quality of ♂. (See "High" under Fever; Intensity, Quick, Severity, Sudden).

**FUMES**—Gas—Gases—(See Gas).

**FUNCTIONS**—The ☽ is the chief index of functional integrity, and is at the head of the functional group. The ☽ is functional, and denotes affections and functional disturbances from external causes, as food, clothing, habits, climate, environment, etc. The nature of functional and structural disorders can be inferred from the combination of the sign, planet, house and aspects. The ☽ has chief rule over the bodily functions, and is the source of natural power, as the natural powers of each organ of the body depend upon the regular and proper functions of such part. The ☽ is more powerful and benefic over the functions when in-creasing, and more weak and malefic when decreasing in light. Functions, as ruled by the ☽, are to be designated as the particular power or activity of the organ ruled by the sign which contains the ☽ at B. For the functions ruled by each Sign see the Sign in the alphabetical arrangement, as Aries, Taurus, etc. Also for the functions of the various organs and parts of the body, their disorders and disturbances, see the part in the alphabetical arrangement, as Brain, Heart, Kidneys, Liver, Stomach, etc. The following subjects and paragraphs have to do with the various functions of the body, their normal and abnormal activities.

**Ablation**—Of Functions—(See Ablation, Remote, Removal, Suppression).

**Activities**—Functional Activities— The aspects and position of the ☽ govern the general habits of life and the functional activities. (See Habits. Also note the various paragraphs in this section).

**Arrangements**—The ☽ rules the functional arrangements, the functional activities, and the feminine functions, as the menses and childbirth. The functional arrangement is also governed by the cardinal signs.

**Atrophy**—Of Function—Atrophy of Process Thru Cessation of Function— The work of ♆ and ♄, and by their afflictions to the hyleg. (See Atrophy; "Suppressed" in this section).

**Augmented**—The good asps. between the ☉ and ☽ tend to augment the functional and vital energies, but the evil asps. between them tend to disturb and retard them. (See "Increased" under Vitality).

**Bowels**—(See "Functions" under Bowels).

**Brain**—(See "Functions" under Brain).

**Cells**—Functions of—(See the various paragraphs under Cells).

**Cerebral**—(See "Cerebral Functions" under Cerebral).

**Cessation** — Of Function—♄ in evil asp. to the ☽; ♄ influence and affliction. (See Atrophy, Depleted, Impeded, Slow, Suppressed, in this section).

**Childbirth**—The Functions of—Ruled by the ☽. (See "Causes of Birth" under Birth; Parturition).

**Cold**—Functions Prevented By—(See "Privation" in this section).

**Congestions**—Of the Functions—(See Congestion).

**Conserving Of**—(See Conservation).

**Constitution**—(See "Functions" under Constitution).

**Constructive Functions**—(See Constructive).

**Crystallization**—In the Body—Function of—The work of ♄. (See Crystallization, Deposits, Hardening).

**Deficient**—(See "Regular" in this section).

**Depletion Of**—(See Depletion; Disordered, Impaired, Low, Retarded, Suppressed, in this section).

**Depressants**—Functional Depressants —(See Anaesthetics, Anaphrodisiacs, Sedatives).

**Deranged Functions**—(See "Disordered", and the various paragraphs in this section; "Functions" under Constitution; Deranged).

**Diet**—The Functions Impeded by Wrong Diet—(See "Ailments" under Diet).

**Difficult**—The Feminine Functions Difficult and Slow—(See "Difficult" under Menses).

**Digestive Functions**—(See Digestion, Indigestion).

**Directions**—The Effects of Directions Upon the Functions—(See Directions).

**Discomfort**—From Painful, Excessive, Impaired and Irregular Functions—(See Discomfort; Irregular, Painful, in this section).

**Disordered Functions**—The Functions Disordered—Disturbed—Impaired—Impeded — Weakened — Retarded, etc. Are due to afflictions to the planets, whereas organic diseases are caused by afflictions to the signs; caused by Directions (see Directions); the ☉ affl. by the ☽; ☽ affl. in the 6th H.; the ☽ affl. in ♏ or ♑; the ☽ affl. in a fiery sign; afflictions to the ☽ or ♃; the ☽ afflicting the Asc.; ♃ in □ or ☍ the ☉. The nature of the functional disorder can be inferred from the combination of sign, house, and aspects. (See the various paragraphs in this section).

**Dispersal**—Of the Functional Energy —(See Dispersions).

**Dissipation**—Of the Functional Energy—A ♆ disease. (See Dispersals; "Energy Dissipated" under Dissipation; Neptune).

**Disturbed Functions**—(See "Augmented", "Disordered", and the various paragraphs in this section).

**Dropsy**—From Disturbed Bodily Functions—(See Dropsy).

**Efficient**—The ☽ in the water signs ♋ or ♓, the functions are more efficient, strong and regular. (See Regular, Strong, in this section).

**Elimination**—The Functions of—(See Elimination).

**Energy**—The Functional Energies—(See Dissipation Of, Strong, Weak, and the various paragraphs in this section).

**Exaltation Of**—(See "Excito-Motory" in this section).

**Excessive**—And Painful—Discomfort —The ☽ affl. by ♂ or ♀. (See "Discomfort", "Profuse", in this section).

**Excito-Motory Function**—Exaltation of—(See Exaltation).

**Excretion**—The Functions of—(See Excretion).

**Expansion Of**—Warmth of—(See Electric).

**Fear**—The Functions Suppressed Thru Fear—(See "Functions" under Fear).

**Female Functions**—The Feminine Functions—Disorders of—(See "Functions" under Female; "Difficult", and the various paragraphs under Menses; "Impeded" in this section).

**Generative Function**—Abuse of—Strong—Weak, etc.—(See Barren, Creative, Fruitful, Generation, Passion, Perversions; "Clandestine", "Sex Powers", under Sex).

**Gestation**—Functions of—(See Conception, Gestation, Pregnancy).

**Harmony**—The various functions of the body are kept in greater harmony when the ☉ or ☽ are in ☌, ⚹ or △ asp. the Asc. at B., and by dir. (See Harmony).

**Heart**—The Functional Activities of —(See "Functions", and the various paragraphs under Heart).

**Hindered**—The Functions Hindered—♄ influence. (See "Suppressed", and the various paragraphs in this section).

**Impaired**—♄ afflictions; the ☽ affl. by ♄. At the 1st Quarter, Full Moon, 3rd Quarter of the ☽, the functions and the constitutional activities tend to be impaired. (See Depletion, Slow, Suppressed, and the various paragraphs in this section; "Quarters" under Moon).

**Impeded**—The functions are impeded when the ☽ is in fiery signs, and often prevented, and the feminine functions espec. tend to be difficult and slow. (See "Ailments" under Diet; Irregular, Prevented, Retarded, Slow, Suppressed, Weakened, in this section).

**Inhibited**—♄ influence. (See "Functions" under Inhibitions; Retarded, Slow, Suppressed, and the various paragraphs in this section).

**Irregular**—And Painful—The ☉ and ☽ in bad asp. to each other; functional irregularities are ruled by the ☽, and caused by afflictions to the ☽, or the ☽ in incongenial signs; the ☽ affl. by ♄, irregular, stoppage, or suppression thru cold or privation; the ☽ affl. by ♃ or ♂, irregular and profuse; the ☽ afflicted in ♉; the ☽ affl. in ♏, irregular and painful female functions; the ☽ affl. in ♑, irregular, impeded, and uncertain, and due to depression, worry, and anxiety; the ☽ below the earth in a nocturnal nativity; the ☽ ruler of the 6th H., or in the 6th, and the planet afflicting the ☽ be ruler of the 1st, 6th, or 8th H., the functions are disturbed or irregular; ♀ □ or ☍ ☽, disturbed or irregular; ♀ □ or ☍ ☽, painful and irregular, causing discomfort, and usually due to loose living; ☿ □ or ☍ ☽, thru mental strain or anxiety. (See Anxiety, Depression, Discomfort; "Free Living" under Free; Irregularities, Menses. Also note the various paragraphs in this section).

**Liver**—Functions of—(See Liver).

**Low**—Lowered—The Functions Lowered—The functional activities tend to be lower at the New ☽, the 1st Quarter, Full ☽, and 3rd Quarter, and if it be an eclipse of the ☉, the Solar activity is equally depleted and low. The adverse asps. of ♄ to the ☽ tend to lower, retard, and suppress the functions for the time. (See "Full Moon", "New Moon", under Moon; Impeded, Retarded, Slow, Suppressed, in this section).

**Maternity** — The Functions of — (See Maternity).

**Menses** — Functional Disorders of — (See "Female Functions", "Irregular", in this section).

**Natural Functions** — The Natural Functions in the body are ruled by the ☽, and espec. in the female. (See Females, Menses, Natural; "Disordered", and the various paragraphs in this section).

**Nature** — Of Functional Disorders — (See "Disordered" in this section).

**Normal** — The Functions Normal and Regular—The ☉ well-asp. by the ☽; the ☽ well-asp. in ♋ or ♓, and free from the serious afflictions of the ☉ and planets; the ☽ elevated above the earth in a nocturnal nativity, or below the earth in a day geniture. (See Elevated, Normal, Regular; Efficient, Regular, Strong, in this section).

**Obstructed** — The Functions Obstructed—Caused by ♄, and ♄ afflictions to the ☽. (See Impeded, Retarded, Slow, Suppressed, and other paragraphs in this section; Obstructions).

**Organic Functions**—Ruled by the ☽. The ☽ rules the functions of the various organs of the body. Thus the ☽ in ♋ rules the functions of the stomach; in ♌, the functions of the heart, etc. The ♍ sign, which rules the abdomen and its organs, is recognized as being the algebraic common denominator of all organic diseases and functions, due to the different states and conditions of the digestive and bowel tracts, and their contents, and that nearly all diseases have their origin under the ♍ sign rule. For this reason purging has been held to from Ancient Times as one of the first things to do to relieve and remove the causes of disease in the bowel tract. (See Physic, Virgo). The ☉ is organic, while the ☽ is functional, and afflictions to the ☉ or ☽ in ♍, and espec. when in the 6th H., tend to serious disturbances of organic functions. (See Organic, Organs).

**Over-Activity** — Of the Functions — The ☽ ☌ ♂ at B. and by dir., may cause. Also ♃ tends to, and to surfeits and congestion of the parts ruled by the sign he is in at B., or by dir. or tr. (See Congestion; Augmented, Excessive, Profuse, Strengthened, in this section).

**Painful** — And Irregular — The ☽ affl. in ♏ with females; the ☽ affl. by ♂. (See Discomfort, Excessive, Irregular, in this section).

**Painless**—The ☽ well-asp. by ♂ or ♀. (See Normal, Regular, in this section).

**Parenchyma**—The Functioning Structure of an Organ—(See Parenchyma).

**Parturition** — Childbirth — The Functions of—(See Parturition).

**Perfect** — (See "Regular" in this section).

**Perversion**—Of Function—♆ □ or ☍ ☽, perversion of function of some organ, or the natural function rejected and refused, such as in Sex Perversions, Sodomy, etc. (See Perversions).

**Prevented**—The Functions Prevented —Retarded—Impeded—(See "Impeded" in this section).

**Privation** — The Functions Retarded or Suppressed thru Privation or Cold— The ☽ affl. by ♄. (See "Irregular" in this section; Privation).

**Profuse** — The Functions Profuse — (See "Irregular" in this section).

**Properly Performed** — (See Efficient, Normal, Regular, Strong, in this section).

**Psychopathic Functions**—(See "Functions" under Psychic).

**Quarters of the Moon**—As Related to the Functions—(See "Quarters" under Moon).

**Recuperation**—The Powers of Recuperation to Recover from Disordered Functions—(See Recuperation, Resistance, Vitality).

**Regular**—The Functions are Regular, Efficient, Normal, and Strong—The ☉ well-asp. by the ☽; the ☽ below the earth in a day nativity, and above the Earth in a night one; the ☽ well-asp. in ♉, ♋, or ♓; the ☽ well-asp. by ♄, ♃, ♂, and ♀; the ☽ ⚹ or △ the Asc.; the ☽ well-asp. by ♄, regular, but apt to be slow, weak, and deficient; the ☽ well-asp. by ♃, and free from adverse afflictions, the functions are regular and perfect. (See Efficient, Normal, Strong, in this section).

**Resistance** — The Vital Resistance Good to Disordered Functions — Well Able to Fight Against Functional Disorders—The ☉ well-asp. in ♎. (See Recuperation, Resistance, Stamina, Tone, Vitality Good, etc.).

**Retarded**—The Functions Retarded— The ☉ or ♃ □ or ☍ ☽; ♄ affl. the ☽. (See Difficulty, Hindered, Impaired, Impeded, Irregular, Obstructed, Slow, Stopped, Suppressed, in this section).

**Revitalization**—Of the Functions and Fluids—(See "First Quarter" under Moon).

**Secretion**—The Secreting Functions— (See Secretion).

**Sedatives** — Functional Sedatives and Depressants — (See "Depressants" in this section).

**Sensorial Functions** — Impaired—(See "Functions" under Sensation).

**Slow and Difficult**—And Especially In Females—The ☽ affl. in fiery signs; the ☽ affl. by ♄. (See "Difficult" under Menses; Regular, Retardations, Slow, Suppressions, etc.).

**Solar-Lunar Activities** — As Related to the Functions and Health—The ☉ and ☽ should be in good asp. to each other at B. to insure regular and normal functions, and general good health, and afflictions between the Lights at B., and by dir., tend to impair the functional activities, and the welfare of the constitution in general. (See "Good" under Constitution, Health, Vitality; the various paragraphs in this section).

**Stagnation**—Of the Functions—Caused by ♄ afflictions; the ☽ ☌ or ill-asp. ♄ at B., and by dir.; also assisted by an evil asp. between the Lights at B., and with an ill-asp. of ♄ in the configuration. (See Atrophy, Cessation, Destructive, Fear, Impeded, Irregular, Retarded, Suppressed, in this section).

**Stomach**—The Functions of Disordered—(See Diet, Digestion, Eating, Food, Indigestion, Stomach).

**Stoppage**—Of the Functions—Caused by ♄, and the ☽ affl. by ♄. (See Irregular, Suppressed, in this section).

**Storing**—The Storing Functions of the Body—(See Conservation).

**Strengthened**—The Functions Strengthened—The ☉ in good asp. to the ☽; the ☽ below the earth in a day nativity, or above the Earth in a night one; the ☽ well-asp. by the ☉, ♄, ♂, ♀, and ☿; ☿ in good asp. the ☽ acts favorably upon the functions, and with greater power of mind to control them. (See Efficient, Normal, Regular, Strong, in this section).

**Strong**—The Functions Strong, Regular, and Efficient—The ☽ well-asp. by the ☉ and many planets, and free from ♄ affliction; the ☽ in the congenial watery signs ♋ or ♓, and well-asp., the functional activities are strong and efficient. (See Efficient, Normal, Regular, Strengthened, in this section).

**Suppressed**—The Functions Suppressed—Suspended—Hindered—Retarded—Slow—Stopped, etc.—Caused by ♄ and ♄ affl. to the ☽; ♅ □ or ☍ ☽, may be complete suppression, and attended by some incurable disorder. (See Hindered, Impeded, Irregular, Retarded, Slow, Stopped, in this section; Incurable, Stoppages, Suppressions).

**Suspended**—The Functions Suspended—♄ influence. (See "Suppressed" in this section).

**Transforming**—The Transforming Functions of the Body—(See Conservation).

**Uncertain**—And Irregular—(See "Irregular" in this section).

**Vital Functions**—The Vital Functions Suspended—(See "Suppressed" in this section. Also see the various paragraphs under Vital).

**Vitality**—And the Functions—The ☽ affl. in ♏ in females tends to painful, irregular functions, and to lower the tone and vitality. (See the various paragraphs under Vitality).

**Warmth**—The Warmth and Expansion of the Functions—(See Electric).

**Wastings**—Wasting—Functional Disorders Caused By—(See Emaciation, Nutrition, Wastings).

**Weak**—The Functions Weak and Irregular—(See Impeded, Irregular, Regular, Retarded, Slow, Suppressed, Weakened, in this section).

**Weakened**—The Functions Weakened—Impeded—Impaired—Retarded, etc.—The ☉ □ or ☍ ☽, the functions of the organ ruled by the sign containing the ☽ are weakened, impeded, and disturbed; the ☽ affl. in ♏, ♑, or fiery signs; the ☽ below the earth in a nocturnal nativity; the ☽ affl. by ♄, weakened, and may be suppressed and stopped by cold and privation; the ☽ well-asp. by ♄, may be regular, but weak, slow, or deficient; the ☽ affl. by the bad asps. of ♃, the functions weakened and impeded by injudicious diet; ☿ □ or ☍ ☽, weakened, impeded, and irregular thru mental strain, anxiety and worry. (See "Ailments" under Diet; "Weak Body" under Weak; Vitality Low; Impaired, Impeded, Irregular, Slow, Suppressed, in this section).

**FUNDAMENT**—Of the Body—The Base—The Anus—Ruled by ♂, ☿, the ♏ sign, and the 9th H.

**Disorders Of**—Are ♏ diseases, and afflictions to ♂ and ☿; malefics and afflictions in the 9th H. (See Anus, Rectum).

**Knots In**—(See Knots).

**FUNGUS GROWTHS**—Vegetable Growths—Ruled by ♆. Also a ☉ disease. (See Excrescences, Growths, Mushrooms, Sponges, Tumors; "Vegetable Growths" under Vegetable).

**Fungi**—(See Tinea).

**FURY**—Furious—Madness—Frenzy—Violent—Mania—Furious Conduct—Furious Temper, etc.—The ☉ affl. in ♉, ♌, or ♏; ☉ Sig. □ or ☍ ♂; the ☽ Sig. to the ☌ or ill-asps. ♂ by dir., and ♂ ill-dignified; the ☽ to the place of the Bull's Horns by dir.; ♆ affl. in the 12th H.; ♃ Sig. □ or ☍ ♂; ♂ ill-dig. at B., and affl. by ♄ and ☿; ♂ affl. at B., and born under ♂ influence, or ♂ ruler; ☿ causes when the dominion of death is vested in him; ☿ Sig. ☌ or ill-asp. ♂ at B., and by dir.; ♉ on the Asc., furious like the Bull when provoked. (See Anger, Brain Storms, (see Brain); Cruel, Demoniac, Desire Body (see Desire); Epilepsy, Excitable, Frenzy, High Temper (see Temper); Hysteria, Impulsive, Insanity, Madness, Mania, Ravings, Riotous, Savage, Uncontrolled, Vehement, Vicious, Violent, Wild, etc.).

**Beasts**—Injury by Furious Beasts—(See "Furious" under Beasts).

**Death by Fury**—(See "Death" under Madness).

**Enthusiasm**—The Fury of—(See Enthusiasm).

**Fits of Fury**—The combined influence of ♄ and ♂ induces to alternate fits of fury and melancholy.

**Soldiers**—Soldiers Become Furious and Cruel—(See Soldiers).

**FUSIONS**—Adhesions—Union of Parts—Coalition—(See Coalition).

**FUTURE EVENTS**—The Times of Possible Accidents, Disease, Injury, Death, etc.—Future events are of the nature of the planet, or planets, causing them. Mars ☌ or ill-asp. the ☉, ☽, Asc., M.C., or Hyleg, by dir. tends to accidents, cuts, injury, fever, inflammations, quarrels, violent death, etc. The afflictions of ♄ tend to chronic ill-health, sorrow, trouble, misfortune, reverses, or even death, if the vitality is low thru worry. And so on with each of the planets. Raphael's Ephemeris of the Major Planets from the year 1900 to the year 2000 should be in the hands of every student who wishes to look ahead over the planetary influences for many years to come. (For further discussion of this subject see Character, Directions, Events, Fate, Prognostication, Time).

# G

**GAIT**—Carriage—Locomotion—Step—Walk—Tread—Motion In the Body, etc.—This subject is also largely considered under "Walk", as Gait and Walk are both quite frequently referred to in the Textbooks of Astrology, and for convenience of reference some of the subjects are given here, and some under Walk. See the following subjects in the alphabetical arrangement when not considered here—

**Action**—(See the various paragraphs under Action).

**Active Body**—(See Active).

**Ankles Knock**—(See Ankles).

**Automatic Action**—(See Automatic).

**Awkward Gait**—Or Walk—♄ Sig. in ♑; ♑ on the Asc. (See Awkwardness, Clumsiness. Also note the various paragraphs in this section).

**Awry Gait**—Treading—Twisted—Turned to One Side, Distorted, etc.—♄ in the Asc. or M.C. at B., in earthy signs.

**Bad Gait**—♄ in ♑ in partile asp. the Asc.

**Balanced Movement**—(See Balance, Coordination, Dexterity).

**Bow Legs**—(See this subject under Legs).

**Brisk Gait**—(See "Energetic" in this section).

**Carriage**—(See the various paragraphs in this section, and under Walk).

**Claw Feet**—(See Feet).

**Club Feet**—(See Feet).

**Clumsy Gait**—(See Clumsiness; "Dragging", and the various paragraphs in this section).

**Commanding Gait**—Majestic—♌ influence; ♌ on Asc. (See Commanding).

**Coordination Of**—(See Coordination, Incoordination).

**Crippled**—In the Legs or Feet—(See Crippled, Extremities, Feet, Legs, Limbs, Lower).

**Defective Gait**—Defects In—♄ in the Asc.; caused by ♄ afflictions. (See Defects; "Defective" under Walk).

**Deformities**—In Legs or Feet—(See Deformities, Distortions, Feet, Legs).

**Dexterity**—In Gait—☿ and ♊ influence. (See Dexterity; "Energetic" in this section).

**Distorted Gait**—(See Distortions; "Awry" in this section).

**Downward Look**—(See "Downward" under Look; Stooping).

**Dragging Gait**—Shuffling—♄ ascending at B. (See "Knocking" under Ankles; "Club Feet" under Feet; "Knock Knees" under Knees).

**Energetic Gait**—Brisk Walk—Light, Quick, Smart, and Nimble Step—♊ gives; ☿ Sig. of the person in Hor'y Q.; ☿ ascending at B., and free from the afflictions of other planets. (See Action, Active, Energy, Motion, Movement, Nimble, Quick, Rapid).

**Equilibrium Disturbed**—(See Balance, Coordination, Equilibrium, Incoordination; "Equilibrium" under Walk).

**Erect; Feet**—The Feet Strike Together—♄ ascending at B. (See "Dragging" in this section).

**Festination**—The Peculiar Walk of Paralysis Agitans—(See "Festination" under Walk).

**Firm Step**—Firm, Commanding, Proud and Majestic—♌ gives; ♌ on the Asc.

**Flat Feet**—(See "Splay Foot" under Feet).

**Forward**—Pitches Forward—(See "Equilibrium" under Walk).

**Genteel Carriage**—A Good Carriage—♊ and ♌ give; ♀ Sig. in ♎. (See Genteel).

**Gouty**—(See "Feet" under Gout).

**Heavy Gait**—♓ gives; ♓ on Asc. (See Heavy, Stooping).

**Incoordinated**—(See "Equilibrium" in this section).

**Intoxicated Gait**—Drunken—(See Drunkenness, Intoxication).

**Knock Knees**—(See Knees).

**Lameness**—In the Legs or Feet—(See Lameness; "Lameness" under Feet, Legs).

**Legs**—Defects In—Crooked—Deformed—Lameness In—(See Legs).

**Light Walk**—Nimble—Quick—Energetic—(See "Energetic" in this section; "Active Body" under Active; Motion, Movement, Nimble, Quick, Rapid, etc.).

**Limping**—(See "Gout", "Lameness", and the various paragraphs under Feet, Knees, Legs, Limbs).

**Locomotion**—Defects of—(See Action, Locomotion, Motion, Movement, Muscles).

**Majestic Gait**—(See Commanding, Firm, in this section).

**Malformations**—In Legs and Feet—(See Crippled, Deformities, in this section; Distortions, Malformations).

**Motion**—Of the Body—(See Action, Motion, Movement, Quick, Rapid, Slow, etc. Also note the various paragraphs in this section).

**Movement**—Of the Body—(See Movement. Also see the various paragraphs in this section).

**Muscles**—(See "Muscles" under Legs; Muscles).

**Nimble Step**—Light—Quick—(See "Energetic" in this section; "Quick Motion" under Motion; Quick).

**Paralysis Agitans**—Peculiar Gait of—(See "Festination" under Walk).

**Peculiar Gait**—(See "Festination" under Walk).

**Pitches Forward**—(See "Equilibrium" under Walk).

**Posture**—(See the various paragraphs under Posture).

**Proud Gait**—(See Proud; Commanding, Firm, in this section).

**Quick Walk**—(See "Energetic" in this section).

**Rough In Carriage**—♄ Sig. in ♉ (Hor'y).

**Shuffling Gait**—(See "Dragging" in this section).

**Slow Gait**—(See Dull, Feeble, Inactive, Inertia, Lassitude; "Slow Motion" under Motion; "Dragging", and the various paragraphs in this section).

**Smart and Quick**—(See "Energetic" in this section).

**Splay Foot**—(See "Splay" under Feet).

**Staggering Gait**—Swaying—Tottering—Due to afflictions to ☿, and Incoordination. (See Clumsy, Equilibrium, Intoxicated, in this section).

**Step Firm**—Majestic—(See Commanding, Firm, in this section).

**Stooping**—Heavy—(See Downward Look, Heavy, in this section; Stooping).

**Stoppage Gait**—♄ influence; ♄ affl. in ♓; Subs at LPP (4, 5L); also may be caused by ♅ influence, and due to incoordination, partial paralysis, etc. (See Coordination, Incoordination, Stoppages, Suppressions; "Festination" under Walk).

**Strutting Gait**—Swaggering—♅ setting at B., and not in a strong sign or house; ♄ rising and affl. at B.; ♄ Sig. of the party in Hor'y Q., and one who knocks his ankles together, or who may be bow-legged or knock-kneed. (See Dragging, Equilibrium, Proud, in this section).

**Swaggering**—(See "Strutting" in this section).

**Swaying**—Tottering—(See Equilibrium, Staggering, in this section).

**Tottering**—(See "Staggering" in this section).

**Treading Gait**—(See "Awry" in this section).

**Turned to One Side**—(See "Awry" in this section).

**Twisted Gait**—(See "Awry" in this section; Contortions, Twistings).

**Unsteady**—(See "Staggering" in this section).

**Waddling Gait**—♓ on the Asc. (See Dragging, Heavy, in this section).

**GALEN**—Galen taught the same theories about the cure of disease as did Hippocrates. (See Antipathy, Hippocrates).

**GALL**—Bile—Gall Bladder—Choler—Gall Stones, etc.—(See Bile).

**GALLOWS**—Death On by Sentence—(See Hanging, Judges).

**GAMBLING**—Gamblers are born under severe mental affliction, and Gambling is practically a mental disease. The 5th H. rules largely over gambling and speculation. The watery signs predominating at B., and also malefics in ♊ or ♐, or with these signs upon the Asc., and afflicted, tend to. The ☉ Sig. in ♓; ♅ in strong asp. to the cusp of 5th H., or a planet in the 5th; the ☽ in the 5th H., and afflicted; ♄ Sig. ☌ ♀; ♂ ruler at B., and afflicted, and also afflicting ☿; ♂ Sig. in ♉ or ♊; ♂ or ♀ in the 5th H.; ☿ Sig. ☌ ♂; ☿ in the 5th H., and affl. by ♄ or ♂, and espec. when ☿ is in a water sign; lord of the 5th H. in the Asc., and afflicted; ♐ on the Asc., and the 5th H. affl. by ♂; the 6th face of ♌ on the Asc. (See Cheating, Deceitful, Dishonesty, Forgers, Riches, Speculative, Shrewdness, Thieves, etc.).

**GAMES**—Fond of Outdoor Sports and Games—Danger of Injury or Death By—(See Amusements, Exercise, Hunting, Sports).

**GANGLION**—Ganglia—Nerve Centers—Chronic diseases begin their action in the Ganglionic Centers, while acute diseases start with disturbances of the peripheral nerves. (See Acute, Chronic, Peripheral). The action of ♄ by cold and chill, and by causing internal congestions, disturbs the ganglionic centers. (See Centripetal, Cold, Congestions, Saturn).

**Basal Ganglia**—The ☉ and ☽ acting thru the ♏ sign, by way of the Lumbar and Intestinal branches of the Solar Plexus, affect and influence the Basal Ganglia of the brain, and also the Medulla, the Pituitary Body, Ductless Glands, Genito-Urinary System, Bladder, Rectum, Anus, Uterus, Large Intestines, and give way to the Hepatic Diathesis. (See Diathesis, Ductless, Liver; "Ribes", in this section).

**Central Ganglia**—(See "Vaso-Dilator" under Vaso).

**Cerebral Ganglia**—(See Brain, Cerebral).

**Cervical Ganglion**—The ☉ and ☽ acting thru the ♉ sign affect the Superior Cervical Ganglion, the pharyngeal plexus, the eustachian tubes, the throat and neck, and give way to the Renal Diathesis. (See "Cervical Ganglion" under Cervical; "Lumbar", "Middle", in this section).

**Fifth Thoracic Ganglia**—(Spinal)—Influenced by the ☉ and ☽ acting thru the ♋ sign. The 5th thoracic (spinal) ganglia, the left coronary, the hepatic, splenic, diaphragmatic, and gastric plexuses, affect the organs of digestion, the pleura and their dependencies, and give way to the Cranio-Abdominal Diathesis. (See "Middle Cervical" in this section; Diaphragm).

**Impar**—The Ganglion Impar (in front of the Coccyx)—Acted upon by the ☉ and ☽ in ♐. Also the ☉ and ☽ in this sign, acting thru this ganglion and the inferior hypogastric plexus, affect the heart, the bladder, the muscular system, the hips, thighs, the gastro-intestinal tunics, and give way to the Thoracic Diathesis. (See Chest, Thorax).

**Lumbar Ganglia**—The ☉ and ☽ in ♎ act upon this ganglia, and also by acting thru the aortic, hypogastric, and renal plexuses, affect the hypogastrium, the renal system, the bladder in infants, uterus in pregnant women, the small intestine, and give way to the Renal Diathesis. (See "Cervical" in this section).

**Middle Cervical Ganglion**—The ☉ and ☽ in ♊, acting thru this ganglion, and the thoracic (spinal) ganglia, the right coronary plexuses, the deep cardiac, the post-pulmonary plexuses, affect the upper limbs, the respiratory system, and give way to the Cranian Diathesis. (See "Fifth Thoracic", "Splanchnic", in this section).

**Pathological Formation**—Of Ganglion—♀ in ♊.

**Ribes**—The ☉ and ☽ acting thru ♈, thru the ganglion of Ribes, and also thru the cavernous and carotid plexuses, affect the head and its dependencies, and the cerebro-spinal nervous system, and give way to the Hepatic Diathesis. (See "Basal" in this section).

**Semilunar Ganglion**—Ruled by the ♋ sign.

**Spinal Ganglion** — (See "Fifth Thoracic", "Middle Cervical", in this section).

**Splanchnic Ganglia** — The ☉ and ☽ acting thru the ♍ sign, thru the Splanchnic ganglia, the solar and mesentric plexuses, affect the abdominal organs and their dependencies, the lower part of the stomach, and give way to the Cranian Diathesis. (See "Middle Cervical" in this section; Cranium, Diathesis, Nerves, Plexuses).

**Vaso-Dilator Action** — (See "Central" in this section).

**GANGRENE** — The Mortification and Death of Soft Tissue — Gangrenous Sores—A ♄ disease, and caused usually by chill and cold, driving the blood inwards, causing congestion and mortification; Subs at CP and Local. (See Carcinoma, Centripetal, Cold, Congestion, Crusts, Decay, Malignant, Mortification, Necrosis, Sores, Ulcers).

**Mouth** — Gangrenous Sores In — Cankers — Cancrum Oris — Aphthae — A ♄ disease; ♄ in the 6th H.; ♄ affl. the hyleg or Asc. (See "Mouth" under Aphthae).

**Pus**—Malignant Gangrene with Pus—(See "Gangrene" under Pus).

**GAS**—Gases—Fumes—Air—Atmosphere—Ether—Vapor, etc.—Gases are ruled by ♅, as this planet rules the Ether, the Air, the Atmosphere, etc. Also ruled and influenced by the Airy Signs, and espec. the ♒ sign, the strong sign of ♅. The following subjects and paragraphs have to do with Gas, Gases, their compounds, influences, and effects in and out of the human body, which subjects see in the alphabetical arrangement when not considered here.

**Abdomen** — Gaseous Distention of — Meteorism—♅ affl. in ♍. (See Abdomen, Bowels, Distentions, Flatulence, Inflation, Tympanites; "Bowels" under Wind).

**Air; Aquarius; Asphyxia; Belching;**

**Bloating; Borborygmus** — (See this subject under Bowels).

**Bowels** — Gas In — (See "Gas" under Bowels).

**Caisson Disease**—(See Caisson).

**Carbon; Colic; Compressed Gases**—Compressed Air — Ruled by ♅. (See Caisson, Compressed).

**Cramps; Death** — By Escaping Gas — Suffocated By — Case—See "Knights", No. 270, in 1001 N.N.

**Distentions; Dyspnoea; Emphysema;**

**Escaping Gas** — Death By — (See "Death" in this section).

**Ether; Explosions; Fermentation;**

**Flatulence; Foul Gases**—(See Foul).

**Fumes; Gastralgia**—(See Stomach).

**Hydrogen; Indigestion; Inflations;**

**Meteorism** — (See "Abdomen" in this section).

**Miasma; Nitrogen; Noxious; Odors;**

**Oxygen; Poisoning** — Poison Gases — Death By—♅ in the 8th H., and affl. the hyleg; also Subs at Lu.P. (3D) make the effects of Poison Gases more depressive and dangerous. (See Poison).

**Pressure**—Gas Pressure—Compressed Gas—Ill Effects of—(See Caisson, Compressed; "Atmosphere" under Pressure).

**Puffing; Pungent; Spinal Gas** — The Gas In the Spinal Canal—(See "Canal" under Spine).

**Stomach**—Gas In—Bloating—Indigestion—Fullness At Stomach—Caused by afflictions in ♋, ♍, and ♑; ♋ on cusp the 6th H.; the ☽ in ♋ □ or ill-asp. any of the malefics as promittors; the ☽ affl. in ♋ tends to bloating from gas; ♅ affl. in ♋ or ♍; ♄ affl. in ♋; ♃ affl. in ♉ or ♋; a ♃ disease, due to surfeits; ☿ affl. in ♋ tends to windiness in stomach, and due to worry and anxiety; ☿ affl. in ♍ or ♑; the Asc. to the place of ☋ by dir. (See Bloating, Belching, Flatulence, Indigestion, Plethora, Pressure; "Wind" under Stomach).

**Suffocation** — By Escaping Gas — (See "Death" in this section).

**Sun Spots** — And the Gases of Our Atmosphere—(See "Sun Spots" under Spots).

**Swellings** — Caused by Gases, Wind, etc., In the Body — (See Distentions, Flatulence, Inflations, Swellings, Tympanites, etc. Also note the various paragraphs in this section).

**Tympanites**—(See "Abdomen" in this section; Tympanites).

**Uranus**—(See "Influence of ♅" under under Uranus).

**Vapors; Wind**—(See "Bowels"; "Stomach" under Wind).

**GASTRIC** — Gastro — Gastronomical — Gastro-Abdominal Disorders—Stomach Disorders—Gastro-Intestinal Disorders—The subject of Gastric is largely considered under Stomach, as Gastric means pertaining to the Stomach. A few subjects concerning the Stomach, which are especially referred to in the Textbooks as Gastric, will be listed in this section, and also referred to in the section on Stomach. See the following subjects in the alphabetical arrangement, or under Stomach, when not considered here.

**Abdominal**—(See "Gastro-Abdominal" in this section).

**Acids** — The Gastric Acids — Gastric Acidity — Hydrochloric Acid — (See Acids, Digestion, Fluids, Indigestion, Juices, etc.).

**Cancer**—Gastric Cancer—(See "Stomach" under Carcinoma).

**Catarrh** — Gastric Catarrh — (See "Catarrh" under Stomach).

**Deficient**—The Gastric Juices Deficient—(See "Stomach Juices" under Deficient).

**Disorders** — Gastric Disorders — (See the various paragraphs in this section, and under Stomach).

**Fever** — Gastric Fever — Fever with Gastric Derangement — The ☉ affl. in ♋; a ♋ disease; afflictions in ♋; the ☽ hyleg, and to the ☌ or ill-asp. ♄ by dir.; ♂ in ♋ in the 6th H.; ♂ affl. in ♋ or ♍. Case—See Chap. 13, page 97, in Daath's Medical Astrology. (See Fever).

**Gastralgia** — Pain In the Stomach — The ☉ to the ☌ ☽ by dir.; ♂ affl. in ♋; Subs at SP (7D). (See "Pain" under Stomach).

**Gastritis**—Inflammation of the Stomach—The ☉ ☌ ♂ in ♋; the ☉ or ♂ affl. in ♋; ♅ and ♂ action in ♋; ♂ in ♋ in the 4th H. These influences tend to Acute Gastritis. Chronic Gastritis is caused by ♄ affl. in ♋. or affl. the hyleg therefrom. Subs at SP and KP tend to the various forms of Gastritis, as the acute Catarrhal form, with excessive secretion of mucus, the Phlegmonous form, with excessive redness and swelling, the toxic form from swallowing poison. Case—See "Gastritis", Chap. 13, page 91, in Daath's Medical Astrology. (See Inflammation).

**Gastro-Abdominal Disorders**—Due to the combined action of planets in the ♋, ♍, and ♓ signs, and in the 4th and 6th H. (See the Introduction under Disease; "Sixth House" under Sixth; "Innervation" in this section).

**Gastroenteritis**—Inflammation In Both Stomach and Bowels—♂ affl. in ♍. (See "Inflammation" under Bowels; Enteritis).

**Gastro-Intestinal** — (See "Tunics" in this section).

**Gastronomical** — (See "Indiscretions" in this section).

**Indiscretions** — Gastronomical Indiscretions—(See "Evil Diet" under Diet; Eating, Food, Gluttony; "Diet" under Indiscretions).

**Inflammation** — Gastric Inflammation —(See "Gastritis" in this section).

**Innervation** — Gastro-Abdominal Innervation—The physiological action of the ☿ Group of Planets and Herbs tends to produce, and by acting thru the Solar Plexus. (See "Mercury Group" under Herbs).

**Intestinal Tunics** — Gastro-Intestinal Tunics—(See "Tunics" in this section).

**Juices**—Gastric Juices—Are ruled by the ♋ sign. Saturn affl. in ♋ or ♑ tends to disturbances of these juices, deficiency of, abnormality of, lack of, obstructions of, restraint of, sluggish action or production of, etc. Also Subs at SP (8D) tend to disorders of. (See "Fluids" under Digestion).

**Migraine**—(See Migraine).

**Neuroses** — Gastric Neuroses — (See "Neuroses" under Stomach).

**Obstructions**—Gastric Obstructions—(See "Juices" in this section; "Obstructions" under Stomach).

**Pepsin** — Lack of In Stomach — (See "Pepsin" under Stomach).

**Plexuses** — Gastric Plexuses — Ruled by the ♋ sign. (See "Fifth Thoracic" under Ganglion).

**Troubles** — Gastric Troubles — Afflictions in ♋ or ♑. (See the various paragraphs in this section, and under Digestion, Indigestion, Stomach. Also see Migraine).

**Tumor** — Gastric Tumor — Tumor In the Stomach—Afflictions in ♋; a ♋ disease; the ☉ in ♋ and affl. by ♄; ♃ or ♀ affl. in ♋. (See Tumors).

**Tunics** — Gastro-Intestinal Tunics — (See "Impar" under Ganglion).

**Ulcer** — Gastric Ulcer — Imposthumes —Abscess or Ulcer In the Stomach— ♄ in ♋; ♂ in ♋ or ♑. (See Abscess, Ulcers).

**Vein** — The Gastric Vein — Ruled by the ♋ sign. (See Veins).

**GEMINI**—The Gemini Sign—This is the Third Sign of the Zodiac, and is affiliated with the Third House. It is ruled by ☿. The Symbol of this sign is "The Twins". Gemini is hot, moist, and mental in nature, and disturbs the nervous system. Gemini is in an airy, barren, bi-corporeal, changeable, commanding, common, dexterous, doublebodied, dual, fortunate, hot, human, masculine, mental, moist, motive, mutable, nervous, northern, positive as a masculine sign, yet given to negativeness and passivity as a common sign; restless, sanguine, speaking, sweet, vernal, western, whole sign. This sign corresponds to the atmospheric vibrations, and has affinity with the sense of hearing. The Hebrew letter Zain is connected with the ♊ sign, the sign which rules the arms and hands, the instruments by which thoughts are executed. Breathing is a function of this sign. It is a sign of Speech, along with ☿, the ruler of the sign. The ☽ directed to the Right Foot of Gemini, in the Constellation Gemini, is said to bring good health. This sign on the Asc. at B. tends to give a tall, slender body, with long fingers, a straight nose, fine expressive eyes, and with good vitality. For the Countries and Nations ruled by ♊ see "Gemini" under Nations. The Colors ruled by ♊ are white mixed with red. (See "Air Signs" under Signs).

**GEMINI RULES** — Each Sign of the Zodiac has an external, internal, and structural rulership over the parts of the body ruled by the sign. Externally, ♊ rules the shoulders and upper arms. Internally, the breath, nerve fibres, and upper lobes of the lungs. Structurally, the clavicle, scapula, humerus, or bones of the part. The following is an alphabetical and classified list of the parts of the body, and other matters ruled by ♊, as listed and mentioned in the various Textbooks of Astrology. See these subjects in the alphabetical arrangement—Air, Arms, Atmosphere, Blood Making (see Haematopoiesis); Breathing (Breath);

Bronchial Tubes; Bryonia Alba, a typical drug of this sign; Capillaries; Chloride of Potassium, the Zodiac Salt ruled by this sign (see Potassium); Clavicle (Collar Bone); Colors, white and red mixed; Countries (see Nations); Dorsal Nerves and Dorsal Region of the Spine; Drugs (see Bryonia, Potassium); Fingers, Function of Breathing, Gases, Haematopoeisis, Hands, Hearing, Humerus; Lungs (upper lobes of); Mentality, Mind; Nations (see "Gemini" under Nations); Nerve Fibers; Nerves in General, the upper Dorsal, the upper Spinal; Nervous System; Oxygenation of the Blood (see Oxygen); Potassium Chloride, Radius, Respiratory System; Ribs (Upper); Scapula, Shoulders and Shoulder Blades, Speech; Spine (Dorsal Region of); Thymus Gland, Trachea, Twins; Ulna, Upper Dorsal and Spinal Nerves and Upper Ribs.

**GEMINI DISEASES** — The Diseases and Afflictions Ruled by Gemini—The ☉ afflicted in this double-bodied sign tends to two diseases at the same time. The pathological action of ☐ tends to Negativeness, Passivity, Nervousness, and Restlessness. However, ☐ is the strongest of the common signs to control and fight off disease. See the following disease subjects in the alphabetical arrangement when not considered here—

**Abdomen**—Disorders In—(See "Diseases" under Abdomen).

**Accidents**—To the Arms, Shoulders, or Hands—(See "Accidents", "Fractures", under Arms; Clavicle, Hands, Humerus, Radius, Shoulders, Ulna).

**Anaemia; Arms**—Diseases of—Fractures—(See Arms).

**Asthma; Bilious Complaints** — (See "Biliousness", "Obstruction", under Bile).

**Blood**—Blood Disorders—Impure Blood—(See Blood, Impure).

**Bowels**—Disorders of—(See Bowels).

**Brain Fever**—(See Brain).

**Breathing**—Disorders of — (See Breath).

**Bronchitis**—(See Bronchial).

**Capillaries**—Disorders of—(See Capillaries).

**Chest**—Disorders In—(See Chest, Lungs).

**Clavicle**—Collar Bone—Fracture of—(See Clavicle).

**Consumption**—Of the Lungs—(See Consumption, Phthisis, Tuberculosis).

**Corrupted Blood**—(See "Impure Blood" under Impure).

**Dorsal Region** — Disorders of — (See Dorsal).

**Fancy**—All Disorders and Evils of the Fancy—(See Fancies).

**Feet**—Disorders of—(See Feet).

**Flatulence; Fractures**—(See "Accidents" in this section).

**Gout**—In the Arms—(See "Arms" under Gout).

**Hands**—Diseases In—Fractures, Hurts, Injuries To—(See Hands).

**Head**—Diseases In—Accidents To—(See Head).

**Hearing**—Disorders of—(See Hearing).

**Hips**—Disorders of—(See Hips).

**Imagination**—Disorders of—Deranged—(See Imagination).

**Impure Blood**—(See Impure).

**Liver**—Disorders of—(See Liver).

**Lower Limbs**—Disorders of — (See Feet, Legs, Thighs).

**Lungs**—Disorders of—Consumption——(See Consumption, Lungs, Phthisis, Tuberculosis).

**Mental Disorders**—Diseases of the Mind—(See Intellect, Mental, Mind).

**Muscles**—Disorders of—(See Muscles).

**Nervous Diseases**—(See Nerves).

**Oxygenation**—Of the Blood—Disorders of—(See Oxygen).

**Pericardium**—Inflammation of — (See "Pericarditis" under Heart; Pericardium).

**Phthisic**—(See Asthma, Consumption).

**Phthisis; Pleurisy**—(See Pleura).

**Pneumonia; Pulmonary Disorders**—(See Lungs, Pulmonary).

**Respiratory Disorders**—(See Breath).

**Rheumatism**—In the Arms, Hands, Shoulders—(See "Rheumatism" under Arms, Hands, Shoulders. Also see Rheumatism).

**Ribs**—Upper Ribs—Injury or Fracture of—(See Ribs).

**Scapula**—Fracture of—(See Scapula, Shoulders).

**Shoulders**—Disorders of—Hurts, Fractures of—(See Shoulders).

**Thighs**—Disorders of—(See Thighs).

**Thymus Gland**—Disorders of — (See Thymus).

**Torpid Liver**—(See Liver).

**Trachea**—Disorders of—(See Trachea, Windpipe).

**Tuberculosis; Two Diseases**—At the Same Time—The ☉ affl. in ☐. (See "Two Diseases" under Disease).

**Veins**—Windiness In—(See Veins).

**Wasting Diseases** — Wasting of the Lungs — (See Consumption, Lungs, Phthisis, Tuberculosis, Wastings). For collateral study see Castor, Double-Bodied, Dual-Minded, Mercury; "Mutable Signs" under Mutable; Pisces, Pollux, Sagittarius, Third House, Triplets, Twins, Virgo.

**GEMMATION** — Budding—Reproduction by Gemmation is under the rule of ♀, and by division of cell, under ♃. (See "Division", "Gemmation", under Cells; Fecundation; Ovaries, Proliferation, Reproduction).

**GENERAL**—

**Actions**—General Actions—(See Conduct, Habits, Manners, Morals, etc.).

**Ailments**—General Ailments and Disorders—(See "Disorders" in this section).

**Blood**—General Debility of — (See "Blood" under Debility).

**Debility**—(See "General Debility" under Debility; "Debility" under Nerves; "Weakness" in this section).

**Disorders**—General Disorders and Ailments—Are governed by the 6th H., the sign on the cusp, or planets in the 6th. (See Ailments, Disease, Disorders, Sixth House).

**Dropsy**—General Dropsy—(See "Anasarca" under Dropsy).

**Eruptions**—General On the Face or Over the Body—(See Eruptions; "Eruptions" under Face; Measles, Scarlet Fever, Smallpox, etc.).

**Headaches**—General Over the Head—(See "General" under Headaches).

**Health**—General Health—(See "General" under Health).

**Ill-Health**—General Ill-Health—General Weakness—(See Debility, Feeble; "General", "Ill-Health All Thru Life", under Ill-Health; Infirm, Invalids, Sickly; "Much Sickness" under Sickness; "Low" under Vitality; "Weak Body" under Weak, etc.).

**Malaise**—General Malaise—(See Malaise).

**Relaxation**—General Relaxation—Laxity—(See Relaxation).

**Weakness**—General Weakness—(See "Ill-Health" in this section).

**Whole Body**—The Disease or Weakness Is General Over the Whole Body—(See Whole).

**GENERATIVE SYSTEM**—Generative Organs—Generation—Organs of Regeneration—Sex Organs—Genitals—Reproductive Organs—Privy Parts—Secret Parts, etc.—Are ruled by ♂, ♀, the ♍, ♎, and ♏ signs, and the 8th H. The external organs of generation are ruled by ♂, the ♎ and ♏ signs. The internal organs of generation are ruled by ♀ and the ♍, ♎, and ♏ signs. Malefics in ♍, and espec. in ♍ in the 6th H., tend to greatly affect and disturb the uterus and internal generative organs. The following subjects have to do with the organs of Generation, which see in the alphabetical arrangement when not considered here.

**Abscess In**—(See "Abscess" under Secrets).

**All Diseases In**—Signified by the 7th and 8th H., and the ♎ and ♏ signs; afflictions in ♏, and are ♏ diseases; ☽ diseases, and caused by afflictions to the ☽, and espec. with the ☽ in ♏; ♂ diseases, either in men or women; ♀ affl. in ♏. (See Genitals; "All Diseases" under Secrets).

**Barrenness**—Wholly Unfit for Generation—(See Barrenness).

**Cancer Of**—(See "Generative Organs" under Carcinoma).

**Chancre; Chancroid; Death**—From Disorders of—Afflictions in the fixed signs, and espec. in ♏.

**Deformities Of**—(See Eunuchs; "Sex Channels" under Genitals; Hermaphrodites, Maimed, Virile).

**Diseases Of**—Afflictions in ♍, ♎, ♏, the 6th, 7th or 8th H.; Subs at LPP (4, 5L). (See the various paragraphs in this section, and under Females, Genitals, Men, Privates, Reproduction, Secret Parts, Sex, Venereal, Women).

**Distempers In**—Infirmities In—Members of Generation Afflicted—(See "Diseases" under Genitals; "Distempers" under Secrets).

**Eruptions In**—♃ affl. in ♏; ♃ in ♏ in the 6th H., and affl.; ♃ in ♏ and affl. the ☽ or Asc. (See Eruptions).

**Excessive Members**—(See Virile).

**External Organs**—Of Generation—Diseases of—Afflictions To—Hurts To—Afflictions to ♂; ♂ affl. in ♎ or ♏. (See Genitals).

**Female Organs**—Of Generation—Diseases of—Afflictions To—(See Females, Genitals, Ovaries, Vagina, Vulva, Womb, Women, etc.).

**Fruitfulness; Functions**—The Generative Functions—Abuse of—(See "Passional Excesses" under Passion; Perversions; "Solitary" under Vice, etc.).

**Genitals**—(See the various paragraphs under Genitals).

**Genito-Urinary System**—Disorders of—(See Genito-Urinary).

**Gestation; Glands Of**—(See Glands, Glans Penis (see Penis); Muciparous, Ovaries, Testes, etc.).

**Gonorrhoea; Hydrocele; Impotent;**

**Infirmities In**—(See All Diseases, Diseases, Distempers, and the various paragraphs in this section).

**Inflammatory Disorders Of**—♂ affl. in ♏; ♀ in ♉ or ♏ in ☌, □, or ☍ ♂. (See "Inflammatory" under Genitals, Secrets).

**Injuries To**—(See Maimed).

**Internal Organs**—Of Generation—Disorders of—Afflictions in ♍ or ♏; ☽ affl. in ♏ with females; ♂ affl. in ♍ or ♏, and espec. when in the 6th or 8th H.; afflictions to ♀. (See Ovaries, Womb).

**Leucorrhoea; Maimed; Male Organ**—Of Generation—(See Penis).

**Malformations**—♆ and ♄ in ♉ or ♏. (See "Deformities" in this section).

**Masturbation**—(See "Solitary" under Vice).

**Men**—(See "Mens' Genitals" under Genitals).

**Menses; Muciparous Glands**—(See Muciparous).

**Nervous Disorders Of**—(See "Nerves" under Secrets).

**Obstructions In**—The ☉ or ♄ affl. in ♏. (See Obstructions).

**Ovaries; Pains In**—(See "Pains" under Secrets).

**Parturition; Passional Excesses**—(See Passion).

**Penis; Perversions; Powers Of**—Strong—Weak, etc.—(See Amativeness, Apathy, Barren; "Signs Of" under Children; Creative, Fruitful, Impotent; "Powers" under Sex).

**Pregnancy; Prenatal; Privates;**

**Procreation; Propagation**—(See Amative).

**Pudic; Puerperal; Regeneration;**

**Reproduction; Scandalous Diseases**—(See Scandalous).

**Scrotum; Secrets**—Secret Parts—Note the various paragraphs under Genitals, Reproductive Organs, Secrets, Sex, as they are supplemental to this section).

**Self-Abuse** — (See "Solitary" under Vice).

**Semen**—Seminal—(See Semen).

**Sensitive** — (See "Generative Organs" under Sensitive).

**Sensuality; Sex** — Sex Organs — Sex Diseases—(See Sex).

**Spermatozoon**—(See Semen).

**Sterility; Strong Powers Of** — (See "Powers" in this section).

**Swellings In**—(See "Inflammation" in this section; "Swellings" under Secrets).

**Testes; Tumors In**—♃ or ♀ affl. in ♏. (See Tumors).

**Ulcer In**—(See "Genitals" under Ulcer).

**Undeveloped**—The Generative Organs Undeveloped—♄ influence; ♄ affl. in ♉ or ♏; ♄ ☌ ♆ in ♉ or ♏; the ♆ influence tends to undevelopment in the part ruled by the sign he is in at B. (See Defects, Deficient, Diminished, Undersized, Undeveloped, etc.).

**Unfit**—Wholly Unfit for Generation—(See Barrenness).

**Urethra; Uterus**—(See Womb).

**Vagina; Varicocele** — (See Scrotum, Varicose).

**Venereal Diseases**—(See Venereal).

**Virile** — Excessive Virile Members — (See Virile).

**Vulva; Weakness**—Of the Generative System—Planets in the fixed signs, and afflicted, tend to weaken the Generative System; planets in ♉ by reflex action to ♏, and in ♌ and ♒ by their □ aspects to ♏; malefics in ♏ at B., and affl. the hyleg; the ☽ hyleg in ♏, and afflicted, tends to weaknesses and afflictions of the female generative organs; ♀ affl. in ♏. (See the various paragraphs in this section).

**Womb**—Note the various paragraphs under Womb).

**Women**—See the various paragraphs under Females, Women).

**GENEROUS**—Generosity—♃ influence; ♃ well-aspected in ♐ or ♓; ♃ in the Asc. or M.C.; the ☽ ☌ ♃ in ♐, ♓, the Asc., or M.C. (See Humane, Kind, Riches, Sympathetic).

**GENITALS**—Genital Organs—The Genitalia—Pudic—Privities — Members of Generation — Secrets — Reproductive Organs — External Sex Organs, etc. — Denoted by ♂, ♏, and the 8th H. The subjects of Generative Organs, Genitals, Secret Parts, Sex Organs, Reproductive Organs, Privates, etc., are practically one and the same, but are divided into several Sections and Articles in this book for handy reference, and under the headings mentioned prominently in Astrological Literature. See the following subjects in the alphabetical arrangement when not more fully considered here.

**Accidents To**—Injury—Hurts — (See "Mens' Genitals" in this section; Maimed).

**Any Disease** — Of the Genitals — Caused by afflictions to ♀. (See "All Diseases" under Generation).

**Castration**—(See Testes).

**Cervix**—Of the Womb—(See "Cervix" under Womb).

**Chancre**—(See Syphilis).

**Chancroid**—(See Gonorrhoea).

**Channels and Vents**—Lack of Proper Sex Channels—♄ and ♀ in the 4th or 7th H., and afflicted. (See Eunuchs; "Deformities" under Generation).

**Circumcision; Clitoris; Contortions**—♅ affl. in ♏. (See Contortions, Distortions).

**Deformities** — (See "Deformities" under Generative).

**Diseases** — Of the Genitals — Disturbances of—Distempers In—Caused principally by ♂, the ruler of the Genitals, thru passional excesses and irregularities, and also by ♀ thru excess of amorous indulgence; the ☉ affl. in ♉, ♏, ♒, or ♓; the ☉ in ♏ or ♓ in ☌ or ill-asp. any of the malefics as promittors; the ☽ affl. at B.; the ☽ affl. in ♉ or ♏, or afflicting the hyleg therefrom; the ☽ in ♋ in ☌ or ill-asp. ♄ (or ☿ if he be of the nature of ♄) at the beginning of an illness or at decumb.; the ☽ affl. in ♒; ♆ in ♏ and affl. the ☉ or ☽; ♅ affl. in ♏ in evil asp. the ☉ or ☽ tends to produce sex disorders, venereal diseases, genital disturbances, and of a deep-seated nature; ♅ affl. in ♉; ♄ or ♂ affl. in ♏; ♄ in ♋, ♌, or ♍; ♂ in ♏ ☌ or ill-asp. the ☉; ♂ diseases; ♂ □ or ☍ the ☽; ♂ affl. in ♊, ♎, or ♏; ♂ in an angle, occi. of the ☉ and ori. of the ☽; ♃ affl. in ♊, ♋, ♎, or ♏; ♀ diseases; ♀ affl. in ♉, ♏, or ♐; caused by an afflicted ♀; the diseases of ♀ are principally those of the members of generation, and of the matrix, or womb; ☿ affl. in ♎ or ♏; ☿ and the ☽ in ♏ or ♓, ☌ or ill-asp. any of the malefics as promittors; ☿ affl. in ♈, ♉, ♎, ♏, ♐, ♑, or ♓; ♉ or ♏ upon the cusps of the 6th, 8th, or 12th H.; malefics conjoined in ♉ or ♏; many planets, as a Stellium, in ♏ or the 8th H. at B., and afflicted. Diseases of the Sex Organs, or Genitals, are never as severe unless ♉ (the sign opposite to ♏), and the throat and larynx, ruled by ♉, are also afflicted, or with progressed influences in ♉. (See the various paragraphs in this section; "All Diseases In", "Weaknesses", and the various paragraphs under Generation; Secrets; "Sex Diseases" under Sex). Cases of Disorders of the Genitals—See Figures 9, 10, 11, and 34, in the book, "Message of the Stars" by the Heindels.

**Disorders Of** — (See "Diseases", and the various paragraphs in this section).

**Distempers Of** — (See "Diseases" in this section).

**Erections; Eunuchs;**

**External Genitals** — Ruled by ♂, ♏, and ♎. (See "External" under Generation).

**Female Genitals**—Disorders of—(See the various paragraphs under Females, Women, Vagina, Venereal, Vulva).

**Generation**—Generative System—Disorders of—(See Generative).

**Genital Pole**—Of Paracelsus—The ♏ sign. (See Paracelsus, Scorpio).

**Genito-Urinary**—(See the various paragraphs under Genito-Urinary System).

**Gonorrhoea; Hermaphrodites;**

**Hydrocele; Inflammation**—Inflammatory Diseases of—♂ affl. in ♏. (See "Inflammatory" under Generative, Secrets).

**Injuries To**—(See "Accidents" in this section).

**Leucorrhoea; Losses**—Seminal Losses—(See Semen).

**Maimed**—(See Maimed; "Accidents" in this section).

**Male Organ**—(See Penis).

**Mens' Genitals**—Diseases of—Accidents or Injury To—♂ diseases; caused by an afflicted ♂; ♂ affl. in ♏. (See Castration, Gonorrhoea, Maimed, Penis, Scrotum, Testes, Venereal).

**Menses; Nervous Affections Of**—♅ or ☿ affl. in ♏. (See Pudic; "Nerves" under Secrets).

**Pain In**—♄, ♂, or ☿ affl. in ♏; ♏ on the Asc. and afflicted, or on the cusp of 6th or 8th H., and containing malefics.

**Paracelsus**—Genital Pole of—(See "Genital Pole" in this section).

**Parturition**—(See Parturition, Puerperal).

**Passional Excesses**—(See "Passional Excesses" under Passion).

**Penis; Pole**—(See "Genital Pole" in this section).

**Priapism**—(See Penis).

**Pudic; Reproduction; Res Venereae;**

**Scandalous Disease**—(See Scandalous).

**Scrotum; Secret Parts; Semen; Sex**—Sex Channels—Sex Diseases—(See "Channels", and the various paragraphs in this section, and under Generation, Secrets, Sex).

**Stricture; Swellings Of**—(See "Swellings" under Secrets).

**Syphilis; Testes; Trouble**—With the Genitals—The ☽ affl. in ♉, by reflex action in ♏. (See "Diseases", and the various paragraphs in this section).

**Ulcer—In the Genitals**—(See "Genitals" under Ulcer).

**Undeveloped**—The Genitals Undeveloped—(See "Undeveloped" under Generative).

**Urethra; Vagina; Varicocele;**

**Venereal; Vents**—And Channels—(See "Channels" in this section).

**Virile Members**—(See Virile).

**Vulva; Whites**—(See Leucorrhoea).

**Womb; Women**—(Note the various paragraphs under Females, Women).

**GENITO-URINARY SYSTEM**—The Genito-Urinary System, Tract, or Organs, are ruled by the ♏ sign, and are strongly affected for good or evil by the ☉, ☽, and planets acting thru this sign, according to the aspects. The ♂ Group of Herbs have a pathological action on the Genito-Urinary System. The nerves of the Genito-Urinary System are ruled by ♅ and ☿, and the arteries and veins by ♃. The Glands of are ruled by ♆.

**Genito-Urinary Diseases**—The ☉ affl. in ♏; the ☽ affl. in ♏, or affl. the hyleg therefrom; ♄ in ♏, occi., and affl. the ☉, ☽, or Asc.; ☿ affl. in ♉; ♏ on the Asc.; a Stellium in ♏ or the 8th H., and containing malefics; afflictions in ♉, by reflex action in ♏. (See "Cervical Nerves" under Cervical).

**Nervous Affections Of**—♅ in ♏; ☿ affl. in ♉ or ♏. (See Bladder, Genitals, Urine, Varicocele, Varicose).

**GENIUS**—Geniuses—Evolved Types—Prodigies—Precocious, etc.—The ♆ and ♅ vibrations are usually strong at B., and in good asp. to ☿, the mental ruler. The map of birth does not always account for Genius, and the Prenatal influences, the map for the time of conception, should be studied. (See Prenatal). Also the qualities inherent in the Ego have much to do with Genius, or Prodigies, such as expert Mathematicians, Lightning Calculators, Chess Players, Inventors, Cranks, Musical Geniuses, etc. (See Ego).

**Calculators**—Lightning Calculators—Mathematical Geniuses—Cases—(See Mathematical).

**Chess Players**—(See Mathematical).

**Child Prodigies**—(See Mathematical, Music, Precocious, Premature, Prodigies).

**Dull**—The Genius Is Dull—The ♓ influence predominating at B.; ☿ affl. in ♓; in Hor'y Q., the Sig. of the party in ♓. (See Dull).

**Ingenious**—Inventive—Clever—Skillful—Of Unusual Mental Abilities—Constructive—Original, etc.—The ☉ Sig. ☌ ☿ gives ingenuity; the ☉ Sig. in ♍ or ♏; the ☽ in ♊, ♍, ♏, or ♒; the ☽ ☌, P, and good asp. ☿; the ☽ angular at B., or in ♉ or ♋; the ☽ Sig. in ♒; ♅ configurated with ☿; ♅ ascending at B.; ♄ in ♊, ♏, ♑, or ♒; ♄ Sig. in ✱ or △ ☿; ♃ Sig. in ♑; ♂ Sig. in ♊ or ♑; ♀ Sig. in ♍ or ♓; ♀ ✱ or △ ☿; ☿ ascending in ♍; ☿ Sig. in ♒; ☿ Sig. ✱ or △ ♂; ☿ Sig. in ♊, an ingenious, pregnant fancy; ♋ and ♑ influence strong at B.; ♑ on the Asc. When the ☽ is Sig. in ♑ the native is not ingenious. (See "Judgment Good" under Judgment; Learning, Mathematical, Mechanical; "Quickened" under Mental; "Good Mind" under Mind).

**Inventors**—(See Mathematical).

**Mathematical**—(See Mathematics).

**Mechanical**—(See Mechanical).

**Musicians**—Musical Geniuses—(See Music).

**Not Ingenious**—The ☽ Sig. in ♑. (See Dull).

**Pig**—A Performing Pig—Case—See "Performing Pig", No. 781, in 1001 N.N. (See Swine).

**Precocious**—Premature Mental Development—(See Premature).

**Pregnant Genius**—♄ Sig. in ♒; ♂ Sig. in ♏; ☿ Sig. in ♊, a pregnant and ingenious fancy. (See "Ingenious" in this section).

**Premature**—(See "Precocious" in this section).

**Reading**—Child Reads at three years of age, studies Darwin, Huxley, at eight years of age. See Case, "Wiener", No. 353, in 1001 N.N. (See "Child Prodigy" under Prodigy).

**Two Things at Once** — A Male can write a letter and solve a problem at the same time—Case—See "Neptune", No. 352, in 1001 N.N.

**GENTEEL**—

**Genteel Body**—(See Beautiful, Handsome, Well-Proportioned).

**Genteel Carriage**—(See "Genteel" under Gait).

**Genteel In Manner**—The ☉ ☌ ☿ at B.; the ☽ Sig. ☌ or good asp. to ♀.

**Not of Genteel Form**—(See Crooked, Deformed; "Ill-Formed" under Ill; Ugly, etc.).

**GENTLE**—Harmless—Peaceful—

**Gentle Disposition**—Harmless—People born under strong ♀ influence; ♀ Sig. in ♐, ♒, or ♓; the ☉ Sig. in ♋ or ♓; the ☽ strong at B., and well-placed and aspected; the ☉ Sig. in ♉, ♋, or ♒; the ☽ Sig. ⚹ or △ ♀; ♃ Sig. ☌ ☿ and free from ill-asps. of malefics; ♃ Sig. in ♓; the ♒ influence tends to. (See Harmless, Mild, Temper).

**GEOCENTRIC** — The System of Astrology which takes the Earth as a center, and the movements of the planets as seen from the Earth, and in the Earth's Zodiac. The most of the influences in this Work are based upon this System. The Planetary Tables, used by Astronomers and Astrologers in general, and by the Navies of the World, are Geocentric. Also Raphael's Ephemeris gives the Geocentric positions and Longitudes of the planets for each current year. See Earth, Heliocentric).

**GERMS** — Microbes — Bacteria — Germinal—Pestilential Virus, etc.—(See Air, Cholera, Epidemics, Microbes, Microzymasis, Miasma; "Virus" under Pestilence; Zymotic, etc.).

**Germinal**—(See Protoplasma).

**Morbid Germs** — (See Day, Night; "Night Action" under Moon).

**GESTATION**—Pregnancy—The Prenatal Period—Maternity—The State of a Woman with Child—The Puerperal State, etc. — The ☽ rules the mother during Gestation. The ☉, ☽, and Asc. at B., and their relation to each other, indicate whether the period of gestation has been normal, or plus or minus, according to whether the ☽ is above or below the horizon at B., increasing or decreasing in light. (See Prenatal Epoch). The period of gestation is seven or nine months, at which times the ☽ forms the □ and △ aspects to her place at conception, and children born at these times live, but children born at the 8th month do not survive, as the ☽ forms no special aspect to her place at the 8th month. (See "Eight Months Children" under Children). The state of a woman with child is judged by the 5th H. and its influences. The subject of Gestation is also considered under Pregnancy. (See Pregnancy). The following subjects have to do with Gestation, the Prenatal Period, Pregnancy, the Foetus, etc., which subjects see in the alphabetical arrangement when not considered here.

**Abortion; Abnormal Gestation** — Afflictions in ♍, ♎, or ♏, and also in the 5th H. Also caused by Subs at PP (2, 3, 4L). (See Abortion; "Death" under Children; Foetus, Pregnancy, Premature, Prenatal, Stillborn).

**Birth; Children; Conception;**

**Eight Months Children** — (See this subject under Children).

**Embryo; Foetus; Fruitful; Maternity** —(See Maternal, Maternity, Mother).

**Miscarriage; Monsters; Moon** — (See "Gestation", and the various paragraphs under Moon).

**Parturition; Pregnancy;**

**Premature Birth**—(See Abortion, Premature).

**Prenatal Epoch** — The Conditions Which Prevail from Conception to Birth—(See Prenatal).

**Quickening; Seven Months Children**—(See "Eight Months Children" under Children; Parturition, Premature).

**Two Weeks Before Time**—Born Two Weeks Early, etc.—Case—(See Cases under Premature).

**GESTICULATION**—Gestures —Characteristic of the Fixed Signs, and especially of ♉. (See Speech).

**GHASTLY LOOK** — (See Pale, Sickly, White).

**GHOSTS** — (See "Astral Shells" under Astral).

**GIANTS**—Abnormally Tall—The tallest people, as a rule, are produced by the ♐ sign, and espec. when this sign is upon the Asc. at B., and with the ☉ and ♃ rising in this sign. The 26° ♐ on the Asc., a physical prodigy. Also ♅ rising tends to abnormal tallness. It is not always easy to determine the height from the natal map, and the prenatal conditions should be considered, heredity, ancestry, and also the inherent qualities of the Ego may enter into the matter. (See Enlarged; "Abnormal Growth" under Growth; Height; "Body" under Large; Pituitary, Tall, etc.).

**GIDDINESS**—Dizziness—(See Dizziness, Fainting, Vertigo).

**GIFTED** — Highly Accomplished — (See Excellent, Genius; "Good Mind" under Mind; "Natural Abilities" under Natural).

**GINSENG**—A Typical Drug of ♃. (See "Typical Drugs" under Jupiter).

**GIVER OF LIFE** — Hyleg — Apheta — Prorogator—(See Hyleg).

**Givers of Children** — (See "Givers of Children" under Children).

**GLANCES**—The Look of the Eyes—(See Expression; "Glances" under Eyes; Look).

**GLANDS**—Glandular System—Glans—Gonads—Organs of Secretion—The Glands are under the rulership of the ☉, ☽, ♆, the mutable signs, and the internal rulership of ♓. The glands as a whole are under the rule of the

☉ and ♃, but individual glands are also under the rule of other planets. The glandular processes generally are ruled by the ☽. Also ♀ acts strongly upon the glands, causing glandular, and other swellings, at fixed points. The Glands are one of the manifestations of the Vital Body, and are the organs of secretion. (See "Body" under Vital). The Glands are subject to the physiological action of the planets and herbs ruled by ♀. The Glands of the different parts of the body are ruled also and affected by the sign of the Zodiac ruling the part, and the lord of such sign, and are stimulated or suppressed according to the nature of the planets in such signs, and the aspects to them at B., and by dir. The principal glands of the body are listed and mentioned in this Article. See the following subjects in the alphabetical arrangement when not more fully considered here.

**Addison's Disease**—(See Adrenals).

**Adrenals; Affected** — The Glands Affected — Caused principally by afflictions to the ☉, ☽, ♃, and with afflictions in ♓ and the common signs. ♆ rules the glandular system, and when in signs which rule the arms, hands, legs, and feet, tends to shrinking and withering of the limbs, and wasting of the tissues of the parts. (See "Diseases" in this section; the Introduction under Aneurysm).

**Aneurysm; Arms**—Glands of Affected —(See "Affected" in this section; Aneurysm).

**Bowels**—The ☽ in ♍ rules the glands and functions of the bowels, and the ☽ affl. in ♍ tends to glandular troubles in the bowels. ♆ in ♍ tends to wasting of the glands of the bowels. (See "Glandular" under Bowels).

**Bubo; Cervical Glands** — (See Cervical).

**Cervix** — Glands of Affected — (See "Cervix" under Womb).

**Clitoris** — The Glans Clitoris — (See Clitoris).

**Cowper's Glands**—(See Cowper).

**Cysts**—(See Aneurysm, Cysts).

**Develops**—The Glands—♆ in ⚹ or △ the Asc. develops the Glandular System.

**Digestion**—The Digestive Glands— (See Digestion, Gastric, Juices, Stomach).

**Diseases Of**—Disorders of—The ☉ in water signs tends to disorders of; afflictions to ♃ or the ☽; afflictions in ♓ and the common signs; Subs at SP (7D). (See the various paragraphs in this section).

**Disorders Of**—(See "Diseases" and the various paragraphs in this section).

**Ductless Glands**—(See Ductless).

**Endocrine Glands**—(See Ductless).

**Feet**—Glands of Affected—(See "Affected" in this section).

**Fever**—Glandular Fever—The ☉ or ☽ affl. by ♂; ♂ in the various signs tends to glandular fever in the part ruled by such sign; Subs at CP, KP, and Local. (See Fever).

**Fixed Points** — Glandular Swellings at Fixed Points — ♀ diseases. (See "Swellings" in this section).

**Gastric Glands**—(See Digestion, Stomach, in this section).

**Genito-Urinary Organs** — The glands of are ruled by ♆, and ♆ affl. in ♎ or ♏ tends to disorders of. (See Genito-Urinary).

**Glans**—Glans Clitoris—Glans Penis— (See Clitoris, Penis).

**Gonads**—(See "Reproductive" in this section).

**Groins** — Glands In Affected — Enlarged—(See Bubo, Groins).

**Hands**—Glands of—(See "Affected" in this section).

**Head**—Glands of—The Glands of the Head are affected and disturbed by the ☽ or ♆ in ♈. (See Pineal, Pituitary, in this section).

**Inguinal Glands**—(See Bubo, Groins).

**Intestines**—Bowels—Glands of—(See "Bowels" in this section).

**Kidneys**—Glands of—Afflictions in ♎ tend to disorders of. (See Kidneys).

**Lachrymal**—(See Tears).

**Lacteals**—(See Milk).

**Legs**—Glands of—(See "Affected" in this section).

**Limbs**—Glands of—(See "Affected" in this section).

**Liver; Lymphatic Glands**—(See Lymph).

**Mammary Glands** — (See Breasts, Milk).

**Mesenteric Glands**—(See Mysentery).

**Milk Glands**—Lacteals—(See Breasts, Milk).

**Mouth**—Glands of—(See Mouth, Salivary).

**Muciparous** — Mucus — (See Muciparous, Mucous).

**Mumps**—The Parotid Glands Affected —(See Parotid).

**Neck**—Glands of Affected—Glandular Swellings In the Neck and Throat— (See "Glandular Swellings" under Throat).

**Ovaries; Pancreas; Parenchyma;**

**Parotid; Penis** — Glans Penis — (See Penis).

**Pineal; Pituitary; Prostate;**

**Racemose**—(See Pancreas).

**Reproductive Glands** — Sex Glands — Gonads—Ruled by ♂ and the ♏ sign. (See Ovaries, Ovum, Reproduction, Semen, Sex, Testes, etc.).

**Salivary; Sebaceous; Secretory**—(See Secretions).

**Sex Glands** — Gonads — (See "Reproductive" in this section).

**Skin**—Glands of—Ruled by ♎ and ♑. Disorders of caused by afflictions in these signs, and also by an afflicted ♄ or ♀. (See Skin, Sweat).

**Softening**—Of the Glandular Tissues —A ♀ and ♓ disease. (See Softening).

**Spleen; Stomach**—Disorders of Glands of—The ☽ in ♋ rules the glands of the stomach. Also ♆ in ♋ rules the glands and secretions of the stomach. The ☽, ♆, ♄, and other planets afflicted in ♋ tend to disorders of the glands and secretions of the stomach. Also caused by Subs at SP (7D). (See "Digestion", "Diseases", in this section; "Glands" under Stomach).

**Sudoriferous**—(See Sweat).

**Suprarenals**—(See Adrenals; "Uremic Coma" under Coma; Suprarenals).

**Sweat Glands**—(See Sweat).

**Sweetbread**—(See Pancreas).

**Swellings** — Glandular Swellings—Caused by ♆ and ♀ and these planets afflicted at B., and by dir. (See Fixed Points, Neck, Throat, in this section).

**Testes; Throat** — Swellings of the Glands of—(See "Neck" in this section).

**Thymus; Thyroid; Tissues**—Softening of the Glandular Tissues—(See "Softening" in this section).

**Tonsils; Tumors** — Glandular Tumors —(See Adenoma, Scrofula).

**Urethra** — Glands of — (See "Genito-Urinary" in this section).

**Vagina** — Glands of — Disorders of — Ruled by ♏, and caused by afflictions in ♏. (See Vagina).

**Wasting Of** — ♆ influence and diseases. ♆ in any sign, and afflicted, tends to wasting of the glands of the part ruled by such sign. (See Affected, Bowels, in this section).

**GLASS**—Case—Swallows Glass, Iron, Nails, etc. See "Human Ostrich", No. 986 in 1001 N.N. (See Deglutition, Freaks).

**GLAUCOMA**—A Disease with Intraocular Tension—A ☉ disease; the ☉ affl. in ♈; the ☽ or Asc. in Nebulous parts, and affl. by ♄, tends to blindness from Glaucoma. (See "Glaucoma" under Eyes).

**GLEET**—Gleets—Chronic Gonorrhoea—(See "Chronic" under Gonorrhoea).

**GLOOM** — Gloomy — Caused principally by ♄ influence and afflictions, and by the ♄ signs ♑ and ♒, and espec. by ♑ on the Asc., and with ☿ affl. in ♑; ♄ ☌ or ill-asps. ☿, the mental ruler; ♄ afflicting the Asc. or M.C.; ♄ ℞, and in ♐r. over, or in □ or ☍ ☿; ♄ affl. in the 3rd or 9th H.; ♄ ☌ the ☉ in the 12th H.; ♄ ☌ or ill-asp. the ☽; ♄ in ♑ or ♒ and afflicted; ♄ ☌ ☿ in ♏ in the 8th H.; the ☉ in ♑, and affl. by ♄; the ☉ hyleg, and ☌ or ill-asp. ♄ at B., or by dir.; the ☽ at B., or the prog. ☽, in ☌ or ill-asp. ♄; ☿ in ♓ and affl. by ♄; caused by afflictions in ♋; the 3rd dec. of ♑ on the Asc. (See Anguish, Anxiety, Brooding, Dejected, Depressed, Despair, Despondent, Discontentment, Fears, Forebodings, Grave, Grief, Hope, Hypochondria, Introspection, Low Spirits (see Low); Melancholy, Misery, Morose, Obsessions, Optimism, Repining, Sad, Sorrow, Suicide, Worry, Wretched, etc.).

**GLOSSY**—Shiny—Oily— (See "Glossy" under Hair; "Oily" under Face, Skin).

**GLOTTIS**—Involuntary Closure of—Spasmodic Action of—Hiccough—A ♅ affliction; ♅ affl. in ♒. (See Hiccough, Spasmodic).

**GLUTEAL REGION**—(See Buttocks).

**GLUTTONY**—A Greedy Eater—Overeating—Engorgement—Repletion—Gormandizing—Feasting—Voracity—Insatiable Appetite—Ravenous Appetite —Intemperate In Eating, etc. Gormandizing habits are given by ♃ and ♀, and also by the ☽, the ruler of ♋, the stomach sign; ♋ on the Asc., and the ☽ as ruler of the Asc., afflicted, or in evil asp. to the Asc., tends to direct the mind to the stomach and cause over-eating, gluttony, obesity, etc., and people of this type, and who also have many planets in ♋ at B., should avoid over-eating. Other causes are—the ☉ affl. by ♃ or ♀; the ☉ Sig. in ♓, ruins himself by feasting; the ☉ affl. in ♉; the ☽ affl. at B., and to the evil asps. the Asc. by dir.; the ☽ affl. in ♓, given to the pleasures of the table; the ☽ in the 6th H., and ill-aspected by ♃ or ♀; the ☽ in ♐ and affl. by the ☉ or ♂ when taken ill, tends to some violent disease caused by gluttony or repletion (Hor'y); the Prog. ☽ in □ or ☍ the radical ♃; ♆ affl. in ♉; ♄ ill-dig. at B.; ♄ ☌ ♃ in ♍; ♃ affl. in ♉, ♋, ♍, ♏, or in the 1st or 6th H.; ♃ in ♋ in the Asc. and afflicted; ♃ □ or ☍ the ☉; ♂ to the ☌ or ill-asp. ♀; ♂ Sig. □ or ☍ ♃ or ♀; ♂ Sig. in ♉; ♀ affl. in ♎; ♀ in ♉ or ♋, ill-asp. by ♂, and espec. if the 6th H. is involved; ♀ Sig. in ♑, love their belly; ☿ affl. in ♉, or ☿ Sig. in ♉, loves ease and gluttony; ☿ affl. in ♑; the ♉ sign strong at B. tends to make great eaters; the Asc. to the ill-asps. the ☽, and the ☽ affl. at B., tends to dire results and diseases from over-eating; the 2nd face of ♉, the 4th face of ♌, the 16° ♑, and the 22° ♓ on the Asc. (See "Causes" under Apoplexy; Appetite, Congestion, Cramps, Cravings, Diet, Distentions, Drink, Eating; "His Own Worst Enemy" under Enemies; Epicureans, Excesses, Extravagance, Feasting; "Large Quantities" under Food; Gastric; "High Living" under High; Idle and Dull (see Idle); Indiscretions, Indulgence, Intemperance; "Enlarged" under Liver; Luxuries, Obesity, Over-indulgence, Pleasure, Plethora, Puffing, Redundant, Ringworm, Stomach, Surfeits, etc.).

**GLYCOGEN**—Animal Starch Found In the Blood and Liver—Ruled by ♃. Glycogen is formed and stored in the Liver by ♃, and is also in the blood, and is drawn upon by ♂ for fuel during muscular activity. Under stress and strain of the body Glycogen is released in large quantities to restore the equilibrium. The wastes of the Portal Blood stream are converted into Glycogen in the Liver by ♃ to act as fuel for the body. (See Liver, Starches).

**GLYCOSURIA**—Sugar In the Urine—(See Diabetes; "Sugar" under Urine).

**GNAWING PAINS**—Over the Whole Body—☿ affl. in ♒. (See "Pains" under Whole).

**GOATS**—Are ruled by the 6th H. in the native's map, as this house rules small animals.

**Death Of**—Epidemics Among—Eclipses in ♑, or malefics in this sign at the Vernal, and lord of the year, and especially if occurring in the 6th H.;

many eclipses occurring the same year, the death of goats, sheep, and many small animals in the territory afflicted by the eclipse, and espec. if the eclipses occur in four-footed, quadrupedal signs. (See "Small Animals" under Animals; "Virus" under Pestilence; Pets, Quadrupeds, Sheep).

**Goat's Back**—Constellation—For the evil effects of when the ☉ or ☽ are directed to it, see "Threatened" under Disease; Disgrace, Hircus, Sickness).

**GODFATHERS**—Ruled by ♃. Godmothers are ruled by ♀. (See "Godfathers" under Father).

**GOGGLE EYES**—Large, Protruding Eyes—Exophthalmos—(See "Abnormal Protrusion" under Eyeballs; "Exophthalmic" under Goiter).

**GOITER**—Goitre—Enlargement of the Thyroid Gland—A Crystallization and Obstruction in the Throat and Neck, affecting the Thyroid Gland—Bronchocele—Goiter is larger during the increase of the ☽, and decreases in size during the decrease of the ☽. Goiter is a ♉ disease, and caused by afflictions in ♉; ♀ affl. in ♉; ♀ in ♉, and affl. the ☽ or Asc.; ♀ in ♉ in the 6th H.; ♄ or ☋ in ♉; ♄ occi. in ♉, and affl. the ☉, ☽, or Asc.; ♄ affl. in ♏, by reflex action; ♄ ☌ the Pleiades, and malefics in ♉;; ♂ ☌ ♄ in ♉; ♂ affl. in ♉, or affl. the ☉, ☽, or Asc. from this sign; afflictions in or to the 16°♉; a result of the Algol influence in ♉; the ☽ hyleg in ♉ with females; Subs at LCP (6C), SP (7D), and at KP. Cases—See Fig. 3D, 3E, in the book, "Astro-Diagnosis", and Fig. 29 in "Message of the Stars", books by the Heindels. (See Cretinism, Crystallization, Myxoedema, Obstructions, Thyroid, Tumors).

**Exophthalmic Goiter**—Exophthalmos—Goggle Eyes—♀ affl. in ♉. (See Goggle Eyes" under Eyeballs).

**GOLD**—Aurum—Ruled by the ☉. A Typical Drug and Metal of the ☉. (See Sun, Therapeutics).

**GONADS**—Reproductive Glands—(See "Reproductive" under Glands).

**GONAGRA**—Gout In the Knees—(See "Gout" under Knees).

**GONORRHOEA**—Urethritis—Gleets—Running of the Reins—Inflammation of the Urethra—Chordee—Chancroids, or Soft Chancres, often accompany Gonorrhoea, and these same influences will also apply to Chancroids. Gonorrhoea is caused principally by afflictions to ♀, and is a ♀ disease; ♀ affl. in ♎ or ♏; ♀ affl. in ♏ in the 6th H.; ♀ or ☿ affl. in ♏ or ♓; ♀ in ♏ and affl. by ♂; the ☽ affl. in ♏; the ☽ in ♏, ☌, or ill-asp. ♄ (or ☿ if he be of the nature of ♄) when taken ill (Hor'y); the ☽ affl. by ♂ when taken ill (Hor'y); the ☽ to the ☌ or ill-asp. ♂ by dir., if indiscreet; ♅ ☌ ♄ or ♂ in ♏; ♂ affl. in ♏; a ♂ disease; ♂ □ or ☍ ♀; a ♏ and ♓ disease, and with afflictions in these signs; Subs at PP (2, 3, 4L), and at KP. (See Bubo, Penis, Scandalous, Urethra, Venereal).

**Chancroids**—A Small Sore, or Ulcer on the Genitals Which Often Accompanies Gonorrhoea—(See the first part of this section).

**Chordee**—Painful, Down-Curved Erection In Gonorrhoea—Caused by the same influences as Gonorrhoea, Chordee, and Chancroids, and tends to accompany the more severe forms of Gonorrhoea. (See the Influences in the first part of this section. Also see "Chordee" under Urethra).

**Chronic Gonorrhoea**—Gleet—A ♀ disease; ♀ affl. in ♏ in the 6th H. Also a severely afflicted ♀ denotes death by Gleet in some cases, where unusual indiscretions are carried on over a long period of time, and where ♀ afflicts the hyleg, and also holds the dominion of death. Also caused and aggravated by Subs at PP (2, 3, 4L), and at KP (11D).

**Gleet**—(See "Chronic" in this section).

**GOOD**—The term "Good" is found in many sections and Articles in this book. Good and Evil, the Positive and Negative, the Active and Passive influences, etc., are constantly working over Humanity, and the ever changing aspects of the planets tend to expansion and contraction; tend to disease, ill-health, worries, etc., by their evil aspects, and to good health, success, peace of mind, etc., by their favorable aspects. It would require too long a list to enumerate all the good conditions here, as related to the mind and body, and you are advised to look for the paragraph "Good" under whatever subject you have in mind. (See "Good" under Chemists, Children, Circulation, Complexion, Conduct, Constitution, Digestion, Eyes, Face, Figure, Health, Journeys, Judgment, Mind, Morals, Personality, Recuperation, Resistance, Shape, Sight, Stature, Surgeons, Teeth, Understanding, Vitality, etc. Also see Aspects, Beautiful, Clear, Comely, Dishonest, Evil, Favorable, Favored, Fine, Form, Handsome, Healers, Honest, Periods, etc.).

**Sudden Good or Ill**—The ☽ to the place of ♅ by tr. or dir., according as to how ♅ is dignified. (See "Sudden Evils" under Evil; Sudden, Uranus).

**GORGON'S HEAD**—(See Algol).

**GORMANDIZING**—Ravenous Appetite—(See Appetite, Carbuncles, Gluttony).

**GOUT**—Goutish Humours—Gouty—Arthralgia—Pain In the Joints—Rheumatic Gout—Is caused by the retention of Urea by ♄, and is a periodic disease. (See Saturn).

**Arms**—Gout In—(See the ♄ influences under "Causes" in this section).

**Arthralgia**—Pain in a Joint Due to Gout and the Deposits of Urea by ♄—(See "Pain" under Joints).

**Arthritis**—Inflammation of a Joint Due to Gout and Urea Deposits, etc.—(See "Arthritis" under Joints).

**Atonic Gout**—The ☽ to the ☌ or ill-asps. ♄ by dir. (See Atonic).

**Causes of Gout**—Planetary Indications—The ☉ in ♉ and affl. by ♃; the ☉ affl. in ♏; the ☽ affl. in airy signs; the ☽ affl. in ♊, or afflicting the hyleg therefrom; the ☽ hyleg, and to the ☌ or ill-asp. ♄ by dir.; the ☽ affl. in ♐; the ☽ in ♊ or ♑, ☌ or ill-asp. any of the malefics as promittors; a ☽ disease; the ☽ to the ☌ ♄ by dir.; the ☽ in ♍, ☌ or ill-asp. ♄ (or ☿ if he be of the nature of ♄) at the beginning of an illness, or at decumb. (Hor'y); ♆ in ♓ and affl. the ☉; ♆, H, or ♄ in ♎, and affl. the ☉ or ☽; ♄ in ♉, ♌, ♎, ♐, ♑, or ♓, and affl. the hyleg; a ♄ disease; ♄ in ♌, gout in the heart; ♄ in signs which rule the arms, hands, legs, and feet tend to gout and rheumatism in these parts; ♄ affl. in ♏; ♄ in ♏ or ♐, occi., and affl. the ☉, ☽, or Asc.; ♄ affl. in the 6th H., or affl. the hyleg therefrom; ♄ affl. the hyleg or Asc.; ♃ affl. in ♉ or ♐; ♂ in ♏ and affl. the ☽ or Asc.; ♂ in ♏ in the 6th H.; ♂ in ♑; ♀ affl. in ♐ or ♑; ☿ in ♑, ☌ or ill-asp. any of the malefics as promittors, and due principally to worry and melancholy; a ♉, ♏, ♐, ♑, ♒, and ♓ disease, and by afflictions in these signs; the Asc. to the □ or ☍ ♄ by dir.; lords of the 1st or 6th H. in airy signs; malefics angular and occi. of the ☽, and in the last degrees of ♊ or ♐, and if the benefics are with the malefics, or ori., or angular, and cast any ray to the Lights, they will be cured, but incurable if the benefics are very weak, and do not assist; the 25° of mutable signs is usually afflicted; the 5th H. and ♀ are frequently involved, denoting the cause; airy signs on the Asc. or 6th H., or the ☽ in airy signs at B., or at decumb.; earthy signs on the Asc.; Subs at KP and Local.

**Chalk Stones**—Of Gout—(See Chalk).

**Curable**—The Gout Is Curable—(See "Causes" in this section).

**Death by Gout**—Afflictions in cardinal signs dispose to.

**Extremities**—Gout In the Upper or Lower Extremities—♄ in signs which rule the arms, shoulders, hands, tends to gout in the upper extremities, and when ♄ is in ♐, ♑, ♒, ♓, to affect the lower extremities; also by reflex action to ♊ when ♄ is in ♐, the upper extremities are often afflicted with gout or rheumatism. The lower extremities are especially afflicted with gout when the ☽ is afflicted in ♐, and affl. the ☉, ☽, or Asc.; ♄ in ♑, and occi., and affl. the ☉, ☽, or Asc.; ♄ affl. in ♓, gout in the feet. (See Arms, Feet, Hands, Knees, Legs, Lower, Shoulders, in this section. Also see "Humours" under Extremities).

**Feet**—Gout In Feet and Toes—Podagra—Also the Hands are often affected by reflex action to ♍, the sign ruling the Hands—The ☽ affl. in ♊, ♐, or ♓; the ☽ in ♐, ☌, or ill-asp. ♄ (or ☿ if he be of the nature of ♄) at the beginning of an illness or at decumb., a spice of Gout (Hor'y); the ☽ in ♐, and affl. by the ☉ or ♂ when taken ill (Hor'y); the ☽ affl. in ♊, wandering gout in the feet; ♄ affl. in ♏, ♑, or ♓; ♄ in the Asc. or M.C., in ♊ or ♐, occi. of the ☉ and ori. of the ☽, and in the latter degrees of the sign; ♄ ☌ ♂ in the Asc. or M.C., in the latter degrees of ♓; ♂ in ♓ and affl. the hyleg therefrom; ♀ affl. in ♓; ☿ affl. in ♓; ☿ affl. at B.; a ☿, ☽, and ♄ disease; a ♓ disease, and by afflictions in ♓; ♓ on the Asc.; ♓ ascending at the Vernal Equi., People ruled by ♓, and in Countries under ♓, suffer grievous infirmities in the head, feet, and with gout and dropsy; also caused by afflictions in ♍, and by the ☉ and ☽ acting thru ♍; Subs at LPP (4, 5L) and at KP. (See "Feet" under Dropsy; Fiber; "Disorders" under Head; "Hands", "Wandering Gout", in this section).

**Fingers**—Gout In—(See "Hands" in this section).

**Flying Gout**—(See "Wandering" in this section).

**Hands**—Fingers—Gout In—Also May Occur In the Feet Under These Influences—Goutish Humours In the Hands—The ☽ affl. in ♊, a wandering gout in the hands; the ☽ in ♐ and affl. by the ☉ or ♂ when taken ill (Hor'y); the ☽ in ♐, ☌, or ill-asp. ♄ (or ☿ if he be of the nature of ♄) when taken ill, or at decumb.; a ♄ disease; ♄ affl. in ♊, ♏, ♐, or ♓; ♄ ☌ ♂ in the 1st or 7th H., ori. of the ☉ and occi. of the ☽, and in the latter degrees of ♊ or ♐; ♄ in the Asc. or M.C., occi. of the ☉, and ori. of the ☽, in the latter degrees of ♊ or ♐; ♃ affl. in ♉; ♂ in ♐; a ☿ disease; ☿ affl. at B.; ☿ affl. in ♊ or ♐. (See "Arms", "Feet", in this section; "Rheumatism" under Hands, Feet).

**Head**—Gout In—Gouty Pains In—☿ affl. in ♊.

**Heart**—Gout In—♄ affl. in ♌, or affl. the hyleg therefrom. (See Heart).

**Hips and Thighs**—Gout In—A ♐ disease, and afflictions in ♐; the ☽ in ♐; ☌, or ill-asp. ♄ (or ☿ if he be of the nature of ♄) at the beginning of an illness, or at decumb. (Hor'y); ♄ affl. in ♊ or ♐; ♄ in ♐ in the 6th H.; ♃ affl. in ♊ or ♐; ♃ affl. in ♐ in the 6th H.; ♃ in ♐, and affl. the ☽ or Asc.; ♀ affl. in ♐, hip gout; ♀ affl. in ♑, gout in thighs; ♀ in the 6th H., and afflicted, or ♀ in this house and affl. the ☽ or Asc. (See Hips, Thighs).

**Humours**—Goutish Humours—(See Arms, Causes, Feet, Hands, Knees, and the various paragraphs in this section. Also see Humours).

**Impure Blood**—Caused by Gout—(See "Impure Blood" under Impure).

**Incurable Gout**—Classed as Incurable Ordinarily—(See "Causes" in this section).

**Joints**—Gout and Pain In—Caused principally by ♄, and in the joints and parts ruled by the sign containing ♄ at B. (See "Gout" under Joints).

**Knees**—Gout In—Flying Gout In the Legs or Knees—♂ affl. in ♑; ♄ in ♑, the gout or rheumatism are more endurable until the causes are removed. (See "Gout" under Knees, Legs.)

**Legs**—Gout In—Flying Gout In—(See Causes, Knees, in this section; "Gout" under Legs).

**Limbs**—(See Arms, Causes, Extremities, Feet, Hands, Knees, in this section).

**Lower Extremities**—Lower Parts—Gout In—♄ in ♐ and affl. the ☉, ☽, or Asc.; the ☽ affl. in ♐, or affl. the hyleg therefrom; ♄ in ♑, occi., and affl. the ☉, ☽, or Asc. (See "Extremities" in this section).

**Melancholy**—Gout From—☿ affl. in ♑. (See Melancholy).

**Pains** — Gouty Pains — Generally caused by an afflicted ♀, and with ☿ in the configuration causing the gout, and where the nerves are affected by mineral deposits, etc. (See Head, Joints, Legs, and the various paragraphs in this section).

**Podagra** — Gout In the Feet — (See "Feet" in this section).

**Rheumatic Gout**—Caused principally by afflictions in ♐. (See "Causes" in this section, Rheumatism).

**Shoulders**—Gout In—♄ or ☿ affl. in ♊. (See "Arms" in this section) .

**Spice of Gout** — (See "Feet" in this section).

**Surfeits**—Gout Resulting From—(See "Gout" under Surfeits).

**Swellings** — From Gout — Principally In the Joints — (See "Joints" in this section; Swellings).

**Tendency to Gout**—Principally by afflictions in ♐; ♃ affl. in ♐; earthy signs on the Asc. (See "Causes" in this section).

**Thighs** — Gout In — (See "Hips and Thighs" in this section).

**Toes**—Gout In—♄ in ♓. (See "Feet" in this section; Toes).

**Wandering Gout** — Flying Gout — In the Arms, Hands, Legs and Feet—The ☽ affl. in ♊ when the ☽ is the afflictor in the disease; ♄ affl. in ♓, in the toes. (See Arms, Feet, Hands, Knees, Legs, in this section).

**Wrists**—Gout In—(See "Gout" under Wrists). For further study along the line of Gout, and its causes, see Crystallization, Deposits, Minerals, Moon, Periodic, Precipitation, Pressure, Retentions, Saturn, Urea, Uric Acid, Wastes, etc.

**GRACEFUL**—Graceful Body, Form, and Manner — The ♎ and ♀ influences strong at B., and well-asp. by the ☽; ♎ on the Asc. gives a tall, graceful and slender body, but the last few degrees of ♎ rising tend to a shorter and stouter body, and not as graceful or comely. The active and strong planets tend to destroy grace of body and manner, and espec. when acting thru the positive signs. (See Beautiful, Comely, Coordination, Dexterity, Form, Handsome, Harmony, Manner, Shape, Well-Formed, Well-Proportioned).

**GRADUAL**—Gradual Emaciation—Progressive Emaciation — (See Consumptions, Emaciation; "Malnutrition" under Nutrition; Tabes, Tuberculosis, Wasting, etc.).

**GRAIN**—Corn—Wheat—Scarcity of—(See Corn, Drought, Dryness, Famine, Fountains, Fruit, Rottenness, Scarcity, Starvation, Vegetation, Wheat).

**GRAND**—

**Grandchildren**—(See this subject under Children).

**Grand Mal**—(See Epilepsy).

**Grand Man** — The 12 Parts, or Divisions of the Body, and as ruled by the 12 Signs of the Zodiac. Planets in the Signs at B., and by dir., and the Sign upon the Asc. at B., tend to affect the part ruled by the Sign for good or evil. (See Aries, Taurus, Gemini, etc.; Houses, Signs, Zodiac).

**Grandparents**—(See this subject).

**GRANDEES** — Nobles — Noblemen — Suffering or Death of—(See Nobles).

**GRANDPARENTS**—

**Grandchildren**—(See this subject under Children).

**Grandfather** — Death of the Grandfather, or an Aged Male In the Family —♂ to the ☌ or ill-asp. ♄ by dir. The 7th H. rules the grandfather, according to the sex of the nativity. Male relatives are ruled by ♂. (See "Male" under Relatives; Seventh House, Uncles).

**Grandmother** — Death of the Grandmother, or an Aged Female In the Family — (See "Death" under Aunts, Family, Mother; "Female Relatives" under Relatives; Sister).

**GRANULATIONS**—The Healing Process —The Small Elevations on a Healing Surface—This is a benevolent indication and influence, and carried on by the benefic, constructive, and healing influences of the good aspects of the ☉, ♂, and ♃. If the ♄ influence is stronger than the Benefics, and the vitality low and weak, then decay, suppuration, ulceration, or mortification may set in instead of healthy granulations. (See Curable, Incurable).

**Eyelids** — (See "Granulated" under Eyelids).

**Joints** — (See "Granulations" under Joints).

**GRAPE** — Vitis Vinifera — (See Sun Group under Herbs. Also see Carcinoma).

**GRAPHITE**—A Native Form of Carbon — Plumbago — A Mineral of ♄. (See "Minerals", "Metals", under Saturn).

**GRATIFICATION** — Of the Appetites — (See Amorous, Appetites, Drink, Eating, Excesses, Epicureans, Feasting, Food, Gluttony, Luxuries, Passion, Pleasure; "Sex Excesses" under Sex; Venery, etc.).

**GRAVE** — Gravity — Thoughtful — Serious—Sober—Taciturn—A ♄ and ♑ influence; ♄ Sig. in ♑; ♄ ☌ ☿; ♄ in ♍ in partile asp. the Asc., tends to a grave countenance, or appearance; ♄ in the 3rd, 9th, or 12th H.; the ♄ sign ♑ on the Asc. at B.; the ☉ in ♑ and affl. by ♄; the ☉ or ☽ to the ☌ or ill-asp. ♄ by dir.; the earthy signs on the Asc., and strong at B., tend to gravity, and to make one more serious, thoughtful, and melancholic. (See Austere, Depressed, Despondent, Gloomy, Melancholic, Quiet, Reserved, Responsibility, Serious, Taciturn).

**The Grave**—Ruled by ♄ and the 4th H. Also Grave Diggers are ruled by ♄. (See Burial, Corpse, Death, Terminal).

**GRAVEL**—A Sand-Like Deposit In the Urine — Sand — Concretions — Calculus, etc.—Gravel is crystallized in the kidneys by the ♄ influence, as ♄ has his exaltation in ♎, the kidney sign.

**Bladder**—Gravel In—♄ affl. in ♎ or ♏; Subs at KP, PP (2, 3, 4L). (See "Bladder" under Stone)

**Causes**—The ☉ affl. in ♎, ♏, or ♒; the ☉ or ☽ affl. in the 6th H. in a fixed sign; the ☽ to the ☌ or ill-asp. ♂ by dir.; the ☽ in ♉ and affl. by the ☉ or ♂ when taken ill (Hor'y); ♄ in ♎ or ♏; ♄ in the 6th H. in a fixed sign; a ♄ disease; ♂ in ♉, ♎, or ♏; ♂ in ♌ when ♂ is the afflictor in the disease; ♂ in ♌, ☌ or ill-asp. the ☉; ♂ in the 6th H. in a fixed sign; a ♎ and ♏ disease, and indicated by afflictions in these signs; fixed signs show, and espec. when in the 6th H.; ♏ on the Asc., and with the ☽ at the same time in ♒, tends to the formation and voiding of red gravel. Cases of Gravel—See Fig. 8 in "Message of the Stars" by the Heindels. Also see "Gravel", Chap. 13, page 90, in Daath's Medical Astrology. (See Calculus, Crystallization, Deposits, Elimination, Hardening, Lime, Minerals, Retarded, Retention, Sand, Stone, Suppressions, Urea, Uric Acid, Wastes, etc.).

**Death by Gravel**—Denoted by ♂, and when ♂ is one of the afflictors, and holding the dominion of death.

**Kidneys**—Gravel and Sand In—♄ affl. in ♎; Subs at KP (11D). (See "Kidneys" under Stone).

**Liver**—Gravel In—♄ affl. in ♍, ♎, or ♏; ♄ affl. in ♋, gravel in the upper lobes; ♄ affl. in ♍, gravel in the lower lobes; Subs at Li.P. (4D). (See Liver; "Liver" under Stone).

**Red Gravel**—(See "General Causes" in this section).

**Sand**—(See Sand).

**Stone**—(See Stone).

**GRAY**—The color Gray is ruled by the 8th H. (See Colors).

**Brain**—Gray Matter of—(See Cortex).

**Gray Hair**—(See "Gray" under Hair).

**GREAT**—Greatness—

**Great Ability**—☿ Sig. in ♍, great mental abilities; ☿ Sig. in ♎, great natural ability; ☿ in ♍ in the Asc., and in ✱ or △ asp. ♃ and the ☽; ☿ Sig. in ☌ or good asp. the ☽ and Asc.; ♂ Sig. ☌ ☿, considerable ability; ♂ Sig. ✱ or △ the ☉, a great mind. (See Excellent, Genius, Gifted, Mathematician, Mechanical; "Abilities" under Mind; "Natural Abilities" under Natural; Prodigies, Reputation, Scholar, Science, etc.).

**Great Beasts**—Great Cattle—Large Animals—Danger From—Attacks By—Great Beasts and Animals are ruled by the 12th H., and ♂ in the 12th H., and affl. by ♅ or ♄, makes the native liable to injury from large beasts. Also Ceti or Menkar joined with the Luminaries at B. (See Animals, Beasts, Cattle, Elephants, Four-Footed, Horses, Quadrupeds, etc. Also see "Great Cattle" in this section).

**Great Cattle**—Great Beasts—Danger From, or Attacks By—The ☉ to the cusp the 12th H. by dir.; the ☽ to the place of Ceti; lord of the 6th H. in the 12th; a malefic ruler of the 12th H. at B., and in the 12th at a Solar Rev. (See "Great Beasts" in this section; "Cattle" under Large).

**Great Dangers**—Subject To—(See "Great" under Danger).

**Great Energy**—(See "Great" under Energy).

**Great Events**—(See "Great" under Events).

**Great Eyes**—(See "Great" under Eyes).

**Great Learning**—(See "Great" under Learning. Also see "Great Ability" in this section).

**Great Lips**—(See Lips).

**Great Men**—Death of—An Eclipse of the ☉ or ☽ in a fiery sign signifies the death of Great Men, or of Kings and Rulers; an eclipse of the ☉ in the 2nd Dec. of ♓, death of famous and excellent men; an eclipse of the ☽ in ♊, ♌, ♎, or ♓; Comets appearing in ♉, ♋, ♌, ♎, ♏, ♑, or ♒. (See Assassination, Famous, Kingdoms, Kings, Lady; "Power" under Men; Nobles, President, Princes, Queens, Renown, Rulers, etc.).

**Great Mind**—(See "Great Ability" in this section; "Elegant Mind" under Elegant).

**Great Mortality**—(See Mortality).

**Great Mouth**—(See Mouth).

**Great Physical Powers**—(See Athletic).

**Great Recuperative Powers**—(See Recuperation).

**Great Resistance**—To Disease—(See Resistance).

**Great Vitality**—(See Vitality).

**Great Women**—Death of—(See Lady, Queens).

**Greatness**—Sickness by Aiming At, or Great Struggle For—Lord of the 10th H. in the 6th H. at B.

**The Great**—Much Mortality Among—The ☉ in the 8th H. at the Vernal, and Lord of the Year, and espec. if the ☉ is evilly aspected by lord of the 8th; the ☉ in the Asc., and afflicted, and Lord of the Year at the Vernal Equinox; an eclipse of the ☉ or ☽ in a fiery sign; ♄ Lord of the Year at the Vernal, in ♓, and oriental; ♄ in ♉ in an angle, afflicted, and direct in motion at a Vernal Ingress; ♂ in ♎, ℞, and Lord of the Year at the Vernal. (See "Great Men" in this section).

**GREEN**—Is the color of ♄ in the Solar Spectrum. Is represented by the 2nd, 8th, 9th, and 12th Houses. Is ruled by the ☽ in ♋ or ♌. Red mixed with green is denoted by ♃; ♋ denotes green or russet; ♌, red or green; ♐, light green or olive. Green, ruled principally by ♄, tends to relieve inflamed eyes, and is a restful color to the eyes, and to live in a green room, wear green glasses, etc. Green color predominates in Nature, and is also the color of the Human Intellect. (See Colors, Conjunctivitis; "Treatment" under Eyes; "Solar Spectrum" under Solar).

**Green Sickness**—(See Chlorosis).

**GRIEF**—Dolens—Griefs—Lamentations—Sorrow, etc.—The ☉ to the ☌ or ill-asp. ♄ by dir.; the ☉ to the ☌ ☽ by dir.; the ☽ to the ill-asps. ♄ or ♀ by dir.; the 2nd Dec. of ♊ on the Asc.;

♄ in ♌, and in evil asp. the ☽; ♄ to the bad asps. ♀ or ☿ by dir. (See Anguish, Anxiety, Bereavement, Dejected, Depressed, Despondent, Disgrace, Gloom, Melancholy, Ruin, Sadness, Sorrow, Trouble, Worry, etc.).

**Death By** — Denoted by ☿; ♄ ☌ ☿ in ♑, and espec. when in the 12th H., as the 12th H. rules Grief.

**Females**—Grief To—(See "Grief" under Females).

**Full of Grief**—Full of Sorrow—The ☌ or ill-asps. of ♄ to the ☉ by dir. or tr.; in Hor'y Q., ♄ afflicting the Sig. (See Complaining, Murmuring, Repining, Sorrow,

**Heart Afflicted by Grief**—(See "Grief" under Heart).

**Legs** — Phlegmatic Grief In — Phlegmatic Dolens—(See "Milk Leg" under Legs).

**Men** — Grief To — (See "Grief" under Men).

**Mind** — Grief of Mind — Lord of the Asc. and the ☽ much afflicted at B., and by dir. (See Anguish, Anxiety, Despondent, Worry; the various paragraphs in this section).

**Much Grief Generally**—Much Sorrow Prevalent—♄ to the bad asps. his own place at B. by tr. or dir., with people so affected; ♄ sole ruler at a Solar Eclipse; an eclipse of the ☉ in the 3rd Dec. of ♈; ♑ ascending at the Vernal, and ♄ afflicted, grief to Peoples and Countries ruled by ♑. (See "Capricorn" under Nations).

**Phlegmatic Grief**—In the Legs—(See "Legs" in this section).

**Public Grief** — Public Sadness and Sorrow—An eclipse of the ☉ in the 1st Dec. of ♒; ♀ elevated above, and configurated with ♄ at a Solar Eclipse or Ingress. (See Eclipse, Ingresses, Public; "Much Sadness" under Sadness; Sorrow; "Much Grief" in this section).

**Women** — Grief To — (See "Grief" under Females, Women).

**GRIEVOUS**—Distressful—Heavy—

**Colds**—Grievous Colds In the Head—(See "Colds", "Disorders", under Head).

**Diseases** — Grievous Diseases — Distressful—Difficult to Cure—Serious Illnesses—Heavy and Prolonged Illnesses —The ☉ to the ill-asps. the ☽ by dir., and the ☽ hyleg, or affl. at B., according to the sign the ☉ is in; the ☉ or ☽ to the ☌ or ill-asps. ♄ by dir.; ♅ ☌ ♄ in the 6th H.; lord of the 6th H. affl. by the □ or ☍ of the lord of the Asc.; lord of the 6th affl. in the 6th, 8th, or 12th H., or a malefic in the 6th, not easily cured; lord of the 1st in the 4th or 8th H., and afflicted; malefics afflicted and elevated above the ☉ or ☽. (See Chronic; "Maladies" under Distressful; "Duration of Disease" under Duration; Epilepsy; "Sick" under Escape; Extraordinary, Fatal, Fierce; "Affliction" under Heavy; Incurable, Lingering, Painful, Poignant, Prolonged, Public (see "Grievous" under Public); Serious, Severe, Sharp, Slow, Tedious, Vehement, Violent, etc.).

**Feet**—Grievous Infirmities In—(See "Weakness" under Feet).

**Head** — Grievous Colds In — (See "Colds", "Disorders", under Head).

**Mortality** — Grievous Mortalities — (See Mortality).

**GRIPINGS** — Cramps — Spasmodic Pains In the Bowels or Stomach—(See "Gripings", "Pain", "Spasmodic", under Bowels, Stomach; Colic, Cramps, Gas, Spasmodic, Wind, etc.).

**GRIPPE**—La Grippe—(See Influenza, La Grippe).

**GRISTLE**—Cartilage—(See Cartilage).

**GROINS**—Inguinal Region—The Inguinal Canal — The Depression between the Thigh and Trunk—Ruled by the ♏ Sign.

**All Diseases In**—Signified by the 8th H., and espec. in Hor'y Q.

**Bubo**—Tumor In—Inguinal Tumor—(See Bubo).

**Diseases In**—Afflictions in ♏, and are ♏ diseases; malefics in the 8th H., or affl. the lord of the 8th.

**Enlarged Glands Of**—Afflictions in ♏ and the 8th H.; Subs at KP and PP (4, 5L). (See Bubo, Enlarged, Glands).

**Hernia** — Inguinal Hernia — Rupture In the Groin—(See "Inguinal" under Hernia).

**Injuries In** — Accidents To — Wounds To—Afflictions in ♏ or the 8th H.; ♂ affl. in ♍, ♏, or the 6th and 8th H.

**Lymphatic Glands Of** — Swelling of — (See Bubo).

**Pain In Groins**—A ♏ disease, and afflictions in ♏; ♂ affl. in ♏.

**Tumors In Groins**—♄ affl. in ♏. (See Bubo).

**GROOVES**—(See Channels, Fissure).

**GROSS**—Coarse—Unrefined—

**Gross Blood**—(See "Too Much Blood" under Blood; "Impure Blood" under Impure).

**Gross Humours**—The Body Is Full of Gross Humours — (See "Gross" under Humours).

**Gross Manners** — Coarse Manners — Lack of Refinement — ♂ strong and prominent at B., and ♀ weak; many planets in the earthy and watery signs, and the airy signs especially weak and unoccupied. (See Manners, Rough, Unrefined).

**GROWTH** — Increase — Expansion — Enlargement—Increment—Growth of the Mind and Body, etc.—♅ and ♀ govern the functions of growth, and nutrition of the body. ♀ rules growth until adolescence, and then ♅ takes charge. The ☽ has much to do with the growth and development of the body. Assimilation, and the growth of the body are furthered by the work of ♃. The growth of the mind depends much upon the aspects and position of ☿ at B. The Solar Forces focussed thru the ☽ stimulate the growth of the body.

**Abnormal Growth** — Of the Body — Strange and Abnormal Growth — Diminished or Increased Growth of the Body — Diminutive growth is due to decreased Pituitary secretion, and enlarged growth to increase of this secretion. The Pituitary Body is ruled by ♅, and the action of ♅ by his various aspects and influences on the Pituitary secretion tends to either increase or diminish the secretion, and to produce Giants, Freaks of Nature, Dwarfs, etc. Abnormal growth and freaks of nature, are produced by ♅ ☌ ♀. (See Diminished, Dwarfed, Enlarged, Giants; "Over-Developed" under Organs; Pituitary; "Abnormally Tall" under Tall).

**Arrested Growth**—Cessation of—(See Arrested, Atrophy, Deformities, Diminished, Dwarfed, Obstructions, Paralysis, Pituitary, Retarded, Suppressions, Thyroid, etc.).

**Bone**—Outgrowth of—Exostosis—(See "Bones of Arms" under Arms).

**Cessation Of**—(See "Arrested" in this section).

**Increase of Growth**—Incrementitions—Due to the tonic, or plus action of ♂. (See "Tonic Action" under Mars).

**Mind**—Growth of the Mind—Arrested Mental Development—Precocious—Rapid Mental Development, etc.—The Mind is but a temporary part of Man, and is one of the Vehicles thru which he acts on the Material, or Earth Plane, and by acting thru the brain. Afflictions at B., and also during the prenatal period, tend to place limitations and restraints upon the brain cells, so that the mind is crippled and hampered in its action, and these afflictions, and espec. to ☿, the mental ruler, may cause idiocy, imbecility, a foolish mind, bad judgment, and also to give the various bad traits of temperament, whereas the favorable asps. to ☿, the ☽, the Asc., and with ☿ well-asp. by the ☽, and also in good relation to the Asc., tend to give a better brain, and a more free action of the mind thru the brain. The Pineal Gland, and the Pituitary Body in the brain, have more to do with spiritual growth than with mental growth. The 12th H. conditions at B. also indicate largely the freedom of expression that the mind will have over the brain and body, and a badly afflicted 12th H. at B. tends to restraint of the senses, to deafness, and also to bring limitations upon the brain and body for the present life, so that the native may find it impossible to make much mental progress. The same influences which tend to Deformities, Hunchback, Idiocy, Poor Judgment or Memory, etc., tend to retard the mental growth and development. (See these subjects. Also see "Active Mind" under Active; "Arrested", "Quickened", under Mentality).

**Miscellaneous Subjects**—The following subjects have to do with Growth in its various phases, which see in the alphabetical arrangement—Abnormalities, Acromegaly, Arrested, Assimilation, Atrophy, Augmented, Backwardness, Blight, Cells, Cessation, Congenital, Corpulent, Crooked, Decrease, Defects, Deficient, Deformed, Development, Deviations, Diminished, Dwarfed, Enlarged, Exaggerated, Exostosis, Expansion, Extremities, Fat, Fleshy, Foetus, Form, Freaks, Genius, Gestation, Giants, Hair, Height, Hermaphrodites, Hindered, Humpback, Idiocy, Ill-Formed, Imbecile, Imperfections, Increase, Inhuman, Irregularities, Large, Limbs, Malformations, Medium, Members, Mental, Mind, Monsters, Muscles, Nutrition, Obesity, Obstructions, Organs, Outgrowth (see Excrescences, Exostosis); Overgrowth (see Over); Perversions, Physical, Pituitary, Precocious, Premature, Prenatal, Retarded, Shape, Short, Small, Stature, Stout, Suppressions, Tall, Thin, Undersized, Undeveloped, Unnatural, Uvula, Weight, Withering, etc.

**Never Grew Up**—At Age of 25 Had the Mind of a Child—Case—See "Never Grew Up", No. 720, in 1001 N.N.

**Normal Growth**—Of the Body depends largely upon the action of the Pituitary Gland, and whether or not it is functioning properly. (See Pituitary).

**Retarded Growth**—(See "Arrested" in this section).

**GROWTHS**—New Growths—Excrescences—Lumps—Growths are caused by ♄ influence, and resulting from concretions, deposits, etc. Also caused by ♃, and ♂ afflictions to ♃; ♂ prog. ☌, P, □ or ☍ the radical ♃, or vice versa, due to impurities in the blood. (See Concretions, Deposits). Growths generally appear in parts and organs of the body ruled by the Sign of the Zodiac containing malefics at B., and espec. the sign containing ♄, due to deposits, or the sign containing ♃, due to congestions, and resulting from plethora or surfeits. For Growths affecting the different organs, or parts of the body, see "Growths" under the Organ or Part, in the alphabetical arrangement, as "Growths" under Head, Face, etc.

**Blindness from Growths**—(See "Growths" under Blindness; "Defects" under Eyes).

**Bone**—Outgrowth of—(See Exostosis).

**Fatty Growths**—(See "Lardaceous" under Carcinoma; Cysts, Degeneration, Fat, Sarcoma, Sebaceous, Steatoma, Waxy, Wen, etc.).

**Fleshy Growths**—(See Caruncle; "Growths" under Fleshy).

**Fungus Growths**—Vegetable Growths—(See Fungus, Vegetable).

**Hairy Growths**—(See Moles, Naevus).

**Harmful Growths**—(See Malignant, Noxious, Poisonous).

**Harmless Growths**—(See Moles, Warts, Wens; "Non-Malignant" in this section).

**Horny Growths**—(See Horny).

**Malignant Growths**—(See Carcinoma, Malignant, Tumors).

**Morbid Growths**—♂ influences overlaid and intermixed with other planets, as with ♆, ♅, ♄. Also formed by ♃, due to Plethora, Excesses, Impure Blood, etc. (See Fungus, Morbid).

**New Growths**—Neoplasm—(See Tumors, Warts, Wens).

**Non-Malignant Growths**—Ruled mostly by ♀, and are Venus diseases.

**Noxious Growths**—Poisonous and Harmful—♃ affl. in ♒, from over-eating; ♃ □ or ☍ the ☉. (See "Over-Eating" under Eating; Noxious).

**Obstructing Growths**—(See Cataracts; "Defects" under Eyes; Goiter, Obstructions, Tumors, etc.).

**Outgrowth**—(See "Bone" in this section).

**Overgrowth** — Excessive Growth — (See Enlarged, Giants, Overgrowth).

**Poisonous Growths**—(See Malignant, Noxious, in this section).

**Tumors**—(See Tumors).

**Ulcers**—(See Ulcers).

**Vegetable Growths** — (See Fungus, Vegetable). For further study along this line see Abnormalities, Carcinoma, Caruncle, Cataract, Cells, Concretions, Congestions, Crystallization, Cysts, Decay, Defects, Deformities, Degeneration, Deposits, Epithelioma, Excessive, Excrescences, Exostosis, Eyes, Face, Feet, Goiter, Hardening, Head, Hypertrophy; "Impure Blood" under Impure; Lipoma, Lumps, Minerals, Moles, Naevus, Plethora, Retentions, Sarcoma, Scales, Sebaceous, Skin, Steatoma, Suppressions, Surfeits, Swellings, Venereal, Warts, Wens, etc.

**GUARDIANS**—Godfathers—Are governed by ♃, and the aspects to ♃ at B., and by dir., indicate the conditions affecting them for good or ill. Godmothers are ruled by ♀. (See "Godfather" under Father).

**GUILLOTINE** — Death by Sentence of Law—Beheaded—♂ affl. in ♉. (See Beheaded, Executed, Hanging, Judge). Case of Death by Guillotine — See "Princess", No. 697, in 1001 N.N.

**GULLET**—(See Oesophagus).

**GUMS**—The Gums—Gingiva—

**Bleeding Gums**—Spongy—Ulcerated—♂ afflicted in ♈ or ♉; Subs at MCP (4C). (See "Ulcerated" in this section).

**Gum Boils**—An ♈ disease. (See Boils).

**Inflamed Gums**—Sore Gums—Gingivitis—♂ afflicted in ♈ or ♉. The upper Gums are ruled by ♈, and the gums around the lower teeth by ♉. (See "Lower", "Upper", under Teeth).

**Putrid Gums** — ♄ afflicted in ♈ or ♉. (See Putrid).

**Pyorrhoea** — (See Jaws, Pyorrhoea, Teeth).

**Sore Gums** — (See Bleeding, Inflamed, in this section).

**Spongy Gums**—(See "Bleeding" in this section).

**Tumor**—Of the Gums—Elastic Tumor —Epulis—♃ or ♀ in ♈ or ♉, and afflicted by ♄. (See "Tumors" under Mouth).

**Ulcerated Gums**—♃ afflicted in ♈, of the upper gums; ♃ afflicted in ♉, of the gums of the lower jaw. (See Ulcers).

**Wounds To**—♂ afflicted in ♈ or ♉.

**GUNSHOT** — Guns — Danger by Fire Arms — Powder Burns — Pistols—Shotguns — Weapons, etc. — Guns are ruled by ♂ in general, and accidents, injury, or death by are usually caused by ♂ afflictions.

**Accidents by Fire Arms**—♂ affl. at B.; the ill-asp. of ♂ by dir. to the ☉, ☽, Asc., or M.C.; fire signs dispose to. (See the various paragraphs in this section).

**Blindness** — By Gunshot Wounds — (See "Gunshot" under Blindness).

**Danger from Fire Arms** — Danger of Injury By—The ☽ to the ☌ or ill-asps. ♂ by dir.; ♂ affl. at B.; ♂ ☌ the Asc. by dir.; the Asc. to the ☌ the ☉, and the ☉ ☌ ♂; the Asc. to the place of the Aselli or Capricornus. (See the various paragraphs in this section).

**Death by Gunshot**—Danger of—Death by Accidental Gunshot — Suicide By—The ☉ or ☽ hyleg, and to the ☌ or ill-asp. ♂ by dir.; ♂ in a fiery sign, and ☍ the Asc., and espec. when in ♌ near the Ascelli; ♂ affl. the hyleg at B., and by dir., and holding the dominion of death, and when a violent death is indicated by the radix. Cases—(1) Shot Himself Accidentally—See "Shot Himself", No. 177, in 1001 N.N. (2) Shot Himself—See "Puzzle Horoscope", No. 672, in 1001 N.N. (3) Death by Accidental Pistol Shot — See "Gambetta", No. 736, in 1001 N.N. (4) Shot to Death —See "Mexico", No. 758, in 1001 N.N. (5) Shot Himself to Death—See "Haydon", No. 818, in 1001 N.N. (See Suicide; "Death" under Violent).

**Gunshot Wounds**—Danger of—Liable To—The ☉ hyleg, and the ☉ to the ☌ or ill-asps. ♂ by dir.; the ☉ or ☽ affl. by ♂ from ♊, ♐, or ♒; the ☉, ☽, and other planets in the Asc. with Regulus, and evilly aspected; the ☉ directed to Praesepe; the Prog. ☉ or ☽ ☌, □, or ☍ the radical ♂; the ☽ ☌ or ill-asps. ♂ by dir.; the ☽ in an airy sign, and to the ☌ or ill-asp. ♂ by dir.; the ☽ at a Solar Rev. passing over the place of ♂ at B.; caused by the ☉ or ♂, the positive, electric, and heat-producing planets; ♂ afflictions make liable to, and usually to the part of the body most afflicted by ♂ at B.; ♂ ☌ or ill-asp. the ☉, ☽, Asc., or M.C. by dir.; ♂ affl. in the 6th H.; ♂ affl. in ♐, and also affl. the hyleg; ♂ affl. in ♊ or ♍, and in ☌ or ill-asp. the Asc. by dir.; ♂ by Periodic Rev. to the ☌, □, or ☍ ♅; caused and ruled by ♂; fire signs dispose to; afflictions in ♐.

**Hunting** — Shooting — Fond of — (See Exercise, Hunting, Sports). For further influences along this line, see Assassination, Battle, Contests, Cuts, Disputes, Duels, Fighting, Feuds, Instruments, Iron, Murder, Quarrels, Sports, Stabs, Sword, War, Weapons.

**GUSTATIVENESS** — Gustativeness Large—(See Diet, Eating, Epicureans, Feasting, Food, Gluttony).

**Gustatory Process**—Ruled by ♉. (See Taste).

**GUTTA SERENA**—Amaurosis—Partial or Total Blindness—The ☽ in the 1st, 4th, or 7th H., decr. in light, and in ☌ or ☍ ♅, ♄, or ♂, and the malefics ascend after her, occi., and at the same time the malefics be in ☌ or ☍ the ☉, and ori. of the ☉ and ascend before him,—under these circumstances, with ♄ as the special afflicting planet, Amaurosis tends to result. Saturn especially tends to cause blindness by Amaurosis. Also caused by Subs at MCP (3 and 4C). (See Amaurosis).

# H

**HABIT**— Habits—Disposition — Habitual—Tendency to Repetition—Diathesis—Hexis—Hectic — Permanent Habit —Bad Habits— Good Habits—Tendencies—Practices—Vices—Virtues, etc.— The ♄ influence tends greatly to make people governed by habit, as ♄ rules over habits, and tends to make them fixed. Habit is also the result of automatic action by the ☽. The aspects and position of the ☽ govern the general habits of life, and the functional activities. The ☽ has an important influence over the personal habits. The ☽ well-asp. in ♉ gives methodical habits. The ☉ influence leads to tendencies which are later taken up by the ☽ action and made automatic, and result in unconscious behavior. (See Automatic). The influences of the negative signs and planets tend to the formation or habits, whether good or bad, being more related to the unconscious, or the subconscious realms of the mind. The following subjects have to do with Habits, their causes, nature, etc., which see in the alphabetical arrangement when not more rfully considered here.

**Abnormalities; Acquired Habits**—Are generally acquired under the action and influences of the ☽, and strong ☽ characters are greatly influenced by environment and external conditions. (See Acquired).

**An Ill Habit**—Of the Body—(See "Ill-Health All Thru Life" under Ill-Heath).

**Appearance**—The Habits As To Appearance — (See Appearance, Cleanliness, Clothing, Cosmetics, Dirty, Dress, Filthy, Neat, Uncleanly, etc.).

**Appetites; Automatic Action** — Tendency to Form Habits by Repetition— (See Automatic).

**Bad Habits**— Wrong Habits—Tendency To, and especially along the lines of Eating, Drinking, Pleasure, Appetites, etc.—♄ ☌ or ill-asp. ♂ or ♀ by dir.; ♃ □ or ☍ the ☉; ♀ affl. at B.; ♀ affl. by ♂; ♀ affl. in ♍, and espec. in the 6th H. With ♀ affl. in ♍ carelessness in the habits should be avoided. (Note the various paragraphs and subjects in this section).

**Better**—The Habit Better—The ☉ configurated with the lord of the Asc., the native is more comely and the habit better. (See Comely).

**Blackheads** — Due to Bad Habits of Living — (See "Comedo" under Sebaceous).

**Body**—Ill Habits of—An Ill Habit of —(See An Ill Habit, Drink, Dissipation, Narcotics, and the various paragraphs in this section).

**Careless Habits** — Careless of Habits and the Health—♀ affl. in ♈; common signs on the angles. (See Careless; "Bad Habits", and the various paragraphs in this section).

**Conduct**—(See the various paragraphs under Conduct, Manners, Temperament).

**Cosmetics**—Ill Habits and Indiscretions In the Use of—(See Cosmetics, Lotions).

**Creatures of Habit** — Fixed Habits — The ☉, ☽, and many planets in fixed signs at B., or with fixed signs on the angles; the ♉ and ♍ signs tend to make creatures of habit. (See "Fixed Habits" under Fixed).

**Death**—Death from Bad Habits—(See Death, Drink, Eating, Excesses, Gluttony, Passion, Pleasures, Sex; "Dry Habit" in this section).

**Diathesis** — The Hexis, or Permanent Habit In Disease—(See Diathesis).

**Diet** — Habits of — (See Diet, Eating, Epicureans, Excesses, Feasting, Food, Gluttony, Intemperate, Luxuries, Moderate, Temperate, etc.).

**Directions** — Temporary or Transient Habits may arise under the influence of Directions, but the influences of the radical map indicate habits of a more permanent and fixed nature. (See Directions).

**Dirty**—(See Dirty, Filthy, Uncleanly).

**Diseases** —From Bad Habits—The ☽ □ or ☍ the Asc., diseases brought on by loose living and bad habits; ♀ affl. in ♈. (See "Bad Habits", and the various paragraphs in this section; "High Living" under High; "Loose Living" under Loose, etc.).

**Dress** — Habits of — (See Clothing, Dress, Neat, etc.).

**Drink** — Dissipated Habits In — (See Drink, Drunkenness, Intoxication).

**Drug Habit**—(See Narcotics).

**Drunkenness**—Habitual Drunkenness —(See Drunkenness).

**Dry Habit**—Of the Body—Death From —(See "Dry Habit" under Dry).

**Eating** — Evil Habits In — (See Diet, Eating, Excesses, Food, Gluttony, etc.).

**Environment**—As Related to Habits— (See Environment, External, Negative, Positive).

**Eruptions** — Due to Bad Habits and Improper Living — (See Eruptions; "Eruptions" under Face; Pimples).

**Evil Habits** — (See Drink, Narcotics, Passion, Perversions, Secret, Vices).

**Excesses** — From Evil Habits — (See Excesses).

**Expense** — Expensive Habits — (See Expense, Extravagant, Luxuries, Prodigal, etc.).

**External Conditions**—As a Factor In the Formation of Habits — (See Acquired, Environment, External).

**Extravagant Habits** — (See Expense, Extravagance, Luxuries, Prodigal).

**Fevers**—Habitual Fevers—(See "Habitual" under Fever).

**Filthy Habits** —(See Dirty, Filthy, Uncleanly).

**Fixed Habits** — Creatures of Habit — (See "Creatures Of" in this section).

**Food**—Habits Concerning the Eating and Use of—(See Diet, Eating, Food).

**Formation of Habits**—(See the Introduction to this section).

**Full Habit**—Diseases Arising from Too Full a Habit—Denoted by ♃. (See Full, Plethora).

**Good Habit and Size**—♂ ruler of the Asc., and ori.

**Good Habits**—(See Moderate, Temperate, in this section).

**Governed by Habit**—♄ influence, and ♄ strong at B., and ♄ tends to make the habits fixed. (See "Creatures Of" in this section).

**Habitual**—(See Drunkenness, Fevers, Melancholy, and the various paragraphs in this section).

**Hexis**—The Permanent Habit In Disease—(See Diathesis, Directions; "Certain" under Disease; Hexis).

**Ill Habit**—Of the Body—Ill Habits of the Body—(See An Ill Habit, Body, Narcotics, and the various paragraphs in this section).

**Immoderate Habits**—(See Excesses, Intemperance).

**Immoral Habits**—(See "Loose Morals" under Morals; Passion, Sex, etc.).

**Improper Habits**—Illness From—♀ affl. in ♏.

**Impulsive Habits**—Ill-Health From—♀ affl. in ♈. (See "Careless" in this section; Impulsive, Recklessness).

**Intemperate Habits**—(See Drink, Excesses, Intemperance, etc.).

**Irregular Habits**—The ☽ to the ill-asps. ♀ by dir. (See Erratic, Irregular).

**Loose Habits**—(See Loose).

**Luxurious Habits**—(See "Expense" in this section).

**Melancholy**—Habitual Melancholy—(See Melancholy).

**Methodical Habits**—The ☽ well-asp. in ♉. (See Methods).

**Moderate In Habits**—(See Moderate, Temperate).

**Morals**—The Habits and Morals—(See Morals).

**Narcotic Habit**—(See Narcotics).

**Natural Habits**—The ☉ well-asp. in ♍. (See Natural).

**Nature's Wants**—Careless Concerning—(See "Requirements" under Nature).

**Overcoming Bad Habits**—The ☉ in ♍ gives good power and ability to overcome any undesirable habit, and to make one careful of the body. (See Virgo).

**Passion**—The Passional Habits—(See Excesses, Passion, Sex, Venery, etc.).

**Permanent Habits**—Fixed Habits—Indicated by the influences of the radical map; many planets in fixed signs at B., and with fixed signs on the angles. (See "Creatures Of" in this section).

**Personal Habits**—The ☽ has an important influence over the personal, acquired, and temporary or transitory habits.

**Perverted Habits**—(See Perversions).

**Pleasures**—Habits Concerning—(See Pleasure).

**Plethoric Habit**—(See Plethora).

**Questionable Habits**—(See Loose, Morals).

**Regular Habits**—Should be cultivated when ☿ is in ♍. (See Regular).

**Repeated Action**—Repetition In the Formation of Habits—(See Automatic).

**Secret Bad Habits**—(See Perversions, Secret, Sex, Solitary).

**Sedentary Habits** (See Sedentary).

**Sex Habits**—(See Amorous, Excesses, Passion, Sex).

**Skin Eruptions**—(See "Eruptions" in this section).

**Solitary Habits**—(See Secret, Solitary).

**Studious Habits**—Not Studious—(See Dull, Examinations, Genius, Knowledge, Learning; "Quickened" under Mental; Reading, Science, Study, etc.).

**Temperaments**—The Various Temperaments and Habit—(See Temperament).

**Temperate Habits**—(See Moderate, Temperate).

**Tendencies**—(See Heredity, Tendencies).

**Tobacco Habit**—(See Tobacco).

**Too Full a Habit**—(See "Full Habit" in this section).

**Transient Habits**—Temporary—Caused by Directions. (See Directions; "Fixed" in this section).

**Uncleanly Habits**—(See Dirty, Filthy, Uncleanly).

**Unconscious Behavior**—(See the Introduction to this Article).

**Unsettled Habits**—(See Changes, Mutable, Restless, Residence, Travel, etc.).

**Unsteady Habits**—(See "Unsettled" in this section).

**Vices; Women**—The Habits of Women—(See Females, Women).

**Wrong Habits**—(See "Bad", and the various paragraphs in this section). For further study see Behavior, Celibacy, Conduct, Cosmetics, Debauched, Depraved, Dishonest, Disposition, Dissipated, Gormandizing, Health; "High Living" under High; Improvident, Indiscretions, Lascivious, Licentious, Love Affairs, Lustful, Manners, Men, Obesity, Practices, Quarrelsome, Self-Indulgent, Slovenly, Spendthrift (see "Expense" in this section); Tendencies, etc. Many other subjects may also occur to your mind as related to Habits. Look for them in the alphabetical arrangement.

**HAEM**—The Prefix Haem—For words not listed under "Haem", see "Hem". In present-day Medical Dictionaries, words beginning with "Haem" are usually listed under "Hem". Also words like "Anaemia" are often found under "Anemia", as the shortened spelling is becoming more prevalent.

**HAEMATEMESIS**—(See Haemoptysis; "Blood" under Vomiting).

**HAEMATIDROSIS**—Bloody Sweat—(See "Haematidrosis" under Sweat).

**HAEMATOMA**—Blood Tumor—A Tumor Containing Blood—Caused by ♄. (See Hemorrhoids).

**HAEMATOMYELIA**—Hemorrhage Into the Spinal Cord—(See this subject under Spine).

**HAEMATOPOIESIS** — Haematosis — Blood Making—Blood Formation—The physiological action of the ☉ contributes to blood making. This process is also presided over by ♃ and ♂. Disturbances and diseases which concern blood making and formation are the diseases of ♃ and ♂, and caused by their afflictions, and also by afflictions to these planets. Pulmonary Haematosis is aided by the physiological action of the ☿ Group of Herbs. (See Blood, Haemoglobin, Iron, Oxygen).

**HAEMATOSIS**—(See Haematopoiesis).

**HAEMATURIA**—Blood in the Urine—(See "Blood" under Urine).

**HAEMOGLOBIN**—The Coloring Matter of Red Corpuscles—♂ assimilates Iron from the food and turns it into Haemoglobin. (See Haematopoiesis, Iron, Mars; "Blood" under Red).

**HAEMOPHILIA**—Hemophilia—Abnormal Tendency to Hemorrhage—(See "Haemophilia" under Hemorrhage).

**HAEMOPTYSIS**—The Spitting of Blood —Expectoration of Blood—A disease of the ☽ and the ♋ sign; the ☽ in ♊ or ♋, and affl. by the ☉ or ♂ when taken ill; attacks are apt to come when the ☽ is in ☌, □, or ☍ ♂; more apt to occur at the Full ☽ when the fluids of the body are at high tide; ♂ causes when the dominion of death is vested in him, and he afflicts the hyleg; ♂ in ♉, ♊, or ♋, and espec. when in the 6th H.; ♂ in an angle, occi. of the ☉ and ori. of the ☽.

**Death**—Death from the Spitting of Blood—♂ denotes; ♂ affl. the hyleg and holding the dominion of death; ♂ occi. at B., and affl. the hyleg. (See Effusions, Expectoration, Hemorrhage; "Epistaxis" under Nose; "Blood" under Vomiting).

**HAEMOSTATICS**—Styptics—Having the Property of Checking Hemorrhage —A therapeutic property of ♄ remedies. (See Astringent; "Therapeutic Qualities" under Saturn).

**HAIL**—Hailstorms—Furious and Tempestuous Hailstorms—An eclipse of the ☽ in ♎, and espec. in the 1st Dec. of ♎, and with suffering or loss of life, injury by, etc.; ♅ in an angle at an Equinox or Solstice; Comets appearing in ♑. (See Cold, Ice, Snow, Weather).

**HAIR**—The Hirsute Appendage of the Skin—Pilary—Hairy—The Hair in a general way is ruled by ☿, and ☿ in ♈ rules and affects the hair. Is also ruled by ♀. Being an appendage of the skin, is ruled by ♑. The Hair is also connected with the ♍ Sign, and Potassium Sulphate, the ♍ Salt. (See Potassium). The greater part of this Article will be taken up with the description, color, and condition of the Hair, and a few paragraphs will be given to disorders of the Hair, or Hair Follicles. (See Alopecia, Baldness, Barber's Itch, Beard, Brittle, Disorders, Follicles, Inhibited Growth, Lotions, No Hair, Shrunken, in this section).

**Absence Of**—(See Baldness).

**Abundance of Hair**—Heavy—Luxuriant—Much Hair—Plentiful—Thick—The ☉ Sig. in ♍; the ☽ gives; ♄ Sig. in ♍, plentiful and dark hair; ♄ in ♍ in partile asp. the Asc.; ♄ Sig. in ♏, usually dark, short and thick; ♄ in N. Lat. gives a body with much hair, but if in S. Lat. more smooth and fleshy; ♃ strong at B., or ♃ Sig. in Hor'y Q., denotes thick hair; ♃ in the Asc.; ♀ in the Asc., and strong at B.; ♀ Sig. in ♉ in her own term, soft and luxuriant; ♀ in ♏; ☿ strong at B. and rising; ☿ Sig. in ♉, dark, short and thick; ♏ gives much hair, and curling, crispy, or bushy; ♏ on the Asc., plentiful and curly; the earthy and watery signs give; people born under the Southern Parallels, and who have the ☉ continually in their Zenith, and constantly scorched by it, have plentiful and thick hair, which is protective from the heat and rays of the ☉. (See "Growth" in this section).

**Alopecia**—Loss of the Hair—(See Baldness, Falling Out, Loss Of, No Hair, in this section).

**Auburn Hair**—♄ in ♎; ♃ in the Asc., auburn brown; ☿ indicates auburn, or light brown; ♎ gives; ♎ on the Asc., light auburn or flaxen. (See "Red" in this section).

**Baldness**—(See Baldness; Falling, Little, Loss Of, No Hair, in this section).

**Barber's Itch**—(See Barbers).

**Beard**—(See the various paragraphs under Beard).

**Beautiful Hair**—The ☉, ☽, ♀, or ♃ in ♉, and espec. near the 18°, and Medusa's Head; the ☽ or ♀ in the 5° of ♈ or ♐. (See Beautiful; Abundant, Lovely, in this section).

**Black Hair**—The ☉ in ♈, ☌ or near Cauda; the ☽ in ♉, ♍, ♏, or ♑, in partile the Asc., black or brown; the ☽ Sig. in ♏, and espec. when in the terms of ♄ or ♃; the ☽ in ♏, black and curly; the ☽ Sig. in ♉, ♍, ♏, or ♑; the ♄ influence tends to darken the hair, and with ♄ strong at B., rising in the Asc., ♄ as ruler, ♄ as Sig. of the person in Hor'y Questions, and with a ♄ sign upon the Asc. at B., such as ♑ or ♒; ♄ or ♑ ascending at B., black, lanky hair; ♄ Sig. in ♊, ♍, ♏, ♑, or ♓ in Hor'y Q.; ♄ Sig. in ♊, black or dark brown; ♄ Sig. in ♓, black or a coal, or sad black; ♄ Sig. in ♏, black or dark, and usually short or thick; ♄ lord of the Asc., ori., between the Asc. or M.C., or between the 7th H. and the Nadir; ♄ Sig. in ♎ a comely brown; ♄ in ♊, ♍, ♏, ♑, or ♓, in partile asp. the Asc.; ♃ Sig. in ♍; ♃ combust; ♃ in ♍ in partile asp. the Asc., blackish or brown; ♂ Sig. in ♉, ♊, ♍, ♏, or ♑, or in these signs in partile asp. the Asc.; ♂ in ♉ partile the Asc., black, rugged; ♂ in ♊ or ♍, partile the Asc., black or dark brown; ♂ in ♏, partile the Asc., or ♂ Sig. in ♏, black, curly; ♂ in ♑ partile the Asc., or ♂ Sig. in ♑, black, lank hair; ♀ Sig. in ♉, in the term of ♃, shining black; ♀ in ♍, black or sad brown; ♀ in ♑, partile the Asc., dark or black; ♀ Sig. in ♏, black, unless ♀ be in the terms of ♂ or ♀; ☿ Sig. in ♍ in the terms of ♃ or ♄; ☿ Sig. in ♌; ☿ rising at B., and with a ☿ sign upon the Asc.; ☿ in ♍ in partile asp. the Asc., black or dark brown; ☿ ruler of the Asc., and occi., long black hair; ♈, ♉, ♊, ♍, ♎, ♏, or ♑ on the Asc.; ♋ on Asc., sometimes black; ♎ on the Asc. sometimes gives jet black, glossy hair, ♎ being the exalted sign of ♄; ♉ on the Asc. gives dark or black hair; ♊ gives blackish hair; ♍ gives black hair, and espec. the latter half of the sign; ♑ gives black, lanky hair; ♑ on cusp the 7th H. Sulphur, ruled by ♄, darkens the hair, and ♄ rising produces black hair. Lilly says the hair is black when ♑ descends and light when ♑ ascends. (See Black, Dark, Sulphur. Also in this section see Brunettes, Dark).

**Blondes**—(See "Light" in this section; "Light Complexion" under Complexion).

**Body**—(a) Hairy Body—Very Hairy Body—♄ strong at B.; ♄ when ori. makes the body more hairy and tall than when occi.; ♄ in N. Lat., more hairy than when in S. Lat.; denoted by ♄ as Sig. in Hor'y Q.; the ☽ influence gives much hair on the body; ♂ rising and ori. of the ☉; ♂ ruler of the Asc., and ori.; ☿ Sig. in ♓, very hairy body when in the term of ♄; ☿ in ♓ in partile asp. the Asc.; ♏ gives a hairy body; ♏ on the Asc., a short, hairy, coarse body. (See "Abundance" in this section. (b) Little Hair On the Body—Smooth Body—The ☽ ascending at B.; ♄ or ♂ occi. of the ☉ at B.; ♄ lord of the Asc., and occi., as between the M.C. and Desc., or between the Nadir and Asc.; ♄ in S. Lat. at B., the body is more smooth, and with less hair; ♂ ruler of the Asc., and occi., little or no hair on the body; born in cold climates, as in the Arctic Regions; the Quadrant from the Winter Tropic to the Vernal Equinox tends to, and to give straight hair. (See Loss Of, No Hair, in this section). (c) Some Hair On the Body—♄ occi. of the ☉, and ♄ in N. Lat.; ♂ ori. at B.

**Brittle and Dry**—(See "Dry" in this section).

**Brown Hair**—The ☉ Sig. in ♉, ♊, ♋, ♍, ♏, ♐, or ♑; the ☉ Sig. in ♒, dark brown when in the term of ♄; the ☉ rising at B., light brown; the ☉ Sig. in ♌, ♐, ♒, or ♓, light brown; the ☉ in ♑ partile Asc., lank brown; the ☉ Sig. in ♐, light brown, but of a dark brown when in the first eight degrees of this sign; the ☉ Sig. in the first six degrees of ♑, light brown; the ☉ in ♊, ♍, ♏, or ♑, in partile asp. the Asc.; the ☉ in ♍ partile Asc., much bright brown; the ☽ Sig. in any sign except ♏ or ♑; the ☽ Sig. in ♈, ♌, ♎, or ♓, light brown; the ☽ in ♎, smooth light brown; the ☽ in ♑, lank dark brown; the ☽ in ♉, ♍, or ♏, dark brown; the ☽ in ♋ or ♍, sad brown; the ☽ Sig. in ♐ or ♓, bright brown; the ☽ in ♉, ♊, ♋, ♏, ♐, ♑, ♒, or ♓, partile the Asc.; the ☽ in ♐ or ♓, partile the Asc., bright brown; the ☽ ♑, partile Asc., brown or black; ♄ in ♋, sad brown; ♄ in ♊, ♋, ♌, ♍, ♎, ♐, or ♒, partile Asc.; ♄ Sig. in ♒, sad brown; ♄ in ♊, dark brown or black; ♄ in ♍, very dark brown; ♄ Sig. in ♎, comely brown; ♄ Sig. in ♌ or ♐; ♃ indicates dark brown or chestnut; ♃ in ♉ partile the Asc., brown rugged; ♃ in ♊, glossy brown; ♃ in ♊, ♋, ♍, ♑, or ♒, partile the Asc.; ♃ Sig. in ♋ or ♑, dark brown; ♃ Sig. in ♌, light brown, or yellowish brown and curly; ♃ Sig. in ♍, dark or sad brown; ♃ Sig. in ♎ or ♓, light brown; ♃ in the Asc., thick brown; ♃ in the Asc., auburn brown, and espec. when ♂ is also rising and strong; born under ♃, soft, thick brown; ♂ in ♉ partile Asc., brown or black rugged; ♂ Sig. in the first seven degrees of ♊, the term of ☿, light brown; ♂ Sig. in ♊, ♋, ♌, ♍, ♎, ♒, or ♓; ♂ Sig. in ♋, or ♂ in ♋ in partile the Asc., thick brown; ♂ in ♊ or ♍, dark brown; ♂ Sig. in ♌, ♎, ♒, or ♓, light brown; ♂ Sig. in ♍, very dark brown, but lighter when in the first seven degrees of ♍; ♂ in ♐ partile Asc.; ♂ Sig. of the person, and ♂ in earthy signs, dark or sad brown; ♂ in earthy signs and near fixed stars of his own nature, dark or sad brown; ♂ Sig. of the person, light brown, and espec. when ♂ is in a watery sign; ♀ in the Asc., bright brown or chestnut; ♀ in the Asc., and strong at B., light brown; ♀ indicates light brown hair; in Hor'y Q. ♀ as Sig. denotes a party with smooth, soft, brown hair; the ⚹ or △ asps. of ♀ give brown, or light brown hair; ♀ in ♉, ♊, ♍, ♎, ♏, ♐, ♒, or ♓, in partile asp. the Asc.; ♀ Sig. in ♉, ♊, or ♎, soft brown; ♀ in ♍, sad brown or black; ♀ Sig. in ♍ or ♑, dark brown if in her own term; ♀ in ♏, dark brown; ♀ in ♒, light brown; ☿ Sig. in any of the signs may give brown hair, according to aspects; ☿ in ♉, ♊, ♋, ♍, ♏, ♐, ♑, or ♒, in partile Asc.; ☿ Sig. in ♈, ♌, or ♎, light brown; ☿ indicates light brown or auburn hair; ☿ in ♉ partile Asc., short, thick, brown hair; ☿ in ♊, ♌, or ♍, dark brown; ☿ in ♋, sad or dark brown; ☿ Sig. of the party, sad or dark brown; ☿ rising and strong at B., sad or dark brown; ☿ Sig. in ♏, curly, bushy sad or dark brown; ☿ in ♍ partile the Asc., brown curling; ♈ on the Asc., brown or sandy; ♊, ♋, ♍, ♎, ♏, ♐, or ♓ on the Asc.; ♊ gives dark brown; ♊ on the Asc. tends to brown or blackish hair, but the first seven degrees to a lighter brown; ♋ on the Asc. gives sad or dark brown; ♍ on the Asc., a dark brown, except lighter in the 1st Dec.; ♎ on the Asc., brown and glossy; ♏ on the Asc. gives a dark or sad brown, plentiful, curly and bushy; ♐ on the Asc., a bright brown, but darker brown in the first eight degrees. (See Brown. Also see Auburn, Chestnut, Dark, Light, Tawny, in this section).

**Brunettes**—♀ Sig. in ♉, often handsome brunettes, a perfect beauty, and with a Venus de Milo figure. (See Beautiful, Black, Dark, in this section).

**Bushy Hair**—(See "Curly" in this section).

**Chestnut Hair**—The ☽ Sig. in ♐, shining, oily, glossy, chestnut hair; ♃ indicates chestnut or dark brown; ♃ Sig.

in ♐, or ♃ in ♐ in partile asp. the Asc.; ♃ in the Asc., but liable to be bald, and espec. about the temples; ♂ in earthy signs and near fixed stars of his own nature; born under ♀, chestnut or light hair; ♀ in the Asc., chestnut or bright brown; ☿ in ♐, chestnut, and growing off the temples; ☿ ascending at B., and free from the rays of other planets; ♐ gives light chestnut; ♐ on the Asc., light brown or chestnut, and growing back from the temples.

**Coarse Hair**—Stiff—Wiry—Rough—Rugged—Harsh—Strong—♄ Sig. in ♉, rough, dark; ♃ Sig. in ♉; ♃ Sig. in ♏, dark and coarse; ♂ Sig. of the person in Hor'y Q.; ♂ tends to make the hair stiff, coarse, strong and wiry; ♂ Sig. in ♉, rough and coarse; ♂ Sig. in the last six degrees of ♎; ♂ occi. at B.; ♂ in the 5° ♈ or ♐ tends to make the hair coarse and stiff; ♈ gives wiry hair; ♉ gives harsh, dark and curling hair; ♉ on the Asc., rough and curly. (See Hard, Rough, Rugged, Wiry, in this section).

**Color of the Hair**—The color of the hair depends upon the planets aspecting the Asc., the sign rising, and the ruler of the term ascending. Also the color is usually that given by the planet near to, or aspecting the degree on the Asc., or in Hor'y Q. the planet on the cusp, or ruling the cusp of the house which signifies the party. The hair is of a lovely and beautiful color when the ♀ influence is strong at B. (See the various paragraphs in this section, such as Black, Brown, Dark, Light, Red, etc.).

**Comely Hair**—♀ gives when strong at B.; ♄ Sig. in ♎, a comely brown. (See "Beautiful" in this section).

**Cosmetics**—(See Cosmetics, Lotions).

**Crisping**—(See "Curly" in this section).

**Curly Hair**—Crisping—Bushy—Frizzled—Shaggy—Kinky—Given principally by the ♏ sign; ♏ gives plentiful, bushy, and curly hair, and espec. with ♏ on the Asc.; ♏ on the Asc., brown curly, or plentiful sad brown; the ☉ strong at B.; the ☉ in ♏ or ♐; in Hor'y Q. the ☉ or ♂ as Sig. of the person; the ☉ gives light, sandy, curling hair; the ☽ in ♏, black and curly; ♄ ori. at B.; ♄ lord of the Asc., and ori., as between the Asc. and M.C., or between the Desc. and Nadir; ♄, ♃, or ☿ in ♏ tend to bushy and curly hair, and espec. when rising and in the Asc.; ♃ influence strong at B., the hair curls gently, and espec. if in a fiery sign; ♃ Sig. in Hor'y Q. denotes moderate curling hair; ♃ in ♉ partile the Asc., inclined to curl, or rather frizzle; ♃ Sig. in ♉ or ♌; ♃ in ♌ partile Asc., light brown, or yellowish curling hair; ♃ in ♏, dark, curling and bushy; ♂ Sig. of the person, curling or crispy, and espec. when ♂ is in an airy sign; ♂ strong at B., and ruler; ♂ in ♈ partile Asc., light or red curling hair; ♂ in ♏ partile the Asc., black curly hair; ♂ Sig. in ♈ or ♏; ♀ in ♏; ☿ Sig. in ♈ or ♏; ☿ in ♈ partile Asc., light brown, curling; ☿ in ♏ partile Asc., brown curling; ♉ gives dark, harsh, rough and generally curling hair; ♉ on the Asc., dark curled; ♉ on the Asc., often curly in front; ♌ gives bushy or curling yellowish hair; ♏ on the Asc., brown curling, or dark curling and plentiful; the 3rd face of ♒ on the Asc.; people born under Southern Parallels, and who have the ☉ continually in their Zenith, and who are continually scorched by it; the Quadrant from the Summer Tropic to the Autumnal Equi., and the Quadrant from the Winter Tropic to the Vernal Equi., tend to produce curly hair.

**Dark Hair**—Dark Brown—Dark Brown or Black—Darkish—Swarthy—Sulphur, ruled by ♄, darkens the hair, and ♄ rising produces black hair; the ☉ Sig. in ♍, dark and abundant; the ☽ in ♍ or ♏, partile the Asc., dark, dark brown, or black; the ☽ in ♉, ♍, ♏, or ♑; ♄ rising at B.; ♄ Sig. in ♈, ♉, ♊, ♋, ♍, ♏, ♑, ♒, or ♓, or in these signs in partile asp. the Asc.; ♄ Sig. in ♉, rough dark; ♄ in ♊, dark brown or black; ♄ Sig. in ♍, dark and plentiful; ♄ Sig. in ♏, short, thick, and dark; ♄ in ♑ or ♒; ♄ Sig. in ♓, dark black; in Hor'y Q. an asp. of ♄ to the Sig., or the Sig. in ☌ ♄, denotes a dark-haired person; ♃ in ♋, ♍, or ♏, partile Asc.; ♃ Sig. in ♍; ♃ Sig. in ♏, dark, coarse, curling and bushy; ♂ Sig. in ♉, ♊, ♍, ♏, or ♑, or in these signs in partile the Asc.; sometimes given by ♂; ♂ in ♊ or ♍, partile the Asc., dark brown or black; ♀ Sig. in ♈ if in the term of ♃; ♀ Sig. in ♉, often handsome brunettes; ♀ Sig. in ♍ or ♑, or in these signs in partile the Asc.; ♀ Sig. in ♏ unless ♀ be in the terms of ♂ or ♀; ☿ Sig. of the person in Hor'y Q.; ☿ Sig. in ♉, ♋, ♍, or ♏, or in these signs in partile the Asc.; ☿ Sig. in ♉ or ♏, dark, short, and thick; ♈ gives dark, wiry hair; ♉ gives dark, harsh, and generally curly; ♉ on the Asc., dark or black; ♊, ♋, ♍, or ♓, when on the Asc., give dark, or dark brown; ♊, ♍, or ♓ give when on the Asc., or strongly occupied; ♋ on the Asc., generally dark brown; ♌ gives dark yellow hair; ♍ on the Asc., darkish, dark brown, or black; ♏ on the Asc., dark, curly, and plentiful; ♑ on the Asc., dark and lanky; ♒ on the Asc., a dark flaxen; ♓ on the Asc., a soft, dark brown. (See Black, Complexion, Dark; Black, Brunettes, Hazel, in this section).

**Disorders**—Of the Hair—The Hair Affected—The Follicles Affected—Afflictions in or to ♈ or ♑; the Asc. afflicted; ♂ affl. in ♈ or ♑, in the Asc. or 6th H.; afflictions in cardinal signs, and espec. in the 28° of card. signs; afflictions in the 18° ♉ near Gorgon's Head (Algol); ☿ affl. in ♈ tends to affect the hair; ♃ affl. in ♐, or ♐ upon the Asc., tends to falling out of the hair. (See Baldness; "Barber's Itch" under Barbers; Follicles. Also note the various paragraphs in this section).

**Dry and Brittle**—♄ in ♈; Subs at AT and AX. (See Dry, Fragile).

**Eyebrows**—Eyelashes—(See Eyebrows, Eyelids).

**Fair Hair**—Light—Blondes—(See "Fair", "Light", under Complexion; "Light" in this section).

**Falling Hair**—Baldness—Loss of—Alopecia—♐ influence; ♐ on the Asc.; ♃ in ♐. (See Baldness; "Loss Of", "No Hair", in this section).

**Fine Hair**—Soft—Silky—The fiery signs give fine hair, but tend to early loss of the hair, due to their heat; the airy signs give fine hair, and tend to gray rather than baldness. (See "Soft" in this section).

**Flaxen Hair**—Soft—Light Golden—The ☉ Sig. in ♈; the ☉ in ♈ partile Asc., flaxen or yellow; the ☉ in ♓ partile Asc.; the ☉ Sig. in the first eight degrees of ♓, flaxen and soft; the ☽ in ♈ partile the Asc., or the ☽ Sig. in ♈; ♃ Sig. in ♈, or in ♈ partile Asc.; ♃ occi., a dark flaxen; ♂ rising at B.; ♂ gives flaxen, light brown, or red; in Hor'y Q., ♂ as Sig. in watery signs denotes hair more light and flaxen; ♂ in ♌; ♂ in water signs and near fixed stars of his own nature; ♀ in ♌ partile the Asc., light flaxen; ♀ Sig. in ♌ in the term of ♀; ♀ in ♒ partile Asc., flaxen or light brown, and with a fair complexion; ♀ Sig. in ♒ in her own term; ♀ Sig. in ♓; ♀ in ♓ partile Asc., sometimes flaxen; the ♌ sign gives a dark flaxen; ♎ gives flaxen, light yellow, or light auburn, shining, smooth, and long, and espec. when on the Asc.; ♒ gives a sandy or dark flaxen, and espec. when on the Asc. (See Golden, Light, Soft, in this section).

**Follicles**—The Hair Follicles—Disorders of—(See "Disorders" in this section).

**Frizzled Hair**—(See "Curly" in this section).

**Glossy Hair**—Oily—Shiny—The ☽ in ♈, and espec. in the Asc.; the ☽ in ♎, smooth and glossy; the ☽ Sig. in ♐, shining, oily, glossy chestnut; ♃ in ♊, brown glossy; ♀ in the Asc.; ♀ Sig. in ♉ in the term of ♃, often a shining black; ♎ on the Asc., shining, glossy, smooth, long, brown hair, and sometimes a glossy jet black. (See Oil).

**Golden**—The ☉ indicates golden hair. (See Flaxen, Light, Yellow, in this section).

**Gray Hair**—Hoary—Ruled by ♄, the ruler of old age; the airy signs strong at B., and many planets in them, tend to fine hair, and to gray hair early in life, and do not tend to baldness; the ♒ sign on the Asc., or the ☉ in ♒, and many planets in the signs of ♄, tend to gray hair early in life, and often before middle life the hair is a pure silvery white, considered very beautiful, and the face is young looking. (See "White" in this section).

**Growth**—Of the Hair—The fiery signs when strong at B., and well occupied, tend to early loss of the hair. The earthy and watery signs strong at B., to abundant and plentiful, and espec. ♉, ♋, and ♓. The growth of the hair is inhibited when the ☉ or ♄ are in the 5° of ♈ or ♐. A moderate growth of hair is given by ♂ ascending at B., and also by the Quadrant from the Autumnal Equi. to the Winter Tropic when well occupied at B. (See Abundance, Baldness, Loss Of, Scanty, in this section).

**Hairy Body**—(See "Body" in this section).

**Hard Hair**—Rugged—♄ ascending at B., hard and rugged; ♃ in ♉, brown rugged; ♉ gives black rugged. (See "Coarse" in this section).

**Harsh Hair**—(See Coarse,Hard,Rough, in this section).

**Hazel Hair**—Dark Brown—☿ ascending at B., and free from the rays of other planets; ♊ influence. (See Brown, Dark, in this section; "Hazel" under Eyes).

**Head**—Hair of the Head Darker Than the Beard—(See Beard).

**Heavy**—Much—Plentiful—(See "Abundance" in this section; "Heavy" under Beard).

**Hoary**—(See Gray, White, in this section).

**Inflamed**—The Hair Follicles Inflamed—(See "Barber's Itch" under Barbers).

**Inhibited Growth**—(See "Growth" in this section).

**Kinky**—(See "Curly" in this section).

**Lank**—Lanky—Lean—Shrunken—The ☉ in ♑ in partile asp. the Asc., lank brown; the ☽ in ♑ partile Asc., lank dark brown; ♄ ascending at B., dark brown or black lanky; ♂ in ♑ partile Asc., black lanky; ♑ on the Asc., lanky dark or black hair.

**Legs**—Coarse and Hairy Legs—(See "Coarse" under Legs).

**Light Hair**—Light Brown—Blondes—Golden—Yellowish—Flaxen—Gray—White—Bright, etc.—The ☉ indicates light, or golden hair; the ☉ gives light, sandy curly hair; the ☉ rising at B., light brown; the ☉ Sig. in ♈ or ♎; the ☉ in ♌, partile the Asc., light brown or yellow; the ☉ in ♎ partile Asc.; the ☉ in ♐, ♒, or ♓, partile Asc.; the ☉ Sig. in the first six degrees of ♑, light brown; the ☽ Sig. in ♈, ♌, ♎, or ♓, light brown; the ☽ in ♈, ♌, or ♎, partile the Asc.; the ☽ in ♎, partile Asc., smooth light brown; ♄ Sig. in ♌ in Hor'y Q.; ♄ in ♌, partile Asc., light brown; ♃ in ♈ or ♎, partile Asc., light brown; ♃ in ♌ partile Asc., light brown or yellowish curly; ♃ in ♓, partile Asc., light brown, but with a dark complexion; born under ♃, and ♃ occi., light brown near the temples and forehead; ♂ in ♈, partile Asc., light or red curly; ♂ gives flaxen, light brown or red hair; ♂ occi., light or red; ♂ Sig. in watery signs in Hor'y Q., more light and flaxen; ♂ in ♊ in the beginning of the sign, and in partile the Asc., light brown; ♂ Sig. in the first seven degrees of ♊, the term of ☿, light brown; ♂ Sig. in ♌, ♎, ♒, or ♓, light brown; ♂ in ♎, partile Asc., light brown; ♀ gives light hair; ♀ in the Asc., and strong at B., light brown; ♀ Sig. in Hor'y Q. indicates and signifies a person with light hair, or a blonde; ♀ Sig. in ♈ or ♋, or in these signs in partile the Asc.; ♀ Sig. in ♋, and the ☽ with ♀, very light; ♀ in ♌, partile Asc., light flaxen or red; ♀ in ♒, partile Asc., flaxen or light brown; born under ♀, light hair; ♀ in the Asc., a bright or light brown; the ✱ or △ asps. of ♀ give bright or light brown; ☿ indicates light brown or auburn; ☿ Sig. in ♈, ♌, or ♎, light brown; ☿ in ♈, partile the Asc., curly light brown; ☿ in ♌ or ♎, partile Asc., light brown; ☿ in ♎, partile Asc., smooth light brown; ♋ on the Asc., light brown; ♌ on the Asc., light, yellow, or tawny; ♎ on the Asc., light, flaxen, light yellow, or auburn; ♑ on the Asc., more light than dark, and may be light and fair, but Lilly says that when ♑ descends the hair is usually black; ♐ on the Asc., light brown or chestnut, and growing back from the temples; ♒ on Asc., fair, light, flaxen, sandy, or white. (See Beard, Brown, Fair, Light; "Light Complexion" under Complexion; Auburn, Brown, Chestnut, Color, Curly, Fair, Flaxen, Golden, Gray, Sandy, Tawny, White, Yellow, in this section).

**Little Hair**—(See Body, Scanty, in this section).

**Long Hair**—The Hair Grows Long—♃ ruler of the Asc., and occi.; ♀ Sig. in ♎, the hair grows long, but is not very thick or abundant; ☿ ruler of the Asc. and occi., long black hair; ♎ on the Asc., long, smooth, light and shining hair. (See Flaxen, Glossy, Lank, in this section).

**Loss of Hair**—Alopecia—Baldness—Cases—See "Aqueous Tumour", No. 120, and "Loss of Hair", No. 121, in 1001 N.N. (See Baldness; "No Hair", "Scanty", in this section).

**Lotions**—Hair Lotions—Indiscreet Use of—(See Cosmetics; "Lotions" under Face; Lotions).

**Lovely Color**—♀ influence strong at B. (See Beautiful, Brunettes, Color, in this section).

**Luxuriant Hair**—(See "Abundance" in this section).

**Moderate**—Moderate Curling—Moderate Growth—(See Curly, Growth, in this section).

**Much Hair**—(See "Abundance" in this section).

**No Hair**—♄ influence and afflictions tend to; ♄ affl. in ♈; ♄ affl. the Asc. (See "Loss Of" in this section. Also see Case, "No Hair or Teeth", Chap. 8, page 49, in Daath's Medical Astrology).

**Oily Hair**—Glossy—Shiny—(See "Glossy" in this section).

**Plentiful**—(See "Abundance" in this section).

**Pubes**—Hair of—(See Pubes).

**Red Hair**—♂ exactly rising at B., and the greater the amount of iron the redder the hair; ♂ rising in ♈ gives fiery red hair, and usually red curly; ♂ ascending, strong at B., and ruler; born under ♂, and characteristic of ♂ people; ♂ in ♈, partile asp. the Asc., light or red curly; in Hor'y Q. ♂ as Sig. of the person; ♂ occi., light or red; ♂ Sig. in ♈; ♂ Sig. in the last six degrees of ♎, wiry and reddish; ♂ near the Lion's Heart (Cor Leo) at B.; ♂ in ♊ if ♂ be near Aldebaran; ♂ in fiery or airy signs, and with fixed stars of his own nature, a deep sandy red; ♀ in ♌ partile Asc., red or light flaxen; ♈ on the Asc., red, brown, or sandy. (See "Red Beard" under Beard; Freckles, Iron, Red; Auburn, Curly, Sandy, in this section).

**Rough Hair**—♈ on the Asc., rough and wiry; ♉ on the Asc., rough and curly. (See Coarse, Hard, Rugged, Wiry, in this section).

**Rugged**—Coarse—Hard—Wiry—Rough—♉ gives rugged hair; ♃ Sig. in ♉, or in ♉ partile Asc.; ♂ in ♉ partile Asc., brown or black rugged. (See Coarse, Hard, Rough, Strong, Wiry, in this section).

**Sad Hair**—Sad Brown—Sad Black—♄ ascending at B., sad hair; ♄ in ♋ partile Asc., sad brown; ♄ Sig. in ♓, sad black; ♃ combust., very sad or black; ♃ Sig. in ♍, dark or sad brown; ♂ in earthy signs as Sig. of the person, sad brown; ♂ in earthy signs and near fixed stars of his own nature, dark or sad brown; ♀ in ♍ or ♏, sad brown or dark; ☿ rising and strong at B., sad or dark brown; ☿ Sig. of the party in Hor'y Q., sad brown or dark; ☿ in ♋ partile Asc., sad brown; ☿ Sig. in ♋ or ♏, sad or dark brown; ♋ or ♏ on the Asc., sad or dark brown; ♏ on Asc., sad brown, curling and plentiful. (See Black, Brown, Dark, in this section).

**Sandy**—Sandy Colored—The ☉ gives light, sandy, curling hair; the ☉ Sig. in ♈; ♂ strong at B., and ♂ ruler; characteristic of ♂ people; ♂ rising at B.; ♂ in ♌, ♒, or ♓; the ♂ sign ♈ on the Asc.; ♂ in fiery or airy signs and with fixed stars of his own nature, a deep sandy red; ☿ ori. of the ☉ except when ☿ is in ♊; ♈ on the Asc., red, brown, or sandy; ♒ on the Asc., a sandy or dark flaxen. (See "Red" in this section).

**Scanty Hair**—Baldness—Thin—Loss of—Fewer Hairs on Head or Body—♀ Sig. in ♎, scanty, but grows long. (See Baldness, Beard; Body, Disorders, Falling, Loss Of, No Hair, in this section).

**Shaggy**—Bushy—(See "Curly" in this section).

**Shiny Hair**—Oily—Glossy—(See "Glossy" in this section).

**Short and Thick**—Abundant—♄ Sig. in ♏, usually short and thick, black or dark; ☿ Sig. in ♉, dark, short and thick; ☿ in ♉ partile the Asc., short, thick brown hair. (See "Abundance" in this section).

**Shrunken**—(See "Lank" in this section).

**Silky Hair**—Fine Texture—(See Fine, Soft, in this section).

**Smooth Hair**—The ☽ or ☿ Sig. in ♎, smooth light brown; the ☽ Sig. in ♎, or ♎ on the Asc., smooth and glossy; the ☽ or ☿ in ♎ in partile Asc., smooth light brown; ♀ in the Asc., and strong at B., smooth and soft; ♎ on the Asc. gives flaxen, light yellow, light auburn, shining, smooth, long hair.

**Soft Hair**—Fine—Silky—The ☉ Sig. in ♑; the ☉ Sig. in the first eight degrees of ♓, soft and flaxen; ♃ in the Asc., or born under ♃, soft thick brown; ♂ Sig. in ♎, except in the last six degrees; ♀ influence strong at B., soft and smooth; ♀ Sig. in ♉, in her own term, and espec. when in the Asc., soft and luxuriant; in Hor'y Q., ♀ as Sig. denotes a party with soft, smooth, brown hair; ♀ Sig. in ♉, ♊, or ♎, soft brown; ♓ on the Asc., soft dark brown. (See "Fine" in this section).

**Some Hair**—On the Body—(See "Body" in this section).

**Stiff Hair**—(See "Coarse" in this section).

**Straight**—Straight Hair occurs with those born in cold climates, or in Arctic Regions. Produced by the Quarter between the Winter Tropic and the Vernal Equi.; the ♄ influence strong at B., and ♂ weak or setting; ♂ occi. to the ☉ tends to. (See Coarse, Hard, Lank, Rugged, Strong, Wiry, in this section).

**Strong**—Strong and Wiry—In Hor'y Q. ♂ Sig. of the person. (See "Wiry" in this section).

**Sulphur**—The Effect of On the Hair—(See Sulphur).

**Swarthy**—(See "Dark" in this section; Swarthy).

**Sycosis**—(See "Barber's Itch" under Barbers; "Disorders" in this section).

**Tawny**—Tan—Brownish Yellow—♌ on the Asc., light, yellow, or tawny. (See Brown, Light, Yellow, in this section).

**Temples**—Hair Growing Off the Temples—(See "Temples" under Baldness).

**Thick Hair**—(See Abundance, Curly, in this section; "Much Beard" under Beard).

**Thin**—Scanty—(See "Scanty" in this section).

**Tonics**—Hair Tonics—Cantharides, a typical drug of ♂, is one of the principal ingredients in hair tonics. For the indiscreet use of Hair Tonics, Cosmetics, and Lotions, see Cosmetics.

**White Hair**—Hoary—Whitish Gray—The ☉ and ♀ in the ♒ sign, or with ♒ on the Asc., tend to give a beautiful white hair in youth or middle age; ♂ in watery signs, and near fixed stars of his own nature, often tends to a bright, whitish hair; ♑ on the Asc. (See "Gray" in this section). Case—Hair Turns White In a Day—See "Strange Case", No. 405 in 1001 N.N.

**Wiry and Strong**—Wiry and Rough—♂ tends to make the hair strong, stiff, wiry and coarse; ♂ Sig. of the person in Hor'y Q.; ♂ in the last six degrees of ♎, wiry and reddish; ♈ on the Asc., a dark wiry and rough. (See Coarse, Hard, Rugged, Strong, in this section).

**Yellow**—Yellowish—The ☉ gives; the ☉ Sig. in ♈ or ♌; the ☉ rising at B.; the ☉ in ♈, partile the Asc., yellow or flaxen; the ☉ in ♌, partile Asc., yellow or light brown; ♃ Sig. in ♌, or ♃ in ♌ partile the Asc., yellowish or light brown, curly; ♂ occi.; ♂ ruler of the Asc., and occi.; the ♌ sign, and with ♌ on the Asc., gives bushy or curling yellowish hair; ♎ gives; ♎ on the Asc., light yellow, light, auburn or flaxen, and usually shining and glossy. (See Yellow; Flaxen, Golden, Light, Tawny, in this section).

**HALITOSIS**—Foul or Disagreeable Breath—(See "Foul Breath" under Breath).

**HALLUCINATIONS**—A False Perception or Image—A ♆ disease and affliction; afflictions to ♆ or ☿; ♅ in ♎, and affl. ☿ or ♆; a ♄ disease and affliction; ♂ affl. in ♌; the 3rd Decan. of ♒ on the Asc., ruled by the ☽. Mild forms, as "Imagining Things", are a ♆ and ♓ condition, and also ☿ is usually afflicted by ♆; Subs at AT. (See Anguish, Anxiety, Chaotic, Clairaudience, Clairvoyant, Delirium, Delusions, Demoniac, Dreams, Fancies, Fears, Fits, Forebodings, Hearing, Horrors, Hysteria, Ideals, Idiocy, Illusions, Imaginations, Insanity, Mediumship, Melancholy, Morbid, Notions, Obsessions, Paranoia, Perceptions, Premonitions, Spirit Controls, Superstitions, Terrors, Visions, Weird, Worry, etc.).

**HALTER**—Death By—Malefics in ♉. (See Execution, Hanging, Judge, Law, Suffocation).

**HAMS**—Hamstrings—Thighs—(See Thighs).

**HAND OF MAN**—Human Means—Death By—Injury By—(See Ambushes, Assassination, Assaults, Attacks, Common People, Cuts, Duels, Enemies, Execution, Homicide, Human; "Hand of Man" under Man; Mobs, Murder, Poison, Robbers, Stabs, Treachery; "Death" under Violent).

**HANDS**—The Hands are under the external rulership of the ♍ sign. The hands correspond to, and are opposite to the feet, ruled by ♓. Also ruled by ☿, ♃, the ♊ sign, and affected by all the common signs. Ruled and affected by the 3rd, 6th, 9th, and 12th Houses. The Bones of the hands are under the structural rulership of ♊ and ♍. The Arms, Shoulders, Hands, Legs, and Feet should be studied together, as all these parts are ruled by the common signs, and what affects one may adversely affect all to a greater or lesser degree, according to the planets and afflictions in these signs at B. Also see the Articles on Fingers, Nails, Toes, Feet, Wrists, etc. The Wrists are said to be ruled by the ♌ sign, being opposite to, and corresponding to the ankles, ruled by ♒. The hands are especially denoted by the 3rd H., the house of ☿. The Forehand is governed by ♂. This Article will be divided into two Sections. Section One, Description of the Hands. Section Two, Diseases of the Hands.

**— SECTION ONE —**

**DESCRIPTION OF THE HANDS—**

**Ambidextrous**—(See Ambidextrous).

**Arms**—Long or Short Arms usually indicate the same conditions with the hands and fingers. (See the various paragraphs under Arms).

**Broad Hands**—Broad, Thick and Short—Given by the ♉ influence strong at B.; ♉ on the Asc., or the ☉ and other planets in ♉, broad, plump and short hands; the ☽ gives thick hands and feet. (See Fleshy, Short, Thick, in this section).

**Club Hands**—(See "Clubbed Fingers" under Fingers).

**Dexterity**—(See Dexterity).

**Elbows**—The Hands Growing From—No Forearm—Cases—(See "Missing" under Forearm).

**Fingers**—(See the various paragraphs under Fingers).

**Fleshy and Short**—(See Broad, Short, in this section).

**Four Hands** — Case — Has two heads, four arms, and four hands, and with one body — (See "Twins", No. 236, in 1001 N.N.).

**Frog Child**—Right Forearm and Hand Missing from Birth — (See "Missing" under Forearm).

**Gross and Large**—♉ gives, and with ♉ on Asc. (See "Broad" in this section).

**Large Hands** — (See "Gross" in this section).

**Left-Handed**—(See "Left-Handed" under Left).

**Long Hands** — Long Fingers — ♊ ascending at B.; ☿ ascending at B., and free from the rays of other planets; ♊ gives, and with ♊ on the Asc.; ♍ on the Asc.; the 3rd or 4th face of ♎ on the Asc. (See "Long" under Arms, Legs, Feet).

**Nails**—The Finger Nails—(See Nails. Also see "Nails" under Fingers, Toes).

**No Hands**—Case—See "Born Incomplete", No. 281, in 1001 N.N. See "Missing" under Forearm.

**Plump Hands** — (See "Broad" in this section).

**Right-Handed** — (See Ambidextrous, Dexterity. Also see "Left" in this section).

**Short Hands**—♉ gives; ♊ tends to in many cases, and to give short and fleshy hands and feet; ♊ on the Asc., short and fleshy hands, but with long arms and legs, but some say the fingers are long. (See "Broad" in this section).

**Thick Hands**—And Feet—The ☽ gives. (See "Broad" in this section).

## — SECTION TWO —

**DISEASES OF THE HANDS—**

**Abscesses**—♃ affl. in signs ruling the hands, as in ♊ or ♍. (See Abscesses; "Felons", "Whitlows", under Fingers).

**Accidents To** — All Accidents, Hurts, Wounds, or Injuries to — ♊ signifies; afflictions in ♊, ♍, or ♐; ♄ or ♂ in the Asc. or M.C. in the latter degrees of ♊, ♍, or ♐; ♂ affl. in ♊ or ♍. (See Cuts, Fractures, in this section).

**Acromegaly**—Abnormal Development and Enlargement of the Hands—The ☉, ♄, ♆, ♃, or ♂ affl. in ♍. (See "Enlargement" under Arms, Extremities, Feet; Enlargements).

**All Diseases In**—Signified by the 3rd H., and afflictions in ♊ or ♍. (See "Diseases" in this section).

**All Hurts To** — (See Accidents, Cuts, Fractures, in this section).

**Aneurysm**—In the Hands—(See Aneurysm).

**Ankylosis**—In the Joints—(See Ankylosis; "Ankylosis" under Fingers).

**Atrophy Of**—Claw Hands—♄ affl. in ♊, ♍, or the 3rd or 6th H. (See Atrophy).

**Blisters** — Bullas — Of the Hands and Feet—(See Blisters, Dysidrosis).

**Blood Impurities** — (See "Corrupt Blood" in this section).

**Claw Hands** — (See "Atrophy" in this section).

**Cold Hands**—Cold Fingers—♄ influence; ♄ in ♊ or ♍; Subs at LCP, AP and HP. (See Cold; "Cold" under Extremities; Fingers).

**Corrupt Blood** — Blood Impurities — Disorders In the Hands From—The ☉ or ♃ in signs which rule the Arms, Hands, Legs and Feet, govern the blood of these parts, and tend to blood poisoning, blood impurities, and blood disorders in these parts, which may lead to swellings, eruptions, and skin disturbances of the hands. (See "Blood" under Arms; "Impure Blood" under Impure).

**Cramps In**—Writer's Cramp—Incoordination—Spasmodic Disorders—♅ affl. in ♊ or ♍; ☿ in ♊ or ♍ in the 3rd or 6th H., and affl. by ♅; Subs at LCP, AP and HP. (See "Hands" under Cramps).

**Cuts to Hands**—Wounds—Injuries—♂ affl. in ♊ or ♍; ☿ in ill-asp. to ♂, slight cuts. (See "Accidents" under Arms; "Arms" under Cuts; Accidents, Fractures, in this section).

**Cysts In**—(See Cysts).

**Deformities Of**—Malefics in ♊ or any of the common signs; common signs on the angles and containing malefics; afflictions between ♅ and ♂, or between ♄ and ♂ in common signs. (See "Hands" under Deformities; "Clubbed Fingers" under Fingers; "Missing" under Forearm; "Atrophy" in this section).

**Diseases In**—Humours In—Infirmities In—Afflictions in ♊ or ♍, with these signs on the Asc., 3rd or 6th H., and containing malefics; many planets, a Stellium, in ♊, ♍, the 3rd or 6th H., and containing malefics; ♄ or ♂ in the 1st, 3rd, 6th, or 7th H., in the latter degrees of any common sign, and ori. of the ☉ and occi. of the ☽; signified in Hor'y Q. by ♂ in ♐; signified by the 3rd and 6th H., and afflictions therein; Subs at LCP, AP, and HP. (See "Diseases" under Extremities. Also note the various paragraphs in this section, and under Arms, Extremities, Fingers, Feet).

**Dysidrosis**—(See Blisters, Dysidrosis).

**Eczema In**—(See Eczema).

**Elephantiasis** — Enlargement — (See "Arms" under Elephantiasis; Enlargements, Hypertrophy, Oedema; "Acromegaly" in this section).

**Enlarged** — (See Acromegaly, Enlarged, Elephantiasis, Gout, Swelling, in this section).

**Eruptions**—♃ or ♀ affl. in ♊ or ♍. (See "Arms" under Eruptions; "Corrupt Blood" in this section).

**Erysipelas** — In the Hands and Extremities—♂ affl. in ♊ or ♍; Subs at LCP, HP. (See "Arms", "Extremities", under Erysipelas).

**Extremities** — Diseases In — (See Extremities, Feet, Legs, Limbs. Also note the various paragraphs in this section).

**Feet**—Due to the correspondences between the hands and feet, see the various paragraphs under Feet.

**Felons**—(See "Felons" under Fingers).

**Fingers**—(See the various paragraphs under Fingers, Nails).

**Fractures**—♂ affl. in ♊, ♍, or ♐; afflictions in the common signs denote. (See Fractures).

**Glands** — The Glands and Vesicles of the Hands Affected—Ruled and affected by ♆ when this planet is in signs which rule the hands. (See the Introduction under Aneurysm).

**Gout In** — Gouty Humours — Wandering Gout—(See "Hands" under Gout; Joints, Lameness, Rheumatism, Swelling, in this section).

**Hand of Man**—Injury or Death By—(See Hand of Man).

**Humours In**—(See "Humours" under Fingers; Diseases, Gout, in this section).

**Hurts** — (See Accidents, Cuts, Fractures, in this section).

**Hypertrophy**—(See Elephantiasis, Enlarged, in this section).

**Incoordination**—(See "Cramps" in this section).

**Infirmities In**—(See "Diseases" in this section).

**Injury To**—(See Accidents, Cuts, Fracture, in this section).

**Joints** — Swelling or Inflammation In —(See "Joints" under Fingers; "Gout" in this section).

**Lameness In** — The ☽ in ♊, ♍, or ♐, and affl. by the ☉ or ♂ at the beginning of an illness (Hor'y); ♂ in ♊, ♍, or ♐, and espec. when in the 1st, 3rd, or 6th H.; ♂ in ♑ when ♂ is the afflictor in the disease. (See Gout, Humours, Joints, Rheumatism, Swelling, in this section).

**Leprosy In**—(See "Leprosy" under Extremities; Leprosy).

**Man**—Hand of Man—Injury or Death By—(See Hand of Man).

**Metacarpus** — Bones of the Palms of the Hands — Disorders of — Afflictions in ♊ or ♍; Subs at AP.

**Missing**—One or Both Hands Missing —Congenital Deformity— (See "Missing" under Forearm; "No Hands" in Sec. 1 of this Article).

**Motor Nerves**—The Motor Nerves Affected or Partially Paralyzed, Causing Cramps or Spasm—♅ affl. in ♊ or ♍. (See Cramps; "Cramps" under Feet; "Nerves" under Motor; Spasmodic Diseases; "Cramps" in this section).

**Muscles** — The Muscles of the Hands Affected—♂ affl. in ♊ or ♍; ♅ in ♊ or ♍, due to disturbed nerve supply to the muscles; Subs at AP, HP. (See Atrophy, Cramps, Motor, Paralysis, in this section).

**Nails** — (See the various paragraphs under Nails; "Nails" under Fingers, Toes).

**Nerves**—Nerve Pains In—The ☉ affl. in ♎; the ☽ to the Bull's Horns; ♂ affl. in ♊ or ♍; ☿ affl. in ♊. (See "Pains" under Arms; "Motor" in this section).

**Neuralgia In**—☿ affl. in ♊ or ♍. (See Cramps, Motor, Nerves, in this section; Neuralgia).

**No Hands**—(See "Missing" in this section).

**Oedema**—(See Elephantiasis, Enlarged, Swelling, in this section; Oedema).

**Pains In**—(See Cramps, Motor, Nerves, Neuralgia, in this section).

**Palms** — Of the Hands — (See "Metacarpus" in this section).

**Paralysis** — Cramps — Spasms In — ♅ affl. in ♊ or ♍; Subs at AP, HP (2D). Case—The Hands Paralyzed—Unable to Move Them, and Writes with Aid of the Tongue — See "Tunison", No. 113, in 1001 N.N. (See Cramps, Motor, Muscles, in this section; Paralysis).

**Perspiring Hands**—(See Dysidrosis).

**Rheumatism** — ♄ in ♊ or ♍; ♄ or ♂ angular, in the 1st or 7th H., in the latter degrees of ♊ or ♐, and ori. of the ☉, and occi. of the ☽. (See "Gout" in this section).

**Shoulders** — (See the various paragraphs under Shoulders).

**Skin** — Skin Disorders and Eruptions Due to Bad Blood — (See "Corrupt Blood" in this section).

**Spade-Like Hands** — Accompanies Myxoedema—(See Myxoedma).

**Spasms** — Spasmodic Disorders In — (See Cramps, Motor, Muscles, Paralysis, in this section).

**Swelling In**—The ☽ in ♊, ♍, the 3rd or 6th H., and affl. by the ☉ or ♂; the ☽ in ♐, ☌ or ill-asp. ♄ (or ☿ if he be of the nature of ♄) at the beginning of an illness, or at decumb.; ♃ affl. in ♊ or ♍. (See Abscesses, Acromegaly, Corrupt Blood, Enlarged, Gout, Humours, Joints, Lameness, Oedema, Rheumatism, in this section).

**Thumb**—The Thumb Nearly Cut Off—Case—See Chap. 13, page 97, in Daath's Medical Astrology.

**Ulcers**—The ☽ affl. in ♊ or ♍. (See "Ulcers" under Feet; "Arms" under Ulcers).

**Varicose Veins** — (See "Arms" under Varicose).

**Verruca**—Warts—(See "Arms" under Warts).

**Vesicles**—Disorders of the Glands and Vesicles — (See Aneurysm; "Affected" under Glands; Vesicles).

**Wandering Gout**—(See "Gout" in this section).

**Warts**—(See "Arms" under Warts).

**Wasting**—Of the Hands—♆ in signs which rule the hands. (See Wasting).

**Whitlows**—Phlegmonous Inflammation—(See "Whitlows" under Fingers).

**Wounds To**—(See Accidents, Cuts, Fractures, in this section).

**Wrists**—(See Wrists).

**Writer's Cramp** — (See "Cramps" in this section).

**Writes with Tongue** — Hands Paralyzed—(See "Paralysis" in this section).

**HANDSOME**—Beautiful—Good Looking —Elegant Form, etc.—The ♉, ♎, and ♒ signs are the most favored for beauty and handsomeness, and also ♓ if ♀ be therein. The ♒ sign gives more beauty than any other sign except ♎. The ♍ and ♐ signs also tend to make the body well-proportioned and handsome; ♐ on the Asc., ruddy and handsome; ♎ on the Asc.; the ☉ Sig. in ♍; the ☉ Sig. in ♐, tall and handsome; the ☽ Sig. in ♊, comely; the ☽ in ♎ or ♐, partile asp. the Asc.; the ☽ Sig. in ☌ ♀, and ♀ well-dignified; ♄ in ♎, partile the Asc., rather handsome but not beautiful; ♃ Sig. ☌ ♀, great personal beauty unless ♀ be in ♏ or ♑; ♃ Sig. ☌ ☿, and ☿ well-dig., and free from affliction, and espec. if both are in angles; born under ♃; ♃ Sig. in ♌ or ♍; ♃ Sig. in ♒ with females, a perfect beauty; ♃ Sig. in ✶ or △ ♀; ♀ in the Asc. in one of her own signs; ♀ Sig. in ✶ or △ ♂, a handsome man; ♀ Sig. in ♉ or ♎; ♀ Sig. ☌ ☿, handsome and well-shaped; born under ♀, very handsome altho rather short and stout if occi.; the ✶ or △ aspects of ☿, if ☿ be well-dig., give a very handsome body if ☿ is not combust; all Constellations of human form tend to give a very handsome shape. (See Beautiful). The following subjects have to do with a handsome and beautiful body, form, appearance, face, complexion, eyes, hair, etc., which subjects see in the alphabetical arrangement when not considered here.

**Appearance**—(See the various subjects under Appearance).

**Beautiful; Body**—A Handsome Body—(See the first part of this section).

**Carriage** — (See Carriage, Commanding, Erect, Upright).

**Comely; Complexion**—Handsome Complexion—♃ in the Asc. at B., and ♃ in ♈ or ♎, the complexion is rosy and handsome. (See Beautiful, Rosy, Ruddy, under Complexion).

**Countenance** — A Handsome Countenance — (See "Beautiful" under Complexion, Eyes, Face; Countenance, Expression, Look; "Face" in this section).

**Dimples; Elegant; Expression;**

**Eyes** — Handsome Eyes — Full and Handsome—(See Beautiful, Full, under Eyes).

**Face**—(1) Handsome Face—♃ Sig. in ♎, oval and handsome; ♀ Sig. in ♉ or ♎; ♎ gives a round and lovely face; ♐ gives a long and handsome face; ♐ on the Asc., an open and handsome countenance. (See "Beautiful" under Face). (2) The Face Not Handsome—The ☽ ill-dignified at B., or in watery signs and afflicted; ♃ Sig. in ♉; ♍ on the Asc., well-favored but not handsome; ♑ on the Asc., usually an ugly face. (See Face, Freckles, Marks, Moles, Pimples, Scars; "Face" under Smallpox; Ugly, etc.).

**Fair; Features; Figure; Fine;**

**Forehead** — (See "Handsome" under Forehead).

**Fresh-Colored**—And Handsome—(See Fresh, Ruddy).

**Genteel; Graceful; Hair**—(See Beautiful, Lovely, under Hair).

**Lovely; Middle Stature** — And In No Way Handsome—♍ on the Asc. at B.

**Neat; Not Handsome** — The ☽ Sig. in Hor'y Q.; ♃ in ♉, partile the Asc., stout, well-set, but not handsome; ♍ on the Asc., well-favored body, but not handsome; ♑ on the Asc., usually crooked body, ill-favored, and ugly. (See Crooked, Deformed, Ill-Formed, Ugly).

**Pleasing Body** — Attractive — (See Pleasing).

**Shape**—Of the Body—(See the various references under Shape).

**Skin** — Handsome and Pure Skin — ♒ on the Asc. Also ♍ on the Asc. gives a thin, delicate, tender and beautiful skin. (See "Beautiful" under Complexion, Face).

**Stature**—Note the various paragraphs and subjects under Stature).

**Tall and Handsome**—The ☉ Sig. in ♐; born under ♀ and ♀ ori.; ♎ on the Asc. (See "Tall and Elegant" under Elegant. Also note the various paragraphs under Tall).

**Ugly** — (See "Not Handsome" in this section).

**Well-Composed** — Well-Favored Body —Well-Formed—Well-Made and Handsome — Well-Proportioned — Well-Shaped—(See these subjects).

**HANGING** — Death On the Gallows — Death by the Halter or Noose—Strangulation—The ☉ Sig., □ or ☍ ♄, and espec. if either be in the 10th H.; the ☉ directed to, or joined with the Ascelli; the ☽ with Antares, and ☍ ♄ with Aldebaran; caused by the □ and ☍ asps. of the ☽; ♄ in a fixed sign, ori., □ or ☍ the ☽, and contrary in condition, or ♄ occi., and the ☽ be succedent to him; ♄ ori. in a fixed sign, and in □ or ☍ the ☉, or when occi. in a fixed sign, and in □ or ☍ the ☽, tends to death by suffocation, hanging, or trodden by a mob in a tumult; ♄ to the ☌ or ill-asp. ♂ by dir.; ♂ affl. the ☽ from the 10th or 4th H., or near Cepheus or Andromeda; ♂ affl. in ♉ or ♏ in the 10th or 4th H. denotes hanging; ☿ in □ or ☍ ♄ at B., and otherwise affl. by malefics, the native is said to inherit the Gallows; the fixed signs and the earthy signs dispose to, and espec. when in the 10th or 4th H., and containing the malefics ♄ and ♂, and with these planets affl. the hyleg, either of them holding the dominion of death in a nativity otherwise showing a violent death. (See Beheaded, Execution, Guillotine, Halter, Homicide, Ignoble, Impalement, Judges, Lynching, Mobs, Murder, Riots, Strangulation, Suffocation, Tumults; "Death" under Violent).

**Fears of Hanging**—Haunted by Visions of Hanging—Case—See "Haunted", No. 299, in 1001 N.N. Also for Cases and Birth Data of people hanged for crime, see "Hanged", No. 540, and "Murderer", No. 636, both in 1001 N.N.

**Overhanging Eyebrows**—(See "Beetle Brows" under Eyebrows).

**HAPPINESS** — Happy — Happy Disposition—Contentment—Peace of Mind, etc. —The ☉ to the ☌ or P. Dec. Arista by dir.; the ☽ to the ☌ and good asps. ♀ by dir.; the ☽ ☌ ♀ or ☿ in the 3rd or 9th H., the houses of mind, and these planets free from the afflictions of the malefics; the ☽ decr., separating from ♀ and applying to ♃; the ☽ sepr. from ☿ and apply. to ♃; the ☽ Sig. ☌ ♀, a happy disposition; the ☽ at full in a nocturnal geniture, sepr. from ☌ and apply. to ♀, an increase of happiness; ♆ by his good aspects tends to favorable spiritual and interior states, religious ecstasy; ♄ by his unfavorable aspects to the Sigs. tends to destroy peace of mind, and lead to melancholy and morbid fears; ♃ in the Asc. near the cusp; ♃ Sig. ☌ ♀ promises the greatest happiness; ♀ ruler at B., and well-aspected, tends to happiness, and a joyful nature; ♀ in the 3rd or 9th H. in ☌ the ☽ or ☿; the Asc. to the place of Crater. (See Arista, Cheerfulness, Comforts, Contentment, Crater; "Fortunate" under Fortune; "Good Health" under Health; Jovial, Joy, Juvenility; Mild; "Peace of Mind" under Mind; Optimistic, Prosperity, Religion, Unhappy).

**Happy Death** — A Peaceful and Easy Death — (See "Easy Death" under Death).

**Happy Disposition** — The ☽ Sig. ☌ ♀, an easy and happy disposition, and with little care beyond the enjoyment of the present moment. (See Contentment, Ease, Smiling).

**HARD**—Hardening—Hardness—Indurations—Sclerosis, etc.—Hardening is the work of ♄. Also called the destructive work of ♄, and caused by the pathological deposits and wastes retained by ♄. Also the work of the ♄ sign ♑, and of ☋, which is of the nature of ♄. The hardening of the bones, also the work of ♄, may be considered an exception to the rule, and a normal process up to a certain point. Hardening is carried on by the mineral deposits carried by the blood, which minerals are ruled by ♄. These minerals, when carried to excess, become pathological, and the unusual hardening of any part of the body, of an organ, joint, tissue, membrane, etc., takes place when these minerals, wastes, and acids are deposited in excess, and where elimination is at fault. (See Saturn). The following subjects have to do with Hard, and Hardening, which see in the alphabetical arrangement when not considered here.

**Adipose Tissue** — Hardening of — (See "Hardness" under Fat).

**Arteries** — Hardening of — Arterio-Sclerosis — (See Arteries).

**Articulations** — Joints — Hardening of — (See Joints).

**Atrophy; Bones** — Hardening of — Ossification — Bone Building — The work of ♄. (See Bones, Osseous).

**Bunions**—Corns—(See Corns).

**Calculus; Carcinoma** — Hard Carcinoma—(See "Scirrhus" under Carcinoma).

**Chancre**—Hard Chancre—(See "Chancre" under Syphilis).

**Cirrhosis** — Thickening — (See Cirrhosis).

**Clots; Complexion** — The Complexion Hard and Dull — (See "Dull" under Complexion).

**Concretions; Condensation;**

**Congestions; Connective Tissue** — Hardening and Induration of—Thickening of—The work of ♄, and ♄ afflicted in the sign ruling the part. (See Cirrhosis, Connective, Sclerosis).

**Consolidation; Consumptions** — As Hardening of the Lungs, or other Organs, in Tubercular Conditions—Caused by ♄, and ♄ in the sign ruling the part, or organ. (See Consumptions; "Hardening" under Lungs; Tuberculosis).

**Cornification; Corns; Corrosions;**

**Costiveness; Cough**—(See "Dry Hard Cough" under Cough).

**Crusts; Crystallization; Cure** — The Disease Is Hard to Cure—(See Chronic, Curable, Difficult, Grievous, Incurable, Prolonged, Slow, Tedious, Wastings).

**Decay; Degeneration; Density;**

**Deposits; Destructive; Deterioration;**

**Disposition** — A Hard and Cruel Nature—(See Cruel).

**Ears**—(See "Hardening" under Ears).

**Enlargements; Faeces** — Hard Faeces —(See "Hardening" under Faeces).

**Fat**—(See "Hardness" under Fat).

**Gall Stones**—(See Bile).

**Gout; Gravel; Growths**—Hard Growths —(See Bunions, Growths, Horny, Stone; "Hard Tumors" under Tumors; Warts).

**Hair**—(See "Hard Hair" under Hair).

**Hemachromatosis** — The Skin Turns Hard — (See Hemachromatosis; "Skin" in this section).

**Horny; Inhibitions; Joints** — (See "Hardening" under Joints; Synovial).

**Kidneys**—(See Cirrhosis, Stone, under Kidneys).

**Lesions; Lithemia; Liver**—(See Cirrhosis, Hardening, under Liver).

**Lungs** — (See "Hardening" under Lungs).

**Membranes** — Hardening of — (See Cirrhosis, Membranes, Sclerosis, Synovial, Thickening, Tissues. Also note the various paragraphs in this section).

**Moles; Naevus; Nature**—A Hard and Cruel Nature—(See Cruel, Savage, Vicious).

**Nerves**—(See Atrophy, Decay, Lesions, Nerves, Optic, Paralysis, Sclerosis, Spinal Cord (see Spine).

**Obstructions; Optic Nerve** — Hardening of — (See Crystallization, Optic, under Eyes).

**Organs**—Hardening of—(See Kidneys, Liver, Optic, and the various paragraphs in this section; Cirrhosis, Crystallization, Sclerosis).

**Ossification**—(See Bones, Osseous).

**Petrifaction; Retentions;**

**Rheumatism; Sand; Scales; Scirrhus;**

**Sclerosis; Skin**—Hard and Rough Skin —♄ strong at B., or ♄ Sig. of the person, represents one of a rough, hard skin; the 2nd face of ♒ on the Asc. (See Hemachromatosis; "Thick" under Skin).

**Spinal Cord**—Hardening of—♄ affl. in ♌. (See Sclerosis; "Cord" under Spine).

**Stone** — Gravel — Sand — (See Gall Stones" under Bile; Gravel, Sand, Stone).

**Suppressions; Synovial Membranes**— Hardening of—(See Joints, Synovial).

**Thickening** — (See Cirrhosis, Hypertrophy, Thickening).

**Tissues** — Thickening of — Hardening of—(See Adipose, Membranes, in this section; Cells, Hypertrophy, Sclerosis, Tissues).

**Tumors**—(See "Hard" under Tumors).

**Urea; Uric Acid; Vessels**—Blood Vessels — Hardening of — (See "Arterio-Sclerosis" under Arteries; Vessels).

**Warts; Wastes; Wasting.**

**HARELIP**—A Congenital Fissure of the Lip—(See Lips).

**HARLOTS** — Prostitutes — The Lower Order of Women—Wench—Danger of Becoming—♄ and ♀ ill-affected, or ill-dignified at B.; ♀ Sig. □ or ☍ ♂; ♀ in ♏ and affl. by ♄ and ♂; ♀ Sig. ☌ ♂, and given to brawling in low public houses. (See Debased, Depraved, Disgrace, Dissolute, Drink, Immodest, Infamous, Lewd, Loose, Low, Nymphomania, Obscene, Scandalous, Shameless, Taverns, Venery, Vile, etc.).

**Injured By**—Disgrace Thru—♄ and ♀ both ill-dig., and ill-affected in the map; ♄ Sig. □ or ☍ ♀; ♂ Sig. □ or ☍ ♀; ♀ Sig. □ or ☍ ♂. (See "Harlots", "Injured", under Men).

**HARMFUL**—

**Harmful to Others** — (See Brutish, Cruel, Dangerous, Destructive, Fierce, Inhuman, Murderous, Savage, Vicious, Violent, etc.).

**Maladies**—Harmful Maladies and Diseases — (See Fierce, Grievous, Malignant, Pernicious, Severe, Vehement, Violent, etc.).

**Not Harmful**—Harmless to Others—The Disease Is Slight and Mild, and Not Dangerous—(See Harmless, Mild, Slight).

**To Himself** — (See "His Own Worst Enemy" under Enemies).

**HARMLESS**—Inoffensive—A Mild and Even Disposition—Quiet—The ☽ Sig. in ♎ or ♒; ♃ Sig. in ♓; ♀ Sig. in ♐, ♒, or ♓; people born under strong ♀ influence have a quiet and mild disposition; the 4th face of ♎ on the Asc. (See Gentle, Kind, Mild, Peaceful, Quiet).

**Harmless Diseases**—Not Dangerous—(See Mild, Slight).

**HARMONY** — Harmonious — The principle of the ☽ is harmony, and also of ♀. In whatever sign or house ♀ is found in at B., it is her mission to restore harmony and balance to the affairs, or part of the body ruled by such sign or house, and to help overcome the afflictions. (See Balance, Coalition, Coordination, Correspondences, Dexterity, Equilibrium, Graceful, Libra, Rhythm, Signature, Sympathy).

**Body and Mind**—More Harmony Between—Given by the ⚹ and △ aspects of ☿ to the Asc. at B.

**Constitution** — A Harmonious Constitution—The ☉ or ☽ ☌, ⚹, or △ the Asc. at B., and by dir.; ♀ in the 6th H., and well-aspected, the health is good if not abused, but easy to become an invalid if excesses are engaged in. (See "Good" under Constitution, Health).

**Disturbed**—The Harmony of Body and Mind Disturbed—(See Disease, Fevers, Ill-Health, Insanity, Melancholy, Suffering, Sickness, Worry, etc.).

**Functions**—(See "Harmony" under Functions).

**Muscular Action**—Harmonious Muscular Action—(See Coordination, Dexterity).

**Physical Harmony**—Perfect Physical Development — Comes from planetary harmony and good configurations at B.; a predominance of the ⚹ and △ aspects in the radical map; the benefics strong at B., and the malefics weak. (See Beautiful, Comely, Graceful; "Harmony" under Functions; Handsome, Well-Proportioned).

**HARROW**—The Harrow of ♐—(See Arrow Head).

**HARSHNESS** — Of the Voice — (See Coarse; "Hoarseness" under Larynx; Rough).

**HASTY**—Hasty Disposition—The ☽ in fire signs at B., hasty and excitable. (See Anger; "Brain Storms" under Brain; Choleric, Erratic, Excitable, Explosive, Fierce, Foolhardy, Forethought, Improvident, Impulsive, Quarrelsome, Precipitate, Rashness, Recklessness, Riotous; "High Temper" under Temper; Uncontrolled, etc.).

**HATE** — Hatred — Hated — Aversion — Animosity—Enmity—This is a ♏ characteristic, and the result of the extreme vibrations of ♂, and usually mixed with ♅ and ♄ influences. The Benefics are also usually weak and obscurely placed. The hatred, malice, and revenge tend to be retained when ♄ enters into the configuration with the ♂ influence. Violence in connection with hatred may result when ♂ is also affl. by ♅. (See Anarchists, Anger, Antipathy, Aversions, Duels, Emotions, Enemies, Enmity, Execrated, Feelings, Feuds, Jealousy, Malice, Misanthropic, Murderous, Plots, Poison, Relatives, Resentful, Revenge, Riotous, Treachery, Vicious, Violent, etc.).

**Females** — Has the Hatred of — The Love of a Female Turned to Hate—The ill-asps. of the ☽ to the ☉ or ♀ by dir. (See Jealousy; "Grief" under Love Affairs; "Injured" under Men; Treachery).

**Hated by Others** — The ☽ to the ill-asps. the ☉ by dir.; ♄ Sig. □ or ☍ the ☉; ♃ Sig. ☌ ♄, generally hated by every one because of his mean and deceitful ways; ☿ Sig. □ or ☍ ♂, despised by others for his infamous conduct. (See Deceitful, Dishonesty, Execrated, Infamous, Mean, Outcast, etc.).

**Hatred Prevalent**—An eclipse of the ☉ in ♏. (See Prevalent, Public).

**HAUNCHES**—The Region Including the Hips, Hip Bone (Ilium), and the Buttocks—Ruled by ♎ and the 7th H. Also influenced largely by ♐.

**Boils On** — (See "Buttocks" under Boils).

**Diseases In** — (See "Diseases" under Buttocks, Flanks, Hips).

**Heats** — In the Haunches — Humours In—(See "Heats" under Buttocks).

**Hurts To** — (See "Hurts" under Buttocks; Cuts, Fractures, Injuries, under Hips; Ilium).

**HAUNTINGS** — Haunted by Visions of Hanging — (See "Fears" under Hanging). See Dreams, Fears, Forebodings, Hallucinations, Imaginations, Obsessions, Premonitions, Spirit Controls, Terrors, Visions, etc.

**HAY FEVER**—Hay Asthma—Rose Cold —(See "Hay Asthma" under Asthma; Colds; "Coryza", "Hay Fever", under Nose).

**HAZEL** — Dark Brown — (See "Hazel" under Eyes, Hair).

**HEAD** — The Upper Part of the Body Containing the Brain—Cephalic—Cranium—Skull—The Head, and the Organs of the Head, are ruled by ♂ and the ♈ sign. (See Aries, Mars). The Head is especially under the external rule of ♈. The Encephalon, the Skull, and its contents are ruled by ♈. The Brain is under the internal rulership of ♈, and the bones of the head under the structural rulership of ♈. (See Brain, Cranium). The 1st H. represents and rules the head and face of Man. The Head is also affected and influenced by all the cardinal signs, and planets in such signs at B., and by dir. The Head and Brain correspond to the cardinal signs and the Mental Temperament. (See Decanates, Temperament). The lower back part of the head, the Occipital Region, is ruled by the ♉ sign. (See Occipital). For the various subdivisions of the Head, see the subject in the alphabetical arrangement, such as Brain, Cranium, Cerebellum, Cerebral, Cerebro-Spinal, Cheeks, Chin, Ears, Eyes, Forehead, Face, Hair, Jaws, Mouth, Nose, Scalp, Skin, Teeth, Temples, etc. This Article will be divided into Two Sections. Section One, Description of the Head. Section Two, Diseases of the Head. See the following subjects in the alphabetical arrangement (in both sections) when not more fully considered here.

— SECTION ONE —

**DESCRIPTION OF THE HEAD—**

**Bent Forward** — ♓ on the Asc. (See Crooked; "Downward Look" under Look; Stooping).

**Big Head**—(See "Large" in this section).

**Cheeks; Chin; Complexion; Dimples;**

**Downward Look** — (See "Downward" under Look).

**Ears; Expression; Eyebrows;**

**Eyelids**—Eyelashes—(See Eyelids).

**Eyes; Face; Flat on Sides** — (See "Square" in this section).

**Forehead; Glances; Great Head**—(See "Large" in this section).

**Hair; Horse-Shaped Head** — ♐ on the Asc. (See Horses).

**Jaws; Large Head**—Big Head—Great Head—Produced by the ☉ influence; ♄ Sig. in ♒ or ♓; ♄ in ♒ in partile asp. the Asc.; ♄ in ♓ in partile the Asc., large head and eyes; ♌ on the Asc., large and round. Case of Very Large Head—See "Dwarf", No. 669, in 1001 N.N. (See "Large" under Eyes, Face).

**Lips; Little Head** — (See "Small" in this section).

**Long Head** — ♄ in ♍ when Sig. in Hor'y Q. (See "Long" under Chin, Face).

**Look; Marks**—Moles—Planets in ♈ at B. indicate; ♈ on the Asc., and containing one or more planets; ♂ rising in ♈ in the Asc. (See "Marks" under Face; Marks, Moles, Naevus, Scars, Warts).

**Mouth; Naevus** — Birthmarks — (See Naevus).

**Nodding** — To One Side — Skippish Manner—The native jumps forward when speaking, and nods the head to one side like a goat when it butts—♑ influence; the ☉ in ♑, or ♑ on the Asc. at B. (See "Falls To One Side" in Sec. 2 of this Article).

**Nose; Occiput; Peculiar Shaped**—(See "Falls To One Side" in Sec. 2 of this Article).

**Red**—Ruddy—(See Complexion, Face).

**Round Head**—Great Round Head—♌ on the Asc.

**Scalp; Scars** — (See Accidents, Cuts, Pockmarked, Scars, in Sec. 2 of this Article).

**Skull**—(See Cranium, Skull).

**Small Head**—Little Head—♃ or ♂ Sig. in ♑, or in ♑ in partile asp. the Asc.; ♂ occi. For Case of Small Head of an Idiot, see "Microcephalic Idiot", No. 086 in 1001 N.N. (See Idiocy).

**Square Head**—Characteristics of the Motive Temperament; the 1st Decan. of mutable signs on the Asc. (See Decanates; "Square" under Face).

**Stooping Head** — (See "Downward Look" under Look; Stooping).

**Temples; Two Heads**—Has Two Heads and One Body—Case—See "Twins", No. 236 in 1001 N.N. Also see Case in British Journal of Astrology for Oct., 1931. Born June 23, 1919, 6:30 A.M., Antwerp. Died at birth. (See "United Twins" under Twins).

— SECTION TWO —

**DISEASES OF THE HEAD—**

Troubles in the head are largely dependent upon the ♓ sign, the Plantar System, and ♍, the Abdominal Organs, and troubles originating in these parts are quickly reacted to the head, causing a great number of head and brain disturbances.

**Abscesses** — (See "Brain" under Abscess).

**Accidents To** — Hurts — Wounds — Injuries—Cuts—Blows—Bruises—Fractures, etc.—The ☉, ☽, or malefics afflicted in ♈, and espec. when in the 1st H.; the prog. ☉ or ☽ to the places of malefics in ♈; the ☉ by dir. to the ill-asps. ♂ in ♈ in the 8th H. at B.; ♅ affl. in the 1st H., by machinery; ♅ in ♈ at B., and affl. by ♂; ♄ in ♈, ☌, □, or ☍ the Asc. by dir., and espec. if ♄ be in the Asc. at B.; ♄ ☌ ☋ in ♈; ♂ in ♈, ♎, the Asc., or 1st H. at B., and afflicted;

♂ on the Asc. at B., slight hurts or cuts to the head or face; afflictions in the 1st H. at B., and by dir.; afflictions in ♈ or ♎; ♈ or ♎ on the Asc., and containing malefics; the 1st Decan. of ♈ on the Asc., ruled by ♂; malefics in any of the cardinal signs at B., and in ☌, □, or ☍ the prog. ☉ or ☽; the 1st face of ♊ on the Asc., and the ☽ therein with ♄ or ♂; afflictions in ♊, fractures of the head or skull; the 30° ♍ on the Asc. (See Blows, Bruises, Cuts, Fractures, Injuries, Wounded, in this section; "Accidents" under Eyes, Face, Jaws, Nose).

**Acne; Acute Diseases In**—Acute Neuralgic Pains In—Acute Pains In—(See Darting, Headaches, Neuralgia, Pain, and the various paragraphs in this section. Also see Acute, Brain, Eyes, Nose, and the various diseases under these subjects).

**Affected**—The Head Affected—The ☉ and ☽ acting thru the ♈ sign affect the head. (See "Ribes" under Ganglion). All the cardinal signs affect the head, and planets in such signs, as they form the cardinal cross, and all the cardinal signs, of which ♈ is one, are in adverse aspect to each other. The head is affected by disorders in the abdominal organs, ♍, and in the Plantar System, ♓. Any planet when in its own sign tends to affect the head, as the sign ruled by each planet is considered as influencing the head and the ♈ sign. When in a sign next to, or following the sign it rules, it affects the throat and neck and influences the ♉ sign, and so on around thru the 12 signs. Thus the head is affected by the ☉ in ♌; the ☽ in ♋; ♄ in ♑ or ♒; ♃ in ♐ or ♓; ♂ in ♈ or ♏; ♀ in ♉ or ♎; ☿ in ♊ or ♍, as these are the home and strong signs of these planets. (See Table 196 in Simmonite's Arcana, Chap. IX, page 68, which is a Table of these influences).

**Afflicted**—The Head Afflicted—(See the various paragraphs in this section).

**All Diseases In**—Signified by the 1st H., and afflictions in ♈, or with ♈ on the Asc.

**Apoplexy; Arteries**—Of the Head Affected—♃ affl. in ♈. (See "Head" under Arteries).

**Baldness; Beard; Beheaded;**

**Blemishes**—Afflictions in ♈. (See "Blemishes" under Face; "Marks" in Sec. 1 of this Article).

**Blood**—Rush of—Flow of—Determination of Blood to the Head—The ☉ or ♂ in ♈ at B., or ♈ on the Asc., and accompanied by high fever when ill; the the ☽ or Asc. ☌ ♂ at B.; the ☽ to the ill-asps. ♃, the direction occurring from cardinal signs, and espec. with females; ♄ in ♌, ☌, □ or ☍ ♃ or ♀; ♃ affl. in ♈; ♃ affl. in ♈, ill-blood in the veins of the head; ♂ rising in ♈; a ♂ disease; ♂ tends to cause Insanity by a rush of blood to the head; the Asc. to the place of Regulus; an ♈ disease. (See Apoplexy).

**Blows**—To the Head—Strokes To—♄ or ♂ affl. in ♈; ♄ in ♈, ☌, □, or ☍ the Asc. by dir., and espec. if ♄ be in the Asc. at B.; ♄ or ♂ affl. in ♈ in the Asc. at B., and with these planets affl. the Asc. by dir. (See Blows; Accidents, Bruises, Cuts, Fractures, in this section).

**Brain**—Disorders of—(See Brain, Cerebral).

**Bruises To**—♄ in the Asc. at B., and espec. when in ♈. (See Bruises; "Accidents" in this section).

**Cancer**—Carcinoma—(See "Face", "Head", under Carcinoma).

**Catalepsy; Catarrh**—In the Head—The ☽ in ♈, ☌, or ill-asp. any of the malefics as promittors; ♄ in ♈ or ♎; ♄ occi. in ♈, and affl. the ☉, ☽, or Asc.; ♄, ♆, or ♅ in ♈ or ♓, and in ill-asp. to the ☉ or ☽; ♀ affl. in ♈. (See "Frontal" under Abscesses; Catarrh; "Catarrh" under Nose).

**Central Part**—Of the Head—Depression In—(See "Malformation" in this section).

**Cephalic; Cerebellum; Cerebral;**

**Cerebro-Spinal; Cerebrum;**

**Chronic Diseases**—In the Head—♆ or ♄ affl. in ♈. (See Catarrh, Chronic, Nose; "Chronic" under Stomach).

**Circulation**—Impeded—Disturbed—♄ in ♈, ☌ ♃ or ♀. (See Apoplexy; "Impeded" under Circulation; "Blood" in this section).

**Colds In**—The Head Disordered by Cold—Cold or Watery Diseases In—The Head Affected by Diseases of a Cold and Watery Nature—♆, ♅, or ♄ in ♈ in ill-asp. to the ☉ or ☽; the ☽ ☌ the Asc. by secondary direction; the ☽ in ♏ and affl. by the ☉ or ♂ when taken ill, stoppage in the head by grievous colds; ♄ in the Asc.; signified by ♄ in ♈ when ♄ is the afflictor in the disease; ♀ affl. in ♈ when ♀ is the afflictor in the disease. (See Catarrh, Cold, Colds, Congestion; "Coryza" under Nose; Saturn).

**Coma; Complexion; Congestions;**

**Coryza**—(See "Coryza" under Nose).

**Countenance; Cranium; Cuts To**—(See "Accidents" in this section; "Cuts", "Hurts", under Face).

**Danger To**—The ☉ directed to Praesepe. (See "Accidents" in this section; Ascelli; "Accidents" under Eyes, Face; Praesepe).

**Darting Pains In**—Acute Pains—Shooting Pains—♅ in ♈, ♎, or the 1st H.; ♅ rising in ♉, darting pains; ♂ in ♈, ♎, or the 1st H. (See "Pain" in this section).

**Defluxions**—Of Rheum From—(See "Rheum" in this section; Defluxions).

**Deformities Of**—Malefics in cardinal signs and afflicting each other, and espec. from angles. (See "Small Head", "Two Heads", in Sec. 1 of this Article; Hydrocephalus, Malformations, in this section).

**Delirium; Depression In**—(See "Malformation" in this section).

**Determination**—Of Blood to the Head—(See "Blood" in this section).

**Diseased**—The Head Much Diseased—The ☽ in P. Dec. an Infortune tends to a disease in the head, and if ☿ also be affl. by a malefic the disease will be very severe; the ☽ in partile ☍ ☿ at decumb., the head is deeply affected (Hor'y); ☿ at B. in P. Dec. a malefic, or in □ to the ☽ from the 1st or 7th H.; ☋ or malefics in the Asc. at decumb. (Hor'y).

**Diseases Of**— (See "Diseased", "Disorders Of", and the various paragraphs in this section).

**Disorders of the Head**—Diseases In—Distempers In—Infirmities In—Maladies In—The Head Disturbed—The Disease Lies In the Head or Brain—The ☉ or ☽ affl. in ♈; the ☉ affl. in ♎; the ☉ evilly aspected at B., and the ☉ in bad asp. the Asc. by dir.; the ☉ to the ☌ or P. Dec. the ☽ by dir.; the ☉ to the ☌ or ill-asps. ♄ or ♂ by dir.; the ☉ or ☽ in the 6th H. in cardinal signs, and afflicted; the ☉ in ♈ in the 6th H., ☌, or ill-asp. any of the malefics as promittors; the ☉ in the 6th H., lord of the year, and afflicted at the Vernal Equi., a prevalence of head troubles; the ☽ affl. in ♈ or ♎, and espec. when in the Asc. or 6th H.; the ☽ to the ☌ or ill-asp. ♅ by dir.; the ☽ in ♎, ☌ or ill-asp. ♄ (or ☿ if he be of the nature of ♄) at the beginning of an illness, or at decumb.; the ☽ P. ♄, diseases in the head and stomach; the ☽ affl. in the 6th H.; the ☽ ☌ ♂ in the Asc. when taken ill; the ☽ hyleg, and afflicted, and espec. with females; the ☽ ☌ the Asc. by secondary dir.; the ☽ in P. asp. ♄ or ♂ at B., and by dir.; ♄ in ♈ or ♎ in the 1st or 6th H.; ♄ affl. in ♒; ♃ affl. in ♈ or ♐; ♂ affl. in ♈, ♎, the 1st or 7th H.; ♂ diseases and afflictions; ♂ in ♈ in the 6th H.; mad and sudden distempers in the head are a ♂ disease and affliction, and caused by ♂ affl. in ♈, and also ♅ in ♈; ♀ or ☿ affl. in ♈; ☿ diseases; ☿ □ the ☽ from the 1st or 7th H., and ☿ ☌ ♄ or ♂; born under ☿; ☿ in ♈, ☌, or ill-asp. any of the malefics as promittors; a malefic or ☋ in the Asc. denotes diseases in the head, or in the part of the body signified by the sign ascending; malefics in the 1st H., or in the sign ascending; malefics, or the afflicting planets, in cardinal signs; any malefic in the Asc. when taken ill; planets in the Asc., as the Asc. rules the head; cardinal signs show, and espec. afflictions in ♈; ♈ on the Asc., and afflicted, and cardinal signs on the angles; ♈ denotes; afflictions in ♈ or ♎; ♈ or ♎ on the Asc.; the Asc. to the ☌ ☉ by dir., and the ☉ affl. at B.; ♒ ascending at the Vernal, People and Countries under ♒ so suffer; ♐ ascending at the Vernal Equi., and ♃ afflicted, People born under ♐, and in Countries ruled by this sign, are afflicted with infirmities in the head and legs, and with fevers; ♓ ascending at the Vernal, People ruled by ♓, and in Countries ruled by ♓, suffer grievous infirmities in the head, feet, and with Gout and Dropsy. In Hor'y Q. if the Asc. is afflicted by a malefic, ℞, slow, combust., peregrine, or in □ or ☍ to the lord of the 6th, 8th, or 12th, tends to trouble in the head, or to the parts signified by the sign ascending, and the planet, or planets, in the ascending sign. An Example—♋

on the Asc. and ♄ therein, trouble in the head, or parts signified by ♋, as in the bowels, reins, secrets; also cough, as ♄ rules cough, and ♋ rules the breast. Judgment is more certain if the ☽, lord of the Asc. or 6th, or sign on the 6th, signify the same member or parts as signified by ♄. See Table in Lilly's Astrology, Chap. XXIX, page 179, showing what parts of Man's body every planet signifies in the 12 Signs. (See "Disordered Brain" under Brain. Also note the various paragraphs in this section).

**Distempers In**—(See "Disorders Of" in this section).

**Disturbed** — Disturbances Of — The Head Is Disturbed — (See "Disorders Of", and the various paragraphs in this section).

**Dizziness; Downward Look**—Stooping Head—(See "Downward Look" under Look; Stooping).

**Dropsy Of**—(See Hydrocephalus).

**Dry and Hot Diseases**—In the Head —(See "Hot and Dry" in this section).

**Dull Pains In**—A ☿ disease; ☿ affl. by ♄. (See "Pains" in this section).

**Ears; Eczema Of**—(See Eczema).

**Electric Pains In**—☿ in ♈ and affl. by ♅; ☿ affl. by ♅. (See "Pains" in this section).

**Encephalitis**—(See Encephalon).

**Enlarged**—The Head Enlarges and Swells—(See "Tumor" under Brain; Enlarged, Hydrocephalus).

**Eruptions**—(See Eruptions; "Eruptions" under Face).

**Erysipelas**—(See "Head" under Erysipelas).

**Excrescences**—(See "Malformations" in this section; "Head" under Excrescences).

**Expression; Eyes**—(See Eyeballs, Eyebrows, Eyelids, Eyes).

**Face**—(See the various paragraps under Face).

**Faintings; Falls**—Hurts to Head By —♄ affl. in ♈, and espec. in the Asc. (See Accidents, Bruises, Cuts, Fractures, in this section; "Falls" under Infancy).

**Falls To One Side**—(See "Heavy" in this section).

**Females**—The Head Afflicted In—The ☽ hyleg, and afflicted, and espec. when in ♈. (See "Women" under Headaches).

**Feverish Diseases**—Which Affect the Head—The ☉ affl. in ♈; ☿ affl. by ♂, fevers in the head; ♈ on the Asc. (See "Hot Diseases" in this section).

**Fixity**—Of the Head—♄ affl. in ♈; Subs at AT.

**Flow of Blood To**—(See "Blood" in this section).

**Fontanelles**—Slow Closure of—Lack of Ossification of—The ☽ affl. in ♈; ♄ weak and affl. at B., and many planets in watery signs, and the earthy sign influences weak at B.; Subs at AT, AX. (See Ossification).

**Forehead; Fractures**—(See "Fractures" under Skull).

Freckles; Giddiness—(See Dizziness).

Glands—Of the Head Affected—(See "Head" under Glands).

Gout In—Gouty Pains In—(See "Head" under Gout).

Grievous Colds In—Grievous Infirmities In—(See Colds, Disorders, in this section).

Growths In—Tumorous Growths In—♀ affl. in ♈; ♀ ☌ ♅ in ♈, and in □ or ☍ malefics; Subs at MCP (5C). Case—See "Tumorous Growth", Chap. XIII, page 91, in Daath's Medical Astrology. (See Growths; "Growths" under Face, Eyes, Tumors).

Guillotined; Headaches—This subject, and the various kinds and causes of Headaches, are given in the section on Headaches, just following this Article. Also see "Pain" in this section).

Headstrong—(See Obstinate).

Heaviness In—Heavy Feeling In—The ☽ in ♈, ☌, □, or ☍ ♄ (or ☿ if he be of the nature of ♄) at the beginning of an illness, or at decumb. (See Dull Pains, Headaches, Heavy, Pain, in this section).

Heavy—The Head Is Heavy and Falls to One Side—Case—See "Unfortunate Case", No. 351 in 1001 N.N. (See Heaviness, Hydrocephalus, Large, Nodding, in this section).

Hemicrania—Neuralgia of Half the Head—♅ affl. in ♈; Subs at AT. (See "Neuralgia" in this section).

Hemispheres—Hemispherical Excrescences—(See "Malformations" in this section).

Hemorrhage In—(See "Blood" in this section; Apoplexy).

Hot Diseases In—Hot Humours In—Feverish Diseases In—The Asc. to the ☌ the ☉ by dir.; the Asc. to the ☌ stars of the nature of ♂; ♈ on the Asc. (See "Feverish" in this section; "Hot Diseases" under Heat; "Mars Group" under Stars).

Hot and Dry Diseases—In the Head—♈ on the Asc., as the head is classed as hot and dry, being ruled by the hot and dry, masculine, and positive sign ♈. (See "Dry and Hot Diseases" under Heat).

Humours In—Humour In—The ☉ to the ☌ or P. the ☽ by dir., and the ☽ ill-asp. at B.; the ☽ in the 1st or 7th H. at B., and P. ♄ or ♂, and if ☿ also be afflicted by ♄ or ♂ the disease will tend to be very severe; ♄ affl. in ♈, copious flow of humours from the head; ♀ or ☿ affl. in ♈. Wilson has observed that those who have a copious flow of humours from the head are remarkable for shallowness of intellect and for dishonesty. (See Defluxions, Hot Diseases, Moist Humours, Rheum, in this section; Catarrh, Colds, Rheum).

Hurts To—(See Accidents, Blows, Cuts, Falls, Fractures, Injuries, Wounds, in this section).

Hydrocephalus; Idiots—Small Head—Microcephalic Head—(See Idiots).

Ill-Blood—In Veins of Head—(See "Blood" in this section).

Imaginary Diseases In—☿ affl. by ♆. (See Imagination).

Impeded Circulation—In the Head—(See "Circulation" in this section).

Infirmities—Grievous Infirmities In—(See Colds, Disorders, and the various paragraphs in this section).

Inflammations In—♂ affl. in ♈. (See Catarrh, Colds; Encephalitis; "Inflamed" under Eyes; "Coryza" under Nose; Feverish, Hot Diseases, in this section).

Injuries To—Wounds—Hurts—♄ or ♂ affl. in ♈, and espec. when in the Asc. Cases—See "Sebastian", No. 576 in 1001 N.N. See Fig. 28 in the book, "Message of the Stars", by the Heindels. (See Accidents, Blows, Bruises, Cuts, Falls, Fractures, in this section).

Insanity—From Rush of Blood to the Head—(See "Blood" in this section; Insanity).

Insomnia; Jaws; Large Head—Very Large Head—(See Hydrocephalus; "Large Head" in Sec. 1 of this Article; "Heavy" in this section).

Longitudinal Depression—(See "Malformation" in this section).

Machinery—Hurts to Head By—(See Machinery).

Mad Distempers—(See the ♂ influences under "Disorders" in this section).

Maladies In—(See "Disorders", and the various paragraphs in this section).

Malformation Of—Malformation of the Skull—Soft, Watery, and Hemispherical Excrescences—Longitudinal Depression In the Central Part—The ☉ in the Asc., and affl. by malefics; the ☽ in the 1st H., or on the cusp of the 1st, and affl. by ♅; ♈ or ♎ on the Asc. (See Deformities; "Head", "Skull", under Excrescences; Idiots, Malformations, Monsters, Prenatal Epoch; "Deformities" in this section).

Marks—Moles—Scars—Blemishes—(See "Marks", "Scars", in Sec. 1 of this Article; Accidents, Blemishes, Cuts, Pockmarked, in this section).

Medulla; Megrims—(See Migraine).

Membranes—Of the Head Disordered—(See "Membranes" under Brain; Catarrh, Cerebral, Frontal, Meninges, Nose, etc.).

Men Suffer—With Affections of the Head—♂ ℞ in ♐ at the Vernal Equi., and Lord of the Year. (See Men).

Meninges; Mercury Remedies—These remedies are cephalic, and affect the head. (See "Mercury" under Herbs; "Remedies", "Therapeutic Properties", under Mercury).

Microcephalic Head—(See "Small Head" in Sec. 1 of this Article; "Idiots" in this section).

Migraine; Mind—Disorders of—(See Mental, Mind).

Moist Humours—Watery Humours—The Head Afflicted by Abundance of Moist Humours—Snuffling—The ☽ ☌ the Asc. by secondary dir.; ♄ affl. in ♈; ♀ affl. in ♈ or ♉; ♀ affl. in ♉ when ♀ is the afflictor in the disease, and also causing swellings in the neck; a ☿ disease, and ☿ affl. at B. (See "Humours" in this section; "Humours", "Moist Humours", under Moist; "Humours" under Watery).

**Moles**—(See Moles; "Marks" in Sec. 1 of this Article).

**Mouth; Movement** — Of the Head Abnormal—(See "Nodding Spasm" in this section; Erratic, Jerky, Movements, Spasmodic).

**Much Diseased** — (See "Diseased" in this section).

**Mucus**—Mucous Discharges—The ☽ or ♀ affl. in ♈. (See Catarrh, Colds, Humours, Moist, Rheum, in this section; Mucus).

**Muscles** — ♂ affl. in ♈ tends to affect the muscles of the head. (See Muscles).

**Naevus; Navamsa** — (See "Subdivisions" in this section).

**Nervous Affections**—Of the Head—♅ or ☿ affl. in ♈; ☿ in ♈ and affl. by ♅ or ♂; ☿ affl. by ♂. (See Neuralgia, Nodding, Pain, Spasmodic, in this section; Headaches, Nerves).

**Neuralgia**—In the Head or Face—The ☉, ☽, or ♅ affl. in ♈; the ☉ affl. in ♌; a ♅ disease, as neuralgia is the province of ♅; ♅ affl. in ♈; ♂ affl. in ♈, ♊, or ♎; ☿ affl. in ♈; an ♈ disease. (See Acute, Darting, Dull, Hemicrania, Pains, in this section; "Neuralgia" under Face; Headaches, Neuralgia). Case—Of Acute Neuralgic Pains in the Head — See "Pains In the Head", Chap. XIII, page 90, in Daath's Medical Astrology.

**New Growths**—(See Growths, Tumors, Warts, Wens, in this section).

**Nodding Spasm** — The Head Nods to One Side—A ♅ affliction, and due to incoordination; ♅ affl. in ♈ or ♉; Subs at AT. (See "Heavy" in this section; "Nodding" in Sec. 1 of this Article; Erratic, Incoordination, Jerky, Spasmodic).

**Noises In** — Rumbling In the Head — The ☽ in ♒, ☌, or ill-asp. ♄ (or ☿ if he be of the nature of ♄) at the beginning of an illness, or at decumb.; the ☽ ☌ ♄ (or ☿ if he be of the nature of ♄) at decumb., rumbling noises in the head; ☿ in ♈, ☌, or ill-asp. any of the malefics as promittors, noises arising from indigestion, or excesses of any kind. (See Catarrh, Colds; "Tinnitus" under Ears).

**Nose**—Obstructions In—Stoppages In the Head—Stoppages by Colds—♄ affl. in ♈, ♎, ♑, or the Asc.; the ☽ in ♏ and affl. by the ☉ or ♂ when taken ill, stoppages in the head by grievous colds; ☿ diseases, and ☿ affl. in ♈. (See Obstructions, Stoppages; "Colds" in this section).

**Obstructions In** — Stoppages In the Head—Stoppages by Colds—♄ affl. in ♈, ♎, ♑, or the Asc.; the ☽ in ♏ and affl. by the ☉ or ♂ when taken ill, stoppages in the head by grievous colds; ☿ diseases, and ☿ affl. in ♈. (See Obstructions, Stoppages; "Colds" in this section).

**Occiput; One Side**—The Head Falls to One Side—(See Heavy, Nodding, in this section).

**Operations On**—Do not perform surgical operations upon the head when the ☽ is in ♈, the sign ruling the head. (See Operations).

**Organs Of**—Disorders of—(See Brain, Ears, Eyes, Mouth, Nose, and the various paragraphs in this Article).

**Pains In** — ♅, ♂, or ☿ affl. in ♈, and espec. when in the 1st H.; ♅ affl. in ♈, acute and spasmodic pains in; ♅ rising in ♉, acute neuralgic, and darting pains in; ♅, ♆, or ♄ in ♋, and affl. the ☉ or ☽; the ☉ affl. at B., and ☌ or P. asp. the Asc. by dir.; the ☉ to the ☌ the ☽ by dir., and the ☽ affl. at B.; the ☉ affl. in ♌ when the afflictor in the disease, violent pains in; the ☉ in ♌, ☌, or ill-asp. any of the malefics as promittors; ♃ affl. in ♈, and caused by ♃ when the dominion of death is vested in him; ♂ affl. in ♈, violent and distracting pains in; ♂ in ♈ or ♏, ☌, or ill-asp. the ☉; ♂ affl. in ♎; ♂ by periodic rev. to the evil asps. ♅; ♂ in the Asc., and affl. the ☉ or ☽ in ♈; ♀ affl. in ♈ or ♉; ☿ affl. in ♈, ♊, or ♓; ☿ in ♈, and affl. by ♅, electric pains in the head; ☿ in ♍ or ♓, ☌, or ill-asp. any of the malefics as promittors; ☿ affl. in ♊, gouty pains in the head; a ♎ disease, and afflictions in ♎; ☋ in the Asc.; fixed stars of the nature of ♂ ascending at B.; ♋ ascending at a Vernal Equi., and the ☽ weak and afflicted, people born under ♋, and in Countries ruled by ♋, suffer pains in the head. (See Acute, Darting, Dull, Electric, Gouty, Hemicrania, Neuralgia, Spasmodic, in this section; Headaches, Neuralgia; "Neuralgia" under Face; Pain).

**Pale; Pimples; Pineal; Pituitary;**

**Pockmarked** — (See "Face" under Smallpox).

**Prevalence**—Of Head Disorders—The ☉ in the 6th H., and Lord of the Year at the Vernal Equi. (See "Disorders" in this section).

**Remedies**—Remedies Affecting the Head—(See Cephalic; "Mercury" in this section).

**Rheum** — Defluxions of Rheum from the Head — The ☽ affl. in ♈; a ♓ disease; ♄ affl. in ♈ or ♓. (See Defluxions, Rheum. Also see Humours, Moist Humours, in this section).

**Ringing**—In the Head—(See "Noises" in this section; "Tinnitus" under Ears).

**Rumbling Noises** — (See "Noises" in this section).

**Rush of Blood** — To the Head — (See "Blood" in this section).

**Scalp; Scars** — (See "Marks" in this section).

**Sickly Looking** — (See "Pale" under Face; Pale, Sickly).

**Sight**—(See Blindness, Eyes, Sight).

**Skin** — Of the Head and Face — (See "Skin" under Face; Scalp).

**Skull; Small Head**—(See "Microcephalic" in this section).

**Snuffling** — In the Head and Nose — (See "Moist Humours" in this section; "Snuffling" under Nose).

**Soft Excrescences** — (See "Malformation" in this section).

**Spasmodic Pains In**—♅ affl. in ♈. (See "Pains" in this section).

**Spasms In** — ♅ or ☿ affl. in ♈. (See "Nodding Spasm" in this section).

**Stomach**—The Head Affected by Stomach Trouble— ♂ affl. in ♋. (See Dizziness, Headaches).

**Stoppages In**—By Colds—(See Colds, Obstructions, in this section).

**Strokes To**—(See "Blows" in this section).

**Subdivisions**—Of the Head—Disorders of—The subdivisions of the Head, and disorders in such parts, as in the Eyes, Ears, Forehead, Nose, are shown by the sub-influences of the Navamsa divisions of the ♈ sign. (See Navamsa).

**Sudden Distempers**—Sudden and Mad Distempers in the Head—♅ affl. in ♈; a ♂ disease and affliction; ♂ affl. in ♈, mad and sudden distempers in the head. (See Distempers; "Diseases" under Sudden; "Disorders" in this section).

**Swells**—The Head Swells—Swellings In—The Head Enlarged—(See "Tumor" under Brain; Hydrocephalus).

**Swoonings**—(See Fainting).

**Teeth; Temples; Tissues**—(See "Membranes" in this section).

**Tongue; Trance; Troubles** — In the Head — (See "Disorders Of", and the various paragraphs in this section).

**Tumors In** — (See "Growths" in this section).

**Two Heads**—(See "Two Heads" in Sec. 1 of this Article).

**Ulceration**—(See "Ulcers" under Face; "Ulceration" under Forehead; Ulcers).

**Veins** — Of the Head — Ill Blood In—(See "Blood" in this section).

**Ventricles; Vertigo; Violent Pains** — In the Head—♂ affl. in ♈. (See "Pains" in this section; "Violent" under Headaches).

**Visage**—(See Face, Visage).

**Vision** — (See Accommodation, Eyes, Sight).

**Warts** — (See "Marks" under Face; "Marks" in Sec. 1 of this Article).

**Watery Diseases**—(See Excrescences, Humours, Moist Humours, Snuffling, in this section).

**Wens; Wounds To** — Wounded In the Head—(See Accidents, Blows, Bruises, Cuts, Fractures, Injuries, in this section).

**HEADACHES** — Pains In the Head — Neuralgia In—It may not always be possible Astrologically to detect or locate the cause of a headache, as the causes are many, and often complicated and mixed under various planetary afflictions. However, as a fundamental rule, the ♈ sign, the Asc., ♅ and ♂ are usually involved in the configurations, and strong afflictions from the malefics to the ☉, ☽, Asc., or hyleg. There are cases where people may have malefics in ♈ in the Asc., and afflicted by other malefics, who have never had a headache, and other influences, aspects, house and sign positions of the planets would need to be studied, and also the special idiosyncrasies, or a diathesis, be considered. Headaches may occur with most any disease, and also from Dissipation, Bad Habits, Gluttony, Excesses, Drink, Loss of Sleep, Insomnia, Irregularities, Feasting, Loose Morals, Over-Exertion, Over-Study or Reading, Eye Trouble, Indigestion, Sex Excesses, etc. (See these subjects). The various kinds and varieties of Headaches, and their planetary causes, are listed in the paragraphs which follow.

**All Over the Head**—General Over the Head—Many planets, or a Stellium, in ♈ at B., and scattered out thru the various faces and decanates of ♈; Subs at AT and AX.

**Amative Tract** — Headache In — (See Amative).

**Anaemic Headaches**—♄ affl. in ♈; Subs at AT, MCP, and HP. Also given by the general influences causing Anaemia. (See Anaemia; "Thin Blood" under Blood; Chlorosis).

**Bilious Headache**—♆, ♅, ♄, or ♂ promittors, and ☌, or ill-asp. the ☉ in ♈. (See Bile).

**Blood Impure**—Headaches from Corrupt and Impure Blood — The ☉ in ♈, and affl. by ♃. (See Impure).

**Catarrhal**—Nasal—Headaches From—♄ affl. in ♈, ♎, or ♏; Subs at MCP (3, 4C). (See Catarrh; "Catarrh" under Head, Nose).

**Causes of Headaches**—The following influences have been listed in the various textbooks as causes, or as existing at the time of headaches — An ♈ disease; afflictions in ♈, or ♎ by reflex action to ♈; any planets in ♈ at B., and afflicted; ♈ on the Asc., and afflicted; ♈ on the cusp the 6th H., or in the 6th H., and containing ☉, ☽, or malefics, and affl. by □ or ☍ aspects; the ☉ affl. in ♈; the ☉ to the ☌ the ☽, ♂, or the Asc. by dir.; the ☽ affl. in ♈ or ♎; the ☽ in ♈, ☌, or ill-asp. ♄ (or ☿ if he be of the nature of ♄) when taken ill, or at decumb.; the ☽ in the 6th H. in cardinal signs, and afflicted; the ☽ hyleg in ♈ and afflicted, and espec. with females; the ☽ in ♈, ☌, or ill-asp. any of the malefics as promittors; the prog. ☽ in ♈, and ☌ any planets in ♈ at B.; the ☽ directed to the Ascelli; ♅ affl. in ♈ or ♎; ♄ affl. in ♈ or ♎; ♄ in ♈ in ☌ ♃ or ♀; ♄ ☌ the Asc. by dir.; ♃ affl. in ♈; ♃ ☌ ♄ in ♈; ♂ affl. in ♈; ♂ in the 6th H. in a cardinal sign, and affl. the ☉ or ☽; ♂ affl. in ♈ in the Asc. or 6th H.; ♀ affl. in ♈, ♉, or ♎; ☿ affl. in ♈ or ♎; ☿ in ♈ or ♊, ☌, or ill-asp. any of the malefics as promittors; a ☿ disease; born under ☿.

**Center of Head**—Headaches In—The ☉ in ♈.

**Constipation** — The Headaches of — (See Constipation).

**Continual Headache**—Complains Continually of Headache—The ☽ ☌ or ill-asp. ♄ (or ☿ if he be of the nature of ♄) at the beginning of an illness, or at decumb.

**Darting Pains** — In the Head — (See "Darting" under Head).

**Frequent Headaches** — In Women — (See "Women" in this section).

**Frontal Headaches**—♆ in ♈, and affl. by the ☉, ♄, or ♂; ♄ affl. in ♈; Subs at AT and AX. (See "Abscess" under Frontal).

**General**—(See "All Over the Head" in this section).

**Hyperaemic Headaches**—The ☉ affl. in ♈. (See Hyperaemia).

**Impure Blood**—Headaches From—(See "Blood" in this section).

**Internal Headaches**—The ☉ affl. in ♈.

**Migraine** — Paroxysmal Headaches — Megrims In the Head—(See Migraine).

**Nasal Catarrh**—Headaches From—♄ affl. in ♏. (See "Catarrh" in this section).

**Nervous Headaches**—Nervous Strain and Headaches From—The ☉ in ♈, ☌, or ill-asp. any of the malefics as promittors; ☿ affl. in ♈, and espec. from nervous strain, or overstudy; ☿ affl. in ♎. (See "Strain" under Nerves).

**Neuralgia**—In the Head—(See "Neuralgia" under Head).

**Occipital Headaches**—♀ affl. in ♉. (See Occiput).

**Ocular Headaches** — The ☽ or ☿ affl. in ♈; Subs at AT, MCP, SP, and KP. (See "Eyestrain" under Eyes; Reading, Study).

**Organic Headaches**—The ☉ affl. in ♈. (See Organic).

**Pain**—In the Head—(See "Pain" under Head).

**Paroxysmal Headache**—(See Migraine, Paroxysms).

**Periodic Headache**—Headaches at the Menstrual Periods—The ☽ or ♄ affl. in ♏; Subs at AT, and PP (2, 3, 4L). (See Menses).

**Reading and Study**—Headaches From —(See "Ocular" in this section).

**Regular Headache**—Periodic—Caused by the ☽. (See Periodic; "Periodic" in this section).

**Rheumatic Headache**—♄ in ♈, and affl. the ☉, ☽, or Asc. (See Rheumatism).

**Shooting Pains** — In the Head — (See "Darting" under Head).

**Sick Headache**—Afflictions in ♈ and ♎; ♄ affl. in ♎; Subs at KP, and due to retained poisons, and improper kidney action.

**Spasmodic Pains**—In the Head—♅ in ♈. (See "Spasmodic" under Head; Migraine).

**Sudden Headaches**—♅ affl. in ♈ or ♎, and espec. when in the Asc. or 6th H. (See Sudden).

**Temporal Headaches** — ♃ affl. in ♈; Subs at Li.P. Caused mostly by liver disorders, and afflictions to ♃, the ruler of the liver. (See Temples).

**Toxaemic Headache** — Uremic Headache — ☿ affl. in ♈. (See Toxaemia, Uremia).

**Unilateral Headache**—(See Migraine).

**Uremic Headache** — (See "Toxaemic" in this section).

**Violent Headaches**—The ☽ in ♈ and affl. by ♂; ♅ affl. in ♎; ♂ in ♈. (See "Pains", "Violent", under Head).

**Women**—Frequent Headaches In—The ☽ to the ill-asps. ♃ by dir.; the ☽ hyleg in ♈, and affl. by ♃; the ☽ affl. in ♏, or malefics in ♏ afflicting the ☉, ☽, or Asc., from female disorders, and disturbance of the female functions.

**HEALERS**—Healing—The Healing Powers — The planetary influences at the birth of individuals endow various Healing Powers, and to suit the various needs, beliefs, peculiarities, and idiosyncrasies of the twelve fundamental classes of Humanity, as represented by the 12 Signs of the Zodiac. All Schools of Healing have their place in the World, have their followers, and it is the duty of a patient to call upon the Healer in whom he has faith, no matter of what School. This Book, and also this Article, are not a treatise upon the merits of the various Schools of Healing, but merely to help you understand the causes and philosophy of disease, why people are sick, the nature of the sickness, its duration, possible termination, etc., and to list those influences which tend especially to endow one with successful Healing Powers, and also to list those influences which tend to make one a failure as a Healer. For the welfare of the patient, it is important that the Healer called upon should be compatible with the patient, for the best success, and that the star maps of the Healer and patient have agreeable exchanges. Otherwise, the Healer may injure the patient. The following subjects have to do with Healers, Healing, Treatment, the care of the Sick, and those connected with such work in various ways, or the preparation of Foods or Remedies for the Sick. The Sixth House rules strongly over the Healing Powers, and the Healing Service.

**Absent Healing**—(See "Metaphysical" in this section).

**Allopathy**—The treatment of the sick by using remedies which oppose, and are in antipathy with the planetary influences causing the disease. (See Antipathy, Hippocrates, Opposites).

**Antipathy**—Healing By—(See Antipathy).

**Asylums**—Care of the Sick In—Confined In—(See Asylums).

**Avoid** — Healers for the Patient to Avoid—Those who have ♄ in the Asc. or 6th H. of the patient. (See "Compatability" in this section).

**Bath House Keepers**—Good Influences For—(See Bathing).

**Biochemists**—Those who use the 12 Zodiac, or Tissue Salts, in the treatment of disease, and to supply the lacking chemical constituents of the body. (See Biochemistry; "Salts" under Zodiac).

**Black Magicians**—Those who use Occult Powers for evil purposes in the treatment of the sick, and to defraud —(See Magical).

**Chemists**—(See Chemists).

**Chiropodist**—One Who Treats the Feet and Hands — The ♊, ♍, and ♓ people are especially adapted to this work, and espec. the ♊ people, as ♊ gives unusual skill and ability in the use of the hands.

**Chiropractors**—The best Chiropractors are born under ☿ and ♊, as a rule, ♊ on the Asc., or the ☉, ☽, ♂, or ☿ in ♊. A keen and sensitive touch is needed for correct palpation by the hands, and this is given especially by the □ sign, and where the hands are to be used in a more delicate and scientific manner. (See Subluxations, Touch, Vertebrae).

**Color**—Healing By—(See Color).

**Christian Science**—(See "Spiritual" in this section).

**Compatibility**—Of Healer and Patient —Incompatibility of—Rules For—The Compatibility of the Healer and Patient is determined by the rising sign in each map, whether in harmony or not; by the exchanges in the 6th H. in each map, whether of benefics or malefics, and also by the relation existing between ♄ in each map. The 7th H. also rules the Physician in the case. The first important rule is that the rising signs in both maps, the signs on the Asc., should be in harmony, belong to the same triplicity, and be in ✳ or △ aspect to each other. If the patient has ♈ on the Asc. at B., his Healer, for the best success, should also have a fiery sign on the Asc., as ♌ or ♐. If the Healer employed in this case should have ♋, ♎, or ♑ upon the Asc. at B., he would tend to affect the patient adversely, or cause him to get worse. If the patient should start out with an adverse Healer, and continue to get worse, by changing to a Healer whose map is in harmony, the patient would tend to improve rapidly. The ✳ and △ aspects between the rising signs of the two maps tend to naturally inspire faith and confidence between the patient and Healer, whereas the □ or ☍ aspects between them tend to an aversion, the same as between people who marry under such conditions and separate. (See "Enemies", "Healers", under Antipathy. Also see Death, Poisoned, Sympathy, in this section).

**Cure of Disease**—Curable Diseases— Incurable Diseases — (See Curable, Drugs, Incurable, Medicines, Moderation, Treatment. Also note the various paragraphs in this section).

**Death**—The Patient May Die by Having the Wrong Healer—The rising sign of the patient being in □ or ☍ to the Asc., or rising sign of the Healer; ♄ in the Healer's map in the sign occupying the 6th H. in the patient's map of birth. (See "Compatibility" in this section).

**Diagnosis**—(See Diagnosis, Judgment, Prognosis).

**Diet and Hygiene**—♍ is the sign which rules these matters, and people who have ♂, and other planets in ♍ at B., or who are born under ♍, make good Dieticians, Teachers, Lecturers, and Healers, by the direction of a well-balanced and regulated Diet for their patients. The ♍ people, however, tend to hold onto disease when sick, and espec. if they are unenlightened, and live in their lower minds. (See Virgo). Case of a Diet Specialist—See "Wallace", No. 292, in 1001 N.N. (See Diet; "Health Foods" under Food; Hygiene, Prevented (Disease Prevented); Sanitation; "Hygiene" in this section).

**Divine Healers**—Faith Healers—Spiritual Healers—Metaphysical Healers— Drugless Healers—♅ strong at B., and well-aspected; ♅ rising, in the Asc. or M.C., and in ☌ the ☉, gives strong powers for the study and practice of these forms of healing, and to go deeply into the Occult and Recondite Sciences. (See Faith, Hypnotic, Magnetic, Metaphysical, Psychic, Spiritual, in this section).

**Doctors** — (See "Physicians", and the various paragraphs in this section).

**Drugs**—(See Drugs).

**Drugless Healers**—(See Chiropractors, Divine, Faith, Mental, Metaphysical, Nature, Naturopaths, and other paragraphs in this section).

**Eclectic Physicians** — This School is quite universal in its methods and practices, and tends to choose the best from many Schools of Healing, and to not be bound by any one method. Eclectics tend to be versatile, and to have their planets at B. well-scattered out thru the Signs of the Zodiac, and with a desire to delve into many subjects, and to gather Truth wherever it may be found. In addition to this, the best Eclectic Healers usually have ♂, the ♍ and ♏ signs strong and prominent at B. (See "Physicians" in this section).

**Electricity**—(See "Healing" under Electricity).

**Enemas**—Healing By—(See Enemas).

**Enemies** — The general influences which would tend to make certain classes and types of people an enemy to the native also tend to make the Healer adverse to him, and the magnetic and vibratory exchanges between the two maps, and natures, rather evil, and to not benefit each other. (See Enemies; "Compatibility" in this section).

**Failures As Healers**—Do Not Make Good Healers—♄ in the 6th H. of the Healer at B.

**Faith Healing**—Spiritual Methods, as by Religious Rites, Christian Science, Prayer, Laying On of Hands, etc. — ♆ strong at B., and well-aspected, makes the Healer more susceptible to the inflow of Spiritual Powers in Healing, and also ♆ strong and favorably aspected in the map of the patient makes him more amenable to the spiritual powers of healing. Such methods, however, may become dangerous when ♆ is weak and badly afflicted in the maps of both Healer and patient, and lead to obsessions, and dangerous mental and spiritual states, black magic, etc. Also ♅ strong at B. in both the maps, of Healer and patient, tend to increase the powers, knowledge, and beliefs necessary for successful healing by faith and spiritual power. (See Divine, Metaphysical, and the various paragraphs in this section).

**Foods**—Health Foods—(See Diet, Hygiene, Specialties, in this section).

**Good Healers** — Make Good and Successful Healers—The ☉ in a fiery sign at B.; the ☉ well-aspected in ♏; born under ♏. (See "Magnetic", and the various paragraphs in this section).

**Health Specialties** — (See Diet, Food, Hygiene, Specialties, in this section).

**Herbs**—The Use of Herbs In Healing —(See Herbs).

**Homeopathy** — Treating Disease by Sympathy and Similars — (See Homeopathy, Sympathy).

**Hospitals**—(See Hospitals).

**Hygiene** — And Diet — (See "Diet" in this section; Hygiene).

**Hypnotism** — Hypnotic Powers of Healing—(See Hypnotism).

**Incompatibility** — Of the Healer and Patient — (See Antipathy, Compatibility, Death, Enemies, Poisoned, in this section).

**Incurable Diseases**—(See Curable, Incurable).

**Injured**—By the Healer—(See Antipathy, Compatibility, Death, Enemies, Death, Poisoned, in this section).

**Judgment of Disease**—(See "Diagnosis" in this section).

**Laying On of Hands** — A Religious Rite In Healing—(See "Faith" in this section).

**Length of the Illness**—(See Duration, Grievous, Incurable, Invalids, Long, Prolonged, Slow, Tedious, etc.).

**Magic Powers** — In Healing — (See Magic).

**Magnetic Healers**—Born under ♏, and the ♏ influence strong at B.; the ☉ in ♏. (See "Healers" under Magnetic).

**Massage**—Manipulation—Kneading—Friction—Methodic Pressure—Healers born under ♏, the ☉ in ♏, are especially adaptated to this work, due to their strong magnetism and healing powers. (See "Osteopathy" in this section).

**Medicines** — The Use of Medicines In Healing—(See Antipathy, Drugs, Herbs, Medical, Medicines, Remedies, Sympathy, Treatment).

**Mental Healing** — (See "Psychic" in this section).

**Metaphysical Healing** — Absent Healing—Healing at a Distance thru Prayer, Concentration, Realization, Spiritual Power, etc., or the use of these same methods in the presence of the patient —♆ and ♅ strong at B. in the maps of the Healers tend to make the best Practitioners along this line, and with those who have Occult and Metaphysical knowledge, and who understand the healing and magnetic forces and currents which are operating in the Universe. (See Divine, Faith, Prayer, Spiritual, in this section).

**Midwives** — (See Midwives, Obstetricians).

**Mineral Waters** — Healers Making a Specialty of—Healers born under ♓, the ☉ in ♓, and many planets in watery signs at B. tend to be especially fortunate in this work. Also people born under ♄ make good Healers, and Managers of Mineral Water Sanitariums, as ♄ rules strongly over minerals, and the mineral products of the Earth. The Occult Masters of Wisdom teach us that we get sufficient mineral nourishment from vegetable foods, and that after 40 years of age, distilled water is more healthful for drinking purposes, and tends to prevent the excess of minerals in the system, causing Gout, Rheumatism, etc., later in life. One Occult Axiom is, "Internally undistilled water is Man's worst enemy, but used externally on the skin is his best friend." (See Minerals; "Water" under Skin).

**Mud Baths** — These baths are especially helpful to strong ♄ persons, those born under ♄, and who thru melancholy and mental depression have so lowered their vital forces as to allow poisons to accumulate in the body. Mud baths help to open the pores of the skin, and to extract the excess of mineral deposits and wastes in the system. Also Healers who practice these methods are apt to be born under ♄, and to resort largely to material and physical means of healing.

**Nature**—The Healing Powers of—The Defensive Forces of Nature—Nature is said to do the healing, and all we can do is to assist Nature. (See Phagocytes, Recuperation, Resistance, Stamina, Tone, Vis Conservatrix, Vitality).

**Nature Cure** — A Nature Cure Physician, and Author of a book on the subject. See "Kleinshrod", No. 690, in 1001 N.N. (See "Curing" under Nature).

**Naturopaths**—Naturopathy—Good Healers along this line are born under ♍ and ♏, and whose planets at B. also indicate versatility, adaptability, magnetic powers, and with considerable knowledge of Universal Truth, the Occult and Metaphysical Wisdom, and of the Laws of Health. The Naturopaths use what are called natural methods in healing, such as by regulating the diet, habits, and also by the use of massage, electricity, baths, waters, and the various forces in Nature, but are classed as Drugless Healers, and do not use drugs internally. (See Medical Astrology).

**Nurses**—Influences Which Make Good Nurses—(See Nurses).

**Nut Butters**—A Maker of as a Health Specialty — (See "Specialties" in this section).

**Obstetricians**—(See this subject).

**Opposites**—Healing by the Use of Opposite Forces—By Antipathy—(See Antipathy, Opposites).

**Orthopedist**—(See this subject).

**Osteopathy**—The most successful Osteopaths are born under ♏, and with the ☉ and many planets in ♏, and whose magnetic powers of healing are strong. (See Magnetic, Massage, in this section).

**Patient and Healer**—Compatibility of —(See "Compatibility" in this section).

**Periods of Success**—As Healers—The ☉, ☽, Asc., or M.C. to the good asps. ♂ by dir., and espec. as Surgeons. (See Surgeons).

**Phagocytes** — Healing and Defending Forces of the Body—(See Phagocytes).

**Physicians**—A Successful Physician—Success as a Doctor of Medicine—These influences apply largely to Healers in general, and to all who have to deal with the sick in the treatment and cure of patients, the alleviation of human suffering, no matter by what method, or by what School of Healing administered—The ☉ in ♏ at B., and well-asp. by ♃ and ♂; the ☉ Sig. in ♏; the ☉ well-asp. in ♏; the ☉ P. ✳ or △ ♃ at B.; the ☽ incr. in light, sepr. from ♄ and apply. to ☿; the ☽ ruling the employment, or in her decr., configurated with ☿, and in ♉, ♊, ♋, ♐, ♑, or ♓, and with ♓ strong, and aspected by ☿ or the ☽; the ☽ Sig. ☌ ♂, and ♂ well-dignified; ♃ ruler of the horoscope; ♃ Sig. ☌ ♂; ♃ well-asp. in ♏; ♃ well-asp. in the 6th H., the house of health; ♂ and ♀ together rulers of the employment; ♂, ♃, or ♀ in the 6th H.; ♂ lord of the 6th, and in the 6th; any asp. of ♂ to the ☽ or ☿ inclines to the study of Medicine, Surgery, or Chemistry; to have success as a Physician ♂ should be strong at B., and in good asp. to the ☉, ☽, or ☿; ♂ a strong ruler at B.; ♂ ☌ ♀ in the 6th H. usually makes good Physicians; ♀ alone ruler makes good Medical Doctors; ♀ well-asp. in the 6th H.; ☿ in ♏, well-asp. by ♃ and ♂; in Hor'y Q., the Sig. in a fiery sign denotes; born under ♍, good healers along the lines of Diet and Hygiene, but apt to be failures in surgery, and where courage is needed; born under ♏, good Medical Doctors and Surgeons; any benefic in the 6th H. tends to make good Healers; in Hor'y Q., the Sig. in ♏; benefics in the 12th H.; lord of the employment in ♏, and well-asp.; lord of the Asc. in the 6th H.; lord of the 2nd in the 6th, may gain a fortune in the Practice of Medicine; lord of the 2nd in the 12th H., success in Hospitals, Prisons, Asylums, and Institutions of Healing where patients are confined; lord of the 4th in the 6th, and well-asp.; lord of the 5th in the 6th; lord of the 6th in the 2nd, gains as a Physician; lord of the 6th in the 6th; lord of the 7th in the Asc.; lord of the 10th a benefic, in the 6th H., and well-asp.; lord of the 12th a benefic, in the 6th, and well-asp.; the Asc. or M.C. ✳ or △ ♂; the 6th face of ♋, the 4th face of ♌, the 2nd face of ♏, or the 2nd face of ♐ culminating on the M.C.; the 10° ♊ on the Asc., a degree of healing and sympathy, and makes strong Healers. Cases of Eminent Healers and Physicians—See "Massari", "Nunn", "Quain", in 1001 N.N. (See Chemists, Surgeons; "The Sick" under Sick. Also note the various paragraphs in this section).

**Poisoned** — May Be Poisoned by the Healer or Physician — Incompatibility between Healer and Patient—The patient having the lord of the 8th in the 6th H. at B.; lord of the 6th in the 11th; ♄ in the Healer's map in the 6th H. of the patient, or in the sign occupying the 6th H.; the rising signs in the maps of Healer and patient in □ or ☍ asp. to each other. (See Compatibility, Death, in this section; "Ill-Treatment" under Sickness).

**Powers**—The Healing Powers Strengthened—♆ in ✳ or △ asp. to ♅.

**Practice of Healing**—Disposed to the Study and Practice of Healing, Whether It be by Medicine, Diet, Hygiene, or any Other System—The ♍ sign and the 6th H. deal with healing matters and hygiene, and ♍ and the 6th H. strong at B., and well-occupied, tend to turn

the attention to Healing. Also the ♏ sign strong at B., and containing the ☉, ♂, or ☿, disposes to healing along the lines of drugs, surgery, massage, magnetism, etc. The ☉ in ♍ or ♏, and espec. when in the 6th H.; the ☉ or ☿ in the 6th H.; the ☉ well-asp. by ♂; ♆, ♅, or ♂ in ♍ or the 6th H.; ♂ well-asp. in the 10th H.; the 3rd Decan. of ♍ on the Asc., which is ruled by ☿; any aspect of ♂ to the ☽ or ☿.

**Prayer** — Healing by Prayer — (See Divine, Faith, Metaphysical, Psychic, in this section).

**Prevention of Disease**—By the Patient, or thru the Advice of the Healer — (See Diet, Hygiene; "Disease Prevented" under Prevention; Sanitation, Spiritual Power (see Spiritual); Suggestion, Thinking, etc.).

**Process** — The Healing Process — (See Granulations).

**Prognosis**—(See this subject).

**Psychic Healing** — Divine Healing — Mental Healing—Healing by Faith, etc. —A Good Psychic Healer—The Patient More Susceptible To—♅ strong at B., or ruler of the horoscope. The best time for Psychic Healing is when the ☽ is in ♋ or ♓. (See Divine, Faith, Hypnotism, Metaphysical, in this section; Psychic).

**Reformer** — A Hygienic Reformer — Case and Birth Data of—(See Hygiene).

**Religion** — Religious Rites — Healing By—(See Divine, Faith, in this section).

**Remedies** — (See Antipathy, Color, Cure, Drugs, Herbs, Medicines, Metals, Minerals, Opposites, Sympathy, Treatment, etc. Also see the various paragraphs in this section).

**Sanitariums**—(See Asylums, Confinement, Hospitals, Prison, Twelfth House; "Mineral Waters" in this section).

**Sanitation**—(See Cleanliness, Hygiene, Prevention, Sanitation).

**Sick**—The Treatment and Care of the Sick — (See Cure, Hospitals, Nurses, Sick. Also note the various paragraphs in this section).

**Sixth House**—The House which is strongly related to Health and Healers—(See Sixth House, Virgo).

**Skillful Healers**—(See "Good Healers" in this section).

**Specialties**—Makers of Health Foods and Specialties—Nut Butters—♂ well-asp. in ♍ gives success in the preparation of Health Foods and Specialties. Case—A Maker of Health Specialties and Nut Butters—See "Mapleton", No. 1000, in 1001 N.N. (See Diet, Hygiene, in this section; "Health Foods" under Food).

**Spiritual Healers**—♆ is the planet which rules strongly over spiritual matters, the spiritual nature, and people born under the strong influence of ♆, and also ♅, and with ♆ ☌ the ☉, or ♆ in the 1st or 10th H., and well-asp., tend to make good Spiritual Healers. Also ♆ in ✳ or △ asp. ♅ at B. tends to strengthen these powers, and to give greater spiritual insight, and a greater consciousness of spiritual power in the healing work. (See Divine, Faith, Metaphysical, in this section).

**Strengthened**—The Healing Powers Strengthened—(See "Powers" in this section).

**Study of Healing**—Disposed To—(See "Practice of Healing" in this section).

**Success As Healers**—Periods of Success As Healers—(See Good Healers, Periods, Physicians, and the various paragraphs in this section).

**Suggestion**—Healing By—(See Hypnotism; "Psychic" in this section).

**Surgeons**—Makes a Good Surgeon—(See Surgeon).

**Sympathy**—Healing by Methods of—(See Homeopathy, Sympathy).

**Treatment of Disease**—(See Cure, Remedies, Treatment. Also note the various paragraphs in this section).

**Unfortunate**—As Healers—♄ in the 6th H. of the Healer at B.; lord of the 7th H. a malefic, and in the 6th H., and afflicted; lord of the 12th a malefic, and in the 6th H., and afflicted. The ♍ sign people tend to take on the diseases of other, and are not good Healers in the presence of dangerous illnesses and fevers, or as Surgeons, but they make good Healers along the lines of Diet, Food, Hygiene, Prevention, Sanitation, etc.

**Vibration**—As a Factor In Healing—(See Vibrations).

**Waters**—Healing By—(See Bathing; "Mineral Waters" in this section).

**Wealth**—Gains Wealth As a Healer, or In the Practice of Medicine—Lord of the 2nd H. in the 6th, or lord of the 6th H. in the 2nd H. (See Periods, Physicians, in this section).

**Zodiac Salts**—Biochemistry—Healers Who Make Use of the 12 Tissue Salts, Known as the Schuessler Tissue Remedies—(See "Biochemists" in this section; "Salts" under Zodiac).

**HEALTH**—The State of the Health—The General Health—Rules for Judging the Health—Good Health—Bad Health, etc.—The 6th H. and ♍ denote the state of the health. Also the 1st H. rules the health and constitution. The ☽ governs the health, and has significance over health matters, and espec. with females, while the ☉ is a strong indicator of health with males. However, the ☉ and ☽ are important factors in the health of both sexes. The rising sign also governs the health and the life. The Part of Fortune (⊕) does not affect the health, but has more to do with finance. When ♄ or ♂ both afflict the ☉, the health is not as bad as when ♄ alone afflicts the ☉, for the aspects of ♂ to the ☉, whether good or bad, tend to strengthen the system. The planet ♅ does not exercise any great influence over the health except when in the 6th H., and there tends to nervousness, suicide, or accidents. Ill-asps. between the ☽ and ♂, and between the ☉ and ♄, tend to greatly injure the health because of their opposite and dissimilar natures. The ill-asps. between the ☉ and ♂, and between the ☽ and ♄, do not injure as much, as their natures are more in common with each other. Health is largely indicated by the ☉ and ☽ at B.,

their positions, signs, and aspects, as they are the fountains of life on the Earth. In health every cell of the body is polarized in subjection to the central will. Therefore, health is obedience, government, and order in the system, while disease is rebellion, insubordination, and disunion. Remember, the stars only incline and show tendencies, and that your health can be improved and modified by self-control, right thinking, spiritualization, and by control of the passional and sex nature. Read the various paragraphs of this Article for the many and manifold considerations concerning health, as regards yourself, your family, your relatives, and also the Public Health in general. The rules for judging the normal state of the health from the star map of birth are given in the paragraph, "Judging The Health" in this section. See the following subjects in the alphabetical arrangement when not considered here—

**Absent Party**—State of the Health of An Absent Party in Hor'y Questions—(See Absent).

**Abundance of Health**—Good Health All Thru Life—Rarely Ill—Little Sickness All Thru Life—The ☉ in ♐ and well-aspected, physical ailments rare; the ☽ hyleg with females does not conduce to many ailments; ♂ ☌, P., ⁎, or △ the ☉; ♀ well-asp. in the 6th H. if the health is guarded; ♌ on the Asc., rarely ill; lord of the 8th H. in the 8th, little sickness all thru life, but slightly threatened with illness at times. (See "Good Health" in this section).

**Affected**—The Health Affected—The Health Suffers—(See "Bad Health" in this section. Also see the various paragraphs under Ill-Health, Sickness).

**Aged**—Aged People—State of the Health In—(See Old Age).

**Air**—Healthy Air—(See "Healthy Air" under Air).

**Always Ailing**—(See "Bad Health" in this section; "Ill-Health All Thru Life" under Ill-Health).

**Analeptics**—An Agent Restoring Health and Strength—(See Analeptic).

**Anxiety**—Concerning the Health—(See Hypochondria).

**Asthenia**—Loss of Strength—(See Adynamia, Asthenia).

**Aunts**—Health of—(See Aunts).

**Bad Health**—The Health Suffers—Ill-Health—Impaired Health—Delicate Health—Poor Health—Disordered System—Weak Constitution—The Vitality Low, etc. There are two classes of planetary influences, those which cause general ill-health and weakness from birth, and those which cause periods of bad health along thru life. In this paragraph the influences will be listed which tend to general, fundamental, and prolonged bad health, and further along, in the paragraph, "Periods of Ill-Health", will be given the Directions, Transits, etc., which tend to periods of ill-health, or temporary bad health. The following are the General Influences which tend to Bad Health, and a weak constitution from birth, and with lower vitality and resistance to disease, etc.—The SUN □ or ☍ the ☽ at B.; the ☉ or ☽ affl. by malefics; the ☉ □ ♄ and the ☉ hyleg; the ☉ or ☽ in the 6th H., and affl.; the ☉ in the 6th H., and affl. by malefics or the ☽; the ☉ or ♄ in the 6th H. in ☌, □, or ☍ each other, which is one of the worst positions for bad health; the ☉ in the 6th H. in cardinal signs, and affl. by the ☽ or ♄; the ☉ occi., and affl. by ♄; the ☉ Sig. in ♋ or ♑; in male horoscopes when the ☉ is affl. by both ♄ and ♂ the health will not be exceptionally bad, as ♂ in any asp. to the ☉ tends to increase the animal heat; the MOON sepr. from ♂ and apply. to the ☉ or ♄; the ☽ Sig. □ or ☍ ♄ (Hor'y); the ☽ hyleg and ☌ a malefic, and espec. when in the 6th H.; the ☽ (or the ☉) affl. by malefics, and the malefics elevated above the Lights; the ☽ Sig. in ♑; the ☽ weak and affl. at B., the health is rarely good, and espec. with females; the ☽ in the 6th H., and affl., the disease is in the part signified by the sign on the cusp of the 6th; the ☽ ill-asp. by ♃; the ☽ affl. in the 1st H., the health not good, and the life precarious; the ☽ affl. by ♄ at B., and tends to ill-health every seven years; the ☽ □ or ☍ the ☉ at B.; the ☽ in bad asp. to the ascending degree at B., and by dir.; in female nativities the ☽ is the strong ruler in health matters, and no matter how severely the ☽ may be afflicted, if there are good asps. of the benefics to the ☽ the health is improved, and also the health does not tend to be as bad under planetary afflictions along thru life; NEPTUNE in the 1st H., and affl. the ☉ or ☽; ♆ in the 6th H., and affl. the ☉, ☽, or hyleg; ♆ □ or ☍ ♄, bad health thru obsessions, and the taking of drugs, medicines, or narcotics; SATURN in the 6th H. at B., conjoined with the ☉, or affl. the ☉; ♄ or ♂ in the Asc. at B., and affl.; ♄ affl. in the 6th H., and espec. if the mind dwells on selfish aims; ♄ in the 6th H. in ☌, □, or ☍ the ☉.; ♄ in the 10th H., affl. the hyleg, and espec. if ♄ be affl. by ♅ and ♂, always ailing; ♄ Sig. ☌ the ☉; ♄ □ or ☍ ♃; ♄ in the Asc., bad for the health in infancy and childhood; ♄ ffl. in ♏ or ♑; ♄ rising at B.; ♄ ruler of the 6th H. at B., and in ☌ or evil asp. the Asc. by dir.; ♄ rising at B., and affl. the hyleg; ♄ in the 10th H., and affl. the hyleg; ♄ in an angle, ori. of the ☽ and occi. of the ☉; ♄ Sig. in ♋, indicates a sickly person in Hor'y Q.; JUPITER in the 6th H. at B. in a cardinal sign, and affl.; ♃ affl. in the 6th H.; ♃ affl. in the Asc., ill-health thru corrupt blood; ♃ Sig. ☌ the ☉; ♃ Sig. in ♋ or ♑; MARS affl. in the 6th H., and also affl. the hyleg; ♂ ☌ ♀, and affl. by the □ and ☍ of planets; VENUS affl. in the 6th H.; ♀ affl. in the 5th H., thru pleasure and dissipation; ♀ Sig. in ♋ or ♑, sickly and feeble; ♀ Sig. ☌ the ☉, too sickly as a rule to make much exertion; MERCURY Sig. in ♑, sickly and feeble; malefics in the 6th H. at B., and affl. the hyleg; a malefic in an angle, rising before or after the ☉ or ☽; common signs on the Asc. and angles, and containing malefics and many afflictions; FIXED STARS of the nature or ♄ or ♂ ascending at B.; ♋, ♑, or ♓ on the Asc., and with afflictions to the hyleg and 6th H.; the ASCENDANT hyleg and ☌, □ or ☍ a malefic; lord of the Asc. in the 1st, and affl. by malefics or lords of the 6th, 8th, or 12th; lord of the Asc. in the 6th, 8th, or 12th, and affl.; lord of the 4th in the 6th, and affl.; lord of the 6th in the Asc., is seldom strong or robust in early years and has poor health, and the nature of the sickness is indicated by the planets in the 6th, the sign on the 6th, and lord of the 6th; lord of the 8th in the 6th; lord of the 11th a malefic, and in the 6th; lord of the 11th in the 6th; lord of the 12th a malefic, and affl. in the 6th H. (See Disease; "Ill-Health" under Females, Males; Ill-Health, Infirmities; "Public Health Bad" under Public; Sickness, etc. Also see "Periods of Bad Health" in this section).

**Benefitted**—The Health Benefitted—(See Better, Improved, in this section).

**Better**—The Health Better—The Health is generally better when the ☉ is rising at B., and weaker when setting. (See "Better" under Disease; Immunity, Resistance, Strong, Vitality; Good, Improved, Promoted, in this section).

**Blood**—Bad Health from Impure Blood—From Too Much Blood, etc.—♃ affl. in the Asc. (See Impure, Pressure, Too Much, under Blood).

**Breakdown In Health**—Principally caused by an afflicted ♀; ♀ in ♏ ☌ ♂ or the ☽, and thru sex abuses and excesses; ♀ affl. in the 6th H., thru luxuries and abuses; ♀ □ or ☍ ♂; the ☉ or ☽ to the ☌ or ill-asp. the malefics by dir., and espec. among those with weak vitality, frail constitutions, and among the aged; may be caused by a train of evil directions to the hyleg, the evil directions of malefics to the hyleg, the ☉, ☽, or Asc., and espec. among the aged and the feeble. (See Chronic, Consumptions, Directions, Dissipation, Drink, Excesses, Feasting, Habits, Ill-Health, Invalids, Sickness, Wastings, etc. Also note the various paragraphs in this section).

**Brothers**—Health of—(See Brothers).

**Careless**—Of the Health and Habits—(See "Careless" under Habits).

**Changes**—Changes Detrimental to Health—Changes Which Interfere with Health and Comfort—♅ in the 6th H. (See Comforts).

**Cheerfulness**—As An Asset of Good Health—(See Cheerfulness).

**Childhood**—The Health In—(See Childhood, Children, Early Years, Infancy).

**Children**—Health of—(See Childhood, Children, Early Years, Infancy).

**Comforts and Health**—(See Comforts).

**Common People**—The Health of the Common People—The Public Health—(See Common, Mankind; "Health" under Public).

**Complexion; Constitution**—(See the various paragraphs under Constitution.

**Contentment; Corrupt Blood** — Bad Health From — (See "Blood" in this section).

**Damage**—To the Health—(See "Bad Health", and the various paragraphs in this section).

**Daughter**—Health of—(See Daughter).

**Debility; Delicate Health**—(See "Bad Health" in this section; Pale, Sickly, Vitality Low; "Body" under Weak).

**Depressed**—Depressed Concerning the Health—(See Depressed, Hypochondria).

**Detrimental**—Has a Detrimental Effect Upon the Health—The ☉ ☌ or P. ♄, and especially in common signs. (See "Bad Health" in this section).

**Directions**—Effect of Upon the Health —(See Directions).

**Diseased Body**—Diseased Mind—(See "Bad Habits", and the various paragraphs in this section. Also see the various subjects under Disease, Ill-Health, Mental, Mind, Sickness).

**Disordered System**—(See Disorders; "Disordered" under System; "Bad Health", and the various paragraphs in this section).

**Dissipation**—Bad Health From—(See Dissipation).

**Dissolute; Distempers; Drink;**

**Drug Habit**—Drugs—Bad Health from Use of—(See Drugs, Medicines, Narcotics).

**Drunkenness**—(See Drink, Drunkenness, Intoxication).

**Early Years** — The Health In — (See Early, Childhood, Children, Infancy, Youth).

**Eating**—Disorders from Wrong Eating—(See Diet, Eating, Excesses, Food, Gluttony).

**Elderly People**—The Health of—(See Grandparents, Middle Life, Old Age).

**Emaciation; Enemies**—Health of—Death of—(See Enemies).

**Enfeebled Health**—(See "Bad Health" in this section; Emaciated, Feeble, Infirm, Infirmities, Invalids, Sickly, etc.).

**Enhanced**—The Health Enhanced—The ☽ well-asp. by ♃ and ♀. (See Abundance, Improved, Promoted, in this section).

**Epidemics; Excesses**—The Health Injured By—(See Excesses).

**Family**—The Health of—(See Family).

**Father**—Health of—(See Father).

**Fears**—About the Health—(See Hypochondria).

**Feasting**—Ill Health From—(See Feasting, Gluttony, etc).

**Feeble Health**—(See Emaciated, Feeble, Infirm, Invalids, Sickly; "Bad Health" in this section).

**Females** — Women — The Health of—(See Aunts, Daughter, Females, Mother, Sister, Women; the ☽ influences under "Bad Health" in this section).

**Foods**—Health Foods—(See "Health Foods" under Food; "Specialties" under Healers).

**Friends**—Health of—(See Friends).

**Functions**—And the Health—(See Functions).

**General Debility**—(See Debility; "Debility" under Nerves; "Low" under Vitality; "Body" under Weak).

**General Health**—The General Health and the constructive functions are governed by the ☽. The General Health is much affected by the ☽, her aspects, sign and house position. The ☽ in ♉ or ♍ are good influences for the general health, and benefit it. Also ♃ and ♀ in good asp to the ☽ enhance the general health. (See General. Also for the Rules to Judge the General Health see "Judging the Health" in this section).

**General Ill-Health**—(See Ill-Health).

**General Malaise**—(See Malaise).

**Gluttony**—Bad Health By—(See Gluttony).

**Good Health** — Very Good Health — Healthy — Strong — Robust — Rarely Ill —Vitality Good—Signs of Good Health —Marks of—Periods of Good Health, etc.—The SUN, ☽, and Asc. free from affliction; the ☉, ☽, or ♃ in the Asc. or M.C. at B., strong by sign, and in good asp. to the hyleg; the ☉ in ♐ unless the hyleg is afflicted; the ☉ well-asp. by the ☽, ♂, and the benefics, and free from the strong afflictions of the malefics; the ☉ in a fire sign in the Asc. or M.C., and well-aspected; the ☉ to the ☌ ♃ by dir.; the MOON hyleg in the 1st or 10th H., well-asp. by the ☉ and benefics, and free from the ill-asps. of the malefics, and espec. with females; the ☽ free from affliction, well-asp. by ♃ or ♀, and also the Asc. free from malefic planets; the ☽ free from affliction, angular, and espec. in the 1st or 10th, not combust or evilly aspected by the lords of the 4th, 6th, 8th or 12th; the ☽ to the ☌ ♃ by dir.; the ☽ to the ☌ ♀ by dir. if ♀ be well-dignified at B.; the ☽ (or ☉) to the ✶ or △ asps. of ♃ or ♀ by dir.; the ☽ to the place of Canis Majoris; for the best of health, and location for health, follow the direction of the ☽ at B., or the lord of the Asc.; the ☽ well-asp. in ♉ or ♍; the ☽ angular and the Lights free from affliction; the ☽ ✶ or △ the ☉ or Asc. at B.; the ☽ to the △ asp. the Asc. in the Zodiac; the ☽ directed to Markab, Bull's North Eye, or the Right Foot of ♊; ♄ △ the Asc., and in good asp to the hyleg; JUPITER in the 6th H. unless much afflicted by position and aspects; ♃ ☌ or good asp. the ☉; ♃ hyleg in the Asc. or M.C., and well-aspected; ♃ Sig. ☌ ♀, very good health; ♃ well-asp. in the 1st H.; ♃ or ♀ in the 1st H., well-aspected, and with a strong sign upon the Asc.; ♃ or ♀ in the Asc. at B., and free from □ and ☍ asps.; ♃ in good asp. to the ☽; ♃ ☌ the Asc. by dir.; ♃ or ♀ to the ☌ or good asp. the M.C. by dir.; MARS ☌ or any asp. the ☉, usually strong and healthy; VENUS well-asp. in the 6th H., the health is good if not abused; the ASCENDANT well-asp. by the ☉, ☽, and many planets; a strong sign upon the Asc., and with ♃ or ♀ in the 1st H., and well-asp.; the ruler of the Asc. strong; the sign on the Asc., and the lord thereof, free from affliction, swift in motion, not combust or adversely aspected by the lords of the 4th, 6th, 8th, or 12th, dignified, angular, as in the 1st or 10th, and if in the 9th or 11th H., to be well-asp. by ♃, ♀, or the ☉, or in the terms of ♃ or ♀; lord of the Asc. in the 1st H., and well-asp.; the Asc. ✱ or △ the ☉, ☽, or ♃; fiery signs upon the Asc., the vitality is strong and the health tends to be good if dissipation and excesses are avoided; ♒ on the Asc., healthy and strong; the signs of the Summer Quarter on the Asc., as ♋, ♌, or ♍, or the ☉ or ☽ in these signs at B., tend to give a healthy, strong and vigorous body; ♋ on the Asc., altho classed as a weak sign, tends to give a stronger and healthier body when the ☉ is in ♋ in the Asc. at B., as the ☉ adds vitality to any sign he is in at B., and espec. when in the Asc.; the 14° ♓ on the Asc.; the Asc. to the place of Crater (see Crater); the Asc., the ☉ and ☽ free from affliction; the Asc. ☌ ♃ by dir.; the hyleg strong and well-asp. by the benefics, and free from the serious afflictions of the malefics; all good asps. to the hyleg benefit the health, but good asps. to the ☉, ☽, or Asc., espec. from the 6th or 8th Houses, or their rulers, are very efficacious; the Asc. well-asp. by the ☉, ☽, and many planets; a strong SIXTH HOUSE, even tho the hyleg be afflicted; the 6th H., the sign thereon, and its ruler, free from the presence or evil asps. of malefics; lord of the 6th in the 6th, unless much afflicted; Arista ascending at B. (See "Abundance", "Prospects", in this section; Cheerfulness; "Good" under Constitution, Recuperation, Resistance, Stamina, Tone, Vitality; Contentment; "Good Health" under Females, Males; Harmony; "Abundance of Health" under Health; "Long Life" under Life; "Peace of Mind" under Mind; Optimism; "Public Health Good" under Public; Robust, Ruddy; "Body" under Strong; Vigor, Vivacious, etc.).

**Grandparents**—Health of—(See Grandparents).

**Habits**—And the Health—(See "Careless", and the various paragraphs under Habits).

**Harmony** — A Harmonious Constitution—(See "Good" under Constitution; Harmony).

**Health Affected**—(See "Bad Health", and the various paragraphs in this section).

**Health Bad**—(See "Bad" in this section).

**Health Foods**—Health Specialties—(See "Foods" in this section).

**Health Good**—(See "Good" in this section).

**Healthy**—Healthy Air—Healthy Constitution—(See Air; "Good" under Constitution; "Public Health Good", under Public; "Good Health" in this section).

**Heat**—The Animal Heat—Lack of, and Tending to Ill-Health—(See "Animal Heat" under Heat).

**Husband**—Health of—(See Husband).

**Hypochondria**—Morbid Fears Concerning the Health—(See Hypochondria).

**Ill-Health**—Tendency To Ill-Health—(See the various paragraphs under Ill-Health; "Bad Health", in this section).

**Immunity**—From Illness—(See Immunity).

**Impaired Health**—(See "Bad Health" in this section. Also note the various paragraphs under Disease, Ill-Health, Sickness).

**Improved**—Improved State of the Health—The Health Promoted—The ☉, ☽, or Asc. afflicted, but well-asp. by the benefics; the ☽ in ♉ or ♋, and well-asp.; the ☽ to the P. Dec. ♃; the ☽ combust, and sepr. from ☌ the ☉, and ♃ aspect the place in any way, the health will improve, but the eyes are generally left weak and out of order; ♃ or ♀ well-asp. in the 6th H.; the mundane ✱ of ♃ or ♀ to the M.C.; the favorable asps. of the benefics to the hyleg. (See "Better" under Disease; "Increased" under Vitality; Better, Enhanced, Good, in this section).

**Impure Blood**—Ill-Health From—(See "Blood" in this section).

**Indicators of Health**—Significators of Health—The ☉, ☽, Asc., planets in the 1st H., or just above the Asc.; planets in the 6th H., and the ruler of the 6th, their signs, aspects, etc.; lord of the 6th, or the strongest or most afflicted planet in the 6th; also the M.C., the Midheaven, and how aspected at B., and by dir., and planets in the 10th H. at B. (See "Significators" under Disease, Form; "Judging the Health", and the Introduction to this Article).

**Indifferent State**—Of the Health—The ☽ to the ☌ or ill-asps. ♆, indifference of mind to life's duties; the Asc. to the □ or ☍ ♃ by dir., often due to plethora. (See Apathy, Careless, Dull, Indifferent, Indisposition; "Periods of Bad Health" in this section).

**Indisposition; Infancy**—The Health In—(See Infancy).

**Infirm; Infirmities; Injury**—To the Health—The Health Menaced—Planets in their signs of detriment or fall tend to injure the health when they are the afflictors in the disease; the ☉ affl. by ♄; the ☽ affl. by ♂. (See the Introduction, Bad Health, and the various paragraphs in this Article).

**Invalidism; Judging the Health**—Rules For—(1) The rising sign is the first to be considered, whether strong or weak, and the aspects to the degree ascending, and judge accordingly. (2) Consider the ☉, its sign and strength, the aspects to the ☉, and whether or not the ☉ is hyleg. (3) Consider the ☽, her sign and aspects, and whether strong or weak, or hyleg. These are the three sensitive points in the map, the ☉, ☽, and Asc., and govern the constitution, physical strength, and functions, and the constitutional powers, the vitality, stamina, the regularity or irregularity of the functions, and the general health, depend upon these three vital centers. (4) Consider next the planets in the 6th and 8th H., and whether they afflict any of these three vital centers, as the parts of the body ruled by the signs in which planets are posited will tend to be disordered according to the nature of the afflicting planet. (5) If no planets in the 6th H., then consider the sign on the cusp of the 6th, as the part of the body ruled by such sign will tend to be a center of physical disturbance, and the part of the body so affected will be a center, or seat from which many other disorders may arise. (See "Indicators" in this section).

**Liable**—To Ill-Health—(See "Ill-Health All Thru Life" under Ill-Health; "Slow" under Recuperation; "Low" under Resistance, Vitality; Sickly; "Body" under Weak). For influences which tend to make the native less liable to Disease or Ill-Health, see "Good Health" in this section; Immunity; "Good" under Constitution, Resistance, Vitality).

**Little Sickness**—(See Abundance, Good Health, Immunity, in this section).

**Location**—Residence—The Health As Affected by Location—(See Altitude, Abroad, Foreign Lands (see Foreign); Location, Native Land (see Native); Place of Birth (see Place); Residence; "Health" under Travel).

**Long Life**—(See Life).

**Loss of Health**—Loss of Strength—The ☉ in a weak sign at B., and afflicted; ♄ affl. in ♒; afflictions to ♃; ♀ □ or ☍ ♂, due to sex excesses unless controlled; ♀ in ♏, ☌ the ☽ or ♂, thru sex excesses. (See Asthenia, Bad Health, Periods of Bad Health, Undermined, and the various paragraphs in this section).

**Lust**—Bad Health thru Inordinate Lust—(See Lust).

**Malaise; Males**—The Health of—(See Males).

**Malnutrition**—(See Nutrition).

**Marriage Partner**—The Health of (See Marriage Partner).

**Medicines**—Ill-Health from the Use of —The Use of Medicines In Restoring Health—(See Drugs, Medicines, Narcotics, Poisons, Remedies, Treatment).

**Men**—The Health of—(See Brother, Father, Grandfather, Males, Men, Uncles).

**Menaced**—The Health Menaced—(See "Injury" in this section).

**Middle Life**—The Health In—(See Middle Life).

**Mind**—Disorders of—The Health and Peace of the Mind—(See the various paragraphs under Intellect, Mental, Mind).

**Morbid Fears**—About the Health—(See "Morbid" under Fears; Hypochondria, Morbid).

**Mother**—The Health of—(See Mother).

**Much Sickness**—(See "Many Diseases" under Disease; "Much Sickness" under Sickness).

**Narcotics; Nerves**—Disorders of—Health Affected By—(See Nerves).

**Obsessions**—Health Disordered By—(See Obsessions, Spirit Controls).

**Old Age**—Health In—(See Old Age).

**Opposite Sex**—The Health Injured Thru—(See Opposite).

**Passion**—The Health Injured by Passional Excesses—(See Amorous, Excesses, Lust, Passion, Sex).

**Peace of Mind**—The Health Benefitted By—(See Contentment, Happiness; "Peace of Mind" under Mind).

**People**—The Health of the People—(See "Common People" in this section).

**Periodic Diseases**—(See Periodic).

**Periods of Bad Health**—The Health Suffers—The Adverse Influences of Directions, Progressions, and Transits over the Health, etc.—Of course, the degree of suffering which may come to the native at these times will depend upon his knowledge, wisdom, self-control, spiritual understanding, etc. We are taught that we must conquer the Monsters of the Zodiac, to walk the gauntlet of the Zodiacal influences undaunted, and to not be affected by them, but at this stage of human evolution there are only a few who can do it successfully, such as the Masters, the Initiates, the Adepts, etc. The influence of ♄, for instance, in his lower vibrations, is to chastise, afflict, bring suffering and death upon all those who are living in sin, evil, and wickedness, but to those who have conquered, ♄ is our best friend, our Protector, and he is the Bridge over which we pass from this Earth Plane to higher states of spiritual consciousness. So, in considering the following influences, remember they apply only to those who are drifting in life, who are unawakened, unregenerated, and who have not as yet discovered themselves, their real mission and place in life, and who may be classed as "Misfits", failures to a large extent so far in life. A study of the Occult and Metaphysical books which we already have, and to know the plan of the Universe, why we are here, where we came from, and where we go from here, will help us all to be better Masters of our Destiny, and a good book for us all to digest is "The Tarot of the Bohemians", by Papus. Also the books, "The Key to the Universe", and "The Key of Destiny", by Dr. and Mrs. Homer Curtiss; Wilde's Chaldean Astrology, and many others. The following planetary influences tend to Periods of Bad Health—The SUN to the ☌ or ill-asp. ♄ by dir., and the ☉ hyleg at B., and with danger of a fatal illness; the ☉ to the ☌ or ill-asp. the ☽ by dir., and the ☽ hyeg and affl.; directions of the ☉ affect the health if the ☉ be hyleg, and also the father; the ☉ to the □ or ☍ ♃ or ♀ by dir.; the ☉ affl. at B., and ☌ the Asc. by dir.; the ☉ to the ☌ or ill-asp. the ☽ and the direction falling in the 8th H., and espec. if the ☉ or ☽ rule the 8th at B., and be afflicted radically by ♄ or ♂; the ☉ to the cusp the 6th, 7th, or 8th H.; the ☉ to his own ill-asps. by dir., according to the sign the ☉ is in, and in which the aspect falls; the ☉ by dir. to the ill-asps. the ☽, Asc., or M.C., or to his own place; the ☉ to the bad asps. ☿ by dir., and espec. by the □ aspect, if ☿ also be affl. at B.; the ☉ hyleg, and the ☉ to the ☌, P., □ or ☍ any of the malefics by dir.; the ☉ in the 6th or 8th H. at B., and to the ☌ or ill-asp. ♄ by dir.; the ☉ or ☽ occupying the 6th

H. by dir., and espec. if the ☉ and ☽ were in evil asp. to each other at B., or either occupied the 6th H.; adverse asps. of the ☉ to ♆, ♅, ♄, or ♂ by dir., and espec. among the aged and those of frail constitution; the Prog. ☉ to the ☌, P., □ or ☍ the ☽, ♄, the Asc., or any malefic; the Prog. ☉ to the □ or ☍ ♃ or ♀; the ☉ directed to Antares and all stars of the nature of ♂ and ☿ combined; the ☉ hyleg, and to the ☌ or P. Dec. Regulus; the ☉ by Periodic Rev. to the ill-asps. the radical ☽; the ☉ □ or ☍ ♄ at a Solar Rev. presignifies illness; the ☉ hyleg, and ♅ ☌ or P. the ☉ at a Solar Rev., ill-health of a peculiar nature; cross aspects to the ☉ by Promittors or Non-Promittors when the horoscope is an unfortunate one; when several aspects of non-promittor malefics are formed to the ☉ simultaneously, then considerable ill-heath usually follows; a total eclipse of the ☉ falling on the place of the ☉ at B., or a malefic, and espec. when the ☉ is badly affl. at B., or by dir.; the MOON to the ☌, P., □ or ☍ the ☉, Asc., or any malefic by dir., and more so if the ☽ be badly affl. at B.; the directions of the ☽, if the ☽ be hyleg, affect the health, both mentally and physically, and also affect the family affairs, the mother, sister, or wife; the ☽ or Asc. receiving evil asps. by dir. tend to adversely affect the health whether the ☽ is hyleg or not, but when the ☽ is hyleg or within 5 degrees of a hylegiacal place, evil directions to her tend to greatly endanger the health; the ☽ to the ☌ or ill-asp. ♄ by dir., and espec. if the direction fall in the 6th H.; the ☽ in the 6th H. at B., and to the ☌, P., or ill-asp. any of the malefics by dir.; the ☽ to the ☌ or ill-asp. ♂ by dir., diseases according to the sign ♂ is in; the ☽ affl. at B., and to the ☌ or ill-asp. ♀, usually from indiscretions and excesses; the ☽ affl. the rising degree or the Asc. by dir.; the ☽ affl. at B., and to the cusp of the 6th, 8th, or 12th H.; in Hor'y Q. the ☽ Sig. in ♑ indicates bad health of the party, a thin, weak, and small body; the ☽ Sig. ☌ the ☉ by dir., and espec. if the ☽ be applying, and it happens in the 8th H., or the ☉ be lord of the 8th; the ☽ to the ☌ the ☉ by dir., and espec. if in ☌ or ill-asp. the ☉ at B., and either occupied the 6th H.; the prog. ☽ to the □ or ☍ the ☉, ♃, ♀, the Asc., or to the ☌ or ill-asp. any of the malefics; the prog. ☽ to the ☌ or ill-asp. ♂, and espec. with females; the prog. ☽ to the ☌ or ill-asp. ♆, and espec. if ♆ be affl. at B.; the ☽ by periodic rev. to the ☌ or ill-asp. ♄ or ♂; the ☽ passing over the place of ♄, ♂, or ♀ at a Solar Rev., and these planets affl. at B.; the ☽ to the place of Ceti, Rigel, or Hercules; the ☽ to the ☌ or P. South Scale or Regulus if the ☽ be hyleg; NEPTUNE ☌ or P., the ☉ at a Solar Rev. if the ☉ be hyleg; ♆ passing the place of the radical ☽ by tr., or in ☌ the ☽ at a Solar Rev.; ♆ or ♅ in evil asp. the ☉ or ☽ by dir.; ♆, ♅, or any malefic falling in the 6th H. by dir., and affl. the hyleg; ♅ affl. at B., and to the ☌ or ill-asp. the Asc. by dir.; the ill-asps. of ♅ to the ☉ by dir.; URANUS by periodic rev. to the ☌ ♄ or ♂ radical; SATURN ☌ or ill-asp. the ☉, ☽, Asc., or hyleg by dir.; ♄ ruler of the 6th H. at B., and in ☌ or evil asp. the Asc. by dir.; ♄ ori. of the ☉ at B., and in ill-asp. the Asc. by dir., and the Asc. be hyleg at B.; ♄ to the ill-asps. his own place by dir. or tr., or to the place of the ☉, ☽, or any planet; ♄ ruler of the 6th H. at B., and the M.C. to the ☌ or ill-asp. ♄ by dir.; ♄ ruler of the 6th H. at B., and to the ☌ or ill-asp. the Asc. by dir.; ♄ to the ill-asps. ♃ or ♀; ♄ to the ☌ or ill-asp. the ☉ or ☽ if the ☉ or ☽ are hyleg, or either ruler of the 1st, 6th, 8th, or 12th H.; ♄ ☌, □, or ☍ the ☉ at B., and when ♄ comes to the next evil asp. the ☉ by dir.; the prog. ♄ in ☌ or ill-asp. the ☉, ☽, ♃, ♀, ☿, or the Asc.; ♄ by tr. in the 1st, 6th, 8th, or 12th H.; transits of ♄ over the Asc., M.C., or the places of the ☉ and ☽ at B., and espec. if ♄ affl. the ☉ or ☽ at B., or the Asc. or M.C.; transits of ♄, ♅, or ♂ coming to the evil asps. the progressed places of the ☉ or ☽, and espec. if these aspects coincide with an evil dir.; the tr. of ♄ or other malefics thru the 6th H. if in the 6th at B., and afflicted, or afflicting the 6th, or lord of the 6th; ♄, ♅, or ♂ on the cusp of the 6th or 7th H. at B., and such degrees ascending at a Solar Rev.; ♄ at a Solar Rev. ☌ or P. asp. the radical ☉ if the ☉ be hyleg; ♄ passing over the place of the radical ☽ by tr., or in ☌ the ☽ at a Solar Rev.; ♄ passing over the place of ☿ at B., if ☿ be weak and afflicted, or ♄ ☌ ☿ at a Solar Rev.; the periodic directions of ♄ to the radical ☉, and espec. if the ☉ be hyleg; JUPITER ruler of the 1st H. at B., and to the ill-asps. ♄ by dir.; ♃ by periodic rev. to the ill-asps. the ☉ or ♂ at B.; the bad asps. of ♃ and ♀ to the prog. places of the ☉ or ☽; ♃ or ♀ prog. in □ or ☍ asp. the Asc.; bad asps. of the progressed ♃ or ♀ to the places of the radical ☉ or ☽; MARS to the cusp of the 1st, 6th, 8th, or 12th H.; ♂ to the ☌ or ill-asps. ♄ by dir.; ♂ to the place of ☋; ♂ ☌ the Asc. by dir.; ♂ to the ☌ or ill-asp. the ☽ or ♀, and generally thru abuses or debauchery; ♂ by periodic rev. to the evil asps. ♅; ♂ rising at B., and again at a Solar Rev.; ♂ on the cusp of the 6th or 7th H. at B., and such degree ascending at a Solar Rev.; ♂ at a Solar Rev. passing the place of the radical ☽, ♄, or ♀, and espec. if the ☽ and ♀ were affl. at B.; the tr. of ♂ as promittor over the place of the ☉ or ☽ at B., or in ☍ thereto; VENUS affl. at B., and to the ☌, P., or evil asp. the Asc. by dir.; ♀ Sig. to the ☌ the ☉, and the ☉ ill-dig. at B., tends to become unhealthy; the bad asps. of the prog. ♀ to the places of the prog. ☉ or ☽; ♀ prog. to the ☌ or ill-asps. ♄; ♀ by periodic rev. to the ill-asps. ♄, ♂, the ☽, or M.C. in the map of birth; MERCURY affl. at B., and to the ill-asps. the ☽; the ASCENDANT meeting the bad directions of planets; evil directions falling in the Asc.; directions of the Asc. affect the health if the Asc. is hyleg; the Asc. to the evil asps. ♃ by dir., and diseases according to the sign in which ♃ is placed; malefics in the Asc., or 1st H., at a Solar Rev.; the Asc. by dir. to the ☌ or ill-asps. ♅; the Asc. to the place of ☋ by dir.; transit of the ruler of the 1st H., or Asc., when a malefic, over the radical M.C., or ruler of the M.C.; the Asc. by dir. to the evil asps. the ☉ or ☽; the Asc. to the ☌ the ☉ by dir.; the Asc. to the ☌, P., □ or ☍ any of the malefics; the Asc. to the □ or ☍ ♀, ill-health thru excesses, pleasures, etc.; the directions to or by the Asc. are more powerful for good or evil when the Asc. is hyleg at B.; the Asc. to the ☌ or ill-asp. ♂ by dir., sickness of the nature of ♂ and the sign he is in, considered with that of the Asc.; a malefic ☌ the Asc. by dir.; the MIDHEAVEN to the ☌ or evil-asp. the ☽ by dir., and espec. if the ☽ be affl. at B., afflicted in both mind and body; malefics ☌ the M.C. by dir., according to the nature of the malefic and the sign on the M.C.; lord of the 10th a malefic, and falling in the 6th or 8th H. by dir.; lord of the 10th a malefic, and to the ☌ the ☉, ☽, Asc., or hyleg; MALEFICS by tr. over the place of the ☉ or ☽ at B. if they afflict the Lights in the radical map; ill-asps. of the malefics to the ☉ by dir., or by tr., even tho they do not afflict the ☉ at B.; a malefic by dir. or tr. falling on the place of another malefic, evil for the health, and according to the sign occupied, and the nature of the conjoined planets; malefics in the 1st or 6th H. at a Solar Rev.; the tr. of malefics thru the 6th H. if in the 6th at B., or lord of the 6th; a train of evil DIRECTIONS affl. the hyleg, and with little assistance from the benefics, and death may result; a train of good directions, if accompanied by a very evil dir. to the hyleg at the same time, may cause ill-health; an evil dir. to the hyleg signifies illness; an evil dir. falling in the Asc. or 6th H. usually affects the health adversely, and espec. if a malefic. (See "Bad Health" in this section; "Periods Of" under Acute; Directions; "Threatened with Disease", "Time of the Disease", under Disease; Events; "Signs of Ill-Health" under Ill-Health).

**Periods of Good Health**—The influences at birth, and along thru life, which tend to Good Health—(See "Good Health" in this section).

**Pestilence; Pleasure**—The Health Injured by Excessive and Inordinate Pleasures — (See Excesses, Lust, Passion, Pleasure, Sports, etc.).

**Plethora; Poor Health** — (See "Bad Health" in this section. Also see Chronic, Emaciated, Feeble, Ill-Health, Infirm, Invalid, Sickly, Sickness, Wastings; "Body" under Weak, etc.).

**Premature** — Premature Ill-Health — Short Life— (See "Early Death" under Early; "Short Life" under Life; "Dies Before Middle Life" under Middle Life).

**Promoted** — The Health Promoted — (See Better, Enhanced, Improved, Strengthened, in this section).

**Prospects**—Of Good Health and Long Life—The prospects of good health and long life are based upon the positions of the ☉ and ☽ at B., the hyleg and its aspects, the ☉ hyleg in a male nativity, and the ☽ hyleg in the female, and with many good asps. to the ☉, ☽, Asc., or hyleg. (See Hyleg, Immunity; "Long Life" under Life; Vitality Good. Also see Abundance, Good Health, in this section). For Prospects and Indications along the lines of ill-health see "Bad Health" in this section; Ill-Health, Invalids; "Much Sickness" under Sickness; Vitality Low; "Weak Body" under Weak.

**Public Health**—(See Epidemics; Pestilence, Prevalent; "Health" under Public).

**Rarely Good**—The Health Rarely Good —Rarely Bad—(See "Ill-Health All thru Life" under Ill-Health; Bad Health, Good Health, Improved, Promoted, Prospects, and the various paragraphs in this section).

**Recuperative Powers**—(See Recuperation).

**Relatives** — Health of — (See Aunts, Brothers, Children, Daughter, Family, Father, Grandparents, Husband, Mother, Relatives, Sister, Son, Uncles).

**Residence**—The Effect of the Location and Residence upon the Health—(See "Location" in this section).

**Resistance**—The Powers of Resistance Against Disease—(See Resistance).

**Restoratives** — Of Health — (See Analeptics, Cure, Diet, Drugs, Food, Healers, Medicines, Remedies, Tonics, Treatment, etc.).

**Robust Health**—(See Robust, Ruddy, Strong, Vitality Good. Also see "Good Health" in this section).

**Ruddy; Rugged Health**—(See Robust, Ruddy).

**Rules**—For Judging the Health—(See "Judging the Health" in this section).

**Seven Year Periods** — Danger of Ill-Health Every Seven Years—The ☽ affl. by ♄ at B. tends to ill-health every seven years, due to the new evil asps. formed between them; the □ and ☍ of ♄ to his own place by transit occurs about every seven years, tending to ill-health, and which may become chronic for a time. (See Periods).

**Short Life**—(See "Death" under Childhood, Children, Infancy; "Early Death" under Early; "Short" under Life; Untimely).

**Sickly; Sickness** — (See the various paragraphs under Disease, Ill-Health, Sickness. Also see the various paragraphs in this section).

**Significators**—Of Health—(See "Indicators" in this section).

**Signs** — Signs of Bad Health — Signs of Good Health—Signs of Death—Signs of Long and Short Life, etc.—(See Bad Health, Good Health, and the various paragraphs in this section. Also see Death, Disease, Ill-Health, Life, Sickness, etc.).

**Sister**—Health of—(See Sister).

**Sixth House**—The House of Health—(See Sixth, Virgo).

**Son** — Health of — (See "First Born", "Sons", under Children; Males, Sons).

**Sound Body** — Sound Constitution — Sound Mind In a Sound Body — (See "Good Health" in this section; "Good" under Constitution; "Sound Mind" under Mind; Sound).

**Specialties** — Health Specialties — Makers of — (See "Specialties" under Healers).

**Stamina**—(See Endurance, Recuperation, Resistance, Stamina, Strength, Tone, Vitality, etc.).

**State of the Health**—The 6th H. and the ♍ sign, and the influences in each, indicate the state of the health in the ordinary course of human life. Also the ☉ and ☽, their sign, house positions and aspects, have much to do with the state of the health, and when the Lights are strong, dignified, well-placed, and free from affliction, the constitution is strong and better able to resist disease. The ☉ rising tends to a better state of health. The Lights, when afflicted, or afflicting each other at B., tend to more frequent sickness and to poorer health. (See Bad, Enhanced, Good, Improved, Strengthened, Weakened, and the various paragraphs in this section).

**Strength**— Loss of—Much Strength— (See "Loss Of", and the various paragraphs in this section. Also see the various subjects under Strength, Strong, Vitality, Weak).

**Strengthened** — The Health Strengthened—♂ in aspect to the ☉ tends to strengthen the system, and give greater vitality. (See Abundance, Enhanced, Improved, in this section. Also see "Increased" under Strength, Vitality).

**Strong Body** — (See "Body" under Strong).

**Stronger**—The health is stronger when the ☉ is elevated above the Earth, and well-aspected in a day nativity, and also when the ☽ is above the horizon in a night nativity, as the ☉ rules by day, and the ☽ by night; the ☉ rising and elevated in the East at B., and espec. when in his own sign ♌; fiery or airy signs upon the Asc. (See Day, Good Health, Improved, Night, Strengthened, in this section).

**Suffers**—The Health Suffers—(See Bad Health, Impaired, Opposite Sex, Weak, Weakened, in this section).

**System Disordered**—(See "Bad Health", and the various paragraphs in this section. Also see "Disordered" under System).

**Tendency** — To Ill-Health—(See "Bad Health" in this section. Also see Tendency" under Disease, Ill-Health).

**Tolerably Healthy** — Tolerably Good Health—♀ well-aspected in the 6th H. if the health is not abused by excesses and indiscretions; the ☽ angular, and the Lights nearly free from affliction; ♑, ♒, or ♓ on the Asc., or the ☉ or ☽ in these signs, the Winter signs. (See "Medium Vitality" under Vitality).

**Tone** — (See Stamina, Tone, Vitality).

**Transits** — The Effects of upon the Health—(See Transits).

**Travel** — Traveling for the Health — Where To Go—If the 9th H. of the radical map shows favorable conditions for Foreign Travel, travel Abroad in those Countries ruled by the Signs in which you have ♃ or ♀ at B., unless these planets are badly aspected. If short journeys are taken, and the 3rd H. at B. is well-aspected and fortunate, travel in the directions in which you have the benefics at B., if they are well-aspected. Much travel will be apt to be engaged in for the health when ☿ is affl. in the 6th H. at B. (See Location; "Native Land" under Land; Residence; "Health" under Travel).

**Uncertain Health**—The ☽ affl. in the 6th H.

**Uncles**—Health of—(See Uncles).

**Undermined**—The Health Undermined and Injured by Abuses, Debauchery, Dissipation, Excesses, Extravagance, High Living, Sex Excesses, etc.—♂ to the ☌ or ill-asp. the ☽ or ♀; ♀ affl. in the 2nd, 5th, or 6th H.; ♀ in ♏ ☌ ♂ or the ☽, and generally thru sex excesses; ☿ affl. in the 6th H., from over-study or over-work. (See Debauchery, Depraved, Dissipation, Drink, Excesses, Extravagance, Feasting, Gluttony, High Living (see High); Passion, Pleasures, Plethora, Reading, Sex Excesses (see Sex); Sports, Study, Surfeits, Venery).

**Unfortunate** — As to Health and In General — (See Fate; "Ill-Health All Thru Life" under Ill-Health; "Much Sickness" under Sickness; Unfortunate. Also see "Bad Health" in this section).

**Unhealthy** — (See Feeble, Infirm, Invalids, Pale, Sickly, Vitality Low; "Body" under Weak. Also see "Bad Health", and the various paragraphs in this section).

**Venery**—Bad Health Thru—(See Venery).

**Virgo Sign**—The Sign of Health—(See Virgo. Also see "State of the Health" in this section).

**Vital Forces** — Depletion of — (See Vital).

**Vitality**—(See the various paragraphs under Vitality).

**Wards Off Disease**—(See "Wards Off" under Disease).

**Weak Body** — Weak Health — (See Sickly, Vitality Low; "Body" under Weak; "Bad Health" in this section).

**Weakened** — The Health Weakened — The Health Weaker—(See "Short Life" under Life; "Lessened" under Vitality; "Weakened", "Weaker" under Weak. Also see Bad Health, Impaired, Enfeebled, Undermined, and the various paragraphs in this section).

**Wife**—The Health of—(See Husband, Wife).

**Will Improve** — The Health Will Improve — (See "Improved" in this section).

**Women** — The Health of — (See Females, Mother, Opposite Sex, Sister, Women).

**Worries** — Is Worried and Anxious About the Health—♆ affl. in the 6th H. (See Hypochondria).

**Worry** — Ill-Health Thru Worry — ☿ affl. in the 6th H. (See Dejected, Depressed, Despondency; Low Spirits (see Low); Melancholy, Worry, etc.).

**Worse**—The Health Worse—The Disease Turns for the Worse — (See Chronic, Crises; "Worse" under Disease; Worse. Also see Bad Health, Undermined, Weakened, in this section).

**Worst Position**—For the Health—The ☉ ☌ ♄ in the 6th H., or in □ or ☍ with either in this house, is one of the worst positions and aspects at B. for the health. (See "Ill-Health All Thru Life" under Ill-Health; "Much Sickness" under Sickness; Vitality Low; "Body" under Weak).

**Years** — Good and Bad Years for the Public Health—(See Public).

**Youth**—Health In—(See Youth). For other subjects concerning the health, and which may not be listed in this Article, look for the subject in the alphabetical arrangement.

**HEALTHY**—Strong—Robust—Ruddy—

**Appearance** — Healthy Appearance — (See "Good", "Red", under Complexion; Robust, Ruddy, etc.).

**Body** — Healthy Body — (See Robust, Ruddy, Strong, Vitality Good. Also see "Abundance", "Good Health", under Health).

**Children** — Healthy Children — (See "Healthy" under Children).

**Constitution**—A Healthy Constitution —(See "Good", and the various paragraphs under Constitution; Robust, Ruddy, Strong, etc.).

**Healthy Make**—Strong, Robust, Plump, and Well-Set—A Healthy Make—♒ on the Asc. at B. (See Well-Made).

**Healthy and Strong** — Fire Signs on the Asc. at B.; ♒ on the Asc. (See "Body" under Strong; Vitality Good).

**Tolerably Healthy**—(See "Tolerably" under Health).

**Year**—A Healthy Year for the People — (See "Public Health Good" under Public).

**Unhealthy**—(See Sickly, Unhealthy).

**HEARING**—The Sense of Hearing—The Hearing is ruled by ☿, the ♊ sign, and the 12th H. The sense vibrations are ruled by ☿. Also ☿ rules the speech. The ♊ sign, ruled by ☿, corresponds to the atmospheric vibrations, and has affinity with the sense of hearing. In the Hindu System of Astrology the Hearing is ruled by the 3rd H. The Hebrew letter Vau, which letter is connected with the ♉ sign, is predominant in Mind and Hearing, and is also closely related to the transformation of thought into speech. The Ears are the organs of Hearing, and the Ears have special affinity with ☿ and the ♉ sign. The 12th H., and its conditions at B., tend to especially affect the hearing, as this house is closely connected with the Senses, and limitations upon them, and in cases of deafness, ☿ and the 12th H., are usually badly afflicted. In our system of Astrology the 1st H. also rules and affects the ears, and the ♈ sign also has some influence over the ears and hearing, as ♈ rules the head. The hearing of the right ear is more especially affected by ♄, and that of the left ear by ♂. (See the various paragraphs under Ears). In this Article the Hearing, its condition, defects, impediments, deafness, etc., will be considered.

**Acute**—The Hearing Very Acute—☿ in ♊, ♎, or ♒, and well-aspected by ♂.

The hearing becomes less and less acute by the clogging of the Auditory Nerve. (See "Auditory" in this section).

**Auditory Nerve** — Clogging of — This nerve, and the organs of hearing, and the sense of hearing in general, are ruled by ☿. Clogging and inhibition of the Auditory Nerve are due to mineral deposits by ♄, and espec. when ☿ is affl. in the 12th H., and the hearing becomes less and less acute; Subs at AT and AX.

**Blood**—Deafness Due to Ill-Blood In the Veins of the Ears, or Congestion In the Blood Vessels—♃ influence; ♃ in ♈, and affl. by ♄. (See Circulation, Deafness, in this section).

**Bones of the Ears**—Deafness Due to Hardening of—♄ influence; ♄ affl. in ♈. (See "Deafness" in this section).

**Born Deaf**—Born Deaf, Dumb, Imbecile, Blind and Lame—Case—See "Arundel", No. 159, in 1001 N.N. Being born deaf is due to prenatal afflictions, as a rule. Natal aspects and conditions also may concur, as ♄ affl. in ♈ or ♉ at B.; ♄ ☌ ☿ in ♈ in the 12th H. (See Congenital, Prenatal; "Deaf and Dumb" in this section).

**Catarrh**—Deafness From—Catarrhal Deafness—♄ affl. in ♉; ♄ affl. in ♉ in the 12th H.; ♄ affl. in ♈. (See Catarrh, Eustachian).

**Circulation Obstructed** — Causing Deafness—♃ in ♈, and affl. by ♄; ♀ in the 12th H., and affl. by ♄, ☿ or ♂, the venous circulation in the ears obstructed, tending to deafness. (See "Blood" in this section).

**Clogging** — Of the Auditory Nerve — Deafness From — (See "Auditory" in this section).

**Colds or Chills** — Deafness From — ♄ affl. in ♈. (See Colds).

**Congestion of Blood** — In the Ears — Deafness From — (See Blood, Circulation, in this section).

**Danger To the Hearing**—☿ affl. in the 12th H. tends to bring dangers to the ears and the sense of hearing, and denotes a limitation upon the Spirit in its manifestation thru the senses on the material plane of life. (See "Disordered" under Ears; Limitations, Twelfth House).

**Deafness**—Liable to Deafness—Debility of Hearing—Impediment In the Hearing—The ☉ ☌ ☿ in the 12th H. in ♊ or ♍, and affl. by malefics; the ☉, ♀, and ☿ in ☌ in ♓ in the 12th H., and affl. by ♄, ♅, or ♂; the ☉ or ☽ in ☌ with ☿ in any part of the map, and affl. by ♄ or ♂; the ☽ decr. in light, sepr. from ♄ and apply. to ☿; the ☽ incr. in a day nativity, sepr. from ☿ and apply. to ♄; the ☽ sepr. from ☿ and apply. to the ☉; the ☽ ☌ ☿ in the 12th H., and affl. by ♄ or ♂; ♄ afflictions tend to; ♄ in the houses or terms of ☿; ♄ □ or ☍ ☿, and espec. if ☿ be lord of the 6th or 12th H.; ♄ tends to deafness by hardening of the bones of the ears, and interfering with vibration; ♄ afflictions tend to deafness by deposits of minerals along the auditory nerve, clogging this nerve and stopping vibration; ♄ occi. in ♈ and affl. the ☉, ☽, or Asc.; signified by

♄ in ♈ when he is the afflictor in the disease; ♄ in the 6th H., and afflicting ☿; ♄ in the 12th H. in ☌ or ill-asp. ☿; ♄ affl. the hyleg or Asc.; ♄ in ♑, thru colds or chills; ♄, ♅, or ♆ in ♒ and affl. the ☉ or ☽, slight deafness; ♄ affl. in ♒; ♄ in ♉; ♆ or ♅ in ♑ or ♒, and affl. the ☉, ☽, or ☿; ♅ in the 12th H. ☌ ☿; ♃ in ♈ and affl. by ♄, due to congestion in the blood vessels, or ill blood in the head and ears, but mostly of a slight and temporary nature; ♂ in ♈ and affl. ☿, and both ♂ and ☿ affl. by ♄, and espec. when the 12th H. is also concerned in the configuration; ♀ in the 12th H. in the terms of ☿, and affl. by ♄, ♂, or ☿, the venous circulation in the ear is obstructed; ☿ affl. in ♈, ♉, ♏, or ♓; ☿ affl. in ♉ in the 12th H.; ☿ weak and affl. at B.; ☿ ☌ the ☉ in the 12th H., and affl. by malefics; afflictions to ☿ in ♓, the 12th sign; ☿ affl. in the 12th H., or combust the ☉, congestion in the ears may follow, and with lack of nerve force and the vital fluids to the ears; ☿ affl. in the 12th H.; ☿ in the 12th H. in ☌ ♆ and in □ or ☍ ♃, tends to poor circulation in the ears; ☿ in the 12th H., and affl. by ♄; ☿ in the 12th H., and espec. in earthy or watery signs, and affl. by ♅, ♄, or ♂; ☿ ruling the 12th H., and in ☌ the ☉, or affl. by ♅, ♄, or ♂, or with ☿ in the 12th and so afflicted (☿ ruling the intellect is thus held in bondage thru the 12th H. influence); ☿ in the 5th H. in ♋, ♏, or ♓, in the map of a parent or of the child, the infant may be deaf, insane, or deformed; ☿ lord of the 6th H., and affl. by ♄; ☿ lord of the 6th or 12th, and ☿ posited in the 6th; ☿ in a sign of ♄, and in the 10th or 12th H., and affl. by ♄, ♅, or ♂; in deafness ☿ is nearly always afflicted by a malefic, and is usually in the 12th H.; afflictions in the ♍ sign are also quite common and conspicuous in deafness, and espec. with ♍ upon the Asc., the 6th or 12th H.; ♊ or ♍ on the cusp of the 12th H., and with ☿ affl. in any part of the map. Cases—See Fig. 7, 8, 30, 31, in "Message of the Stars", and Fig. 17C, in "Astro-Diagnosis", books by the Heindels. (See "Deaf and Dumb", and the various paragraphs in this section).

**Deaf and Dumb**—Deaf Mute—This condition is caused by a combination of the influences which cause deafness and inability of speech, and as ☿ rules both the hearing and the speech, this planet is usually heavily afflicted either during gestation, or at birth. The 12th H., the house of limitations, is also strongly involved. The following planetary influences tend to produce this double affliction,—☿ is usually afflicted by ♄ or ♂, and also the 12th H. is involved; ☿ ruler of the Asc., and affl. in the 12th H.; ♄ and ♂ ☌ ☿ in the 12th H., and espec. when in ♈; malefics and afflictions in the mute signs ♋, ♏, or ♓. This affliction, when congenital, may be caused by afflictions to the ☽ and ☿ at the time of the monthly return of the ☽ to the central line of impulse during gestation, and the planetary positions at B. may not enter into its causes at all. Also the map for the time of conception may give some clue to the disorder, and the conditions over the 12th H. and ☿ at conception, and a study [illegible] the Prenatal Epoch should be made in [illegible]. There is also an Occult [illegible] back of these cases, as involved in the doctrine of Karma, the Laws of Cause and Effect, of Consequence, of [illegible]ity, and as taught in Theosophy and Rosicrucianism, and it would be [illegible] for the advanced student to read the Chapter on "The Law of Consequence" in the book "Cosmo-Conception" by Max Heindel. Also read [illegible] on "Prenatal Abnormalities" [illegible] the book "The Prenatal Epoch" by [illegible] H. Bailey. Cases—Birth Data [illegible] of Deaf and Dumb—(1) Jan. [illegible], 10:55 P.M., London, Eng. [illegible] See "Arundel", No. 159, and "Deaf and Dumb", No. 166, in 1001 N.N. (See Congenital, Defects, Deformities, [illegible], Imbecility, Limitations, [illegible], Mutes, Prenatal, Speech, Twelfth House, Born Deaf, Deafness; Deaf, Dumb and Blind; Deaf, Dumb and Idiot, in this section).

**Deaf, Dumb and Blind**—Caused by the combined influences which [illegible] Deafness, Dumbness, and Blindness, and with such configurations [illegible] during the prenatal life, and [illegible] may also be concerred in [illegible] birth in congenital cases of this kind. May also be caused, or concurred in, when the ☉ or ☽ are in ☌ Nebulous [illegible] at B., such as the Hyades, Pleiades, [illegible]. Many afflictions in and to [illegible] at B. or during gestation, would tend to such extreme limitations [illegible] senses and physical organism, as such a Stellium in the 12th H., [illegible] and malefics in the 12th H., [illegible] sibly in ♓ in the 12th, as ♓ is also the 12th sign, and the sign of [illegible] sorrows, etc. Also if Nebulous Stars be there with the [illegible] in the 12th [illegible] at the time, the sight would be [illegible] endangered, and the blindness [illegible]. (See "Born Blind", "Deaf and Dumb", in this section).

**Deaf, Dumb and Idiot**—In idiocy [illegible] also the principal planet to be considered, and also the 12th H., the house of limitations, and idiocy [illegible] only another of the physical [illegible] tal limitations which can be added [illegible] deafness, dumbness, blindness, [illegible]cility, etc., at B. Case—See "Deaf and Dumb", No. 166 in 1001 N.N. [illegible] Born Jan. 27, 1906, 3:50 [illegible] 2 deg. W. Died Jan. 16, 19[illegible]. (See Idiots, Mutes; Deafness, [illegible] Dumb, in this section).

**Deaf, Dumb, Blind and Lame**—[illegible] Lameness afflictions to [illegible] important part, and afflictions [illegible] 12th H., which house corresponds [illegible] the 12th sign ♓, and which may [illegible] in serious disability to the [illegible] and feet, causing lameness. Such [illegible] tions, combined with those [illegible] Blindness, Deafness, Mutes, [illegible] cause such a combination of [illegible] nate limitations. Case—See [illegible] No. 159 in 1001 N.N. (See [illegible] under Blindness; [illegible] Lameness; Born [illegible] in this section).

**Debility of Hearing**—[illegible] and the various [illegible] section).

**Defective Hearing**—(See the various paragraphs in this section; "Defects" under Ears).

**Delusions**—Of Hearing—Hallucinations of—A ♆ disease and affliction; ♆ affl. in ♈; ♆ ☌ or ill-asp. ☿, and espec. in the 12th H.; a ♄ disease, and caused by the afflictions of ♄ to ☿. (See Clairaudience, Delirium, Delusions, Hallucinations, Illusions, Paranoia).

**Destroyed**—The Hearing Destroyed On One Side—Case—Run Over and Skull Fractured at Five Years of Age—See "Run Over", No. 853, in 1001 N.N. (See Deafness, Loss Of, and the various paragraphs in this section).

**Dulling**—Of the Sense of Hearing—(See Auditory Nerve, Deafness, Slight, in this section).

**Dumb and Deaf**—(See "Deaf and Dumb" in this section; Mutes).

**Ears**—(See the various paragraphs under Ears).

**Eustachian Tubes**—The Hearing Impeded Thru Disorders of—(See Eustachian).

**Fever**—The Hearing Affected Thru High Fevers, as in Delirium, the Hearing of Voices, etc.—(See the influences under Delirium; "High Fevers" under Fever; "Delusions" in this section).

**Gestation**—The Hearing Affected During—Born Deaf, etc.—(See Born Deaf, Deaf and Dumb, in this section).

**Hallucinations**—Of Hearing—(See Delusions, Fever, in this section).

**Hardening of Bones**—Of the Ears—Deafness Due To—(See "Bones" in this section).

**Hears Voices**—(See Delusions, Fever, Voices, in this section).

**High Fevers**—Disturbances of the Hearing By—(See "Fever" in this section).

**Idiot**—Born Deaf, Dumb, and Idiot—(See "Deaf, Dumb, and Idiot" in this section).

**Ill-Blood**—In the Veins of the Ears—Deafness From—(See "Blood" in this section).

**Imbecility**—Case—Born Deaf, Dumb, and Imbecile—(See "Born Deaf" in this section).

**Impediment**—In the Hearing—(See "Deafness", and the various paragraphs in this section; Impediments).

**Infancy**—Deafness In—(See "Deformed" under Infancy).

**Inhibition**—Of the Hearing and Auditory Nerve—(See Auditory, Bones, Deafness, in this section; Inhibitions).

**Insanity**—And the Hearing—The same ♆ influences which are involved in Insanity, and also in Epilepsy, are also listed as causes of Deafness, and the delusions of Hearing in Insanity, the hearing of voices, are usually caused by an afflicted ♆, and also where the 12th H. is afflicted at the same time, or ♆ affl. by ♄ and ♂. (See Delusions, Hallucinations; "Causes" under Insanity).

**Left Ear**—The left ear is ruled by ♂, and the afflictions of ♂ to ☿ tend to deafness and impediments in this ear. (See "Left Ear" under Ears; "Ears" under Left; "Right Ear" in this section).

**Liable to Deafness**—Tendency To—Danger of—(See Danger To, Deafness, and the various paragraphs in this section).

**Limitations**—Upon the Senses, and Upon the Hearing—(See Limitations, Twelfth House; Auditory, Bones, Impediment, Inhibition, and the various paragraphs in this section).

**Loss of Hearing**—Case—See Fig. 7 in the book, "Message of the Stars" by Max Heindel. (See Deafness, Destroyed, and the various paragraphs in this section).

**Malformations**—In the Ears—Deafness Due To—♄ affl. in ♈. Also may be due to prenatal influences. (See Defects; "Defects" under Ears; Malformations; Bones, Deafness, Deaf and Dumb, in this section).

**Monstrosities**—Defective Births—Congenital Deformities—(See Monstrosities; Born Deaf; Deaf and Dumb; Deaf, Dumb and Blind, in this section).

**Mutes**—A Deaf Mute—(See "Deaf and Dumb" in this section; Mutes).

**Nerves**—The Auditory Nerves Affected—(See "Auditory" in this section).

**Obstructed**—The Circulation In the Ears Obstructed—The Auditory Nerve Clogged—Deafness From—(See Auditory, Blood, Circulation, Impediment, Inhibition, in this section).

**One Ear**—Loss of Hearing In One Ear—On One Side—The afflictions of ♄ tend especially to deafness in the right ear, and the afflictions of ♂ to loss of hearing in the left ear. Case—Hearing Destroyed in One Ear—See Destroyed, Left, Right, in this section).

**Paranoia**—The Hearing Affected In—The same influences which tend to Paranoia also tend to affect the hearing, and cause delusions of hearing. (See Paranoia; Delusions, Voices, in this section).

**Partial Deafness**—Slight—Temporary—♆ affl. in ♈, and resulting from an abscess in the frontal sinuses; ♆ in ♈ and affl. by the ☉, ♄, or ♂; ♆ in ♈ or ♉ in ☌ ♄; ♄ affl. in ♉; ♄, ♆, or ♅ in ♒, and affl. the ☉ or ☽, slight deafness; ☿ in ♑, ☌, □, or ☍ ♄, and espec. when in a cardinal sign. (See Left, Right, in this section).

**Prenatal Epoch**—Many causes of Deafness may arise during gestation, or the Prenatal Period. For a general study along this line see Congenital, Defects, Deformities, Malformations, Monstrosities, Prenatal. Also see Deafness, Deaf and Dumb, in this section).

**Right Ear**—Ruled by ♄, and the ♄ afflictions to ☿, the Asc., and the 12th H. tend to deafness and defects in the right ear. (See "Ear" under Right; "Left" in this section).

**Sense of Hearing**—Dulling of—(See "Dulling" in this section).

**Slight Deafness**—(See "Partial" in this section).

**Speech**—And the Hearing—Both are ruled by ☿. (See the Introduction, and "Deaf and Dumb" in this section; Speech).

**Temporary Deafness**—(See "Partial" in this section).

**Tendency**—To Deafness—(See Danger, Deafness, and the various paragraphs in this section).

**Twelfth House**—The Effect of Upon the Hearing—(See the Introduction, Deafness, and the various paragraphs in this Article).

**Vibration**—Vibration In the Ear Stopped, Tending to Deafness—(See Auditory, Bones, Deafness, in this section; Vibration).

**Vital Fluids**—Lack of In the Ears—Deafness From—(See the ☿ influences under "Deafness" in this section; "Circulation" under Ears).

**Voices**—Hears Voices—This may be due to highly developed clairvoyant and clairaudient faculties, and also to planetary afflictions causing disturbances in the vibratory apparatus of the ears, and may be caused by the afflictions of ♆ or ♄ in the ♈ or ♉ signs, and also with the 12th H. badly afflicted, and also ☿ involved in the configuration. (See Delusions, Fever, Vibration, in this section; Clairvoyance, Clairaudience, Insanity, Mediumship, Neptune, Obsessions, Spirit Controls).

**Weak Hearing**—Weak Ears—The ☉, ☽, and ☿ in ☌, and affl. by ♄ or ♂; ☿ affl. in the 12th H. (See the various paragraphs under Ears, Weak).

**HEART**—The Heart—Cardia—Cardiac—The Heart is ruled by the ☉, the ♌ sign, and the 5th H. Is under the internal rulership of ♌. All the fixed signs, as ♉, ♌, ♏, and ♒ tend to affect and influence the heart and its action for good or ill, as these signs make up the Fixed Cross, and all are in □ or ☍ asp. to each other. The ☉ in ♌ rules the structure of the heart. The ☽ in ♌, the functions of the heart, and the pericardium; ♆ in ♌, the depressor nerve; ♅ in ♌, the valves; ♄ in ♌, the left auricle and the endocardium; ♃ in ♌, the arteries and right auricle; ♂ in ♌, the muscles; ♀ in ♌, the veins and aorta; ☿ in ♌, the nerves. The left ventricle and the arterial blood are ruled and influenced by ♃, and ♀ rules the right ventricle and the venous blood. The ventricles are also ruled by ♌ in a general way, and the valves by ♅. The heart in the male is ruled by the ☉, and in the female is strongly influenced by the ☽, her aspects, and espec. when the ☽ is in ♌ at B., or in a fixed sign. The ☉ and ☽ acting thru the ♌ sign, and thru the Splanchnic Ganglia, tend to affect the Cardia, the Heart, the 5th, 6th, 7th, 8th, and 9th dorsal vertebrae, the upper part of the stomach, and give way to the Cardiac Diathesis. (See Cardiac). In Hor'y Q. the heart is signified by planets in the following signs—the ☉ in ♏ or ♐; the ☽ in ♎ or ♏; ♄ in ♉ or ♊; ♃ in ♈, ♋, or ♓; ♂ in ♌, ♒, or ♓; ♀ in ♌, ♍, ♑, or ♒; ☿ in ♍, ♎, ♐, ♑, or ♒. (See Table in Chap. XXIX, page 179, in Lilly's Astrology, showing the signification of each of the planets in the 12 Signs). The ♃ Group of Herbs tend to have a pathological action on the cardiac muscle. The therapeutic properties of ☉ remedies are cardiac, and affect the heart action. The following subjects have to do with the heart, its structure, action, functions, diseases, etc., which subjects see in the alphabetical arrangement when not considered here—

**Accelerated Action**—Rapid Pulse—High Pulse—The ☉ ☌ or ill-asp. ♂; the ☽ in ♈ or ♊, and affl. by the ☉ or ♂ when taken ill; the ☽ in ♉, ☌, □, or ☍ ♄ (or ☿ if he be of the nature of ♄) when taken ill, or at decumb., and occasioned by surfeits, high living, etc. (See "High" under Pulse).

**Action of the Heart**—Good Heart Action—The Action Disturbed—(See the various paragraphs in this section).

**Affected**—The fixed signs, and espec. the ♌ sign, tend to affect the heart. The heart is affected when the ☉ is in ♌, ♏, and fixed signs; the ☽ in ♎; ♅ in ♊; ♄ in ♉; ♃ in ♋ or ♓; ♀ in ♌, ♍, or ♒; ☿ in ♍, ♎, or ♒. This is according to the plan as given in Table 196 in Simmonite's Arcana. For explanation of the Table see "Affected" under Head. The heart is also affected by any planet in ♌, and afflicted, and also when ♌, or a fixed sign, may be upon the Asc. at B., and afflicted. (See the various paragraphs in this section).

**Afflicted**—Affliction At the Heart—The Heart Afflicted—The ☉ or ☽ affl. in ♌ or ♒; afflictions in ♌ or ♒, and the fixed signs. (See "Heart Trouble", and the various paragraphs in this section).

**All Diseases**—Of the Heart—Are signified by ♌ and the 5th H., and afflictions therein.

**Aneurysm**—Of the Aorta—♂ affl. in ♌. (See Aneurysm, Aorta).

**Angina**—Angina Pectoris—Pain and Oppression About the Heart—(See Angina).

**Aorta**—Diseases of—Aneurysm—(See Aneurysm, Aorta).

**Arteries**—Of the Heart—Disorders of—♃ affl. in ♌. (See Aneurysm, Aorta, Arteries).

**Arythmia Cordis**—(See "Rhythm" in this section).

**Asthma**—(See "Heart Asthma" under Asthma).

**Atrophy Of**—♄ affl. in ♌. (See Atrophy).

**Auricles**—Auricular Disorders—♃ affl. in ♌ tends to disorders of the right auricle; ♄ in ♌, the left auricle, and also to organic auricular weakness. (See "Organic" in this section).

**Blood Obstructions**—Obstruction of the Blood Thru the Heart—♅ affl. in ♌, thru valvular trouble; ♄ affl. in ♌, due to organic heart weakness, muscular weakness, poor circulation, etc.; ♄ ☌ ♃ or ♀ in ♌. (See "Obstructions" under Blood; "Poor Circulation" under Circulation; Obstructions; Arteries, Fever, Leaky, Valves, Veins, in this section). For Spasmodic Gushing of the Blood thru the Aorta, see Aorta.

**Blood Vessels**—Of the Heart—(See Aneurysm, Aorta, Arteries, Auricles, Blood, Veins, in this section).

**Bradycardia**—Abnormally Slow Action of the Heart—Slow Pulse—(See "Slow" under Pulse).

**Broken Heart**—Dies of a Broken Heart—(See Broken).

**Cardiac**—Cardiac Diathesis—Cardiac Disease—Cardiac Dropsy—Cardiac Inhibitions—Cardiac Orifice—Cardiac Sedatives—(See Cardiac; Diathesis, Dropsy, Heart Trouble, Inhibitions, Orifice, Sedatives, and the various paragraphs in this section).

**Cardialgia**—(See Angina, Heartburn, Pain, in this section).

**Carditis**—Inflammation of the Heart—The ☽ or ♂ affl. in ♌. (See Endocarditis, Inflamed, Pericarditis, in this section).

**Cases of Heart Trouble**—Birth Data, etc.—See "Heart Disease", No. 082, and No. 104, in 1001 N.N. See Figures 5A, 5B, 5C, 5D, 5E, in the book "Astro-Diagnosis" by the Heindels. See Figures 19, 24, 25, 33, in "Message of the Stars", by the Heindels. See Case, Male, Chap. 8, page 48, in Daath's Medical Astrology. (See all the paragraphs in this section for the various forms and manifestations of heart trouble).

**Chronic Disease**—Of the Heart—The ☉ hyleg, and to the ☌ or ill-asp. ♄ by dir.; ♄ affl. in ♌. (See "Chronic" under Back; Chronic, Stomach).

**Circulation**—The Circulation Thru the Heart Disturbed—(See "Blood" in this section; "Poor Circulation" under Circulation).

**Constrictions**—(See Constrictions; "Orifice" in this section).

**Contractions**—(See Orifice, Valves, in this section; Constrictions, Contractions).

**Coronary Plexuses**—(See Coronary; "Middle Cervical" under Ganglion).

**Cramps**—In the Heart—♅ in ♌. (See Cramps).

**Cyanosis**—Due to Heart Trouble—Incomplete Heart—(See the Case under Cyanosis; "Incomplete" in this section).

**Death**—From Heart Trouble, or Heart Failure—Fixed signs dispose to; fixed signs on angles, and many planets in fixed signs at B.; many afflictions in fixed signs, and espec. in ♌ and ♒; ♃ much afflicted at B., and affl. the hyleg by dir., tends to death from heart failure. (See Death).

**Debility**—Of the Heart—(See Heart Trouble, Weak, and the various paragraphs in this section).

**Deformity**—Of the Heart—(See Incomplete, Malformation, in this section).

**Degeneration**—(See "Fatty" in this section).

**Depleted Action**—Weak Heart—♄ in ♌. (See Feeble, Impeded, Weak, in this section).

**Depressor Nerves**—Of the Heart—Ruled and affected by ♆ in ♌. (See "Nerves" in this section).

**Deranged Heart**—(See "Heart Trouble", and the various paragraphs in this section).

**Diet**—Ailments of the Heart Due to Wrong Diet—♃ affl. in ♌. (See "Ailments" under Diet).

**Dilatation**—Of the Heart—Cardiectasis—The ☽, ♃, ♂, or ♀ affl. in ♌. (See Aneurysm, Aorta; "Dilatation" under Arteries; "Too Much Blood" under Blood; Dilatations, Distentions).

**Disease**—Heart Disease—Diseases—(See "Heart Trouble", and the various paragraphs in this section).

**Disorders Of**—(See "Heart Trouble", and the various paragraphs in this section).

**Displacement Of**—(See "Right Side" in this section).

**Distention Of**—(See "Dilatation" in this section).

**Disturbed Action**—♅ ☌ ☽ in ♋, and □ ♂ tends to disturbed heart action from gas in the stomach. (See Affected, Heart Trouble, Irregular, Rapid, Rhythm, Suspended, Weak, and the various paragraphs in this section).

**Dorsal Region**—The Dorsal Region of the Spine, and the Middle Dorsal Nerves, are ruled by the ☉ and ♌, and afflictions in ♌ tend to affect this region, the back, and the heart, and also to cause Subs of the Dorsal Vertebrae. (See Back, Dorsal, Spine).

**Dropsy**—Of the Heart—Dropsy from Heart Trouble—Dropsy from Weak Heart Action—An ♒ disease, and many planets affl. in ♒ at B.; the ☉ in ♒ in ☌, P., or ill-asp. ♄; ♆ affl. in ♎ or ♓ in the 6th H., or affl. the Asc., or hyleg; Subs at HP, Lu.P., KP. (See Dropsy; Blood, Weak, in this section).

**Drought**—♌ ascending at the Vernal Equi., tends to Drought, and suffering from heart disorders among People in Countries ruled by ♌. (See "Disease" under Drought).

**Drug Heart**—♆ affl. in ♌ tends to suspension of the heart action thru drugs, sleeping potions, opiates, and narcotics; ♆ in the 5th H., or on cusp the 5th, or in ☍ thereto. (See "Drug Habit" under Narcotics).

**Drugs**—Herbs—The Action of on the Heart—The therapeutic properties of ☉ remedies are cardiac, and affect the heart action. The ♃ Group of Herbs tend to have a pathological action on the cardiac muscle. (See "Jupiter Group", "Sun Group", under Herbs; "Typical Drugs" under Jupiter, Sun. Also see "Remedies" in this section).

**Endocarditis**—♄ in ♌ rules and affects the endocardium; ♂ affl. in ♌; ♂ in ♋ in the 5th H. (See Carditis, Pericarditis, in this section).

**Enlarged Heart**—Hypertrophy of—♆ in ♌ and affl. by ♄; ♅ affl. in ♌; ♃ influence tends to an enlarged heart by the formation of fat and adipose tissue; ♃, ♂, or ♀ affl. in ♌; ♂ in ♌, and affl. the hyleg; ♂ in ♌ in the 6th H. tends espec. to hypertrophy of the heart; Subs at HP. Case—Of Enlarged Heart—See "Hypertrophied", No. 082, in 1001 N.N. (See Enlarged, Expansions, Hypertrophy).

**Excesses**—Palpitation, and Disturbed Heart Action Thru Excesses—♀ affl. in ♌. (See Excesses; "Palpitation" in this section).

**Excitement**—Palpitation Due to Haste and Excitement—The ☽ in a fire sign at B., and espec. in ♌. (See Excitable, Hasty; "Palpitation" in this section).

**Exhaustion**—Of the Heart—♄ affl. in ♌; afflictions in ♌. (See "Weak" in this section).

**Failure**—Heart Failure—(See Death, Exhaustion, Faintings, Feeble, Heart Failure, Heart Trouble, Weak, in this section. See Fig. 24 in "Message of the Stars" by the Heindels).

**Faintings**—At the Heart—Syncope—Swoonings—The ☽ in ♌ or ♒, ☌, □, or ☍ ♄ (or ☿ if he be of the nature of ♄) at the beginning of an illness, or at decumb., and death often occurs when the ☽ comes to the exact ☍ of ♄ (Hor'y); the ☽ in ♈, and afflicted under similar conditions, tends to a weak pulse; ♅ affl. in ♌ or ♒. (See Faintings; "Weak Pulse" under Pulse; "Weak Heart" in this section).

**Fatty Degeneration**—Of the Heart—Fatty Heart—A ♃ disease; ♃ affl. in ♌ or the 5th H.; ♃ in ♌ and affl. by ♂ tends to this disease; Subs at HP, Lu.P., and KP. (See Degeneration, Fat; "Enlarged" in this section).

**Feeble**—The Heart Action Feeble—Slow and Weak Pulse—(See "Feeble" under Pulse; Depleted, Impeded, Morbid, Weak, in this section).

**Fever**—Fever from Obstructions Near the Heart and Lungs—The Heart and Lungs Oppressed—The ☽ in ♉, ☌, □, or ☍ ♄ (or ☿ if he be of the nature of ♄) at the beginning of an illness or at decumb. (Hor'y). This is usually occasioned by surfeits, high living, etc., and if the ☽ be not supported by benefics there is danger of death within 14 days. (See "High Living" under High; "Fever" under Lungs; Obstructions, Surfeits).

**Fifth House**—This house rules the heart, along with ♌, the 5th sign, and the ☉, the ruler of ♌. Afflictions in this house tend to disturb the heart. (See Fifth House; "Heart Trouble", and the various paragraphs in this section).

**Fluttering**—Of the Heart—(See Rapid, Spasm, in this section).

**Functions**—Of the Heart—The ☽ in ♌ rules the functions of the heart, and the ☽ affl. in ♌ tends to irregular and disturbed heart functions. (See Functions; "Heart Trouble", and the various paragraphs in this section).

**Gases**—The Heart Disturbed by the Pressure of Stomach Gases and a Distended Stomach—(See "Disturbed" in this section).

**Good Heart Action**—The ☉, ☽, ♃, or ♀ in ♌, and free from affliction, and also with no malefics in or afflicting the 5th H., the cusp of the 5th, or ruler of the 5th.

**Gout**—In the Heart—♄ in ♌. (See "Heart" under Gout, Rheumatism).

**Grief In**—The Heart Afflicted by Grief, Debility, and Weakness—♄ in ♌ when ♄ is the afflictor in the disease; ♄ in ♌ and affl. the ☽. (See "Weak", and the various paragraphs in this section).

**Gushing of Blood**—Thru the Aorta—(See Aorta).

**Haste**—Palpitation from Haste and Excitement—(See Excitement, Palpitation, in this section).

**Heartburn**—A Burning Sensation at the Epigastrium and Lower Part of the Chest—Pain In and About the Heart—Cardialgia—A ♋ and ♌ disease; a Stellium in ♌ or the 5th H., and espec. many planets in the 5th H. in a fixed sign; a ♀ disease, and caused by afflictions to ♀; the ☽ in ♌, ☌, □, or ☍ ♄ (or ☿ if he be of the nature of ♄) at the beginning of an illness or at decumb. (Hor'y). (See Angina, Belching, Paraesthesia; "Burning" under Sensations; "Pain" in this section).

**Heart Failure**—The ☉ in ♌ or ♒, and affl. by ♄; ♄ or the ☽ affl. in ♌; many planets in ♌ or ♒; ♂ affl. in ♒. (See Death, Exhaustion, Faintings, Feeble, Heart Trouble, Weak, in this section).

**Heart Trouble**—Heart Disease—Disturbed Heart Action—The Heart Distempered—The ☉ gives; the ☉ affl. in ♉, ♌, ♏, ♐, or ♒; the ☉ affl. in ♏ tends to heart trouble of a violent or inflammatory nature; the ☉ affl. in the 5th H.; the ☉, the ruler of the heart, ☌ ☋, or a malefic in ♌ in any part of the map; the ☉ ☌ ♀ in ♌, and also affl. by the ☽ and ♄; the ☉ □ or ☍ the Asc.; the ☉ affl. in ♉, thru rich foods, gormandizing, and surfeits; the ☉ or ☽ in the 6th H. in fixed signs and afflicted; the ☉ ☌ ♄ in fixed signs at B., and espec. if the ☉ or ☽ be affl. by ♅ or ♂; the ☉, ☽, and planets in ♉, and other fixed signs, and afflicting the ♌ sign or the hyleg; the ☉ affl. in ♌, danger of organic heart trouble; the ☽ affl. in ♌, or affl. the hyleg therefrom; the ☽ in ♉, ♌, ♎, ♏, or ♒, in ☌ or ill-asp. any of the malefics as promittors; the ☽ in ♌ on the M.C., and afflicted by malefics; the ☽ ☌ ♄ or ♂ in ♌; ♆ or ♅ in ♌ or ♏, and affl. the ☉ or ☽; ♅ affl. in ♌; ♅ in ♌ on the Asc., and affl. by the □ or ☍ ♂; ♄ affl. in ♌ or ♒; ♄ in ♌, occi., and affl. the ☉, ☽, Asc., or hyleg; ♄ ☌ ☽ in ♌; ♄ in ♉ or ♊ signifies heart trouble in Hor'y Q.; ♄ or ♂ in the 6th H., in fixed signs, and affl. by the ☉ or ☽; ♄ in ♏ and affl. the ☉ or ☽; ♄ affl. in the 5th H.; ♄ ☌ or ill-asp. the ☉ in a fixed sign; ♃ in ♈, ♋, or ♓ in Hor'y Q.; ♃ in ♌, and affl. by ♂; ♂ in ♌, ♒, or ♓ in Hor'y Q.; ♂ in the 6th H. in a fixed sign, and affl. the ☉ or ☽; ♂ affl. in the 5th H.; ♂ affl. in ♓ when ♂ is the afflictor in the disease; ♂ in ♏, ☌, or ill-asp. the ☉; ♂ in ♉, ♌, or ♏ in the 6th H., and affl. the ☉, ☽, Asc., or hyleg; ♂ in a fixed sign at B., and affl. the hyleg; ♀ affl. in ♌ or ♒; ♀ affl. in ♌ in the 6th H.; ♀ in ♌, ♍, ♑, or ♒ in Hor'y Q.; ♀ in ♌, and affl. the ☽ or Asc.; ☿ affl. in ♌ or ♒; ☿ in ♍, ♎, ♐, ♑, or ♒, in Hor'y Q.; caused by afflictions in ♋, by distended stomach and pressure against the heart, over-indulgence of the appetite, etc.; ♉, ♊, ♌, ♎, ♏, or ♒ on the Asc.; fixed signs show when on the Asc., or cusp of 6th H., and containing afflictions; fixed signs on angles, and containing many planets in □ and ☍; the malefics, or afflicting planets, in fixed signs; malefics on the cusp the 5th H., or in exact ☍ thereto; Subs at HP, Lu.P., and KP. ♌ rising at the Vernal Equi., and afflictions in ♌ and the fixed signs, tend to an increase of, and prevalence of heart troubles and weaknesses. For the Periods and Times when heart trouble may come, be renewed or aggravated, see "Periods", "Prevalance", in this section.

**Heat**—The Heart Affected by Extreme Heat—♌ ascending at the Vernal Equi., and the ☉ afflicted. (See "Extreme Heat" under Heat; "Prevalence" in this section).

**Herbs**—The Effect of on the Heart—(See "Drugs" in this section).

**Heredity**—The Heart Affected by Hereditary Transmission—(See "Organic" in this section).

**High Living**—The Heart Affected By—(See "Fever" in this section).

**Horary Questions**—The Heart Signified In—Heart Affections Denoted In—(See the Introduction to this Article. Also note the various Horary influences in the different paragraphs in this section).

**Hypertrophy**—(See "Enlarged" in this section; Hypertrophy).

**Ill-Affected Heart**—(See "Heart Trouble", and the various paragraphs in this section).

**Impeded Action**—Slow—Suspended—Feeble—Weak—The influence of ♄ impeding the work of the Pneumogastric Nerve; a ♌ disease, and afflictions in ♌; ♄ affl. in ♌. (See Impeded; Drug Heart, Morbid, Obstructed, Slow, Stoppage, Weak, in this section).

**Incompetency**—(See Leaky, Mitral, Regurgitation, Valves, in this section).

**Incomplete**—The Partition Between the Right and Left Side of the Heart Incomplete, Resulting In Cyanosis—Case of a Male—(See the Case under Cyanosis; "Malformation" in this section).

**Incoordination**—Lack of Coordination of the Heart Action—♅ in ♋ or ♌ in the 5th H., and afflicted. (See Incoordination; "Rhythm" in this section).

**Indiscretions**—Heart Disturbances From—(See Diet, Excesses, Fever, High Living, Lacing, Narcotics, Palpitation, in this section).

**Inefficiency**—Muscular—Mitral—Valvular—♄ affl. in ♌; ♅ or ♂ affl. in ♌. (See Heart Trouble, Impeded, Mitral, and the various paragraphs in this section).

**Inflamed Heart**—Heart Trouble of a Violent or Inflammatory Nature—The ☉ affl. in ♏. (See Carditis, Endocarditis, Myocarditis, Pericarditis, in this section).

**Inhibition**—Cardiac Inhibition—♄ affl. in ♌, or in fixed signs. (See Inhibitions).

**Insufficiency**—(See Mitral, Regurgitation, Valves, in this section).

**Interrupted**—The Heart-Beat Irregular—Rhythm Interrupted—(See Incoordination, Rhythm, in this section).

**Irregular**—The Heart Action and Functions Irregular—The ☽ affl. in ♌; the Prog. ☽ ☌ the radical ♅ in ♌; ♅ affl. in ♌; ♅ in ♌ in the Asc., and in ☍ ♂ in the 7th H.; ♃ or ♀ in ♌, and in □ or ☍ H. (See Incoordination, Functions, Rhythm, Spasms, in this section).

**Jupiter Group**—Of Herbs—Action of On the Heart—(See "Drugs" in this section).

**Lacing**—Tight Lacing—Causing Palpitation—♀ in ♌. (See Lacing; "Palpitation" in this section).

**Leaky Valves**—♅ affl. in ♋ or ♌, and espec. when in the 5th H.; ♄ affl. in ♌, due to blood obstruction, accumulation, and pressure; ♄ affl. in the 5th H. (See Blood, Mitral, Regurgitation, Valves, in this section; Valves).

**Left Auricle**—(See "Auricles" in this section).

**Left Coronary Plexus**—(See "Plexus" in this section).

**Lesions**—Valvular Lesions—♅ affl. in ♋ or ♌ in the 5th H. (See Leaky, Mitral, Regurgitation, Valves, in this section).

**Lining**—Inflamed Linings of the Heart—(See "Inflamed" in this section).

**Lower Heart**—The Lower Part of the Heart Affected—Afflictions in the 3rd Decan. of ♌; Subs at Lu.P. (See "Upper" in this section. Also see Lower, Middle, Navamsa, Upper).

**Malformation Of**—Many planets in fixed signs, or in the 5th H., and afflicted; malefics conjoined in ♌ or the 5th H., and afflicted; afflictions in ♒. (See "Incomplete" in this section).

**Medicines**—And the Heart—(See Medicines, Remedies; "Drugs" in this section).

**Mitral Insufficiency**—Stenosis—Leaky Valve—Regurgitation—Inefficiency—Incompetency—A ♌ disease; ♅ or ♄ affl. in ♌; malefics in the 5th H., and afflicted; Subs at HP, Lu.P. (See Leaky, Regurgitation, Valves, in this section).

**Morbid Action**—Of the Heart—Impeded—Slow—Caused by ♃ when the dominion of death is vested in him; ♃ affl. in ♌. (See Impeded, Slow, Weak, in this section; Morbid).

**Muscular Action**—The Muscular Action Weak and Inefficient—♄ affl. in ♌. (See Inefficiency, Myocarditis, in this section).

**Myocarditis**—Inflammation of the Cardiac Muscles—♂ affl. in ♌. (See "Inflamed" in this section).

**Nails**—Blue and dark discolorations of the half-moons of the finger nails indicate heart weakness, valvular trouble, and are indicative of afflictions in ♌, malefics in ♌, or ♌ on the Asc. at B., and afflicted. (See Nails).

**Narcotic Drugs**—The Heart Action Weak, Irregular, or Suspended By—(See "Drug Heart" in this section).

**Navamsa**—The different parts of the heart are shown by the Navamsa subdivisions of the ♌ sign. Thus afflictions in the different faces and degrees of ♌ locate the part of the heart afflicted, weak, or disturbed. (See Navamsa).

**Nervous Affections**—Of the Heart—♅ in ♌ or the 5th H., and afflicted; ♅ on the cusp the 5th H., or in ☍ thereto, and afflicted; ☿ affl. in ♌. (See Angina, Depressor, Heartburn, Neuralgia, Pain, Palpitation, Spasm, in this section).

**Neuralgia Of**—☿ affl. in ♌ or ♒. (See Angina, Heartburn, Nervous, Pain, in this section).

**Obstructed** — The Heart Action Obstructed—The ☉ in ♌, ☌, □, or ☍ ♄; ♄ affl. in ♌. (See Obstructions. Also see Blood, Fever, Impeded, Inhibition, Lacing, Mitral, Regurgitation, Stoppage, Suspended, Valves, in this section).

**Opiates**—Harmful Action On the Heart —(See "Drug Heart" in this section).

**Oppression**—About the Heart—Pain and Oppression—(See Angina, Cyanosis, Fever, Heartburn, Neuralgia, Pain, in this section).

**Organic Weakness** — Of the Heart — Organic Heart Trouble—Organic Weak Heart — Structural Disorder — The Heart Affected by Hereditary Transmission—The ☉ in ♌ in ☌, □, or ☍ ♄; the ☽ in the 6th H. in fixed signs, and affl. by malefics; ♅ in ♌ and affl. by ♄; ♄ in ♌, and affl. the ☉; ♄ ☌ or ill-asp. the ☉. (See Heredity, Organic, Structural; Auricles, Incomplete, Malformation, Weak, in this section. See Fig. 3 in "Message of the Stars", by the Heindels for a Case record).

**Orifice**—Cardiac Orifice Constricted—♄ in the first degrees of ♋, or in the last degrees of ♊, and affl. by ♆. (See Constrictions, Contractions; "Valves" in this section).

**Pain In** — Cardialgia — ☉ and ♌ disease; the ☉ in ♌ and affl. by ♂; the ☽ in ♒, and affl. by the ☉ or ♂ when taken ill, and the ☽ slow in motion and decr. in light (Hor'y); the ☽ in ♓, ☌, □, or ☍ ♄ (or ☿ if he be of the nature of ♄) at the beginning of an illness or at decumb. (Hor'y); ♂ affl. in ♌; ♂ affl. in ♌ in the 5th H. (See Angina, Heartburn, Neuralgia, Oppression, in this section).

**Palpitation**—Trembling of the Heart — Passion of the Heart — Tremors — Violent Pulsation—Throbbing—Thrills —Caused by afflictions in ♌, ♒, and the 5th H.; the ☉ affl. in ♌ or ♒; the ☉ rising in ♌, and affl. by ♂; the ☉ in ♌, and affl. by ♃; the ☉ or ☽ in ♌ or ♒ in ☌ or ill-asp. any of the malefics as promittors; the ☉ affl. by ♄; the ☉ in ♌ or ♒ in the 6th H., and afflicted; the ☉ in ♌, and affl. by ♂ by dir. or progression, violent palpitation; a ☉ disease; the ☽ in ♌ or ♒ in the 5th or 6th H., and affl. by malefics; the ☽ affl. in ♏; the ☽ in a fiery sign, and espec. in ♌, due to haste and excitement; the ☽ ☌ ♂ in ♌; palpitation is best relieved when the ☽ is in decr., and in good asp. the radical ♃ or ♀, or when the transits of ♃ or ♀ are in good asp. to the radical ☽; ♆, ♅, or ♄ as promittors in ☌ or ill-asp. the ☉ or ☽ in ♌, or in the 5th or 6th H.; ♅ ☌ the ☽ in ♌; ♅ affl. in ♌ or ♒; ♅, ♆, or ♄ in ♌, and affl. the ☉ or ☽, and over-exertion and excitement should be avoided; ♄ ☌ ♃ and ♀ in ♌; ♄ ☌ ♃ and in ☍ ♀; ♃ affl. in ♌ or ♒; a ♃ disease; ♃ in ♌ or ♒, and in ☍ the Asc. by dir.; ♂ affl. in ♌ or ♒; ♂ in ♌, or afflicting planets in ♌ or ♒, tends to palpitation, as his dynamic action leads to tremors; ♂ promittor in ♒, ☌, or ill-asp. the ☉; ♂ in ♌ or ♒ in the 6th H., and afflicted; ♂ in ♌ or ♒, and affl. the ☉, ☽, or Asc.; ♀ in ♌ or the 6th H., and afflicted, or affl. the ☉, ☽, or Asc., and usually caused by tight lacing, indiscretions, or excesses of some kind; ☿ affl. in ♌ or ♒; ☿ in ♏, ☌, or ill-asp. any of the malefics as promittors; ♌ on the Asc., and afflicted; afflictions in ♋, from distended stomach and pressure against the heart; Subs at HP, Lu.P. Case—See Fig. 11A in "Astro-Diagnosis", by the Heindels. (See Passion, Spasm, in this section).

**Partition Incomplete** — (See "Incomplete" in this section).

**Passion**—Of the Heart—Trembling of —♃ in ♌ or ♒, and ☍ the Asc. by dir.; ♅ or ♂ in ♌; ☿ affl. in ♌. (See Palpitation, Spasm, in this section).

**Pathological Action**—(See "Drugs" in this section).

**Pericarditis** — Inflammation of the Pericardium — A ♊ disease, and afflictions in ♊; ♂ in ♌. The ☽ in ♌ has special rule over the functions of the heart and the pericardium, and the ☽ ☌ ♂ in ♌ tends to inflammation of the pericardium. Also caused by Subs at Lu.P. (See Carditis, Endocarditis, Inflamed, in this section; Pericardium).

**Periods of Heart Trouble**—The Times and Periods When Heart Trouble Is Apt to Come — The Directions and Transits Causing—The ☉ to the ☌ or ill-asp. ♄, or other malefics, by dir.; the ☉ in ♌ or ♒, and to the ☌ or ill-asp. ♂ by dir.; the ☉ and ♂ in fixed signs at B., and by dir., and espec. if the ☉ or ☽ be affl. by ♄ or ♂; the ☽ in ♌, and affl. by the ☉ or ♂ when taken ill (Hor'y); ♄ to the ☌ or ill-asps. the ☉ by dir.; malefics passing thru ♌ by tr. or dir., and espec. if there were malefics in ♌ at B., or affl. the ♌ sign; ♌ the prog. Asc., and containing malefics; the prog. ☉ in ☌ a malefic in the radical map, and espec. in fixed signs, and the nature of the heart disturbance may be judged according to the influence of the malefic; malefics in the 5th H. at B., and by dir. (See Heart Trouble, Prevalence, in this section).

**Plexus**—(See "Coronary" in this section; "Cardiac Plexus" under Cardiac).

**Poison**—The Heart Afflicted by Poison—♄ in ♌ when ♄ is the afflictor in the disease. (See "Gout" in this section).

**Poor Action**—Of the Heart—♆ in ♌, and affl. by ♄; ♅ or ♄ affl. in ♌; ♀ and ☿ in ♌, and affl. by the □ or ☍ ♄; Subs at HP. (See Blood Obstructions, Heart Trouble, and the various paragraphs in this section).

**Pressure Upon**—(See Pressure).

**Prevalence**—Of Heart Trouble—General—Due to influences at the Equinoxes. (See "Extreme Heat" under Heat).

**Pulse** — Rapid Pulse — Slow — (See Pulse. Also see Accelerated, Faintings, Palpitation, Rapid, Slow, Weak, in this section).

**Rapid Heart Action** — Tachycardia — ♅ affl. in ♌. (See Accelerated, Palpitation, Passion, Spasm, in this section).

**Regurgitation** — Mitral Regurgitation —Leaky Valves—Caused by afflictions in ♌; the ☉ rising in ♌ and affl. by ♄, unless strain is avoided in early years; ♅ affl. in ♒; ♅ in ♒ in the 5th H.; ♄ in ♌, due to obstruction of the blood, blood accumulation and pressure; ♄ affl. in the 5th H. (See Blood, Leaky, Mitral, Obstructions, Strain, Valves, in this section).

**Remedies** — Heart Remedies — Action of Drugs On the Heart—(In this section see Drug Heart, Drugs; the ☽ influences under Palpitation; Sedatives, Stimulants).

**Remits** — The Pulse Remits and Is Slow—(See "Slow Pulse" under Pulse; Interrupted, Irregular, Obstructed, Slow, in this section).

**Restricted** — The Heart Action Restricted — Obstructed — Sluggish — The ☉ in ♌ in ☌, □, or ☍ ♄. (See Impeded, Inhibition, Obstructed, Poor Action, Slow, Stoppage, in this section).

**Rheumatic Heart** — Rheumatism Around the Heart—♄ affl. in ♌. (See Gout, Poison, in this section).

**Rhythm** — The Rhythm Interrupted — Disturbed — Arythmia Cordis — Afflictions in ♌ or ♒; the ☽ afflicted in ♌; ♅ ☌ ☽ in ♌ or ♒; ♅ afflicted in ♌ or ♒; ♅ in ♌ in ☍ to planets in ♒; ♅ in ♌ or ♒, ☌, □, or ☍ ☿; ♅, ♄, ♂ and ☿ in fixed signs, and especially when in ♌ or ♒; ♃ and ♀ in ♌, and in □ or ☍ ♅; Subs at HP. (See Drug Heart, Incoordination, Irregular, Obstructed, Palpitation, Passion, Spasm, and the various paragraphs in this section).

**Right Side**—Of the Heart—The Heart On the Right Side—Right Auricle—Right Coronary Plexus — (See "Auricles" in this section; "Middle Cervical" under Ganglion). Case of Heart on the Right Side—See "Heart", No. 981, in 1001 N.N.

**Sedative**—Heart Sedative—(See Aconite, Sedatives; Drug Heart, Drugs, Remedies, Sleeping Potions, Tobacco, in this section).

**Sensitive**—The Heart the Most Sensitive Organ—♌ on the Asc.

**Sleeping Potions** — And Narcotics — Are harmful when ♆ is in ♌ or the 5th H. at B., and afflicted. (See Drug Heart, Tobacco, in this section).

**Slow Action** — Bradycardia — (See "Slow" under Pulse; Impeded, Morbid, Obstructed, Restricted, Stoppage, Suspended, Weak, in this section).

**Smoking** — Effect of on the Heart in Some Cases — (See "Tobacco" in this section).

**Spasm**—Spasmodic Action of the Heart —Tachycardia — Paroxysm of — Fluttering—♅ affl. in ♌ or ♒; ♅ in ♌ in ☍ to planets in ♒; ♅ ☌ ☽ in ♌, and more apt to prove fatal; ♄ in ♌ and in ☌, □, or ☍ ♅; ♀ in ♌ in □ or ☍ ♅; ☿ affl. in ♌; Subs at HP. (See Irregular, Palpitation, Passion, Rapid, Rhythm, in this section). For Spasmodic Gushing of Blood Thru the Aorta, see Aorta.

**Stenosis**—Of the Mitral Valve—(See Mitral, Regurgitation, Valves, in this section).

**Stimulants**—Heart Stimulants should be used with caution during the decr. of the ☽, and espec. if the ☽ is in evil asp. to the radical ♃ or ♀. Use heart stimulants when the ☽ is in incr., and in good asp. to the places of ♃ or ♀ at B. (See Stimulants; Drug Heart, Drugs, Remedies, in this section).

**Stomach Distention**—The Heart Disturbed By—(See "Gases" in this section).

**Stoppage** — Suspension of the Heart Action—♅ affl. in ♌; ♆ affl. in ♌, due to the action of a drug, opiate, narcotic, tobacco, etc.; ♆ in ♌, and affl. the ☉, ☽, Asc., or hyleg; ♆ affl. in the 6th H. in ♌. (See "Drug Heart" in this section).

**Strain** — Damage to the Heart from Strain or Over-Exercise—♂ on the cusp of 5th H.; ♂ affl. in ♌. (See "Regurgitation" in this section).

**Strength**—Of the Heart—The ☉ has affinity with the heart, and the strength or weakness of the heart is largely denoted by the sign position of the ☉ at B., and the aspects to the ☉.

**Structural Disorders**—(See "Organic" in this section).

**Sudden Death**—From Heart Trouble —The ☉ or ♂ in fixed signs at B., or by dir., and afflicted, and especially if the ☉ or ☽ at B. were affl. by ♄ or ♂.

**Suspension** — (See Impeded, Obstructed, Stoppage, in this section).

**Swoonings**—(See "Faintings" in this section. Also see Fainting).

**Syncope**—From Heart Trouble—(See "Faintings" in this section).

**Tachycardia** — (See "Spasm" in this section; "Troubled" under Pulse).

**Thrills** — (See "Palpitation" in this section; Spasmodic, Uranus).

**Throbbing**—(See "Palpitation" in this section; "High Pressure" under Blood).

**Tight Lacing**—Heart Disturbed By—(See "Lacing" in this section).

**Tobacco Heart**—♆ affl. in ♌ or in the 5th H. at B., and also when in ♌ or the 5th H. by dir. or tr., tends to affect the heart action adversely under the strong and persistent use of tobacco or narcotic drugs of any kind. (See "Drug Heart" in this section).

**Treatment** — (See "Remedies" in this section).

**Trembling** — Tremors — (See Palpitation, Passion, Spasm, in this section).

**Trouble** — Heart Trouble — Troubled Heart and Pulse — (See Drug Habit, Heart Trouble, and the various paragraphs in this section; "Troubled" under Pulse).

**Uncertain Action**—The ☉ in ♌ or ♒, ☌, P., □, or ☍ ♅. (See "Heart Trouble", and the various paragraphs in this section).

**Upper Part**—Of the Heart—The upper part of the heart is more affected when planets are in the 1st Dec. of ♌, and with Subs. at UHP, the 1st Dorsal;

the middle part affected with malefics and afflictions in the 2nd Decan. of ♌, and with Subs at HP, the 2nd Dorsal. (See Lower, Navamsa, in this section).

**Valves** — Valvular Trouble — Weak Valvular Action—♅ rules the valves of the heart, and ♅ affl. in ♌ tends to valvular trouble, leaky valves, mitral insufficiency, regurgitation, etc., and espec. if ♄ also afflict ♌ or the 5th H.; the ☉ rising in ♌ and affl. by ♄; ♄ affl. in ♌ or the 5th H., or affl. the lord of 5th, or cusp of 5th H. (See Leaky, Lesions, Mitral, Nails, Orifice, Regurgitation, in this section).

**Veins Of**—♀ affl. in ♌ tends to affect the veins of the heart, and the venous blood. (See Aorta).

**Ventricles** — (See the Introduction to this Article).

**Violent Inflammation** — Of the Heart —(See "Inflamed" in this section).

**Weak Heart** — Weakened Heart Action—Depleted Heart Action—Debility of the Heart—Exhaustion of—Feeble Action—Morbid Action—Afflictions in ♌ or ♒, and in the 5th H., or to the cusp of the 5th; a ☉ disease; born with the ☉ as ruler; the ☉ rising in ♌ at B., and affl. by ♄, and to the ☌ or ill-asp. ♄ by dir.; the ☽ affl. in ♌ or ♏, or affl. the hyleg therefrom; the ☽ affl. in fixed signs; ♄ on the cusp of 5th H., or in exact ☍ the cusp; ♄ affl. in ♌, organic weakness, and weak and depleted heart action; ♃ affl. in ♌; a ♌ and ♒ disease, and with afflictions in these signs; malefics in ♌ or ♒; planets in ♌ in the 5th or 6th H., and afflicted; afflictions in the 5th H., or to the cusp of 5th. (See Depleted, Exhaustion, Feeble, Heart Trouble, Impeded, Morbid, Obstructed, Organic, Weakness, Valves, and the various paragraphs in this section; "Weak Pulse" under Pulse).

**Weakness**—Of the Heart—Denoted by the sign position of the ☉ at B., and the aspects to the ☉. (See Auricles, Organic, Strength, Valves, Weak, in this section).

**Wind**—Around the Heart—☿ affl. in ♌.

**HEARTBURN**—(See this subject under Heart).

**HEAT**—Hot—Warm—Warmth—Heats—Heated—Caloric—Parched—The ☉ and ♂ are hot, denote heat, and are caloric, while ♃ and ♀ are warm. Heat and expansion in the body are produced by the positive and electric planets, the ☉, ♃, and ♂. The ☽ also reflects the heat from the ☉. A warm influence is exerted over the body by ♃ and ♀, and not a hot influence. Heat and moisture are prolific, nutritive, and benefic influences, while cold and dry are more malefic. Heat and cold are active, and masculine qualities. Dryness and Moisture are passive and feminine. The distribution of heat in the body is ruled by the ☉ and ♂. Heat predominates in the right side of the body, and cold in the left side, and espec. in males. (See Benefics, Cold, Dryness, Fire, Jupiter, Left, Malefics, Mars, Moisture; "Operations" under Nature; Right, Sun, Venus).

**Abundant Heat** — Diseases Arising from Excessive Heat—(See Excessive, Extreme, Over-Indulgence, Plenty, in this section).

**Accidents By**—(See Burns. Fire, Liquids, Scalds).

**Acids**—(See "Hot" under Acids).

**Acute Hot Diseases**—Acute Fevers—(See "Hot Diseases" under Fever).

**Adhesions** — Due to Melting and Excessive Heat—(See Adhesions).

**Air** — Hot and Dry Air — (See "Corrupt Air", "Hot and Dry", under Air; Drought, Famine, Pestilence; "Warm" under Weather; "Hot Winds" under Wind).

**All Hot Diseases**—And Inflammations —Are diseases of the ☉ and ♂, and also of the fiery signs, and espec. of ♌.

**Animal Heat** — The animal heat is ruled over by the Asc. (1) Increased—The Animal Heat Increased—♂ in good asp. the ☉ or the Asc. (2) Excess Of—♂ ☌, P., □ or ☍ Asc. (See "High Fever" under Fever). (3) Lack of—The Animal Heat Lacking in the Earlier Years —The ☉ or ☽ in ♑; ♑ on the Asc. The earthy signs are cold, and many planets in them at B. tend to lower the heat of the body, and give a cold body, and also make the native more affected by cold, and diseases arising from cold. (See "Cold Body" under Cold; "Early Years" under Early; Excessive, Heats the System, Lack Of, Over-Abundance, Plenty, in this section).

**Blasting Hot Winds**—(See "Hot Blasting Winds" under Wind; "Extreme Heat" in this section).

**Blood**—Overheated Blood—Hot Blood —Feverish Blood — (See "Overheated" under Blood).

**Body**—The Bodily Heat—Hot Bodily Temperament—(See Animal Heat, Disposition, Excessive Bodily Heat, Hot Bodily Temperament, in this section).

**Breast**—Heat In — (See "Heat" under Breast).

**Burns**—(See Burns, Fire, Scalds; "Hot Liquids" in this section).

**Buttocks** — Heats In — (See "Heats" under Buttocks).

**Center**—The Heat Center In the Spine —CP, the 5th Dorsal, is the Heat Mere, and also corresponds to the ♌ sign. To reduce fever, Chiropractors adjust this vertebra. (See "Fifth Dorsal" under Vertebrae; "Excessive Bodily Heat" in this section).

**Cholera**—(See Cholera, Epidemics).

**Climate** — (See Excessive Heat, Extreme Heat, Summers, Tropical, Warm, Weather, Winds, in this section).

**Cold and Heat**—Suffers from Extremes of Heat and Cold — Heat and Cold — The ☽ in ♐, ☌, or ill-asp. ♄ (or ☿ if he be of the nature of ♄) at the beginning of an illness, or at decumb. (Hor'y); the ☽ in ♊ and affl. by the ☉ or ♂; the ☽ affl. by ♄ or ♂ in airy signs; ♆, ♅, or ♄ in ♒, and affl. the ☉ or ☽. (For the influences of Internal Heats and Externally Cold, see "Internal Heats" in this section; Centrifugal, Centripetal).

**Danger by Heat** — Prejudice by Heat —(See Burns; "Injury by Fire" under Fire; Scalds).

**Death by Heat**—By Hot Diseases—♂ causes death of all hot diseases, high and burning fevers. Also caused by the ☉, as in sunstroke, and with the ☉ and ♂ affl. in ♈. (See "Death" under Burns; Electricity; "High Fevers" under Fever; "Death by Fire" under Fire; Lightning, Scalds; "Sunstroke" under Sun; Excessive Heat, Extreme Heat, Hot Diseases, Hot Liquids, in this section).

**Decrease**—Of the Heat In the Body— Low Caloric—(See Animal Heat, Lack Of, in this section).

**Diseases from Heat**—(See Epidemics; "Hot Eruptions" under Eruptions; Fever, Excessive Heat, Extreme Heat, Sunstroke, and the various paragraphs in this section).

**Disposition**—Hot In Disposition—(See "Choleric Temperament" under Choleric; "Hot and Dry Body" in this section).

**Distempers**—Hot Distempers—(See Blood, Hot Diseases, and the various paragraphs in this section).

**Distribution of Heat**—In the Body— Is carried on by the ☉ and ♂.

**Drought** — Suffering from Extreme Heat and Drought—(See Drought; "Extreme Heat" in this section).

**Dry and Hot Air**—(See Drought, Epidemics, Famine, Fountains, Summer; "High Temperature" under Weather; "Hot Blasting Winds" under Wind; "Extreme Heat" in this section).

**Dry and Hot Body**—(See "Hot and Dry" in this section).

**Dry and Hot Diseases**—Subject To— People born under a fiery sign, with a fiery sign upon the Asc., or the ☽ or lord of the Asc. in a fire sign, the illnesses are of a hot and dry nature; diseases of the ☉ and ♂; the ☽ in ♌, and affl. by the ☉ or ♂ when taken ill, the disease is of a hot and dry nature, and with high fever. (See "Dry Body" under Dryness; Fevers; "Fevers" under Moon; Heats, Hot Bodily Temperament, Hot Diseases, Humours, in this section).

**Epidemics**—Thru Excess of Heat— (See "Corrupt Air" under Air; Atmosphere, Cholera, Epidemics, Pestilence).

**Eruptions**—Hot Eruptions—(See "Fevers", "Hot", under Eruptions).

**Excessive Heat**—Immoderate Heat— Intemperate Heat — Diseases Arising From—The ☉ denotes when the ☉ afflicts the ☽ or Asc., as in fevers, sunstroke; caused by ♂ when the dominion of death is vested in him. (See "Extreme Heat" in this section).

**Excessive Bodily Heat**—The ☉ and ♂ are heating pathologically, and their afflictions tend to fevers and rise of temperature. The ♂ influence especially tends to focussed heat in the body, and to localized inflammation. Excess of bodily heat is given with ♈ on the Asc. at B. The Bilious Temperament is hot in quality. Subs at CP, the 5th Dorsal vertebra, the Heat

Mere, tend to excessive heat in a part, general excessive heat over the body, and with Subs also at KP to excessive heat with Rash. (See "Choleric Temperament" under Choleric; Fever, Inflammation; Animal Heat, Body, Heats, Hot Bodily Temperament, Hot Diseases, Humours, Internal, Over-Abundant, Plenty, in this section).

**External Heat**—Suffers from Much External and Internal Heat—The ☽ in ♌ ♂ or ill-asp. ♄ (or to ☿ if he be of the nature of ♄) at the beginning of an illness or at decumbiture, and they frequently die when the ☽ comes to the ☍ ♄ if no good asp. prevents it (Hor'y); ♂ in aspect to the ☉ at B., and by dir.; fiery signs upon the Asc. (See Heats, Internal Heats, in this section).

**Extreme Heat**—Violent Heat—Suffering from Extremely Hot and Dry Weather—An eclipse of the ☉ in ♈; ♄ ♂ ♂ in fiery signs; ♂ in ♊, and lord of the year at the Vernal Equinox.; ♈ ascending at a Solar or Vernal Ingress, and ♂ be afflicted, then Countries and People ruled by ♈ suffer from extreme heat and drought; ♌ ascending at the Vernal Equi., and the ☉ afflicted, ♌ people, and Countries under ♌, suffer from extreme heat, drought, pestilential air, and from diseases of the heart and brain. (See Dry and Hot Air, Excessive Heat, in this section). For Extreme Heat in the Mouth and Throat see "Heat" under Mouth, Throat. For Extreme Heat in a localized part of the body see "Excessive Bodily Heat" in this section. Also see Inflammation.

**Extremes of Heat and Cold**—Suffers From—(See "Cold and Heat" in this section).

**Eyes**—Hot Diseases In—Hot Humours In—(See "Hot Diseases" under Eyes).

**Famine**—From Extreme Heat and Drought—(See Drought, Famine, Fountains, Pestilence, Rivers, Weather, Winds).

**Fevers**—Hot Diseases—(See Fever; Hot Diseases, Overheated, in this section).

**Fiery**—Hot and Fiery Diseases— Caused by ♂. (See Burning, High, Pernicious, under Fever).

**Fire**—Injury or Death By—(See Burns, Fire).

**Flushings**—Hot Flashes—☉ diseases; the ☉ affl. by ♂; the ☉ ♂ ♂ in ♈; ♈ on the Asc. (See Flushings).

**Focussed Heat**—In the Body—♂ influence. (See Inflammation; "Excessive Bodily Heat" in this section).

**Fomentations**—Hot Fomentations— (See Emollient).

**Full of Heat**—The Body Full of Heat —(See Animal Heat, Excessive Bodily Heat, Over-Abundance, Plenty, in this section).

**Functions**—The Warmth and Expansion of the Functions—(See Electric).

**Fusions** — Resulting from Extreme Heat In a Part—(See Adhesions).

**General Excessive Heat** — (See "Excessive Bodily Heat" in this section).

**Haunches**—Heats In—(See "Heats" under Buttocks).

**Head**—Hot Diseases In—Hot Humours In—(See "Hot Diseases" under Head).

**Heart**—The Heart Affected by Extreme Heat—(See "Extreme Heat" in this section; "Heat" under Heart).

**Heat and Cold**—Suffers from Extremes Of—(See "Cold and Heat" in this section).

**Heat of the Body**—(See Animal Heat, Excessive Bodily Heat, in this section).

**Heat Prostration**—(See "Sunstroke" in this section).

**Heated Flushings**—(See "Flushings" in this section).

**Heats**—Hot Humours—♂ affl. in the sign ruling the part. (See "Heats", "Humours", under Buttocks, Eyes, Head, Hips, Reins, Thighs; Animal Heat, Excessive Bodily Heat, Heats the System, Humours, Internal Heats, in this section).

**Heats the System**—♌ influence; fiery signs on the Asc. (See Animal Heat, Heats, in this section).

**Hips and Thighs**—Heats In—(See "Heats" under Hips).

**Hot Blasting Winds**—(See "Blasting" in this section).

**Hot Bodily Temperament**—Hot Body—Hot In Disposition—This is a positive temperament. It is given by the ☉ in a fiery sign at B., or a fiery sign upon the Asc.; many planets in fiery signs at B.; ♂ strong and rising at B., or in the Asc. or M.C.; ☿ oriental at B. The Choleric, or Bilious Temperament is hot in quality. Those born in the Tropics and hot climates, born under the Southern Parallels, and who have the ☉ continually in their Zenith, and who are continually scorched by it, have a hot bodily temperament. (See Animal Heat, Dry and Hot Diseases, Excessive Bodily Heat, Hot and Dry Body, in this section).

**Hot and Dry Air**—(See "Air" in this section).

**Hot and Dry Body**—Hot and Dry Bodily Temperament—Heat and Dryness are positive. The Quadrant from the Summer Tropic to the Autumnal Equinox tends to produce a bodily temperament abounding in heat and dryness. Given by the ☉ and many planets in fiery signs at B., or with a fiery sign upon the Asc.; ♂ strong and rising at B., as in the Asc. or M.C. The ☉ and ♂ are hot and dry, and the ☉ and ♂ Groups of Planets and Herbs are hot and dry. The Choleric Temperament is hot and dry. (See "Choleric Temperament" under Choleric; "Mars Group", "Sun Group", under Herbs; "Dry and Hot Diseases", "Hot Bodily Temperament", in this section).

**Hot and Dry Diseases**—(See "Dry and Hot Diseases" in this section).

**Hot and Dry Head**—(See "Hot and Dry" under Head).

**Hot and Fiery Diseases**—(See "Fiery" in this section).

**Hot and Moist Body**—(See this subject under Moisture).

**Hot and Moist Diseases**—Hot and Moist Distempers—The ☉ or ☽ Sig. ☌ ♂ tends to putrid and hot distempers; the ☽ ☌ ♂ during the increase and First Quarter of the ☽, as the ☽ is considered hot and moist from the New ☽ to the 1st Quarter; ♃ diseases; ♃ when ori. causes heat and moisture, hot and moist diseases; ♀ causes when ori. (See "Hot and Moist" under Moisture; "Moist and Warm" in this section).

**Hot Body**—(See "Hot Bodily Temperament" in this section).

**Hot Diseases**—Hot Distempers—The ☉ directed to Aldebaran, Antares, Regulus, Deneb, Betelguese, Bellatrix, and Frons Scorpio; the ☉ or ☽ Sig. ☌ ♂, and danger of death by; caused by ♂, and the ☉ affl. by ♂; ♈ or ♌ on the Asc.; Subs at CP. (See "Overheated Blood" under Blood; Fever; "Hot Bodily Temperament" under Temperament; Dry and Hot Diseases, Heats, in this section).

**Hot Flashes**—(See "Flushings" in this section).

**Hot Humours**—♂ diseases; ♂ affl. in the sign ruling the part. (See Fevers, Heats, Hot Diseases, Humours, in this section).

**Hot Liquids**—Hot Water—Hot Fluids—Danger By—Injury or Death By—The ☉ to the ☌ or ill-asp. ♂ by dir.; the Asc. to the place of the Ascelli or Capricornus. (See Burns, Liquids, Scalds).

**Hot Signs**—Hot and Moist Signs—(See "Signs" in this section).

**Hot Weather**—(See Blasting, Excessive Heat, Extreme Heat, in this section; Drought, Epidemics, Famine, Fountains, Pestilence, Weather).

**Humours**—Hot Humours—♂ diseases. (See Heats, Hot Diseases, Hot Humours, in this section; "Heats", "Humours", under Buttocks, Eyes, Head, Hips, Loins, Thighs).

**Ilium**—Heats In—The same as for "Heats" under Buttocks.

**Immoderate Heat**—Ills Arising From—(See Excessive Heat, Extreme Heat, in this section).

**Increased Animal Heat**—(See Animal Heat, Excessive Bodily Heat, in this section).

**Inflammation**—Excessive Heat In a Part—Localized Heat—(See Inflammation; "Excessive Bodily Heat" in this section).

**Injuries by Heat**—(See Burns, Fire, Scalds; "Hot Liquids" in this section).

**Insufficient Heat**—In the System—(See Animal Heat, Lack Of, in this section).

**Intemperate Heat**—Ills Arising From—(See Dry and Hot Air, Excessive Heat, Extreme Heat, in this section).

**Internal Heat**—(See "External" in this section).

**Internal Heats**—And Externally Cold—The ☽ in ♈, □ or ☍ ♄ (or ☿ if he be of the nature of ♄) when taken ill, or at decumb. (Hor'y). (See Cold and Heat, External Heat, Heats, in this section).

**Lack of Animal Heat**—Decreased—Low Caloric—The earthy signs are cold, and these signs on the Asc., and espec. ♑, or with the ☉ or ☽, and many planets in these signs at B., tend to lack of animal heat, and espec. in the early years of life; ♄, and the ♄ sign ♑, tend to unusual coldness in the body, and to cause ills arising from cold, such as chills and internal congestions. (See "Animal Heat" in this section; "Diseases Arising from Cold" under Cold; "Congestions" under Internal).

**Left Side of Body**—Cold predominates in the left side of the body, and heat in the right side, and espec. in male nativities. (See Left, Right).

**Liquids**—Danger by Hot Liquids—(See "Hot Liquids" in this section).

**Localized Heat**—In a Part—(See "Inflammation" in this section).

**Loins**—Heats In—(See "Heats" under Buttocks, Loins).

**Low Caloric**—(See "Lack of Animal Heat" in this section).

**Melting**—Of the Tissues by Excessive Heat—(See Adhesions, Ankylosis, Coalition).

**Moist and Hot**—(1) Moist and Hot Bodily Temperament—(See "Hot and Moist" under Moisture. (2) Hot and Moist Diseases—(See "Hot and Moist Diseases" in this section).

**Moist and Warm**—(1) Moist and Warm Diseases—♆, ♃, and ♀ diseases, as these planets are warm and moist in influence. (See "Relaxation and Moisture" under Moisture). (2) Moist Warmth In Body—☽ influence, and the ☽ well-asp. by ♃ or ♀. (See "Warmth" under Moisture). (3) Moist and Warm Signs of the Zodiac—♎ and ♒. (See Moisture; "Moist and Hot" in this section).

**Mouth**—Extreme Heat In—(See "Heat" under Mouth).

**Much Heat**—(See Animal Heat, Excessive Heat, Excessive Bodily Heat, Extreme Heat, External Heat, in this section).

**Over-Abundance of Heat**—Sharp and Sudden Diseases Caused from An Over-Abundance of Animal Heat—♂ diseases; ♂ in the 6th H., and affl. the ☉ or ☽. (See Excessive Bodily Heat, Fevers, Hot Diseases, in this section).

**Over-Heated**—The Asc. to the □ or ☍ ♂ by dir., and with violent fever. (See Blood, Excessive Bodily Heat, Sunstroke, in this section).

**Parched**—Parched Air—Parched Body—(See "Parched" under Air; Fevers; Air, Excessive Bodily Heat, Extreme Heat, Hot Diseases, in this section).

**Part**—Excessive Heat In a Part—(See "Inflammation" in this section).

**Pestilential Warm Air**—(See "Pestilential Air" under Air).

**Plenty of Heat**—In the Body—The ☉, ☽, and many planets in fiery signs at B.; fiery signs on the Asc. (See Animal Heat, Excessive Bodily Heat, in this section).

**Prejudice by Heat**—(See "Injury by Fire" under Fire).

**Prostration**—By Heat—(See Excessive Heat, Sunstroke, in this section).

**Putrid Hot Diseases**—(See "Hot and Moist Diseases" in this section).

**Pyrexia**—(See Fever).

**Rashes**—Heat Rashes—♂ the afflictor in the disease; Subs at CP and KP. (See Eruptions).

**Reins**—(See "Heat" under Reins).

**Right Side of Body**—(See "Left Side" in this section).

**Scalds**—(See Scalds; "Hot Liquids" in this section).

**Searing Burns**—(See "Searing" under Burns).

**Sensations**—Heat Sensations—(See "Flushings" in this section; "Sensations" under Burning).

**Signs**—The Hot Signs—♈, ♊, ♌, ♐. The ♊, ♎ and ♒ signs are classed as moist and warm, and hot and moist.

**Stomach**—Overheated Stomach—(See "Hot" under Stomach).

**Suffering from Heat**—(See Excessive Bodily Heat, External Heat, Extreme Heat, in this section; "High Fever" under Fever; Sunstroke).

**Summers Warm**—(See Excessive Heat, Extreme Heat, in this section; Summer).

**Sunstroke**—Heat Prostration—(See "Sunstroke" under Sun; Excessive Heat; Extreme Heat, in this section).

**Super-Abundance of Heat**—In the Body and Externally—(See Animal Heat, Excessive Heat, Excessive Bodily Heat, Extreme Heat, Hot Diseases, Overheated, Sunstroke, in this section).

**Thighs**—Heats In—Hot Humours In—(See "Heats", "Hot Humours", under Hips, Thighs).

**Throat**—Extreme Heat In—(See "Heat" under Mouth, Throat).

**Tropical Heat**—In Cold Climates—(See Tropical).

**Urine Hot**—(See "Hot Urine" under Urine).

**Violent Heat**—(See "Extreme Heat" in this section; "Death" under Burns).

**Vital Heat**—(See "Heat" under Vital).

**Warm**—(1) Moist and Warm—(See "Moist and Warm" in this section. (2) Warm Pestilential Air—(See "Pestilential" under Air). (3) Warm Signs—(See "Signs" in this section). (4) Warm Summers—(See "Summers" in this section).

**Weather**—Hot Weather—Warm Weather—The ☉ ☌, or in any strong asp. to ♃, except when the ☉ is also in asp. with ♄ or ♅. (See Drought, Dry and Hot Air, Epidemics, Excessive Heat, Extreme Heat, Famine, Sunstroke, in this section).

**Winds**—Hot and Blasting Winds—(See "Blasting" in this section).

**HEAVY**—Heaviness—Dull—The afflictions of ♄ tend to deaden the Senses, and slow up the functions of the body, causing a feeling of heaviness and weight in different parts of the body, and to cause dullness, lethargy, lassitude. See the following subjects in the alphabetical arrangement when not considered here—

**Aches**—Heavy Aches and Pains—(See "Heavy Aches" under Aches).

**Affliction**—Heavy Afflictions—(See "Sad Sickness" in this section; Affliction).

**Apathy; Appearance**—Heavy Appearance—In Hor'y Q. ♄ Sig. in ♉. (See Appearance).

**Beard**—Heavy Beard—(See "Much Beard" under Beard).

**Blood**—The Blood Heavy with Wastes —(See "Foul", "Gross", under Blood; "Impure Blood" under Impure).

**Body**—Heavy Body—♏ on the Asc., a strong and heavy body. (See Corpulent, Fat, Fleshy, Giants, Large, Obesity, Stout).

**Breast**—Heaviness of the Breast—(See "Heaviness" under Breast).

**Dull**—Dull and Heavy Appearance—Dull and Heavy Mind—(See the various paragraphs under Dull; Appearance, Mind, in this section).

**Eyes**—Heavy, Dull, and Sleepy Eyes —(See Dull Eyes, Sleepy Eyes, under Eyes).

**Functions**—The Functions Dull and Heavy—(See Hindered, Retarded, Slow, under Functions).

**Gait**—Heavy Gait—(See "Heavy" under Gait).

**Hair**—Heavy Head of Hair—Heavy Beard—Much Hair On the Body—(See "Much Beard" under Beard; Abundance, Body, under Hair).

**Head**—Heavy Feeling In—The Head Heavy and Falls to One Side—(See Heaviness In, Heavy, under Head).

**Heaviness All Over Body**—The ☽ in ♌, and affl. by the ☉ or ♂ when taken ill. (Hor'y).

**Heavy Sickness**—The Sickness Heavy and Prolonged—♅ ☌ ♄ in the 6th H. (See Chronic, Grievous; "Long Diseases" under Long; Prolonged, Severe, Slow, Tedious, Wastings; "Heavy and Sad" in this section).

**Heavy and Sad Sickness**—The ☉ or ♄ in the 6th H., and in ☌, □, or ☍ each other; ♄ affl. in the 6th H. (See "Heavy Sickness" in this section).

**Inactive; Indifferent; Inertia;**

**Jaw**—Heavy Jaw—(See Chin, Jaws).

**Lassitude; Lethargy; Listless;**

**Melancholy; Mind**—The Mind Is Heavy and Dull—Habitual Drowsiness and Sleepiness—Mental Lethargy—♄ influence; ☿ affl. by ♄ at B.; ☿ in ♑ in ☌ or ill-asp. ♄; ☿ affl. by ♄ at B., and by dir.; the Asc. to the ☌ or ill-asp. ♄ by dir. (See "Mind" under Dull; "Drowsiness" under Sleep).

**Pains**—Heavy Pains—(See "Body Suffers", "Heavy", under Aches).

**Repletion; Retarded; Retentions;**

**Sad and Heavy Sickness**—(See "Heavy and Sad" in this section).

**Senses**—The Senses Heavy and Dull—(See Dull; "Dulling" under Senses; "Mind" in this section).

**Sickness**—Heavy Sickness—(See Heavy Sickness, Heavy and Sad, in this section).

**Sleepiness**—(See Drowsiness, Sleepiness, under Sleep; "Mind" in this section).

**Slow; Sluggish; Stomach**—Heaviness of—(See "Heaviness" under Stomach).

**Suppressions; Tired Feeling**—(See Apathy, Dull, Fatigue, Inactive, Inertia, Lassitude, Lethargy, Listless, Malaise, Rouse, Tired, Weariness, etc.).

**Weariness**—(See Weariness; "Tired Feeling" in this section).

**Weak**—(See "Weak Body" under Weak).

**HEBETUDE**—Dulling of the Senses and of the Intellect—(See Apathy, Dull; "Mind" under Heaviness; Lethargy; "Dulling" under Senses).

**HECTIC**—Habitual—The Hectic Fever of Phthisis—Hectic Fever—(See "Hectic Fever", "Low Fever", under Fever).

**HEELS**—Heel Bone—The Os Calcis—Ruled by ♓.

**Bruises To**—♄ affl. in ♓. (See "Accidents", "Bruises", "Hurts", under Feet).

**Disorders Of**—(See "Os Calcis" under Feet).

**Lump Growing On**—Case—(See "Lump" under Feet).

**HEIGHT OF BODY**—The position of the Nodes of the ☽ are said to partly determine the height of a person. Height is also largely influenced and determined by the Decanate rising. A tall Sign upon the Asc. at B. tends to give a tall body, and a short sign rising, a short body, etc. The planetary influences causing the various heights of the body are given under the subjects referred to in this section.

**Abnormal Growth**—(See Growth).

**Abnormally Tall**—(See Giants, Tall).

**Above Average Height**—♈, ♌, or ♐ on the Asc. at B. (See Giants, Tall).

**Above Middle Height**—The ☉ Sig. in ♊ or ♌ (Hor'y); the ☽ Sig. in ♊, ♌, ♍, ♎, or ♐ in Hor'y Q.; ♄ Sig. in ♌ or ♎; ♃ Sig. in ♊; ♃ in the Asc. at B.; ♂ rising or ori. of the ☉ at B.; ♀ Sig. in ♈, ♊, ♌, ♍, ♎, or ♐; ♀ in the Asc., or rising; ☿ ascending at B.; ☿ Sig. in ♍; ♈, ♌, ♐, or ♒ on the Asc. (See "Stature" under Middle).

**Diminished Stature**—(See Diminished, Dwarf, Growth, Mean, Medium, Middle, Short, Small).

**Low Stature**—(See Diminished, Dwarfed, Mean; "Short Body" under Short; Small).

**Mean Height**—(See Mean, Middle).

**Medium Height**—(See Mean, Medium, Middle).

**Middle Stature**—(See Middle).

**Short Body**—(See Short). For further influences along the lines of Height, see Appearance, Commanding, Contracted, Decanates, Diminished, Dwarf, Enlarged, Erect, Figure, Form, Giants, Growth, High, Large, Long, Mean, Medium, Middle, Portly, Shape, Short, Size, Small, Stature, Tall, Undersized, Weight, etc.

**HEIGHTS**—High Places—Precipices—High Buildings—

**Buildings**—Falls From—Death or Injury By—(See "Buildings" under Falls).

**Death** — By Falls from Heights or Precipices—♄ in the M.C. in ☌ or ☍ the ☉ or ♂, and espec. if in an airy sign and affl. the hyleg; malefics in the 9th H., and affl. the ☉, ☽, or hyleg, death by falls from heights during a voyage, or in Foreign travel; malefics in the 3rd H., affl. the ☉ or ☽ in airy signs, danger of on an inland, or short journey. (See "Heights" in this section; "Travel" under Falls).

**Distortions**—By Falls from Heights—(See Distortions).

**Excrescences**—By Falls from Heights —(See Excrescences).

**Heights**—High Places—Precipices—Danger of Falls From — Death or Injury By—The ☉ hyleg at B. and to the ☌ or ill-asp. ♄ by dir.; the ☽ in an airy sign, hyleg, and to the ☌ or ill-asp. ♂ by dir.; the ☽ to the ☌ or ill-asp. ♅ by dir.; ♅ or ♄ in the M.C., in ♈, ♋, ♎, or ♑, and in ☌ or ☍ the ☉ or ♂; ♅ to the ☌ or ill-asp. ♄ by dir.; ♄ in quadrupedal or tropical signs in ☌ or ☍ the ☉ or ♂, and with ♄ in the M.C.; ♄ in an airy sign ☌ or evil asp. the Asc. by dir.; ♄ and ♂ controlling the Lights, the malefics being in fixed signs and distant from each other; ♄ in the M.C. in ☌ or ☍ the ☉ or ♂, and espec. if in an airy sign and affl. the hyleg; the malefics ♄ and ♂ in the M.C., and elevated above the Luminaries; the Asc. to the ☌ or ill-asp. ♂ by dir., and ♂ in an airy sign at B.; malefics in the 3rd or 9th H., and affl. the ☉ or ☽, falls from heights during inland travel, short journeys, or on voyages and in Foreign travel; if during travel the Sigs. of travel are in the 12th H., in a fixed sign, and afflicted, there is danger of falls from heights, and with great danger of fatal injuries and death. (See "Death", and the various paragraphs in this section).

**Lameness** — By Falls from Heights — (See Distortions).

**Paralysis** — By Falls from High Places—(See Distortions).

**Travel** — Journeys — Danger of Falls from High Places During Home or Foreign Travel—(See Death, Heights, in this section; "Travel" under Falls; "Danger", "Death", under Travel).

**HELIANTHUS**—Sun Flower—A typical plant and drug of the ☉. (See "Sun Group" under Herbs; "Typical Drugs" under Sun).

**HELIOCENTRIC**—The Heliocentric System of Astrology takes the ☉ as a center, and the indications of the planets, including the Earth, in the great Zodiac around the ☉. These influences are important, and often help to explain the nature and cause of diseases and afflictions which are not clearly shown or accounted for by merely consulting the Geocentric map of birth, or the planets as they move in the Earth's Zodiac. It is well for the student of Medical Astrology to understand the Heliocentric System, and to have a Heliocentric Table of the planets for each year. Compare your star map of birth also with a Heliocentric map for your time and year of birth, and also the directions, transits, and movements of the planets during the current year, in both systems. This Book and Work is based upon the Geocentric System of Astrology, using the Earth's Zodiac. A study of the Heliocentric System would require a separate large treatise. The System of Solar Biology, as taught by Hiram Butler, of the Esoteric Brotherhood of Applegate, California, is a good System of the Heliocentric Method, and they also can furnish you with the Heliocentric Tables of Planets for any year. (See Geocentric). The Heliocentric map for the day of your birth is said to especially show the Soul, its stage of advancement, and the problems to be faced in Earth Life for further development. The Geocentric Map of Birth shows this Soul with its limitations, acting thru the prison house of the physical body, and the relation of the native to the outer and material world for an Incarnation. Some Writers also claim that the map for the time of Conception shows the Soul, the Character, and the nature of the incoming Ego, and the student of Advanced Astrology should study all three maps if he wishes to investigate the spiritual phases of the native, as well as the physical and mental. This book, however, is limited more to the planetary influences as they affect the individual in a physical body (the diseases, afflictions, and experiences he is apt to encounter in Earth life), and we cannot take the time or space to go into the various and important matters on the spiritual side of life, or out of Incarnation, as would be indicated by the Heliocentric Map for the time of birth. It is the hope of the Author, however, that such matters and study may be added to future Editions of this Volume.

**HELLEBORUS** — A typical drug of ♄. (See "Saturn Group" under Herbs; "Drugs" under Saturn).

**HELPLESSNESS**—Helpless Creature—♂ weak at B., and considerably out of power and dignity; ♃ Sig. in ♑; many planets at B. in the negative, feminine, and mutable signs of the Zodiac; mutable signs on the angles at B., and also with the ☉ and the majority of the planets setting below the western horizon, and with many also in common signs. (See Mutable, Negative).

**HEM** — For words not listed under "Hem" see "Haem".

**HEMACHROMATOSIS**—The Skin Turns Hard, Cold, Yellow, and Leathery—A ♄ disease. (See Cold, Hardening, Skin).

**HEMATEMESIS** — (See "Blood" under Vomiting).

**HEMATOSIS** — Hematopoiesis— Blood Making—Blood Formation—(See Haematopoiesis).

**HEMIANOPIA** — Blindness of One-Half of the Visual Field — (See "Hemianopia" under Sight).

**HEMIATROPHY**—Impaired Nutrition of One Side of the Body—Facial Hemiatrophy—(See Atrophy; "Atrophy" under Face).

**HEMICRANIA**—Neuralgia of Half of the Head—(See "Hemicrania" under Head).

**HEMIPLEGIA**—Paralysis In One Side of the Body—(See "Hemiplegia" under Infancy, Paralysis).

**HEMISPHERES**—(See "Cerebral Hemispheres" under Cerebral, Head).

**HEMLOCK**—Conium—A Typical Drug of ♄. (See "Saturn Group" under Herbs; "Drugs" under Saturn).

**HEMOPHILIA**—Abnormal Tendency to Hemorrhage—(See "Haemophilia" under Hemorrhage).

**HEMORRHAGE**—Loss of Blood—Flow of Blood—Effusion of Blood—Bleeding—Bloodshed—Caused by ♂; a ♂ disease and affliction; ♂ too much in evidence at B., and by dir. or tr., and worse at the full ☽; ♂ tends to the rupture of blood vessels; ♂ causes death by violent hemorrhage; ♂ affl. in any sign brings greater danger of hemorrhage in the part, or parts, ruled by such sign; ♂ □ or ☍ the ☉; ♂ in ♌, □ or ☍ the ☉; ♂ ori. at B., and affl. the hyleg by dir.; ♂ sole ruler at an eclipse; ♂ ☌ the ☉ at a Solar Rev.; both internal and external hemorrhages are denoted by ♂; the ☉ afflicted tends to; a ☉ disease; the ☉ hyleg, and the ☉ to the ☌, □, or ☍ ♂ by dir.; the ☽ to the ill-asp. ♂ by dir.; the Prog. ☽ to the ☌ or ill-asp. ♂ by dir.; ♄ in ♏, occi., and affl. the ☉, ☽, or Asc.; a ♃ disease, due to plethora of the blood vessels; ☿ sole ruler at an eclipse. (See "Loss of Blood" under Blood; "Blood" under Effusions. Also note the various paragraphs in this section).

**Abnormal Tendency To**—Haemophilia—Due to ♂ afflictions to the ☉, ☽, Asc., or hyleg; also caused indirectly by ♃ in cases of Plethora and abnormal fullness of the blood vessels; Subs at AT, CP, KP, and Local. (See "Pressure", and "Too Much Blood", under Blood; Flooding, Plethora; "Vascular Fullness" under Vascular).

**Accidents**—Injuries—Wounds—Cuts—Hemorrhages By—(See "Lesions" in this section; "Shedding" under Blood; Cuts, Effusions, Stabs, Wounds, etc.).

**Apoplexy**—Cerebral Hemorrhage—(See Apoplexy).

**Arteries**—Danger of Hemorrhage From—(See Aneurysm, Apoplexy, Arteries, Plethora; "Abnormal Tendency" in this section).

**Bleeding**—Blood Letting—(See Bleeding, Effusions; "Epistaxis" under Nose; the various paragraphs in this section).

**Blood Letting**—(See Bleeding).

**Bloodshed**—(See "Shedding" under Blood).

**Blood Vessels**—Rupture of—(See Apoplexy; "Rupture" under Vessels).

**Bloody Discharges**—(See Discharges, Flux, Spitting, in this section).

**Bowels**—Hemorrhage of—(See "Hemorrhage" under Bowels).

**Bronchial**—Broncho-Pulmonary Hemorrhage—(See "Hemorrhage" under Bronchial, Lungs).

**Cerebral Hemorrhage**—(See Apoplexy, Cerebral).

**Childbirth**—Excessive Hemorrhage At Time of—Fever or Death From—The ☽ affl. by ♂ at B., and with the ☽ hyleg, or in the 8th H. (See "Hemorrhage" under Parturition).

**Clots**—(See Clots).

**Cutis**—The Derma—Hemorrhage In—(See Purpura, Scurvy).

**Death by Hemorrhage**—Death by Loss of Blood—♂ shows; ♂ the afflicting planet in violent signs and affl. the hyleg; ♂ causes death by violent hemorrhage; ♂ in ♌ in the 8th H., and affl. by the □ or ☍ of the ☉ or ☽; the ☉ or ☽ to the ☌ or ill-asp. ♂ by dir.; afflictions in fixed signs; afflictions in ♒, as this sign rules the blood. Case—Case of Death by Internal Hemorrhage after a Miscarriage—(See "Death from Hemorrhage", No. 168, in 1001 N.N. (See "Loss Of" under Blood; Cuts, Effusions, Flooding, Stabs, Sword, Weapons, etc.).

**Diathesis**—The Hemorrhagic Diathesis—Given by the Sanguine Temperament, which is ruled by ♃ and the Airy Signs. (See Diathesis, Sanguine).

**Discharges**—Bloody Discharges—Sanguineous Discharges—Caused by ♂, the afflictions of ♂, and ♂ entering into the configuration. The discharges are more profuse at the Full ☽. (See "Bloody Discharges" under Discharges. Also note the various paragraphs in this section).

**Duels**—Hemorrhage From—(See Duels, Sword).

**Effusion of Blood**—(See "Shedding" under Blood; Effusions).

**Epistaxis**—Nose Bleed—(See "Epistaxis" under Nose).

**Expectoration of Blood**—Spitting of Blood—(See Haemoptysis).

**External Hemorrhage**—Denoted by ♂; the ☉ or ☽ to the ☌ or ill-asp. ♂ by dir., both external and internal hemorrhages may result. (See Cuts, Epistaxis, Flooding, Injuries, Menses, Stabs, Weapons, Wounds, etc.).

**Flooding Hemorrhage**—Of Women During Menses—(See "Flooding" under Menses; Miscarriage, Parturition).

**Flux**—Bloody Flux—(See Flux).

**Fracture**—Hemorrhage With—(See "Compound" under Fracture).

**Full Moon**—Bloody Discharges, or a Hemorrhage, are more profuse at the Full ☽. (See "Full Moon" under Moon).

**Haematemesis**—(See Haemoptysis; "Blood" under Vomiting).

**Haematomyelia**—Hemorrhage Into the Spinal Cord—(See "Spine" in this section).

**Haemophilia**—(See "Abnormal Tendency" in this section).

**Haemoptysis**—Spitting and Expectoration of Blood—(See Haemoptysis).

**Haemostatics**—Agents to Arrest Hemorrhage—Styptics—Astringents—(See Astringents, Haemostatics).

**Hemorrhagic Diathesis**—(See "Diathesis" in this section).

**High Blood Pressure**—As a Cause of Hemorrhage and Rupture of Blood Vessels — (See Apoplexy; "Pressure" under Blood).

**Incised Wounds** — Hemorrhage From —(See Cuts).

**Injuries**—Lesions—Loss of Blood from Accidents or Injuries—(See Accidents, Lesions, in this section; Cuts, Stabs, Weapons, etc.).

**Internal Hemorrhage** — (See Death, External, in this section).

**Kidneys** — Hemorrhage of — Renal Hemorrhage—(See "Hemorrhage" under Kidneys).

**Lesions**—Hemorrhage from Accidents, Injuries, Cuts, etc. — ♂ influence and afflictions; ♂ affl. in the 1st H. at B., and ☌ the Asc. by dir. or tr.; the ☉ or ☽ to the ☌ or ill-asp. ♂ by dir., and espec. in watery signs. (See "Loss Of", "Shedding", under Blood; Cuts, Effusions, Instruments, Sharp Instruments (see Sharp); Weapons).

**Loss of Blood**—(See "Loss Of" under Blood; "Lesions", and the various paragraphs in this section).

**Lungs**—Hemorrhage of—(See "Hemorrhage" under Bronchial, Lungs).

**Menses** — Flooding of — (See "Flooding" under Menses).

**Miscarriage** — Excessive Hemorrhage Attending—(See Miscarriage; "Death" in this section).

**Much Bloodshed**—(See "Blood" under Effusions; "Much Slaughter Everywhere" under Slaughter).

**Nose Bleed** — (See "Epistaxis" under Nose).

**Operations**—Greater Loss of Blood In — Blood Letting — Hemorrhage from the incisions of operations are greater if performed at the time of the Full ☽. (See Bleeding; "Rules For Operations" under Operations).

**Parturition**—Much Hemorrhage During—(See "Childbirth" in this section).

**Piles**—Bleeding Piles—(See Hemorrhoids).

**Plethora**—Hemorrhage Due To—(See Plethora; "Abnormal Tendency" in this section).

**Prevalent**—Effusion of Blood Prevalent—Much Bloodshed Prevalent—(See "Shedding" under Blood; "Blood" under Effusion; Shedding, Slaughter, War, etc.).

**Profuse Hemorrhage**—Hemorrhage is more profuse at the Full ☽, which is the time of high tide of the fluids of the body. (See Discharges, Effusions, Flooding, Full Moon, Violent, in this section).

**Purpura**—Hemorrhage Into the Skin —(See Purpura).

**Remedy**—To Help Stop Hemorrhage— (See "Haemostatics" in this section).

**Renal Hemorrhage** — (See "Hemorrhage" under Kidneys).

**Rupture**—Of Blood Vessels—(See Abnormal Tendency, Blood Vessels, Plethora, in this section).

**Sanguinary Discharges**—(See Bloody Discharges, Discharges, Lesions, and the various paragraphs in this section).

**Scurvy** — Hemorrhage In — (See Purpura, Scurvy).

**Sharp Instruments** — Cuts by and Hemorrhage—(See Cuts, Duels, Instruments, Sharp, Stabs, Sword, Weapons).

**Shedding of Blood**—(See "Shedding" under Blood; Cuts, Effusions; Shedding, Slaughter, Stabs, War. Also note the various paragraphs in this section).

**Skin** — Hemorrhage into — (See Purpura, Scurvy).

**Spine**—Haematomyelia—Hemorrhage Into the Cord—♂ afflicted in ♌.

**Spitting of Blood**—(See "Expectoration" in this section).

**Stabs**—Hemorrhage From—(See Cuts, Duels, Stabs, Sword).

**Stomach** — Hemorrhage of — (See "Hemorrhage" under Stomach).

**Styptics**—(See "Haemostatics" in this section).

**Sword**—Stabs and Cuts By—Hemorrhage From—(See Duels, Stabs, Sword).

**Tendency To**—(See "Abnormal Tendency" in this section).

**Veins**—The Abstraction of Blood by Opening a Vein—(See Bleeding).

**Vessels**—Rupture of Blood Vessel— (See Apoplexy, Plethora; "Rupture" under Vessels; "Abnormal Tendency" in this section).

**Vicarious Hemorrhage**—(See "Vicarious" under Menses; "Epistaxis" under Nose; "Blood" under Vomiting).

**Violent Hemorrhage**—Death From— ♂ causes death by violent hemorrhage. (See "Death" in this section).

**Vomiting of Blood**—(See Haemoptysis; "Blood" under Vomiting).

**War**—Bloodshed In—(See "Shedding of Blood" under Blood; Slaughter; Sword, War).

**Womb** — Flooding of — (See Flooding Hemorrhage, Profuse, in this section; "Hemorrhage" under Womb).

**Women** — Suffer Hemorrhages — (See "Womb" in this section).

**Worse**—Hemorrhages Worse and More Profuse—(See Flooding, Profuse, in this section).

**Wounds**—The Hemorrhages of—(See the various paragraphs under Cuts, Injuries, Stabs, Wounds).

**HEMORRHOIDS**—Piles—A Small Blood Tumor at the Anal Orifice—Ruled by ♏ and the 8th H.; a ♏ disease, and afflictions in ♏ or the 8th H.; a common ♏ disease, and almost any planet affl. in ♏ tends to; ♏ on the Asc. or 6th H.; a ♉ disease, and espec. with ♉ on the Asc. and affl. by ♂; afflictions in ♉, the sign opposite to ♏; the ♍ and ♒ signs are often involved; a ♐ disease, and caused by afflictions in this sign; the ☉, ☽, and other planets afflicted in ♏; the ☽ affl. in ♏, and espec. affl. by the ☉ or ♂ when taken ill; the ☽ in ♏, and in ☌ or ill-asp. ♄ (or ☿ if he be of the nature of ♄) at the beginning of an illness or at decumb.; ♆, ♅, or ♄ in ♏ and affl. the ☉ or ☽; ♆ ☌ ♄ in ♉ or ♏, painful hemorrhoids; ♄ affl. in ♏, and espec. when also affl. the ☉, ☽, Asc., 6th, or 8th H.; a ♄ disease;

♄ in ♏ tends to obstruct the blood circulation, which combined with the dynamic energy of ♂ in ♏ causes bleeding piles; ♄ in ♌ or ♏, and affl. ♀, tends to too much flux of the hemorrhoids; ♃ affl. in ♏, or affl. a planet in ♏, a common cause; ♃ affl. in ♎, from too much blood; a ♂ disease; caused by ♂, the ruler of the ♏ sign, and shows the activity of ♂ in the blood; ♂ affl. in ♏; ♂ in an angle, occi. of the ⊙, and ori. of the ☽; ♂ influence at birth overlaid and intermingled with the influence of the other malefics ♆, ♅, and ♄; ♂ in ♏ in the 6th H., and affl. the ☽ or Asc.; ♂ in ♏ and affl. by malefics, danger of hemorrhage, and the likelihood of an operation; ♂ taking part in any configuration causing piles, and with danger of hemorrhage, and the necessity of an operation; Subs at KP, LPP (4, 5L), and at Sac. and Coc. (See Anus, Constipation, Fistula, Haematoma, Rectum).

**Bleeding Piles**—Hemorrhage From—Caused by the combined influences of ♄ and ♂ in ♏; ♄ in ♏ and □ ♂.

**Blind Piles**—Itching Piles—Protruding Piles—Caused by ♄ affl. in ♏, due to congestion and stagnation of blood in the parts. Also caused by Subs at LPP (4, 5L).

**Cases of Hemorrhoids**—Birth Data, etc.—See Figures 7 and 32 in Message of the Stars, and Fig. 18D in Astro-Diagnosis, books by the Heindels.

**Discharges From**—The Discharge More Profuse—They are more profuse at the Full ☽. (See "Full ☽" under Moon).

**Flux**—Too Much Flux of the Hemorrhoids—♄ in ♌ or ♏ and afflicting ♀.

**Hemorrhage Of**—(See "Bleeding", and also the opening part of this Article).

**Itching Piles**—(See "Blind" in this section).

**Operations On**—Hemorrhoids should not be operated on while the ☽ is passing thru the ♏ sign. Mars in ♏ and afflicted by malefics, or ♂ in any configuration causing piles, and with danger of hemorrhage, may make an operation necessary. (See "Rules" under Operations).

**Painful Hemorrhoids**—♆ ☌ ♄ in ♉ or ♏.

**Plexus**—The Hemorrhoidal Plexus—(See "Ductless Glands" under Ductless).

**Protruding Piles**—(See "Blind" in this section).

**Too Much Blood**—Hemorrhoids From —♃ affl. in ♎. (See "Too Much Blood" under Blood).

**HEMP**—Indian Hemp—(See Cannabis; "Saturn Group" under Herbs).

**HEPATIC DIATHESIS**—(See "Basal Ganglia" under Ganglion; the Introduction under Liver).

**Hepatic Plexus**—(See "Fifth Thoracic" under Ganglion).

**Hepatic Process**—(See "Alterations" under Cells; the Introduction under Liver).

**HERBS**—Plants—Trees—Roots—Bulbs —Berries—Vegetation—Seeds—Flowers —Leaves—Barks—Fruit—Nuts—Resins, etc.—

**Herbs as Remedies**—In every locality on the Earth, Nature has provided an Herb, Plant, Flower, Leaf, Root, etc., with medicinal properties to combat the diseases peculiar to that locality. Herbs to be highly efficient as remedies should be gathered during the Planetary Hour ruled by the planet which rules the Herb, and when the Herb is at its prime, green, and juicy. Read the Chapter on "Medicines and Planetary Influence" in Pearce's Textbook of Astrology, which gives the rulership of Herbs, and the rules for gathering them. The large textbook known as "Culpepper's Herbal", very fully treats of Herbs, their rulerships, and as remedies. Also see Chapters IV, V, and VI, on "Herbal Remedies", in Raphael's Handbook of Medical Astrology. Also read Chap. V, in Daath's Medical Astrology, on "How the Planets Crystallize in Organic and Inorganic Life". Herbs are used as remedies on the principles of sympathy or antipathy. Thus diseases caused by ♂ may be combatted by the Herbs and Remedies of ♄, by antipathy, or if the Herbs of ♂ are used, by sympathy. (See Antipathy, Culpepper, Cure, Drugs, Healers, Hippocrates, Homeopathy, Medicines, Polarity, Remedies, Sympathy, Treatment). The Physiological Action, the Pathological Action, the General Action, the Elementary Qualities, the Chemical Affinities, the Therapeutical Affinities, the Diathesis, etc., of the Planets and Herbs are very nicely arranged in the book called "Astral Medicine" by Dr. Duz, of Paris, France, and on pages 130 to 141 of the said book. In this Article will be listed the principal Herbs of each Planet, and the Therapeutic Properties given at the end of each Group. Also see "Drugs", Therapeutic Properties", "Typical Drugs", under each of the planets as given in the Articles on each planet. A more exhaustive list of the Herbs ruled by each planet is to be found in the book, "Culpepper's Herbal", which is quite a large volume in itself. A most interesting little Booklet on Herbs, their Therapeutic Qualities and value as remedies, is published by Heath and Heather, Herb Specialists, of St. Albans, England, which booklet is sent free to those writing for it. This Firm claims to gather Herbs at the right time, and to prepare them for the Market in their most valuable and efficient form. Their booklet contains a list of Herbs for sale, with Price List, etc. Raphael's Ephemeris and Almanac annually carries the advertisement of this Firm, and they are, no doubt, reliable.

**Jupiter Group**—Typical Herbs Ruled by ♃—Acer Campestre, Agrimonia Eupatoria, Alexander, Aloe (American), Aniseed, Apricots, Asclepias Vincetoxicum, Asparagus Officinalis, Avens, Balm, Balsam, Beet (White), Beta Vulgaris, Betonica Officinalis, Betony, Bilberry, Bloodwort, Borago Officinalis (Borage), Blue Flag, Castanea Vesca, Chaerophyllum Sativum, Chervil, Chestnut Tree, Cichorium Endivia, Cinnamon, Cinquefoil, Cochlearia Officinalis and Anglica, Costmary, Crithmum Maritumum, Dandelion, Dianthus Caryophyllus, Dock, Dog Grass, Endive, Eupatorium, Ficus Carica, Fig Tree, Flag (Blue), Fumitoria Officinalis, Geum Urbanum, Gilliflowers, Ginseng, Hart's Tongue, Hissopus Officinalis (Hyssop), Houseleek, Iceland Moss, Iris, Jessamine, Lapsana Communis, Lichen Caninus and Islandicus, Lime Tree, Liverwort, Lungwort, Maple, Marchantia Polymorpha, Melilotus Officinalis, Melissa Officinalis, Melitot, Moss (Iceland), Myrrh, Nailwort, Oak, Peppermint, Pinks (Wild), Polybody, Potentilla Reptans, Pulmonaria Officinalis, Roses (Red), Saccharum Officinalis, Sage, Salvia Officinalis, Samphire (Small), Scurvy Grass, Sempervivum Tectorum, Smyrnium Olusatrum, Succory (Wild), Swallow-wort, Tanacetum Vulgare, Taraxacum Densleonus (Dandelion), Thistle, Thorn Apple, Tomato, Tormentil, Triticum Repens, Vaccinium Myrtillus, Wild Pinks, Wild Succory. The Therapeutic Properties of the ♃ Group are Alexipharmic, Analeptic, Anthelmintic, Antispasmodic, Balsamic, Emollient. (See "Therapeutic", "Typical Drugs", under Jupiter).

**Mars Group**—Typical Herbs Ruled by ♂—Ajuva Chamaepitys, Alexandrian Senna, All-heal, Allium Sativum, Aloes, American Centaury, Anemone, Arnica, Arsmart, Artemisia Absinthium, Arum Maculatum, Barberry, Basil, Bayberry, Berberis Vulgaris, Boxtree, Briony, Brooklime, Broom, Broomrape, Bryonia Dioica, Butcher's Broom, Capsicum, Capers, Carduus Benedictus, Cassia Obovata, Catmint, Cayenne Pepper, Centaurea Calcipitra, Centaury (American), Cinchona, Civet, Cochlearia Armoracia, Cooko-pint, Corlander, Cotton Thistle, Cranesbill (Wild), Crataegus Oxyacantha, Cresses (Various), Crowfoot (Marsh), Daisy (English), Dove's-foot, Dragon's Flaxweed, Dyer's-weed, Flaxweed (Dragon's), Furzebush, Garden Cress, Garlic, Gentian (Yellow), Geranium Robertianum and Columbinum, Gratriola Officinalis. Hawthorn, Honeysuckle, Hope, Hops, Horseradish, Horsetongue, Humulus Lupus, Hyssop (Hedge), Juniperus Sabina, Lady's Thistle, Lead Wort, Leeks, Linum (Various Species of), Madder, Marsh Crowfoot, Masterwort, Mousetail, Mustard, Myrtle (Wax), Nettles (Small Stinging), Ocymum Basilicum, Onions, Oregon Grappe, Pepper (Red), Peppermint, Peruvian Bark, Peucedanum Ostruthium, Pine, Pineapple, Plantain, Poison Nut, Quaker Button, Ranunculus Aquatilis, Rheum Rhaponticum and Undulatum, Rhubarb, Rocket, Rubia Tinctorum, Sarsaparilla, Savin, Senna (Alexandrian), Sisymbrium Sophia, Savin, Smilax, Snake Root (White), Star Thistle, Strychnos Nux Vomica, Thistle (Lady's), Tobacco, Ulex Europaeus, Urtica (Urens, Dioica, and Pilulifera), Valeriana Officinalis, Wakerobin, Wax Myrtle, White Snake Root, Witch-hazel, Wormwood (Common), Yellow Gentian. The Therapeutic Properties of the ♂ Group are

Aphrodisiac, Caustic, Escharotic, Resolvent, Rubefacient. Stimulant. Tonic, Vesicant. (See "Therapeutic", "Typical", under Mars).

**Mercury Group**—Typical Herbs Ruled by ☿—Amara-duicis, Anethum Graveolens, Anise, Aniseed, Apium Gravolens, Artemisia Abrotantum, Avena, Azaleas, Balm (or Melissa), Bitter Sweet, Bryonia Alba (ruled by ☐), Calamintha Officinalis, Caraway, Carrot.(Wild), Carum Carui, Celery (Wild), Convallaria Majalis, Coraline, Corylus Avellana, Cow Parsnip, Cynoglossum Officinale, Daucus Carota, Dill, Elecampane, Elfwort, Endive, Fennel, Fern, Foeniculum Vulgare, Germander, Glycerrhiza Glabra and Enchinata, Hare's Foot, Hazel Nut, Horehound (White), Hound's Tongue, Inula Helenium, Lavandula Vera, Lavender of Our Gardens, Lily of the Valley, Liquorice, May Apple, Maidenhair (White and Golden), Male Fern, Mandrake, Marjoram (Common, Wild and Sweet), Marrubium Vulgare, Melissa, Mulberry, Myrtle, Nailwort, Nephrodium Felix Mas, Nux Vomica, Oats, Olive Spurge, Organum Vulgare, Parietaria Officinalis, Parsley (Wild), Pastinaca Sativa, Pellitory of the Wall, Petroselinum Sativum, Podophyllin, Satureia Hortensis, Savory, Savoy, Scabiosa Succisa, Smallage, Southern Wood, Starwort, Teucrium Scorodonia, Trefoil, Valerian, Wild Carrots, Winter Savory. The Therapeutic Properties of the ☿ Group are Alterative, Antiperiodic, Cephalic, Nervine. (See Haematopoiesis, Innervation; "Innervation" under Gastric; "Therapeutic", "Typical Drugs", under Mercury).

**Moon Group**—Typical Herbs Ruled by the ☽—Acunthus Mollis, Adder's Tongue, Agaricus, Anthemis Pyrethrum, Betony Stone-crop, Brassicae, Buck's Meat, Cabbage, Caltrops, Cardamine Pratensis, Cheiranthus Cheiri, Chickweed, Clary, Cleavers Coralwort, Colewort, Colocynth, Convolvulus Coeruleus, Cress, Cuckoo Flowers, Cucumbers, Cucumis Sativis, Cucurbito Pepo, Daisy Dogtooth, Duck's Meat, Duckweed, Flaf (Sweet), Geranium Triste, Honey-Suckle, Iris, Lactucas, Ladysmock, Lemnae, Lettuce, Lily (Meadow), Livelong, Loose-strife, Mercurialis Annua, (Mercury), Moonwort, Mouse-ear, Ophioglossum Vulgatum, Orpine, Pearlwort, Pellitory, Peplis Portula, Portulaca Oleraceae, Privet, Pumpkin, Purslane, Pyrethrum, Rattle Grass, Salices (many of the Salices), Salvia Verbenaca, Saxifrage (Winter), Spunk, Stellaria Media, Stonecrop, Trefoil, Utricularia Vulgaris, Wallflowers, Water Arrowhead, Watercress, Waterflag, Water Lily (Yellow), Water Violet, White Lily, White Poppy, White Rose, White Saxifrage, Whitlow Grass, Wild Wallflower, Willows, Wintergreen, Woodbine. The Therapeutic Properties of the ☽ Group are Alterative, Attenuant, Emetic. (See "Therapeutic", "Typical Drugs" under Moon).

**Neptune Group** — (♆). This planet is said to have rule over Herbs which are of a narcotic, soporific and sleep-producing, anaesthetic nature, such as Opiates, Tobacco, Cocaine, Morphine,

Heroin, etc. The Therapeutic Properties assigned to ♆ are Analgesic, Anodyne, Hypnotic, Soporific, and Suggestive. The Poppy Plant, Papaver Somniferum, from which Opium is made, is undoubtedly strongly ruled or influenced by ♆. The Poppy is also listed under the ♀ Group. Cocaine is the alkaloid taken from the Coca Plant (Cuca), known as Erythroxylon Coca, and is similar in its action to Caffeine, the active alkaloid of Coffee, altho Cocaine is much stronger in its deleterious effects upon the nervous system. Coffee also undoubtedly comes under the rule of ♆. Mosses, Mushrooms, Sponges, and Vegetable Fungus Growths, are also ruled by ♆. (See "Drugs", "Therapeutic", "Typical Drugs", under Neptune; Narcotics).

**Rottenness of Herbs** — And Seeds — (See Decay, Fruit, Rottenness).

**Saturn Group** — Typical Herbs Ruled by ♄ — Aconite, Aegopodium, Podagraria, Amaranthus Blitum, Aspen Poplar, Asplenium Ceterach, Atropa Belladonna, Barley, Barrenwort, Beach Tree, Beet, Belladonna, Birdsfoot, Bistort, Black Hellebore, Blackthorn, Blue Bottle, Boneset, Buckthorn, Cannabis Sativa, Capsella Bursa-pastoris, Carduus Heterophyllus, Centaurea Nigra, Clown's Woundwort, Comfrey, Conium Maculatum, Crosswort, Cydonia Vulgaris, Equisetum Vulgaris, English Oak, Fagus Sylvatica, Flaxweed, Fleawort, Fumitory, Gladwin, Goutwort, Ground Moss, Hawkweed, Heartsease, Hedera Helix, Helleborus Niger, Hemlock, Hemp (Indian), Henbane, Holly, Hordeum Species, Horsetail, Hyoscyamus Niger, Ilex Aquifolium, Illecebrum Verticillatum, Indian Hemp, Isatis Tinctoria, Ivy (Common), Jew's Ear, Knapweed, Knotgrass, Lolium Parenne, Mangel, Medlar, MespilusGermanica, Mosses, Mullein (Great), Navelwort, New Jersey Tea, Oak (English), Onion, Ornithopus Perpusillus, Pansies, Persicaria Urens, Plantago Psyllium, P. Coronopus, Plantain (Plantago), Polygonatum Multiflorum, Polypod (Rock), Polypodium Dryopteris, Poplar (Aspen), Populus Nigra, Prunus Spinosa, Purus Torminalis, Quince, Rhus Toxicodendron, Rock Polypod, Rupture Wort, Rushes, Rye, Sciatica Wort, Service Tree, Shepherd's Purse, Sloes, Solomon's Seal, Spleenwort, Symphytum Officinalie, Tamarix Anglica, Taxus Baccata, Tea (New Jersey), Thistle, Tulsan, Ulmus Campestris, Verbascum Thapsus, Wolfsbane. The Therapeutic Properties of the ♄ Group are Antiphlogistic, Antipyretic, Astringent, Febrifuge, Refrigerant, Sedative, Styptic. (See "Drugs", "Therapeutic", under Saturn).

**Sun Group** — Typical Herbs Ruled by the ☉ — Almond, Anagallis Arvensis, Angelica Sylvestris, Anthemis Nobillis, Ashtree, Bay Tree, Calendula Officinalis, Celandine, Centaurea Nigra, Chamomile, Chelidonium Majus, Citrus Aurantium, Colchicum Autumnale, Corn Hornwort, Drosera Rotundifolia, Echium Vulgare, Euphrasia Chamomilla, Eyebright, Fraxinus Excelsior, Grape (Vitis Vinifera), Heart Trefoil, Helianthus, Hypericum Androsaemium,

Juniperus Communis, Laurel, Lemon, Ligusticum Scoticum, Male Peony, Marigold, Meadow Rue, Mistletoe, Mustard, Olive, Orange, Passion Flower, Peppermint, Petasites Vulgaris, Pimpernel, Potentilla Tormentilla, Rice, Rosmarinus Officinalis, Rue, Saffron, Sanguisorba Officinalis, Sinapis Nigra and Alba, St. John's Wort, St. Peter's Wort, Sun Dew, Sun Flower, Tormentil, Turnsole, Vine (Vitis Vinifera), Viper's Bugloss, Walnut. The Therapeutic Properties of the ☉ Group are Cardiac, Anticachectic, Sudorific. (See "Drugs of the ☉" under Sun).

**Uranus Group** — (♅). The rulerships of the more distant planets ♅ and ♆ over Plants and Herbs, if they have such rulership on the Earth Plane, have not as yet been very clearly defined or listed. Their influences are observed so far as being mainly mental, or spiritual, and to affect the mind and nervous system. The Therapeutic action of the drugs and herbs of ♅, or the effects of ♅ action, are observed to be electric and vibrational. Of the Herbs, Croton Oil, the oil expressed from the seed of the Croton Tiglium tree, is listed as a typical herb of this planet. More of the minerals and metals are listed than herbs, as being ruled by ♅. (See "Therapeutic", "Typical", under Uranus. Read carefully the entire Article on Uranus).

**Venus Group** — Typical Herbs Ruled by ♀ — Acillea Ptarmica, Ajuga Reptans, Alder Tree (Black and Common), Alehoof, Alkanet, Alnus Glutinosa, Althaea Officinalis, Apples, Archangel (Wild and Stinking), Arctium Lappa, Arrack, Artichoke, Asparagus, Beans, Bear Berry, Bellis Perennis, Birch, Bishop's Weed, Black Alder, Blites, Bramble, Bugle Holly, Bunium Flexuosum, Burdock, Cherry, Chestnut (Earth), Chickpease, Cloves, Cock's-Head, Coltsfoot, Columbines, Couchgrass, Cowslip, Crabsclaw, Cranesbill, Crosswort, Cudweed, Daisy, Devil's-Bit, Dipsacus Sylvestris, Dropwort, Elder, Eryngium Maritimum, Featherfew, Figwort, Foxglove, Fumitory, Galium Cruciatum, Golden Rod, Gooseberry, Gromel, Ground Ivy, Groundsel, Herb Robert, Holly (Sea), Ivy (Ground), Indigo Plant (Indigofera), Kidney Bean, Kidney Wort, Ladies' Bedstraw, Ladies' Mantle, Leonurus Cardiaca, Ligustrum Vulgare, Lithospermum Arvense, Little Daisy, Mallow (Common), Marshmallow, Matricaria Parthenium, Mentha Pulegium, Mercury (Dog and French), Meum Athamanticum, Mint-money-wort, Mints, Motherwort, Mugwort, Nepeta Cataria, Nepeta Glechoma, Obione Portulacoides, Okro Gombo Pods, Orchis, Oxalis Acetosella, Parsley, Peachtree, Peartree, Penny Royal, Penny Wort, Peppermint, Plantago Major, Plantain (Greater), Plums, Poppy, Primula Veris, Prunella Vulgaris, Pulsatilla, Queen of the Meadows, Ragwort, Red Cherries, Rose (Damask), Rubus Fruticosis, Rye, Sanicle, Sanicula Europaea, Saponaria Officinalis, Scrophularia Nodosa and Aquatica, Sea Holly, Secale Cereale, Selfheal, Senecio Jacobaea, Sibthorpia Europaea, Silverweed, Soapwort, Sonchus Arvensis, Sorrel, Sow-thistle, Spearmint, Spignel, Strawberry, Tansy, Teasel, Throatwort, Thyme, Tussilago Farfara, Verbena Officinalis, Vervain, Violets, Wheat, Yarrow. The Therapeutic Properties of the ♀ Group are Antinephritic, Diuretic, Demulcent, Emetic. (See "Therapeutic", "Typical Drugs", under Venus).

For further and collateral study along the lines of Herbs, their use, etc., see Antipathy, Cure, Drugs, Fruits, Healers, Medical, Medicines, Metals, Minerals, Plants, Remedies, Rotten, Seeds, Sympathy, Treatment, Vegetation, etc.

**HERCULES**—The Star—Caput Herculis —Pollux—(See Pollux).

**HEREDITY** — Hereditary — Inherent— Innate—Inherited Tendencies—Constitutional, Organic, and Structural Tendencies of Body — Hereditary Transmission is often explained by the Figure of the Heavens for the moment of Conception rather than by the Figure for the moment of birth, and in this connection you should make a thorough study of the Prenatal Epoch, and how to erect Maps for the time of conception when the birth hour is known approximately. In the Natal Map the ⊙ is the Sig. of the inherent tendencies and hereditary transmissions, while the ☽ denotes acquired conditions, as the ⊙ is Organic, and the ☽ Functional. In many diseases the Map of Birth does not fully account for the condition, whereas the map for the time of conception does explain and account for the disease condition more fully. A person may be bothered with bowel and abdominal disorders, and the map of birth not show any afflictions in ♍ or the 6th H., but in the map for the time of conception, ♄ or ♂, or both, may be in ♍ in the 6th H., which would account for such an inherent tendency. So also in cases of Deafness, Blindness, Idiocy, and many congenital conditions, the map for the time of conception, and the influences of the ☽ at the time of her monthly return to the central line of impulse during gestation, account for many defects and congenital deformities. Inherent Mania is an affliction especially indicated by the map of conception, and may not be shown by the map of birth. In making a study of the star maps of birth of many individuals in the same family, considering their Aunts, Uncles, Grandparents, Cousins, etc., there is a noted similarity between the maps, and the same Rising Sign, or some particular Sign of the Zodiac, is usually prominent in all of them, and all are similarly afflicted or benefitted, and either the ⊙, ☽, or the Asc., are in the same sign or triplicity. (See "Likenesses" under Family). However, an inherited trait may be represented by any part of the nativity, and by antenatal maps from the time of conception, and on down to birth. Heredity also must be considered to account for the differences in people born at the same time, and in the same vicinity, although the times, seasons, and appointments of their lives will be very similar. The 4th H. in the map of birth also denotes and shows heredi-tary tendencies. The Occult side of heredity is a big subject, the incoming Ego, the effects of Karma, the age of the Soul, the stage in Evolution, etc., and these subjects are well-discussed in the book, "Cosmo-Conception", by Max Heindel, and also in the books, "The Key to the Universe", and "The Key of Destiny", by Dr. and Mrs. Homer Curtiss. Also in the book, "The Tarot of the Bohemians", by Papus, the plan of Destiny, Fate, Heredity, and how the Universe is builded and conducted: the Past, Present, and Future of the Human Race, are well defined and explained. (For collateral study see the references at the end of this section).

**Hereditary Diseases**—And Tendencies —These are especially indicated by the ⊙, his position and afflictions at B. Also indicated by the fixed signs, and with many planets and afflictions in them at B. The 4th, 8th, and 10th H., the Lights and ♄, are espec. concerned with hereditary influences and transmissions. (See Eighth House; "Fixed Signs" under Fixed; Fourth House, Moon, Saturn, Sun, Tenth House).

**Well-Descended Body**—♃ in an earthy sign at B.; the Ruler or Sig. in his own triplicity, and well-aspected, one well descended. Nature and the Higher Powers so rule, arrange and manage the incarnation of an individual, and by the Law of Attraction and Similars, lead an incoming Ego to parents, ancestors, and a line of descent, which is more or less bound up with the native from out of the Past, and to cause the birth to take place at a time and place which gives a star map of birth considerably in harmony with such relationships. The parents give to the maturing embryo and child a body much like their own, as a rule, or similar to some relative or ancestor in the line, but the Occult Masters and Initiates teach that the mind and character of the child are not directly transmitted from the parents, but that the incoming Ego, or Spirit, brings such character with it. It is said that the star map of birth shows the character and attainments which the native had at his death in the physical body in his material incarnation previous to this one, and that in the present life he is forming and building the map which will be his star map of birth at his next incarnation. Also by right living, right thinking, attainment, wisdom, knowledge, understanding in the present life, by obeying the laws of health, the native is also largely determining the kind and quality of his next physical body. People who are ignorant, negative, passive, receptive, given to worry, brooding, and who are constantly thinking in terms of disease, tend to attract disease, ill-health, and to be born into a family with weak and sickly bodies, as into a family afflicted with Consumption, Asthma, Tuberculosis, and various constitutional and organic diseases, whereas a native now given to right and constructive thinking, thoughts of good and perfect health, is gradually building a body, a prototype, for his next body, and a more perfect, healthful, handsome, strong and efficient body. These matters are discussed in the books mentioned in this section, and it is well for all students of Astrology to study deeply into the Occult side of life, know The Mysteries, if you ever expect to understand the Philosophy of Life and Destiny, and not follow along ignorantly in the trails of Exoteric Schools of Thought, Religion, or Philosophy, or allow yourself to be governed by the superstitions and false traditions, and false interpretations of Truth, such as prevail over the Earth today. (For further and collateral study along this line see Acquired, Ascendant, Astral, Birth, Blindness, Character, Children, Conception, Congenital, Constitutional, Deafness (see Hearing); Deaf and Dumb (see Hearing); Defects, Deformities, Destiny, Deviations, Diathesis, Ego, Environment, Epilepsy, Events, External, Family, Fate, Father, Form, Functions, Genius, Gestation, Hexis, Idiocy, Idiosyncrasies, Imperfections, Innate, Insanity, Latent, Mania, Map, Monsters, Mother, Mutes, Nativity, Natural, Organic, Parents, Personality, Praeincipients, Prenatal, Prodigies, Remarkable, Soul, Spirit, Structural, Susceptibility, etc., and other subjects which you may have in mind which may be connected with heredity).

**HERMAPHRODITES** — Androgynous—Dual-Sexed—Bisexual—Male and Female Organs Developed In the Same Body — The human body in the early stages of its evolution was bisexual, hermaphrodite, and with the male and female organs equally developed in the one physical body. Then came the separation of the sexes into two bodies, a more distinct male and female body, of which Adam and Eve are regarded as the first types of the separated sexes. (See the book, "Cosmo-Conception", by Max Heindel, on this subject of the Separation of the Sexes). Remnants of this early hermaphrodite type still appear on Earth. In the remote future it is said by the Occult Masters that the male and female bodies will again be reunited into one form, or body. The word Hermaphrodite originated from the word "Harpocrates", the God of Silence, and Ptolemy used the word at times to refer to Stammerers, those who had some defect of speech, and were silent and unable to speak. The common signs strong at B. are said to predominate at the birth of a hermaphrodite. Also the ☽ in the 1st H., with ♄ and ☿, and espec. if ♂ also give testimony, a hermaphrodite, or perhaps have but one passage. (For further planetary influences which tend to this condition see Eunuchs; "Foolish Mind" under Foolish; "Hermaphrodites" under Men; "Excessive Virile Members" under Virile).

**HERMES** — The Greek name for Mercury, the Messenger of the Gods—(See Mercury).

**HERNIA**—Rupture—The Protrusion of a Viscus from Its Normal Position—Hernia is classed as a ♄, ♂, ♍, and ♏ disease. Also a ♀ disease when ♀ is affl. by ♄; afflictions in ♍ or ♏, and espec. when these signs occupy the 6th H.; ♄ in ♍ or ♏ in the 6th H.; ♂ affl. in ♍ or ♏, and espec. in the 6th H.; ♀ in ♍ or ♏, and affl. by ♄; the Asc. to the □ or ☍ ♄ by dir.; Subs at PP. (See the various paragraphs in this section).

**Abdominal Hernia**—♄ or ♂ affl. in ♍; ♂ in ♍ in the 6th H.; ♀ affl. in ♍, in some cases, and espec. if affl. by ♄; Subs at PP (2, 3, 4L). (See Abdomen).

**Aneurysm** — Hernial Aneurysm — The ☽ affl. in ♏. (See Aneurysm).

**Brain**—Hernia of—Encephalocele — ♄ or ♂ affl. in ♈; Subs at AT. (See Brain).

**Death by Hernia** — ♂ the afflicting planet.

**Diaphragm**—(See "Hernia" under Diaphragm).

**Encephalocele**—Hernia of the Brain—(See "Brain" in this section).

**Exaggerated Action** — Hernia Resulting From—(See Exaggerated; Influence Of" under Mars, Uranus).

**Groin**—Hernia In—(See "Inguinal" in this section).

**Inguinal Hernia**—Hernia In the Groin, and Thru the Abdominal Ring — A ♏ disease, and afflictions in ♏; ♏ on the Asc. at B.; the ☉ or ☽ in ♏, and affl. by ♂ at B., and by dir.; a ♅ disease; ♅ affl. in ♏, and espec. in the 6th H.; a ♄ disease; ♄ affl. in ♌ or ♏, or ♄ in evil asp. to ♀; denoted by ♂; a ♂ disease and affliction; ♂ exactly rising in ♏; ♂ ☌ or ill-asp. ♅, and espec. when in ♏ and fixed signs; ♂ in ♍, ♏, or ♐, and affl. the hyleg; ♂ affl. in ♍ in the 6th H.; a ♀ disease, and espec. when ♀ is affl. by ♄; ♀ in ♏ in ☌ or ill-asp. ♄; ♀ in ♏ in the 6th H., and affl. by ♄; Subs at PP (3, 4L). (See Groins).

**Lacerations**—(See Lacerations).

**Motion** — (See "Accelerated Motion" under Motion).

**Rupture**—(See the various paragraphs under Rupture. Also see Bursting, Lacerations, Pressure. Note the various paragraphs in this section).

**Scrotal Hernia**—(See "Hernia" under Scrotum).

**Strangulated Hernia** — A ♄ disorder and affliction; ♄ affl. in ♍ or ♏, and espec. in the 6th H., and with danger of constriction of the bowel, and interferring with the passage of faeces; Subs at PP (2, 3, 4L). (See Inguinal, Ventral, in this section; Scrotum).

**Umbilical Hernia**—(See Navel).

**Ventral Hernia**—Hernia Thru the Abdominal Wall—♂ affl. in ♍ or ♓, and espec. in the 6th H. (See Belly; "Abdomen" in this section).

**HERPES**—A Skin Disease with Patches of Distinct Vesicles—

**Face**—Herpes On—The ☽ or ♂ affl. in ♈; an ♈ disease; ♈ on the Asc. at B., and espec. when ♂ or the ☽ are in ♈ in the Asc., and afflicted; Subs at MCP (4C), and at KP. (See Face).

**Herpes Zoster**—Shingles—The ☽ affl. in ♋, ♌, or ♍; a ♂ disease; ♂ affl. in ♌; an ♈ disease, and afflictions in ♈, or ♈ on the Asc., and afflicted.

**Ringworm** — The Circling Tinea or Herpes—(See Ringworm).

**Tetter**—A Form of Herpes—Ringworm—Eczema—(See Eczema, Ringworm, Tetter). For collateral study see Barber's Itch (see Barbers); Eczema, Eruptions, Psoriasis, Skin, Spotted Fever (see Spotted); Tinea, Vesicles.

**HEXIS**—The Permanent Habit In Disease—(See Diathesis, Directions; "Certain" under Disease; Heredity, Organic, Praeincipient, Structural).

**HICCOUGH**—Hiccup—Involuntary Closure of the Glottis—An Interrupted Spasmodic Inspiration—Caused by afflictions in ♋; a ♋ disease; a ☽ and ♅ disease; ♅ affl. in ♋ or ♍, and due to the erratic action of the Diaphragm; ♅ ☌ ☽ in ♋; ♅ affl. in ♉, and afflicting the organ of Coordination, located in ♉; Subs at SP (7, 8D), and at Spl.P. (9D). (See "Interference" under Breathing; Diaphragm, Glottis, Spasmodic).

**HIGH**—Highly—

**Altitudes**—High Altitudes—Falls From—(See Heights).

**Blood Pressure**—High Blood Pressure—(See "Pressure" under Blood).

**Body**—A High Body—(See Giants, Tall).

**Disease Runs High**—(See "High" under Fever).

**Excitable**—Highly Excitable—(See Excitable).

**Fever**—High and Burning Fever—(See "High Fever" under Fever).

**Forehead**—A High Forehead—(See Forehead).

**High Strung**—(See "Strung" in this section).

**Living**—High Living—Disease, Fever, or Plethora From—The ☉ affl. by ♃ or ♀; the ☉ □ or ☍ ♃; the ☽ affl. by ♃; the ☽ in ♉ at B., and to the ☌ or ill-asp. ♄ by dir. (or to ☿ if he be of the nature of ♄), at the beginning of an illness, or at decumb., fevers from; ♃ causes complaints from high living and injudicious diet; ♃ □ or ☍ the Asc.; ♃ affl. in ♉, ♍, or ♎; ♃ affl. in ♉, or ♃ affl. the ☉, ☽, or ♀ from this sign, plethora from; ♀ diseases; ♀ affl. at B., and to the ☌ or ill-asp. the Asc. by dir.; ☿ affl. in ♌; ♌ on the cusp the 6th H. tends to disorders from inharmonious living; lord of the 6th or 10th H. in the 5th H., and afflicted. (See Appetites, Debauched, Depraved, Diet, Dissipation, Dissolute, Drink, Drunkenness, Eating, Epicureans, Excesses, Extravagance, Feasting, Fever (see "Slight Fever" under Fever); Food; Free Living (see Free); Gluttony, Indigestion, Indiscretions, Indulgences, Inflation, Intemperance, Luxuries, Obesity, Plethora, Riotous Living (see Riotous); Surfeits, etc.).

**Mortality High**—High Death Rate—(See Mortality).

**Nervous Tension**—High Nervous Tension—High Strung—Highly Neurotic—(See "Nerves" under Excitable; "Neurotic" under Nerves; Tension; "Strung" in this section).

**Nose**—A High Nose—(See "High" under Nose).

**Places**—High Places—Heights—Falls From—(See Heights).

**Pulse**—High Pulse—(See "Accelerated" under Heart; "High" under Pulse).

**Sensitive**—Highly Sensitive—(See Hyperaesthesia, Sensitive).

**Strung**—High Strung—The ☉ in ♊; the ☉ in any asp. to ♅, or vice versa; ♆, ♅, ☿, and the ☽ tend to make the body high strung and nervous. (See "Nerves" under Excitable; "Full Moon" under Moon; "Neurotic" under Nerves).

**Temper**—(See Anger; "Even Temper", "High Temper", under Temper).

**Tension**—High Nervous Tension—(See "Nervous Tension" in this section).

**Tides**—Tide—High Tide—The Fluids of the Body At High Tide—(See Fluids; "Full Moon", under Moon).

**Urine**—Highly Loaded Urine—(See "Highly Loaded" under Urine).

**Winds**—High Winds—Suffering From—(See "High" under Winds).

**HIGHWAYMEN**—Injury or Death By—♄ Lord of the Year, and afflicted at the Vernal Ingress, causes many highway robberies, and thieves to be active generally, and with much public anxiety, sadness, and tribulation; Comets appearing in ♎. (See Bandits, Crime, Rapine, Robbers, Thieves).

**HINDER PARTS**—Of the Body—(See Back, Buttocks, Dorsal, Loins, Rear, Spine, etc.).

**HINDRANCES**—Hindered—The influence of ♄ by his afflictions is to hinder, impede, retard, suppress, and to slow up the functions of the body, and to do so by retaining the wastes of the body, by hardening, crystallization of the tissues, suppressions of the fluids of the body, etc. (See Arrested, Clogging, Crystallization, Deposits, Functions (see "Hindered" under Functions); Hardening, Impeded, Impediments, Minerals, Obstructions, Restrictions, Retarded, Retention, Rigid, Slow, Stoppages, Suppressions, Wastes, etc.).

**HINDU ASTROLOGY**—This System of Astrology differs somewhat from the European System of Astrology, as used in this Work, and it would take a separate volume to go into the Hindu Methods. There is a good Treatise on Hindu Astrology in the book, "Sepharial's Manual of Astrology". Also the British Journal of Astrology, of London, and edited by Mr. E. H. Bailey, is devoting a large amount of time and space to the Hindu Methods. Also see Alan Leo's New Dictionary of Astrology. It is very evident that the Hindu interpretations of Astrology are very valuable in explaining the planetary and Zodiacal causes of many diseases and afflictions, and are an aid in diagnosis, and it is well for the student of Medical Astrology to study into the Hindu System. In future Editions of this Encyclopaedia, an elaborate treatise of the Hindu System will, and should be added, as well as many other subjects which may not appear in the First Edition. My desire is to see this Work added to as the years and Generations go by, and until it becomes a large Library of Volumes on the subject of Medical Astrology, but such a great and complete Work is too much to be done by any one person, and during the lifetime of one individual. In the Hindu System, the rulership of the Eyes and Ears is placed under different Houses than in our System. Also the rule concerning the Father and Mother is different, and is not elastic, according to sex, as in our System. (See Ears, Eyes, Father, Mother). Also, in the Hindu System, each Sign of the Zodiac is divided into nine equal parts, known as "Navamsa", and this finer division helps to locate the part of an organ afflicted, and to account for the various deteriorations of a complicated organ, such as the Heart. In this Work, I am giving you a brief Article on Navamsa, which should be enlarged upon in future Editions. (See Hyleg, Memory, Navamsa, Senses).

**HIPPOCRATES**—Called the "Father of Medicine". Born about 460 B.C., and died about 357 B.C. He advocated Antipathy in the cure of disease, which System is now advocated by Allopathy. (See Antipathy, Cure, Galen, Healers, Homeopathy, Medicines, Opposites, Paracelsus, Remedies, Sympathy, Treatment).

**HIPPUS** — Clonic Spasm of the Iris — (See "Hippus" under Eyeballs, Iris).

**HIPS**—The Upper Part of the Thigh—Hip Joint — The Hips are ruled by ♐ and the 9th H. They are under the external rulership of ♐. The arteries and nerves of this region are under the internal rulership of the ♐ sign. The hip bones, and the femur, are under the structural rulership of ♐. (See Sagittarius). The Locomotor Muscles of the Hips and Thighs are ruled by ♐.

**Accidents To**—Hurts, Injuries, Wounds To—♄ or ♂ affl. in ♐; ♄ ☌ ♂ in ♐; afflictions in ♐; ♐ on the Asc. (See Bruises, Cuts, Fractures, in this section).

**Aches**—In the Hips and Thighs—Old Aches In—♄ in ♐ when ♄ is the afflictor in the disease; the ☽ in ♍ in ☌ or ill-asp ♄ (or ☿ if he be of the nature of ♄) at the beginning of an illness, or at decumb. (Hor'y). (See Aches).

**Ailments In**—(See "Diseases", and the various paragraphs in this section).

**All Diseases In**—Signified by the 9th H. and ♐, and afflictions therein.

**Ankylosis**—Of the Hip Joint—The ☉ or ♂ affl. in ♐, or the ☉ ☌ ♂ in ♐, by excess of heat; ♄ affl. in ♐, by deposits. (See "Case" under Ankylosis).

**Arthritis** — Of Hip Joint — Hip Joint Disease—♄ ☌ ♂ in ♐, and also otherwise afflicted by the ☉, ☽, or malefics. (See "Arthritis" under Joints; "Hip-Joint Disease" in this section).

**Bones Of** — Are under the external rulership of ♐. Disorders and injuries of the hip bones are caused by afflictions in ♐, and also Subs at PP (4L). (See Dislocation, Fracture, Joint, in this section).

**Broken Hip**—(See "Fracture" in this section).

**Bruises To**—Contusions—♄ affl. in ♐. (See Bruises).

**Circulation Poor In**—♄ in ♐, ☌ or ill-asp. ♃ or ♀.

**Cold In** — Cold and Chill In the Hips and Thighs—♄ in ♐. (See Cold).

**Cold and Moist Humours**—In the Hips and Thighs—♀ affl. in ♐ when ♀ is the afflictor in the disease. (See "Cold and Moist" under Humours).

**Contusions** — (See "Bruises" in this section).

**Coxalgia**—(See "Pain" in this section).

**Cramps In**—♅ in ♐. (See Cramps).

**Cuts To**—Afflictions in ♐; ♂ affl. in ♐; ♐ on the Asc. (See Cuts).

**Diseases In**—Hip Diseases—Diseases in Hips, Thighs, and Haunches—Afflictions in ♐; ♐ diseases; ♐ on the Asc.; malefics in the 9th H.; a Stellium in the 9th H., or in ♐; the ☉, ☽, ♄, ♂, or ♀ affl. in ♐; ♄ affl. in ♊, by reflex action; ♄ in ♐ in the Asc., and afflicted. (See "Hip Joint", and the various paragraphs in this section; "Impar" under Ganglion).

**Dislocation**—Of the Hip Joint—Afflictions in ♐, or ♐ on Asc.; ♄ or ♂ affl. in ♐. (See Dislocations).

**Drying Up**—(See "Synovial Fluid" in this section).

**Feverish Ailments In**—♐ on the Asc.; ♂ in ♐. (See "Hot Humours" in this section).

**Fluid**—Of the Hip Joint—(See "Synovial" in this section).

**Fracture**—Broken Hip—♄ or ♂ affl. in ♐; the ☽ affl. in ♐; ♂ affl. in ♊, by reflex action; ♐ on the Asc., 6th, or 12th H.; ♐ ruler of the 6th or 12th H., and afflicted by the progression or transit of planets. (See Femur, Fractures).

**Gout In**—(See "Hips and Thighs" under Gout).

**Hams**—Hamstrings—(See Thighs).

**Haunches**—(See Buttocks).

**Heats In**—Hips and Thighs—The ☉ or ♂ afflicted in ♐; ☉ ☌ ♂ in ♐; ♐ on the Asc., and espec. if the ☉ or ♂ are also in ♐ in the Asc. (See "Heats" under Heat).

**Hip-Joint Disease** — Arthritis — A ♐ disease, and afflictions in ♐; ♐ on the Asc.; the ☉ in ♐, ☌ or ill-asp. ♄; the ☉ ☌ ♂ in ♐; the ☉ and other important planets in ♐, and affl. by the ☌, □, or ☍ of ♄ and ♂; ♄ in ♐, occi., and affl. the ☉, ☽, or Asc.; ♄ afflicting the ☉, or other important body, in ♐, and with ♂ usually forming an aspect; ♄ ☌ the ☉ in ♐, and the ☉ also affl. by ♂; ♄ and ♂ both in ♐ in ☌ ☉; ♄ affl. in ♐ may result in some permanent disability of the hip joint, causing lameness, and inability to walk. Case—Hip Joint Disease—See Chap. XIII, page 85, Daath's Medical Astrology. (See Accidents, Ankylosis, Arthritis, Dislocation, Fracture, Gout, Heats, Lameness, Pain, Synovial, in this section; "Inability" under Walk).

**Hot Humours**—In Hips and Thighs—The ☉ or ♂ affl. in ♐ when either of these planets are the afflictors in the disease; ♐ on the Asc. (See Feverish, Heats, Humours, in this section).

**Humours In**—In Hips or Thighs—♂ affl. in ♐, pain and ulcers in the hips and thighs by humours settled in those parts. (See Cold and Moist, Hot Humours, Pain, in this section).

**Hurts**—To Hips and Thighs—♄ or ♂ affl. in ♐; malefics affl. in the 9th H., or in the Asc. in ♐. (See Accidents, Bruises, Cuts, Dislocation, Fracture, Lameness, in this section).

**Ilium**—The Upper Part of the Innominate, or Hip Bone—Injuries and Afflictions to this part of the Hip Bone tend to result when malefics are in the last face of ♏, and in the 1st Decan. of ♐. (See Ilium; Bone, Fracture, Ischium, Pubes, in this section).

**Injuries To**—Hips and Thighs—(See Accidents, Bruises, Cuts, Dislocation, Fracture, in this section).

**Innominate Bone**—The Hip Bone, and including the Ilium, Ischium, and Pubis—The Pelvis—Injuries To—Ruled by ♐, and also partly influenced by ♏. Afflictions and malefics in ♐ tend to injuries to. (See Ilium, Ischium, Pelvis, Pubes, in this section).

**Ischium**—The Inferior Part of the Hip Bone—Accidents and Injuries to may result when the afflictions are in the 3rd Decan. of ♐, or in the first face of ♑. (See Ischium, Pubes. Also see Ilium, Innominate, in this section).

**Joint**—The Hip Joint—Disorders of—(See Ankylosis, Arthritis, Dislocation, Gout, Heat, Hip-Joint Disease, Lameness, Pain, Synovial, in this section).

**Lameness**—In the Hips and Thighs—The ☽ affl. in ♐. (See Dislocation, Fracture, Gout, Hip-Joint Disease, Rheumatism, Swellings, Weakness, and the various paragraphs in this section).

**Locomotor Muscles**—Of the Hips and Thighs—Ruled by ♐. Disorders of are caused by afflictions in ♐.

**Men Suffer**—With Hip and Thigh Diseases—♂ in ♐, ℞, and Lord of the Year at the Vernal Equinox. (See Men).

**Moist and Cold Humours**—In the Hips —(See "Cold and Moist" in this section).

**Muscles**—(See Locomotor, Rheumatism, in this section).

**Narrow Hips**—(See "Small" in this section).

**Nervous Pains In**—(See "Pains In" under Thighs; "Pain" in this section).

**Old Aches In**—(See "Aches" in this section).

**Operations On**—Should not be made when the ☽ is passing thru ♐. (See Operations).

**Pain**—In the Hips and Thighs—Coxalgia—Nervous Pains In—The ☽ in ♎ or ♐, ☌, or ill-asp. ♄ (or ☿ if he be of the nature of ♄) at the beginning of an illness, or at decumb. (Hor'y); ♃ affl. in ♐; ♂ in ♐ and affl.. the ☉; ♂ affl. in ♐ tends to pains and ulcers in the hips or thighs due to humours settled in those parts; ☿ affl. in ♊ or ♐; nervous pains in. (See "Pain" under Thighs).

**Pelvis**—Disorders In—(See Pelvis; "Innominate" in this section).

**Pubes**—Pubis—The Anterior Portion of the Innominate Bone—(See Pubes; "Innominate" in this section).

**Restrictions**—In the Region of the Hips and Thighs—♄ affl. in ♐. (See Restrictions. Also note the various paragraphs in this section).

**Rheumatism In**—Hips or Thighs—Rheumatic Pains In—Afflictions in ♊ or ♐; ♐ on the Asc.; the ☽ affl. in ♐; ♆, ♄, or ♅ in ♐, and affl. the ☉, ☽, or Asc.; ♄ affl. in ♐; ♄ in ♐ in the 1st or 6th H.; ♃ affl. in ♊ or ♐; Subs at PP (2L). (See Gout, Lameness, in this section; Gout, Rheumatism).

**Sacrum**—(See Sacrum).

**Small Hips**—Narrow Hips—♄ ascending at B.

**Strong Hips**—Strong and Well-Proportioned Hips, Thighs, and Legs—♃ in the Asc.; ♐ on the Asc.

**Swellings**—In the Hips or Thighs—The ☽ in ♐, ☌, or ill-asp. ♄ (or ☿ if he be of the nature of ♄) at the beginning of an illness, or at decumb. (Hor'y); ♃, ♂, or ☿ affl. in ♐; ♃ affl. in ♐ in the 6th H.; ♀ affl. in ♑. (See Swellings).

**Synovial Fluid**—Drying Up of In Hip Joint—♄ affl. in ♐. (See Ankylosis, Arthritis, Hip Joint Disease, Lameness, in this section; Joints, Synovial).

**Tumors**—In Hips or Thighs—A ♐ disease, and afflictions in ♐; ♄ or ♀ affl. in ♐; ♂ affl. in ♒. (See the ☽ influence under "Swellings" in this section; Tumors).

**Ulcers In**—(See Humours, Pain, in this section; Ulcers).

**Walk**—Inability to Walk Due to Hip Diseases or Injury—(See "Hip-Joint Disease" in this section; Walk).

**Weakness**—In Hips or Thighs—The ☽ hyleg in ♐, and afflicted, and espec. with females; ♄ affl. in ♍ or ♐; ♂ or ☿ affl. in ♐; ♐ on the Asc. or 6th H., and containing malefics, and espec. ♄. (See "Lameness" and the various paragraphs in this section).

**Well-Proportioned**—Hips and Thighs —Well Formed—Strong—♃ in the Asc.; ♐ on the Asc. (See Well-Proportioned).

**Wounds**—To Hips or Thighs—(See Accidents, Cuts, Dislocation, Fracture, Hurts, in this section).

**HIRCUS**—Capella—The Goat—An eminent fixed star of the 1st magnitude in 20° ♊, of the nature of ♂ and ☿. (See Calamity, Capella, Dishonest).

**HIVES**—Urticaria—Nettle Rash—A Vesicular Cutaneous Eruption—(See Urticaria, Vesicles).

**HOARSENESS**—Dysphonia—(See "Hoarseness" under Larynx).

**Hoarse Signs**—Of the Zodiac—♈, ♉, ♌, ♑. Those born under them are said to have a hoarseness, or roughness of the voice, and those born under ♑ to be more weak and feminine, and to have a whistling sound in speaking. (See Throat, Voice).

**HOGS**—Swine—Ruled by the 6th H. in the map of the native. (See Swine).

**A Performing Pig**—See "Performing Pig", No. 781, in 1001 N.N.

**HOLLOW**—Sunken—(See "Hollow" under Cheeks, Chest; "Sunken" under Eyeballs).

**Tumor**—Hollow Tumor and Cystic Formations—(See "Hollow" under Cysts).

**HOME**—The Home—Ruled by the ☽ and the 4th H.

**Death**—Dies In His Own Home—Lord of the 8th H. in the 4th H. at B.

**Fire**—Burns, Scalds In the Home—♂ in the 4th H. at B., and by dir., in a fiery sign, and affl. the ☉, ☽, or Asc. (See Burns, Fire, Scalds).

**No Home**—No Home or Friends—A Wanderer—Vagabond—The ☉ Sig. in □ or ☍ ☽. (See "Many Changes" under Residence; Roaming; Wandering; "Wandering" under Travel; Vagabond).

**Worry**—Thru Home Conditions—☿, or malefics, affl. in the 4th H. (See "Worries" under Children; Environment, Family, Love Affairs, Marriage).

**HOMEOPATHY**—A School of Medicine founded by Dr. Hahnemann, and on the theory of treating disease by Sympathy and Similars. Thus ♄ diseases are treated by ♄ remedies; ♂ diseases by ♂ remedies, etc. Their Motto is "Similia Similibus Curantur". However, Paracelsus, a Swiss Physician and Astrologer, born in 1493, was the first to advocate the doctrine of treating by Similars. Most of the Astrological Doctors and Writers on Medical Astrology in Modern Times have been Homeopaths, and say much in support of the Homeopathic Theory. (See Antipathy, Cure, Galen, Healers, Opposites, Paracelsus, Sympathy, Treatment; "Zodiac Salts" under Zodiac). For the birth data of a leading Homeopathic Physician, see "Kali, Dr. C. S.", No. 894, in 1001 N.N.

**HOMICIDE**—Homicidal—Tendency To—Danger of—♄ Sig. □ or ☍ ♂, or vice versa; the Asc. to the ☌, P., □ or ☍ ♂ by dir., and ♂ in a sign of human form at B., as in ♊, ♍, the 1st half of ♐, and in ♒. The ☉ is also usually severely afflicted, and the ♈ and ♌ Signs, the strong signs of the ☉. The 0° of ♌ and ♒; the 5° of ♈ and ♎, and the 9° of mutable signs, are often involved and afflicted by malefics. (See Assassination, Criminal; "Patricide" under Father; Murder). Case of a Homicide—See "Who Was This", No. 560, in 1001 N.N.

**HOMOSEXUALITY**—Sodomy—The Attraction of Persons of the Same Sex—Caused by ♅ influence, and afflictions of ♅ to the ☉, ☽, or ♀ at B. Even the good aspects of ♅ to the ☉ or ♀ may lead to sex perversions and abnormalities. Also caused by ♆ affl. in 7th H. (See "Licentious" under Men; Perversions, Unnatural, Vices).

**HONEST**—Honesty—Upright—Honourable—Frank—Sincere—Open-Minded—Trustworthy, etc.—The ☉ in ♌, or the ☉ Sig. in ♌, and well-aspected; the ♌ influence tends to, being the sign of the ☉; ♌ on the Asc., and with the ☉ as ruler; the ☉ Sig. in ♒; the ☽ incr. in light, and apply. to ♃, unless ♂ be in □ or ☍ ♃, which would modify; ♄ Sig. in ♐; ♃ rising at B., well-aspected and dignified; ♃ ruler and well-aspected; ♃ in the Asc., well-aspected and dignified; ♃, ♄, and ☿ well-placed and well-aspected; ♃ in the M.C., near the Meridian, well-aspected, and in a strong sign, honourable, and also confers honors and dignity; ♀ Sig., and in ⚹ or △ ♃; ♀ on the Meridian, dignified and well-aspected, unless affl. by ♄; ♀ Sig. in ♊; the 1st face of ♎ or ♐ on the Asc. (See Character, Cheating, Conduct, Criminal, Deceitful, Dishonest, Evil, Forgers, Gambling, Good, Honour, Hypocritical, Liars, Libelers, Morals, Noble, Principles, Recreations, Reliable, Responsibility, Robbers, Sincere, Trustworthy, etc.).

**Honourable Things**—Strives After—☿ Sig. in ♐, but seldom attains them.

**Tolerably Honest**—The ☽ Sig. □ or ☍ ☿, and ☿ well-asp. by ♃. (See Dual, Miserly, Selfishness).

**HONOUR**—Honor—Honorable—The Honour is ruled by the 10th H. (See Tenth).

**Death**—In Affairs of Honor—(See Contests, Duels).

**Honorable**—The Native Is Honest and Honourable—(See Honest).

**Loss of Honour**—The Honor is affected by the directions to the Midheaven, and the M.C. afflicted by the evil aspects of planets tends to loss of honor; the ☉ directed to the Ascelli; ♄ or ♂ to the cusp the 10th H. by dir.; ♄ to the ☌ or ill-asp. the radical ☉ by dir.; the periodic direction of ♄ to the radical ☉; ♃ by periodic revolution to the ill-asps. the radical ☉. (See Anxiety, Disgrace, Misfortune, Renunciation, Reputation, Reversals, Ruin, Scandal, Sorrows, Trouble, etc.).

**HOOKED FORWARD**—(See Bending; "Downward Look" under Look; "Stoop Shoulders" under Shoulders; Stooping).

**HOPE**—Hopes—Hopeful—Ambitions—Desires—Hope is ruled by the 11th H. conditions. (See Ambition, Desires, Eleventh House).

**Hopeful**—Sanguine—Cheerful—Optimistic—(See Cheerfulness; "Peace of Mind" under Mind; Optimistic; "Sanguine Temperament" under Sanguine).

**Hopes Cut Off**—Lack of Hope—In a Weak and Hopeless State—Malefics in the 11th H.; lord of the 11th a malefic, and espec. ♄, and in the 12th H. (See Dejected, Despair, Despondency, Insanity, Invalids, Low Spirits (see Low); Melancholy, Mutable Signs (see Mutable); Optimism, Worry, etc.).

**Life**—Small Hope of Life—The Sick Will Hardly Escape—(See "Hope" under Life; "Sick" under Escape).

**HORARY QUESTIONS**—A Horary Map is a Map of the Heavens made up for the time of an incident, a worry, an anxiety, or the beginning of a disease, at decumbiture, at the taking to bed in illness, etc., and the aspects, sign and house positions of the planets at such a time usually give the key to the situation, and the possible outcome for good or ill. Many of the influences listed in this Encyclopaedia are Horary. The Rules of Horary Astrology are given in Lilly's Astrology,

Wilson's Dictionary of Astrology, Simmonite's Horary Astrology, Alan Leo's New Dictionary of Astrology. Also a short Article in Sepharial's New Dictionary of Astrology. (See Cardinal, Course, Cure, Decumbiture, Diagnosis, Duration; "Fixed Signs" under Fixed; Long Diseases (see Long); Mutable Signs (see Mutable); Prognosis; Querent, Quesited, Recovery; "Diseases" under Short).

**HORAS**—These are the positive and negative halves of Signs, and are known as the Solar and Lunar Horas. The Solar Horas are the positive halves, and the Lunar Horas are the negative halves. Malefics in the positive, or Solar Horas, are very powerful, and weak when in the negative, or Lunar Horas. Benefics are stronger when in the Negative Signs, and Negative Horas, and weaker when in the positive, or Solar Horas. In the odd, or positive signs, the first half is positive, or Solar, and the second half negative, or Lunar. In the even, or negative signs, the first half is negative, or Lunar, and the second half positive, or Solar. It is well to bear these distinctions in mind in judging of the force of the benefics or malefics in disease or health, and in the matter of the duration of disease, prognosis, etc. Mr. E. H. Bailey, in his Journal, The British Journal of Astrology, is devoting considerable time and space to the subject of Horas, and their influences. (See "Negative Signs" under Negative; "Positive Signs" under Positive).

**HORNY GROWTHS**—Cornifications—♄ influence. (See Bunions, Cornifications, Corns, Growths, Hardening, Nails, Scales).

**Venereal**—Horny Venereal Growths—(See Venereal).

**HOROSCOPE**—The Star Map, or Figure of the Heavens, made up for the time, place, year, day, month, and hour of birth. It shows what is hidden in our auric atmosphere; shows our weaknesses of mind and body, as well as our tendencies and strong points, our talents, possibilities, suitabilities, likes and dislikes, antipathies, aversions, sympathies; shows what diseases are liable to come from birth to death, their nature and possible time, or the event; the parts of the body more liable to be afflicted, and the possible outcome of any diseases; shows the crises in disease, when they are due; shows our relation to Nature, environment, and the Will of The Higher Powers for us during the present life in the physical body. To follow the leadings of the Natal Map, its good and strong points, insures greater success with less effort, and to avoid failures and unnecessary illnesses, sorrows, reversals, downfalls, etc. The influences of the Horoscope begin at birth, and endure until the death of the body. Congenital defects belong to the Antenatal Period. The Map, or Figure of the Heavens, for the time of Conception, also indicates and shows the tendencies of the native, and the Prenatal Map, the map for time of Conception, should also be studied along with the Natal Map. (See Conception, Character, Destiny, Fate, Map, Medical Astrology, Natal, Nativity, Power, Prenatal Epoch, Radix).

**HORRORS**—Terrors—Fears—

**Nervous Horrors**—The Asc. to the □ or ☍ ♄ by dir. (See "Nervous Fears" under Fears). For collateral study along the lines of the Horrors that can come to mind and body, see Darkness; "Delirium Tremens" under Delirium; Demoniac, Dreadful, Dreams, Fears, Forebodings, Hallucinations, Insanity, Mania, Nightmare (see Dreams); Obsessions, Portentous, Premonitions, Solitude, Spirit Controls, Terrors, Visions, Weird, etc.).

**HORSES**—Mules—Horses are denoted by, and ruled by the 12th H. in the map of the native, and this house shows his relation and fortune with them, and also with all large animals. Mules (Hybrids), a cross between the Horse and Ass, are barren. (See Barren). Horses are also ruled by ♃ and the ♐ sign, and people born under ♐ are usually fond of horses, and horseback riding, and all sports wherein horses are used.

**Accidents**—Caused by Horses, or In Their Use—Injuries By—Death By—Falls From, etc.—(See "Injuries" and the various paragraphs in this section).

**Bites By**—(See "Animals" under Bites).

**Danger By**—(See the various paragraphs in this section).

**Death Of**—(See "Many Horses Die" in this section).

**Falls from Horses**—Hurts, Injury or Death By—Afflictions in ♐; the ☽ in ♐, and affl. by the ☉ or ♂; ♅ or ♂ in the 12th H. (See Falls).

**Head**—The Native Has a Horse-Shaped Head—♐ on the Asc.

**Hurts By**—(See "Injuries", and the various paragraphs in this section).

**Hybrids**—(See Barrenness).

**Injury By**—Accidents, Hurts, Injuries by Horses—Injury by Large Animals—The ☉ or ☽ affl. by ♂ at B., and the Lights to the ☌ or ill-asp. ♂ by dir.; the ☉ or ☽ ☌ ♂ in ♐ in the Asc.; the ☽ in ♐ and affl. by the ☉ or ♂; the ☽ affl. at B., and to the ☌ cusp of 12th H. by dir.; the Prog. ☽ ☌ ♄ or ♂ in ♐; ♅ or ♂ affl. in the 12th H. at B., and affl. the cusp of 12th H. by dir., or planets in the 12th; ♄ in ♐, and affl. by ♅ or ♂; ♂ in ♊, ♍, or ♐, and ☌ or ill-asp. the Asc. by dir.; ♂ ☌ the Asc. by dir.; ♂ in ♐ in the Asc., and afflicted; ♂ in ♐ in the Asc., 6th, 8th, or 12th H., and afflicted; ♂ ruler of the 5th H., and affl. in ♐; ♐ on the Asc., 6th, 8th, or 12th H., and afflicted; ♐ on the Asc., and ♃ ruler in the 6th, 8th, or 12th H., and in ☌ ♄ or ♂. (See Bites, Falls, Kicks, Thrown, and the various paragraphs in this section; Animals, Beasts, Bites, Cattle, Elephants; "Great Beasts" under Great; Quadrupeds).

**Kicks By**—Thrusts—(See Kicks).

**Large Animals**—Horses, Cattle, Elephants, Great Beasts, etc.—Injuries By—(See "Injuries" in this section).

**Many Horses Die**—Destruction of—Horses and Mules Die—An eclipse of the ☉ in the 3rd Decan. of ♐, or an eclipse of the ☽ in 2nd Decan. of ♐; an eclipse of the ☉ in ♐; ♂ in ♋ at the Vernal Equi., and lord of the year; ♂ in ♐, direct in motion, at the Vernal, and lord of the year. (See "Death of Animals" under Animals; "Virus" under Pestilence).

**Mules**—Hybrids—(See Barrenness).

**Races**—The Winning Horse In Races—(See the Article on "Colours" in Wilson's Dictionary of Astrology. Also see "Race Horses" under Colors in this book. Also see the book, "The Silver Key", by Sepharial).

**Riding**—Fond of Horseback Riding—Fond of Horses and Outdoor Sports—The ☉ or ☽ in ♐; ♃ Sig. in ♐; a ♐ influence; ♐ on the Asc. at B. Malefics in ♐ add to the dangers, and may result in injury or death. (See Falls, Injury, Thrown, in this section; Exercise, Hunting; "Death" under Sports).

**Thrown**—Thrown From a Horse While Riding—Injury or Death By—The ☉ or ☽ ☌ ♂ in ♐ in the Asc.; the Prog. ☽ ☌ ♄ or ♂ in ♐; ♂ in ♐ in the Asc., and afflicted; ♐ on the Asc., and ♃ ruler in the 8th H. in ☌ ♄ or ♂. (See Falls, Injury, Riding, in this section).

**Thrusts**—Kicks—(See Kicks).

**Veterinary Surgeon** — Adapted To—(See Veterinary).

**HOSPITALS**—Sanitariums—Asylums—Are ruled by ♆ and the 12th H. The same influences which tend to place people in an Asylum, or Hospital, with illness or mental derangement, also tend to self-undoing, and to make the native his own worst enemy, and to undermine the health by dissipation and wrong living, and if people would live right, and obey the Laws of Health, there would be little need for Hospitals. Perfect health can only be attained when people become spiritualized, and more conscious of their Inner and Divine Powers, and of the presence of The Christ within them. It would be a strange sight to see one of the Great Masters, Adepts, or Initiates, lying sick in a Hospital, as they have learned how to conquer and prevent disease, and to rule their Stars, instead of being ruled by them.

**Confinement In**—Danger of Being Confined In a Hospital—The 12th H. prominent at B., and probably containing the ☉, ☽, ♄, or an afflicting planet; the ☉ or ☽ affl. in the 12th H.; the ☉ is usually affl. by ♀, and the ☽ by ♄; the Prog. ☽ ☌ or ill-asp. ♆ by dir., if ♆ is afflicted at B.; ♄ in ♓, or in the 12th H., and afflicted, danger of being confined by some chronic disease; ♆ affl. at B.; ♆ or ♅ affl. in the 12th H.; ruler of the Asc. in the 12th H.; afflictions in the 12th H. (See "Causes" under Chronic; Confinement; "Asylums" under Insanity; Invalids, Pisces, Prisons, Twelfth House).

**Death In Hospital**—Liable To—The ☽ affl. in the 8th H. at B., and also affl. by ♄ by dir. (See "Death" under Prison).

**Employment In**—Successful In Hospital Work—The ☉, ☽, ♄, ♃, or ♀ in

the 12th H., and well-aspected; ♃ well-asp. in ♓; ♂ in ♓ in the 12th H., and well-aspected, tends to success as a Surgeon in Hospitals, Asylums, or Prisons. (See Healers, Nurses, Prisons, Surgeons, Twelfth House).

**HOT**—Heat—Warmth—(See the various paragraphs under Fire, Heat, Warmth).

**HOUR**—Hours—

**Hour of Death**—Probable Time of—(See "Hour" under Death).

**Planetary Hours**—(See "Hours" under Planets).

**Womb**—Hour-Glass Contraction of—(See "Hour-Glass" under Womb).

**HOUSES**—The Twelve Mundane Houses of the Heavens—The Houses have an effect on the body in accordance with their correspondence with the Signs of the Zodiac. Thus ♈ and the 1st H. rule the head; ♉ and the 2nd H., rule the neck and throat, and so on around thru the signs and houses. The Houses rule the same parts of the body as ruled by its corresponding Sign, but in a secondary way. In matters of health, diagnosis, and prognosis, it is important to know the house position of planets, and the influence of each house at B., and especially of the 6th H., the house of health, and also of the 1st H., or Asc., the house which rules largely over the physical form. The Houses are positive and negative, masculine and feminine, the same as the Signs. The Odd Houses, as the 1st, 3rd, 5th, etc., are positive and masculine. The Even Houses, as the 2nd, 4th, 6th, etc., are negative and feminine. The Houses are also classed as Angular, Succedent, and Cadent. (See Angles, Cadent, Cardinal; "Fixed Signs" under Fixed; Mutable, Negative, Positive, Signs, Succedent; "Odd and Even" in this section). Good Articles on the influences of the Houses are to be found in Wilson's Dictionary of Astrology; Sepharial's New Dictionary of Astrology; Alan Leo's New Dictionary of Astrology; Sepharial's Manual of Astrology; Lilly's Astrology.

**Angles**—The 1st, 10th, 4th, and 7th Houses, the houses on the East, South, North and West places of the map. (See Angles).

**Ascendant**—The sign rising on the Eastern horizon at B., and also known as the 1st H. (See Aries, Ascendant, First House).

**Cadent Houses**—The 3rd, 6th, 9th, and 12th H. (See Cadent).

**Eighth House**—Known as the House of Death. Corresponds to the ♏ sign. (See Eighth House, Scorpio, Terminal).

**Eleventh House**—The House of Friends, Children, Hopes, Wishes, etc. (See Eleventh).

**Even Houses**—(See "Odd and Even" in this section).

**Feminine Houses**—The Even Houses, as 2nd, 4th, etc. (See "Odd and Even" in this section).

**Fifth House**—The House of Children, Amusements, Speculation, Love Affairs, Women, Pleasure, etc. (See Fifth).

**First House**—(See Angles, Aries, Ascendant, First House).

**Fourth House**—The House of the Close of Life, a Terminal House—(See Fourth, Nadir, Terminal).

**Masculine Houses**—The Odd numbers, as the 1st, 3rd, 5th, etc. (See "Odd and Even" in this section).

**Negative Houses**—The Even Houses —(See "Odd and Even" in this section).

**Ninth House**—The House of the Higher Mind, of Philosophy, Religion, and also of Foreign Travel or Residence. (See Ninth).

**Odd and Even Houses**—The Positive and Negative—The Masculine and Feminine—The 1st, 3rd, 5th, 7th, 9th, and 11th Houses are the odd, positive, and masculine houses, and rule the left side in a male, and the right side in a female. The even, negative, and feminine houses are the 2nd, 4th, 6th, 8th, 10th, and 12th Houses, and rule the right side in a male, and the left side in the female. The house position of the afflicting planet shows which side of the body is afflicted, according to the sex of the native. (See Feminine, Left, Masculine, Negative, Positive, Right).

**Positive Houses**—(See "Odd and Even" in this section).

**Second House**—(See Second House).

**Seventh House**—(See Descendant, Seventh).

**Signs of the Zodiac**—The Signs As Related To the Houses—(See each Sign in the alphabetical arrangement, as Aries, Taurus, Gemini, etc.).

**Sixth House**—The House of Health, and related to the ♍ Sign. (See Sixth).

**Succedent Houses**—The 2nd, 5th, 8th, and 11th Houses, those following an Angle. (See Angles, Cadent, Succedent).

**Tables of Houses**—The Tables by Joseph G. Dalton are much in use, showing the cusps of the houses for places between the Latitudes of 22° to 56° North. Also a Table of Houses for the same degrees of Latitude is published by the Rosicrucian Fellowship, of Oceanside, Calif. A Table of Houses published by Raphael gives the cusps for each degree of Latitude from the Equator to 50° North, and also for 59° 56′ N.

**Tenth House**—The Midheaven—(See Tenth).

**Terminal Houses**—Those having to do with Death, and the End of Life. They are the 4th, 8th, and 12th Houses. (See Eighth, Fourth, Terminal, Twelfth).

**Third House**—(See Third).

**Twelfth House**—(See Confinement, Limitations, Terminal, Twelfth).

**HUMAN**—

**Human Form**—Signs of—Articulate Signs—(See Articulate; "Nature of Events" under Events; Mankind; "Human Shape" in this section).

**Human Hands**—Human Means—Accident, Death, or Injury By—(See "Hand of Man" under Man).

**Human Ostrich**—Eats Glass, etc.— Case—See "Human Ostrich", No. 986 in 1001 N.N.

**Human Race**—Humanity—Every Evil To—(See "Every Evil" under Evil; Humanity).

**Human Shape**—Of Human Shape, Yet of Beastly Form and Savage In Disposition—(See "Resembles Animals" under Animals; "Beastly Form" under Beasts; Inhuman, Monsters, Savage, Wild).

**Human Signs**—Signs of Human Form —Speaking Signs—♊, ♍, ♒, and the 1st half of ♐. Also ♎ is included by some Authors. The Airy Signs are especially classed as Human Signs because they give a kinder and more human, or humane disposition, and this is especially true of the ♒ sign. When the lord of the geniture, or the Asc., is in one of these signs at B., the native is of humane disposition. The lord of an eclipse falling in a Human Sign, its evil effects will fall upon Humanity. (See Articulate; "Air Signs", "Whole Signs", under Signs).

**HUMANE**—Kind—Sympathetic—Spiritual—A special characteristic of the ♒ sign. Abraham Lincoln, the Emancipator, was born with the ☉ in this sign. Also given by ♃ when this planet is ruler at B., strong and well-aspected. (See Aquarius, Ideals, Jupiter, Noble, Philanthropic, Pity, Sympathy).

**HUMANITY**—Mankind—The Public—

**Every Evil Upon**—(See Calamities, Comets, Drought, Earthquakes (see Earth); Epidemics; "Every Evil" under Evil; Famine, Floods; "Human Signs" under Human; Mankind, Pestilence, Plague, Prevalent, Public, Storms, Volcanoes, etc.).

**HUMERUS**—The Large Bone of the Upper Arm—Is under the structural rulership of the ♊ Sign.

**Atrophy Of**—♄ affl. in ♊; Subs at LCP (6C), and at AP. (See Atrophy).

**Exostosis Of**—♄ or ♂ affl. in ♊; Subs at LCP (6C), and AP. (See "Bones of Arm" under Arms).

**Fracture Of**—♄ or ♂, or both, affl. in ♊. (See "Accidents", "Broken Arms", under Arms).

**HUMIDITY**—Humid—Moisture—Humidity is ruled by the ☽.

**Much Affected by Humidity**—Increased Moisture In the Body—Denoted by the ☽, and when the ☽ afflicts the ☉ or Asc. (See "Bodily Temperament", and the various paragraphs under Moisture).

**HUMMING**—Droning—Buzzing—A Low, Murmuring, Monotonous Sound—Ruled by ♆. (See Singing, Speech, Voice).

**Humming Bird**—The Humming of Bees—Buzzing—Said to be ruled by ♆. (See Bees).

**HUMOURS**—Humors—Humor—Any Fluid of the Body—Ruled by the ☽ in general, as the ☽ rules the Fluids of the body. Corrupt and Disease Humors are ruled by ♄ and ♂, and also caused by the afflictions of the malefics to the ☉, ☽, and Asc. (See Fluids).

**Abounding**—Humours Abounding— Brings Humours by Directions—The ☉ to the ☌, P., □, or ☍ the ☽ by dir., and the ☽ hyleg or afflicted at B.; the ☽ to the ☌ or ill-asp. ♄ by dir.

**Aqueous Humor**—(See Aqueous; "Aqueous Humor" under Eyes).

**Bloody Humour**—(See "Bloody Flux" under Flux).

**Bowels**—Humours In—The ☉ affl. in ♍ when the ☉ is the afflictor in the disease. (See Bowels, Diarrhoea, Dysentery, Flux).

**Breast**—Humours Falling Into—(See "Humours" under Breast).

**Brings Humours**—(See "Abounding" in this section).

**Choleric Humours**—(See Choleric).

**Cold Humours**—Caused by ♄, and are ♄ diseases. (See Cold. For Cold Humours in the Stomach see "Raw Humours" under Indigestion).

**Cold and Moist Humours**—Diseases Which Proceed from Cold and Moisture—Cold and Moist Distempers—Cold and Watery Diseases—The ☉ or ☽ to the ☌ or ill-asps. ♄ by dir., and the Lights affl. at B.; the ☽ to the ☌ or ill-asp. ♅ by dir.; the ☽ ☌ the Asc. by secondary dir.; ☽ diseases; watery signs on the Asc. and 6th H. at B., or at decumb., or the Sigs. of the disease in them at the beginning of an illness; afflictions in ♓, as the feet are cold and moist; ♀ affl. in ♐. The right or left sides of the body are more subject to, according to the sex. (See Cold; "Odd and Even" under Houses; Left; "Cold and Moist" under Moisture; Right).

**Corrupt Humours**—The ☽ affl. at B., and to the evil asps. the Asc. by dir.; ♄ diseases; ♂, and other afflictions in ♓, corrupt humours in the feet. (See Corrupt, Decay, Discharges, Gangrene, Impure, Mortification, Putrefaction).

**Defluxion of Humours**—Downward Flow of—(See Defluxion).

**Dropsical Humours**—(See "Danger Of", "Humours", under Dropsy).

**Dry Humours**—(See "Humours" under Dry).

**Dysentery**—(See Dysentery).

**External Humours**—Internal Humours—The External and Internal Humoural Secretions—♂ and the ♏ sign preside over the plexuses and the intestinal ganglia which rule the external and internal humoural secretions. The Humoural Secretions are also especially affected by the physiological action of the ♀ Group of Plants. (See "Venus Group" under Herbs; "Physiological Action" under Venus).

**Extremities**—Humours In—(See "Humours" under Extremities).

**Eyes**—Humourous Discharges From—(See "Discharges", "Hot", under Eyes).

**Father**—The Father Suffers From—(See "Humours" under Father).

**Feet**—Corrupt Humours In—(See "Humours" under Feet).

**Fingers**—Humours In—(See "Humours" under Fingers).

**Flow of Humours**—A ♓ disease; the Asc. to the ☌ the ☉ by dir., and the ☉ in a watery sign. (See Catarrh; "Humours" under Flow, Head).

**Fluids**—(See the various paragraphs under Fluids).

**Fluxes**—(See Flux).

**Flying Humours**—☿ diseases. (See Flying).

**Gross Humours**—The Body Full of—The ☽ in ♓ and afflicted by the ☉ or ♂ when taken ill (Hor'y). (See "Gross Blood" under Blood).

**Goutish Humours**—(See "Humours" under Gout).

**Hands**—Humours In—(See "Gout", "Humours", under Fingers, Hands).

**Head**—Humours In—(See "Humours" under Head).

**Hips and Thighs**—Humours In—(See "Humours" under Hips; "Hot" in this section).

**Hot Humours**—In the Head, Eyes, Hips, Thighs—♂ influence; ♂ in the sign which rules the part. (See "Hot Humours" under Eyes, Head, Heat, Hips).

**Humoural Changes**—Those which interfere with the economy of the system are ruled over by the ☽.

**Internal Humours**—(See "External" in this section).

**Lachrymal Humours**—(See "Humours" under Tears).

**Legs**—Humours In—(See Gout, Humours, Rheumatism, under Legs).

**Moist Humours**—Moist and Cold Humours—(See "Moist Humours" under Moisture; "Cold and Moist" in this section).

**Morbid Humours**—(See "Offensive" in this section).

**Nose**—A Humour In—(See Catarrh, Colds; "Coryza", "Humour", under Nose).

**Offending Humours**—The principal Humour offending is indicated by the 6th H., planets in the 6th, the rulership of the cusp of the 6th at B., or at decumb. (See Sixth House).

**Offensive Humours**—Peccant—Morbid—Unhealthy—Those which accompany infections, and the presence of ptomaines, leucomaines, toxins, etc. The ♄ influence and afflictions encourage such action, and accompanied by lowered vitality. (See Offensive).

**Peccant Humours**—(See "Offensive" in this section).

**Principal Humour Offending**—(See "Offending" in this section).

**Raw Humours**—(See "Raw Humours" under Indigestion).

**Rheum**—Watery or Catarrhal Discharge—(See Rheum).

**Secretions**—Humoural Secretions—(See "External", and the various paragraphs in this section; Secretions).

**Splenic Humour**—(See Spleen).

**Stomach**—Raw Humours In—(See "Raw" under Indigestion).

**Thighs**—Humours In—(See "Humours" under Hips).

**Throat**—Humours Falling Into—(See "Humours" under Throat).

**Undigested Humours**—(See "Raw Humours" under Indigestion).

**Unhealthy Humours**—(See "Offensive" in this section).

**Vitreous Humor**—(See "Vitreous" under Eyes).

**Watery Humours**—(See Catarrhs, Colds, Discharges, Fluxes, Rheum; "Humours" under Watery).

**HUMPBACK**—Hunchback—Angular Curvature of the Spine—(See "Humpback" under Spine).

**HUMUS**—A Dark Material from Decaying Vegetable Matter—(See "Decay" under Vegetation).

**HUNGER**—Cravings—Desire for Food—(See Appetite, Cravings, Diet, Drink, Eating, Epicureans, Excesses, Feasting, Gluttony, High Living (see High); Indulgence, Intemperate, Obesity, Plethora, Surfeits, etc.).

**HUNTING**—Injury In, and In Sports While Hunting, and Especially While Riding Horses—Afflictions in ♐. (See Gun-shot; "Riding" under Horses. Also see Amusements, Exercise, Pleasure, Recreation, Shooting, Sports, etc.).

**HURRICANES**—Tornadoes—Wind Storms—Suffering, Injury, or Death From—(See High Winds, Storms, Tornadoes, under Wind).

**HURRIED**—Rapid—Accelerated—

**Heart Beats**—Hurried Heart Beats—(See "Accelerated" under Heart; "High Pulse" under Pulse).

**Respiration Hurried**—(See "Rapid" under Breath).

**Speech**—Hurried Speech—(See "Rapid" under Speech). See Accelerated, Exaggerated, Intense, Rapid.

**HURTFUL**—Causing, or Tending to Cause, Hurt or Injury—The result of the adverse action of the malefic planets, and of the evil aspects between the ☉, ☽, and planets, afflictions to the Asc., and Hyleg. (See Accidents, Affliction, Blows, Bruises, Burns, Cuts, Hurts, Injuries, Wounds, etc.).

**Hurtful Signs**—Of the Zodiac—Obnoxious Signs—♈, ♉, ♎, ♏, and ♑. Planets in them at B. tend to Distortions. These Signs on the Asc. at B. make the native more liable to Blows, Falls, Wounds, and other Injuries. (See Distortions, Lameness, Obnoxious).

**Hurtful to No One**—Harmless—Inoffensive—(See Harmless).

**HURTS**—Trauma—Injury—Wounds, etc.—This word covers a wide range of subjects, as disease, affliction, accidents, injuries, wounds, etc., which are classed as Hurts in Astrology. The various Hurts that can occur to the native are also listed largely under Accidents, Disease, Injury, etc. The influences and afflictions of the malefic planets, and especially when they are afflicting the ☉, ☽, Asc., or Hyleg at B., and by direction, tend to Hurts and Injuries. Hurts by Drowning, Plots, Trance, Treachery, Water, are caused by ♆. Sudden Hurts, as by bathings, water, electricity, explosions, machinery, etc., are caused by ♅. Hurts by falls, bruises, contusions, are caused by ♄. Hurts by violence, cuts, stabs, injuries, loss of blood, wounds, etc., are caused by ♂. There are also the many sources of Hurts, as by the hand of Man, by beasts, animals, hurts in battle, war, hurts by insects, reptiles; by bites, kicks; by machinery, in travel and on railroads or on ships; by burns, scalds, fire, chemicals, liquids, etc. Then the Hurts to the different parts of the body. If you do not find in the following list the particular injury, or part of the body hurt, look in the alphabetical arrangement for the subject, or part, you have in mind, and look for "Accidents", "Hurts", "Injuries", "Wounds", under the part, as under Arms, Head, Face, Hips, Legs, etc. The following list of subjects is more abstract, and giving the causes, the sources, and kinds of Hurts. People born with the Hurtful Signs on the Asc., or with planets in them, are more liable to hurts and violence. (See "Hurtful Signs" under Hurtful, the Article before this one). In judging of the liability to Hurts, Wounds, Accidents, Disease, Injury, etc., the Asc., or the 1st H., and its opposite house, the 7th H., and the planets afflicting the Hyleg, are to be considered, and judgment given by their general character. See the following subjects in the alphabetical arrangement when not considered here—

**Accidents**—Note the various paragraphs under Accidents).

**Acids; Aeroplanes; Air; Amelioration of Hurts**—The benefics elevated above the malefics which produce them, and also to cause a moderation in disease. (See Amelioration).

**Amusements; Animals**—(See Animals, Beasts, Quadrupeds).

**Assassination; Assaults, Automobiles**—(See Vehicles).

**Bathing**—(See Bathing, Drowning).

**Battle**—(See War).

**Beasts**—(See Animals, Beasts, Four-Footed, Quadrupeds).

**Bites; Blemishes**—From Hurts—(See Blemishes, Blindness, Crippled, Deformities, Disfigurements, Lameness, Limbs, Scars, etc.).

**Blood**—Loss of Blood by Hurts—(See Cuts; "Loss of Blood", under Blood; Hemorrhage, Stabs, etc.).

**Blows; Brother**—Hurts To—(See Brother).

**Bruises; Buildings**—Hurts by the Fall Of—(See Buildings).

**Burns; Calamities; Carelessness;**

**Casualties; Catastrophies; Cattle**—(See "Attacks By" under Cattle).

**Chemical Action**—Hurts By—(See Acids, Chemical, Drugs, Narcotics, Poisons, etc.).

**Childhood**—Hurts In—(See Childhood).

**Children**—Hurts to Women and Children—The ☽ to the ☌ or ill-asp. ♂ by dir., and the ☽ affl. by ♂ at B., and hurts to women especially. (See "Accidents" under Childhood, Children, Females, Women).

**Chronic Hurts**—Given by ♄, and espec. to that part of the body ruled by the sign or house in which ♄ was placed at B. (See Chronic).

**Cold**—Hurts By—(See Cold).

**Concussion; Constitutional Hurts**—(See "Hurts" under Constitution).

**Contests; Contusions**—(See Bruises).

**Curable Hurts**—(See Curable; "Amelioration" in this section).

**Cuts; Danger of Hurts**—(See "Liable To" in this section).

**Dangerous Hurts**—(See "Dangerous" under Accidents; "Violent" in this section).

**Death by Hurts**—(See "Death" under Accidents, Injuries, Violence. Also note the various paragraphs in this section, and under Death).

**Diseases**—Hurts By—(See the various paragraphs under Disease, Ill-Health, Sickness).

**Dislocations; Distortions; Drink;**

**Duels; Early Years**—Hurts In—The ☉ or ☽ to the ☌ or ill-asp. ♂, or other malefics, by dir. during childhood; ♂ coming to the ☌, □, or ☍ the Asc. or Desc. in early life usually causes hurts, wounds, injuries, or fevers if the nativity denotes them. (See "Accidents" under Childhood, Children; "Early Years of Life" under Early; "Early Youth" under Youth).

**Earthquakes**—(See this subject under Earth).

**Eating**—Hurts from Wrong Eating—(See Diet, Eating, Food).

**Electricity**—(See Electricity, Lightning).

**Employment**—Hurts In—(See Employment).

**Enemies**—Hurts By—(See Enemies).

**Escapes**—Narrow Escapes from Hurts—(See Escape).

**Exercise**—Hurts During—(See Exercise, Sports).

**Falls; Family**—Hurt to Some Member of the Family—(See Family).

**Father**—Hurts To—(See Father).

**Females**—Hurts To—(See "Accidents" under Females, Women; "Children" in this section).

**Fire**—Hurts By—(See Burns, Fire).

**Fire Arms**—(See Gunshot).

**Floods**—Hurts By— (See Floods).

**Four-Footed Beasts**—Hurts By—(See Animals, Beasts, Four-Footed, Quadrupeds).

**Fractures; Friends**—Hurts To—(See "Absent Party" under Absent; Friends).

**Gases; Gunshot; Habits; Hand of Man**—Hurts By—(See Hand of Man).

**Healers**—Hurts By—(See "Injured By" under Healers).

**Heat**—Hurts By—(See Burns, Fire, Heat, Scalds).

**Heights**—Hurts by Falls From—(See Heights).

**Hemorrhage; Highwaymen**—Hurts By—(See Highwaymen).

**Homicide; Horses**—Hurts By—(See Horses, Kicks).

**Human Hands**—Human Means—Hurts By—(See "Hand of Man" in this section).

**Hunting**—Hurts and Injuries While Hunting—(See Hunting).

**Hurtful Signs**—(See "Hurtful Signs" under Hurtful).

**Husband**—Hurts To—(See Husband).

**Ill-Health**—(See the various paragraphs under Ill-Health).

**Incisions**—(See Cuts, Duels, Instruments, Stabs, Sword, Weapons).

**Incurable Hurts**—Without Remedy—Permanent In Effects—(See Crippled, Incurable, Permanent).

**Indiscretions; Infancy**—Hurts In—(See "Accidents" under Infancy).

**Injuries**—(See the various paragraphs under Injuries).

**Insects**—Hurts By—(See Adder, Bites, Insects, Stings, Venomous).

**Instruments**—Hurts By—(See Instruments).

**Iron**—And Steel—Hurts By—(See Iron).

**Judging of Hurts**—(See the Introduction to this Article).

**Kicks; Lacerations; Lameness**—From Hurts—(See Crippled, Lameness).

**Liable to Hurts**—Danger of—Tendency To—Susceptible To—The malefics oriental tend to hurts and injuries, and when occi. to disease. A planet in evil asp. to a Sig. at B. promises hurt, and espec. when by transit or dir. it thereafter affects the same Significator; the ☉ or ☽ affl. by ♂, or other malefic, at B., and to the ☌ or ill-asp. ♂ by dir.; the ☉ to the ill-asps. ☿ by dir., and ☿ afflicted at B.; ♆ or ♅ affl. the ☉, ☽, Asc., or hyleg at B., and by dir.; ♄ rising at B., and affl. the ☉ or ☽; ♄ ☌ or ill-asp. ♂, and espec. if either planet be oriental; ♂ □ or ☍ the ☉ or ☽ at B.; ♂ in evil asp. to ♄ at B.; ♂ on the Asc. at B., and affl. the ☉, ☽, Asc., or hyleg by dir.; the transits of ♂ as promittor over the place of the ☉ and ☽ at B.; ♂ to the ☌ or evil asp. of ♄ by tr. or dir., and espec. when ♂ was affl. by ♄ at B., and the danger is increased if ♂ be stationary or ℞ at the time; malefics in the 8th H. at B., and to the ☌ the Desc. by Oblique Descension. (See "Danger Of", "Tendency To", under Accidents, Injuries).

**Lightning**—Hurt, Injury or Death By—(See Lightning).

**Liquids**—Hurts By—(See Acids, Bathings, Drowning; "Hot Liquids" under Heat; Liquids, Scalds).

**Loss of Blood**—From Hurts or Accidents—(See "Loss Of" under Blood; Cuts, Duels; "Lesions" under Hemorrhage; Instruments, Stabs, Sword, Weapons, etc.).

**Machinery**—Hurts By—(See Employment, Machinery; "Accidents" under Uranus).

**Maiming; Males**—Hurts To—(See Brother, Father, Husband; "Accidents" under Male; Men, Son, Uncle).

**Maritime Pursuits**—Hurts In—(See Drowning, Maritime, Navigation, Sea, Ships, Shipwreck).

**Men**—Hurts To—(See the various paragraphs under Men).

Mobs Hurts By—(See Mobs).

Mother—Hurts To—(See Mother).

Murdered—(See Murder).

Navigation — Hurts In — (See "Maritime" in this section).

Operations — Surgical Operations—Hurts By—(See Operations, Surgeons).

Parents — Hurts To — (See Father, Mother, Parents).

Permanent Hurts—The Effects Incurable—(See Incurable, Permanent).

Pleasure—Hurts In the Pursuit of—(See Amusements, Exercise, Hunting, Pleasure, Recreations, Sports, Theatres).

Plots—Hurts By—(See Plots).

Poison—Hurts By—(See Poison, Plots, Treachery).

Quadrupeds—Hurts By—(See "Four-Footed" in this section).

Quarrels — Hurts In — (See Assaults, Blows, Contests, Cuts, Duels, Enemies, Gun-Shot, Quarrels, Stabs, etc.).

Railroads — Hurts On — (See Railroads).

Rash Acts—Hurts From—(See Hasty, Rashness).

Recreations — Hurts During — (See Bathings, Exercise, Hunting, Pleasure, Recreation, Sports, Theatres, Travel).

Relatives — Hurts To — (See Family, Relatives).

Remedy — Hurts Without Remedy — (See Blemishes, Crippled, Deformed, Distortions, Incurable, Maimed, Permanent, Remedy, etc.).

Reptiles; Reputation — Hurts To — (See Disgrace, Honour, Reputation, Ruin, Scandal, etc.).

Riding—Hurts In—(See Horses).

Robbers—Hurts By—(See Robbers).

Ruptures; Scalds; Scars; Sea—Hurts On the Sea—(See "Maritime" in this section).

Searing—(See "Searing" under Burns).

Serpents; Sharp Instruments — (See Cuts, Duels, Instruments, Stabs, Weapons).

Ships — Hurts On — (See Sea, Ships, Shipwreck).

Shipwreck; Signs—The Hurtful Signs of the Zodiac — (See "Hurtful Signs" under Hurtful; Obnoxious).

Sister—Hurts To—(See Sister).

Snow—Suffering From—(See Snow).

Sports—Hurts In—(See Amusements, Exercise, Horses, Hunting, Sports).

Stabs; Steel and Iron — Hurts By — (See Iron).

Stings; Stones—Hurt by Flying Stones —(See "Assaults" under Stone).

Storms—(See Blizzards, Floods, Lightning, Rain, Storms, Thunder, Weather, Wind).

Strange Hurts — Sudden and Unexpected— Extraordinary—Unusual—Denoted by ♅ and his afflictions to the ☉, ☽, Asc., or hyleg at B., and by dir. Also caused by ♆. (See Extraordinary, Mysterious, Peculiar, Strange, Sudden, Tragical, Uncommon, Unusual).

Strangulation; Sudden Hurts — ♅ influence. (See "Strange" in this section).

Suffocation; Surgeons — Danger To — (See Surgeons).

Susceptible—To Hurts—(See "Liable To" in this section).

Sword; Tendency — To Hurts — (See "Liable To" in this section).

Theatres—Hurts, Injury, or Death In —(See Theatres).

Thieves—Hurts By—(See Highwaymen, Pirates, Robbers, Thieves).

Time of Hurts — When Apt to Occur —The Periods by Directions and Transits Which Bring Such Dangers—The ☉ or ☽ to the ☌ or ill-asp. ♂ or other malefics by dir.; ♂ ☌ the Asc. by tr. or dir.; malefics to the ☌ or ill-asp. the ☉, ☽, Asc., M.C., or hyleg by dir. (See "Time" under Accidents, Death, Disease, Evil. Also see Comets, Crises, Critical, Directions, Eclipses, Epidemics, Escapes, Events, Ingresses, Periods, Prognosis, Prognostication, Progression, Secondary Directions (see Secondary); Time, Years).

Tornadoes—Hurricanes—Hurts By—(See "Tornadoes" under Wind).

Trampled—(See Crushed, Mobs, Trampled).

Trance; Travel—(See "Accidents" under Abroad, Journeys, Travel, Voyages).

Treachery; Unexpected Hurts — (See "Strange" in this section; Unexpected).

Vehicles—Hurts By—(See Vehicles).

Violent Hurts—(See Violent).

Volcanoes; Voyages—Hurts On—(See Maritime, Navigation, Sea, Ships, Shipwreck, Travel, Voyages).

War; Water — Hurts By — (See Bathing, Drowning; "Hot Liquids" under Heat; Scalds, Sea; "Accidents" under Water).

Weapons; Weather; Wife — Hurts To — (See Husband, Marriage Partner, Wife).

Wild Animals—Hurts By—(See "Wild Animals" under Animals; Beasts; "Dangers" under Travel; Wild).

Wind — (See "High Wind", "Tornadoes", under Wind).

Women—Hurts By—Hurts To—(See "Injured by Women" under Men; Treachery; "Injuries To" under Women).

Wounds—(See the various paragraphs under Accidents, Injuries, Wounds, and also the paragraphs in this section).

Youth — Hurts In — (See Childhood, Children; "Early Years" under Early; Youth).

HUSBAND — Fiance — The ☉ rules the husband, or fiance, in a female nativity, and also the 7th H., the house of marriage, the marriage partner, and partnerships, and afflictions to the ☉, or to planets in the 7th H., indicate his fate, health, etc. Remember that all the influences in this section are in the wife's map, and affect her relations to the husband, and in the Article on "Wife", the influences given there will be taken from the map of the Husband.

Accident to Husband—Danger of—♂, or other malefics, to the ☌ or ill-asp.

the ☉ by dir., and espec. those falling in the 7th H.; the ☉ in a female nativity to the ☌ or ill-asp. ♂, or other malefic, and the accident or hurt will be of the nature as given by the malefic; ♂ to the ☌ or ill-asp. the ☉ by dir., and espec. if it fall in the 7th H., there is danger of a serious accident to the husband, death by the accident, or to have an illness with a very high fever; ♂ or ♅ affl. in ♎ or the 7th H. in a female nativity. (See "Accident" under Wife).

**Afflicted**—The Husband Afflicted—The directions of the ☉ in the wife's map afflict and affect the husband for good or ill; ♄ affl. in ♎ or the 7th H. (See "Afflicted" under Wife).

**Anchorite**—The Husband An Anchorite — A Celibate — Averse to Having Children—The ☉ affl. by ♄ in a female nativity; ♄ in the 11th H.; ♀ affl. by the ☽ and ♄, and ♀ in a sign of ♄, and the ☽ in the sign of ♀. This may also lead to sterility. (See Barren, Celibacy).

**Barrenness In**—Sterility—(See Barrenness).

**Celibacy Of**—(See "Anchorite" in this section).

**Children** — Averse To — Children Not Wanted—(See "Anchorite" in this section).

**Danger To** — The ☉ in the 7th H. in the wife's map, and eclipsed at a Solar return, and the ☉ also afflicted by malefics; ♄ in the 7th H. at B., and near the cusp, and again in the 7th H. at a Solar Revolution. (See "Danger To" under Wife).

**Death Of**—Danger of Death of Husband, or of Fiance—The ☉ affl. by ♅, ♄, or ♂ at B., and by dir.; the ☉ to the ☌ or ill-asp. ♄ by dir., or other malefics; the ☉ affl. by malefics, and a malefic in the 7th H. at B.; the ☉ apply first to ♃, and then to ♅, and espec. if ♅ or ♄ be in the 7th H.; the ☉ to the ☌ or ill-asp. ♅ by dir., the husband may die within the following year; ♅ affl. in the 7th H., danger of sudden death of; ♄ ☌, □, or ☍ the ☉ at B., or by dir.; ♄ affl. in the 7th H. at B.; ♄ at a Solar Rev. passing the place of the radical ☉, and espec. if the ☉ be hyleg, and ♄ be stationary; ♂ in the 7th H. at B., danger of death by violence, accident, or fever; ♂ in evil asp. the ☉ at B., and under the adverse direction of ♂ to the ☉ after marriage; lord of the 6th or 8th H. in the 7th H. (See Dies Before Wife, Pleurality, Sudden, in this section; "Death Of" under Fiance, Marriage Partner, Wife; Widows).

**Delicate In Health**—Sickly—(See "Ill-Health Of" in this section).

**Dies Before Wife**—Will the Husband Die Before the Wife?—One of the best ways to get at this question is to erect a Horary Figure unless the Artist is thoroughly familiar with the age, constitution, habits, and stamina of the Querent, but the information should not be revealed. In Hor'y Q., the lord of the 1st H. and the ☽ are taken for the man, and the lord of the 7th and the ☉ for the woman, and judge of the nature of the aspects to them. An-

other method is to measure the distance in degrees between the lords of the 1st and 7th H., and the lord of the 8th, and then predict that the one will die first whose Sig. is nearest the lord of the 8th. The following influences, if they exist in the map of the wife, indicate the death of the husband before the wife,—Malefics in the 7th H. at B.; the planet to which the ☉ first applies being a malefic; malefics afflicting the ☉, or the Sig. of the wife; ruler of the 7th a malefic, and ℞. For a woman to marry when the ☽ is combust is a bad sign, and indicates the possible death of the husband within two years after marriage. (See Widowers, Widows; "Dies Before Husband" under Wife).

**Drink**— Drunkard— Dissolute Habits — Husband May Be Given To — The Husband Improvident and Profligate— ♂ in the 11th H. in map of wife; ♂ in a watery sign and affl. the ☉; ♂ ☌ or ill-asp. the ☉; ♄ □ or ☍ the ☉ in the wife's map, the husband improvident. (See "Husband" under Drunkenness; "Dissolute", "Drink", under Wife).

**Dull and Timid**—♀ connected with ♄ in the wife's horoscope. (See Dull).

**Early Death Of**—Malefics in the 7th H. in map of wife, danger of; lord of the 6th in the 7th, and espec. if ♂ be in the 7th H. (See "Early Death" under Wife).

**Fever**—The Husband Subject to Fevers—Death by High Fever—♂ affl. in the 7th H.

**Fiance** — Death or Illness of — (See Fiance).

**Fruitful** — The Husband Fruitful — Signs of—♃ in the 11th H. of the wife. The wife's nativity must also show fruitfulness. (See Fruitfulness; "Fruitful" under Wife).

**Grave and Morose** — Troublesome — The ☉ applying to ♄ in the wife's map. (See "Grave" under Wife).

**Habits**—(See "Drink" in this section).

**Hasty**—Unfaithful—Untrue—♅ in the 7th H. in wife's map, and in □ or ☍ the ☉, danger of; ♂ ☌ or ill-asp. ♀ in wife's map. (See "Free Love" under Free; "Liaisons" under Love Affairs; "Clandestine" under Sex).

**Ill-Fortune To** — The ☉ to the ☌ or ill-asp. malefics by dir. in wife's map.

**Ill-Health Of**—The Husband Delicate In Health—The ☉ at B., or the Prog. ☉, in ☌ or P. ♄ in the map of the wife; the ☉ affl. by malefics, and a malefic in the 7th H. at B.; the ☉ to the ☌ or ill-asp. malefics by dir.; to marry when ♅, ♄, or ♂ are in the Asc. of the wife's nativity; ♅, ♄, or ♂ in the 7th H. of the wife. Directions of the ☉ in the wife's horoscope affect the husband for good or ill. (See "Sickly" under Marriage Partner; "Ill-Health" under Wife).

**Imprisoned Thru Wife** — (See "Wife" under Prison).

**Improvident** — (See "Drink" in this section).

**Killed by Accident** — (See "Accident" in this section).

**Marriage** — Bad Time For, and the Health Affected—To marry when the ☉ is badly aspected by directions in the wife's map, or when malefics are in the Asc. or 7th H. of her map. Also the husband should not marry when the directions of ♄ badly afflict the ☉, ☽, Asc., or hyleg in his own map. (See "Best Time to Marry" under Marriage).

**Marriage Partner** — (See the various paragraphs under Marriage Partner).

**Men** — Males — (See the various paragraphs under Males, Men).

**Murders His Wife**—Murders His Wife, Fiancee, or Sweetheart — Danger of — ♂ □ or ☍ ♀ in the map of the lady. Case—See "Holloway", No. 189, in 1001 N.N. (See "Strangles" in this section).

**Older Than Himself**—Marries a Lady Older Than Himself—(See "Older Than Himself" under Marriage).

**Plurality of Wives**—The ☽ applying to several planets at the same time in the map of the man. Also ♀ and many planets in the double-bodied signs at B. tend to, and espec. ♀ affl. in ♊; ♄ affl. in the 7th H. of the husband may result in the death of several wives. The tendency is for the wife to share the fate of the husband's map, and if a woman does not want to die an early death by marriage, she should know the map of the fiance beforehand, and not go into the marriage relation blindly, and in ignorance of his horoscope. These same influences also indicate several marriages for the wife, and a wife so born may separate from, or bury several husbands. (See Widowers, Widows).

**Poison**—Husband Commits Suicide by Poison—Case—See "Husband", No. 162, in 1001 N.N.

**Profligate**—(See "Drink" in this section; "Dissolute" under Wife).

**Relatives** The Husband's Relatives The Relatives of the marriage partner, with both husband and wife, are said to be ruled by the 9th H. of the map. The male relatives are ruled by ♂, and the female relatives by the ☽ and ♀. Malefics in the 9th H., or lord of the 9th a malefic, indicates trouble with the marriage relatives, or their ill-health. Benefics in the 9th, good relations, and good health for them. (See Relatives; "Relatives" under Marriage Partner, Wife).

**Several Marriages** — (See "Plurality" in this section).

**Sickness Of**—(See "Ill-Health" in this section).

**Sterile** — (See Barrenness, Impotent; "Anchorite" in this section).

**Strangles Wife**—Death of Wife—Case —See "Beach Murder", No. 134, in 1001 N.N.

**Sudden Death**—The ☉ to the ☌ or ill-asp. ♅ or ♂ in the wife's map; ♅ or ♂ afflicting the 7th H.; ♂ afflicting the ☉ by ☌, P., or ill aspect. (See "Death" in this section).

**Suffers**—The Husband Suffers — (See Accident, Afflicted, Drink, Ill-Health, in this section).

**Suicide Of**—(See "Poison" in this section).

**Timid and Dull**—(See "Dull" in this section).

**Unfaithful** — Untrue—(See "Liaisons" under Love Affairs; "Hasty" in this section).

**Unfruitful** — (See "Anchorite" in this section).

**Unsteady**—(See Drink, Hasty, in this section).

**Untrue**—(See "Hasty" in this section).

**Widowers** — (See Widowers; "Plurality" in this section).

**Wife** — Note the various paragraphs under Wife).

**Wives** — May Have Several Wives — (See "Plurality" in this section).

**HYACINTH**—A Mineral or Stone ruled by the ☉. (See "Metals and Minerals" under Sun).

**HYADES**—Seven stars of the 3rd magnitude, a Nebulous cluster, in the first part of ♉, in the Bull's Head, violent in nature, and of the nature of ♂ and the ☽, and said to bring most every evil upon the native when directed to the ☉, ☽, or Asc. Their influences when with the ☉ or ☽ at B., or afflicting the Lights, tend to eye disorders, weak sight, blindness, hurts to the eyes or face, to measles, death from fevers, or a violent death. The ☉ with the Hyades at B. is indicative of evil, and liable to a violent death. The ☉ directed to them brings the danger of blindness in one or both eyes. The ☽ Sig. in ☌ the ☉ near the Hyades, likely to be nearly blind. The ☽ to the place of, great defect in the sight, and often blindness. The Asc. to the place of, wounds or hurts to the eyes, cuts, danger from sharp instruments, and often death from fever. The Fixed Stars and Nebulous Groups of the nature of ♂ and the ☽ are the Ascelli, Castor, Pollux, Hyades, Deneb, Pleiades, Praesepe. The Hyades are frequently listed and mentioned in this book. See such subjects as Beheaded, Blindness, Blows, Disgrace, Evil, Eyes, Face, Ill-Health, Imprisonment (see Prison); Murder, Nebulous, Pirates, Ruin, Shipwreck, Stabs, Stars, Violent Death (see "Death" under Violent); Wounds.

**HYBRIDS** — Mules — (See the Introduction under Barrenness. Also see Horses).

**HYDATID CYSTS**—A Cyst of the Tenia in its Larval State — (See "Cyst-Like Tumor" under Brain; Cysts).

**HYDRAEMIA** — Hydrohaemia — (See "Thin Blood" under Blood).

**HYDRA'S HEART** — Cor Hydra — Alphard—A star of the 2nd magnitude in the 1st face of ♌, and of the nature of ♄ and ♀. Tends to bring many evils upon the native when directed to the ☉, ☽, Asc., or hyleg. For some of the influences of this star see "Animals" under Bites; Calamity, Disgrace, Drowning; "Malice of Fortune" under Fortune; Intemperance; "Injured by Women" under Men; "Ill-Fortune" under Wife and Mother; "A Murderer" under Murder; "Death" under Poison; Riotous, Ruin).

**HYDROCARBONATES**—Carbohydrates, Starches, Sugars, Cellulose, etc.—Ruled by ♃. (See Jupiter, Starches, Sugar).

**HYDROCELE**—Caused by the ☽ affl. in ♏. (See Scrotum, Testes).

**HYDROCEPHALUS** — Dropsy of the Brain—Water On the Brain—A ☽ disease; the ☽ affl. in ♈, and espec. when in the Asc. or 6th H.; a ♆ disease; ♆ affl. in ♈; ♆ in ♈ and affl. by ♄; ♆ in ♈, ☌ the ☉ or ♂, and affl. by ♄; lords of the 1st or 6th, or the ☽, in watery signs; Subs at AT, KP (11D). Cases—See "Hydrocephalus", Nos. 147, 148, in 1001 N.N. See Fig. 17C in "Astro-Diagnosis", by the Heindels. (See Dropsy, Enlarged; "Large Head", "Swells", under Head).

**HYDROCHLORIC ACID** — One of the principal Digesting Juices of the Stomach. A lack of is caused by ♄ affl. in ♋, and resulting in Indigestion. Also caused by ♄ ☌ ☽ in ♋, as the ☽ rules the juices of the stomach in general. (See Acids, Digestion, Fluids, Indigestion, Juices; "Hydrochloric" under Stomach).

**HYDROCYANIC ACID**—A Typical Drug of ♄. (See Acids; "Drugs" under Saturn).

**HYDROGEN** — Ruled by ♄, and has affinity with Cold. (See Cold, Gases, Saturn). Hydrogen is also related to the 4th Ternary of the Signs of the Zodiac, the ♋, ♏, and ♓ Signs, the watery signs, and is the dominant element of these signs. (See "Operations" under Nature; "Signs" under Water).

**HYDROHAEMIA**—(See Hydraemia).

**HYDRONEPHROSIS**—(See this subject under Kidneys).

**HYDROPHOBIA**—Fear of Water. Also a Symptom of Rabies.

**Fear of Water**—A ♆ influence; ♆ ☌ or ill-asp. ♄ at B., and by dir.; ♆ affl. in the 8th H., and may cause death by water, as by drowning; Subs at AT, SP, and KP. (See Fears).

**Hydrophobia**—Rabies—Death or Injury from Mad Dog Bite—The ☉ or ☽ to the ☌, □, or ☍ ♂ by dir.; ♂ afflicting the hyleg by dir.; afflictions in common signs show, and espec. by evil aspects to the ☉ or hyleg. (See Bites, Dogs, Lock-Jaw).

**HYDROSALPINX**—(See "Dropsy" under Fallopian).

**HYDROTHORAX**—Water On the Chest —(See "Dropsy" under Chest).

**HYGIENE** — Disposed to the Study of Hygiene, Diet, Sanitation, Medicine, etc.—The ♍ Sign strong at B.; ♍ upon the Asc. or 6th H.; the ☉ or ♂ well-asp. in ♍, and also with increased interest in Sanitation; the ☉ in the 6th H., the house of ♍, and espec. with the ☉ in ♍. (See Cure, Diet, Food, Healers, Prevention, Remedies, Sanitation).

**Hygienic Reformer** — See "Lybeck", No. 212, in 1001 N.N.

**Hygiene Specialist** — See "Wallace" No. 292, in 1001 N.N. See "Health Foods" under Food; "Diet and Hygiene", "Specialties", under Healers.

**HYLEG**—The Giver of Life—Apheta—Prorogator — The ☉, ☽, and Asc. are the principal Prorogators, or Givers of Life. Also ♃, ♀, and the Part of Fortune (⊕) may become the Hyleg if they are in a hylegiacal place at B., strong, dignified, and well-aspected, and the ☉, ☽, or Asc. are not in such places. The ☉ is the Giver of Life in a day nativity if in a hylegiacal place, dignified, and well-aspected, and the ☽ is the Prorogator by night if similarly strong by sign, aspect, and house position. The Significator should be in one of the Aphetical places in order to be strong. In a male nativity the ☉ or Asc. should be taken as Hyleg if they are so situated, and in a female horoscope, the ☽ or Asc. are the first to be considered for hyleg, and if the ☽ is not strong, then ♀ should be taken as hyleg in a female nativity if in an aphetic place. In a male horoscope, ♃ may well be taken as hyleg if this planet is in dignity, and qualified for such a position, and the ☉ or Asc. are out of proper dignity. In cases of extreme emergency for a hyleg, the Part of Fortune is mentioned by some Authors as permissible to be taken as Hyleg if in a hylegiacal place, and all the other Significators are weak, and not in such places. The Asc. may be taken as Hyleg with either sex. It is advocated by some Writers that the ☉, ☽, or Asc. may become Hyleg at some time after birth by progressing into one of the hylegiacal places soon after birth, but this theory is not very strongly upheld, and does not account for the death in many instances where the supposed progressed ☉, ☽, or Asc. have been so taken. The degree rising on the Asc. at B. is always a most vital place, and is usually afflicted and badly involved in every death, whereas any other degree which may be taken after birth does not show such vital importance in accounting for death. The duration of life depends upon the Hyleg, the Hylegiacal Places, and the rulers of these places, for long life, and the ☉, ☽, Asc., or Benefics in such a place indicate long life, and strong vitality, whereas the malefics in such places weaken the strength and prospect of long life. (See Anareta; "Long Life", "Short Life", under Life). The question of death is ruled over by the afflictions to the Hyleg, the Terminal Houses, and the planets therein. (See Terminal). The Hyleg when coming to the ☌ of malefics is always weakened, and with danger of disease or death. A Hyleg which is badly afflicted by malefics at B., or in an Anaretic Place, should be avoided, and some other one chosen, as ♃, ♀, the Asc., or ⊕, if the ☉ or ☽ cannot be taken as Hyleg. When the Hyleg sets, death ensues, and the West Angle becomes Anareta. It usually takes a train of evil directions to the Hyleg to produce death, and one adverse direction is rarely considered as strong enough to cause death. (See "Arguments for Death" under Death; Directions).

**Hylegiacal Places**—These are the parts of the map, or Houses of the Heavens at B., which give greater vitality and endurance to the native when the ☉, ☽, Asc., or Benefics, are found in these places. The majority of Writers ascribe the following places and degrees to be the Hylegiacal Places,—(1) From 25 degrees below the Asc. (rising degree), to 5 degrees above the Asc. (2) From 5 degrees below the cusp of the 9th H. to the middle of the 11th House. (3) From 5 degrees below the cusp of the 7th H. to 25 degrees above the Descendant. There is a picture of the Hylegiacal Places in Sepharial's New Dictionary of Astrology, in the Article on Hyleg, showing the Hylegiacal Places in black, but with a little variation from the figures and degrees given for the 11th H. Sepharial gives the 2nd Hylegiacal Place as extending from 5 degrees below the cusp of 9th H. to extend over to the 25th degree of the 11th H. The student should also read the Articles on the Hyleg in the various standard Textbooks and Dictionaries of Astrology.

**The Hindu Hyleg** — The Hylegiacal Places In the Hindu System—These differ some from those used in the Western Astrology, but are strongly advocated by Mr. Bailey, the Editor of the British Journal of Astrology, and Mr. Bailey considers them more correct than the ones given as authentic in this Article. In the Hindu Astrology the Hylegiacal Places are as follows,—(1) From the middle of the Asc. to the middle of the 12th House. (2) From the middle of the 11th H. over to the middle of the 8th H. (3) From the middle of the 7th H. down to the middle of the 6th H. In any event, in either System, these places are calculated by Oblique Ascension. Mr. Simmonite, in his Arcana of Astral Philosophy, says that "No degrees under the Earth are eligible to the rule of Hylegiacal locus." The 6th and 8th Houses are classed as evil houses in the Western Astrology, and to allow one-half of these Houses to stand as a Hylegiacal Place, as is done in the Hindu System, would seem to be contrary to the facts in cases of disease and death. (For further study along this line see such subjects as Ascendant, Decumbiture, Descendant, Incurable, Jupiter; "Duration of Life" under Life; Moon, Part of Fortune, Prognosis, Sun, Terminal, Venus; "Centers" under Vital; Vitality; "Weak Body" under Weak, etc.).

**HYMEN**—Imperforate Hymen—(See "Hymen" under Vagina).

**HYOID BONE**—The Bone at the Root of the Tongue—(See "Hyoid" under Tongue).

**HYOSCYAMUS**—A Typical Drug of ♄. (See "Saturn Group" under Herbs; "Drugs" under Saturn).

**HYPERACIDITY**—An Abnormal Amount of Acid In the Body—Excess Deposits of Wastes and Poisons—Caused by the afflictions of ♄, and especially after middle life, and in old age. Also this condition is more common and prevalent with people born under negative Signs, and who have many planets at B. in the negative Signs and Houses, and with an earthy or watery sign upon the Asc., and also with the negative planets ♆, ♄, ♀, and the ☽ strong and predominant. A certain amount of acidity in the body is normal, but with age, under the influences and afflictions of ♄, the tissues begin to harden, crystallize, and deposits of Urea, Uric Acid, and other waste minerals, are made by ♄ in order to gradually bring on the death of the body, otherwise people would live too long, and overpopulate the Earth. Threescore years and ten are long enough for people to live in a physical body unless they are enlightened, highly spiritualized, and have some special mission to teach and help Humanity. An alkaline body, if not too excessively alkaline, is a healthy body, and when an excess of acidity predominates, and the body is no longer able to keep the balance between acidity and alkalinity, death ensues. The negative people, who are more susceptible to this condition, tend also to conditions of hyperacidity by worry, brooding, introspection, and morbid states of mind, which tend to lower the vital forces, and the resistance against disease, and negative people who are also born under the strong influence of ♄, tend to die an earlier death, and many of them commit suicide, and such people usually are over-charged with acidity, whether they be young or old. Acid conditions in the body are also hastened, and brought on, by excesses in diet, and the use of too much sweets and pastries, starches and sugars. This condition can be remedied by living upon a non-starchy diet, and the free use of fruit juices, such as of the lemon, orange, and grapefruit. Also the daily use of a soda drink, such as Upjohn's Citrocarbonate Effervescent Powder, helps to neutralize the over-acid conditions in the body, and to prolong life, and to keep the body in a healthy and balanced condition. (See Acids, Alkaline, Crystallization, Death, Decay, Deposits, Elimination, Gout, Hardening, Minerals; "Negative Nature", "Negative Planets", "Negative Signs", under Negative; Retention, Rheumatism, Saturn, Stoppages, Suppressions, Urea, Uric Acid, Wastes, etc.).

**HYPERACTIVITY** — Excessive — Exaggerated—

**Body**—Hyperactivity of—♂ influence, and ♂ strong at B.; due to the plus or tonic action of ♂. (See Accelerated, Action, Active, Energy, Enlarged, Exaggerated, Excessive; "Over-Exercise" under Exercise; Exertion, Growth, Increase, Motion, Movement, Muscles; "Over-Activity" under Over, etc.).

**Disease**—Fevers—Inflammations—The Hyperactivity of—(See "Causes" under Disease, Fever, Inflammation, Spasmodic, etc.).

**Mind**—The Psychic Powers—Hyperactivity of—(See "Over-Active Mind" under Active; Hypnotism; "Hyperactivity" under Psychic).

**HYPERAEMIA**—A Condition of Plethora—Due to the tonic, or plus action, of the ☉; a ☉ disease; the ☉, ♃, and afflictions in ♌; the ☉ ☌ or ill-asp. ♂; a ♃ disease; ♃ affl. in ♌; afflictions in

♌, general hyperaemia. (See "Too Much Blood" under Blood; Congestion, Dilatations, Distentions, Plethora, Surfeits, Swelling; "Vascular Fullness" under Vascular; "Pressure" under Vessels, etc.).

**Headaches**—Hyperaemic Headaches—(See Headaches).

**Liver** — Plethora Of — (See "Hyperaemia" under Liver).

**Lungs**—(See "Hyperaemia" under Lungs).

**HYPERAESTHESIA** — Excessive Sensibility—Hypersensitive—Supersensitive—Due principally to afflictions to ☿, as ☿ rules vibration, and afflictions to ☿ tend to increase the rate of mental and nerve vibrations, causing hypersensitiveness and nervous affections, or to cause a slower vibration, resulting in dullness, lethargy, lassitude, dulling of the senses, crawling and creeping sensations, etc. The ☉ □ or ☍ the ☽ tends to make one hypersensitive, quick to take offense; the ☉ affl. in ♐ or ♒; ☿ afflicted; ☿ affl. in the 6th H., hypersensitive to the condition of others, and liable to worries thru servants and subordinates, tending to affect the health. (See Augmented, Emotions, Excitable, High Strung (see "Strung" under High); Irritable, Mercury; "Neurotic" under Nerves; Sensation, Senses, Sensibility, Sensitive, Strain, Tension, Vibration, etc.).

**HYPERAMNESIA**—(See "Amnesia" under Memory).

**HYPERCHLORHYDRIA**—(See this subject under Stomach).

**HYPERIDROSIS** — Hyperhidrosis — Excessive Sweating—(See "Sweating" under Axillae, Feet; Dysidrosis; "Night Sweats" under Phthisis; "Excessive Sweating" under Sweat).

**HYPERKINESIA**—Exaggerated Muscular Contraction—(See "Hyperkinesia" under Muscles).

**HYPEROPIA**—Hypermetropia—Far-Sighted — (See "Hyperopia" under Sight).

**HYPERPYREXIA**—(See "High Fevers" under Fever).

**HYPERSENSITIVENESS** — (See Hyperaesthesia).

**HYPERTROPHY** — Abnormal Increase in the Size or Part of an Organ—♂ influence; a ♂ disease, and due to the tonic or plus action of ♂. Also ♃ presides to the Hypertrophic Process, and conditions of Plethora. (See Cirrhosis, Elephantiasis; "Organs" under Enlarged; Expansion, Plethora, Thickening; "Planets" under Tonic).

**Cells** — (See "Hypertrophy" under Cells).

**Heart**—(See "Dilatation", "Enlarged", under Heart).

**Skin**—Hypertrophy of Papillae of—(See Papilloma).

**HYPNOTISM** — Hypnotic — Odic Force —A Predominance of the Psychic Powers Over the Physical—The State of Artificial Somnambulism—Mesmerism—Magnetism—♆ is hypnotic in Nature, and Hypnotic is a Therapeutic Property of this planet. Also ♆ gives hypnotic powers. (See Clairvoyance, Magic, Magnetism, Mediumship, Negative, Neptune, Occult Powers (see Occult); "Sleep-Walking" under Sleep; Uranus).

**Best Time to Hypnotize**—When the ☽ is in airy sign, and especially in ♒.

**Hypnotic Drugs** — (See Anaesthetics; "Neptune Group" under Herbs; Narcotics).

**Hypnotic Subject**—Easily Hypnotized—Born under the strong influence of ♆, and also being a negative person; ♆ ☌ the ☉, ☽, or ☿ at B., or by progression; ♆ in the Asc., 10th, or 12th H.; the afflictions of ♆ to the ☉, ☽, Asc., or hyleg tend to; ♆ progressed to the ☌, P., □ or ☍ ♀, or vice versa; the Prog. ☉ or ☽ to the ☌ or ill-asp. ♆ by dir., and espec. if ♆ is afflicted at B. People who have many planets in the positive and masculine signs of the Zodiac at B., and who are highly individualized, are usually not hypnotic subjects. (See Impressionable, Mediumistic, Negative, Obsessions, Passive, Prophetic, Psychic, Spirit Controls, Suggestion, Susceptibility).

**Hypnotic Troubles**—Subject To—Born under the strong influence of ♆; ♆ affl. in the Asc., 6th, 8th, 10th, or 12th H.; ♆ affl. in ♓ in the 12th H.

**Mesmerist**—A Phrenologist and Mesmerist—Case—Birth Data of—See "Moores", No. 816 in 1001 N.N.

**Practices Hypnotism** — And Black Magic—♂ ☌ or ill-asp. ♆, and espec. the ☌, the native practices hypnotism or black magic, or may become the victim of such. (See "Black Magic" under Magic).

**Treatment**—Successful In Giving Hypnotic Treatment—Has Hypnotic Powers of Healing—The Hypnotic Powers of Healing are ruled by ♆, as ♆ is hypnotic in nature, and people who are born under the strong influence of ♆, and with ♆ well-aspected by ♂, and who also have fortunate influences in ♏, ♓, and the 8th or 12th Houses, make fortunate Hypnotic Healers, and in the use of Hypnotism for the treatment of Obsessions, Insanity, Spirit Controls, etc., and to use White Magic in their work. Also ♅ strong at B. gives such powers, and espec. when ♅ is well-aspected by ♆ and ♂; also ♅ ☌, ⚹, or △ the ☽. (See "Magnetic Healers" under Magnetic).

**HYPOCHONDRIA** — Hypochondriasis — Extreme Depression, and with Morbid Anxiety Concerning the Health—Brooding Over Disease and Ill-Health—Atrabiliary—Low Spirits—Vapors—Melancholy, etc.—The ☉ affl. in ♍ or the 6th H.; the ☉ hyleg, and to the ☌ or ill-asp. ♄ by dir.; a ☽ disease and afflictions to the ☽; the Prog. ☽ to the ☌ or ill-asp. ♄; a ♆ disease; ♆ affl. in ♊, ♋, ♍, or the 6th H.; ♆ in ♋ in the 6th H.; ♆ in ♋ and affl. the ☉, ☽, Asc., or hyleg; ♅ affl. in ♍; a ♄ disease; ♄ ruler of the Asc. at B.; ♄ to the ill-asps. his own place by tr. or dir.; ♄ ascending and affl. the ☉, ☽, Asc., or ☿; ♄ afflicting the ☽ or ☿; ♄ affl. in ♍ or ♑; a ♋ disease, and afflictions in ♋, or ♋ on the Asc.; a ♑ disease; ♑ upon the Asc. The color Red has a curing effect upon Hypochondria, and patients enclosed in a room surrounded by red glass have been greatly benefitted, and soon take on a more hopeful and cheerful spirit, and with increased appetite. (See Anxiety, Atrabile, Brooding, Dejected, Delusions, Depressed, Despondency, Fears, Gloom, Illusions, Imagination, Introspection, Melancholy, Morose, Obsessions, Stone, Suicide, Worry, etc.).

**HYPOCRITICAL**—Hypocrites—Hypocrisy—Presenting a Good Outside—Insincere—Deceitful—Duality, etc.—♄ Sig. in ♓; ♄ in the 9th H.; ♄ ☌ or ill-asp. ♀ or ☿, and espec. when ♄ is in the 9th H.; ♀ Sig. in ♋, puts best side outward, and seems to be in earnest when not; ☿ Sig. □ or ☍ ☽. (See Deceitful, Dishonest, Dual-Minded, Liars, Mockery, Treachery, etc.).

**Religion**—Hypocritical In—False Religionists—The ☉ Sig. ☌ ♃ and ♃ ill-dignified and badly aspected at B.; ♄ ☌ or ill-asp. ♀; ♄ affl. in the 9th H.; ♄ Sig. in ♓; ♂ affl. in the 9th H.; ☿ affl. by ♂; malefics in the 9th H.; the 4th face of ♊ on Asc. (See "False Religionists", "Fanatical", under Religion; "Impoverished" under Riches).

**HYPOGASTRIUM**—The Lower Anterior Portion of the Abdominal Region—Ruled and influenced principally by the ♎ sign.

**Affected**—The Hypogastrium Affected—(See Abdomen, Belly, Bowels; "Lumbar Ganglia" under Ganglion).

**HYPOPHYSIS CEREBRI**—(See Pituitary).

**HYSTERIA**—Hysterics—Hysterical—Vapors—The ☉ rules the emotional nature in women, and afflictions to the ☉ tend to this trouble. A ☉ disease; the ☉ ☌, □, or ☍ ♅ at B., and by dir.; the ☉ afflicted denotes hysterics in women; a ☽ disease; afflictions in the ☽ sign ♋; the ☽ □ or ☍ ☿; the ☽ hyleg in ♒ in female nativities, and afflicted; the ☽ affl. in ♒, or affl. the hyleg therefrom; the ☽ in ♒, ☌, or ill-asp. any of the malefics as promittors; the ☽ in ♒, ☌, or ill-asp. ♄ (or ☿ if he be of the nature of ♄) at decumb., or the beginning of an illness, and tends to the danger of suffocation in hysterical fits (Hor'y); hysterical patients are worse at the Full ☽; a ♆ disease; ♆ □ or ☍ ♃; ♆ in evil asp. to ☿; afflictions to ♆; ♆ in ♈ in the 9th H., and in □ or ☍ ♅, ♄, or ♂; ♆ in ♈ in ☌ ♅ or ♂, exaggerated hysteria; ♆ in ♈ in □ ♄, for selfish reasons; ♅ affl. in ♒; ♄ denotes death by; a ♂ disease; ♀ affl. in ♒ in the 6th H.; ♀ in ♒ and affl. the ☽ or Asc.; ☿ affl. in ♒; a ♑ disease, and afflictions in ♑, Subs at AT, AX, CP, and PP. Cases—See "Nymphomania", No. 306 in 1001 N.N. See Fig. 14E in "Astro-Diagnosis" by the Heindels. (See "Brain Storms" under Brain; Coma, Delirium, Delusions, Emotions, Exaggerated, Excitable, Fainting, Fits, Frenzy, Fury, Hallucinations; "Low Spirits" under Low; "Neurotic" under Nerves; "Psychic Storms", under Psychic; Vapors; "Spirit" under Vital).

**Mother**—The Mother Afflicted with Hysteria—The ☽ in the 4th or 7th H., and affl. by ♄. (See Mother).

# I

**ICE**—Ruled by ♄. (See Cold, Frost, Hail, Saturn, Snow, Winter).

**ICTERUS**—(See Jaundice).

**IDEALS**—Idealism—The Idealistic Temperament—The fiery signs, and especially ♐, tend to give Ideals, and the Idealistic Temperament, and to be interested in Utopianism. The earthy signs and ♄ have least to do with Ideals. As a rule ♉ and ♍ are the least Idealistic.

**High Ideals**—A special trait of the more spiritual sign ♒, and with the ☉ well-aspected in ♒ at B., or with ♒ on the Asc.; the 1st face of ♑ on the Asc. (See Honest, Humane, Noble; "Pious" under Religion).

**Impractical Ideals**—The afflictions of ♆ tend to, and to give wild-cat, radical, extreme ideals and notions, and to influence people to try the impossible and unreasonable way of doing things, and to lead the imagination beyond the limitations of reason. Where the horoscope indicates Humanitarian tendencies, the action of ♆ often leads to Utopianism, and espec. if the malefics ♄ and ♂ are obscurely placed, and weak in influence at B. The ♆ and ♂ influences combined tend to discontent with the present conditions in the World, and with a desire to create an ideal condition, or Utopianism. The ♅ influence combined with that of ♆ tends to a desire for rapid and sweeping Reforms. The earthy signs and ♄ give a more practical idea of things, but with tendency to endurance, and a more slow and plodding existence, get and keep what they can of material things, and to put up with things and World Conditions as they are. The ♓ sign in regard to Ideals is considered dreamy and impractical, and people with ☿ affl. in ♓ tend to be fanatical, scattering of their mental forces, and full of vagaries. (For collateral study see Anarchists, Chaotic, Conduct, Confused, Delusions, Destructiveness, Dreamy, Eccentric, Enthusiasm, Erratic, Fanatical, Fancies; "Fixed Ideas" under Fixed; Flightiness, Habits, Hallucinations, Ideas, Illusions, Imagination, Incoherent, Incoordination, Judgment, Misunderstood, Morals, Neptune, Notions, Novelties, Obsessions, Opinions, Peculiar, Reactionary, Reformers, Religion, Riotous, Strange, Uranus, Utopianism, Vagaries, Visionary, etc.).

**IDEAS**—Notions—Ideals—

**Extraordinary**—In Their Ideas—Extraordinary Pursuits and Objects—♅ influence; ♅ strong at B., ascending, rising; ♅ ☌ the ☉ or ☿ in the 10th H.

**Fixed Ideas**—Many planets in the fixed signs at B., and not easily changed. (See "Anxiety Neuroses" under Anxiety; Fixed; "Fixed Signs" under Fixed; Monomania, Obstinate).

**Flight of Ideas**—Confusion of Ideas—Mixed Ideas—(See "Chaotic Mind" under Chaotic; Confused, Dreamy, Erratic, Flightiness, Impulsive, Incoherent; "Bad" under Judgment; "Shallow Mentality" under Mental; Projects).

**Revolutionary Ideas**—(See Anarchists, Ideals, Nations, Reformers, Revolutionary, Riotous, etc.).

**IDENTITY**—Loss of—Disorientation—The ⊙ affl. in ♈. Subs at AT or AX. (See Memory).

**IDIOCY**—Idiots—Phrenasthesia—Imbecility—Extreme Mental Deficiency—Feeble-Minded—Loss of Reason—

**Born an Idiot**—Congenital Idiocy—This is caused by lack of proper adjustment in prenatal life between the Vital Body and the Physical Body, and the head of the Vital Body may be several inches above the skull, and very noticeable after birth to one who is clairvoyant. The angle of the Stellar Ray is thrown out of proper adjustment to the mother's body during gestation in cases of congenital idiocy. During the prenatal period there are also very serious afflictions in the ♈ sign, the sign which rules the head and brain, and which tend to stop, hinder, and suppress the proper growth and development of the encephalon, head, and skull, etc. There is also an Occult cause for congenital Idiocy, which the deeper students of the Occult Mysteries will find in their reading. Some Idiots are only human animals, and with no human soul. The book, "Cosmo-Conception" goes into these matters, and from the Rosicrucian standpoint, written by Max Heindel. The planetary aspects and influences at B. usually also conform to prenatal conditions, but do not always account for the condition if it existed at B. The configurations at B. indicate conditions which may arise after birth, as a rule, and to loss of mind or reason after birth, and to imbecility. Cases—Birth Data of Congenital Idiots—See "Idiot from Birth", No. 742, in 1001 N.N. See Fig. 12 in "Message of the Stars", by the Heindels. Case—Male Born Nov. 28, 1910, 1 p.m., New York City, N.Y. Other cases are listed under "Deaf and Dumb", and "Microcephalic" in this section. (See Congenital, Hereditary, Organic, Prenatal Epoch, Structural).

**Causes at Birth**—Influences which conduce to Idiocy at B., or after, or which may concur with prenatal conditions, are as follows,—☿ is the principal planet to be considered, and afflictions to ☿, the houses of ☿, as the 3rd and 6th H., and also the house position of ☿; ☿ unconnected with the ☽ or Asc. at B., and afflicted (see Epilepsy and Insanity, in which diseases these influences also predominate); ☿ ☌ ♂, and with the ☽ in ☍ ♄ culminating may tend to; ☿ combust and affl. by malefics, the ☽ also weak and afflicted, the Asc. afflicted by the presence or ill-asps. of malefics, no good asp.

between the ☽ or ☿, or between them and the Asc., the native is apt to be an Idiot or go insane. This may also happen when ☿ is not combust; ☿ ruler of the Asc., and in the 12th H., and affl. by ♂ (see Case of "Deaf, Dumb and Idiot" under Hearing); ☿ affl. at B., "a very idiot or ass", says one Author; ♃ in good asp. to ☿ at B. may preserve the faculties for some years, but with the danger of losing the reason under evil directions if the foregoing conditions exist at B.; ♆ affl. in the 3rd H.; ♅ affl. in the 6th H., danger of Idiocy, and if other afflictions to ☿ concur; ♅ ☌ the ☽ at B., and by tr. or dir., tend to a mild form of Idiocy for the time if other conditions in the map of birth so indicate; the 28° ♑ on the Asc.; Subs at AT and AX. Degeneration of the Thyroid Gland, ruled by ☿, also tends to Idiocy. (For other influences along this line, and collateral study, see Cretinism, Dwarf, Epilepsy, Foolish, Hallucinations, Imbecility, Incoordination, Insanity, Irrational; "Mental Deficiency", "Weak Mentality", under Mental; Myxoedema; "Loss of Reason" under Reason; Saint Vitus Dance, Thyroid; "Body" under Vital, etc).

**Deaf, Dumb, and Idiot**—Influences and Case Record—(See this subject under Hearing).

**Microcephalic Idiot**—With a Very Small Head—Case Record—See "Microcephalic", No. 086, in 1001 N.N. (See "Small Head" under Head).

**Unfortunate Case**—To a Great Extent An Idiot—Head Falls to One Side—See "Unfortunate Case", No. 351, in 1001 N.N.

**IDIOPATHY**—An Inborn Peculiarity—A Primary Disease—A Morbid State of Mind or Body—An Idiosyncrasy—An Individual Characteristic or Affection—(See Idiosyncrasies; "Morbid Mind" under Mind).

**IDIOSYNCRASIES**—Peculiarities of Constitution or Temperament—(See Congenital, Constitution, Diathesis, Heredity, Idiopathy, Morbid, Organic, Peculiar, Praeincipients, Structural, Susceptibility, Temperament, etc.).

**IDIOTS**—(See Idiocy).

**IDLE AND DULL**—Indolent—Easy Going—Ergophobia—Slothful—Lazy—Inert—Lassitude, etc.—The ⊙ weak at B., and badly aspected; the ⊙ or ☽ as Sigs. in ♋ or ♓ in Hor'y Q.; the ☽ weak and affl. at B., and in no asp. with ♂; the ☽ or ♃ Sigs. in ♑; the ☽ ill-dig. at B.; the ☽ cadent and afflicted, and with no good aspects from ♃, ♂, or ♀; ♆ in the 3rd or 9th H., and in asp. to the ☽ or ☿, indolent; ♄ ☌ the Asc. by dir.; a weak ♂ at B., of no spirit; ♂ affl. in ♓, or Sig. in ♓; ♀ ill-dig. at B., a lazy companion; ♀ Sig. in ♋; ☿ Sig. in ♉, idle, slothful, loves ease and gluttony; the ♉ influence strong at B., a lover of ease; ♓ influences tend to a dull and indolent disposition, and espec. ♓ on the Asc., or planets as Sigs. in ♓; the earthy and watery signs strong at B. tend to an inactive and indolent nature; the 22° ♋ on the Asc.; the 4th face ♑ on the Asc.; the cardinal signs weak at B. (See "Of No Ambition" under Ambition; Apathy, Careless, Dull, Ease; "Lack of Energy" under Energy; Exertion; "Resigned to Fate" under Fate; Gluttony, Imbecility, Improvident, Inactive, Indifferent, Inertia, Labour, Lassitude, Lazy, Lethargy, Listless, Negative, Neglect, Procrastination, Rouse, Sedentery, Work, etc.).

**IGNOBLE DEATH**—Ignominious Death —♄ ruler of the horoscope and afflicted by malefics; ♄ affl. in 10th H. (See Banishment, Beheaded, "Burned At Stake" under Burns; "Electrocution" under Electricity; Execution, Exile, Fugitive, Guillotine, Hanging, Impalement, Judges, Lynching, Mobs, Murdered; "Death In Prison" under Prison; "Public Death" under Death).

**Ignoble Life** — (See Conduct; "Low and Base" under Low; Morals).

**Ignominious and Violent Death**—The ☉ or ☽ Significators in ☌ ♂, and ♂ ill-dignified; the ☽ weak and ill-dig. at B., and to the ☌ the M.C., if there be symptoms of a violent death in the radix; a malefic in the 10th H., in □ or ☍ the Lights, if there are signs of a violent death in the figure. (See "Causes His Own Death" under Death; "Death" under Violent).

**ILEAC PASSION**—A Disease with Pain In the Abdomen, Faecal Vomiting, and Spasm of the Abdominal Muscles — Caused by ♄, and also ♄ causes death by; ♄ affl. in ♍; a ♍ disease, and afflictions in ♍; ♀ affl. in ♌ or ♍. (See Abdomen, Spasmodic).

**ILEUM**—The Lower Half of the Small Intestine. Ruled by ♍.

**Obstructions In**—Disorders of—♄ affl. in ♍; afflictions in ♍; Subs at PP. (See "Small Intestines" under Bowels; Obstructions).

**Ileo-Caecal Valve**—Obstruction In—♄ affl. in ♍.

**ILIAC** — Pertaining to the Ilium or Flanks. (See Flanks, Ilium, Sides).

**ILIUM** — Iliac — The Upper Part of the Innominate Bone—Hips—The Iliac Regions are ruled by ♏. The Iliac Arteries and Veins are ruled by ♐.

**Diseases In** — Afflictions in ♏, ♐, and the 7th H. (See Buttocks, Flanks; "Ilium" under Hips).

**ILL**—Bad—Evil—Misfortune—Not Advantageous, etc.—Due to its many subdivisions, the subject of "Ill-Health" is made up separately in the Article following this one. (See the various paragraphs under Bad, Evil, Fate, Fortune, Good).

**Ill-Affected**—(See Disease, Ill-Health, Indisposed, Sickness, etc.).

**Ill Blood**—(See Corrupt, Foul, Poor, under Blood).

**Ill Company** — Fond of Low and Bad Company—(See "Low Company" under Low).

**Ill Complexion** — (See "Bad" under Complexion).

**Ill-Disposed**—A Bad Disposition—The ☽ Sig. in ♍ or ♏; ♃ Sig. in ♏. (See Conduct, Cruel, Hatred, Judgment, Malicious, Revengeful, Temper; "Ill-Natured" in this section).

**Ill Events**—(See Directions, Events).

**Ill Fame** — (See Disgrace, Honour, Reputation, Scandal, etc.).

**Ill-Fated**—See Fate; "Malice of Fortune" under Fortune; Unfortunate).

**Ill-Favored Body** — ♄ in his second station at B. (See Crooked, Deformed, Ill-Health; "Much Sickness" under Sickness; "Ill-Formed" in this section).

**Ill-Formed Body**—Ill-Made Body—Ill Figure—Ill-Shaped—Ill-Proportioned — Crooked — Ugly — Misshaped — Ungainly—Ill-Composed—Disfigurements, etc.—All Constellations of human form tend to give a handsome shape and due proportions to the body. Constellations not of human form tend to vary the proportions, and incline towards their own shape by making the body larger, smaller, crooked, unshapely, stronger, or weaker. The ♄ and ♑ influences especially tend to give a crooked and misshaped body, and with ♄ in the Asc. at B., or with ♑ on the Asc. However, ♄ lord of the Asc. and occi., as between the M.C. and Desc., or between the Nadir and Asc., tends to give a good shape. In Hor'y Q. any planet as Sig. in ♑ indicates that the person inquired of is usually of an ugly, crooked, bony, thin, ungainly, and rather unpleasant appearance, stooped, and usually not handsome. The ♋ sign also tends to a misshaped body, and espec. when the ☉, ♄, ♃, or ♂ are Sigs. in this sign; ♄ Sig. in ♋ in partile asp. the Asc.; ♄ Sig. in ☍, an ill-made body, and awkwardly formed; ♄ Sig. in ♑ or ♓; ♄ Sig. in ♑, or with ♑ on the Asc., tends to make one thin and ungainly; the ☉ in ♋ partile the Asc., a mean and ill-made body; the ☽ ill-dig. at B., not handsome, but apt to be a muddling creature; the ☽ Sig. in ♏ or ♑; the ☽ Sig. in ♏, an ill-shaped, thick and short person; the ☽ □ or ☍ ♄; the ☽ when occi. gives a lean, short, and ill-formed body; ♂ in ♋ in partile asp. the Asc., short, crooked, and ill-made; ♂ Sig. in ♋, ill-made and misshaped body, and espec. if ♂ is afflicted by the ☉ or ☽; ☿ in ♏ or ♑ in partile the Asc.; ♓ on the Asc., an ill figure, crooked, stooping, and with head bent forward. (See Abnormal, Awkward; "Beastly Form" under Beasts; Blemishes; "Dogs" under Children; Contortions, Crooked, Defects, Deformities, Disfigurements, Distortions, Face; "Club Feet" under Feet; Imperfections, Incomposed, Incurvating, Inhuman; "Knock Knees" under Knees; "Bow Legs" under Legs; Malformations, Missing, Monsters, Stooping, Teeth, Ugly, etc.).

**Ill-Fortune** — (See Directions, Disgrace, Events; "Malice of Fortune" under Fortune; Miseries, Misfortune, Reputation, Reversals, Ruin, Sorrow, Trouble, Unfortunate, etc.).

**Ill Habits of the Body**—Thru the Use of Drugs or Narcotics—♆ diseases and afflictions. (See Disease, Habits, Hexis, Ill-Health, Narcotics, Sickness, Vices).

**Ill-Health**—(See the next Article after this one).

**Ill-Humour** — Out of Sorts — (See Irritable, Temper; "Ill-Natured" in this section).

**Ill-Made Body**—(See "Ill-Formed" in this section).

**Ill-Mannered**—(See Manners).

**Ill-Natured**—Ill-Disposed—Ill Temper—Bad Disposition—Turbulent Nature, etc.—The ☽ Sig. in ♈, ♍, ♏, ♑, or ♓; the ☽ Sig. □ or ☍ ♄; ♄ Sig. in ♈ in Hor'y Q.; ♄ Sig. □ or ☍ the ☽; ♄ Sig. ☌, □, or ☍ ♂, or vice versa, and espec. when in angles; ♄ ☌ the Asc. by dir.; ♂ Sig. in ♉; ☿ affl. at B., and in evil asp. the Asc. by dir.; ☿ Sig. in ♈, ♋, ♌, ♑, or ♓. (See "Ill-Disposed" in this section; "High Temper" under Temper).

**Illness** — (See Disease, Health, Ill-Health, Sickness).

**Ill-Placed** — (See "Right Side" under Heart; "Floating" under Kidneys; Organs; "Ill-Placed" under Teeth).

**Ill-Proportioned** — (See "Ill-Formed" in this section).

**Ill-Treated**—(See Beaten, Cruel; "Injured By" under Healers; "Ill Treatment" under Sickness).

**ILL-HEALTH** — Illness — Illnesses — Sickly—Diseased, etc.—The subject of Ill-Health is also largely treated and considered under "Disease", and "Sickness", and the subjects in this Article are largely a repetition, but arranged for ready reference, as disease, sickness, suffering, etc., are so often referred to as "Ill-Health" in the Textbooks of Astrology. See the following subjects in the alphabetical arrangement when not considered more fully here—

**Abroad** — Ill-Health Abroad — (See Abroad, Foreign, Travel).

**Absent Party**—Ill-Health or Death of—(See Absent).

**Accidents**—Ill-Health Due To—(See "Illness" under Accidents).

**Acute Diseases**—(See Acute).

**Ailing**—Is Always Ailing—(See Ailing).

**Ailments; Air** — Ill-Health from Bad Air—(See "Corrupt" under Air).

**Anxiety**—Ill-Health Thru—(See Anxiety).

**Attracts Disease**—(See Attracts).

**Aunts**—Ill-Health of—(See Aunts).

**Bad Health** — (See Chronic; "Bad Health" under Health; Invalids, Sickly, Sickness, Vitality Low; "Weak Body" under Weak; the various paragraphs in this section).

**Begins** — Ill-Health Sets In — (See "Time Of" in this section; "Time" under Disease; "Periods of Bad Health" under Health).

**Better** — The Health Is Better — (See "Better" under Disease, Health).

**Blood**—Ill-Health from Impure Blood—(See Impure).

**Bodily Ailments**—(See Ailments, Disease, Infirmities, Sickness; the various paragraphs in this section).

**Brings Disease Upon Himself** — (See "Brings Disease" under Disease).

**Brother**—Ill-Health of—(See Brother).

**Business Cares** — Ill-Health From — (See Cares).

**Cares** — Ill-Health From — (See Anxiety, Cares, Troubles, Worry).

**Causes**—Causes of Ill-Health—Causes His Own Illnesses — (See "Causes", "Brings Disease", under Disease).

**Childhood**—Ill-Health In—(See Childhood, Children, Infancy).

**Children** — Ill-Health of — (See Childhood, Children, Early Years, Infancy, Youth).

**Chronic Ill-Health** — ♄ rising at B. tends to chronic ill-health, and espec. in the latter part of life. (See Chronic, Invalids, Lingering; "Ill-Health" under Old Age; Prolonged, Sickly, Tedious, etc.).

**Cold Water**—Craving for In Illness—(See Cravings).

**Colds**—Illness From—(See Colds).

**Complaints; Complications** — Ill-Health from a Complication of Diseases—(See Complications).

**Contagious Diseases**—Ill-Health By—(See Contagions).

**Continued Ill-Health** — (See Chronic, Continuity, Duration, Incurable, Invalids, Lingering, Permanent, Prolonged, Slow, Tedious, Wastings, etc.).

**Course**—The Course of Disease In Ill-Health—(See Course).

**Crises; Critical**—The Critical Periods of Life, Tending to Ill-Health — (See Critical, Periods, Years).

**Curable; Dampness**—Ill-Health By—(See Dampness, Moisture).

**Dangerous Illnesses** — (See Dangerous, Fatal, Fierce, Grievous, Severe, Sharp, Violent, etc.).

**Days** — Crises and Critical Days In Disease—(See Better, Crises, Critical, Days; "Worse" under Disease).

**Death**—Danger of Death from the Illness—(See "Arguments for Death" under Death; "Danger to Life" under Life).

**Debauchery** — Ill-Health From — (See Debauchery, Dissipation, Drink, Excesses, Intemperance, etc.).

**Decay** — Ill-Health Due to Decay In the System—(See Decay).

**Decrepitude; Delirium; Diet** — Ill-Health Due to Wrong Diet—(See Diet, Eating, Excesses, Food, Gluttony, Indigestion, Indiscretions, etc.).

**Directions**—As the Cause of Ill-Health—(See Directions).

**Disease**—(See the various paragraphs under Disease, Sickness, and also in this Article).

**Disorders** — (See Disease, Disorders, Sickness, etc.).

**Dissipation** — Ill-Health From — (See Dissipation).

**Distempers**—Ill-Health By—(See Distempers).

**Distress** — Suffering and Ill-Health Thru — (See Anguish, Anxiety, Cares, Distress, Trouble, Worry, etc.).

**Drink; Drunkenness; Early Years** — Ill-Health In—(See Early).

**Eating** — Ill-Health Thru Wrong Habits of Eating—(See Diet, Eating, Food, Gluttony, etc.).

**Emaciation; Enemies**—Ill-Health of—(See Enemies).

**Enneatical**—The 9th day of an Illness. (See Enneatical).

**Entire Body**—The Ill-Health Is Thru the Entire Body — (See "Whole Body" under Whole).

**Events** — The Event of Ill-Health — Time of—(See Directions; "Time" under Disease; Events).

**Excesses** — Ill-Health Due To — (See Excesses).

**Excitement** — (See "Ill-Health" under Excitement).

**Exercise** — Ill-Health from Over-Exercise—(See "Inordinate" under Exercise).

**Exposure**—Ill-Health From—(See Exposure).

**Family**—Ill-Health of—(See Family).

**Fatal Illness**—(See "Certain", "Sure", under Death; Fatal).

**Father**—Illness of—(See Father).

**Feasting** — Ill-Health From — (See Feasting).

**Feeble; Females**—Ill-Health of—(See Aunts, Daughters; "Ill-Health" under Females, Mother, Sister, Wife, Women).

**Fevers; Fiance**—Fiancee—Ill-Health of—(See Fiance).

**Folly**—Ill-Health By—(See Folly).

**Food**—Illness from Improper or Rich Food—(See Diet, Eating, Food).

**Frequent Ill-Health**—(See "Ill-Health All Thru Life" in this section; "Much Sickness" under Sickness).

**Friends**—Ill-Health of—(See Friends).

**General Ill-Health** — General Weakness—The ☉ or ☽ hyleg at B., and to the ☌ or ill-asp. ♄ by dir.; the ☽ affl. in ♑, and espec. when young; ☿ affl. in ♓; ♍ on the Asc., general weakness and debility from dyspeptic action. (See Debility, Dyspepsia, Sickly; "Much Sickness" under Sickness; Vitality Low; "Weak Body" under Weak; "Ill-Health All Thru Life" in this section).

**Gluttony** — Illness From — (See Gluttony).

**Grandparents** — Ill-Health of — (See Grandparents).

**Grievous Illness**—(See Grievous).

**Growths** — Ill-Health By — (See Growths, Tumors).

**Habits** — Ill-Health From — An Ill Habit of Body—(See Habits; "Ill-Health All Thru Life" in this section).

**Health** — (See "Bad Health" and the various paragraphs under Health).

**Heat**—Ill-Health from Excess of Heat —(See Fevers; "Suffering" under Heat).

**High Living**—Ill-Health Thru—(See "Living" under High).

**Humours; Husband** — Ill-Health of — (See Husband).

**Ill-Health All Thru Life** — Is Always Ailing — Frequent Ill-Health — Much Sickness — An Ill Habit of Body — Liable to Ill-Health — Sicky — The ☉ in the 6th H. unless well-aspected; the ☉, ☽, or Asc. hyleg, and ☌ or ill-asp. a malefic, and espec. with ♄; the ☉ ☌ ♄ in the 6th H., or in □ or ☍ if either are in this house; the ☉ and ☽ much afflicted at B.; the ☽ affl. in ♑, often ailing, and espec. in childhood; the ☽ hyleg in ♑, and afflicted, the health is seldom good, and espec. with females; ♄ in the 10th H. in evil asp. to the hyleg, the native will always be ailing unless very powerful aspects counteract; ♄ in the 10th H. in □ asp. the hyleg, and ♄ evilly aspected by ♅ or ♂, except the Benefics favorably aspect both ♄ and the hyleg; the malefics ♅, ♄, or ♂ joined with the hyleg, and espec. if ♅ and ♂ also afflict ♄; a malefic planet joined with the hyleg; a malefic tends to afflict all thru life that part of the body ruled by the sign and house of the malefic, and espec. if afflicted by one or more of the other malefics, in which case the special ailments tend to be aggravated, and to predominate all thru life under evil transits and directions, and to eventually be the cause of death. Good aspects from the Benefics to ♄ and the hyleg will tend to bring much relief, and mitigate the disease. (See "Unhealthy" under Health; Incurable, Sickly; "Much Sickness" under Sickness; Vitality Low; "Weak Body" under Weak).

**Imaginary Ills**—(See Imagination).

**Imbecility of Body**—(See Imbecility).

**Immunity to Disease** — (See Immunity).

**Imprudence**—Ill-Health By—(See Imprudent).

**Impulsiveness** — Ill-Health From — (See Impulsive).

**Incurable; Indifferent; Indigestion;**

**Indiscretions**—Ill-Health From—(See Conduct, Diet, Excesses, Habits, Indiscretions, etc.).

**Indisposition; Indulgences; Infants**—Ill-Health of—(See Infancy).

**Infirmities; Inflammation;**

**Intemperance**—Ill-Health From—(See Intemperance).

**Invalids; Journeys**—Travel—Voyages —Ill-Health During, or the Results of —(See Abroad, Foreign Lands, Journeys, Railroads, Travel, Voyages).

**Less Liable to Ill-Health**—(See "Good Health" under Health; Immunity, Recuperation, Resistance, Stamina; "Body" under Strong; Tone, Vitality Good).

**Liable to Ill-Health**—(See Directions; "Bad Health", "Periods of Bad Health", under Health; Ingresses, Lunations, Pale, Progressions; "Low" under Resistance; Sickly, Sickness, Transits, Vitality Low; "Ill-Health All Thru Life" in this section).

**Lingering Illness**—(See Chronic, Lingering, Long, Prolonged, Slow, Tedious, Wastings).

**Lives Thru Illness**—(See "Lives Thru Serious Illnesses" under Serious).

**Location** — Ill-Health Due To — (See "Ill-Health" under Residence).

**Long Siege**—Of Ill-Health—The ☉ to the ☌, P, □ or ☍ ♄ by progression or dir., and espec. if the nativity shows weak vitality, and the patient is given to worry, fear, bad thinking; the ☉ in P. asp. to ♄ by progression may bring ill-health for a period of ten years; the ☉ progressed to the □ or ☍ ♄, ill-health for three years. (See Chronic, Consumption, Invalids; "Long Illnesses" under Long; Prolonged, Tedious, etc.).

**Low Spirits**—Ill-Health Due To—(See "Low Spirits" under Low).

**Lust**—Ill-Health From—(See Amorous, Excesses, Lust, Passion, Venery).

**Luxuries**—Ill-Health Due To—(See Extravagance, Luxuries).

**Maladies**—(See Disease).

**Malaise; Males**—Ill-Health of—(See Father, Grandfather, Husband; "Ill-Health" under Males; Son, Uncles).

**Malice of Fortune**—Ill-Health Due To—(See "Malice" under Fortune).

**Many Illnesses**—Many Long Illnesses—(See "Ill-Health All Thru Life" in this section; "Long Illnesses" under Long; "Much Sickness" under Sickness).

**Meat**—Ill-Health Due to Use of—(See "Cooked Foods" under Food; "Raw Humours" under Indigestion; Meat).

**Melancholy**—Ill-Health Due To—(See Melancholy).

**Men**—Ill-Health of—(See Men).

**Middle Life**—Ill-Health At Time of—(See Middle Life).

**Mild Illnesses**—(See Colds, Mild, Slight).

**Mind**—Ill-Health Due to Mental Disorders, Bad Thinking, Overstudy, etc.—(See the various paragraphs under Mental, Mind, Reading, Study).

**Moisture**—Moist Humours—Ill-Health Due To—(See Exposure, Humours, Moisture, Water, Wet).

**Mortal Illness**—Danger of—(See "Arguments for Death", "Certain", "Sure", under Death; Fatal; "Small Hope of Life" under Life).

**Mother**—Ill-Health of—(See Mother).

**Much Sickness**—(See "Much" under Sickness; "Ill-Health All Thru Life" in this section).

**Nature of the Ill-Health**—(See "Disease", "Nature of the Disease", under Nature).

**Neglect**—Ill-Health From—(See Neglect, Poverty).

**Nervous Disorders**—(See Nerves).

**Old Age**—Ill-Health In—(See Adults, Grandparents, Old Age).

**Old Maladies Return**—(See Return).

**Opposite Sex**—Ill-Health Thru—(See Amorous, Excesses, Harlots, Lascivious, Lewd, Licentious, Lust; "Injured" under Men; Opposite Sex; "Passional Excesses" under Passion; "Diseases" under Sex).

**Over-Eating**—Ill-Health From—(See Diet, Eating, Feasting, Food, Gluttony).

**Over-Excitement**—Ill-Health From—(See Excitable).

**Over-Exertion**—Of Mind or Body, and Ill-Health From—(See Exercise, Exertion, Reading, Study).

**Pain; Pale**—(See Pale, Sickly).

**Passional Excesses**—Ill-Health From—(See "Passional", "Sex", under Excesses).

**Periodic Illnesses**—(See Periodic).

**Periods of Ill-Health**—(See Aspects, Directions; "Periods of Bad Health" under Health; Ingresses, Lunations, Periods, Progressions, Secondary, Solstices, Transits, Vernal, Years).

**Plethora; Poison**—(See "Sickness" under Poison).

**Poverty**—Ill-Health From—(See Neglect, Poverty).

**Privation**—Ill-Health From—(See Neglect, Poverty, Starvation).

**Prolonged Illness**—(See Chronic, Long, Prolonged, Tedious).

**Rash Acts**—Ill-Health From—(See Anger, Rashness).

**Reading**—Ill-Health from Too Much Reading and Study—(See "Brain Fag" under Brain; Fatigue, Reading, Study)

**Recovery from Illness**—(See Crises; "Better" under Disease; Moderation, Recovery, Recuperation).

**Recuperation**—From Illness—(See "Recovery" in this section).

**Relapses; Relatives**—Ill-Health of—(See Family, Relatives).

**Resistance**—To Disease—(See "Good Health" under Health; Immunity, Resistance, Strong, Vitality, Weak, etc.).

**Serious Illnesses**—(See Grievous, Incurable, Pernicious, Serious, Severe, Vehement, Violent, etc.).

**Seven-Year Periods**—Tending to Chronic and Lingering Illness Every Seven Years—(See "Seven-Year Periods" under Periods).

**Severe Illness**—(See "Serious" in this section).

**Short Life**—(See "Short" under Life).

**Sick**—The Sick—State of the Sick—(See Sick).

**Sickly**—The Health Not Good—(See "Bad Health" under Health; Sickly).

**Sickness**—(See the various paragraphs under Sickness).

**Signs of Ill-Health**—The Native Is Apt To Suffer Much Ill-Health If These Conditions Exist at Birth, and by Direction—The ☉ or ☽ in the 6th H., and affl. by malefics; the ☉ or ☽ on or near the cusp. of the 7th H. at B., and afflicted; the ☉ conjoined at B., or by dir., with Antares, Aldebaran, Hercules, Hyades, Regulus, or any eminent star of the nature of ♂; ♄ in the 6th H. at B., and affl. by the ☉ or ☽; ♄ or ♂ affl. the ☉, ☽, or Asc. by body or aspect, or by dir.; ☿ affl. in the 6th H.; lord of the 1st H. in the 6th, 8th, or 12th H., and afflicted, combust, □ or ☍ lords of the 4th, 6th, 8th, or 12th H., slow in motion, out of dignity, and with no assistance from Benefics Hor'y. (See "Causes of Disease" under Disease; "Bad Health", "Periods of Bad Health", under Health; "Much Sickness" under Sickness; "Ill-Health All Thru Life" in this section).

**Sister**—Ill-Health of—(See Sister).

**Slight Indisposition**—(See Mild, Slight).

**Slow Diseases**—(See Chronic, Lingering, in this section; Slow).

**Sores; Sports**—Ill-Health By—(See Exercise, Sports).

**Stamina; Study**—Ill-Health from Overstudy—(See "Brain Fag" under Brain; "Eyestrain" under Eyes; Reading, Study).

**Succumbs Easily**—To Disease—(See "Succumbs Easily" under Disease, Sickness; Negative, Succumbs; the Introduction under Virgo; "Low" under Vitality).

**Suffering**—(See the various paragraphs under Suffering).

**Surfeits; Symptoms; Tedious Illness**—(See Tedious).

**Ten Years of Ill-Health**—Danger of—(See "Long Siege" in this section).

**Tendency to Ill-Health**—(See "Liable To" in this section).

**Three Years of Ill-Health**—Danger of—(See "Long Siege" in this section).

**Time of Ill-Health**—Time When Due Under Ordinary Conditions—(See "Time" under Disease).

**Tone; Travel**—Ill-Health During Travel—(See "Journeys" in this section).

**Treatment**—Various Lines of Treatment for Ill-Health—(See Antipathy, Cure, Drugs, Healers, Medicines, Opposites, Remedies, Sympathy, Treatment).

**Tumors; Ulcers; Uncles**—Ill-Health of—(See Uncles).

**Vexations**—Ill-Health Due To—(See Cares, Disgrace, Reversals, Ruin, Sorrow, Trouble, Vexations, Worry, etc.).

**Violent Diseases**—(See Pernicious, Severe, Sharp, Vehement, Violent, etc).

**Vitality**—Ill-Health Due to Low Vitality—(See "Low" under Vitality; "Weak Body" under Weak).

**Vitiated In Body**—(See "Low" under Vitality; Vitiated).

**Voyages**—Ill-Health On—(See Abroad, Foreign Lands, Ships, Shipwreck, Travel, Voyages).

**Wards Off Disease**—(See "Wards Off" under Disease).

**Wastings; Weak Body**—Invites Disease. (See "Attracts Disease" under Attracts; "Low" under Vitality; "Weak Body" under Weak).

**Weather**—Ill-Health Due to Weather—(See Cold, Heat, Storms, Weather, Wind, etc.).

**Wet Feet**—Colds, Disease, and Ill-Health Due To—(See "Wet Feet" under Feet).

**Whole Body**—The Illness Is Over the Whole Body—(See Whole).

**Wife**—Ill-Health of—(See Wife).

**Wine**—Ill-Health from Surfeit of Wine—(See Wine).

**Women**—Ill-Health of—(See Aunts, Females, Mother, Sister, Wife, Women).

**Worse**—The Health Is Worse—(See "Worse" under Disease).

**Young Men**—Ill-Health of—(See "Young Men" under Young).

**Youth**—Ill-Health In—(See Youth).

**ILLAQUEATIVE**—Ensnaring—Enticing—♆ influence. (See "Action Of" under Neptune).

**ILLEGITIMATE**—Illegitimate Children—(See Bastards).

**ILLICIT**—Illicit Appetites—Illicit Practices—Given To—(See "Ilicit" under Appetites).

**ILLNESS**—Illnesses—(See the various paragraphs under Disease, Ill-Health, Sickness).

**ILLUSIONS**—A False Perception of An External Object—Illusions are under the rule of the ☽.

**Illusory Appetites**—(See "Appetites" under Peculiar).

**Illusory Diseases**—And Troubles—Brooding Over—♂ affl. in ♍. (See Brooding, Hypochondria, Imaginary).

**Mental Illusions**—♅ affl. in ♋; ☿ affl. by ♅; Subs at AT and AX. (See Anguish, Anxiety, Brooding, Chaotic, Delirium, Delusions, Demoniac, Dreams, Fancies, Fears, Forebodings, Hallucinations, Horrors, Ideals, Imaginations, Insanity, Mania, Mental; "Diseased Mind" under Mind; Obsessions, Phenomena, Premonitions, Pseudo, Spirit Controls, Strange, Terrors, Worry).

**ILLUSTRIOUS MAN**—Death of—(See Famous; "Great Men", "The Great", under Great; Kings, Lady, Nobles, President, Princes, Queens, Rulers).

**IMAGINATION**—Imaginary—Imaginative—Imaginations—The Imagination is ruled by ♆, ♂, ☿, and the ☽. The Hebrew letter Heth is connected with the ♋ sign, and also rules the Imagination. Artistic, or Poetic Imagination, is largely the influence of the fiery and watery signs, but ♎ and ♒ may also be included. The influences of ♆ and the ♓ sign tend to Imaginations bordering on Hallucinations, and the afflictions of ♆ to Involuntary Clairvoyance. The afflictions of ♆ also tend to imaginations which may be classed as false fears, obsessions, a chaotic mind, and mental perversions, etc. The influence of ♅ has to do more with the Intuitions than with the Imagination, altho the afflictions of ♅, when configurated with ♆ or ☿, tend to disordered imaginations, eccentricities, and peculiarities of Temperament.

**Deluded Imagination**—(See "Disordered" in this section).

**Deranged Imagination**—A Diseased Imagination—A ♊ affliction, and afflictions in ♊; the ☽ affl. at B., and espec. if the ☽ is in ♊, and ☿ in ♓ at the same time; ☿ affl. at B.

**Disordered Imagination**—Weak or Deluded—♋ influence, and afflictions in ♋; the ☽ affl. at B.; the ☽ in the 6th H., and affl. by ☿. (See Ideals).

**False Imagination**—The ☽ in bad asp. to ♂.

**Fancies**—(See Fancies).

**Fearful Imaginations**—☿ affl. at B., and in □ or ☍ the Asc.

**Flighty Imagination**—(See "Vain" in this section).

**Fond Imaginations**—(See Flighty; "Vain" in this section).

**Head**—Imaginary Diseases In—(See "Imaginary" under Head).

**Imaginary Diseases**—Imaginary Ills—Illusory—Pretended—The ☉, ♆, ♄, or ♂ affl. in ♍; ☿ in ♉ ☍ ♆ or ♄ in ♏; ☿ affl. in ♓; ☿ affl. by ♆, imaginary diseases in the head, and pretended ailments; ♂ affl. in ♍ tends to brooding over illusory diseases and troubles; ♋ on the Asc., and afflictions in ♋, imagine themselves suffering from ailments which may not exist; ♄ affl. in ♉. (See Brooding, Hypochondria, Illusions, Pseudo).

**Imagination Runs Away**—Inclined to Strange Methods, and Outside the Limitations of Reality—♆ prominent at B., and afflicted, or the ☉, ☽, ☿, or the Asc. affl. by ♆. (See Peculiar, Strange, in this section).

**Imaginative**—The ☽ influence strong at B.; a ♆ trait; ♆ in ♈, ♋, or ♒.

**Lugubrious Imagination**—(See "Melancholy" in this section).

**Melancholy Imagination**—Lugubrious—Doleful—Sad—The ☉, ☽, or ☿ in the signs of ♄; the ☽ in ♑ or ♒ and affl. by ♄; ♅ in ♒ and affl. by the ☽; ♄ strong at B., and afflicting ☿. (See Doleful, Gloom, Grief, Melancholy, Sadness).

**Morbid Imaginations**—Perverted—Unhealthy—The ☉ or ☽ ☍ ♆, and espec. along sex lines; ♆ afflicted in ♋ or ♒, the imagination should be kept pure, and morbid tendencies fought against; ♆ affl. in ♍; ♆ in the 12th H., and in ☍ ☽ in the 6th; ♂ ☌ ♀, and espec. in sex, social, and love affairs; ☿ affl. in ♋. (See "Erotic" under Mania; "Morbid" under Mind; Morbid, Nymphomania, Perversions; "Imaginations" under Puberty).

**Peculiar Imagination**—♆ in ♈ or ♋; the 3rd Decan. of ♒ on the Asc., ruled by the ☽. (See Peculiar).

**Perverted**—(See "Morbid" in this section).

**Powerful Imagination**—Strong—♄ in ♎, ♑, or ☿, well-dignified and aspected; ♊ gives; the 2nd Decan. of ♉, or the 3rd Dec. of ♋ on the Asc., which are ruled by the ☽.

**Sensuous Imaginations**—The ☽ affl. by ♀, and espec. at the age of puberty; the ☽ in ♑ and in ☍ ♄ in ♋, and espec. if ♄ afflict ♀ at the same time, or ♀ afflict ♄. (See Amorous, Lascivious, Lewd, Licentious, Lust, Nymphomania, Passion; "Imaginations" under Puberty; Sensuality, Sex).

**Strange Imaginations**—♆ in ♈, ♋, or ♒; ♃ affl. in ♈. (See "Peculiar" in this section; Demoniac, Peculiar, Strange).

**Strong Imagination**—(See "Powerful" in this section).

**Unhealthy Imagination**—(See "Morbid" in this section).

**Vain Imaginations**—Fond Imaginations—Flighty—A ☿ disorder; afflictions to ☿ at B. (See "Vain Fears" under Fears; Flighty).

**Weak**—The Imagination Weak and Deluded—(See "Disordered" in this section). In addition to the references already given in this Article, see Anarchists, Chaotic, Clairvoyant, Dejection, Delirium, Delusions, Depressed, Despondent, Dreamy, Eccentric, Emotions, Erratic, Hallucinations, Hypnotism, Hysteria, Ideas, Insanity, Intuition, Jealousy, Mania, Mediumship, Memory, Mental Disturbances (see Mental, Mind); Notions, Obsessions, Paranoia, Perceptions, Persecution, Pretenses, Psychic, Reformers, Religion, Sensitive, Spirit Controls, Vagaries, Visions, Worry, etc.

**IMBECILITY**—Imbecile—Feeble In Mind or Body—Phrenasthesia—Weak Mind, etc.—

**Imbecility of Body**—Weakness of—Ill-Health—If the sign of the radical 6th, 8th, or 12th H. be in the 1st H. in a Revolutionary Figure, then sickness and trouble during the year to follow is apt to come, and imbecility of body. Also when the Asc. of a Revolutionary Figure is in evil asp. to the Angles of the Radix. (See Feeble; "Periods of Bad Health" under Health; Ill-Health; "Low" under Vitality; "Weak Body" under Weak).

**Imbecility of Mind**—Phrenasthesia—The ☽ affl. in ♑; the ☽ in ♑ in partile asp. the Asc., one who is imbecile, idle, dull and mean. CASES of Imbecility—Birth Data, etc.—See "Arundel", No. 159; "Seventeen Years In Bed", No. 843; "Weak Mind", No. 673, all in 1001 N.N. Also see "Female" in Chap. 8, page 49, in Daath's Medical Astrology. (See Congenital, Dementia, Deranged, Dwarf, Foolish, Growth, Idiocy, Insanity; "Arrested Mental Powers" under Mental; "Weak Mind" under Mind; Monstrosities, Prenatal; "Void of Reason" under Reason; Retarded, Thyroid).

**Moral Imbecility**—(See "Imbecility" under Morals).

**IMMEDIATE**—Immediate Causes of Death, Disease, Events, Accidents, Hurts, Injuries, etc.—

**Death**—Immediate Cause of—When the train of Directions which cause death fall together, and none follow, for the quality of the death, and the disease which may cause it, observe those directions which precede, although at a distance; the aspects and positions of the malefics, and especially as they affect the hyleg. Also notice the positions and aspects of the Benefics, as the Benefics, altho they tend to preserve life when concurring in a train of directions, often specify the disease which is the immediate cause of death. In death by violence observe the Genethliacal positions of the ☉ and ☽, how they are affected by the malefics, and how the ☉ and ☽ are concerned in the quality of the death. (See "Quality of the Death" under Death; Directions; "Fatal Illness" under Fatal; Quality, Species; "Death" under Violent).

**IMMINENT**—Impending—Dangerous and Close at Hand—

**An Accident Imminent**—(See Accidents).

**Death Imminent**—(See "Arguments for Death", "Certain", "Sure", under Death; "The Sick Will Hardly Escape" under Escape; "Fatal Illness" under

Fatal; "Danger to Life", "Small Hope of Life", under Life; "Impossible" under Recovery).

**Death Not Imminent**—(See Amelioration; "Better" under Disease; "Spared" under Life; Moderation; "Patient Will Recover" under Recovery).

**Disease Imminent** — (See Directions; "Time Of" under Disease; "Periods of Ill-Health" under Ill-Health). For the various kinds of afflictions and events which may be impending and imminent see the subject in the alphabetical arrangement. See "Danger Of" under Accidents; Blows, Cuts, Dangers, Directions, Events, Hurts, Injuries, Misfortune, etc.

**IMMOBILITY**—Of the Body—(See Action, Cold, Locomotion, Motion, Movement, Paralysis, Rigid, Rigors, Stiff).

**IMMODERATE**—Excessive—Exceeding Reasonable Bounds—

**Eating**—Immoderate Eater—(See "Immoderate" under Eating).

**Habits**—Immoderate In Habits—(See Diet, Drink, Eating, Excesses, Feasting, Habits, Indulgence, Intemperance, Pleasure, Sports, etc.).

**Heat**—Diseases Which Proceed from Immoderate Heat — (See "Excessive Heat" under Heat; "Hot Blasting Winds" under Wind).

**Menses**—Immoderate Catamenial Discharges — (See "Profuse" under Discharges, Menses).

**Pulse**—Immoderate Pulse—(See "High Pulse" under Pulse).

**Respiration** — (See "Immoderate" under Breathing). For other study and subjects see Abnormalities, Amorous, Drunkenness, Excess, Excesses; "High" under Fever; Inordinate, Intoxication, Over-Exertion, Passion, Rapid, Rashness, Venery, etc.

**IMMODEST**—♄ ☌ or ill-asp. ♀ at B., and the immodesty becomes more pronounced and shameless under the afflictions of ♄ to ♀ by dir. if ♀ was affl. by ♄ at B. (See "Sex Organs" under Exhibition; Harlots, Indecent, Lewd, Modesty; "Loose Morals" under Morals; Notoriety, Obscene, Shameless, etc.).

**IMMORALITY** — Immoral — (See Conduct; "Loose Morals" under Morals).

**IMMUNITY** — Proof Against Attacks of Disease — Wards Off Disease Easily — Less Liable to Disease—Vitality Strong —Resistance to Disease Strong, etc.— The ☉ well-aspected in ♈ or ♌; the ☉ well-asp. in ♌, less liable to disease than in any other sign; the ☽ hyleg in ♐ in female nativities does not conduce to many ailments; ♃ and ♀ both rising, and supporting the Lights by good aspects, such often pass unharmed thru Pestilence, Plague, Cholera, Yellow Fever, or Diphtheria Epidemics; ♃ well-asp. in the 6th H., and not afflicted by malefics. (See "Less Liable To" under Accidents; "Immunity" under Fevers; "Abundance of Health", "Good Health", under Health; "Long Life" under Life; Recuperation, Resistance, Resources, Scarlet Fever, Smallpox, Stamina, Strong, Vitality Good, etc.).

**IMPAIRMENT** — Impairments — Impaired—

**Eyes Impaired** — (See "Eye Trouble", and the various paragraphs under Eyes; Sight).

**Functions**—The Bodily Functions Impaired—(See Functions).

**Head Impaired**—(See "Disorders" under Head).

**Health Impaired**—(See Disease; "Bad Health" under Health; Ill-Health, Invalids, Sickly, Sickness, etc.).

**Mental Abilities Impaired**—☿ ℞ at B., and otherwise weak and afflicted; ☿ combust, some Authors say; ☿ affl. by the ☽; ☿ in no asp. to the ☽ or Asc.; ☿ setting and out of dignity, less apt to be studious. (See Comprehension; "Mind" under Erratic; Faculties, Foolish, Idiocy, Imbecility, Intellect; "Bad" under Judgment; "Shallow", "Weak", under Mentality; "Weak Mind" under Mind; Perception, Study, Understanding).

**Mental Faculties Impaired**—The ☉ ☌ or P. ☿; ☿ rising after the ☉ at B.; ♒ on the 6th H. (See "Mental Abilities" in this section).

**Sensorial Functions Impaired** — (See "Functions" under Sensation).

**Vitality Impaired**—(See Vitality). For the various impairments of the different organs and parts of the body, or of the Mind, see in the alphabetical arrangement the subject you have in mind. Also see Blemishes, Decay, Defects, Deformities, Degeneration, Deterioration, Detriment, Disabilities, Disease, Hurts, Ill-Health, Impediments, Imperfections, Injuries, Mental, Mind, Sickness, etc.

**IMPALEMENT**—Death By, or by Crucifixion. Danger of Such a Death. ♂ in the 10th or 4th H., near the places of Andromeda or Cepheus (within 5°), and ♂ in □ or ☍ the ☉ or ☽. (See Aldebaran, Cepheus, Hanging).

**IMPAR** — The Ganglion Impar (See "Impar" under Ganglion).

**IMPEDIMENTS** — Impeded — Impeded Action of Mind or Body — The influences and afflictions of ♄ tend to impede and suppress the functions, and the action of the various organs of the body. The influence of ♄ with ☿, the mental ruler, is to make the mind dull, melancholic, and with fears. Saturn in any sign or house tends to impediments and weakness of the parts or organs ruled and influenced by such sign or house, and worse at times according to the aspects, transits, and directions of ♄ in afflicting his own radical place. Also ♄ afflicted in the 6th H., or ♄ afflicting the ☉, ☽, Asc., or Hyleg, tends to many impediments in the body which may adversely affect the health and mind. Nearly every subject in this book has to do with some impediment, detriment, hurt, or injury to the body and mind, and it would take too much space to list them here. (See "Hindered", "Impeded", "Impediment", "Inhibitions", "Obstructions", "Retarded", "Suppressed", etc., under each Organ, or Part of the Body, and look in the alphabetical arrangement for the subject you have in mind. However, the more general and abstract subjects along this line are listed here, which also see in the alphabetical arrangement when not more fully considered here.

**Action** — Impeded Action In the Body —(See Action, Motion, Movement, Retarded, Slow, etc.).

**Air**—(See "Impediment" under Air).

**Arrested Growth** — Arrested Mental Powers—(See Arrested).

**Blindness**—Due to Impediments—(See Blindness, Cataract; "Growths" under Eyes).

**Blood** — The Blood Impeded — (See "Corrupt", "Pressure", "Too Much Blood", under Blood).

**Bowel Action Impeded**—(See Bowels, Constipation, Costiveness, Faeces).

**Circulation Impeded** — (See Circulation; "Circulation" under Heart).

**Disease**—Note the various paragraphs under Disease).

**Ears**—Impediments In—(See "Left", "Right", under Ears; "Deafness" under Hearing).

**Fluids**—(See "Impeded" under Fluids).

**Functions**— (See "Impeded" under Functions).

**Growth**—The Growth Impeded — (See Diminished, Dwarf, Growth).

**Head**—Circulation In Impeded — (See "Circulation" under Head).

**Hearing**—The Hearing Impeded—(See "Deafness", "Deaf and Dumb", under Hearing).

**Heart**—(See "Impeded" under Heart).

**Memory Impeded** — (See "Forgetful" under Memory).

**Mind**—Impediments to the Mind—(See Chaotic, Dull, Idiocy, Insanity, Intellect, Judgment, Memory, Mental, Mind, Perceptions, Understanding).

**Mineral Deposits** — The System Impeded By — (See "Gall Stones" under Bile; Concretions, Deposits, Gout, Gravel, Joints, Minerals, Sand, Stone, Uric, Wastes, etc.).

**Secretions Impeded** — (See Fluids, Glands, Secretions).

**Senses**—The Senses Limited and Impeded—(See Hearing, Limitations, Senses, Sight, Smell, Taste, Touch, Twelfth House).

**Speech**—Impediments of—(See Dumbness, Mutes; "Impediment", "Stammering", under Speech; Tongue). For further study see the following subjects,—Cirrhosis, Clogging, Clots, Condensation, Congestions, Consolidation, Corrosion, Crippled, Crystallization, Deafness (see Hearing); Decay, Defects, Deficiencies, Deformities, Delayed, Density, Destructive, Elimination, Embolism, Excretion, Growths, Hardening, Hurts, Idiocy, Ill-Health, Imbecility, Imperfections, Indigestion, Infarcts, Inhibitions, Injuries, Irregular, Lameness, Motion, Movement, Mutes, Obstructions, Ossification (see Osseous); Poisons, Prevented, Retarded, Retentions, Rheumatism, Rigidity, Sand, Saturn Influence (see Saturn); Sclerosis, Sickness, Slight, Slow, Sluggish, Stiffness, Stomach (see "Stopped"

under Stomach); Stone, Stoppages, Suppressions, Teeth (see "Impediments" under Teeth); Thickening, Thrombus, Tumors, Twelfth House, Wastes, Weak, etc.

**IMPERFECT**—Imperfections—This is a very broad and large subject, and practically every subject in this book is related to some imperfection of the mind or body. For the Imperfections which may exist in any Part, or Organ of the body, see "Defects", "Imperfect", "Imperfections", etc., under the Part, Organ, and Subject you may have in mind, as the list and references would be too many to incorporate here in this Article. However, the more abstract subjects which are related to Imperfections, and also some of the more prominent Imperfections over the body, will be listed here in the paragraphs which follow. People born under the Imperfect Signs, ♌, ♏, or ♓, are apt to be broken, imperfect, or mutilated in some way. (See Broken, Mutilated). Imperfections are also caused by the influences and afflictions of the Malefics, and especially of ♄ and ♂, and the imperfection, defect, deformity, disease, affliction, blemish, weakness, etc., is usually in that part, or parts of the body, ruled by the Signs containing the malefics. The Signs the ☉ or ☽ are in may also indicate the source and location of imperfections and weaknesses when the Lights at B. are seriously afflicted by the malefics.

**All Over the Body**—Imperfections All Over the Body—The ♋ sign gives, and when strongly afflicted at B. (See Whole).

**Children** — Imperfect Children — (See "Imperfect" under Children).

**Conception** — The Conception Imperfect and Defective — (See Conception, Inhuman).

**Congenital**—The Imperfection Is Congenital, and Exists from Birth — (See Congenital, Diathesis, Heredity).

**Deafness** — Deaf and Dumb — Deaf, Dumb and Blind — Deaf, Dumb and Idiot—(See Blindness, Hearing, Idiocy, Mutes).

**Imperfect Signs** — ♌, ♏, and ♓. (See Broken, Mutilated).

**Imperfectly Formed**—Case—See "Imperfectly Formed", No. 303 in 1001 N.N. (See "Beastly Form" under Beasts; "Ill-Formed" under Ill; Incomplete, Inhuman, Missing, Monsters, etc.).

**Incomplete** — Born Incomplete — (See "Incomplete" under Birth; Incomplete, Missing, Monsters, etc.).

**Inhuman** — Inhuman In Shape — (See "Beastly Form" under Beasts; Inhuman, Monsters).

**Legs**—Case—The Legs Imperfect, and Also Without Rectum — (See "Bad Legs", "Crooked", "Imperfect", under Legs).

**Limbs Imperfect** — (See Arms, Congenital, Feet, Hands, Knees, Legs, Limbs, Malformations).

**Menstruation** — (See "Imperfect" under Menses).

**Missing Members** — (See "Armless Wonder" under Arms; "Missing" under Forearm; Incomplete, Missing).

**Mutes**—(See "Deaf and Dumb" under Hearing; Mutes).

**Mutilated Signs** — (See "Imperfect Signs" in this section).

**Prenatal Epoch**—Many Imperfections are accounted for by prenatal conditions, and afflictions during Gestation. (See Conception, Congenital, Foetus, Gestation, Prenatal).

**Signs** — The Imperfect Signs — (See "Imperfect Signs" in this section).

**Speech** — Imperfections In — (See "Stammering", and the various paragraphs under Speech).

**Stomach**—(See "Imperfections" under Stomach).

**Teeth**—Imperfections In—(See Teeth).

**Tongue** — (See "Imperfections" under Tongue).

**Walk**—Gait—Imperfections In—(See Gait, Walk). For further study along this line see Animals (see "Resembles" under Animals); Birthmarks (see Naevus); Blemishes, Blindness (see "Born Blind" under Blindness); Blotches, Breasts (see "Imperfections" under Breasts); Broken Signs (see Broken); Cloaca, Club Feet (see Feet); Crooked, Defects, Deficient, Deformities, Disfigurements, Distortions, Dogs (see "Resembles" under Dogs); Dumb, Dwarf, Excrescences, Eyes, Face, Fancies, Feet, Fissures, Foolish, Freckles, Genitals, Head, Hermaphrodites, Humpback (see Spine); Hurtful Signs (see "Hurtful Signs" under Hurtful); Idiocy, Imbecility, Impairments, Impediments, Incomplete, Insanity, Irregular, Lameness, Marks, Members, Mind, Moles, Nipples, Organs, Peculiar, Pockmarked (see "Face" under Smallpox); Savage, Scars, Spine, Triplets, Ugly, Warts, Wild, etc.

**IMPERFORATE** — Without Opening — Closure of the Different Orifices of the Body, either Congenital or Acquired—Caused by ♄ influence, as this planet contracts and limits. Saturn in any sign may cause imperforate conditions in any orifice, or opening ruled by that sign, according to the aspects and afflictions of ♄. (See Contractions, Limitations, Orifices, Saturn).

**Imperforate Anus** — (See "Imperforate" under Anus).

**Imperforate Hymen** — (See "Hymen" under Vagina).

**IMPETIGO**—Acute Pustular Inflammation of the Skin—A ♑ disease; ♑ on the Asc. (See Pimples; "Pustular Diseases" under Pus; Skin).

**IMPETUOUS**—Choleric—Hasty—Impulsive—(See Anger, Choleric, Excitable, Hasty, Impulses, Rashness).

**Impetuous Winds** — High Winds and Suffering From — (See "High" under Winds).

**IMPORTANT**—

**The Disease Is Important**—(See Grievous, Serious, Severe, etc.).

**The Disease Is Not Important** — (See Mild, Slight).

**IMPOSSIBLE**—Recovery Almost Impossible — (See "Arguments For Death", "Certain", "Sure", under Death; Escape (see "Sick" under Escape); Fatal, Grievous, Incurable; "Hope" under Life; Malignant, Pernicious, Recovery, Recuperation, Resistance, Serious, Severe, Vehement; "Diseases" under Violent; Vitality Low).

**IMPOSTHUMES** — Imposthumations — Abscesses—(See Abscesses, Ulcers).

**IMPOTENT**—Impotency—Barrenness—Sterility—The general influences causing Impotency are listed in the Article on Barrenness. Impotency may largely be considered a ♀ disease, and caused by afflictions to ♀. Also the 17° ♊, a barren sign, on the Asc. at B. is a degree of Impotency and loss of Faculties. Also caused by Subs at PP.

**Females** — Barrenness In — Impotency In—Lack of Sexual Power In—These influences are given under "Causes" in the Article on Barrenness. For influences which tend to cause Females to remain childless and unprolific see "Males Born Maimed" under Maimed; "Never Occur" under Menses; "Unfruitful" under Wife.

**Males**—Impotency In the Male—Sexual Debility In — ♀ in an angle, and espec. in the Western angle, and ♄ be in ☌, or in configuration with her, or in mutual reception, and ♂ elevated above ♀, or ♂ ☍ ♀, tends to produce impotence in the male; ♀ in a feminine sign alone; ♄ and ♀ in the 7th H., and ♂ elevated above them. (See "Causes" under Barrenness; "Mutilation Of" under Foetus; "Unfruitful" under Husband).

**Males Nearly Impotent**—If the ☉ and ☽ be configurated together in feminine signs with ♂ and ♀, and ♀ be in a feminine sign, if a male, will be nearly impotent, but if a female very lustful, but if ♂ be feminine and ♀ masculine, males will have more strength and vigor. Mars and ♀ so configurated, when ori. and diurnal, make men more robust, but if vespertine and occi., more debilitated. If ♄ be configurated with them all, they are more prone to unnatural and violent desires. Their lust is added to by ☿, but ♃ configurated with them also moderates the desires and makes them more circumspect.

**IMPOVERISHED**—

**Impoverished Blood** — (See Anaemia; "Thin Blood" under Blood; "Impure Blood" under Impure).

**Impoverished Body** — (See Consumption, Decrepitude, Emaciation, Feeble, Infirm, Invalids, Malnutrition (see Nutrition); Pale, Sickly, Thin, Vitality Low; "Weak Body" under Weak).

**IMPRACTICAL** — (See Erratic, Ideals; "Bad" under Judgment; Notions, Practical).

**IMPREGNATION** — (See Conception, Fecundation, Fertilization (see Fertile); Pregnancy).

**IMPRESSIONABLE** — (See Influenced, Negative, Receptive).

**IMPRISONMENT** — Danger of — Fear of — Long Imprisonment—Time of—(See these subjects under Prison. Also see Banishment, Confinement, Exile, Fugitive; "Asylums" under Insanity; Limitations, Punishment, Restraint, etc.).

**IMPROPER**—

**Associates**—Improper Associates and Companions—Given To—(See Companions, Criminals, Environment, Gambling, Harlots; "Liaisons" under Love Affairs; "Low Company" under Low; Sex Relations (see Sex); Social Relations).

**Conduct** — Improper Conduct — (See Conduct).

**Eating** — Feeding — Improper Feeding —(See Appetite, Diet, Eating, Feeding, Feasting, Food, Gluttony, Indigestion, Indiscretions, Plethora, Surfeits, etc.).

**Habits** — Improper Habits — (See Habits).

**Living**—Improper Living—(See Appetites, Conduct, Drink, Eating, Excesses; "Free Living" under Free; Habits; "High Living" under High; "Loose Morals" under Morals; Passion, Sex, Vices, etc.).

**IMPROVED**—Improvement—

**Conditions In Life**—A Change for the Better In Life — (See "Better" under Change).

**Constitution** — The Constitution Improved — (See "Strengthened" under Constitution).

**Disease**—The Disease Is Improved—Changes for the Better — (See Abatement, Amelioration, Crises; "Better" under Disease; Moderation, Modification, Recovery, Recuperation, Resolution).

**Health Is Improved** — (See "Good Health", "Improved", "Promoted", under Health).

**Mind Is Improved** — (See Character, Destiny, Events, Fate, Fortune; "Good" under Judgment; "Quickened" under Mentality; "Sound Mind" under Mind; Riches, Wealth, etc.).

**Vitality Improved** — (See "Strengthened" under Constitution; "Increased" under Vitality).

**IMPROVIDENT** — Lack of Foresight or Thrift—The ☉ to the ☌ or P. asp. the ☽; the Prog. ☽ to □ or ☍ ♃; the ☽ afflicted and cadent, in ♑ or ♏, and with no good asps. of ♃ or ♀; ♂ ⚹ or △ ♀, thoughtless and improvident. (See Careless, Drink, Drunkenness, Dull, Idle, Judgment Bad (see Judgment); Erratic, Folly, Foolhardy, Forethought, Hasty; "Improvident" under Husband; Imprudent, Inactive, Indifferent, Lazy, Lassitude, Lethargy, Neglectful, Poverty, etc.).

**IMPRUDENT** — Imprudence — Rashness — Heedless — Lacking Discretion — Characteristic of the Choleric, or Bilious Temperament, ruled by the ☉, ♂, and the fiery signs; the ☉ to the ☌ or P. the ☽; the ☉ to the ☌, P., □ or ☍ ♂; the periodic direction of ♄ to the radical ♀; ☿ affl. in ♐; lord of the 1st and 8th H. being the same planet (Hor'y). (See Anger, Careless, Choleric, Cruel, Erratic, Excitable, Folly, Foolhardy, Forethought, Hasty, Improvident, Impulsive, Judgment Bad (see Judgment); Rashness, Recklessness, High Temper (see Temper); Unchaste, Uncontrolled, etc.).

**Death from Imprudence**—☿ affl. in ♐; lord of the 1st and 8th being the same planet (Hor'y).

**Disease from Imprudence** — (See "Brings Disease Upon Himself" under Disease; "His Own Worst Enemy" under Enemies; "Diseases" under Excesses; "Disease and Sickness" under Folly; Indiscretions, Rashness).

**Excess of Prudence** — (See "Excess" under Prudent).

**Females**—Imprudent Conduct of—The Asc. to the place of Markab. (See Markab; "Conduct" under Women).

**Not Remarkable for Prudence**—♀ Sig. ⚹ or △ ♂, not remarkable for prudence or principle; ♀ Sig. □ or ☍ ♃, void of prudence and virtue. (See Companions, Conduct, Debauched, Depraved, Disgrace, Drink, Excesses, Forethought, Love Affairs, Low Company (see Low); Passion, Principles, Sex, Shameless, Wanton, etc.).

**IMPUDENT** — ♂ influence; ♂ rising in the Asc. (See "Bold" under Look; Saucy).

**IMPULSE** — The Central Line of Impulse—(See Prenatal Epoch).

**IMPULSES** — Impulsiveness — ♅ and ♂ have special rule over the Impulses.

**Accidents** — From Impulsiveness and Precipitated Rash Actions — ♂ in the 1st H., afflicted, and in □ or ☍ the ☉ or ☽. (See Anger; "Animal Instincts" under Animal; Foolhardy, Forethought, Hasty, Imprudent, Judgment, Rashness, Recklessness).

**Blind Impulses**—Governed by Impulse Rather Than by Reason—The ☉ to the ☌, P., □ or ☍ ♂ by dir.; ♆ affl. in ♌; ♆ ☌, P., □ or ☍ ♂; ♅ influences tend to.

**Habits** — (See "Impulsive" under Habits).

**Ill-Health** — From Outbursts of Impulsive Expression—The ☉ affl. in ♈; ♀ affl. in ♈, ill-health from impulsive habits. (See Expression, Hasty, Precipitate, Rashness).

**Impulsiveness**—The ☉ ☌ or ill-asp. ♅; ♆ affl. in ♌; ♅ in ♈; ♅ affl. the ☉; ♅ or ♂ influences, and espec. when acting thru the cardinal signs; ♄ when prominent and strong at B. tends to counteract impulsiveness, and to steady the nature; ♃ affl. in ♈; ♂ affl. in the 1st H.; ♂ afflicting ☿; ♂ affl. in ♏, ♐, or ♑; ♂ ☌, □, or ☍ ☿; ♂ in ♈; ♂ to the cusp the 1st H. by dir.; ♂ ☌ ☋ by dir.; ♂ progressed ☌ or ill-asp. ♄ or ♀ in the radix, or vice versa; ☿ in ♐; ☿ progressed ☌ or ill-asp. ♂ or ♅ in the radix, or vice versa; the 3rd Decan. of ♈ on the Asc.; the 16° ♌ on the Asc.; a ♐ influence. The fire and water signs and elements incline to impulsiveness, due to emotional excitement. Fixed signs, as a class, are not as impulsive. (See Emotions, Excitable, Feelings).

**Morbid Impulses** — ♄ influence; ♄ strong at B.; ♄ affl. the ☉, ☽, ☿, or Asc. at B., and by dir. (See "Morbid" under Fears and Imagination; Morbid).

**Nerve Impulses** — (See Innervation, Nerves).

**Sudden Impulses**—The ☉, ☽, or ♂ affl. in ♈; the ☉ ☌ ♅ or ♂; ♅ ☌ or ill-asp. ♂; ♅ in the Asc. or 10th H.; ♂ in the 1st H. in evil asp. to the ☉ or ☽ tends to accidents, injuries, wounds, etc., from impulsive, precipitate, sudden and rash actions.

**Uncontrolled Impulses**—♅ afflicting ☿.

**Violent Impulses** — (See "Murderous" under Murder; "Tendency to Violence" under Violence). For further study along this line see Chaotic, Choleric, Dangerous, Desires, Dispersions, Eccentric, Effervescent, Erratic, Fire Signs (see Fire); Folly, Frenzy, Furious, Ideas, Notions, Peculiar, Reason, Temper, Uncontrolled, Vicious, Water Signs (see Water); etc.

**IMPURE**—Impurities—Corrupt—Foul—Impure Blood—Impure Conduct—Impure Morals, etc.—See "Blood", "Causes of Impure Blood", and the various paragraphs in this Article, with reference to Impure Blood, and Disorders Arising therefrom.

**All Diseases** — Arising from Impure Blood—Ruled by ♃, and are ♃ diseases; ♄ in ♊ when ♄ is the afflictor in the disease; ♀ diseases.

**Arms** — Hands, Legs, and Feet—Corrupt Blood In—The ☉, ♃, or ♀ afflicted in signs which rule these parts. (See "Blood" under Arms; "Blood" under Feet, Legs; "Corrupt Blood" under Hands).

**Blood**—Impure Blood—Corrupt Blood — Foul Blood — Gross Blood — Heavy Blood—Coarse Blood—Depraved Blood —Stagnant Blood—Poisoned Blood—Polluted Blood — Ill Blood, etc. — Corrupt Blood is due principally to the influence of ♃, and afflictions to or from this planet, as ♃ rules strongly over the blood. Impure blood is also caused by various other planetary and sign influences, which are listed under "Causes of Impure Blood", and the various paragraphs in this Article.

**Boils**—From Corrupt Blood—(See Abscesses, Boils).

**Brain**—Ill Blood In Veins of the Brain and Head — (See "Ill Blood" under Brain, Head; "Brain" under Congestion).

**Causes of Impure Blood** — Corrupt Blood—Foul Blood—Ill Blood—Heavy and Coarse Blood — Polluted Blood — Poisoned Blood — Toxic Blood — Blood Impurities, etc.—The ☉ in ♈, ♊, ♋, ♎, ♐ ♒, or ♓, and affl. by ♃; the ☉ in ♋ ☌ or ill-asp. any of the malefics as promittors; the ☉ ill-aspected by ♃ in any part of the map; the ☉ to the ill-asps. ♃ by dir.; the ☉ in ♌ or ♒, ☌, P., □ or ☍ ♅ or ♄, the blood is heavy and poisoned with waste materials; the ☽ in ♊, ♏, or ♑, and affl. by the ☉ or ♂ when taken ill, or at decumb. (Hor'y); the ☽ affl. in an airy sign at B., or at decumb., indicates corrupted blood, Gout, or Cutaneous affections; the ☽ hyleg and affl. in ♎ in female nativities; the ☽ to the ill-asps. ♃ by dir., the blood is gross or corrupted; ♆ or ♅ in ♊, ♋, ♍, ♎, or ♒, and affl. the ☉ or ☽; ♅ in the 6th H.; ♅ ☌ ♂ in ♊, and in □ or ☍ ♃ and ♀; ♄ in ♊, ♍, ♎, or ♒, and affl. the ☉ or ☽; ♄ to the ☌ ♃ by dir.; ♄ ☌ ♃ or ♀, stagnant and polluted blood; ♄ in ♊, ☌, □, or ☍ ♃ and ♀; ♄ affl. in ♎, or ♄ in ♎ in □ or ☍ ♃ and ♀, the blood and body are charged with impurities; ♃ affl. in ♋, the result of over-eating, surfeits and plethora; a ♃ disease; ♃ causes death by impure and foul blood; ♃ on the Asc. at B., and afflicted, the result of over-eating; ♃ affl. the ☉ at B., and by dir.; caused by the pathological action of the ♃ Group of Herbs (see "Jupiter Group" under Herbs); ♃ affl. in ♉, ♊, ♋, ♍, ♎, ♐, or ♒, or affl. the ☉ or ☽ from these signs; ♃ affl. in ♉, ♊, or ♋ tends espec. to foul and corrupt blood, and blood heavy with poisons and waste materials; ♃ affl. in ♎, from too much blood; ♃ affl. by ♂; ♃ affl. in ♒, the blood abounds too much, and is thereby corrupted; ♃ affl. in the Asc.; ♃ in the 6th H. at B., and affl. by the ☉; ♃ ☌ ♄, and in ☍ the ☽ and ♀; ♂ affl. in ♊, ♒, or ♓; ♂ to the ☌ or ill-asp. ♃ by dir., or by progression; ♂ in ♊, ☌, or ill-asp. the ☉; ♂ in ♊ in the 6th H.; ♀ affl. in ♊ or ♒; ♀ is nearly always afflicted by a malefic in bad blood conditions, leading to excesses in pleasures, habits, eating, and conduct; ☿ affl. in ♎ or ♒; the airy signs ♊, ♎, or ♒ on the Asc. at B., and afflicted; a ♊, ♎, ♒, and ♓ disease, and afflictions in these signs; airy signs on the Asc. or 6th H. at B., or the ☽ in an airy sign at B., or at decumb., or the Sigs. in airy signs at the beginning of an illness; a ♊ disease, and afflictions in ♊; ♐ on the Asc. at B., and afflicted; an ♒ disease, as ♒ rules the blood, and afflictions in this sign tend to impure and foul blood, disturbed circulation of the blood, to blood poisoning and morbid changes in the blood, and also insufficient oxygenation; afflictions in ♓; afflictions in or about the 25° ♌ or ♒, or the 21° ♎; lords of the 1st, 6th, or the ☽ in airy signs; Subs at SP and KP. Cases of Impure Blood—See Fig. 11G in "Astro-Diagnosis", by the Heindels. For other subjects along this line, and for the effects of Impure, Foul, and Corrupt Blood, see Abscesses, Acidity, Alkalinity, Anaemia, Aneurysm, Aquarius, Arteries, Auto-intoxication, Blood (see the various paragraphs under Blood); Boils, Breathing, Chlorosis, Circulation (see the various paragraphs and references under Circulation); Corrupt, Deposits, Dizziness, Elimination, Eruptions, Excretions, Faintings, Fetid, Fevers, Foul, Gout, Headaches, Heart (see the various paragraphs under Heart); Inflammation, Jupiter, Minerals, Obstructions, Oxygenation, Pimples, Plethora, Poisons, Pulse, Rheumatism, Septic, Skin Diseases, Sores, Stiffness, Stomach (see "Blood" under Stomach); Toxaemia, Ulcers, Urea, Uric, Varicose, Veins, Venus, Vessels, Wastes, etc. Also see other subjects you have in mind, and which are not listed here. Impure blood is usually acid blood, and too much acidity in the body means the death of the body. Pure blood is more alkaline than acid, and alkaline blood is maintained by proper diet, by avoiding excess of starches and sugars, and by eating plenty of fruits, oranges, lemons, grapefruit, vegetables, etc. Also a good and quick way to make the blood, urine, and other secretions of the body alkaline, is to take frequent doses of Citro-Carbonate (Upjohn), which is an effervescing drink, and also to take daily Epsom Salts Baths, one pound of Epsom Salts to half a tub of water in the bath tub, and soak in this solution for 10 or 15 minutes. Also, after 40 years of age, drink distilled water. Every student should make a scientific study of Diet, and the nature and food value of each article of food, in order to feed the body properly, and to maintain health, and avoid acidity of the blood, and corrupt and foul blood, etc. When the body is wholly acid, death results. Remember that excessive acidity of the body is injurious, and alkalinity of the right proportion is health and life. (See Hyperacidity).

**Death from Impure Blood**—♃ causes; ♃ afflicting the hyleg by dir., and ♃ much afflicted at B., and holding the dominion of death.

**Digestive Disorders** — From Impurities In the Blood and System—(See "Impurities" under Digestion).

**Feet**—(See "Feet" under Blood).

**Flying Pains**—From Corrupt Blood—(See "Flying Pains" under Flying).

**Foul Blood**—Especially an ♒ disease, and caused by afflictions in ♒. (See "Causes" in this section).

**Hands** — Corrupt Blood In — (See "Arms" in this section).

**Head**—Ill Blood In Veins of the Head —(See "Brain" in this section).

**Headaches** — From Bad Blood — (See "Blood" under Headaches).

**Impoverished Blood** — (See Anaemia, Haemoglobin, Oxygenation).

**Impure Blood** — (See Blood, Causes, Foul, in this section).

**Impurities** — Blood Impurities—The Body Charged with Impurities—♄ affl. in ♎, and due to inactive and disordered kidney action; ♄ in ♎, □ or ☍ ♃ or ♀. (See "Causes" in this section).

**Legs**—(See "Arms" in this section).

**Many Diseases** — From Impure Blood —♃ affl. in ♒, due to the blood being corrupted by too much blood, and by plethora, surfeits, etc. (See "Too Much Blood" under Blood; "Many Diseases" under Diseases; "Ill-Health All Thru Life" under Ill-Heath; Plethora; "Much Sickness" under Sickness; Surfeits).

**Morals** — Impure In Morals — Lewd Conduct—(See Lewd, Licentious; "Loose Morals" under Morals).

**Morbid Blood**—Morbid Changes In the Blood—(See "Morbid" under Blood).

**Pains** — Flying Pains from Corrupt Blood—(See "Flying Pains" under Flying).

**Poisoning** — Blood Poisoning — Poisoned Blood — Toxic Blood — (See "Causes" in this section; "Blood Poisoning" under Poisons; Toxaemia).

**Poor Blood** — (See Anaemia; "Poor Blood", "Thin Blood", under Blood).

**Putrefaction**—In the Blood—A ♃ disease. (See "Putrefaction" under Blood; Putrefaction).

**Reins** — Bad Blood In — (See "Blood" under Reins).

**Sex Relations** — (See "Impure" under Sex).

**Sickness** — The Illness Arises from Corrupt Blood—The ☽ ☌ or ill-asp. ♄ in ♌ (or ☿ if he be of the nature of ♄) at the beginning of an illness, or at decumb., and they frequently die when the ☽ comes to the ☍ ♄ if no good aspects prevent (Hor'y).

**Sluggish Blood** — (See "Sluggish" under Blood).

**Stagnant Blood**—(See "Stagnant" under Blood).

**Stomach Trouble** — From Corrupt Blood—(See "Blood" under Stomach).

**Too Much Blood** — And with Corruption of the Blood — (See "Too Much Blood" under Blood).

**Ulcers**—Proceeding from Bad Blood—(See "Corrupt Blood" under Ulcers).

**Veins**—Ill Blood In Veins of the Head —(See "Brain" in this section).

**Women** — Corrupt Blood In — (See "Blood" under Women).

**INABILITY**—Lack of Power or Ability—

**Concentration** — Inability to Concentrate—(See Concentration).

**Disease**—Inability to Throw Off Disease — A characteristic of the ♍ sign class of people. (See "Low" under Recuperation, Resistance, Vitality; Virgo; "Weak Body" under Weak).

**Study**—Inability to Do Deep Study—(See Dull, Examinations, Imbecility; "Mental Abilities Impaired" under Impaired; "Incapable" under Learning; "Deficiency", "Incompetency", "Shallow", "Weak", under Mentality; "Weak Mind" under Mind; Study, etc.).

**INACTIVE**—Inaction—Inactive State of the Body or Mind—♄, ♅, or ♆ in ♊ at B., and affl. the ☉ or ☽; lack of strong ♂ influence at B.; the water signs strong at B.; Subs at AT, AX, SP. (See Action, Ambition, Apathy, Careless, Clumsiness, Debility, Dull, Energy, Exertion, Feeble, Idle, Indifferent, Inertia, Labour, Languid, Lassitude, Lazy, Lethargy, Listless, Low Spirits (see Low); Malaise, Motion, Movement, Retarded, Rouse, Sedentary, Sickly, Slow, Sluggish, Suppressed, Torpor, Vitality Low, Walk, Weak Body, etc.).

**INARTICULATE** — Incapable of Proper Articulation—Mute—Dumb—

**Inarticulate Signs** — ♈, ♉, ♌, and ♑. (See Articulate).

**Inarticulate Speech** — (See Dumb, Mutes; Impediment, Inarticulate, Stammering, under Speech; Tongue).

**INCAPABLE**—Incapacity—

**Mental Incapacity** — (See Dementia, Idiocy, Imbecile; "Study" under Inability; Insanity).

**Physically Incapacitated**—(See Feeble, Inefficiency, Infirm, Invalids, Sickly, Vitality Low, Weak Body).

**Remedy**—Incapable of Remedy—(See Incurable, Permanent; "Incapable" under Remedy).

**INCENDIARISM**—Pyromania—Arson—The Malicious Burning of a Building —☿ in ♊ and affl. by ♂; ☿ in ♊ ☌ ♂ at the Vernal Equinox tends to a prevalence of fires by Incendiarism.

**Death by Incendiarism**—♅ in a human sign at B., setting, and in ☍ to a Luminary, tends to under the evil directions of ♅ to the ☉ or ☽, and espec. when the 8th H. is involved in the configuration. (See "Death" under Fire.)

**INCEST** — (See "Incest" under Perversions).

**INCIPIENT** — Incipient Diseases — (See Praeincipients).

**INCISED WOUNDS** — Danger of Injury By — (See Cuts, Duels, Instruments; "Accidents" under Iron; Operations, Stabs, Sword).

**INCISORS** — (See "Incisors" under Teeth).

**INCLINED** — Incline — Inclined To — Tendencies — The Star Map of Birth, and also the Prenatal Epoch Map for the time of Conception, show the inclinations and tendencies of the body and mind. These influences show the more natural lines of expression for the native, but, of course, the evils in any map can be resisted, overcome, transcended, and controlled. The Stars only incline, and do not rule the human Will. The inclinations of the Native may be congenital, or acquired. For the various inclinations and tendencies, which operate over, and thru the native, see Acquired, Conduct, Character, Congenital, Destiny, Diathesis, Directions, Disease, Excesses, Fate, Habits, Idiosyncrasies, Ill-Health, Mental, Mind, Passion, Perversions, Propensities, Temper, Temperament, Tendencies, Vices, etc. Also look in the alphabetical arrangement for the subject you have in mind.

**INCOHERENT** — Incongruous — Confused — Disconnected — Lack of Coordination, etc. — (See Chaotic, Confused, Coordination, Delirium, Delusions, Dementia, Deviations, Disease, Dreamy, Erratic, Fears, Gait, Hallucinations, Ideals, Ideas, Idiocy, Imaginations, Incoordination, Insanity, Involuntary, Mania, Mind (see the various paragraphs under Mental and Mind); Notions, Paralysis, Perversions, Reason, Spasmodic, Unnatural, Walk, etc. Also look in the alphabetical arangement for the subject you have in mind).

**INCOMPATIBILITY** — Discordant — Antagonistic — Inharmonious, etc. — (See Antipathy, Aversions, Balance, Compatibility, Cure of Disease (see Cure); Enemies, Equilibrium, Friends, Harmony, Hatred, Healers (see "Incompatibility" under Healers); Incurable, Magnetism, Medicines, Opposites, Quarrels, Remedies, Resentful, Sympathy, Temperaments, Treatment, etc.).

**INCOMPETENCY** — Inability — Lack of Capacity —

**Bodily Incompetency** — (See Debility, Decrepitude, Deformities, Feeble, Infirm, Invalids, Sickly, Vitality Weak (see Vitality); "Weak Body" under Weak, etc).

**Mental Incompetency** — (See Idiocy, Imbecility; "Study" under Inability; Inefficiency, Insanity).

**Mitral Incompetency** — (See "Mitral" under Heart). For other parts or organs of the body which may be affected with incompetency, look in the alphabetical arrangement for the subject you have in mind.

**INCOMPLETE** — Imperfect — Not Fully Developed —

**Born Incomplete** — (See "Incomplete" under Birth; "Born Blind" under Blindness; Cloaca, Congenital, Cyclops, Deaf and Dumb (see Hearing); Defects, Deformities, Distortions, Dwarf, Frog Child, Hermaphrodites, Idiocy, Imbecile, Imperfect, Inhuman, Malformations, Members, Missing, Monsters, Organs, Prenatal Epoch, Toes, etc.).

**Mental Development Incomplete** — Mental Defects — (See Foolish Mind (see Foolish); Idiocy, Imbecile, Insanity; "Arrested", "Deficiency", under Mental; "Weak Mind" under Mind).

**Oxygenation Incomplete** — (See Oxygen).

**Physical Development Incomplete** — (See Diminished, Dwarf, Growth, Idiocy, Members, Organs, Undersized, etc. Also note the references under "Born Incomplete" in this section).

**INCOMPOSED** — Disturbed — Disordered

**Body** — The Body Incomposed — The 5th face of ♋ on the Asc. (See Deranged, Disease, Disordered, Ill-Health, Infirm, Weak, etc.).

**Mind** — The Mind Incomposed — (See Anger, Anguish, Anxiety, Despondency; "Irritations" under Mental; "High Temper" under Temper).

**INCONSTANT** — (See Changes; "No Home" under Home; "Light In Mind" under Mind; Mutable, Negative, Residence, Restless; "Wanderer" under Travel; Unstable, Vacillating, Vagabond).

**INCONTINENCE** — (See "Incontinence" under Urine).

**INCOORDINATION** — Of Action — Incoherent — Lack of Coordination — Caused by ♅ influence and afflictions to the organ of Coordination situated in the ♉ region of the body, and also caused by reflex action from ♏, the exalted sign of ♅; ♅ ☌, □, or ☍ the ☉ at B., and by dir.; a ☿ disease; afflictions to ☿, the mental ruler, or to a ☿ sign, or the malefics in evil asp. to the ☉ in a ☿ sign, as in ♊ or ♍.

**Heart Action** — Incoordination of — (See "Incoordination" under Heart).

**Muscles** — Incoordinated Action of — Ataxia — Case — See Fig. 1 in the book, "Message of the Stars", by the Heindels. (See Ataxia; "Incoordination" under Muscles).

**Nerve Action** — Incoordination of — (See such subjects as Contractions, Cramps, Involuntary, Jerky, Nausea, Nerves, Paralysis, Rhythm, Saint Vitus Dance, Spasmodic, Speech, Strabismus (see Eyes); Tetanus, Tics, Tremors, Twitchings, Vomiting, Walk, Winking (see Eyelids). Also, for further study along this line, see Action, Balance, Chaotic, Confused, Contraction, Coordination, Disease, Elephantiasis, Energy, Equilibrium, Erratic Movements (see Erratic); "Athetosis" under Fingers; Gait, Harmony, Ideals, Ideas, Idiocy, Ill-Health, Incoherent, Insanity, Mental, Mind, Motion, Movement, Nystagmus (see Eyeballs); Opisthotonos, Sickness, Spine, Subluxations, Unbalanced, Vertebrae, etc. Nearly every subject in this book is related to lack of proper coordination and harmony between mind and body, and between the various parts and functions of the body, and for subjects not listed here look in the alphabetical arrangement for the subject you have in mind.

**INCREASE** — Increased — Increasing — Augmentation, etc.—The plus, or tonic action, of the planets, when operating favorably, and by their good aspects, tends to increase of health, strength, vitality, and mental power. The unfavorable influences of the planets, by their plus or tonic action, tend to increase of disease, ill-health, fevers, inflammations, mental unbalance, etc. The great majority of the subjects in this book have to do with some increased or abnormal and pathological action of the planets, and all subjects which have to do with Increase cannot be listed here in this Article, but only the more important and suggestive ones, and for subjects not listed, look for it in the alphabetical arrangement.

**Abscesses Increased**—(See Abscesses).

**Abundance**—(See the various paragraphs under Abundance).

**Acidity**—The Acidity of the Body Increased—(See Acidity, Deposits, Gout, Hyperacidity; "Impure Blood" under Impure; Minerals, Uric, Wastes, etc.).

**Action**—The Action of the Mind or Body Increased—(See Accelerated, Action, Active, Hasty, Motion, Movement, Quick, Rapid, etc.).

**Augmented**—(See the various paragraphs under Augmented).

**Bile**—Blackness of Bile Increased—(See "Black Bile" under Bile).

**Birth Rate**—(See "Increased" under Birth).

**Blood Increased**—(See "Too Much Blood" under Blood).

**Cold**—Cold In the Body Increased—(See "Body" under Cold).

**Death Rate Increased**—(See Mortality).

**Discharges Increased**—(See Discharges, Exudations, Fluids, Flux).

**Disease**—The Disease Will Increase—The Disease Is Increasing—The ☽ or lord of the 6th applying to the ill-asps. the lord of the Asc.; lord of the 6th stronger than the lord of the 1st; lord of the 6th in the 8th or 12th H.; when the afflicting planets are angular and out of their dignities. (See Chronic, Crises, Directions, Fatal; "Increased" under Fevers; Grievous, Lingering, Prolonged, Relapses, Serious, Severe, Sick (see "Sick" under Escape); Vehement, Violent Maladies (see Violent); Worse).

**Dropsy**—(See "Increased" under Dropsy).

**Dryness**—The Dryness of the Body Increased—(See "Increased" under Dryness).

**Energy**—Increase of—(See "Increase" under Energy).

**Enlargements**—(See the various paragraphs under Enlarged).

**Epilepsy Increased**—(See Epilepsy).

**Erysipelas Increased**—(See Erysipelas).

**Evils Increased**—(See "Much Evil" under Evil).

**Exaggerated Action**—(See Exaggerated).

**Excess Of**—(See the various paragraphs under Excess, Excesses).

**Expansion**—Of the Bodily Tissues—(See Expansion).

**Fat**—Increase of—(See Fat, Obesity).

**Fever Increased**—(See "High Fever" under Fever).

**Flesh**—Increase of—(See Corpulent, Fat, Fleshy, Stoutness).

**Fluids**—The Fluids of the Body Increased—(See "Excessive", "High Tide", under Fluids).

**Flux**—Increase of—(See "Violent" under Flux).

**Functions**—The Functional Activities Increased—(See "Over-Activity" under Functions).

**Growth**—Growth of the Body Increased—(See Enlarged, Expansion, Giants, Growth).

**Hair**—Abundance of—Loss of Hair Increased—(See Baldness; "Abundance" under Hair).

**Health**—The Health Increased—(See "Good Health" under Health; Immunity; "Body" under Strong; Vitality Good).

**Heat**—The Heat of the Body Increased —Fevers—(See Fever; "Body" under Heat).

**Height**—Height of the Body Increased —(See Giants, Height, Tall).

**Hyperaesthesia**—Excessive Sensibility—(See Hyperaesthesia).

**Hypertrophy**—Abnormal Increase In the Size of An Organ—(See Hypertrophy).

**Improved**—(See the various paragraphs under Improved).

**Incrementations**—Increase or Growth —(See Enlarged, Growth).

**Inflammation Increased**—(See "Increased" under Inflammation).

**Insanity Increased**—(See "Increased" under Insanity).

**Mobility Increased**—(See Accelerated, Action, Exaggerated, Motion, Movement, Rapid, Spasmodic, etc.).

**Moisture**—The Moisture of the Body Increased—(See "Moist Constitution" and the various paragraphs under Moisture).

**Moon**—Increase of—(See Fluids, Functions; "Increase Of" under Moon).

**Mortality Increased**—Death Rate Higher—(See Mortality).

**Motion**—Movement—(See these subjects).

**Mucus**—The Mucus In the Body Increased—(See Catarrhs, Colds, Expectoration, Mucus, Phlegm).

**Nervousness Increased**—(See Erethism; "Increase", "Neurasthenia", under Nerves).

**Over-Abundance**—(See the various paragraphs under Hyper, Over, Super).

**Pain Increased**—(See Pain).

**Phlegm**—Increase of — (See "Mucus" in this section).

**Plentiful**—(See the paragraphs under Plenty).

**Promoted**—(See the paragraphs under Promoted).

**Recuperation** — The Recuperative Powers Increased—(See Recuperation).

**Relapses**—The Danger of a Relapse In Disease Increased—(See Relapse).

**Resistance**—The Powers of Resistance to Disease Increased—(See Resistance, Stamina, Tone, Vitality).

**Rheumatism Increased**—(See "Promoted" under Rheumatism).

**Secretions Increased** — (See Discharges, Fluids, Glands, Juices, Secretions).

**Sensibility Increased**—(See Hyperaesthesia, Sensibility, Sensitive).

**Spasmodic Action Increased** — (See Convulsions, Exaggerated, Fits, Hyperactivity, Spasmodic, Tics, Twitchings).

**Strength**—The Strength of the Constitution Increased—(See "Increased" under Constitution; "Improved" under Health; Strength, Vitality).

**Suffering Increased**—(See Pain, Suffering, Worse).

**Superabundance** — (See the various paragraphs under Superabundance).

**Sweat**—(See "Excessive" under Sweat).

**Swellings**—(See Swellings, Tumors).

**Temperature**—Increase of—High—(See "High" under Fevers; Temperature).

**Tetters Increased**—(See Tetter).

**Thickening**—(See the paragraphs under Thick).

**Too Much** — (See the various paragraphs under Abundance, Excess, Hyper, Over, Superabundance).

**Tumors**—(See the various paragraphs under Growths, Tumors).

**Ulcers Increased**—(See Ulcers).

**Urine Increased**—(See "Polyuria" under Urine).

**Vitality Increased**—(See Vitality).

**Wastes**—Of the Body Increased—(See Deposits; "Impure Blood" under Impure; Minerals, Urea, Uric, Wastes).

**Weakness Increased**—(See "Body" under Weak).

**Weight**- The Weight Increased—(See Corpulent, Fat, Fleshy, Stout, Weight).

**Worry**—Increase of—(See Cares; "Low Spirits" under Low; Miseries, Reversals, Ruin, Troubles, Worry, etc.).

**Worse**—The Disease Is Worse or Increased—(See "Worse" under Disease; Relapses, Worse). Also see such subjects as Abnormal, Anger, Appetites, Conduct, Corpuscles, Decreased, Deposits, Diminished, Dissipation, Drink, Gluttony, Habits; "High Living" under High; Immoderate, Intemperate, Passion, Pleasures, Riotous, Sex, Temper, etc.

**INCREMENTATIONS**—Increase or Growth—(See Enlarged, Expansion, Growth, Increase, Large, etc.).

**INCURABLE**—Incurable Diseases—The Disease, Affliction, or Malady Is Incurable, or Without Apparent Remedy— Many planets in the fixed signs, ♉, ♌, ♏, or ♒ at B., and afflicted, tend to deep-seated and incurable diseases. The influences of the malefics, and their afflictions, are the principal causes of prolonging a disease and making it incurable, and especially the influence of ♄ at B., and by dir. If the malefics are angular, ori., and elevated above the Lights, and the benefics are occi., weak, and lend no assistance, the disease tends to be tedious, prolonged, or incurable, and the more ori. or angular the planet is, whether malefic or benefic, the more powerful will be its effects. The malefics in angles at B., well fortified, and in elevation above the Lights and Benefics, and the latter in weak signs; malefics in angles at B., occi. of the ☉, and ori. of the ☽, and the benefics in no way connected with the malefics, nor with the ☉ or ☽; the malefics strong, and holding dominion in angles, or above the Lights, and evilly aspected by ♃ or ♀, or the malefics with the ☉ or ☽ in angles, and the Luminaries receiving no help from the benefics; the malefics holding dominion, and afflicting the hyleg, and with no assistance to the hyleg from benefics, and the malefics elevated above the Luminaries at B., provided the ☉ or ☽ are not in angles, and the malefics receive no good asp. from ♃ or ♀; when a malefic in a sign and house is afflicted by two or more malefics at B., then the part of the body afflicted is apt to develop an incurable malady, and predominate more or less all thru life, and eventually cause death under a train of evil directions, and especially if at B. the malefic is in the 6th, 8th, or 12th H.; the ☉ or ☽ in the 6th H. at B., and affl. by malefics; the ☉ or ☽ in angles, and affl. by malefics elevated above them; the ☽ and many planets in fixed signs at the beginning of an illness (Hor'y); ♅ affl. in the 1st or 6th H.; ♅ diseases are mostly nervous, and often incurable; ♅ □ or ☍ ♄ in fixed signs; ♅ □ or ☍ the ☽, and often with complete suppression of the functions; ♅ □ or ☍ the Asc.; ♄ afflicted in fixed signs; ♄ in the 6th H., and afflicting the hyleg; ♃ afflicted in ♓, due to tendency to dropsy and swellings; indicated by the 6th H. conditions; lord of the 6th affl. by the □ or ☍ the lord of the Asc., grievous and hard to cure; lord of the 8th in the 6th; lord of the 1st in an Azimene degree, and affl. by lord of the 6th. (For further influences along this line see Azimene, Birth (note the various paragraphs under Birth); Blemishes, Blindness, Changes, Chronic, Complications, Congenital, Continuous, Course of Disease (see Course); Crippled, Crises, Cure, Deafness, Death (see "Arguments for Death", "Certain", "Sure", under Death); Decay, Defects, Deformities, Dementia, Directions, Distortions, Duration of Disease (see Duration); Epilepsy, Escape (see "The Sick Will Hardly Escape" under Escape); Extraordinary, Fatal, Fixed Signs (see Fixed); Functions (see

"Suppressed" under Functions); Gangrene, Grievous, Healers (see "Death" under Healers); Hereditary, Ill-Health (see "Ill-Health All Thru Life" under Ill-Health); Invalids, Lameness, Latent Diseases (see Latent); Lingering, Long Diseases (see Long); Malformations, Malignant, Malnutrition, Mania, Monsters, Morbid, Mysterious, Narcotics, Negative, Organic, Paralysis, Passive, Peculiar, Prolonged, Recovery, Recuperation, Resistance, Saturn, Sick (see the paragraphs under Sick); Sickly, Slow Diseases (see Slow); Strange Diseases (see Strange), Structural, Suppressions, Tedious, Treatment, Uranus, Wastings, Weak Body (see Weak); Worse, etc.).

**Conspicuous Diseases**—The Disease Is Conspicuous and Less Liable of a Cure —(See Chronic, Conspicuous, Deformities, Dementia, Demoniac, Epilepsy, Exhibitionism, Face, Feet, Foolish Mind (see Foolish); Head, Hydrocephalus, Idiocy, Imbecility, Insanity, Lameness, Leprosy, Limbs, Malformations, Monsters, Siamese Twins (see Twins); Skull, Spine, Walk, etc.).

**Deep-Seated**—The Disease Is Deep-Seated and Incurable—(See Chronic, Death, Fatal, Lingering, Malignant, Morbid, Tedious, etc.).

**Difficult to Cure**—(See Chronic; "Difficult" under Cure; Environment, Extraordinary, Grievous, Invalids, Long, Malignant, Native Land, Prolonged, Residence, Slow, Tedious, Wastings).

**Drunkards**—(See "Incurable" under Drunkenness).

**Hurts Incurable**—(See Crippled, Permanent; "Hurts" under Remedy).

**Incapable of Remedy**—(See Fatal, Incapable, Permanent; "Hurts" under Remedy. Also see the first part of this Article, and the various references herein).

**Mental Diseases**—Incurable Diseases of the Mind — The ☽ and ☿ unconnected with each other or the Asc., and with ♄ and ♂ in angles ruling the scheme, but the disease will not be conspicuous or openly displayed. The ☽ and ☿ unconnected with each other or the Asc., and the malefics in the Eastern Parts, and in the Asc. or M.C., and the benefics occi., then the disease becomes incurable and also conspicuous. (See "Curable", "Incurable", under Brain; Chaotic, Conspicuous, Dementia, Demoniac, Fears, Foolish, Frenzy, Idiocy, Imbecility, Insanity, Madness, Mania; "Derangement" under Mental; "Diseased Mind" under Mind; Obsessions, Paranoia, Spirit Controls).

**Old Age** — Incurable Infirmity In — (See "Incurable" under Old Age).

**Remedy** — The Disease or Hurt Is Without Remedy — (See "Certain", "Sure" under Death; Fatal, Permanent; "Hurts" under Remedy).

**Rheumatism Incurable**—(See "Death", "Incurable", under Gout, Rheumatism).

**Sudden and Incurable Diseases**—♅ □ or ☍ the ☉ at B., and by dir. For further subjects along this line, and which may not be listed here, look for the subject in the alphabetical arrange-

ment. Also remember that many diseases are classed as "Incurable" in the ordinary sense, which may become curable when the native becomes awakened, more highly spiritualized, and learns how to think correctly, and to live in accordance with the Laws of God, and of Health, Longevity, etc.

**INCURVATING BODY** —Crooked — Not Straight—♄ strong at B., in the Asc., or rising; a ♄ sign on the Asc., as ♑; ☿ Sig. in ♑, a crooked make; ♓ gives a body not very straight, but incurvating. (See Crooked; "Ill-Formed" under Ill; Stooped).

**INDECENT** — An Abandoned Person — Profligate—Unrestrained—Morally Perverted — Without Virtue — Shameless, etc. — (See Debauched, Depraved, Lascivious, Lewd, Licentious, Lustful; "Loose Morals" under Morals; "Unbridled Passion" under Passion; Perversions, Profligate, Shameless, Virtue, Wanton, etc.).

**INDEPENDENT** — Independence of Thought and Opinion—♆ and ♅ influence; ♅ ascending at B.; ♅ in the 3rd or 9th H.; ♅ ☌ the ☉, ☽, or ☿ at B.; ♅ in the Asc. or 10th H. at B., in ☌ the ☉, ☽, or ☿; the ☽ applying to the ☌ or any aspect of ♆ or ♅. These influences tend to make the native unorthodox, to be much misunderstood in life, persecuted, and to be fond of Astrology, the Esoteric, Occult, Metaphysical, and Ancient Wisdom, and with a deep desire to know the Truth about Life, Death, Destiny, The Hereafter, The Mysteries, The Secret Doctrines, Religion, The Soul, Salvation, Redemption, etc. (See Eccentric, Ideals, Ideas, Metaphysics, Misunderstood, Occult, Opinions, Peculiar, Persecution, Philosophy, Positive, Nature, Reactionary, Reformers, Religion, Revolutionary, Saucy, Science, Truth, etc.).

**INDIAN HEMP**—A Typical Drug of ♄. (See Cannabis; "Saturn Group" under Herbs).

**INDICATIVE CRISES** — In Disease — Those which occur at the half aspects in every Quadrate of the ☽ from her place at seizure or decumbiture, as at 45°, 135°, 225°, or 315°. (See Crises).

**INDICATORS OF DISEASE**—Indicators of Health — (See Anareta; "Significators" under Disease; "Indicators" under Health; Hyleg, Malefics, Significators, Sixth House).

**INDIFFERENT**—Indifference—Neutral —Disinterested—Ill or Sick—Poorly—

**Blood** — Indifferent State of — (See "Poor", "Thin", under Blood).

**Complexion** — (See "Indifferent" under Complexion).

**Disposition** — An Indifferent Disposition — Indifference — Many planets in bicorporeal signs at B. tend to an indifferent disposition; lack of strong ♂ influence at B.; mutable signs on the Angles at B.; many planets cadent. (See Dreamy, Dull; "Lack Of" under Energy; Idle, Inactive, Inertia, Labour, Lassitude, Lethargy, Listless, Manner, Negative; "Temperament" under Phlegmatic; Rouse).

**Duty**—Indifferent To—(See "Of No Ambition" under Ambition; Carelessness, Debauched, Improvident, Neglectful, etc.).

**Expression**—Indifferent Expression of the Face—Born under ♄; ♄ rising at B.; ♄ in the Asc. (See Countenance, Dull; "Dull" under Eyes; "Sad" under Face; Grave, Melancholic; "Mind" in this section).

**Face**—An Indifferent Face—(See "Expression" in this section).

**Health**—(See "Indifferent State" under Health).

**Marriage**—Indifferent To—(See "Indifferent" under Marriage).

**Mind**—Indifferent State of Mind—Indifferent Expression — Apathy — Dull, etc.—The ☽ to the ☌ or ill-asp. ♆ by dir., indifference of the mind to life's duties; the 3rd face of ♉ on the Asc., careless and indifferent. (See Apathy, Dull, Languid, Lethargy, Listless, Procrastination; "Disposition", "Expression", in this section).

**Passion**—Indifferent Passions—(See Apathy, Bachelors, Celibacy; "Free from Passion" under Passion).

**Signs of Zodiac**—The Indifferent Signs —(See "Indifferent" under Signs).

**Stature**—Indifferent Stature—Not Distinctive—The ☽ Sig. in ♈; ☿ in ♒. (See Crooked, Form, Mean, Small, Stature, Stooping, Ugly, etc.).

**Teeth**—Indifferent Teeth—(See "Indifferent" under Teeth).

**INDIGENT**—Destitude—Without Comforts—In Poverty—(See Comforts, Idle, Improvident, Misery, Penurious, Poverty, Property, Reversals, Riches, Ruin).

**INDIGESTION**—Indigested—Undigested—Caused ordinarily by afflictions in ♋, or its opposite sign ♑ by reflex action. Also afflictions in cardinal signs show, or cardinal signs upon the angles, as the cardinal signs ♈, ♋, ♎, and ♑, are all in adverse aspect to each other, and form the cardinal cross. Also caused by the ☉ affl. in ♋, and espec. when affl. by ♄; the ☽ in ♋, and affl. by ♄; the ☽ in ♋ or ♍, and in □ or ☍ ♃ or ♀; the ☽ ☌ ♅ in ♋ or ♍; the prog. ☽ in ♋ or ♍, and in ☌, □, or ☍ malefics; ♆ in ♋ in the 6th H.; ♄ affl. in ♋ or ♑; ♃ or ♂ affl. in ♋; Subs at SP. (See Acids, Alimentary, Aphthae, Diet; "Digestive Disorders", "Inability to Digest Food", "Weak Digestion", under Digestion; Dyspepsia, Flatulence, Food, Gas (see "Stomach" under Gas); Gastric, Hydrochloric, Juices, Nutrition, Stomach; the various paragraphs in this section).

**Anxiety**—Indigestion from Anxiety and Worry—(See "Anxiety" under Digestion).

**Chronic Indigestion**—Inability to Digest Food—♄ affl. in ♋; ♄ in the 6th H. at B., in a cardinal sign, and affl. by the ☉ or ☽. (See "Inability" under Digestion; Emaciation; "Malnutrition" under Nutrition; Wasting).

**Cold**—Indigestion from Taking Cold —A ☽ disease; the ☽ affl. in ♋. (See Cold, Colds).

**Cramps**—From Indigestion—♅ affl. in ♋ or ♍. (See Cramps).

**Food**—Indigestible Food—Desire For —(See "Indigestible" under Food).

**Head**—Noises In the Head Arising from Indigestion—(See "Noises" under Head).

**Illness from Indigestion**—The ☽ in ♍, ☌, □, or ☍ ♄ (or ☿ if he be of the nature of ♄) at the beginning of an illness or at decumb., and the patient is apt to be sick for a long time (Hor'y).

**Impaired Digestion**—Imperfect—(See Digestion, Dyspepsia; the various paragraphs in this section).

**Inability to Digest Food**—(See "Chronic" in this section).

**Intestinal Indigestion**—♅ in ♑ in ☍ ♆ in ♋, and also in □ ♄, the food is often undigested and appearing in pieces in the stools; ♄ affl. in ♍; ☿ in ♍, and affl. the ☽ or Asc.; ♀ affl. in ♍ in the 6th H.; ☿ affl. in the 6th H., and due to overwork or overstudy; ♍ on the cusp the 6th H.; afflictions in the 6th H. (See Chyle).

**Meat**—Ill-Digested Meat and Illness From—(See Meat; "Raw Humours" in this section).

**Nervous Indigestion**—♅ affl. in ♋; ♅ ☌ ☽ in ♋; ☿ affl. in ♋ or ♑. (See Nerves).

**Poor Digestion**—Suffers from Indigestion—The ☉ affl. in ♋; the ☉ in ♋ and affl. by ♃; the ☽ affl. in ♋; a ☽ disease; the ☽ in ♍ ☌ ♄, etc. (See "Illness" in this section); ♆, ♅, or ♄ in ♋ or ♑, and affl. the ☉ or ☽; ♄ in ♋ in the Asc. or 6th H., and espec. when affl. the ☉ or ☽; ♃ affl. in ♋; ♂ in the 6th H. in card. signs, and affl. the ☉ or ☽; ♂ in ♋, ☌, or ill-asp. the ☉; ♂ □ or ☍ ☉ at B., and by dir.; ♀ affl. in ♋ in the 6th H., and affl. the ☽ or Asc.; ☿ in ♋, ♐, ♑, ☌ or ill-asp. any of the malefics as Promittors; cardinal signs on the 6th H.; card. signs show, and afflictions in them; afflictions in ♋; ♋ on the Asc. or 6th H., and containing malefics and afflictions. (See "Chronic" in this section).

**Raw Humours**—The Stomach Offended with Cold, Raw, and Undigested Humours—♄, ♅, or ♆ in ♊, and affl. the ☉ or ☽; ♄ affl. in ♋, a cold stomach; ♀ affl. in ♋ when ♀ is the afflictor in the disease; the Asc. affl. by the ☉ or ☽. (See Meat).

**Stomach**—(See the various paragraphs under Digestion, Stomach).

**Weak Digestion**—(See "Weak" under Digestion).

**Worry and Anxiety**—Indigestion From —(See "Anxiety" under Digestion). For collateral study see Acids, Alimentary, Belching, Cachexia, Diet, Digestion, Dyspepsia, Emaciation, Emetics, Feasting, Fermentation, Fluids, Gastric, Gluttony, Juices, Nausea, Nutrition, Vomiting, etc.).

**INDIGO**—A color ruled by ♄ and ♀. Indigo is not blue, but a color in itself, and represents Spiritual Mind, and Intellect over-shadowed by Divine Mind. (See Colors, Copper; "Venus Group" under Herbs).

**INDISCRETIONS**—Indiscreet—Tending to Injure the Health—

**Actions**—Indiscretions In—(See Conduct, Habits; the various paragraphs and references in this section).

**Conduct**—Indiscretions In—(See Conduct).

**Cosmetics** — Indiscretions In the Use of—(See Cosmetics, Lotions).

**Death**—From Indiscretions—(See "Causes His Own Death" under Death; Debauchery; "Death" under Eating; "His Own Worst Enemy" under Enemies; Folly, Imprudence, Intemperance, Intoxication, Narcotics, Rashness, etc.).

**Diet**—Indiscretion In—Gastronomical Indiscretions—Due to an afflicted ♃ or ♀, or afflictions by these planets; ♃ and ♀ diseases; ♃ affl. in ♉ or ♋; ♃ or ♀ in the 6th H., and afflicted; ♀ affl. in ♋ or ♓; the Asc. affl. by ♃ or ♀. (See "Evil Diet" under Diet; Drink, Eating, Excesses, Food, Gluttony, Indigestion, etc.).

**Diseases Arising From**—♀ □ or ☍ the Asc. (See "Fever", and the various paragraphs in this section).

**Drugs**—Indiscretions In the Use of—(See Drugs, Narcotics).

**Fever and Sickness**—From Indiscretions—The ☉ affl. by ♃ or ♀; the ☽ affl. by ♀, irregularities and ailments arising from indiscretions, excesses, and carelessness; the ☽ affl. by ♃; ♃ diseases, and indiscretions in diet especially. (See "Ailments" under Diet; Excesses; "Indiscretions", "Slight", under Fever; Folly; "Free Living" under Free; "High Living" under High; Plethora, Surfeits, etc.).

**Gastronomical Indiscretions**—(See "Diet" in this section).

**Habits**—Indiscreet Habits—(See Conduct, Drink, Drunkenness, Gambling, Habits, Luxuries, Morals, Narcotics, Passion, Perversions, Vices, etc.).

**Sex Life**—Indiscretions and Excesses In—(See Amorous, Harlots, Intercourse, Lascivious, Lewd, Licentious; "Loose Morals" under Morals; "Excesses" under Passion; Sex, Venery).

**Slight Disorders**—From Indiscretions —♀ affl. the ☉ at B., and by dir. (See Ephemeral, Mild, Slight).

**Sports** — Indiscretions In and Suffering From — (See Amusements, Exercise, Pleasure, Sports).

**Volitional Power** — Will-Power — Indiscretions Thru Loss of, or Weakness of—♆ influence; ♆ affl. in ♐. (See Involuntary, Volition, Will).

**Wounds** — Accidents, Hurts, Injuries or Wounds from Indiscretions — (See Accidents, Blows, Cuts, Falls, Folly, Foolhardy, Hasty, Hurts, Injuries, Quarrels, Rashness, Stabs, Violence, Wounds, etc.). For further and collateral study see Anger, Appetites, Carelessness, Cravings, Deposits, Depraved, Disease, Disgrace, Dissipation, Dissolute, Epicureans, Erratic, Feasting, Ill-Health, Improvident, Imprudent, Indulgences, Irregularities, Judgment, Love Affairs, Meat, Neglectful, Obesity, Poisons, Poverty, Prodigal, Profligate, Recklessness, Recreations, Riotous, Ruin, Sickness, Temper, Tumors, etc.).

**INDISPOSITION**—Indisposed—Ailing—

**Cold Temperament**—Indisposed By—(See "Temperament" under Cold).

**Febrile Indisposition**—♂ affl. in ♒; ♂ to the ill-asps. his own place at B., or by dir., or to the place of the ☉ or ☽. (See "Liable To" under Fever).

**Indisposed** — The transits of malefics over the place of the ☉ or ☽ at B. if they afflict the Lights in the radix; the ☉ directed to Aldebaran; the ☽ affl. in ♋ at B. and by dir.; ♄ to the ill-asps. his own place by tr. or dir., or to the place of the ☉ or ☽, or any planet; ♂ to the cusp the 1st H. by dir.; ♀ Sig. in ♌, frequently indisposed, altho not seriously. (See "Bad Health" under Health; Ill-Health, Mild, Sickly, Slight).

**Lingering Indisposition**—(See Chronic, Lingering, Long, Prolonged, Slow, Tedious, Wastings).

**Mental Indisposition** — (See "Low Spirits" under Low; Melancholy; "Irritations" under Mental; Worry, etc.).

**Occasional Indisposition** — ♀ affl. the ☽ at B., and by dir. or tr.; ♀ affl. in the 5th or 6th H. at B., and thru pleasures, dissipation, or wrong eating; ♀ affl. in ♌.

**Parents Indisposed** — (See "Afflicted" under Parents).

**Slight Indisposition** — Temporary Indisposition—Ill aspects of the ☉ to the malefics if the malefics did not afflict the ☉ at B.; the tr. of the ☉ over the radical ♆ when ♆ is Promittor; the ☽ to the ill-asps. her own place at B.; the ☽ to the ill-asps. ♆ or ♅ by dir., as by Colds; the ☽ to the bad asps. ♀ by dir., temporary disorders; ♄ ☌ or ill-asp. the ☽, and both occi., temporary derangement of the health; caused by directions which are brief in duration; benefics in the 6th H., and well-aspected, the indisposition will be slight and soon overcome. (See Colds, Fatigue, Headaches, Mild, Minor, Recovery, Slight, Temporary, etc.).

**INDIVIDUALITY**—The Sign the ☉ is in at B. represents the Individuality, or the Higher Mind. Also many planets in the positive and masculine signs at B. give a strong Individuality, and the native is not as liable to worry and brood so much over disease or trouble. People who are strongly individualized at B. have more resistance, will-power, and ability to overcome disease and obstacles, and do not give up as easily. (See Character, Fate, Negative, Personality, Positive).

**INDOCILE**—Child Born With a Wild, Indocile, and Savage Nature—(See "Beastly Form" under Beasts; "Dogs" under Children; "Animal Forms" under Monsters; Savage, Wild).

**INDOLENT** — (See Carelessness, Dull, Idle, Inactive, Improvident, Inertia, Labour, Lassitude, Lazy, Lethargy, Listless, Lymphatic, Neglectful, Poverty, Uncleanly, etc.).

**INDULGENT**— Indulgences — Improper Living, and Tending to Disorders of Mind and Body—

**Amorous Indulgences** — Excess of — (See Amorous).

**Blood Disorders** — Through Excesses and Indulgences — ♃ affl. in ♒. (See "Poor Blood", "Too Much Blood", under Blood; Excesses, Impure, Plethora).

**Drink and Intoxicants**—Too Much Indulgence In — (See Alcoholism, Drink, Drunkenness, Intoxication, Wine).

**Drugs** — Narcotics — Over-Indulgence In—(See Drugs, Narcotics).

**His Own Worst Enemy**—Thru Indulgence and Extravagance — (See "His Own" under Enemies).

**Over-Indulgences** — (See Over-Indulgence).

**Passional Nature**—Sickness from Excessive Indulgence of—(See Amorous, Excesses, Passion, Sex, Venery).

**Pleasure** — Excessive Indulgence In, and With Injury to the Health—(See the various paragraphs under Pleasure).

**Self-Indulgent**—(See this subject).

**Sports** — Exercise — Excessive Indulgence In—(See Exercise, Sports). For collateral study see such subjects as Debauched, Depraved, Diet, Dissipated, Extravagance, Feasting, Free Living, Food, Gluttony, High Living, Imprudent, Indiscretions, Luxuries; "Loose Morals" under Morals; Perversions, Profligate, etc.

**INDURATIONS** — The Hardening of a Tissue or Part—(See Hardening, Sclerosis).

**INEBRIATION** — A Drunken Condition —(See "Delirium Tremens" under Delirium; Drink, Drunkenness, Intoxication).

**INEFFICIENCY**—Incapacity—Want of Sufficient Power or Energy—

**Heart**—Muscular Inefficiency of—(See "Inefficiency" under Heart).

**Lungs** — Pulmonary Inefficiency — ♀ affl. in ♊. (See Lungs, Pulmonary). See Defects, Deficient, Incapable, Incompetent, Insufficiency, Lack Of, Loss Of).

**INEQUALITY**—Of the Pupils—(See Iris, Pupils).

**INERTIA** — Inert — Apathy — Sluggishness—Inactivity—Absence of Contractility—The ☽ gives; lack of strong ♂ influence at B.; ♂ setting in the West, weak, and ill-dignified, and in no aspect to the ☉ or ☽. (See Apathy, Dull, Idle, Inactive, Lassitude, Lethargy, Listless, Sluggish).

**Inactive and Indolent**—(See Carelessness, Duty Energy, Exertion, Fatigue, Improvident, Indifferent, Labour, Malaise, Vitality Low, Weak Body; the references in the first part of this section).

**Mind** — Inactive State of Mind — (See Chaotic, Clogging, Clouded, Dreamy, Dull, Inactive; "Arrested" under Mental; "Weak" under Mind).

**System** — Inactive and Inert State of the System — (See Apathy, Debility, Dull, Feeble, Inactive, Infirm, Lassitude, Lethargy, Retardations, Sedentary, Sluggish, Suppressions, Weak, Weakened).

**INFAMOUS** — Base — Vile — Shameless— The ☽ Sig. in ♏, infamous in her desires if a female, and openly scandalous if the ☽ be affl. by the □ or ☍ of ♄ or ♂; the ☽ Sig. in the 10th H. in ♑, and affl. by ♄, ♂, or ♀; the ☽ to the left hand of Ophiucus, given to debauchery and infamy; ♄ Sig. □ or ☍ the ☉, the aspect of infamy, and to be held in contempt; ♄ and ♂ in the 4th H.; ☿ Sig. □ or ☍ ♂, despised by every one for his infamous life. (See Debased, Debauched, Depraved, Disgrace, Dissolute, Drink, Drunkenness, Execrated, Hatred, Honour, Lewd, Low; "Loose Morals" under Morals; Obscene, Passion, Perversions, Profligate, Reputation, Scandalous, Sex, Shameless, Vile, Wanton, Wench, etc.).

**INFANCY** — Infants — Infantile — The Early Years of Childhood—Life from the cradle to the grave is divided into Planetary Periods, and each period ruled by a different Planet. (See Periods). The first to fourth years of life are ruled by the ☽, and during this period the evil directions of the ☽, or afflictions to the radical ☽ by transits or directions, make this period especially dangerous to the native, or to cause sickness or early death. Therefore, it is well to make a study of the star map of every infant, and note the influences of and to the ☽ during the first few years of life, and if any evil directions are found, or a train of evil directions, to be forming and culminating during this period, greater care and protection should be given the child during the infantile stage. With every new-born child the prospect of life is an important thing to know, for if early death is indicated, and the directions forming soon after birth are of a fatal nature, and also the vitality weak at B., then all else in the life of the child comes to naught as far as the physical and Earth life is concerned for the time. The death of infants, the causes of early death, their destiny, the future course of the Ego, etc., are explained from an Occult standpoint in the book, "Cosmo-Conception", by Max Heindel. Some Writers and Authorities also say that the first seven years of life in childhood are ruled by the ☽. In the Kabala, Infancy was dedicated to the ☉. The following paragraphs and subjects have to do with the beginnings, birth, the early life, diseases and afflictions of the child, and during the period of Infancy, which subjects see in the alphabetical arrangement when not considered here. Also many of the subjects along this line are listed and considered under the subjects of Birth, Childhood, Children, Conception, Congenital, Early Years (see Early); Foetus, Gestation, Pregnancy, Prenatal Epoch, etc. See these subjects.

**Accidents at Birth**—In Delivery, and Perhaps by the Use of Instruments—♅ in ♏; ♅ or ♂ in the 5th H. of the mother. (See "Accidents" under Childhood, Children, Parturition; "Early Years" under Hurts).

**Adopted** — Separated from Parents — (See Adoption).

**Afflicted In Infancy**—(See Poor Health, Sickly, Weak, and the various paragraphs in this section).

**All May Die In Infancy** — Or Early Life — But Few Live — Malefics in the 5th or 11th H. of the parents, and afflicted; lord of the 5th in the 6th or 8th H., and afflicted; lord of the 5th in the 8th, and affl. by lord of the 8th; lord of the Asc. in the 6th, and affl. by lord of the 8th, and with no assistance from the benefics. (See "Death of Children", under Children; "Early Death" under Early).

**Animal Heat**—Lack of In Infancy and Early Years—(See "Animal Heat" under Heat).

**Asphyxiated at Birth**—(See Asphyxia; "Delayed Births" under Children).

**Beastly Form**—(See "Beastly Form" under Beasts).

**Birth** — (See the various paragraphs under Birth; Accidents, Death Soon After Birth, Infections, in this section).

**Bladder In Infants**—(See Bladder).

**Blindness In**—Born Blind—Blind from Birth—(See "Born Blind" under Blindness).

**Blue Baby**—(See Asphyxia).

**Born Alive**—Lives But a Few Hours —(See "Death Soon After Birth" in this section).

**Born Almost Dead**—(See "Death Soon After Birth" in this section).

**Born Dead** — (See Abortion. Miscarriage, Stillborn).

**Bowel Complaint**—(See "Cholera Infantum" under Cholera; Diarrhoea).

**Boys**—Male Infants—(See Male, Males, Son, in this section).

**Bronchitis In**—(See Bronchitis).

**Buries His Children** — (See "Buries His Children" in Sec. 3 under Children).

**But Few Live** — Lord of the 10th a malefic in the 5th H. (See "All May Die" in this section).

**Childhood** — (See the various paragraphs under Childhood, Children, Early Years; also see the subjects in this section).

**Children**—(See the various paragraphs under Childhood, Children).

**Cholera Infantum**—(See Cholera).

**Club Feet**—(See Feet).

**Colic; Conception; Congenital Defects** —(See Birth, Congenital, Defects, Deformities, Malformations, Monsters, Prenatal Epoch).

**Conjunctivitis**—Case of In Infancy— (See Conjunctiva; "Ophthalmia" in this section).

**Constitution In**—(See Good Constitution, Poor, Sickly, Weak, under Constitution; Stamina, Strength, Strong, Weak, and the various paragraphs in this section).

**Continuance of Life** — After Birth — (See "Continuance" under Life; "Nurture", and the various paragraphs in this section).

**Convulsions**— (See Convulsions, Fits; "Dentition" under Teeth).

**Cough; Cramps** — (See Colic, Cramps, Flatulence; "Stomach" under Gas).

**Crippled from Birth** — (See Crippled, Deformities, Distortions, Lameness, Missing).

**Daughter Born** — (See Daughter; "Birth of a Female" under Female).

**Deaf**—Deaf and Dumb—Deaf, Dumb and Blind — Deaf, Dumb and Idiot — (See Blindness, Deaf, Dumb, Hearing, Idiocy, Mutes).

**Death At Birth**—(See "Birth" in Sec. 3 under Children; "Death Soon After" in this section).

**Death by Accident** — Danger of — ♂ coming to the ☌ the Asc. or Desc. soon after birth. (See "Death" under Accidents; "Accidents" in this section).

**Death In Infancy** — Danger of — The Premature Death of Infants—Signs of Death In Infancy—In death in Infancy, it is necessary, in order to understand the causes, to study the Prenatal Epoch Chart, and the Chart of Descent, in connection with the Natal Map. For the Rules which indicate death in Infancy see "Signs of Death" in this section. Also note the following general influences—The hyleg much afflicted by malefics; one of the malefics in ☌ the ☉ or ☽ in an angle; the malefics in angles, and with ☉, ☽, and Asc. afflicted, and with no assistance from the benefics; the ☉, ☽, Asc., and hyleg all afflicted, and with malefic planets in angles, and their evil aspects close, and with no assistance to the hyleg from benefics; those born with the ☉ ☍ ♄ live thru infancy with difficulty, and espec. if both are in angles, and the hyleg severely afflicted; the ☽ between ♂ and the ☉, or the ☽ ☌ ♂ and the ☉, will almost exchange the cradle for the grave; ♅, ♄, or ♂ near the rising degree, and affl. by the ruler of the 8th H., and the ☽ at the same time affl. by the ☉; ♄ in power and elevation at B., and affl. the hyleg, and such almost invariably die in infancy, and thus the Fable that "Saturn Devours His Own Children." In the map of the parent, if the 5th H. promises children and the 11th H. deny them, or if the 11th H. promises them and the 5th H. deny, the children are more apt to die in infancy; ♄ afflicted in the 5th H. of a parent; ♄ or ♂ in ☍ ♃ in the map of a parent destroys some; ☿ in the 5th H. in a barren sign, and afflicted. (See "Death" under Childhood; Destroys, Early Death, First-Born Child, Short Life, under Children; "Early Death" under Early; Eclipses; "Full Moon" and "New Moon", under Moon; "Death Soon After Birth", "Signs of Death", and the various paragraphs in this section). Cases—Birth Data and Cases of the Death of Infants and Children at Various Ages— (1) Death at Birth — (See "Death at Birth" in this section). (2) Death Soon After Birth—(See this subject in this section). (3) Lives 12 Hours — (See "Short Life", No. 775, in 1001 N.N. (4) Lives Three Weeks — (See "Short Life", No. 786, in 1001 N.N.). (5) Lives Two Months—(See "Born In a Flood", No. 227, in 1001 N.N.). (6) Lives Three Months—(See "Convulsions", No. 155;

"Morrison", No. 188; "Short Life", No. 776, all in 1001 N.N.). (7) Lives Four Months—(See "Short Life", No. 371, in 1001 N.N.). (8) Lives Six Months—(See "Heart", No. 981, in 1001 N.N. (9) Lives Nine Months — (See "Short Life", No. 778, in 1001 N.N.). (10) Lives Fourteen Months—(See "Short Life", No. 777, in 1001 N.N.). (11) Lives Twenty Months —(See "Short Life", No. 779, in 1001 N.N.). (12) Lives Seven Years — Or Dies During the First Seven Years— (See "Signs of Death" in this section). Also see Case, "Strangled at Birth", No. 922 and No. 923, in 1001 N.N. See Daath's Medical Astrology, Chap. 14.

**Death Soon After Birth**—Born Almost Dead—Lives Only a Few Hours—The ☉ or ☽ hyleg, and ♄ afflicting both the ☉ and ☽, lives but a short time, and the closer the aspects the shorter the life; the ☉ and ☽ both affl. by malefics, and one of them the hyleg; the Asc. hyleg, and with ♄ on the Asc., M.C., Desc., or Nadir, and with no assistance from the benefics to the hyleg, seldom lives long; ruler of the Asc. in the 6th or 8th H., and malefics in the Asc., and with ♋, ♑, or ♓ on the Asc.; ♋, ♑, or ♓ on the Asc., and the hyleg affl. by malefics. (See "Born Almost Dead" under Children; "Early Death" under Early; "Continuance of Life", "Short Life", under Life; "Incapable of Nurture" under Nutrition; "Low" under Vitality; "Weak Body" under Weak; "Death In Infancy", "Signs of Death", in this section).

**Defective Births** — (See "Defective Births" under Birth; Congenital, Defects, Deformities, Hearing, Idiocy, Inhuman; "Birth" under Lameness, Paralysis; Malformations, Missing, Monsters, Prenatal Epoch, Savage, Virile).

**Deformed from Birth** — ☿ in the 5th H. in ♋, ♏, or ♓ in the map of a parent, or of the child, and espec. if ♄ or ♂ afflict ☿, may be deaf, deformed, or insane. (See Blindness, Congenital, Crippled, Deformities, Distortions, Feet, Hearing, Idiocy, Insanity, Limbs, Malformations, Monsters, Parturition, Prenatal Epoch; "Defective" in this section).

**Delivery**—Birth—Injuries at Birth— Unusual Delivery—(See "Excision" under Foetus; "Injury", "Mangled", and the various paragraphs under Parturition).

**Dentition**—Fits During— (See "Dentition" under Teeth).

**Destroys the Children** — (See "Destroys" under Children; "Death In Infancy", "Death At Birth", "Death Soon After Birth", in this section).

**Diarrhoea** — (See "Bowel Complaint" in this section).

**Die Before Maturity** — (See "Death" under Childhood; Early Death (see Early); "Short Life" under Life; Maturity; "Death In Youth" under Youth).

**Dies Soon After Birth** — (See "Death Soon After" in this section).

**Dies Young** — (See "Death" under Childhood; "Early Death" under Children; "Short Life" under Life; "Death Before Maturity" under Maturity).

**Directions Kill** — The First Train of Evil Directions Kill—The ☉, ☽, or ♄ affl. in the 6th H. at B., and the hyleg severely afflicted. (See Directions; "Low" under Vitality; "Weak Body" under Weak).

**Diseases and Infections**—(See "Infections" in this section).

**Diseases of Infancy**—(See "Disease", and the various paragraphs under Children. Look for the name of the disease in the alphabetical arrangement, such as Cholera Infantum, Colic, Convulsions, Diarrhoea, Eruptions, Measles, Mumps, Scarlet Fever, etc. Also note the various paragraphs in this section).

**Distortions**—(See "Moment of Birth" under Calamity; Contortions, Deformities, Distortions, Excrescences).

**Duration of Life** — (See Duration; "Early Death" under Early; "Continuance", "Long", "Short", under Life; the various paragraphs in this section).

**Early Death Of**—(See "Death In Infancy", "Death Soon After Birth", and the various paragraphs in this section; "Death" under Childhood, Children; "Early Death" under Early; "Short Life" under Life).

**Early Years**—Accidents, Hurts, Sickness In — (See "Early Years" under Early).

**Eclipses** — Death of Infants Born at Time of—(See Eclipses; "Full Moon", "New Moon", under Moon).

**Eleventh House** — One of the Houses of Children—(See Eleventh).

**Embryo** — (See Conception, Embryo, Foetus, Gestation).

**Eyes**—Affections of the Eyes In Infants—(See "Born Blind" under Blindness; Conjunctivitis, Infections, Ophthalmia, in this section).

**Fall In Infancy**—See Case, "Religious Melancholia", No. 976, in 1001 N.N.

**Female Infant**—Birth of a Female— Death of At Birth—(See "First-Born Child" under Children; Daughter, Eclipses; "Birth Of", "Death Of", under Females).

**Females Predominate** — (See "Sex of Children" under Children; "Birth of a Female" under Females).

**Fevers In Infancy**—♂ coming to the ☌ or ill-asp. the Asc. tends to fevers, hurts, inflammations, wounds, or injuries, if the nativity denotes such, (See "Fevers" under Childhood, Children).

**Few Children** — (See "Few" under Children).

**Few Live**—(See "All May Die" in this section).

**Fifth House**—The House of Children —(See Fifth House).

**Fits**—(See Convulsions, Fits; "Dentition" under Teeth).

**Foetus** — (See Abortion, Conception, Embryo, Foetus, Gestation, Miscarriage, Pregnancy).

**Fontanelles** — Slow Closure of — (See this subject under Head).

**Foolish** — The Child Born Foolish — (See Foolish, Idiocy, Imbecile, Inhuman, Savage).

**Gestation; Girls**— A Girl Born— Daughters—(See "Female", "Females", in this section).

**Good Constitution**—Good Health of— Stamina and Vitality Good — Weak Constitution — (See "Constitution" in this section).

**Health Poor**—(See Poor, Sickly, Weak, in this section).

**Healthy Infants**—Healthy and Long-Lived Children — (See "Long-Lived" under Children; "Good" under Constitution, Health; Immunity, Vitality).

**Heat**—Lacking In Animal Heat—(See "Animal Heat" under Heat).

**Hemiplegia** — Infantile — The ☉ or ♄ affl. in ♈; the ☉ coming to the ♂ ♅ soon after birth; Subs at AT, AX, and CP. (See Hemiplegia; "Hemiplegia" under Paralysis).

**Hermaphrodites; Hurts** — (See "Accidents" in this section; "Accidents", "Hurts", under Children; "Early Years" under Early, Hurts).

**Husband An Anchorite**—Does Not Desire Children—(See "Anchorite" under Husband).

**Hydrocephalus; Idiocy;**

**Ill-Formed Body**—(See "Beastly Form" under Beasts; "Dogs" under Children; Crooked, Deformed; "Ill-Formed" under Ill; Inhuman, Monsters, etc.).

**Ill-Health**—(See Poor, Sickly, Weak, in this section; "Sickly", "Unhealthy", under Children).

**Imbecility; Infant May Not Survive**— (See Death In Infancy, Death Soon After Birth, Early Death, Eclipses, and the various paragraphs in this section).

**Infantile Paralysis**—(See Hemiplegia, Paralysis, in this section; Distortions, Excrescences).

**Infections at Birth**—Unusual Diseases at Childbirth—♅ afflicted in the 5th H. of the mother. (See the various paragraphs under Parturition).

**Inflammations**—Inflamed Eyes — (See Conjunctivitis, Eyes, Fevers, Ophthalmia, in this section; "Fevers" under Childhood; Inflammation).

**Injury At Birth**—(See "Accidents" in this section; "Injury At Birth" under Parturition).

**Instrumental Delivery**—(See "Injury" in this section).

**Lame from Birth** — (See Congenital, Crippled, Deformities, Distortions, Excrescences, Feet, Lameness, Legs, Paralysis).

**Liable to Disease** — (See Ill-Health, Poor, Sickly, Weak, in this section; "Ill-Health All Thru Life" under Ill-Health; "Low" under Recuperation, Resistance, Vitality; "Weak Body" under Weak).

**Life Spared** — (See "Spared" under Life; "Signs of Death", "Will Live", in this section).

**Lives But a Short Time**—(See Death In Infancy, Death Soon After Birth, Nurture, in this section).

**Lives Thru Sickness**—(See "Stamina" in this section; "Lives Thru" under Serious).

**Long Life**—(See "Long-Lived" under Children; "Long Life" under Life).

**Maimed At Birth**—Males Born Maimed —(See Maimed).

**Male Infant**—A Male Born—Death of a Male—(See "Male Children Born" under Children; Eclipses; "Births" under Males).

**Males Predominate**—(See "Male Children Born", "Sex", under Children; Predetermination, Triplets, Twins).

**Maturity**—Will Live To—Will Not Live To—(See Maturity; the various paragraphs in this section).

**Measles; Middle Life**—Will Live To— (See Middle Life).

**Miscarriage; Monsters;**

**Mortality Among**—(See "Mortality Great" under Children).

**Mother**—The Infant Affected by the Conditions of the Mother—(See Mother, Parents, Parturition).

**Mouth**—Cankerous Sores In—(See Aphthae; "Thrush" under Mouth).

**Much Sickness**—In Infancy—The ☉ or ☽ affl. in ♋; the ☽ affl. in the 6th H.; the hyleg much afflicted by malefics; ♄ on the Asc. (See Poor, Sickly, Weak, in this section; "Sickly", "Unhealthy", under Children; "Early Years" under Early; "Ill-Health All Thru Life" under Ill-Health; "Much Sickness" under Sickness).

**No Duration of Life**—(See Death At Birth, Death In Infancy, Death Soon After Birth, Dies Young, in this section; "Death" under Chidhood, Children; Duration; "Early Death" under Early; "No Duration", "Short Life", under Life; "Incapable of Nurture" under Nutrition).

**Not Strong or Robust**—(See Ill-Health, Much Sickness, Sickly, Weak, in this section; "Low" under Resistance, Vitality; Robust, Strength; "Not Strong" under Strong; "Weak Body" under Weak).

**Nursing Of**—(See Milk).

**Nurture**—Incapable of Nurture—Dies Immediately After Birth—(See "Incapable of Nurture" under Nutrition; Death At Birth, Death Soon After Birth, in this section).

**Ophthalmia**—Inflamed Eyes—Conjunctivities—Case of Inflamed Eyes two days after birth and Defective Sight— See "Sight Defective", No. 684 in 1001 N.N. (See Conjunctiva; "Inflamed" under Eyes).

**Paralysis**—Infantile Paralysis—Paralyzed from Birth — (See Distortions, Excrescences; "Birth", "Infantile", under Paralysis).

**Parental Love**—And Affection—(See "Love and Affection" under Parents).

**Paroxysms**—Fits During Dentition— (See "Dentition" under Teeth).

**Parturition**—Childbirth—Accident, Hurt, Disease, Infection, or Death to Child During—(See the various paragraphs under Parturition; Accidents, Delivery, Infection, Injury, in this section).

**Poor Constitution**—(See "Weak" under Constitution; Vitality Low; "Weak

Body" under Weak; Poor Health, Sickly, Weak, and the various paragraphs in this section).

**Poor Health**—Weak signs on the Asc. at B., as ♎, ♑, or ♓, and the hyleg afflicted by malefics; the ☉ or ☽ angular, and affl. by a malefic; the ☽ affl. in the 6th H.; ♄ affl. in the Asc., bad health during infancy and childhood. (See Ill-Health, Poor Constitution, Much Sickness, Sickly, Weak, in this section; Childhood, Children; "Early Years" under Early).

**Premature Birth**—Premature Death—(See Abortion; "Death under Childhood; "Death", "Eight Months Children", under Children; "Early Death" under Early; Foetus; "Short Life" under Life; Miscarriage, Premature, Prenatal Epoch, Untimely; "Death" in this section).

**Prenatal Epoch**—(See Prenatal).

**Resistance to Disease**—Good and Bad—(See Immunity, Recuperation, Resistance, Stamina, Tone, Vitality; "Weak Body" under Weak).

**Rickets; Robust**—The Infant Robust—Not Robust—(See Robust; "Not Strong", and the various paragraphs in this section, and under Children).

**Savage**—Of a Savage and Wild Disposition—(See "Beastly Form" under Beasts; Inhuman, Savage, Wild).

**Scarlet Fever**—Scarlatina—(See Scarlet).

**Separated from Parents**—(See Adoption).

**Seven Years of Life**—Or Dies During First Seven Years—(See "Signs of Death" in this section).

**Sex of Children**—Predetermination of—(See "Sex of Children" under Children; Predetermination).

**Short Life**—(See "Death" under Childhood, Children, Youth; "Early Death" under Early; "Short Life" under Life; "Death In Infancy" in this section. See Chap. XIV in Daath's Medical Astrology).

**Shorter Will Be the Life**—The greater the affliction of the Significators of Life, as the ☉, ☽, Asc., or lord of the Asc., the shorter will be the life.

**Sickly**—(See "Sickly" under Children; Poor Health, Much Sickness, in this section).

**Sickly But Recovers**—If the ☽ separate from a malefic and apply to a benefic at B., the child may be sickly for a time after birth, if the map otherwise indicated weakness, but will recover. (See Recovery, Recuperation, Resistance).

**Sight**—Defective Sight—(See "Born Blind" under Blindness; Conjunctivitis, Eyes, Sight; "Ophthalmia" in this section).

**Signs of Death**—In Infancy—Rules for Judging—Will the Child Live or Die?—Indications in the map of a parent are—Lord of the 5th H. ℞, combust, in fall or detriment, and affl. by lord of the 8th or 12th H., signs of an early death; lord of the 5th weak, affl. by a malefic in the 8th or 12th H., unless opposite testimonies concur, the child will speedily die; lord of the Asc. in the 5th H., and afflicted, or ♅, ♄, or ♂ be in the 5th H., and ℞, or ☋ in the 5th H., are signs of death. Also notes the following RULES and Influences—Signs of Death—

(1) the ☉ just below the Asc. or Desc., malefics in the ♓ Navamsas of signs, and with the negative Hora of a sign rising. (See Navamsa, Horas).

(2) The ☽ ☌ a malefic, with no assistance from a benefic, and with malefics in the Asc. or Desc.

(3) Three malefics in three angles, and the ☽ in the 4th angle, and the ☽ and malefics all in evil aspect to each other.

(4) The ☽ afflicted, and also the ruler of the 8th H. afflicting a malefic in the Asc., or just above the Asc.

(5) The ruler of the 4th or 8th H. afflicting the ruler of the Asc. in the 6th H., and with no good asp. from the benefics.

(6) The ☉ or ☽ in an angle in ☌ a malefic, or if the malefic be an equal distance from the ☉ and ☽, and without the assistance of good asps., and the rulers of the Lights also in malefic places, the child will die immediately or soon after birth.

(7) The ☉ or ☽ angular in ☌ or ill-asp. a malefic, and without the assistance of good asps.

(8) The ☽ in the 12th H., decr. in light, with no benefics in angles, with malefics rising, and also malefics in the 8th H.

(9) The ☉, ☽, and Asc. afflicted, malefics in angles, and the hyleg without assistance from the benefics.

(10) The ☉ and ☽ in ☍ asp., and in □ asp. to malefics which are also in ☍ to each other.

(11) Malefics in the 1st, 7th, 8th or 12th H. in ☌ or ill-asp. the ☽, with no good asps. to the ☽, and no benefics angular.

However these rules will not hold good, and the infant will be spared if

(A) If the benefics ♃ and ♀ are in the Asc., in strong signs, well-aspected, and not afflicted by malefics.

(B) Lord of the Asc. strong, not afflicted, and well-aspected.

(C) The benefics in good asp. to, and ruling the hyleg.

(D) The hyleg assisted by the good asps of ♃ or ♀.

(E) The ☽ in the decanates of ♃ or ♀ in the 6th or 8th H.

(F) The positive horas of signs rising, and espec. those of positive signs. If these last six rules, or conditions, prevail, the child will live beyond the 7th year, but may not live a long life. If the first eleven rules prevail, and with no offsetting good influences, the child generally dies during the first seven years of life. An old Kabalistic rule is that the 7th hour after birth indicates and decides whether or not the child will live, and a star map erected for a time exactly seven hours after the moment of birth, and studied as to the aspects and positions of the planets, and judged accordingly, will give valuable information as to the prospect of life. These rules apply to the map of birth only, and the Prenatal Epoch map should also be studied along with the map of birth. (See Death At Birth, Death In Infancy, Death Soon After Birth, in this section; "Death" under Childhood, Children; "Symbols of Death" under Death; "Early Death" under Early; "Short Life" under Life).

**Snuffles**—(See Nose).

**Some Will Die In Infancy**—If the 5th H. promises children, and the 11th H. deny them, and vice versa, some will die in infancy. (See "Death In Infancy" in this section).

**Sons** — The Birth or Death of — (See Male, Males, in this section).

**Spared**—The Life of Is Spared—(See the six rules, A, B, C, etc., under "Signs of Death" in this section; "Spared" under Life).

**Stamina Good**—In Infancy—The fiery signs on the Asc. at B., and next to them are the airy signs, and ♍ and ♏, and children born under these signs live thru illnesses that would ordinarily prove fatal to those born under weaker signs. (See Stamina, Tone, Vitality; "Healthy", "Long Life", in this section).

**Stillborn; Strangled At Birth**—Cases —(See Asphyxia, Strangulation).

**Strength Increased** — The benefics or the ☽ in the 5th or 11th H., and with fiery signs on the Asc. in the map of parent; ♂ in the Asc., and well-aspected, and in a strong sign in the map of the child, has much power to bring them thru infancy even tho the map is otherwise weak. (See "Strength" under Children; Strength).

**Strong In Infancy**—(See Constitution, Stamina, Strength, Vitality, in this section; Strength, Strong).

**Suffers Much** — (See Much Sickness, Poor Health, in this section).

**Suffocated At Birth**—(See Asphyxia, Suffocation).

**Summer Complaint** — (See "Cholera Infantum" under Cholera).

**Survival**—May Not Live—Will Live— (See Death, Spared, Will Live, and the various paragraphs in this section).

**Teething**—(See "Dentition" under Teeth).

**Thrives and Lives** — (See Long Life, Stamina, and the various paragraphs in this section).

**Thrush** — (See "Mouth" in this section).

**Triplets; Twins; Ulcers**—Of the Mouth —(See "Mouth" in this section).

**Unhealthy**—(See Ill-Health, Much Sickness, Poor Health, Sickly, Vitality, Weak, and the various paragraphs in this section).

**Untimely Death**—(See Death At Birth, Death In Infancy, Death Soon After Birth, and the various paragraphs in this section).

**Unusual Diseases** — At Birth — (See "Infections" in this section).

**Vitality** — (a) Good Vitality — (See Constitution, Healthy, Long Life, Stam-

ina, Strength, in this section; "Good" under Vitality). (b) Vitality Less — Low In Infancy—Born with ♋, ♑, or ♓ on the Asc.; the ☉ affl. in ♑; many evil directions to the ☉, ☽, Asc., or hyleg at B., and during infancy. (See Death, Ill-Health, Much Sickness, Poor Health, Sickly, Weak, in this section; "Sickly Children" under Children; "Low" under Vitality; "Weak Body" under Weak).

**Weak**—Weak Body—Weak Constitution — Weak and Sickly — (See Death In Infancy, Ill-Health, Much Sickness, Poor Health, Sickly, Vitality, in this section; "Weak Body" under Weak).

**Weaning; Wild Disposition** — (See "Savage" in this section).

**Will Live**—And Be Healthy—Thrives and Lives Thru Disease — (See Long Life, Spared, Stamina, Strong, Vitality, in this section; "Long-Lived" under Children; Endurance; "Little Sickness" under Health; Immunity; "Lives Thru" under Serious).

**Will the Child Live or Die?** — (See Death In Infancy, Healthy, Long Life, Short Life, Sickly, Spared, Stamina, Strength, Strong, Weak, Vitality, and the various paragraphs in this section).

**Worms In Children**—(See Worms).

**INFARCTS** — A Plug or Obstruction — Clot — Embolus — (See Clots, Embolus, Obstructions, Thrombus).

**INFECTIONS**—Infectious Diseases— Contagions—Invasions, etc.—Amulets were worn by the Ancients as a protective measure against Infections, and Infectious and Contagious diseases. The moderate use of Tobacco, if it does not debilitate the system, is also said to be a protection against Infections. The pathological action of the ♃ Group of Herbs tends to Infection and Toxaemia. (See Amulets, Contagions; "Jupiter Group" under Herbs; Tobacco, Toxaemia).

**Birth**—Infections At—(See Infancy).

**Death from Infections**—And Infectious Fevers—(See "Death" under Contagious).

**Diarrhoea**—Infectious Diarrhoea— (See "Cholera Infantum" under Cholera).

**Eyes**—(See "Infections" under Infants).

**Infectious Diseases**—Infectious and Contagious Fevers — Liable To — Predisposed To — The ☽ people contract these diseases easily. Also the ♏ people, those born under ♏, as ♏ is a magnetic sign and attracts infectious complaints. The ☉ affl. in ♏ or ♓; the ☉ affl. in ♓ gives much receptivity to infectious complaints; the ☉ Sig. to the ☌ ♂; the ☽ hyleg in ♏ or ♓, and espec. with females; ♂ diseases and afflictions, and the ♂ influence tends to death from such, and very violent and severe attacks; ♂ affl. in ♋, ♍, ♎, ♏, or ♓, infectious and contagious diseases and fevers should be guarded against; ♂ in ♓ and affl. the ☽ or Asc.; ♂ affl. in ♓ in the 6th H.; ♂ Sig. ☌ the ☉; ♀ affl. in ♏; a ♏ disease; ♏ or ♓ on the Asc. and afflicted. (See Chickenpox, Cholera, Endemic, Epidemics,

Eruptions, External, Germs; "Offensive" under Humours; Leprosy, Magnetic, Measles, Mumps, Pandemic, Perihelion, Pestilence, Plague; "Blood Poisoning" under Poison; Pus, Scarlatina, Scorpio, Smallpox, Septic, Syphilis, Toxaemia, Venereal, etc.).

**INFERIOR**—Inferiority—

**Belly**—Inferior Part of—(See Abdomen, Belly, Bowels, Groins, Hernia).

**Inferiority Complex**—A Strong Feeling of Inferiority—The Apologetic Attitude—♄ prominent at B., and strong afflictions of ♄ to the ☉, ☽, ☿, or Asc.; preponderance of the ☽ and ♀ influences over the more forceful planets; ♋ sign influence, as this sign tends to timidity, over-sensitiveness, and dreads disturbing and discordant conditions; ♎ influence, from a desire for agreement and concord. (See Fears, Mind, Negative, Obsessions, Self-Confidence).

**Inferior Hypogastric Plexus**—(See "Impar" under Ganglion).

**Inferior Mentality**—(See Arrested, Dwarfed, Foolish, Idiocy, Imbecility, Insanity; "Inferior" under Mentality; "Weak Mind" under Mind).

**Inferior Parts of Body**—(See Lower).

**Inferior Physique**—(See Body, Crippled, Crooked, Defects, Deformed, Dwarfed, Form; "Ill-Formed" under Ill; Infirm, Invalids, Monsters, Stature; "Weak Body" under Weak).

**Inferior Planets**—♀, ☽, ☿.

**Inferior Vena Cava**—(See "Vena Cava" under Veins).

**INFILTRATIONS** — (See Effusions, Osmosis, Serum).

**INFIRM**—Infirmities—Infirmity—

**Bodily Infirmities**—Infirm Body—♅, ♄, and ♂ occi. at B. tend to disease and bodily infirmities; ♅, ♄, or ♂ on the cusp of the 1st, 6th, or 7th H. at B., or in exact evil asp. to these degrees, and espec. if the ☉ is ☌ the ☽, or ☍ the ☽ in the 1st or 7th H. If only one Luminary be with ♅, ♄, or ♂ in the 1st or 7th H. the infirmities will be produced in those parts of the body ruled by the signs on the cusps of the 1st and 7th; ♄ in ♋ and in bad asp. the Asc.; the 3rd Decan. ♍ on the Asc. (See Adynamia, Asthenia, Death, Debility, Decay, Decrepitude, Delicate, Disease, Emaciation, Fading, Feeble; "Health Bad" under Health; "Ill-Health All Thru Life" under Ill-Health; Invalids; "Low" under Resistance; Sickly; "Much Sickness" under Sickness; "Low" under Vitality; "Weak Body" under Weak, etc.).

**Grievous Infirmities**—Grievous Infirmities Generally—Much Sickness Generally—(See Grievous; "Public Health Bad" under Public).

**Mental Infirmities**—Liable To—The ☉ or ☿ in common signs, and affl. by the ☌ or ill-asps. the malefics; the ☉ or ☽ to the ☌ or ill-asp. ♄ by dir.; mental infirmities are produced by afflictions to the ☽ and ☿, or both, in certain signs of the Zodiac, as in ♑ or ♓; ♆ affl. in the 9th H.; born under the strong and adverse influence of ♄; ☿ diseases and afflictions; ☿ in no asp.

to the ☽ or Asc. at B.; ♒ on the cusp the 6th H., and afflicted. (See Idiocy, Imbecility, Insanity, Intellect, Memory; "Deficiency", "Diseases", and the various paragraphs under Mental; "Weak Mind", and the various paragraphs under Mind; Perception, Understanding).

**Much Infirmity**—Often Ailing—The ☽ sepr. from ♄ and applying to ♂ at B. (See Ailing, Chronic; "Ill-Health All Thru Life" under Ill-Heath; "Much Sickness" under Sickness; "Low" under Vitality; "Weak Body" under Weak). Infirmities may occur in any organ or part of the body, and in the mind, and for the subject, or disease, you have in mind, look for it in the alphabetical arrangement, as nearly every subject in this book has to do with some Infirmity of Body or Mind. Also see such subjects as Brothers, Congenital, Defects, Deformities, Dissolution, Enemies, Extremities, Father, Females, Friends, Heredity, Limbs, Males, Men, Mother, Nobles, Old Age, Parents, Reins, Relatives, Secrets, Serious, Severe, Sister, Women, etc.

**INFLAMMATION** — Inflammatory— Inflammations — The termination "Itis" to words indicates Inflammation. The Inflammatory Process without alteration of tissues is presided over by ♃. The Inflammatory Process with degeneration of tissues is presided over by ♄. Inflammation and Fever are the work of ♂ to cleanse and burn out the accumulated wastes and filth of the body, and in this way ♂ is untimately constructive in his work, altho destructive for a time in the process. (See Cleansing, Combustion, Constructive, Destructive, Energy, Fever). Inflammation is brought on by ♂, and mostly because of rash and uncontrolled thinking. Also ♂ is rubefacient, reddening, and inflammatory, and tends to bring the blood to the surface. (See Centrifugal, Congestion, Rubefacient). Acute diseases under ♂ are inflammatory. (See Acute). The ☉ is also inflammatory, and tends to inflammation, and especially when afflicting ♂ in the 1st H. Inflammation is produced by the ☉ and ♂, the positive, electric, and heat-producing planets. (See Mars, Sun). People born under the Bilious and Choleric Temperaments are more subject and susceptible to inflammations and fevers. (See Bilious, Choleric). In any sign ♂ tends to inflammation in the part of the body ruled by the sign he is in at B., or is now passing thru by transit, progression, or direction. The same influences which tend to inflammations also tend to fevers. (See Fever). Inflammation may attack any organ or part of the body, and for inflammation in the part, or organ, you have in mind, see the subject in the alphabetical arrangement. The following subjects are related to inflammation, and when not more fully considered here, see the subject in the alphabetical arrangement. (See "Causes" in this section).

**Abscesses; Accidents**—(See Accidents, Blows, Cuts, Falls, Fractures, Hurts, Injuries, Stabs, Wounds, etc., as Inflammation may attend any of these conditions).

**Acute Diseases**—(See Acute).

**All Kinds**—Of Inflammation—A ☉ disease and affliction. Also ♂ diseases; ♌ diseases. (See the various paragraphs in this section).

**All Over the Body**—The ☽ in ♎ and affl. by the ☉ or ♂ when taken ill (Hor'y). (See "Whole Body" under Whole).

**Aneurysm; Antiphlogistic**—An Agent Reducing Inflammation—(See Antiphlogistic).

**Appendicitis**—(See Appendix).

**Arteritis**—(See "Inflammation" under Arteries).

**Arthritis**—(See Joints, Synovial).

**Bites; Blepharitis**—(See Eyelids).

**Blood Inflamed**—(See "Inflamed" under Blood).

**Bronchitis**—(See Bronchial).

**Bruises; Business Partner**—Suffers Inflammatory Disease—(See Partner).

**Carditis**—(See Heart).

**Catarrhal**—(See Catarrh).

**Causes of Inflammation**—Liable To—Susceptibility To—Inflammatory Distempers—Danger of—Subject to Inflammatory Complaints—In addition to what is said in the first part of this Article, the following influences are listed,—The ☉ or ☽ affl. by ♂ at B., and by dir.; the ☉ or ☽ to the ☌ or ill-asp. ♂ by dir., and affl. by ♂ at B.; the ☉ ☌ ♂ at B., and espec. in the 6th H.; the ☉ or ♂ affl. in the Asc.; the Prog. ☉ or ☽ to the ☌ or ill-asp. ♂; the ☉ or ☽ to the ☌ or ill-asp. ♂ by dir., and ♂ ruler of the 6th H. at B.; the afflictions of the ☉ tend to fever and inflammation; the ☽ in the 6th H. in a cardinal sign, and affl. by ♂; the ☽ to the Bull's Horns; ♅ to the ☌ or ill-asp. the ☉; ♃ affl. in ♎, from too much blood; ♂ □ or ☍ the ☉; ♂ in ♌, □, or ☍ the ☉; ♂ diseases; ♂ in a watery sign, and to the ill-asps. the Asc. by dir.; ♂ in the 6th H., and affl. the ☉ or ☽; ♂ in common signs and affl. the ☉, ☽, or Asc.; ♂ affl. in the 1st, 4th, or 6th H.; ♂ affl. in ♈ or ♌; ♂ to the ☌ or ill-asp. the ☉, ☽, or Asc., and espec. if affl. by ♂ at B.; ♂ affl. in fiery signs, and to the ☌ or ill-asp. the Asc. by dir.; ♂ to the ☌ or ill-asps. ♅ by dir.; ♂ ☌ the ☉ at B., and espec. in the 6th H.; the transits of ♂ over the places of the radical ☉ or ☽, or in ☍ to them; the evil directions of ♂ if ♂ is strongly afflicted at B.; ♂ too much in evidence at B.; ♂ in the 6th H., in bowels, and in parts ruled by the sign ♂ is in; the Asc. to the place of Cor Leonis (Regulus); Asc. to the □ or ☍ ♂ by dir.; fiery signs on the Asc.; ♈ is especially inflammatory when on the Asc.; a ♌ disease, and afflictions in ♌. (See the Introduction and the various paragraphs in this section).

**Caustics; Cells and Tissues**—(See "Inflammation" under Cells).

**Chronic Inflammation**—A ☉ disease. The inflammatory action of the ☉ is of the chronic type. (See Chronic).

**Cleansing; Colitis**—(See Colon).

**Color**—(See "Treatment" under Red).

**Congestive Inflammation**—♄ ☌ or ill-asp. ♃, and espec. if ♃ be more dominant. (See Congestion).

**Conjunctivitis**—(See Conjunctiva).

**Constructive; Cuts; Cystitis**—(See Bladder).

**Danger of Inflammation**—(See "Causes" in this section).

**Death By**—Caused by the afflictions of ♃. (See "Death" under Jupiter).

**Destructive; Diathesis**—(See Diathesis; "Causes" in this section).

**Diseases**—Inflammatory Diseases—(See "Causes", and the various paragraphs in this section).

**Distempers**—Inflammatory Distempers—(See "Causes" in this section; Distempers).

**Elimination; Encephalitis**—(See "Inflammation" under Brain).

**Endocarditis**—(See Heart).

**Energy**—(See Constructive, Destructive).

**Enteritis**—(See "Inflammation" under Bowels).

**Entire Body**—Inflammation In—(See "All Over" in this section).

**Eruptions; Excretory System**—(See "Disorders" under Excretion).

**Eyes Inflamed**—(See Conjunctiva; "Inflamed" under Eyes).

**Face**—(See Eruptions; "Red" under Face; Irritated).

**Fallopian Tubes**—Salpingitis—(See "Disorders" under Fallopian).

**Falls; Father**—(See "Inflammatory Attacks" under Father).

**Females**—Inflammatory Troubles In—The ☉ to the ☌ the ☽ by dir.; the ☽ to the ☌ the ☉ by dir. (See Females).

**Fevers**—Inflammatory Fevers—The ☽ directed to the Ascelli; ♂ □ or ☍ the Asc. by dir.; a ♌ disease and afflictions in ♌, and they grow worse towards sunrise. (See Fever).

**Fever and Inflammation**—The Two Combined—(See "Scope" under Enlarged).

**Fingers**—Toes—(See "Whitlows" under Toes).

**Folliculitis**—(See "Hair Follicles" under Follicles).

**Gastritis**—(See Gastric).

**Genitals**—(See "Inflammatory" under Genitals).

**Glands**—(See "Swelling" under Glands).

**Gums**—(See "Inflamed" under Gums).

**Heat; Hemorrhoids; Hepatitis**—(See "Inflammation" under Liver).

**Hexis; Hot Diseases**—(See Fever, Heat).

**Hurts; Increased**—The Inflammation Is Increased—The ☉ ☌ or ill-asp. ♂, the susceptibility to inflammation is increased.

**Infections; Injuries; Intestines**—(See "Inflammation" under Bowels).

**Iritis**—(See Iris).

**Kicks; Kinds of Inflammation**—(See the various paragraphs in this section).

**Laryngitis**—(See Larynx).

**Left Side**—Inflammations and Disorders In—(See Left).

**Liable To**—(See Causes, Increased, in this section).

**Lower Parts**—(See Lower).

**Lymphangitis**—(See Lymphatics).

**Mastitis**—(See Breasts).

**Mastoiditis**—(See Mastoid).

**Membranes; Meningitis**—(See Meninges).

**Middle Parts**—(See Middle).

**Mother**—(See "Inflammations" under Mother).

**Mucous Membranes**—(See "Inflammation" under Mucous).

**Mumps**—(See Parotid).

**Naso-Pharynx**—Inflammation In—(See Nose, Pharynx).

**Nephritis**—(See Kidneys).

**Neuritis**—(See Nerves).

**Ophthalmia** — Conjunctivitis — (See Conjunctiva).

**Osteitis**—(See Bones).

**Ovaritis**—(See Ovaries).

**Pain; Parents**—(See "Inflammation" under Father, Mother).

**Parotiditis**—Mumps—(See Parotid).

**Pericarditis**—(See Heart).

**Peritonitis**—(See Peritoneum).

**Pharyngitis**—(See Pharynx).

**Phlegmonous**—(See Phlegmon).

**Piles**—(See Hemorrhoids).

**Pleuritis**—(See Pleura).

**Pneumonia; Poisons**—(See "Body" under Poison).

**Predisposition To**—(See Causes, Increased, in this section).

**Privates; Process**—The Inflammatory Process—(See the first part of this Article).

**Prostatitis**—(See Prostate).

**Pustular Inflammation**—(See Phlegmon, Pus).

**Red Color**—(See "Treatment" under Red).

**Reins**—(See "Inflammation" under Reins).

**Remedies For**—(See Anodyne, Antiphlogistic; Emollient; "Treatment" under Red; Resolvent).

**Right Side**—Inflammations and Disorders In—(See Right).

**Rubefacients; Salpingitis**—(See Fallopian).

**Secrets**—Inflammations In—(See Generative, Genitals, Privates, Secrets, Sex Organs, Venereal, Womb).

**Skin; Sores; Sthenic Inflammation**—Strong and Active Inflammation—♂ ☌ or ill-asp. ♃. (See Sthenic, Strong).

**Stomatitis**—(See Aphthae).

**Suppurative Inflammation**—(See Phlegmon, Pus).

**Susceptibility To**—(See Causes, Increased, in this section).

**Swellings; Tendency To**—(See "Causes" in this section).

**Tissues**—(See "Cells" in this section).

**Toxaemia; Treatment Of**—(See "Remedies" in this section).

**Ulcers; Upper Parts**—(See Upper).

**Vascular**—(See Vascular, Vessels).

**Veins**—(See "Phlebitis" under Veins).

**Venereal; Vesicants; Vessels**—See Vascular; "Inflammation" under Vessels).

**Violent Inflammation**—The Asc. □ or ☍ ♂ by dir., if ♂ is in airy or earthy signs, threatens violent inflammation. (See Violent).

**Whole Body**—(See "All Over the Body" in this section.

**Wounds**—(See Hurts, Injuries, Wounds).

For subjects along this line, and which may not be included in this Article, look in the alphabetical arrangement for the subject you have in mind.

**INFLATION**—The Body Inflated—The ☽ in ☍, ☌, or ill-asp. ♄ (or ☿ if he be of the nature of ♄) when taken ill, or at decumb., and caused by surfeits, high living, etc. (Hor'y). (See Distentions, Flatulence, Gas, Puffing, Tympanites, etc.).

**INFLEXIBLE**—Rigidity—Stiffness—(See Cold, Rigid, Rigors, Stiff). Many planets at B. in fixed signs, or fixed signs upon the angles, tend to give an inflexible, unbending, uncompromising temperament. (See "Fixed Signs" under Fixed; Obstinate).

**INFLUENCED EASILY**—Impressionable—More Difficult to Cure—More Susceptible to Disease—Convinced on Slight Evidence—Negative—Receptive, etc.—♃ Sig. ☌ the ☉; ☿ weak and afflicted at B., and often in a watery sign; ♋ on the Asc., and the ☽ remote in a common sign, tends to make the native light, credulous and inconstant. (See "Difficult to Cure" under Cure; "Light In Mind" under Mind; Negative, Plastic, Receptive, Sensation, Susceptible).

**INFLUENZA**—Grippe—La Grippe—Contagious and Epidemic Catarrhal Fever—First called Influenza in Italy in the Seventeenth Century because attributed to the "Influenze of the Stars", and this name has passed into Medical use. This disease occurs in Countries at the time of an Eclipse, and where the Eclipse is visible, and espec. in Parts under the Central Line of the Shadow. Occurs when three or four superior planets are in ☌ or ☍. Said to be caused by electrical conditions in the atmosphere, due to planetary influence. Caused by cross aspects of Promittors, or Non-Promittors, to the ☉ when the horoscope is an unfortunate one. Catarrhal Fevers grow worse towards sunset. Also caused by the ☉ and ☽ badly aspected at B., or by dir.; the ☉ in ♉, and affl. by malefics; an eclipse of the ☉ in ♊, and the ☉ badly afflicted by malefics; the ☽ ☌, □, or ☍ ♄ at a Solar Rev.; the ☽ hyleg, and to the ☌ or ill-asp. ♄ by dir.; a ♆ disease; ♆ ☌., □, or ☍ ☉; ♄ □ ♅, and this aspect existed in 1918 during the great Influenza Epidemic of that year; ♄ □ ♆; ♄ ☌ ♃ if in the same Lat., or ♄ have higher Lat. than ♃, and tends to a malignant form; a ♅ disease, and caused by the afflictions of ♅; ♉ and ♏ are frequently afflicted, showing infection thru the throat; afflictions in ♊ at B., or by dir.; afflictions in common signs, or these signs upon the angles; Subs at MCP, CP, SP, and KP. (See Atmosphere, Catarrh, Colds, Epidemics, La Grippe, Lethargy, Nose; "Sleeping Sickness" under Sleep).

**Malignant Influenza**—Caused by ♃ ☌ ♄ if of the same Lat. If ♄ have higher Lat. than ♃, and these planets in ☌, Influenza and terrible diseases prevail. (See Malignant).

**Nose**—The Nose Affected In Influenza —(See "Influenza" under Nose).

**INFORTUNES**—Malefics—(See Malefics).

**INGRESSES**—These are the times when the ☉ passes the Equinoxes and Solstices, and the positions of the planets in the Signs and Houses at these times are very important to note in health matters, as they are times when disease is apt to come. Ingresses are frequently referred to in this book. Students of Medical Astrology should make a careful study of Ingresses, Equinoxes, and Solstices in the Textbooks of Astrology. (See Air, Catarrh, Cholera, Enemies, Epidemics, Epilepsy, Equinoxes, Fruit, Mania, Mutilated, Prevalent, Rheumatism, Scarlatina, Solar, Solstices, Tropical, Vernal).

**INGUINAL**—(See Groins).

**Inguinal Hernia**—(See Hernia).

**INHARMONY**—(See Antipathy, Discord, Enemies, Incompatibility, Quarrels).

**INHERENT**—Innate—Hereditary—(See Heredity, Innate).

**INHERITANCE**—Sickness from Loss of —Lord of the 6th in the 4th H., and much vexation from. (See Property, Reversals, Riches).

**INHIBITIONS**—Restraint of Organic Activity—Due to ♄ influence and afflictions; ♄ tends to bind, hinder, retard, and suppress the functions of both body and mind by his afflictions, or to dwarf and disorganize the different organs of the body and cause disease, improper elimination and excretion, etc. (See "Saturn Influence" under Saturn).

**Auditory Nerve**—Inhibition of—(See "Auditory" under Hearing).

**Faculties Inhibited**—♄ afflictions to the ☉, ☽, ☿, or Asc., and the Faculties inhibited or restrained are those ruled over by the sign ♄ is in at B., or by the planet, or planets, which are especially afflicted by him, and according to the signs they occupy. (See Dull, Faculties; "Arrested" under Mental).

**Functions Inhibited**—♄ influence, and to the parts ruled by the sign he is in at B., or in temporarily by tr. or dir., and tends to lack of vital activity and circulation of vital forces in the part. (See Functions, Stoppages, Suppressions).

**Growth**—Growth of Body and Mind Inhibited—(See Dwarfed, Growth, Idiocy, Imbecility; "Arrested" under Mental; "Weak Mind" under Mind; Undersized, etc.).

**Hair**—Growth of the Hair Inhibited—(See Hair).

**Hearing**—The Hearing Inhibited—(See "Deafness", "Inhibition", under Hearing).

**Heart**—The Heart Inhibited—(See "Inhibition" under Heart).

**Memory**—The Memory Inhibited—(See Memory).

**Mental Inhibitions**—(See Apathy, Arrested, Dull, Examinations, Foolish, Idiocy, Imbecility, Insanity, Intellect, Memory, Mental, Mind, Perception, Understanding, etc.).

**Optic Nerves**—Inhibition of—(See Blindness, Optic, Sight). For further and collateral study see Atrophy, Binding, Cessation, Confinement, Crystallization, Defects, Deficient, Difficult, Diminished, Elimination, Excretion, Hardening, Hindrances, Limitations, Morbid, Restraint, Retarded, Shrinkage, Twelfth House, etc. Inhibitions can occur in any part or organ of the body, due to the presence of ♄, or other malefic, in the sign ruling the part afflicted, and for subjects not listed here, look in the alphabetical arrangement for the subject, part, or organ you have in mind.

**INHUMAN**—Not Perfectly Human In Shape—When the ruler of the last New or Full ☽ before birth, and the rulers of the ☉ and ☽ are unconnected with the preceding New or Full ☽, tends to unnatural conformities, and monstrous births. If in addition to this absence of connection, ♅, ♄, or ♂ be in angles, and the ☉ and ☽ be in ♈, ♉, ♌, ♐, or ♑, in Quadrupedal and Bestial Signs, then the conception will tend to be defective. (See "Beastly Form" under Beasts; "Dogs" under Children; Conception, Congenital, Deformities, Disfigurements, Distortions, Monsters, Savage, Wild, etc.).

**Inhuman Disposition**—♂ ill-dignified at B., and afflicted by ♄. (See Brutish, Criminal, Cruel, Merciless, Pity, Savage; "High Temper" under Temper; Vicious, Violent, Wicked, etc.).

**INIMICAL TO HIMSELF**—(See "Brings Disease Upon Himself" under Disease; Disgrace; "His Own Worst Enemy" under Enemies; Reversals, Ruin, Scandal, Self-Undoing).

**INJECTIONS**—(See (Enema).

**INJUDICIOUS**—Indiscreet—Imprudent —Heedless—Void of Discretion—

**Cosmetics**—Injudicious Use of—(See "Indiscreet" under Cosmetics).

**Diet**—Sickness from Injudicious Diet —(See "Evil Diet" under Diet; Digestion, Excesses, Gluttony, Habits, Imprudent, Indigestion, Indiscretions).

**Judgment**—(See "Bad Judgment" under Judgment).

**INJURIES**—Traumatism—Wounds—Hurts—Accidents—Detriment—The subject of Injuries is also largely considered in this book in the Articles on Accidents, Hurts, Wounds. For Injuries to the various parts, or organs of the body, see the subject in the alphabetical arrangement. For convenience of reference many subjects are relisted here. In a general way malefics oriental at B. tend to Injuries, Accidents, Hurts, etc., and when occidental to disease. The malefics in the signs at B. indicate danger of accidents, hurts, and injuries to the part, or parts, of the body ruled by the signs containing them, and especially when under the directions or transits of the malefics to such signs. (See "Danger of Injuries", and the various paragraphs in this section. Also see the Introduction under Accidents, Hurts, Wounds). See the following subjects in the alphabetical arrangement when not considered here—

**Abortion; Abrasions; Accidents**—And Attended with Injury—(See the various paragraphs under Accidents, Hurts, Violence, Wounds).

**Aeroplanes; Air**—(See the various paragraphs under Air).

**Ambushes; Anarchists; Animals**—(See the various paragraphs under Animals, Beasts, Bites, Cattle, Horses, Kicks, Quadrupeds).

**Assassins; Assaults; Athletics**—Injuries In—(See Athletics, Exercise, Sports).

**Authority**—Injured by One In Authority—(See Kings, Rulers).

**Automobiles**—Injury By—(See Vehicles).

**Avalanches; Badly Injured**—But Lives—♂ or ☊ in the Asc., and ♄ affl. the lord of the 1st H., may be badly injured and nearly killed; a malefic with the lord of the Asc., and a benefic in the Asc. (Hor'y).

**Bathings**—(See Bathing, Drowning, Water).

**Battle**—Injured In—(See Contests, Duels, Quarrels, Slaughter, War).

**Beasts**—(See "Animals" in this section).

**Bites; Blasts of Wind**—(See the various paragraphs under Wind).

**Blindness**—From Injury—(See "Injury" under Blindness).

**Blood**—Injuries with Loss of Blood—(See "Injuries" under Blood; Cuts, Stabs, etc.).

**Blows; Brother**—Injury To—(See Brother).

**Bruises; Buildings**—Injury by Fall of —Falls From—(See Buildings, Crushed, Falls, Heights).

**Burglars**—Injury By—(See Burglars, Highwaymen, Robbers, Thieves).

**Buried Alive**—(See Avalanches, Burial, Crushed).

**Burns; Calamities; Cattle**—Injury By —(See Cattle).

**Causes of Injury**—♂ tends to cause all injuries which are attended by a flow of blood; ♂ ☌, □, or ☍ the ☉, ☽, Asc. or hyleg by dir., and the radical map a violent one, showing tendency to injuries, accidents, or a violent death; ♄ causes injuries where blood does not flow, as blows, bruises, concussions, falls, etc. (See the Introduction, "Danger Of", "Tendency To", and the various paragraphs in this section).

**Childbirth**—Injury In—(See Birth, Infancy, Parturition).

**Childhood**—Injury In—(See Childhood, Children, Infancy).

**Children**—Injury To—(See Children).

**Cold**—Injuries By—(See Blizzards, Cold, Snow, Storms, Winter).

**Common People**—Injury To—(See Common).

**Concussions; Contests**—Injured In—(See Contests, Duels, Quarrels, Sword).

**Contusions**—(See Bruises).

**Convicts**—Prisoners—Injured By In Prison—(See Prison).

**Crippled**—By Injury—(See Crippled, Fractures, Lameness, Limbs).

**Crushed; Cuts; Daggers**—Injured By —(See Cuts, Stabs).

**Danger of Injury**—Tendency To—Liable To—Predisposed To—Susceptible to Injuries—Injuries are caused principally by the ☉ and ♂, the positive, electric, and caloric-producing planets; the ☉ or ☽ hyleg, and to the ☌ or ill-asp. ♂ by dir.; the ☽ to Aldebaran by dir.; the ☽ to the ☌ or P. Dec. Regulus if the ☽ be hyleg; ♅ causes injuries by shock, electricity, accidents by machinery, explosions, sudden events; ♅ ☌ ♂ in the 7th H.; ♅ ☌ ♂ in ♈, or in angles; ♄ causes injuries by falls, blows, bruises, concussions, fractures, revenge, treachery, etc.; ♄ ☌ or ill-asp. ♂, and espec. if either planet be ori.; ♄ or ♂ in the Asc. or 7th H., or in □ or ☍ to these houses, and also the ☉ be in □ or ☍ the ☽, and either of them in angles; ♂ causes injuries by cuts, burns, violence, loss of blood, by attacks of enemies or robbers, by recklessness, gun-shot, stabs, the sword, and in battles or war; ♂ coming to the Asc. or Desc. early in life causes injuries and accidents; ♂ and the ☋ by their afflictions cause injuries by rash and self-motived acts; caused by the malefics ori. at B., and affl. the ☉, ☽, Asc., or hyleg; a malefic rising in an angle, going before or after the ☉; the 22° ♌ on the Asc. tends to; fiery signs on the Asc., and affl. by ♂; the airy signs on the Asc. at B. make the native less liable to injuries and accidents. Those born under the Hurtful Signs ♈, ♉, ♋, ♏, or ♑ are more liable to injuries. (See "Danger Of" under Accidents, Hurts, Wounds. Also in this section see the Introduction, "Causes", "Tendency To", and the various paragraphs).

**Dangerous Injuries**—Or Accidents—(See "Dangerous" under Accidents).

**Daughter**—Injury To—(See Daughter).

**Death By**—The ☉ and ☽ in evil asp. to ♂ at B., and by dir.; ♂ on the Asc., and afflicted. (See "Death" under Accidents, Hurts, Violent, Wounds; "Death" under the various subjects listed in this Article).

**Demoniacs**—Injure and Wound Themselves—(See Demoniac).

**Detriment; Diet**—Injury by Wrong Diet—(See Diet, Food, Indigestion).

**Directions**—As the Cause of Injury—(See Directions, Events).

**Disablements** — From Injury — (See Disabilities).

**Disease**—Injury By—(See the various paragraphs under Disease).

**Distortions; Dreadful Injury** — Terrible—Meets With—♂ affl. the ☉ at B., and by dir., and the ☉ weak and ill-dignified.

**Drugs** — Injured by Use of — (See Drugs, Medicines, Narcotics).

**Duels; Early Years**—Injury In—(See Early).

**Earthquakes**—(See Earth).

**Eating**—Injured by Wrong Eating—(See Diet, Eating, Food).

**Effusion of Blood**—Injured By— (See "Loss of Blood" under Blood; Effusions).

**Electricity; Elements**—Injured By, as by Storms, Weather, etc. — (See Air, Cold, Electricity, Elements, Fire, Heat, Lightning, Storms, Weather, Wind).

**Elephants** — Injured By — (See Elephants).

**Employment**—Injured In—(See Employment, Machinery).

**Enemies**—Injured By—(See Enemies).

**Enmity; Escapes** — Has Narrow Escapes from Injury—(See Escapes).

**Events; Excesses; Excoriations**—(See Abrasions).

**Exercise** — (See Athletics, Exercise, Hunting, Sports).

**Explosions; Extraordinary Injuries**—(See Extraordinary, Peculiar, Unusual).

**Extravagance; Extremities**—Injuries To — (See Ankles, Arms, Extremities, Feet, Hands, Legs, Limbs, Wrists).

**Falls; Father**—Injury To—(See Father).

**Females** — Injury To — (See Aunts, Daughter, Females, Mother, Sister, Wife, Women).

**Feuds; Fire**—(See Burns, Fire, Heat, Liquids, Scalds).

**Fire Arms**—(See Gun-Shot).

**Folly; Food**—Injured by Wrong Use of—(See the various paragraphs under Diet, Drink, Eating, Food).

**Foreign Land**—Injured In — (See Abroad, Foreign).

**Four-Footed Beasts** — Injured By — (See Animals, Beasts, Cattle, Elephants, Four-Footed, Horses, Quadrupeds).

**Fractures; Friends** — Injury To — Injury By—(See Friends).

**Gases; Genitals; Groins; Gun-Shot;**

**Habits; Hand of Man** — Injured By — (See Ambushes, Assassins, Assaults, Blows, Cuts, Hand of Man, Murder, Stabs, etc.).

**Harlots**—Injured By—(See Harlots).

**Haunches; Healers**—Injured By—(See Healers).

**Heat**—(See Burns, Fire, Heat, Scalds).

**Heights**—Falls From—(See Heights).

**Hemorrhage; High Places**—Injury by Falls From—(See Buildings, Heights).

**Highwaymen**—Injured By—(See Highwaymen).

**Himself**—Injures Himself—♂ people. (See Demoniac, Inimical, Suicide).

**Homicide; Honour** — Injured In Affairs of—(See Contests, Duels, Honour).

**Horary Maps**—Horary Questions—Injury Indicated In — ♄, ♂, or ☋ in the 8th H.

**Horses** — Injured By — (See Bites, Horses, Hunting, Kicks).

**Hunting** — Injury In — (See Horses, Hunting).

**Hurtful Signs**—(See Distortions, Hurtful, Obnoxious).

**Hurts** — (See the various paragraphs under Hurts).

**Husband**—Injury To—(See Husband).

**Ill-Health**—Injury By—(See the various paragraphs under Ill-Health).

**Immunity** — Less Liable to Injury or Accident — (See "Less Liable" under Accidents; Immunity).

**Incised Wounds** — (See Cuts, Duels, Instruments, Sharp, Stabs, Sword).

**Incurable** — The Injury Is Without Remedy—(See "Incapable of Remedy" under Remedy).

**Infants** — Injury To — (See Birth, Infancy, Parturition).

**Insects** — Injury By — (See Bites, Insects, Obnoxious, Stings, Venomous).

**Instruments**—Injury By—(See Blows, Cuts, Duels, Instruments, Machinery, Parturition, Sharp, Stabs, Sword, Weapons).

**Inventions** — Injuries By — (See Employment, Inventions, Machinery).

**Iron and Steel**—Injury By—(See Instruments, Iron, Sharp, Steel, Weapons).

**Journeys**—Injuries On—(See Abroad, Foreign Lands, Journeys, Railroads, Ships, Travel, Vehicles, Voyages).

**Kicks; Kings**—Injury To—Injury By —(See Kings, Rulers).

**Lacerations; Lack Of**—(See the various paragraphs under Lack).

**Lameness; Landslides** — (See Avalanche, Crushed; "Earthquakes" under Earth; "Landslides" under Land).

**Left Side**—Of the Body—Accidents or Injuries To—(See Left).

**Less Liable**—To Injuries—Airy signs on the Asc. at B. (See "Less Liable" under Accidents; Immunity).

**Liable to Injury**—In Greater Danger of—(See Danger Of, Tendency To, in this section; "Liable To" under Accidents, Hurts).

**Lightning; Liquids**—(See Acids, Liquids, Poisons, Scalds).

**Loss of Blood** — Injuries By — (See "Loss Of" under Blood; Cuts, Effusions, Flow, Hemorrhage, Instruments, Shedding, Stabs, Sword).

**Lower Order of Mankind**—Injured By —(See Mankind).

**Luxuries** — Injured By — (See Appetites, Extravagance, Habits, Luxuries).

**Machinery** — (See Employment, Machinery).

**Maimed; Males** — Injury To — (See Brother, Father, Grandfather, Husband, Males, Son, Uncle).

**Mankind**—Injured by Lower Order of —(See Mankind).

**Maritime People**—Sailors—Injury To —(See Maritime, Navigation, Sailors, Ships, etc.).

**Marriage Partner** — Injury To — (See Husband, Marriage, Marriage Partner, Wife).

**Medicines**—Injured By—(See Drugs, Medicines, Narcotics).

**Men** — Injury To — (See the various paragraphs under Men).

**Middle Life**—Injuries In—(See Middle Life).

**Middle Parts**—Of Organs—Injury To —(See Middle, Navamsa).

**Mind**—Injuries To—(See Idiocy, Imbecile, Insanity; the various paragraphs under Mental, Mind).

**Mindful of Injuries**—Retains Anger— (See Anger, Enmity, Revenge, Treachery).

**Mines**—Injuries In—(See Mines).

**Mischief; Mob** — Injured By — (See Mobs).

**Mother**—Injury To—(See Mother).

**Murder; Narcotics; Narrow Escapes**— From Injury—(See Escapes).

**Navigation** — Injured In —(See Maritime, Navigation, Sea, Ships, Shipwreck, etc.).

**Neglect** — Injury By — (See Neglect, Poverty, Privation, Starvation).

**Nobles**—Injury To—(See Nobles).

**Obnoxious** — Injury by Obnoxious Creatures—(See Obnoxious).

**Paralysis** — From Injury — (See Distortions, Paralysis).

**Parents** — Injury To — (See Father, Mother, Parents).

**Part of Body Injured**—(See "Parts of Body" under Accidents).

**Parturition** — Injury to Mother or Child In— (See Birth, Infancy, Parturition).

**Peculiar Injury**—(See Extraordinary, Peculiar, Unusual).

**Perils; Permanent In Effect** — (See Permanent).

**Pirates**—Injury By—(See Pirates).

**Plots** — Injury and Treachery By — (See Enemies, Enmity, Plots, Poison, Treachery).

**Popular Tumult** — (See Lynching, Mobs, Tumults).

**Poverty; Power** — Injured by One In Power and Authority — (See Judges, Kings; "Power" under Men; Princes, Rulers).

**Precipices** — Falls From — (See Heights).

**Predisposed**—To Injuries—(See Danger Of, Liable To, Tendency To, in this section).

**Prison**—Injured In—(See Prison).

**Private Injury** — Blindness From— (See "Total" under Blindness; Treachery).

**Private Members**—Injured In — (See Genitals, Maimed, Privates, Secrets, Testes).

**Prostitutes** — Injured By — (See Harlots).

**Quadrupeds**—Injured By—(See Animals, Beasts, Cattle, Elephants, Four-Footed, Horses, Quadrupeds).

**Quarrels**—Injured In—(See Contests, Duels, Enemies, Feuds, Quarrels, War).

**Railroads**—Injured On—(See "Short Journeys" under Journeys: Railroads, Travel).

**Rash Acts** — Injured As Result of — (See "Rash In Action" under Action; Folly, Hasty, Imprudent, Rash).

**Recklessness** — Injured Because of — (See Recklessness).

**Reins**—Injury In—(See Reins).

**Relatives** — Injury To — (See Family, Relatives).

**Religion**—Injured Because of—(See "Injured" under Religion).

**Remedy** — The Injury Incapable of Remedy — (See "Incurable" under Hurts; Incurable, Permanent; "Incapable" under Remedy).

**Reptiles; Retains An Injury** — (See "Mindful Of" in this section).

**Reversals; Riding** — Injured While Riding—(See Horses).

**Right Side**—Of the Body—Injury To —(See Right).

**Robbers**—Injured By—(See Robbers, Thieves).

**Ruin; Rulers** — Injured By — (See Kings; "Power" under Men; Princes, Rulers).

**Ruptures; Sailors**—Injury To—(See Maritime, Navigation, Sailors, Ships, Shipwreck).

**Scalds; Scandal; Sea**—Injured At Sea —(See Sea, Ships, Shipwreck, Voyages).

**Secret Enemies** — Injured By — (See Ambushes; "Secret" under Enemies; Feuds, Plots, Revenge, Treachery).

**Secret Parts**—Injury To—(See Genitals, Privates, Secrets).

**Self-Inflicted Injury**—(See "Himself" in this section).

**Self-Motived**—Injury from Rash Acts —(See "Rash Acts" in this section).

**Serious Injury** — (See "Dreadful" in this section; "Dangerous" under Accidents).

**Serpents; Sharp-Edged Tools**—Injured By — (See Cuts, Duels, Instruments, Stabs, Sword, etc.).

**Ships**—Injured On—(See Ships).

**Shipwreck; Shock** — (See Electricity, Fright, Shock, Uranus).

**Sickly; Sickness** — (See the various paragraphs under Sickness).

**Sister**—Injury To—(See Sister).

**Slander**—(See Disgrace, Libel, Reputation, Ruin, Scandal, Slander, etc.).

**Slight Injury**—(See Ameliorated, Mild, Mitigated, Moderation, Slight, etc.).

**Snakes; Son**—Injury To—(See Son).

**Spontaneous Injury** — Sudden — (See Spontaneous; "Accidents" under Sudden).

**Sports** — Injury In — (See Exercise, Gunshot, Horses, Hunting, Sports).

**Stabs; Steel**—(See Cuts, Instruments, Iron, Stabs, etc.).

**Stings; Stones**—Injured by Flying Stones—(See "Flying" under Stones).

**Storms**—(See Lightning, Storms, Wind).

**Strokes**—(See Blows).

**Sudden Injury**—(See Spontaneous, Sudden).

**Suicide; Sword; Tendency to Injuries**—Or Accidents, Hurts, Wounds, etc.—The ☽ to the ill-asp. the ☉ by dir., or transit; the Prog. ☽ to the ☌ or ill-asp. ♂; ♅ to the ☌ or ill-asp. ♂ by dir.; ♂ □ or ☍ the ☉, ☽, or ♅; ♂ affl. in ♊ or ♍, and ☌, P., □, or ☍ the Asc. by dir. (See Causes, Danger Of, Liable To, in this section).

**Terrible Injury**—(See Dreadful, Serious, in this section).

**Thieves**—Injured By—(See Highwaymen, Pirates, Robbers, Thieves).

**Time of Injuries**—(See "Time Of" under Accidents; Directions, Events, Time).

**Tornadoes**—(See Wind).

**Trampled; Travel**—Injury During—(See Abroad, Foreign Lands, Journeys, Railroads, Ships, Shipwreck, Travel, Vehicles, Voyages, etc.).

**Treachery**—Injured By—(See Ambushes, Enemies, Enmity, Feuds, Plots, Poison, Treachery).

**Treatment Of**—(See Resolvent).

**Tumults**—(See Lynching, Mobs; "Flying Stones" under Stones; Tumults).

**Uncle**—Injury To—(See Aunts, Uncle).

**Unusual Injury**—(See Extraordinary, Mysterious, Peculiar, Strange, Sudden, Unusual).

**Upper Parts**—Of the Body or Organs—Injury To—(See Navamsa, Upper).

**Various Injuries**—♂ affl. in ♓, and ☌, □, or ☍ the Asc. (See Various).

**Venomous Injuries**—(See Adder, Bites, Obnoxious, Reptiles, Serpents, Venomous).

**Violent Injuries**—(See Violent; "Death", and the various paragraphs in this section).

**Volcanoes**—Injury By—(See Volcanoes).

**Voyages**—Injury On—(See "Long Journeys" under Journeys; Maritime, Navigation, Sea, Ships, Shipwreck, Travel, Voyages).

**War**—Injury or Death In—(See War).

**Water**—Injury By—(See Bathing, Drowning, Floods; "Hot Liquids" under Heat; Liquids, Rain, Scalds, Sea, Ships, Shipwreck, Storms, Water).

**Weakness**—Injured by Weakness and Low Vitality—(See "Low" under Vitality; "Weak Body" under Weak).

**Weapons**—Injury By—(See Blows, Contests, Cuts, Duels, Gunshot, Instruments, Sword, Weapons, etc.).

**Weather**—Injured By—(See Drought, Famine; "Excessive Heat" under Heat; Storms, Weather, Wind).

**Wife**—Injury To—(See Wife).

**Wild Beasts**—Injury By—(See "Wild" under Animals; "Danger" under Travel; Wild).

**Wind**—(See the various paragraphs under Wind).

**Women**—Injured By—Injury To—(See "Women" under Men; also the various paragraphs under Females, Women).

**Wood**—Injured by Wood or Stone—(See "Assaults" under Stone).

**Wounds**—Injury By—(See Accidents, Cuts, Hurts, Stabs, Wounds; the various paragraphs in this section).

**Young Men**—Injury To—(See Young).

**Youth**—Injury In—(See Youth).

**INNATE**—(See Congenital, Constitution, Diathesis, Heredity, Natural, Organic, Structural, Temperament, etc.).

**INNER PARTS**—All Diseases In—(See Inward, Kidneys, Reins).

**INNERVATION**—The Function of the Nervous System—A Discharge of Nervous Force—Nerve Impulses—Principally under the rule of ☿, and influenced by the ☿ Group of Herbs, which are Nervine and Periodic. The physiological action of the ☿ Herbs, by their action on the Solar Plexus, tend to Gastro-Abdominal Innervation. By their action thru the Brachial Plexus, and by Pulmonary Haematosis, Pulmonary Innervation takes place. The ☿ Herbs tend to Periodicity and the Nervous Influx by their physiological action. (See Enervation; "Innervation" under Gastric; Haematopoiesis; "Mercury Group" under Herbs; "Full Moon" under Moon; Nerves, Periodic, Periodicity; "Solar Plexus" under Plexus).

**INNOMINATE BONE**—The Hip Bone, including the Pubis, Ilium, and Ischium—Ruled by ♐. (See Haunches, Hips, Ilium, Ischium, Pelvis, Pubes).

**INOFFENSIVE**—(See Gentle, Harmless, Humane, Kind, Quiet, etc.).

**INORDINATE**—Immoderate—Excessive—Unrestrained—

**Affections**—Inordinate Affections—(See Affection, Amorous, Excesses, Free Love, Passion, etc.).

**Drugs**—Inordinate Use of—(See Drugs, Narcotics).

**Exercise**—Inordinate Exercise—Disease Resulting From—(See Exercise, Exertion, Fatigue, Sports).

**Growth**—Inordinate and Excessive—(See Corpulent, Enlarged, Giants, Growth, Large, Stout, Tall, etc.).

**Lust**—Inordinate Lust, and Diseases Therefrom—(See Lust).

**Pleasures**—Inordinate and Lustful Pleasures, and Ill-Health From—(See Debauchery, Dissipation, Drink, Excesses; "High Living" under High; Lust; "Loose Morals" under Morals; Pleasure, Venery, etc.).

**Pulse**—Inordinate Pulse—(See "High Pulse" under Pulse). For further study see Abnormal, Appetites, Deportment, Eating, Habits, Immoderate, Indiscretions, Morals, Passion, Perversions, Sex, etc.

**INSANITY**—Lunacy—Mental Derangement—Madness—From a planetary standpoint this disease is very closely related to Epilepsy, varying according as to whether ♄ or ♂ are the afflictors in a day or night nativity. In a disease of this magnitude the configurations and aspects in the natal map must necessarily be very severe, and also during prenatal life. In studying this disease the ☽ and ☿ should be primarily considered, their afflictions, their relation to each other and to the Asc. Mental weakness is more apt to result when there is no aspect at B. between the ☽ and ☿, and also when neither form an asp. to the Asc., and at the same time be severely afflicted by malefics. In this case if ♄ be the afflictor in a day nativity, Epilepsy is more apt to occur, but in a night nativity, if ♄ be the afflictor, Insanity may follow, and espec. if the ☽, ♄, ♂, and ☿ be found in ♋, ♍, or ♓. On the other hand when ♂ is the afflicting planet, there tends to be Insanity by day, and Epilepsy by night. Also when the ☉ and ☽ are conjoined, and ill-aspected by ♄, or opposed and afflicted by ♂, Insanity may occur, and espec. if the Lights be found in ♎, ♐, or ♓, and such infirmities will tend to be incurable if there are no good asps. to the ☉, ☽, or ☿ from the benefics. In Insanity the Asc. is not necessarily afflicted, but in cases of Epilepsy the Asc. is usually badly aspected and afflicted by the ☽, ☿, and malefics. (See "Causes" in this section).

**Agitated**—The Insane More Agitated —(See "Full Moon" under Moon).

**Asylums**—Insane Asylum—Confined In An Insane Asylum or Prison, and Often by the Work of An Enemy—♆, ♅, or ♂ affl. in the 12th H.; ♆ affl. in the 4th H., and apt to end days in an Asylum; ♆ in the 12th H., in □ or ☍ ☿; ♄ affl. in the 12th H.; afflictions in the 12th. Case—See "Obsession", No. 130, in 1001 N.N. (See Confinement, Hospitals, Limitations, Prison, Restraint, Twelfth House).

**Cases of Insanity**—(1) Insane At Age of 40, and Committed Suicide—See "Suicide", No. 137, in 1001 N.N. (2) Insane At Age of 27 from Self-Abuse and Smoking—See "Self-Indulgence", No. 229, in 1001 N.N. (3) Committed Suicide When Insane—See "Bavaria", No. 823, in 1001 N.N. (4) Other Cases—Figures, Birth Data, etc.—See Figures 13, 14, and 23, in "Message of the Stars", and Figures 19A, 19B, and 19C, in "Astro-Diagnosis", both books by the Heindels. (See Cases under Lunacy).

**Causes of Insanity**—In addition to what has been said in the Introduction to this Article, note the following planetary influences—The SUN is also generally afflicted; the ☉ above the horizon at B., and ☿ affl. by ♂; the ☉ below the horizon and ☿ affl. by ♄; the ☉ and ☿ in common signs, and affl. by the ☌ or ill-asps. the malefics, and espec. afflictions from angles, or by planets out of dignity; the ☉ and ♂ contribute to Insanity when they rule ♅, ☿, the ☽, or 1st H., and espec. if the ☽, ☿, and Asc. be unconnected with each other or the Asc.; the MOON, ☿, and the Asc. in no relation or aspect to each other, and ☿ affl. by the ☌ or ill-asp. the malefics, and espec. if the affliction is from angles; the Prog. ☽ ☌ ♄ or ☋ in the 12th H.; the ☽ and ☿ both badly aspected by ♄, ♅, or ♂; a ☽ disease; NEPTUNE in the configuration plays an important part in this disease, and espec. when his ill-aspects are added to those of ♄ or ♂, in which case Obsessions and Demoniacal affections may also occur; an afflicted ♆; ♆ affl. in the 12th H.; ♆ □ ☿, and espec. if ♆ is in the 12th H.; ♆ ☌ ♂ in ♈, and affl. by ♅ and the ☽, and the map otherwise indicating mental weakness; ♆ in ♈, and in □ asp. the ☉, ♅, ♂, and ☿; ♆ affl. in ♈ in the 12th H.; a ♆ disease; ♆ affl. in the 4th H., may end life in an Insane Asylum; ♆ affl. in the 3rd or 9th H.; URANUS elevated above, and afflicting the ☽ and ☿ at the same time; ♅ afflicting one or both Luminaries, and ♄ or ♂ afflicting the mental rulers; ♅ and ♂ afflictions tend to produce violent forms of Insanity, and where there is great muscular activity; ♅ affl. in the 6th or 12th H.; ♅ affl. in ♓; ♅ by transit in ☌ ♂, ☿, or the ☽ in the radical map, almost to the point of Insanity in some cases; ♅ in ♒ and affl. by the ☽, danger of, and espec. when other configurations indicate the disease; SATURN the afflictor in a night nativity; ♄ and ♂ in an angle, occi. of the ☉, and ori. of the ☽, and ☿ in familiarity with ♂; ♄ ☌, □, or ☍ the Asc. in a night nativity, and espec. when in ♋, ♍, or ♓, and with ☿ and the ☽ in no relation to each other, or to the Asc.; ♄ ☌ ♃ in or near the 22° ♍, and affl. by ♆, and other configurations concording; MARS affl. in the 12th H.; ♂ □ or ☍ ☿; ♂ ☍ ☿ from the 6th and 12th H.; a ♂ disease; ♂ afflictions tend to the violent forms; ♂ the afflictor in the configuration in a day nativity tends to, and to epilepsy in a night map; ♂ affl. in the 3rd H., and espec. when in a water sign; ♂ in ♏ in the 3rd H., and in □ to the ☽ if other aspects and afflictions concur; ♂ ☌, □, or ☍ the Asc. in a day nativity, with other influences in accord, as stated; ♂ and ☿ holding dominion at B., and in familiarity with each other, and ♂ affl. the hyleg and elevated above the Luminaries, the Insanity is increased; ♂ afflicts the mental rulers, and espec. in a day nativity; MERCURY and the ☽ unconnected with each other or the Asc.; a ☿ disease; ☿ affl. in the 12th H.; ☿ badly afflicted at B., ☌, or evil asp. the malefics, and with no assistance to ☿ from the benefics; ☿ in ♉ in ☍ ♅, ♄, and the ☽ in ♏; ☿ combust and affl. by malefics, etc. (This sentence and configuration is finished in full under Idiots). Mutable signs on the angles, and also greatly afflicted, tend to insanity, and also to lack of hope; cardinal and fixed signs on the Asc. and the angles lessen the chanes of insanity; the 22° ♍ or ♓ on the Asc., or containing afflictions, tend to, and are sensitive degrees for this disease, and also sometimes by the exact □ aspects of the malefics, or of ☿ and the ☽ to these degrees; the 12th H. is also generally prominent and afflicted, as this house indicates confinement, limitation, restriction, and suppression of the faculties; the 12th H. is more afflicted in Insanity, while the 3rd H. is more prominent in Epilepsy, which helps to differentiate the two diseases; the Asc. unconnected with ☿ or the ☽, and otherwise afflicted by the malefics ♄ or ♂, as stated; the 28° ♑ on the Asc. tends to, and to give a weak mind or intellect; Lunations falling on the place of a badly afflicted radical ☽ tend to, and to give a temporary attack of insanity. (See Lunacy). The following paragraphs give classified conditions concerning Insanity and further influences not listed in this one, and in the Introduction to this Article. For Cases of Insanity, Birth Data, etc., see "Cases" in this section.

**Children** — Children May Become Insane—☿ in the 5th H. in the map of a parent, afflicted in ♋, ♏, or ♓, and espec. if ♄ or ♂ afflict ☿ at the same time. (See "Deformed" under Infancy).

**Confined In Asylum**—(See "Asylums" in this section).

**Curable Cases**—Hope of Remedy—The Insanity will tend to be mitigated, or curable, if the benefics are elevated at B. above the malefics which produce it, and espec. under favorable directions to the ☽ and ☿. The more oriental and angular the benefics or malefics may be, the more powerful their effect for good or evil. There is also hope of remedy when ☿ is in good asp. to the ☽ or Asc. (See Curable, Incurable, Lunacy).

**Dangerous Lunatics** — Violent Lunatics — Those under ♂ influence, and where ♂ is the causative agent. (See Fury, Madness; "Violent" under Mania; Causes, Outrageous, Violent, in this section).

**Day**—Insanity In a Day Nativity—♂ is the cause and afflicting planet. (See the Introduction to this Article).

**Delusions**—Insanity with Delusions—(See Paranoia).

**Immunity From** — Cardinal or Fixed Signs on the angles of the map lessen the liability to. (See Immunity; "Curable" in this section).

**Increased**—The Insanity Is Increased —(See the ♂ influences under "Causes" in this section).

**Incurable** — Lasting — The afflictions causing the affliction being in the Fixed Signs. (See "Fixed Signs" under Fixed; Incurable, Lunacy).

**Mitigated** — (See "Curable" in this section).

**Muscular Activity In** — Produced by the afflictions of ♅ and ♂. (See "Causes" in this section).

**Night** — Insanity In Night Nativities —♄ the afflictor in a night nativity. (See the Introduction to this Article).

**Not As Susceptible To** — Less Liable To—The cardinal or fixed signs on the Asc. or angles of the map at B.

**Outrageous** — The Patient Becomes Outrageous, Unmanageable—☿ and the ☽ unconnected with each other or the Asc., with ♄ and ♂ in angles ruling the scheme, ♂ by day or ♄ by night, and espec. if the malefics be in ♋, ♍, or ♓, and under these conditions if the malefics be in the Eastern Parts in angles, and the benefics in the West, the insane become unmanageable, outrageous, raving, breaking away from their homes, and wandering in nakedness. (See Demoniac; "Violent" in this section).

**Periodic**—Insanity At Periods—♅ afflicting the ☽ and ☿ at the same time, and elevated above them. (See "Temporary" in this section).

**Postponed**—☿ and the ☽ at B. unconnected with each other or the Asc., but having the good asps. of the benefics, the insanity may not appear as early in life, but wait for a train of evil directions to ☿ and the hyleg.

**Puberty** — Insanity sometimes occurs at puberty if at birth the sex sign ♏ was afflicted by ♂, and the ☽ and ☿ in evil aspect and afflicted by malefics. (See Puberty).

**Raving**—The Insane Rave—(See "Outrageous" in this section).

**Rush of Blood to Head** — Insanity Caused By—A ♂ disease. (See "Blood" under Head).

**Self-Abuse** — Insanity From — Case— See "Self-Indulgence", No. 229, in 1001 N.N. (See "Solitary" under Vice).

**Suicide** — Commits Suicide While Insane—(See "Cases" in this section).

**Surgeon** — Successful As Surgeon In Asylum—(See "Hospitals" under Surgeons).

**Temporary Insanity**—♅ ☌ ☽ in 9th H., and in □ or ☍ ♂ and ♆. (See Periodic, Violent, in this section; "Delirium Tremens" under Delirium; Frenzy, Fury, Madness, Mania, Temporary).

**Treatment Of** — The Blue Color, and to be confined in a Blue Room, with blue window panes, tends to soothe the most violent maniac or insane person. Also Insanity is caused by Obsessions, Evil Spirit Controls, Morbid Fears, Fixed Ideas, etc., which could be largely relieved or mitigated, and possibly cured, by Suggestion in the Hypnotic State, or by commanding the Evil Spirit to depart, as did The Christ in some cases. (See Curable, Incurable, in this section).

**Unmanageable**—(See "Outrageous" in this section).

**Violent Forms**—Caused by ♅ and ♂ afflictions; Subs at AT and AX, and attended also with ♅ or ♂ affliction, often causes violent temporary insanity. (See Lunacy; Dangerous, Outrageous, Temporary, in this section). For further and collateral study, and in which many of the same influences predominate as in Insanity, see Anxiety, Congenital, Coprolalia, Delusions, Demoniac, Derangements, Dreamy, Emotions, Epilepsy, Fanatical, Fancies, Fears; "Fixed Ideas", "Fixed Signs", under Fixed; Foolish, Frenzy, Fury, Hallucinations, Heredity, Idiocy, Illusions, Imbecile, Intellect, Irrational, Irresponsible; "Low Spirits" under Low; Lunacy, Madness, Mania, Melancholy, Memory, Mental Derangement (see Mental, Mind); Morbid, Noisy, Obsessions, Paranoia, Perceptions, Permanent, Prenatal, Reason, Spirit Controls, Suicide, Terrors, Understanding, Unsound Mind (see Mind); Weak Mind (see "Weak" under Mind); Worry, etc.

**INSATIABLE**—Insatiable Appetite—(See Appetites, Diet, Eating, Feasting, Gluttony, Hunger, etc.).

**INSECTS**—

**Insect Bites**—(See Adder, Bites, Obnoxious, Stings, Venomous).

**Insect Pests**—(See Comets, Floods, Venomous, Vermin).

**INSENSIBILITY**—See Anaesthetics, Analgesia, Carus, Catalepsy, Coma, Consciousness, Delirium, D r e a m s, Epilepsy, Fainting, Feelings, Fits, Hypnotism, Narcotics, Neptune (the influences and afflictions of ♆ tend to conditions of Insensibility—See Neptune); Paralysis, Sleep, Trance, etc.

**INSOLATION**—(See "Sunstroke" under Sun).

**INSOMNIA** — Sleeplessness — Wakefulness—(See "Insomnia" under Sleep).

**INSPIRATION**—Inhalation —Inbreathing—(See "Inspiration" under Breathing).

**INSTABILITY**—Unstable—Changeable

**Emotions**—Instability of — (See Emotions).

**Health**—Instability of—(See the various paragraphs under Health, Ill-Health, Sickness).

**Mind**—Instability of — (See Changes, Chaotic, Confusion; "Dreamy" under Dreams; Flightiness; "Instability", "Unstable", under Mind; Mutable, Negative, Receptive, Restless, Roaming, Susceptibility, Unstable, Vacillating, Vagabond, Wandering, etc.).

**INSTINCTS**—The ☽ is instinctive and rules the Instincts. (See Faculties).

**Animal Instincts**—(See "Animal Instincts" under Animal).

**Maternal Instincts**—(See Maternal).

**Self-Preservation**—Instincts of—(See Self-Preservation).

**INSTITUTIONS** — Confinement In— Afflictions in the 12th H. (See Hospitals; "Asylums" under Insanity; Prison).

**INSTRUMENTS**—Weapons—

**Instrumental Delivery** — Injury At Birth by Instruments — (See "Accidents" under Infancy; Parturition).

**Sharp Instruments**—Danger By—Injury By—Wounds By—The ☉ and ♂ afflictions tend to, they being the positive, electric, and caloric-producing planets; ♂ afflictions to the ☉, ☽, Asc., or Hyleg at B., and by dir.; ♂ in the 8th H., and affl. the ☉, ☽, or Hyleg; the Asc. to the place of the Pleiades, Hyades, or Castor. (See Cuts, Duels, Iron, Stabs, Sword, Weapons).

**INSUFFICIENT**—Insufficiency—

**Heat**—Insufficient Heat In the System —(See "Animal Heat" under Heat).

**Mitral Insufficiency**—(See Inefficiency, Mitral, under Heart).

**Oxygenation** — Insufficient Oxygenation—(See Oxygen).

**INTELLECT**—Intellectual—Intelligence —Intelligent—Mind—Understanding, etc.—This subject is mostly considered under the subjects of Mental, Mind. See the various paragraphs under Mental, Mind. The Intellect is ruled by ☿, which planet is designated as the Mental Ruler in general. The ♈ sign also rules the Intellect. The Asc. is said to rule the brain, and to have great influence over the mind and intellect, and each of the planets as they aspect and influence the ☽, ☿, and the Asc., tend to give their peculiar qualities to the mind for good or evil. Green is the color of the Human Intellect. (See Green). The study of intellectual ability is a deep and far-reaching one, and with many things to be considered which are not always shown and indicated by the map of birth. Heredity, the Age of the Soul, past experiences and causes, the aspects and influences of the prenatal period, etc., and others, are factors which have to be considered, and which play an important part in the state and quality of the Intellect. (See "Judging the Mind" under Mind).

**All Evils**—Of the Intellectual Parts— All evils of these parts, and diseases of the Mind proper, are ☿ diseases fundamentally, with ☿ weak and afflicted at B., or afflictions to the parts of the natal map partaking of the ☿ influences, etc. (See "Diseases of the Mind" under Mind).

**Diseases of the Intellect**—Disordered Mind—(See the various paragraphs under Mental, Mind. Also note the various references at the end of this Article).

**Dull Intellect**—(See Dull, Smoky).

**Good Intellect**—A Strong and Powerful Intellect—A Good Mind—A Clear Intellect—☿ well-aspected by the ☽ at B., and also in favorable relation to the Asc., and in one of his own signs, as in ♊ or ♍, or with one of these signs on the Asc. at B., and also the 3rd and 9th Houses, the houses of mind, strong and well-aspected at B., tend to give a good and strong intellect, whereas the opposite conditions tend to give a weaker understanding, or poor judgment, a shallow mind. However, ☿ may be rather weak at B., and yet the native have a strong intellect, or be a Genius, if the 3rd H. and Asc. be strongly influenced by ☿, or a ☿ sign. This was the case with some very great men and scholars, as Sir Isaac Newton, Spencer, Huxley, and others. In some cases a strong 9th H. gives a great intellect, as with Kant. Mars in the Asc. in △ asp. the ☉ tends to give a powerful intellect. (See "Active Mind" under Active; Genius; "Good" under Judgment; "Quickened" under Mental; "Sound Mind", "Strong Mind", under Mind).

**Powerful Intellect**—(See "Good" in this section).

**Shallow Intellect**—(See "Humours" under Head; "Shallow" under Mental).

**Solidarity**—Of the Intellect—Any aspect of ♄ to ☿ tends to give solidarity of intellect.

**Sound Intellect**—The 3rd Decan. of ♑ on the Asc. at B. denotes. (See "Sound Mind" under Mind).

**Strong Intellect**—(See "Good" in this section).

**Weak Intellect**—A weak Intellect, Insanity, Imbecility, Mental Defects, etc., usually result from a weak and afflicted ☿, ☽, and Asc. at B., and with ☿ in no aspect with the ☽ or Asc., and also with weak and afflicting influences over the 3rd, 9th, and 12th Houses. The weaknesses of the Intellect are governed by ☿ and the ☽, their relation to each other and the Asc., and the aspects to them. (See Foolish, Idiocy, Imbecility, Insanity; "Weak" under Mental, Mind). For further and collateral study along the lines of Intellect and Mind see such subjects as Chaotic, Comprehension, Confusion, Congenital, Defects, Deficiencies, Dull, Eccentric, Emotions, Epilepsy, Erratic, Examinations, Expression, Faculties, Fancies, Feelings, Fury, Hebetude, Ideals, Ideas, Knowledge, Learning, Look, Mania, Mathematical, Memory, Mental, Mind, Monsters, Notions, Perception, Precocious, Prenatal, Prodigies, Psychic, Reading, Reason, Senses, Study, Talents, Temper, Temperament, Understanding, Will, etc.).

**INTEMPERANCE**—Intemperate—Immoderate and Excessive In Eating, Habits, Conduct, Drink, Pleasures, Sex Matters, etc.—

**Causes of Intemperance**—General Causes of—The ☉ ☌ ♀ in ♏ or ♓, and afflicted; the ☉ Sig. in ♓; the ☉ to the ill-asps. the ☽, ♂, or ♀ by dir.; the ☉ afflicting ♀ by asp. at B.; the ☽ affl. at B., and to the evil asps. the Asc. by dir.; the ☽ to the evil asps. ♀ by dir.; ♆ afflictions tend to make one exceedingly intemperate, and liable to moral lapsing; ♄ ☌ or ill-asp. ♀ at B., or by dir., and espec. if ♄ is out of dignity; ♃ Sig. in □ or ☍ ♀ at B., and by dir., given to all kinds of intemperance and debauchery; ♂ affl. in ♓, intemperance should be guarded against; ♂ to the ☌ or ill-asp. ♀ by dir.; ♀ affl. in ♎; ♀ affl. in ♓ in the 6th H.; ♀ in ♓ and affl. the ☽ or Asc.; ♀ affl. in ♏; caused espec. by an afflicted ♀; ♀ affl. by the ☉ at B., and by dir.; ♀ affl. at B., and to the ☌ or ill-asp. the Asc. by dir.; ☿ ill-posited and in □ or ☍ ♂; the Asc. to the ill-asps. ♀ by dir., and ♀ afflicted at B.; the Asc. to the ill-asps. the ☽ by dir., and the ☽ affl. at B.; the 10 and 11° ♌ on the Asc., given to intemperance. (See Appetites, Conduct, Cravings, Debased, Debauched, Depraved, Diet, Dissipation, Drink, Drunkenness, Eating, Epicureans, Excesses, Fanatical, Feasting, Food, Gluttony, Habits, Immoderate, Indiscretions, Indulgent, Intoxication, Lascivious, Lewd, Lust; "Loose Morals" under Morals; Passion, Perversions, Pleasures, Plethora, Profligate, Sex, Sports, Surfeits, Temperance, Venery, Wanton, etc.).

**Death**—Death by Intemperance—Danger of—(See "Causes His Own Death" under Death; "Brings Disease Upon Himself" under Disease; "His Own Worst Enemy" under Enemies).

**Diseases Proceeding From**—Distempers From—Caused principally by afflictions to ♀; ♀ affl. in ♓ in the 6th H.; ♀ in ♓ and affl. the ☽ or Asc.; ♀ ∠ ☉ at B., and by dir.; the ☽ in the 6th H., and in ill-asp. to ♀; diseases of ♃, due largely to over-eating, excesses, and plethora; ♃ Sig. □ or ☍ ☉; ♂ affl. in ♓, and espec. when ♂ is in the 6th H., or affl. the ☽ or Asc.; the Asc. to the ill-asps. the ☽ by dir., and the ☽ affl. at B., according to the sign the ☽ is in at B.; many planets in watery signs, and espec. in ♓. (See "Death" in this section).

**Heat**—Intemperate Heat—Diseases and Suffering From—(See "Excessive Heat" under Heat).

**Ruins Himself**—By Intemperance—The ☉ Sig. in ♓. (See Ruin).

**Sex Life**—Intemperate In—(See Amorous; "Passional Excesses" under Passion).

**Sports**—Intemperate In—Injuries or Disease Caused By—(See Exercise; "Intemperate" under Sports).

**INTENSE**—Intensity—Intensive—Intensification—♂ tends to intensify and accelerate the actions in body and mind. The opposite effect is produced by ♄, as his action tends to slow up, denude and deplete, yet the action of both ♄ and ♂ are needed in the human economy to give balance. (See Malefics, Muscles, Nerves, Temper).

**Intensive Action**—Over the Body—♂ influence. (See Accelerated, Action, Violent).

**Intensity of Disease**—Severity of—(See Direct, Fulminating; "Disease" under Increase; Severity).

**Intense Itching**—(See Itching). For other phases of Intensity, or Excess, see Desire, Emotion, Exaggerated, Excess, Excesses, Passion, etc.).

**INTERCELLULAR**—Intercellular Spaces—Are connected with the Air Signs. (See Cells; "Air Signs" under Signs).

**INTERCHANGE**—The ♌ sign is significant of interchange of the forces of the body. (See Leo).

**INTERCOSTAL**—Between the Ribs—Affected by the ♉, ♊, and ♋ signs. (See Breathing, Chest, Diaphragm, Ribs).

**Bulging**—Intercostal Bulging—The ☉, ♃, or ♂ affl. in ♊; Subs at Lu.P., and KP. (See Expansion).

**Muscles**—The Intercostal Muscles Affected—♂ affl. in ♉, ♊, or ♋. (See "Diseased" under Diaphragm).

**Neuralgia**—Intercostal Neuralgia—♅, ♂, or ☿ affl. in ♉, ♊, or ♋; Subs at Lu.P. (3D). (See Neuralgia).

**Pain**—In the Intercostal Muscles—Pleurodynia—♂ affl. in ♉, ♊, or ♋; Subs at Lu.P., and CP. (See Pain).

**INTERCOURSE**—Sex Relations—

**A Criminal Intercourse**—♄ ruler of the 5th H at B., and by dir. in ☌ or evil asp. the Asc., and espec. if ♄ afflict ♂ and ♀ at B. (See Love Affairs; "Loose Morals" under Morals; Perversions).

**Little or No Desire**—(See Apathy, Aversion, Celibacy, Cohabitation, Deviations; "Indifferent" under Marriage; "Free from Passion" under Passion).

**Sickness from Excesses In**—(See Amorous, Excesses, Indulgent, Passion, Sex, Venery, etc.).

**Social Intercourse**—(See Companions, Environment, Friends, Love Affairs, Marriage, Social, etc.).

**INTERFERENCES**—In the Functions and Parts of the Body—Usually ♄ influences. (See Deformities, Functions, Hardening, Interrupted, Lameness, Paralysis, Retarded, Rhythm, Spasmodic, Suppressions, etc.).

**INTERMITTENT**—Occurring at Intervals—

**Cramps**—Intermittent Cramps—♂ affl. in ♒, and espec. in the 6th H.; ♂ in ♒ and affl. the ☽ or Asc. (See Cramps, Erratic, Muscles, Organs, Spasms, Tetany, Tics, etc.).

**Fever**—Intermittent Fever—Ague—Malaria—Periodic Fever—Fever at Intervals, etc.—♂ in ♌ or ♒, and espec. in the 6th H., and afflicted, or affl. the ☽ or Asc.; earthy signs on the Asc. and 6th H. at B., or at decumb., or Significators in, signify in Hor'y Q. (See Ague, Ease, Malaria, Quartan, Quotidian, Relapsing, Remission, Remittent, Semitertian, Tertian).

**Organs**—Intermittent Action of—Irregular Action of—(See "Irregular" under Heart; Incoordination, Irregular; "Intermittent" under Kidneys; Spasdomic).

**INTERNAL**—Internal Parts of the Body—The ☉ rules all internal, organic, and constitutional diseases. The Internal Generative and Excretory System are under the internal rulership of the ♏ sign. The Internal Generative System and Organs are ruled by ♀. The sign on the Asc. at B. rules the part, or organ of the body designated by such sign, both internally, externally, and structurally. (See External, Organic, Structural).

**Carotids**—The Internal Carotid Arteries—(See Carotid).

**Chill**—Cold—Internal Diseases Arising from Chill, Cold, Neglect, or Privation—(See "Internal Diseases" under Chill).

**Congestions**—Internal Congestions—Caused by ♄ influence, chilling the surface of the body by the influence of cold, which is ruled by ♄, and by constricting the blood vessels of the extremities and surface, being centripetal in influence. (See Centripetal, Cold, Congestions, Saturn).

**Constitutional**—Internal Constitutional Diseases—Ruled and presided over by the ☉, and by the ☉ afflicted at B., and by dir. (See Constitution).

**Diseases**—Disorders—Internal Disorders—The ☉ affl. in ♎ tends chiefly to internal disorders. (See the various paragraphs in this section. Also see Constitution, Functions, Organic, and the various diseases affecting the Internal Organs and Tissues).

**Ears**—Internal Disorders of—(See Deafness, Ears, Hearing).

**Ease**—Internal Ease In Disease—(See Ease).

**Excretory System**—Disorders of the Internal Excretory System—Afflictions in ♏. (See Excretion).

**Force**—(See "Internal" under Force).

**Generative Organs**—Disorders of the Internal Generative Organs and System—(See "Internal" under Generative).

**Headaches**—(See "Internal" under Headaches).

**Heats**—Internal Heats—(See "Internal" under Heat).

**Hemorrhages**—Internal—Denoted by ♂. (See "Internal" under Hemorrhage).

**Humoural Secretions**—(See "Internal" under Humours).

**Neglect**—Internal Disorders From—(See "Chill" in this section).

**Organic Diseases**—Internal and Organic—(See Organic).

**Privation**—Internal Disorders From—(See "Chill" in this section).

**Sex Organs**—Internal—Ruled by ♀, and afflictions to ♀ tend to disorders of. (See "Internal" under Generative).

**Structural Diseases**—Internal—(See Organic, Structural).

**Women**—Females—Internal Complaints of—The ☽ to the □ or ☍ ♀ by dir.; the Asc. to the ☌, P, □, or ☍ ♄ by dir., and ♄ occi. at B., dangerous internal complaints. (See the various paragraphs under Females, Women).

**Zodiac Signs**—Internal Rulership of—(See "Internal" under Signs).

**INTERRUPTED**—Interrupted Sequence In Disease—A planet turning ℞ during the course of a disease tends to somewhat disorganize the disease for the time, cause interrupted sequence until it becomes direct in motion again. Planets direct in motion tend to continuity of the disease. (See Amelioration, Better, Continuity, Course, Crises, Ease, Retrograde, Sequence, Worse). Also interruptions may take place in the action of any organ of the body. See the different organs in the alphabetical arrangement, as Bowels, Heart, Kidneys, Lungs, Stomach, etc. Also see Breathing, Elimination, Excretion, Fever, Functions, Motion, Movement, Pulse, Retention, Rhythm, Secretion, Spasmodic, Stoppages, Suppression.

**INTERSTITIAL**—(See Connective; "Cornea" under Eyes; Intercellular, Tissues).

**INTERVALS**—Of Ease and Amendment In Disease—(See Amelioration, Better, Course, Crises, Ease, Moderation, etc.).

**INTESTINES**—Intestinal Canal or Tract—Enteric—(See Bowels).

**INTOXICATION**—Intoxicating—Intoxicants—Intoxicating Liquors—

**Auto-Intoxication**—(See this subject).

**Danger from Intoxication**—The ☽ affl. in ♓, or affl. the hyleg therefrom; the ☽ to the place of the Bull's Horns.

**Death by Intoxication**—Death from Drink—♅ or ♄ in ♋, ♍, ♏, or ♓, and affl. the ☽; ♓ on the Asc. (See Drink; "Death" under Eating).

**Strong Intoxicants**—Strong Liquors—Given to the Use of—♆ affl. in ♍ or the

6th H., or afflicting the hyleg therefrom. (See "Delirium Tremens" under Delirium; Diet, Dipsomania, Drink, Drunkenness, Eating, Excesses, Food, Intemperance).

**INTRACTABLE**—

**Intractable Diseases**—Difficult to Cure (See "Difficult to Cure" under Cure, Difficult).

**Intractable Disposition**—(See Erring).

**INTROPULSION**—Intropulsive—Intropulsive Congestion—The action of Cold, ruled by ♄, tends to chill the surface, drive the blood inwards, causing internal congestions by Intropulsion. Also caused by ♄ ☌ or ill-asp. the ☽ at B., or by dir. (See Centripetal, Cold, Congestion).

**INTROSPECTION**—Subjectivity—Introversion—The watery signs tend to an active inner life, introspection, subjectivity, brooding, melancholy, etc., and also the airy signs. The earthy and fiery signs tend more to fix the mind and attention upon outer and material things, as in extroversion, and to brood more over worldly cares, business, finance, and earthly things. Ill-Health and mental disturbances result from either of these courses if the ideas become too fixed, or the nature be unadaptable to environment. (See Brooding, Dejected, Depressed, Despondent, Fears; "Fixed Ideas" under Fixed; Gloom, Hallucinations, Hypochondria; "Low Spirits" under Low; Melancholy, Moods, Retrospective, Self-Absorbed, Worry, etc.).

**INTROVERSION**—Turning Inward—(See "Squint" under Eyes; "Club Feet" under Feet; Introspection).

**Moral Introversion**—The bad aspects of ♆ to the Significators tend to. (See Morals).

**INTUITION**—Intuitions—Intuitive—♆ rules the psycho-physical processes which induce to intuitive perception. Also ♅ gives intuitive powers, and intuition is the principle of ♅. (See Uranus).

**Impaired Intuitions**—Heavy afflictions to ♆, ♅, ♃, or ☿ at B.

**Intuitive**—The ☽ in the 1st H.; ♆ or ♅ in the 3rd or 9th H., and in good asp. to ☿, or the Significators; ☿ strong at B., and well-aspected, and espec. when in the 3rd H.; the 1st decan. of ♉ on the Asc., which is ruled by ☿; the 3rd face of ♎ on the Asc.; the 1st face of ♏ on the Asc.

**Spiritual Intuition**—♆ or ♅ strong at B., and favorably aspected. (For further and collateral study see Dreams, Faculties, Fancies, Ideals, Ideas, Imagination, Judgment, Mental, Mind, Perception, Pineal, Prophetic, Retrograde, Spirit, Spiritual, Understanding).

**INTUSSUSCEPTION**—(See this subject under Bowels).

**INUNDATIONS**—(See Floods, Rain, Storms, Waters).

**INVALIDS**—Invalidism—

**Chronic Invalidism**—The ☉ affl. in ♍, or with ♍ on the Asc. or cusp the 6th H., apt to court and hold onto disease; the ☉ or ♄ in the 6th H., and afflicted; ♀ in the 6th H., and afflicted, if excesses are indulged in; ☿ in the 6th H., and affl. by ♄; ♉, ♍, or ♑ on the Asc., thru fear of disease. (See Asthenia, Chronic, Confinement; "Constitution" under Harmony; Hospitals, Ill-Health, Lingering; "Long Illnesses" under Long; Prolonged, Sickly, Slow, Tedious; "Low" under Vitality; Wastings; "Weak Body" under Weak).

**Hopeless Invalids**—The ☉ ☌ ♄ at B., and by dir.; the ☉ ☌ ♄ in the 6th H., danger of many years of ill-health or invalidism, and espec. if there is a fixed sign on the cusp the 6th H. at B.; many planets in common signs at B.; common signs on the Asc. and angles. (See "Sick Bed" under Confinement).

**INVASIONS**—The Onset of a Disease—(See Decumbiture, Directions; "Beginning" under Disease; Events, Infections, Progression, Time, Transits).

**INVENTIONS**—Devices—Machinery—Danger of Accident, Injury, or Death By—(See Employment, Machinery, Weapons, etc.).

**Inventors**—(See Genius, Learning, Mathematical, Novelties).

**INVERTED**—Inverted Feet—(See "Club Feet" under Feet).

**INVIGORATION**—The Invigoration of the System Increased—♂ in good aspect to the Asc. at B., and by dir. (See "Good Health" under Health; Robust, Stamina, Strong, Tone, Vigor, Vitality, etc.).

**INVOLUNTARY**—Independent of the Will—Involuntary disorders in the body are caused by ♅ or ♂, such as contractions, spasmodic action of muscles, twitchings, etc. For the Involuntary Processes and Functions of the body, such as Assimilation, Digestion, Elimination, Excretion, Functions, Growth, Heart Action, Nutrition, etc., see these subjects in the alphabetical arrangement.

**Clairvoyance**—Involuntary Clairvoyance—(See Clairvoyance).

**Contractions**—Involuntary Contractions of Muscles—(See Contractions, Erratic, Hiccough, Jerky, Movements, Muscles, Saint Vitus, Spasmodic, Tics, Vomiting, etc.).

**Discharges**—(See "Involuntary" under Discharges).

**Faeces**—Involuntary Discharge of—(See Faeces).

**Glottis**—Involuntary Closure of—See Glottis, Hiccough).

**Mediumship**—Involuntary—(See Clairvoyance, Mediumship).

**Muscular Excitement**—Involuntary—(See Muscles).

**Nervous System**—Involuntary Nervous System—(See Sympathetic).

**Trance**—Involuntary—(See Trance).

**Urine**—Involuntary Discharge of—(See "Incontinence" under Urine). For other study along this line see Accelerated, Action, Breathing, Clonic, Constrictions, Contortions, Coordination, Cough, Cramps, Epilepsy, Exaggerated, Fainting, Fits, Gait, Incoordination, Insanity, Irregular, Motion, Pain, Pulse, Rapid, Rigidity, Spasmodic, Strictures, Tetanus, Tonic, Tremors, Twistings, Twitchings, Winking, etc.

**INVOLUTION** — A Rolling or Turning Inward—The Principle of ♆. (See Neptune).

**INWARD PARTS** — The Reins — (See Reins).

**Inward Faculties**—The Phantasies or Inward Faculties Prejudiced — (See "Prejudiced" under Fancies).

**IODINE** — Ruled by ♆. (See "Typical Drugs" under Neptune).

**IPECAC** — A typical Polycrest Remedy corresponding to the ♋ Sign. Used much as an Emetic. (See Cancer Sign, Emetics; "Therapeutic" under Moon).

**IRASCIBLE**—Vicious—High-Tempered —Wilson has observed that people who have lost one eye are usually very vicious and irascible. (See "One Eye" under Eyes; "High Temper" under Temper; Vicious).

**IRIDIN** — Iris — Blue Flag — A Typical Drug of ♃. (See "Typical Drugs" under Jupiter).

**IRIS**—The Colored Membrane of the Anterior Part of the Eye—Pupils—The Aperture, or Opening In the Iris — The Iris comes under the influence of the ♈ and ♉ Signs.

**Anisocoria**—(See "Inequality" in this section).

**Aperture** — Pupil — Disorders of—(See the various paragraphs in this section).

**Argyll-Robertson Pupil** — Failure of the Pupil to Respond to Light—Paralysis of the Iris — A Condition In Locomotor Ataxia—A ♄ disease. (See Mydriasis, Paralysis, in this section; Locomotor Ataxia).

**Blue Flag**—Iris—Iridin—(See Iridin).

**Clonic Spasm**—Of the Iris—Hippus— ♅ affl. in ♈ or ♉; Subs at MCP (4C), and at SP (7D). (See "Clonic" under Spasmodic).

**Dilatation**—Of the Pupils—(See "Mydriasis" in this section).

**Disorders Of**—(See the various paragraphs in this section).

**Hippus** — Clonic Spasm of the Iris — A Spasmodic Pupillary Movement, and Independent of Light — (See "Clonic" in this section, and under Eyeballs).

**Inequality**—Of the Pupils—Anisocoria —♄ ☌ the ☉ or ☽ in ♈, and may tend to a permanent contraction in the pupil of the eye affected. (See "Left Eye", "Right Eye", in Sec. 1 under Eyes).

**Inflammation**—Of the Iris—(See "Iritis" in this section).

**Iridoplegia**—(See "Paralysis" in this section).

**Iris**—The Plant Blue Flag—(See Iridin).

**Iritis**—Inflammation of the Iris—A ☉ disease; the ☉ affl. in ♈, and usually in the eye ruled by the ☉, according to the sex. (See "Left", "Right", under Eyes).

**Light** — Lack of Adaptation to Light —Iridoplegia — (See Argyll-Robertson, Mydriasis, Paralysis, in this section).

**Mydriasis** — Abnormal Dilatation of the Pupils—A ♄ disease; ruled by ♄ and the ♑ Sign, which influences rule the Peripheral Nerves, and their afflictions tend to morbid manifestations in the action of these nerves. (See Peripheral). Large and dilated pupils occur in the later stages of Locomotor Ataxia, and are known as the "Argyll-Robertson Pupil", and due to paralysis of the centers of Accommodation for the eye. (See Locomotor Ataxia). The Argyll-Robertson pupil, in the early stages of the disease, as in Locomotor Ataxia, responds to accommodation, but not to light, but in the more advanced stages of the disease does not respond either to light or accommodation, due to the strong influence of ♄ afflictions, as ♄ tends to retard function, crystallize and harden the tissues, deposit wastes, etc. (See "Saturn Influence" under Saturn). The general planetary influences listed under Locomotor Ataxia tend to Mydriasis, and abnormalities of the pupils as to accommodation, or failure to react to light. (See "Light Rays" under Light).

**Mydriatics**—An Agent causing Mydriasis, or Dilatation of the Pupil—Belladonna and Atropin, which are ruled by ♄, are the principal Mydriatics used. (See Belladonna).

**Paralysis**—Of the Iris—Iridoplegia— ♅ or ♄ ☌ the ☉ or ☽ in ♈; Subs at MCP (4C), and SP (7D). (See "Argyll", "Mydriasis", in this section; Paralysis).

**Pupils** — Disorders of — (See the various paragraphs in this section).

**Spasm of Iris** — (See "Clonic" in this section).

**Tremulous Contraction**—Of the Iris— Spasm of—(See Clonic, Hippus, in this section).

**IRON**—Ferrum—Steel—Iron is ruled by ♂, along with Oxygen, ruled by the ☉. The Iron in the blood is ruled by ♂. Iron and the ♂ influences maintain the heat of the blood. Also Iron Color is ruled by ♂. Mars assimilates the iron from the food and converts it into Haemoglobin. (See Haematopoiesis, Haemoglobin; "Fires of Life" under Life; "Mars Influence" under Mars). In the child, from birth to puberty, the Thymus Gland has charge of the work of assimilating iron from the food, and forming Haemoglobin for the blood. At adolescence ♂ and the Desire Body take charge of the work. Mars in the Asc. at B. tends to increase the iron in the system, giving a ruddy complexion, and usually red hair. (See "Red" under Hair; "Blood" under Red). Iron is a stock remedy in ♄ complaints. (See Therapeutics).

**Accidents by Iron**—Accidents, Injury, or Death by Iron or Steel — Wounds, Hurts, or Cuts By, etc.—The ☉ to the ☌, P., □, or ☍ ♂ by dir.; a ♂ influence; in Hor'y Q., ♂ in the Asc., and a malefic planet with the lord of the 1st H. (See Cuts, Instruments).

**Blood**—The Iron In the Blood—(See the first part of this Article).

**Death by Iron**—Danger of—The ☉ to the ☌ or ill-asp. ♂ by dir.; the ☉ to the place of Praesepe.

**Injury By**—(See Accidents, Death, in this section).

**Iron Phosphate** — The ♓ Sign Zodiac Salt, and supplies the blood and vital energy. (See "Vital Energy" under Energy; "Salts" under Zodiac).

**Irons**—Put In Irons In Prison—(See "Beaten In Prison" under Prison).

**Marcassite**—Crystallized Iron Pyrites —Ruled by the ☽.

**Swallows Iron**—Swallows Iron, Nails, and Glass—Case—(See Glass).

**IRRATIONAL** — Impaired Reason — Weakened Understanding—The ☽ and ☿ have strong rule over the rational faculties, and the ☽ and ☿ afflicted, afflicting each other, and also have no aspect or relation to the Asc., tend to impairments of the rational and reasoning faculties, and to irrational manifestations. The Sensitive, or irrational faculties are ruled by the ☽. The ☽ Sig. in ♏ in Hor'y Q. indicates one who tends to be brutish, gross, sensuous, or irrational. (See Brain Storms, Brutish, Chaotic, Confusion, Cruel, Delirium, Erratic, Erring, Faculties, Fanatical, Foolish, Frenzy, Fury, Idiocy, Imbecile, Insanity, Intellect, Judgment, Madness, Mania, Mental, Mind, Perception, Reason, Understanding, etc.).

**Irrational Fears** — (See Anxiety, Dejected; "Morbid Fears" under Fears; Hypochondria, Melancholy, Morbid, Worry, etc.).

**IRREGULAR** — Irregularities — Irregularities of the system are denoted by the ☽ when the ☽ afflicts the ⊙ or Asc.; caused by an afflicted ♅; the Asc. afflicted by the ⊙ or ☽.

**Bowels** — Bowel Action Irregular — (See "Irregular" under Bowels).

**Breathing** — The Breathing Irregular —(See "Irregular" under Breathing).

**Circulation**—Of the Blood—(See "Irregular" under Circulation).

**Course of Disease**—Irregular Disease — ☿ diseases. (See Course, Erratic, Peculiar, Variable, Various, etc.).

**Death**—By Irregularities—Lord of the 8th in the 1st, death by irregularities or suicide. (See "Death" under Indiscretions).

**Disease**—Irregular Course of—Disease from Irregularities — Irregular Maladies — (See Carelessness, Course, Debauched, Depraved, Diet, Dissipation, Drink, Eating, Excesses, Food, Imprudent, Indiscretions, Love Affairs, Lust, Morals, Passion, Variable, Venery, etc.).

**Erratic**—(See the various paragraphs under Erratic).

**Feet**—Irregular and Ill-Made Feet—(See "Ill-Made" under Feet).

**Females** — Irregular Functions In — (See "Functions", "Irregular", under Females; "Irregular" under Functions, Menses).

**Fevers**—Irregular Fevers—(See "Irregular" under Fevers).

**Fluids** — Of the Body — Irregularities of—(See Fluids).

**Food** — Irregularities In — (See Diet, Drink, Eating, Food, Gluttony, etc.).

**Forethought** — (See "Painful Complaints" under Forethought).

**Functions** — (See "Irregular" under Functions).

**Habits**—(See "Careless", "Irregular", under Habits).

**Heart Action**—(See "Irregular" under Heart).

**Kidneys**—(See "Irregular Action" under Kidneys).

**Maladies** — Irregular Maladies — Irregular Course of—Maladies from Irregularities — (See "Disease" in this section).

**Menses**—(See "Functions" under Females; "Irregular" under Functions, Menses).

**Movements** — Irregular — (See Movement).

**Organs**—Irregular and Spasmodic Action of—♅ influence. (See Action, Erratic, Intermittent, Jerky, Spasmodic).

**Painful Irregularities** — (See Forethought).

**Parts**—Of the Body—Irregular Action of—♅ influence. (See "Organs" in this section; Uranus).

**Periodic Irregularities** — (See Periodic).

**Pulse** — Irregular — (See "Irregular" under Heart; "Troubled" under Pulse).

**Rash Acts**—Illness from Irregularities and Rash Acts—(See Foolhardy, Rashness, Recklessness).

**Sickness** — Due to Irregularities — Lord of the 6th H. in the 1st, much sickness thru Irregularities. (See "Disease" in this section).

**Spasms** — Spasmodic Action — (See Contractions, Cramps, Spasmodic).

**Stomach**—(See "Irregularities" under Stomach).

**Womb** — Irregular Contractions of — (See "Hour Glass" under Womb).

**Women** — Irregular Functions In — (See "Females" in this section).

**IRRESPONSIBLE**—Disregardful of the Consequences of Action — Caused by the □ and ☍ aspects of ♅; also caused by the afflictions of ♂ to the ☽ and ☿, and espec. when ♂ is rising at B., and with the map otherwise weak as to mentality; the 3rd Decan. of ♓ on the Asc. (See Idiocy, Imbecility, Insanity, Irrational; "Weak Mind" under Mind; Respect, Responsibility).

**Irresponsible Medium**—(See Mediumship).

**IRRITABLE**—Irritability—

**Mental Irritability** — Out of Sorts — Ill-Humor — Peevish — Fretful — The ⊙ ☌ ☽ at B., or within three degrees of the ☌, out of sorts, listless, and dispirited at every New ☽; the Prog. ⊙ to the ☌ or ill-asp. ♅; the ☽ □ ♂; the ☽ to the ☌ or ill-asp. ♂ by dir., and espec. if ♂ afflict the ☽ at B.; the Prog. ☽ to the □ or ☍ ♅, ♄, or ♂ in the radical map; ♅ affl. in ♎ or ♍; ♄ ☌ the Asc. by dir., ill-humored; ♂ afflicted in ♌ or ♍; the bad aspects between ♂ and ♅, and espec. when ☿, the ☽ and Asc. are also involved; pronounced in the fiery and watery signs. (See Anger, Choleric, Excitable, Fretful; "High Strung" under High; Irascible, Peevish, Quarrelsome, Sensitive; "Sun Spots" under Spots; "High Temper" under Temper).

**Nervous Irritability** — Irritability of the Nerves—(See Erethism, Hyperaesthesia; "Irritability", "Neurasthenia", under Nerves).

**Stomach**—Irritability of the Stomach Walls — (See "Irritable" under Stomach). See Irritations.

**IRRITANTS**—Agents Producing Irritation — ♂ drugs and remedies. Also some Herbs of the ☉ are irritant. Counter-Irritants are ruled by ♂. (See Applications, Cantharides, Caustics; "Typical Drugs" under Mars; Mustard, Rubefacient, Stimulants, Vesicant).

**IRRITATIONS**—Dryness in the body is attended with diseases causing friction and irritation, as the diseases of the ☉, ♅, ♄, ♂, and ☿. (See Dryness, Friction).

**Allaying Irritation**—(See Demulcent).

**Bronchial Irritation**—(See Bronchial, Cough).

**Cellular Irritation**—(See Cells).

**Cosmetics**—Irritations Due To—(See Cosmetics).

**Diarrhoea**—Irritative Diarrhoea—(See Diarrhoea, Dysentery).

**Intestinal** — (See "Irritations" under Bowels).

**Irritants**—(See Irritants).

**Mental Irritations**—(See "Mental Irritability" under Irritable; "Irritations" under Mental).

**Renal Irritations** — (See "Irritation" under Kidneys).

**Skin Irritations**—(See Eruptions, Itch, Skin).

**Stomach Irritations**—(See "Irritable", "Irritations", under Stomach).

**Sympathetic Irritations**—(See Sympathetic).

**Throat Irritations**—(See Throat). The influences of the malefics, and the evil aspects of the planets tend to cause irritations to the various organs, and parts of the body. For other subjects along this line, look in the alphabetical arrangement for the subject you have in mind.

**ISCHIUM**—The Inferior Part of the Hip Bone — Ruled by ♐. Also under the structural rulership of ♏.

**Ischiatic Affections**—The ☽ affl. in ♐.

**Ischiatic Pains**—And Rheumatism—♄ affl. in ♐. (See "Ischium" under Hips).

**ISCHURIA** — Retention or Suppression of Urine—(See "Ischuria" under Urine).

**ISSUE**—Children—(See Children).

**No Issue**—(See Barren, Impotent).

**ITCH**—Itching—Generally considered a ♑ disease.

**Barber's Itch**—(See Barbers).

**Intense Itching** — (See "Pruritis" in this section).

**Nettle Rash**—Urticaria—An Ephemeral Skin Eruption with Itching—(See Urticaria).

**Piles** — Itching Piles — (See "Blind Piles" under Hemorrhoids).

**Pruritis** — Intense Itching — A ♑ disease; ♂ or ☿ afflicted in ♑; ♂ in ♊ when ♂ is the afflictor in the disease. The itching is more intense at the Full ☽. (See "Full Moon" under Moon).

**Scabies** — The Itch — A Contagious Parasitic Disease—(See Scabies).

**The Itch**—Scabies—(See Scabies).

**Thighs** — Itching In — (See "Itching" under Thighs).

**Urticaria** — Nettle Rash — (See Urticaria). See Eruptions, Exanthema, Paraesthesia, Skin Diseases.

**IVY POISON**—Poison Ivy—Rhus Toxicodendron—Ruled by ♄, and Ivy Poisoning is caused by ♄. One person in 18 is susceptible to it.

# J

**JAUNDICE**—Icterus—A Yellow Coloration of the Skin—Caused by functional disturbance of the Liver. Is principally a disease of the ☽, ♄, and ♂.

**Black Jaundice**—A ♄ disease; ♄ in ♊ when ♄ is the afflictor in the disease, and dark brown or greenish black in exceptional cases; the ☽ in ♌, ☌ or ill-asp. ♄ (or ☿ if he be of the nature of ♄) at the beginning of an illness, or at decumb. (Hor'y). (See "Black Bile" under Bile).

**Causes**—Afflictions in ♋, and to the ☽, the ruler of the ♋ sign; ♄ affl. in ♊, ♋, ♌, or ♑; ♄, ♅, or ♆ in ♊, and affl. the ☉ or ☽; ♄ in an angle, occi. of the ☉ and ori. of the ☽; ♃ affl. in ♋, ♍, ♑, or ♓; ♂ in ♐, and affl. the ☽ or Asc.; a ♂ disease; ♂ affl. in ♐ in the 6th H.; a ♌ disease, and caused by afflictions in ♌; connected with the 7th degree of ♈ and ♎, and espec. if the ☽ is therein, and affl. by ♄ or ♃; Subs at Li.P. (See Bile; "Yellow" under Complexion, Face; Liver; "Complexion" under Yellow).

**Death By**—Caused by ♃, his adverse aspects, and afflictions to ♃.

**Jaundiced Look**—In Hor'y Q., ♄ Sig. indicates such a person. (See "Yellow" under Face).

**Obstructive Jaundice** —Toxaemic —A ♄ disease; ♄ afflicted in ♐; ♄ ☌ ♃, and espec. when in signs which affect the liver; Subs at Li.P.

**Toxaemic Jaundice** — (See "Obstructive" in this section).

**Weil's Disease**—Enlarged Spleen, with Jaundice—(See "Weil's Disease" under Spleen).

**Yellow Jaundice** — The ☽ in ♑, and affl. by the ☉ or ♂ when taken ill; a ♂ disease; a ♌ disease, and afflictions in ♌.

**JAWS** — Maxillary — The upper Jaw is ruled by ♈. The lower Jaw, or Mandible, is ruled by ♉. (See Appearance, Face).

**Accidents To** — Injuries, Fracture, Hurts, or Wounds To — ♄ or ♂ affl. in ♈ or ♉ at B., and by dir., and espec. when these signs were on the Asc. at B.

**Diseases Of** — (See Gums, Necrosis, Pyorrhœa, Teeth).

**Lock-Jaw** — (See Lock-Jaw).

**Lower Jaw** — Mandible — Ruled by ♉, and afflictions in ♉ tend to disorders of, and to decay of the teeth of the lower jaw. (See Chin, Gums, Teeth).

**Swollen Jaw** — ♂ afflicted in ♉ or ♏; afflictions in ♉ or ♏.

**Upper Jaw** — The Superior Maxillary — Ruled by ♈, and afflictions in ♈ tend to disorders of. The upper jaw tends to overhang the lower jaw when the 5th face of ♒ is on the Asc. at B.

**JEALOUSY** — A ♄ affliction; ♄ Sig. in ✶ or △ the ☽; ♄ Sig. in ♋; ♄ ☌, P., □, or ☍ ♀, a demon of jealousy in the married life; the evil directions of ♄ to the ☉, ☽, ☿, Asc., or M.C.; the ☉ affl. in the ♄ sign ♑; ♅ affl. in ♉ or ♏; ♂ in the 6th H. in ♉, ♌, or ♏, and affl. by the ☉, ☽, or ♄; ♀ affl. in ♏; ♀ well-dig. at B. tends to jealousy, and often without cause; ⊕ to the ill-asps. ♀ by dir., jealous of his wife; the 2nd face of ♈ on the Asc. (See Delusions, Doubts, Fears, Hallucinations, Hate; "Grief", "Jealousy", under Love Affairs; Malice; "Injured" under Men; Mistrustful, Obsessions, Poison, Suicide, Suspicious, Treachery, etc.).

**JEJUNUM** — The Upper Two-Fifths of the Small Intestine — Ruled by ♍. Obstructions in are caused by ♄ in ♍, and espec. when ♄ is in the 6th H. in this sign; Subs at UPP. (See "Small Intestines" under Bowels; Colon, Ileum).

**JERKINGS** — Spasmodic Movements — Incoordinations, etc.—

**Jerky Movements** — A ♅ disease; caused by ♅ influence, and afflictions to the Organ of Coordination situated in ♉, and ruled by the ♉ Sign. Also caused by ♅ affl. in the 6th H. (See Contractions, Convulsions, Coordination, Cramps, Epilepsy, Erratic; "Nystagmus" under Eyeballs; Fits, Hiccough, Incoordination, Involuntary, Irregular, Motion, Motor, Movements, Muscles, Nerves, Spasmodic, Tics, Twitchings, etc.).

**Jerky Respiration** — Irregular Respiration or Breathing — (See "Jerky" under Breathing).

**JOINTS** — Articulations — The Joints in general are ruled by ♄ and the ♑ Sign. The subjects in this Article have to do more with the abstract conditions which affect the Joints, Diseases of the Joints, etc. For the various Joints of the body, such as those of the Arms, Ankles, Elbows, Feet, Fingers, Hands, Hips, Knees, Legs, Shoulders, Wrists, etc., see these subjects in the alphabetical arrangement.

**Accidents To** — Injuries To — Hurts To, etc. — Caused generally by ♄ afflictions, and to a joint, or joints, in the part of the body afflicted by ♄ at B., and by dir. (See Bones, Dislocations, Fractures).

**Ankylosis** — (See Ankylosis; "Inflammation", "Stiff", in this section).

**Arthralgia** — (See "Gout", "Pain", in this section).

**Arthritis** — Inflammation of a Joint — Pain In — Excessive Heat In — Gout In — Arthritis Deformans — Rheumatoid Arthritis — ♄ ☌ or ill-asp. ♂; ♂ ☌ or ill-asp. ♄ or ♃. Arthritis Deformans, and also Rheumatoid Arthritis, are caused by ♄, and in the part afflicted by ♄ at B., and thru the retention of wastes, by mineral deposits, by crystallization, thickening, and hardening. (See Deformities, Gout, Inflammation, Pain, Rheumatism, in this section; "Arthritis" under Hips).

**Articular Rheumatism** — (See "Rheumatism" in this section).

**Atrophy** — Articular Muscular Atrophy of the Legs — (See Atrophy, Legs).

**Bones** — Of the Joints — Ruled by ♄, and the afflictions of ♄, or afflictions to ♄, tend to disorders of the bony structure of the joints. Also the bones of the joints are affected by the excessive heat of ♂, tending to melting of the joint, adhesions, and ankylosis, resulting in a stiff joint. (See Ankylosis).

**Bursa** — Bursitis — A Small Sac Formation In the Joint — (See Bursa).

**Chronic Inflammation** — In a Joint — (See "Inflammation" in this section).

**Deformities Of** — Arthritis Deformans — Chronic Inflammation of a Joint, with Deformity — Caused by mineral deposits, and the retention of Urea by ♄. (See Arthritis, Gout, Rheumatism, in this section).

**Diseases Of** — Joints In the Different Parts of the Body Are Liable to Disease — The ☉, ☽, or ♄ affl. in ♑; ♑ ascending at the Vernal Equinox, and ♄ afflicting People and Countries under ♑, great sufferers with the joints. (See the various paragraphs in this section).

**Dislocations** — Luxations — (See Dislocations).

**Elbow Joints** — (See Elbows).

**Enlarged Joint** — (See Deformities, Gout, Rheumatism, Swollen, in this section).

**Fingers** — (See "Ankylosis" under Fingers).

**Fluids Of** — (See Synovial).

**Fracture Of** — (See Fractures).

**Gout In** — Pains In — Afflictions to the ☽; ♄ strong at B., as in the Asc. or M.C., or in one of his own signs, as in ♑, and affl. the ☉, ☽, Asc., or hyleg. (See Arthritis, Deformities, Inflammation, Rheumatism, in this section; "Joints" under Gout).

**Granulations In** — ♄ influence. (See "Joints" under Feet).

**Hardening** — Crystallization — The work of ♄ by pathological and abnormal mineral deposits and the retention of wastes. A destructive process of ♄. The ♄ influence and afflictions tend to the hardening of the synovial membrane, and lack of secretion of the synovial fluid, tending to stiffen and dry up the joints. (See Crystallization, Fluids, Hardening, Synovial).

**Heat**—Excessive Heat In the Joints—(See Ankylosis, Arthritis, Bones, in this section).

**Hip-Joint Disease**—Arthritis of—(See "Hip-Joint Disease" under Hips).

**Inflammation Of**—Arthritis—(See "Arthritis" in this section). Chronic Inflammation in the Joints is due to ♄ afflictions, and with ♑ especially strong and afflicted at B. (See "Arthritis" in this section).

**Injuries To**—(See "Accidents" in this section).

**Knee Joint**—(See Knees).

**Large Joints**—Well-Set—(See "Body" under Large; "Large" under Limbs).

**Leg Joints** — Arthritis of — Arthritic Muscular Atrophy In—(See "Arthritis" under Legs).

**Lubrication; Luxations**—(See Dislocations).

**Muscles**—Arthritic Muscular Atrophy In Legs—(See "Arthritis" under Legs).

**Pain In**—Arthralgia—The ☽ in airy signs and affl. by ♄ or ♂; the ☽ in ♊ and affl. by the ☉, ♄, or ♂; the ☽ in ♎ or ♐, in ☌ or ill-asp. ♄ (or ☿ if he be of the nature of ♄) at the beginning of an illness or at decumb.; ♄, ♅, or ♆ in ♒ and affl. the ☉, ☽, or Asc. The pains tend to be in the joints over the entire body if at decumb., or when first taking sick, the ☽ is under the Sun's beams, or in ☌ with ♄, ♅, or ♂. (See Arthritis, Dengue, Gout; "Pains" under Whole; Arthritis, Gout, Inflammation, in this section).

**Rheumatism In** — Articular Rheumatism — Chronic Deformans — A ♄ disease; the work of ♄ deposits of Urea in the joints; a ♑ disease, and afflictions in ♑; ♄ in ♑; the ☽ affl. in ♑; the ☉ affl. in ♐. (See Gout, Rheumatism; Arthritis, Gout, in this section).

**Sac**—A Small Sac Formation In the Joint—(See Bursa).

**Shoulder Joint** — Disorders of — (See Shoulders).

**Stiff Joints**—Ankylosed—Hardened—Enlarged—Swollen—Crystallization of—♄ influence. Caused by the retention and deposit of Urea in the joints by ♄. (See Ankylosis; Arthritis, Deformities, Gout, Hardening, Inflammation, Rheumatism, in this section).

**Subluxations**—A Partial Dislocation—(See Subluxations).

**Swollen Joints**—Enlarged—Inflamed—Gout In—Stiff Joints, etc.—(See Dengue; Arthritis, Gout, Inflammation, Rheumatism, Stiff, in this section).

**Synovial Fluid**—Synovial Membranes—Disorders of—(See Lubrication, Synovial; "Hardening" in this section).

**Thickening**—(See "Arthritis" in this section).

**Union of Bones**—(See "Bones" in this section).

**Well-Jointed Body**—☿ oriental at B.

**Well-Set Joints**—(See "Large" in this section).

**Whole Body**—Pains In the Joints Over the Whole Body—(See "Pain" in this section).

**Wrists**—(See Wrists).

**JOURNEYS**—Short Journeys—Long Journeys—Travel—Inland Journeys—Travel In the Native Land—♅ is the principal planet causing journeys. Also the 3rd and 9th H. are the houses of Travel and Journeys, the 3rd H. indicating inland travel and short journeys, and the 9th H. Foreign Travel, Voyages, etc. Malefic planets in these houses at B., or a malefic as lord of these houses, indicate danger in travel, while the benefic planets in these houses tend to benefits and gain by travel, either in business or health matters. These matters are further considered under the subjects of Abroad, Foreign Lands, Location, Native Land, Railroads, Residence, Ships, Travel, Vehicles, Voyages, etc. The following subjects and paragraphs are listed here, as they have to do with the welfare of the native, the health, environment, business success, the mental and spiritual welfare, etc., and to assist with fore-knowledge to avoid dangers which may lead to accidents, injuries, ill-health, sickness, or death thru journeys, by traveling or locating in a wrong direction from the birthplace. Some people, according to their maps of birth, should remain at their birthplace all thru life for the best of success and health, while others should remove, or even locate in a Foreign Land. People born in Northern Latitudes, and who have nearly all their planets below the horizon at B., can, by removing to the South Latitudes, reverse their maps and bring their planets above the Earth, and near the Zenith, and into greater power, and thus a career which would have been obscure in the land of birth may become very notable, powerful, and successful in the opposite Hemisphere.

**Abroad**—(1) Avoid Journeys Abroad—The ☉ hyleg, and the ☉ to the ☌ or ill-asp. ♂ by dir.; the ☽ in the 9th H. in a Solar Rev., and affl. by ♄ or ♂; the ☽ to the ☌ or ill-asp. ♂ by dir., and ♂ affl. the ☽ at B., or ♂ occupying the 9th H.; ♆, ♅, ♄, or ♂ ruler of the 8th H. at B., and any of them in the 9th H. at a Solar Rev.; ♄ ascending at B., and the ☉ to the ☌ or ill-asp. ♄ by dir.; ♂ ☌ the ☉ at a Solar Rev.; malefics in the 9th H. unless they be strong by sign and aspect; ruler of the 9th H. at B. in the 4th H. at a Solar Rev., and afflicted; the M.C. to the ☌ or evil asp. the ☽ if the ☽ be weak and afflicted at B.; lord of the 2nd H. in the 9th H., and afflicted. (See Abroad, Drowning, Foreign Lands, Shipwreck; the various paragraphs in this section). (2) Should Take Journeys Abroad, or Live Abroad—Benefics in the 9th H. at B., and with malefics in the 4th H., or in the Sign ruling the Native Land. (See "Health" under Abroad; Foreign Lands, Location, Native Land; "Place of Birth" under Place; Residence, Travel, Voyages).

**Accidents On Journeys**—Danger of—Injuries—Hurts—Malefics in the 3rd or 9th H. at B. (See "Travels" under Falls; Railroads, Robbers, Ships, Shipwreck; "Accidents" under Travel; "Injuries" under Voyages; Long Journeys, Short Journeys, Voyages, in this section).

**Avoid Journeys**—A Bad Time for Journeys—The ☽ to the ill-asps. ☿ by dir.; ♅ to the bad asps. the ☽, and espec. if either rule the 3rd or 9th H.; ♄ to the ill-asps. ♃ if either be ruler of the 3rd or 9th H.; the M.C. to the ☌, P., □, or ☍ the ☽ if the ☽ be weak and afflicted at B. (See "Abroad", and the various paragraphs in this section; "Avoid", "Bad Time For", under Travel; "Danger" under Voyages).

**Bad Time For**—(See "Avoid", and the various paragraphs in this section).

**Bites**—On Journeys—(See "Journeys" under Bites).

**Brings a Journey**—Or Voyage—The M.C. to the ✶ or △ ♂. (See "Disposes To", "Voyage Soon Follows" under Voyages).

**Burns**—On a Journey—(See "Journeys" under Burns).

**Cuts**—On a Journey—(See "Travel" under Cuts).

**Dampness**—(See "Wet Journeys" in this section).

**Danger On Journeys**—(See Maritime, Navigation, Ships, Shipwreck; "Danger" under Travel; Voyages; "Accidents", and the various paragraphs in this section).

**Death On a Journey**—Death During Travel—(See Drowning; "Death" under Railroads, Sea, Ships, Shipwreck, Travel, Voyages).

**Drowned**—On a Journey—(See Drowning, Shipwreck; "Death" under Sea, Voyages, Water).

**Exposure**—On Journeys—And the Health Suffers From—(See "Travel" under Exposure).

**Fatigue**—(See "Sickness" under Travel).

**Fever**—(See "Fever" under Voyages).

**Fire**—On Short Journeys or At Sea—(See "Ships", "Short Journeys", under Fire).

**Food**—Lack of On Journeys—(See Desert; "Privations" under Sea; "Food" under Travel).

**Good Time**—For Journeys—Good Time for Short Journeys and Inland Travel—The ☉ to the good asps. ♂, and the ☉ or ♂ ruler of the 3rd H. at B.; the ☉ to the P. or good asps. the ☽; the ☉ to the cusp the 3rd H. by dir.; the ☉ by Periodic Rev. to the good asps. ☿; the ☽ by dir. to the good asps. the Asc. if the ☽ was well-aspected at B.; the ☽ incr. in light, and free from affliction of malefics, and well-aspected by ♃ or ♀; the ☽ in the 3rd H. at B., and to the good asps. ♅ by dir.; the ☽ in the 5th H., and well-aspected by benefics; the ☽ to the good asps. the ☉, and espec. if the direction fall in the 3rd H.; the ☽ to the ☌ ☿ by tr. or dir., and the aspect fall in the 3rd H., or the ☽ or ☿ be in the 3rd H. at B.;

the ☽ to the ☌ or good asp. ⊕; the ☽ to the cusp the 3rd H. by dir.; the ☽ to the ☌ ♃ by tr. or dir.; the Periodic Direction of ♄ to the good asps. the radical ♂; ♃ to the ☌ the ☽ in the 3rd H.; ♃ by Periodic Rev. to the ☌ the radical ☽; ♂ by Periodic Rev. to the good asps. the ☽; the M.C. to the ☌ or P. asp. the ☽ if the ☽ rule the 3rd H. at B.; the M.C. to the good asps. the ruler of the 3rd H.; the M.C. to the ☌, P., or good asp. ☿; ☿ to the good asps. the ☽ by dir. or tr.; the ruler of the 1st H. by tr., when a benefic, to the cusp the 3rd H., or to the good asp. the ruler of the 3rd H. at B.; when ♂, the ☽ or ☿ are in the 3rd H. at B., a journey is usually made when the ☽, or planet, comes to the cusp the 3rd H. by Periodic Direction in Mundo; a benefic in the Asc. or an angle. (See "Good Time For" under Voyages).

**Health**—(1) The Health Suffers On a Journey—The native is liable to sickness and a fever on a journey if it is started in a ♄ or ♂ hour, or with ♄, ♂, or other malefics in the 3rd or 9th H. at B., or by dir., and the malefic afflicting the ☉, ☽, Asc., M.C. or Hyleg; taking, beginning, or returning from a journey when the ☽ is in the Asc. (See "Sickness" under Travel). (2) Journeys On Account of Health—Travels for His Health—☿ affl. in the 6th H. at B., travels on account of the health. Travel for the health should be made in the directions in which ♃ and ♀ are posited at B., and avoid the directions and Countries indicated by the directions and sign positions of malefics at B. (See "Travel" under Health).

**Illness On a Journey**—(See "Health" in this section).

**Injury On a Journey**—(See "Accidents" in this section).

**Inland Journeys**—Land Journeys—Short Journeys by Rail or Other Vehicle—Are governed principally by ☿. The ☽ to the ☌ ♃ inclines to. (See "Short Journeys" in this section).

**Land Journeys**—(See "Inland", "Short", in this section).

**Long Journeys**—Are governed by ♃; ♃ in the 9th H., and favorably aspected, tends to success and good health on long journeys. There is danger of accidents or death on long journeys when the ruler of the 8th H. at B. is in the 7th at a Solar Rev., and espec. if the nativity be a violent one. (See "Accidents", "Sickness", under Abroad; Drowning, Foreign, Sea, Ships, Shipwreck; "Foreign Travel" under Travel; "Good Time" under Voyages).

**Many Journeys**—(See "Many Changes" under Residence; "Love Of", "Wanderer", under Travel).

**Ocean Journeys**—(See Sea, Ships, Shipwreck. Voyages; "Fortunate", "Perils", under Water).

**Pirates**—Danger or Death By On Journeys—(See Pirates).

**Privation On Journeys**—(See "Privations" under Seas).

**Railroad Journeys**—Injury or Death By—(See "Short Journeys" in this section).

**Ships**—Journeys By—Injury, Death, or Discomfort By—(See Maritime, Navigation, Sea, Ships, Shipwreck, Voyages).

**Short Journeys**—Inland Journeys—Railroad Travel—Danger of Injury or Death By—The 3rd H., and planets therein, rule short journeys. Short journeys should not be made at these times, or under the following aspects and influences—The ☽ to the ☌ or ill-asp. ♅ by dir., and the ☽ in the 3rd H. at B.; the ☽ in the 3rd H. at the Vernal Equi., lady of the year, and afflicted; ♅ in the 3rd H. at B., and afflicted; ♅ afflicted in ♊; ♅ affl. at B., and to the ☌ or ill-asp. the Asc. by dir.; ♅ influence and afflictions in the 3rd H. at B., and by dir., tend to death on railways or rolling stock if the map of birth shows a violent end; ♅ setting at B., and in ☍ the Luminaries, and when ♅ again afflicts the Lights by dir.; ♄ by tr. or dir. in ☌, □, or ☍ the radical ☿; ♃ in the 3rd H., and afflicted, may be in an accident, but escapes injury (see "Escapes" under Travel); ♂ in the 3rd H., and afflicted; ♂ in the 1st H., and affl. by ♃; ♂ affl. in ♊; ♂ in the 3rd H., and affl. the ☉ or ☽; ♂ to the cusp the 3rd H. by dir.; ♂ by Periodic Rev. to the ill-asps. the ☽, or to the ☌ or ill-asp. ♅, and espec. if ♂ be in the 3rd or 9th H. at B.; ♂ progressed to the ☌ or ill-asp. ☿, or vice versa; ☿ in the 8th H. at B., and afflicted, avoid short journeys; ☿ in the 3rd H. at B. in ☌ ♄, ♅, or ♂, and otherwise afflicted by the ☽, ♃, or ♀; malefics in the 3rd H., and afflicted, or afflicting the ☉ or ☽; lord of the 8th or 11th H. a malefic, in the 3rd H., and afflicted; the 2nd Decan. of ♊, ruled by ♂, on the cusp of the Asc. at B. (See Railroads, Travel, Vehicles; Accidents, Avoid, Inland, and the various paragraphs in this section).

**Sickness**—On Journeys—(See "Health" in this section).

**Stings**—Bites or Stings On Journeys—(See "Journeys" under Bites).

**Sudden Journeys**—The ☽ by Periodic Rev. to the aspects of ♅ in the radical map.

**Travel**—(See the various paragraphs under Maritime, Navigation, Sea, Ships, Shipwreck, Travel, Voyages; "Brings a Journey", "Health", and the various paragraphs in this section).

**Unfavorable Journeys**—(See "Avoid", and the various paragraphs in this section; Railroads, Sea, Ships, Shipwreck, Travel, Voyages).

**Voyages**—(See the various paragraphs under Sea, Ships, Shipwreck, Voyages).

**Wet Journeys**—Health Suffers By—♄ in the 3rd H. at B. (See "Journeys" under Moisture).

**Wind Storms**—Danger From On Journeys—(See "Storms" under Wind).

**JOY**—Joviality—Jolly—Mirth—Gladness—Cheerfulness—Joy and life come from the ☉. Also ♀ is the author of mirth and cheerfulness, and espec. with ♀ in the Asc. or M.C. at B., or in ☌ with ☿. Jupiter rising at B. also gives a cheerful disposition, and joviality is a ♃ trait. Other influences which produce joy and gladness are the ☽ in ♎ or ♓, and well-aspected; the ☽ incr. in light, and applying to ♃ unless ♂ be in □ or ☍ to ♃; ♃ Sig. in ♒; ♂ well-aspected in ♐; ♐ on the Asc. (See Cheerfulness, Contentment, Happiness, Life, Mild, Mirth; "Peace of Mind" under Mind; Optimistic, Sanguine).

**Life Robbed of Its Joy**—The ☉ or ☽ in the 12th H., and affl. by malefics; the ☉ or ☽ ☌ ♄; the ☉ ☌ ♄ in 12th H.; the ☽ in ☍ ♄ or ♀; ♆ □ ☿, due to obsessions, hallucinations, morbid fears, and adverse Astral influences; ♄ □ the ☉, ☽, or ♀; ♄ affl. in the 12th H.; ♃ or ♀ affl. in the 12th H. (See Confinement, Dejected, Depressed, Despondent, Hypochondria; "Low Spirits" under Low; Melancholy, Morbid, Obsessions, Sadness, Smiles, Sorrow, Worry).

**JUDGES**—Magistrates—The Law—Sentence by Law—Punishment by Law—Judicial Condemnation—Death or Imprisonment by Sentence of Law—See the following subjects in the alphabetical arrangement when not considered here—

**Beheaded; Burned At Stake**—(See "Stake" under Burns).

**Death**—By Sentence of Law—Judicial Condemnation—Judicial Execution—Judicial execution is strongly denoted by the 17° ♊ and ♐, and planets which may occupy these degrees, or degrees also in □ to them. Death by Law is denoted when ♃ is involved in configurations otherwise indicating a violent death, as ♃ is said to rule Judges and the Law. The mutable signs, and espec. ♊ and ♐, indicate the homicidal tendency, or Judicial Execution. Fixed signs also indicate such a death, and espec. when ♄ is in a fixed sign, such as ♉, and afflicting the hyleg. Other testimonies are as follows—The ☉ Sig. □ or ☍ ♂; the ☽ to the ill-asps. ☿ by dir., and ☿ or the ☽ afflicted by malefics at B.; the ☽ incr., or at Full, sepr. from ☿ and applying to ♂; ♅ ☌ ♂ in ♈; ♄ or ♂ with Caput Algol, and the ☽ with Deneb.; ♄ in a fixed sign □ or ☍ the ☉, and contrary in condition, or ♄ occi. of the ☽, and the ☽ be succedent to him; ♃ bearing testimony to ♂, and ♃ afflicted at B.; ♃ affl. the hyleg by dir.; ♃ affl. at B., and afflicting the hyleg by dir., and holding the dominion of death, and espec. where a violent death is indicated; ♂ in a human sign, and afflicting ♃; ♂ just setting in ☍ the Asc.; ♂ Sig. in □ or ☍ the ☉, and ☿ □ ♂, death by a Public Executioner, and espec. if the ☉ is in the 10th H.; lord of the 8th H. a malefic, and in the 10th, and espec. if the lord of the 8th or 10th afflict the lord of the Asc. from fixed signs; lord of the 10th in the 12th H.; the M.C. to the ill-asps. the ☉, ☽, or ♂ by dir. (See the various paragraphs in this section).

**Decapitation**—(See Beheaded).

**Electrocution**—(See Electricity).

**Enemies**—Has Many Enemies Among Magistrates—♀ Sig. □ or ☍ ♃.

**Execution**—(See the various subjects and references under Execution).

**Fortunate Among Magistrates**—The ☽ Sig. ☌ ♃.

**Fugitives; Gallows**—Sentenced to Death On—(See Hanging).

**Guillotine; Halter**—Death By—(See Hanging).

**Hand of Man**—Death By—(See "Hand of Man" under Man).

**Hanging; Ignoble Death**—(See Ignoble).

**Impalement; Imprisonment**—(See Prison).

**Law**—Sentenced and Punished by the Law—(See the various paragraphs in this section).

**Many Enemies**—Among Magistrates —(See "Enemies" in this section).

**Murderer**—Convicted and Sentenced for Murder—(See Assassins, Homicide, Murder).

**Officers of the Law**—(See Officers).

**Prisons**—(See "Imprisonment", and the various paragraphs under Prison).

**Public Death**—Public Execution—♂ Sig. □ or ☍ the ☉, and ☿ also □ ♂, and espec. if the ☉ be in the 10th H. (See "Death" in this section; Execution; "Public Death", under Public).

**Punishment**—By Law—(See Punishment; the various paragraphs in this section).

**Strangulation**—Suffocation by Law—(See Hanging).

**Tragical Death**—(See Tragical).

**Untimely Death**—(See Untimely).

**Violent Death**—(See Execution, Hanging; "Death" under Violent; the various paragraphs in this section. Also for other influences which contribute to sentence and punishment by Law, see Cheating, Criminal, Depraved, Disgrace, Dishonest, Downfall, Drunkenness, Evil, Gambling, Highwaymen, Honour, Liars, Libelers, Perjury, Perversions, Pirates, Plots, Poison, Reputation, Reverses, Robbers, Ruin, Scandal, Sedition, Self-Undoing, Thieves, Treachery; "Tendency to Violence" under Violent, etc.

**JUDGMENT**—The Act of Judging—The Decisions—The Mental Faculties—Discrimination, etc.—

**Bad Judgment**—Errors of Mind—Erratic Judgment—Void of Solid Judgment—Poor Judgment—Lack of Discrimination and Foresight—Lack of Tact—A Prejudiced or Biased Mind—The ☉ ☌ ☿, combust, or in □ or ☍ ♅, ♄, ♃, or ♂; the ☉ afflicted and ill-dignified at B.; the ☉ Sig. ☌ ☿, not much sound judgment; the ☽ □ or ☍ ☿; the ☽ and ☿ unconnected with each other or the Asc.; the ☽ Sig. ☌ ♄, commits many errors of judgment; ♃ Sig. □ or ☍ ☿; ♃ to the ill-asps. ☿ by dir., wrong opinions; ♂ afflicted in the 10th H., lacks discrimination; ☿ alone ruler of the mind, and also tends to be ill-disposed; ☿ □ or ☍ ♄, weak judgment, and views things thru a false medium; ☿ ☌ or combust the ☉, and ☿ receiving no assistance from the benefics; ☿ Sig. ☌ ☉; ☿ ill-dignified at B., of little judgment, and lacking in tact; ☿ in evil asp. to ♂ tends to false judgment; the 1st Decan. of ♊ on the Asc. tends to perverted judgment. (See Anarchists, Chaotic, Confused, Cruel, Delusions, Deviations, Dull, Eccentric, Emotions, Erratic, Examinations, Faculties, Fanatical, Fancies, Forethought, Hallucinations, Hasty, Ideals, Ideas; "Ill-Disposed" under Ill; Illusions, Imaginations, Imbecility, Impairments, Impractical, Improvident, Impulsive, Incompetency, Indiscretions, Injudicious, Intellect, Memory, Mental (see "Shallow" under Mentality; Mind (see "Weak" under Mind); Notions, Opinions, Peculiar, Perception, Perversions, Reason, Temper, Uncontrolled, Understanding, Vicious, Violent, Void Of).

**Body**—Judging the Body—(See Appearance, Body, Form, Physical, Shape, Stature, etc).

**Disease**—The Judgment and Diagnosis of Disease—In order to judge of the disease, its mildness or severity, and its possible outcome, the following parts and influences of the map of birth should be considered—The ☉, ☽, and Asc., and their strength and afflictions; the Hyleg, its strength, aspects and afflictions; the power of the malefics and their afflictions to the Hyleg; the mutual afflictions among the planets; planets elevated, rising, or setting; malefics elevated above the benefics or hyleg (which tend to make the disease more forceful); planets in the 6th H., the House of Health; the house position of the lord of the 6th H., his nature, whether benefic or malefic, and aspects. Also the degree of the vitality should be studied, the powers of recuperation and resistance to disease, and the quality of the disease; the Significator of the disease; the nature of the planet causing the disease, and the transits, progression, directions, house and sign position of such planet at birth and now, and how the afflicting planet affects the radical map, etc. Diseases not shown, indicated, or accounted for by the radical map, can oftentimes be found and indicated in the prenatal map, the map for the time of conception, or the aspects to the ☽ at the monthly periods during gestation. Also the Heliocentric positions of planets may help to explain the nature and cause of the disease. (See Acquired, Acute, Anareta, Chronic, Constitution, Course, Curable, Diagnosis, Diathesis, Directions; "Causes" under Disease; Disturbances, Duration, Events, Fatal, Heredity, Hyleg, Incurable, Long, Majority, Mild, Modification, Nature, Organic, Parts, Prenatal, Prognosis, Quality, Recovery, Recuperation, Remedy (see "Incapable" under Remedy); Resistance, Severe, Short, Sixth House, Slight, Structural, Type, Vitality, etc.).

**Good Judgment**—Sensible—Sound Judgment—Tactful—Has Good Foresight, Forethought, and Discrimination—Practical—An Accurate Reasoner —The ☉ well-dignified at B.; the ☽ well-aspected, dignified, and in good relation to ☿ and the Asc.; ♃ strong at B., and well-aspected; ♃ Sig. in ♐; ♃ Sig. ✱ or △ ☿; ☿ Sig. ✱ or △ ♃, possesses solid sense; ☿ in the Zodiac in P. asp. ♄, accurate judgment; the 3rd face of ♏ on the Asc.; ♂ a strong ruler at B., and well-aspected, gives moderately good judgment. (See "Active Mind" under Active; "Mental Energy" under Energy; Learning; "Quickened" under Mentality; "Brightened", "Clear", "Judging", "Quality", "Sound", "Strong", under Mind; Practical, Prudent, Sagacious).

**Health** — Judging the Health — (See "Judging the Health" under Health).

**Mind**—Judging the Mind—(See "Judging the Mind" under Mind).

**JUGULAR VEINS**—Ruled by the ♌ sign. (See Veins).

**JUICES**—Fluids—

**Digestive Juices** — (See "Fluids" under Digestion; "Juices" under Gastric). See Acids, Fluids, Glands, Secretions.

**JUMPING SPASM** — (See "Jumps Forward" under Manner; "Jumping" under Spasmodic).

**JUPITER** — The Planet Jupiter — The Greater Benefic. The general influence of ♃ is benevolent, and his aspects never kill unless configurated with malefics in a train of evil directions. By nature he is positive, masculine, electric, warm and moist. (See "Qualities" in this section). He is the Author of Justice, and when the ruling planet at B. tends to make the native just, generous, kind, jovial, and religious. In order that the student can the more quickly refer to the various influences of this planet, I have arranged this Article into three Sections. Section One—The Influences of Jupiter; Section Two—Jupiter Rules; Section Three—The Diseases of Jupiter.

## — SECTION ONE —

**THE INFLUENCES OF JUPITER**—In this section the influences with which ♃ has to do, and over which he presides, are arranged alphabetically under subjects for quicker reference.

**Activity** — Seat of — The Liver is the seat of ♃ activity. There he forms Glycogen which is used as fuel for the body during muscular activity. (See Glycogen, Liver).

**Afflictions Of**—Evil Aspects of—♃ afflicts only by his □ and ☍ aspects, but the good influence of ♃ is vitiated by his ☌ with ♄. By his bad aspects, ♃ has the evil effect of producing congestion, undue blood pressure, apoplectic conditions, diseases arising from surfeits, gormandizing habits, clogging of the system, and indicates overfunctional activity of the parts ruled by the sign he is in at B., or by tr. or dir. The evil aspects of ♃ to the ☉, ☽, and planets tend to have a very evil and detrimental influence. (See "Aspects" in this section; "Death" in Sec. 3 of this Article).

**Anareta** — ♃ can act as Anareta in morbid deaths. (See Anareta).

**Angel Of**—Zadkiel.

**Aspects Of**—For the influences of his evil aspects see "Afflictions Of" in this section. The good influences of ♃, by his favorable aspects, are the preservation of life, restoration of health, elaboration, conservation of energies, and to insure fruitfulness, temperateness, etc. No aspects of ♃ or ♀ alone

cause disease, but only as configurated with malefics. In diseases caused by ♄ the good aspects of ♃ help more than those of ♀. (See "Directions" in this section).

**Assimilation**—And Growth—Are aided and furthered by the work of ♃. (See Assimilation, Growth).

**Astral Body**—In the Astral Body, ♃ has direct relation to the breath, lungs, liver, and Blood. (See Astral).

**Author Of**—♃ is the author of justice, temperance, and moderation.

**Benefics**—♃ and ♀ are called the benefic planets. (See Benefics).

**Births**—Normal births are ruled by ♃. (See Birth).

**Children** — ♃ is fruitful, and a giver of children. His good directions to the Midheaven, or to the fruitful places in the map, promise a child. (See "Birth of a Child" under Children; Fruitfulness).

**Classification Of** — ♃ is classed as a hot, airy, moist, fruitful, positive, masculine, and benefic planet. (See "Qualities" in this section).

**Cold and Dry**—♃ exerts a temperate influence between the extremes of cold and dry, and tends to warmth and moisture.

**Colors** — ♃ rules violet in the Solar Spectrum. Also said to rule blue, purple; red mixed with green. (See Color).

**Conservation**—♃ and ♀ both have to do with the nourishing, supporting, conserving, and aphetic processes, the storing of various cell substances, selection, transformation, filtration, and reservation.

**Directions Of** — The good directions of ♃ to the M.C. promise a child. The good directions of ♃ to the hyleg at B., and by dir. tend to good health, and also to spare life in a severe sickness. (See Benefics, Directions; "Good Health" under Health; "Spared" under Life).

**Dominates**—♃ dominates the Arterial System. (See Arteries).

**Dry and Cold** — (See "Cold" in this section).

**Energies** — The influence of ♃ is to conserve the energies by his good aspects.

**Evil Aspects Of**—(See "Afflictions Of" in this section).

**Expansion and Heat**—♃ being a positive and electric planet tends to produce heat and expansion in the body, and to give a positive, confident, forceful state of mind.

**Fat**—♃ has charge of the disposition and distribution of Fat in the body. Also, ♃ adds the fatty constituents to the milk, and other fluids. (See Fat).

**Filtration** — (See "Substance" under Cells).

**Foetus** — The Foetus becomes enveloped with the Amniotic Fluid under ♃ influence. (See Foetus).

**Fuel** — Of the Body — (See "Activity" in this section).

**Full Effects Of** — The full effects of the ♃ influence for good or ill are not felt until middle life, and especially when he is in ♋ or the 4th H. at B. (See Middle Life).

**Glycogen**—♃ forms the Glycogen in the Liver. (See "Activity" in this section).

**Good Influences Of** — (See "Aspects" in this section).

**Greater Fortune**—Greater Benefic—♃ is called the Greater Fortune, or Greater Benefic, and ♀ is called the Lesser Benefic. (See Benefics).

**Growth and Assimilation**—(See "Assimilation" in this section).

**Heat and Expansion** — (See "Expansion" in this section).

**Herbs** — The Herbs Ruled by ♃ — Typical Plants of — (See "Jupiter Group" under Herbs, Muscles; "Typical Drugs" in this section).

**Hour** — ♃ Hour — (See Bleeding; "Hours" under Planets).

**Hyleg** — ♃ as Hyleg — (See Hyleg). When ♃ is not Hyleg, his good aspects to the ☉, ☽, Asc., or Hyleg are a powerful protective agent.

**Justice**—(See "Author Of" in this section).

**Life-Saving Power** — Neither of the Benefics will save life if the lords of the 6th and 8th Houses are in evil aspect to each other. (See "Aspects", "Directions", in this section).

**Metal Of**—Tin. (See Therapeutics).

**Middle Life** — (See "Full Effects Of" in this section).

**Milk** — ♃ adds the fatty constituents to milk. (See Milk).

**Mind**—The positive and good aspects of ♃ tend to give a forceful state of mind.

**Moderation**—♃ is the Author of. (See "Author Of" in this section).

**Moisture and Warmth** — (See "Cold and Dry" in this section).

**Muscular Activity** — (See "Activity" in this section).

**Normal Births**—(See "Births" in this section).

**Nourishing** — (See "Conservation" in this section).

**Pathological Action** — (See "Pathological" in Sec. 3 of this Article).

**Physiological Action**—The Physiological Action of ♃ is Cell Development. (See Cells).

**Plants and Herbs**—(See "Herbs" in this section).

**Preservation**—The Principle of ♃. (See Preservation).

**Principle Of**—Preservation.

**Processes Of**—(See "Conservation" in this section).

**Protective Agent** — (See "Hyleg" in this section).

**Qualities** — Aggregative, Airy, Alexipharmic, Alterative, Analeptic, Anthelmintic, Antispasmodic, Apoplectic, Balsamic, Benefic, Beneficent, Benevolent, Buoyant, Clogging (by evil aspects), Confident, Conservative, Cor-

pulent, Diurnal, Elaborating, Electric, Emollient, Enriching, Expansive, Forceful, Fortunate, Fruitful, Fullness (gives Fullness), Generous, Guttonous (by evil aspects), Gormandizing, Health-Restoring, Heat-Producing, Hot, Just, Masculine, Moderation, Moist, Nourishing, Optimistic, Opulent, Overflowing, Plethoric, Positive, Preserving, Redundant, Religious, Reverent, Sanguine, Self-Indulgent, Sociable, Supporting, Temperate, Warm, etc.

**Reservation**—(See "Conservation" in this section).

**Seat of Activity** — (See "Activity" in this section).

**Selection**—(See "Conservation" in this section).

**Sidereal Body**—Relation of ♃ To— (See Astral Body).

**Signs**—Of the Zodiac—For the influence of ♃ in each of the Signs see the classified lists of ♃ in Signs in the various Textbooks and Dictionaries of Astrology.

**Social Planet**—♃ is called the Social Planet, due to the joviality and good nature he gives when well-placed, well-aspected, and strong at B.

**Storing**—(See "Conservation" in this section).

**Supporting** — (See "Conservation" in this section).

**Teeth** — ♃ gives good teeth when strong and well-aspected at B. Also distorted teeth are attributed to his evil aspects. (See "Foreteeth" under Teeth).

**Temperament** — The Sanguine Temperament is given by ♃. (See Sanguine).

**Temperance**—(See Temperance; "Author Of" in this section).

**Therapeutic Qualities**—Therapeutic Properties of ♃ — Alexipharmic, Analeptic, Anthelmintic, Antispasmodic, Balsamic, Emollient. (See these subjects).

**Tonic Action Of**—(See Plethora).

**Transformation**—(See "Conservation" in this section).

**Typical Drugs** — Of Jupiter — Eupatorium, Ginseng, Iridin, Pepperment (Mentha), Stannum. (See "Jupiter Group" under Herbs).

**Warmth** — ♃ tends to warmth and moisture. (See "Cold and Dry" in this section).

— SECTION TWO —

**JUPITER RULES** — Governs—Dominates—See the following subjects in the alphabetical arrangement—Absorption; Adipose Tissue (see Adipose, Fat); Adrenals, Aluminum, Amniotic Fluid (see Foetus); Aphetic Process (see "Conservation" in Sec. 1 of this Article); Arms, Arteries, Arterial Blood and Circulation (see Arteries); Assimilation; Auricle, the Right Auricle of the Heart (see "Auricles" under Heart); Births, Normal Births; Blood, the Arterial Blood and Circulation, Blood Enrichment, Blood Making, the Fibrin of the Blood (see Blood, Fibrin, Haematopoiesis); Blue Color; Blue Flag (see Iridin); Bowels—Arteries of

— (see Bowels); Breath; Carbohydrates (see Hydrocarbonates); Cells—Cell Development, Cell Division, Cell Reproduction by Division, Storing of Cell Substance, Cellular Tissue Building, Cellulose (see Cells); Circulation—Of the Arterial Blood (see Arteries, Circulation); Clergymen; Colors (see "Colors" in Sec. 1 of this Article); Conservation of Energies and Tissues; Defensive Forces of the Body (see Defensive, Phagocytes); Devotion (see Religion); Digestive Organs and Functions (see Digestion); Domestic Pets; Duties; Ear—♃ in ♈ rules the Right Ear; Energy—Conservation of Energy; Eupatorium; Fat — Disposition of In the Body, the Fatty Constituents of Milk and other Fluids of the Body (see Fat); Father's Relatives; Feet; Fibrin of Blood; Filtration; Generosity; Genito-Urinary Organs — the Arteries and Veins of; Ginseng; Glycogen; God Fathers; Good Fortune; Green Color mixed with Red; Growth; Guardians; Haematopoiesis; Hams (see Thighs); Hands; Heart—♃ in ♌ rules the Arteries of the Heart (see Heart); Herbs of ♃ (see "Jupiter Group" under Herbs); Hydrocarbonates; Increase; Iridin; Journeys (Long Journeys); Legal Affairs; Legs (Arteries of); Life from 45 to 57 Years of Age (see Periods); Liver; Long Journeys (see Journeys); Lungs; Metal (Tin); Nutrition; Peppermint; Pets — Domestic Pets; Phagocytes; Pisces Sign; Plants (see "Jupiter Group" under Herbs); Pleura; Processes—(see "Conservation" in Sec. 1 of this Article); Purple Color (see Colors); Red Mixed with Green; Reins; Relatives of the Father (see Father); Religion; Reservation (see Cells); Ribs; Right Ear; Ritual; Sagittarius Sign; Sanguine Temperament (see Sanguine); Seed (see Seed, Semen); Selection (see Cells); Sides of the Body; Signs—♃ in Signs Rules (see "Signs" in Sec. 1 of this Article); Stannum; Starches; Stomach—Arteries of (see "Arteries" under Stomach); Storing Functions of the Body (see Conservation; "Storing" under Cells); Sugar In the Body (see Sugar, Sweets); Support of the Body (see "Conservation" in Sec. 1 of this Article); Suprarenal Capsules (see Adrenals); Sweets — Sweet Foods — Sweet Things In Merchandise (see Sugar, Sweets); Teeth; Thursday; Tin; Tissues—Conservation of (see Conservation); Transforming Functions In the Body (see Conservation, Transforming); Veins of the Genito-Urinary Organs (see Genito-Urinary); Violet Color In the Solar Spectrum (see Colors); Vis Conservatrix; Viscera; Wealth, etc.

— SECTION THREE —

THE DISEASES OF JUPITER — The most of the diseases of ♃ arise from indiscretions in eating or drink, causing indigestion, distempers, distentions, plethora, fullness, too much blood, corrupt blood, etc. No aspects of ♃ or ♀ cause disease, but only as configurated with malefics. Jupiter does not in himself cause any disease, but afflictions to ♃ affect the Blood, Lungs, Liver, and indirectly the Heart, as ♃ rules the Blood. Also afflictions to ♃ cause Apoplexy, Abscesses, Boils, Cramps, Pleurisy, etc. (See the Introduction, "Afflictions", "Aspects", "Directions", in Sec. 1 of this Article). The following diseases and conditions are attributed to the afflictions of ♃, and when this planet is ill-dignified at B., or afflicting the ☉, ☽, Asc., or Hyleg, and the various houses of the map of birth. See these subjects in the alphabetical arrangement when not more fully considered here—

**Abscesses; Adipose Tissue** Adiposis —Formation of Adipose Tissue In Excess—Adipose Sarcoma—(See Adipose, Fat, Sarcoma).

**Adrenals**—Suprarenals—Disorders of —(See Adrenals).

**Air** — Diseases from Superabundance of—Diseases from Corrupt Air—(See Air).

**Albumen**—Waste of, and Excess of In the Urine—Albuminuria—(See Albumen).

**Alterations**—In the Red Blood Particles, and in the Tissues—(See Alterations, Blood; "Alterations" under Cells; "Blood" under Red).

**Aneurysm; Apoplexy; Arms** — Disorders In—(See "Circulation", "Diseases Of", under Arms).

**Arteries** — Arterial Blood — Disorders of — (See Arteries; "Arterial Circulation" under Circulation).

**Assimilation**—Imperfect Assimilation —(See Assimilation).

**Back**—Disorders In—♃ afflicted in ♌. (See "Pains" under Back).

**Backbone**—Disorders In—(See Spine, Vertebrae).

**Bladder**—Stone In—Abscess In—(See Bladder, Stone).

**Blood**—Alterations In—Corrupt Blood —Determination of Blood to the Head —Discharges of Blood with Watery Humours—Disorders of the Blood, and especially the Arterial Blood—Fevers Due to Too Much Blood—Foul Blood—High Blood Pressure — Impure Blood and All Diseases Arising From—Low Blood Pressure — Blood Making, Disturbances of—Morbid Changes In the Blood — Obstructions from Too Much Blood—Changes In the Blood Particles; Poisoning of the Blood—Putrefaction In the Blood — Red Blood Particles, Changes In — Sugar In the Blood and Urine—Thin and Watery Blood — Too Much Blood, Fevers and Obstructions From—Urine, Sugar In—Blood Vessels, Fullness of—Watery and Thin Blood— (See the various paragraphs under Blood).

**Boils; Bowels** — (See Arteries, Circulation, Gripings, Spasm, under Bowels).

**Breast**—Cancer of—(See "Breast" under Carcinoma).

**Breathing** — (See Immoderate, Labored, Obstructed, under Breathing).

**Bronchitis**—(See Bronchial).

**Calculus** — (See "Stone" in this section).

**Cancer** — Carcinoma — Cancer of the Breast—Death by Cancer—Fatty, Lardaceous, and Waxy Cancer—Cancer of the Pancreas—(See Carcinoma).

**Carotid Arteries**—Fullness of—(See Carotid).

**Cellular Inflammation**—(See "Inflammation" under Cells).

**Cerebral Congestion** — (See "Brain" under Congestion).

**Changes**—In the Red Blood Particles —(See "Blood" under Red).

**Chest**—Tightness of—(See Chest).

**Choleric Distemper**—(See Choleric).

**Circulation**—Of the Blood—Disorders of—(See Arteries, Circulation).

**Clogging**—Of the System—(See Clogging).

**Cold and Dry Liver**—(See Liver).

**Colic; Congestions**—Cerebral Congestion — Congestion of the Blood — Congestion In the Lungs — (See Blood, Circulation, Congestion, Lungs).

**Consumption; Corpulence;**

**Corrupt Blood**—(See Impure).

**Cramps; Cysts**—In the Arms, Hands, Legs and Feet—(See the Introduction under Aneurysm).

**Death**—♃ causes death by Apoplexy, Cancers, Decayed System, Enlarged Heart, Foul Blood, Foul System, Heart Disorders (Enlarged Heart), Impure Blood, Inflammations, Inflammation of Lungs, Jaundice, Judge (By Sentence of), Liver Diseases, Lung Diseases, Morbid Deaths (♃ as Anareta In), Plethora, Quinsy, Spasms, Stomach (Foul Stomach), Surfeits, Swellings, Toxaemia, Tumors. (See these subjects).

**Decayed System**—♃ Causes Death By —(See Decay).

**Degeneration**—Fatty Degeneration of the Muscles of the Heart—(See Degeneration; "Fatty Degeneration" under Heart).

**Dental Maladies**—(See Teeth).

**Deposits** — Of Fat Over the Body — (See Fat).

**Determination of Blood**—To the Head — Rush of Blood to the Head — (See "Blood" under Head).

**Diabetes Mellitus**—(See Diabetes).

**Diathesis** — (See "Thoracic" in this section).

**Diet** — Improper Diet and Diseases Arising From—(See Diet).

**Digestive Disorders** — Defects In the Digestive Organs — (See Defect, Disorders, under Digestion; Indigestion).

**Distempers**—Choleric Distemper— Distempers In the Throat—(See Choleric, Distempers, Throat).

**Distentions**—(See Distentions, Flatulence, Fullness, Plethora).

**Dreams** — Strange Dreams — (See Dreams).

**Dropsy; Dry and Cold Liver** — (See Liver).

**Ear** — Affections of the Right Ear — (See "Right Ear" under Ears).

**Eating** — Excesses In — (See Diet, Drink, Eating, Excesses, Food, Gluttony, Indiscretions).

**Eczema; Enlargements** — (See Enlarged; "Enlarged" under Heart).

**Epidemics** — (See Epidemics; "Sun Spots" under Spots).

**Epistaxis** — (See "Epistaxis" under Nose).

**Excesses** — In Diet and Eating, and Diseases Proceeding From—(See "Eating" in this section).

**Face**—Swellings In—(See Face).

**Faintings; Fat** — Fatty Deposits In Excess Over the Body—Fatty Degeneration of the Heart and Muscles— Fatty, Sardaceous Cancer—(See Fat).

**Feet**—Cysts In—(See "Arms" in this section).

**Fever**—From Too Much Blood—(See "Too Much Blood" under Blood).

**Flatulence; Fluids** — The Accumulation of In the Different Parts of the Body—(See Accumulative, Fluids).

**Flying Pains**—(See Flying).

**Food** — Excesses and Indiscretions In the Use of—(See "Eating" in this section).

**Foul Blood** — Foul Stomach — (See Foul, Impure; "Foul" under Stomach).

**Fullness** — Of the Arteries and Blood Vessels—Of the System—(See Fullness, Plethora).

**Functions** — Over-Activity of — (See Functions).

**Habit**—The Plethoric Habit—Hyperaemia—(See Plethora).

**Hands** — Cysts In — Eczema In — (See Cysts, Eczema).

**Head** — Determination of Blood To — Rush of Blood To—Fullness of Veins of—(See "Blood" under Head).

**Heart**—Enlarged Heart and Death By —Fatty Degeneration of—Morbid Action of—Trembling of—(See Heart).

**Hemorrhoids; High Blood Pressure**— (See "Pressure" under Blood).

**High Living**—Diseases Arising From —(See "Living" under High).

**Hot and Moist Diseases** — (See "Hot and Moist" under Heat).

**Imaginations** — (See "Strange" under Imagination).

**Immoderate Breathing**—(See "Breathing" in this section).

**Impure**—Impure Blood and Death By —Impure Respiration—(See "Impure" under Breathing; Impure).

**Indigestion; Indiscretions**—In Diet— (See Eating, Injudicious, in this section).

**Inflammation** — Death by Inflammation—Inflammation of the Lungs—Inflammatory Process—(See "Bronchitis" under Bronchial; the Introduction under Inflammation; "Inflammation" under Lungs).

**Injudicious Diet**—Diseases Arising From—(See Injudicious; "Eating" in this section).

**Inward Parts**—Disorders of—(See Reins).

**Jaundice**—And Death By—(See Jaundice).

**Judges**—Sentenced to Prison or Death by a Judge, The Law—(See Judges).

**Kidneys** — Disorders of — Tumor of— (See Kidneys).

**Knees**—Pains and Swelling In—(See Knees).

**Lardaceous Cancer**—(See "Fatty" under Carcinoma).

**Lithiasis**—(See Calculus, Stone).

**Liver**—All Diseases In—Cold and Dry Liver—Congestion In—Death by Liver Diseases—Inflammation and Death By — Derangements and Infirmities In — Obstructions In and Torpid Liver — (See Liver).

**Localized Swellings** — (See Plethora, Swellings).

**Low Blood Pressure**—(See "Pressure" under Blood).

**Lumbago; Lungs** — Congestion In — Inflammation In, and Death By—Obstructions In—(See Lungs).

**Mammary Cancer**—(See "Breast" under Carcinoma).

**Many Diseases**—Due to Corrupt Blood, or Too Much Blood—(See "Many Diseases" under Complications, Diseases).

**Melancholy; Metal**—The Metal ruled by ♃ is Tin, or Stannum. The Pathological action of Tin is poisonous if absorbed in too large quantities. Albumen, Milk, and Oils, are antidotes for Tin Poisoning. (See "Pathological" in this section).

**Milk Glands** — Disturbances of — (See Breasts, Milk).

**Moist and Hot Diseases** — (See "Hot and Moist" under Heat).

**Morbid Conditions** — Morbid Changes In the Blood—Morbid Deaths—Morbid Growths—Morbid Action of the Heart —(See "Morbid" under Blood, Death, Growths, Heart).

**Muscles** — Fatty Degeneration of — (See Degeneration, Fat; "Degeneration" under Muscles).

**Neck**—Disorders of—(See Neck).

**Obstructions** — In the Liver, Lungs, and Throat—(See "Obstructions" under Liver, Lungs, Throat; Obstructions).

**Organs**—Enlargement of—Excessive Functional Activity — (See Enlargements; "Over-Activity" under Functions).

**Pains** — In the Backbone (Spine) — In the Bowels—Spasmodic Pains In the Bowels— Pains In the Head, Knees— Flying Pains — (See "Spasm" under Bowels; Flying; "Pain" under Head, Knees).

**Palpitation**—Trembling of the Heart —(See Heart).

**Pancreatic Cancer**—(See Pancreas).

**Pathological Action** — Of ♃ Herbs — Tend to have a pathological action on the heart muscle and the Pulmonary Parenchyma. (See "Drugs" under Heart; "Jupiter Group" under Herbs; "Metal" in this section).

**Piles**—(See Hemorrhoids).

**Plethora**— Plethoric Habit—Plethoric and Sthenic Distentions—(See Plethora).

**Pleurisy**—(See Pleura).

**Pneumonia; Poisoning**—Of the Blood —(See "Poisoning" under Blood).

**Potato-Like Cancer**—(See "Solanoid" under Carcinoma).

**Pressure**—High and Low Blood Pressure—(See "Pressure" under Blood).

**Process**—Thoracic and Inflammatory Process of the Tissues — (See Inflammation, Thorax).

**Putrefaction** — In the Blood — (See Blood, Putrefaction).

**Quinsy**—And Death By—(See Tonsils).

**Red Blood**—Changes In the Red Blood Particles — (See "Red Blood" under Blood; "Blood" under Red).

**Reins**—Inward Parts—Disorders of— (See Reins).

**Renal Calculi**—Stone In the Kidney— (See "Kidneys" under Stone).

**Respiration** — Disorders of — Immoderate and Impure Respiration — (See Breath).

**Ribs**—All Diseases Lying In the Ribs —(See Ribs).

**Rush of Blood**—To the Head—Flow of To—(See "Blood" under Head).

**Sarcoma** — Adipose Sarcoma — (See Sarcoma).

**Scrofula; Scurvy; Sentence of Judge** —And Death By—(See Judges).

**Short Diseases** — (See "Illnesses" under Short).

**Signs**—Diseases of ♃ in Signs—(See "Signs" in Sec. 1 of this Article).

**Solanoid Cancer**—(See Carcinoma).

**Spasmodic Pains** — In the Bowels — (See "Spasm" under Bowels).

**Spasms**—Death By—(See "Death" under Fits).

**Spine** — Backbone—Vertebrae—Pains In—(See "Pain" under Spine).

**Sthenic Plethora**—(See Plethora).

**Stomach** — Disorders of — Foul Stomach and Death By—Stomach Surfeits— Tumors of—(See Gastric, Stomach).

**Stone**—In the Bladder—In the Kidney —Renal Calculi—(See Stone).

**Strange Dreams**—And Imaginations— (See Dreams, Imagination).

**Strangury** — (See Strangury; "Micturition" under Urine).

**Sugar**—Waste of In the Body—Excess of In the Blood and Urine—(See Diabetes, Sugar; "Sugar" under Urine).

**Superabundance**—Of Air, and Diseases Arising From — Superabundance of Blood and Diseases Arising From — (See "Superabundance" under Air; "Too Much Blood" under Blood).

**Surfeits**—Death By—Diseases Arising From—(See Surfeits).

**Swellings** — Death By — Localized — Swellings In the Arms, Face, Feet, Knees, Legs, Throat—(See "Swellings" under these subjects; also see Plethora, Swellings).

**Swoonings**—(See Fainting).

**Thin Blood**—Thin and Watery—(See "Poor Blood" under Blood).

**Thoracic Diathesis**—Thoracic Process —(See Thorax).

**Throat**—Distempers In—Obstructions and Swellings In—(See Throat).

**Tightness**—Of the Chest—(See Chest).

**Tissues** — Alterations In — Inflammatory Process of—(See Alterations, Inflammation, Tissues).

**Too Much Blood** — (See "Too Much" under Blood).

**Torpid Liver**—(See Liver).

**Toxaemia**—And Death By—(See Toxaemia).

**Trembling**—Of the Heart—(See Heart).

**Tumors** — Death By — Tumor In the Kidneys — (See "Tumor" under Kidneys; "Death" under Tumors).

**Urine**—Urinary Disorders—Excess of Albumen or Sugar In—(See Albumen, Diabetes, Sugar, Urine).

**Vascular Fullness**—(See Vascular).

**Veins**—All Diseases Lying In—Fullness of the Veins In the Head—Disorders of the Veins of the Respiratory System — (See "Blood" under Head; Veins).

**Vertebrae**—Pains In—(See "Pain" under Spine).

**Vessels**—Fullness of Blood Vessels—(See "Dilatation" under Arteries; "Pressure", "Too Much Blood", under Blood; Distentions; Fullness, Plethora, Vascular, Vessels).

**Viscera**—Diseases of—(See Viscera).

**Vomiting; Waste** — Of Albumen and Sugar In the Body — (See Albumen, Diabetes, Sugar).

**Watery Blood**—Watery Humours with Discharges of Blood—(See "Poor" under Blood; "Humours" under Watery).

**Waxy Cancer** — (See "Fatty" under Carcinoma).

**JUSTICE**—Just—

**Death**—Death by the Hand of Justice—By The Law—(See Judges, Law).

**Fugitive**—The Fugitive from Justice Is Dead—(See Fugitive).

**Just Men** — Much Mortality Among — (See "Just Men" under Mortality; Noble; Nobles).

**Just Nature** — (See Honesty; "Good Morals" under Morals; Noble, Sincere).

**JUVENILITY**—Young Looking—Youthful—Well-Preserved—The ☉ hyleg, and ☌ or good aspect ♃. Venus keeps one youthful thru a placid, calm, joyful, and cheerful mind. The adverse influences of ♄ tend to age both mind and body, and this planet strong at B. tends to premature old age, and the contraction and drying up of the body. The ♊ Sign strong at B. tends to preserve the mental faculties to an extreme age, and to keep the mind young and buoyant. The influences of the ♐ Sign tend to preserve the freshness of youth even to an advanced age. (See Well-Preserved; "Youthfulness" under Youth).

# K

**KARMA** — Law of — (See "Ripe Fate" under Fate; Monsters; "Deaf and Dumb" under Hearing).

**KEEN**—Sharp—

**Keen Sight**—(See "Keen" under Eyes, Sight).

**Keen-Edged Tools**—Cuts and Injuries By — (See Cuts, Duels, Instruments, Sword).

**KEPLER**—The Great Astronomer. After his study of Astrology and the effects of the Planetary influences, he said—"A most unfailing experience of the excitement of sub-lunary natures by the conjunctions and aspects of the planets has instructed and compelled my unwilling belief." He believed in the influence of Comets over human affairs, and at the time of the appearance of a Comet predicted the rise and fall of Wallenstein. Kepler was born at Weil on Dec. 7th, 1571, and died Nov. 15th, 1630, at Regensberg.

**KERATITIS** — (See "Cornea" under Eyes).

**KICKS** — The Kicks of Animals — Thrusts—

**Kicks by Animals** — Thrusts — The ☽ to the ☌ or ill-asps. ♂ by dir.; ♂ afflicted in the 12th H., and usually attended with effusion of blood. (See "Hurts" under Animals; "Injury By" under Horses).

**Kicks by Horses** — ♄ or ♂ affl. in ♐; ♐ on the Asc. or 6th H., and afflicted. (See "Animals" under Bites; "Injury By" under Horses).

**Kicked by Husband**—Woman Kicked by Husband, Rendering Her Unfruitful — Case — See "Human Document", No. 929, in 1001 N.N.

**Kicks On Voyages** — Or In Travel — Malefics in fiery signs in the 3rd or 9th H., and affl. the ☉ or ☽. (See "Journeys" under Bites; "Kicks" under Voyages).

**KIDNAPPED** — A planet, or malefic, in the 12th H. at B., and afflicting the ☽; ♆ affl. in the 12th H.; the ☽ ☌ or ill-asp. ♆, and the ☽ otherwise afflicted by malefics at the time of the disappearance. The influence of ♆ is that of mystery, and also of treachery. (See Neptune, Plots, Seduction, Twelfth House).

**KIDNEYS** — The Renal System — Renal Nerves — Renal Circulation — Reins — The Kidneys are under the internal rule of the ♎ Sign. They are also ruled by ♀ and the 7th H. Libra rules the outer and upper part of the kidneys, the medullary and cortical substance, distillation, filtration, and the functional activity of secreting urine. The Distillatory Processes of the kidneys are under the joint rule of ♀ and ♎. (See Distillation, Filtration). The Medullary and Cortical substances are also under the rule of ♀. The renal papillae are ruled by ♀. Venus adds to or subtracts from the Renal Process, modifying the influence of the ☉ or ☽ over the kidneys. Being strongly under the influence of ♀, the kidneys play an important part in the nutrition of the body, as well as in the elimination of wastes. The ☉ and ☽ in ♎ act upon the Lumbar Ganglia, and also by acting thru the Renal Plexuses affect the Renal System, and give way to the Renal Diathesis. (See "Lumbar Ganglia" under Ganglion). The Circulation in the kidneys is ruled and controlled largely by ♅ acting thru the posterior lobe of the Pituitary Body. (See Pituitary). The ♏ Sign rules the under and lower portion of the kidneys, the Sinus, or Pelvis, and also indirectly affects the kidneys by ruling the bladder and urethra, thru which the elimination of urine takes place. Excretion in the kidneys is ruled by ♏. All of the fixed signs rule and affect the kidneys by planets in them, by their internal government. The cardinal signs also greatly influence the kidneys, and denote the kidneys, as they are in □ and ☍ aspect to ♎, and form the cardinal cross, of which ♎ is a part. Wilson, in his Dictionary of Astrology, also says that ♂ has rule over the kidneys, as ♂ rules the ♏ Sign. The ♂ Group of Herbs and Metals tend to have a pathological action on the kidneys, and Gentian, a ♂ remedy, is one of the principle ingredients in kidney medicines and diuretics. Mars is opposed to ♀ therapeutically, and ♂ remedies combat ♀ diseases. (See Opposites). The following subjects have to do with the Diseases, Disorders, and Afflictions of the Kidneys.

**Abscess of Kidneys**—Imposthumes—Pyonephrosis—A ♎ disease, and afflictions in ♎; the ☽ or ♃ affl. in ♎; Subs at KP. (See Abscesses).

**Action**—Of the Kidneys—(See Intermittent, Sluggish, Spasmodic, in this section).

**Acute Bright's Disease**—(See Bright's Disease; Inflammation, Nephritis, in this section).

**Affected**—The Kidneys Affected—(See the various paragraphs in this section; "Affected" under Reins).

**Albuminuria**—(See Albumen).

**All Diseases Of**—All Diseases In the Reins of the Kidneys—Signified by ♎ and the 7th H., and afflictions therein. Also ♂ diseases.

**Amyloid Kidneys**—♃ affl. in ♎; Subs at KP (11D).

**Anasarca**—(See Dropsy).

**Antinephritic**—A Remedy for Inflammation of the Kidneys—(See Antinephritic).

**Anuria**—(See "Suppression" under Urine).

**Back**—Disorders of—(See Back).

**Bladder**—(See "Abscess", "Ulcers", and the various paragraphs under Bladder).

**Brick Dust Deposit**—In Urine—(See Urine).

**Bright's Disease**—(See Bright's Disease; "Diseased", "Inflammation", "Nephritis", in this section).

**Calculus**—Renal Calculus—(See "Kidneys" under Stone).

**Cases**—Of Kidney Trouble—Birth Data, etc.—(See "Diseased Kidneys" in this section).

**Chronic Bright's Disease**—Chronic Kidney Trouble—♄ affl. in ♎. (See "Chronic" under Bright's Disease; "Nephritis" in this section).

**Circulation**—The Renal Circulation Disturbed—The ☽ in ♎, □ or ☍ ♃ or ♀; ♄ affl. in ♎; ♄ in ♎, ☌, □, or ☍ ♃ or ♀. The renal circulation is ruled and controlled largely by ♅ acting thru the posterior lobe of the Pituitary Body, which ♅ rules, and an afflicted ♅ may tend to disturb the renal circulation, and also produce various other incoordinations. (See Circulation).

**Cirrhosis**—Of the Kidneys—Thickening—♄ affl. in ♎, and especially in the 6th H.; ♄ ☌ ♀, and with ♃ also afflicting ♀ by □ or ☍; many afflictions in fixed signs, and with a fixed sign rising. (See Cirrhosis). Case of Cirrhosis of Kidney—See Case No. 4, Chap. XIII, page 93, in Daath's Medical Astrology.

**Colic**—Renal Colic—Nephritic—Calculus In Ureter—The Ureter Obstructed—♄ or ☿ affl. in ♎; ♄ affl. in ♎ or ♏; usually ♄ afflicted in the last degree of ♎; Subs at KP. Case—See Fig. 7D in the book, "Astro-Diagnosis", by the Heindels. (See Colic).

**Coma**—Uremic Coma—(See "Uremic" under Coma).

**Congestion**—Of the Kidneys—The ☉ affl. in ♉, from rich foods and gormandizing; ♀ affl. in ♈, by reflex action in ♎. (See Congestion).

**Death**—From Kidney Diseases—Afflictions in cardinal signs dispose to, and espec. ♄ in these signs and affl. the hyleg.

**Deranged Kidneys**—(See "Diseased", and the various paragraphs in this section).

**Desquamative Nephritis**—(See "Nephritis" in this section).

**Diabetes**—Diabetes Insipidus—Diabetes Mellitus—(See Diabetes).

**Diathesis**—The Renal Diathesis—(See "Lumbar Ganglia" under Ganglion).

**Diseased Kidneys**—Deranged Kidneys—Renal Affections—Kidney Trouble—Distempered Kidneys—Diseases of ♎ and the 7th H., and ♈ diseases by reflex action to ♎; ♎ on the Asc.; ♎ on the cusp the 6th H., and afflicted; afflictions in all the cardinal signs show, ♎ being included in the cardinal cross; cardinal signs on angles and containing malefics; the ☉ affl. in an airy sign, and espec. in ♎; the ☉ affl. in ♎, ♏, or ♓; the ☉ in ♌, ♎, ♏, or ♒, ☌ or ill-asp. any of the malefics as promittors; the ☉ ☌ ♄ in ♎, and in □ or ☍ ♆; the ☽ affl. in an airy sign; the ☽ affl. in ♎, or affl. the hyleg therefrom; the ☽ in ♉, and affl. by the ☉ or ♂ when taken ill (Hor'y); the ☽ in the 6th H., in cardinal signs, and affl. by ♂; the ☽ hyleg in ♎, and afflicted, and espec. with females; the ☽ in ♎ or ♑, ☌, or ill-asp. any of the malefics as promittors; the ☽ to the ☌ or ill-asp. ♂ by dir., and espec. if ♂ afflict the ☽ at B., or ♂ occupy the 6th H.; ♅ affl. in ♎; ♄ affl. in ♈ or ♎; ♄ in ♎ in an angle, and espec. in the Asc.; ♄ in ♎, ☌, □, or ☍ the ☉ or ☽; ♄ in ♎, occi., and affl. the

☉, ☽, or Asc.; ♄ in ♎, ☌ ☽; ♄ in ♎, ☌, □, or ☍ ♃; ♄, ♅, or ♆ in ♌, and affl. the ☉ or ☽; ♄ in ♎ when ♄ is the afflictor in the disease; ♄ affl. in the 6th H. in a mutable sign; ♄ or ♂ in ♎ tend to upset the kidneys; ♃ affl. in ♎, and espec. in the 6th H.; ♃ in ♎, and affl. the ☽ or Asc.; ♂ in ♎ when ♂ is the afflictor in the disease; ♂ in ♎, □ or ☍ ♄; caused by ♂ when the dominion of death is vested in him; ♂ in ♌ and affl. the hyleg; ♂ in ♉, ♌, or ♎, ☌, or ill-asp. the ☉; ♂ in the 6th H. in a cardinal sign; ♂ ☌ or ill-asp. ♀; ♀ diseases and afflictions; caused by afflictions to ♀; ♀ affl. in ♎; ♀ affl. in the Asc.; ♀ affl. in ♎ in the 6th H.; ♀ in ♎, and affl. the ☽ or Asc.; born under ♀ as ruler; ♀ in ♎, □ or ☍ ♄; ♀ is usually associated with ♄ in kidney diseases; ☿ in ♎, ♐, or ♓, ☌, or ill-asp. any of the malefics as promittors; ♎ on angles and afflicted; ♈, ♊, ♎, or ♒ on the Asc.; cardinal signs on the 6th H.; the malefics or afflicting planets in cardinal signs; many planets, or a Stellium, in ♎ or the 7th H.; Subs at KP (10, 11, 12D). Cases—Of Kidney Trouble—Birth Data, etc.—See Figures 5B, 6B, 6D, 7A, 7B, 7C, 7D, 7E, 7F, 7G, 7H, 18B, in "Astro-Diagnosis", by the Heindels; Figuers 3, 8, 21, 25, and 36, in "Message of the Stars", by the Heindels; "Marriage", No. 834, in 1001 N.N.; Chap. XIII in Daath's Medical Astrology. (See the various paragraphs in this section).

**Distempered Kidneys**—(See "Diseased Kidneys" in this section).

**Diuretics** — A Medicine to Act Upon the Kidneys and Increase the Flow of Urine—(See Diuretics).

**Dropsy**—Hydronephrosis—Dropsy of the Kidneys by Obstruction—Urine In the Pelvis of the Kidneys—♄ affl. in ♎; Subs at KP (11D). (See Dropsy).

**Dysuria**—(See "Strangury" under Urine).

**Elimination** — Faulty Elimination of Urine—Suppression of Urine—(See "Elimination" under Urine).

**Eruptions**—Skin Eruptions Due to Faulty Elimination of Urine, and Retention of Poisons—♄ affl. in ♎. (See Eruptions).

**Excretion**—Of Urine—Disorders of—(See "Excretion" under Urine).

**Faulty Secretion** — Of Urine — (See "Suppression" under Urine).

**Fevers**—From Kidney Diseases—♂ affl. in ♎; ♂ in ♎ and afflicting the ☽ or Asc.; ♂ in ♎ in the 6th H. (See Fever).

**Floating Kidney**—A ♀ disease, and caused by afflictions to ♀, and espec. ♀ affl. by ♄; ♅ affl. in ♎.

**Glands**—Of the Kidneys—Disorders of —(See "Kidneys" under Glands).

**Gravel**—(See Gravel).

**Hemorrhage**—In the Kidneys—♂ affl. in ♈ or ♎.

**Hydronephrosis** — (See "Dropsy" in this section).

**Imposthumes**—(See "Abscess" in this section).

**Inflammation**—Of the Kidneys—Nephritis—Inflamed Pelvis—A ♎ disease, and afflictions in ♎; ♎ on the Asc.; ♂ affl. in ♈ or ♎; ♂ in ♎ in the 6th H.; ♂ in ♎ and afflicting the ☽ or Asc. (See Bright's Disease; "Chronic", "Nephritis", in this section).

**Intermittent Action**—Irregular—Spasmodic—♅ affl. in ♎.

**Irritation Of**—♂ ☌ or ill-asp. ♀.

**Ischuria** — (See "Ischuria" under Urine).

**Kidney Trouble**—(See "Diseased Kidneys" and the various paragraphs in this section).

**Libra**—Diseases of—(See Libra).

**Lithiasis** — (See "Kidneys" under Stone).

**Loins**—(See the paragraphs and influences under Loins).

**Lower Part**—Of the Kidneys—Affected by planets in the 3rd face of ♎, and by Subs at KP (11, 12D).

**Lumbar Region** — Also ruled by ♎. (See Lumbar).

**Nephritis**—Inflammation of the Kidneys — Desquamative, Interstitial, or Parenchymatous Nephritis—Bright's Disease—May be Acute or Chronic—♂ in ♎ tends to acute forms, and ♄ in ♎ to chronic forms of nephritis; a ♎ disease, and afflictions in ♎, or ♎ on the Asc. or 6th H., and containing malefics; the ☉ badly aspected by ♃; the ☽ afflicted in a watery sign; ♃ □ or ☍ the ☉; ♀ badly aspected by ♄ or ♃; fixed signs prominent, and espec. ♌, ♏, and ♒; a fixed sign rising on the Asc.; Subs at KP (11D). (See Bright's Disease; Colic, Inflammation, Pyelitis, in this section).

**Nephrolithiasis**—(See "Kidneys" under Stone).

**Nephroptosis** — (See "Prolapsed" in this section).

**Nervous Disorders Of**—☿ affl. in ♈ or ♎.

**Neuralgia Of**—A ♎ disease; ☿ affl. in ♎. (See "Pain" in this section).

**Obstructions**—♄ affl. in ♎, and espec. when in the Asc. or 6th H.; ♃ or ☿ affl. in ♎; ♃ in ♎ in the 6th H., and afflicted, or afflicting the ☽ or Asc. (See Obstructions; Colic, Dropsy, Suppression, Stone, in this section).

**Operations On**—Avoid when the ☽ is in ♎. (See Operations).

**Over-Worked**—The Kidneys Overworked, and Elimination Retarded—♃ in ♎, ☌, □, or ☍ ♄. (See "Elimination" under Urine).

**Pain In**—The ☽ in ♉ and afflicted by the ☉ or ♂ when taken ill (Hor'y). (See Colic, Neuralgia, in this section).

**Parenchymatous Nephritis**—(See "Nephritis" in this section).

**Paroxysms**—Renal—☿ afflicted in ♎. (See Paroxysms, Spasmodic).

**Pathological Action**—On the Kidneys —The ♂ Group of Herbs has such action. (See "Mars Group" under Herbs; "Pathological Action" under Mars).

**Pelvis**—Of the Kidney—Inflammation of—Pyelitis—Urine In—(See Dropsy, Inflammation, Pyelitis, in this section).

**Polyuria** — Excessive Secretion of Urine—(See Diabetes; "Polyuria" under Urine).

**Prolapsed Kidney** — Nephroptosis — ♄ affl. in ♎; Subs at KP (11D).

**Ptosis Of**—(See "Prolapsed" in this section).

**Pyelitis**—Pyelonephritis—Inflammation of the Pelvis of the Kidney—♂ affl. in ♎; Subs at KP (11D). (See Inflammation, Nephritis, Pyelonephritis, in this section).

**Pyelonephritis**—Inflammation of the Kidney and Its Pelvis—(See "Pyelitis" in this section).

**Pyonephrosis** — Suppuration Within the Kidney—Pus In the Kidney—Abscess In—Inflammation In—Ulceration In—A ♎ disease, and afflictions in ♎; a ♄, ☿, and ♃ disease; ♄ ☌ ♃ in ♎, due to disturbed circulation; ♄ affl. in ♎, due to suppression of function, or obstructions; ♂ affl. in ♎, from inflammation; Subs at KP (11D). (See Abscesses, Inflammation, in this section).

**Reins**—Of the Kidneys—Disorders of —(See "All Diseases Of" in this section; Reins).

**Remedies**—Kidney Remedies—(See Antinephritic, Diuretics, and the Introduction to this Article).

**Renal**—Pertaining to the Kidneys— Renal Affections—Renal Calculi—Renal Circulation—Renal Colic—Renal Diathesis—Renal Hemorrhage—Renal Paroxysms—Renal Process—Renal Stones —(See the Introduction, and the various paragraphs in this Article).

**Retarded**—The Kidney Action Retarded—(See Elimination, Obstructions, Over-Worked, Retention, Stone, Suppression, in this section).

**Retention** — Of Urine — (See "Retention" under Urine).

**Sand**—In the Kidneys—(See Sand).

**Secretions**—Faulty Secretion of Urine —Excessive Secretion—Secretion Obstructed—(See Diabetes; Excess, Obstructions, Polyuria, Suppression, under Urine).

**Skin Diseases**—Due to Kidney Trouble —(See Eruptions, Pimples, Skin).

**Sluggish Kidney Action**—♄ or ♃ afflicted in ♎; ♄ ☌ ♃ in ♎. (See Sluggish).

**Spasmodic Action** — Irregular — Intermittent—The ☉ ☌ ♅ in ♎; ♅ affl. in ♎; ♅ in ♎, ☌, P., □, or ☍ ♂. (See Spasmodic).

**Spurious Ischuria** — (See "False Retention" under Urine).

**Stone**—Renal Calculus—(See Gravel, Sand; "Kidneys" under Stone).

**Stoppage**—Of the Urine—(See "Suppression" under Urine).

**Strangury** — (See "Strangury" under Urine).

**Sugar**—In the Urine—Waste of Sugar —(See Diabetes, Sugar; "Sugar" under Urine).

**Suppression**—Of Urine—(See "Suppression" under Urine).

**Suppuration**—In the Kidneys — (See "Pyronephrosis" in this section).

**Supra-Renals** — Adrenals — Disorders of—(See Adrenals).

**Thickening**—Of the Kidneys—(See "Cirrhosis" in this section).

**Tuberculosis Of**—Planets afflicted in ♎; the ☽ in ♎, □, or ☍ ♄ and ♂; ♄ afflicted in ♎; Subs at KP. (See Tuberculosis).

**Tumor**—Of the Kidneys—♃ affl. in ♎. Case—Died after an Operation for Tumor of the Kidney—See "Marriage", No. 834, in 1001 N.N. (See Tumors).

**Ulceration**—(See "Pyronephrosis" in this section).

**Upper Kidneys**—Afflictions in the first face of ♎ tend to disorders of; Subs at KP (10D).

**Uremia**—Uremic Coma—(See Coma, Uremia).

**Ureters**—Obstruction of—Colic In— Stone In—(See Colic, Obstructions, Stone, in this section; Ureters).

**Urethra**—Disorders of—(See Urethra).

**Uric Acid**—Excess of Over the System—Afflictions in ♎. (See Uric).

**Urine**—Retention of—Suppression of —(See "Suppression" under Urine).

**Wastes**—Deposit of Over the System Due to Disordered Kidneys—♄ affl. in ♎. (See Deposits, Poisons, Toxaemia, Wastes).

**Weak Kidneys**—Cardinal signs on the 6th H.; ♄ affl. in ♎. (See "Diseased", and the various paragraphs in this section).

**Weakest Part** — The Kidneys the Weakest Part, or Organs—The ☉ affl. in ♎, or ♎ on the Asc. at B.; ♄ affl. in ♎.

**KILL**—Killing—

**Primary Directions Kill**—(See "Primary Directions" under Directions).

**The Killing Planet**—(See Anareta).

**KILLED**—Danger of Being Killed— Meeting with a Violent End—See such subjects as Accidents, Ambushes, Animals, Assassination, Avalanches, Battle, Beasts, Bites, Blows, Buildings, Burns, Contests, Cuts, Death, Disputes, Duels, Earthquakes, Enemies, Electricity, Execution, Falls, Fire, Foreign Lands, Gunshot, Heat, Heights, Highwaymen, Homicide, Hurts, Injuries, Instruments, Journeys, Lightning, Liquids, Machinery, Mangled, Mobs, Murdered, Pirates, Poison, Prison, Quadrupeds, Railways, Robbers, Scalds, Sentence of Judge (see Judges); Stabs, Stings, Stones (Flying Stones); Storms, Sudden, Sword, Thieves, Travel, Treachery, Untimely Death (see Untimely); Violent Death (see Violent); Water (see Bathing, Drowning, Liquids, Scalds, Shipwreck, Voyages); Wild Animals (see Wild); Wind, Women (see Treachery, Women); Vehicles, Venomous, Volcanoes, Voyages, etc.

**KILLING**—

**Killing Directions** — (See "Primary Directions" under Directions).

**Killing Illnesses**—(See "Arguments for Death" under Death; Fatal; Malignant, Pernicious, Severe, etc.).

**Killing Planet**—Anareta—The Killing Planet is the one forming the most malevolent directions in a train of evil directions, and especially if it is the Anareta at birth, and severely afflicting the Hyleg. (See Anareta).

**KIND**—

**Kind of Death**—(See the various subjects listed under Death, Disease, Killed; "Nature of the Death" under Nature; "Death" under Quality, Species).

**Kind of Disease**—(See "Nature of the Disease" under Nature; Quality, Type).

**Kind Disposition**—Kind Face and Countenance—Warm-Hearted—♃ ruler, strong, and well-aspected at birth. (See Generous, Humane; "Obliging" under Manner; Promises, Smiling; "Even Temper" under Temper).

**KINDRED**—(See Brethren, Family, Relatives).

**KINETIC**—

**Kinetic Force**—Motor Power—Producing Motion—(See Energy, Motion).

**Kinetic Points**—Of the Planets in the Map—For Figure, Map, Case Record, and Explanations of the Static and Kinetic Points in the Nativity, see Daath's Medical Astrology, Chap. XII. (See "Kinetic" under Planets).

**KINGDOMS**—The Destruction of Kingdoms, etc.—Danger of—The appearance of a Comet in the Sign of the Zodiac ruling the Kingdom. (See Assassination; "Death of Great Men" under Great; "Death of Kings" under Kings; Misery, Nobles, Princes, Public, War).

**KINGS**—Queens—Princes—Monarchs—Rulers—Presidents—Great Men, etc.—Are ruled and denoted by the 10th H. Also the ♌ sign rules Kings. At Ingresses and Eclipses the conditions affecting the 10th H. should be especially noted and studied, as it is at such times that some calamity is apt to overtake a King, Kingdom, Nation, or Republic, according to the rulership of the Sign in which the Eclipse occurs. (See Comets, Eclipses, Ingresses, Kingdoms).

**Assassination**—Danger of—♄ ascending at B., and the ☉ to the ☌ or ill-asp. ♄ by dir.; ♄, ♃, or ♂ conjoined in ♓; ♄ ℞ in ♋ or ♌, and lord of the year at a Vernal Equinox; ♂ elevated above, and configurated with the ☉ at a Solar Ingress or an Eclipse; ♂ in ♓, lord of the year at the Vernal, and ori., presignifies the slaughter of Great Men. (See Assassination; "Death of Great Men" under Great; Nobles, President, Queens, Roman, Rulers).

**Bites To**—♄, ♂, and ♀ conjoined in ♏. (See "Adder" under Bites).

**Danger to Kings**—The ☉ in the 10th H., or ♌ on the M.C., and the ☉ affl. by ♄ or ♂ at a Solar Ingress or Vernal Equinox.

**Death of Some King**—Or Reigning Monarch—Danger of Untimely Death of—An Eclipse of the ☉ or ☽ in a fiery sign; an eclipse of the ☉ in ♌, ♍, or ♎, and in Countries ruled by the Sign falling under the central line and shadow of the eclipse; an eclipse of the ☉ or ☽ in ♌, as ♌ rules Kings, Princes, Rulers; an eclipse of the ☉ in the 2nd Decan. of ♈, the 1st Dec. of ♍, the 2nd Dec. of ♎, or the 3rd Dec. of ♑, and in a Country ruled by these Signs; ♌ on the 10th H. at a Vernal Equi., and the ☉ afflicted by the ☌, □, or ☍ ♂, and ♂ in the 8th H., or ruler of the 8th, or ♂ in ☌ or ☍ ♄; Comets appearing in ♌, ♑, or ♒; the ☽ to the □ or ☍ ☉ by dir., death of some King who may be under such a direction. (See Anarchists, Assassination, Famous; "Great Men" under Great; Monarchs, Nobles, President, Princes, Roman, etc.).

**Death by Wrath Of**—By Wrath of Kings, Princes, or Rulers—♂ just setting at B., ☍ the Asc., and ♃ bearing testimony to ♂, and ♃ afflicted at B.

**Dethroned and Murdered**—The ☉ to the ☌ ♂ by dir., murdered or poisoned, or death by treachery; ♂ afflicted at B., and to the ☌ the M.C.

**Diseases to Kings**—An eclipse of the ☽ in ♍; the 1st Decan. of ♍ on the Asc., diseases and infirmities to the King in Countries ruled by ♍.

**Injury To**—♃, ♂, ♀, and the ☽ conjoined in ♉; ♄, ♂, and ♀ conjoined in ♏, wounds to.

**King's Evil**—(See the next section after this one).

**Stings To**—Bites To—(See "Bites" in this section).

**War Amongst Kings**—Comets appearing in ♌.

**Wounds To**—(See "Injury" in this section).

**KING'S EVIL**—Scrofula—Struma—Scrofulous Tumors—(See Scrofula).

**KLEPTOMANIAC**—Light-Fingered—Having a Morbid Desire to Steal—♂ afflicted in ♊; ☿ Sig. in ♋; ☿ afflicted by ♂. (See Cheating, Criminal, Deceitful, Dishonest, Forgers, Gambling, Robbers, Thieves).

**KNAVISH**—A Knave—Trickster—Dishonest—Unprincipled—A Rogue—♄ ill-dignified at B. indicates a foul, nasty, slovenly knave; ♄ to the body or ill-asp. ☿ by dir. (See Conduct, Dishonesty, Habits, Mischief, Morals, Obscene, Unclean, etc.).

**KNEES**—Knee Joint—Knee Cap—Patella—The Knees are under the external and structural rulership of the ♑ Sign, and are also ruled by the 10th H., the house of ♑. In the lower limbs the knees correspond to the elbows, ruled by the opposite sign ♋. (See Elbows). The Knee Joint and the Knee Cap (Patella) are ruled by ♑. The Hebrew letter "Ayin" (GH) is connected with the ♑ sign, the sign which rules the knees. The ☉ and ☽ acting thru the ♑ sign, thru the connective tissues and the peripheral nerves, affect the knees, thighs, cutaneous system, the osseous and mucous systems, and give way to the Splenic Diathesis. (See Capricorn, Tenth H.).

**Accidents to Knees**—Hurts To—Injuries—Wounds—♅, ♄, or ♂ affl. in ♑; a ♑ affliction, and with afflictions in this sign; ♑ on the Asc., and containing malefics, and espec. when ♂ is afflicted in ♑ in the Asc.; ♂ afflicted in ♑ in the 6th H. These influences also tend to fractures of the knees. Saturn in ♑ tends to bruises and contusions in the knees, hurts, falls on the knees, blows to the knees, and also to some weakness, deformity, or permanent injury to the knees. (See "Accidents" under Knees).

**Affected**—The Knees Affected—Afflictions in ♑, or ♑ on the Asc.; affected by the cardinal signs, to which class ♑ belongs; affected when the ☉ is in ♉; the ☽ in ♈; ♅ in ♏; ♄ in ♎; ♃ in ♌, ♍, or ♐; ♀ in ♎ or ♒; ☿ in ♊. See Table 196 in Simmonite's Arcana. (See the various paragraphs in this section).

**All Diseases In**—Affected At the Knees—Signified by ♑ and the 10th H., and afflictions in them; a Stellium in the 10th H.; ♑ on the Asc. (See "Diseases In", and the various paragraphs in this section).

**Ankylosis**—Of the Knee Joint—♄ affl. in ♑, due to deposits; ♂ afflicted in ♑, or ☌ ☉ in ♑ in the Asc., due to excess of heat in the joint, and melting of the joint. (See Ankylosis).

**Blows To** — Contusions — Bruises — ♄ affl. in ♑; ♑ on the Asc.

**Bruises To**—Contusions—(See Accidents, Blows, in this section; Bruises).

**Bursitis**—(See Bursa).

**Capricorn**—(See "Capricorn Diseases" under Capricorn).

**Castor and Pollux**—Knee of—(See Castor).

**Chronic Trouble In**—In the Knee Joint—♄ affl. in ♑, and espec. when ♑ is on the Asc., M.C., or 6th H.

**Cold In**—Colds In—♄ affl. in ♑; ♀ affl. in ♒; ☿ affl. in ♋. (See Cold).

**Consumptive Pains In**—♄ in ♎ when ♄ is the afflictor in the disease. (See "Consumptive" under Thighs).

**Contusions**—(See Blows, Bruises, in this section.

**Cramps In**—♅ in ♑ or ♒. (See Cramps).

**Crooked Knees**—♑ on the Asc. (See Ill-Made, Knock-Knees, in this section).

**Cuts To**—♂ affl. in ♑; ♂ in ♑ in the Asc. (See "Accidents" in this section).

**Decayed Bone Cells**—(See "Knee Cap" in this section).

**Defects In** — ♄ or the ☽ affl. in ♑; ♑ on the Asc.

**Deformities In**—♅ or ♄ affl. in ♑; ♑ on the Asc.

**Diseases In**—Trouble with the Knees—The ☉ affl. in ♉ or ♑; the ☽ affl. in ♈ or ♑; signified by ♄ in ♎, ♏, or ♑; ♃ affl. in ♌, ♍, ♐, or ♑; ♂ affl. in ♌ or ♑; ♂ in ♑, ☌, or ill-asp. the ☉; ♀ affl. in ♋, ♑, or ♒; ♀ in ♑, and afflicting the ☽ or Asc.; ☿ affl. in ♊, ♋, ♑, or ♓; ♑ on the Asc.; Subs at LPP. (See the various paragraphs in this section).

**Falls On**—♄ or ♂ affl. in ♑, and espec. when in the Asc. (See "Accidents" in this section).

**Fractures**—Afflictions in ♑; ♄, ♅, or ♂ affl. in ♑. (See "Accidents" in this section).

**Gout In**—Gonagra—Goutish Humours Above the Knees—The ☽ affl. in ♑; ♂ in ♑ and affl. the hyleg; ♂ in ♑, ☌, or ill-asp. the ☉; ♄ or ♀ affl. in ♑; ☿ affl. in ♑, Gout in, or above the knees; ♑ on the Asc., and espec. if ♄ is also afflicted. (See Gout).

**Humours In**—Goutish Humours—(See "Gout" in this section).

**Hurts To** — (See "Accidents" in this section).

**Ill-Made** — Crooked — ♄ ascending at B.; ♑ on the Asc. (See "Knock-Knees" in this section; "Crooked Body" under Crooked; "Ill-Formed Body" under Ill; "Crooked Legs" under Legs).

**Inflammation In**—♂ in ♑; ♂ in ♑ in the Asc. or 6th H., and afflicted; ♂ in ♑ or ♒, and afflicting the ☽ or Asc. (See Bursitis, Gout, Joint, Lameness, Pain, Rheumatism, Swellings, Synovitis, in this section).

**Injuries To** — (See Accidents, Cuts, Fractures, in this section).

**Joint**—The Knee Joint—Diseases of—Bursitis—Synovitis—Inflammation of—♄ affl. in ♑ tends to chronic inflammation in the knee joint; ♄ and ♂ both in ♑, and afflicted, tend to painful affections in the knee joint and knees in general; ♂ affl. in ♑. (See Ankylosis, Bursitis, Inflammation, Synovitis, in this section).

**Knee Cap** — Patella — Decayed Bone Cells of — Slaughter's Disease — Fracture of—♄ affl. in ♑ tends espec. to a decayed and chronic ailment in the Patella, and also to possible fracture of by blows, falls, accident, etc.; ♂ affl. in ♑, to fracture of by injury, accident. (See "Accidents" in this section).

**Knee Jerk**—Absence of—A ♄ disease; ♄ affl. in ♌ or ♎. This affliction is usually present in cases of paralysis of the legs, and in Tabes Dorsalis, or Locomotor Ataxia. (See Locomotor Ataxia).

**Knee Joint**—(See "Joint" in this section).

**Knock-Knees**—Overlapping of the Knees—A ♄ affliction; ♄ ascending at B.; ♄ in ♑ in the 6th H.; the ☉ or ♄ in ♑; ♑ on the Asc. In Hor'y Q. ♄ as Sig. indicates a person knock-kneed, bow-legged, or one who knocks the knees or ankles together, or who shuffles in his gait. (See Gait; "Bow-Legged" under Legs; Crooked, Defects, Ill-Made, in this section).

**Lameness In**—Lameness In or About the Knees—The ☉ affl. in ♑; the ☉ in ♑, ☌, or ill-asp. any of the malefics as promittors; ♄ or ♂ affl. in ♑; ☿ affl. in ♋, lameness from colds, or cold in the knees. (See "Lameness" under Legs).

**Legs** — (See the various paragraphs under Legs).

**Limbs**—(See the subjects and references under Limbs).

**Lower Extremities**—(See Lower).

**Mark or Mole** — On the Knee — ♑ on the Asc., and a malefic therein. (See Marks, Moles).

**Operations On**—Avoid when the ☽ is passing thru ♑. (See Operations).

**Overlapping Knees** — (See "Knock-Knees" in this section).

**Pains In**—The ☽ affl. in ♈, or afflicting the hyleg therefrom; the ☽ in ♎, ☌, or ill-asp. ♄ (or ☿ if he be of the nature of ♄) at the beginning of an illness or at decumbiture (Hor'y): ♆, ♅, or ♄ in ♎, and affl. the ☉ or ☽; ♂ in ♌, ☌, or ill-asp. the ☉, and caused thru the spinal nerve; ♂ affl. in ♑ in the 6th H.; ♃ affl. in ♐; ♀ affl. in ♒, pain and swellings in the knees from a cold cause; ☿ in ♑, ☌, or ill-asp. any of the malefics as promittors. (See Consumptive, Gout, Inflammation, Joint, Rheumatism, Swellings, in this section).

**Patella**—(See "Knee Cap" in this section).

**Pollux**—Knee of—(See Castor).

**Rheumatism In**—♄ affl. in ♑; ♂ affl. in ♑ in the 6th H.; ☿ affl. in ♑; ♑ on the Asc. (See Gout, Inflammation, Joint, in this section).

**Rickety Knees** — Weak or Wobbly Knees—♑ on the Asc. (See "Weak" in this section).

**Saturn** — (See the influences under Saturn).

**Scars On**—♂ affl. in ♑; ♂ in ♑ in the Asc. or 6th H. (See Scars; "Marks" in this section).

**Slaughter's Disease**—(See "Knee Cap" in this section).

**Stiff Knee**—(See Ankylosis, Gout, Inflammation, Joint, in this section).

**Strains In** — A ♑ disease, and afflictions in ♑; ♄ or ♂ affl. in ♑.

**Strike Together**—(See "Knock-Knees" in this section).

**Swellings In**—♄ or ♂ affl. in ♑; ♃ affl. in ♐; ♀ affl. in ♒, from a cold cause or an afflicted heart. (See Gout, Inflammation, Joint, Pain, in this section).

**Synovitis**—♂ affl. in ♑. (See Synovial; Bursitis, Inflammation, Joint, Pain, in this section).

**Tenth House** — Rulerships and Influences of—(See Tenth).

**Tumors In**—The ☉ afflicted in ♉ when the ☉ is the afflictor in the disease. (See Tumors; "Affected" in this section).

**Weak Knees**—Weakness In—A ♑ influence, and afflictions in ♑, or ♑ on the Asc.; the ☉, ☽, ♄, or ♂ affl. in ♑; the ☽ Sig. in ♑; ♄ ☌ ♂ in ♑; ♄ affl. in ♑ in the 6th H.

**Wounds To**—(See Accidents, Cuts, in this section).

**KNIFE WOUNDS**—Caused by ♂ afflictions. (See Cuts, Incised, Instruments, Stabs).

**KNOCKING** — Knock—(See "Knocking" under Ankles; "Knock-Knees" under Knees).

**KNOTS** — In the Fundament — ♂ in an angle occi. of the ☉, and ori. of the ☽. (See Fundament). For Knotted Veins see Varicose.

**KNOWLEDGE**—Learning—

**Acquires Knowledge Easily** — Has Depth of Mind — ☿ in ♊, ♍, or ♒, and well-aspected by the ☽, or in good relation to the Asc.; ☿ Sig. in ♎; ☿ Sig. ☌, ✱, or △ the ☽; ♃ in good asp. to ☿; ♃ Sig. in ♊; ♃ Sig. ☌ ☽; ♂ Sig. ☌ ☿, has considerable mental ability; ♂ Sig. ✱ or △ the ☉, a great mind. (See "Active Mind" under Active; Learning; "Quickened" under Mentality; "Sound", "Strong", under Mind; Reading, Scholar, Study).

**Little Desire for Knowledge**—Of Dull Mental Capacity—(See Dull, Idle, Inactive, Inertia; "Void Of" under Learning; "Arrested Mentality", "Shallow", under Mentality; "Weak Mind" under Mind; Pretender; "Void Degrees" under Void).

**KNUCKLES**—Joints of the Phalanges—(See Fingers, Toes).

**KYPHOSIS**—Humpback—Angular Curvature of the Spine—(See "Humpback" under Spine).

# L

**LABOR**—

**Childbirth**—Parturition—(See Parturition).

**Labor**—Labour—Work—Fear of Work—Hating Work—Ergophobia—The influences which tend to Fear of Work, or Ergophobia, are the ☉ Sig. in ♋; the ☽ ill-dignified at B. (See Dull, Idle, Inertia, Lassitude, Lazy, Lethargy, Rouse).

**Labored** — Labored Breathing — (See "Labored" under Breath).

**Laborious** — Plodding — Tends to a Laborious and Plodding Life—♄ strong at B., as in the Asc. or M.C.; ♄ in any aspect to ☿; ☿ combust, well-fitted for any kind of plodding business, but with little ability for Science or the Higher Learning.

**LACERATIONS** — Tears — Rending — Rupture of Tissues—The Bursting and Rending of Parts—Caused by the tonic action of ♅, and by ♂ in ☌ or ill-asp. ♅. (See Bursting, Cuts; "Exaggerated Action" under Exaggerated; Hernia, Rupture).

**LACHRYMAL**—The Lachrymal Apparatus—Pertaining to the Tears—(See Tears).

**LACING** — Tight Lacing, and Diseases From—♀ afflicted in ♉, ♊, or ♋; ♀ affl. in ♌ in the 6th H., or afflicting the ☽ or Asc., and tends to palpitation of the heart. (See "Indiscretions" under Dress; "Palpitation" under Heart; Tight).

**LACK OF** — Deficiencies — Diminished — Insufficient—Void of, etc.—Any part or organ of the body is subject under the afflictions of the planets to a lack of secretion, or to have its functions disturbed, and the afflictions of the planet ♄ have much to do with these disturbances. It would take too much space here in this Article to list all these conditions, and you are asked to look in the alphabetical arrangement for the subject you have in mind. Many of these conditions are listed and considered under such subjects as Defects, Deficient, Diminished, Insufficient, Loss Of, Missing, Void Of, etc. See these subjects. Some of the more abstract subjects along this line are listed here, or which the student may overlook.

**Adrenal Secretion** — Lack of — (See Adrenals).

**Animal Heat**—Lack of In Early Years—(See "Animal Heat" under Heat).

**Circulation**—Lack of Circulation In a Part — (See "Deficiency" under Circulation).

**Cohesion**—Lack of Cohesion of Parts—(See Cohesion).

**Energy**—Lack of—(See "Lack Of" under Energy).

**Feeling** — Want of — (See Apathy, Cruel, Feeling, Feelings).

**Firmness** — Lack of Firmness, Courage, Decision, Resolution, etc. — (See Fears, Negative; "Lacking" under Resolution; "Weak Will" under Will).

**Fluids** — Lack of In the Body — (See "Lack Of" under Fluids).

**Gastric Juice**—Lack of—(See "Stomach Juices" under Deficient; Gastric).

**Health**—Lack of Good Health—(See "Bad Health" under Health; Invalids, Sickly; "Much Sickness" under Sickness).

**Heat** — Lack of Animal Heat — (See "Animal Heat" under Heat).

**Men**—Lack of Firmness and Resolution In—(See Effeminate; "Resolution" under Men).

**Mental Power** — Lack of — (See Dull, Feeble, Idiocy, Imbecile; "Weak Mind" under Mind).

**Moisture** — Diseases Arising from a Lack of Sufficient Moisture In the Body—(See "Dry Body" under Dry; "Excessive Bodily Heat" under Heat; Moisture).

**Moral Balance**—Lack of—(See "Balance", and the various paragraphs under Morals).

**Muscles**—Lack of Control of—Muscular Power Weak—(See Muscles).

**Nerve Force**—Lack of—(See "Nerve Force" under Nerves; "Force" under Vital).

**Passion**—Lack of—(See Apathy, Aversions, Celibacy, Deviations; "Free from Passion" under Passion; Perversions).

**Resolution** — Lack of — (See "Firmness" in this section).

**Sports**—Want of Care In—(See Exercise, Sports).

**Tone**—Lack of—(See Atonic, Debility, Feeble, Sickly, Stamina, Tone, Vitality; "Weak Body" under Weak).

**Vital Fluid**—Lack of—(See Vital).

**Vitality**—Lack of—(See Vitality).

**Void Of**—(See Void).

**Will Power** — Lack of — (See "Firmness" in this section; Will).

**LACTATION** — Lacteals — The Milk — Mammary Glands—(See Milk).

**LADY**—Death of a Prominent and Eminent Lady—An eclipse of the ☉ in the 3rd Decan. of ♈; the appearance of a comet in ♒. (See Queens).

**LA GRIPPE** — Influenza — This disease usually travels around the world once in about every fifteen years when ♃ is in his perihelion, and ♂ in perigee at the same time. The disease may also travel around the world once or twice in a year or two until ♃, or some other planet, gets out of perihelion. It is caused by disturbed and vitiated atmospheric conditions, and is more prevalent when the major planets, and especially ♄ or ♃, are in perihelion, and these same influences also tend to cause Typhus Fever. (See Colds, Epidemics, Influenza, Pestilence, Typhus).

**LAKES**—(See Rivers, Sea).

**LAMENESS**—Limping—Impediments In the Gait or Walk — Crippled In the Limbs—Certain Degrees of the Zodiac, known as the Azimene or Mutilated Degrees, when rising on the Asc. at B., or the ☽ in, or ruler of the Asc. in, cause lameness. (See Azimene, Mutilated). If the malefics are in angles ☌ or ☍ the Lights, and the ☽ in her node in a hurtful sign, as in ♈, ♉, ♎, ♏, or ♑, the native will be lame or distorted. The defect will be from birth if the malefics are joined to the Lights, but if in ☍ to them, or if they have a □ to them from the 10th H., it will be by falls, blows, or stabs. Caused by the □ or ☍ aspects of the ☽; ♄ and ♂ joined anywhere in the map, and especially in angles, or in their own nodes, or in the Lunar nodes, tend to. Lameness is also caused by afflictions, or the malefics, in the signs which rule the legs, as in ♐, ♑, ♒, or ♓, or when these signs are on the Asc. at B., and afflicted; a ♐, ♑, ♒, and ♓ disease; ♄ in one of the signs which rule the legs, knees, ankles, or feet, and also where ☿, ♊, and the 3rd H. are also involved by afflictions at the same time, is a very common indication of this disability; afflictions to ♊, the 3rd H., to ♐ and the 9th H., and where ☿ is also afflicted, tend to lameness; ☿ affl. in ♑. (See the various paragraphs in this section).

**Accidents**—Lameness Resulting From — (See Fractures; "Injuries" under Ankles, Arms, Extremities, Feet, Hands, Knees, Legs, Limbs, Lower, Thighs).

**Action**—Of the Body—(See the various paragraphs under Action, Motion, Movement).

**Ankles**—Lameness In—(See Ankles).

**Ankylosis**—Stiff Joint—Lameness By—(See Ankylosis).

**Arms**—Lameness In—(See Arms).

**Atrophy** — Lameness By — (See Atrophy).

**Azimene Degrees**—The Lame Degrees—(See Azimene, Mutilated).

**Birth**—Lame from Birth—Born Lame — Distortions from Birth — Ptolemy gives a number of influences under this heading, which are listed in this book under "Distortions", and "Excrescences". Also see Congenital, Deformities, Malformations. Case—Born Lame—See "Arundel", No. 159, in 1001 N.N.

**Blows**—Lameness By—(See "Causes" under Distortions; the Introduction to this Article).

**Born Lame**—(See "Birth" in this section).

**Burns**—Lameness By—♂ afflicted in signs which rule the limbs. (See Burns).

**Case** — Born Lame — (See "Birth" in this section).

**Club Feet**—(See Feet).

**Colds**—Lameness From—(See "Lameness" under Colds).

**Congenital Lameness**—(See Congenital; "Birth" in this section).

**Coordination**—Lameness Due to Lack of—(See Coordination, Incoordination).

**Crystallization**—Lameness Due To—(See Ankylosis, Crystallization, Deposits. Hardening, Joints, etc.).

**Cuts**—Lameness From—(See "Lameness" under Cuts).

**Defects**—Lameness Due To—(See Defects, Missing).

**Deficiencies**—(See Deficient).

**Deformities**—(See Deformities).

**Degrees**—The Lame Degrees of the Zodiac — (See Azimene, Mutilated; "Signs" in this section).

**Disabilities**—(See "Bodily" under Disabilities).

**Disablements**—(See Disabilities).

**Distortions**—(See "Causes" under Distortions).

**Excrescences**—Lameness By—(See Excrescences).

**Falls from Heights**—Lameness By—(See Distortions, Excrescences, Heights).

**Feet**—Lameness In—(See Feet).

**Fractures**—Lameness By—(See Fractures).

**Gait**—Walk—(See the various paragraphs under Gait, Walk).

**Gout**—Lameness By—(See Gout).

**Hands**—Lameness In—(See "Lameness" under Hands).

**Hardening** — Lameness By — (See "Crystallization" in this section).

**Heights**—Falls from, and Resulting In Lameness—Falls from High Places —(See "Falls" in this section).

**High Places** — Falls From — (See "Falls" in this section).

**Hips**—Lameness In—(See "Lameness" under Hips).

**Hurtful Signs**—Planets and afflictions in them at B. tend to lameness and distortions. (See the Introduction to this Article; Distortions; "Hurtful Signs" under Hurtful).

**Impediments** — (See Hindrances, Impediments, Limitations).

**Imperfections**—(See Defects, Impairments, Imperfections).

**Incised Wounds** — Lameness From— (See Cuts, Incised).

**Incoordination**—Lameness By — (See Coordination, Incoordination, Paralysis).

**Injuries**—Lameness By—(See Accidents, Blows, Cuts, Hurts, Injuries, Wounds; the various paragraphs in this section).

**Knees**—Lameness In—(See Knees).

**Legs**—Lameness In—(See Ankles, Calves, Knees, Legs, Thighs).

**Limbs**—Lameness In—(See Arms, Extremities, Legs, Limbs, Lower).

**Locomotion**—Disorders of—(See Gait, Locomotion, Motion, Movement, Walk).

**Malformations**—(See Deformities, Malformations, Missing, Monsters).

**Missing**—Limbs Missing—Congenital Deformities—(See Missing).

**Monsters**—Monstrosities—(See Monsters).

**Motion** — Disturbances In Motion— (See Action, Motion, Movement).

**Movement**—Disturbances of—Lameness From—(See Action, Gait, Locomotion, Motion, Movement, Walk, etc.).

**Mutilated Degrees**—Planets in them at B. tend to Lameness. (See Azimene; "Broken Signs" under Broken; "Degrees" under Mutilated).

**Paralysis**—Lameness From—(See Paralysis).

**Prenatal Epoch** — Lameness Due to Prenatal Conditions — Congenital Defects—Born Lame, etc.—(See "Birth" in this section; Congenital, Prenatal).

**Quadrupeds**—Lameness Due to Injuries By—(See Distortions, Quadrupeds).

**Rheumatism**—Lameness From — (See Rheumatism).

**Robbers**—Lameness from Injuries By —(See Distortions, Robbers).

**Shipwreck**—Lameness from Injury In —(See Distortions, Shipwreck).

**Shoulders**—Lameness In—(See Shoulders).

**Signs**—Of the Zodiac—The Broken Signs—Imperfect Signs—Planets in them at B. tend to Lameness. (See "Broken Signs" under Broken; "Signs" under Imperfect; "Degrees" in this section).

**Stabs**—Lameness From—(See the Introduction to this Article; Cuts, Stabs).

**Thighs**—Lameness In—(See Thighs).

**Walk**—A Lame Walk—(See Gait, Walk).

**Wounds**—Lameness Due To—(See "Injuries", and the various paragraphs in this section).

**LAMENTATIONS**—Lamenting—(See Complaining, Exhibition, Grief, Murmuring; "Lamentations" under Public; Satire).

**LAND**—Journeys by Land—(See "Land" under Journeys).

**Landed Interests**—(See Property, Riches).

**Landslides**—Death or Injury By— Caused by ♄ afflictions at B., and by dir., and with ♄ affl. the hyleg. (See Avalanches; "Buried Alive" under Burial; Crushed, Earthquakes).

**LANGUAGE**—(See Speech).

**LANGUID**—Languor—Languishing— (See Apathy, Dull, Idle, Inactive, Inertia, Lassitude, Lazy, Lethargy, Listless, Weak, etc.).

**Languid Eyes**—(See "Dull Eyes" under Eyes).

**Languishing**—The ☽ to the ☌ or ill-asp. ♄ by dir.; the 3rd Decan. of ♍ on the Asc., ruled by ♄. (See Apathy, Dull, Fading, Feeble, Invalids, Lassitude, Lethargy, Sickly, Weak, etc.).

**LANK**—Thin—Lean—Spare.

**Lank Body**—(See "Thin Body" under Thin).

**Lank Hair**—(See "Lank" under Hair).

**LAPSING**—A Falling Away—

**Moral Lapsing**—Diseases Arising From—♆ diseases, and caused by afflictions of ♆ to the ☉, ☽, ♀. (See Excesses, Morals).

**LARDACEOUS**—Fatty—Waxy—(See "Fatty Cancer" under Carcinoma; Fat).

**LARGE**—Big—Great—

**Abdomen**—Large and Prominent—(See Abdomen).

**Animals**—Large Animals—Hurts, Injury, or Death By—(See Animals, Beasts, Elephants; "Great Beasts" under Great; Horses, Quadrupeds).

**Birth**—Large at Birth—Case—See "Short Life", No. 371 in 1001 N.N.

**Body**—Large Body—Large Stature—Of Full Size—Large Frame—Large Limbs and Joints—Cold climates and the Arctic Regions tend to. Many planets matutine, or strong in the Asc., in signs of dignity, or conspicuous; a tall sign on the Asc., and many planets rising just before the dawn; the Quadrant from the Asc. to the Nadir tends to produce a large, strong and healthy body; ♌, ♍, and ♐ tend to enlarge the body; the influence of the Constellations not of human form, both within and without the Zodiac, tend to enlarge the body, diminish its size, increase or diminish its strength. In Hor'y Q. the party is of large body and stature if the Sig. be ori., and in ♌, ♍, or ♐. The ☉ strong at B., and dignified, usually presents a person of good, strong, tall, fleshy, large frame and corporature; the ☉ gives a large, strong and bony body; the ☉ Sig. in ♌; the ☉ rising at B.; the ☽ Sig. in ♌; the ☽ gives a full-sized person, and with full stature; ♄ in ♐ or ♒ in partile asp. the Asc.; ♄ Sig. in ♐ in Hor'y Q.; ♃ in ♊, ♌, ♍, ♎, or ♐; ♃ in an airy sign, and rising, large and strong body; ♃ in ♍ in partile asp. the Asc., a full-sized person; ♃ as Sig. in Hor'y Q. denotes a person of a large make; ♃ as Sig. in earthy signs in Hor'y Q. denotes a large body; ♃ in the Asc., or a ♃ sign on the Asc., tends to add to the bulk of the body, and also to increase the vitality; ♂ ascending at B.; ♂ when close to the horizon tends to give a larger body than that indicated by the rising sign; ♂ Sig. in ♌; ♂ in ♌ in partile asp. the Asc., large, tall, and strong body; ♀ Sig. in ♒; ☿ in ♌, partile the Asc.; ☿ Sig. in ♌, a large, full body; ♈ on the Asc. gives a large, strong, and bony body. (See Commanding, Corpulent, Enlarged; "Fat Body" under Fat; Fleshy, Full, Giants, Growth; "Large" under Limbs; "Body" under Strong; Tall, etc.).

**Bones**—Large-Boned—The ☽ Sig. in ♌; ♄ Sig. in ♌ in Hor'y Q; ♂ Sig. in ♈; Martialists have large bones; born under the strong rule of ♂ and ♂ ruler; ☿ Sig. in ♐; ♈ gives, and espec. when on the Asc., and with the ☉ in ♈. (See "Large" under Bones; "Body" in this section).

**Cattle**—Large Cattle—Hurts, Injuries, or Death By—The ☉ to the ☌ ♂ by dir.; the ☽ affl. at B., and to the ☌ the cusp the 12th H. by dir.; malefics in the 12th H. (See Cattle; "Injury By" under Horses).

**Chest**—Large Chest—(See Chest).

**Ears**—Large Ears—(See Ears).

**Eyes**—Large Eyes—(See Eyes).

**Face**—Large Face—Big Face—(See Face).

**Family**—Large Family—(See "Many" under Children; Family, Fruitful, Husband, Wife).

**Feet**—Large Feet—(See Feet).

**Forehead**—(See "Large" under Forehead).

**Hands**—(See "Large" under Hands).

**Head**—A Large Head—(See Head).

**Hips**—Large Hips—(See "Strong" under Hips).

**Intestines**—The Large Intestines—(See Bowels).

**Joints**—Large Joints—(See Joints; Body, Bones, in this section).

**Legs**—Large Legs—(See Legs).

**Lips**—(See "Thick" under Lips).

**Moderately Large**—In Size—(See Mean, Medium, Middle, Moderate, Moderately).

**Mouth**—Large Mouth—(See Lips, Mouth).

**Muscles**—(See "Large" under Muscles).

**Nose**—(See "Large" under Nose).

**Shoulders**—(See Broad, Large, under Shoulders).

**Size**—Large Size—(See Fat, Giants, Tall; "Bones" in this section).

**Stout and Large**—Oriental planets in their first orientality cause large and stout bodies. (See Corpulent, Fat, Fleshy, Stout).

**Strong and Large**—♌ gives; ♌ on the Asc.; the ☽ or ♃ in ♌ in partile asp. the Asc., and also to give a tall body. (See Strong; "Bones" in this section).

**Strong, Large and Tall**—(See "Strong and Large" in this section; Tall).

**Tall, Large and Strong**—(See "Strong and Large" in this section; Strong, Tall).

**Upper Parts of Body**—Upper Parts Large—(See "Body" under Upper).

**LARVAL STATE**—(See Hydatid).

**LARYNX**—Organ of Voice—The Vocal Organ and Containing the Vocal Cords—The Upper Part of the Windpipe—Under the internal rulership of the ♉ sign. Also ruled by ☿. Also ruled and affected by the ♏ sign by reflex action, as ♉ and ♏ are opposite and complementary signs. The Laryngeal Plexus is ruled by the ♉ sign. It is said the Larynx was taken from ♏, and built by taking from the sex force. The earliest types of humanity did not have a larynx. The origin of the Larynx is quite thoroughly discussed in the book, "Cosmo-Conception", by Max Heindel. The Larynx being so closely connected with the sex nature is the reason the voice changes at puberty, and especially in the male. Sex abuses in either sex change the voice, and affect the larynx and vocal cords. (See Effeminate, Voice). The air which stirs the vocal cords into action is ruled by

♉, and ☿ well-placed in a sign of Voice, and well-aspected by benefics, gives good voice expression, and even though ♉ is afflicted, and throat trouble exists.

**Aphasia**—Loss of Speech—(See "Aphasia" under Speech).

**Aphonia**—Whispering Voice—(See "Aphonia" under Voice).

**Castration**—The Larynx and Vocal Organs Affected By—(See Castration).

**Catarrh Of**—♄ affl. in ♉; Subs at LCP and SP. (See Catarrh).

**Consumption**—Of the Larynx—Phthisis of—Laryngeal Consumption—♅ ☌ ♄ in ♉ in the 8th H., and affl. the hyleg, and possible death from this disease.

**Cords**—The Vocal Cords—Disorders of —(See Vocal).

**Croup**—(See Croup; "Laryngitis" in this section).

**Diseases Of**—Laryngeal Affections— —♄ in ♉, occi., and affl. the ☉, ☽, or Asc. (See the various paragraphs in this section).

**Dysphonia**—Difficulty In Phonation—(See "Hoarseness" in this section; Speech; "Aphonia" under Voice).

**Dyspnoea**—(See Croup, Dyspnoea).

**Expression**—Difficulties In Speech—(See Expression, Speech, Voice).

**Functional Disorders**—Afflictions to ☿.

**Glottis**—Disorders of—(See Glottis).

**Hoarseness** — Dysphonia —Harshness of Voice from Disease In the Larynx—The ☉ affl. in ♋; the ☽ in ♉ and affl. by the ☉ or ♂ when taken ill (Hor'y); the ☽ in ♋ or ♎, ☌, or ill-asp. ♄ (or ☿ if he be of the nature of ♄) at the beginning of an illness, or at decumb., and if the ☽ be decreasing, or near the body of ♄, the disease may continue for a long time (Hor'y); ♄ affl. in ♉, due to an obstructed throat; ♄ affl. in ♏; a ☿ disease, and caused by afflictions to ☿ at B., and by dir.; ☿ affl. in ♉ or ♏; ☿ in ♉, ☌, or ill-asp. any of the malefics as promittors; afflictions in ♉ or ♏; many planets in ♉ or ♏, and in fixed signs; ♉ or ♏ on the Asc. or 6th H., and containing afflictions; born under one of the hoarse signs of the Zodiac, as under ♈, ♉, ♌, or ♑; Subs at LCP. (See "Hoarse Signs" under Hoarseness).

**Inflammation**—Of the Larynx—Laryngitis—A ♉ and ♏ disease, and with these signs on the Asc., and afflicted; the ☽ affl. in ♉; ♅ in ♉ and affl. the ☉, ☽, or Asc.; ♄ in ♉ in the 6th H.; ♂ affl. in ♉ or ♏; Subs at LCP and KP. (See Croup).

**Laryngismus**—A Spasmodic Affliction of the Larynx—♅ or ☿ affl. in ♉.

**Laryngitis**—(See "Inflammation" in this section).

**Organic Diseases Of**—Afflictions in or to ♉ and ♏; the ☉ affl. in ♉ or ♏.

**Phlegm**—In the Larynx—♄ affl. in ♉; the ☽ hyleg in ♉ with females. (See "Catarrh" in this section; Mucus, Phlegm).

**Puberty**—The Larynx and Vocal Cords Affected at Time of—(See the Introduction to this Article; Puberty, Voice).

**Spasmodic Affections**—(See "Laryngismus" in this section).

**Speech**—(See the various paragraphs under Speech).

**Suffocation**—Thru Closure and Swelling, or Obstruction In the Larynx—♄ or ♂ affl. in ♉. (See Croup, Dyspnoea).

**Swollen Larynx**—The ☽ ☌ ♂ in ♉; ♂ afflicted in ♉ or ♏; afflictions in ♉ or ♏.

**Throat**—(See the various paragraphs under Throat).

**Trachea**—(See Trachea, Windpipe).

**Tumors Of**—Afflictions in ♉; ♄ affl. in ♉; Subs at LCP. (See Tumors).

**Vertical Larynx**—(See "Vertical" under Spine).

**Vocal Cords**—Voice—(See Voice. Also note the various paragraphs in this section.

**Windpipe**—(See Trachea, Windpipe).

**LASCIVIOUS**—Lascivious Habits—The ☉ ill-dignified at B., privately lascivious and prone to many vices; in Hor'y Q. the ☉ Sig. of the person, and ill-dig. and afflicted, one outwardly decent but secretly vicious and lascivious; ♆ affl. the ☽ or ♀; ♂ ☌ or ill-asp. ♀, or ♀ affl. by ♂. (See Desire, Lewd, Licentiousness, Lust; "Loose Morals" under Morals; Wanton).

**LASSITUDE**—Languor—Dullness—Debility—Flagging of Energy—Relaxation—Tired Feeling—Weariness—Lethargy, etc.—The Lymphatic Temperament tends to give Lassitude; the 8th deg. of ♉ on the Asc., a degree of lassitude; the ☽ ☌ or ill-asp. ♆ or ♄ by dir.; the Prog. ☽ to the ☌ or ill-asp. ♆ in the radical map, and espec. if ♆ is afflicted at B., and produces both mental and physical lassitude; ♄ ☌ the Asc. by dir.; ♃ □ or ☍ ☉ at B. and by dir. (See Apathy, Debility, Dull, Dynamic, Energy, Ennui, Fatigue, Feeble, Hyperaesthesia, Idle, Inactive, Indifferent, Inertia, Languid, Lethargy, Listless, Negative, Procrastination, Weariness, etc.).

**LATENT DISEASES**—Constitutional Diseases—Hereditary—Organic, etc.—Are usually caused by the ☉, and afflictions to the ☉ with the male, and by the ☽ and ♀ afflicted in female nativities. (See Constitutional, Heredity, Organic).

**Mother**—Death of the Mother from Some Latent Disease—(See "Latent" under Mother).

**LATITUDE**—Of the Planets—In disease the influence of the planets, and especially of the malefics, is more pronounced when the afflictors in the disease have the same Latitude, North or South of the Ecliptic, as the hyleg, or the planets afflicted. A wide Latitude between them lessens their evils. (See Nodes).

**LATTER PART OF LIFE**—(See Fourth House, Old Age; "Terminal Houses" under Terminal).

**LAUGHTER**—Is said to be ruled by ♆. (See Cheerfulness, Happiness, Joy, Mirth, etc.).

**LAVENDER COLOR**—Ruled by ♆. (See Colors).

**LAW** — Laws — The Law— Sentence by Law — Social and Moral Laws — Laws of Nature, etc.—

**Death** — By Sentence of Law — (See Execution, Judges).

**Fugitive**—From the Law—(See Fugitive).

**Imprisonment**—By Law—(See Prison).

**Judge** — Sentenced by a Judge — (See Judges).

**Justice**—Death by the Hand of Justice—Fugitive from Justice—(See Fugitive, Judges, Justice).

**Lawsuits**—Many Lawsuits Generally — (See "Lawsuits" under Public; Riches).

**Lawyers**—(See Pettifogging).

**Moral Laws**—Breaks the Moral Laws —(See "Moral Laws" under Love Affairs; "Loose Morals", and the various paragraphs under Morals).

**Nature's Laws** — Outrages Nature's Laws and Suffers Disease Thereby— The ☽ affl. in ♏.

**Officers**—Killed by Officers of the Law —(See Officers).

**Prison**—Imprisoned by Law—(See Prisons).

**Sentence of Law**—(See Judges).

**Social Laws** — Disregard For — (See Love Affairs, Low, Morals, Society).

**Success At Law**—♂ Sig. ☌ ♃.

**LAX**—Laxity—

**Fibre**—Laxity of Fibre and the Tissues—(See Fibre, Flabby, Relaxation, Tissues).

**Laxatives**—(See Psychic).

**Laxness** — (See Carelessness, Dull, Idle, Indifferent, Lethargy, Listless).

**Morals**—Lax Morals—(See Debauched, Depraved, Dissipated, Low, Lust; "Loose" under Morals; Wanton, etc.).

**LAZY**—(See Apathy, Carelessness, Dull, Filthy, Idle, Improvident, Inactive, Inertia, Lassitude, Lethargy, Procrastination, Rouse, Sedentary, Slovenly, Uncleanly, etc.).

**LEAD**—The Metal Lead — Plumbum— Ruled by ♄, and is a typical drug of ♄. (See Therapeutics). Tinctura Saturnina is a preparation of Lead, ruled by ♄, and is used in Hectic Fevers, and the Low Fever of Phthisis. (See "Hectic Fever" under Fever; Mucous; "Night Sweats" under Phthisis; "Remedies" under Saturn).

**Lead Colic**—Painter's Colic—A ♄ disease, and caused by strong ♄ afflictions at B., and by dir. (See "Lead Colic" under Colic).

**Lead Colour Complexion** — ♄ strong at B. indicates such a person, and ♄ Sig. in Hor'y Q. (See "Swarthy" under Complexion).

**Marks**—Pale, Lead-Colored Mark On the Body—(See Marks).

**Poisoning**—Lead Poisoning—Susceptible To — Born under the strong affliction of ♄; Subs at KP (11D), and at PP (3, 4L). (See Poison).

**Sugar of Lead**—Lead Acetate—Ruled by ♄. Used as a Collyria in inflamed eyes, and as an ingredient in liniments and ointments for ulcers, skin diseases, excoriations, etc. (See Abrasions, Collyria, Ointments, Resolvent).

**LEAKAGES** — (a) Nervous Leakage — (See "Leakage" under Nerves). (b) Urine — Leakage of — (See "Incontinence" under Urine). (c) Valves—Leakage of—(See "Leaky" under Heart; Valves).

**LEAN**—Leanness—Thin—Slender, etc.—

**Body**—Lean Body—Denoted by ♄; ♄ in ♌ in partile asp. the Asc., rather lean; ♄ in ♑, partile the Asc.; ♂ in ♑, partile the Asc., small, lean and thin; ☿ ruler of the Asc., and occidental: the second, or latter parts of ♈, ♉, or ♌ ascending make the body more lean; the latter parts of ♋ or ♑ ascending make the body more lean than the first parts; the first part of ♐ on the Asc. gives a lean and spare body. (See Slender, Spare, Thin).

**Bony**—Bony, Lean and Muscular Body —Born under ♂, and given by ♂. (See "Bony", "Raw-Boned", under Bones).

**Complexion**—(See "Lean and Sallow" under Complexion).

**Dry and Lean Body**—(See "Lean and Dry Body" under Dry).

**Face**—(See "Lean" under Face).

**Ill-Formed** — Lean, Ill-Formed and Short—The ☽ gives when occi. at B. (See "Ill-Formed" under Ill).

**Legs** — When ♄ builds the body he gives lean, thin and small legs. (See "Lean" under Legs).

**Middle-Sized** — A Lean and Middle-Sized Body—♃ in ♈ in partile asp. the Asc. (See "Middle Stature" under Middle).

**Muscular**—Lean, Muscular, and Bony —(See "Bony" in this section).

**Short**—Lean, Ill-Formed and Short— (See "Ill-Formed" in this section).

**Small**—Lean, Thin and Small—♂ in ♑, partile the Asc.; ☿ in ♐, partile the Asc., some Writers say small, lean, and thin; the latter part of ♌ on the Asc. makes the body more thin and small. (See Small, Thin).

**Thighs** — Lean and Small Thighs — (See "Small" in this section).

**Thin** — Lean, Small and Thin — (See "Small" in this section).

**Visage** — Lean Visage — (See "Lean", "Long", under Face). For further study along this line see "Long Arms" under Arms; Atrophy, Emaciation; "Long Hands" under Hands; Sickly, Slender, Tabes, Tall, Thin, Wasting.

**LEAPING SPASM** — Jumping Spasm — (See "Saltatory" under Spasmodic).

**LEARNING**— Research — Knowledge— Reading—Study, etc.—

**Acquires Knowledge** — (See Knowledge, Reading, Study).

**Arts and Sciences** — Fondness For — Proficiency In—The ☽, ♄, or ☿ Sig. in ♒; ☿ Sig. in ✶ or △ ♄ or ♀. (See Science).

**Aversion to Study** — (See "Fails" under Examinations; "Aversion" under Study).

**Bad Aspects** — For Learning — (See Dull, Examinations; "Shallow" under Mentality; "Weak Mind" under Mind; "Void Of" in this section).

**Depth of Mind**—(See Genius, Knowledge, Mathematical; "Quickened" under Mental; Metaphysics; "Deep and Profound" under Mind; Occult, Reading, Science, Study; the various paragraphs in this Article).

**Examinations**—Fails In—(See Examinations).

**Fond of Learning** — (See "Studious", and the various paragraphs in this section).

**Great Learning**—Has Great Learning and Knowledge — ♄, ♃, or ♂ as Sigs., and in ☌ ☿; ♃ or ♂ as Sigs., in ✶ or △ ☿. (See "Great Ability" under Great; "Good Mind" under Mind; Renown; the various paragraphs in this section).

**Incapable of Learning** — Wholly Unqualified for Study—☿ Sig. ☌ ☉, unqualified for study, and has a contracted and superficial mind; ☿ Sig. ☌ ♄, gains knowledge with great difficulty. (See "Bad Aspects" in this section).

**Inventive Mind**—Ingenius—Constructive—Original—The ☽ or ☿ Sigs. in ♒; the ☽ Sig. ☌ or good asp. ☿; the ☽ well-asp. in ♍; ♅ configurated with ☿; ♅ ascending at B., inventive, and strikes out many novelties; ♄ or ♀ Sigs. in ✶ or △ ☿. (See Genius).

**Learns Easily** — Quickly Acquires Many Sciences Without a Teacher—The ☽ Sig. ✶ or △ ☿, or vice versa, the best aspects for learning and scientific speculation and investigation. (See "Quickened" under Mentality; "Good Mind" under Mind; "Depth of Mind" in this section).

**Literature**—Addicted To—☿ Sig. ☌ ♃; ☿ in the Asc. or M.C. at B., and well-asp. and dignified; ♀ Sig. ☌ ☿, fond of the elegant branches of Literature if free from the afflictions of malefics. (See Reading, Study).

**Little Depth of Mind** — Small Desire for Knowledge—(See Apathy, Dull, Examinations, Idle, Inactive, Indifferent; "Shallow" under Mentality; "Incapable", "Void Of", in this section).

**Loses Interest**—In Studies and Learning—(See Chaotic, Dreamy, Examinations; "Little Depth" in this section).

**Lover and Promotor** — Of Learning — ♂ Sig. ✶ or △ ☿; ☿ Sig. in ♎.

**Metaphysics**—Occult Learning—Given To—♅ strong at B.; ♅ in the Asc. or M.C.; ♅ in ♒; ♅ ☌ or good asp. the ☉, ☽, ☿, or the Asc.

**Much Attached** — To Learning — (See "Great Learning", "Studious", in this section).

**Novelties** — Creates Many — (See "Inventive" in this section; Novelties).

**Occult Learning**—(See "Metaphysics" in this section).

**Reading** — Fond of — (See Reading, Study).

**Science** — Little Ability For — (See Science).

**Scientific Mind**—(See Science).

**Studious Mind** — Fond of Learning — Given to Study—♊ and ♍ influence; ☿ strong at B., and well-aspected; ♃ at a Solar Rev. passing the place of the radical ☿. (See "Quickened" under Mentality; "Cultivation", "Good Mind", under Mind; Scholar, Study; "Great Learning" in this section).

**Superficial In Learning**—A Contracted and Shallow Mind—(See "Shallow" under Mentality; "Little Depth", "Void Of", in this section).

**Uncommon Pursuits** — Seeks Unusual Learning — ♅ ascending at B. (See "Metaphysics" in this section).

**Void of Solid Learning** — The ☉ ☌ or P. Dec. ☿ at B., and both in ♓, and is usually a pretender to all kinds of knowledge; ☿ ill-dig. at B.; ☿ Sig. ☌ the ☉ or ♄. (See "Incapable", "Little Depth", in this section; "Void Degrees" under Void).

**Well Informed** — Has a Wide Range of Learning — (See "Great Learning", "Metaphysics", "Studious", in this section). For further and collateral study along this line see "Active Mind" under Active; Comprehension, Faculties, Intellect, Intuition, Judgment, Mathematical, Mechanical; "Educational Mind" under Mind; Perception, Precocious, Prodigies, Profound, Scholar, Talents, Truth, Understanding, etc.

**LEATHERY SKIN** — (See Hemachromatosis).

**LEAVES** — (See Herbs, Plants, Trees, Vegetation).

**LEERING EYES**—(See "Leering" under Eyes).

**LEFT** — The Left Side of the Body — Taken as a whole, the ☽ rules the left side of the body. It is also ruled by Cold, and the Cold and Moist Elements. The odd, positive, and masculine signs and houses correspond to the left side of the body in a male, and the even, negative, and feminine signs and houses to the left side of the body in a female. (See Cold, Houses, Negative, Positive, Right, Signs).

**Appendix**—The Appendix Vermiformis On the Left Side — Case — (See "Left Side" under Appendix).

**Arm**—Left Arm—Fracture of—Case—(See "Left" under Radius).

**Auricle**—The Left Auricle—(See "Auricles" under Heart).

**Blindness** — In the Left Eye — (See "Eyes" in this section; "Left Eye" under Blindness).

**Caecum** — On the Left Side — Case — (See "Left" under Appendix).

**Cerebral Hemispheres**—The left ruled by ♂. (See Cerebral).

**Chin**—A Mark Near the Left Side of the Chin—(See "Marks" under Chin).

**Cold and Moist Humours**—In Left Side of Body—(See "Cold and Moist" under Humours).

**Coronary Plexus**—The Left Coronary —(See "Fifth Thoracic" under Ganglion).

**Diseases of Left Side** — In the male they are diseases of the ☉, and ruled by the ☉. In the female they are diseases of the ☽, and ruled by the ☽.

**Ears**—Left Ear—Pain and Disease In —(See "Left" under Ears).

**Eyes**—The Left Eyes—The left eye of a woman is ruled by the ☉, and the left eye of a man by the ☽.

(a) Abscesses of Left Eye—The ☉ or ☽ near the Ascelli, and coming to the ☌, and the ☉ or ☽ affl. by the ☌, □, or ☍ malefics.

(b) Accidents to Left Eye—Hurts—Injuries—Wounds—Danger To—Loss of Sight—Blindness In—The ☉ or ☽ near Nebulous Stars at B., and affl. by ♄ or ♂; the ☉ to the ☌ malefics by dir., danger of blindness in the left eye of a female, or in the right eye of a male; the ☉ or ☽ to the ☌ malefics by dir.; the ☉ or ☽ to the ☌ ♂ by dir, and espec. if ♂ be in ♈ at B., and affl. the Lights; the ☉ or ☽ in an airy sign at B., and afflicted, and espec. when affl. the Asc. by dir.; the ☉ or ☽ in the 12th H., and afflicted by Nebulous stars, or malefics (the 12th H. is said to rule the left eye); the ☉ or ☽ affl. at B., and in evil asp. the Asc. by dir, and espec. if the Lights were near Nebulous Stars at B., and otherwise afflicted by malefics; the ☽ to the ☌ the Pleiades, Praesepe, or Ascelli; ♀ ruler of the 12th H., and in the 2nd H., and affl. by ♅ or ♃ (the 2nd H. rules the eyes in Hindu Astrology). Case—See "Left Eye" under Blindness.

(c) Blindness—In the Left Eye—(See "Accidents" (b) in this paragraph).

(d) Danger—To Left Eye—(See (b) in this paragraph).

(e) Defects—In Left Eye—Impediments In—Born under the ☉ or ☽ as rulers, to the left eye of a woman when the ☉ is ruler, and to the left eye of a male when the ☽ is ruler at B.; the ☉ or ☽ affl. at B., and to the ☌ ☋ by dir. (See "Defects" under Eyes).

(f) Hurts to Left Eye—(See (b) in this paragraph).

(g) Impediments—In Left Eye—(See "Defects" (e) in this paragraph).

(h) Larger—The Left Eye Larger Than the Right—(See "Larger" under Eyes).

(i) Marks—Moles—Scar Near Left Eye—The ☉ Sig. of the party, and near, or in ☌ the ☽ or ♂ in a female nativity, and the ☽ likewise in a male horoscope.

(j) Sight—Of the Left Eye—Loss of, or Sight of Affected—♄ between the 24° and 30° of ♒. (See (b) in this paragraph).

(k) Women—Hurts to Left Eye of—Afflictions to the ☉ at B., and by dir.; the ☉ to the ☌ ♄ or ♂ by dir., and by blows, accident, falls, etc.; the ☉ to the place of Antares. (See (b) in this paragraph). See Antares, Ascelli, Nebulous, Pleiades; "Right Eye" under Right; Sight.

**Face**—Left Side of—Marks, Moles, or Warts On—Burns To—(See "Face" under Burns; "Left Side" under Face).

**Feeble**—On the Left Side—The dry and moist elements are more feeble on the left side of the body, and also cold, while the right side of the body is hot. Planets, signs, and houses which predominate in the cold elements at B. therefore tend to affect the left side more. Saturn is cold in nature, and when in a positive sign at B. tends to affect the left side of a male, and when in a negative and feminine sign, the right side of a male, etc. (See the Introduction to this Article).

**Feet**—The Left Foot—Marks, Moles, or Scar On—(See "Marks" under Feet).

**Females**—Accidents, Hurts, or Injury to Left Side—Blindness In Left Eyes—(See "Eyes" in this section; "Blind", "Eyes", "Hurts", "Left", under Females).

**Fracture**—Of the Left Arm—Case—(See "Left Arm" under Radius).

**Heart**—Left Auricle of—(See "Auricles" under Heart).

**Humours**—In the Left Side—(See "Cold and Moist" in this section).

**Hurts**—To Left Side of Body—♄ or ♂ afflicted in the positive and masculine signs or houses with a male, and in the negative and feminine signs or houses with females. (See the Introduction, "Eyes", "Feeble", and the various paragraphs in this Article).

**Left-Handed**—A predominance of planets in the masculine signs in male nativities, or such signs on angles, or the majority of planets at B. in the feminine signs with females. The opposite of these conditions tends to right-handedness. (See Dexterity, Right).

**Left Side**—Of the Body—Disorders In —Hurts To—Peculiarities of—(See "Eyes", "Feeble", "Hurts", and the various paragraphs in this section).

**Leg**—Left Leg—(a) Fracture of—Hurts To—♄ or ♂ afflicted in a positive and masculine sign with males, as in ♐ or ♒, and in a feminine sign with females, as ♄ affl. in ♑ or ♓. (See "Hurts" in this section). (b) Left Leg Shorter Than Right—Case—See "Unfortunate Case", No. 351, in 1001 N.N.

**Lungs**—Lower Left Lobe of—Ruled by ♎. (See Lungs).

**Males**—Left Eye of—Left Side of—(See the Introduction, Eyes, Feeble, Hurts, and the various paragraphs in this section).

**Marks**—Moles—Scars On the Left Side—Marks or Scar On the Left Eye —Feminine planets and signs when prominent at B. tend to Marks, Moles, and Scars on the left side of the body in females, and in males when masculine signs and planets predominate. (See Marks, Moles, Scars; Eyes, Face, Feet, in this section).

**Moisture**—Moist and Cold Humours In Left Side—(See "Cold and Moist" under Humours). Moisture is more feeble in the left side of the body. (See Moisture).

**Moles**—On the Left Side—(See "Marks" in this section; Moles).

**Neck**—Left Side of Face and Neck Burned—Case—(See "Face" under Burns).

**Ovary**—The Left Ovary—Ruled by the ☽. (See Ovaries).

**Radius**—Of the Left Arm—Fracture of—Case—(See "Left" under Radius).

**Scars**—On Left Eye—On Left Side—(See "Eyes", "Marks", in this section; Marks, Moles, Scars).

**Side**—Left Side of Body—Afflictions To—(See "Left Side" in this section).

**Sight** — Of the Left Eye — Loss of — (See "Eyes" in this section).

**Testicle**—Left Testicle—Ruled by the ☽. (See Testes).

**Toes**—Missing On Left Foot—(See Toes).

**Women**—Hurts to Left Eye of—Hurts to Left Side—(See "Eyes", "Hurts", in this section; "Left Eye" under Blindness).

**LEGITIMATE**—Is the Child Legitimate? (See "Horary" under Bastards).

**LEGS**—Lower Limbs—Lower Extremities—The Legs from the hips to the feet are divided into Thighs, Knees, Calves, Ankles, Feet, etc., and are ruled by the different planets and signs which rule these parts. The Thighs are ruled by ♃, ♐, and the 9th H. The Knees are ruled by ♄, ♑, and the 10th H. The Calves, and the Tibia, Fibula, Ankles, and the parts of the leg between the knees and feet, are ruled by ♒, the 11th H., and also influenced by ♄, the ruler of the ♒ sign. The Feet are ruled by ♓ and the 12th H. The Legs as the lower extremities correspond to the arms as the upper extremities, and each part of the arms is ruled by the sign in opposition to the corresponding parts of the lower limbs. (See Arms). The legs correspond to the common, or mutable signs, and to Motion and the Motive Temperament.

**— SECTION ONE —**

**DESCRIPTION OF THE LEGS**—

See the following subjects in the alphabetical arrangement when not more fully considered here.

**Achilles Tendon**—(See Achilles).

**Action Of**—(See Gait, Lameness, Locomotion, Motion, Movement, Quick, Slow, Walk, etc.).

**Ankles; Arteries** — Of the Legs — ♃ rules the Arteries of the Legs, and ♀ the Veins.

**Bad Legs**—Unsound Legs—Caused by ♄ afflictions; ♄ affl. in the 6th H. in a mutable sign. (See Bent, Crooked, Ill-Formed, Knock-Knees, in this section).

**Bandy Legs**—(See "Bow Legs" in this section).

**Bent Legs**—The 5th face of ♈ on the Asc. (See Bow Legs, Ill-Formed, Knock-Knees, in this section).

**Bones and Joints**—Ruled by ♄.

**Bow Legs**—Bandy Legs—Caused principally by ♄ affliction; the ☉ or ♄ in ♑ and afflicted; ♑ on the Asc.; ♄ as Sig. in Hor'y Q. denotes one bow-legged, or one who knocks his knees or ankles together, or has a shuffling gait; ♃ in ♏ in □ to planets in ♒; ☿ Sig. in ♑; ♏ gives; ♏ on the Asc.; common to natives of ♏; the 1st face of ♊ on the Asc. (See Bad, Bent, Crooked, Ill-Formed, Knock-Knees, in this section).

**Calves; Coarse and Hairy** — ♏ gives, and with ♏ on the Asc. (See "Hairy Body" under Hair).

**Crooked Legs**—♄, ♑, and ♏ influences; ♑ or ♏ on the Asc. (See Bent, Bow Legs, Ill-Formed, Knock-Knees, in this section).

**Extremities; Feet; Femur; Fibula;**

**Fin-Like and Short**—(See "Short" in this section).

**Foetus**—Limbs of—Developed by ♂. (See Foetus).

**Frog Child** — Both Legs Missing Below the Knees—(See Frog).

**Gait; Hairy and Coarse**—(See "Coarse" in this section).

**Hams**—(See Thighs).

**Hips; Ill-Formed** — ♑ influence; ♏ or ♑ on the Asc.; the 3rd face of ♋ on the Asc. (See Bent, Bow Legs, Crooked, Knock-Knees, in this section).

**Imperfect and Distorted**—Case—See "Twins", No. 241, in 1001 N.N.

**Joints**—Ruled by ♄. (See Joints).

**Knees; Knock-Knees**—(See "Knock-Knees" under Knees).

**Large and Well-Set** — (See "Large" under Limbs).

**Lean**—Small, Lean, Thin and Slender Legs—♄ ascending at B.; ♄ gives when he builds the body; denoted by ☿ in Hor'y Q. (See "Slender" in this section).

**Left Leg Shorter** — (See "Leg" under Left).

**Legless** — Both Legs Missing Below the Knees—Case—(See "Missing" under Forearm).

**Length of Limbs** — (See "Long", "Short", under Bones, Limbs; Brevity, Dwarfed, Giants; "Body" under Short; Tall).

**Limbs; Locomotion; Long Legs**—Long and Slender — ☿ ascending at B., and free from the rays of other planets; ☿ gives, and shorter if ☿ is ori.; ♃ indicates long legs and feet; ♊ on the Asc.; the 1st or 4th faces of ♍ on the Asc. (See "Long" under Arms, Bones, Feet, Limbs; Giants, Tall).

**Lower Extremities** — Lower Limbs — (See Lower; the various paragraphs in this section).

**Malformations** — (See Sec. 2 of this Article).

**Marks**—Moles—Scars—(See "Marks" under Left, Right; Marks, Moles, Scars).

**Members; Missing; Moles** — (See "Marks" in this section).

**Motion; Muscles**—Of Legs—Ruled by ♂. (See Muscles).

**Nerves**—Of Legs—Ruled by ☿. (See Nerves).

**One Leg Shorter**—Case—(See "Leg" under Left).

**Patella**—Knee Cap—(See Knees).

**Quick Walk**—(See "Energetic" under Gait).

**Scars** — On Legs — Caused especially by ♂ in the signs which rule the legs. (See Cuts, Scars).

**Shank**—(See Tibia).

**Shin Bone**—(See Tibia).

**Short Legs**—Short and Fin-Like—Short and Thick—Brevity of Limb—The ☿ and ♍ influences tend to short legs; the 2nd face of ♏ on the Asc., short and thick; ♓ on the Asc., short and fin-like. (See Brevity, Dwarfed; "Body" under Short).

**Shorter**—Left Leg Shorter—(See "Leg" under Left).

**Shuffling Gait**—Dragging Gait—(See Gait).

**Slender Legs**—Thin—Lean—Slender and Small Legs—♄ ascending at B.; a ☿ person; ☿ Sig. of the person in Hor'y Q.; ☿ occidentally posited as regards the ☉ except when ☿ is in ♊. (See Lean, Long, in this section; "Tall and Thin" under Tall, Thin).

**Slow Movement**—(See "Slow" under Motion).

**Small Legs**—Small and Slender—Small and Lean—(See "Slender" in this section).

**Stout Legs**—Stout and Strong—♃ in the Asc.; ♂ in ♌ in partile asp. the Asc.; ♈ gives, and ♈ on the Asc.

**Strikes Legs Together**—♄ influence and affliction. (See "Knocking Together" under Ankles; "Knock-Knees" under Knees).

**Strong Legs**—(See "Stout" in this section).

**Tendo Achilles**—(See Achilles).

**Thick and Short**—Given by ♏, and with ♏ on the Asc. (See "Short" in this section).

**Thighs; Thin Legs**—Thin and Lean—Thin and Long—(See Long, Slender, in this section).

**Tibia; Toes; Veins Of**—Ruled by ♀.

**Walk**—(See Gait, Walk).

**Well-Proportioned**—Large and Well-Set—♃ in the Asc. (See "Large" under Limbs; "Stout" in this section).

## — SECTION TWO —

### DISEASES OF THE LEGS—

**Accidents To**—Injuries—Hurts—Fractures—Wounds, etc.—The ☉ or ☽ in ♑ or ♒ and afflicted by ♄ or ♂; ♅, ♄, or ♂ in ♐, ♑, or ♒, and afflicted. (See "Accidents" under Extremities).

**Aches In**—Leg-ache—An ♒ disease and affliction; ♄ affl. in ♒. (See Aches; "Pain" under Limbs, and in this section; Pain).

**Action Of**—The Action Disabled or Abnormal—(See "Action" in Sec. 1 of this Article; Deformed, Distortions, Lameness, Weak, and the various paragraphs in this section).

**Affected**—The Legs tend to be affected when the ☉ is in ♊; the in ♉ or ♒; ♅ in ♒; ♄ in ♏ or ♐; ♃ in ♑; ♂ in ♑ or ♒; ♀ ♌; ☿ in ♈ or ♋. (See Table 196 in Simmonite's Arcana of Astral Philosophy. Also see "Affected" under Head).

**Affections**—Of the Legs—♄ in ♑ or ♒; afflictions in ♒, or ♒ on the Asc. (See "All Diseases", and the various paragraphs in this section).

**All Diseases In**—All Infirmities In—Afflictions in ♑ or ♒, or with these signs upon the Asc., and containing malefics; the 18° ♑ on the Asc., unfortunate in the legs. (See "Affections", and the various paragraphs in this section).

**Amputations**—Operations—Avoid Amputations of the legs when the ☽ is passing thru ♐, ♑, or ♒. (See Operations).

**Aneurysm**—(See Aneurysm).

**Ankles**—Disorders of—Injuries To—(See Ankles).

**Arterial Blood**—Obstructions of the Circulation of In the Legs—Caused by afflictions to ♃ when ♃ is in signs at B. which rule the legs; ♄ ☌ ♃ in ♐; ♄ in ♐ in □ or ☍ ♃; ♃ ☌ ♅ in ♐, and affl. by the □ or ☍ ♄. (See Arteries).

**Arthritis**—Of the Joints—Arthritic Muscular Atrophy—♄ in ♐, ♑, or ♒, ☌ ♂, and affl. also by ♆; ♄ and ♂ afflicted in signs which rule the legs. Case—See Fig. 15B in the book "Astro-Diagnosis" by the Heindels. (See Arthritis, Atrophy).

**Atrophy**—Arthritic Muscular Atrophy—(See Arthritis, Muscles, Paralysis, in this section).

**Bad Legs**—Unsound Legs—(See "Bad Legs" in Sec. 1 of this Article).

**Bent Legs**—(See "Bent Legs" in Sec. 1 of this Article).

**Beriberi**—(See "Beriberi" under Dropsy).

**Blood In**—(a) Arterial Circulation Obstructed—(See "Arterial" in this section). (b) Corrupt Blood In—(See "Corrupt Blood" under Hands; "Arms" under Impure). (c) Lack of Blood In—Poor Circulation In—♄ afflicted in signs which rule the legs; few or no planets in signs which rule the lower half of the body. (See "Arterial Blood" in this section). (d) Blood Vessels—Constriction of—♄ in ♐, ♑, or ♒, and resulting from Cold, a ♄ affliction. (See Cold, Constrictions).

**Bones Of**—Ruled by ♄, and ♄ afflicted in signs which rule the legs tends to affections and diseases of the bones. Also they are affected by Subs at LPP, the 4, 5 Lumbar Vertebrae. (See Bones).

**Bow Legs**—(See "Bow Legs" in Sec. 1 of this Article).

**Broken Legs**—(See "Fractures" in this section).

**Bruises In**—♄ or ♂ in ♑ or ♒. (See Bruises).

**Calves**—Disorders of—(See Calves).

**Circulation Obstructed**—Poor Circulation—(See "Blood" in this section).

**Cold In**—Cold and Numb—♄ affl. in ♐, ♑, or ♒; ♀ affl. in ♒; ☿ affl. in ♎. (See Cold; "Numbness", in this section).

**Congenital Defects**—(See Crippled from Birth" under Birth; Congenital, Deformities, Distortions; "Club Feet" under Feet; "Birth" under Lameness; "Deformities" in this section).

**Constriction**—Of the Blood Vessels—(See "Blood" in this section).

**Contractions In**—♄ affl. in ♐, ♑, or ♒. (See Contractions).

**Control**—Lack of Control Over—♆ in ♊ or ♌ in □ ☉, and with ♄ affl. in ♐,

♑, or ♒; ♅ in ♐ ☌ ☽; ♄ affl. in ♑, and espec. if ♄ afflict ♆ at the same time, and may be due to spinal complications; ♄ □ or ☍ ♆, and the Prog. ☽ ☌ ♄, sometimes loses control of the legs. (See "Paralysis" in this section).

**Corrupt Blood In**—(See "Blood" in this section).

**Cramps In**—♅ in signs which rule the legs; ♄ affl. in ♒; afflictions in ♒. (See Cramps).

**Crippled In**—(See Accidents, Atrophy, Congenital, Deformities, Lameness, Paralysis, and the various paragraphs in this section).

**Cuts**—Danger of—♂ afflicted in signs which rule the legs. (See Cuts).

**Deformities**—♉, ♏, or ♑ on the Asc.; afflictions between ♅ and ♂, or ♄ and ♂, and these planets in common signs; ♄ in the Asc., and afflicted, and espec. if ♄ be in one of the signs ruling the legs. (See Deformities, Distortions; "Frog Child" under Frog; Malformations; "Paralysis" in this section).

**Diseases Of**—(See "All Diseases", and the various paragraphs in this section).

**Distortions**—(See Distortions; "Deformities" in this section).

**Drawn Up**—Under the Body—(See "Paralysis" under Limbs).

**Dropsy Of**—Afflictions in ♌ or ♒, and often due to a weak heart, and disturbed circulation. (See "Dropsy" under Ankles, Feet; Dropsy; "Swellings" in this section).

**Enlarged Veins**—(See Varicose).

**Eruptions On**—♀ afflicted in signs which rule the legs, and due to wrong habits of eating and living. (See Eruptions; Sores, Ulcers, in this section).

**Erysipelas**—♂ afflicted in ♒. (See Erysipelas).

**Extremities**—(See Extremities, Feet, Limbs, Lower).

**Falls**—The Limbs Distorted by Falls—The ☉ Sig. ☌ ♄, and ♄ ill-dignified, the limbs distorted and broken; ♄ affl. in ♑ or the 10th H.; ♑ on the Asc. (See Distortions; "Limbs" under Falls; "Fractures" in this section).

**Feet**—(See the various paragraphs under Feet).

**Femur**—Fracture of—(See Femur).

**Fibula**—Fracture of—(See Fibula).

**Fractures**—Broken Legs—Broken Limbs—Afflictions in ♐, ♑, or ♒; ♄ affl. in ♐, ♑, or ♒; ♂ affl. in ♊, ♍, ♐, ♑, or ♒, and ♂ ☌ or evil asp. the Asc. by dir.; ♂ in ♐ in the 6th or 12th H.; ♐ on the Asc. or cusp of 6th or 12th H., or intercepted in these houses. (See Fractures; "Fractures" under Arms, Feet, Knees, Limbs; Accidents, Falls, in this section).

**Frog Child**—(See Frog).

**Gait**—Walk—Disorders of—(See Gait, Locomotion, Movement, Walk).

**Glands**—Vesicles of—Disorders of—♆ rules and affects the glands of the legs when in signs which rule the legs.—(See Aneurysm; "Affected" under Glands).

**Gout**—In the Legs—The ☽ affl. in ♐, or afflicting the hyleg therefrom; the ☽ affl. in ♊ when the ☽ is the afflictor in the disease, wandering gout in; ♅ in ♐, and affl. the ☉, ☽, or Asc.; ♄ in ♑, occi., and affl. the ☉, ☽, or Asc.; ♄ affl. in ♓, wandering gout in; ♂ in the Asc. or M.C., and in the latter degrees of ♊, ♐, or ♓; ♂ affl. in ♑, flying gout in the legs; ♂ in ♒ and afflicting the hyleg; ♃ afflicted in ♐; ♃ in ♐ in the 6th H., and afflicted. (See Gout).

**Hams**—Disorders of—(See Thighs).

**Hips**—Disorders of—(See Hips, Thighs).

**Humours In**—♂ in ♍ when ♂ is the afflictor in the disease. (See Humours).

**Hurts To**—(See Accidents, Fractures, in this section).

**Hypertrophy**—Of the Muscles—♃ or ♂ afflicted in signs which rule the legs; Subs at LPP (4, 5L). (See Hypertrophy; "Muscles" in this section).

**Ill-Formed**—(See Sec. 1 of this Article).

**Impure Blood In**—(See "Blood" in this section).

**Incoordination In**—(See "Incoordinated" under Gait; "Walk" in this section).

**Infirmities In**—(See "All Diseases", and the various paragraphs in this section).

**Injuries To**—(See Accidents, Fractures, in this section).

**Jerk**—Knee Jerk—Absence of—(See "Knee Jerk" under Knees; Locomotor Ataxia).

**Joints**—Disorders of—(See "Arthritis" in this section; Joints, Synovial).

**Knees**—Disorders of—(See Knees).

**Knock-Knees**—(See Knees).

**Lack of**—Lack of Blood In—Lack of Control Over—(See Blood, Control, in this section).

**Lameness In**—The ☉ or ☽ in ♑, ♒, or ♓, and afflicted; ♄ or ♂ in ♐, ♑, ♒, or ♓, and afflicting the ☉, ☽, or Asc.; ☿ affl. in ♋ or ♑, and usually from colds settling in the legs; ♐, ♑, ♒, or ♓ on the Asc., and containing malefics, or the Asc. afflicted by them by aspect; malefics in ♐, ♑, ♒, or ♓, and affl. the ☉, ☽, or Asc. (See "Lameness" under Feet, Knees; "Gout", and the various paragraphs in this section).

**Legless**—(See Sec. 1 of this Article).

**Leprosy In**—(See Leprosy).

**Locomotion**—Disorders of—(See Gait, Lameness, Locomotion, Motion, Movement, Paralysis, Walk; "Lameness", and the various paragraphs in this Article).

**Locomotor Ataxia**—Absence of Knee Jerk In—(See "Knee Jerk" under Knees; Locomotor Ataxia; "Paralysis" in this section).

**Lower Limbs**—Lower Extremities—The Legs—(See Ankles, Calves, Extremities, Feet, Knees, Limbs, Lower, Thighs. Also note the various paragraphs in this Article).

**Malformations**—(See "Malformations" under Limbs).

**Members**—Parts of the Lower Members Missing—Disorders of the Lower Members — (See Extremities; "Frog Child" under Frog; Limbs, Members, Missing. Also note the various paragraphs in this Article).

**Milk Leg**—Phlegmasia Alba Dolens —Venous Obstruction and Oedema In the Leg—The ☉ afflicted in ♏ when the ☉ is the afflictor in the disease; ♃ affl. in ♒.

**Missing**—The Legs Missing Below the Knees—Case—(See "Frog Child" under Frog).

**Monstrosities**—(See this subject).

**Motion**—In the Legs—Disorders of— (See Gait, Motion, Movement, Walk; Lameness, Paralysis, in this section).

**Motor Nerves**—♅ in signs which rule the legs tends to cramps, spasms, paralysis, and affections of the motor nerves of the legs. (See Motor).

**Movement**—Disorders of the Movement of the Legs—(See "Motion" in this section).

**Moving Parts**—(See Moving).

**Muscles**—Of the Legs—Ruled by ♂. Afflictions to ♂ when he is in signs which rule the legs tend to disorders of the muscles of the legs. Saturn in signs which rule the legs tends to atrophy of the leg muscles, stiffness of, gout and rheumatism in. The leg muscles are also affected and disturbed by Subs at PP (4, 5L). (See Arthritis, Atrophy, Gout, Hypertrophy, Lameness, and the various paragraphs in this section).

**Mutilation Of**—(See "Degrees", "Limbs", under Mutilated).

**Nerves Of**—Disorders of—♅, ♄, or ☿ in signs which rule the legs; afflictions in ♒. (See Aches, Neuralgia, Pain, Paralysis, and the various paragraphs in this section).

**Neuralgia In**—Pain In—Aches In—☿ afflicted in ♐, ♑, or ♒. (See Aches, Pain, in this section; Neuralgia).

**Numbness In**—♅ in signs which rule the legs tends to a numbness and prickling sensation in the legs; ♄ affl. in ♐, ♑, ♒, or ♓ tends to a numbness in the lower limbs, and accompanied by a coldness of the parts, and lack of circulation and the proper supply of nerve force at times; ♄ ☌ ♃ or ♀ in ♐, ♑, or ♒, numbness and disturbed circulation. (See Cold, Numbness; "Cold" in this section.

**Obstruction In**—(See Blood, Numbness, in this section; "Obstructions" under Limbs; Obstructions).

**Operations On** — (See "Amputations" in this section).

**Pain In**—The ☉ affl. in ♊; the ☽ affl. in ♉ or ♒, or afflicting the hyleg therefrom; the ☽ in ♒, ☌, or ill-asp. any of the malefics as promittors; ♃ in the 6th H., and afflicted; ♂ in the 12th H.; ♂ promittor in ♒, ☌, or ill-asp. the ☉; ♂ affl. in ♐, ♑, or ♒; ♀ affl. in ♌ or ♒; ♀ affl. in ♒ tends to pain and swelling in the legs from a cold cause. (See "Pain" under Extremities, Feet, Knees, Limbs, Thighs; "Neuralgia" in this section).

**Paralysis In**—Paraplegia—♅ afflicted in signs which rule the legs. (See "Beriberi" under Dropsy; "Paralysis" under Limbs; Paralysis).

**Paraplegia**—(See "Paralysis" in this section).

**Patella**—Fracture of—(See Knees).

**Phlegmasia Alba Dolens**—(See "Milk Leg" in this section).

**Poor Circulation In**—(See Blood, Numbness, in this section).

**Rheumatism In**—Caused by ♄, and with ♄ afflicted in ♐, ♑, or ♒. (See "Gout" in this section; "Rheumatism" under Extremities; Rheumatism).

**Rigidity**—Of Muscles—♄ affl. in ♐, ♑, or ♒, the result of cold, or excess of mineral deposits and wastes. (See Gout, Lameness, Muscles, Numbness, Pain, Rheumatism, Swellings, in this section; Rigid, Stiff).

**Scars On** — (See "Scars" in Sec. 1 of this Article).

**Sciatica**—(See Sciatic).

**Shins**—(See Tibia).

**Skin Diseases**—Eruptions—♄ and ♑ rule the skin, and ♄ affl. in ♑ tends to skin disorders of the legs; ♂ affl. in ♑ or ♒, and with eruptions; ♀ affl. in ♐, ♑, or ♒. (See "Eruptions" in this section; Eruptions, Skin).

**Sores On**—♄ affl. in ♒, and usually due to impure blood, obstructed circulation. (See Sores; Eruptions, Ulcers, in this section).

**Spasms In**—Spasmodic Diseases of— ♅ affl. in signs which rule the legs. (See Contractions, Cramps, Incoordination, Motor, Nerves, Numbness, Paralysis, in this section; Spasmodic).

**Sprains**—♄ in ♑ or ♒; afflictions in ♑ or ♒; ♒ on the Asc. (See "Sprains" under Ankles; Sprains).

**Stand**—Inability to Stand or Walk— Legs Drawn Up Under Body—(See "Paralysis" in this section; "Inability" under Walk).

**Stiffness In**—(See "Rigidity" in this section; Ankylosis; "Stiffness" under Calves; Joints).

**Swellings In**—The ☽ affl. in ♒ or ♓; ♄ affl. in ♒; ♃ affl. in the 6th H. in ♐; ♃ in ♐, and affl. the ☽ or Asc.; ♀ affl. in ♒, from a cold cause or heart trouble; ♀ affl. in ♓. (See Blood, Dropsy, Gout, Pain, in this section).

**Synovial Fluid**—Disturbances of—♄ affl. in ♐, ♑, or ♒. (See Joints; "Joint" under Knees; Synovial).

**Tendo Achilles**—(See Achilles).

**Thighs**—Disorders of—(See the various paragraphs under Thighs).

**Tibia**—Shin Bone—Fracture of—(See Tibia).

**Torsion**—Torsalgia—(See "Twistings" in this section).

**Tumors In**—♄ in signs which rule the legs, and the Asc. to the ☐ or ☍ ♄ by dir. (See Tumors).

**Twistings In**—Torsion—Torsalgia— Contortions—♅ afflicted in signs which rule the legs; Subs at LLP (4, 5L). (See Contortions).

**Ulcers In**—The ☉ in ♐, ☌, or ill-asp. any of the malefics as promittors; the ☽ affl. in ♒, or afflicting the hyleg therefrom; ♂ in ♒ in the 6th H., and afflicted, or afflicting the ☽ or Asc. (See Ulcers; "Milk Leg" in this section).

**Unable to Stand**—(See "Stand" in this section).

**Unfortunate**—In the Legs—(See "All Diseases In", and the various paragraphs in this Article).

**Unsound Legs**—The ☽ affl. in ♑, ♒, or ♓; ♑ on the Asc. (See "Bad Legs" in Sec. 1 of this Article).

**Upper Parts Of**—Behind the Knees—All diseases in are signified by the 10th H.

**Useless**—The Legs Useless—(See "Paralysis" in this section; "Inability to Walk or Stand" under Walk).

**Varicose Veins**—(See Varicose).

**Veins Enlarged**—(See Varicose, Veins).

**Vesicles Of**—Glands of—Disorders of—(See "Glands" in this section).

**Walk**—Unable to Walk or Stand—(See "Stand" in this section).

**Wandering Gout**—(See "Gout" in this section).

**Wasting Of**—♆ in signs which rule the legs. (See "Legs" under Wasting).

**Weak Legs**—Weakness In—The ☉ affl. in ♊; the ☽ affl. in ♑; the ☽ in ♍, and afflicted by the ☉ or ♂; ♄ or ♃ affl. in ♑; ☿ affl. in ♓; ♑ or ♒ on the Asc. Case—See Fig. 30 in the book "Message of the Stars", by the Heindels. (See "Weak" under Limbs).

**Wounds To**—(See "Accidents" in this section).

**LENGTH**—Lengthening—

**Body**—Length of—Lengthening of—(See Diminished, Dwarfed, Giants, Growth, Height, Medium, Short, Tall).

**Disease**—Length of—(See Acute, Chronic, Course, Crises, Duration, Long, Prolonged, Short, Slow, Tedious).

**Life**—Length of—(See "Death" under Childhood, Infancy, Youth; "Early Death" under Early; "Long Life", "Short Life", under Life).

**LENTIGO**—(See Freckles).

**LEO**—The Leo Sign—The Fifth Sign of the Zodiac, and is affiliated with the 5th H. Leo is ruled by the ☉, and is the day and night house of the ☉. The symbol of this sign is the Lion. Leo is classed as a fixed, fiery, electric, positive, masculine, active, vital, constructive, barren, hot and dry sign. This sign is classed as barren because the ☉ is barren. The ☉ is strong in this sign, and ♌ on the Asc. at B. gives great vitality. Leo represents the heart of the physical organism, and is significant of vital force, vital power, generation, interchange and ardency, and the sphere of ♌ is a deep-seated and extensive one. As ♌ is a hot sign, it heats the system, and also under affliction tends to cause loss of equilibrium in mind and body. Leo belongs to the trinity of fiery signs, as ♈, ♌, and ♐, and these are considered the signs of greatest vitality when on the Asc. at B., and also well-occupied by planets, and especially when rising and elevated in the East at B. Leo draws its strength largely from and thru the Spleen, which is ruled by the ☉. Leo on the Asc. at B. tends to give a tall, commanding figure, strong vitality, fiery and expressive eyes, a good complexion, strong and broad shoulders, a fearless and proud nature. (See Cor Leonis, Lion, Mane of Leo). The Hebrew letter Teth (T) is connected with the ♌ sign, and Teth is predominant in love. Gold is the Metal ruled by ♌. The Colors of ♌ are Gold, Red and Gold, Red and Green. For the Countries and Nations ruled by ♌, see "Leo" under Nations. The Typical Remedy of ♌ is Gold. Magnesium Phosphate is the Salt ruled by ♌. (For further details about the ♌ sign see the classified Articles on Leo in the various Textbooks and Dictionaries of Astrology).

**LEO RULES**—For a classified list of the influences of each of the planets in ♌, see the Textbooks of Astrology. The principal rulership of ♌ is over the Heart, and the Circulation thru the Heart. Also, ♌ rules the Back, and that part of the Spine back of the Heart, and the Heart Place in the Spine, HP, the 2nd Dorsal Vertebra. Each sign has an external, internal, and structural rulership. Externally, ♌ rules the Back and Forearm. Internally, ♌ rules the Heart, Blood, and Liver. Structurally, ♌ rules the Dorsal Vertebrae, the Radius and Ulna of the Arm, and the Wrists. The following is an alphabetical and classified list of the parts of the body, and other matters ruled by ♌, as listed and mentioned in the various Textbooks of Astrology. See these subjects in the alphabetical arrangement—Aorta; Ardency (see Amorous); Back; Blood; Chamomilla; Children; Circulation of the Blood (♌ and ♎ are concerned with Circulation and Distillation); Circulatory System; Constructive Forces of the Body, along with ♂; Creative Powers; Distillation; Dorsal Region of the Back and Spine; Dorsal Nerves (Middle); Dorsal Vertebrae; Equilibrium in the Body; Fifth House; Forearm; Gall and Gall Bladder; Generation; Gold; Heart; Inferior Vena Cava; Interchange of Forces in the Body; Liver; Magnesium Phosphate Salt; Marrow of the Spine; Middle Dorsal Nerves; Nerve Sheaths; Nerves of the Spine; Offspring; Radius; Salt (Magnesium Phosphate); Spinal Cord; Spine—Dorsal Region of—Marrow and Nerves of); Spleen; Superior and Inferior Vena Cava; Ulna; Vena Cavae; Vital Fluids, Vital Forces, and Vital Power of the Body; Wrists. By aspect and reflex action, the ♌ sign also influences all of the other fixed signs, and the parts of the body ruled by them, and is a part of the Fixed Cross, made up of ♉, ♌, ♏, and ♒.

**Leo Qualities**—Active, Affectionate, Amorous, Animal, Ardent, Arrogant, Autocratic, Barren, Bitter, Broken, Brutish, Changeable, Choleric, Commanding, Conjugal, Constructive, Convulsive, Diurnal, Dry, Eastern, Electric, Eruptive, Feverish, Fierce, Fiery,

Fixed, Fortunate, Four-Footed, Hasty, Hoarse, Hot, Hot and Dry, Impulsive, Inflammatory, Masculine, Northern, Oppressive, Passionate, Positive, Romantic, Savage, Sharp, Strong, Summer, Violent, Vital.

**LEO DISEASES** — The Diseases and Afflictions Ruled by Leo—
The Pathological Qualities of ♌ are Ardor, Arrogance, Fixity of Purposes, Impulse, Vitality. Gold is the Typical Remedy of the ♌ Sign, and of the ☉. (See "Sun Diseases" under Sun). The principal diseases of ♌ are those of the Heart and Circulation, and diseases resulting from heart and blood disturbances. Also diseases resulting from Excesses, Pleasures, Amusements, Love Affairs, Passional Excesses, etc. The following are Diseases ruled by the ♌ Sign, which see in the alphabetical arrangement—

**Acute Fevers**—Acute Diseases—(See Acute).

**Anaemia; Aneurysm; Angina Pectoris** —(See Angina).

**Apoplexy; Arterio-Sclerosis**—(See Arteries).

**Back**—All Diseases and Affections of —Injuries To—(See Back, Spine).

**Blood Disorders**—The Blood and Circulation Disturbed—(See Blood, Circulation).

**Burning Fevers**—High Fevers—Sharp — Violent — (See "High Fever" under Fever).

**Cardialgia** — (See "Heartburn" under Heart).

**Carditis**—(See "Carditis" under Heart).

**Circulation of Blood**—Disorders of— (See Arteries, Blood, Circulation, Veins).

**Convulsions; Curvature of Spine**—(See Curvature, Spine).

**Cutaneous Affections** — Due to Blood Disorders — (See "Skin" under Blood; Cutaneous; "Skin Diseases" under Skin).

**Dizziness; Dropsy; Effusion of Blood** —(See Effusions).

**Endocarditis**—(See Heart).

**Enlargement** — Of the Heart — (See "Enlarged" under Heart).

**Epidemics; Eruptions** — Eruptive Fevers—(See Eruptions).

**Eyes**—Sore and Inflamed Eyes—(See Eyes).

**Fainting; Fatty Degeneration**—Of the Heart—(See "Fatty" under Heart).

**Fevers** — High, Violent and Burning Fevers—(See "High" under Fever).

**Gout**—In the Heart—(See "Gout" under Heart).

**Hardening**—Of the Arteries—(See Arteries).

**Heart Troubles**—Various Forms of— (See Heart).

**Heartburn**—(See Heart).

**High Fevers**—(See "High" under Fever).

**Hot Diseases**—(See Fevers; "Dry and Hot Diseases" under Heat).

**Hydraemia**—(See "Thin Blood" under Blood).

**Hyperaemia; Hypertrophy** — Of the Heart—(See Heart).

**Inflamed Eyes** — (See "Inflamed" under Eyes).

**Inflammations**—Inflammatory Fevers —(See "Fevers", and the various paragraphs under Inflammation).

**Injuries**—To the Back or Spine—(See Back, Spine).

**Jaundice** — Yellow Jaundice — (See Jaundice).

**Locomotor Ataxia**—(See Locomotor).

**Marrow of Spine**—Diseases of—(See "Marrow" under Spine).

**Measles; Meningitis** — Spinal — (See Meninges).

**Mitral Disorders** — (See "Mitral" under Heart).

**Neuralgia**—Of the Heart—(See "Neuralgia" under Heart).

**Oppression** — About the Heart — (See "Oppression" under Heart).

**Palpitation** — Of the Heart — (See Heart).

**Passion** — Of the Heart — (See Palpitation, Passion, under Heart).

**Pericarditis**—(See Heart).

**Pestilence; Plague; Pleurisy; Regurgitation**—(See Heart).

**Rheumatism** — In the Back — (See Back).

**Ribs**—Pains In—(See Ribs).

**Sclerosis**—Arterial—(See Arteries).

**Sharp Fevers** — (See "High" under Fever).

**Shingles**—(See Herpes).

**Sides** — All Diseases of — (See Ribs, Sides).

**Slow Heart Beat**—(See Impeded, Slow, under Heart).

**Smallpox; Sore Eyes**—(See "Inflamed" under Eyes).

**Spine** — Disorders of — (See Back, Spine, Subluxations, Vertebrae).

**Sunstroke** — (See this subject under Sun).

**Swoonings**—(See Fainting).

**Syncope**—Swooning—(See Fainting).

**Tachycardia**—(See Heart).

**Trembling** — Of the Heart — (See Heart).

**Valves**—Of the Heart—Disorders of— (See Heart, Valves).

**Vertigo; Violent Fevers** — (See High, Violent, under Fever).

**Weak Back**—(See Back).

**Weak Heart**—(See "Weak" under Heart).

**Yellow Fever**—(See Yellow).

**Yellow Jaundice**—(See Jaundice).

**LEPROSY** — This disease is caused by disorders of the Pituitary Body, ruled by ♅, and by a disordered Thyroid Gland, ruled by ☿. The disease is caused by filth of body, uncleanness, sex excesses, moral depravity, and venereal diseases, which disturb the functioning of the Pituitary Body. It is also an endemic, chronic, and infectious disease.

**General Causes**—The ☽ in the Autumnal Equinox at B., and afflicted by ♄; the ☽ in the sign of the Vernal Equi. at B. tends to white leprosy; the ☽ affl. in ♈, ♉, or ♊, white leprosy; the ☽ affl. in ♎, ♏, or ♐; ♆ in ♑ in the 6th H., or afflicting the hyleg or Asc. from this sign; ♅ afflicted at B., and by dir.; a ♄ and ♑ disease; ♄ or ♂ in the 1st or 7th H. in ♋, ♑, or ♓, in signs ascribed to animals or fishes, and especially when in the latter degrees of the signs containing them; ♄ ☌ ♂ in the 1st or 7th H., in the latter degrees of ♊, ♐, or ♓, ori. of the ☉ and occi. of the ☽, tends to leprosy in the extremities, as in the hands, legs and feet; ♄ in the latter degrees of ♊, ♐, or ♓, and one of them in the 1st or 7th H., and espec. when ♄ is occi. of the ☉ and ori. of the ☽, tends to leprosy in the extremities; ☿ affl. at B., and by dir.; lords of the 1st, 6th H., or the ☽ in airy signs; Subs at CP and KP. Cases—See "Child of a Leper", No. 355 in 1001 N.N. Also see Fig. 12A in the book, "Astro-Diagnosis", by the Heindels. (See Depraved, Endemic; "Diseases" under Extremities; Filth, Infections; "Loose Morals" under Morals; Pituitary; "Sex Excesses" under Excesses, Passion, Sex; Thyroid, Uncleanly, Venereal).

**Treatment of Leprosy**—The use of Chaulmoogra Oil is said to be a cure for this disease. In Guayaquil, Ecuador, 300 cases are said to have been cured by the use of Colodial Salts of Antimony. For information as to the Cure, write to the Department of Agriculture, Washington, D.C.

**LEPTOMENINGITIS**—(See Meninges).

**LESIONS**—Structural Tissue Changes from Disease or Injury, and caused principally by ♅ influence. Also, ♄ and ♂ are prominent in causing Lesions.

**Bowels**—Lesion In—(See Typhoid).

**Corrosions**—(See Corrosions).

**Cortical Lesion**—(See Cortical).

**Heart**—Valvular Lesion of—(See "Lesions" under Heart).

**Nerves**—Nervous System—Lesion of—(See Corrosion; "Lesions" under Nerves; Paralysis).

**Paralysis**—Nerve Lesions—(See "Nerves" in this section).

**Peripheral Lesion**—(See "Aphonia" under Vocal).

**Valvular Lesions**—(See "Lesions" under Heart).

**LESS**—Lessened—

**Less Liable to Disease**—(See "Less Liable" under Disease).

**Less Power**—To Throw Off Disease—(See "Less Power" under Disease).

**Resistance Less**—To Disease—Recuperative Powers Low—(See Recuperation, Resistance, Vitality Low).

**Vitality Lessened**—(See Vitality).

**LETHARGY**—A Condition of Drowsiness—The ☉ and ♂ unaspected at B.; the ☽ affl. in ♈ with females; the ☽ affl. in ♈, or afflicting the hyleg therefrom; the ☽ in ♈, ☌, or ill-asp. any of the malefics as promittors; the ☽ Sig. in ♑ or ♓; the ☽ in ♓, an easy-going and inactive disposition; the ☽ to the ☌ or ill-asp. ♄ by dir.; a ♆ disease; caused by ♆ when the bodily powers are in abeyance, and the psychic powers are in a state of hyperactivity; ♄ ☌ the Asc. by dir., and to cause drowsiness; ♃ Sig. in ♑; ♀ affl. in ♈; a ☿ disease, and caused by afflictions to ☿ as ☿ rules vibration, and a lessened rate of vibration tends to dull the senses; ☿ denotes death by lethargy; ♋ on the Asc. at B. tends to give a lethargic disposition. Encephalitis, with great lethargy, accompanies Influenza and Sleeping Sickness. Lethargy, attended by short remissions, is caused by ♆. (See Apathy, Cataphora, Depressed, Dull, Encephalon; "Lack Of" under Energy; Ennui, Fatigue, Hyperaesthesia, Idle, Inactive, Indifferent, Inertia, Influenza, Lassitude, Lazy, Listless, Pituitary, Rouse; "Drowsiness", "Sleeping Sickness", under Sleep; Weariness).

**LEUCEMIA**—(See Leukocytes).

**LEUCO**—See words beginning with Leuko.

**LEUCOMAINES**—Leokomain—(See "Offensive" under Humours).

**LEUCORRHOEA**—Leukorrhea—Fluor Albus—Whites In Women—Catarrh of the Womb—A ♏ disease, and caused by afflictions in ♏; the ☽ affl. in ♎, ♏, or ♑; the ☽ in ♎ or ♑, ☌, or ill-asp. any of the malefics as promittors; the ☽ in any of the fixed signs and afflicted by ♆, ♅, or ♄; the ☽ in the 6th H. in evil asp. to ♀ in ♏, in Hor'y Q. denotes a person suffering with this trouble; the ☉ in ♉, ♌, or ♒, and afflicted by ♆, ♅, or ♄ when attended by profuse menstruation; ♄ affl. in ♋ in the 8th H.; ♄ affl. in ♏; a ♀ disease; ♀ affl. in ♏; Subs at KP, and PP (2, 3, 4L). (See "Profuse" under Menses; Vagina; "Catarrh" under Womb).

**LEUKEMIA**—(See Leukocytes).

**LEUKOCYTES**—Leukemia—Leucaemia—White Blood Corpuscles. These are said to be destroyers of the body, and to form a nucleus for mineral deposits. They are manufactured in the Spleen, and are principally the work of ♄. During anger, and also during disease and various afflictions, they pass thru the walls of the blood vessels, and deposit themselves in weakened or diseased tissues, and form a nucleus for the increased deposit of mineral wastes of the body, forming tumors, ulcers.

**Increase Of**—Leukemia—Leukocytosis—Caused by ♄ afflicted at B., or ♄ afflicting the hyleg; ♄ affl. in ♍, as ♍ rules the Spleen; ♄ in ♍ and afflicting the ☉, ☽, Asc., or Hyleg; ♄ afflicted at B., and ♂ weak; Subs at CP, SP, and KP. (See Anaemia, Deposits, Lymph, Minerals, Spleen, Tumors, Wastes).

**LEUKOCYTOSIS**—(See Leukocytes).

**LEOKOPLASIA BUCCALIS**—(See Tongue).

**LEWD**—Libidinous—Lustful—Lascivious—Given to Lewd Companies of Women or the Opposite Sex—The ☉ afflicted in watery signs; the ☽ afflicted in ♏ or ♑; the ☽ decr., separating from

♂ and applying to ♀, disgrace thru wantonness; ♂ ill-dig. at B., and affl. the ☽ or ♀; ♂ in the house of ♀; ♂ Sig. ☌ ♀, often associates with women of no respectability; ♂ Sig. ⚹ or △ ♀; ♂ ☌ or afflicting ♀; ♂ and ♄ to the ill-asps. ♀ by dir.; ♀ in bad asp. to ♂ at B., and by dir; ♀ to the ill-asps. ♄ by dir.; ♀ in ♈, ♍, ♏, or ♑, and afflicted by ♂, and espec. ♀ in ♏; ♀ to the ☌ ♂ or ☋ by dir., disgrace thru lewd courses; ♀ ill-dig. at B. (See Debauched, Depraved, Disgrace, Dissipated, Excesses, Exhibitionism, Harlots, Improvident, Lascivious, Licentious, Lust; "Loose Morals" under Morals; Nymphomania, Parents; "Passional Excesses" under Passion; Perversions, Sex, Shameless, Virile, Wanton, Wench).

**LIABLE**—Liability To—Tendency To—Danger of, etc.—

**Accidents**—Hurts, Injuries, Wounds—Liable To — (See "Danger Of", "Liable To", "Tendency To", etc., under Accidents, Hurts, Injuries).

**Disease**—Liable To—(See Directions; "Liable To" under Disease; "Bad Health", "Periods of Bad Health", under Health; Invalids, Lunations, Progressed; "Low" under Resistance, Vitality; Sickly; "Much Sickness" under Sickness; Sixth House; Transits; "Weak Body" under Weak).

**Less Liable to Disease** — (See "Good Health" under Health; Immunity; "Strong" under Recuperation; "Good" under Resistance, Vitality; Robust, Ruddy, Stamina; "Body" under Strong; Tone). The ills to which humanity are subject are legion, and too numerous to list here. Look in the alphabetical arrangement for the subject you have in mind. See Character, Destiny, Disgrace, Dishonour, Fate, Pain, Reversals, Ruin, Sorrow, Suffering, Trouble; "Free Will" under Will. A person may be liable to many evils, according to the indications of their star maps, especially if they are drifting in life, lacking in wisdom, self-control, discretion, discrimination, and the knowledge of Astrology, but the student of the Occult, of Astrology, the Metaphysical, etc., can usually by his foreknowledge forestall many evils that would naturally overtake the ignorant, the uninitiated, and those who are not ruling their stars. Ripe Fate may be the exception, which is discussed under "Fate".

**LIARS**—Lying—Falsifiers—☿ affl. at B., and the ☽ to the ☌ or ill-asp. ☿; ☿ ill-dig. at B.; ☿ □ or ☍ ☽; ☿ Sig. in ♈; ☿ to the ☌ or ill-asp. ♂ by dir., and ♂ weak; ♄ and ♂ afflicting ☿; ♄ Sig. □ or ☍ ☿; ♂ to the ☌ or ill-asp. ☿; ♂ Sig. □ or ☍ ☿, his most solemn protestations are not to be believed. (See Artifice, Character, Cheating, Deceitful, Dishonest, Dual, Forgers, Gambling, Hypocrites, Knavish, Libel, Mischief, Perjury, Pettifogging, Principles, Shrewdness, Swindlers, Thieves, Treachery, Truth).

**LIBEL** — Libellers — Given to Libel — Blackmailers — Slanderers — Defames the Character of Others — Writers of Libel—Liars, etc.—☿, the mental ruler, ill-dig. at B., afflicted by malefics, and the ☽ to the ill-asps. ☿ by dir.; ☿ at a Solar Rev. passing the place of the radical ♂; ☿ Sig. □ or ☍ ♄, much given to villifying the character of others, and is apt to suffer lawsuits for libel and blackmail; the ☽ incr. in light, sepr. from ♄ and apply. to ☿; ♃ to the ill-asps. ☿ by dir., and ☿ afflicted by ♃ at B.; ♂ to the ill-asps. ☿ by dir., and ☿ affl. by ♄ or ♂ at B.; the M.C. to Algenib, danger of imprisonment thru libel. (See Character, Dishonesty, Liars; "Scandalmongers" under Scandal).

**LIBERTY**—At Liberty to Travel Where You Will—(See "Home or Abroad" under Travel).

**LIBIDINOUS**—Violently Libidinous—(See Lewd, Lust, Nymphomania, Virile).

**LIBRA** — The 7th Sign of the Zodiac, the day and home sign of ♀, and is related to the 7th H. Libra is classed as an airy, cardinal, positive, masculine, hot, warm, moist, humane, and nervous sign. It is the exalted sign of ♄, and the fall of the ☉. When afflicted it causes inharmony and want of tone by disturbances in the system, and disordered kidneys. Libra implies sublimation, which is vaporization and recondensation. The Symbol of this sign is "The Balance", and the influence of the sign is to help keep the balance in the system by the work of secretion, excretion, elimination, and separating the poisons which are carried off in the urine. Libra and ♒ are considered the weakest of the positive signs. Externally, ♎ rules the external Generative and Urinary Organs, and the Anus. Internally, it rules the Kidneys. Structurally, this sign rules the Lumbar Vertebrae. Libra rules the outer or upper portion of the Kidneys, the Medullary and Cortical Substances. Libra and ♌ are concerned with Distillation and Circulation, and ♎ especially rules Distillation and Filtration. Libra and ♏ are closely associated in the work of the kidneys, secretion and excretion of urine. (See Kidneys, Scorpio, Urine). Libra is a rather fruitful sign because of ♀. For the Nations and Countries ruled by ♎ see "Libra" under Nations. The Colors ruled by ♎ are Black, and Dark Crimson. The Hebrew letter "Lahmed" (L) is connected with the ♎ sign, and also with Sleep and Dreams. When on the Asc. at B. the ♎ sign gives a tall, graceful, slender body, but the last few degrees rising, the body is shorter and stouter due to the influence of the next sign ♏. The Pathological Qualities of ♎ are Jealousy, Melancholy, Self-Centeredness, Sensitiveness. (See Seventh House, Venus). The following are the Qualities ruled over, or given by ♎ —Airy, Artistic, Autumnal, Beauty, Cardinal, Changeable, Diurnal, Equinoctial, Fortunate, Fruitfulness, Graceful, Hot, Humane, Masculine, Moist, Moveable, Musical, Nervous, Obeying, Positive, Sanguine, Southern, Speaking, Sweet, Warm, Western, Whole, etc.

**LIBRA RULES**—For the external, internal and structural rulerships of ♎ see the Introduction to this Article. The following is an alphabetical list of the parts of the body, and other matters ruled by ♎. Look for these subjects in the alphabetical arrangement—Adrenals; Anus; Back — Lower Part of; Balance — Poise and Equilibrium; Black or Dark Brown in Hor'y Q; Black or Dark Crimson Colors; Bladder; Blue and Dark Crimson; Circulation; Colors—Black or Dark Brown —Black or Dark Crimson—Swarthy or any Dusky Color—Blue and Dark Crimson—Tawny; Cortical Substances of the Kidneys; Crimson Color; Dark Brown Color in Hor'y Q.; Dark Crimson or Black; Distillation of Urine; Dusky Colors; Equilibrium, Equipose; Fallopian Tubes; Filtration, Distillation and Sublimation of Urine; Functional Activity of Secreting Urine; Generative Organs — External; Haunches to the Buttocks; Hypogastrium; Jealousy; Kidneys—Outer and Upper Parts of; Liver; Loins; Lower Part of the Back; Lumbar Region in General, Including the Lumbar Nerves, the Lumbar Vertebrae, Lumbar Region of the Spine, and the Kidneys; Medullary and Cortical Substances of the Kidneys; Melancholy; Mouth (Duz); Nerves (Lumbar); Outer and Upper Part of the Kidneys; Ovaries; Poise; Recondensation; Reins of the Back; Remedy —Rhus Toxicodendron; Renal System (see Kidneys); Rhus Toxicodendron (see "Saturn Group" under Herbs); Secretion of Urine; Self-Centeredness; Sensitiveness; Skin; Sodium Phosphate Salt; Spine (Lumbar Region of); Sublimation of Urine; Suprarenals; Tawny Color; Tongue (Duz); Upper Part of Kidneys; Ureters; Urinary Organs (External); Urine — Distillation, Filtration, Secretion, and Sublimation of; Vaporization; Vaso-Motor System; Veins; Vertebrae (Lumbar).

**LIBRA DISEASES**—The Afflictions of —Pathological Effects of—See the following subjects in the alphabetical arrangement when not considered here—

**Abscess** — (Imposthumes) — Of the Bladder—Of the Kidneys—Of the Reins —(See "Abscess" under Bladder, Kidneys, Loins, Reins).

**Anuria** — Suppression of Urine — (See Urine).

**Atrophy** — Wasting— (See Atrophy, Wasting).

**Back** — All Diseases In — Injuries or Weakness In the Lower Part of the Back—Disorders In Reins of the Back —(See Back, Reins).

**Bladder** — Disorders of — All Diseases In — Abscess, Imposthumes, or Ulcers In—(See Bladder).

**Blood**—Corrupt Blood—(See Impure).

**Bright's Disease**—(See Bright's).

**Calculus** — Renal — In the Kidneys — (See "Kidneys" under Stone).

**Colic**—Renal—(See "Colic" under Kidneys).

**Coma; Corruption**—Of the Blood—(See Impure).

**Debility**—Weakness—(See Debility).

**Diabetes; Diseased Kidneys**—Distempered Kidneys—(See Kidneys).

**Distillation** — Of Urine—Disturbances of—(See Distillation, Filtration, Sublimation, Urine).

**Eczema; Emaciation** — (See Emaciation, Tabes).

**Filtration** — Of Urine — Disturbances of — (See Filtration, Distillation, Sublimation, Urine).

**Floating Kidney**—(See Kidneys).

**Functions** — Functional Disturbances of the Kidneys — (See "Diseased Kidneys" under Kidneys; "Suppression" under Urine).

**Gravel**—In the Bladder or Kidneys— (See Gravel).

**Haunches**—Heats In—(See Buttocks, Haunches).

**Head** — Pains In or Injury To — (See Head).

**Health**—Of Libra People—The Health of ♎ People, and in Countries ruled by ♎, tends to be good when the ☉, ☽, ♃, or ♀ are in ♎ at the Autumn Quarter, and free from affliction, but poor and afflicted in health when the malefics so occupy ♎.

**Heats**—(See "Heats" under Buttocks).

**Imposthumes**—(See "Abscess" in this section).

**Inflammation** — Of the Kidneys and Ureters—(See Kidneys, Ureters).

**Inharmony**—In the System—And Disturbances—Afflictions in ♎. (See "Disordered" under System).

**Insomnia**—(See Sleep).

**Ischuria**—False Ischuria—(See Ischuria).

**Kidneys**—All Diseases In—(See Kidneys).

**Liver**—Disorders of—(See Liver).

**Loins** — Abscess In — Pains and Diseases In—(See Loins).

**Lower Part of Back**—Pains and Diseases In—(See Back).

**Lues**—(See Syphilis).

**Lumbago; Lumbar Region** — Of the Spine—Diseases In—(See Lumbar).

**Malnutrition**—(See Nutrition).

**Nephritis**—(See Kidneys).

**Neuralgia**—Of the Kidneys—(See Kidneys).

**Pains** — In the Back and Kidneys — (See "Pain" under Back, Kidneys).

**Pathological Action**—Of the ♎ Sign— (See the Introduction to this Article).

**Polyuria** — (See Diabetes; "Polyuria" under Urine).

**Poor Health** — (See "Health" in this section).

**Pyelitis**—(See Kidneys).

**Reins** — All Diseases In — Abscesses, Imposthumes, and Ulcers In — (See Reins).

**Renal Disorders** — Renal Calculus — Renal Colic—(See Kidneys).

**Sand**—(See Gravel, Sand, Stone).

**Skin Diseases**—(See Skin).

**Sores; Spurious Ischuria**—(See "Ischuria" under Urine).

**Stone** — In the Bladder or Kidneys — (See Stone).

**Suppression of Urine**—(See Urine).

**Syphilis; Tabes; Tone**—Lack of—(See Tone).

**Tumors**—Of the Kidneys—(See Kidneys).

**Ulcers**—In the Bladder or Reins—(See "Ulcers" under Bladder, Reins).

**Uremia; Ureters**—Inflammation and Obstruction In—(See Ureters).

**Urine**—Disturbances of—(See Urine).

**Veins**—All Diseases of—(See Veins).

**Wasting Diseases**—(See Atrophy, Consumptions, Emaciation, Tabes, Wasting).

**Weakness**—In the Back—General Weakness and Debility—(See "Weak" under Back; Debility, Weak).

**LICENTIOUSNESS**—Lascivious—Lewd—Wanton—Loose—Dissolute, etc.—Ruled and indicated by the 5th H.; the ☽ sepr. from ♄ and applying to ♀; ♆ affl. in the 5th H., licentious habits; ♅ in □ or ☍ to planets, and espec. to ♀; ♂ with ♀ alone, and ♄ absent; ♂ Sig. □ or ☍ ♀; in a female horoscope ♂ and ♀ in masculine signs, and in ☌, or evilly configurated, tend to make women licentious beyond nature, and espec. if the Luminaries also be in masculine signs at B.; ♀ ill-dig. at B.; ♀ affl. at B., and to the ☌ or ill-asp. the Asc. or ♂ by dir.; ♀ Sig. □ or ☍ ♂; the 3rd Decan. of ♎ on the Asc. (See Amorous, Debauched, Depraved, Dissipation, Dissolute, Harlots, Indecent, Lascivious, Lewd; "Licentious" under Men; "Loose Morals" under Morals; Nymphomania, Obscene, Passion, Perversions, Scandal, Shameless, Wanton, etc.).

**LIFE**—Prospects of Life—Length of Life, etc.—The expression of life, continuity, and the giving of life, are the most salient characteristics of the ☉, and the ☉ has significance of life and the constitution. The 1st H. also has signification of the life of Man, and his physical body and appearance. The ☉ gives the life force, and life and joy are said to come from the ☉. The fiery signs are life-giving signs. Life also corresponds to the fixed signs, and to the heart and Vital Temperament. Life manifests as motion, or vibration. Saturn afflicts and suppresses life and joy by his evil aspects to the ☉, ☽, Asc., or Hyleg. The following subjects have to do with life, and the planetary influences as they affect and influence life for good or ill, which subjects see in the alphabetical arrangement when not considered here—

**Accidents; Anareta**—The Destroyer of Life—(See Anareta).

**Average Life**—The ☉ well-aspected in the Asc. at B. indicates an average length of life, and a strong constitution in Hor'y Q. (See "Long Life" under Life; Middle Life).

**Benefics**—The Benefics As Givers and Preservers of Life—(See Benefics).

**Birth**—Continuance of Life After Birth—(See "Continuance' in this section).

**Change of Life**—(See "Menopause" under Menses).

**Changeable Life**—(See Changes, Instability, Location, Residence, Restless, Roaming, Travel, Unstable, Wandering).

**Childhood**—Life In—(See Childhood).

**Close of Life**—(See Close, Fourth House, Old Age, Terminal).

**Conscious Life**—(See Consciousness).

**Continuance of Life**—Continuity of Life—The continuance and continuity of life after birth are expressed by the ☉; the ☉, ☽, and Asc., and one of them hyleg, well-aspected by benefics, and with good aspects among them, and free from the evil asps. of malefics, promote life and give a strong constitution; the benefics ♃ and ♀ angular, free from affliction, and in good asp. to the hyleg, as by ☌, ⚹, △, or P., is a good sign of the continuance of life; the ☉ hyleg in a male nativity, and well-aspected, and the ☽ hyleg in a female nativity, well-aspected, and free from the afflictions of malefics, indicate a continuance of life, and long life. The last aspect formed between the ☉ and ☽ before birth, whether a good or evil asp., is important to be considered when judging of the influences as to continuance and duration of life. Also, in considering whether the child will live, the Asc., its ruler, and the ruler of the 8th H., the house of death, should be noted, and their aspects and relations to each other, whether good or bad. The lord of the 8th H., and especially when a malefic, and afflicting the lord of the Asc. at B., is not favorable for a continuance of life, and the child may soon die. (See "Death" under Childhood, Children, Infancy; "Early Death" under Early; "Nurture" under Infancy; "Long Life", "Short Life", and the various paragraphs in this section).

**Corresponds To**—Life Corresponds To—(See Introduction to this Article).

**Danger to Life**—The Life In Danger—Danger of Losing the Life—In Danger of Death—May Cause Death—Death Threatened, etc.—The ☉ to the ☌ or ill-asp. ♄ or ♂ by dir., and the ☉ hyleg at B.; the adverse asps. of the ☉ to ♄, ♆, ♅, or ♂ by dir., and espec. among the Aged, or those of a frail constitution; the ill-asps. of several malefic promittors to the ☉ tend to double or treble the danger to life, cause a breakdown in health, disaster or death; a total Eclipse of the ☉ falling on the place of the ☉ at B., and espec. when the ☉ is badly afflicted at B., or by dir.; the ☉ in the 6th or 8th H. at B., and to the ☌ or ill-asp. ♄ by dir.; the ☽ hyleg and to the ☌ or ill-asp. ♄ by dir.; the ☽ Sig. in ☌ the ☉ by dir., and espec. if the ☽ be applying, and it happens in the 8th H., or the ☉ be lord of the 8th; the ☽ hyleg and afflicted, and to the cusp the 8th H. by dir.; the ☽ to the ☌, P., or ill-asp. ♂ by dir., and the danger is by accident, blow, cut, stab, fever, or violence; the ☽ sepr. from the ☉ and apply. to ☿ in a night nativity; the ☽ at Full, or incr. in a nocturnal nativity, sepr. from ♀ and apply. to ♂; the ☽ at a Solar Rev. passing over the place of ♂ at B., and the ☽ afflicted at the Revolution; the ☽ to the □ or ☍ ☿ if the ☽ be hyleg, and ☿ afflicted at B.; the ☽ apply. to the ☍ ♂ in the 8th H., and when in exact ☍; the ☽ hyleg and to the ☌ the ☉ by dir., and the ☉ and ☽ afflicted at B.; the New ☽ implies death, disintegration, and preparation for a new Cycle, and a New ☽, or Lunation, badly afflicted just previous to birth, or just before a disease sets in, is very evil for a continuance of life; ♅ afflicting the hyleg by dir.; ♅ passing over the place of ♂ at B. by transit, and if afflicting the ☉ at the same time; taken sick in a ♄ hour; operating evil primary and secondary directions bring danger of death when the hyleg is evilly aspected at B., but supported by the benefics. (See "Danger of Death" under Children; Danger; "Arguments for Death" under Death; Directions, Eclipses, Fatal, Lunations; "New Moon" under Moon; Old Age, Transits, etc.).

**Death** — (a) Death Threatened — See "Arguments for Death", "Threatened", under Death. (b) Death Not Imminent —(See "Spared" in this section).

**Destiny** — (See Character, Destiny, Events, Fate).

**Destroyed**—Life Destroyed—The hyleg setting on the Western Angle, death ensues; the hyleg ☌, □, or ☍ ♄ or ♂ in the Zodiac or Mundane P. when they are equally distant from any angle, is said to destroy life. It takes a train of evil directions to the hyleg to destroy life, and one evil direction seldom kills, and espec. if the native be young, vigorous and healthy. (See "Certain Death", "Sure Death", under Death; Directions, Fatal).

**Destroyers of Life** — (See Anareta, Malefics).

**Dies Soon After Birth** — (See Abortion, Birth, Infancy, Parturition).

**Directions**—The Effect of Directions On Life—(See Directions).

**Does Not Live to Old Age** — (See "Death At Middle Life" under Middle Life; "Old Age Seldom Attained" under Old Age).

**Duration of Life** — (See Continuance, Long Life, No Duration, Probable, Short Life, and the various paragraphs in this section; "Death" under Childhood, Children, Early, Infancy, Middle Life, Old Age, Youth, etc.).

**Early Death**—(See Early).

**Early Life** — (See Childhood; "Early Years" under Early; Infancy).

**End of Life**—Ruled principally by the 4th H. (See Death, Eighth House, End, Fatal, Fourth House, Old Age, Terminal, Twelfth House).

**Evils of Life**—(See Evil).

**Excess of Life Force** — (See "Life Force" in this section).

**Expression of Life** — (See Introduction to this Article).

**Extravagant Life**—(See Extravagant, Luxury).

**Fatal to Life**—(See Fatal).

**Father** — The Father Long-Lived — Short Life For—(See Father, Parents).

**Few Hours of Life**—Lives But a Few Hours—(See "Death Soon After Birth" under Infancy).

**Fires of Life**—They are kept burning by the life-giving ☉, and the Iron given by ♂, and the cleansing power of ♂ in eliminating wastes and filth. (See Iron; "Constructive" under Mars).

**First Half of Life**—Is said to be ruled by the ☽. (See Periods).

**Force**—Forces—The Life Force—(See "Excess", "Life Force", under Force; Vital).

**Giver of Life** — Giving of Life — (See Hyleg; the Introduction to this Article).

**Hazards Life** — To Rescue Others — (See Rescue).

**Hope of Life**—Small Hope of Life—The Sick Will Hardly Escape—The ☽ in ♈, afflicted by the ☉ or ♂ when taken ill, and espec. if the ☽ leaves the ☌ of ♂ and goes to the ☌ or ☍ ♄ during the illness, or if the ☽ decr. in light and be slow in motion (Hor'y). (See "Destroyed", "Spared", in this section; "Certain Death" under Death; "Sick" under Escape; Fatal).

**Hyleg**—The Giver of Life—(See Hyleg).

**Idle Life**—(See Idle).

**Ill-Health All Thru Life** — (See this subject under Ill-Health).

**Indigent Life**—(See Indigent).

**Infancy** — Dies In — (See "Death" under Infancy).

**Joy and Life**—Come from the ☉. (See Joy).

**Judging of Life**—Judging the Length of Life—(See "Length" in this section).

**Killed** — Sudden End to Life — (See Killed).

**Lease On Life**—A New Lease On Life —Is given by the fevers and inflammations brought by ♂ to burn out the dross and accumulated impurities, provided the system has enough fundamental vitality to withstand his severe cleansing fires. (See Cleansing; "Constructive" under Mars).

**Length of Life**—Judgment on this is formed on the ☉, ☽, Asc., and lord of the Asc., their aspects, etc., and also the strength of the hyleg. (See Duration, Length; Continuance, Duration, Long, Probable, Short, in this section).

**Life Destroyed**—(See "Destroyed" in this section).

**Life Force** — The ☉ gives the life force. Also ♂ aids in giving force, activity, and energy. The ☉ ☌ ♄ at B., the life forces are obstructed, sapped and undermined. (See "Force" in this section).

**Life-Giving Signs**—The Fiery Signs—(See "Fire Signs" under Fire).

**Life Saved**—The Life Will Be Spared —Will Not Be Saved—(See "Spared" in this section).

**Long Life**—Signs of—Marks of—Dies In Old Age—Marks of Long Life—The SUN, ☽, Asc., and hyleg strong at B., well-aspected, and free from evil asps. of malefics; the ☉ rising in ♈, ♌, or ♋, well-placed, and not afflicted; the ☉ well-aspected in ♉ at sunrise; the ☉ in the 1st H., well-aspected and dignified; the ☉ or ☽ in the 1st, 10th, 11th, or 2nd H., and well-aspected by ♃ and ♀; the less the ☉ is afflicted at B., and espec. with males, and the less the ☽ is afflicted with females, the greater the prospects of long life; the ☉ hyleg and well-aspected with males, and the ☽ hyleg, and well-asp. with females, promises long life; the ☉ strong in male nativities; the ☉ in ♑ gives longevity, and to cling to life to the very last; the ☉ and ☽, and the ♌ and ♋ signs, the signs of the ☉ and ☽, well-placed in the map, long lease of life is assured; the ☉ elevated, ♃ and ♀ angular, and in greater power than the malefics; the ☉ well-aspected by the ☽ and benefics, and free from the affliction of malefics; the ☉, ☽, Asc., or hyleg not vitiated by malefics, or lords of the 6th or 8th H.; the ☽ sepr. from the △ of ♀, and applying to the △ of ♃, and with ♃ in the Asc. or M.C., and well-aspected by malefics; the MOON in good asp. to the ☉; the ☽ free from affliction, and well-aspected by ♃ or ♀, and also the Asc. free from malefic planets; the ☽ free from affliction, not combust, or evilly aspected by lords of the 4th, 6th, 8th, or 12th H.; the ☽ and lord of the Asc. direct in motion, swift, angular, and especially in the 1st or 10th H., or in the 8th or 11th., well-aspected by ♃, ♀, and the ☉, or in terms of ♃ or ♀; the ☽ well-asp. in the 8th H., but with danger of drowning; SATURN in ♎ or ♏, and well-aspected; ♄ well-asp. in the 8th H., and espec. when in ♎ or ♑ in the 8th; ♄ moderately fortified in the 1st H., and well-asp. by the ☉, ☽, ♃, or ♀; JUPITER or ♀ in the 8th H. and well-aspected; ♃ and ♀ in good asp. to the hyleg, and not afflicted by malefics; ♃ ☌ or good asp. the ☉, usually long life; ♃ in the 1st H. near the cusp, long life and happiness; MARS ✶ or △ the ☉, usually long life; the ASCENDANT, its lord, and planets there, be well-dignified, free from affliction, well-posited, and increasing in light and motion; if the Asc., lord of the Asc., and the ☉ or ☽, or the majority of them, are strong, free from affliction, not combust or ℞, not near any violent fixed stars, not besieged by malefics, or having the declinations of malefics, and not impeded by the lords of the 4th, 6th, 8th, or 12th H., these are signs of long life, and most or all of these conditions reversed denote short life or great danger to the native; the Asc., and the ☉ and ☽ free from affliction; lord of the 1st H. and the ☽ in no way afflicted, and no malefic, nor the lord of the 8th, nor ☋ ascending, are considered marks of a long life; lord of the 1st and the ☽ in ☌, or well-aspected by a benefic, or a benefic in the Asc.; the distance between the lords of the 1st and 8th H., allowing one degree for a year, indicate the length of life of the native, as a rule, or the event of some serious illness or accident, but as the body of the ☉ may be considered Anareta, if the lord of the 1st become combust before he reaches the lord of the 8th, then reckon according to the number of degrees between him and the ☉ (Hor'y); lord of the Asc. in the 1st H.; lord of the 8th a benefic, in the 8th, and not afflicting the hyleg; lord of the 8th in the 8th H., even if a malefic, and not afflicted; the 1st Decan. of ♍ on the Asc., ruled by the ☉; the 3rd face of ♐ on the Asc.; the 6th face of ♒ on the Asc.; the 4° ♍, the 3° ♑, the 2° ♒, the 10° ♓ on the Asc. indicate long life. (See Duration; "Long Life" under Females, Males; "Good Health", "Prospects", under Health; Hyleg, Immunity; Majority, Maturity, Old Age, Recuperation, Resistance, Stamina; "Body" under Strong; Vitality; "Continuance", "Seldom", and the various paragraphs in this section).

**Maintenance of Life** — Life Is Maintained by the ☉, the giver of life, and by ♂, the giver of iron in the blood. (See "Fires of Life" in this section).

**Malefics** — Destroyers of Life — (See Anareta, Malefics).

**Man** — Life of Man — The 1st H. has significance of the life of man, his body, and physical appearance.

**Manifests**—Life Manifests as Motion and Vibration. (See Motion, Vibration).

**Manner of Life**—Manner of Living—(See Conduct, Habits, Manner, Morals).

**Many Illnesses**—All Thru Life—(See "Ill-Health All Thru Life" under Ill-Health; "Much Sickness" under Sickness).

**Maturity** — Lives To — (See Maturity, Middle Life).

**Middle Life** — Lives To — (See Middle Life).

**Military Life** — Injury or Death In — (See Military).

**Miserable Life**—(See Miserable).

**Mother** — Long Life For — Short Life For—(See Mother).

**Motion and Life**—(See "Manifests" in this section).

**Night Life**—Disposed To—(See "Nocturnal" under Night).

**No Duration of Life**—(See "Death At Birth" under Birth; "Early Death" under Early; Eclipses; "Death", "Death Soon After Birth", under Infancy; "Incapable of Nurture" under Nutrition; "Short Life" in this section).

**Nurture**—Incapable of—(See "Incapable" under Nutrition).

**Obstructed Life Forces**—Caused by ♄ influence and affliction; the ☉, ☽, Asc., or hyleg ☌ ♄ at B., and by dir.; the ☉ in ♌, ☌, □, or ☍ ♄. (See Obstructions, Retarded, Suppressions; "Life Force" in this section).

**Old Age**—Lives To—Seldom Lives To—(See Old Age).

**Parents** — Long or Short Life For — (See Parents).

**Periods of Life**—(See Critical, Cycles, Periods, Years).

**Poverty**—A Poverty-Stricken and Indigent Life—(See Idle, Indigent, Poverty).

**Precarious Life** — The ☽ affl. in the Asc., the health not good, and the life precarious (Hor'y).

**Preserved**—The Life Preserved—(See "Spared" in this section).

**Preservers of Life** — (See Benefics, Preservation).

**Probable Length of Life**—Of the Querent (Hor'y)—Observe the Asc., lord of the Asc., and the ☽; also lord of the 8th, and malefics in the 8th; the planet to whom the ☽, or lord of the 1st H. be joined by a ☌, □, or ☍ aspect. The time of death and the duration of life may be determined by the number of degrees between the Significator and the aspect of the afflicted planet. Years are denoted if the lord of the Asc. be in ☌ the lord of the 8th in an angle. Angles show strength and vitality and do not hasten death. Half years and half months of life are denoted if the Sig. be in fixed signs; if in succedent houses, months; if in cadent houses, weeks. In this case, the lord of the Asc. is more to be considered than the ☽, and the ☌ of the lord of the Asc. with the ☉ or lord of the 8th is to be feared the most. The lord of the Asc. being sorely afflicted in this question does not denote health or life. Only aspects by application are to be considered. (See Continuity; "Time of Death" under Death; Duration; Continuance, Duration, Length, Long, Short, in this section).

**Prolonged**—Life Prolonged—(See "Life Prolonged" in Sec. 3 under Children; Endurance, Prolonged).

**Regulator**—Of the Life Forces—The ☉ is the chief source and regulator of the life forces. (See Sun).

**Rescues Life of Others**—(See Rescue).

**Roaming Life**—Leads a Roaming and Wandering Life—(See "Changeable" in this section).

**Sad Life**—(See Sadness).

**Sapped**—The Life Forces Sapped and Undermined—(See "Life Force" in this section).

**Saved**—The Life Saved—Not Spared—(See "Spared" in this section).

**Second Half of Life**—Ruled by the ☉. (See "First Half" in this section).

**Seldom of Long Life**—The ☉, ☽, Asc., or hyleg afflicted by malefics at B. (See "Death" under Early; "Short Life" in this section).

**Short Life**—Signs of—Early Death—The SUN and ☽ both afflicted at B.; the ☉ badly aspected by the ☽ at B.; the ☉ or ☽ in the 6th H. at B., afflicted, and the rising sign a weak one; born at the time of a total eclipse of the ☉ with males, or an eclipse of the ☽ with females, seldom of long life or strong constitution (see Eclipses); the ☉ or ☽ Sig. ☌ ♂, and ♂ ill-dig., and usually early death thru quarrels, fury, accident, etc.; the ☉ Sig. □ or ☍ ♄ if he be in the Asc., unless a good asp. of ♃ intervene, the native is diseased and short-lived; the ☉ Sig. □ or ☍ ☽ if the ☽ be hyleg, and the aspect close; if the ☉, ☽, Asc., or lord of the Asc., or the most of them, are weak, afflicted, besieged by malefics, or occupying the same declination as malefics, if they be combust or ℞, and impeded by lords of the 4th, 6th, 8th, or 12th H., these are signs of short life or of great danger; the ☉ besieged by ♄ and ♂, cadent, and afflicted by lords of the 6th or 8th, or stars of their nature; the ☉ or ☽ affl. in common signs, and espec. in ♓; the ☉ afflicted in signs of low vitality, as in ♋, ♑, or ♓; the ☉ ☌ several malefics in ♑; the ☉, ♆, ☽, and ☿ conjoined in a sign of low vitality; the MOON nearly in ☌ with the ☉ at B., not well-aspected, and also the hyleg weak and afflicted by malefics; the ☽ sepr. from ♂ and apply. to the ☉; the ☽ ruler of the 1st H., being in the 6th, 8th, or 12th H., and afflicted, combust, ☌, □, or ☍ lords of the 6th, 8th, 12th, or 4th H., and also being slow in motion, out of dignity, and with no assistance from benefics; the ☽ cadent and unfortunate, and afflicted by lords of evil houses; the ☽ or ☉ Significators, in □ or ☍ ♄, according to the sex of the native (see Males, Females); the greater the affliction of the Significators of life, as the ☉, ☽, or Asc., the shorter the life will be; the ☽ ☌ or evil asp. a malefic in the 4th, 6th, 8th, or 12th H., or besieged by ♄ and ♂; the ☽ Sig. ☌ the ☉, very close to the ☉, combust, or applying to the exact ☌; the ☽ Sig. □ or ☍ ♂, and the ☽ hyleg; born at exactly the New or Full ☽ except the ☽ have great Lat.; NEPTUNE culminating and afflicted; URANUS, ♄, or ♂ near the rising degree, afflicted by lord of the 8th, and the ☽ afflicted by the ☉ at the same time; SATURN rising, and the ☉ afflicting the ☽ at the same time; ♄ and ♂ both afflicting the ☽ in female nativities, or the ☉ in male horoscopes; ♄ or ♂ afflicting the ☉, ☽, or Asc. by body or aspect; ♄, ♂, or ☋ in the Asc. or 7th H., peregrine, ℞, or in detriment (Hor'y); ♄ Sig. ☌ the ☉, seldom healthy or of long life; ♄ or ♂ in the Asc., and afflicting the hyleg; ♄ in the 1st H. near the cusp; ♄ in the 7th H.; ♄ culminating and affl. the hyleg; ♄ near the cusp of the 4th H. at B.; MARS afflicted in the 1st H. near the cusp generally cuts the life short, and smallpox is apt to occur when he arrives at the horizon; VENUS Sig. ☌ ☉, and the ☉ ill-dig., and usually due to prodigality; ♀ afflicted at B. tends to short life; born under ♀ influence, and with ♀ afflicted, tends to ill-health, excesses, bad habits which shorten life; ♀ Sig. ☌ ☉; lord of the Asc. combust, ℞, or peregrine, and the cause will be shown by the house that the afflicting planet is lord of, and in which he is posited; ruler of the ASCENDANT in the 6th or 8th H., and malefics in the Asc., and with ♋, ♑, or ♓ on the Asc.; lord of the Asc. under the beams of the ☉, or going to combustion if hyleg; lord of the 6th H. in the 8th or 12th, and afflicted, and espec. if the lord of the Asc. apply to the □ or ☍ lord of the 6th; lord of the 8th in the Asc. if a malefic and afflicted; many planets, and espec. malefics, near cusps of angles at B.; many planets afflicted in signs of low vitality, as in ♋, ♏, or ♓, or these signs on the Asc., and afflicted; the Significators, the lord of the 1st, or the ☽, afflicted by malefics, or by the lords of the 4th, 6th, 8th, or 12th H., or jointed to ☋, denotes short life according to the degree of affliction, and the degrees between the Sig., and the chief afflicting planet, are said to denote the weeks, months, or years of life for the Querent, and as the Promittor may be in Cardinal, Fixed, or Common Signs (Hor'y); the life tends to be short, or with some grave danger of misfortune near, according to the quality of the Significators, and of the houses those planets are lords of, and which afflict the ☽ (Hor'y). A number of Cases and birth data of Short Life, and Death in infancy, are given under Infancy. (See "Death" under Childhood, Children, Infancy; "Early Death" under Early; "No Duration of Life" in this section).

**Shorter**—The Shorter Will Be the Life —(See "Shorter" under Infancy).

**Signs**—Life-Giving Signs—The fiery signs ♈, ♌, and ♐.

**Signs of Long Life**—Of Short Life— (See "Long", "Short", in this section).

**Small Hope of Life**—(See "Hope" in this section).

**Source of Life**—(See "Regulator" in this section).

**Spared** — (a) The Life Is Spared — Death Not Imminent—The Life Saved —Life Preserved, etc.—Life will not be destroyed, or end in death from disease, unless the hyleg is sorely afflicted. The life is spared when there is no train of evil directions, as one direction rarely kills, no matter how malevolent it is. Life is always spared as long as the hyleg remains strong. When the ☽ is hyleg and directed to the ☌ of a malefic planet, if her Lat. when the aspect is completed differs greatly from that of the afflicting planet at B., life will generally be spared, altho a serious illness may result. A good direction of ♃ or ♀ to the hyleg in an otherwise train of evil directions, the life will be spared if the benefics were not badly aspected at B.; a benefic in good asp. to the Anareta; ♃ or ♀ within orb of the Anareta, and with ♃ within 12°, or ♀ within 8° of the anaretic point, life is spared; a malefic in the term of a benefic; the Anareta in the term of a benefic; a benefic in the term of a malefic will do less good, and renders it vicious; if an evil direction of ♃ or ♀ are within the orb of the anaretic point they help to save life; when the hyleg is ☌ the Anareta, but differing widely in Declination, life will be saved; in the World, or Mundane, even one degree of difference in Lat. between the hyleg and Anareta may save if the Anareta is in the term of a benefic, and espec. if the native has a good constitution, but severe indisposition may follow for a time; if the benefics cast a ray of any kind, good or evil, to the anaretic point, the life will be saved unless they are outnumbered by the malefics, and if two malefics are opposed to one benefic there is little hope except the benefics be strong in an angle, and the malefics cadent; if the Anareta falls in the term of a benefic almost any aspect of a benefic will save life. Ptolemy says a ray of either ♃ or ♀, of any kind, falling on the Anareta will save life, but Wilson in his Dictionary thinks ♀ cannot do so alone unless ♃ assists. (See Amelioration, Crises, Directions, Moderation, Recovery, Recuperation).

(b) Life May Not Be Spared—The hyleg ☌ the Descendant, death usually

results, and espec. if the hyleg is under evil directions of malefics; an assisting benefic in the term of a malefic, or the place of the anareta in the term of a malefic; a benefic is vitiated by being in the house, exaltation, or triplicity of a malefic, but most vitiated when in the term of a malefic; a benefic alone, not strong or dignified, has little power to save when threatened by two malefics. Life may be prolonged for a time, but the two malefics will prevail in time.

(c) Life Not Spared—Death Certain— A benefic in the term of a malefic; the anareta in the term of a malefic; a benefic in the term, house, exaltation, or triplicity of a malefic, death is practically certain unless both benefics intervene with good asps. to the hyleg; a benefic alone, afflicted and undignified, and threatened by two malefics; the hyleg and anareta in ☌, yet differing greatly in declination. (See "Arguments for Death", "Certain Death", "Fatal", "Sure Death", "Threatened", under Death; "Destroyed", "No Duration", in this section).

**Sudden End to Life**—(See Accidents, Assassination, Killed, Murdered; "Death" under Sudden; Suicide; "Death" under Violent).

**Suppressed** — Life Suppressed, Retarded and Hindered—♄ influence. (See Saturn, Suppressions).

**Sustains Life**—The Hyleg is the Giver of Life, and when well-placed and strong, sustains and upholds life. (See Hyleg).

**Terminal Houses**—Houses Which Denote the End of Life—(See Terminal).

**Trials of Life**—(See Adversity, Affliction, Anxiety, Fate, Misery, Misfortune, Reverses, Ruin, Sadness, Sickness, Sorrow, Trials, Trouble, Worry, etc.).

**Troubles of Life** — (See "Trials" in this section).

**Undermined**—The Life Forces Undermined—(See "Life Force" in this section).

**Unsettled Life**—(See "Changeable" in this section).

**Upholds Life**—(See "Sustains" in this section).

**Vibration** — (See "Manifests" in this section).

**Vital Forces**—Life Force—Vital Spark of Life—(See "Force" in this section; "Force", "Spark", under Vital).

**Vitality**—The Vital Principle of Life —(See Vitality).

**Wandering Life** — (See "Changeable" in this section).

**Will Not Live** — Will Not Live to a Great Age—Early Death—Short Life, etc.—(See "Seldom" in this section).

**Youth** — Death In — Life In — (See Youth).

**LIGAMENTS**—Sinews—Tendons—The Ligaments are ruled by ♄ and ♂, and ♄ tends especially to harden and crystallize them, and to cause loss of strength in the ligaments, and ♄ in any sign tends to affect the ligaments in the part ruled by the sign he is in at B. Thus ♄ afflicted in ♌ tends to loss of strength and elasticity in the ligaments of the spine. The ligaments are affected also by the ♓ sign, and the ☉ or ☽ in ♓, and acting thru ♓ and the Plantar Nerves tend to influence and affect the fibro-ligamentous system, the respiratory and synovial systems, the os calcis, the feet, toes, etc., and give way to the Thoracic Diathesis. Uranus in ♎ warns against over-straining of the sinews. (See Fiber, Muscles, Sinews, Tendons).

**LIGHT**—Lightness—Fair—Light Color, etc.—

**Action** — Light In Action — Quick In Action — (See "Quick" under Action; Active, Agile, Athletics, Brisk, Gait, Motion, Movement, Nimble, Quick, Sports, Walk, etc.).

**Adaptability**—Lack of Adaptability to Light—(See "Light" under Iris).

**Beard**—Light Beard—(See Beard).

**Brain**—Lightness In—(See Dizziness, Fainting; "Shallow" under Mentality; Vertigo).

**Colors** — Light Colors and White are ruled by the 1st H. (See Colors).

**Complexion**—Light Complexion—(See "Light" under Complexion).

**Degrees** — Light or Fair Degrees of the Zodiac—If the Asc., or its lord, are in one of these degrees at B. the native tends to be of fair and light complexion—♈ 8, 20, 29; ♉ 7, 15, 28; ♊ 4, 12, 22; ♋ 12, 18; ♌ 30; ♍ 8, 16; ♎ 5, 18, 27; ♏ 8, 22; ♐ 9, 19, 30; ♑ 10, 19; ♒ 9, 21, 30; ♓ 12, 22, 28. (See Degrees).

**Eyes**—Light-Colored—(See Blue, Gray, under Eyes).

**Feature**—Lightness of — (See "Lightness" under Features).

**Fingered**—Light-Fingered — (See Kleptomaniac).

**Hair**—Light Hair—(See "Light Hair" under Hair).

**Mind**—Light In—Shallow Mind—(See "Fails In" under Examinations; "Shallow" under Mentality; "Weak Mind" under Mind).

**Rays** — Light Rays — Light Rays are transmitted by ♅, which planet rules the Ether. Uranus thus indirectly tends to affect the eyes thru the light rays, and cause eye diseases or blindness. (See Ether, Mydriasis; "Operations" under Nature; Uranus).

**Time**—Light of Time—The ☉ is called The Light of Time. (See Sun).

**Walk** — Light Walk — Quick Walk — (See "Action" in this section; Gait; "Quick" under Walk).

**Weight**—Light In—(See Diminished, Dwarfs, Emaciated; "Small Body" under Small; Thin, etc.).

**LIGHTNING**—

**Blindness By** — (See "Lightning" under Blindness).

**Calculator**—Lightning Calculator—(See Mathematical).

**Casualties** — By Lightning — ♃ in ♊, lord of the year at the Vernal, and in asp. with ♂, many casualties by lightning; ☿ in ♊ ☌ ♂ at the Vernal Equi., and lord of the year; Comets appearing in ♒. (See Thunder).

**Child**—Struck by Lightning—Case—See "Struck by Lightning", No. 796, in 1001 N.N.

**Death By** — ♅ setting in ☍ to the Luminaries at B. shows danger of, and espec. under evil directions of ♅ to the ☉ or ☽. Also cardinal signs predominant and prominent at B. show, and espec. when they contain several malefics afflicting the hyleg by dir.; ♂ afflicting the Significators. (See "Battle" under Abroad; "Injury" in this section).

**Injury By**—Accidents By—Death By —The fiery signs strong at B. dispose to; ♅ afflicted in ♏; ♅ ☌ or ill-asp. the ☉; ♅ afflicting the hyleg by dir.; the ♅ influences cause accidents by electricity, as ♅ rules the Ether; ♄ in ♊, direct in motion and angular at the Vernal E., much lightning and danger from; ♂ afflicted in fiery signs, and ☌ or ill-asp. the Asc. by dir.; ♂ sole ruler at an eclipse of the ☉; ♂ Sig. ☌ the ☉. (See Clouds; "Fountains" under Dry; Electricity, Ether, Rain, Thunder, Weather, etc.).

**Sea**—Shipwrecks—Damage by Lightning At Sea—(See "Fountains" under Dry; "Lightning" under Ships; "Voyages" in this section).

**Voyages** — Danger by Lightning On Voyages — Malefics in the 9th H. in airy signs, and afflicting the ☉ or ☽. (See "Sea" in this section; "Ships" under Fire).

**LIKES AND DISLIKES**—♅ in ♌ tends to. (See Antipathy; "Dislikes" under Food; Hate, Opposites, Sympathy, etc.).

**LILLY** — William Lilly, the Astrologer, and Author of Lilly's Grammar of Astrology. One of the great Astrologers of his day. For a Biography of Mr. Lilly see Sepharial's Dictionary of Astrology.

**LIMBER** — Nimble — (See Athletics; "Quick In Motion" under Motion).

**LIMBS**—The Legs and Arms—The Extremities—In the Textbooks of Astrology many influences which affect or describe the Arms and Legs are referred to as "Limbs", and this Article is arranged for convenience of reference. These subjects are also considered in the Articles on Arms, Calves, Extremities, Feet, Fingers, Hands, Knees, Legs, Lower, Members, Motion, Movement, Moving Parts, Thighs, Upper, Walk, etc. (See these subjects). Also see the following subjects in the alphabetical arrangement when not more fully considered here—

**Accidents To** — Hurts — Injuries — Wounds—(See "Accidents" under Arms, Extremities, Legs).

**Afflictions In**—(See "Diseases" under Arms, Extremities, Legs).

**Amputations**—Avoid when the ☽ is in ♊ or ♐. (See Operations).

**Ankles**—Disorders of—Injuries To—(See Ankles).

**Arms**—Disorders In—♆ in signs which rule the arms, hands, and feet tends to wasting of the tissues, shrinking, and withering of the limbs. (See the various paragraphs under Arms).

**Atrophy In**—♄ in signs which rule the limbs. (See "Atrophy" under Arms, Feet, Hands, Legs).

**Birth**—The Limbs Distorted from Birth—Lame from Birth—(See Birth, Congenital, Crippled, Deformities, Distortions, Lameness, Paralysis; "Paralysis" in this section).

**Blood Vessels**—Constriction of—Impure Blood In—Lack of Circulation In—(See "Blood" under Arms, Legs).

**Brevity of Limbs**—♍ influence. (See Brevity, Short).

**Broken Limbs**—(See "Fractures" under Arms, Legs).

**Calves**—Disorders of—(See Calves).

**Circulation In**—(See Circulation; "Blood Vessels" in this section).

**Cold Limbs**—♄ in ♊, ♐, ♑, ♒, or ♓; ☿ afflicted in ♓. (See Cold, Constrictions; "Coldness" under Extremities, Legs).

**Congenital Defects**—(See Birth, Congenital, Deformities, Malformations; "Birth" in this section).

**Constriction**—Of Blood Vessels—(See "Blood" under Legs; "Cold" in this section).

**Contractions In**—♄ influence. (See Contractions; "Father" in this section).

**Cramps In**—(See "Arms" under Cramps; "Cramps" under Legs).

**Crippled In**—(See "Birth" in this section).

**Crooked Limbs**—(See "Ill-Formed" under Ill; Knees; "Crooked" under Legs).

**Defects In**—Defective from Birth—(See "Birth" in this section).

**Deformities**—Of Limb—(See the various paragraphs under Arms, Feet, Hands, Knees, Legs, Thighs; Birth, Congenital, Deformities, Malformations, Paralysis, and the various paragraphs in this section).

**Diseases Of**—(See "Afflictions", and the various paragraphs in this section).

**Distortions**—From Birth—Common signs rising at B., and usually with an adverse aspect between ♅ and ♂ in common signs. (See "Causes" under Distortions; Excrescences).

**Drawn Up Under Body**—(See "Paralysis" in this section).

**Dropsy Of**—(See "Dropsy" under Legs).

**Elbows**—Disorders of—(See Elbows).

**Erysipelas In**—(See Erysipelas).

**Extremities**—Disorders In—(See Arms, Extremities, Feet, Legs).

**Falls**—The Limbs Fractured or Distorted by Falls—The ☉ Sig. ☌ ♄, and ill-dignified; ♄ affl. in ♑ or the 10th H.; ♑ on the Asc. (See Distortions, Falls, Fractures).

**Father**—Contractions of the Limbs of the Father—(See "Muscles" under Father).

**Feet**—Disorders In—Afflictions To—(See the various paragraphs under Feet; "Arms" in this section).

**Femur**—Fracture of—(See Femur).

**Fibula**—Fracture of—(See Fibula).

**Foetus**—The Limbs of are developed by ♂. (See Foetus).

**Fractures Of**—(See "Fractures" under Arms, Knees, Legs, Thighs).

**Gait**—Disorders of—(See Gait, Walk).

**Glands Of**—(See "Affected" under Glands).

**Gout In**—(See "Extremities" under Gout).

**Hands**—Disorders In—(See Hands).

**Humerus**—Fracture of—(See Humerus).

**Humours In**—(See "Humours" under Extremities, Hands, Legs).

**Hurts To**—(See "Accidents" in this section).

**Ill-Shaped**—(See "Crooked" in this section; "Knock-Knees" under Knees; "Bow Legs" under Legs).

**Immobility**—(See "Rigidity" in this section).

**Imperfect**—Imperfections In—(See Arms, Feet, Forearms, Hands, Knees, Legs; Birth, Crooked, and the various paragraphs in this section).

**Infirmities In**—(See the various paragraphs under Arms, Extremities, Legs, and in this section).

**Injuries To**—(See "Accidents" in this section).

**Knees**—Disorders In—Hurts To—(See Knees).

**Lameness In**—(See Crippled, Gout, Paralysis, and the various paragraphs in this section).

**Large Limbs**—Large Joints—Well-Set and Large—☿ orientally posited of the ☉ except when ☿ is in ♊. (See "Large" under Joints, Legs; "Bones" under Large; "Long" in this section).

**Legs**—Disorders In—Hurts To—(See Legs).

**Length of Limb**—(See Long, Short, in this section; "Body" under Length).

**Leprosy In**—(See "Diseases" under Extremities; "General Causes" under Leprosy).

**Long Limbs**—♅ or ☿ ascending; ♅ in the Asc., or close thereto, tends to give length of limb, and a slender body. (See "Long" under Arms, Extremities, Legs; Slender, Tall).

**Loss Of**—Malefics afflicted in signs which rule the limbs, and especially ♂ in such a sign, and making amputation necessary. (See "Amputations" under Legs).

**Lower Limbs**—Disorders In—Afflictions To—(See Ankles, Calves, Extremities, Feet, Knees, Legs, Lower, Thighs; "Paralysis", and the various paragraphs in this section).

**Malformations**—♂ in the 3rd or 9th H. in common signs, and afflicting ☿; ♓ on the Asc., and espec. if ♅, ♂, or ☋ afflict the Asc. (See Arms, Crippled, Deformities, Feet; "Ill-Formed" under Ill; Legs, Malformations; "Paralysis" in this section).

**Members**—Brevity of—Length of—Disorders of, etc.—(See Arms, Brevity, Legs, Members; Long, Short, and the various paragraphs in this section).

**Missing**—Part of Limbs Missing from Birth—(See "Missing" under Forearm).

**Motion In**—(See Action, Crippled, Lameness, Locomotion, Movement, Quick, Slow, Walk; Birth, Distortions, Paralysis, in this section).

**Movement In**—(See "Motion" in this section).

**Moving Parts**—Ruled by ☿. (See Moving).

**Muscles**—Of the Limbs—(See "Muscles" under Arms, Extremities, Legs, Thighs; Muscles).

**Mutilation of Limb**—(See Beheaded, Mutilation).

**Nerves of Affected**—☿ affl. in signs which rule the limbs. (See "Neuralgia" under Arms; "Nerves" under Feet, Hands, Legs).

**No Limbs**—No Arms or Legs—There are such cases, as I saw such a lady in a Museum, and her trunk and head were set up on a pedestal for view. Her birth data I did not obtain. Such cases of congenital deformity are caused by prenatal conditions, and afflictions in ♊, ♐, the 3rd and 9th H. at the time of the return of the ☽ to the central line of impulse during gestation. Also such deformity is said to be caused by ♊ or ♐ on the Asc., the common signs on the angles at such a time during pregnancy, and containing malefics, and also the ☉, ☽, and Asc. being badly afflicted at the same time. The case of the Frog Child has the forearms missing, both legs missing below the knees. (See Forearm, Prenatal Epoch).

**Obstructions In**—Weakness In—Weak Limbs—The ☉ in ♊ or ♐, and to the ☌ or ill-asp. any of the malefics as promittors; the ☉ or ☽ in the Asc. in ♑, ♒, or ♓, and afflicted; the ☽ affl. in ♊ or ♐. (See "Obstructions", "Weak", under Legs).

**Operations On**—(See "Amputations" in this section).

**Pain In**—The ☽ in ♒, ☌, or ill-asp. any of the malefics as promittors; ♄ in ♐, ♑, or ♒, ☌, □, or ☍ ♃ or ♀; ♂ promittor in ♒, ☌, or ill-asp. the ☉; ♂ in the 12th H. (See "Pain" under Arms, Feet, Hands, Legs).

**Paralysis In**—Paraplegia—The ☉ affl. in ♐; ♅ and ☿ affl. in signs which rule the limbs; ♄ affl. in ♐ or ♑ on the M.C., or in the Asc., and affl. the ☉; ♄ in ♑ on the upper Meridian, and affl. the ☉, tends to paralysis, defective limbs from birth, or the lower limbs to be drawn up under the body in some cases, and espec. where afflicting prenatal conditions concur. Cases of Paralysis in Limbs—See "Tunnison", No. 113, in 1001 N.N., a case of Paralysis in every Limb; "Seventeen Years In Bed", No. 843, in 1001 N.N., a case of Partial Paralysis; "Von Kothen", No. 211, in 1001 N.N., a case of Legs Paralyzed; Figures 13 A, B, C, D, F, G, and 14A, in the book, "Astro-Diagnosis", by the Heindels. (See "Paralysis" under Arms, Hands, Legs; Lameness, Motor, Palsy, Paralysis; "Festination" under Walk).

**Radius**—Fracture of—(See Arms).

**Rheumatism In**—Rheumatic Pains In—♄ in signs ruling the limbs. (See "Rheumatism" under Extremities; Gout, Rheumatism).

**Rigidity Of**—Stiff Limbs—Caused by the afflictions of ♄ in signs which rule the limbs, and by the hardening of the synovial membranes. (See Hardening, Immobility, Rigidity, Stiffness).

**Short Limbs**—(See "Short" under Arms, Legs; Brevity, Dwarfed; "Body" under Short).

**Slender Limbs**—(See "Small" in this section).

**Small Limbs**—Small and Slender—☿ occidentally posited as regards the ☉ except when ☿ is in ♊. (See "Slender" under Legs).

**Stiffness Of**—(See "Rigidity" in this section).

**Stout Limbs**—Strong Limbs—♂ in ♌ in partile asp. the Asc. (See "Strong" in this section).

**Strong Limbs**—Stout—Muscular—♃ in the Asc.; ♂ Sig. in ♌; ♈ on the Asc. (See "Stout" under Legs; "Body" under Strong).

**Swellings In**—(See "Swellings" under Arms, Extremities, Feet, Hands, Legs).

**Thick Limbs**—(See "Thick" under Hands, Legs).

**Thighs**—Disorders In—Accidents and Hurts To—(See Thighs).

**Throbbing In**—♃ affl. in ♑. (See "Pain" in this section; Throbbing).

**Tissues**—Wasting of—(See "Wasting" in this section).

**Ulcers In**—(See "Arms" under Ulcers).

**Ulna**—Fracture of—(See "Ulna" under Arms).

**Upper Limbs**—(See Arms, Hands, Upper).

**Varicose Veins**—(See Varicose).

**Walk**—Disorders of—(See Gait, Walk).

**Wasting**—Of the Limbs—Of the Tissues—(See "Arms" in this section).

**Weak Limbs**—(See "Obstructions" in this section). Case of Weak Limbs—See Fig. 30 in the book, "Message of the Stars", by the Heindels.

**Well-Proportioned**—Well-Set Limbs—♃ in the Asc. (See "Strong" in this section).

**Withering Of**—(See "Arms" in this section).

**Wounds To**—(See "Accidents" in this section).

**Wrists**—Fracture of—(See Wrists).

**LIME**—Calcium—Chalk—Calcareous Substances—Coral is a form of Calcium. Lime Fluoride, or Calcium Fluoride, is ruled by the ♋ sign, and supplies the teeth and elastic fibre. (See Calces, Coral, Fiber). Calcium Phosphate is ruled by ♑ and supplies the bones. (See Bones, Minerals, Phosphate; "Salts" under Zodiac). Calcium Sulphate is ruled by the ♏ sign, and is connected with tissue cleansing. Lime and Chalk formations in the body are ruled by ♄. (See Chalk, Crystallization, Deposits, Gout, Hardening, Osseous, Rheumatism, Saturn, Sclerosis, Stone, Sulphates, Suppressions, Wastes).

**LIMITATIONS** — Restrictions—Impediments—Hindrances, etc.—Limitation is the principle of ♄, the ♄ sign ♑, and of the 12th H.

**The Body**—Limitations Upon the Body—The ☉, ☽, ♄, or ☿ afflicted in the 12th H. (See Asylums, Barren, Binding, Birth, Blindness, Confinement, Congenital, Deafness, Defects, Deformities, Disease, Dumb, Hearing, Hindrances, Hospitals, Idiocy, Ill-Health, Imbecile, Impediments, Imperforate, Invalids, Malformations, Missing, Monsters, Mute, Paralysis, Prison, Restraint, Saturn Influence, Senses, Servitude, Sickness, Sight, Speech, Tongue, Twelfth House, etc.).

**The Mind**—Limitations Upon—The ☉, ☽, ♄, or ☿ in the 12th H., and afflicted. Conditions become worse under the evil directions of these planets, and espec. when afflicted at the Vernal Equinox, and Lord of the Year. (See Anguish, Anxiety, Dejection, Depression, Despondency, Fears, Idiocy, Imbecility, Insanity, Melancholy; "Weak Mind" under Mind; Worry, etc.).

**LIMP BODY**—Drooping—Relaxation—Caused by the ♂ influence weak at B.; the 20° ♓ on the Asc. at B.; ♓ on the Asc. tends to weak bodily action, and uncertain walk. (See Action, Apathy, Drooping, Feeble, Inactive, Indifferent, Inert, Lethargy, Motion, Movement, Prolapse, Ptosis, Relaxation, Slow, Stooping; "Weak Body" under Weak; "Low" under Vitality, etc.).

**LIMPING** — (See Crippled, Deformities, Feet, Gait, Hips, Knees, Lameness, Legs, Paralysis, Thighs, Walk, etc.).

**LINE**—The Line of Central Impulse—(See Pranatal Epoch).

**LINEN** — Diseases from Wet Linen—Colds, etc.—(See "Linen" under Colds; "Wet Feet" under Feet; "Colds" under Moisture; "Pain" under Nipples; "Linen" under Wet).

**LINGERING**—Slow—Prolonged—Tedious—

**Lingering Death**—♄ causes a lingering death; ♄ affl. in the 8th H., and espec. afflicting the hyleg; ♄ in the 6th H., death by a lingering disease; ♆ in the 8th H., and affl. the hyleg. (See "Lingering" under Death).

**Lingering Diseases**—Lingering Pains—The ☉ or ☽ affl. by ♄; ♄ diseases and afflictions; ♄ affl. the hyleg at B., and by dir.; ♄ ☌ the ☉ or ☽ in the 6th H. (See Aches, Chronic, Consumptions; "Low Fever" under Fever; Grievous; "Long Siege" under Ill-Health; Incurable, Invalids; "Diseases", "Long Ascension", under Long; Prolonged, Slow, Tedious, Wasting).

**LINIMENTS**—(See Collyria, Lead, Lotions, Rubefacients).

**LION**—The Lion is the Symbol of the ♌ Sign.

**Lion's Heart**—Cor Leonis—Regulus—A Fixed Star—(See Regulus).

**Lion's Tail**—Cauda Leonis—Deneb—A Star of the nature of ♄ and ♅, and brings disgrace and ruin by adverse aspects. The ☉ directed to tends to danger of putrid fevers, and public disgrace; the ☽ directed to, danger of misfortune, mischief and great anxiety; the Asc. to the place of, melancholy, trouble, and discontent. (See "Death by Sentence" under Judge; Putrid; "Defect In Sight" under Sight; Vehicles). For influences of the Back, Mane, Neck, or Wing of the Lion, see Blindness; "Threatened" under Disease; Disgrace, Melancholy, Military, Ruin; "Fixed Stars" under Stars).

**Mane of Leo**—(See Mane).

**LIPOMA**—Fatty Tumor—♂ ☌ or ill-asp. ♃. (See "Tumors" under Fat).

**LIPS** — Labia — The Upper Lip is ruled by ♈ and ♊, and is especially influenced by ♀ in ♈. The lower lip, the lower teeth, and the chin, are ruled by ♉. Also the under lip is influenced by ☿ in ♈.

**Diseases** — Of the Lips — Planets afflicted in ♈ and ♉; Subs at MCP, and SP (7D). (See Mouth).

**Full Lips**—Given by ☿.

**Harelip**—A Congenital Fissure of the Lip—An ♈ affliction.

**Large Lips**—(See "Thick" in this section).

**Lower Lip**—(a) Drawn to One Side—Case — See "Extraordinary Accident", No. 192, in 1001 N.N. (b) The Lower Lip Thicker, or Larger Than the Upper One—In Hor'y Q. ♀ as Sig. of the party; ♀ influence at B. signifies; ☿ in ♑, thick lower lip.

**Mouth**—(See "Broad", and the various paragraphs under Mouth).

**Plump Lips** — ♀ Sig. of the person signifies.

**Red Lips**—Ruddy—Ruby—Cherry—♀ in the Asc. at B., and well-dignified; ♀ as Sig. of the party in Hor'y Q.

**Rolling Lips**—♓ on the Asc.

**Scabbed Lips**—The ☽ in ♑, ♒, or ♓.

**Thick Lips**—Large Lips—Great Lips—♄ signifies great lips like those of the Negro; in Hor'y Q. ♄ signifies; ♄ ascending at B.; given by ♄ when he forms the body; ☿ in ♑, thick lower lip; ♉ on the Asc.

**Thin Lips**—☿ gives; ☿ ascending at B. and free from the rays of other planets.

**Upper Lip**—Ruled by ♈, and especially affected and influenced by ♀ in ♈. (See Articulate, Inarticulate, Speech).

**LIQUIDS** — Liquors—♆ and the ☽ have strong influence over liquids. In the body the ☽ rules liquids and fluids in general.

**Burns**—By Hot Liquids—(See "Hot" in this section).

**Craving for Liquors**—The ☽ affl. in ♓ and water signs. (See Alcoholism; "Drink" under Cravings; Dipsomania, Drink, Thirst, etc.).

**Death by Liquids**—The ☉ to the ☌ or ill-asp. ♄ by dir., and one or both in watery signs. (See Bathing, Drowning, Scalds, Water).

**Delirium Tremens** — From Excessive Drink—(See Delirium).

**Drink** — (See the various paragraphs under Drink; "Liquids" under Food).

**Drunkenness**—(See this subject).

**Excesses** — Excessive Use of Liquors and Drink — (See "Excess" under Drink).

**Fluids**—(See Fluids).

**Hot Liquids**—Burns, Injury, or Death By—(See "Hot Liquids" under Heat; Scalds).

**Intoxication**—(See this subject).

**Meals**—Liquids with Meals and Food —(See Drinking, Liquids, under Food).

**Pursuits**—Liquid Pursuits—Are ruled and indicated by the ☽; the ☽ in the 10th H. at B., or a watery sign on cusp of 10th; many planets in watery signs. (See Business, Employment, Vocation).

**Scalds** — (See "Hot Liquids" under Heat; Scalds).

**Strong Liquids** — Uses Too Strong Liquids — (See "Strong Drink" under Drink).

**Sweets and Liquids** — (See "Liquids and Sweets" under Food).

**Thirst**—(See Cravings, Drink, Thirst).

**Water** — (See the various paragraphs under Bathing, Floods, Fountains, Ocean, Rain, Rivers, Sea, Water).

**Wine** — (See Wine). For collateral study, see Blood, Fluxes, Glands, Humours, Juices, Milk, Moisture, Moon, Neptune, Osmosis, Saliva, Secretions, Serums, Ships, Shipwreck, Sweat, Tears, Tides, Urine; "Signs" under Water).

**LISPING** — Imperfect Pronunciation of Letters and Words—♂ gives the lisp and ♄ the stammer. In Hor'y Q. ♄ in ♈ or a bestial sign, afflicting ☿ when the Significator, and the ☽ also be afflicted; ☿ in a weak sign, as in ♋, ♐, or ♓, and affl. by ♄ or ♂, in which case ♂ gives the lisp and ♄ the stammer; ☿ ruler of the 6th H., in a watery sign, and affl. by ♂; ☿ in a watery sign, in any house, and affl. by ♄ or ♂, lisps and pronounces words badly. (See "Stammering" under Speech).

**LISTLESS**—Dull—Vapid—Apathetic—Inactive—No Animation, etc.—The ☉ ☌ ☽ at B., and within 3°, listless all thru life at each New ☽; the ☉ and ♂ unaspected at B.; the ☽ in ♓, easy and inactive disposition; the ☽ Sig. in ♓, not inclined to action unless of the worst kind; the ☽ Sig. in ♑, inactive and dull; the ☽ Sig. in ♒; ♀ in ♏, inert; ☿ in ♉, inert disposition; ♓ on the Asc.; earth and water signs tend to give inactive and indolent natures; lords of the nativity in N. Lat. (See Apathy, Dull, Energy, Ennui, Fatigue, Idle, Inactive, Indifferent, Inertia, Irritable, Lassitude, Lethargy; "Low Spirits" under Low; Moping, Rouse, Slow, Sluggish, Weariness, etc.).

**LITERATURE** — Addicted To — (See "Literature" under Learning).

**LITHEMIA**—Excess of Uric Acid In the Blood — ♄ influence. (See Deposits, Gout, Rheumatism, Stone, Urates, Urea, Uremic, Uric).

**LITHIASIS** — The Formation of a Calculus — ♄ influence. (See Calculus, Lime, Stone).

**LITTLE**—

**Little Bear** — A Star — When joined with the ☉ in an angle is said to cause much sickness, disgrace, great affliction, and trouble. (See "Much Sickness" under Sickness).

**Little Beard**—(See Beard).

**Little Body** — (See Diminished, Dwarfed, Short, Small).

**Little Eyes**—(See Eyes).

**Little Head** — (See "Small" under Head; Idiots).

**Little Mind**—(See Idiocy; "Shallow" under Mentality; "Light", "Weak", under Mind).

**Little Recuperative Power**—(See Recuperation; "Low" under Vitality; "Weak Body" under Weak).

**Little Resistance**—To Disease—(See Resistance).

**Little Sickness** — Rarely Ill — (See "Good Health" under Health; Immunity; "Good" under Recuperation, Resistance, Vitality).

**Little Slender Body**—(See Slender).

**Little Stature**—(See "Little Body" in this section).

**Little Stamina**—(See Stamina).

**Little Suffering** — At Death — (See "Easy Death" under Death).

**Little Vitality** — (See "Low" under Vitality). See Lack Of, Loss Of, Void Of.

**LIVELIHOOD**—Lives In a Mean Way—Exercises Wits For a Livelihood—♂ Sig. in ♊, but the good aspects of the ☉, ♃, and ♀ mitigate. (See Gambling, Poverty).

**LIVELY**—Active—Spirited—Healthy—

**Lively Complexion**—(See "Red" under Complexion).

**Lively Disposition**—(See Action, Active, Brisk, Energy, Quick, etc.).

**LIVER**—Hepatic—The Liver is an organ and gland which is acted upon and influenced by a number of planets and Signs of the Zodiac. The liver is the largest gland in the body, and is the seat of the Animal Soul, or Desire Body. (See "Desire Body" under Desire). In the Astral Body ♃ has direct relation to the liver, and the liver is also the central vortex of the Desire Body, and the seat of the passional desires. (See "Astral Body" under Astral). Jupiter is the main ruler of the liver. It is also under the internal rulership of the ♌ sign. The liver is affected by planets in any of the cardinal signs, as in ♈, ♋, ♎, ♑. The liver is also ruled by ♎, ♏, ♐, and presided over by ♍. The 5th H. denotes the liver. Ptolemy and Wilson say that ♀ rules the liver. Mars also rules the liver, the bile and gall. The upper lobes of the liver are ruled by ♋, and the lower lobes by ♍. The Liver Place in the spine is the 4th Dorsal vertebra, designated as Li.P. The waste products of the Portal Blood Stream are converted into Glycogen in the liver by ♃. (See Glycogen). Saturn forms Uric Acid, Urea, and the Gall in the liver. (See Bile, Urea, Uric). The afflictions of ♄ have an adverse influence over the action of the liver, and infirmities in the liver are given by ♃, while the 5th H., its ruler, and planets therein, signify all diseases in the liver. Mars adds or subtracts to the Hepatic Process, and the ♂ group of herbs act upon and modify the Hepatic Diathesis, and oppose the ♄ diseases of the liver. (See Hepatic). Also the remedies of ☿ have a specific action upon the liver, and relieve its congestion, and especially of the Gall Bladder. Podophyllin (May Apple Blossom), a ☿ remedy, is one of the best remedies to act upon the liver, and to relieve biliousness. Calomel, a ☿ remedy, has also been greatly used as a liver remedy. The ☉ and ☽ acting thru the ♈ sign, thru the ganglion of Ribes, and thru the cavernous and carotid plexuses, affect the cerebro-spinal nervous system, the head and its dependencies, and give way to the Hepatic Process, and also acting thru the ♏ sign. (See Ductless Glands, Fifth House, Ganglion, Hepatic, Jupiter, Mars, Mercury, Saturn, Venus). The following are the diseases and afflictions of the liver, as mentioned in the various Textbooks of Astrology, which see in the alphabetical arrangement when not more fully considered here.

**Abscess of Liver**—♃ affl. in ♍; Subs at Li.P. and KP. Case—See Fig. 10A in "Astro-Diagnosis" by the Heindels. (See Abscesses).

**Affected** — The liver is affected by planets in any of the cardinal signs. (See the various paragraphs in this section).

**All Diseases Of**—Signified by the 5th and 6th H., and by ♄ and ♃ afflictions.

**Amyloid Liver**—Caused by ♃ afflictions; ♃ affl. in ♋ or ♍. (See Amyloid).

**Asiatic Cholera**—The Liver Afflicted In—A ♍ disease; ♂ affl. in ♍. (See Cholera).

**Atrophy Of**—♄ affl. in signs which rule the liver; Subs at Li.P. (See Atrophy).

**Bile**—Disorders of—(See Bile).

**Biliousness**—(See Bile).

**Cancer Of**—(See "Cancer" under Carcinoma).

**Catarrh Of**—The ☉, ☽, or ♄ affl. in ♋ or ♍; ♄ affl. in ♍ in the 5th or 6th H.; Subs at Li.P. (See Catarrh).

**Cirrhosis Of**—Hardening—Thickening—♄ affl. in ♍; Subs at Li.P. (See Cirrhosis).

**Cold and Dry Liver**—♃ affl. in ♍. (See "Cold and Dry" under Dry).

**Colic Of**—♂ affl. in ♍ in the Asc. or 6th H. (See "Cholic" under Bile).

**Congestion Of**—♄ affl. in ♍; ♃ affl. in ♍, due to bad circulation. (See Congestion).

**Death** — From Liver Trouble — ♃ shows; ♃ affl. the hyleg by dir., and ♃ much afflicted at B., and holding the dominion of death; ♀ much afflicted at B., and affl. the hyleg in a train of fatal directions; cardinal signs dispose to.

**Degeneration Of**—(See "Fatty" in this section).

**Deranged Liver**—Disorders of the Liver—Liver Complaints—Infirmities In the Liver—Diseased Liver—The ☉ in ♍ and affl. by ♃; the ☉ to the ill-asps. ♃ by dir.; the ☉ affl. in the 6th H. in cardinal signs; the ☉ in ♋ and affl. by malefics; ☽ diseases and caused by the ☽ affl. at B.; the ☽ to the ill-asps. ♃ by dir., and espec. if ♃ be in ♌ or the 6th H. at B.; the ☽ in the 6th H., and affl. by ♃; ♄ people are subject to, brought on by worry, fretting and moping; ♄ in ♌ or ♍; ♄ in ♌, occi., and affl. the ☉, ☽, or Asc.; ♄ or ♂ in ♎; ♄ affl. in ♎ in the 6th H., great derangement of the liver; ♄, ♅, or ♆ in ♏, and affl. the ☉ or ☽; ♄ affl. in ♈; ♃ affl. in ♊, ♋, ♍, or ♑; ♃ affl. in the 6th H.; ♃ ☐ or ☍ ☽, and espec. with women; ♃ affl. the ☉; ♃ affl. in ♍, and espec. in the 6th H.; ♐ on the 6th, and with afflictions in ♐; ♃ in ♌ or the 6th H. at B., and affl. the ☽ by dir.; ♃ afflicted by ♂; ♂ ☐ or ☍ ♃; ♂ affl. in ♍; caused by ♀ when the dominion of death is vested in her; ♀ affl. in ♍; the Asc. to the ♂ or any aspect ♃ by dir., and ♃ affl. at B., and espec. if ♃ be in ♌ or ♒; cardinal signs show, and espec. afflictions in ♎; Subs at Li.P. The ☉ affl. in ♎ tends to diseases which affect the liver. (See the various paragraphs in this section).

**Diseased Liver**—Diseases of—(See "Deranged", and the various paragraphs in this section).

**Dropsy Of**—The ☽, ♄, or ♃ affl. in signs which rule the liver; Subs at Li.P., and KP. (See Dropsy).

**Dry and Cold Liver**—(See "Cold" in this section).

**Enlarged Liver**—The ☉ affl. in ♉, thru the use of rich foods; ♃ affl. in ♋ in the Asc., the result of gluttony; ♃ affl. in ♍ or ♓; ♃ affl. in the 6th H., caused by overeating. (See Eating, Enlargements, Feasting, Food, Gluttony).

**Fatty Degeneration**—Of the Liver—Fatty Liver—Fatty Transformation of—A ♃ disease; ♃ affl. in ♊, ♍, or ♑; Subs at Li.P. (See Degeneration, Fat).

**Fever**—From Obstructions Near the Liver—Arising from Surfeits, High Living, etc.—The ☽ ☌ or ill-asp. ♄ (or ☿ if he be of the nature of ♄) when one is first taken ill, or compelled to take to his bed, and if the ☽ be not supported by benefics there is danger of death within 14 days (Hor'y). (See "Fever" under Heart).

**Flexure**—Hepatic Flexure—♄ affl. in ♍, and in signs which rule the liver, due to weakening of the parts; Subs at PP (3L). (See Flexure).

**Gall**—Gall Bladder—Gall Stones—(See Bile).

**General Diseases Of** — Afflictions in cardinal signs, and in signs which rule the liver; Subs at Li.P.

**Glands**—The Liver is a Gland, and for disorders of the Glands in general see Glands.

**Glycogen**—Disorders of—Formation of—(See Glycogen).

**Gravel In**—(See "Liver" under Gravel).

**Hardening Of** — (See "Cirrhosis" in this section).

**Hobnail Liver**—The Result of Atrophic Cirrhosis—♄ affl. in ♍; Subs at Li.P. (See Atrophy, Cirrhosis, in this section).

**Hyperaemia Of**—A ♃ disease; ♃ affl. in ♍; Subs at Li.P., and KP. (See Hyperaemia).

**Inactive Liver**—(See "Torpid" in this section).

**Infirmities In**—Given especially by an afflicted ♃, and with ♃ affl. in ♍. (See "Deranged", and the various paragraphs in this section).

**Inflammation Of** — Hepatitis — The ☽ in ♈ and afflicted by the ☉ or ♂ when taken ill (Hor'y); ♂ affl. in ♍; Subs at Li.P. tend to an inflamed liver, and also Perihepatitis, inflammation of the Peritoneal Covering of the Liver.

**Jaundice**—(See Jaundice).

**Liver Complaints** — (See "Deranged", and the various paragraphs in this section).

**Liverishness** — (See "Biliousness" under Bile).

**Lobes**—Disorders In—Afflictions in ♋, in the upper lobes, and in the lower lobes by afflictions in ♍.

**Nerves**—Nerves of Affected — ♅ or ☿ afflicted in signs which rule the liver. (See Colic, Pain, in this section; "Hepatic Plexus" under Hepatic).

**Obstructions** — (See "Fever" in this section; "Obstructive Jaundice" under Jaundice).

**Pain In** — (See "Nerves" in this section; "Cholic" under Bile).

**Perihepatitis**—(See "Inflammation" in this section).

**Peritoneal Covering**—Of the Liver—Inflammation of—(See "Inflammation" in this section).

**Portal Blood Stream**—(See Portal).

**Remedies** — For Liver Diseases — (See "Treatment" in this section).

**Rickets** — The planetary influences and afflictions which cause Rickets tend to changes in the liver and spleen. (See Rickets, Spleen).

**Sluggish Liver**—Torpid—Inactive—♄ affl. in ♍; ♄ ☌ or ill-asp. ♃; ♃ affl. by ♅; ♃ affl. in the 6th H.; Subs at Li.P. (See "Torpid" in this section).

**Spots** — Liver Spots — Cholasmus — Caused by ♄; ♄ affl. in ♍; afflictions in cardinal signs. (See "Biliousness" under Bile; Constipation, Jaundice).

**Stenosis** — Of the Bile Ducts — (See "Ducts" under Bile).

**Thickening Of** — (See "Cirrhosis" in this section).

**Torpid Liver** — Inactive — Sluggish — The work of ♄; ♄ affl. in ♍; caused by the excessive use of any drug ruled by ☿ and ♊, as ♊ is the opposite sign to ♐, the sign which rules the liver. (See "Sluggish" in this section).

**Toxaemic Jaundice**—(See Jaundice).

**Transformation**—(See "Fatty" in this section).

**Treatment** — Of Liver Disorders — In the use of Colors the purple is a good remedy for blood and liver disorders. Also in the way of drugs, use podophyllin. Adjustments of the 4th Dorsal Vertebra, Li.P., are also quite necessary to give fuller and complete nerve supply to the liver. (See the Introduction to this Article).

**Tuberculosis Of** — ♄ afflicted in signs which rule the liver; Subs at Li.P. (See Tuberculosis).

**Ulcerated Liver**—♃ affl. in ♍, and also to Abscess. (See Ulcers; "Abscess" in this section).

**Urea**—(See Urates, Urea, Uric Acid).

**Uric Acid**—(See Uric).

**Wasting Of**—♄ affl. in ♌. (See Wasting).

**Waxy Liver**—Waxy, or Fatty Degeneration—(See "Fatty" in this section).

**Women** — Liver Disorders of — ☽ diseases, and by afflictions to the ☽ at B.; ♃ □ or ☍ ☽. Afflictions to the ☉ would tend more to liver disorders in males.

**Wort** — Liverwort — A ♃ herb. (See "Jupiter Group" under Herbs).

**Yellow Jaundice**—(See Jaundice).

**LIVES**—Lives Thru Disease—The Disease Is Not Fatal—(See "Spared" under Life; "Lives" under Serious).

**LIVING** — (See Conduct, Debauchery, Dissipation, Drink, Eating, Excesses, Food; "Free Living" under Free; Habits, Life, Loose, Luxuries, Men; "Loose Morals" under Morals; Passive, Pleasures, Poverty, Prodigal, Riotous, Sports, Women, etc.).

**LOADED**—Highly Loaded Urine—(See Urine).

**LOATHING** — At the Stomach — (See "Loathing" under Stomach).

**LOBES**—A Rounded Division of An Organ—(See "Lobes" under Liver, Lungs).

**LOCAL PARTS**—

**Deformities Of** — The work of ♄ by retention and crystallization of wastes, and thickening of tissue. (See Crystallization, Gout, Hardening, Joints, Wastes).

**Localized Swellings** — (See Abscess, Boils, Carbuncles, Cysts, Fullness, Hyperaemia, Infections, Inflammation, Plethora, Tumors, Ulcers, etc.).

**LOCATION**—Residence—Locality, etc.—It is said for good health and success, locate in the direction of the ☽ at B., or lord of the Asc. Also locate in places ruled by signs which contain the benefics at B., or in the direction of the benefics. This subject is more fully discussed under Abroad, Altitude, Foreign Lands, Nadir, Native Land, Place of Birth (see Place); Polarity, Residence, Travel, etc. Also see Changes, Climate, Discontentment, Environment, External, Removals, Roaming, Wanderer, etc.).

**Disease** — Location of — (See Diagnosis).

**LOCK-JAW** — Trismus — Spasm of Muscles of Mastication—Malefics in ♉ at B., and affl. the ♉ sign by dir.; the ☉ or ☽ in ♉, and affl. by ♅ or ♄ at B., and by dir.; ♉ on the Asc. at B., and containing malefics by dir.; Subs at MCP (4C). Case—See "Lockjaw", No. 913, in 1001 N.N. (See Hydrophobia, Jaws, Spasmodic).

**LOCOMOTION** — Disorders and Defects of—♄ influence; ♄ ☌ or ill-asp. the ☉ or ☽ at B.; ♄ rising and affl. the ☉, ☽, or Asc.; ♄ in ♐, ♑, ♒, or ♓. (See Action, Ankles, Carriage, Crippled, Deformities, Deposits, Feet, Gait, Gout, Knees, Legs, Limbs, Locomotor Ataxia, Motion, Movement, Paralysis, Rheumatism, Swellings, Walk, etc.).

**LOCOMOTOR ATAXIA**—Tabes Dorsalis —A ♄ disease; ♄ in ♌ or ♎; a ♌, ♎, and ♐ disease, and caused by afflictions in these signs; a ☿ disease, and caused by afflictions to ☿, and by the afflictions of ☿, and espec. when ♀ partakes of the nature of ♄. This disease is the result of Tabes Dorsalis of the spine, a disease of the posterior columns of the spinal cord, attended by incoordination, and lack of sensation. The Knee-Jerk is also absent. Also caused by Subs at AT, AX, CP, and KP. Case — See "Locomotor Ataxia", No. 255, in 1001 N.N. (See Ataxia, Argyll; "Argyll Pupil' under Iris; Paralysis, Tabes).

**Locomotor Muscles** — (See "Locomotor" under Hips).

**LOCUST PEST**—(See Comets).

**LODESTONES**—Magnetized Iron Ore—Ruled by ♅. (See Iron, Magnetism).

**LOGORRHOEA**—Abnormally Rapid Speech—(See "Rapid" under Speech).

**LOINS**—Lower Part of the Back—Reins —Ruled by ♎ and the 7th H.

**Disorders In**—Diseases In—♀ diseases, and caused by afflictions to ♀, the ruler of ♎ and the 7th H. Also the afflictions of ♄ tend to as ♄ has his exaltation in ♎; Subs at UPP and PP. (See "Diseases" under Back; "Disorders" under Reins).

**Heats In**—♂ afflicted in ♎ or the 7th H. (See "Heats" under Buttocks, Reins).

**Imposthumes In** — A ♎ disease, and afflictions in ♎. (See "Abscess" under Back).

**Pain In** — (See "Pains" under Back; Lumbago).

**Ulcers In**—A ♎ disease. (See Ulcers).

**Weak Loins** — Weakness In — Weak Back — The ☉ affl. in the 6th H. in a fixed sign; ♂ in ♉ when ♂ is the afflictor in the disease. (See "Weak" under Back, Kidneys; "Lumbar Region" under Lumbar).

**Wounds In**—♂ affl. in ♎ or the 7th H.

**LONELINESS**—♄ influence; ♄ strong at B., rising, in the Asc. or M.C., and especially afflicting the ☉, ☽, or ☿. (See Recluse, Secretive, Solitude).

**LONG**—Lengthy—Prolonged—

**Arms**—Long Arms—(See Arms).

**Ascension** — Signs of Long Ascension —The ♋, ♌, ♍, ♎, ♏, ♐ signs, and so-called because they take longer in ascending. The signs of short ascension are ♑, ♒, ♓, ♈, ♉, ♊, and these signs take less time in ascending. A ✱ aspect in a sign of long ascension has the same effect as a □, and the disease is prolonged when the afflictors are in signs of long ascension, and shorter when in signs of short ascension.

**Body** — Long Body — ♈, ♉, ♎, and ♏ when on the Asc. give a rather long body, but moderate in stature. (See Giants, Growth, Height, Length, Tall).

**Chin**—(See "Long" under Chin).

**Diseases**—Long Diseases—Long Distempers — Signs of a Long Disease — The Disease Will Be Long — Diseases related to the ☉ usually become chronic and of long duration, and resist treatment; caused by the afflictions of ♄ to the hyleg at B., and by dir.; ♄ in the 6th, or lord of the 6th, and afflicting the hyleg; ♄ ☌ ☽ at the beginning of a disease; ♄ ☌, P., □ or ☍ ☉; the ☽ in a fixed sign (Hor'y); all the Significators in fixed signs, or if they be slow of motion. (See Chronic, Consumptions, Continuity, Course, Crises; "Long" under Disease, Ill-Health; Duration; "Low" under Fever; Incurable, Invalids, Lingering, Prolonged; "Low" under Recuperation, Resistance, Vitality; Rising Sign, Slow, Tedious, Wasting, etc.).

**Face**—Long Face—(See Face).

**Father**—Long Life For—(See Father).

**Feet**—Long Feet—(See Feet).

**Fingers** — Long Fingers — (See Fingers).

**Hair**—(See "Long" under Hair).

**Hands**—(See "Long" under Hands).

**Head**—(See "Long" under Head).

**Illnesses**—Long Illnesses—(See "Diseases" in this section).

**Imprisonment**—(See "Long Imprisonment" under Prison).

**Journeys** — (See "Long" under Journeys, Voyages).

**Legs** — (See "Long" under Legs, Thighs).

**Life** — Long Life — (See "Long Life" under Life).

**Limbs** — (See "Long" under Arms, Legs, Limbs, Thighs).

**Mother** — Long Life For — (See "Long Life" under Mother).

**Nails**—Long Nails and Fingers—(See "Long" under Fingers, Hands, Nails).

**Neck**—(See "Long" under Neck).

**Nose**—(See "Long" under Nose).

**Sight** — Long-Sighted — (See "Hyperopia" under Sight).

**Thighs** — (See "Long" under Legs, Thighs).

**Upper Half of Body** — Upper Part Longer—(See "Body" under Upper).

**Uvula**—(See "Long" under Uvula).

**Visage** — Long Visage — Long Face— (See "Long" under Face).

**LONGINGS** — (See Appetites, Cravings, Desires, Wishes, etc.).

**LOOK**—Glances—Expression—Aspect—Visage—

**Active Look**—Sharp Look—♊ on the Asc.

**Angry Look**—Fierce Look—♂ Sig. in fiery signs. (See Anger).

**Austere Look**—(See Austere).

**Bold Look**—♂ rising in the Asc. (See Boldness, Resolute).

**Commanding Look** — (See Commanding).

**Countenance** — (See the various subjects under Countenance).

**Debauched Look**—(See Debauched).

**Dissipated Look** — (See Debauched, Dissipated).

**Downward Look**—Lowering Aspect—Eyes Looking Downward — Stooping Forward — A strong ♄ characteristic; ♄ in the Asc.; ♄ Sig. □ or ☍ ☽, and tends to stoop forward; the ☽ strong at B., a little lowering; ♅ influence tends to hold the head down when walking, and to a stooping, heavy gait. (See Bent, Downcast, Stooping).

**Dull and Idle Look** — (See Dull; "Sleepy Eyes" under Eyes; Idle, Weariness).

**Effeminate Look**—(See Effeminate).

**Enquiring Look**—☿ rising in the Asc.

**Expression**—(See the paragraphs under Expression).

**Eyes** — Expression of — (See Dull, Glances, Piercing, Quick, Sharp, Sleepy, and the various paragraphs under Eyes).

**Face** — (See the various paragraphs under Complexion, Countenance, Expression, Face, Features).

**Features**—(See Chin, Face, Features, Jaws, Lips, Mouth, Nose, etc.).

**Fierce Look** — (See "Angry" in this section).

**Foolish Looking**—(See Fools).

**Gentle Look**—(See Gentle, Kind).

**Ghastly Look** — (See Pale, Sickly, White).

**Inquiring Look**—☿ rising in the Asc.

**Intellectual Look** — Refined Expression—☿ in ♊ or ♍; ☿ Sig. in ♊; ☿ rising in the Asc., and espec. when in his own signs, and well-aspected by the ☽; ♀ in ♊. (See "Strong Mind" under Mind).

**Jaundiced Look**—(See Jaundice).

**Lowering Look** — Lowering Aspect — (See "Downward" in this section).

**Penetrating Look**—(See "Penetrating" under Eyes).

**Piercing Look**—(See Piercing, Sharp, under Eyes).

**Quick and Active Look** — Quick Sight —(See "Quick" under Eyes).

**Sardonic Look**—♆ rising in the Asc.

**Saucy Look**—♂ rising in the Asc. (See Boldness, Independent).

**Sharp Look** — ♊ on the Asc. (See "Sharp" under Eyes).

**Sickly Look** — (See Anaemia, Chlorosis, Pale, Sickly).

**Smart and Active Look** — ♊ on the Asc.

**Sober Look**—Grave Aspect—♄ influence; ♄ in the Asc. (See Despondent, Grave, Melancholic, Serious, Worry).

**Stern Look**—(See Austere).

**Surly Look**—♄ in ♌ in partile aspect the Asc.

**Visage** — (See Complexion, Countenance, Expression, Face).

**Wanton Look** — ♊ gives. (See Wanton).

**Weary Look** — (See Depressed, Dull, Fatigue, Weariness, etc.).

**LOOSE**—Looseness—

**Loose Habits** — Loose Living — Free Living—The ☉ or ☽ to the bad aspects ♀ by dir.; ♄ to the bad asps. ♂ by dir.; ♀ on the Meridian at B., and ill-aspected by ♂; the ☽ to the □ or ☍ the Asc. by dir., illnesses from loose living and bad habits; ♃ afflicted also tends to loose living, bad habits, and espec. along lines of eating, causing plethora and bad blood. (See Debauchery, Dissipation, Drink, Eating; "Free Living" under Free; Gluttony; "High Living" under High; "Loose Morals" under Morals).

**Loose Morals** — (See "Loose" under Morals).

**Loose Women** — (See Harlots, Nymphomania, Shameless).

**Looseness In Bowels** — (See Cholera, Diarrhoea, Dysentery).

**LOSS OF** — Detriment — Losses — There are quite a number of paragraphs throughout this book indicating the loss of something, as loss of health, of comforts, of friends, of loved ones, or property, fortune, honour, etc., and subjects too numerous to list here, and you are requested to look in the alphabetical arrangement for the subject you have in mind. However, the following are prominent suggestions as to subjects along this line. The afflictions and adverse aspects of the planets at B., and by dir., usually tend to the loss of something as regards the individual, while the good aspects of the planets by transit, progression, and direction tend to the restoration of that which was lost, if restorable, as health, wealth, comforts, ease, peace of mind, success, etc. Look for the heading, "Loss Of", under the following subjects, or others you may have in mind—Appetite, Arms, Aunt, Blood, Character, Cheer, Children, Citizenship (see Banishment, Exile); Comforts, Credit (see Cheating, Deceitful, Dishonesty, Forgers, Thieves, etc.); Daughter, Death, Equilibrium, Eyes, Faculties (see Idiocy, Imbecility, Insanity); Family, Father, Feeling, Feet, Finger, Flesh, Fluids, Fortune, Friend, Hair, Hands, Happiness, Health, Hearing, Honour, Husband, Identity, Infant, Inheritance, Integrity (see Cheating, Criminal, Deceit, Disgrace, Dishonour, Forgers, Liars, Libel, Reputation, Ruin, Thieves, etc.); Joy, Legs, Liberty (see Prison); Limbs, Manhood (see the various paragraphs under Men); Marriage Partner, Memory, Modesty, Money, Mother, Passion, Peace of Mind (see "No Peace" under Mind); Position (see Disgrace, Dishonour, Poverty, Property, Reverses, Ruin, Wealth); Property, Reason, Relatives, Reputation, Riches, Seed (see Semen); Sex Desire (see Apathy, Celibacy; "Free From" under Passion); Sight (see Blindness, Sight); Sister, Smell, Son, Speech, Stamina, Stimulus, Strength, Taste, Teeth, Tone, Uncle, Virtue, Vitality, Voice, Volitional Power, Wealth, Weight, Wife, Womanhood (see Harlots, Shameless). Also see Detriment, Diminished, Lack Of, Less, Lessened, Void Of, Wasting, etc.

**LOTIONS**—Face and Hair Lotions—Ill Effects of—(See Cosmetics; "Lotions" under Face).

**LOUD SPEAKING** — (See "Loud" under Speech, Voice).

**LOVE AFFAIRS**—Love—Dealings with the Opposite Sex—The 5th H. and the ♌ sign are predominant in love affairs, and also ♎ and the 7th H. Venus is the principle of love, and it is afflictions to ♀ that tend to disturbances in the love nature, and to diseases and ill-health by its abuses. The afflictions of ♆, ♅, and ♂ to ♀ tend to excesses, abuses, and irregularities of the love nature, leading to weakness, exhaustion of the vital forces, sorrow, suffering, or death. The afflictions of ♄ to ♀ also cause carelessness in love affairs, or make one unnatural, or given to excessive illegal practices, or abnormal affections. The good aspects of the planets to ♀ tend to make the affections and love nature true and genuine, and to be properly used, and also restrained. The question of love affairs is a large one, and cannot be gone into here except along lines where the love nature is afflicted, abnormal, perverted, and which tends to ill-health, suffering, injury, or death. The unrestrained use of the love and sex nature, and passional displays, excesses, and the use of the sex nature for pleasure and gratification, are undoubtedly the causes of much of the sin, suffering, sorrow, and misery in the World today, and often lead to an untimely death, whereas if the vital forces were saved, used only for propagation, and the nature spiritualized, people would live longer, have better health, and be spared much of the suffering that now overtakes them. The Occult side of love, and love affairs, is very fully considered in the books, "The Key of Destiny", by Dr. and Mrs. Homer Curtiss, and also the book, "Cosmo-Conception" by Max Heindel.

**Addicted To Women**—(See "Addicted" under Men).

**Adulterous Tendencies** — Covets Unlawful Beds—The lower vibrations of ♅ tend to irregularities of the affections and passions, and lead to unconventionalities, chafing under vows and restraints. The afflictions of ♅ to the ☽ in a male horoscope, and the afflictions of ♅ to the ☉ in a female nativity, tend to make one adulterous. Also ♅ in, or afflicting the 7th H., the house of marriage; ♅ affl. ♀ at B., and by dir., tends to many irregularities among young people; ♀ ill-dignified at B.; ♀ with, or afflicted by the malefics at B.; the ☽ sepr. from ♂ and applying to ♀ by aspect; ♂ and ☿ lords of the employment. (See Amorous; "Free Love" under Free; Intercourse, Lascivious, Lewd, Lust, Passion, Sex, etc.).

**Affections** — (See Affections, Inordinate; "Unlawful" in this section).

**Amativeness**—(See Amative).

**Amorous**—(See Amorous).

**Amours**—Illicit Amours—Precipitancy in, and unrestrained impetuosity, caused by the evil directions of ♀; the ☉ or ☽ to the ill-asps. ♀ by dir.; ♆ affl. in the 5th H.; ♆ affl. the ☽ or ♀; ♅ to the ill-aspects ♀ by dir.; ♅ to the good asps. ♀ by dir., but escapes detection. (See "Free Love" under Free; Adulterous, Clandestine, Liaisons, in this section).

**Ardent** — Over-Ardent — Ardency is given by the ☉, the ♌ sign, ♀, and ♀ afflicted or aspected by ♂; ♂ afflicting ♀ tends to ardent passions, and ♂ influence gives ardency; the 3rd decan. of ♈ on the Asc., ruled by ♀. (See Affections, Amorous, Passion).

**Astray** — Women Liable to Be Led Astray—(See Seduction).

**Attachments** — Indiscreet In — Keeps Bad Company—Fond of Low Company —(See Harlots; "Low Company" under Low).

**Bohemian Pleasures** — Fond of—(See "Bohemian" under Pleasures).

**Celibacy** — (See Apathy, Bachelors, Celibacy, Deviations; "Free From" under Passion).

**Chastity** — (See "Chaste" under Females).

**Clandestine Affairs** — (See "Clandestine" under Sex).

**Cohabitation**—Excesses In—Little Desire For—(See Amorous, Celibacy, Cohabitation, Excesses, Passion).

**Covets Unlawful Beds**—(See Adulterous, Amours, in this section).

**Death** — Sudden Death Thru a Love Affair—The ☽ at Full, or incr., sepr. from ♀, and applying to ♂ in a day geniture. (See "Causes His Own Death" under Death).

**Disease** — Thru Love Affairs — (See "Health Suffers" under Opposite Sex).

**Energies Wasted**—Energies and Substance Wasted On the Opposite Sex—♂ afflicting ♀. (See Amorous; "Wasted" under Energies; "Passional Excesses" under Passion; "Ruined" in this section).

**Engagement**—(See Fiance).

**Entanglements**—Has Many Unwise Entanglements With the Opposite Sex —♀ affl. at B. by the malefics ♅, ♄, or ♂.

**Fiance**—Fiancee—(See Fiance).

**Fickle** — The Affections Fickle and Changeable—♀ weak at B., and afflicted, and espec. with ♀ in ♋ or ♍; the ☽ in the Asc. at B., or ruler of the Asc., and afflicted; the ☽ □ or ☍ ☿; the ☉ by Periodic Rev. to the ill-asps. the radical ☽; ♄ Sig. in ♓; ♃ in ♊; ♂ affl. in ♊ or ♎; ☿ rising in ♍ and afflicted; ♊ or ♍ on the Asc.; the influences of the bicorporeal signs strong at B.

**Fixation**—Mother Fixation—Tendency of a Man to Marry a Woman Like His Mother, and Much Older Than Himself —(See "Mother Fixation" under Marriage).

**Flirting** — (See "Fickle" in this section; "Unwomanly Freedom" under Morals).

**Foolish In Love Affairs**—Fixed Stars of the nature of ♄ and ♃ ascending at B., easily mislead by their love nature and passions.

**Fornication**—(See "Adulterous" in this section; "Clandestine" under Sex).

**Free Love**—Free Living—(See Free).

**Genuine**—The Affections True and Genuine, Fixed and Stable—Depth of Affection—♀ well-aspected in ♉; ♀ in the Asc. in a strong sign, and well-aspected. (See "Affections" in this section).

**Grief**—Trouble, Grief, Scandal, or a Downfall Thru the Opposite Sex—♅, ♄, ♂, or the ☽ to the ill-asps. ♀ by dir., and espec. if ♀ or the ☽ be greatly afflicted by malefics at B.; the ☽ to the place of Hydra's Heart; the periodic direction of ♄ to the radical ♀; Fixed Stars of the nature of ♂ and the ☽ ascending at B.; the ill-asps. of the ☽ to ♀ at B. tend to give males the hatred or ill-favor of the fair sex, and the ill-asps. of the ☽ to the ☉ by dir. tend to turn the love of some female to hate. (See Jilted, Ruined, in this section; "Females" under Hate; "Grief", "Women", under Men; Treachery).

**Hate**—The Love of a Woman Turns to Hate—(See "Grief" in this section).

**Health Suffers**—Thru the Opposite Sex—(See "Injury", "Women", under Men; "Health" under Opposite Sex; "Energies" in this section).

**Illicit Amours**—(See Adulterous, Amours, Clandestine, Free Love, in this section).

**Imaginations**—(See "Morbid" under Imagination).

**Immorality**—(See "Loose Morals" under Morals; Perversions, Shameless, Vices).

**Incest**—Inclined To—(See "Incest" under Perversions).

**Indiscreet Attachments**—(See Harlots; "Low Company" under Low).

**Intrigues**—(See Adulterous, Clandestine, Fornication, Liaisons, in this section).

**Jealousy**—In Love Affairs—The ☉ affl. in ♑; ♅ affl. in ♉ or ♏; ♄ ☌ or ill-asp. ♀; ♄ Sig. in ♒; ♄ Sig. ⚹ or △ the ☽; the ill-asps. of ♄ to the ☉, ☽, ☿, the Asc. or M.C. by dir.; ♂ in the 6th H. in ♉, ♌, or ♏, and affl. by the ☉, ☽, or ♄; ♀ affl. in ♏; ♀ greatly afflicted at B., and espec. by ♄; ♀ also well-aspected and dignified at B. may tend to jealousy, and often without cause; the ⊕ to the ill-asps. ♀ by dir., jealous of his wife. (See Jealousy).

**Jilted**—By the Opposite Sex—♄ to the ☌ or ill-asps. ♀ by dir., and may tend to great weakness, sorrow, and ill-health at the time.

**Liaisons**—Illicit Intimacy—Intrigue—The ☉, ☽, or ♀ to the ill-asps. ♅ by dir., and espec. if afflicted by ♅ at B. (See Adulterous, Clandestine, Free Love, in this section).

**Love Passion**—♀ affl. in ♌, and often of bad consequence. (See Amorous, Amours; "Passional Excesses" under Passion).

**Love Potions**—Philtres—Ruled by ♀.

**Low Company**—Fond of—(See "Low Company", "Low Pleasures" under Low).

**Many Love Affairs**—(See "Fickle" in this section).

**Moral Laws**—Little Respect for Social or Moral Laws—♆ afflicted in the 5th or 7th H.; ♂ ruler at B., and afflicted, and espec. when they interfere with his liberty of action. (See "Free Love" under Free; "Loose Morals" under Morals; Unconventional, Vows, in this section).

**Mother Fixation**—(See "Fixation" in this section).

**Opposite Sex**—Dealings With for Good or Ill—(See the various paragraphs under Opposite Sex, and also in this Article).

**Passion**—Passional Excesses—Free from Passion—(See Apathy, Celibacy; "Excesses", "Free From", under Passion).

**Philtres**—(See "Love Potions" in this section).

**Platonic Love**—(See Marriage).

**Pleasures**—Fond of Bohemian and Low Pleasures—(See Low, Pleasures).

**Prostitutes**—(See Harlots).

**Promiscuity**—(See "Clandestine" under Sex).

**Respect**—Has Little Respect for Moral Laws or Social Customs—(See "Moral Laws" in this section).

**Romance**—Love of—Born under ♅; ♅ ☌ or afflicting ♀ at B.; ♅ in the 5th H. (See Romantic).

**Ruined by Women**—♂ ☌ or ill-asp. the ☽ or ♀ at B., and by dir.; ♂ Sig. in ♌ or ♎; ☿ Sig. in ♉, ruins himself among the female sex. (See Energies, Grief, Health, in this section; "Injured", "Women", under Men).

**Scandal**—Danger of—(See Disgrace, Dishonour; "Loss of Honor" under Honor; Scandal).

**Scatters the Affections**—(See "Fickle" in this section).

**Seduction**—(See Seduction).

**Seeks Female Company**—♀ to the good aspects the ☽ by dir. or transit. (See "Addicted To Women" under Men).

**Sex Disorders**—Thru Excesses and Love Affairs—(See Genitals, Private, Scandalous; "Sex Diseases" under Sex; Venereal, Venery).

**Sexual Immorality**—(See Adulterous, Amours, Fornication, Illicit, in this section; Harlots, Lewd; "Loose Morals" under Morals; Perversions, Shameless, Vices, etc.).

**Social Laws**—Little Respect For—(See Moral Laws, Unconventional, Vows, in this section).

**Substance Wasted**—(See "Energies" in this section).

**Sudden Death**—Thru a Love Affair—(See "Death" in this section).

**Suffers In Health**—Thru Love Affairs—(See Grief, Health, in this section).

**Suicide**—On Account of a Love Affair—(See Suicide).

**Trouble** — Thru the Opposite Sex— (See "Grief", and the various paragraphs in this section).

**True Affections**—(See "Genuine" in this section).

**Unconventional**—In Love Affairs—Little Respect for Vows, Restraints, and Social Laws—♆ affl. in the 5th or 7th, or in ♎; ♅ affl. in ♌ or ♎; ♅ ☌ or ill-asp. ♀. (See "Free Love" under Free; "Moral Laws" in this section; Perverse).

**Unfaithful**—In Love Affairs and Sex Relations ♅ or ♂ affl. in ♎; ♅ to the ☌ or ill-asp. ♀ by dir. (See Adulterous, Amours, Clandestine, Fickle, Unconventional, in this section).

**Unlawful Affections**—The ☉ to the ☌ ♀ if ♀ be weak at B. (See "Free Love" under Free; Adulterous, Clandestine, Liaisons, Moral Laws, in this section).

**Unwise Entanglements** — (See "Entanglements" in this section).

**Unwomanly Freedom** — (See "Unwomanly" under Morals).

**Vows and Restraints**—Chafes Under —♅ affl. in the 5th or 7th H.; ♅ ☌ or ill-asp. ♀. (See Moral Laws, Unconventional, in this section).

**Wandering Affections**—(See "Fickle" in this section).

**Wastes Energies** — (See Energies, Health, in this section).

**Women**—(See Addicted To, Astray, Fond Of, Grief, Hate, Health, Jealousy, Opposite Sex, Ruined, Scandal, Seduction, and the various paragraphs in this section; "Poison Death" under Poison; Treachery).

**Zealous**—In Love Affairs and In Affection—♀ in ♌ or the 5th H. (See Amorous, Ardent, in this section). For further and collateral study along this line see Companions, Conduct, Debauched, Depraved, Dissipated, Drink, Excesses, Expense, Females, Habits, Harlots, Husband, Immodest, Indecent, Indiscretions, Lascivious, Licentious, Lust, Marriage, Marriage Partner, Obscene, Prodigal, Renunciation, Riotous, Social Relations, Suicide, Virile, Wanton, Wench, Wife, Wine, Women, etc.).

**LOVED ONES**—Death of—♄ progressed ☌, P, □ or ☍ the radical ♀, and vice versa. (See "Death" under Brother, Children, Daughter, Family, Father, Husband, Mother, Relatives, Sister, Son, Wife, etc.).

**LOVELY**—Beautiful—Elegant, etc.—

**Lovely Body**—♍ gives, but not necessarily beautiful. (See Beautiful, Comely, Elegant, Handsome).

**Lovely Complexion** — (See Complexion).

**Lovely Eyes**—(See Eyes).

**Lovely Face**—(See "Beautiful", "Lovely", under Complexion, Face).

**Lovely Hair**—(See Brunettes, Color, Lovely, under Hair).

**LOW**—

**Low Altitudes**—Residence In—(See Altitude).

**Low and Base** — Vile — Miscreant — Sordid—♂ Sig. □ or ☍ ☽; ♀ Sig. □ or ☍ ♂; ☿ Sig. ☌ ♂, a treacherous miscreant; ♄ Sig. □ or ☍ ☿. (See Degenerate, Depraved, Infamous, Treachery, Vile).

**Low and Cunning**—The ☽ Sig. □ or ☍ ☿. (See Cheating, Deceitful, Dishonest, Forgers, Thieves, Treacherous, etc.).

**Low Blood Pressure**—(See "Pressure" under Blood).

**Low Business** — Follows Some Low Business—♄ Sig. ☌ ♂, engages in some public calling of the lowest order, and often ends days in prison; ♂ Sig. in ♋, usually employed in some low business, and incapable of better. (See Character, Cheating, Deceitful, Dishonest, Evil, Forgers, Libel, Morals, Murderous, Prison, Thieves, Wicked).

**Low Caloric**—Low Animal Heat—(See "Lack of Animal Heat" under Heat).

**Low Character** — (See Low and Base, Low Business, in this section; "Loose Morals" under Morals).

**Low Company**—Fond of—Keeps Bad Company — The ☽ sepr. from ♀ and apply. to the ☉; ♄ to the ill-asps. ♀ or ☿ by dir.; the periodic direction of ♄ to the radical ♀; ♂ by periodic direction to the ill-asps. the ☽ or ♀; ♂ Sig. □ or ☍ the ☽ or ♀; ♂ to the ill-asps. the ☽, ♀, or ☿ by dir.; ♀ Sig. in ♋; ♀ Sig. ☌ ♂; ♀ to the ☌ ♂ by dir.; ♀ Sig. in ♓, and affl. by ♄ or ♂. (See Low and Base, Low Business, Low Women, in this section; Depraved, Debauched, Dissipated, Harlots, Lewd, Lust; "Harlots" under Men; Prodigal, Venery).

**Low Desires**—(See Desires; Low and Base, Low Company, and other paragraphs in this section).

**Low Fellow** — (See "Low and Base" in this section).

**Low Fevers**—(See "Low Fevers" under Fever).

**Low Mentality**—Mind of a Low Order—(See "Low and Base", and other paragraphs in this section; Criminal, Deviations; "Low" under Mind; "Loose Morals" under Morals; Obscene, Perversions, etc.).

**Low Morals**—(See "Low and Base" in this section; Depraved, Infamous; "Loose" under Morals; Obscene, Perversions, Shameless, etc.).

**Low Pleasures** — Given to Low and Sensuous Pleasures — (See "Low" under Pleasures).

**Low Public Houses**—Frequenter of— (See Harlots, Taverns).

**Low Resistance** — To Disease — (See "Low" under Recuperation, Resistance, Vitality).

**Low Spirits** — Sad — Disspirited — Dejected — Cast Down — Melancholic — Vapours—The ☉ ☌ ☽ at B., within 3 degrees, disspirited all thru life at each New ☽; the ☉ or ☽ to the ☌ or ill-asps. ♄ by dir. or tr.; the ☽ Sig. □ or ☍ ♄; ♄ to his own bad asps. by dir.; ♄ Sig. □ or ☍ ☽; ♄ by tr. in ☌, □, or ☍ ☉, ☽, ♃, ♀, or ☿ radical; ♀ afflicted, and espec. by ♄ or ♄ sign influence, tends to ennui, dissatisfaction, discontentment, languor of spirits, lack of interest in life, weariness, etc.; ☿ Sig. in ♑; ♓ on the Asc., and affl. by

♄, or with ♄ rising at B. and afflicting the hyleg. (See Anguish, Anxiety, Apathy, Brooding, Chaotic, Dejected, Depressed, Despondent, Discontentment, Dissatisfied, Doleful, Ennui, Fears, Fretful, Hope, Hysteria, Imaginations, Indifferent, Introspection, Irritable, Joy, Languid, Lassitude, Lethargy, Listless, Melancholia; "No Peace of Mind" under Mind; Morbid, Peevish, Pensive, Psychic, Restless, Sadness, Suicide, Vapors, Weariness, Worry, etc.).

**Low Stature**—The ☽ in her decrease tends to give a low, short, and squat stature. (See Decreased, Diminished, Dwarf, Growth, Height; "Short Body" under Short; Squab).

**Low Vitality**—(See "Low" under Vitality).

**Low Women**—Given To—(See "Low Company" in this section; Harlots, Lewd; "Women" under Men). See Lack Of, Less, Lessened, Loss Of, Lower, Lowered, Lowering, Lowest, Void Of.

**LOWER—**

**Arm** — The Lower Arm — (See Forearm, Hands).

**Back**—Lower Part of the Back—(See Back, Loins, Lumbar).

**Belly**—Lower Belly—(See Belly).

**Bowels**—The Lower Excretory Bowels — (See "Lower Excretory" under Bowels).

**Desires**—Lower Desires—(See Animal, Desires, Instincts, Passion, etc.).

**Dorsal Nerves**—Lower Dorsal Nerves —(See Dorsal).

**Extremities** — Lower Extremities — Lower Limbs — Disorders In — (See Ankles, Calves, Extremities, Feet, Femur, Fibula, Fractures, Gout, Knees, Legs, Limbs; "Neuritis" under Nerves; Rheumatism, Sprains, Swellings, Thighs, Tibia).

**Gout** — In the Lower Limbs — (See Gout; "Gout" under Extremities, Feet, Knees, Legs, Limbs).

**Head**—The Lower Back Part of the Head—(See Occipital).

**Jaw**—Lower Jaw—(See Jaws).

**Kidneys** — The Lower Portion of — Ruled by ♏. (See the Introduction under Kidneys).

**Limbs**—Lower Limbs—Disorders In—Accidents or Hurts To—(See the references under "Extremities" in this section).

**Lip**—Lower Lip—(See Lips).

**Lobes** — Lower Lobes — (See "Lobes" under Liver, Lungs).

**Mankind**—Lower Order of Mankind—(See Mankind).

**Mind**—The Lower Mind—(See "Animal Instincts" under Animal; "Lower Mind" under Mind; Personality).

**Nature** — The Lower Nature — (See "Mind" in this section; Conduct, Desires, Habits, Low, Passion, etc.).

**Organs**—Lower Parts of—(See "Parts of Body" under Accidents; "Marks" under Face; Marks; "Organs" under Middle; Moles, Navamsa; "Lower Part" under Organs; Upper).

**Parts** — Lower Parts of the Body — Diseases and Suffering In— ♀ rules the lower part of the body in general; ♀ diseases and afflictions; born under ♀; ♄ affl. in ♍ in the 6th H. The ♋ sign on the Asc., the lower part of the body is shorter and smaller, and the upper part rounder. (See References under "Extremities" in this section; Abdomen, Belly, Bladder, Bowels, Genitals, Marks, Organs, Rectum, Sex Organs).

**Passions**—The Lower Passions—(See Amorous, Amours, Animal, Appetites, Desires, Excesses, Love Affairs, Passion, Sex, Venery, etc.).

**Teeth** — Lower Teeth — (See "Lower Jaw" under Jaws; Teeth).

**Women**—Lower Order of—(See Harlots, Nymphomania, Shameless, Treachery, etc.).

**LOWERED** — The Vitality Lowered — (See Recuperation, Resistance, Stamina, Tone; Lessened, Lowered, under Vitality).

**LOWERING—**

**Lowering Brow** — (See "Lowering" under Forehead).

**Lowering Look**—Lowering Aspect—Downward Look—♄ gives. (See "Downward" under Look).

**LOWEST**—Vitality At Its Lowest—(See "Force" under Vital; "Lowest" under Vitality).

**LUBRICATION** — Is carried on by the Synovial Fluid, ruled by the ☽. The afflictions of ♄ to a part tend to lack of, and a dry condition of the joints. Thus ♄ affl. in ♑ tends to dryness, pain, and trouble in the knee joint. Saturn affl. in ♌ tends to lack of lubrication between the dorsal vertebrae, which may result in ankylosis. (See Ankylosis, Fluids, Joints, Juices, Mucous Membranes, Oils, Serums, Synovial, etc.).

**LUCIDA MAXILLA** — Ceti — A Star of the nature of ♄. (See Ceti).

**LUCK**—(a) Bad Luck—(See Accidents, Banishment, Calamity, Disgrace, Enemies, Execution, Exile, Fate, Fire; "Malice" under Fortune; Honour, Hurts, Ill-Fortune, Ill-Health, Injury, Judges, Miseries, Misfortune, Plots, Poverty, Prison, Reputation, Reverses, Ruin, Scandal, Shipwreck, Sorrow, Treachery, Trouble, Unfortunate, Vehicles, Water, Wounds, etc.). (b) Good Luck — (See Comforts; "Good Fate" under Fate; "Fortunate" under Fortune; "Good Health" under Health; "Popular" under Reputation; Wealth).

**LUES**—Lues Venereae—Syphilis—(See Syphilis).

**LUGUBRIOUS**—Sad—Solemn—Mournful — (See Imaginations, Melancholy, Mournful, Sadness).

**LUMBAGO**—Pain In the Loins—Pain In the Back—The ☉ in ♉, ☌, or ill-asp. a malefic; the ☉ in ♒ and affl. by ♃; the ☽ hyleg in ♎ with females; ♅ affl. in ♎, spasmodic lumbago; a ♎ disease; ♄ affl. in ♎; ♃ affl. in ♒; ☿ affl. in ♈ or ♎; afflictions in ♎; ♌ or ♎ on the Asc.; the 7th H. involved, and ♄ afflicting ♀, provided the map otherwise shows a rheumatic constitution. (See "Pain" under Back; Gout, Loins, Lumbar, Rheumatism).

Printed in the United States
86927LV00005B/3/A